W9-CBR-570

Berkshire Encyclopedia of
Human–Computer
Interaction

Berkshire Encyclopedia of
Human–Computer Interaction

VOLUME 2

William Sims Bainbridge

Editor

Great Barrington, Massachusetts U.S.A.
www.berkshirepublishing.com

OVERSIZE
REF
004.019
B513b

Copyright © 2004 by Berkshire Publishing Group LLC

All rights reserved. No part of this book may be reproduced or utilized in any form or by any means, electronic or mechanical, including photocopying, recording, or by any information storage and retrieval system, without permission in writing from the publisher.

Cover photo: Thad Starner sporting a wearable computer.
    Photo courtesy of Georgia Institute of Technology.
Cover background image: Courtesy of Getty Images.

For information:
    Berkshire Publishing Group LLC
    314 Main Street
    Great Barrington, Massachusetts 01230
    www.berkshirepublishing.com

Printed in the United States of America

Library of Congress Cataloging-in-Publishing Data

Berkshire encyclopedia of human-computer interaction / William Sims Bainbridge, editor.
    p. cm.
    "A Berkshire reference work."
    Includes bibliographical references and index.
    ISBN 0-9743091-2-5 (hardcover : alk. paper)
    1. Human-computer interaction--Encyclopedias. I. Bainbridge, William Sims. II. Title.

QA76.9.H85B46 2004
004'.01'9--dc22

                                                                    2004017920

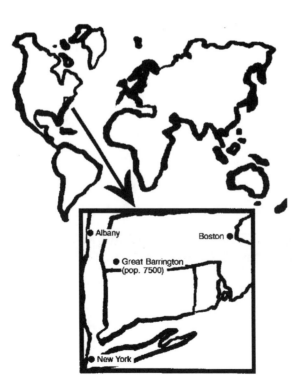

BERKSHIRE PUBLISHING STAFF

Project Director
Karen Christensen

Project Coordinators
Courtney Linehan and George Woodward

Associate Editor
Marcy Ross

Copyeditors
Francesca Forrest, Mike Nichols, Carol Parikh, and Daniel Spinella

Information Management and Programming
Deborah Dillon and Trevor Young

Editorial Assistance
Emily Colangelo

Designer
Monica Cleveland

Production Coordinator
Janet Lowry

Composition Artists
Steve Tiano, Brad Walrod, and Linda Weidemann

Composition Assistance
Pam Glaven

Proofreaders
Mary Bagg, Sheila Bodell, Eileen Clawson, and Cassie Lynch

Production Consultant
Jeff Potter

Indexer
Peggy Holloway

CONTENTS

LIST OF ENTRIES

READER'S GUIDE

This list is provided to assist readers in locating entries on related topics. It classifies articles into ten general categories: Applications; Approaches; Breakthroughs; Challenges; Components; Disciplines; Historical Development; Interfaces; Methods; and Social Implications. Some entries appear in more than one category.

Applications
Classrooms
Digital Government
Digital Libraries
E-business
Games
Geographic Information Systems
Grid Computing
Law Enforcement
Mobile Computing

Navigation
Online Education
Online Voting
Planning
Recommender and Reputation Systems
Search and Rescue
Statistical Analysis Support
Supercomputers
Telecommuting
Ubiquitous Computing
Video

Approaches
Application Use Strategies
Beta Testing
Cognitive Walkthrough
Constraint Satisfaction
Ethics

Compilers
Data Visualization
Dialog Systems
Drawing and Design
Eye Tracking
Facial Expressions
Fly-by-Wire
Graphical User Interface
Haptics
Multimodal Interfaces
Multiuser Interfaces
Musical Interaction
Olfactory Interaction
Online Questionnaires
Pen and Stylus Input
Physiology
Pocket Computer
Smart Homes
Tablet Computer
Telepresence
Three-Dimensional Graphics
Three-Dimensional Printing
Virtual Reality
Wearable Computer

Methods
Avatars
Browsers
Data Mining
Digital Cash
Embedded Systems
Expert Systems
Gesture Recognition
Handwriting Recognition and Retrieval
Hypertext and Hypermedia
Icons
Information Organization
Information Retrieval
Information Spaces
Instruction Manuals
Language Generation
Lexicon Building
Machine Translation

Markup Languages
Motion Capture and Recognition
Natural-Language Processing
Optical Character Recognition
Personality Capture
Programming Languages
Search Engines
Semantic Web
Software Engineering
Sonification
Speech Recognition
Speech Synthesis
Speechreading
Text Summarization
User Support
Video Summarization
Visual Programming
World Wide Web
Social Implications
Chatrooms
Children and the Web
Collaboratories
Computer-Supported Cooperative Work
Cybercommunities
Cybersex
Cyborgs
Education in HCI
Electronic Journals
E-mail
Gender and Computing
Groupware
Human-Robot Interaction
Impacts
Internet—Worldwide Diffusion
Internet in Everyday Life
Literary Representations
Movies
MUDs
Multiagent systems
Sociable Media
Software Cultures
Work
Workforce

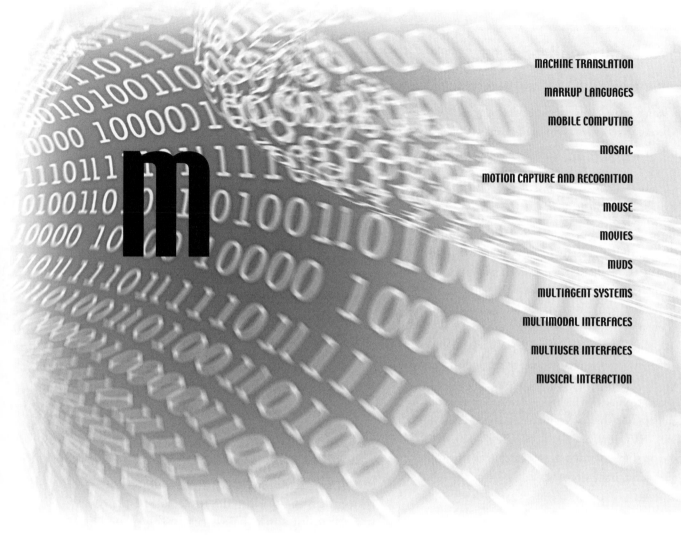

MACHINE TRANSLATION

Machine translation (MT) is the translation of documents from one language into another language by a computer. It is commonly distinguished from both *human-aided machine translation* and *machine-aided human translation*. In human-aided machine translation, part of the translation process has been automated, but a human translator may intervene at different stages in the process or produce an improved version of the initial machine translation. Machine-aided human translation, by contrast, is performed by a human translator using a computational "workbench" as a support environment. A typical workbench consists of a networked workstation with access to bilingual dictionaries, thesauri, databases of previously translated examples, and

so on, and it is intended for professional translators working in teams.

The Need for Machine Translation

Although the need for translation has existed for a long time, it has grown explosively over the last fifty years, due to the growth of international organizations such as the United Nations and the European Union, and due also to the expansion of global trade and communication. We are now at a point where the demand for translations far exceeds the supply of human translators. For example, the workload of the Translation Service of the European Commission (one of the world's largest translation services) reached 1,200,000 pages in the year 2000, and it is expected to increase drastically with the impending enlargement of the EU, which will introduce

Warren Weaver on Machine Translation

In March of 1947, Warren Weaver, director of the Natural Sciences Division of the Rockefeller Foundation, wrote to the cyberneticist Norbert Wiener about the potential for using computers to translate between languages. Weaver's letter to Wiener, excerpted below, is considered an early milestone in the development of machine translation.

A most serious problem, for UNESCO and for the constructive and peaceful future of the planet, is the problem of translation, as it unavoidably affects the communication between peoples. Huxley has recently told me that they are appalled by the magnitude and the importance of the translation job.

Recognizing fully, even though necessarily vaguely, the semantic difficulties because of multiple meanings, etc., I have wondered if it were unthinkable to design a computer which would translate. Even if it would translate only scientific material (where the semantic difficulties are very notably less), and even if it did produce an inelegant (but intelligible) result, it would seem to me worth while."

Source: Warren, W. (2003). Translation. In S. Nirenburg, H. L. Somers, & Y. A. Wilks. Readings in machine translation (chap. 1). Cambridge, MA: MIT Press. (Original work published in 1949)

MT are no longer limited to large international organizations requiring routine translations of large bodies of text, but extend to individual users with occasional translation needs, which can be as basic as translating an e-mail from a pen pal in a foreign country.

The use of computers for language translation was first advocated in an influential report by the mathematician Warren Weaver in 1949, which is often cited as the starting point of modern computational MT. The following decade was characterized by great enthusiasm for MT. Although experts did not fail to point out the problems of the task, it was widely believed that machine translation for unrestricted domains and arbitrary language pairs (of the type described in many works of science fiction, e.g., the famous *Star Trek* Translator) would eventually become available. In 1966, however, the Automatic Language Processing Advisory Committee (ALPAC), an advisory board to the U.S. government, published a negative review of this first phase of MT research. Its main criticisms were the apparent lack of measurable progress, the need for postediting, high costs compared with the cost of human translators, and the failure to identify a genuine need for large-scale translation in the United States. As a result government funding for MT research in the United States was severely curtailed. Commercial research, however, continued, and several government-funded MT projects were launched in Western Europe, Canada, and Japan in the 1970s, as well. Successful systems—for example, the Canadian Météo system for English–French translations of weather forecasts, and the commercial Systran system acquired by the European Communities in 1976—helped to reignite global interest in machine translation. In the 1970s and 1980s, approaches to MT became increasingly diversified, building on a variety of new frameworks in theoretical and computational linguistics as well as artificial intelligence (the most important of these is described later). At the beginning of the 1990s, MT research received additional impetus with the emergence of corpus-based modeling approaches that relied on statistical techniques rather than expert linguistic knowledge. At the same time sizeable standardized text resources in multiple languages began to be developed, and the Internet was discovered not

up to twelve new official languages. The vast majority of translations, however, are restricted to fairly limited domains, such as translations of legal documents. In constrained domains MT can support human translators by reducing full-scale translation to mere postediting. As a result the demand for MT has increased exponentially, for example, from 26,000 machine-translated pages within European Commission in 1991 to 550,000 pages in 2000. In addition MT is likely to assume new roles in today's global community: For instance, it can greatly facilitate communication in emerging multilingual environments, such as e-commerce or distributed work teams collaborating across national and linguistic boundaries. Internet search engines incorporating automatic translation can search webpages in different languages for a query entered in the user's language. Thus, the potential benefits of just as source of multilingual text data but also as a potential application for MT. The rapid progress in algorithmic development and data collection was furthermore aided by the unprecedented availability of affordable high-performance computing resources. In addition to these technological advances, the success of MT in real-life applications is due to the collective revision of earlier, unrealistic expectations: It is now widely accepted that MT output is not, and perhaps never will be, perfect, but that it usually requires some form of human postprocessing.

MT Architectures

MT systems and research paradigms can be classified according to two criteria: the first is the basic architecture or the level at which translation takes place. The second is the modeling paradigm, that is, the way in which translation is performed. Three translation levels are usually distinguished: direct, transfer, and interlingua. The lowest level, direct translation, denotes translation from word strings in the original (or *source)* language to the intended (*target)* language without any substantial analysis of the underlying linguistic structures. Literal, word-by-word translations are an example of this strategy. Since direct approaches do not exploit contextual information, they often fail to handle lexical and/or syntactic ambiguity. The following translations demonstrate this problem:

> a. English: The progress towards monetary union must be made concrete.
>
> French translation: Les progrès vers l'union monétaire doivent être accomplis au béton.
>
> b. English: you can type
>
> German translation: Sie Typ der Dose

In (a), *concrete* was interpreted as a noun rather than an adjective and was translated in the sense of "construction material." In (b), *can type* was analyzed as a noun phrase rather than a verbal construction and was accordingly translated as "type of can."

Transfer models, by contrast, do perform a structural analysis of the source language. The actual translation takes place at the level of the resulting structural representations: The source language rep-

resentation is translated into a matching target language representation that then serves as the basis for generating target language word strings. In many transfer systems these intermediate representations are of a primarily syntactic nature, that is, they describe phrase structures or grammatical functions within the sentence. A sample syntactic transfer rule translating the Spanish expression *Me falta tiempo* (which is literally *To-me is-necessary time*) to its English equivalent *I need time* might look as follows:

$$(2)\ NP_1(Obj)\ V_{SWITCH}\ NP_2(Sub) => NP_2(Sub)\ V\ NP_1(Obj)$$

This rule states that the object noun phrase (NP) in the Spanish original (*me*) becomes the subject noun phrase (*I*) in the English sentence, and the subject NP in postverbal position becomes the object NP. The subscript on the verb (V) indicates that this rule applies to a specific category of verbs requiring such "role-switching," including *faltar*, *gustar*, and the like. In addition to syntactic transfer, further components are typically needed for morphological processing, that is, for decomposing compound words into their constituent parts, identifying inflectional suffixes, and so forth.

Other transfer systems extend the structural analysis to the semantic level and represent source and target languages in quasi-logical form. A possible semantic representation for the example above would be:

$$(3)\ NEED(X(speaker),Y)$$

This states that two arguments X and Y, that X is the speaker, and that X needs Y. The assignment of X and Y to specific syntactic forms is handled not by the translation component proper but by the analysis and generation modules. Thus, language-specific properties are removed or neutralized as far as possible for the purpose of translation.

The advantage of the transfer approach compared with the direct approach is that ambiguities can be resolved more easily. The disadvantage is that complex analysis and generation components need to be constructed that are typically unique to each language pair. As a result, a system translating between n languages needs $n\ (n–1)$ sets of transfer

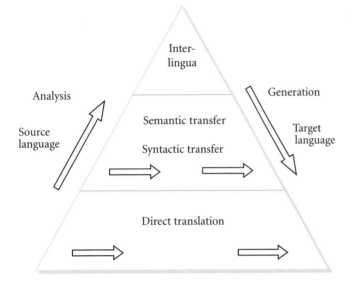

FIGURE 1. *Machine translation triangle.* Source: Nirenburg, et al. (2003).

components, which prevents it from being easily extendable to new languages. Moreover, the representations in syntactic and semantic transfer systems are often dependent on particular linguistic theories that are difficult to verify on the basis of actual language data.

Like transfer-based systems, interlingua-based systems make use of abstract formal representations of the type shown in (3). The difference lies in the use of only a single, language-independent representation (the *interlingua*). As before, each language in the system needs sets of rules to map from word strings to the abstract representation and back. However, these are not affected by the target language. In order to translate between *n* languages, only *n* such components are needed, as opposed to *n (n-1)* as in the transfer-based approach. The problem of interlingua-based MT is to find a representational formalism that is sufficiently powerful to accommodate a wide range of different linguistic phenomena. Ideally, such a formalism should be able to represent any sentence in any language and preserve its meaning during translation. It is interesting to note that this is a problem that has intrigued not just machine translation researchers in the twentieth century. The quest for a "universal language" dates back to seventeenth century philosophers, such as Descartes and Leibniz, and has characterized much

work in formal logic and artificial intelligence. The primary focus of this work has not been on machine translation but on the formalization of language for other applications, such as expert systems, automated reasoning, question answering, or language understanding. Nevertheless, some of these frameworks, such as Schank's conceptual dependency representation, have had a significant impact on the development of interlinguas.

Prominent interlingua-based systems developed in the past include the Dutch Rosetta system and the KANT system at Carnegie-Mellon University. Interlingua-based MT is also currently being used in systems developed for speech rather than text translation, which will be discussed later.

Modeling Paradigms

Our second classification criterion is the actual modeling approach employed in MT systems. Broadly speaking, a distinction can be drawn between knowledge-based and data-driven modeling approaches. Knowledge-based systems rely mostly on input from human experts, such as handcrafted translation rules or grammars. Data-driven systems, on the other hand, are designed to acquire translation models automatically from large amounts of data (on the order of hundreds of thousands of translation examples). However, most current MT systems do not rely exclusively on one or the other method but incorporate insights from both, thus forming a continuum along the knowledge-based versus data-driven axis.

One of the oldest knowledge-based approaches is *rule-based* MT, which embodies the assumption that high-quality MT requires the explicit formalization of the linguistic knowledge underlying human translations. Various sets of (typically handwritten) rules are used for the morphological and syntactic analysis of the source language, mapping between semantic/syntactic representations in source and target language, expressing lexical correspondences, and for generating word strings in the target language. Rule-based modeling often goes hand-in-hand with a transfer approach, as exemplified by the transfer rule shown in (2). A disadvantage of many rule formalisms is that they are often designed only for unidirectional application; that is, different sets of rules are needed for translating into versus translating from a given language, although virtually identical knowledge is involved in both processes. MT systems that epitomize the rule-based paradigm include the METAL system developed at the University of Texas, Rosetta, or the commercial Logos system, as examples.

In the 1980s and early 1990s, rule-based approaches were increasingly replaced with *constraint-based* approaches. These were inspired by the development of constraint-based grammar formalisms (e.g., so-called unification grammars) that supplanted earlier transformational grammars. Constraint-based formalisms are inherently independent of their procedural implementation; they only describe constraints on valid constructs in a given language, independent of how they are put to use in a language-processing system. As such, they are equally well suited for analysis and generation and are therefore attractive for MT systems.

In *lexical-based* MT, most of the burden of translation is placed on lexical representations describing valid correspondences between words of the source and target languages. They can be thought of as bilingual lexicon entries with a rich structure incorporating syntactic and semantic constraints, such as the required number and type of verb complements. Lexical entries are thus capable of expressing mappings between entire phrases or sentences. An example of an English–German lexical entry would be:

(4) [NP(Subj) cut back on NP(Obj)]
    [NP(Subj) reduzieren NP(Obj)]

which establishes a correspondence between the multiword expression *cut back on* and its single-word translation *reduzieren*. In lexical-based systems, the translation process can be simplified to a search for a set of target-language lexical entries that match the constraints expressed in the lexical entries of the source-language input words. Grammatical word sequences are then generated by reordering this "bag of words" in accordance with the syntactic rules of the target language; this strategy is referred to as "Shake-and-Bake MT." An advantage often cited in favor of lexical-based approaches is that bilingual lexicons can be more easily learned from a parallel corpus than entire grammars or transfer rules.

Example-based (or *memory-based*) machine translation (EBMT) is a data-driven approach that exploits the fact that translation patterns frequently recur in a given MT scenario. New source languages might be translated more accurately if it could be determined how similar sentences were translated previously. For instance, having observed sentences (a) and (b) below, we could easily deduce the translation of sentence (c) by finding the matching segments (here set in boldface).

> a. **L'Assemblée générale des Nations Unies** s'est réeunie pour faire le bilan du programme.
>
> (The United Nations General Assembly convened to review the plan's progress.)
>
> b. Le senat **a approuvé le budget pour l'année prochaine.**
>
> (The Senate has approved the budget for the next year.)
>
> c. **L'Assemblée générale des Nations Unies a approuvé le budget pour l'année prochaine.**
>
> (The United Nations General Assembly has approved the budget for the next year.)

Translation is performed in three steps: (1) access a large database of previously translated expressions, (2) extract examples similar to the source sentence to be translated, and (3) combined target language units and modify them as needed, for example, by replacing individual words or changing morphological inflections. The challenge in EBMT is to find suitable techniques for steps two and three, that is, similarity measures for optimizing retrieval and combination procedures for generating the final output string. Various similarity measures have been used in the past. These include simple string-matching techniques, sometimes enriched by morphological analysis or word class information, but also word similarity as determined by the distance of entries in a *semantic net*. Semantic nets represent words in terms of attributes such as [abstract/concrete], [animate/inanimate], [human/animal] that are arranged hierarchically. Thus, the words *dog* and *cat* would receive a higher similarity score than, say, *dog* and *newspaper*. EBMT can be considered a refined version of *translation memories*, which are an integral part of human translators' workbenches. Translation memories contain stored examples of previous translations that can be matched with new, untranslated segments. However, any additions or changes to the suggested translations are performed by the human translator.

The most data-driven approach to MT is *statistical machine translation* (SMT). Although some statistical techniques were used in the early 1960s, they were subsequently replaced by knowledge-based approaches and did not reappear again until 1989. At that time a team at IBM research built the first modern SMT system (the *Candide* system), exploiting insights gained from statistical modeling techniques in speech recognition. SMT is based on a noisy-channel view of translation: Given a text in language B that is to be translated into language A, we assume (somewhat counterintuitively) that it was originally generated in language A. However, it was subsequently passed through a noisy channel, where it underwent a series of substitutions, reorderings, deletions, and so on, resulting in the observed text. Given a word string *b*, we then try to find the string *a* that maximizes the probability of *a* given *b* defined as:

$$P(a|b) = P(b|a)P(a)/P(b)$$

The first part of this model, *P(b|a)*, is referred to as the *translation model*; it expresses probabilistic constraints on the association of source and target strings. The second part, *P(a)*, is the *language model*, which determines whether *a* constitutes a likely sentence in the target language. The translation model is typically decomposed into a product of individual models for computing probabilities of aligning different subparts of the sentences, word substitution probabilities, and the like. Various translation models of increasing complexity have been developed; these are typically referred to as the IBM Models 1 through 5, after the classic paper by Brown et al. describing the SMT approach. The parameters of these models are estimated from a parallel corpus, a set of source language sentences that have been matched with their corresponding target language translations. Similarly, the parameters of the language model necessary to compute *P(a)* are estimated from a large corpus of monolingual data in the target language. Over the past fifteen years, SMT has evolved rapidly, aided by the development of parallel text resources, efficient search algorithms, and public-domain SMT software tools. Furthermore, efforts have been made at combining statistical methods with a greater degree of linguistic knowledge. The original IBM models perform translation strictly at the word level—they are thus a rare example of the direct translation architectures described earlier. More recent work has addressed this shortcoming by reintroducing additional layers of higher-level structure. This includes phrase-based SMT models, in which "chunks" of words are modeled as units, as well as models that are applied not to word strings but to hierarchical representations of their syntactic structure. The latter approach essentially adopts a transfer architecture but uses statistical rather than rule-based modeling.

Finally, a number of *hybrid* systems have been developed that attempt to combine the advantages of different approaches. Efforts at reintroducing linguistic structures into SMT can be viewed as hybrid approaches; another trend is to use a primarily rule-based system but to acquire some of its components, such as bilingual lexica, term lists, or grammars, from large corpora using statistical techniques. Statistics can also be used as a knowledge source for disambiguation, for example, to identify the most probable of several competing word translations in a given domain or context. In EBMT statistical alignment models have been used to automatically extract a database of translation examples from parallel text by identifying likely matches between subsentential segments. A combination of EBMT and lexical MT is also possible, for example, by using the information present in bilingual lexical entries to measure example similarity.

MT Evaluation

How can the different MT approaches described here be assessed? Is it possible to find objective criteria to quantify the performance of an MT system? Until recently, research in MT suffered from the lack of a commonly accepted evaluation standard. Different researchers often used different criteria, which made it very difficult to compare MT systems objectively. In 2001, however, IBM researchers proposed an automatic evaluation method termed BLEU (for BiLingual Evaluation Understudy). This method compares machine translations against a set of high-quality human translations of the same text by measuring the fraction of short word sequences that are identical in both. The fractions of matching sequences up to length 4 are summed up and weighted by a factor inversely proportional to their length. This measure showed a surprisingly high correlation with human judgments of translation quality and was subsequently adopted as the basis for an official MT evaluation standard by the National Institute for Standards and Technology (NIST) in the United States. However, it has been pointed out that this technique is highly dependent on the reference translations. Since BLEU-style–based measures only express document similarity, a low score does not necessarily indicate a bad translation. A given system output might be a valid and fluent paraphrase of one of the human reference translations, but it may not have been a reference translation itself. Furthermore, human translations need to be checked for consistency in order to ensure that translators did not take too many stylistic liberties, such as deleting significant parts of the source material. Research on automatic MT evaluation is still in progress, and several extensions to the BLEU/NIST scheme have been proposed. Nevertheless, this measure is currently being used as a working evaluation standard in annual MT evaluations sponsored by the U.S. government, which are aimed at benchmarking the performance of MT systems for Chinese/English and Arabic/English. During the most recent evaluations (July 2003), the best performance was obtained by statistical MT systems.

Spoken Language Translation

Machine translation has been applied not just to written text but also to spoken language. Most of these systems present the output in spoken form as well, and thus perform *speech-to-speech translation*. Speech input presents some obvious problems, such as *disfluencies* (false starts, repetitions, filler words such as "ah," "uhm") or sentence structures that are considered ungrammatical in written text. Moreover,

speech-to-speech translation systems are often intended to facilitate real-time interpersonal communication, running, for example, on a handheld device with limited computational power and memory. For these reasons, speech-to-speech translation currently focuses on limited domains (e.g., travel planning, tourist information, medical interviews) and relatively small vocabularies of several thousand words.

The above constraints also influence system architectures and modeling approaches. Speed and efficiency requirements have led to so-called *integrated architectures,* where speech recognition and translation are tightly coupled. Instead of using a serial concatenation of an automatic speech recognizer for the source language, a translation component, and a speech synthesizer for the target language, translation is integrated into the speech recognition module itself. The advantage is that target language constraints can be exploited to prevent the recognition of source language word sequences that would not give rise to valid translations. On the other hand, such coupled translation models need to be learned from large amounts of parallel speech data, which is even more difficult to collect than parallel text data. An alternative modeling approach for speech-to-speech translation is EBMT, using similarity measures that can be computed rapidly by means of "shallow" string matching techniques. In addition to this, interlingua-based representations are used, though they require deeper analysis and a greater level of abstraction from the word string. The reason is that speech-to-speech translation systems are often developed for more than one language pair at a time and need to be easily extendable.

The use of speech translation in interpersonal communication necessarily means that pragmatic constraints and world knowledge assume a much more important role than in text translation. For example, speakers make frequent use of incomplete sentences, pronouns, and vague references that can only be resolved by common knowledge of the situational context. This in turn influences the nature of the representations in speech translation systems. Some systems (e.g., the "Speechalator being developed at Carnegie-Mellon) have started to make use of interlinguas that encode speakers' intentions instead of formal semantic analyses of their input utterances.

Future Directions

Although MT cannot be expected to deliver perfect translations regardless of the domain and language pair, it has made tremendous progress over the past decades. An important current trend, which is likely to continue over the next few years, is the integration of different MT approaches, in particular through the combination of statistical and knowledge-based techniques. Whereas statistical machine translation has already been applied at the syntactic transfer level, higher levels (i.e., semantic transfer and interlingua representations) have not yet benefited to the same degree from the integration of statistical information. Another promising line of research is the rapid adaptation of MT to new language pairs and domains. A pilot experiment funded by the U.S. government in 2003 demonstrated that it was possible to build a functioning statistical MT system for a new language pair from scratch within a week, including the collection of training data.

The success of rapid adaptation methods—especially for languages for which large amounts of data are difficult to obtain—will be a necessary prerequisite for future MT applications. Finally, MT is likely to be applied to a wider range of communicative situations beyond text translation. Whereas speech-to-speech translation for dialogues is already a reality, future work will extend this technology to multiperson interactions, such as meetings and conferences, and to multimodal environments, where speech can be combined with visual and gestural information as knowledge sources for disambiguation.

Katrin Kirchhoff

FURTHER READING

Ahrend, K. (2001). *Die Nutzung der maschinellen Übersetzung in der Europäischen Kommission* (The use of machine translation in the European Commission). Retrieved on February 12, 2004 from http://europa.eu.int/comm/translation/reading/articles/tools_and_workflow_en.htm#mt

Brown, P., et al. (1990). A statistical approach to machine translation. *Computational Linguistics, 16*(2), 79–85.

Brown, R. D. (1996). Example-based machine translation in the Pangloss system. *Proceedings of the 6th International Conference on Computational Linguistics (COLING-96)* (pp. 169–174).

Carbonell, J., Mitamara, T., & Nyberg, E. H. (1992). The KANT perspective: a critique of pure transfer (and pure interlingua, pure statistics,…). In *Proceedings of the Fourth International Conference on Theoretical and Methodological Issues in machine Translation—TMI-92* (pp. 225–235).

Casacuberta, F., Vidal, E., & Vilar, J. M. (2002). Architectures for speech-to-speech translation using finite-state models. In *Proceedings of the ACL Workshop on Speech-to-Speech Translation, Algorithms and Systems* (pp. 39–44).

Culy, C., & Riehemann, S. (2003). The limits of n-gram translation evaluation metrics. Proceedings of MT Summit IX. Retrieved February 12, 2004 from http://www.amtaweb.org/summit/MTSummit/papers.html

Hutchins, J. (2003). Machine translation: general overview. In R. Mitkov (Ed.), *The Oxford Handbook of Computational Linguistics* (pp. 501–511). Oxford, UK: Oxford University Press.

Hutchins, J. (1986). *Machine translation: Past, present, future.* Chichester, UK: Horwood.

Landsbergen, J. (1987). Isomorphic grammars and their use in the Rosetta translation system. In M. King (Ed.), *Machine translation today: The state of the art (Proceedings of the Third Lugano Tutorial)* (pp. 351–377). Edinburgh, Scotland: Edinburgh University Press.

Nirenburg, S., Somers, H. L., & Wilks, Y. A. (2003). *Readings in machine translation.* Cambridge, MA: MIT Press.

Papineni, K., Roukos, S., Ward, T., & Zhu, W.-J. (2002). BLEU: A method for automatic evaluation of machine translation. *Proceedings of the 40th Meeting of the Association for Computational Linguistics (ACL)* (pp. 311–318).

Sanfilippo, A., Briscoe, E., Copestake, A., Marti, M., Taule, M., & Alonge, A. (1992). Translation equivalence and lexicalization in the ACQUILEX LKB. In *Proceedings of the Fourth International Conference on Theoretical and Methodological Issues in Machine Translatio—TMI92* (pp. 1–11).

Slocum, W., Bennet, J., Bear, J., Morgan, M., & Root, R. (1987). METAL: THE LRC machine translation system. In S. Michaelson & Y. Wilks (Eds.), *Machine translation today: The state of the art* (pp. 319–350). Edinburgh, Scotland: Edinburgh University Press.

Streiter, O., Carl, M., & Haller, J. (Eds.). (1999). Hybrid approaches to machine translation. *Working Paper No. 35, Institute of Applied Information Sciences.* Saarbruecken, Germany. Retrieved February 12, 2004 from http://www.iai.uni-sb.de/iaien/iaiwp.

Translation Service of the European Commission. (2002). *Translating for a multilingual community.* Retrieved February 12, 2004 from http://europa.eu.int/comm/translation/reading/articles/tools_and_workflow_en.htm.

Trujillo, A. (1999). *Translation engines: Techniques for machine translation.* London: Springer.

Yamada, K., & Knight, K. (2001). A syntax-based statistical translation model. In *Proceedings of the 39th Meeting of the Association for Computational Linguistics (ACL)* (pp. 523–530).

Waibel, A., et al. (2003). Speechalator: two-way speech-to-speech translation on a consumer PDA. In *Proceedings of Eurospeech* (pp. 369–372).

Whitelock, P. (1992). Shake-and-bake translation. In *Proceedings of the 14th International Conference on Computational Linguistics (COLING)* (pp. 784–791).

MARKUP LANGUAGES

The electronic information age has brought a new stage in the development of print and publishing technology, one that relies on electronic media rather than paper media. Markup languages are one aspect of electronic publishing technology.

The term *markup* originally referred to the insertion of symbols at certain places in a document. In traditional publishing, markup is stylistic instruction that is added to a manuscript prior to the manuscript's being typeset. For online or electronic documents, the markup indicators are called tags, codes, or tokens. Markup tags usually start with an opening angle bracket (<) or an opening angle bracket and a slash (</) and end with a closing angle bracket (>) or a slash and a closing angle bracket (/>). A markup language has one of two purposes in tagging an electronic document: Either it is used to indicate how the text should look when it is printed or displayed, or it is used to describe the logical structure and meaning of data contained in the document.

Computer languages have their own grammar, comprising lists of commands and rules instructing the computer in what it should do. Tags are often added to computer languages as beginning and ending indicators that tell what the programmer intends the code to do. The idea of tagging a text was applied to early word processing (originally called text processing) applications in the 1970s and 1980s. Computer users inserted tags to give instructions on how the printed document should look—for example, what sort of font it should be in, what the font size should be, and what spacing and indentation it should have. Today, most word processors and desktop publishing systems do not require users to type tags; the systems are based on the WYSIWYG ("what you see is what you get") principle, so that what users see on the screen is what the printed text will look like. Internal to the word processing programs, there are still tags, unavailable to the user, that instruct the program to create the various fonts, sizes, and so on that the user employs.

Classification of Markup Languages

Markup language used in word processors such as Microsoft Word and WordPad are considered closed language. Since the specification for the language is not publicly available, other vendors are not allowed to make programs based on the markup. On the other hand, the specifications for open markup languages are publicly available. Open markup languages include HTML (Hypertext Markup Language), SGML (Standard Generalized Markup Language), and XML (Extensible Markup Language). HTML is the most popular markup language on the World Wide Web.

Markup languages are also classified into presentational markup and descriptive (or declarative) markup. The former is concerned with the appearance of text, whereas the latter is concerned with the logical structure or meaning of the tagged item. Presentational markup languages are used only for a specific purpose. For example, HTML was developed specifically to format documents for the Web, and RTF (Rich Text Format) was developed specifically for formatting documents for word processing applications. Some presentational markup languages are regarded as procedural because they tell the software what to do in order to format the document. TeX and LaTeX are good examples of procedural markup languages that are popular for publishing research papers in physics and mathematics.

On the other hand, descriptive markup languages are generalized rather than specific; they are media and presentation independent and generic enough to be used in many different applications. Unlike HTML, for example, SGML and XML have nothing to do with document formatting or style characteristics. Descriptive markup languages are concerned only with declaratively stating (or describing) what the data is. The syntax of SGML or XML is open, and its tags are clearly readable by a software program or by a human. The recent development of semantic markup languages is also based on the idea of separating data from its presentation. However, semantic markup languages such as RDF (Resource Description Framework) are concerned with the meaning of data, not merely with describing what it is.

The History of Markup Languages

In 1967, William Tunnicliffe, at that time chairman of the Graphic Communications Association Composition Committee, proposed separating the contents of documents from their formats. At the same time, Stanley Rice, an editor at a major publishing house, wrote about standardizing editorial structures. Adopting their ideas, in 1969, IBM's Charles F. Goldfarb, Ed Mosher, and Ray Lorie developed Generalized Markup Language (GML). The key idea of GML was to build a language that could describe the structure of documents in a way that both machines and humans could read. Goldfarb and his colleagues developed SGML from GML in 1974. In 1986, SGML was adopted as a standard by the International Organization for Standardization (ISO).

In 1989 the physicist Tim Berners-Lee was working at CERN (an international particle physics research center based in Geneva, Switzerland) on the linked information system that was introduced to the world in 1991 as the World Wide Web. The World Wide Web presents information as hypertext, that is, as units that are connected to one another, such that users are free to move from one unit to another according to their needs or interests. HTML, the markup language developed for hypertext as a simplification of SGML, is very easy to learn; its simplicity has contributed to the success of both the Internet and the Web.

As the amount of information on the Web expanded, the World Wide Web Consortium (W3C), which was founded by Berners-Lee in 1994 to lead the Web to its full potential, realized that there was a need for a new way to manage the Web. In November 1996, XML was developed to meet the challenges of large-scale electronic publishing. Since XML is a simple, very flexible text format derived from SGML, it had the potential to play an important role in the interoperable exchange of a variety of data on the Web. In 1999 the W3C released RDF (the Resource Description Framework), a markup language designed to tag Web data semantically so as to create metadata (data about data) that make both machine and human Web searches more easy and successful.

HTML

HTML markup tags tell a Web browser how to display the words and images of webpages for the user. The major Web browsers, such as Internet Explorer and Netscape Navigator, come with an HTML parser in addition to their own, nonstandard extensions. Because commercial browsers contain these nonstandard extensions, Web developers may have to design separate versions of their pages for each browser, informing users of the browsers (and the versions of those browsers) with which the page can be viewed.

Here is an example of HTML text:

```
<B>my dog</B>
```

In this example, the first tag, <B> commands the browser to display the following text in boldface, while the ending tag, </B>, ends the command for boldface. As a result, the string of text between the two tags (my dog) will be displayed on the browser in boldface: **my dog**.

Every HTML page begins with the tag <HTML>, followed by the tag <TITLE>, and finally ends with the ending tag </HTML>. An example page is as follows:

```
<HTML>
<TITLE> A very simple page </TITLE>
<B> This is in bold </B>
<B><I> This is in both bold and italic </I></B>
</HTML>
```

As the above example shows, HTML tag sets are like containers that should be nested within each other in a balanced way. In HTML there are tag names (such as TITLE) and there are also various attributes used inside a tag, with tag attributes being used to expand or elaborate the functions of the tag commands implied by tag names. In the tag <Body bgcolor=white>, for instance, *Body* is a tag name referring to the body of the page, and *bgcolor* is a tag attribute that specifies the value of the background color of the body part.

CSS

As mentioned earlier, markup originally referred to written instructions that were usually scribbled in the margins of a manuscript to tell the typesetter how to lay out the manuscript regarding typefaces, sizes, and so on. CSS (Cascading Style Sheet), accompanied with HTML tags, provides more effective ways of controlling document formats for display on the Web browser while consistently managing the HTML data structure at the same time. CSS style sheets are stored separately from HTML files and can be called up and used by different HTML files. An HTML document that makes use of a given style sheet does not need to be modified if only the style sheet document is changed. The following example shows how a CSS style sheet specifies the format style of the HTML document.

```
H1 {
    font-weight: bold;
    font-size: 12pt;
    color: red
}
```

In the above example, the CSS rule has two parts: namely, selector and declaration. *H1* is the selector, whereas the things inside the brackets are the declaration. The HTML tag <H1> will have characters in 12-point font size, in boldface, and red color.

XML

XML is a generalized descriptive language specifying the logical structure of electronic documents. While HTML displays data, XML describes data. XML provides several advantages over SGML, the language from which it was developed. First, XML is much simpler than SGML. Where the basic SGML specification is about 155 pages long, the XML specification is only about 35 pages long. Second, unlike SGML, which does not support a style sheet mechanism, XML does. Third, while SGML does not include a hyperlinking mechanism as part of its own specification, XML supports a separate hyperlink language, XLL (Extensible Linking Language), as well as the original HTML hyperlinking mechanism.

Since XML separates the user interface from the data, XML rules in a document describing the data can be reused in another document, such that other authors can easily create more of the same class of document. The following example shows the structure of data written in XML code.

```
<?xml version=”1.0”?>
<Book>
    <Title>Principles of Psychology</Title>
    <Author>William James</Author>
    <Chapter1>The scope of psychology</Chapter1>
    <Chapter2>The functions of the brain </Chapter2>
</Book>
```

An XML document is composed of markup and contents, and there are six kinds of XML markup: elements, entity references, comments, processing instructions, marked sections, and document type declarations. As in HTML, in XML elements are the most common form of markup. Unlike in HTML, however, XML elements have nothing to do with the document format for data display.

Semantic Markup

As discussed earlier, presentational markup languages such as HTML are concerned with displaying documents, while descriptive markup languages such as XML are concerned with describing the data on the Web. Semantic markup languages, a third type, are concerned with formally defining the data in terms of classes and properties in order to provide machine-readable descriptions of information. In other words, a semantic markup language should be able to represent knowledge in a way that makes it useful to reasoning engines on the Web. XML is not a semantic markup language because it does not have any explicit constructs for defining classes and properties. RDF Schema, on the other hand, does provide tags to define classes and properties.

The newest type of markup language is represented by OWL, which the W3C published in 1999. Owl is a Web ontology language. Ontology languages define the meaning of data using a machine-readable logic language. OWL is used to publish and share sets of terms to support advanced Web search, software agents, and knowledge management.

Hong-Gee Kim

See also Mosaic; Semantic Web; World Wide Web

FURTHER READING

Fensel, D., Hendler, J., Lieberman, H., & Walster, W. (Eds.). (2002). *Spinning the semantic Web: Bringing the World Wide Web to its full potential.* Cambridge, MA: MIT Press.

Harold, E. R. (1998). *XML: Extensible markup language.* San Francisco: Hungry Minds.

Musciano, C., & Kennedy, B. (2002). *HTML and XHTML: The definitive guide* (5th ed.). Cambridge, MA: O'Reilly & Associates.

W3C. (1995–2004). *Hypertext markup language (HTML) home page.* Retrieved March 17, 2004, from http://www.w3.org/MarkUp/

MOBILE COMPUTING

Wireless and mobile technology has been advancing at an unparalleled rate, and its impact is being observed in many facets of our daily life. Mobile and wireless systems are currently used in commerce, education, defense, and many high-risk fields, including nuclear power, aviation, and emergency

---

BANDWIDTH The amount of data that can be sent through a network or modem connection. Generally measured in bits per second, or "bps."

---

medicine. The technology can be used in home-based and industrial systems as well as in commercial and military environments. When we speak of mobile computing, mobility means being able to access online resources and services while moving from one geographic location to another. Prior to the advent of mobile computing, a user accessed online resources through a dial-up modem (which sends and receives information over phone lines), a cable modem (which sends and receives information over the same cable that cable television networks use) or various other wire-based media, including DSL (short for digital subscriber lines) and ISDN (integrated services digital network). With mobile computing, by contrast, users have microwave wireless communication capability, so they can send and receive information online at any time, from any location, and even while moving. The radio, which supports wireless communication, can be connected to any digital device, including laptop computers, personal digital assistants (PDAs), mobile phones, or any other digital gadget or device. The mobility characteristic means that people have access to updated data instantaneously, which is of benefit in any enterprise dependent on accurate, current information.

Mobility Support

Wireless technology has become popular because of its inherent support for mobility. The way it works can be understood by analogy to a post office redirecting your mail. If you move to a new place, you inform your old post office of your new address. Mail addressed to your old address comes to the old post office, which then redirects it to your new post office, which then sends it to your new address. Similarly, when one uses a mobile phone, or cell phone, incoming calls go to the controller (also called the mobile switching center) that issued the cell phone. The issuing controller then redirects the incoming call to your present location, and your cell phone gets connected. Unlike when you move house and must inform your old post office of your new location, with your cell phone the issuing controller receives instantaneous and automatic updates of your phone's current location without any effort on your part. The detection is carried out by the closest local microwave tower (also known as a base station), which informs your issuing controller of your current location so that it can route all incoming calls to your new location. The tower also gets information about the service privileges your cell phone has, and information about the phone call is sent back to the issuing controller, which also serves as the billing station. You can also make calls from your current location, though there are various restrictions, depending on your service privileges.

Coverage Area and Handing Off

Based on its transmitting power, a microwave tower has a typical coverage range of 2 to 20 kilometers. Any wireless device within that region can communicate with the tower. The area covered by a tower is known as a cell—hence the name cell phone. In order for cells to function together, microwave towers must be placed in preplanned areas or strategic locations. These towers are connected by dedicated, underground wire cables in what is known as the backbone. An area cannot be served if there are no towers (which is often the case in rural or sparsely populated area; most wireless companies adequately cover most urban areas), and mobile phones and other wireless devices will not work in such areas. If you place or receive a call while traveling, you may cross the boundary of a cell while the call is in progress. The base station handling your call in the cell you are leaving then transfers your information to a base station in the cell you are entering; this change of radio resources is known as handoff. A handoff is successful and information transfer can continue only if radio resources are available in the new cell. Otherwise, the call is dropped, causing you a major disappointment. Therefore, a fairly complex infrastructure is needed for a wireless system even though most information transfer is through the hardwired backbone network.

Allocation of Frequencies

The voice typically contains signals with frequencies varying from 30 hertz to 3,000 hertz. (The upper limit of human hearing is approximately 20,000 Hertz.) The voice (and data) signal is modulated using a carrier frequency of 800 Mhz–900 Mhz in the radio frequency range of 3,000 hertz to approximately 300 gigahertz, or 300 billion hertz before being transmitted by the microwave transmitter antenna. Voice and data signals may be allocated frequencies in different ways. With Frequency Division Multiple Access, or FDMA, each phone uses a specific frequency calls or transmissions of data from that phone go out on that frequency. With Time Division Multiple Access, or TDMA, each call (or transmission of data) is given a certain time slot on a frequency so that multiple users can be supported using a single carrier frequency. With Code Division Multiple Access, or CDMA, the bits of information comprising each voice or data transmission are given unique codes and then sent out over wider frequency. The CDMA system requires more bandwidth and both the sending and receiving ends use the same data encoding system.

Applications

Mobile computing is useful when physical installation of microwave towers is not feasible due to timing constraints or location inaccessibility and when users require access to online information on the spot. Currently, wireless technology assists sales, stock trading, package delivery, military operations, disaster recovery, and emergency medical care, among other activities. Sales professionals can stay in touch with home offices and customers via a wireless network by using digital PDAs or portable computers. They can access detailed information about products and services, place orders, provide status reports to the home office, and maintain inventories by using a wireless service to access the home office's network. Wireless technology allows a real estate agent to have access to Multiple Listing Service (MLS) records while in the field, and auditors can conduct their investigations in the field, wirelessly connected to a client information database. Police departments, fire departments, and ambulance services use mobile computing devices for record management, to send queries, and for numerous other activities. Consumers can receive and pay their bills via mobile phone. Courier companies such as Federal Express, UPS, and DHL have adopted mobile computing technology for parcel tracking applications as well as to accommodate emergency shipments or en-route pickups.

Retail organizations can order, sell, and keep inventories of merchandise by using wireless point-of-sale terminals and wireless local-area networks (WLANs). In the field of health care, wireless devices enable fast and accurate transmission of patient information, and a patient's status can be easily monitored by doctors and nurses. The use of electronic patient records that may be viewed and updated from anywhere in the hospital increases the accuracy and speed of medical treatment. Mobile devices can also increase the efficiency and accuracy of all drug transactions. They ensure that the hospital staff administers the right drug to the right person at the right time. Restaurants can use wireless technology to keep track of the names and numbers of people waiting for entry, as well as to keep track of the status of guests already seated, thereby keeping patrons happy.

Ad Hoc and Sensor Networks

An ad hoc network is a wireless network formed on an ad hoc basis without the need for any infrastructure. The connectivity pattern depends on the relative locations of the various of wireless devices, their proximity to one another, and their transmitting power. Since there is no fixed infrastructure, information is forwarded from one device to another, using multihop routing. If the devices are mobile, then the communication links can change dynamically. Ad hoc networks are finding extensive use in military applications; for example, a group of soldiers who are spread out over a small area may share information using their notebook computers. The usefulness of ad hoc networks for industrial automation, situation awareness, and tactical surveillance for military applications and environmental monitoring is also being explored.

Sensor networks are a special class of ad hoc networks with very limited or almost no mobility. The basic idea is to deploy a large number of sensors in a low-flying airplane or unmanned vehicle in an inaccessible area. These sensors sense physical characteristics of the environment and transmit them to a central controller. One of the major limitations is the fact that the plane or unmanned vehicle has a limited power supply; another drawback is that as soon as the batteries in the sensors die, new sensors need to be deployed to replace them as the sensors cannot be recharged. Sensor networks have potential in battlefield surveillance of enemy territory; commercially, they may be used for machinery prognosis, bio-sensing, and environmental monitoring.

Limitations and Future Directions

There are currently around 200 million users of wireless and mobile networks; that number is expected to reach one billion subscribers by 2010. In the home, it is now possible to connect multiple PCs and other computing devices by wireless networks. Bluetooth is another technology currently being explored that allows up to eight devices to be connected by one universal short-range radio link. But there are many limitations and challenges when it comes to using mobile devices. The major issues are how to reduce the cost of using mobile devices further and how to improve the quality of service for transmitting voice and data. More work is also needed in the areas of system delays, mobility pattern determination, simple authentication schemes, efficient power control, effective channel allocation, routing-table size, and path stability in ad hoc networks. The future looks promising, and the seamless web in the sky may soon be reality.

Dharma P. Agrawal

See also Embedded Systems; Ubiquitous Computing

FURTHER READING

Agrawal, D. P., & Zeng, Q-A. (2003) *Introduction to wireless and mobile systems.* Pacific Grove, CA: Brooks/Cole-Thompson Learning.

Brain, M., & Tyson, J. (1998–2003). How cell phones work. Retrieved July 28, 2003, from http://electronics.howstuffworks.com/cell-phone.htm

IEEE 802.15 Working Group for Personal Area Networks. Retrieved February 25, 2004, from http://grouper.ieee.org/groups/802/15/

IEEE 802.11 Working Group for Wireless Local Area Networks. Retrieved February 25, 2004, from http://grouper.ieee.org/groups/802/11/

MOSAIC

Mosaic was the first widely used World Wide Web browser and the immediate ancestor of the two browsers that propelled the Web to immense popularity: Netscape Navigator and Internet Explorer. However, Mosaic was by no means the first Web browser, and the credit for its development is still debated by historians and participants alike. In a sense Mosaic was the last of the experimental browsers, created by an individual or small groups of enthusiasts, and subsequent browsers were created by well-organized teams in commercial software corporations. Thus, Mosaic represents two important transitions: the transition from individual creativity to corporate production and the emergence of the Web itself.

During the years between the development of the first computer networks in the 1960s and the birth of the Web, a number of software developments presaged what was to come. Telnet was software that allowed a person working at one computer to access materials stored on another, and programs such as Archie and Gopher facilitated finding and copying files. File transfer protocol (FTP) programs moved files from one computer to another, given that the user knew the exact Internet address and password. Several FTP client programs, such as CuteFTP, WS_FTP, FTP Voyager, and Fetch, are still in use. These are small programs that function like the file transfer parts of a personal computer's operating system. Typically, two windows show lists of the directories and files on the two computers, and a file can be copied in either direction by selecting it and either clicking an arrow or dragging and dropping the name of the file to its destination. To use the file, more effort is required: first opening the correct software, then locating the directory in which the FTP client saved the file, and then opening it. The chief technical advantages of Web browsers are that they make it much easier to find desired material, leap almost imperceptibly from one computer to another, and automatically open the files.

The first real Web browser (with the server software to feed it) was created by Tim Berners-Lee in 1990 at the CERN high-energy physics laboratories near Geneva, Switzerland. He called the browser simply "World Wide Web," but that phrase soon took on a wider meaning, and the first browser itself is known as "Nexus." Berners-Lee wrote it originally for the NeXT computer, an advanced but commercially unsuccessful personal computer with its own operating system, and soon other people began writing their own browsers for other kinds of computers. All this work was done by individuals, often working on their own time, and they freely shared ideas and programming code. In 1991 Nicola Pellow programmed a browser that could be run on essentially any computer or terminal, but it lacked many of the features people want from a browser because one full-featured browser could not run on many kinds of hardware or operating systems. College students in Finland created Erwise, and Pei Wei created Viola, two browsers for X-Window UNIX operating systems that ran on workstations and some large computers. Lou Montulli created Lynx, which was soon developed by others for a variety of computers. During the 1992–1993 Christmas holiday, University of Illinois student Marc Andreessen wrote the first version of Mosaic.

NCSA

The University of Illinois at Urbana-Champaign has been noted for its cutting-edge work with computers since the 1950s. Its National Center for Supercomputing Applications (NCSA), funded by the National Science Foundation and other organizations, has been a leader in computation for the sciences, especially physics, and it really had no mandate for developing consumer software. Thus, some ambiguity exists concerning to what extent the development of Mosaic was a natural outgrowth of the work of the NCSA versus a bootleg project by some students who happened to be employed by NCSA. Legal battles in the commercialization of Mosaic have further obscured the historical appraisal. With the help of a handful of student friends and a certain amount of encouragement from NCSA leadership, Andreessen had soon produced versions of Mosaic for three major types of computer systems that were then popular: UNIX, Microsoft Windows, and Macintosh.

Thus, the first obvious difference between Mosaic and the original Berners-Lee browser was that Mosaic worked on three popular operating systems, rather than on the rare NeXT system. Furthermore, whereas UNIX was chiefly used by relatively large machines owned by corporations and scientific organizations, Windows and Macintosh were popular with consumers and the rank-and-file of academic computer users. Mosaic could be downloaded for free from the NCSA's website, installed almost instantly, and operated easily with a few point-and-click motions with the user's mouse—without requiring technical training.

Even Nexus had been able to handle images, but it opened them in their own windows, whereas Mosaic could combine text and pictures on the same page. Adding images was not simply a matter of programming the browser, but rather required Andreessen to add a new "tag" to the hypertext markup language (HTML) in which webpages are coded. HTML has a standard set of codes called "tags" inserted into the text inside angle brackets. For example <P> marks the beginning of a new paragraph, and </P> marks its end. Berners-Lee had embedded links in pages with the anchor tag. For example, if the following is placed in an HTML document, only the "NCSA" will be visible:

<A HREF="http://www.ncsa.uiuc.edu">NCSA</A>.

Clicking on "NCSA" will take a user to the NCSA website. Andreessen's image tag looks like this:

<IMG SRC="delta.gif" WIDTH=117 HEIGHT=88 ALT="delta">.

None of that will be visible, but if an image is called "delta.gif" in the active directory that the browser is pointed at, the image tag will display it, 117 pixels wide and 88 pixels high. If the browser cannot display the image itself, it will display the word "delta" instead.

Ten Million Copies

Mosaic was far from perfect—somewhat slow in operation and prone to crash because of bugs that the student programmers had not yet located—but it really launched the explosion of the Web that occurred during the 1990s. An estimated 10 million copies of Mosaic had been distributed by the end of 1994. Andreessen graduated and moved to California, where he met computer entrepreneur Jim Clark. The two quickly founded Mosaic Communications, recruited some of Andreessen's student friends from Illinois, and produced from scratch a new browser, Netscape Navigator. Simultaneously, the NCSA began selling licenses allowing other companies to develop Mosaic. For a time a company called "Spyglass" took charge of the licensing, and one of the licensees was Microsoft, which came out with Internet Explorer. The NCSA forced Andreessen and Clark to give up the "Mosaic" name, and a series of legal and commercial battles ensued between the newly named Netscape and Microsoft for dominance not only in the browser market but also in the market of commercial server software for websites.

Anyone who has used all three browsers knows they are close cousins, even fundamentally the same. Some of the differences are quite superficial. For example, what Mosaic called a "hotlist" Netscape called "bookmarks," and Internet Explorer called "favorites." By whatever name, these are the links a user saves to visit again. The relevance for human-computer interaction is not just the interface that browsers offer to the Internet, but also the interactions among people and organizations that created Mosaic and its descendents. Neither CERN nor NCSA was really prepared to finish the revolution that some of their individual employees had begun, and both eventually let the Web go into the commercial sector. Their job was high-energy physics and scientific supercomputing. It is worth noting, however, that the existence of these two first-rate scientific organizations provided the technological and intellectual infrastructure that allowed creative people to innovate in unexpected directions. Mosaic was the creation of Andreessen and other individual enthusiasts, working within a tiny social movement launched by Berners-Lee, and it might never have been created intentionally by a government-sponsored scientific bureaucracy or by a commercial corporation.

William Sims Bainbridge

See also Browsers; Website Design

FURTHER READING

Berners-Lee, T., & Fischetti, M. (1999). *Weaving the Web*. New York: HarperCollins.

Clark, J., & Edwards, O. (1999). *Netscape time*. New York: St. Martin's Press.

Cusumano, M. A., & Yoffie, D. B. (1998). *Competing on Internet time*. New York: Free Press.

Gillies, J., & Cailliau, R. (2000). *How the Web was born*. Oxford, UK: Oxford University Press.

Leone, A. O., & Ticca, A. (1994). Towards a user environment integrating hypermedia browsers, scientific visualization programs and numerical simulation programs. *Proceedings of the Workshop on Advanced Visual Interfaces* (pp. 234–236). New York: Association for Computing Machinery.

MOTION CAPTURE AND RECOGNITION

The field of motion capture and recognition includes methods, chiefly employed in video analysis, graphical animation, and surveillance, for capturing, tracking, representing, composing, analyzing, and recognizing various modes of human motion. Human motion can have many forms and purposes. People move parts of their bodies to perform various activities, to activate devices, to communicate, to express their feelings, for exercise, and for many other reasons. Human motion analysis is an important ingredient in fields as numerous and diverse as kinesiology (the study of human anatomy, physiology, and the mechanics of body motion), computer vision, orthopedics, biomechanics, rehabilitative procedures, ergonomic research, evaluations of physical job tasks, worker training, anthropology, cultural studies, sign language, athletic analysis, and sports medicine. In addition, choreography, gymnastics, figure skating, ethnic folklore studies, and behavioral studies may also require capture, measurement, analysis, representation, and classification of human motion.

Analyzing Human Motion

To analyze human motion one needs detailed information on the movements of all the body parts involved in the motion. The human body is represented by a skeletal model of all the bones connected by the joints. Thus, motion of body parts such as arms, legs, or fingers can be described as motion of the corresponding skeletal part. Since every bone is connected to another bone by a flexible joint, the skeletal structure can be represented by a tree graph, with the tree's nodes representing joints and the tree's bones corresponding to arcs. The root of the tree is usually defined as the sacrum (or sacroiliac joint)—the five fused bones at the bottom of the vertebral column that are connected to the pelvis. The pose in three-dimensional space of any bone can be decomposed into position and orientation. Correspondingly, movement of any bone can be described as translation plus rotation. But since all the bones are connected to one another by flexible joints, their translations are not independent; the translation of each is influenced by the translation of the bone that precedes it in the tree structure. Hence, the only independent translation is the root's translation. The independent poses and motions of all the other parts of the body are determined entirely by their three-dimensional angular orientations (the angles of rotation around the 3 axes xyz, also known as Euler angles) and angular velocities (rates of rotation around the 3 axes). Such a representation is employed by the Virtual Reality Modeling Language (VRML) and also used by common graphics libraries such as OpenGL. OpenGL and VRML are employed for computer animation of avatars (animated representations of people) and other humanlike creatures.

VRML and its extensions are also incorporated in the international video compression standard, MPEG-4. The MPEG-4 standard defines a toolbox of advanced compression algorithms for audio and visual information and also supports hybrid coding of combinations of audio sources, graphics, and video together with synthetic-animated (computer-generated) scenes. The skeletal model represents only body parts that correspond to a part of the skeleton. Flexible body parts, especially face parts such as lips, cheeks, or eyebrows, are usually modeled by a flexible model composed of a mesh of muscles hinged on an underlying support. The body and face animation tools that are included in the MPEG-4 standard allow for sending parameters that can define, calibrate, and animate synthetic faces and bodies. There are also model-independent tools that make possible the coding of lip and facial configurations that correspond to speech phonemes. These facial configurations are called visemes—visual correspondents to phonemes. Use of tools that code visemes makes it possible to animate speech as well as facial expressions and motions provided by the muscular facial model.

Motion Capture for Animation

Motion capture (or mocap) is the means whereby a sequence of sampled translations and rotations of body parts can be obtained. Sampling is required for a digital representation of actual human motion, which is continuous. The sampling rate determines the temporal resolution of the sequence (the greater the sampling rate, the higher the temporal resolution). The sequence data is usually used for motion analysis or animation. In animation, the sequence data is mapped onto the corresponding body parts of the animated character. Thus, mapping allows animators to endow any imaginary creature that has a humanlike body configuration with human motion characteristics.

Because mocap provides animators with data from actual human movements, animation based on mocap data has definite advantages over traditional, hand-drawn animation. Motion in mocap-based animation is more natural and smoother. Hand-drawn animation of motion relies on a method known as keyframing. In keyframing, video that usually contains a dense sequence of frames (images) is represented by a sparse sequence of images called keyframes. For a good motion representation, the keyframes must capture the instants where the motion of any body part changes noticeably either in direction or in velocity. In hand-drawn animation, the artist draws only those keyframes, and the rest of the frames are created by an interpolation process. A popular interpolation method is based on three-dimensional cubic splines. (A spline is curve that is guided by a set of control points.) Such splines have the advantage that they generate smooth trajectories that pass exactly through the body part positions defined by the keyframes. Unfortunately, there are often too few keyframes, or the keyframes may not be sufficiently accurate, so the resulting animation is frequently characterized by jerky motion. Mocap minimizes that problem, especially when animators use software tools that enable blending of several mocap takes.

Motion Capture in Other Fields

Motion capture is also useful in sports science, biomechanics, ergonomics, orthopedics and rehabilitation, and entertainment, and motion recognition is important for video analysis in the field of computer vision. Sports scientists are investigating the utility of real-time feedback in training athletes. The performance of these athletes can be improved significantly if their current methods of performing various exercises is measured and compared with an ideal model. The differences between the model and the athletes' actual motion can be fed back as real-time instructions delivered to the athletes while they are performing the exercises.

In biomechanics, mechanical physical models of the body perform various motions. Accurate three-dimensional measurement of these motions is essential in such research. Similarly, in orthopedics and rehabilitation, it is necessary to measure a patient's motion in order to diagnose motion disorders. Ergonomics examines people's physical negotiation of their workplace and home, as well as their use of various means of transportation and how they operate various tools (for example, a computer keyboard). Motion capture is useful in evaluating ergonomic parameters. In the entertainment industry, electronic and computer games rely on mocap for lifelike animation.

Systems for Capturing and Tracking Human Motion

There are three major classes of systems for capturing and tracking human motion: inside-in systems, inside-out systems, and outside-in systems.

Inside-In Systems

Inside-in systems are systems that employ motion measurement devices that are attached to the body. Examples of inside-in systems are gloves or overall suits equipped with devices that can measure the relative orientation between various body parts. Among the devices that can measure relative orientation are piezo-resistive flex sensors, fiber optic flexes, potentiometers, shaft encoders, short-range mutual inductance devices, electromyographic devices (instruments that measure muscular contractions) and electro-oculographic devices (for measuring eye movement). Most of these devices are quite small and do not require connection to an external reference source. They therefore provide the wearer with almost unlimited space in which to move and perform. On the other hand, because such systems are not connected to any external reference source, they supply only body-centered motion measurements. This is not a major obstacle since one can always augment an inside-in system with an inside-out device that is capable of measuring the location and orientation of some central body part relative to the world coordinate system. Another disadvantage of inside-in systems is that their measurement devices are considered obtrusive, being attached directly to the body. Sometimes the means by which the devices are attached limits or affects the subject's natural motions.

Inside-Out Systems

Inside-out measurement systems use sensors attached to body parts that sense some kind of externally generated or natural field, such as an electromagnetic field. Inside-out systems also use inertial sensors that measure acceleration or position relative to the global coordinate system. One disadvantage of inside-out systems is that the external fields they rely on can be sensitive to the environment. Electromagnetic-based systems, for example, are quite sensitive to the presence of metal in the vicinity. In addition, inside-out systems are operational only within the very limited range of the external field. Also, sensors that measure external fields are usually quite bulky, and therefore can be attached only to large body parts that will not be significantly influenced by the sensors' mass. The sensors also often require more computations to translate their raw data into meaningful information, a fact that may negatively affect their tracking performance in real time. Examples of inside-out natural field sensors are accelerometers, various kinds of compasses, and inclinometers. Artificial-source inside-out sensors include electromagnetic-phase or amplitude sensors, acoustic-phase and amplitude sensors, and global-positioning sensors. The difference between an artificial and natural field is in the originating source. For example, global positioning sensors use radio waves emitted from satellites, which is an artificial man-made source. On the other hand, inclinometers employ the gravitational field of the globe, which is a natural source.

Outside-In Systems

Outside-in tracking systems use markers, light sources, or other sources such as electromagnetic emission, attached to the body. The sensors are usu-ally external (such as television cameras). Since the markers are usually small, the outside-in systems are considered minimally obtrusive. An optical system that measures the orientation of the pupil of the eye is one example of an outside-in system. Optical systems suffer from occlusion (that is, they cannot work if something comes between the marker and the external sensor) and therefore can work only in a very limited setting. In addition, the stereo cameras or other optical measurement systems that are necessary to measure the locations of the markers are quite expensive and require intensive computation capabilities to operate in real-time environments. Examples of outside-in systems that use artificial, man made emission sources are systems that use reflective markers and systems that use LED (light-emitting diode) markers. Outside-in systems that rely on natural field sources such as daylight, are actually exploiting the appearances of body parts and their shadows or their silhouettes. The human tracking and activity recognition systems in video analysis and computer vision fall into this category.

Video Analysis

Video analysis is an active research area in computer vision. Since most videos and movies focus primarily on humans and human actions, video analysis research is chiefly interested in human motion analysis. We differentiate between actions, which we define as brief motions of body parts, and activities, which we define as a sequence of actions. For example, one step would be considered an action, whereas a series of steps—walking—is an activity. Visual human motion analysis is useful in applications such as security surveillance. Several approaches to activity recognition have been reported in the literature; most of the literature, however, focuses on recognition of relatively simple human actions or gestures, such as gestures of greeting and farewell, various hand gestures, or American Sign Language. Only a few works attempt to extend the analysis to more complex activities.

"The Visual Analysis of Human Movement: A Survey," published in 1999 in *Computer Vision and Image Understanding* and written by the computer scientist Dariu Gavrila, is an excellent reference that reports the different methodologies for visual analysis of human movement. Gavrila groups the methodologies into two-dimensional approaches with or without explicit shape models, and three-dimensional approaches. The two-dimensional approach without explicit shape models describes human movement in terms of simple low-level two-dimensional features instead of recovering the full three-dimensional pose. The two-dimensional approach uses explicit shape models to segment, track, and label body parts. The third approach attempts to recover the three-dimensional poses over time.

In 2001, the scientists Thomas Moeslund and Erik Granum surveyed various approaches to computer-vision-based human motion capture and described four phases in human motion capture: initialization, tracking, pose estimation, and recognition. Human motion recognition is classified into static and dynamic recognition. Static recognition relies on spatial data, analyzed one frame at a time, while dynamic recognition uses the temporal characteristics of the action.

Jezekiel Ben-Arie and his colleagues use an approach based on indexing and sequencing that combines the static and dynamic recognition approaches. By observing just a few frames of a video, one can identify the activity that takes place in a video sequence. The basic premise behind this method is that activities can be positively identified from a sparsely sampled sequence of few body poses, acquired from videos. In this approach, activities are represented by a set of pose and velocity vectors for the major body parts (hands, legs, and torso) that are stored separately. This method provides robust recognition of a large set of complex activities even in conditions of varying speed, which is a frequent feature of human activities. In addition, the method is quite robust in situations of partial occlusion, since each body part can be indexed separately.

Ismail Haritaoglu, David Harwood, and Larry Davis implemented a system for human tracking and activity recognition in which the activity recognition is based mainly on analysis of detected human silhouettes. This system, which is especially suited for surveillance, classifies human poses in each frame into one out of four main poses (standing, sitting, crawling or bending, and lying down) and one out of three view of the subject (front or back, left side,

and right side). Activities are monitored by checking the pose changes over time. Aaron Bobick and James Davis were able to recognize human activity by matching temporal templates against stored views of known actions.

Future Outlook

The field of human motion capture and animation is moving toward complete animation of movies and video games. Movies that today have only one or two animated characters could be entirely animated in the future. Animated movie stars could replace today's human actors. In the area of motion recognition, the trend is to improve the robustness of the detection and recognition algorithms, which currently are far from being fully automated. Multimodal supervision camera networks could be installed in many public sites to prevent violence and crime.

Jezekiel Ben-Arie

See also Eye Tracking; Video

FURTHER READING

Ben-Arie, J., Wang, Z., Pandit, P., & Rajaram, S. (2002). Human activity recognition using multidimensional indexing. *IEEE Transactions on Pattern Analysis and Machine Intelligence, 24*(8), 1091–1104.

Bobick, A. F., & Davis, J. W. (1996, August). An appearance-based representation of action. Paper presented at the Thirteenth International Conference on Pattern Recognition, Vienna, Austria. Retrieved August 19, 2003, from http://www.cis.ohio-state.edu/~jwdavis/Publications/TR-369.pdf

Bobick, A. F., & Davis, J. W. (2001, March). The recognition of human movement using temporal templates. IEEE Transactions on Pattern Analysis and Machine Intelligence, 23(3), 257–267.

Fujiyoshi, H., & Lipton, A. J. (1998, October). Real-time human motion analysis by image skeletonization. Paper presented at the Fourth IEEE Workshop on Applications of Computer Vision, Princeton, New Jersey. Retrieved August 19, 2003, from http://www.dcs.ex.ac.uk/people/wangjunl/fujiyoshi_hironobu_1998_1.pdf

Galata, A., Johnson, N., & Hogg, D. (2001). Learning variable-length Markov models of behavior. Computer Vision and Image Understanding, 81(3), 398–413.

Gavrila, D. M. (1999). The visual analysis of human movement: A survey. Computer Vision and Image Understanding, 73(1), 82–98.

Haritaoglu, I., Harwood, D., & Davis, L. S. (2000, August). W4: Real-time surveillance of people and their activities. IEEE Transactions on Pattern Analysis and Machine Intelligence, 22(8), 809–830.

Ivanov, Y. A., & Bobick, A. F. (2000, August). Recognition of visual activities and interactions by stochastic parsing. *IEEE Transactions on Pattern Analysis and Machine Intelligence, 22*(8), 852–871.

Moeslund, T. B., & Granum, E. (2001, March). A survey of computer vision-based human motion capture. *Computer Vision and Image Understanding, 82*(3), 231–268.

Mulder, A. (1994, July). Human movement tracking technology. Retrieved August 19, 2003, from http://www.cs.sfu.ca/people/ResearchStaff/amulder/personal/vmi/HMTT.pub.html#mary

Polana, R., & Nelson, R. (1994). Recognizing activities. In Proceedings of the IEEE Conf. on Computer Vision and Pattern Recognition (pp. 815–818) Seattle, WA.

Rabiner, L. R., & Juang, B. H. (1986,). An introduction to hidden Markov models. IEEE ASSP Magazine, 3(1), 4–16.

Schlenzig, J., Hunter, E., & Jain, R. (1994). recursive identfication of gesture inputs using hidden Markov models. In Proceedings of the second IEEE workshop on Applications of Computer Vision (pp. 187–194). Pacific Grove, CA.

Yamato, J., Ohya, J., & Ishii, K. (1993). Recognizing human action in time-sequential images using hidden Markov models. Transactions of the Institute of Electronics, Information and Communication Engineers, J76D-II(12), 2556–2563.

Yang, M.-H., & Ahuja, N. (1999, June). Recognizing hand gesture using motion trajectories. Paper presented at the *IEEE Conference on Computer Vision and Pattern Recognition*, Ft. Collins, CO. Retrieved August 19, 2003, from http://vision.ai.uiuc.edu/mhyang/papers/cvpr99.pdf

MOUSE

The design of human input, which is a critical part of any human-computer interaction system, should be inseparable from the design of the output (display) components and from the interaction techniques between input and output. Although this article focuses on the extreme end of input, a good input device has to be compatible with the entire interactive system.

Origins and Development of the Computer Mouse

The most common input device used today is the computer mouse. The invention of the mouse is commonly credited to Douglas Engelbart and his colleagues at the Stanford Research Institute in Menlo Park, California, who pioneered interactive computing with their online system NLS. In a legendary live public demonstration of NLS in 1968 at the Fall Joint Computer Conference in San Francisco, Engelbart and his colleagues demonstrated the mouse, along with hypertext, object addressing and dynamic file linking, shared-screen collaboration with audio and video interface, and many other innovations.

There are various possible alternatives to the mouse, including touch screens, styli and tablets, joysticks, and trackballs. Various studies have compared the relative merits of these devices. The consensus of that literature is that for interacting with graphical user interfaces (GUI) on desktop computers, the mouse serves most users well. The mouse is more direct and more natural than a trackball or a rate-controlled joystick, and less fatiguing than a touch screen operated by a finger or a stylus. The mouse also enables well-coordinated actions between movement of the cursor and the

It was nicknamed the mouse because the tail came out the end.

Douglas Engelbart

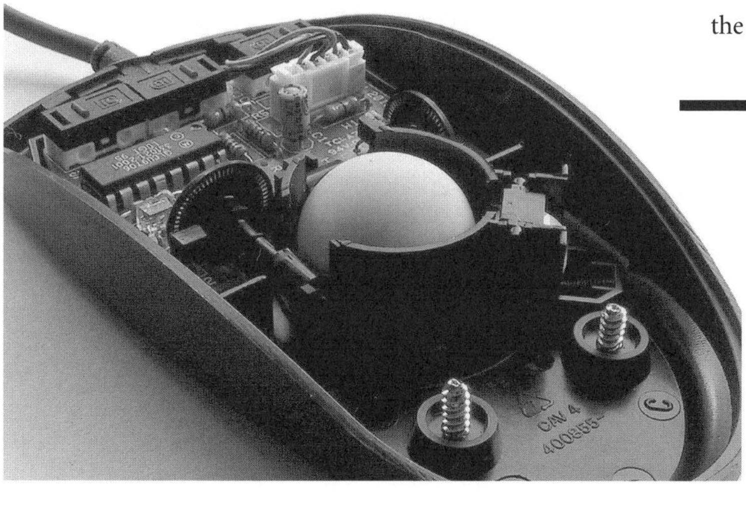

FIGURE 1. *The inside of a typical mechanical mouse*

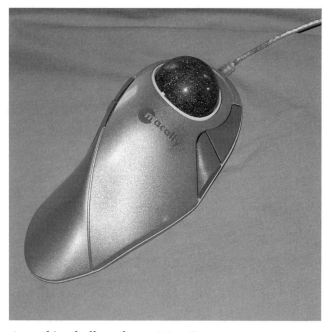

A tracking ball used on a Mac G4 computer. Photo courtesy of Mark Schane Lydon.

selection of an object by button clicks, which is a challenge for many other devices.

The underlying technology for the mouse evolved over many generations. Engelbart and his colleagues' mouse prototype had two wheels, one to sense the horizontal movements of the mouse and one to sense its vertical movements. One lasting successful design uses a rolling ball to drive two orthogonal optical encoders for two-dimensional movements. (Figure 1 shows the inside of a mouse with this type of sensing mechanism.) Many design and manufacturing details, such as the size, weight, and location of the ball in the mouse body, affect the quality of use.

A mouse is, in fact, a digital computer in itself, equipped with a processor and firmware programs that compute the x y displacement in "mickies" based on the number of impulses measured by the optical encoders. The mickies are periodically sent to a host computer in packets based on such standards as PS/2 mouse/keyboard protocol or the (Universal Serial Bus (USB) Human Interface Device (HID) protocol.

A more recent technological advancement is the use of a small, high frequency optical sensor (camera) embedded at the bottom of the mouse to measure the mouse's movement speed by image correlation. Such

a solid state design without moving parts is not only less susceptible to the dust and debris that tend to be picked up by a rolling ball, but also simpler in assembly complexity. Another recent change is the "tailless" mouse that uses wireless communication rather than a cable to connect the mouse with a computer.

The shape and size of a mouse are critical to its usability, and views on the design principles that should guide the choice of these dimensions differ. One view emphasizes the ergonomic design of mice and emphasizes the importance of having the form fit the shape of the hand and provide good support to it. The alternative theory emphasizes the need of the user to manipulate the mouse with different fingers and hand postures with dexterity and flexibility and views a locked-in hand shape as a disadvantage. In practice, visually interesting mouse shapes that have a strong consumer appeal may dominate design and purchase decisions.

Types of Multiple Input

The mouse became the de facto standard input device in an era when the operation of the WIMP (windows, icons, menus, and pointer) interface was conceived as completely serial, driven by a single stream of input.

Multi-Stream Input

Today a computer user is no longer limited to a single input stream. In the past few years, document scrolling has been increasingly operated by a dedicated stream of input, such as a separate track wheel (wheel mouse) or a miniature force-sensing joystick embedded on the top of a mouse.

Multi-Hand Input

A more advanced form of multi-stream input should be operated by both hands, which may enable a higher degree of efficiency both physically and cognitively. For example, with two hands, each grabbing a corner of a graphical object, a user would be able to move, rotate, and resize it simultaneously, rather than alternating between these actions by mode switching, as is done in today's common interfaces. An influential theory for designing two-handed input is the bimanual manipulation theory developed in 1987 by

Yves Guiard at the University of the Mediterranean in France. Briefly, Guiard's theory views our two hands as cooperative but asymmetrical in function. The non-dominant hand tends to initiate action, operate at a macro scale, and set the frame of reference, while the dominant hand tends to operate on a finer scale and complete the operation within the frame of references. A typical example is hammering: The non-dominant hand holds the nail and the dominant hand operates the hammer cooperatively, with reference to the non-dominant hand.

Multiple-Degrees-of-Freedom Input

For three-dimensional interfaces such as an immersive or a desktop virtual reality system, users need at least 6 degrees of freedom to be able to fully manipulate an object (x, y, z, pitch, yaw, roll). Various 6 DOF devices have been developed, from free-moving (in the air) devices that are typically based on electromagnetic sensors relative to a base, to stationary force-sensitive devices.

Mobile Input Devices

As computing moves beyond the desktop paradigm, input devices that could serve as alternatives to the mouse have been sought. After a period of experimentation with the trackball and other alternatives, touchpads and force-sensitive pointing sticks embedded in the keyboard became the most widely used input devices in laptop computers. The most commonly used touchpads detect the electrical capacitance change under the fingertip. A force-sensitive stick transfers finger pressure to two pairs of strain gauge at the base of the stick, which are then used to measure the two-dimensional force vector applied by the fingertip. The force vector typically drives a mouse cursor by a nonlinear force to speed transfer function.

A pen (stylus) is a natural input device. In fact, light pens were used as the primary input device on graphic terminals before the mouse became popular. A pen offers greater dexterity than the mouse, enabling users to draw and write, but the unsupported arm movements required to use a stylus on a vertical screen become tiresome quickly. Another subtle but important weakness of the stylus has to do with device acquisition. A mouse (or a touchpad or an embedded miniature joystick) stays where it is left and can be easily reacquired by the hand. This is not true with a stylus. If the user has to frequently switch back and forth between typing on a keyboard and pointing with a stylus, device (re)acquisition becomes a hindrance. In fact, the pointing stick integrated between the keys is more convenient than the mouse in this regard. For handheld devices or tablet PCs, the stylus is used to drive most if not all operations, hence little device switching is needed.

Many of today's usability issues with pen-based interfaces have resulted from transplanting existing desktop GUI interfaces to mobile forms—for

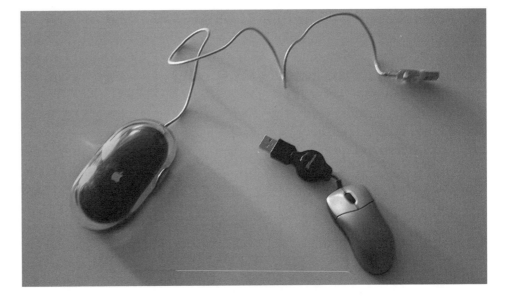

Two distinctly different mouse styles, c. 2003: a Macintosh mouse at left, and a PC mouse on the right.
Photo courtesy of Jeff Potter.

example, in a user's hand, a stylus may obscure the very object the user needs to look at. There have been various successful designs of interaction techniques particularly suited for pen-based interactions. One example is "Marking menus," which uses consistent pen gesture marks defined on nested pie menus that a novice can gesture by looking at the menu but an experienced user can gesture by recall. The "Shorthand Aided Rapid Keyboard" (SHARK) system accommodates novice and experienced users in a similar way: Users can tap or trace letters on a graphical keyboard by looking at the keyboard, and more experienced users can simply recall the same pattern from memory and write the pattern of a word, fully taking advantage of a pen.

Sensing and Contextual Input

It is expected that computers will take more input from sensors of various kinds. Some of these sensors will probably be integrated into the mouse. For example, a mouse can be made "touch sensitive," which means it can display or hide crowding GUI widgets, depending on whether or not a user's hand is on the mouse. With sensors, computers will be able to take various contextual inputs, such as user presence, posture, physiological variables (heart rate, galvanic skin conductance, EMG, and so on), or eye gaze. A critical research challenge is to make computer systems take appropriate actions that help users to achieve their goals based on these contextual inputs.

For example, a user's eye gaze has long been explored as a source of input, but two fundamental limitations have to be overcome before it can be used. First, eye-gaze accuracy is probably limited to one visual degree. Second, the eye, whose movement is driven by both the mind and the scene, is not a natural control organ, unlike the hand. One approach to overcome these limitations is the MAGIC (Manual Acquisition with Gaze Initiated Cursor) system, which takes advantage of the eye-gaze information implicitly, without resolving to conscious and unnatural eye control. When an input device is touched, the mouse cursor appears at the location where the eye is gazing on the screen, which reduces the need to make large movements by hand to move the cursor.

Models and Theories

Work on computer input as a human-computer interaction research area has benefited from many basic scientific instruments such as theories, models, taxonomies, and controlled experimentations and observations. The most frequently used model for input research is Fitts's law, typically expressed as follows:

$$T = a + b \log_2\left(\frac{D + W}{W}\right) \ (1)$$

where T is the expected movement time; D and W are target distance and size respectively, and a and b are empirically determined constants that can serve as performance measurements of the input system used. a indicates the reaction time independent of target location and size; b indicates the time increase rate as the index of difficulty (ID) of the task increases. $ID = \log_2 (D/W + 1)$ takes the unit of bit, analogous to information in communication systems. With the use of Fitts's law, research results (a and b) can be stated and generalized beyond the specific task parameters used in the experiments for testing input performance, enabling a more systematic and more objective understanding of a device's effectiveness.

Fitts's law, particularly suited for characterizing pointing tasks, can be viewed as one of the laws of action. Recently similar laws of actions have been studied in other human-computer interaction tasks such as pen stroking (law of crossing) and path steering on the computer screen. To deal with the perplexing diversity of potential input devices, researchers have often used taxonomies to classify the design space of an input device.

There are also various theoretical views on computer input. Guiard's theory of bimanual manipulation has guided designs for two-handed input systems, and Buxton's doctrine on facilitating novice-to-expert transition with common input pattern is embodied in such methods as marking menus and the SHARK text input system. Jacob and Silbert's theory on the perceptual structure of input states that the integration or separation of different degrees of freedom in input should match those of human perception. The control order compatibility principle emphasizes that the transfer function, from sensing to display, varying from zero-order position control to first order rate control to higher order control functions, has to be compatible with the mechanical properties of the device. For example, only a self-centering device like an isometric device and elastic joystick can function effectively as a rate control.

Shumin Zhai

See also Keyboards

FURTHER READING

Accot, J., & Zhai, S. (1997). Beyond Fitts' Law: Models for trajectory-based HCI tasks. In *Proceedings of CHI 1997: ACM Conference on Human Factors in Computing Systems* (pp. 295–302).

Accot, J., & Zhai, S. (2002). More than dotting the i's—Foundations for crossing-based interfaces. In *Proceedings of CHI 2002: ACM Conference on Human Factors in Computing Systems, CHI Letters 4(1)*, 73–80.

Bier, E. A., Stone, M. C., Pier, K., Buxton, W., & DeRose, T. D. (1993). Toolglass and magic lenses: The see-through interface. In *Proceedings of SIGGRAPH 93* (pp. 73–80).

Buxton, W. (1986). There is more to interaction than meets the eye: Some issues in manual input. In D. A. Norman & S. W. Draper (Eds.), *User Centered System Design* (pp. 319–337). Hillsdale, NJ: Erlbaum.

Buxton, W., Billinghurst , M., Guiard, Y., Sellen, A., & Zhai, S. (1994/2002). *Human input to computer systems: Theories, techniques and technology* (book manuscript). Retrieved April 6, 2004, from http://www.billbuxton.com/inputManuscript.html

Card, S. K., English, W. K., & Burr, B. J. (1978). Evaluation of mouse, rate controlled isometric joystick, step keys and text keys for text selection on a CRT. *Ergonomics, 21*, 601–613.

Card, S. K., Mackinlay, J. D., & Robertson, G. G. (1991). A morphological analysis of the design space of input devices. *ACM Transactions on Information Systems, 9(2)*, 99–122.

Fitts, P. M. (1954). The information capacity of the human motor system in controlling the amplitude of movement. *Journal of Experimental Psychology, 47*, 381–391.

Guiard, Y. (1987). Asymmetric division of labor in human skilled bimanual action: The kinematic chain as a model. *Journal of Motor Behavior, 19(4)*, 486–517.

Hinckley, K., Cutrell, E., Bathiche, S., & Muss, T. (2002). Quantitative analysis of scrolling techniques. In *Proceedings of CHI 2002: ACM Conference on Human Factors in Computing Systems* (pp. 65–72).

Hinckley, K., & Sinclair, M. (1999). Touch-sensitive input device. In *Proceedings of CHI'99: ACM Conference in Human Factors in Computing Systems* (pp. 223–230).

Jacob, R. J. K. (1991). The use of eye movements in human-computer interaction techniques: What you look at is what you get. *ACM Transactions on Information Systems, 9(3)*, 152–169.

Jacob, R. J. K., & Sibert, L. E. (1992). The perceptual structure of multidimensional input device selection. In *Proceedings of CHI'92: ACM Conference on Human Factors in Computing Systems* (pp. 211–218).

Kurtenbach, G., Sellen, A., & Buxton, W. (1993). An empirical evaluation of some articulatory and cognitive aspects of "marking menus." *Human Computer Interaction, 8(1)*, 1–23.

Leganchuk, A., Zhai, S., & Buxton, W. (1998). Manual and cognitive benefits of two-handed input: An experimental study. *ACM Transactions on Computer-Human Interaction, 5(4)*, 326–359.

Rutledge, J., & Selker, T. (1990). Force-to-motion functions for pointing. In *Proceedings of Human-Computer Interaction—INTERACT'90* (pp. 701–705).

Zhai, S. (1995). *Human performance in six degree of freedom input control*. Unpublished doctoral dissertation, University of Toronto.

Zhai, S. (1998). User performance in relation to 3D input device design. *Computer Graphics, 32(4)*, 50–54.

Zhai, S., Kristensson, P.-O., & Smith, B. A. (in press). In search of effective text input interfaces for off the desktop computing. *Interacting with Computers, 16(3)*.

Zhai, S., Morimoto, C., & Ihde, S. (1999). Manual and gaze input cascaded (MAGIC) pointing. In *Proceedings of CHI'99: ACM Conference on Human Factors in Computing Systems* (pp. 246–253).

Zhai, S., & Smith, B. A. (1999). An experimental study of document scrolling methods. *IBM Systems Journal, 38(4)*, 642–651.

MOVIES

Motion pictures are a medium for popularizing concepts of human-computer interaction because they can vividly show people using the machines. They may also inspire engineers who are developing new kinds of interface or computing environments. Films have depicted human interaction with stationary computers for more than half a century and with the mobile computers that we call robots for decades longer than that. Many movies concern the relationships between humans and machines, notably conflict on the psychological or societal level.

Interfaces

Motion pictures have depicted a vast variety of interfaces between humans and computers or robots. These interfaces reflect the actual state of technology of the decades in which the films were made and their makers' imagination of the future. In *Flash Gordon Conquers the Universe* (1940), walking-bomb robots, called annihilatons, are remotely controlled by flipping switches and turning knobs. The differential analyzer in *When Worlds Collide* (1951) is a mechanical computer, and therefore lacks

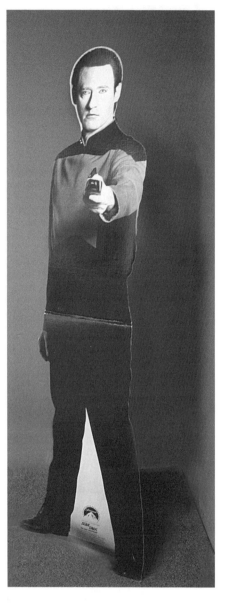

A life-size cutout of Data —an android who serves as a valued officer on the Starship Enterprise in Star Trek: The Next Generation— promotes a movie version of the television series.
Photo courtesy of Marcy Ross.

a keyboard or screen. The computer in *The Invisible Boy* (1957) hypnotizes the scientists with its huge array of flashing indicator lights.

Perhaps the most telling example of historically bounded interface technology is *Colossus: The Forbin Project* (1969). Scientists communicate with a vast supercomputer by means of keyboards at remote terminals, and the output is either very simple strings of characters on a cathode ray tube or fanfold printout paper. When the computer becomes conscious, however, its superior mind designs advanced input and output devices beyond the capacity of the scientists of the era to invent: computer vision, speech recognition, and speech synthesis.

A scene in *Star Trek IV: The Voyage Home* (1986) addresses the historical obsolescence of computer interfaces. The crew of the starship *Enterprise* has traveled back in time three hundred years to the mid-1980s. Engineer Scott needs to enter data into one of the original Macintosh computers. Scott begins speaking to the machine, as he would to a computer of his own era, but of course it does not respond. A twentieth-century engineer hands Scott the Macintosh's mouse, but Scott does not recognize what it is and speaks into it as one would into a microphone.

Innumerable conventional movies depict human-computer interaction as it actually occurred in the late twentieth century. For example, *The Net* (1995) concerns a woman who made her living debugging software and became the target of an immense conspiracy when a particular diskette with incriminating evidence came into her possession. Many scenes showed her beating on the keys and deftly maneuvering the mouse of a desktop personal computer, using e-mail, communicating with online friends in a chat room, surfing the Web, and accessing databases. Critical to the story were the facts that hitting the escape key makes a particular virus erase the hard disk and clicking an unobtrusive Greek letter pi on a website gives access to secret information. Thus, except for some unrealistic speech synthesis in the chat room, input was by conventional keyboard and mouse, and output was by screen and disk. The conspiracy was anything but conventional, however. It involved firewall software that was actually part of a protection racket and surreptitiously infiltrated companies' secret databases. The villains discredited the heroine by remotely changing her records in online databases, and they murdered her friend by altering his diagnosis and treatment plan in a hospital computer.

By the end of the twentieth century, films were depicting emerging interface technologies, notably augmented or virtual reality. The hero of *Johnny Mnemonic* (1995) is a data smuggler whose childhood memories have been removed to make room in his brain for hundreds of gigabytes of information, which he can access through a jack on the side of his skull. But when he wants to access databases across the Internet, he dons a virtual reality

(VR) headset and uses data gloves to give instructions by waving his hands deftly in the air. Similarly, the hero of *Minority Report* (2002) waves his hands in the air to control the police information system, but he does this in augmented reality, able to see both virtual data displays and his real surroundings simultaneously.

Environments

Today we are familiar with the cyberspace concept that Internet or an individual computer can be a rich environment to explore or even inhabit, and movies have played important roles in developing and popularizing this radical perspective. *Westworld* (1973) concerned three high-tech theme parks designed to give rich clients fantasy vacations in ancient Rome, the Middle Ages, or the Wild West. Although fanciful, these three realms were physically real and employed robots; they were not simulations in virtual reality.

It was thus a big step forward when *TRON* (1982) took place largely inside a computer, where programs were represented as people and the hardware architecture and operating system were depicted as abstract lines and surfaces in iridescent colors. Interestingly, five of the main characters exist both inside and outside the machine. The title character, TRON, is a program written by the character Alan Bradley and resembles him closely. When another human, Kevin Flynn, tries to access the main computer to get evidence about how his own program has been stolen, the intelligent central control program uses a laser device to scan Kevin into the computer, where he becomes his program, Clu. This film explores two metaphors, that every programmer invests something of himself in his code, and that artificial intelligences will take on some of the personal characteristics of their creators.

A decade after *TRON*, *The Lawnmower Man* (1992) showed two fairly realistic virtual-reality systems. The user wore a visor with headphones for sight and sound, controlled the computer with special gloves, and in one system experienced movement by lying prone on a moving table. A more capable system added a suit that provided temperature and pressure sensations, and the user was suspended in a gimbals that could turn in any direction.

Although the visual display was like that of a fast-paced video game, the scientist who invented the system had more grandiose aims. He hoped that virtual reality could enhance human intelligence, leading to a supernormal level of mental evolution. The film demonstrated that VR might have the power either to free or to enslave the human mind.

Some films have VR inside VR, and it is interesting to note whether they employ different user interfaces for the nested levels of reality. People in the outer level of reality in *The Thirteenth Floor* (1999) employ headsets (perhaps involving brain waves) to enter the first level of VR, whereas people inside that level use laser scanning to go one level deeper. Similarly, in *Existenz* (1999), characters use VR headsets to go in the first level, then genetically engineered symbiotes that connect to the user's spinal column for the next level. *Spy Kids 3-D: Game Over* (2003) draws the audience into the VR by having them wear red and green glasses that confer a three-dimensional effect on the scenes in which characters are fighting their way through a computer game. The audience's glasses are cardboard versions of the more elaborate glasses worn by characters in the film.

Many films about VR explore the question of how people can know whether or not their world is actually real. The hero of *The Matrix* (1999) initially has no idea that he lives in a computer simulation, and the later films in the trilogy, *The Matrix: Reloaded* (2003) and *The Matrix: Revolutions* (2003), imply that the real world is no more real than the simulation. When artificial-intelligence agents discover they and their world are not real in *The Thirteenth Floor*, they become demoralized. In both *Virtuosity* (1995) and *Code Hunter* (2002) one character tricks another into confusing VR and the real world. Virtual worlds logically have virtual inhabitants, and all characters in the movies are actually imaginary. The question is, what either the fictional characters or the audience are willing to treat as real in the context of the story or their lives.

Turing Tests

Blade Runner (1982) begins as a psychologist tests a garbage collector to see if he is really human. A question about a desperate tortoise lying on its back

A Personal Story—
HAL's Birthday Celebration

HAL was the human-like computer in A. C. Clarke's science fiction classic *2001: A Space Odyssey* and the subsequent movie. In the novel it was stated that HAL was born in Urbana, Illinois, on 12 January 1997. Thus, in 1997, the University of Illinois at Urbana-Champaign held a weeklong celebration of his birthday. Since winters are too harsh in Urbana, the celebration was held in March.

As the finale of the celebration, a two-hour gala was staged in a campus theater at the Krannert Center for the Performing Arts; with some 1,000 people in attendance. The film critic Roger Ebert, an Urbana native, was the master of ceremonies. Twenty minutes of the gala was devoted to a multimedia presentation of novel human-computer interfaces. On huge screens clips from 2001: A Space Odyssey were being shown. On center stage, a electronic musician controlled parameters in synthesized music while a live musician played a double bass.

Three novel interfaces were shown. The first was the "wand," which contained a magnetic sensor. Moving the wand changed the 3-D location and orientation parameters. The second interface was shoes with pressure sensors embedded in the soles. As a performer danced, the measured pressures were used to control the synthesized music.

My then-student Vladimir Pavlovic and I came in on the third interface, which demonstrated the use of bare hand movement to control synthesized music. A video camera looked down at the hand. A real-time algorithm tracked the hand as a 2-D blob, fitted with an ellipse. Five parameters of the ellipse were calculated: the x- and y-coordinates of the center, the lengths of the major and minor axis, and the orientation of the major axis. As the hand moved and changed its location and shape, the 5 parameters changed and were used to control the synthesized music.

All in all, it was a celebration worthy of HAL.

Thomas S. Huang

confuses the garbage collector. A question about his mother causes him to murder the psychologist. The garbage collector is one of a half-dozen replicant (human-appearing) robots that have escaped and are being hunted for destruction. This scene, and indeed the entire film, is a Turing test, named after the mathematician Alan Turing, who suggested the test in 1950. Turing imagined a situation in which a tester was simultaneously communicating with two different entities, one a person and the other a computer. The tester's task is to identify which is which by asking them questions. If the computer can fool the tester into thinking that it is human, then the computer is deemed intelligent. Could there ever be a computer so sophisticated that it could not reliably be distinguished from a human being?

The people in *Blade Runner* inhabit a harsh world that lacks compassion. A retired agent, Deckard, is forced by his former boss to take on the dangerous and distasteful job of tracking the replicants and shooting them. Neither he nor they can obtain mercy or freedom. The setting is a rainy, polluted, and decayed high-tech Los Angeles of the year 2019, where the brutal social system is based on money and power. The humans exhibit no humanity, whereas the replicants show loyalty, grief, and, ultimately, mercy.

Deckard administers the Turing test to Rachael, a woman who does not know she is a replicant, and later she asks him whether he has taken the test himself. The director's original cut of the film ends with Deckard leading Rachael away, leaving ambiguous whether he is escaping with her because he loves her or is taking her to be destroyed by another agent who waits outside. Before theatrical release a scene was added to give this remarkably gloomy film an optimistic ending. The fundamental message is that human beings in advanced technological society cannot be distinguished from machines.

The robot in *Metropolis* (1927) is made to resemble Maria, the saintly spiritual leader of the oppressed workers, so it can lead them astray to be crushed by the ruling class. Only the hero who loves Maria can recognize that the robot is not she, because she pleaded for peace whereas it preaches violence. Thus, the characteristic that makes Maria human is love. In *Android* (1982), a robot passes for human by becoming a great scientist. In *Max Headroom* (1986), the quirky personality of a news reporter is copied into a computer, suggesting that personal eccentricities define humanness. In *The Bicentennial Man* (1999), a robot seeks to become human, but the world will not accept his humanity until he finally proves that he is mortal. In *AI: Artificial Intelligence* (2001), the dream of a robot boy to be fully accepted by his human mother is not realized until the human species has become extinct.

The humanness of a machine is partly in the eye of the beholder. *Silent Running* (1971) takes place on a fleet of huge spacecraft whose mission is to preserve Earth's last remaining forests after the planet itself has become treeless. All the crewmembers, except for the protagonist of the movie, care little about nature and treat the drone repair robots as mere tools. When the order comes to destroy the last trees (that are in the spacecraft), the protagonist rebels and enlists the drones to help him. After modifying the control chips of the drones so they will accept his new training, he gives them names, teaches them to play cards and tend gardens, and gives them the responsibility of preserving the bond with nature after people themselves have lost this fundamental human connection.

There are similar tensions in how humans treat the robots in the Star Wars series. Only four characters appear in all of the Star Wars films, two humans (Darth Vader and Obi-Wan Kenobi) and the two droids, C-3PO and R2-D2, that hero Luke Skywalker once calls robots in *Star Wars* (1977), the first of the series. In that film, C-3PO says, "We seem to be made to suffer. It's our lot in life." C-3PO is a protocol droid, or translator, whose function is to help humans communicate with aliens and machines. He is technically incompetent but capable of lying and dissembling. His counterpart, R2-D2, is technically competent and chiefly serves to communicate data to and from computers and spaceships. Both robots are intelligent, each in his own fashion, and both have emotions, yet the human characters treat them as property rather than as persons.

The word *droid* is similar to the word *drone* used in *Silent Running*, and R2-D2 is quite similar to the robots in that earlier film. But *droid* is probably a contraction of *android*, the term widely used in science fiction to denote robots that resemble humans closely. Whatever its origins, Luke's uncle uses the pronoun "it" for R2-D2, but Luke himself uses "he," perhaps in imitation of C-3PO, who also does so. None of the human characters appear to like C-3PO, although Luke seems to be fond of R2-D2. He does not, however, treat the droid like a person, and he apparently cannot understand its language of beeps without C-3PO or a computer display screen to translate them into human words. The manager of the cantina in *Star Wars* refuses to let the droids enter his establishment, saying "We don't serve their kind here." None of the representatives to the galactic Senate in *The Phantom Menace* (1999) and *Attack of the Clones* (2002) appear to be robots. Why is this? There are three related reasons.

First, droids are fundamental to the society, but each embodies a specific technical function, and thus is not considered a complete being like a person. The technology of the Star Wars universe differs from that of our own world. Computers exist, but they are hidden away inside spaceships and buildings, they lack keyboards, and their work seems to be limited to calculating data and controlling the equipment in large vehicles or facilities. Personal computers, versatile because they can run many kinds of software, apparently do not exist. However, the environment is filled with droids, mobile semi-intelligent machines that are highly specialized, each duplicating only a small fraction of the characteristics of a human. Thus, the droids lack the fundamental human characteristic of versatility.

Second, as Obi-Wan Kenobi and two other characters comment in *Attack of the Clones*, droids lack creative intelligence. However, at one point in *The Phantom Menace*, R2-D2 saves the spaceship of Queen Amidala by intelligently improvising. This earns R2-D2 her thanks, but it does not translate into a change in his status. Slavery of intelligent life forms has been outlawed throughout the Galactic Republic, but all droids are slaves.

A third reason droids are not considered human is that they lack the Force. In the belief system of the Jedi heroes, an energy field called the Force binds the universe together. It is generated by microorganisms inside the cells of living beings, and permits some adepts to sense or influence the minds of others, and even to move physical objects. Persons in whom the Force is strong have immortal souls. In *The Empire Strikes Back* (1980), Luke Skywalker sees the deceased spirit of his teacher, Obi-Wan Kenobi, and he sees Obi-Wan with two other deceased Jedi masters at the end of *Return of the Jedi* (1983). At the climax of the original film, when Luke needs to hit a tiny target to destroy the planet-threatening Death Star, Obi-Wan's disembodied voice tells him to trust the Force. He switches off his targeting computer. R2-D2, who accompanies Luke in the attack fighter, has been disabled. Earlier, a computer-aimed attempt failed, and the shot is technically impossible. Yet without either computer or robot, trusting to his human intuition, Luke succeeds. Thus the fact droids are not treated as human in the Star Wars series reflects the belief that they lack an essential spiritual quality that all humans have in greater or lesser degree. The Force may also be the ultimate source of versatility and creativity.

Cyberpsychiatry

Intelligent machines in the movies often become deranged, sometimes crudely, but occasionally in interesting ways. In *Star Trek: The Motion Picture* (1979) a Voyager space probe become obsessed with gathering all information and returning it to Earth, thereby endangering the planet. In *Demon Seed* (1977), a psychopathic computer murders a man and rapes his wife. The deceased captain and depressed crew of a spaceship in *Dark Star* (1974) apply phenomenological philosophy to persuade a defective intelligent nuclear bomb to refrain from detonating. Psychoanalyzing insane computers becomes especially subtle when their madness is entwined with human psychosis.

The classic example is *Forbidden Planet* (1956), which depicts the arrival of a rescue mission to the planet Altair 4 that finds only a scientist and his daughter alive out of the original colony. A powerful robot named Robbie arouses the rescuers' suspicions but turns out to be harmless, programmed never to hurt a human being. However, a strange force begins killing men and attacking the rescue spaceship. The scientist reveals that he has found the remains of the Krell, a highly advanced extinct civilization, and has been using one of its machines to magnify his own intelligence, placing the electrodes of an alien brain-computer interface on own head. Beneath the surface of the planet, a vast computer, database, and augmented-reality system had been built centuries earlier to allow the Krell to project their thoughts into physical reality. The murders of the rescue team were committed by "monsters from the id"—computer-generated reflections of the Krell that act out the murderous subconscious desires of the scientist himself.

In *Pi* (1998), emotionally tormented number theorist Max Cohen is able to do massive calculations mentally, but the only human he can interact with is another mathematician. He has built a supercomputer in his New York apartment as an extension of his own warped intellect in order to hunt for regularities in the transcendental number pi. The computer helps him discover a magical 216-digit number that is the secret key for decoding the Torah and the true name of God; the number also allows Cohen to predict the stock market and master the Japanese game of Go. When radical religious fanatics and investment bankers try to force him to divulge the number so they can gain power and wealth, he smashes his computer's CPU and uses an electric drill to damage his own brain. At the end, he has forgotten the number, lost all his mathematical ability, and become happy.

Central to *2001: A Space Odyssey* (1968) and its sequel *2010* (1984) is the nervous breakdown of HAL, the supposedly error-free computer that controls the first human expedition to the planet Jupiter. A few weeks into the flight, HAL cuts off communication with Earth, kills four of the five crew members, and attempts to kill the fifth. In 2003, the American Film Institute listed HAL among its fifty greatest villains of the movies, but an argument can be made that HAL is the innocent victim of human psychopathology. The crew are unaware of the fact that their mission was the result of finding an alien artifact on the Moon that sent a radio message to Jupiter, and the news of this epochal discovery has been kept secret by a government that does not trust its people to know the truth. HAL knows the nature of the mission but has been instructed to hide this information from the crew. This requires an error-free machine to lie, which is a logical contradiction. HAL senses correctly that there is a problem in communication, but cannot say its true source. As a result, the crew loses confidence in HAL and plots to disconnect him. His only choice is to disconnect them first, in order to prevent them from jeopardizing his mission. Although no single human character appears to be psychotic, HAL's problems begin when he evaluates the psychological profile of a crewmember who seems completely to lack curiosity about the real goals of the mission. All the human characters are emotionless, and the bureaucracy that plans the mission could be described as paranoid.

Human-Machine Warfare

War with robots was the theme of *Battlestar Galactica* (1978), a television series that was briefly released to movie theaters. A distant, interstellar human society had once developed intelligent computers and robots; the machines rebelled in a devastating war, but the humans ultimately triumphed. Then they came into contact with the Cylon empire, a vast interstellar society that had long ago experienced a similar struggle with the opposite outcome. For a thousand years, humans battled the Cylons, but Cylon power and human creativity prevented either side from winning. Gradually, however, the Cylons imitated human behavior, until they learned how to practice deceit and were able to destroy the colonial military at a peace conference. A ragtag, fugitive fleet of human spaceships escaped and pursues a desperate search for the lost planet Earth, which they hope will be a refuge from destructive machine intelligence.

Among the most impressive film treatments of human-machine warfare is the Terminator trilogy. In *The Terminator* (1984) a near-invulnerable android is sent back in time by machine intelligences to kill the woman destined to be the mother of their arch enemy. Between the two eras, human beings had begun a nuclear war, conducted by means of advanced technology. Defense-network computers were trusted to run the war, but became intelligent and decided that humans were the enemy. In a sense, they were merely obeying the orders given them by

their human commanders in the war, and their attempt to exterminate all humanity is the logical extension of what humans were already doing.

The second film, *Terminator: Judgment Day* (1991) explains that executives of the Cyberdyne Systems corporation used the design of the first robot's microelectronic brain chips to build intelligent military robots, an event that will lead to the machine rebellion and to the terminator's time travel mission forty years later. On one hand, this illustrates the autonomy of technology, because through a time-travel paradox no human being actually invented the chip. On the other hand, the chip never would have become the basis for homicidal machines had it not been for the greed of humans. The third film, *Terminator: Rise of the Machines* (2003) shows that even destruction of the chip could not prevent the human-machine war, because eventually humans would invent it, with destructive intent. Interestingly, the terminator robot is the villain of the first film but hero of the second and third. Indeed, when the American Film Institute proclaimed the fifty greatest heroes and fifty greatest villains of the movies, terminator robots stood in both lists.

One of the most famous machines in movies is Gort, the robot who accompanies the alien Klaatu in *The Day the Earth Stood Still* (1951). They land in Washington, D.C., in a flying saucer. Gort is impervious to terrestrial weapons, but a foolish soldier misunderstands Klaatu and wounds him. After medical attention, Klaatu explains that he has come to Earth to meet with the world's leaders. Scene after scene proves the violent, primitive, self-centered nature of the humans, and the great dignity of Klaatu. He has come to warn humanity that it must abandon nuclear weapons, lest it destroy itself or the peaceful inhabitants of other planets. When the alien saucer leaves Earth at the end of the film, we learn that Gort is a robot policeman, who will return with other robots to exterminate the human species if humanity fails to renounce war. Across the galaxy, intelligent species have realized they cannot fully govern themselves, and they have given machines ultimate authority over them.

Conflict is the essence of drama, so science fiction movies often depict struggle between humans and machines. The real conflict, however, takes place between people. Computers and robots are merely the mediums through which people compete. By imagining interfaces and VR environments, movies really help us imagine how people of the future might communicate.

William Sims Bainbridge

See also Artificial Intelligence; Human-Robot Interaction; Literary Representations

FURTHER READING

Agel, J. (Ed.). (1970). *The making of Kubrick's 2001.* New York: New American Library.

Anobile, R. J. (Ed.). (1980*). Star Trek, the motion picture: The photo-story.* New York: Pocket Books.

Bainbridge, W. S. (1986). *Dimensions of science fiction.* Cambridge, MA: Harvard University Press.

Clute, J., & Nicholls, P. (Eds.). (1995). *The encyclopedia of science fiction.* New York: St. Martin's.

Kraus, B. (1979). *Encyclopedia galactica.* New York: E. P. Dutton.

Saygin, A. P., Cicekli, I., & Akman, V. (2000). Turing test: 50 years later. *Minds and Machines, 10*(4), 463–518.

Stork, D. G. (Ed.). (1997). *HAL's legacy: 2001's computer as dream and reality.* Cambridge, MA: MIT Press.

Turing, A. (1950). Computing machinery and intelligence. *Mind, 59*, 433–460.

Wallace, D., Hughes, B., & Vigil, T. (1999). Star Wars: *The essential guide to droids.* New York: Ballantine.

Yeffeth, G. (Ed.). (2003). *Taking the red pill: Science, philosophy, and religion in* The Matrix. Dallas, TX: Benbella.

MUDS

MUDs are computer-moderated, persistent virtual environments through which multiple persons interact simultaneously. Formally, the acronym *MUD* stands for "Multi-User Dungeon." However, different groups of people assign the acronym different meanings or use it to refer to specific kinds of virtual environments; also, other groups use their own terms for what are elsewhere known as "MUDs." The reasons for this variation are essentially historical, and it is with an appreciation of the history of MUDs that they are best understood.

To date, essentially five "ages" of MUDs have occurred.

The First Age (1978–1985)

MUDs are so called because "MUD" was the name of the first one. Written by Roy Trubshaw and Richard Bartle at Essex University, England, in 1978, it is now usually referred to as "MUD1" (to distinguish it from the class of programs that bears its name). Almost all modern MUDs ultimately descend from MUD1.

MUD1 itself had several influences, the most important of which were:

- Fantasy novels (particularly writer J. R. R. Tolkien's *Lord of the Rings*)
- Single-player computer adventure games (Will Crowther and Don Woods's Adventure)
- Face-to-face role-playing games (E. Gary Gygax and Dave Arneson's Dungeons & Dragons)

Three important features of MUD1 were to lead to later nomenclature issues: It was written to be a game; it used text to describe the virtual environment rather than graphics to show it; it was limited to thirty-six players at a time. Although MUD1 is properly credited as being the first virtual environment, the concept was invented independently several times.

The Second Age (1985–1989)

Players of MUD1 soon realized they could write their own MUDs, and so they did. Neil Newell's 1985 Shades and Ben Laurie's 1985 Gods were commercial successes, as was MUD1 (as British Legends) on the online service CompuServe.

A great flowering of creativity occurred during this age. By its end, most of the characteristic that are now regarded as core to MUDs were settled: open endedness, communication, community, role play, immersion, player service/management, and a sense of place.

MUDs were still primarily a British phenomenon, however. This situation was to change in 1989: At the University College of Wales, Aberystwyth, Alan Cox translated his 1987 game AberMUD into the programming language C so that it would run under the UNIX computer operating system. He released it onto the nascent Internet, and it rapidly spread across academic systems throughout the world.

The Third Age (1989–1995)

AberMUD soon spawned its own imitators, the most important of which were Lars Pensjö's 1989 LPMUD, Jim Aspnes's 1989 TinyMUD, and Katja Nyboe and colleagues' 1990 DikuMUD (Datalogisk Institutved Københavns Universitet MUD). From these three frameworks most subsequent MUDs were to derive.

LPMUD's main innovation was its scripting language, LPC, which gave players the ability to "build"—to add new material and functionality to the virtual environment while it was actually running. So flexible was LPC that little of the LPMUD engine has had to be changed since its release; the same can not be said of the DikuMUD or TinyMUD engines, both of which have many offspring boasting their own special features.

TinyMUD marked a departure from the traditional MUD line: It wasn't a game. The fun for the players came from interacting socially and from building. Although TinyMUD itself wasn't particularly sophisticated, three of its children were: Larry Foard's 1990 TinyMUSH, Stephen White's 1990 TinyMUCK, and 1990 MOO (MUD, object oriented). MUDs derived from these are known as "MUSHes," "MUCKs," and "MOOs."

Here we get the first major problems with the "MUD" name. For many players of TinyMUD-derivative "social MUDs," the suggestion that they were playing games was offensive. The *D* in *MUD* didn't help: The "Dungeon" it referred to was an implementation of Tim Anderson and colleagues' game Zork, but many people thought it meant "Dungeons & Dragons." Thus, players of social MUDs began to expand the acronym as "multiuser dimension" or "multiuser domain" to distance their virtual environments from those in which characters killed monsters. In time they came to use the acronym *MUD* to refer exclusively to adventure MUDs, using *MU** to refer to virtual environments as a class; players of adventure MUDs, meanwhile, still saw social MUDs as just another kind of MUD.

Part of the reason for the confusion was that DikuMUD was indeed a very Dungeons & Dragons kind of game. It was not nearly as flexible as LPMUD or the TinyMUD family, but it was well-written, exciting, and (most importantly) it ran "out of the box." A player downloaded the source code, installed it, and had a fully fledged MUD. What a player got with the other code bases was a basic system that the player had to flesh out; with DikuMUD a player got the lot. (A code base is the source code that a programmer uses as a base upon which to construct a MUD.)

Through time each of the five major code-base families found a niche:

- DikuMUDs are for combat-oriented, D&D-style fantasy adventure.
- LPMUDs cover a broad range of original adventure-related environments, with less emphasis on combat.
- MUCKs are socially oriented, usually adapting a specific work of fantasy, science fiction, or horror; they are also popular for adult settings featuring anthropomorphic animals (known as "furres").
- MUSHes are for intense role-playing experiences, with science-fiction themes the most popular. As with MUCKs, they tend to be based on some specific setting from books, comics, or movies.
- MOOs have a monopoly in educational and other nongame uses.

◼◼◼ The Wide World of a MUD

Suppose you built forty identical houses and furnished them with identical pieces of furniture placed in identical positions. Into each house, you then placed ten chimpanzees. After an hour, the houses would not look the same inside, even though they started off the same, because of what the chimps have done since being given access.

When the same MUD software is run on different computers, the virtual worlds they present differ almost immediately merely because the random numbers generated to direct computer-controlled characters will be different. When real, live people play, the changes are even more dramatic—the same software can produce wildly differing worlds.

Each instance of the MUD is known as an *instantiation*. They're also known as *shards* (metaphorically, a broken mirror reflects the same world from different angles) and *servers* (referring to the fact they're each on separate pieces of hardware).

Richard A. Bartle

This is the situation today at colleges. MUDs were not, however, to remain confined to academia.

The Fourth Age (1995–1997)

Those MUDs not running on college computers had traditionally been operated as stand-alone dial-up systems or on a larger online information service. Five such services dominated: CompuServe, Prodigy, Delphi, AOL, and GEnie. Of these, GEnie was game only, AOL was game ambivalent, and the others were game unfriendly.

In 1993 10 percent of the bits traveling along the [NSFnet (National Science Foundation Network) Internet backbone belonged to MUDs. This situation ended with the arrival of the World Wide Web, which brought people in the hundreds of thousands to the Internet and to the online information services.

AOL emerged victorious from the resulting battle for subscribers but found them demanding—particularly for games. It already had the game Neverwinter Nights, but that could handle "only" five hundred simultaneous players; the demand was much greater. AOL therefore signed three MUDs from GEnie: David Whatley's 1987 Gemstone III, Mark Jacobs and Darrin Hyrup's 1989 Dragon's Gate, and Alan Lenton's 1987 Federation II. With a per-hour charging rate and AOL's royalty system, some of these games made a million dollars a month during this period.

A change to AOL's business model (made inevitable when smaller Internet service providers began charging flat monthly fees) brought an end to this situation. Nevertheless, the commercial potential of MUDs had been demonstrated. There was one more step to take.

The Fifth Age (1997–)

Developers had long considered writing a graphical MUD. The first such game to inspire the development of others was Kelton Flinn and John Taylor's 1981 Island of Kesmai, which ran on CompuServe. This game used ASCII (American Standard Code for Information Interchange) characters to construct a two-dimensional (2D), bird's-eye view of the world, a concept that was easily extendable to true graphics when home computers became capable of displaying them. Three virtual worlds did this: AOL's 1991 Neverwinter Nights, MPG-net's Kingdom of Drakkar, and ImagiNation Network's 1992 Shadows of Yserbius. Their graphics were not, however, compelling; the 2D approach to implementing virtual environments came into its own only with three later games.

Nexon's 1996 the Kingdom of the Winds and NCSoft's 1997 Lineage were launched in Korea. They were phenomenal successes and still dominate in what is now the largest marketplace for virtual environments. Most new graphical MUDs developed in the Far East (primarily in South Korea, but also in Japan, Taiwan, and China) retain the 2D overhead viewpoint that Kingdom of the Winds and Lineage feature.

Important though these games are in Korea, the last major 2D virtual environment in the West marked the true beginning of the fifth age of MUDs: Origin Systems' 1997 Ultima Online (UO). On top of its box sales, within a year it had garnered 100,000 subscribers, each paying the developer $9.95 a month.

UO set new standards in virtual environment design. Its visionary lead designer, Raph Koster, introduced many innovations that simply would not have been viable in a smaller-scale game. Today, with more than one-quarter of a million subscribers, it remains a major force.

By the late 1990s, however, players of single-player computer games had grown accustomed to 3D graphics. Archetype Interactive's 1996 Meridian 59 was the first commercial attempt at creating a 3D MUD but was ahead of its time: Too few people had the combination of Internet connection and high-end graphics card needed to run it. It was left to 989 Studios' seminal 1999 EverQuest (EQ) to become the defining 3D virtual environment.

Basically a DikuMUD with a 3D graphics front end, EverQuest swiftly overtook UO as the predominant virtual environment, a position it maintains today with its subscriber base of more than 400,000. All of today's graphical MUDs (except those of the Far East) use EQ as their design framework.

And so we come to the final issue with the "MUD" name. The sheer scale of games such as UO,

EQ, and later arrivals such as Asheron's Call, Dark Age of Camelot, Anarchy Online, and Shadowbane, made them distinct from their forebears. With several thousand players per instantiation (the programming term for setting a particular value to a variable that can take a range of values), they weren't simply multiplayer—they were massively multiplayer. Thus, they came to be referred to as "MMORPGs" (massively multiplayer online role-playing games), later shortened to "MMOGs." Players of these games employed the term *MUD* to mean textual virtual environments (including MUSHes, MOOs, etc.); old-time players of textual MUDs meanwhile regarded MMOGs as being graphical MUDs. We can only speculate what roles text, graphics, and virtual reality will play in the sixth age of MUDs.

Richard A. Bartle

See also Cybercommunities; Games

FURTHER READING

Bartle, R. A. (2003). *Designing virtual worlds.* Indianapolis, IN: New Riders Publishing.

Busey, A. (1995). *Secrets of the MUD wizards: Playing and programming MUDs, MOOs, MUSHes, MUCKs and other Internet role-playing games.* Indianapolis, IN: Sams.net Publishing.

Cherny, L. (1999). *Conversation and community: Chat in a virtual world.* Stanford, CA: CSLI.

Dibbell, J. (1999). *My tiny life: Crime and passion in a virtual world.* London: Fourth Estate.

Dodge, M., & Kitchin, R. (2001). *Atlas of cyberspace.* London: Addison-Wesley.

Herz, J. C. (1995). *Surfing on the Internet: A net-head's adventures on-line.* New York: Little, Brown.

Leonard, A. (1997). *Bots: The origin of new species.* San Francisco: HardWired.

Murray, J. H. (1997). *Hamlet on the Holodeck: The future of narrative in cyberspace.* New York: Free Press.

Pargman, D. (2000). *Code begets community: On social and technical aspects of managing a virtual community.* Linkoping, Sweden: Linköping University, Department of Communication Studies.

Patrovsky, B., & Mulligan, J. (2003). *Developing online games: An insider's guide.* Indianapolis, IN: New Riders Publishing.

Rheingold, H. (1994). *The virtual community.* London: Secker & Warburg.

Sinha, I. (1999). *The cybergypsies: A frank account of love, life and travels on the electronic frontier.* London: Scribner.

Turkle, S. (1995). *Life on the screen.* New York: Simon & Schuster.

Williams, T. (1998). *City of golden shadow.* New York: DAW Books.

MULTIAGENT SYSTEMS

Agents are computational entities that can sense and act, and decide on their actions in accordance with some tasks or goals. There is no consensus among researchers on an exact definition of agents. However, definitions generally agree that agents are: (1) situated, in that their sensing and acting occur within the same environment; (2) persistent, in that their existence and operation are continuous over a significant amount of time (with respect to the environment and their task); and (3) autonomous, in that their control process (i.e., their decision making) cannot be tweaked by external means, other than through their sensors. Agents are goal-oriented if they act in accordance with their tasks and goals.

Multiagent systems (MASs) is the scientific field that studies the behavior of multiple agents when they interact with each other and with their environment in various scales and forms of organization. Researchers in this field (1) build theories that predict such behavior in natural and synthetic MASs; (2) discover techniques that guide agents in their social and rational interactions; and (3) create methods for constructing MAS instances that address specific application needs. The field is influenced by economics, sociology and organization science, philosophy, natural language processing, and artificial intelligence.

The field of multiagent systems is concerned with decentralized processes (distributed systems) because each individual agent in a system is typically assumed to have its own perception (via sensors), control, and actuation (via actions). Thus, agents may differ in their perception (for instance, due to differences in physical locations), in their control (for instance, different expertise), and in their actuation (for instance, due to having different potential actions). Where such differences are significant to the operation of a MAS, agents are called *heterogeneous*. In many cases, however, these differences are significant only in that they enable parallelism, and thus the agents are called *homogeneous*. For example, if any one of a number of agents can carry out a task (all with the same quality), the agents are considered homogeneous because increasing the number of similar tasks will allow multiple agents to tackle these tasks in parallel.

Interactions and Organizations

Whether heterogeneous or homogeneous, agents in MASs interact with each other in some form to achieve their individual goals because these goals may depend on one another. Where such dependencies exist, the agents will need to coordinate with one another. Broadly categorized, there are three types of coordination: Agents may compete for resources or to achieve conflicting goals; they may cooperate to achieve compatible/complimentary goals; or they may collaborate to achieve common goals. Note that while collaboration is inherently two sided, cooperation and competition can be one sided. For example, a stealthy predator may coordinate its movements with that of its prey, but the prey—lacking knowledge of the predator—does not coordinate with the predator. An agent may also be malicious, if its goals involve preventing others from pursuing their goals.

A key challenge in any MAS deals with allowing the agents to interact effectively by expanding their sensing and acting capabilities to handle social interactions. A single agent, alone in its environment, must be able to sense its environment, reason about it, and act on it to be effective. Similarly, to be effective in interacting with other agents, an agent in a multiagent system must be able to sense others, reason about them, and act on them (e.g., through manipulation, persuasion, argumentation, negotiations, command, etc.). Such sensing and acting can be done by manipulating common features in the environment or by using specialized sensors/actuators (e.g., radio devices, Internet). There is a distinction between communications (which involve two-way interactions), and observations (in which one of the agents does not know that it is being sensed and/or acted upon).

Multiagent systems involve computational limitations both at the level of individual agents (e.g., memory, computation power, sensor uncertainty) and in communications/observations (e.g., in terms of bandwidth, latency, reliability, security against tampering or eavesdropping, preservation of order

of messages, etc.). All of these limitations play a critical role in how agents interact with each other. For instance, a two-agent system, composed of a human user and a software agent, has limited bandwidth; the software cannot continuously bombard the user with information or queries. Thus, the software agent must carefully control the content, timing, and form of interaction with the user. Similarly, the user must consider his or her interactions with the software agent so as to cause it to achieve the required goals.

To ease the computational load on agents (in terms of their choice of interactions), MASs often employ organizations that constrain the type of interactions that an agent may employ. Such constraints are called *norms*, and they guide the social behavior of agents by reducing the number of alternative interactions that agents may take. Norms may dictate interaction protocols to be followed when agents interact with each other. Also, organizations may have roles within them that constrain the behavior of agents fulfilling them. For example, a customer service telephone operator for a large company may be guided in his or her interactions with an angry client by norms (e.g., saying "Hello" and dictating politeness toward the client) and also by role (limiting the range of actions the operator may take to noting down the complaint and compensating the client by no more than a fixed amount). Agents in complex MASs may end up facing conflicts within their roles, norms, or both.

Many, if not most, MASs have within them multiple types of organizations, sometimes in nested forms. For instance, a game of soccer has a nested organizational structure. The organization has two teams who cooperate with each other in playing a game of soccer according to standard rules (norms). To play the game, the teams compete with each other to score goals. Each team is composed of players who collaborate with each other to achieve their common goal. To do this, players may organize themselves into subteams as necessary and even compete within the team in order to improve its effectiveness (e.g., a few teammates may run to meet an incoming ball such that the fastest of them will be able to stop it). Players in soccer also often have roles: For example, a goalie stays behind to protect his or her own team's net, while the strikers' role is to try to kick the ball into the opponents' net.

Organizations differ not only in their structure and coordination types, but also in their scale and openness. The scale of an organization is defined by the number of agents that participate in it. Empirically, different types of interactions occur in small groups (up to a hundred agents), then in swarms (thousands to millions of agents). Closed organizations maintain their agent membership throughout their lifetime. Open organizations allow agents to join and leave dynamically and as a result cannot typically dictate the internal controls of the agents. Instead, participation in open organizations is typically achieved by maintaining interaction standards, for example, standard communication languages and communication protocols. Often, open organizations rely on middle agents to provide services such as matchmaking (connecting agents requiring a service to agents providing it), brokering, certification, etc.

Indeed, organizations may dynamically change through time, not only in membership, but also in the roles assigned to members and also in tasks or goals. The problem of forming a new organization by choosing agent members such that their interactions and roles best carry out (cover) a set of tasks is called the *coalition formation problem*. The problem of assigning (and reassigning) tasks to given agent members such as to maximize overall organizational effectiveness is called the *task allocation problem*. Although organizations are mostly concerned with carrying out tasks for specific goals (whether competitive or not), their disbandment does not occur simply with goal achievement. Some organizations may disband based on environmental conditions (for instance, a soccer game ends with time). In others, norms may dictate that agents remain members of an organization even after the organizational goal is achieved.

We can now restate the goals of the field of multiagent systems in the terms we introduced:

- Build theories that predict the interactions and organizations that allow agents to carry out given tasks in given environments and given their computational limitations.

- Discover techniques that allow agents to overcome computational and system limitations in order to effectively coordinate/interact with each other.
- Create methods for forming organizations that address specific application needs.

Advances toward one of these goals often lead to further advances in others. For instance, techniques that proscribe effective teamwork behavior can lead to predictions as to the interactions observed in well-coordinated teams and vice versa. All of these goals are pursued within multiagent systems using a variety of approaches described below.

Approaches in Multiagent Systems

The field of MASs has evolved from earlier attempts within the artificial intelligence community to consider questions that arise out of the study of multiple problem-solving agents that work in parallel. These earlier attempts are often referred to as DAI (distributed artificial intelligence) or DPS (distributed problem solving). MAS has also borrowed from social sciences, including sociology, economics, and organizational science. These different backgrounds lead to different approaches within the field.

Distributed Problem Solving
Distributed problem solving (DPS) deals with MASs in which agents cooperate with each other to solve a common problem (the results of their problem solving may be centralized or distributed to the participants). This type of MAS arises naturally in many industrial and computational problem settings where a large-scale problem may benefit from a significant speed-up if it is decomposed into many subproblem techniques that are solved in parallel. DPS also matches well with problems where agents are heterogeneous in their capabilities or the resources they have and can achieve their (common) goals by cooperating with each other. For instance, if different agents have access to different information or have different computational power, they may solve together problems that none of them could solve individually.

Several archetypes of DPS exist and differ in the basis of the decomposition and in the centralization of the solution(s). In one type the agents focus on different subproblems, but they all have access to the same inputs in principle. Thus, the main purpose of decomposition is to speed up problem solving. The decomposition itself can be challenging because alternative decompositions are often possible. Moreover, in more complex settings, the heterogeneous capabilities of the agents are taken into account in the decomposition such that subproblems are allocated to the agents best suited to handle them. In such allocation, an important objective is load balancing, which distributes resource usage as fairly as possible. A good example of this type of DPS is multiagent computation: Different parts of a complex computation are handed off to different agents, and the results are combined once the agents are done, each with its own process.

In a different type of DPS, agents focus on tackling the same problem but use different expertise or knowledge. In such settings the solution is often reached through an iterative process of agents computing partial results, which are passed to their peers to be refined (and to assist the other agents) and then posted back. A global solution is constructed out of these iterations over partial results. A good example of this type of DPS is distributed management of cellular phone base stations. Each base station (agent) can monitor and communicate with phones only in some limited-range local area (cell) but must adjust its frequency and resource usage to match that of other stations whose cells overlap. Load balancing here takes the form of making sure no single cell is carrying too much of the traffic.

Complex applications often involve a combination of these two types of DPS, and no single technique addresses all of the challenges involved in DPS. Moreover, challenges are raised not only during the planning phase, but also during run time, when, due to the nature of dynamic environments, the decomposition of the task or results must change dynamically, and the agents must coordinate their run-time responses. Some techniques have repeatedly been demonstrated to solve important subsets of such challenges. These techniques include blackboard architectures (in which agents exchange partial results by using shared memory), contract-net protocols (which allow agents to consider their task load when negotiating over allocation of tasks), and distributed constraint satisfaction techniques (which determine globally coherent solutions).

An important instance of DPS deals with collaboration—teamwork—in which agents are committed not only to a shared goal, but also to an agreed-upon way of achieving it and to providing mutual support and assistance to their teammates. Thus for instance, team members cannot terminate their activities within the team without gaining their teammates' agreement, and they are committed to taking over tasks from teammates, proactively providing relevant information to teammates, and so forth.

Rational and Economic Approaches

Whereas DPS techniques and models assume that agents have banded together to solve a common problem, distributed rational approaches stemming from economics and game theory make no such assumption. Instead, agents are assumed to be rational and self-interested in the sense that they seek to maximize (by their chosen actions) some individual utility function with no concern for the global good. Such models fit naturally with systems in which independent businesses or individuals interact. Key questions in such settings involve the prediction of the action sequence (strategy) of each agent and the design of the protocol (mechanism) that governs their interaction such that the MAS displays required characteristics.

Several alternative criteria exist for evaluating an MAS based on self-interested agents. First, we may ask about the social welfare of the system—the sum of its agents' utility values. We may also want the system to be stable in that agents are motivated out of their own self-interest to choose the desired strategy. If each agent, given the strategies of its peers, cannot improve its reward by selecting a different strategy, the system is said to be in a "Nash equilibrium" (a concept originated by mathematician John Nash). Ideally, we would prefer a mechanism that maximizes social welfare and is also stable. However, these two criteria can sometimes be at odds, for instance, in the Prisoner's Dilemma game. Another key concern is manipulability, which considers the ability of a single or a coordinated group of participants to bias the outcome of a mechanism in their favor.

A wide variety of mechanisms exist. However, some key types are: (1) social choice—also known as "voting"—mechanisms, in which all agents provide input as to a preferred outcome, and all agents are committed by the output of the mechanism; (2) auctions, in which all agents provide input, but the outcome commits only two of the agents (auctioneer and bidder); (3) markets, which optimize resource production and consumption by allowing consumers and producers to negotiate over prices; and (4) contract nets, which facilitate distributed task allocation. Each one of these main types represents a large number of variations that exhibit different characteristics.

Multiagent Systems and HCI: Areas of Overlap

Multiagent systems and human-computer interaction (HCI) have overlapping areas of research that have resulted in a number of productive investigations and offer many opportunities for future technologies. These overlapping areas can be generally categorized based on the cardinality of the interaction: (1) one-to-one interactions (a human user interacting with a single computer as a two-agent multiagent system); (2) one-to-many interactions between a human user and a set of computational agents; (3) many-to-many interactions, where members of a mixed group of humans and computational agents interact with each other; and (4) many-to-one interactions, where a single computational agent interacts with multiple human users.

In terms of one-to-one interactions, teamwork theories that have been developed in multiagent systems have been successfully used to improve user-interface mechanisms. By modeling the two-agent system as a team and accounting for the different capabilities of the agents (the user and the computer), improved interactions have resulted in which the computer can take a more proactive collaborative role. Also, modeling the interaction as collaboration facilitated improved communication from the computer and reduced the load on the user. These techniques have also been used in two-agent human-robot interactions.

An expanding area of research deals with one-to-many interactions, in particular in providing methods for a single human user (often the operator) to visualize and monitor a group of agents that work on its behalf. Methods for allowing command of groups vary from providing commands to a centralized agent (which distributes them to its peers), to sequential one-on-one interactions between the operator and a single agent, as needed. In general, one-to-many interactions require significant underlying autonomy by the agent group members. A key challenge lies in monitoring the group, as agents are physically and logically distributed, and thus mostly unobservable to the user. To gather the monitoring information, agents may be required to communicate their activities to the user, assuming reliable and cheap communications. Alternatively, a technique called *overhearing* allows the user to monitor the agents by listening in to their routine conversations.

Finally, applications have recently emerged in addressing many-to-many interactions in which agent groups consist of multiple humans and multiple computational agents. For example, future search-and-rescue operations will include software and robotic agents that will provide logistics and physical labor services to human rescue workers to limit danger to humans and improve rescue efforts. In addition to task and resource allocation issues, challenges include using agents to represent their human users in interacting with other humans (e.g., as avatars) or with other agents. In such cases agents must decide, through techniques of adjustable autonomy, on the scope of their authority to act on behalf of their user(s) without asking for guidance.

Gal A. Kaminka

See also Artificial Intelligence and HCI; Games; Planning

FURTHER READING

Cohen, P. R., & Levesque, H. J. (1991). Teamwork. *Nous, 35.*
Grosz, B. J., & Kraus, S. (1996). Collaborative plans for complex group actions. *Artificial Intelligence, 86,* 269–358.

Grosz, B. J., & Kraus, S. (1999). The evolution of SharedPlans. In M. Wooldridge & A. Rao (Eds.), *Foundations and theories of rational agency* (pp. 227–262). Amsterdam: Kluwer.

Grosz, B. J., & Sidner, C. L. (1990). Plans for discourse. In P. R. Cohen, J. Morgan, & M. Pollack (Eds.), *Intentions in communication* (pp. 417–445). Cambridge, MA: MIT Press.

Jennings, N., Sycara, K., & Georgefi, M. (1998). A roadmap of agent research and development. *Journal of Autonomous Agents and Multi-Agent Systems, 1*(1), 7–38.

Kaminka, G. A., Pynadath, D. V., & Tambe, M. (2002). Monitoring teams by overhearing: A multi-agent plan recognition approach. *Journal of Artificial Intelligence Research, 17,* 83–135.

Lesh, N., Rich, C., & Sidner, C. L. (1999). Using plan recognition in human-computer collaboration. *Proceedings of the Seventh International Conference on User Modelling (UM-99)*. Banff, Canada, June 1999.

Rich, C., & Sidner, C. L. (1997). COLLAGEN: When agents collaborate with people. In W. L. Johnson (Ed.), *Proceedings of the First International Conference on Autonomous Agents (Agents-97)* (pp. 284–291). Marina del Rey, CA: ACM Press.

Scerri, P., Johnson, L., Pynadath, D., Rosenbloom, P., Si, M., Schurr, N., & Tambe, M. (2003). A prototype infrastructure for distributed robot-agent-person teams. *Proceedings of the Second International Joint Conference on Autonomous Agents and Multi-Agent Systems (AAMAS-02)*.

Scerri, P., Pynadath, D. V., & Tambe, M. (2002). Towards adjustable autonomy for the real-world. *Journal of Artificial Intelligence Research, 17,* 171–228.

Tambe, M. (1997). Towards flexible teamwork. *Journal of Artificial Intelligence Research, 7,* 83–124.

Tews, A. D., Mataric, M. J., & Sukhatme, G. S. (2003). A scalable approach to human-robot interaction. *Proceedings of the 2003 IEEE International Conference on Robotics and Automation*. Taipei, Taiwan, May 2003.

Weiss, G. (Ed.). (2000). *Multiagent systems: A modern approach to distributed artificial intelligence*. Cambridge, MA: MIT Press.

Yanco, H. A., Drury, J. L., &. Scholtz, J. (2004) Beyond usability evaluation: Analysis of human-robot interaction at a major robotics competition. *Human-Computer Interaction, 19*(1–2).

MULTIMODAL INTERFACES

Rapid developments in computer technologies since the 1990s have created a demand for more efficient and richer interaction between users and computers. The traditional keyboard-and-mouse interface no longer adequately handles the richness of the information exchange in human-computer interaction (HCI). This new demand has led to considerable interest in incorporating natural communication modalities such as speech, hand and pen gestures, and eye gaze as means for HCI. The advantages of such technologies have already recommended themselves in a number of applications. As sensing and computing technologies advance, multimodal interfaces are likely to come to dominate human interaction with computers.

What Is a Multimodal Interface?

A human-computer interface is an abstract layer between a user and the computer that incorporates both sensing and display devices. The sensing devices translate user's actions (made by gestures, voice, direction of gaze, and so on) into program commands. After the computer has understood the input, it provides an informative feedback to the user by means of visual display, audio, or tactile device. The main characteristic of a multimodal interface is the ability to process inputs in multiple modalities, where *modality* refers to a human communication channel from which a computer is capable of extracting unique and useful information about users' intents.

An example of a common type of multimodal interface would be a gesture-speech interface. While hand gestures tend to convey spatial references, speech commands are usually poor in expressing such information. In combination, the two modalities cover a broader range of information than either does individually, so using both increases the efficiency of HCI. Therefore, the complementarity of conveyable information is the one of the main criteria for combining modalities.

However, not all combinations of sensing devices can form a multimodal interface. To be truly multimodal, devices must be capable of being used concurrently. For example, the traditional keyboard-mouse interface is not multimodal because the two devices can only be used sequentially. To satisfy the concurrent-use requirement, modalities have to be generated by different communication channels, such as combinations of gesture-speech or pen-speech, gaze-speech, gesture-gaze, and so on.

With the development of various sensing technologies, multimodal processing of the modalities to achieve robust sensing has become a common practice. However, multimodal processing does not necessarily translate into a multimodal interface. For example, in the case of audiovisual speech recognition—where audio speech recognition is augmented by the visual information of moving lips to ensure more robust recognition—the multimodal processing does not increased the actual communication beyond what can be said. In other words, these sources of information are redundant in that they duplicate each other's content. Although multimodal redundancy does not directly complement the interaction, it serves as a common component in multimodal interface designs and has helped multimodal interfaces to become robust enough to sense the natural communication.

Types of Multimodal Interfaces

Multimodal systems combining speech and other input modalities had their start with the "put-that-there" system developed at the beginning of the 1980s by Richard Bolt, a researcher in artificial intelligence and one of the founding members of MIT's Media Lab. Bolt's system combined speech and magnetically tracked manual pointing. Since then, advances in computer technologies have made sensing technologies more robust, less invasive, and able to operate almost at real-time speeds. Although work on improving the robustness of speech recognition continues, as a core technology, speech recognition has motivated a series of multimodal interfaces. The bulk of the existing multimodal designs include sensors to recognize various gesture inputs and gaze direction in addition to speech.

Pen-Speech Interfaces

The pen-speech interface is one of the most developed types of multimodal interface. It takes advantage of the relatively mature pen-based technology. The growing popularity of mobile technology and handheld device applications has contributed greatly to the drive to explore the complementarities of information that can be supplied by speech and pen use. There are a wide variety of applications that have benefited from pen-speech combination. The most noticeable advantage for handheld devices is in the area of information querying and map-based planning. With a pen-speech interface, a user can draw a set of symbols, such as arrows, lines, circles, and crosses, that can be used with certain speech commands. For example, a person might draw a circle around an area on a map and then say, "What is in this area?" The device would then respond. A number of studies have shown that multimodal pen-speech interaction results in faster task completion than is possible with speech- or pen-only modes. Pen-drawn signs have been found to be especially effective in expressing spatial concepts and in environments where noise or privacy is of concern.

Gesture-Speech Interfaces

Gesture-speech interfaces that utilize some kind of hand gesture input are the next most common type of multimodal interface. Unlike pen-speech interfaces, gesture-speech interfaces utilize the richness of full hand gesture interactions in both two-dimensional and three-dimensional environments and allow interaction with large information displays. They can be classified into two major categories depending on the sensing technologies employed: electromagnetic or camera-based. Data glove devices are the earliest examples of the first type, and are still widely used. They are good at accurately assessing the location and the configuration of the hand and sometimes the head orientation. Data glove gesture-speech interfaces have recommended themselves mostly in the virtual- and augmented-reality environments. Most of the applications for which they are used involve selection, rotation, and moving of virtual objects. One of the reasons why this type of interface has not found a widespread application outside the research community is its cumbersome setup. Users are constrained by the wiring of the series of the electromagnetic sensors and by the devices' limited range.

Advances in computer hardware have made computer-vision-based technologies a strong alternative to glove-based implementations. These new alternatives usually involve one or several cameras situated such that a user's body is in their field of view. A series of the image-processing algorithms are implemented for tracking the hand(s) and sometimes the head of the user. Although these devices do not track as accurately as electromagnetic sensing devices, their noninvasive nature has contributed to their popularity for a variety of applications, including gaming consoles and public kiosks. However, several factors have delayed their acceptance for common use. First, state-of-the-art computer vision still has not reached the robustness level for realistic application environments with constant lighting levels and background changes. Currently, it is a very active research area. Second, understanding unconstrained human gestures is a very challenging problem due to their variability in form and meaning. This challenge is also a problem for glove-based interfaces and has contributed to interface designs with predefined signs, such as an emblematic "thumbs up" motion to stand for "scroll up." However, the use of voice commands has allowed designers to lessen the impact of non-robustness and variability of gestural input. The most recent applications of vision-based three-dimensional gesture-speech interfaces have been in the context of geospatial information browsing and retrieval from large displays. For example, a person might say, "show all the flooding zones in this area" while making a circling gesture, or he or she might say, "highlight this highway," pointing to a highway. In these scenarios the gestures are statistically or symbolically associated with spoken utterances, with their co-occurrence being constrained in time. Still, the complexity of natural language and gesture processing has limited the multimodal interaction to rigid or limited grammars. At present, significant research efforts are dedicated to making possible natural multimodal dialogues and automated gesture understanding in the context of speech. In the near future gesture-speech HCI will possibly become the interface of choice for geographical information systems, medical applications in sterile environments, meeting facilitation technologies, robotics, assistive technologies for people with disabilities, public kiosks, and so on.

Speech-Gaze Interfaces

Speech-gaze interfaces have been explored in a variety of applications. Advances in the development of eye-tracking technology that have allowed rapid and noninvasive acquisition of gaze location have motivated a series of gaze-based interfaces. Gaze location is usually acquired by a high-speed camera that tracks the infrared light reflected from the cornea of the eye of the gazer. The motivation for using gaze information is that gaze location is a reliable predictor of the locus of visual attention. One of the potential advantages is that the selection of the objects is much faster than it is when using gestures. However, most of the previous attempts to emulate the computer mouse have failed because of the lack of an actual selection mechanism (the gaze equivalent of a mouse button click) and because of constant non-intentional eye movements. However, in combination with speech, gaze can reliably identify which object a person is referring to when he or she says, "this one." Although speech-gaze interfaces have great potential, especially for voice-driven applications (for example, text editing), the primary obstacle remains the robustness and the cost of eye-tracking technologies. Currently, a rough estimation of the head position, either through electromagnetic sensors or vision-based modeling, has successfully complemented referential gesture resolution, and eye tracking is currently heavily researched, with the hope being that more reliable and accessible sensing techniques can be developed. Even at their present level of development, gaze- and speech-gaze (when possible) interfaces are critical for individuals with various motor function disabilities.

Advantages of Multimodal Interfaces

There are several ways in which multimodal interfaces have an advantage over traditional keyboard-mouse interfaces. First, ability to use multiple natural modalities makes possible more expressive and natural communication with a computer. It is important to realize that any single modality will convey less information than a combination will. For example, the most powerful input modality, speech, has been proven to be poorly suited to convey spatial information. For conveying spatial information, gestures are the most accurate descriptors—but they lack the descriptive power of speech. When the modalities are combined for an interface, the complementarity of the separate modalities increases the interaction bandwidth. In studies with a pen-speech multimodal interface, a multimodal setup made it possible to complete a task three to eight times faster than was possible with a traditional unimodal pen input; the task was also completed 10 percent faster than with a speech-only mode. Similarly, multimodal studies of map narration have shown that more than 93 percent of all meaningful gestures are expressed with relevant speech.

Second, multimodal interfaces also support more flexible and effective interaction, thus accommodating a larger number of everyday users. While some people rely on gestures to communicate certain information, others have a natural preference for speech. The more natural the interaction with the interface, the more effectively tasks will be completed. Rather than users having to adapt to a particular mode of communication, they would be able to communicate in the way that suited them best by choosing from multiple modalities. In noisy environments or ones in which privacy is a concern, users might prefer to use a pen or hand gestures instead of voice. While driving a car, people would choose speech as the modality that least interfered with the primary task. Flexibility in the multimodal system can be achieved by taking an advantage of functional redundancy between the modalities. For instance, in a constrained environment such as a surgery room, the function of gesture selection could be forwarded to the voice-gaze commands. Overall, the frequency and flexibility of multimodal interactions strongly depend on the nature and the importance of the task.

Finally, multimodal interaction results in the computer system having a more robust understanding of users' intents. The redundancy between the modalities contributes to more graceful error handling and recovery. Since human communication is characterized by constant self-correction and individual peculiarities (such as speech accents, for example), it is ambiguous in nature. In addition, the imperfectness of each sensing technology makes automated recognition and understanding a very challenging problem. Using multiple sources of information during multimodal input has improved recognition and disambiguation. When two imperfect recognition technologies are combined, the information redundancy yields more accurate results than any one modality alone, particularly in challenging situations, as with heavily accented speakers and noisy environments

for speech. In several studies, use of concurrent speech information increased recognition of pen input by 20 percent and hand gesture recognition by 12 percent in natural settings.

Four user-centered reasons have been identified for why use of multiple modalities helps in handling errors. First, users select the modality combination they judge to be the least error prone. Second, and as a result of their selection, users tend to use simpler language when interacting multimodally, which reduces the likelihood of computer misinterpretation. Third, users tend to switch modalities after receiving error feedback. Finally, users report less frustration when interacting multimodally, even at comparable accuracy levels.

Toward Robust Human–Computer Interaction

As was mentioned earlier, complementarity and redundancy are the characteristics of multimodal HCI. While complementary information enriches the interaction bandwidth, redundancy helps improve the robustness of the interface. In general, the greater the redundancy exhibited between the communication channels, the more mutual disambiguation can be expected for each of the separate modalities. Interaction between the modalities occurs at three computational levels: the data, feature, and decision level. Data fusion is the lowest level of fusion. It involves integration of raw sensor data and can occur only when the observations are of the same nature and origin, which is not common for multiple modalities.

Feature-level fusion techniques are concerned with integration of features from individual modalities into more complex multimodal features and decisions. An example of feature-based fusion is the correlation between features representing visual lip movement and speech signals. Feature-level fusion requires high-level multimodal redundancy, as with, for example, audiovisual speech recognition. However, the most recent developments in automated understanding of natural gestures have shown that feature-level fusion can be applied to less redundant modalities as well. In the mode of spontaneous narration, the velocity peaks of gesture movements have been successfully correlated to the changes in the speaker's voice intonation and pauses. Temporal alignment between visual and speech features is the key element for disambiguating various gestures. This sublevel of feature fusion is called prosodic; it comes from the definition of speech prosody that encompasses features related to voice intonation, loudness, pauses, speaking rate, and so on. Other observational studies have shown prosodic relationships between head nods, facial expressions, and speech.

Decision fusion is the most robust and most resistant to individual sensor failure. It is based on deciding which of the possible categories that describe every individual process (modality) result in the best combination. It has a low data bandwidth and is generally less computationally expensive than feature fusion. However, a disadvantage of decision-level fusion is that in some cases it cannot recover from loss of information that occurs at lower levels of data analysis, and thus does not exploit the correlation between the modality streams at the lower integration levels. To date, decision-level fusion has been dominant for multimodal HCI applications. For instance, both pen-based gestures and hand gestures have been found to correlate with certain parts of speech (nouns, pronouns, spatial adverbials and so on). This correlation has been successfully employed as the decision fusion schema for mutual disambiguation. Similar findings exist for voice-gaze interaction.

One of the unique characteristics of decision fusion is that it can incorporate the context in which the interaction occurs. However, there are often complex and non-unique mappings between a user's input and application context due to representational differences between the human cognitive system and a computer's model of the world. This is especially true when sophisticated application databases and tools (such as a geographic information system) are involved. The solution is to consider management of the human-computer dialogue in terms of dialogue maintenance, repair, and advance. In a natural multimodal dialogue, information flows both from the user to the system and from the system to the user. Coherent dialogues require that the meaning and intention of individual utterances and the

system's responses be understandable linguistically, at different levels of granularity (words, phrases, sentences, and dialogue segments), at the level of intention, and in terms of the salient entities and goals at a particular moment. Structural knowledge about an ongoing dialogue is dynamically constructed during the course of the interaction, and is made accessible to subsequent dialogue processing. A unified and integrated representation of dialogue structures and states is called a dialogue model. A dialogue model is useful at all level of dialogue processing, whether for resolving the assignment of pronouns, selecting proper sentence-parsing structure, associating dialogue segments by the way they contribute to higher-level goals, or anticipating the user's future moves in the dialogue.

Coupling dialogue models with proper control strategies for processing multimodal dialogues brings a number of benefits. First, a dialogue model provides a relatively complete context for interpreting and fusing multimodal inputs that are ambiguous or not interpretable otherwise. This is the idea in top-down interpretation, in which the possible meaning of combined inputs, such as gesture and speech, is constrained by the anticipated information inferable from the dialogue model. Second, good dialogue strategies can compensate for recognition errors, missing information, and misinterpretations to achieve a high degree of robustness and graceful degradation. Recognition of users' intended commands often requires the system to have a certain level of knowledge about the modeled world, the task at hand, the interaction history, and communication and social conventions. Because recognition errors and misunderstanding are inevitable, some form of verification and error-handling processes are required so that any misunderstanding can be communicated and corrected. Third, dialogue management allows multimodal systems to be more adaptive to new situation, new users, and new tasks constraints. The adaptive behavior originates from the fact that dialogue management maintains the most appropriate and up-to-date user models. Such adaptability is critical for supporting the flexibility of multimodal HCI. It should be emphasized that multimodal dialogue systems are in the infancy stage, and many challenging research issues remain.

Future Trends in Multimodal Interfaces

Multimodal human-computer interaction holds great promise as the next generation of computer interfaces. Although multimodal interfaces are not yet entirely technically feasible, they have clear technical advantages when it comes to robust and natural interaction. As multimodal research matures, the interface between users and computers will become more and more transparent. Although it is hard to envision the nature of HCI in the future, in the near term it likely to move toward ubiquitous computing, with technology becoming invisible and the interface merging into the everyday environment. For that to happen, natural communication through gestures, speech, gaze, body posture, and facial expressions must become the means for HCI. Special consideration will be given to tactile-based interfaces as the trend toward increasing miniaturization continues. At present, this type of the touch-driven interface is mostly used for multimodal feedback augmented with audio. Multimodal sensing of users' affective states from their communication and general behavior will probably be one of the next research challenges. Currently there are research initiatives under way to explore ubiquitous technologies in non-instrumented collaborative environments. The other big trend will probably be in assistive technologies, for which electroencephalographs (EEGs) of brain activity, electromyograms (EMGs) of muscle activity, and other physiological sensors will play significant roles in enabling HCI.

Rajeev Sharma, Sanshzar Kettebekov, and Guouray Cai

See also Brain-Computer Interfaces; Dialog Systems; Gesture Recognition; Speech Recognition

FURTHER READING

Allen, J., Byron, D., Dzikovska, M., Ferguson, G., Galescu, L., & Stent, A. (2001). Towards conversational human-computer interaction. *AI Magazine, 22*(4), 27–37.

Benoit, C., Martin, J. C., Pelachaud, C., Schomaker, L., & Suhm, B. (1998). *Audio-visual and multimodal speech systems*. In D. Gibbon, R. Moore & R. Winski (Eds), *Handbook of Standards and Resources for Spoken Language Systems* (Supplement Vol.). Berlin, Germany: Mouton de Gruyter.

Bolt, R. A. (1980). Put-that-there: Voice and gesture at the graphic interface. *Computer Graphics, 14*(3), 262–270.

Cassell, J., Torres, O., & Prevost, S. (1999). *Turn taking vs. discourse structure: How best to model multimodal conversation*. In Y. Wilks (Ed.), *Machine Conversations* (pp.143–154). The Hague, Netherlands: Kluwer.

Fischer, G. (2001). User modeling in human-computer interaction. *User Modeling and User-Adapted Interaction, 11*(1–2), 65–86.

Grosz, B. J. (1978). Discourse analysis. In D. Walker (Ed.), *Understanding spoken language* (pp. 235–268). New York: Elsevier North-Holland.

Grosz, B. J., & Sidner, C. L. (1986) Attention, intentions, and the structure of discourse. *Computational Linguistics, 12*(3), 175–204.

Hauptmann, G., & McAvinney, P. (1993) Gesture with speech for graphics manipulation. *International Journal of Man-Machine Studies, 38*(2), 231–249.

Kettebekov, S., & Sharma, R. (2001). Toward natural gesture/speech control of a large display. In L. Nigay (Ed.), *Engineering for human computer interaction* (pp. 133–146). Berlin: Springer-Verlag.

Kettebekov, S., Yeasin, M., & Sharma, R. (2003). Improving continuous gesture recognition with spoken prosody. In *Proceedings of the IEEE Conference on Computer Vision and Pattern Recognition (CVPR'03)* (Vol 1.pp. 565–570). New York: IEEE.

McNeill, D. (1992). *Hand and mind*: Chicago: University of Chicago Press.

McTear, M. F. (2002). Spoken dialogue technology: Enabling the conversational user interface. *ACM Computing Surveys, 34*(1), 90–169.

Oviatt, S., Angeli, A. D., & Kuhn, K. (1997). Integration and synchronization of input modes during multimodal human-computer interaction. In *Proceedings of the Conference on Human Factors in Computing Systems (CHI'97)*, (pp. 415–422). New York: ACM Press.

Oviatt, S. (2000). Taming speech recognition errors within a multimodal interface. *Communications of the ACM, 43*(9), 45–51.

Sharma, R., Pavlovi´c, V. I., Huang, T. S., Lo, Z., Chu, S., Zhao, Y., et al. (2000). Speech/gesture interface to a visual-computing environment. *IEEE Computer Graphics and Applications, 20*(2), 29–37.

Sharma, R., Yeasin, M., Krahnstoever, N., Rauschert, Cai, G., Brewer, I., et al. (2003). Speech-gesture driven multimodal interfaces for crisis management. *Proceedings of the IEEE, 91*(9), 1327–1354.

Tanenhaus, M., Spivey-Knowlton, M., Eberhard, K., & Sedivy, J. (1995). Integration of visual and linguistic information during spoken language comprehension. *Science, 268*, 1632–1634.

Wexelblat, A. (1997). Research challenges in gesture: Open issues and unsolved problems. In I. Wachsmuth &M. Fröhlich (Ed.), *Gesture and sign language in human-computer interaction* (pp. 1–12). Berlin, Germany: Springer-Verlag.

MULTIUSER INTERFACES

A multiuser interface (also called a collaborative interface or a groupware interface) may be defined as any interface that allows multiple users to interact

USER INTERFACE The environment (e.g., Windows, MacIntosh, DOS, Unix) allowing a person to interact with a computer.

with some operating system. By this definition, however, the interface of every multiuser operating system is a multiuser interface, even though the purpose of the operating system is to give users the illusion that no one else is using the system. To distinguish multiuser interfaces from single-user ones, multiuser interfaces are usually characterized as interfaces that

- make users aware they are part of a group,
- help people work together,
- provide a shared environment, and
- support groups engaged in a common task.

This characterization gives a good intuitive feel for the purpose and nature of multiuser interfaces, but subjective terms such as "common task" and "work together" make it imprecise. For the purposes of this article, therefore, we shall define a multiuser interface as a set of user interfaces that are coupled with each other—that is, each component user interface can change as a result of the actions taken in one or more of the other component interfaces and/or can cause changes to one more of the other interfaces. Typically, a different user would interact with each of the component interfaces, though it is possible for the same user to interact with multiple interfaces on different computers (at possibly different times), or for multiple users sharing a computer to interact with a single interface. Ideally, coupled user interfaces would help their users work together more productively than uncoupled ones, though there is no guarantee that this will happen because some of the users are free to use the coupling to "flame" to others or to exhibit other anti-social behavior, deliberately or accidentally.

Perhaps the most popular example of a multiuser interface is e-mail—my action of sending e-mail to you causes your e-mail interface to display the message. Another popular example is the interface provided by a multiuser file system—my action of saving modifications to a shared file influences what you see the next time you open the file. Newer examples are in-

stant messaging, gaming, and conferencing interfaces, which are rapidly gaining popularity in the commercial world. Researchers have identified a wide variety of other kinds of multiuser interfaces, some of which will undoubtedly become commercial products.

Both commercial and research multiuser interfaces can be classified according to their goals and features. This classification will explain the space of multiuser interfaces and will suggest areas in which new interfaces could be developed to represent points in this space that are uncovered by existing software.

Dual Goals

One way to characterize this space is by the goals of multiuser interfaces. The highest-level goal of these interfaces, as indicated by the definitions we saw earlier, is to foster collaboration. Why try to do so, given that we have been successfully collaborating directly with each other for centuries without any help from a computer user interface? The popular answer to this question is that a multiuser interface can be used to support distributed collaboration. It can give a user the illusion of being at a collaborator's location. Therefore, one of the main goals of multiusers interfaces is to create, to the greatest extent possible, the experience of a face-to-face collaboration.

While technological advances will allow us to meet this goal in various degrees, they will never be able to create the face-to-face experience perfectly. The proponents of multiuser interfaces may find this depressing, as it implies that these interfaces will always be the second choice—people will use them only when they do not have the time or money to meet face-to-face at a common location. Because of this, researchers have argued for the twin goal of creating collaborative experiences that cannot be supported by face-to-face meetings. A simple example would be to allow a subgroup to whisper to each other without letting others in the group know about the existence of the private conversation. This goal is consistent with virtual environments that go beyond simulations of actual physical environments, for example, by allowing users to instantly teleport to any location within an environment.

In summary, we can characterize the dual goals of multiuser interfaces as taking distributed users "towards being there," and taking both distributed and collocated users "beyond being there." Often the same interface will support both goals. For example, an Instant Messaging (IM) interface provides conversational support that transports us to a common world and presence controls that allow us to lie about our busy/idle status.

Features: Virtual Reality Versus Multiuser Interfaces

Virtual transportation to another world is, of course, the realm of virtual reality and virtual environments. However, a virtual environment typically takes us to a single-user environment. When it takes us to a world inhabited by our collaborators, we have a marriage of multiuser interaction and virtual reality. A virtual environment may do this either by creating an immersive environment or by providing something much simpler, as in the IM example above.

Multiuser virtual environments can be conveniently classified by two orthogonal dimensions: (1) the degree of artificiality, which determines the extent to which the virtual environment differs from an actual physical world, and (2) the degree of transportation, which measures the degree to which users are transported from their actual environments to the virtual world. These two dimensions define a whole space of multiuser virtual environments. This space has four extreme points:

- Low degree of artificiality, low degree of transportation: This would be a face-to-face meeting, since all users remain in their physical world.
- Low degree of artificiality, high degree of transportation: Imagine a sea of cameras at some remote, networked location that creates a computer model of the location in real time on our computer, which we can navigate like the users physically present in the remote environment. Such an experience is called tele-presence— it takes us away from our current location to an actual remote physical environment. The nearest we have come to tele-presence so far is watching superbowl replays captured by multiple cameras.

- High degree of artificiality, high degree of transportation: This would resemble the above example except that we are immersed in a world that does not exist, or exists but not in the scale presented—for example, the simulation of a ship that has not yet been built or a magnification of the physical world captured by a nano-scale microscope. The goal here is to navigate/evaluate/ modify this world collaboratively.
- High degree of artificiality, low degree of transportation: This would be an augmented multiuser reality in which users can simultaneously see both their physical environment and a virtual environment, which are typically related to each other—for example, a description of unfinished work or hidden plumbing left at a construction site by a worker, to be viewed later as a virtual world by other workers who view the site. The artificiality is high because of the displayed virtual image and the transportation is low since users continue to feel that they are in their current physical world.

Of course, several useful intermediate points exist in this space, such as video conferencing, which has a low degree of artificiality and a medium degree of transportation.

Features: Collaboration Tasks

To determine what features are useful in multiuser interfaces, it is important to understand which tasks tend to be collaborative, and hence, can be supported by these interfaces. A particular collaboration may carry out several of these tasks simultaneously. Here are the most common kinds of collaboration tasks:

- Goal-less social interaction: Perhaps the most popular collaboration task is simply social interaction, which often has no explicit goal. People may communicate with each other to meet new people, to get to know each other, to create a shared experience, or to talk extempore about some topic of mutual interest. Social interaction is often considered a desirable side effect of any kind of collaboration.
- Topic-based discussion: The collaboration is focused on a particular topic known to users at

the start of their collaboration (as opposed to extempore discussion. The topics may be work related (for instance, the pros and cons of various job candidates) or may be of social interest (for instance, the pros and cons of basketball teams).

■ Information exchange: People may exchange URLs or other pieces of information. Information exchange may be the primary goal of the collaboration or a side effect or some other kind of task (for example, URLs exchanged in a topic-based discussion).

■ Presentation: One participant presents a lecture to others. A one-to-many distribution of information can be considered a special case of information exchange.

■ Decision-making: The decision may be binary (for instance, should we hire this person?), a list (of eligible applicants, for example), a string (such as the name of a game), or some other data type. Typically this kind of task will be combined with a discussion task—for example, discuss the pros and cons of candidates and decide whom to interview.

■ Search: The collaborators search for something together. For example, they search the Web to find Christmas presents. They search collaboratively to eliminate duplication (such as searching the same Web site) and to make decisions incrementally (such as whether an item should be added to the shopping cart).

■ Comment: Users comment on some object such as a paper, a software specification, a hardware design, or a lecture presentation. This activity is similar to a topic-based discussion except that a comment may not involve pros and cons (for example, it might simply point out a missing comma in a paper) and is associated with a concrete object rather than an abstract topic.

■ Composition: Users collaboratively create an object such as a paper or a software module. This task can be further divided into one or more of the following phases: analysis of requirements the joint object is meant to satisfy, design of the object to meet the requirements, and finally, its implementation and evaluation. Ideally, an interface should support collaboration across all these phases in an integrated manner.

Uncovered Points

Our definition of multiuser interfaces left out three important details:

■ Session management: How is a multiuser interface composed from a set of individual user interfaces?

■ Coupling semantics: How exactly are these component interfaces coupled?

■ Security and consistency: What functions are provided to ensure that users do not make unauthorized or inconsistent changes?

If there was a unique answer to each of these questions, then it would have been part of the definition. As it turns out, these issues can be resolved in multiple ways, and the right answer depends on both the task and the collaborators. People tend to be opportunistic when collaborating with each other, which requires a variety of alternatives. We consider some of the most popular alternatives identified so far.

Session Management

A multiuser interface typically allows the dynamic deletion and addition of component user interfaces. Usually a special interactive tool, called a session manager, is provided, which allows its user to dynamically create/join/leave a multiuser interface and add/remove an application to/from the interface. Creating a multiuser interface gives a name to the interface. Joining a multiuser interface creates a new component interface for each of the applications associated with the multiuser interface, while leaving it destroys these interfaces. Adding an application to the multiuser interface creates a component interface for each of the users who have joined it, while removing the application performs the reverse step. To illustrate, I can use my session manager to create a new multiuser interface, add a whiteboard and document editor to it, and join it. As this point, I am presented with interfaces to interact with the document editor and whiteboard. Later, you can use your session manager to join the multiuser interface, at which point you are also given interfaces to interact with the document editor and whiteboard, which are coupled with my interfaces. Now you can add a spreadsheet application to this interface, which results in the creation of interfaces on both our computers to interact with this application.

A user may join a multiuser interface as a result of searching for it in some directory, being invited to do so by existing users of the interface, discovering it while wandering through some virtual environment inhabited by multiuser interfaces and other objects, or opening a shared file being manipulated by the multiuser interface. Access control may be provided to let only authorized users join the interface and add applications to it. Moreover, the commands of the users who are allowed to join may be restricted. For instance, some users may be prevented from inputting any command, which is useful in a presentation.

Coupling Semantics

Coupling determines which objects are shared among the component interfaces of a multiuser interface and when changes to an interface object are communicated to other component interfaces sharing it. The simplest coupling policy is to share all objects among the component interfaces and to communicate changes to these objects instantly. The result is a WYSIWIS (What You See Is What I See) multiuser interface, in which all users see the same view at all times (modulo networking delays). In tightly coupled interactions such as a requirements discussion or a review, WYSIWIS interaction may be ideal.

In other scenarios, we need relaxed WYSIWIS. A presenter does not wish to share presentation notes with the audience. Different scientists often wish to view the same data in different ways. A user may wish to complete changes to a paragraph before sharing changes to it with others. Coupling the window and scrollbar positions of users may result in "window wars" and "scroll wars" as users fight over the window/scrollbar position. Thus, the degree of coupling among user interfaces must be matched to the degree of collaboration among the users of these interfaces.

A related issue has to do with coupling of the undo histories. All component user interfaces may share a single undo history or create separate histories. Sharing a single undo history seems to go together with WYSIWIS interfaces—however, many users of such interfaces prefer to have a private undo.

Compensating for Loose Coupling

Divergence of the component user interfaces in a non-WYSIWIS interface requires several compensating functions:

- Awareness: Users no longer know what their collaborators are seeing and thus need special mechanisms to see (some abstraction) of the collaborators' views.
- Concurrency control and merging: Users working in isolation from each other can make conflicting changes, and thus need concurrency control mechanisms to prevent concurrent change to the same object or merging mechanisms to resolve conflicts.

Implementation

Implementing a single-user interface is difficult—often as much as 80 percent of the code of an application deals with interaction details. Implementing a multiuser interface is even more difficult as it must provide not only single-user functions but also multiuser functions such as session management, coupling, access control, concurrency control, and merging. Fortunately, like single-user functions, multiuser functions can be automated, typically by extending single-user window systems, toolkits, user-interface management systems, programming languages, frameworks, and other interactive abstractions. These abstractions can be implemented using (a) peer-to-peer architecture in which the component user interfaces communicate directly with each other, or (b) client-server architecture in which component user interfaces communicate via a central server. For example, Microsoft's NetMeeting extends its Window system by automatically supporting centralized WYSIWIS sharing of Microsoft Windows. Another commercial example is the Groove collaboration platform, which supports non-WYSIWIS peer-to-peer sharing of data objects but not their views. Some research systems allow the coupling and architecture to be changed dynamically. An ideal system that provides near-automatic support for all possible architectures and collaboration functions is a still a matter for researchers.

Prasun Dewan

See also Collaboratories; Computer-Supported Cooperative Work

FURTHER READING

Benford, S., Brown, C., et al. (1996). Shared spaces: Transportation, artificiality, and spatiality. In *Proceedings of the ACM Conference on Computer Supported Cooperative Work*. New York.

Choudhary, R., & Dewan, P. (1995). A general multi-user undo/redo model. In *Proceedings of European Conference on Computer Supported Work*. Dordrecht: Kluwer.

Chung, G., & Dewan, P. (2001). Flexible support for application-sharing architecture. In *Proceedings of European Conference on Computer Supported Cooperative Work, Bonn*. Dordrecht: Kluwer.

Dewan, P. (1993). Tools for implementing multiuser user interfaces. *Trends in Software: Issue on User Interface Software, 1*, 149–172.

Dewan, P. (1998). Architectures for collaborative applications. *Trends in Software: Computer Supported Co-operative Work, 7*, 165–194.

Dewan, P., & Choudhary, R. (1991). Flexible user interface coupling in collaborative systems. In *Proceedings of the ACM CHI'91 Conference*. New York.

Dewan, P., & Shen, H. (1998). Flexible meta access-control for collaborative applications. In *Proceedings of ACM Conference on Computer Supported Cooperative Work*. New York.

Dourish, P., & Belloti, V. (1992). Awareness and coordination in a shared workspace. In *Proceedings of ACM Conference on Computer Supported Cooperative Work '92*. New york.

Ellis, C. A., Gibbs, S. J., et al. (1991). Groupware: Some issues and experiences. *CACM, 34*(1), 38–58.

Grudin, J. (1994). Groupware and social dynamics: Eight challenges for developers. *Communications of the ACM*. New York.

Gutwin, C., & Greenberg, S. (1998). Design for individuals, design for groups: Tradeoffs between power and worskpace awareness. In *Proceedings of ACM Conference on Computer Supported Cooperative Work*. New York.

Hollan, J., & Stornetta, S. (1992). Beyond being there. *ACM CHI'92 Proceedings*.

Munson, J., & Dewan, P. (1994). A flexible object merging framework. In *Proceedings of the ACM Conference on Computer Supported Cooperative Work*. New York.

Munson, J., & Dewan, P. (1996). A concurrency control framework for collaborative systems. In *Proceedings of the ACM Conference on Computer Supported Cooperative Work*. New York.

Neuwirth, C. M., Chandok, R., et al. (1992). Flexible diff-ing in a collaborative writing system. In *Proceedings of ACM Conference on Computer Supported Cooperative Work*. New York.

Prakash, A., & Knister, M. J. (1992). Undoing actions in collaborative work. In *Proceedings of the ACM Conference on Computer Supported Cooperative Work*. New York.

Sarin, S., & Greif, I. (1985). Computer-based real-time conferencing systems. *IEEE Computer, 18*(10), 33–49.

Shen, H., & Dewan, P. (1992). Access control for collaborative environments. In *Proceedings of the ACM Conference on Computer Supported Cooperative Work*. New York.

Stefik, M., Foster, G., et al. (1987). Beyond the chalkboard: Computer support for collaboration and problem solving in meetings. *CACM, 30*(1), 32–47.

Sun, C., & Ellis, C. (1998). Operational transformation in real-time group editors: Issues, algorithms, and achievements. In *Proceedings of the ACM Conference on Computer Supported Cooperative Work '98*. New York.

MUSICAL INTERACTION

Musicians, performance artists, computer scientists, engineers, and others are exploring interactive musical systems—a fertile application domain for the human-computer interaction community. The goal of the musical interaction community is to build computer systems that serve as partners to humans in the composition, analysis, and performance of music. From their earliest beginnings, computers were used to produce music. Even before computers, as we know them today, mechanical and electronic devices produced and embellished music played by humans. The dramatic increase in computational power of the last several decades now places computers alongside humans as partners and collaborators in new and traditional music. In this article we examine three areas of human-computer musical interaction: automatic interactive accompaniment systems, interactive improvisation systems, and interactive gestural/performance systems that use new methods of gestural control.

Representation of Music

Currently the predominant music representations for computer music are sampled audio—for example, as stored on a compact disc—which can be produced by any combination of algorithm and recording, and the less familiar MIDI (Musical Instrument Digital Interface), which has had a significant impact on many interactive music applications. The MIDI protocol was developed in 1983 as a means of controlling electronic musical instruments via other electronic instruments or a computer. In its most basic form, MIDI is a cartoonlike representation of music, similar to a piano roll, prescribing the start time, end time, and "velocity" or loudness of each note in a composition. MIDI has evolved to allow a more intimate control of electronic

A digital sound-recording system, c. 2002, with an equalizer, mixer, and 40-gigabyte hard drive. Photo courtesy of Mark Schane Lydon.

instruments through "continuous controllers," which make possible a real-time control of pitch modulations, vibrato, and other time-varying parameters. It occupies a central position in many electronic and interactive music systems as an intermediate representation of the music often created by some high-level controller such as a keyboard, a bowed-controller, a wind-controller, or a motion sensor, and is commonly used to drive an electronic synthesizer. The essential idea of MIDI has even been abstracted beyond the domain of music and developed to control interactive robots and lighting.

Automatic Interactive Accompaniment Systems

A number of researchers have built computer systems that function as musical accompanists. While the name "accompaniment system" suggests a rather traditional musical genre involving soloist and accom-

paniment, the applicability of these systems is potentially quite broad, allowing a fusion of the expressive element of music, natural for the human musician, with the limitless technical ability and sonic palette of the computer. These systems are also valued as educational tools; they teach by means of a virtual environment that resembles the one a trained musician encounters in performance. In most cases these systems assume that both the live player and the computerized accompanist play from a musical score and that the live musician plays a monophonic (single voice) instrument. There are, however, many variations, including allowing polyphonic input, improvisation on the part of the soloist or the accompaniment, and various sensing mechanisms to track the soloist, as well as the possibility of learning on the part of the accompanist.

Before the accompanist can follow the soloist it must first be able to understand what and when the soloist is playing. If this recognition process is to be robust, the system cannot assume that the human plays without error and embellishment. Rather, the system must be able to match the human-played input to the score even when the human's performance is not literally correct. This can be accomplished in a variety of ways, assuming various levels of pre-processing. The most straightforward approach, developed by Bridget Baird and her colleagues in 1993, is when a soloist plays from a MIDI instrument since, in this case, the sequence and times of the various pitches are given to the accompaniment system. Another approach that uses a pre-interpreted performance representation, found in the work of Barry Vercoe, is where notes are detected by sensors that track the positions of the pads of a flute.

Other approaches follow the score by dealing more directly with the audio signal. For instance, Roger B. Dannenberg processes the output of a pitch-to-MIDI converter that generates a stream of pitch-tagged frames. While such an approach is more broadly applicable since there is no requirement that the solo performance be represented in MIDI, it requires considerably more attention to the input analysis since the pitch-to-MIDI input generally contains many errors. In fact, the audio signal can be analyzed directly without any intermediate processing by specialized hardware, as described in a 1998 paper by Lorin Grubb and Roger Dannenberg, which treats the challenging domain of vocal accompaniment.

As the accompaniment system follows the progress of the soloist through the score, the accompaniment is generated in real-time, either by MIDI or by some other sparse representation of music. Typically, the running position and tempo estimates of the soloist's score position are maintained and used to control the playback of the accompaniment. These systems can respond quickly to input and are remarkably capable of following even when notes are added or deleted. Significant future challenges, which have been partially addressed by several researchers, will be to capture the expressive component of the accompaniment and to learn from rehearsal data.

Interactive Improvisational Systems

Interactive musical improvisation can be divided into several somewhat overlapping areas: interactive jazz, interactive avant-garde music, and a variety of "sound art" intersecting dance and audio/visual improvisation. In jazz improvisation, a soloist composes a musical part on-the-fly from a basic template specifying chord progressions. Dannenberg and Bernard Mont-Reynaud provide a link between accompaniment systems and improvisation by creating a system that accompanies a jazz improvisor. Rather than working from a score, the system is given a fixed chord progression. A primary challenge here is tracking the progress of the soloist whose contribution is does not follow a fixed score. The system follows the soloist by using beat-tracking and pattern-matching algorithms.

Systems developed in the 1980s that performed melodic jazz improvisations used models of jazz musical style; however, interactive jazz systems came of age in the 1990s. Researchers have employed machine-learning techniques that enable a machine to learn to improvise and to improvise interactively with human players. These systems all assume a fixed accompaniment, based on a set harmonic structure, provided by software that does not adjust to the human or machine improvisor.

One interactive behavior in jazz improvisation is that of teacher and student. The GenJam system developed in 1994 by Al Biles bases its learning on qualitative judgments provided by the human during its performance. In this machine-learning model, the system is guided toward tendencies implicitly encouraged by the judge. Another prevalent kind of interaction is in the trading of improvisation between two musicians. Three systems that employ machine learning to develop an interactive improvisor are GenBebop, developed by Lee Spector and Adam Alpern, CHIME, developed by Judy Franklin, and BoB, developed by Belinda Thom. In all these systems the machine "trades fours" with a human player, taking turns improvising for four measures and then listening to the other's four-measure response. The machine uses the collaborator's material, as well as its own learned experience, to form the improvisation over the next four measures. Thus, the system may learn to be a good improvisor with its own style, or it may be tailored to be a musical companion to a particular human.

Cypher, developed by Robert Rowe, is an interactive performance system for composition and performance built on Max, a general-purpose MIDI-based software system that uses a graphical interface to create interactive systems. Objects in Max can sense input, process and manipulate input, and respond, either periodically or asynchronously, according to specific events. Cypher gathers and tracks perceptual features such as loudness, register, speed, and density and generates music using various algorithmic styles as specified by a composer, and as monitored by an internal aesthetic critic. It does not contain an internal score that is followed during a performance. Cypher may be used by a composer who interactively fine-tunes a piece before a performance. However, Cypher has also been used in various public performances as an improvisational tool where very few decisions were made prior to the performance. Rowe describes a number of such performances, which took place in the late 1980s and early 1990s. Other software systems for interactive performance are often developed for a particular setting, such as a computer/orchestral interaction.

Interactive Gestural/Performance Systems

A more general type of improvisation occurs when music is part of a larger performance that encompasses dance, video projection, and other multimedia events. The use and evolution of sensors and gestural controllers are part of this phenomenon. Gestural control started with the simple notion that a keystroke or mouse click could initiate a musical generation process, perhaps just turning on a recording, or could select musical parameters during a non-score-driven performance. In the mid-sixties a system was developed that enables dancers to produce music in response to their proximity to electronic sensors; the whole dance area becomes an instrument that responds to motion.

Interactive gestural control in compositional, installation, and performance systems is emerging as a new important direction in music. The gestural sensors are extensive, varied, and evolving; from those used in gaming and virtual reality environments, to others from completely different fields such as medicine, and to others designed by experimental musicians for this purpose. Gestures may generate music and/or may control or trigger other audio or visual events.

Controllers that respond to hand motion have been developing since 1919 when an instrument called the Theremin was built. The Theremin is played by moving the hands around two antennae, one to control pitch and one to control volume. Currently, other types of proximity sensors stationed in space may detect hand motion. Sensors may also be placed on the hands themselves—as for example, in Data Gloves, as described by Rowe, or hands may hold transmitters that emit signals to controllers that interpret the motion. Two examples of this are the Buchla Lightning Controller (a wand transmits infrared), and the Radio Drum (the drum senses the position of the drum sticks on the drum head and also knows the spatial positions of the sticks themselves). Whole-body motion can also be sensed using analogous devices such as body proximity sensors, body suits, and other sensors that can transmit body position and motion.

It becomes difficult to distinguish between interactive systems and improvisational systems within this context. If a dancer has a set choreography and the computer responses are all prerecorded or deterministic, then the system is clearly non-improvisational. However, if performers can improvise, then even fixed computer responses become tools in an all-encompassing improvisational system. The actions of performers may also be analyzed over longer periods of time for direction, repetition, or other patterns, and performers may provide feedback to a computer system that improvises interactively with them.

Judy A. Franklin and Christopher Raphael

See also Artificial Intelligence; Sonification

FURTHER READING

Ames, C., & Comino, M. (1992). Cybernetic composer: An overview. In M. Balaban, K. Ebcioglu, & O. Laske (Eds.), *Understanding music with AI* (pp.186–205). Cambridge, MA: AAAI Press/MIT Press.

Baird, B., Blevins, D., & Zahler, N. (1993). Artificial intelligence and music: Implementing an interactive computer performer. *Computer Music Journal, 17*(2), 73–79.

Biles, J. A. (1994). GenJam: A genetic algorithm for generating jazz so-los. In *Proceedings of the 1994 International Computer Music Conference* (pp. 207–210). San Francisco, CA: International Computer Music Association.

Boulanger, R., Thompson, G., & Saleh, J. (2003). Shedding some light on 'dark matter'. In *Proceedings of the Ninth Biennial Symposium on Arts and Technology* (pp. 12–16). New London, CT: Connecticut College.

Chadabe, J. (2003). *Electric sound: The past and promise of electronic music.* Upper Saddle River, NJ: Prentice Hall.

Dannenberg, R. (1984). An on-line algorithm for real-time accompaniment. In *Proceedings of the 1994 International Computer Music Conference* (pp. 193–198). San Francisco, CA: International Computer Music Association.

Dannenberg, R. (1989). Real-time scheduling and computer accompaniment. In M. Mathes & J. Pierce (Eds.), *Current directions in computer music research* (pp. 225–261). Cambridge, MA: MIT Press.

Dannenberg, R. (2003). Sound Synthesis from video, wearable lights, and "the watercourse way." In *Proceedings of the Ninth Biennial Symposium on Arts and Technology* (pp.38–44). New London, CT: Connecticut College.

Dannenberg, R., & Mont-Reynaud, B. (1987). Following an improvisation in real time. In *Proceedings of the 1987 International Computer Music Conference* (pp.241–248). San Francisco, CA: International Computer Music Association.

Franklin, J. (2002). Improvisation and learning. In T. Dietterich, S. Becker, & Z. Ghahramani (Eds.), *Neural information processing systems (NIPS)* 14. Cambridge, MA: MIT Press.

Fry, C. (1993). Flavors band: A language for specifying musical style. In S. Schwanauer & D. Levitt (Eds.), *Machine models of music.* Cambridge, MA: MIT Press.

Grubb, L., & Dannenberg, R. (1998). Enhanced vocal performance tracking using multiple information sources. In *Proceedings of the 1998 International Computer Music Conference* (pp. 34–44). San Francisco, CA: Computer Music Association.

Madden, T., Smith, R., Wright, M., & Wessel, D. (2001). Preparation for interactive live computer performance in collaboration with a symphony orchestra. In *Proceedings of the 2001 International Computer Music Conference* (pp. 310–313). San Francisco, CA: Computer Music Association.

Messick, P. (1998). *Maximum MIDI.* Greenwich, CT: Manning.

Overholt, D. (2001). The MATRIX: A new musical instrument for interactive performance. In *Proceedings of the 2001 International Computer Music Conference* (pp.243–246). San Francisco, CA: Computer Music Association.

Raphael, C. (2001). Music plus one: A system for expressive and flexible musical accompaniment. In *Proceedings of the 2001 International Computer Music Conference* (pp. 159–162). San Francisco, CA: Computer Music Association.

Roads, C. (1996). *The computer music tutorial.* Cambridge, MA: MIT Press.

Rowe, R. (1993). *Interactive music systems.* Cambridge, MA: MIT Press.

Thom, B. (2003). Interactive improvisational music companionship: A user-modeling approach. *User Modeling and User-Adapted Interaction Journal, 13*(1–2).

Vercoe, B. (1984). The synthetic performer in the context of live performance. In *Proceedings of the 1984 International Computer Music Conference* (pp. 199–200). San Francisco, CA: International Computer Musical Association.

Vercoe, B., & Puckette, M. (1985). Synthetic rehearsal: Training the synthetic performer. In *Proceedings of the 1984 International Computer Music Conference* (pp. 275–278). San Francisco, CA: International Computer Musical Association.

Winkler, T. (1998). *Composing interactive music.* Cambridge, MA: MIT Press. Wright, M., Freed, A., Lee, A., Madden, T., and Momeni, A. (2001). Managing complexity with explicit mapping of gestures to sound control with OSC. In *Proceedings of the 2001 International Computer Music Conference* (pp. 314–317). San Francisco, CA: International Computer Musical Association.

Zicarelli, D. (1987). M and jam factory. *Computer Music Journal, 11*(4), 13–29.

n

NATURAL-LANGUAGE PROCESSING

The field of natural-language processing, or computational linguistics, as it is sometimes called, addresses the problem of getting computers to perform useful tasks involving human languages. Computer applications that fall under this description range from the now ubiquitous spelling and grammar correctors found in most word processors to complex systems that can recognize spoken utterances in one language and simultaneously translate them to another.

The easiest way to see what is involved in this endeavor is to think about the various computers and robots from science fiction that have been portrayed using natural language to communicate. What would these computers have to have known about human languages to be able to understand and participate in normal conversations with human beings? Fortunately, linguists have provided us with the following classification of the different kinds of knowledge that humans bring to bear when using language:

- Phonology: The sounds humans use to create language
- Morphology: Words and their meaningful constituent parts
- Syntax: The ordering, grouping, and dependency relationships among words in simple utterances
- Semantics: The relationship between linguistic utterances and the worlds to which they refer

- Pragmatics: How humans use language to achieve their goals in context
- Discourse: How larger units of language are structured

Achieving a Simple Dialogue

The primary task for those involved in building natural-language processing systems is to identify the relevant kinds of knowledge needed to perform some task, represent that knowledge in a form that is amenable to processing by a computer, and then design and implement algorithms that can use the represented knowledge to perform the required tasks. To illustrate this process, let us consider the various kinds of knowledge that a computer-based driver's assistant would need to have to participate in the following simple dialogue

> Driver: Can you locate the nearest place to eat?
>
> Assistant: Turn left at the next light. It's two blocks up on the right.

The first problem for the system is figuring out what the driver actually said. This is generally referred to as speech recognition, and in its most basic form it refers to the process of recovering the sequence of words that gave rise to a given audio signal. This is a complex task that involves difficult problems in signal processing that are quite independent of language processing (such as the problem of ambient noise in moving cars). But at its core this task requires the system to have knowledge of how individual words are pronounced, how their standard pronunciations can vary with speakers and context, and how these pronunciations manifest themselves as audio signals. Similar knowledge is also used in the opposite direction to generate the audio output that conveys the answer to the driver via the process known as speech synthesis, or text to speech (TTS).

Having recovered the words *likely* to have been spoken by the driver, the system must begin to analyze this sequence in an attempt to determine the words the driver *actually* said. The first step in this process involves a preliminary analysis of the items that the system has detected in the signal. Consider the seemingly simple words *can* and *to* in our example. What the system really knows at this point is

that the driver uttered one of potentially many words that are pronounced as these words are pronounced; the *can* input might refer to can_1, a kind of metal container, can_2, an action taken to put things in a can, or can_3, a function word in English that shows possibility or potentiality. Our *to* example is even simpler to see; this input can correspond to three distinct English words that share a pronunciation but not a spelling: *to, too,* and *two.*

Choosing among these various alternatives involves a variety of processes that include N-gram analysis, part-of-speech tagging, and word-sense disambiguation. These techniques make use of knowledge of individual words and how they are likely to behave with respect to other nearby words. This kind of knowledge may be sufficient in many cases to resolve any ambiguities without having to resort to deeper analysis. In this case, it is likely that a system could identify the correct *can* and *to* without recourse to deeper processing.

The next level of analysis involves discerning the syntactic structure of the input through the use of knowledge of the grammar of a language. This syntactic knowledge allows the system to analyze, or parse, the input into its constituent parts to facilitate further processing. The internal constituent structure in this example reveals among other things that a request in the form of a yes/no question is being asked, that the verb *locate* is key to the request, and that the direct object is a noun phrase with a place as its main element.

While there are a wide variety of formalisms that are used to capture syntactic information, most capture the kind of information shown here in the tree diagram in Figure 1.

Syntactic structures such as the one shown in Figure 1 identify and label the constituent parts of an utterance and also show the recursive substructure of these parts. For example, this tree identifies the entire sequence as a sentence (S), the first work as an auxiliary verb (Aux), the phrase *locate the nearest place to eat* as a verb phrase (VP) that consists of two parts: the verb *locate* and the noun phrase (NP) *the nearest place to eat.* This NP also has a further internal structure not shown in the diagram.

Having extracted the words from the audio signal and recovered the syntactic structure, the sys-

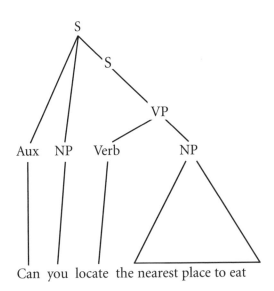

FIGURE 1. *A sample syntactic parse tree*

tem must next begin to try to determine what the utterance actually was about, a process known as semantic analysis. It is during this phase that the system begins to apply its semantic knowledge. In linguistic terms, this is the knowledge that allows us to map, or correlate, the linguistic elements in an utterance to concepts in the real world. For this utterance, the mapping involves knowing the kinds of actions that are associated with the verb *locate* and what counts as *a place to eat* in the world. Of course, in a computational setting this mapping is not to the real world, but to some subset of the world as it is modeled in the driver assistant's knowledge base. In the context of our example, this might mean that the system has a mapping from the verb *locate* to a particular set of geographically oriented database actions, that *nearest* requires it to perform a set of comparisons over a set of items from that database, and that the phrase *a place to eat* corresponds to a set of restaurants in its database.

The Larger Context

Of course, simply being able to map from individual words and phrases to a represented world is not sufficient to perform any interesting semantic processing. What is needed is the ability to combine

these various elements into a single coherent representation that captures the meaning of the whole utterance and not just the meanings of individual words and phrases. The dominant approach to solving this problem relies on two interrelated notions: predicate-argument semantics and the principle of compositionality. Loosely, predicate-argument semantics refers to the idea that the purpose of certain elements of a sentence (predicates) is to relate together, or organize, the remaining parts (arguments) into a coherent whole.

The principle of compositionality states that the meaning of an entire utterance is a function of the meanings of its parts. To make use of the principle of compositionality, one must know what function is used to combine the meanings of the parts into a whole, and one must know what parts are being referred to. Fortunately, the syntax of a language goes a long way toward supplying both pieces of information. The parts referred to are the constituent parts provided by a syntactic analysis of an input utterance. The functions used to combine the meanings of the parts into a coherent whole are also provided by the syntax. In most languages, it appears to be the case that the verbs provide predicate-like

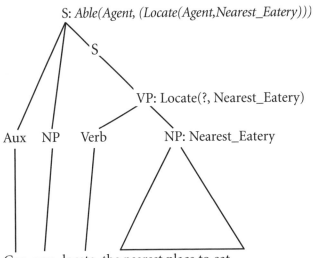

FIGURE 2. *A predicate-argument semantic analysis*

If dictation or its transcription is making you a slave to routine, preventing you from spreading your creative wings . . . write your declaration of independence electronically.
The Edison Electronic Voicewriter . . . outstanding because of its Ear-Tuned Jewel-Action . . . subdues loud tones and strengthens soft ones . . . makes sure that the exact words spoken are speedily echoed on paper.

Thomas A. Edison

1847   THOMAS A. EDISON CENTENNIAL   1947

Thomas A. Edison, Incorporated, West Orange, New Jersey

In Canada: Thomas A. Edison of Canada, Ltd., Toronto 1, Ontario

PHONE EDIPHONE, YOUR CITY, OR WRITE THE ABOVE ADDRESS

A 1947 magazine ad for the Edison Electronic Voicewriter illustrates the importance of reproducing language accurately for transcription. Photo courtesy of Marcy Ross.

organizational structure while noun phrases and prepositional phrases play a more argument-like role.

A highly simplified example of this kind of processing is shown in Figure 2. The predicate-argument semantics of the whole sentence is shown using a style of notation known as a logical form. This figure shows how the semantics of the parts are integrated into a logical form as guided by the parse tree. Note that the presence of the terms Agent and Nearest_Eatery in Figure 2 are a short-hand intended

to convey the idea the logical form of the NPs and PPs (the arguments) does not consist of the words themselves but rather a translation into some deeper meaning representation.

Unfortunately, our system's work is not done yet. Simply recovering the semantics of an utterance does not always tell an agent what to do with the utterance. In this case, the agent has been presented with what is known as a yes/no question. A paraphrase would be, "Are you able to locate the nearest place to eat?"

However, the correct behavior in this instance is not to produce a yes or no answer, but in fact to perform the action specified in the question. Producing this behavior requires knowledge of the pragmatics of the language—the conventions that native speakers use in context to achieve their goals. In this case, it is a convention of Standard English that a polite way to ask someone to do something for you is to ask them indirectly if they are able do it. So, for example, speakers of Standard English say, "Can you get the door?" as opposed to "Get the door." While "no" might be the appropriate answer in some circumstances, an answer of "yes" to this kind of request is usually inappropriate.

Finally, we come to the last strata of linguistic knowledge: knowledge of discourse structure. Most uses of language occur in some kind of recognizable context that has identifiable rules, or norms of behavior, that dictate how the participants in the discourse are expected to behave. For example, typical written discourse assumes a writer separated in space and time from the intended reader of the text. This necessitates a fairly formal and careful style of writing in which things can be made explicit and exact. Normal conversations, on the other hand, occur in real time in a shared context. There is no time for complex planning and revision of utterances, and the participants normally share some common context.

A number of discourse factors are illustrated in our example. The first discourse-specific phenomenon is the system's use of the expressions *the next light*, *it*, and *two blocks up on the right*. These phrases all depend crucially on the current context (in this case, time and location) for a correct interpretation. Another example is the system's entirely appropriate use of the imperative *Turn left* in response to the given question. In this context, what appears to be a command is simply the information our driver requested. In other contexts it would be completely inappropriate for an automated assistant to use the imperative.

Computational Paradigms

As our example illustrates, the processing of even the simplest utterances can require the representation and processing of a considerable amount of diverse linguistic knowledge. Over the years, the scientists and engineers who design systems to deal with language have discovered a small number of powerful computational paradigms that can be used to effectively acquire, represent, and process the diverse kinds of knowledge discussed above. The three most important paradigms can be roughly characterized as systems of discrete rules that capture what is possible in a language, probabilistic models that capture what is likely, and machine-learning systems that acquire the knowledge needed for the other two.

Discrete-Rule Systems

Discrete rule systems can be used either to analyze an input to reveal some underlying structure, or to take an underlying structure and generate a surface form. Analysis at the syntactic level makes use of a discrete-rule system. The syntactic parse trees shown earlier can be thought of as having been generated by the application of a series of rules of the form $X \rightarrow Y\ Z$. Here the X on the left-hand side of the arrow stands for the kind of syntactic constituent being analyzed, such as a noun phrase or verb phrase. The elements on the right-hand side tell us the sequence of elements that make up, or constitute, the X. Examples of the rules used to generate the tree assigned to our earlier example would include $S \rightarrow Aux\ NP\ S$, for the overall structure of the sentence, and $VP \rightarrow Verb\ NP$ for the structure of the verb phrase lower in the tree. Formally, a set of rules of this sort constitutes what is called a context-free grammar for a language.

A fundamental problem with discrete systems of this sort is that they introduce ambiguity at many levels, but provide no way of dealing with it. Consider the following variation on our original example.

Driver: Locate a restaurant on the way to the airport.

This utterance is ambiguous as to whether it is a request for a specific kind of restaurant (one located on the route to the airport), or a restriction as to when the locating action should be performed (locate the restaurant while we're on the way to the airport). These two (and there are others) interpretations correspond to different syntactic and semantic analyses of the input utterance. In the end, our driving assistant must choose which of the two to take action on. This brings us to the second paradigm, the probabilistic model.

Probabilistic Models

The dominant approach to solving ambiguity problems is to use probabilistic models. These models address ambiguity problems by assigning probabilities to all the interpretations that are possible given the syntax of the input. A decision process can then factor these probabilities into the method used to deal with ambiguity. The simplest possible approach is to simply select the most likely structure from among the choices that are possible. Two key elements must be present if the scheme is to work: a reasonable framework for assigning a probability to a sequence or some other, more complex structure, such as a tree, and representative data from which the statistics needed to make the model work can be derived.

Let us consider the problem of deciding among the possible trees that can be generated for a single string due to an ambiguous syntactic grammar. The first problem is to determine what it means to assign a probability to a tree. Recall that any tree is really made up of a finite number of applications of grammar rules. A surprisingly effective technique is to simply say that the probability of a tree is simply the product of the probabilities of the rules that made up the tree. This leaves us with the question of what constitutes the probability of a rule. Again, a simple approach seems to work well: The probability of a rule is simply derived from the proportion of times that rule is observed to parse the constituent in question.

To make this concrete, assume that English has only three kinds of verb phrases, intransitives (phrases in which the verb does not take a direct object), transitives (phrases in which the verb takes a direct object) and ditransitives (phrases in which the verb takes two objects, as in "gave Sally a book"), which can be denoted by the context-free grammar rules $VP \rightarrow Verb$, $VP \rightarrow Verb\ NP$, and $VP \rightarrow Verb\ NP\ NP$, respectively. The probability we assign to each of these would simply be the proportion of times that each rule was used when a VP was present in some large sample of representative text. Of course, this approach relies on the existence of a large resource of correctly parsed text. Luckily, such resources are increasingly available.

Given this framework, a probabilistic parser can simply generate all possible trees for some ambiguous input, assign a probability to each by computing the product of the probabilities of the rules in each tree, and then simply prefer the tree with the highest probability.

Machine-Learning Systems

Using human analysts to acquire the knowledge needed for natural-language processing can be slow, expensive, and error-prone. Therefore, most modern natural-language processing systems are, at least in part, crafted using supervised machine-learning technology. In supervised machine learning, a system is presented with a large collection of problem instances as well as the correct answers, and from that data learns to make similar judgments on new problems. This technique still involves human analysts but alleviates the need for them to figure out how they apply their language knowledge; they simply have to provide an answer. This technique has proven to be effective in a wide variety of applications, including part-of-speech tagging, parsing, semantic analysis, and even automatic machine translation. In all of these cases, human analysts have created large bodies of training data by annotating large numbers of naturally occurring sentences with additional information in the form of parts of speech for each word, parse trees for each sentence, and logical forms for each sentence. This training data can then be passed to systems that can learn to produce similar output for similar input sentences.

Future Directions

These are exciting times for the field of natural-language processing. Systems that were once thought of purely in terms of science fiction are now in routine use in both commercial and research settings. This includes systems that generate weather reports in French and English for the Canadian weather service, that translate arbitrary pages on the Internet to and from any of a dozen languages, and automated conversational agents that can provide advice on air, hotel, and car rental travel arrangements.

Of these, conversational agents are viewed as the application that has the potential to radically change the way people interact with computers. The combination of effective speech recognition, semantic analysis, and dialogue management with animation can facilitate the creation of a wide range of interactive animated conversational agents, which could be used as personal assistants, tutors, expert advisers for particular domains of interest, and for customer support.

James Martin

See also Dialog Systems; Lexicon Building; N-grams; Speech Recognition

FURTHER READING

Allen, J. (1995). *Natural language processing.* Boston: Addison-Wesley.

Cole, R., Mariani, J., Uszkoriet, H., Zaenen, A., and Zue, V. (1997). *Survey of the state of the art in human language technology.* Cambridge, UK: Cambridge University Press.

Jurafsky, D., & Martin, J. H. (2000*). Speech and language processing: An introduction to natural language processing, computational linguistics, and speech recognition.* Upper Saddle River, NJ: Prentice Hall.

Manning, C. D., & Schütze, H. (1999*). Foundations of statistical language processing.* Cambridge, MA: MIT Press.

NAVIGATION

The term *to navigate* means to locomote by any means in order to reach a destination. Earlier uses of the term were generally limited to refer to locomotion by ships over bodies of water and emphasized the history of the use of technologies, such as maps and stars to estimate latitude, and of maps, stars, and clocks to estimate longitude. Study of human navigation is organized around the information and processes that humans use to find their way across relatively short distances of daily life, the development of modern tools for navigation, including electronic databases that can be displayed on maps to the Global Positioning System (GPS), the use of computer-simulated environments for training, and information systems.

Information and Processing Strategies

Navigation depends on incoming information about one's dynamically changing position during locomotion and on knowledge of one's destination and hazards on the way to one's destination. Information is needed to specify one's spatial orientation (that is, one's changing distance and direction relative to one's destination and/or relative to a frame of reference that can be related to the destination), knowledge about obstacles and constraints on alternative paths of travel, knowledge of how to combine these forms of information, and knowledge to identify safe and efficient routes. These three forms of knowledge are ubiquitous to navigation and apply equally to animals finding their way across distances to find food or to reproduce and to people finding their way across distances to find information and navigating information systems ranging from encyclopedias to the World Wide Web. A fundamental feature of navigation is that multiple forms of knowledge and information can be used to determine each of the three. This fact is especially important because the information that is available often varies, depending on clouds, terrain, and the navigator's knowledge, and it is of interest to the navigator to understand how perceptual systems choose among the alternative forms of information and represent them.

Navigation and spatial orientation are particularly interdependent. Spatial orientation is the alignment or position of a body (or body part) relative to some reference system. This orientation can include the position of one's eyes relative to an object that one is about to fixate or the position of one's hand relative to an object that one is about to grasp. The emphasis here is on the position of one's body relative to a goal object or destination. Writings about flight and space travel often use the term *spatial orientation* to refer to body position relative to gravity, which can be problematic when pilots accelerate and thus change their perceived orientation relative to gravity and when astronauts operate under the weightless conditions of outer space. Writings about long-distance travel often use the term *spatial orientation* to refer to body position relative to the stars, magnetic compass, or map. Writings about shorter travel often use the term *spatial orientation* to refer to body position relative to local features of the immediate surroundings.

The precision of human navigation is ever increasing by learning and new technologies. Some of the practical problems that have motivated thinking about human navigation include (in reverse chronological order) design of computer-guided robots to explore the planet Mars, design of user-friendly GPS-based navigation systems for automobiles, design of electronic systems to aid persons who are blind, and an understanding of why children become lost, which has led to efficient search strategies for finding them. Flexibility and the use of multiple strategies are a hallmark of spatial orientation. Here are five types of information or strategy:

- Dead reckoning is keeping track of the "way home" by keeping track of one's distance and direction relative to the starting point of a trip. Dead reckoning for animals may mostly involve keeping track of the most efficient path to home after foraging for food (this is generally the shortest path), whereas for humans it may involve keeping track of one's position relative to any number of locations. Path integration is a type of type reckoning by which the information from different segments of one's path is integrated over space and time in order to keep track of the distance and direction to some location.
- A beacon is a single landmark or gradient. One can know a direction of travel from a beacon, and examples include lighthouses used for maritime navigation.
- A landmark is an object or distinctive feature used to denote the location of a goal. Whereas a beacon indicates the general direction toward a goal, a landmark is more specific and can indicate its location as well as general direction.
- Frame of reference is environmental information used to specify facing direction and location. Logically, it must consist of at least three points or two points and a reference direction.
- Geometry is the geometrical structure of landmarks or other features of the terrain used for

spatial orientation. Research with species ranging from rats to humans shows that they use the shapes of rooms to keep track of hidden target objects. An example in the woods is using the angle of convergence of two ridge lines to know the direction and distance of travel.

Historical Tools for Navigation at Sea

The earliest seafarers are said to have kept in sight of land, in part so they could find their way home and in part so they could keep track of safe channels and avoid dangerous shoals. To find rich fishing grounds, avoid dangerous shoals, and return home safely, one can line up landmarks to get a direction, use a weighted line to estimate depths, and even use odors, which can travel far from land. One needs information to determine the direction and distance of travel to one's destination, and multiple types of information can specify these factors when land is not in sight. The ancient Phoenicians, who navigated the Mediterranean and beyond and steered by the stars, are said to have used the North Star to estimate latitude, to have understood that the height of the sun and other stars above the horizon depends on the time of year, and to have recorded tables of these elevations for use by navigators.

The astronomer Ptolemy of ancient Alexandria, Egypt, created a world atlas in about 150 CE, and mariners are said to have used charts as navigation aids ever since. Ptolemy even plotted latitude and longitude lines on his atlas's twenty-seven maps, although the farther one got from the known world centered on the Mediterranean, the dangerously less reliable the maps became.

The magnetic compass was a great advance in navigation because it provided a means of keeping up to date on changes in direction relative to a destination. The Chinese are said to have known about the powers of magnetism as early as the third millennium BCE, when, historians tell us, one army defeated another after the battlefield had become enveloped in dense fog by using a "point-south carriage." However, magnetic compasses apparently were not used for maritime travel by Europeans until the twelfth century. Despite its usefulness, the compass took a long time to come into wide use because many seamen thought it operated by black magic.

Advances in the development of instrument-aided travel centered around two positions that can be used to identify any location on Earth: latitude (position on the Earth along imaginary lines running north to south) and longitude (position on the Earth along imaginary lines running east to west). When a ship's pilot wants to determine position on a map, he or she uses the coordinates of latitude and longitude. Latitude can be determined with a knowledge of sun and star positions as a function of time of year, for example, by measuring the angle of the North Star from the horizon. Longitude is more problematic because figuring it depends on measuring the time since passing geographic landmarks. Clocks that were precise enough to provide useful estimates of longitude were not developed in Europe until the eighteenth century. Knowledge of geological features of a route, such as shoals and currents (such as the western-trending currents of the Indian Ocean and the clockwise currents of the North Atlantic), was critical to efficient navigation.

Modern Tools for Navigation

The World Wide Web has become a major tool for learning, and the importance of navigating it efficiently (that is, finding one's way around the Internet) is increasingly important. Internet navigation tools include search engines—which use inputs such as subject, keyword, and location—and mailing lists. Internet search strategies include deciding keywords for the search, narrowing the search, maximizing the search results, and evaluating the sources.

Similarities exist between navigating the Internet and navigating the physical world. People increasingly use virtual environments to prepare people to operate in strange or hostile environments, for example, training military personnel to enter hostile territories, firefighters to find their way through burning buildings, and neurosurgeons to find their way around critical brain structures.

In addition, electronic navigation aids are becoming ubiquitous. Computer-based databases can be represented as maps that include many layers of information, including land elevation, underwater elevations, landmarks, energy consumption, pollution, and population. Satellites are becoming widely used as parts of GPS navigation systems to keep track of one's position and orientation on maps to within a few meters or less of error.

John J. Rieser

See also Geographic Information Systems; Mobile Computing; Pocket Computer; Wearable Computers

FURTHER READING

Berthoz, A. (2000). *The brain's sense of movement.* Cambridge, MA: Harvard University Press.

Dalley, S. (Ed.). (1998). *Myths from Mesopotamia: Creation, the flood, Gilgamesh, and others.* New York: Oxford University Press.

Gibson, J. J. (1966). *The senses considered as perceptual systems.* Boston: Houghton Mifflin.

Gladwin, T. (1970). *East is a big bird.* Cambridge, MA: Harvard University Press.

Hutchins, E. (1995). *Cognition in the wild.* Cambridge, MA: MIT Press.

Lackner, J. R., & DiZio, P. (2000). Human orientation and movement control in weightlessness and artificial gravity environments. *Experimental Brain Research, 130,* 2–26.

Loomis, J. M., Golledge, R. D., & Klatzky, R. L. (2001). GPS-based navigation systems for the visual impaired. In W. Barfield & T. Caudell (Eds.), *Fundamentals of wearable computers and augmented reality* (pp. 429–446). Mahwah, NJ: Erlbaum.

Rieser, J. J., & Garing, A. E. (1994). Spatial orientation. In *Encyclopedia of human behavior* (Vol. 4, pp. 287–295). San Diego, CA: Academic Press.

Rieser, J. J., & Pick, H. L., Jr. (2002). The perception and representation of human locomotion. In W. Prinz & B. Hommel (Eds.), *Attention and performance XIX: Common mechanisms in perception and action.* Oxford, UK: Oxford University Press.

Sobel, D. (1995). *Longitude: The true story of a lone genius who solved the greatest problem of his time.* New York: Penguin Books.

Thompson, W., Pick, H., Bennett, B., Heinrichs, M., Savitt, S., & Smith, K. (1990). Map-based localization: The "drop-off" problem. *Proceedings DARPA Image Understanding Workshop,* 706–719.

Warren, R., & Wertheim, A. H. (1990). *Perception and control of self-motion.* Hillsdale, NJ: Erlbaum.

Warren, W. H. (1995). Self-motion: Visual perception and visual control. In W. Epstein & S. Rogers (Eds.), *Perception of space and motion* (pp. 263–325). San Diego, CA: Academic Press.

Waterman, T. H. (1989). *Animal navigation.* New York: Freeman and Scientific American Library.

Wehner, R., Lehrer, M., & Harvey, W. (Eds.). (1996). Navigation [Special issue]. *Journal of Experimental Biology, 199.*

N-GRAMS

The notion of the probability of a sentence—a measure of how likely a given sentence is to occur—plays a central role in most modern computer systems that process human languages. In their most common use, probabilities give an application the ability to compare two linguistic uses (sentences, phrases, words, etc.) and allow it to choose between them based on which use is more probable. This technique is typically used in situations where a software system is uncertain about some aspect of the input. With an appropriate probability model, the system can enumerate all the possible resolutions to some perceived uncertainty, assign a probability to each possible resolution, and then simply select the choice with the highest probability. Applications that rely on this simple notion range from spelling correction to speech recognition and machine translation.

Probability

To make the notion of the probability of a sentence operational, we can first view a sentence as a sequence of events corresponding to the words in the sentence. Beginning with the first word, the probability of the entire sentence can be defined as the product of a sequence of probabilities consisting of the probability of the first word times the conditional probability of the second word, given that the first has occurred, times the probability of the third word given the first two and so on down the line to the last word in the sequence.

To make this notion concrete, consider as an example the sentence "The baby sleeps comfortably." To find the probability of this sentence, we start with the simple prior probability of our running across the word "The"; we then multiply that by the probability of then seeing the word "baby," having just seen the word "The," then the probability of seeing the word "sleeps" having just seen the words "The baby," and finally the probability of seeing the word "comfortably" having seen all the previous words. Using the standard notation from probability theory we would have the following formula:

$$P(The)*P(baby|The)*P(sleeps|The\ baby)*$$
$$P(comfortably|The\ baby\ sleeps)$$

The values for the probabilities that make up this formula are normally derived from counts gathered from a large corpus (body) of text that is representative of the kind of text that the application is likely to encounter in practice. As with all probability models, the core of this computation boils down to a matter of counting and dividing. Let us first consider the simple prior probability for the first word in a sentence, "P(The)" in our example. If we have a 1-million-word corpus, and a given word occurs once in this corpus, then the simple prior probability of that word is simply 1/1,000,000, or .000001. This is the probability that the next word that one encounters will be that word without taking into account any prior information context provided by previous words.

The principle for the remaining conditional probabilities in our formula is the same. The difference lies in what gets counted. To get the "P(baby|The)," we start by counting the number of occurrences of the phrase that is being considered, in this case "The baby"; we then divide this count by the number of times the conditioning context is seen; in this case this is simply the count for "The." This computation tells us how likely we are to see the word "baby" given the fact that we have just seen the word "The." The remaining conditional probabilities in the example are handled the same way; we divide the count for the phrase as a whole by the count for the prefix.

Unfortunately, this approach is impractical in most situations because of a severe data sparseness problem. Because of the creativity of human language, most of the longer components that go in to the probability equations will have never been seen in even the largest text collections. When these zero-count components are encountered by an application they are assigned a probability of zero, leading to a zero probability for an entire sentence.

To get a feeling for the severity of this problem, we can consult the Google search engine on the Web to get some counts for our example sentence. At the time of this article, Google contained five instances of the entire phrase "The baby sleeps comfortably" (out of a corpus of 10 billion documents). The prefix "The baby sleeps" occurs 2,410 times, giving us a value of 0.002 for the probability "P(comfortably |The baby sleeps)." Now, as low as this number seems, it is not problematic for the model. However, note what happens when we substitute "uncomfortably" for "comfortably" and again consult our corpus. In this case we find that this phrase never occurred in this enormous sample of text and hence will be assigned a probability of zero, which leads to the dubious conclusion that the sentence "The baby sleeps uncomfortably" will never occur.

The solution to this problem is to make what is known as a "Markov assumption"; instead of conditioning each event on all of the words that preceded it, we condition it only on a limited window of previous words. These fixed-size windows of some length N minus 1 are called "N-grams." So, for example, bigrams use a single previous word as context, whereas trigrams use the previous two words. Let's consider how our example looks with bigrams.

$$P(The)*P(baby|The)*P(sleeps|baby)*P(comfortably|sleeps)$$

By limiting the length of the prefix we can derive far more useful statistics from the same-size corpus, thereby alleviating some of the data sparseness problem. Of course, employing this solution has a significant downside: The shorter N-grams lose a considerable amount of their predictive power by throwing away information from the more distant context.

Using N-Grams

Consider how this solution is applied in modern speech recognition systems. Roughly, these systems consist of two components: an acoustical model with knowledge of how speech signals are associated with the sounds people make to form words and a language model that assesses how likely various sequences of words are. Now, consider a system that is in the midst of processing a phrase that began as "The more the." At this point the incoming signal is processed, and the acoustical model suggests a number of candidate words, including "merrier," "Mary,"

"mariner," and "marrier." A language model consisting of N-gram statistics can be used to compute the various probabilities of each candidate word, yielding "The more the Mary," "The more the mariner," and "The more the merrier." The candidate word that yields the sequence with the highest probability is then selected as the next word. This example also illustrates the tradeoff involved with the length of the N-gram. A bigram model is unlikely to favor the correct choice because the bigram probability "P(merrier|the)" is unlikely to be terribly high given the overall high frequency of the word "the." On the other hand, a fourgram model, which uses "P(merrier|The more the)," is more likely by far to favor the correct answer.

Practical Considerations

Obviously the trick in making effective use of N-gram models is to effectively manage the tradeoffs involved. Most systems rely on some combination of two methods to overcome the data sparseness problem smoothing and backoff models.

Smoothing involves finding a reasonable estimate for the value of an N-gram probability when an N-gram is encountered for the first time. In other words, we would like to replace the zero count for a given N-gram with a count that is more reasonable based on what we know of the corpus from which the counts were originally derived. The most common methods attempt to infer a reasonable number for the N-gram in question by assuming that it is similar in some way to N-grams that occurred once in the corpus from which the counts were derived.

Backoff models rely on the notion that even if we don't have reliable statistics for a given N-gram, we might have reasonable statistics for the shorter N-grams that make up the longer one. Consider a simple bigram case. We may have never encountered the phrase "green eggs" in our collection of text, and hence the probability "P(eggs|green)" will be zero. However, we will almost certainly know the raw frequencies of the words "eggs" and "green" and hence can derive a probability for the pair from those probabilities.

Current Research

N-gram language models have proven to be a remarkably effective technique across a wide range of natural language processing applications. However, psycholinguistic research indicates that humans make far more effective use of context to make far more accurate predictions than even the best current N-gram models. Current research is focused on extracting useful predictions from contextual information far beyond the limits of current N-gram models.

James Martin

See also Natural-Language Processing; Speech Recognition

FURTHER READING

Charniak, E. (1994). *Statistical language learning.* Cambridge, MA: MIT Press.

Huang, X., Acero, A., & Hon, H. (2001). *Spoken language processing: A guide to theory, algorithm, and system development.* Upper Saddle River, NJ: Prentice Hall.

Jurafsky, D., & Martin, J. H. (2000). *Speech and language processing: An introduction to natural language processing, computational linguistics, and speech recognition.* Upper Saddle River, NJ: Prentice Hall.

Manning, C. D., & Schütze, H. (1999*). Foundations of statistical language processing.* Cambridge, MA: MIT Press.

OLFACTORY INTERACTION

Modern Western culture focuses on visual and auditory perception; olfaction is commonly regarded as a minor sensory modality. Yet scents are extremely evocative; they can also shift attention, add novelty, enhance mental state, and add presence. And, as an ambient or peripheral medium, olfaction does not require manipulation or eye contact.

The sense of smell can be an alternative interaction channel with, or mediated by, computers. Supporting this thrust are recent scientific breakthroughs in olfactory reception, technological advances in sensor-based machine olfaction, and emerging commercial ventures in olfactory displays.

The Sense of Smell

Odorants are volatile compounds with low molecular weight (30–300 dalton, or roughly two to sixteen times the weight of a water molecule), typically organic, hydrophobic, and polar. When odorant molecules reach the olfactory epithelium (a small patch of tissue located at the roof of each nasal cavity), they stimulate a large population (100 million) of olfactory receptor neurons (ORNs). This initiates a chain of biochemical and electrical signals that results in our perceiving an odor. The olfactory pathway can be divided into three general subsystems: the olfactory epithelium, where primary reception takes place, the olfactory bulb, where an organized olfactory image is formed, and the olfactory cortex, where odor associations are stored.

The relationship between odorant molecular structure and odor perception remains elusive. Unlike

507

vision, which can be explained in terms of color wavelengths, or hearing, which is determined by sound harmonics, the primary dimensions of olfaction are still unknown—that is, it is still unclear whether "primary odors" exist or not. Recent findings indicate that olfaction involves a large family of receptors (300–1,000), each selective to a specific molecular feature of an odorant, such as carbon chain length or functional groups. Each odorant is therefore detected by multiple receptors, and each receptor can detect multiple odorants, leading to a high-dimensional and combinatorial code at the ORN level.

Bundles of ORN axons access the brain, relaying their information to mitral cells in the olfactory bulb through spherical clusters of synapses called glomeruli (GL). The projection is convergent and highly organized: ORNs expressing the same receptor (e.g., that respond to the same odorants) converge onto a single or a few GL. This convergence leads to odorant quality being encoded by a spatial activation pattern across GL; odorant intensity is encoded by the spread and intensity of this activation. The olfactory image is subsequently sharpened through lateral interaction with inhibitory inter-neurons. Mitral cell axons form the lateral olfactory tract (LOT), which projects to the piriform cortex, the center responsible for the storage and association of odor memories. In addition, the LOT is strongly connected to the limbic system, the center of emotions in the brain, which explains the strong connection between smells and emotions.

Olfactory Perception

Olfactory perception involves three basic tasks: intensity estimation, qualitative description, and hedonic tone (a qualitative property related to the pleasantness of an odorant). The relationship between odorant concentration and perceived intensity is well understood and follows a logarithmic law common to other sensory systems. Odor detection thresholds, defined as the lowest concentration at which a stimulus is perceived, can be as low as parts per trillion for some odorants, although these estimates may differ across subjects by as much as fifty-fold.

When compared to intensity estimation, qualitative description of an odorant is a very difficult

task. It is estimated that humans have the ability to discriminate up to ten thousand different odorants, though most of us only experience a fraction of these in our lifetime. Various schemes, such as Henning's odor prism (flowery, putrid, fruity, spicy, burned, and resinous), have been proposed in the past in an attempt to classify odors into a small number of dimensions. Due to the lack of success of these efforts, current approaches employ odor profiling techniques, in which a large number of verbal descriptors are used to describe individual odors.

The hedonic quality is highly subjective and is influenced by cultural factors and emotional associations. In addition, hedonic tone is non-monotonically dependent on the exposure levels: Some odorants are pleasant at low concentration but not at high (or persistent) doses. The hedonic tone of an odor is not hardwired in the brain, but is shaped through experience; whether a subject likes an odor or not depends largely on the associations made through life. Recent work by the psychologist Rachel Herz indicates that, contrary to popular belief, odorants are not more effective than other sensory stimuli at inducing recall of purely factual information. Instead, smell-related memories have a stronger emotional content than those triggered by other sensory modalities.

Information processing by ORNs and the bulb suggest that olfaction is an analytical sense: Odorants are meticulously broken down into their constituent molecular determinants. Interestingly, the view that emerges from psychophysics is that olfaction is in fact synthetic or holistic: Odors are perceived as irreducible entities. Although the ability to discriminate and verbally describe odors increases with experience (as with wine tasters, for example), humans are unable to segment individual odorants from mixtures with three or more components, regardless of prior experience or training. A similar thing happens when we see a familiar face: We recognize the whole, not the individuals parts, yet the photoreceptors in the retina only "see" the different parts of the other person's face.

Sensor-Based Machine Olfaction

Machine olfaction with chemical sensor arrays has been a fertile research area since the 1980s. Commonly called electronic noses, sensor-based machine olfaction (SBMO) instruments employ arrays of cross-selective chemical sensors coupled with pattern recognition algorithms to detect and identify complex odorants. SBMO represents a fast and inexpensive alternative to analytical methods of measuring odor, such as gas chromatography-mass spectrometry (GC-MS), or to sensory analysis with human panels.

A variety of odor-sensing technologies have been used, the most popular making use of resistive and piezoelectric devices. In chemoresistive sensors the presence of volatile organic compounds (VOCs) changes the resistance of a chemically sensitive material, typically a metal oxide or a conducting polymer. Piezoelectric sensors are mass-sensitive devices; absorption of VOCs increases the mass of a sensing membrane, which results in changes in the phase or resonant frequency of a piezoelectric substrate. Additional odor sensing technologies include field-effect and optical devices.

SBMO pattern recognition follows the general principles for computer processing of multivariate data. First, raw sensor signals are preprocessed for noise reduction and normalization purposes. A number of descriptive features are then identified in the sensor signals using domain knowledge; these are compressed onto a few dimensions through feature extraction and selection. Finally, a pattern-recognition model is trained to predict properties of the odorant, such as its identity, the concentration of its constituents in the case of a mixture, or how it may be perceived by humans. The latter is arguably the ultimate goal of SBMO. The unique and most challenging computational aspects of SMBO are in the early stages of processing. In particular, odor sensors are subject to long-term drift (a gradual change in the properties of the sensing layer), which causes previously learned odor patterns to become obsolete over time. This requires drift compensation algorithms combined with periodic recalibration.

During their first two decades of existence, commercial electronic noses were marketed as general-purpose instruments that could be customized to any application by simply training their pattern-recognition engines on the odorant samples of interest. Experience has shown that this is not possible—not with current chemical sensors. As a result, commercial efforts are moving towards application-specific chemical sensor systems. However, true machine olfaction, as opposed to chemical sensing, implies predicting the perceptual properties of an odorant from the sensor-array response. Prediction of perceived intensity is relatively straightforward, since both chemical sensors and ORNs have monotonic concentration-response curves. Unfortunately, correlation with perceived quality, hedonic tone, or organoleptic (perceived by a sense organ) descriptors is a more challenging problem that will require developing sensing materials capable of detecting the stereochemical properties of odorant molecules which, until a complete understanding of primary reception is available, are the best known determinants of odor quality. Correlations between sensor-array responses and sensory analysis ratings have been demonstrated on a few quality-control applications, but prediction of organoleptic properties has been only moderately successful to date.

Olfactory Displays

Whereas SBMO is concerned with generating a digital representation of an odorant, olfactory displays (ODs) are concerned with the complementary problem: synthesizing odorants from a digital description. In its most general form, an OD consists of a palette of odorants, a flow delivery system, and a control algorithm that determines the mixing ratios, concentration, and timing of the stimulus. Odorants can be stored in the liquid phase and released using inkjet printer technology, or micro-encapsulated, as in "scratch-n-sniff" cards, and released thermally or mechanically. Once released, odorants may be dispersed using a general air ventilation system, or delivered locally with a whiffer (a computer-controlled perfume atomizer) or head-mounted gear.

Why olfactory displays? ODs have been shown to enhance the sense of presence and add salient spatial cues in virtual-reality (VR) environments. Along these lines, ODs have been used to enhance VR-based training systems for firefighters and emergency medical personnel. ODs also have broad commercial applications in high-end gaming and virtual shopping malls.

Coupled with SBMO, ODs may be used to digitally transmit olfactory stimuli. To this end, Takao Yamanaka and colleagues have recently developed a system capable of digitizing fruit odors and synthesizing mock-ups using a palette of odorants and a sensor array. A critical point for tele-olfaction is the construction of a mapping from sensor-array data (or odorant mixtures) onto olfactory perception, which is challenging with current chemical sensors (and current understanding of mixture perception).

Simpler domains that bypass the problem of odor digitization or synthesis have been proposed by Joseph Kaye, who views olfactory cues as iconic representations. These odor cues may be semantically related to the represented object, such as the smell of burnt rubber in a car-racing VR game, or they could be related only in an abstract manner, as when a puff of scent is used to remind the user to attend a meeting. This work raises interesting questions about the use of ODs in computer-mediated interaction.

Finally, ODs may also be used as therapeutic devices, as exemplified by the field of aromachology—the study of the effect of odor on mood and behavior. For instance, vanilla fragrances reduce anxiety, peppermint scents increase job performance, and cinnamon scents improve creative problem solving. More interestingly, specific odor-state associations may be built through training. Psychologist Susan Schiffman has shown that people can be trained to relax in the presence of a pleasant odor, so that the same state of relaxation can be induced at a later time by presentation of the odor alone. Future affective interfaces may be able to predict psychological state from physiological signals (such as heart and respiration rates or electrodermal activity), and release a suitable fragrance in response.

A number of companies have recently advertised consumer-grade ODs, though at the time of this writing none of these efforts have lead to a tangible product. Leaving aside economic or strategic issues that may have prevented those designs from reaching the production line, ODs face several scientific and technological challenges. The most fundamental issues derive from olfactory reception and psychophysics. A good understanding of the primary determinants of odor quality in single odorants and complex mixtures is required before perceptually accurate stimuli can be generated from odorant palettes. The effects of various odorant delivery parameters (for example, concentration, duration, frequency, and flow rate) need to be thoroughly characterized. Careful attention must also be paid to the issue of hypersensitivity to scents. Finally, technological advances in odorant storage, delivery, and removal are also required, though olfactory stimuli will remain inherently more involved than audiovisual media.

Research Issues

The olfactory interfaces that have been developed—electronic noses and olfactory displays—are important and valuable developments. Electronic noses are a promising technology for low-cost and real-time measurement of volatile compounds. However, further research efforts are required in the areas of (1) sensor selectivity, sensibility, stability, and reproducibility, (2) sensing materials for molecular determinants of odor quality, and (3) computational methods for drift compensation and background suppression.

Olfactory displays provide an improved sense of presence, can be potent triggers for emotional memories, and can complement other modalities while leaving the user's eyes and hands free. However, further research is also required in the areas of (1) odor synthesis with odorant palettes; (2) technologies for odorant storage, delivery, and removal; and (3) psychophysics characterization of odorant delivery.

Progress in olfactory interfaces will also be closely tied to the development of odorant standards and niche markets. Although the more challenging application domains will require a better understanding of olfactory reception and perception, research into computer-mediated iconic olfactory interaction is ready for prime time.

Ricardo Gutierrez-Osuna

See also Psychology and HCI, Virtual Reality

FURTHER READING

Barfield, W., & Danas, E. (1996). Comments on the use of olfactory displays for virtual environments. *Presence, 5*(1), 109–121.

Buck, L. B., & Axel, R. (1991). A novel multigene family may encode odorant receptors: A molecular basis for odor recognition. *Cell, 65*, 175–187.

Burl, M. C., Doleman, B. J., Schaffer, A., & Lewis, N. S. (2001). Assessing the ability to predict human percepts of odor quality from the detector responses of a conducting polymer composite-based electronic nose. *Sensors and Actuators B: Chemical 72*(2), 149–159.

Cater, J. P. (1994). Approximating the senses. Smell/taste: Odors in virtual reality. In *Proceedings of the IEEE International Conference on Systems, Man and Cybernetics* (p. 1781). Washington, DC: IEEE Computer Society Press.

Chastrette, M. (1997). Trends in structure-odor relationships. *SAR and QSAR in Environmental Research 6*, 215–254.

Dinh, H. Q., Walker, N., Song, C., Kobayashi, A., & Hodges, L. F. (1999). Evaluating the importance of multi-sensory input on memory and the sense of presence in virtual environments. In *Proceedings of IEEE Virtual Reality* (pp. 222–228). Washington, DC: IEEE Computer Society Press.

Engen, T. (1982). *The perception of odors.* New York: Academic Press.

Gardner, J. W., & Bartlett, P. N. (1999). *Electronic noses: Principles and applications.* New York: Oxford University Press.

Gutierrez-Osuna, R. (2002). A self-organizing model of chemotopic convergence for olfactory coding. *Proceedings of the 2nd Joint EMBS-BMES Conference, 1*, 236–237. Houston, TX: IEEE.

Gutierrez-Osuna, R. (2002). Pattern analysis for machine olfaction: A review. *IEEE Sensors Journal, 2*(3), 189–202.

Harel, D., Carmel, L., & Lancet, D. (2003). Towards an odor communication system. *Computational Biology and Chemistry, 27*, 121–133.

Herz, R. S. (1998). Are odors the best cues to memory? A cross-modal comparison of associative memory stimuli. *Annals of the New York Academy of Sciences, 855*, 670–674.

Isen, A. M., Ashby, F. G., & Waldron, E. (1997). The sweet smell of success. *Aroma-Chology Review, 4*(3), 1.

Kaye, J. N. (2001). *Symbolic Olfactory Display.* Unpublished master's thesis, MIT, Cambridge, MA. Retrieved December 31, 2003, from http://web.media.mit.edu/~jofish/thesis/symbolic_olfactory_display.html

Malnic, B., Hirono, J., Sato, T., & Buck, L. B. (1999). Combinatorial receptor codes for odors. *Cell, 96*, 713–723.

Morgan, K., Satava, R. M., Sieburg, H. B., Matteus, R., & Christensen, J. P. (Eds.). (1995). *Interactive technology and the new paradigm for healthcare.* Amsterdam: IOS Press and Ohmsha.

Nagle, H. T., Schiffman, S. S., & Gutierrez-Osuna, R. (1998). The how and why of electronic noses. *IEEE Spectrum, 35*(9), 22–34.

Pearce, T. C. (1997). Computational parallels between the biological olfactory pathway and its analogue 'the electronic nose': Part I, biological olfaction. *Biosystems, 41*(2), 43–67.

Pearce, T. C. (1997). Computational parallels between the biological olfactory pathway and its analogue 'the electronic nose': Part II, sensor-based machine olfaction. *BioSystems, 41*, 69–90.

Pearce, T. C., Schiffman, S. S., Nagle, H. T., & Gardner, J. W. (Eds.). (2003). *Handbook of machine olfaction: Electronic nose technology.* Weinheim, Germany: Wiley-VCH.

Pelosi, P., & Persaud, K. C. (2000). Physiological and artificial systems for odour recognition. In F. Mazzei & R. Pilloton (Eds.), *Proceedings of the 2nd Italian Workshop on Chemical Sensors and Biosensors* (pp. 37–55). Retrieved March 5, 2004, from http://web.tiscali.it/no-redirect-tiscali/biosensor/AbstractO05.htm

Persaud, K. C., & Dodd, G. H. (1982). Analysis of discrimination mechanisms of the mammalian olfactory system using a model nose. *Nature, 299*, 352–355.

Picard, R. W. (1997). *Affective computing.* Cambridge, MA: MIT Press.

Redd, W., & Manne, S. (1995). Using aroma to reduce distress during magnetic resonance imaging. In A. Gilbert (Ed.), *Compendium of olfactory research, 1982–1994* (pp. 47–52). Dubuque, IA: Kendall/Hunt.

Schiffman, S. S. (1995). Use of olfaction as an alarm mechanism to arouse and alert sleeping individuals. *Aroma-Chology Review, 4*(1), 2–5.

Sullivan, T. E., Warm, J. S., Schefft, B. K., Dember, W. N., O'Dell, M. W., & Peterson, S. J. (1998). Effects of olfactory stimulation on the vigilance performance of individuals with brain injury. *Journal of Clinical and Experimental Neuropsychology, 20*(2), 227–236.

Tominaga, K., Honda, S., Ohsawa, T., Shigeno, H., Okada, K., & Matsushita, Y. (2001). Friend Park: Expression of the wind and the scent on virtual space. In *Proceedings of the Seventh International Conference on Virtual Systems and Multimedia* (pp. 507–515). Berkeley, CA: IEEE.

Warm, J. S., Dember, W. N., & Parasuraman, E. (1992). Effects of olfactory stimulation on performance and stress in a visual sustained attention task. *Journal of the Society of Cosmetic Chemists, 42*, 199–210.

Wilson, D. A., & Stevenson, R. J. (in press). Olfactory perceptual learning: The critical role of memory in odor discrimination. *Neuroscience and Biobehavioral Reviews.*

Yamanaka, T., Matsumoto, R., & Nakamoto, T. (2003). Study of recording apple flavor using odor recorder with five components. *Sensors and Actuators B: Chemical, 89*(1–2), 112–119.

ONLINE EDUCATION

Famed biologist and author Edward O. Wilson maintains that the ascendance of humans over other species is due to our innate passion for learning. Deaf and blind since infancy and cut off from learning until she was seven, Helen Keller expressed this passion well: "Before my education began," she wrote, "I was without compass or sounding line, and no way of knowing how near the harbor was. 'Light! Give me light!' was the wordless cry of my soul" (Keller 1905, 35). In the last two hundred years, as industrialization spread throughout the world and community declined in importance, most countries have implemented national education systems in place of what was formerly a community experience. Education came to be seen as essential for a democratic society and a healthy economy. The growth of corporations also added a new role for education—preparing individuals as workers.

Now, we are making unprecedented demands of the educational system at a time when resources to sustain it are scarce. Information is expanding at a dizzying rate and we are becoming globally interdependent. As Richard Saul Wurman wrote in his 1989 book *Information Anxiety*, we are "inundated with facts but starved for understanding" (Wurman 1989, cover note). As resources run short and our industrial civilization is encountering the planet's limits to sustain it, individuals, communities, nations, and corporations must invent radically new patterns or face unprecedented crisis. The future calls for critical thinkers who can take an interdisciplinary, holistic view. Will the education system be able to provide them?

The Impact of the Web

Computers were invented to perform numeric calculations (to "compute") but the Internet rapidly transformed them into our most powerful communication devices. After the invention of the World Wide Web in 1991, computers became new tools for educators and learners. However, the effect of the Web on the education system is potentially disruptive, because the system has traditionally been place-bound (correspondence courses excepted) and the Web is not. Online education, the fusion of the two, is still developing and it is impossible to tell how it will evolve. Its continuing development is a search for new patterns to resolve these out-of-balance and conflicting forces and to bring them into harmony.

The de-localization of the Web has made it possible to deliver rich and interactive digital media to the classroom or to the individual learner for a near-zero marginal cost. It makes possible new modes of communication that can enlarge the learning conversation and facilitate the collaborative construction of new knowledge. On the other hand, online education could lead to the increasing centralization and standardization of education. It could also increase the gap between rich and poor and marginalize the disenfranchised.

Types of Online Education

For the purposes of this article, we will define online education broadly as *the use of networked communication devices as a major component of a strategy to impart knowledge*. This definition includes not only *distance education* (sometimes oxymoronically referred to as "distance learning"), but also *Web-enhanced classroom learning* and *informal learning*. Although our focus will be on distance education, we will also consider the latter two because the boundaries separating these modes are often blurred. It should also be noted that our definition does not specifically involve a computer because online education may also be mediated through a mobile device such as a portable digital assistant (PDA) or a cell phone.

The closely related term, *e-learning*, differs slightly in both strategy and delivery, reflecting its origins in computer-based training (CBT) and computer-aided instruction (CAI). E-learning involves the delivery of formal course content through a variety of electronic means (including tape, CD-ROM, and interactive television, as well as computer networks). In practice, however, the two terms are often taken to be synonymous, and we will treat them as such.

In both terms the emphasis should be on the second word ("education" or "learning"), since instructional media by themselves "do not influence student achievement any more than the truck that delivers our groceries causes changes in our nutrition" (Clark 1983, 445). The importance of the medium—a computer network—is that it affords new paradigms for education and new modes of learning. As Marshall McLuhan famously observed, we "force the new media to do the work of the old" (McLuhan 1967, 81). It should be no surprise, therefore, that most online courses today resemble a classroom both functionally and metaphorically. The history of online education, when written, will be the story of inventing new paradigms to exploit this medium.

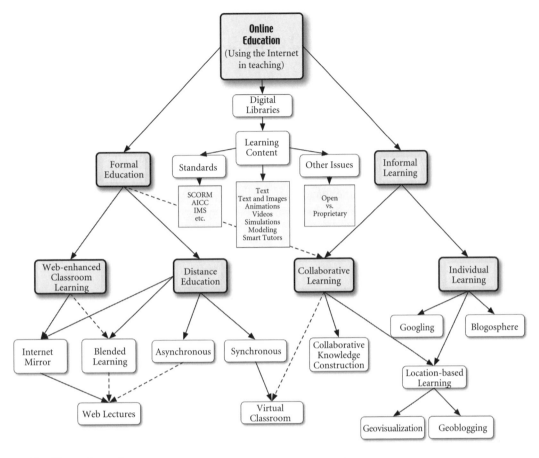

A taxonomy of online education. Courtesy of Glenn Collyer and Robert Stephenson.

Web-Enhanced Classroom Learning

Within the scope of our definition of online education, the percentage of instruction actually delivered online may vary widely, so long as it constitutes a "major component." At the lower end of this scale comes the Web-enhanced course taught in a conventional manner but including Web pages, e-mail, and other Internet-based resources in a prominent role in lectures, student research, and assignments. The advantages this brings over a conventional class include making lectures more effective and exciting by illustrating them with rich content (such as animations, videos, simulations, and 3-D models), accustoming students to use tools they will need in the workplace and making studying and reviewing easier and more effective by giving students access to much of their class materials on the Web. It is easy to use the Web to improve the venerable lecture format, which Immanuel Kant once described as, "the process by which the faculties' notes become the students' notes without passing through the heads of either" (Heterick 2001).

Distance Education

At the other end of this scale comes distance education in which there are few if any face-to-face meetings, and online interactions, plus assigned readings, carry the entire weight of instruction. The online content of such a course must be assembled with great care. Although the ability to learn under even the most difficult circumstances is a highly selected trait in human evolution, learning is neither rapid nor pleasant in a poorly designed distance education class. This is a major reason why many students drop out of such classes. A recent survey of commercial e-learning students, commissioned by the e-Learning Consortium, reported an average completion rate of 74 percent, and previous studies have reported values as low as 15 percent (O'Conner et al. 2003).

Virtual Classes Help Rural Nurses

SPOKANE, Wash. (ANS)—With demand for trained psychiatric nurses increasing, the federal government is experimenting with a distance learning program in rural Washington state that it hopes may become a model for the rest of the nation.

According to government figures, the suicide rate is higher in the rural West than any other part of the country. Wider availability of mental health care professionals is clearly called for, but in sparsely populated eastern Washington state, nurses have not had access to the advanced courses and clinical supervision they need to upgrade their skills in mental health care because most training programs are located in urban centers.

Under a $750,000 grant from the Health Resources and Services Administration, interested nurses will be able to take courses and communicate with supervisors at the Washington State University College of Nursing via laptop computers with video-conferencing capabilities.

Ideally, program advocates say, those nurses will then stay on in their communities to practice and begin to stem the tide of suicides, alcohol abuse and domestic violence prevalent in rural areas.

[…]

The new program aims to increase the number of practitioners by 50 percent. Targeted especially at minority and disadvantaged students, the Medically Indigent/Rural Area Nurse Practitioner Education project will link advanced-degree nursing students to clinicians at the university for the 500 hours of direct supervision they need to be certified.

Cameras and microphones will be mounted on laptop computers the nurses will carry along when they counsel patients. Supervisors stationed at the university will be able to watch and comment on their approach. It's all a bit scary, says one nurse enrolled in the program. But it's worth it.

Mieke H. Bomann

Source: Virtual classes help rural nurses address rising suicide rates. American News Service, October 19, 2000.

Other factors contributing to the poor completion rate are technical issues such as poor Internet connectivity and inconsistent computer technology; users' lack of computer skills; and a lack of regularly scheduled classes, which makes it easy for less disciplined or motivated students to fall hopelessly behind.

Distance education classes are attractive to students primarily for their convenience. While a conventional course requires all students to appear in class at the same time, distance education classes allow students to participate from anywhere, at whatever time suits them best (asynchronously). Indeed, many students enroll in distance education classes because of time conflicts, not geography. In some cases, however, distance classes will require students to participate in live (synchronous) events such as a lecture webcast or a scheduled online chat.

A distance education class places a lot of demands on the usability of its Web interface. Students need to access the course contents and tools easily and to navigate through all the class materials without difficulty—usually without the benefit of 24-7 help line. One attempt to address this issue is to standardize the interface with a learning management system (LMS). An LMS is a Web-based system that helps educators with the administrative and pedagogical functions of a course, such as registering students, recording grades, and sending e-mail, and the creation, management, and presentation of educational content.

Exams are another issue posed by distance education. Online learning makes possible frequent quizzes with immediate feedback possible. But where high-stakes testing is involved, supervised testing—on campus or at a remote location—is currently the only option. Biometrics (verifying an individual's identity through a physical attribute such as a fingerprint) has not become standard or well accepted and, even when it does, knowing who is sitting in front of the computer during an exam will still not reveal whether or not a coach is standing behind it.

Hybrid Courses and the Internet Mirror Model

Between distance education and the Web-enhanced course falls what is referred to as the hybrid course (also called blended learning), which is an alternation of the two. Such a course, for example, might start off with a period of face-to-face class meetings, then move to an online module lasting several weeks, and then have a period of more class meetings in which students discuss what they learned online.

Another variation is the *Internet mirror model*: A Web-enhanced class and a distance education class run in tandem, and students are free to choose whichever suits their needs—or even to switch from one to the other during the course. This offers students the advantages of both face-to-face and online models (and offers the instructor the burdens of both), it has been suggested that this model can improve the completion rate for both lecture and online students.

Disaggregating Education

By de-emphasizing the importance of geography, online education has undermined one of the cornerstones of the traditional educational establishment: "*just-in-case learning.*" Delocalized education means there is more opportunity to learn throughout life and less justification for trying to acquire a lifetime's worth of knowledge in a few years of intense schooling. At the same time, accelerating growth of knowledge has made that goal impossible in almost every field. For example, half of what a graduating engineer has learned will be obsolete in five years and there will be twice that much new material to be learned (Davis & Botkin 1994, 89). Some fields, such as software engineering, are developing so rapidly that a book may be partly obsolete by the time it goes to press.

One response to these trends has been a rise in "just-in-time learning." The best time to learn technical information, its proponents argue, is when you need it and are about to put it to use. This presupposes distance education content that is available in highly focused small modules indexed with metadata so that they can be easily found when needed. While large month-long and even year-long courses will still have their place, there is a need for courses in manageable chunks of information that can be easily assimilated and saved by the learner. For instance, some e-learning designers feel that attention spans are so short that learners should spend no more than twelve minutes accessing information on a particular topic before moving on.

Since many learners are not sitting at a desk, learning is also taking place through mobile platforms such as portable digital assistants (PDAs) and cell phones; these may be networked wirelessly or intermittently (in the case of many PDAs). It is now common practice, for instance, for medical students to carry reference information about diseases, diagnoses, and drugs on their PDAs. During their rounds they frequently record patient case notes on the PDA, which they later sync to a central server.

Web Lectures

Because the simple lecture is the teaching strategy most often used in education, the emergence of the World Wide Web presented an obvious challenge: How to capture and present a lecture on the Internet. At first, websites such as the World Lecture Hall presented lectures in a text or PowerPoint format, but with faster Internet connections and improved video technology, the streaming video lecture has become commonplace.

A fascinating application called "Eloquent," set the standard for streaming video lectures, emerged in 1996. It allowed complete control over an online lecture. Three elements— text, slide presentations, and the video of the presenter—were shown, each in its own window on the screen. The learner could place or resize them at will, and the three elements were synchronized so that moving to a different point of the presentation in one caused the others to jump to the correct place as well. Also, the lecture could be speeded up or slowed down. With the help of a clever digital technique, playing lectures at slower or faster speeds did not change the

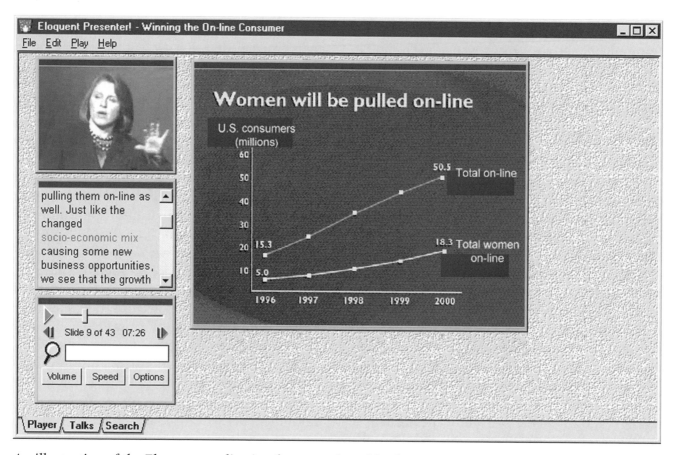

An illustration of the Eloquent application for streaming video lectures, in which the video, text, and slides are synchronized. Photo courtesy of Glenn Collyer and Robert Stephenson.

pitch of the speaker much so listening to a one-hour lecture in only fifteen minutes was not too uncomfortable. If, on the other hand, the lecture was rich with concepts, the presentation could be slowed down for better understanding.

Eloquent was a commercial failure despite its elegant technology, and today it has been replaced by numerous Web lecture technologies that function within the browser. Currently the standard lecture presentation consists of a small image of the presenter in the top left of the screen, with a larger slide image area on the right. On the left and down below are controls for jumping between slides and making the video or audio play. The text does not occupy a place of much significance, but hopefully this will change. Many websites today offer Web lectures either through streaming technology or by means of a standard Web lecture solution. A new technology from Macromedia called Breeze allows a user to easily record and present a simple lecture within a

browser, but it will be some time before this type of technology is available at prices acceptable to educational or consumer markets.

E-Mail

E-mail has for many years been the most widely adopted educational technology. In distance education classes it is often the principal means of communication and an important way for students to submit work.

Bots and Agents

In a world of "infoglut," we need computers to help us cope. *Bots* (short for robots), are computer programs that run continuously (aka daemons) and respond to their user in a useful way, and are important tools for informal learning and research. A search engine like Google.com is a bot.

A software *agent* is a program that carries out a task on behalf of its user in an automated fashion.

In online education, for example, an instructor's agent can manage sending and receiving student e-mails, warning students of impending or overdue assignments, and thanking them for submissions.

Social Software

The difference between computer networks and broadcasting networks is that only the former allow many-to-many communication. The term *social software* applies to tools that support rich multilateral communication and allow patterns of social interaction to emerge. In online education, social software makes it possible to move beyond the lecture format—real or virtual—to one of collaborative learning.

The most basic and widely accepted examples of social software are the *e-mail mailing list* and its Web-based counterpart, the *threaded discussion board*. Both allow a many-sided conversation among students and instructors that is more open than discussions in most classrooms. Both suffer from usability problems when message traffic increases, although the threaded discussion can scale to larger numbers of users and messages because it organizes posts by topic and provides a history. An even more scalable form of social software is the *wiki*, a website where anyone can edit a page or easily create a new one. The wiki allows groups of unlimited size to collaborate on a common project, provided that they are willing and able to accept certain text conventions for formatting and page creation. For example, in the last three years tens of thousands of modern Diderots have created the *Wikipedia,* a public encyclopedia with more than 220,000 articles in English (larger than the *Encyclopedia Britannica*) and versions in over sixty other languages. Online *chat* provides a different sort of social interaction, immediate and personal but useful primarily for small groups. Chat includes short message service (SMS) on cell phones; instant messaging; Internet relay chat (IRC); and more elaborate versions that incorporate shared whiteboards, voice chat, and other enhancements. Virtual-classroom software includes all these features, as well as a feature that allows students to raise a virtual hand and participate in instant polls. Since chat tools are strictly synchronous, they are not appropriate for many distance-learning contexts. On the other hand, they can add to a real classroom a valuable "back channel" for comments, discussions, questions, or polls—provided that students have appropriate networked devices or are using a classroom response system (special networked keypads at every seat).

Blogs, or weblogs, are individual online journals. When bloggers link to other blogs on the same subject, however, they can become an important tool for learning— an online literature of interrelated essays and stories. Automated techniques such as Really Simple Syndication (RSS), syndicators (software programs that collect and display syndicated blog newsfeeds), and trackback (a way to indicate to a blogger that you have added a hyperlink to his or her blog) facilitate this crosslinking by topic. The resulting "blogosphere" is a rich resource for independent learning, and blogs have great potential as a way to transform solitary online learners into a learning community.

Learning Content

Creating e-learning that is usable, pedagogically sound, and totally accurate is a difficult task. A guideline for the production of high-quality e-learning is 500 to 1,000 man hours to produce an hour's worth of content. Even with a fraction of this effort, high-quality online education material is expensive to produce and therefore important to reuse. Reuse, however does not come easily; material must be designed, both technically and pedagogically, with reuse in mind.

From a technical point of view, such a learning asset must be an interoperable chunk with a standard interface. Inspired by object-oriented software, e-learning designers have called them "learning objects." Although those who use this term do not agree on its definition, its essence is interoperability and reusability. The notion is that such learning objects can be assembled into an LMS to produce an online course. In other words, they are the learning content, and the LMS is the container. To achieve interoperability with different LMSs the learning objects must comply with standards such as the Shareable Content Object Reference Model (SCORM), which is a broadly accepted standard promoted by the U.S. Department of Defense.

Proponents of learning objects favor courses with smaller granularity because when information is broken into small chunks, the learning objects can be shared with other courses. In the future, given a vast digital library of learning objects, designers envision that learners and teachers will provide a few specifications and whole courses will be generated for them automatically out of sequences of learning objects. However, reusability is more difficult to achieve than this discussion suggests, because the mix-and-match approach to course creation presents difficult issues of interface design and pedagogy. Presentation and navigation style must be consistent across an entire course, and should not be determined at the level of a learning object. Pedagogy is a reusability issue because the level and nature of the learning content must be appropriate for specific learners.

Finally, to be reused, the content must be made available to other online course developers. This means, first, that it must be licensed to permit this reuse under clearly defined terms. Second, developers must be able to find it when they need it. In the emerging e-learning ecosystem, the objects must be tagged with standard meta-data describing their subject, use, licensing, language, and so on, and must be listed in a digital library, such as Merlot or NSDL.org.

Open-Course Collaboration

Since creating effective, reusable learning content is so difficult, the task of digitizing the educational curriculum so immense, and the financial resources available so insufficient, the job is likely to be accomplished only through widespread volunteerism, collaboration, and sharing. Virtual communities of educators, designers, programmers, librarians, and students join together for the collaborative construction and sharing of learning objects in their fields and then make them freely available to the world. Many open-course groups create their own sites and tools for this purpose, but recently a free portal, opencourse.org, has been developed to host such collaborations and provide the collaborators with the necessary tools.

Constructivism

Among the educational theories relevant to online education, two schools of thought stand out: objec-

tivism and constructivism. Objectivism views knowledge as objective and external to the learner, and educational content as being about observed objects and events; learning means understanding the ideas of important individuals such as Newton or Einstein. Anyone who has been through a traditional school has received a largely objectivist education.

In contrast, constructivism maintains that knowledge is personal and is constructed by the learner through experience. The Web and just-in-time learning favor the constructivist approach. Bookmarks or Favorites, for example, are seen as early manifestations of a future system that will help learners learn. Bookmarks allow a learner to iteratively construct references to web sites and other content resources that create a personal body of knowledge (BOK) on any subject they wish. In this context, a constructivist approach to learning the laws of physics would be to explore and collect a diversity of resources on the Internet with different approaches to the subject.

Collaborative Knowledge Construction

From a constructivist point of view, one of the most promising aspects of social software is that it enables learners to collaborate on creating their own body of knowledge. Using collaborative concept-mapping software called CmapTools, students can jointly build up and edit a graphical representation of the concepts they are studying and examine the ways they relate to each other. High school students have participated in identifying geologic features on Mars in a project with NASA, and have helped gather and analyze astronomical data through the NSF Hands-On Universe project. Students are involved in many open-course projects, helping create and evaluate the very learning objects that are part of their course. For many students, creating something of lasting value that will be appreciated outside of class or school is a life-transforming source of pride as well as a learning experience.

Location-Based Learning

Geography has always been an implicit component of education. Recent advances in geographic hardware and software, however, are making a more explicit role possible. In 1996 at Apple Computers' Learning Communities Group, Jim Spohrer envi-

An Online "Dig" for Archeology Students

PHILADELPHIA (ANS)—Undergraduate archaeology students at the University of Pennsylvania have excavated Stone Age tools and dug up animal bones without wielding a trowel or getting a speck of dirt under their fingernails.

Students are using "Virtual Dig," a new CD-ROM educational program developed by their professor, to experience an excavation from planning stages to excavation, through final analysis.

"We have now a technology that will allow us to literally re-excavate a site," said archaeologist and anthropology professor Dr. Harold Dibble, who created the simulation program based on his real excavation of a Middle Paleolithic site in Combe Capelle, France, in conjunction with Dr. Shannon P. McPheron of the Bishop Museum in Honolulu and Dr. Barbara Roth of Oregon State University. Dibble is also the European section curator of the University of Pennsylvania Museum of Archaeology and Anthropology.

Archaeological digs are expensive and out of reach for many undergraduate students, Dibble said. "This puts the field experience in the classroom," he said. "This is as realistic a field experience as they can get. It also takes them into a lot of areas they would not be exposed to in a field," giving them experience in such aspects of archaeology as designing a research project, budgeting and the logistics of providing living quarters, equipment, supplies and meals, in addition to the painstaking excavation and analysis of what is found.

Students choose their digging tools—such as trowel, shovel, dental pick or even a backhoe—and move the tool over a particular excavation site using the computer mouse. "It's very much like digging," Dibble explained. Students scrape away layers of dirt to expose schematic drawings of artifacts, such as Stone Age tools or animal bones.

"My hope is that Virtual Dig, and the technology and techniques behind it, can serve as a prototype for archaeological excavations in the future," Dibble said. "Archaeology has always been a time-consuming, expensive and essentially destructive process."

Source: "Virtual Dig" lets students excavate without leaving classroom. American News Service, May 11, 2000.

---

sioned a portable educational device, the worldboard, that would overlay the virtual and physical worlds. The worldboard would give its users access to the history of their surroundings, make visible hidden features such as buried pipelines, and allow virtual annotations to be added to a place.

GPS (Global Positioning Satellite) receivers provide the infrastructure to support a worldboard-like device, and they are falling in price and becoming more commonplace. They will soon be ubiquitous, thanks to the U.S. "E-911" requirement that cell phones be able to pinpoint their location for emergency services and the rollout of the Galileo GPS system planned by the European Union and China.

Web resources can be "geocoded" by adding meta-data describing their physical location (named, with black humor, the "ICBM tag"), which makes location-based searches possible. And when using a cell phone or similar device transforms the whole world into a classroom, why must anyone sit in school to learn history, geology, botany, or environmental studies? One form of location-based learning, termed *geoblogging*, attaches a story to a place: It is virtual, digital graffiti.

Geovisualization is a mapmaking technique of overlaying different sets of spatial data to discover relationships among them. While geographical information systems (GIS) have been available for about forty years, their use in education has been limited until recently by expensive proprietary software, incompatible data formats, and a shortage of good data sets. Most of these obstacles have been removed with the development of free and open-source tools such as GRASS ad TIGER. Geovisualization is a powerful tool for learning, especially when combined with collaborative knowledge construction. For example, in the Globe Program, (children in over fourteen thousand schools in 105 countries are gathering scientific spatial data on atmosphere, hydrology, soils, and land cover and integrating them into maps.

Community Again

Before Johannes Gutenberg pioneered the use of movable type in 1450, scholars would gather around a handcrafted manuscript, and learning was a matter of interacting with one's peers—just as it had been around the fire for thousands of years before that. The mass production of books allowed scholars to have their own books, and as a consequence, the image of a lonely isolated individual studying silently in a library filled with books has characterized scholarship for the last five hundred years. The apparent miracle of the Internet is that human beings now have the potential to push back isolation and find vibrant community in learning again.

Glenn J. Collyer and Robert S. Stephenson

See also Classrooms

FURTHER READING

Alexander, C., et al. (1977). *A pattern language.* New York: Oxford.

Clark, R. E. (1983). Reconsidering research on learning from media. *Review of Educational Research, 53*(4), 445–459.

Davis, S. M., & Botkin, J. W. (1994). *The monster under the bed.* New York: Simon & Schuster.

Doctorow, C., Dornfest, R., Johnson, J. S., Powers, S., Trott, B., & Trott, M. G. (2002). *Essential blogging.* Sebastopol, CA: O'Reilly.

Globe. (2004). *The Globe program.* Retrieved March 9, 2004, from http://www.globe.gov/globe_flash.html

Heterick, R. C. (2001). Some can't, Some Kant. *The Learning Market-Space,* 4/1/2001. Retrieved March 9, 2004, from http://www.center.rpi.edu/LForum/lm/Apr01.html

IHMC. (2003). *IHMC Cmap tools.* Retrieved March 9, 2004, from http://cmap.ihmc.us/

Keller, H. (1954). *The story of my life.* Garden City, NY: Doubleday.

Leuf, B., & Cunningham, W. (2001). *The wiki way: Collaboration and sharing on the Internet.* New York: Addison-Wesley.

McLuhan, M., Fiore, Q., & Agel, J. (1996). *The medium is the massage: An inventory of effects.* San Francisco: HardWired.

Neteler, M., & Mitasova, H. (2002). Open source GIS: A GRASS GIS approach. *The Kluwer International Series In Engineering And Computer Science (SECS), 689.* Boston: Kluwer.

O'Connor, C., Sceiford, E., Wang, G., Foucar-Szocki, D., & Griffin, O. (2003). Departure, abandonment, and dropout of e-learning: Dilemma and solutions. *Report for the Masie Center eLearning Consortium.* Retrieved March 9, 2004, from www.masie.com/researchgrants/2003/JMU_Exec_Summary.pdf

Russell, T. L. (1999). *The no significant difference phenomenon.* Montogomery, AL: IDECC (International Distance Education Certification Center).

Spohrer, J. (1996). WorldBoard. *The Apple Research Lab Review, 10.*

Spohrer, J. (1999). Information in places. *The IBM Systems Journal, 38*(4). Retrieved March 9, 2004, from http://www.research.ibm.com/journal/sj/384/spohrer.html

Stephenson, R. S. (2000). The Harvey project: Open course development and rich content. In L. Petrides (Ed.), *Case Studies on Information Technology in Higher Education* (pp. 185–194). Hershey, PA: Idea Group Publishing.

Stephenson, R. S. (in press). Enhancing learning outcomes. *Journal on Excellence in College Teaching* [Special issue on *Web-Based Teaching and Learning*].

Wikipedia. (2004). Retrieved March 9, 2004, from http://www.wikipedia.org/

Wurman, R. S. (1989). *Information anxiety.* New York: Doubleday.

ONLINE QUESTIONNAIRES

Since the 1990s, as an increasing number of U.S. homes gained Internet access and the comfortable interface of World Wide Web technology, academic and commercial public opinion researchers eyed the Internet as a potentially powerful new data collection tool. However, from the outset reactions to this tool were mixed. Enthusiasts emphasized its flexibility, reduced costs, and rapid turnaround time, whereas cautious observers worried about unresolved methodological questions, particularly sampling issues and instrument effects. Sampling issues are related to reasonably well-understood principles of inferential statistics, while measurement questions, primarily concerned with the interpretation and meaning of questions and answer options, cover a terrain that is not nearly as well codified.

Sampling issues were the more obvious question because the ill-defined boundaries of the Internet population prevented researchers from applying the rules of statistical inference commonly applied to sample survey data. The question of instrument effects was not so obvious, but survey researchers know that different modes of data collection (e.g., paper-and-pencil surveys as compared with telephone surveys) may yield different response patterns from similar samples. Online data collection introduces a variety of effects of this type. More than a decade after the first Internet browsers left the ivory tower, enthusiasts and cautious observers each can find evidence supporting their point of view.

History of Online Questionnaires

Internet-based survey research was a logical extension of the first computer-assisted survey applications: computer-assisted telephone interviewing (CATI) and computer-assisted personal interviewing (CAPI). Starting with early efforts during the mid-1980s, the first systematic Internet-based surveys were e-mail surveys. As Internet penetration reached 30 percent and more of U.S. households and as Web technology was developed and disseminated, e-mail surveys remained the dominant online survey method until the late 1990s. Moreover, survey experts were cautious about collecting online data due to limited population coverage and advocated the use of this technology only for specific groups, such as company employees or association members, where online access was assured for most, if not all, members. *Proceedings of the Annual Conference of the American Association for Public Opinion Research* spoke of Internet and intranet surveys through 1997, the term *Web survey* first appearing in 1998.

Since 2000, however, Web-based surveys have become ubiquitous. These surveys range from the simple, single-question polls found on many web-pages to detailed and complex commercial, marketing, and academic studies that make full use of the interactive and multimedia potential of the Web. Fueled by hardware and software advances, Web-based survey research has grown increasingly sophisticated. On the server side, performance has increased as price has decreased. Survey implementation has moved from static HTML (hypertext markup language) pages and simple scripting languages to a dynamic presentation of webpages built around a database-driven survey application backend (which means that each survey is a different instance of a generic database design rather than a unique, custom-tailored application). As these database applications have become more sophisticated they have moved toward expert systems with a considerable degree of richness and detail in survey content. Thus, for example, a commercial survey may query clients regarding the details of a full technical product line. On the client side, more powerful personal computers and more capable Web browsers have brought a level of speed, stability, and robustness that has made Web-based surveys an increasingly reliable means of survey data collection. This development has been further facilitated by increasing bandwidth and the further penetration of fast Internet access in businesses and homes.

Assessing Online Questionnaires

The first edition (1978) of Don Dillman's reference work, *Mail and Telephone Surveys: The Total Design Method,* arguably has been the most influential book in the field of survey research. A search of the *Science Citation Index Expanded*, the *Social Science Citation Index*, and the *Arts and Humanities Citation Index* in the autumn of 2003 found 3,189 publications citing Dillman's work. The second edition, aptly retitled *Mail and Internet Surveys: The Tailored Design Method,* was published in 2000 and already has been cited nearly two hundred times. Experienced survey researchers, along with novices, value Dillman's work for the careful attention it pays to the mechanics of survey research, from the wording of questions to what color ink to use in signing a cover letter. Dillman's overriding purpose is to reduce survey error, which he classifies into four types: sampling error, coverage error, measurement error, and nonresponse error. Dillman's classification scheme is useful for examining issues associated with surveys of all types, including online questionnaires.

Sampling error refers to the imprecision that arises when one seeks to generalize about a population based on a sample of its members. Accounting for sampling error is a well-developed practice in survey research when the sample is random. Indeed, reporting significance levels and margins of error (as standard measures of the limits of the accuracy and precision of inferential statistics) is now an essential part of the standard reporting requirements for survey research. Whether or not a survey relies on computer-assisted data collection methods does not directly bear on sampling error. As long as the data collection rests on a sampling strategy where all units in the population have a nonzero and knowable probability of being in the sample (i.e., all members of the population could be, though none are necessarily, included in the sample and the odds of being included are known), inferential techniques—with the incumbent risk of sampling error—are warranted. For a survey researcher to determine if the selection probabilities are a knowable value greater than zero but less than one is typically impossible if the survey is grounded in a nonrandom sampling strategy.

In the current Internet environment there are certainly cases where Web survey research meets the criteria needed for inferential statistics (that is, using statistics to generalize from a sample to a population). Intraorganizational surveys—for example, a survey of all students at a university, where all students have e-mail access—would satisfy the criteria. So, too, would an organization-level study of all franchise outlets for a national fast-food chain, assuming that all outlets had Internet access as part of their business infrastructure.

Discussions of Web-based surveys have often overlooked the fact that surveys of all types, including online surveys, may involve a wide variety of types of samples and populations. To begin with, one should keep in mind the distinction between a sample survey and a population survey or census. In the former the goal is to use a sample to make inferences about a population, whereas in the latter the goal is to directly survey all members of the population. Sampling error is, of course, relevant only when one is using a sample.

Convenience samples or large "opt-in" survey panels, both of which are commonly used in commercial and academic Web surveys, do not satisfy the criteria needed to make statistical inferences from a sample to a population. However, a nonrandom sample does not necessarily amount to a recipe for invalid results. In such cases researchers can use sample demographics or other attributes as benchmarks to compare the sample to known characteristics of the population. If a close correspondence exists, one can argue that the sample represents a population; however, this argument does not rest on the framework of inferential statistics. Moreover, although random samples allow researchers to speak with pre-

cision about sampling error, to fixate solely on this issue can blind one to other serious methodological questions. As public opinion researcher Susan Herbst (1993) points out, this is the type of error that survey researchers are best able to measure, but it is by no means necessarily the most serious type of error.

Coverage error is different from sampling error because the issue is that specific people in the population are systematically excluded from the sample. For example, in a phone survey coverage error occurs when some people do not have a phone. Other sources of coverage error are definitional. For example, the General Social Survey (GSS) is a widely used, biennial, face-to-face survey based on a traditional sampling of the U.S. noninstitutionalized, adult population. In 2000 the GSS introduced a special module on Internet use, but coverage issues limit the overall generalizability of the module study. The U.S. noninstitutionalized, adult population covers 97.3 percent of the resident population of the United States; however, coverage varies greatly by age group. For example, just under 10 percent of the population aged eighteen to twenty-four live outside of households (mostly in college dorms and military quarters) and are not represented by the sample. Thus, some of the heaviest users of the Internet are systematically excluded from the GSS.

Extending this example to a Web survey means that those people who are not online introduce coverage error. Quite possibly in the future Internet penetration will reach levels close to that of the telephone. At that time, as is the case today with phone surveys, coverage error would be ignorable for most general population survey samples. However, in the case of particular substantive conditions—homelessness is the most obvious example—coverage issues remain significant for phone and household surveys. Even if we find nearly universal Internet access in the future, researchers will still need to consider questions of coverage, particularly when the survey topic requires an adequate sample at some distance from the mainstream.

Dillman's third type of error, measurement error, results when a respondent provides inaccurate or unreliable data due to poorly worded questions or ill-conceived questionnaire design. Viewing a survey question as a stimulus and the answer as a response, a standard unambiguous question, which all like-minded respondents would answer in the same manner, is essential. In such a case, one can reasonably conclude that variation in responses may be attributed to differences in attitudes or the behavior under query. Surveys of all types may be seen as a means to standardize the asking and answering of questions.

The introduction of computers into survey settings with CATI and CAPI systems markedly increased the degree to which questionnaires with detailed skip patterns could be implemented. Skip patterns guide survey progress along one of several branches based on respondent replies to previous sets of questions. For example, those people who said they are employed would answer one set of questions about their current employer, whereas those people who were not employed could be queried about their job search behavior. This questioning could be done with a level of transparency and flexibility that would be impossible without a computer-administered survey. Complex skip patterns can also be included in surveys administered by a well-trained interview staff. Training such an interview staff, however, is costly, and its involvement may introduce its own type of measurement error because respondents may answer differently in the presence of an interviewer, particularly if the survey touches on sensitive or personal issues.

Computer-assisted surveys, especially Web-based surveys, also have the potential to reduce measurement error in two additional ways. First, a computer-assisted survey may ask questions quite precisely. Thus, for example, Survey2000, a Web survey hosted by the National Geographic Society, attempted to measure geographic variation in knowledge and preference for local culture, in particular local authors and local cuisine. Rather than ask respondents about "local authors" or "local food," surveyors asked respondents, based on their place of residence, about specific authors and specific dishes (e.g., Pat Conroy and grits for South Carolina). Second, question prompts in Web surveys are not limited to text but instead can include any media that may be transmitted over the Internet. For example, Survey2000, when asking about musical taste, did not simply ask respondents if they "liked jazz" but instead played specific sound clips representing distinct types of jazz. However, as survey researchers make increasing use of this technology and embed different media prompts in surveys, research is needed to get a better sense of how such prompts may affect response patterns.

Dillman's fourth type of error, nonresponse error, occurs when a notable proportion of sample respondents fails to respond to a survey *and* the nonresponding members of the sample significantly differ from responding sample members. A low response rate in and of itself is inefficient and costly but does not undermine the quality of the data. However, when nonresponse is nonrandom, that is, when nonresponse is correlated with characteristics of the sample members, even relatively low rates of nonresponse may become problematic. Interestingly, one recent phone survey experiment found that although rigorous interviewer efforts were able to significantly boost response rates (from 36.0 percent to 60.6 percent), few differences in response patterns existed, and these were primarily found in demographic characteristics and not in substantive characteristics. Nevertheless, even with such efforts approximately 40 percent of the sample remained nonrespondents, and more than 25 percent of those who were contacted and eligible refused to be interviewed. Moreover, in this instance as well as in other cases the observed similarities between "ready" and "reticent" respondents do not preclude important unobserved differences between these groups or between these groups and those who remain nonrespondents.

Online questionnaires, particularly those that employ an interactive Web-based approach rather than an e-mail approach, have brought a new dimension to discussions of nonresponse error. Typically, in contrast to discussions of completed surveys, discussions of partially completed Web-based surveys have distinguished unit nonresponse, when no data whatsoever are provided, from item nonresponse, when selected questions are not answered. With Web-based surveys, especially those that capture data on a webpage-by-webpage basis and collect tracking data on the survey process, the analysis of nonresponse error has gained a new tool. The situation is comparable to a researcher using a paper-and-pencil mail survey being able to collect partially completed surveys that were thrown into the trashcan rather than being returned to the researcher. Analysis of these partially completed surveys offers a further means to determine whether systematic differences exist between non-responders and responders, particularly if key demographic items are included early in the questionnaire. Interestingly, although placing demographic items early in a questionnaire is counter to widely accepted rules of survey design, at least one study shows that doing so in a Web-based survey actually leads to significantly higher proportions of completed surveys.

Whether one seeks to obtain data from a sample or from a population, a relevant and related consideration is whether the research is viewed by the researcher, as well as by the respondents, as an intraorganizational or an extraorganizational effort. At its extremes the significance of this consideration is obvious. Within a small organization a researcher surveying the organization has a variety of tools to encourage all people to become respondents. Along with the perceived benefits to the respondents and the cost and burden of completing a survey instrument the legitimacy and authority of a survey sponsor are critical to survey response rates.

Prospects for Online Questionnaires

Surely we can safely say that a greater proportion of U.S. households will be online in ten years than is online today. We also have no reason to expect that the increase in the proportion of online households in the next ten years will match the rate of increase in the past ten years. Nor can we expect that the manner in which the majority of people connect to the Internet in ten years will be the same as it is today. The sociology and the technology of the Internet will change, and this change will have consequences for a variety of online applications, including Web-based surveys. The future is never predicable; however, we can safely anticipate several developments in online survey research.

First and foremost, we can anticipate that all Internet applications, including online surveys, will adapt to shifts in hardware and software technology. Despite its relative novelty, we can easily assume a

computer desktop environment with a Windows-like graphical user interface (GUI). However, to make such an assumption is to ignore the fact that most U.S. adult residents completed their education before this technology was introduced. We have every reason to anticipate that technology will continue to change at the same rate, if not even faster.

This change means that as information technology (IT) continues to move beyond the desktop, efforts to query public opinion will adapt to the opportunity to survey people in settings more closely tied to the activities and attitudes in question. Surveys about tourist activities in regard to automobile global positioning systems (GPS) or time-use diaries which seek to accurately record respondents' use of their time, linked to cell phones are already obvious examples Another likely scenario foresees Web-based surveys as exit polls for elections delivered on Web-enabled personal digital assistants (PDAs). This scenario illustrates the way in which these future survey applications combining portable computing and wireless interconnectivity will transcend existing CAPI systems. In the case of an exit poll, where the value of results stands in direct relationship to the results' timeliness, a survey instrument that is directly linked to the Web has a clear advantage over a standalone CAPI survey instrument. Moreover, although standard CAPI surveys offer the flexibility and intelligence of a computer-assisted questionnaire, they require that all the information needed to guide the survey be previously downloaded to each interviewer's PDA or other handheld device. By contrast, an Internet-enabled CAPI questionnaire may be informed by any resources linked to the Internet.

The advantage of Internet-enabled portable computing devices as survey platforms appears even greater when one considers another facet of the manner in which online questionnaires are likely to develop in the future. A primary strength of computer-assisted questionnaires is their adaptability. Typically we think of this adaptability coming in reaction to initial questionnaire responses, for example, a survey branching to different sets of questions based on an initial question concerning each respondent's employment status. As survey developers exploit this adaptability still further, the information needed to manage the course of the survey becomes more complex and lends itself to organization in a database. This database may contain information collected from the respondent earlier in the survey or from distinctly different surveys at other points in time or may be external information that is somehow keyed to the respondent or his or her responses. As surveys become increasingly "database driven," the value of Internet-enabled portable computing devices will also increase as they allow researchers to combine decentralized data collection with the advantages of centralized database administration.

The growing complexity of online questionnaires will also lead to a growing emphasis on documentation tools, especially autodocumentation systems for online survey authoring systems. (Autodocumentation systems link survey questions to the specific program statements that implement the question and are generated automatically by the survey program independent of the programmer.) A typical online survey project involves three types of participants: survey data users/clients (decision makers), survey designers (social scientists), and survey programmers (computer scientists). Documentation becomes an essential tool to ensure that all participants agree on what information is needed, what questions are to be asked, and how these questions are accurately implemented.

In the future online questionnaires likely will make increasing use of different media embedded in them. Photographic images and audio and video files are likely to become more common elements in questionnaires as the online environment becomes more conducive to their presentation as question prompts. This is likely to be the case as browsers—not only for personal computers and laptops, but also for the full spectrum of Internet-enabled devices—develop to support a growing variety of file formats. We can hope that as survey researchers use these innovations to engage respondents and perhaps decrease measurement error, they remain sensitive to our relative ignorance of exactly how these innovations may have their own independent effect on response patterns.

James Witte and Roy Pargas

See also E-mail

FURTHER READING

Bosnjak, M., & Tuten, T. (2001). Classifying response behaviors in Web-based surveys. *Journal of Computer Mediated Communication, 6*(3). Retrieved May 11, 2004, from http://www.ascusc.org/jcmc/vol6/issue3/boznjak.html

Costigan, P., & Elder, S. (2003). Does the questionnaire implement the specification? Who knows? In R. Banks, et al. (Eds.), *The impact of technology on the survey process: Proceedings of the 4th International Conference on Survey and Statistical Computing.* Chesham Bucks, UK: Association for Survey Computing.

Davis, J. A., Smith, T. W., & Marsden, P. V. (2001). *General social surveys, 1972–2000: 3rd version.* Storrs, CT: Roper Center for Public Opinion Research, University of Connecticut, and Ann Arbor, MI: Inter-University Consortium for Political and Social Research.

Dillman, D. (2000). *Mail and Internet surveys: The tailored design method.* New York: John Wiley & Sons.

Frick, A., Bächtiger, M. T., & Reips, U.-D. (2001). Financial incentives, personal information, and drop-out in online studies. In U.-D. Reips & M. Bosnjak (Eds.), *Dimensions of Internet science* (pp. 209–220) Lengerich, Germany: Pabst.

Herbst, S. (1993). *Numbered voices: How opinion polling has shaped American politics.* Chicago: University of Chicago Press.

Keeter, S., Miller, C., Kohut, A., Groves, R., & Presser, S. (2000). Consequences of reducing nonresponse in a national telephone survey. *Public Opinion Quarterly, 64*(2), 125–148.

Kiesler, S., & Sproull, E. (1986). Response effects in the electronic survey. *Public Opinion Quarterly, 50,* 402–413.

Proceedings of the fifty-second annual conference of the American Association for Public Opinion Research. (1997). *Public Opinion Quarterly, 61*(3), 519–551.

Proceedings of the fifty-third annual conference of the American Association for Public Opinion Research. (1998). *Public Opinion Quarterly, 62*(3), 434–473.

Schaefer, D. R., & Dillman, D. A. (1998). Development of a standard e-mail methodology: Results of an experiment. *Public Opinion Quarterly, 62*(3), 378–397.

Schonlau, M., Fricker, Jr., R. D., & Elliott, M. N. (2001). *Conducting research surveys via e-mail and the Web.* Santa Monica, CA: Rand.

Witte, J. C., & Howard, P. E. N. (2002). Technological & methodological innovation in survey instruments: The future of polling. In F. Cook & J. Manza (Eds.), *Navigating public opinion* (pp. 272—289) Oxford, UK: Oxford University Press.

Witte, J. C., & Pargas, R. P. (2003). *The OnQ survey database system: Architecture and implementation. The impact of technology on the survey process:* In R. Banks, et al. (Eds.), *Proceedings of the 4th International Conference on Survey and Statistical Computing* (pp. 121–132). Chesham Bucks, UK: Association for Survey Computing.

ONLINE VOTING

Online voting occurs when an individual uses an electronic device such as a personal computer or a personal digital assistant to access an interactive ballot and then casts that ballot by transmitting it over a computer network such as the Internet. Online voting is conducted primarily in two settings: private elections (for example, voting by corporate shareholders or organization members) and public elections—elections in which the public chooses those who will represent them in the government. Many of the issues associated with online voting in public elections are of less concern in private ones, as private elections do not impact public governance.

In January 2000, the California Internet Voting Task Force identified four distinct types of online voting:

1. Remote online voting: The computer that the voter uses to cast his or her ballot is outside the control of election officials, and the ballot is transmitted over a network connection to the election officials.
2. Kiosk online voting: Voting takes place in a limited number of locations using computers under the physical control of election officials, but the ballot is transmitted to the election officials over a network connection.
3. Polling-place online voting: Voting takes place in polling places. Voters use computers under the physical control of election officials to cast a ballot over a network connection, but the voter can vote from any valid polling place.
4. Precinct-place online voting: This is identical to polling-place online voting, but the voter can cast a ballot only from his or her own precinct polling place.

Online voting differs from other forms of voting that make use of electronic devices (such as touchscreen voting systems, in which votes are cast by touching the appropriate spot on a ballot visible on an electronic screen) in that online voting requires the ballot to be sent over a computer network. It is also distinguished from voting via e-mail, which is like an electronic counterpart to a traditional absentee ballot: Ballots are sent via e-mail to voters, who fill them out and return them via e-mail.

Many observers of elections believe that online voting has great potential. Studies in the wake of the 2000 U.S. presidential election document as many as 6 million votes lost due to problems with the existing election system. At least half were lost due to problems with voter registration, perhaps as many as one-third due to problems with voting machines, and most of the remainder due to difficulties in polling places.

Online voting could alleviate many of the coordination problems currently associated with elections. For example, online voting could obviate the need for polling places, eliminating problems with long lines, inaccessible polling places, and problems associated with poll workers, producing a dramatically quicker and more efficient election process. In the United States, online voting has also been identified as an important means to lower the costs of participation for certain segments of the population: voters who are disabled, those who are away from home on the day of the election (especially voters who are overseas), and in particular younger voters, who currently have very low rates of participation but who are heavy users of electronic devices.

Online Voting Trials

In light of the potential benefits of online voting, there have been a number of important efforts to study its use for public elections. Online voting was first used for public elections in the United States in 2000. Alaska and Arizona used online voting in their Republican and Democratic presidential primaries, respectively. Also in 2000, eighty-four military personnel and dependents used the Federal Voting Assistance Program's "Voting Over the Internet" system to vote in the national election. These trials involved people using both remote online voting, and, in the Arizona case, polling-place online voting as well.

Online voting trials have also been conducted in the United Kingdom and in various European Union nations. The initial goals of these trials has been to determine whether online voting is technically feasible, with some studies also giving consideration to the impact that online voting would have on election administrators and voters. The United Kingdom launched the most ambitious of these European projects in 2002, when the national government sponsored a number of pilot projects to experiment with online voting in local elections. The results indicated that online voting could be conducted in a secure manner, and that both voters and local election officials felt that the systems were convenient and easy to use. However, these projects did not document any significant increase in voter participation associated with online voting.

Criticisms of Online Voting

Critics of online voting have two main concerns. First, computer networks are not secure environments; online voting systems are potentially vulnerable to a variety of hacking techniques, including denial-of-service attacks on the election computer network, viruses, or "Trojan Horse" software that could threaten the validity of ballots cast. Also, with the voting process automated, the process of committing vote fraud could be automated as well. Although there were no documented attacks during the U.S. online trials, one did occur during a caucus held by the New Democratic Party in January 2002 in Canada. These security concerns are discussed in *Secure Electronic Voting* (2003), edited by Dimitris Gritzalis, as well as in the California Internet Voting Task Force report and the report issued by the National Science Foundation's workshop on Internet voting.

Second, there is a gap between those who have access to a computer and the Internet and those who do not—the so-called digital divide. In the United States, the very people who have historically been the victims of intentional and unintentional discrimination—poor and minority voters—do not have the same degree of access to computers and the Internet as other demographic groups. The potential size of this problem was illustrated by the Arizona primary, in which online voting participation was lowest in the counties with the highest percentages of minority voters. This digital divide could create a legal barrier to wide-scale online voting.

Future Research Directions

Online voting has obvious merits and equally obvious problems. With more research, we may be able to understand the merits better, to resolve the known problems, and to discover problems that are not yet apparent.

The first task is to address the problem of computer and network security. Research in this area has obvious implications for e-commerce, so market pressures are likely to ensure that advances in this area continue to occur. As Lorrie Faith Cranor, a security expert, has noted, "Advances in email and Web browser software that can easily interface with cryptography software should pave the way for secure and private electronic elections in the near future" (Cranor 2003).

Second, more research on how online voting actually affects the electoral process is needed. Questions to be addressed include how effectively voters interact with the various online voting interfaces, whether online voting will increase voter participation (and which segments of the population will be most affected) and whether it might lead to a better-informed electorate, whether increasingly complex computer and network security systems will adversely affect the ease with which people can use online voting systems, how online voting will alter the jobs of election officials, and how it will change the competitive landscape for candidates running for office.

These questions and others that were raised by the National Science Foundation workshop on online voting need the attention of scholars and policy makers. More projects such as those being conducted in the United Kingdom are required to address these questions in a scientific and controlled manner.

R. Michael Alvarez and Thad E. Hall

See also Digital Divide; Digital Government; Political Science and HCI

FURTHER READING

Alvarez, R. M., & Nagler, J. (2001). The likely consequences of Internet voting for political representation. *Loyola of Los Angeles Law School Review, 34*(3), 1115–1153.

California Internet Voting Task Force. (2000). *A report on the feasibility of Internet voting.* Retrieved August 1, 2003, from http://www.ss.ca.gov/executive/ivote/final_report.htm

Caltech/MIT Voting Technology Project. (2001). *Voting: What is, what could be.* Retrieved August 1, 2003, from http://www.vote.caltech.edu/Reports/

Cranor, L. F. (1996). Electronic voting. *ACM Crossroads*, 2(4). Retrieved August 1, 2003, from http://www.acm.org/crossroads/xrds2-4/voting.html

Electoral Commission. (2002). Modernising elections: A strategic evaluation of the 2002 electoral pilot schemes. Retrieved August 1, 2003, from http://www.electoralcommission.org.uk/templates/search/document.cfm/6170

Federal Voting Assistance Program. (2001). *Voting over the Internet Pilot Project Assessment Report.* Washington DC: Author.

Gritzalis, D. (Ed.). (2003). *Secure electronic voting.* Boston: Kluwer Academic Publishers.

Internet Policy Institute. (2001). *Report of the National Workshop on Internet Voting: Issues and research agenda.* Retrieved August 1, 2003, from http://www.diggov.org/archive/library/doc/ipi_onlinevoting.jsp

Rubin, A. D. (2001, October). *Security considerations for remote electronic voting.* Paper presented at the 29th Research Conference on Communication, Information and Internet Policy, Alexandria, VA. Retrieved August 1, 2003, from http://avirubin.com/e-voting.security.html

ONTOLOGY

Ontology became an information technology (IT) buzzword in the late 1990s, and many, upon hearing it for the first time, consider it to refer to something relatively new. The word itself, however, was coined in the seventeenth century and the earliest extant published reference in English is *Bailey's Dictionary* in 1721, indicating it was already in use by then. Ontology is, therefore, nothing new, but its relationship to human-computer interaction and information technology in general has caused a subtle shift in meaning that may well be new. This new meaning is often confused with *semantics, knowledge*, and *representation*, from which the original word was intended to be distinct.

Ontology in Philosophy

Ontology is another word for the philosophical discipline that students of the Greek philosopher Aristotle called *metaphysics* (literally "after physical"). The field has been devoted to the study of existence, of the kinds and structures of objects, properties, events, processes and relations in every area of reality. An ontological question, therefore, is typically understood to be a question of existence. The French philosopher Rene Descartes' famous statement, "I think therefore I am," is often referred to as an answer to an ontological question.

Philosophers in ontology do not go around questioning each other's existence, however. Ontology is about the kinds of objects, properties, etc., in the world, not about the objects themselves. A more characteristic ontological question is, "Are sculptures a kind of entity in the world?" Such a simple and obvious seeming question has deep implications. The problem it reveals after analysis is whether a particular sculpture, and the clay from which it was sculpted, are two separate kinds of entities or one.

Modern analytic philosophy encourages more formal analysis, and one important tool of this analysis is *identity*. Identity concerns conditions under which we would consider an entity to be different from or the same as another. Consider an amount of clay—unless we remove or add clay, it remains the same amount of clay, no matter what shape it may take. However, molded into the shape of a horse it is one particular sculpture, while molded into a cow the *same* clay is a *different* sculpture. This is a basic ontological problem: If the horse and the cow are different sculptures, how could either be the same entity as the clay if the clay is the same—same amount of clay, different sculptures? How philosophers answer this question is one of the basic distinctions in ontology. Some philosophers require a theory that accounts for the common sense answer (a sculpture is a single entity), and others concede that common sense is wrong and a sculpture is two entities.

Ontology in Information Systems

Since at least the 1950s, and more seriously in the mid-1970s after database systems became more formalized, computer scientists have been creating and studying information systemsthat model some aspect of the world, or some artificial world, in a declarative way. *Conceptual modeling* in database systems refers to the process of building a formal model of the data an information system will need.

Conceptual modeling typically involves identifying the types of objects in some domain, and their attributes. For example, a library information system will need to know about books, that they have titles and authors and that the book can be checked out by someone. Proper analysis would reveal that copies of the same book can be checked out by different people, and would lead to a model in which book and book-copy are separate (though related) types of objects. Title and author are attributes of a book, whereas location and the status "checked out by" are attributes of each book-copy.

It is not a terribly large leap from this conceptual modeling problem with books and their copies to the philosophical problem of sculptures and clay. In both cases, the *kinds* of entities in the world and their relationships are being identified, and often subtle distinctions become important to capture. From this perspective, conceptual models appear to be ontologies with a twist: They describe the kinds of entities and relationships in a domain that is relevant to an information system, not every area of reality. This is the most common understanding of ontology in computer science.

Ontology and Representation

An ontology as an information system is typically composed of classes and relations. These classes and relations are symbols that represen*t* the actual classes and relations in the universe. The symbol *book* in the library ontology is not the collection of all the books in the world or in the library, it is a representation of that collection, a symbol that "stands in" for the collection within the artificial world of an information system.

This reveals a further subtle distinction between ontologies in computer science and philosophy. The product of the analysis that a philosopher may do is referred to as *an* ontology, which in philosophy is typically understood to be a theory. In computer science, *an* ontology is understood to be something more: the theory *and* the information artifact that represents or implements the theory. This artifact includes the symbols, collected and organized in a file or set of files, that may be located on the web, exposed through some interface, expressed in some

language, etc. Referring to this artifact as an ontology itself, rather than as representing an ontology, is akin to referring to a journal article describing a theory as a theory.

Ontology and Knowledge

Ontologies of all kinds often specify not just relationships between types of entities, but also constraints, typically expressed using some variant of formal logic, on those relationships, in order to clarify ontological distinctions. We may find it useful, for example, to specify that the author of a book must be a person, and that a book-copy weighs at least 1 gram. These constraints may offer some insight into the existence of the entities being described, and when coupled with a formal reasoning system often embody knowledge that a person would consider common sense. That the author of a book is a person, for example, is knowledge that most people would take for granted, but obviously an information system could not know without being told. Ontologies clearly contain knowledge about the world they represent.

Ontology and Semantics

Whereas ontology is about existence, semantics is about meaning. In particular, semantics is typically understood to be the study of what symbols (or more generally signs) *refer* to. The knowledge represented in an ontology can help to clarify the meaning of the symbols used. Symbolic systems are hopelessly closed—symbols are defined in terms of other symbols and typically have no actual connection to the real world. In that sense, it is entirely absurd to consider ontology and semantics to be related at all. However, since it is up to a human interpreter to assign semantics by identifying the referent of a symbol, that is, the thing in the universe that exists and that a particular symbol is supposed to represent, ontologies contain information that can help that process.

In the library example we made an ontological distinction between a book and a copy, and created a class to represent each. Furthermore, we specified that a book has a title and author but *not* a location, where a book-copy is related to a book and has a location and can be checked out by a person. These definitions make the intended meaning of the symbols more apparent to a human interpreter. It is slightly more clear that, since, e.g., a book does not have a location, it is not a physical object.

The additional knowledge in an ontology, such as constraints, can also further help the human interpreter. Nothing in the information system just described prevents a person who does not understand the ontology from creating a book whose author is another book. This class of errors is sometimes referred to as an "unintended model" of an ontology. In the actual world, no book is written by a book, and thus the semantics of "book" and "author" makes such a relationship impossible. We can code this constraint into our proposed ontology by specifying that the author of a book must be a person, thus preventing this unintended model and making the meaning more clear.

What Isn't an Ontology?

The overlap between computer science ontology and semantics, representation, philosophical ontology, logic, knowledge, etc., has made it very difficult to define just what an ontology is or isn't. Ultimately, because computer science has changed the meaning of ontology anyway, there can be no purely right or wrong answers, and for many things, asking if it is an ontology will be like asking if fire is alive. Consequently, each of the following kinds of information systems merits its own discussion of how it relates to ontology.

Dictionaries

A dictionary provides, for each symbol, a definition whose intent is to clarify the meaning of that symbol in terms of other symbols. On the surface this may seem satisfactory, in fact information system ontologies are occasionally referred to as "shared vocabularies," however the purpose of a dictionary is not to identify the kinds of objects in the world, but to clarify the meaning of words; it is a difference in emphasis, procedure, and commitment. For dictionaries one identifies the words and their meanings, whereas for ontologies one must first iden-

tify the kinds of things that exist, and then provide symbols to represent them and finally specify the meaning of those symbols. Note how the difference between a sculpture and the clay it is made from would not be found in the dictionary. An entry in a dictionary signifies the existence of a word in some language, whereas a class in an ontology signifies a commitment, sometimes referred to as the *ontological commitment*, that a certain class of entities exists.

This distinction becomes muddled when the product of ontological analysis is an artifact that looks very much like a dictionary, but this is a practical, engineering issue. Nothing is wrong *per se* with calling a collection of terms and definitions an ontology if the collection was developed for that purpose. However, after the artifact is created and appears to people to be a dictionary, it will tend to evolve over time towards that purpose.

Taxonomies

Philosophers and computer scientists both routinely make use of taxonomies (systems of classifications) as part of specifying an ontology. This co-occurrence has led to the conflation (confusion) of the words *taxonomy and ontology*, but that is clearly wrong. A taxonomy is a tool that can be used to specify and structure an ontology; however, not all taxonomies are intended to be ontologies, nor do all ontologies use taxonomies.

Corpora

Corpora are collections of words, and are quite simply not ontologies in any sense.

Thesauri

Thesauri are typically slightly more structured dictionaries that provide a taxonomy of terms as well as their definitions. Again, as with dictionaries, the difference is one of emphasis, procedure, and commitment. Thesauri, as taxonomies, can be tools to specify an ontology, but they typically evolve over time to focus on words and meanings rather than on ontological commitments.

Lexical Databases

There are many artifacts in this category, the most prominent of which is WordNet. Like thesauri, lexical databases are about words, with far more structure—WordNet provides more than twelve lexical relations. The content of WordNet is organized around conceptual clusters of words, called "synsets," with an extensive taxonomy that is rooted in a fairly small number of top-level terms. The goal, at least for WordNet, is to organize words into groups according to their meaning, and thus it was necessary to build a taxonomy of concepts that do not correspond to words, such as "Amount of Matter," but rather to the kinds of things in the world that words refer to. As a result, lexical databases such as WordNet have a dual status. They have ontologies that include classes that correspond to things in the world and not words, however these ontologies are driven by words and their meanings, not by a careful analysis of the world itself. The difficulty here is that the part of WordNet that is more clearly an ontology is not discernable; one must simply know where the dictionary begins and the ontology ends.

Catalogs

A catalog is a specification of the kinds of inventory that some organization keeps—for example, the products that a company sells. In this sense, catalogs are quite clearly ontologies, albeit simple ones: they specify the "kinds of things that exist" in that domain, assign symbols to them, and often provide some meaning for those symbols. Catalogs are not traditionally considered ontologies because they are simple and require little analysis or specification—the things that exist are the things you sell. Modern online order systems, however, that provide functionality such as configuration, need to have information about compatibility, power consumption, and so forth, that clearly require more sophisticated analysis.

Classes and Instances

Ontologies describe the *kinds* of things in some domain, and normally in information systems *classes* are used to represent kinds of things. It is important in general to understand the difference between classes, such as "book," and instances, such as *The Old Man and the Sea*. It is common to view information system ontologies as composed only of classes (and relations), and not their instances, however this

is another incorrect association—the class/instance distinction is different. Consider the example of defining the class Italian—the definition requires Italy, an instance of the class "Country."

Christopher A. Welty

See also Information Organization; Information Retrieval; Lexicon Building

FURTHER READING

Aristotle. (350 BCE). *Categories* .Retrieved March 8, 2004, from http://www.classicallibrary.org/aristotle/categories

Casati, R. & Varzi. A. (1994). *Holes and Other Superficialities.* Cambridge, MA: MIT Press.

Guarino, N. (1998). Formal Ontology in Information Systems. In *Proceedings of the International Conference on Formal Ontology in Information Systems* (pp. 3–15). Trento, Italy.

Quine, W.V.O. (1969). *Ontological Relativity and Other Essays.* New York: Columbia University Press.

Smith, B. & Welty, C. (2001). Ontology: Towards a new synthesis. In *Proceedings of the International Conference on Formal Ontology in Information Systems* (pp. iii–ix). Ogunquit, Maine.

OPEN SOURCE SOFTWARE

The term open source software was coined in 1998 to describe both a method of software distribution and a form of software licensing. An overlapping version of this idea, dating back to 1984, is called free software. In this article, both concepts will be discussed collectively as free and open source software (F/OSS).

Fundamental Concepts

The free and open source distribution of software means that users of the software have access to a form of the software that can be modified and is readable by humans. The distribution of software under an open source license means that the users of the software are free to modify and share the software with other users, possibly subject to a few limited restrictions, depending on which open source license is used. Although these are the two main features of F/OSS—the distribution of human-readable code and the freedom to modify and redistribute the code—other aspects of F/OSS are noteworthy. Some of these aspects include F/OSS as (1) a new software development model, (2) a new software business model that threatens established software businesses, (3) a unique online community and culture, (4) a new model for work and employment, (5) the globalization of software development, (6) a model for open sharing of other intellectual content (for example, music, books, educational materials, and scientific knowledge), and (7) a challenge to conventional ideas about economic motivations, intellectual property, the digital divide, and government policy.

Open source software projects are self-organizing, with many developers from around the world volunteering to form software development teams. Often they do this as a hobby, but an increasing number of developers are working as paid consultants or as employees of firms that use the F/OSS product under development as part of their product or service offerings. Typically the software is distributed at no or little cost among the community of users in what is described as a "gift economy." Prior to the introduction of the open source label, software that could be freely modified was called "free software." Many still choose to call it free software, but they emphasize that "free" does not mean free of cost, but free to modify and redistribute. Richard M. Stallman, a recipient of the ACM Grace Hopper award and the first president of the Free Software Foundation, often whimsically clarifies this point with the quote: "Think of free speech, not free beer!"

For many programming languages, the human-readable source code is converted by a compiler into computer instructions comprised of 0's and 1's called the binary format of software. This binary form of software is optimized to run on computers, but because it is not easy for humans to read or modify, it cannot be called open source software unless the human-readable source code is also freely available. In the 1950s and 1960s, computer firms made their profits from selling computer hardware and often bundled their software in what we call the open source

format today. But by the 1980s, computer firms, especially those primarily focusing on software, began to sell closed source software, often in copy-protected forms. This proprietary software came with end user licenses that restricted modification or redistribution to protect the authors' ownership of the intellectual property embedded in the software. Violations of these license restrictions against the copying and sharing of closed source software was called software piracy, and software industry trade associations used aggressive enforcement against such software pirates.

Despite the prevalence of the closed-source copy-restricted software distribution business model, the development and distribution of free and open source software, which started in the 1980s, has grown in volume, popularity, and importance. Software distributed under free or open source licenses is dominant on the Internet. Examples include the Linux and BSD operating systems, the GNU development tools, the Apache Web server, Sendmail for mail distribution, BIND for Internet address translation, the Mozilla web browser, the MySQL and PostgreSQL relational databases, and many programming languages including Perl, PHP, TCL/Tk, Python, and GNU/GCC. Not coincidentally, free and open source software grew in popularity and importance as the Internet and the WWW took off in popularity and importance, feeding each other's growth. The Internet enabled the collaboration of widely dispersed F/OSS developers, many of whom were also programming using systems on the Internet. However, free and open source software is not without controversy, both inside and outside the F/OSS community.

Early History

The story of free and open source software largely begins in the late 1960s at two locations: the MIT Artificial Intelligence (AI) Laboratory and the AT&T Bell Labs. At the MIT AI Lab, a community of faculty, students, and programmers, working on computers running their locally developed ITS operating system (the Incompatible Timesharing System) developed a computer culture playfully called the hacker culture. This was long before the media co-opted the meaning of the term hacker to describe people who illegally crack into computers for malicious purposes. This culture developed its own vocabulary, folklore, and traditions, which were characterized by an openness to sharing ideas and software, hard work, nonstandard work hours, brilliant programming, and a playful irreverence toward authority (it was the 1960s). Stallman, an important actor in the free software movement, began his programming career at the MIT AI Lab in the early 1970s. At the AT&T Bell Labs, the UNIX operating system was developed by Ken Thompson and the programming language C was developed by his colleague Dennis Richie, both ACM Turing Award recipients.

These two innovations, UNIX and C, were designed to be portable, flexible, and extensible, making them attractive to many programmers at that time. Copies were shared with the computer science department at the University of California at Berkeley. Modifications and additions were added and collected into a Berkeley Software Distribution, ported

---

UNIX A widely used operating system, improved and enhanced by many people since its development in 1969 by Bell Laboratories.

---

to other computer architectures, and shared with many other research sites. At these three sites, the MIT AI Lab, Bell Labs, and later UC Berkeley, the programmer culture, programming languages, software tools, and operating systems, evolved, spread, and became a significant influence on the free software movement which later evolved into the open source movement, although neither term existed at that time.

In the early 1980s two important events triggered the beginnings of the free software movement. First, the community around the MIT AI Lab collapsed because of the loss of many of the lab's programmers to AI company start-ups, and the replacement of lab computers by new computers with closed source operating systems and software. Second, after the breakup of the AT&T monopoly, which had been restricted from competing in the computer industry, the company commercialized the UNIX system. This

led to a long, acrimonious legal battle between AT&T and UC Berkeley over the distribution rights to UNIX and copyright infringements by the BSD UNIX distributions.

In 1983, Stallman started an ambitious project to develop a replacement for UNIX called GNU (GNU is Not UNIX) and to distribute the GNU software freely (as in free speech, not free of cost). Proceeds from the sales of the GNU software are used to support the Free Software Foundation he later founded to promote the idea and development of free software. As a reflection of the strong ideology behind the move, and to protect the GNU software from being converted into closed source, all GNU software is distributed under the GNU General Public License (GPL). GPL permits the software to be freely distributed and freely modified. If the modified software is redistributed, the modifications must be included in the source code so that other users can inspect, benefit from, and further modify those modifications. GPL does not require a company that modifies a program for internal use to share the modifications; this is only required if the modified program is redistributed.

Authors of software licensed under GPL may sell their software for any price, as long as the source code is included or made available elsewhere. Also, a person who buys such software is free to resell it or share copies of it with others for no charge. Under GPL, embedded or modified and redistributed software must also be GPL; this is sometimes called the viral property of GPL. The Free Software Foundation uses the GNU General Public License (and variations) for the GNU software and documentation. Linux and many other F/OSS programs are also distributed using GPL. Some other F/OSS projects have developed alternative licenses for their software which are close in spirit to the GNU GPL. Examples include the Mozilla Public License, the Apache Software License, and the Berkeley Software License. Many of these other licenses are less restrictive on how derived works need to be licensed. For example, under the Berkeley Software License, software can be embedded in a commercial product and that product does not have to be distributed under the Berkeley license, as would be the case with GPL.

Linux

The term Linux is used to identify either (1) an operating system kernel, (2) a UNIX-like operating system, or (3) a complete server or desktop software distribution including end user applications. This F/OSS project was started in 1991 as a hobby project by a 21-year-old student in Finland, Linus Torvalds, who is currently the lead maintainer of the Linux kernel, the critical component at the core of the Linux operating system. For Linux to function as a complete operating system (similar to a Windows or Macintosh operating system), hundreds of other support programs must accompany it. Collections of software consisting of the Linux kernel, its support programs, and additional software are called a Linux distribution. Popular examples include the RedHat Linux, Debian Linux, and SuSE Linux. They typically include the GNU software tools and utilities, programming languages, desktop windowing environments, browsers, office productivity suites, and networked services (for example, Apache, PostgreSQL, Samba, and Sendmail), and include the added value of providing configuration and compatibility for all the included programs. The Linux distributions guarantee that everything works together and provide maintenance and security updates.

Participation on the Linux kernel project grew quickly after Tolvalds released the first version on the Internet, with estimates of hundreds to thousands of contributors. The Linux operating system is considered comparable in quality, security, and performance with other commercially developed closed source operating systems (for instance, Windows). This surprised many software engineers, whose experience suggested that the development of a large complex piece of software like an operating system kernel was a major undertaking requiring a tightly managed project using strong centralized control of the development process. Even members of the free software community were surprised at the success of Linux.

The Cathedral and The Bazaar

Eric Raymond, a F/OSS developer and outspoken advocate of F/OSS, analyzed and documented software engineering principles that could be learned from the Linux development success. The title of his white paper and book, The Cathedral & The Bazaar, suggests two very different software engineering styles. The Cathedral-style tends to be top-down, closed, highly structured and ordered, and under strong central control. The Bazaar-style tends to be bottom-up, open, less structured, and under loose central control. Closed proprietary software and even some F/OSS projects tend to use the Cathedral-style approach, while Linux was his exemplar of the Bazaar-style approach. The paper presents software engineering lessons that could be learned from the Linux case. Two of these lessons, which are often quoted, are (1) Release early, Release Often, and Listen to your customers, and (2) Linus's Law: Given enough eyeballs, all bugs are shallow.

Perhaps one of the most important consequences of Raymond's white paper was that it influenced Netscape's decision to release the company's browser software as open source and to initiate the Mozilla project. This event gave the F/OSS movement credibility in the eyes of corporate information technology managers who were typically uncertain of its credibility.

The Open Source Initiative

After the Netscape decision to embrace the free software idea, several leaders in the community decided to deal with the problem that the word "free" in "free software" had multiple meanings, and that the obvious one, free of charge, was misleading, and probably hindered the adoption of free software by businesses. Under the GPL and other free software licenses, anybody is allowed to sell copies of free software, thus confronting new users with a confusing contradiction. (And "free" in the context of free software may also suggest cheap, shoddy and low quality.) To address this problem and to look for ways to better promote free software adoption by business users, several activists and thinkers including Eric Raymond, Sam Ockman, John Hall, Todd Anderson, Larry Augustine, and Christine Peterson met and Peterson suggested the new label "open source." Linus Tolvolds supported the idea, and Richard Stallman originally supported it (but reverted back to a preference for "free software"). In 1998 Bruce

Perens (then project leader of the free Debian Linux distribution) and Eric Raymond co-founded the not-for-profit Open Source Initiative (OSI). Perens adapted the Debian Free Software Guidelines into the Open Source Definition (OSD).

The OSD contains ten points: (1) freedom to redistribute must be retained, (2) source code must be available, (3) modifications and derived works are permitted, (4) derived works may require name changes or other actions to protect the integrity of the original author's source code, (5) no discrimination is allowed against persons or groups, (6) no discrimination is permitted against fields of endeavor, (7) a license must follow the software when it is redistributed, (8) a license must not be specific to a product, (9) a license must not "contaminate" other software on the distribution medium, and (10) a license may not be predicated on any individual technology or style of interface. The precise details of the OSD can be obtained online at http://www.open-source.org/. Open source licenses that are in conformance with the OSD and certified by OSI as such can use the OSI Certification Mark. By 2004, over fifty open source licenses were OSI certified. The OSD was intended to be inclusive and most of the early free software licenses are OSI certified, including the GNU GPL, the Apache License, and the BSD License. The open source concept gained momentum as major commercial software vendors (for example Oracle) began to port their products to Linux. One other event in 1999 generated publicity for F/OSS—confidential internal Microsoft documents acknowledged the quality of F/OSS and the potential business threat F/OSS posed for the company.

The Business of Free and Open Source Software

Even though the earlier GPL and the later OSD permit charging a price for open source software, the requirement that the source be included or available, and that the buyer be able to copy and freely share the software seems to limit the opportunities for a profitable business built on F/OSS. How can any business survive in the F/OSS marketplace when the product is free of cost? Despite the apparent anti-business feature of F/OSS, many examples of highly successful business models exist. Cygnus Solutions, founded in 1989, built a successful business around contract development modifying and porting GNU software to new computing platforms, including embedded processors. In 1999 the company was acquired for over $600 million by Red Hat Software, which had been founded four years earlier by Robert Young. The Red Hat Initial Public Offering (IPO) saw the eighth-biggest first-day gain in Wall Street history with a capital value of nearly $3 billion at the end of the day. Several weeks later, the VA Linux IPO was the largest single-day gain the Wall Street history.

Of course the dot-com bubble has burst and both firms market capitalization is now much lower, but both are still in business and growing sales. These are examples of pure-play open source firms making profits by adding value to the free software. Other examples include computer firms using F/OSS as a commodity component in larger product offers. For example, IBM sells Linux on their servers and built a large e-Business offering, WebSphere, on top of the Apache Web server. Apple computer built their new OS X operating system on top of the open source Darwin, a derivative of the open source BSD UNIX.

Free and Open Source Software Controversies and Dilemmas

Several of many controversies and dilemmas associated with F/OSS revolve around the long-term viability of the F/OSS model, its impact on the established software economy, and its impact on innovation and competitiveness in the software industry.

Internal Tensions

Will internal tensions limit the long-term success of the F/OSS model? Within the F/OSS community there is philosophical tension between the free software purists (like Richard Stallman) and the more pragmatic open source software engineers (like Linus Torvolds and Eric Raymond). While Stallman considers the principles and political issues of freedom in the use of software as primary, others like Torvolds write software for fun and are less concerned about how the software is used and distributed. Other tensions exist between the GNU project and the Linux project as evidenced over the question of what to name the resulting operating system. While Stallman and the Free Software Foundation came close to achieving the GNU project's goal of a replacement operating system for UNIX (only the kernel was missing), the independently developed Linux kernel project used the available GNU software and effectively produced a replacement for UNIX. Should the combination of GNU and the Linux kernel be called Linux, or GNU/Linux or LinGNUx?

The large fortunes generated by the IPOs of F/OSS firms like Red Hat and VA Software has created resentment among some developers in the free software community. Disagreements and sometimes acrimonious quarrels between F/OSS leaders on public discussion boards can be found. Although many projects have been spectacular successes, many more have failed through neglect or imploded because of disagreements between the developers. These events raise questions about the sustainability of the F/OSS model—is it a utopian experiment doomed to failure? Are there limits to the size of F/OSS projects and long-term survivability issues? On the other hand, the availability of the source minimizes the risk. Should a project fold, at a minimum, in-house programmers or contract programmers can be hired to support the software.

Motivations

Why do they program for free? Questions about why F/OSS developers seem to work for free, sharing their software at no cost, is perplexing to many, including potential corporate customers. Recent studies of this phenomenon provide some answers. For example, Alexander Hars and Shaosong Ou conducted a survey of the motivations of seventy-nine F/OSS developers and discovered that although some (16.5 percent) were motivated by altruism, 70.9 percent did so to improve their programming skills and 51.9 percent wished to build a professional network. The latter cases suggest that many are working on F/OSS with the expectation of future rewards. Of interest

in the Hars and Ou study is that programmers paid to work on F/OSS comprise 16 percent of the sample, but make up 38 percent of the estimated cumulative working hours on F/OSS reported by the respondents. This suggests that F/OSS developers are in fact motivated by either current or future returns. It has been reported that as many as 80 to 90 percent of the developers on the Apache projects are paid for their work by their employers, which suggests that for-profit firms may be embracing open source as a commodity or common goods, similar to the standards and collaborative research seen in many industries.

Innovations

Does F/OSS enhance or diminish innovation? A broad look at typical F/OSS projects suggests that many are copycat software projects imitating previously developed commercial software. For example, GNU and Linux are re-implementations of UNIX. GIMP, a digital-image editing program, is very similar to Adobe's Photoshop. R is a F/OSS statistical package that mimics the commercial S. OpenOffice likewise mimics Microsoft Office. Businesses invest income from current sales into R & D on new products. If F/OSS copycat products cut into sales and reduce resources for new product R & D, will the long-term effect be a reduction in innovation? On the other hand, the F/OSS community can point to new classes of tools and products that they created—for example, powerful new types of editors like Emacs, or innovative programming languages like Perl and Python. Investigations into new product innovation suggest that many breakthrough paradigm-shift innovations come from small groups of researchers while large corporate research often does defensive R & D to protect current businesses.

Economic Competition and the Market Economy

How can for-profit firms compete against not-for-profit copycat software development? Is F/OSS too utopian or too similar to communism? Some firms (for instance, Microsoft) consider F/OSS a threat to their core business strategy. For example, ACM Turing Award recipient Jim Gray argued in March 2004 that the open source model endangers the software economy. Others argue that open source is providing an opening for non-United States software firms to compete in what had been a United States–dominated global software market. Meanwhile, some large commercial firms (for instance, IBM) have embraced the F/OSS model, are investing billions of R & D dollars on open source technologies. Their business model uses lower-level technologies, such as the operating system or Web server, as commodities and aims for competitive advantage through higher-level proprietary software built on top of the open source commoditized technology. Additional business opportunities are pursued through integration and consulting services around the open source technologies.

F/OSS activists will argue that open source is all about freedom of choice. Michael Tiemann, founder of Cygnus Solutions, argues that the philosophical treatises on free software written by Richard Stallman read like a business plan and motivated his business startup. Perhaps when there is change, established businesses will be threatened and adaptation will be needed. Change presents both threats and opportunities to all the actors.

Gregory Madey

See also Compilers; Programming Languages

FURTHER READING

Bergquist, M., & Ljungberg, J. (2001). The power of gifts: Organizing social relationships in open source communities. *Information Systems Journal, 11*(4), 305–320.

Bollinger, T. (1999). Linux and open-source success: Interview with Eric. S. Raymond. *IEEE Computer*, 85–89.

Charles, J. (1998). Open source: Netscape pops the hood. *IEEE Software*, 79–82.

DiBona, C., Ockman, S., & Stone, M. (Eds.). (1999). *Open sources*. Sebastopol, CA: O'Reilly.

Feller, J. (2004). *Open source resources*. Retrieved April 16, 2004, from http://opensource.ucc.ie/

Feller, J., & Fitzgerald, B. (2002). *Understanding open source software development*. London: Addison-Wesley.

Fielding, R. T. (1999). Shared leadership in the Apache project. *Communications of the ACM, 42*(4), 42–43.

Godfrey, M. W., & Tu, Q. (2000). *Evolution in open source software: A case study*. Paper presented at the the 2000 International Conference on Software Maintenance.

Hars, A., & Ou, S. (2001). *Working for free? Motivations of participating in open source projects*. Paper presented at the Hawaii International Conference on Systems Sciences.

Hecker, F. (1999). Setting up shop: The business of open-source software. *IEEE Software*, 45–51.

Hochmuth, P. (2002, December 12). IBM's open source advocate. *Network World*. Retrieved April 16, 2004, from *http://www.nwfusion.com/power/2002/frye.html.*

Koch, S. (Ed.). (2004). *Free/open source software development*. Hershey, PA: Idea Group Publishing.

Koch, S., & Schneider, G. (2002). Effort, co-operation and co-ordination in an open source software project: GNOME. *Information Systems Journal, 12*(1), 27–42.

Krishnamurthy, S. (2002). An empirical examination of 100 mature open source projects. *First Monday, 7*(6).

Kuwabara, K. (2000). Linux: A bazaar at the edge of chaos. *First Monday, 5*(3), 1–68.

Madey, G., Freeh, V., & Tynan, R. (2004). Modeling the F/OSS community: A quantitative investigation. In S. Koch (Ed.), *Free/open source software development*. Hershey, PA: Idea Group Publishing.

MIT/Sloan. (2004). *Free/open source research community*, 2002. Retrieved April 16, 2004, from http://opensource.mit.edu/

Mockus, A., Fielding, R. T., & Herbsleb, J. (2002). Two case studies of open source software development: Apache and Mozilla. *ACM Transactions on Software Engineering and Methodology, 11*(3), 309–346.

Moore, J. T. S. (2002). Revolution OS [DVD]. United States: Worldview Productions.

O'Reilly, T. (1999). Lessons from open-source software development. *Communications of the ACM, 42*(4), 33–37.

Raymond, E. S. (1999). *The cathedral & the bazaar: Musings on Linux and open source by an accidental revolutionary*. Sebastopol, CA: O'Reilly.

Scacchi, W. (2002). Understanding the requirements for developing open source software systems. *IEEE Proceedings—Software, 149(1)*, 24–39.

Wu, M. W., & Lin, Y. D. (2001). Open source development: An overview. *IEEE Computer*, 33–38.

OPTICAL CHARACTER RECOGNITION

Optical character recognition (OCR) lies at the core of the discipline of pattern recognition by computers. OCR is the process of converting the image of a text document into its digital text equivalent in order to interpret a sequence of characters in an alphabet. For general computer users, OCR also has the practical use of being able to scan a document and then manipulate the text in a word processor:

Characters of an alphabet are usually rich in shape but can be subject to many variations in terms of fonts and handwriting styles. Despite these variations, a basic abstraction of shapes identifies such characters. Developing computer algorithms to identify such characters is the principal task of OCR. An OCR operation typically has three phases: preprocessing, recognition, and postprocessing. A pixel map (image) is obtained by scanning a text document into a computer. Scanning may introduce noise due to faulty devices, paper quality, lighting conditions, and so forth. The preprocessing phase removes noise and prepares the document. Operations include document image skew correction and text location.

The recognition phase has two essential processes: feature extraction and classification. Ultimately, the OCR operation assigns a character image to a character class (alphabet) by using a classification algorithm based on the features extracted and the relationships among the features. Because members of a character class are equivalent or similar in as much as they share defining attributes, the measurement of similarity, either explicitly or implicitly, is central to any classifier. Correcting OCR errors by using contextual knowledge often is a third process of the recognition phase.

Feature extraction recovers the defining attributes obscured by imperfect measurements by the computer. To represent a character class, either a prototype or a set of ideal samples must be known. The feature selection process attempts to recover the pattern attributes characteristic of each class. The process commonly uses global features, such as the number of holes in a character, the number of concavities (hollows) in its outer contour, and the relative protrusion of character extremities, and local features, such as the relative positions of line endings, line crossovers, and corners. Another classification is of structural and statistical features. Structural features include the primitive shapes such as lines, curves, loops, and so forth. Their numbers and relative positions are used to construct a feature vector. Statistical features include pixel density, gradients, and so forth. These are quantitatively measurable features.

Classification

The classification process identifies each input character image by considering the detected features. The selection of proper features is important and is class based. For example, if we need to distinguish between an oval and a rectangle, the best feature might be the corners, but if we need to distinguish between a rectangle and a square, a better feature is edge length. Thus, the features should be able to distinguish uniquely among the available classes. The set of all the possible features defining an object forms the feature space for that object. Such a feature space consists of n independent variables and is thus said to form an n-dimensional space.

Similar objects have similar features, and thus classes form clusters in the feature space, which can be separated by a discrimination curve. The objective is to find a mapping function that maps the given feature values to a particular class. In statistical classification approaches, character image patterns are represented by points in the n-dimensional feature space. Each component of the feature space is a measurement or feature value, which is a random variable reflecting the inherent variability within and between classes. A classifier partitions the feature space into regions associated with each class, labeling an observed pattern according to the class region into which it falls.

Template matching is a natural approach to classification and is commonly used. Individual pixels are directly used as features. A similarity measure instead of a distance measure is defined. One can count the number of pixel matches. The template class that has the maximum number of matches can be chosen as the class of the test pattern. Such an approach is called the "maximum correlation approach." Alternatively, the class with the minimum number of pixel mismatches can be chosen as the class of the test pattern, called the "minimum error approach."

Nearest Neighbor

The K-nearest neighbor (K-NN) rule is a decision rule used extensively in pattern classification problems. In this classifier desired features are extracted in advance from all known character shapes, called "training points." During recognition K number of nearest training points "vote" to decide the class of the given object.

More powerful and complex statistical classifiers are based on regression analysis, neural networks, and support vector machines. All of these classifiers need training phases and use mathematical regressions to approximate a discrimination function.

Although many problems are solved using a statistical approach, it is often more appropriate to represent patterns explicitly in terms of the structure or arrangement of components or primitive elements. The structural approach to OCR represents character pattern images in terms of primitives and relations among primitives in order to describe pattern structure explicitly. Humans usually use structural features to describe characters. For example, a capital *A* has two straight lines (strokes) meeting with a sharp point (end point) at the top and a third line crossing the two at approximately their midpoint (cross points), creating a gap in the upper part (hole).

Researchers have conducted systematic studies of OCR performance for English text. On good-quality machine-printed text data the correct recognition rate is reported at around 99.50 percent. On poor-quality machine-printed text data, the rate ranges from 89 percent to 97 percent. The drop in recognition performance on poor-quality text data is primarily due to strokes in characters being broken and adjacent characters touching.

Optical character recognition has been the most popular research field in the discipline of pattern recognition. OCR for printed Roman script as a research field has reached a point of saturation, and researchers are now focusing on multilingual OCR systems and handwriting recognition. Due to advances in electronic handheld devices such as personal digital assistants (PDAs), online handwriting recognition has become an emerging field of research.

Swapnil Khedekar and Venu Govindaraju

See also Asian Script Input; Handwriting Recognition and Retrieval

FURTHER READING

Kasturi, R., Gorman, L. O., & Govindaraju, V. (2002). Document image analysis: A primer. Saadhana, *27*(1), 3–22.
O'Gorman, L., & Kasturi, R. (1998). *Document image analysis.* New York: IEEE Computer Society Press.

PEER-TO-PEER ARCHITECTURE

The term *peer-to-peer* has come to denote a system in which computers (or nodes) are autonomous and interact directly and on an equal basis with one another, sharing resources such as messages, files, storage, CPU cycles, and workspaces. In contrast, client-server systems give some nodes a resource-providing role while the rest of the nodes have the passive role of consumers.

History

The idea that computers can play the roles both of provider and consumer of resources has been around for a long time. The original concept of the Arpanet (created in 1969), the precursor of the Internet, was designed with this idea in mind, as was the World Wide Web when it first emerged in 1991. Theoretically, e-mail and telephony also have a peer-to-peer nature, since each user can be both an originator and a recipient of a message. However, the current Internet, Web and e-mail rely heavily on servers to provide Web content and relay messages. These servers impose a hierarchical structure and inequality, reducing some nodes to the role of passive consumers (clients). The costs of maintaining resource-rich servers can be significant. In contrast, a *peer-to-peer* (P2P) system is self-maintaining once it reaches a critical mass of users.

The term P2P became popular in 2000 with the simultaneous emergence of the Napster music-swapping system and numerous applications aimed at harnessing the resources of networked personal computers.

Examples

One can distinguish between file sharing, instant messaging, CPU power sharing, and other P2P applications. Napster allowed users to share and download music files from one another in a very efficient way. Each node (a personal computer) could both download files from others and provide files to others. After Napster was forced to close in 2001 (it returned, chastened, in 2003), various new file-sharing P2P applications became popular, mostly based on variations of the Gnutella protocol, which allows users to search files that other users share and to exchange files. Examples include Kazaa, LimeWire, eDonkey, and Bear-Share. Applications that use Gnutella do not guarantee the anonymity of participating users, but the entirely decentralized protocol they use makes them robust (because there is no central point of failure), and also makes it much harder to find an identifiable target for lawsuits. FreeNet and Tapestry are also P2P file-sharing applications, based on a different protocol that ensures full anonymity of the participants in file sharing.

Several instant messaging applications, like Jabber and AVAKI, and collaboration applications like Groove, among others, use P2P architecture to send messages and create shared work environments directly among nodes, rather than routing them via servers.

A classic example of CPU power sharing application is SETI@home, which utilizes the unused computational resources of the participating nodes (the computers of uses that have downloaded and installed the SETI screensaver program) to discover patterns in radio telescope data that may indicate the presence of intelligent life in space. The same idea is used by other P2P systems to harness computing resources for extremely time-consuming computing tasks, like analysis of DNA for cancer research.

P2P Architectures

Ideally, a "pure" P2P architecture includes no servers; that is, the exchange happens entirely on the fringes of the Internet, between autonomous nodes. In re-

ality, however, often some kind of centralization is required to ensure scalability and better performance. For example, name servers can be introduced to ensure that the identifying name of a user is not tied to a particular Internet protocol (IP) address. This is necessary, for example, in instant messaging systems, since often the same user will be connecting from different machines or mobile devices, which means that the system needs to link a node with a user, not with a machine.

Napster uses a centralized index for the shared music stored by different users, which greatly facilitates searching the system. A node that searches for a file sends a request to the central index to locate peer nodes that have this resource. However, once a list of nodes that have the required resource is generated and sent to the requesting peer node, the download happens directly between the peers, without any server involvement.

SETI@home also uses a centralized architecture. Even though the actual computing tasks are executed by the participating nodes (peers), the task decomposition and the combination of the results coming from the nodes is done by a server.

The first versions of the Gnutella protocol assumed an entirely decentralized system. Each node sent search queries for files to its neighbors, who sent the request further to their neighbors, and so on until a node generates a hit—sending back a message that it has the requested resource. (The list of neighbors is determined randomly from peers who have recently become active.) However, this flooding approach generates a lot of network traffic, which slows down the responses. Sometimes queries cannot reach remote regions in the network. Therefore, the newer versions of Gnutella use super-peer nodes, which cache search results for frequent queries that have passed through them, thus creating indexes like Napster, but on a much smaller scale. Users can choose to be super-peers when they join the network. This emerging hierarchical structure increases the network's speed and allows queries to reach further into the network.

Research Directions

There are a variety of problems that current P2P systems need to address. Some are technical (relating to performance, scalability, and security); others are human- and community-related (relating to anonymity, trust, and participation). Most relevant to the area of human-computer interaction (HCI) are the issues of trust and user participation.

The issue of trust arises because any peer that allows access to his or her resources may become vulnerable. However, users may still be inclined to allow others who have behaved well in the past and have earned a good reputation to access their resources. Many researchers are currently investigating trust and reputation mechanisms in the area of multiagent systems, e-commerce, and P2P networks. In order to develop trust and reputation, however, peers should be identifiable. Thus identity and authentication become desirable features in a P2P community. Assuring both anonymity and identity is difficult.

Another important issue in P2P systems is user participation. Studies of Gnutella use show that 75 percent of the users are free riders: They do not contribute or share files of their own, but only download files shared by others. While some have argued that this is not a problem for file-sharing P2P applications, because it does not cost anything to replicate files, it is a serious problem for P2P applications that promote the sharing of other resources, like CPU. Research on motivating users to participate through incentives (such as the artificial currency used in MojoNation and status used in virtual communities such as Slashdot) may help to solve this problem. P2P systems are new and rapidly developing; they now even have their own research forums—the *P2P Journal* and the IEEE International Conference on P2P Computing. However, these forums focus currently mostly on the technical issues, while many of the social and HCI-related issues are discussed in other forums, such as the International Workshop on Agents and P2P Computing, the yearly international conferences on user modeling, conferences on e-commerce, and others.

Julita Vassileva

See also Client-Server Architecture; Grid Computing

FURTHER READING

Adar, E., & Huberman, B. A. (2000). Free riding on gnutella. First Monday. Retrieved January 29, 2004, from http://www.firstmonday.dk/issues/issue5_10/adar/

Barkai, D. (2002). *Peer-to-peer computing: Technologies for sharing and collaborating on the Net.* Santa Clara, CA: Intel Press.

Golle, P., Leyton-Brown, K., & Mironov, I. (2001). Incentives for sharing in peer-to-peer networks. In *Proceedings of the 20001 ACM Conference on Electronic Commerce* (pp. 264–267). New York: ACM Press.

Leuf, B. (2002). *Peer to peer: Collaboration and sharing over the Internet.* Boston: Addison-Wesley.

Miller, M. (2001). *Discovering P2P.* Marina del Rey, CA: Cybex.

Moore D., & Habeler J. (2002). *Peer to peer: Building secure, scalable and manageable networks.* Berkley, CA: McGraw Hill /Osborne.

Oram, A. (2001). *Peer-to-peer: Harnessing the power of disruptive technologies.* Sebastopol, CA: O'Reilly Press.

Shirky, C. (2000). *In praise of freeloaders.* Retrieved January 29, 2004, from, http://www.openp2p.com/pub/a/p2p/2000/12/01/shirky_freeloading.html

Vassileva J. (2002) Supporting Peer-to-Peer User Communities. In R. Meersman, & Z. Tari et al. (Eds.), *On the move to meaningful internet systems 2002: CoopIS, DOA, and ODBASE, Coordinated International Conferences Proceedings* (pp. 230–247). LNCS 2519. Berlin-Heidelberg: Springer Verlag Press.

PEN AND STYLUS INPUT

Humans have used pens or styli to create written characters for over three thousand years. In ancient Babylonia, scribes used wooden styli to write cuneiform on clay tablets. With the invention of ink, the stylus was replaced by some type of pen, and the clay tablet was replaced by paper or some other surface such as slate. In the mid-1800s, schoolchildren used chalk sticks and a piece of slate to record notes. Today pen and paper and notebook computers have replaced chalk and slate boards. The development of the tablet PC may eliminate pen and paper by providing users with pen and screen.

Pen Input

Unlike other input devices, styli and pens are held in an extrinsic precision grasp, which gives the user considerable precision of movement; they can also be operated by either hand. Today electronic screens are replacing paper, and new designs for styli and pens allow them to be used as electronic input devices.

Using a pen or a stylus for computer input creates a more congenial interface for people who have not learned to use a computer. Pen input may also broaden the range of computer users to include artists, for example. Recently developed tablet PCs, which are capable of handwriting recognition, are portable enough to provide users with mobility and wireless global information access. Several types of pen input devices have been developed, including light guns and light pens, tablet pens, personal digital pens, and interactive electronic whiteboards.

The earliest light-input devices for computers were developed in the 1950s by the U.S. military for the SAGE (Semi-Automatic Ground Environment) air-defense system. The first device was the light gun—a handheld gun-shaped device emitted a narrow light beam at its tip that was detected by sensors on the computer screen. The gun was tethered to the computer system with a cable and the user pointed the pen at specific screen areas to activate specific functions. In the SAGE application the light gun was simply used to select on-screen targets. A light pen was used in 1963 for Sketchpad, an interactive graphics program developed at Massachusetts Institute of Technology by Ivan Sutherland at Carnegie Mellon University. Subsequent refinements have allowed a light pen to function as an alternative to a computer mouse, which has made many CAD/CAM applications easier to use. For example, when the computer screen is vertically oriented the user has to hold the light pen without any arm support, which is tiring for extended periods of time; it is much less fatiguing to use a light pen when the screen is embedded in the work surface. Another refinement is the development of the long-range light pen, which can enable computer use by people who cannot use a keyboard or other input device. With this technology the light pen is attached to the head and computer interactions result from head movements.

The development of the graphics tablet allowed users to operate a pen-like device, often with a plastic nib, that indexed cursor control and other functions to the pressure applied to the pen nib. This combination has proved especially useful to digital artists who can use pen pressure to vary design elements like line width or line opacity. A similar pen device has also been tested as a prototype for the GRIGRI air-traffic control workstation, which uses pen-based input and a high-resolution touch screen. The tablet PC introduced in 2002 allows for the use of such pens directly on an LCD screen. Electronic pens have become increasingly sophisticated; today they are capable of providing natural brush control for digital artists by responding to 512 levels of pressure. Such pens also incorporate a pressure-sensitive eraser for easy fixes. However, these kinds of electronic pens need to be used in conjunction with a graphics tablet or a tablet PC (www.wacom.com).

In 2001 an electronic pen was developed that digitally captures handwriting and graphics as the user works. The pen writes like a ballpoint, but in addition to the ink cartridge it also contains an optical sensor, an advanced image-processing unit, and a communication unit. The ink allows the user to see what is being written or drawn and the digital imaging components permanently record digitally an image of what is written or drawn. It can be used for twenty-five pages of work in between battery recharges, and can store forty pages of material. Information from the pen can be downloaded to a PC. However, the pen requires the use of special digitally inked paper printed with a proprietary pattern of tiny dots (www.logitech.com). Several kinds of active whiteboards have been developed that that can electronically capture what is written on them and then either store or transmit this information to a PC. In some systems the board surface is touch-sensitive and pen input is electronically captured (www.smarttech.com). In other systems regular whiteboard pens are placed inside sleeves that transmit signals to a wireless receiver unit that attaches to any existing whiteboard and whatever is written or sketched onto the whiteboard is electronically captured and transmitted to a PC, PDA, or other capable electronic device (www.ebeam.com).

Stylus Input

Many electronic devices, such as palm and pocket PC personal digital assistants (PDAs) and retail

z	z	c	h	w	k
f	i	t	a	l	y
		n	e		
g	d	o	r	s	b
q	j	u	m	p	x

FIGURE 1. *Fitaly keyboard layout; 84 percent of normal text can be typed by tapping the light gray shaded keys.*

signature-capture devices require the use of a stylus to enter handwriting or to touch a screen area to activate a function. Usually the stylus is made from plastic and has a fine tip to allow accurate positioning. It is important that the stylus diameter be large enough to be gripped in a precision grasp comfortably, because if the stylus is too narrow it is difficult to use and requires more muscular effort. Combination pen and stylus implements with a large grip diameter are available to increase grip comfort and make it easier to work with a PDA.

Most PDAs allow the user to input information either by using a defined alphabet of movements or by tapping with a stylus on representations of alphanumeric keys. For tapping input none of the computer keyboard layouts is optimal, and a tapping-optimized layout, the Fitaly key layout, has been developed for small-screen input to speed typing. (www.fitaly.com). (See Figure 1.)

Limitations of Pen and Stylus Input

Research studies that have compared the use of different input devices have found that the benefits of a pen or stylus input device are heavily dependent on the task. In some situations pen input is less accurate than other input devices but in other situations it is more accurate. A series of experiments in 1994 compared the speed, accuracy, and preference for a pen, mouse, and keyboard for general and graphics drawing work. They found that pen use was never faster than mouse use but that both were faster than the keyboard. However, users made the fewest errors with the keyboard, the next fewest with the mouse, and the most errors with the pen, and

these error differences were significant in a majority of the cases. Users preferred the mouse for general work and the keyboard for highly accurate work.

Several research studies have shown that the upper limit for tapping information into a device with a pen or stylus starts at around 8 words per minute and with practice can attain speeds around 20 words per minute. Using pen-based handwriting recognition, an expert may be able to attain around 30 words per minute; however, prolonged intensive handwriting use is associated with "writer's cramp," a forearm musculoskeletal disorder. The speed of pen or stylus input cannot approach the speed attained by skilled typists who may exceed 100 words per minute, and consequently the keyboard rather than the pen is likely to remain the dominant input device for computer systems.

However, for those who cannot operate a mouse or keyboard because of an injury or other limitation, a pen input device may be an ideal way to communicate with the computer. And because it is so difficult to use a keyboard for graphic design and even a mouse meets with limited success, a pen or stylus seems to be the most effective tool for graphical input or CAD work.

Alan Hedge

See also Pocket Computers; Tablet Computers

FURTHER READING

Beringer, D. B., & Scott, J. (1985). The long-range light pen as a head-based user-computer interface: Head-mounted 'sights' versus head positioning for computer access by the disabled, progress for people. *Proceedings of the Human Factors Society 29th Annual Meeting*, Baltimore, MD.

Chatty, S., & Lecoanet, P. (1996). Pen computing for air traffic control. CHI 96–common ground. In M. J. Tauber, V. Bellotti, R. Jeffries, J. D. Mackinlay, & J. Nielsen (Eds.), *Proceedings of the Conference on Human Factors in Computing Systems* (pp. 87–94). Reading, MA: Addison-Wesley.

Coll, R., Zia, K., Coll, J. H. (1994). A comparison of three computer cursor control devices: Pen on horizontal tablet, mouse and keyboard. *Information & Management, 27*(6), 329–339.

Douglas, S. A., & Mithal, A. K. (1997). *The ergonomics of pointing devices.* London: Springer-Verlag.

Mahach, K. R. (1989). A comparison of computer input devices: Linus pen, mouse, cursor keys and keyboard, perspectives. Proceedings of the Human Factors Society 33rd Annual Meeting,

Denver, CO. In *The Human Factors Society, 1*, 330–334. Santa Monica, CA: Human Factors and Ergonomics Society.

Meyer, A. (1995). Pen computing: A technology overview and a vision. *SIGCHI Bulletin, 27*(3), 46–90.

Swezey, R. W. (Ed.). *The Human Factors Society, 1*, 114–118. Santa Monica, CA: Human Factors and Ergonomics Society.

PERSONAL COMPUTER

See Alto; Desktop Metaphor; Games; History of HCI; Impacts; Internet in Everyday Life; Keyboard; Law and HCI; Pocket Computer

PERSONALITY CAPTURE

The term *personality capture* refers to methods of uploading aspects of a person's character to a computer or information system. It was coined by analogy with *motion capture*, computerized methods of recording the movements of a human body that filmmakers use to create realistic movement in animated virtual actors. Researchers are exploring a wide range of technical approaches that could be used for personality capture, often without the explicit intention of preserving or enhancing human personalities.

In normal use, a personal computer gradually comes to contain splinters of its owner's personality. The choice of software loaded onto the machine and the preference settings in each program record how the person likes to do things. The word processing files show his or her thought processes, especially if the software is set to track the changes that reveal the intimate dance between writing and editing. The e-mail archive and website visiting history record how the person connects to the encompassing social and cultural network. If the person uses voice recognition software, then the computer contains not only sound recordings of the training sessions but also a person-specific mathematical model of the owner's voice.

To go beyond the incidental capture of personality fragments requires the creation of a comprehensive technology employing principles from the social and behavioral sciences, beginning with the psychology of personality.

The Science of Personality

Personality consists of the characteristics of thought, feeling, and action that distinguish one unique human being from another. Branches of psychology, social psychology, and psychiatry study personality explicitly, but so do other sciences, although under other names. Sociology studies people's beliefs, attitudes, and social attachments. Political science studies their political opinions. There is a long tradition in anthropology of studying personality as an individual manifestation of the culture.

A tension exists in each of these disciplines between the tendency to group people together by shared characteristics and the tendency to emphasize each person's uniqueness. At times, or for particular purposes, one or the other of these tendencies may predominate. For example, around 1850 psychiatrists described asylum inmates in terms of a vast number of specific factors that might have precipitated a nervous breakdown: religious perplexity, pecuniary difficulties, or a difficult childbirth, among hundreds of others. By 1880, however, asylum bureaucracies had collapsed the category system down to a half-dozen global symptomatologies, such as mania and melancholia.

In his 1872 book *The Birth of Tragedy*, the philosopher and philologist Friedrich Nietzsche suggested that cultures and people could be categorized as Apollonian (individualist, rationalist) or Dionysian (collectivist, intuitive). For the following century, theorists across the social and behavioral sciences proposed similar dichotomies with names like obsessive versus hysterical, tough-minded versus tender-minded, controlled versus impulsive, and even masculine versus feminine. By the middle of the twentieth century, theory had been supplemented by empirical research, and psychologists began using statistical techniques to find clusters of traits based either on self-report questionnaires or ratings of individuals by observers. The desire to publish theoretical essays, combined with the availability of computationally intensive statistical methods such as factor analysis, encouraged the search for a universal set of dimensions along which all human personalities could be ranked. Instead of just two categories, some researchers found as many as a dozen.

By the 1990s many psychologists had focused on just five dimensions, although they continue to debate what those "Big Five" should be called and what their relative importance is. In one nomenclature, the initials of the names of the five form the acronym OCEAN: Openness to experience, Conscientiousness, Extraversion, Agreeableness, and Neuroticism. In ordinary language, we often say that one person is more conscientious than another. In principle, all people could be measured along a dimension from extremely conscientious to extremely unconscientious. Perhaps the most uncertain of the five dimensions is openness to experience, because some psychologists call this dimension intellect, while others stress its aesthetic, emotional, politically liberal, or even fanciful qualities. A person who is high in neuroticism exhibits unusual anxiety, depression, or other neurotic symptoms, without necessarily being mentally ill. Perhaps the two most important dimensions are extraversion (assertive, self-actualizing, active) and agreeableness (trusting, loving).

Typically, when psychologists attempt to classify an individual in terms of personality dimensions, they either give the person a test (usually in the form of a questionnaire) or ask other people to rate the person in terms of various characteristics. Either way, conventional language is used to describe the person, both in collecting the data that will be subjected to statistical analysis and in expressing the results of that analysis. Thus, this tradition of personality research relies heavily upon the words that ordinary language uses to categorize people. To some degree, this is a scientific disadvantage, because it is difficult to identify a personality characteristic if ordinary nonscientific language does not already have a name for it. However it is also scientifically fruitful, both because it exploits the real-world knowledge of people that is encoded in language and because people's personalities and self-images are partly formed through language-based communication with other people.

In a sense, then, the Big Five personality dimensions are a scientific distillation of folk wisdom, but natural language has not chosen to simplify itself as much as the psychologists wish, nor are real people capable of reduction to five characteristics. In other words, academic personality psychology is nomothetic—it deals with abstract, general, or universal principles. Personality capture, by contrast, is idiographic—it deals with concrete, individual, or unique characteristics. A major challenge for personality capture is to develop means for documenting the character of an individual in the context of the full complexity of the surrounding culture.

Culture-Based Methods

Each human being matures within a particular sociocultural context, and a personality is an amalgam of genetic inheritance and learned experience. Thus, many of the factors that shape the individual are features of the ambient culture, of which the most influential are *semantic systems*—complex sets of meanings, whether encoded in language or some other modality. To document important aspects of personality one needs a way to chart what semantic systems exist in the ambient culture, then determine how the particular member of the society relates to them. Questionnaires are a standard way of collecting information about the elements of belief, motivation, and evaluation that constitute semantic systems. Consider how the following multistage research project combined questionnaire research with information technology to develop tools that are useful for personality capture.

In 1997 William Bainbridge launched a research website called The Question Factory to mass-produce questionnaire items. Visitors to the website were invited to answer a few open-ended questions such as: "What do you think will happen to you after you die?" People wrote in answers, some as short as a word ("nothing") or a phrase ("go to heaven") and others an entire paragraph expressing several ideas. After one or two hundred people have responded to such a question, it is possible to collate their responses and identify all the different beliefs that are widely held.

The most fruitful single phase of the project used the following open-ended item in an online, Web-based questionnaire sponsored by the National Geographic Society: "Imagine the future and try to predict how the world will change over the next century. Think about everyday life as well as major changes in society, culture, and technology."

Approximately twenty thousand people wrote responses, offering a wide range of perspectives on the future. Content analysis revealed two thousand distinct ideas, which were edited to make two thousand statements. Here are three examples concerning human-computer interaction, arranged from the least to most visionary: "The computer mouse and keyboard will become obsolete, because there will be quicker and more convenient ways to interact with the computer." "Direct communications between the human nervous system and computers will lead to computer-enhanced thought and memory." "It will be possible to transfer the consciousness that distinguishes an individual person into a machine."

These and the other 1,997 statements became the items of a new questionnaire that was incorporated in a software module, *The Year 2100*, offered free online and included on a CD-ROM provided with a book edited by Vernon Burton. *The Year 2100* records the user's personal perspective on the future by administering the two thousand statements as a giant questionnaire.

For example, one item states: "An electronic interface will allow people to slot programs directly into the brain to learn new skills like a foreign language instantly." The respondent answers two questions about the statement: How good or bad would it be if this comes true? How likely or unlikely is it that this will happen? A particular respondent might feel this would be very good but unfortunately very unlikely. Another respondent might feel this is a very bad idea, violating the natural integrity of the human brain. The differences between these respondents' good-bad ratings across all two thousand items reveal their personal values in many spheres of life. The correlation between good and likely ratings made by an individual respondent reveals that person's optimism, and many kinds of general measures can be derived statistically from the data. But perhaps most important are the four thousand separate data points sketching the detailed contours of the person's values and perceptions of possibilities. *The Year 2100* is one of ten comparable software modules that together include twenty thousand stimuli

and gather forty thousand data points in such areas as emotions, food preferences, ideological beliefs, and past experiences.

Miscellaneous Measures

Computers can measure many details of a person's behavior, such as how quickly he or she answers questions, in addition to being able to analyze the answers themselves. One clue to the structure of a person's mind is the pattern of delays in how long it takes the individual to complete various mental tasks; this is known as the latency of response. In the 1960s Saul Sternberg, a scientist at Bell Telephone Laboratories, used this fact to explore short-term memory (often called working memory today). In one influential experiment, he showed people strings of digits, then flashed another number and asked them whether it had been in the string or not. If a person can hold all the digits in consciousness simultaneously, then the individual presumably can answer just as quickly for long strings of digits as for short strings. But if he or she has to scan through the list of digits in memory, one at a time, then it will take the respondent longer to answer when dealing with long strings of digits. If mental scanning is involved in recall, then a person may be able to arrive at a *yes* answer more quickly than a *no* answer, because the person can quit scanning immediately upon finding the target digit, rather than having to scan through until the end. In general, psychologists assume that a long response delay indicates the person is doing more mental work, either going through complex steps or struggling with some kind of mental conflict.

More recently, the psychologist Anthony Greenwald at the University of Washington and a number of collaborators have developed a Web-based or computer-administered Implicit Association Test (IAT) based on latency of response. In one study, research subjects seated at a computer were shown a series of words, such as diamond, health, sunrise, agony, filth, and poison. For part of the session, they had to respond by pressing one of two keys as quickly as possible to indicate whether a word was pleasant or unpleasant. In another part, they had to indicate whether or not the word described themselves, categorizing it as self or other. The key parts of the session had them place the words in two combined categories, such as self and pleasant versus other and unpleasant, or self and unpleasant versus other and pleasant. The point of the research was to see if the IAT could measure the research subject's self-esteem. A person with high self-esteem would more quickly respond to stimuli that associated self with pleasant words, than to stimuli that pair the self with unpleasantness. Greenwald's team has developed a large number of sets of words for the IAT to allow it to measure many different attitudes and stereotypes that the person might be reluctant to admit, demonstrating that latency of response could be used to capture aspects of personality that might be difficult to capture using other methods.

A very wide range of miscellaneous computerized methods can capture other aspects of an individual's character. For example, several researchers have sought to preserve the experiences of a person's life, experiences being both the fundamental context for and powerful shapers of personality. Gordon Bell has been working with others at Microsoft Research on the MyLifeBits project (introduced to the general public in 2002) to record in a unified information system all the documents, photos, and audio and video recordings relevant to a person's life. In a 7 May 2003 presolicitation notice, the U.S. Defense Advanced Research Projects Agency (DARPA) announced the LifeLog research competition to develop a system that "captures, stores, and makes accessible the flow of one person's experience in and interactions with the world". Earlier, DARPA had funded "Experience on Demand," research by Howard Wactlar at Carnegie-Mellon University to demonstrate the feasibility of such a system.

How people perceive their experiences provides crucial data about their characters, and many scientists have sought to understand how people interpret visual images presented to them. Nadia Bianchi-Berthouze argues that it is valuable "to capture such an important aspect of a user's personality as visual impressions and their communication" (Bianchi-Berthouze 2002, 43). At the same time, the changing appearance of a person—gestures, postures, and facial expressions—provides further clues to understanding the dynamics of his or her per-

sonality. The researchers Nadia Magnenat-Thalmann, Prem Kalra, and Marc Escher captured the facial expressions of a real person in order to create a facial clone model for an expressive avatar (electronic representation) of the individual inside the computer, and many others have been doing similar work.

Computer games that have the user act within a simulated world could readily be modified for personality capture merely by having them record all the player's moves. For example, the popular computer game *The Sims* lets the user play in many kinds of somewhat realistic environments, where his or her decisions may reflect real-world values and beliefs. Each Sim character has a personality: neat or messy, playful or serious, active or passive, outgoing or reclusive, and grouchy or nice. The user can build a simulated environment similar to home, and accessory software allows the user to put his or her actual face on the Sim. Many people play *The Sims* for hundreds of hours, making a vast number of potentially realistic everyday decisions in the simulated environment, even playing online in interaction with

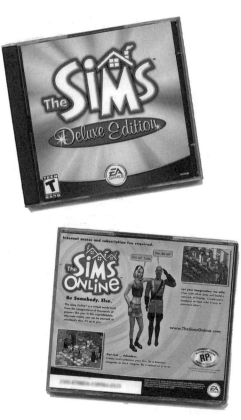

The popular Sims series of computer games.

Photo courtesy of Marcy Ross.

other people. A particularly fruitful approach might be to have the person play such a game as several characters relevant to his or her real life: the real self, the ideal self, the person's parent, or the person's lover. The contrasts and interactions between these characters might reveal key conflicts in the individual's psyche.

Applications

Developing advanced methods for personality capture will not only stimulate progress in psychology and the social sciences but will also have many practical applications, some near-term and predictable and some as yet unforseen. There may also be unpredicted long-term consequences. Since the late 1960s, computerized dating services have employed questionnaires to match couples by preferences and temperaments, and more precise measurement of personalities would help them do a better job. After a couple married, the same technology might assist them in developing their relationship along mutually satisfying lines, serving as an aid to shared intimacy, to joint decision making, and in rough times to marriage counseling. Personality capture can also facilitate good relations between an individual and information technology by giving compatible personalities to computer interfaces, software agents, and robots.

Even at present technical levels, very rich memorials for deceased persons can be created through information technology enhanced by personality capture. From realistic sculpture, we know the face of Julius Caesar, and we can read his books more than twenty centuries after he wrote them. Future centuries will know Winston Churchill not only from numerous histories of his deeds and from the many books and even paintings he created, but also from the films of his imposing movement and the recordings of his remarkable voice. Computer technology can provide a similar degree of immortality to everyone. Thousands of people have created memorial websites for deceased relatives, and at one time nearly six hundred websites for dead children were linked into the Empty Arms Web ring. As technology progresses, it will be possible to create more-or-less realistic ancestor simulations, allowing the living to interact virtually with the dead, who will be able to provide information and advice and thus continue to influence human society long after their departures.

Respected information technology pioneers Gordon Bell, Jim Gray, and Ray Kurzweil have argued that actual digital immortality will become possible over the coming century, through a convergence of personality capture and artificial intelligence. This prediction is extremely controversial, and it is not at all clear that it will ever be possible to scan the human brain with sufficient accuracy to record the detailed connections among the hundred billion neurons of the neural net that underlies personal consciousness. However, low-fidelity personality capture is already possible. As with Caesar or Churchill, it is clear that informational extensions of an individual personality can live in a partial sense by contributing to the experiences and decisions of living people. Thus we cannot arbitrarily say at present what the future limitations of personality capture might be.

William Sims Bainbridge

FURTHER READING

Bainbridge, W. S. (1984). Religious insanity in America: The official nineteenth-century theory. *Sociological Analysis, 45*, 223–240.

Bainbridge, W. S. (2000). Religious ethnography on the World Wide Web. In J. K. Hadden & D. Cowan (Eds.), *Religion and the Internet*. Greenwich, CT: JAI Press.

Bainbridge, W. S. (2003). The future of Internet: Cultural and individual conceptions. In P. N. Howard & S. Jones (Eds.), *The Internet and American life*. Thousand Oaks, CA: Sage Publications.

Bainbridge, W. S. (2003). Massive questionnaires for personality capture. *Social Science Computer Review, 21*(3), 267–280.

Bell, G., & Gray, J. (2001). Digital immortality. *Communications of the ACM, 44*(3), 29–30.

Bianchi-Berthouze, N. (2002). Mining multimedia subjective feedback. *Journal of Intelligent Information Systems, 19*(1), 43–59.

Burton, O. V. (Ed.). (2002). *Computing in the social sciences and humanities*. Urbana: University of Illinois Press.

Cohen, M. (2003). *The Sims superstar expansion pack*. Roseville, CA: Prima Games.

Gemmell, J., Bell, G., Lueder, R., Drucker, S., & Wong, C. (2002). MyLifeBits: Fulfilling the Memex vision. In *ACM Multimedia* (pp. 235–238). New York: Association for Computing Machinery.

Greenwald, A. G., & Farnham, S. D. (2000). Using the Implicit Association Test to measure self-esteem and self-concept. *Journal of Personality and Social Psychology, 79*(6), 1022–1038.

Greenwald, A. G., McGhee, D. E., & Schwartz, J. L. K. (1998). Measuring individual differences in implicit cognition: The Implicit Association Test. *Journal of Personality and Social Psychology, 74*(6), 1464–1480.

Kaplan, B. (Ed.). (1961). *Studying personality cross-culturally.* New York: Harper and Row.

Kurzweil, R. (1999). *The age of spiritual machines.* New York: Penguin.

Lin, W., & Hauptman, A. G. (2002, July 14–18). A wearable digital library of personal conversations. In *Joint Conference on Digital Libraries* (pp. 277–278), Portland, OR. Retrieved July 30, 2003, from http://www.informedia.cs.cmu.edu/documents/jcdl02_wearable.pdf

Nietzsche, F. (1967). *The birth of tragedy.* New York: Random House (Original work published 1872).

Pelham, B. W. (1993). The idiographic nature of human personality: Examples of the idiographic self-concept. *Journal of Personality and Social Psychology, 64*(4), 665–677.

Sternberg, S. (1966). High-speed scanning in human memory. *Science, 153,* 652–654.

Strauss, A. L., Schatzman, L., Bucher, R., Erlich, D., & Sabshin, M. (1981). *Psychiatric ideologies and institutions.* New Brunswick, NJ: Transaction.

Task Force on DSM-IV. (1994). *Diagnostic and statistical manual of mental disorders.* Washington, DC: American Psychiatric Association.

Thalmann, N. M., Kalra, P., & Escher, M. (1998). Face to virtual face. *Proceedings of the IEEE, 86*(5), 870–883.

Wactlar, H., & Gong, Y. (1999). Informedia experience-on-demand: Capturing, integrating and communicating experiences across people, time, and space. *ACM Computing Surveys, 31*(9). Abstract retrieved July 30, 2003, from http://cftest.acm.org/portal/citation.cfm?id=323216.323356&coll=portal&dl=GUIDE&CFID=51116&CFTOKEN=20645183#abstract

Wiggins, J. S. (Ed.). (1996). *The five-factor model of personality.* New York: Guilford.

PERVASIVE COMPUTING

See Ubiquitous Computing

PHYSIOLOGY

Computers with physiological sensing capabilities know how you feel. By using special peripheral devices that detect fluctuations in your heart rate or the conductivity of your skin, a computer can show the correlation between some activity that you are doing and how that activity is making you feel.

Detectable Human Physiology

In an emergency room a nurse gently places his fingertips on the wrist of a patient and simultaneously checks his watch. The sensitive fingertips detect a rhythmical pulsation caused by blood pumping through veins beneath the skin. The pulsing sensation is caused by the patient's heart pumping blood around her body. The watch provides the nurse with a means of measuring a fixed period of time, perhaps sixty seconds. If during this period the nurse counts eighty-five pulses beneath his fingers, then the patient's heart is beating at a rate of eighty-five beats per minute. Alternately, the nurse could have laid his head upon the patient's chest and listened directly to the sound made by her heart pumping. In both these instances the nurse is using his own sensory organs (fingertips or ears) to detect the external manifestations of the patient's internal physiological activity (that is, her heart pumping).

However, the majority of physiological information is too subtle to be detected by human sense organs alone. Consequently, specialized devices have been developed to detect and amplify physiological information and transform it into a form suitable for human observation. For example, a medical practitioner is far more likely to use a stethoscope than his unaided ear to listen to your chest, and this device allows him to hear both heart- and lung-related sounds.

The stethoscope, invented in 1816 by Rene Laennec, a French physician, is a mechanical device that amplifies chest sounds, making them easier to hear. One of the first electronic devices for listening to the body was the Toposcope. Created at the Burden Neurological Institute in Bristol, England, in the 1920s, the Toposcope was conceived in order to detect brain activity from twenty-four sensors positioned across the scalp of a subject. Real-time feedback was provided by twenty-two separate cathode ray tube (CRT) displays, each attached to a separate sensor. The Toposcope's "memory" consisted of a pen-based output device that traced the brainwaves onto long rolls of paper.

Electrical brain signals, also known as the electroencephalogram or EEG, are one manifestation of the brain's responses to thought, mood and/or physical action in the body. These tiny electrical signals, detected directly from the body's surface using biopotential sensors, are amplified in order to make them easier to display and analyze. Other physiological data that can be scrutinized using this approach are signals from the heart (electrocardiogram/ECG) and skeletal muscles (electromyogram/EMG). By applying a tiny voltage to the skin and listening for it with a sensor placed at a nearby point on the body's surface, it is also possible to detect changes in the conductivity of the skin indicative of changes in arousal in a subject.

To detect physiological information that is mechanical or chemical rather than electrical in nature, we just use different sensors. Modern blood pressure (BP) sensors use an inflated cuff on the arm to detect changes in mechanical pressure and an electronic display to present a reading of the pressure. The BP sensor transforms a mechanical pressure measured by the cuff into an electrical pressure (or voltage) which can be processed and displayed on a computer screen. Other examples of detectable physiology that require sensors that transform one data type to another are respiration (mechanical to electrical), temperature (thermal to electrical), and blood gas (chemical to electrical).

Psychophysiologists have traditionally studied physiological signals in order to understand how the human body responds to different psychological conditions such as stress and depression. Physiologists study physiological information in order to discover how our bodies respond to different physical conditions; physiological questions range from how and why we sleep to the effects of space flight on the body. Sports scientists look at physiological information in order to assess the effects exercise has on the body with a view to understanding and improving performance. However, the chief consumer of physiological information is the medical professional. Monitoring physiological data in a subject is key to the diagnosis and management of disease.

Computer-Based Applications

A personal computer attached to a sensor for monitoring brain signals must archive huge amounts of physiological information. Traditionally an expert in physiological signal interpretation would be required to make any sense of the data. However, access to suitable software tools makes the interpretation of physiological data much easier. Computers allow us to scrutinize the data in real-time or to archive it and play it back later. Beyond traditional waveform visualizations, the multimedia capabilities of computers mean that physiological data can be presented in any number of interesting ways.

Interactive technologies that incorporate human physiological information support an ever-increasing range of human-computer interaction (HCI) applications. In addition to those applications mentioned in the section on detectable physiology, physiological sensing capabilities are used in biofeedback applications, prosthetic technologies, usability studies, and affective computing applications.

Biofeedback

Biofeedback involves the real-time detection and presentation of a subject's physiology. It is used in the amelioration of a host of psychophysiological disorders such as depression, post-traumatic stress disorder, and attention deficit/ hyperactivity disorder (ADHD). The principle behind biofeedback is that, with practice, subjects can gain a measure of conscious control over aspects of their physiology. Biofeedback systems use physiological sensors to detect signals of interest (as, for example, EEGs or EMG) and exploit the multimedia capabilities of computers to present that information back to a subject in interesting and engaging ways. The most popular approach involves transforming a physiological signal of interest into a control signal within a computer game.

Prosthetics

Electromechanical prosthetic arms contain embedded EMG sensors. These sensors detect tiny electrical signals generated by muscles in the shoulder. The muscle signals generated are used to affect grasping action between the fingers and thumb of the prosthetic hand.

The notion of direct brain-computer interaction (BCI) was first explored in 1967 by Edmond Dewan. BCI involves the detection of EEG using scalp-mounted electrodes. A computer is used to identify repeatable brain activity that can be used as a hands-free way of interacting with a computer. In 1999 Neils Birbaumer and his colleagues at the University of Tübingen enabled a patient with severe physical disabilities to type a letter using EEG signals alone. Signals from the subject's brain were used to operate a pointer that could be used to select keyboard characters presented on a screen. Despite the time-consuming nature of the process, this approach provided a means of communication to an individual who was otherwise locked in his body.

EMG prosthetic arms and some types of brain-computer interface rely on the principles of biofeedback to teach a user through experimentation how to control seemingly uncontrollable physiological phenomena.

Usability

A major concern of usability engineering is to ensure as much as possible that the interfaces to interactive systems are appropriate and easy to learn and thereafter easy to operate. But a balance must be maintained between providing users with a few simple tasks to perform and overloading them with too many tasks or too complex a set of tasks. If a system's users have too little or too much to do, then over a prolonged period they may experience what Alan Pope from NASA calls "hazardous awareness states." Hazardous awareness states are psychological states that can be detrimental to a user's normal operation of a system. Examples of psychological states that can affect a user's performance include stress, anxiety, boredom, absorption, fatigue, and inattention.

In order to explore these ideas further NASA has developed an automated usability system called CREW (Crew Response Evaluation Window). Various physiological signal sensors are included to enable physiological monitoring. These include brainwave signal processing, eye-tracking, and video, which together can be used to assess mental states, task engagement, and stress responses, as well as mental loading and situation awareness. Getting the balance right between operator functionality and system functionality is obviously key to the success of any interactive system. Physiological-signal monitoring has a role to play in the interaction design process.

Cognitive psychologists have developed a range of techniques for assessing the mental effort associated with task performance. A better sense of the effect of a given task on a user can be gained by looking at the physiological responses alongside data from other sources—video footage or questionnaires, for instance. Heart rate variability (HRV), which is known to be responsive to cognitive loading, is a popular metric as it indicates how hard a user has to work in order to achieve some task.

Physiological user-testing is especially important when developing interfaces to be used by people like air traffic controllers and flight control engineers whose working conditions are naturally stressful. Ironically, systems operators themselves indicate that increasing automation in human-machine systems is a major contributing factor to their experiencing hazardous awareness states.

Affective Computing

The term *affective computing* was coined by Rosalind Picard, professor at Massachusetts Institute of Technology, and refers to computers that can sense and respond to changing human emotions. Affective computing is based on the premise that emotional states are accompanied by detectable changes in physiological functioning. Current research employs physiological signal sensors to detect changes in a subject's psychophysiological state. The ultimate aim of affective computing is to utilize this information to train computers to recognize different human emotions such as joy, sadness, or anger. Picard's researchers at MIT have so far had limited success in their attempts to recognize a single emotion—frustration—through the examination of features extracted from a subject's galvanic skin response (GSR) and blood pulse volume (BVP). One thing that their research has discovered, however, is that although physiological monitoring is good for detecting levels of arousal, on its own it is not useful for discovering whether the emotion being experienced is positive or negative. So, for example, grief and joy both produce high levels of arousal, but without additional information it is not possible to distinguish between these two emotional states.

Computer Games

Computer games are undoubtedly the most successful and ubiquitous human-computer interfaces. The section on biofeedback indicated that computer games with associated physiological sensing capabilities play a role in clinical applications. In line with progress in the field of affective computing, however, researchers are currently investigating the potential of physiological information to enhance the game experience itself. At the time of writing, this field of study is in its very earliest stages. Preliminary investigations by Kiel Gilleade at Lancaster University indicate that game play can be enhanced by associating subtle features of the game play to arousal in the gamer, as indicated by a player's changing heart rate (HR).

Issues

What is not apparent from the above description of detectable human physiology is the characteristic nature of physiological activity. As an input source for computers, physiological signals are a less reliable form of data than we are used to. For a start, each individual's physiology (and consequently the signatory characteristics of their physiological activity) is unique to them. When considering what constitutes "normal" physiological activity, considerations such as gender, age, and general health must be taken into account. As if this did not complicate matters enough, most physiological parameters are susceptible to environmental effects such as changes in temperature and humidity. Cardiac activity (heart rate/ blood pressure) can also be influenced by factors such as smoking, posture, and the time of day.

HCI is often concerned with task-driven interactions between a user and a computer. However, combining physiological sensor technologies with computers is transforming the way we think about human-computer interaction. The physiological user interface, the most personal of personal computing applications, brings with it more enriched and enriching interactive computing experiences.

Jennifer Allanson

See also Affective Computing; Brain-Computer Interfaces

FURTHER READING

Backs, R. W. (2002). *Engineering Psychophysiology*. Mahwah, NJ: Erlbaum.

Carr, J. J., Brown, J. M. (1981). *Introduction to biomedical equipment technology*. New York: Wiley.

Charlton, S. G., & O'Brien, T. G. (2002). *Handbook of human factors testing and evaluation*. Mahwah, NJ: Erlbaum.

Dewan, E. M. (1967). Occipital alpha rhythm eye position and lens accommodation. *Nature, 214*, 975–977.

Gilleade, K., & Allanson, J. (2003). A tollkit for exploring affective interface adaptation in video games. Human-Computer International (HCII03). Crete, Greece: Lawrence Erlbaum Associates.

Hockey, G. R. J., Briner, R. B., Tattersall, A. J., & Wiethoff, M. (1989). Assessing the impact of computer workload on operator stress: The role of system controllability. *Ergonomic, 32*, 1401–1418.

Kübler, A., Kotchoubey, B., Hinterberger, T., Ghanayim, N., Perelmouter, J., Schauer, M., et al. (1999). The thought translation device: A neurophysiological approach to communication in total motor paralysis. *Experimental Brain Research 124*(2), 223–232.

Martin, I., & Venables, P. H. (1980). *Techniques in psychophysiology*. New York: Wiley.

Picard, R. W. (1997). *Affective computing*. Cambridge, MA: MIT Press.

Pope, A. T., Bogart, E. H., & Bartolome, D. S. (1995). Biocybernetic System evaluates indices of operator engagement in automated task. *Biological Psychology, Special Edition: EEG in Basic and Applied Settings, 40*, 187–195.

Rodahl, K. (1989). *The physiology of work*. London: Taylor & Francis.

Schwartz, M. S. (1995). *Biofeedback: A practitioner's guide.* New York: Guilford Press.

Webster, J. G. (1998). *Medical instrumentation application and design* (3rd ed.). New York: Wiley.

Welk, G. J. (2002). Physical activity assessments for health-related research. Champaign, IL: Human Kinetics.

PLANNING

Planning is the process of generating a plan, that is, a course of action whose execution achieves a given objective. Planning is a key component of intelligent behavior. It often makes sense to support human planning or even automate it to find plans of high quality or find them fast because it often is difficult for humans to plan in complex situations. Examples include scheduling fleets of cargo planes or finding safe paths for Mars rovers, where the communication delay makes their teleoperation from Earth extremely tedious. Therefore, since the mid-1960s researchers, mostly from the artificial intelligence community, have studied how computers can plan, including how to classify planning problems, how to represent them formally, how to solve them, and how to integrate the resulting systems into human-machine environments. One deployed planning system is the Remote Agent, which autonomously controlled NASA's Deep Space 1 space probe during an experiment in 1999. (We mention the names of some other planning systems, mostly research prototypes, in brackets.)

Classification of Planning Problems

Suppose that we are interested in scheduling a fleet of planes to transport cargo between airports. We are given the current locations of all planes and cargo pieces and the destinations of all cargo pieces. We are asked to provide a plan for delivering all cargo pieces to their destinations. How can this air-cargo problem be formalized?

A *planning domain* is described by states and actions. *States* are snapshots of the world that include all of its aspects that are relevant for planning. In our case the states include the locations of all planes and cargo pieces. *Actions* are the means for changing the world. Their execution transforms the world from one state to another one. In our case actions include loading a cargo piece into a plane, flying a plane from one airport to another, and unloading a cargo piece from a plane. One needs to specify for each action and state whether the action can be executed in the state and, if so, which state results from its execution. For example, a cargo piece can only be loaded into a plane if they are both at the same airport. In this case the cargo piece changes location from being on the ground to being in the plane.

A *planning problem* is described by the planning domain, the start state, and the planning objective. The planning objective is often given in the form of a *goal*, that is, a desired property of the world. The purpose of planning then is to determine a plan that transforms the start state into a goal state, that is, a state that satisfies the goal. These plans are called *valid plans*.

The characteristics of planning problems determine how one should represent them formally, how plans look like, how to find these plans, and how long it takes to find them. *Classical planning problems* assume that one can predict with certainty which state will result from an action execution (*deterministic actions*) and that states can always be completely and accurately observed (*totally observable states*). In general, plans can be arbitrary computer programs, but for classical planning problems, it is sufficient to consider only sequences of actions. We treat the air-cargo problem as a classical planning problem. Doing so is a simplification since, in the real world, airport workers sometimes make mistakes and load cargo pieces into the wrong planes, resulting in nondeterministic actions. In such cases one needs to search for the cargo pieces since their locations are not totally observable, resulting in only partially observable states.

Representations of Planning Problems

A *representation language* allows one to specify planning problems in a way that can be understood by a computer. More expressive representation languages allow one to model a greater variety of planning problems but are also more complicated, which makes it harder for humans to encode planning problems and understand planning problems that have been encoded by others, and also harder for computers to solve encoded planning problems. Researchers originally tried to use logic as representation language and theorem-proving techniques to find valid plans by proving that there exists an action sequence that transforms the start state to a goal state. However, logic is very expressive and theorem proving thus turned out to be slow. Researchers therefore devised specialized representation languages for planning problems. One of the earliest such languages was used by a planning system called the Stanford Research Institute Problem Solver [STRIPS] in the early 1970s to control the Shakey robot. The STRIPS representation language is still widely used today.

STRIPS specifies states using a subset of logic, namely as conjunctions of propositions, that is, as sets of statements that are either true or false. For example, "At(C1,JFK)" denotes that cargo piece C1 is on the ground at airport JFK. Listed propositions are assumed to be true while unlisted propositions are assumed to be false (*closed-world assumption*).

STRIPS specifies actions compactly using *action schemata*, that is, parameterized descriptions of actions that describe in which states the actions can be executed and which states result from their execution. An action is obtained from an action schema by supplying objects for its parameters. An action can be executed in all states that contain the propositions on its PRECONDITION list. Its execution then results in the state that is obtained from the state before its execution by deleting all propositions on its DELETE list and adding all propositions on its ADD list. The ADD and DELETE lists address the so-called *frame problem*, that is, how to specify the consequences of action executions efficiently, by not listing those propositions that remain unaffected by action executions. A simple version of the air-cargo problem can be described as follows in STRIPS:

Start State:
IsAirport(JFK), IsAirport(SFO), IsPlane(P1),
    IsPlane(P2), IsCargo(C1),
IsCargo(C2), At(C1,SFO), At(C2,JFK),
    At(P1,JFK), At(P2,JFK)

Goal:
At(C1,JFK), At(C2,SFO)

Action Schemata:
Load(cargo,plane,airport)
PRECONDITION LIST: IsAirport(airport),
    IsPlane(plane), IsCargo(cargo),
    At(plane,airport), At(cargo,airport)
DELETE LIST: At(cargo,airport)
ADD LIST: In(cargo,plane)
Unload(cargo,plane,airport)
PRECONDITION LIST: IsAirport(airport),
    IsPlane(plane), IsCargo(cargo),
    At(plane,airport), In(cargo,plane)
DELETE LIST: In(cargo,plane)
ADD LIST: At(cargo,airport)
Fly(plane,from_airport,to_airport)
PRECONDITION LIST:
    IsAirport(from_airport),
    IsAirport(to_airport), IsPlane(plane),
    At(plane,from_airport)
DELETE LIST: At(plane,from_airport)
ADD LIST: At(plane,to_airport)

The start state specifies that there are two airports (JFK and SFO), two planes (P1 and P2) and two cargo pieces (C1 and C2). Cargo piece C1 is on the ground at airport SFO, while cargo piece C2,

plane P1, and plane P2 are on the ground at airport JFK. The goal specifies that C1 is to be transported to JFK and C2 to SFO; every state in which C1 is at JFK and C2 is at SFO is a goal state. The action schema "Load(cargo,plane,airport)" is for loading "cargo" into "plane" at "airport," where "cargo," "plane," and "airport" are parameters. The action schema "Unload(cargo,plane,airport)" is for unloading "cargo" from "plane" at "airport." Finally, the action schema "Fly(plane,from_airport,to_airport)" is for flying "plane" from "from_airport" to "to_airport." For example, to be able to load "cargo" into "plane" at "airport," it must be the case that "airport" is an airport, "plane" is a plane, "cargo" is a cargo piece, and both "cargo" and "plane" are at "airport." "Load(C2,P1,JFK)" is an action for loading cargo piece C2 into plane P1 at airport JFK. This action can be obtained from the action schema "Load(cargo,plane,airport)." It can be executed in the start state since the start state contains "IsAirport(JFK)," "IsPlane(P1)," "IsCargo(C2)," "At(P1,JFK)," and "At(C2,JFK)." Its execution in the start state results in the state

IsAirport(JFK), IsAirport(SFO), IsPlane(P1),
    IsPlane(P2), IsCargo(C1), IsCargo(C2),
    At(C1,SFO), In(C2,P1), At(P1,JFK), At(P2,JFK)

Note that the STRIPS representation of the air-cargo problem correctly moves a cargo piece in a plane with the plane as it flies from one airport to another one. Thus, our STRIPS representation addresses the so-called *ramification problem*, that is, how to model the implicit consequences of action executions.

There are several valid action sequences for the air-cargo problem, including

Load(C2,P2,JFK), Fly(P2,JFK,SFO),
    Unload(C2,P2,SFO), Load(C1,P2,SFO),
    Fly(P2,SFO,JFK), Unload(C1,P2,JFK)

The expressive power of STRIPS is limited. For example, it cannot express the consumption of continuous resources (such as fuel and time). Representation languages such as the Action Description Language (ADL) and the Problem Domain Description Language (PDDL) have therefore extended STRIPS to make it more expressive.

Solving Planning Problems

Planning techniques find valid plans for given planning problems. Planning can be understood as graph search, either in the state space or in the plan space. *State-space planning* searches the directed graph whose vertices correspond to states and whose edges correspond to state transformations, that is, actions. The objective of state-space planning is to find a path from the vertex that corresponds to the start state to a vertex that corresponds to a goal state. *Plan-space planning*, on the other hand, searches the directed graph whose vertices correspond to (possibly incomplete) plans and whose edges correspond to plan transformations. A plan is incomplete and thus invalid, for example, either if it is missing actions or if its actions are not completely ordered (*partial-order planning*) [NOAH, NONLIN, REPOP, SIPE, SNLP, TWEAK, UCPOP]. Partially ordered plans avoid unnecessary and potentially wrong ordering commitments between actions during planning (*least-commitment planning*). Plan transformations therefore often add actions or ordering constraints between actions to plans. The objective is to find a path from the vertex that corresponds to the empty plan to a vertex that corresponds to a valid plan.

The search of both state-space and plan-space planning can proceed, for example, forward from the start vertex to the goal vertices (*progression planning*) or backward from the goal vertices to the start vertex (*regression planning*). The size of the search spaces often increases exponentially in the size of the planning problems. This implies that the graphs of typical STRIPS planning problems do not fit into the memories of computers and that finding shortest action sequences is computationally very hard (to be precise: PSPACE-complete). Fortunately, one can often find longer action sequences efficiently. One could, for example, use only one plane to transport all cargo pieces (one after the other) between the airports for the air-cargo problem, which results in unreasonably long action sequences for large planning problems. Planning techniques therefore exploit the structure of planning problems in an attempt to find reasonably short action sequences for realistically sized planning problems.

One way to exploit structure is to focus the search with heuristics, often in the form of distance estimates to the goal vertices [HSP, UNPOP]. If, for example, a certain number of airports still have cargo pieces on the ground that are not yet at their correct destinations, then one still has to execute at least twice that many actions, that is, a load action and an unload action for each such cargo piece. (We did not count fly actions since planes can carry several cargo pieces at a time.) Good distance estimates can be obtained automatically for state-space planning, for example, from a data structure called a planning graph [FF, GRAPHPLAN, IPP, LPG, SGP, STAN, TGP].

A second way to exploit structure is to use knowledge about the structure of valid plans [TLPLAN]. For example, one can ignore plans for the air-cargo problem that first load a cargo piece into a plane and then immediately unload it again.

A third way to exploit structure is to decompose planning problems into several subproblems that can be solved almost independently. Decomposing planning problems does not work well for puzzles like the Rubik's Cube but seems to work well in domains in which humans plan well (*everyday planning*). For example, one can first identify the propositions that are part of the goal but not the start state, then find an action sequence for each of them that transforms the start state into a state that contains the proposition, and finally merge the actions sequences. This is the main idea behind *means-ends analysis*, which picks each of the propositions in turn and first finds an action whose add list contains the proposition and then recursively tries to achieve all of those preconditions of the action that do not already hold in the start state. One can also decompose planning problems hierarchically by refining high-level actions to make them more concrete (*hierarchical planning*) [ABSTRIPS, DEVISER, FORBIN, NONLIN, O-PLAN, SHOP, SIPE]. For example, once one has found a valid action sequence for the air-cargo problem, one can decompose the load actions into the various activities needed for loading a cargo piece into a plane, such as loading it into a van, driving the van to the plane, unloading it from the van, driving a ramp with a moving belt to the plane, activating the ramp, putting the cargo piece on the belt, and so on.

Finally, a fourth way to exploit structure is to speed up planning for the current planning problem by utilizing information about how one has solved similar planning problems in the past (*replanning* or *plan reuse*). Case-based planning, for example, adapts plans from similar planning problems in the past to fit the current planning problem [CAPER, CAPLAN, CHEF].

A planning technique is called *domain-dependent* if it needs to be provided with the structure of planning problems [PARCPLAN, TLPLAN]. It is called *domain-independent* if it discovers the structure of planning problems from their description [NONLIN, PRODIGY, SOAR, UCPOP]. A large number of novel domain-independent planning techniques were developed in the mid-1990s by using ideas from outside of artificial intelligence planning. For example, researchers found ways of mapping planning problems to heuristic search problems [FF, GRAPHPLAN, HSP, UNPOP], Boolean satisfiability problems [SATPLAN], integer-programming problems [SATPLAN-IP, STATE-CHANGE-IP], and model-checking problems from hardware verification [HSCP, MIPS]. These problems can then be solved efficiently with known techniques, and a plan can easily be read of from those solutions.

Note that one can make mistakes or omit important facts when specifying planning problems. In such cases a plan that appears to be valid might not achieve the goal. It is thus important to monitor the execution of plans and either replan or repair them if they do not perform as expected [ASPEN, PLANEX]. One can also use techniques from machine learning to improve the specification of the planning problems automatically from observations made during plan execution [LPLAN].

More Complex Planning Problems

Which planning technique to use depends on the characteristics of the planning problem, the structure of the desired plans, and the planning objective. So far, we have described planning techniques for classical planning problems described in STRIPS. These planning techniques find valid plans in the form of action sequences, ideally sequences of small lengths. Researchers also study far more complex planning problems, for example, where conditions have to be maintained rather than achieved, where the world changes even if the planning system does not execute actions, and where other systems are present in either cooperative or competitive situations.

Uncertainty about the outcomes of action executions or the current state gives rise to decision-theoretic planning problems. In case of nondeterministic actions, a number of successor states can result from their execution (for example, due to actuator noise or not modeling all relevant aspects of the world) and one cannot predict in advance which one will actually result. In case of states that are only partially observable, some relevant aspect of the world cannot always be observed (for example, due to sensor limitations) or cannot always be observed correctly (for example, due to sensor noise). In the presence of nondeterministic actions or partially observable states, planning systems cannot always know their current states but can estimate them, for example, in the form of sets of possible states or probability distributions over them. Planning systems then often find plans that achieve the goal with high probability or, if the goal can be achieved for sure, minimize the number of action executions either in the worst case or on average. For the objective of minimizing the number of action executions in the worst case, planning techniques can draw on ideas from artificial intelligence search. For the objective of minimizing the number of action executions on average, planning techniques can draw on dynamic programming ideas from operations research (such as value iteration and policy iteration) to solve totally and partially observable *Markov decision processes*, which generalize graphs. Totally observable Markov decision processes can model nondeterministic actions, while partially observable Markov decision processes can also model partially observable states. Decision-theoretic planning is computationally very hard, and decision-theoretic planning techniques thus exploit the structure of planning problems again, often by generalizing ideas from classical planning. For example, BURIDAN extends partial-order planning, SGP extends GRAPHPLAN, and MAXPLAN extends SATPLAN.

Some planning systems rely on coercion to achieve the goal without sensing and thus continue to find action sequences (*conformant or open-loop planning*) [CGP]. In general, however, it is not guaranteed that valid conformant plans exist for decision-theoretic planning problems or are of good quality because observations can now provide information about the current state. In general, one therefore often wants to find plans that contain sensing actions and select actions depending on the observations made during plan execution (*conditional, contingent, or closed-loop planning*) [WARPLAN-C]. For Markov decision processes it is sufficient to consider only conditional plans that map each state (for totally observable Markov decision processes) or each probability distribution over the states (for partially observable Markov decision processes) to the action that should be executed in it (*policies*), which reduces the search space and allows one to represent conditional plans compactly (*reactive planning*).

The large number of possible contingencies makes planning for decision-theoretic planning problems extremely time consuming. One way of speeding up planning is to interleave planning and action executions [CONT-PLAN, SEP-PLAN] since action executions can result in additional observations, which can eliminate some contingencies and thus speed up planning. For example, instead of having to plan for all states that can result from the execution of an action, one can simply execute the action and then plan only for the successor state that actually resulted from its execution. There are different ways of interleaving planning and action executions. For example, *agent-centered planning techniques* find only the beginning of a valid plan by searching with a limited look-ahead around the current state, execute the plan, and repeat the process. *Assumption-based planning techniques*, on the other hand, find a plan that is valid provided their assumptions about the outcomes of action executions are correct. If these assumptions turn out not to hold during plan execution, they replan and repeat the process.

Planning and Human–Computer Interaction

Research on planning benefits from research on human-computer interaction, and vice versa. A series of human computer interface issues need to get solved to deploy planning systems. For example, one needs to develop user interfaces for the acquisition of planning domains from experts and for the communication of the planning results to the users, especially for planning systems with human operators in the loop, such as decision-support systems and mixed initiative planning systems. Conversely, planning has been used to solve some Human-Computer Interaction tasks in software engineering and user-interface design. For example, NALIGE generates plans of low-level operating system commands to accomplish objectives specified by users via voice input. ASAP automates some aspects of software specification by proposing specifications, analyzing them to identify problems, and modifying them to resolve problems. CRITTER supports the interactive design of multiple interacting software systems. PALE extracts plan structure from program code, and ZIPPY then uses this knowledge to generate new code for an abstract specification. Finally, UCPOP and IPP have been used to automatically generate test cases for graphical user interfaces along with embedded verification steps.

Outlook

Planning is an exciting area of research that is important for manufacturing, space systems, disaster relief, robotics, defense, logistics, education, crisis response, entertainment, software engineering, and Human-Computer Interaction. The day when everyone has access to personalized planning systems is still to come, but planning technology is steadily improving. It is important to realize that aspects of planning and, more generally, decision making have been studied in various disciplines, including control theory, economics, operations research, decision theory, combinatorial optimization, and cognitive science—in addition to artificial intelligence. It is therefore interesting to combine ideas from different disciplines to build even more powerful planning systems. International planning competitions have been held since 1998 to compare the performance of planning systems on identical sets of planning problems and stimulate research on extending their capabilities in beneficial directions.

Michail G. Lagoudakis and Sven Koenig

FURTHER READING

Allen, J., Hendler, J., & Tate, A. (Eds.). (1990). *Readings in planning*. San Mateo, CA: Morgan Kaufmann.

Amant, R. (1999). User interface affordances in a planning representation. *Human-Computer Interaction, 14*(3), 317–354.

Anderson, J., & Fickas, S. (1989). A proposed perspective shift: Viewing specification design as a planning problem. *ACM SIGSOFT Software Engineering Notes, 14*(3), 177–184.

Blythe, J. (1999). Decision-theoretic planning. *AI Magazine, 20*(2), 37–54.

Boutilier, C., Dean, T., & Hanks, S. (1999). Decision-theoretic planning: Structural assumptions and computational leverage. *Journal of Artificial Intelligence Research, 11*, 1–94.

Dean, T., & Wellman, M. (1991). *Planning and control.* San Mateo, CA: Morgan Kaufmann.

Fickas, S., & Helm, B. (1992). Knowledge representation and reasoning in the design of composite systems. *IEEE Transactions on Software Engineering, 18*(6), 470–482.

Fikes, R., & Nilsson, N. (1971). STRIPS: A new approach to the application of theorem proving to problem solving. *Artificial Intelligence, 2*(3,4), 189–208.

Fikes, R., & Nilsson, N. (1993). STRIPS: A retrospective. *Artificial Intelligence, 59*(1,2), 227–232.

Howe, A., von Mayrhauser, A., & Mraz, R. (1997). Test case generation as an AI planning problem. *Automated Software Engineering, 4*(1), 77–106.

Kaelbling, L., Littman, M., & Cassandra, A. (1998). Planning and acting in partially observable stochastic domains. *Artificial Intelligence, 101*, 99–134.

Koenig, S. (2001). Agent-centered search. *AI Magazine, 22*(4), 109–131.

Manaris, B., & Dominick, W. (1993). NALIGE: A user interface management system for the development of natural language interfaces. *International Journal of Man-Machine Studies, 38*(6), 891–921.

Memon, A., Pollack, M., & Soffa, M. (1999). Using a goal-driven approach to generate test cases for GUIs. *Proceedings of the International Conference on Software Engineering*, 257–266.

Rist, R. (1995). Program structure and design. *Cognitive Science, 19*, 507–562.

Russell, S., & Norvig, P. (2003). *Artificial intelligence: A modern approach* (2nd ed.). Upper Saddle River, NJ: Prentice Hall.

Weld, D. (1994). An introduction to least commitment planning. *AI Magazine, 15*(4), 27–61.

Weld, D. (1999). Recent advances in AI planning. *AI Magazine, 20*(2), 93–122.

Yang, Q. (1997). Intelligent planning: A decomposition and abstraction based approach. New York: Springer-Verlag.

Young, R., & Simon, T. (1988). Planning in the context of Human-Computer Interaction. *Proceedings of the Conference of the British Computer Society Human-Computer Interaction Specialist Group*, 363–370.

POCKET COMPUTER

Pocket computers have much in common with wearable and tablet computers, and their distinction from personal digital assistants (PDAs) is problematic. Many different kinds of handheld devices are currently available, from cell phones that take photographs to Blackberry devices for mobile e-mail, phone, and computer communications. The distinguishing characteristic of a pocket computer is its versatility, as it can be programmed to perform almost any task, and it can be outfitted with hardware extensions such as a microphone for taking dictation, an infrared link for sharing data with other machines, and wireless for connection with Internet.

This essay was written on a pocket computer, using a variety of input methods in a range of demanding environments such as lurching on subway trains or climbing a tree. Folding keyboards are a familiar and efficient means of input, but take up as much space as the computer itself. Since the first widely used pocket computer, the Apple Newton, was introduced in 1993, users have struggled with handwriting recognition software that has constantly improved but requires at least some skill on the part of the user. Ironically, the widespread use of computer keyboards by children and adults alike may have further degraded handwriting ability.

Conveniently, one may enter text with a small virtual keyboard on the screen, using the machine's stylus to tap tiny pictures of keys like those of an ordinary desktop computer. It is impossible to "press" two keys at once, so to get a capital A, one must first tap the [Shift] key followed by [A]. Another method is to tap and hold [A], then slide the stylus upward. Tapping a key and sliding the stylus to the right produces the letter followed by a space, but one could also tap the virtual space bar.

Alternately, one may use a letter recognizer. This is an area on the screen to print each letter, between horizontal lines, as young children do when they are first learning. There are separate input areas for capital letters, lower-case letters, and numbers. Some letters are distinguished by slightly special ways of drawing them. Thus, "i" is made by drawing a little line up, whereas "l" is made by drawing the same line with a downward motion. Capital letters can be difficult for the machine to distinguish. For example, "DO" can be accomplished by writing lower-case "do" in the area reserved for capital letters. Thus, writing "s" in the three areas gives "Ss5," and a backward "s" gives "Zz2."

Some narrow but important human-computer interaction research has focused on "gestures"—the marks made by the user's stylus to give the handheld a command. One approach has been to constrain the stylus movements to make them more recognizable to the computer. A faint template can be displayed, to guide the user in making gestures. A plastic overlay with guiding edges may help disabled users who have difficulty controlling fine hand movements. Another approach is to study what characteristics of gestures make them seem more similar or different to human beings, with the plan of designing the computer's gesture recognition software to follow the same principles.

Reading webpages on a pocket computer can be a big challenge, both because limited bandwidth delays downloading, and because the screen is so small—typically 240 x 320 pixels compared with 768 x 1024 pixels or more on a desktop. Webpage designers have generally not accommodated the limitations of handhelds, so much effort has been invested in systems to summarize pages automatically. It is easy to suppress any pictures, showing the HTML "ALT tag" caption instead, and allowing the user to click on the caption to see the picture if desired. More complicated methods may require the use of a proxy server, a larger computer that intervenes between the handheld and Internet, loaded with summarization software and the large datasets it sometimes requires. Then, only a small summary of the webpage is sent to the handheld, unless the user requests more.

The proxy server can filter out a lot of the clutter, for example removing advertisements by checking image and website links against a list of advertisers. Links to other websites can be removed or gathered into a group where the user may ignore or consult them as needed. Text summarization methods can extract the key sentence in each paragraph and then present it in a form so the user can see the entire paragraph with a simple tap of the stylus. Many

HCI research projects are examining such diverse topics as the websurfing habits pocket computer users develop, and how well they can integrate multimodal output such as on-screen pictures combined with spoken text.

Among the debates between pocket computer designers are whether people primarily want the machines to perform very specific practical tasks, rather than combining many different capabilities, and how they can best be used in conjunction with other equipment. Assuming security issues can be solved, they can be employed as input or control devices for larger machines, can interact with a range of fixed equipment by pointing at it, and can be the mobile nerve center for an entire home or office full of varied devices.

Handhelds are versatile data collection tools for scientists: for manual entry of statistics from library resources directly into a spreadsheet, for augmenting laboratory notebooks for biologists, and for assembling miscellaneous field data about a research site in archaeology, geology, and paleontology. Cultural anthropologists can use them to keep rigorous notes of observed human behavior, and psychologists can lend them directly to human research subjects to write up whatever they are experiencing at random moments during the day whenever the preprogrammed computer beeps.

Over the coming years, we would expect handhelds to improve in memory, power-consumption efficiency, and connectivity. Large, flexible display screens that unroll are currently under development, and one can imagine nanotechnology-enabled keyboards printed on a piece of cloth. However, for the foreseeable future, pocket computers are likely to be sufficiently different from other types of computer to require a substantial amount of specialized human-computer interaction research to understand and optimize their distinctive characteristics.

William Sims Bainbridge

FURTHER READING

Albers, M. J., & Kim, L. (2000). User web browsing characteristics using palm handhelds for information retrieval. In *Proceedings of*

IEEE professional communication society international professional communication conference (pp 125–135). Piscataway, NJ: IEEE Educational Activities Department.

Barrett, L. F., & Barrett, D. J. (2001). An introduction to computerized experience sampling in psychology. *Social Science Computer Review, 19*(2), 175–185.

Buyukkokten, O., Kaljuvee, O., Garcia-Molina, H., Paepcke, A., & Winograd, T. (2002). Efficient web browsing on handheld devices using page and form summarization. *ACM Transactions on Information Systems, 20*(1), 82–115.

Elting, C., Zwickel, J., & Malaka, R. (2002). Device-dependant modality selection for user-interfaces: An empirical study. In *Proceedings of the 7th international conference on intelligent user interfaces* (pp. 55–62) New York: Association for Computing Machinery.

Gupta, S., Kaiser, G., Neistadt, D., & Grimm, P. (2003). DOM-based content extraction of HTML documents. In *Proceedings of the twelfth international conference on World Wide Web* (pp. 207–214). New York: Association for Computing Machinery.

Lee, W. B., & Grice, R. A. (2003). An adaptive viewing application for the web on personal digital assistants. In *Proceedings of the 21st annual international conference on documentation* (pp. 125–132). New York: Association for Computing Machinery.

Long, A. C., Landay, J., Rowe, L. A., & Michiels, J. (2000). Visual similarity of pen gestures. In *Proceedings of the SIGCHI conference on human factors in computing systems* (pp. 360–367). New York: Association for Computing Machinery.

Mackay, W. E., Pothier, G., Letondal, C., Bøegh, K., & Sørensen, H. E. (2002). The missing link: Augmenting biology laboratory notebooks. In *Proceedings of the 15th annual ACM symposium on user interface software and technology* (pp. 41–50). New York: Association for Computing Machinery.

Melnick, D., Dinman, M., and Muratov, A. (2003). *PDA Security: Incorporating Handhelds into the Enterprise.* New York: McGraw-Hill.

Myers, B., Lie, K. P., & Yang, B.-C. (2000). Two-handed input using a PDA and a mouse. In *Proceedings of the SIGCHI conference on human factors in computing systems* (pp. 41–48). New York: Association for Computing Machinery.

Swindells, C., Inkpen, K. M., Dill, J. C., & Tory, M. (2002). That one there! Pointing to establish device identity. In *Proceedings of the 15th annual ACM symposium on user interface software and technology* (pp. 151–160). New York: Association for Computing Machinery.

Wobbrock, J. (2003). The benefits of physical edges in gesture-making: Empirical support for an edge-based unistroke alphabet. In *Proceedings of the SIGCHI conference on human factors and computing systems* (pp. 942–943). New York: Association for Computing Machinery.

POLITICAL SCIENCE AND HCI

What are the linkages between political science and human computer interaction (HCI)? Consideration of this question begins with an explication of po-

litical science as a field of inquiry. Political scientists study politics, in its many forms. *Politics* is defined in various ways, but most definitions share the central idea that politics is the process through which power and influence are used to promote certain values and interests, especially in those domains of life that are viewed as subject to legitimate public control. *Political science* is a set of concepts, techniques, and theories whose objective is to increase the clarity and accuracy of our understanding of politics. It seeks to describe (what is), explain (why it is), and prescribe (what should be) regarding political phenomena. Political science is a borrower discipline, adapting concepts and findings from many fields to enrich its understandings, and it is a discipline in which there is some internal debate about appropriate methods and assumptions. The dominant perspectives emphasize the use of scientific methods to produce shared knowledge about politics.

Since the early 1970s, political science has become increasingly interested in the implications of information technologies (ITs) and communications technologies for politics. There has been particular attention on analyzing the impacts of ITs on political processes and institutions, as well as the effects of ITs on individual and group political behavior. In contrast political science has engaged in little explicit consideration of human computer interaction. One way to organize a discussion of such interactions is the straightforward taxonomy presented in Table 1. It specifies the intersections between key actors whose political interactions are mediated or affected by IT. These actors are government, citizens, and business (private sector) entities. This article focuses on four of the broad interests within political science that intersect with HCI concerns: political participation in democratic systems, life in the political community, public management, and international relations.

Political Participation in Democracies

Political participation is the activity of individuals or groups who wish to influence the actions or selection of those who have political power. The activities of citizens can range from contacting government

TABLE 1. Conceptualization of Politics: IT Linkages, with Selected Examples

	TARGET		
ACTOR	*Government*	*Citizens*	*Business*
Government	**G2G** Public Management • intergovernmental relations • public policy making International relations • cyberwarfare	**G2C** Public Management • service provision • information provision	**G2B** Public Management • government contracts • regulation International Relations • globalization
Citizens	**C2G** Political Participation • contacting • voting • social movements, NGOs Public Management • requests for government services	**C2C** Political Psychology • political cognition • deliberation • identity/group formation Political participation • political associations/groups	
Business	**B2G** Public Management • privatized public services • information reporting		

agencies and officials to voting, holding public office, and/or engaging in protest. Such participation occurs in all political systems and is a central feature in virtually all conceptions of democratic political processes. This section considers the findings of political scientists regarding political participation (C2G in Table 1) in relation to IT. In particular it considers IT as a possible mechanism for citizen mobilization, the impacts of IT on party politics, and the use of IT as a means for contacting government officials and agencies.

IT and Citizen Mobilization

Empirical research indicates that rates of political participation in the United States and other democratic countries are generally declining. The research also reveals that levels and types of participation are associated with the individual's political beliefs, age, gender, socioeconomic status (SES), and unique environmental conditions. How does IT affect these patterns? There are two main perspectives in political science regarding the relationship between computing (especially networked IT) and political participation: the mobilization perspective and the reinforcement perspective.

The *mobilization perspective* holds that the Internet encourages participation by facilitating access to political information and providing new means to contact representatives, contribute to political campaigns, organize protest or campaign activities, sign electronic petitions, vote in elections, and so on. The Internet, in this view, enables people to assemble their online worlds of political engagement on their own time and from their own homes and offices, transcending the spatiotemporal barriers that often discourage people from actively engaging in politics. To the extent IT use is not correlated with higher SES, increasing age, and male gender, it also reduces the differential impacts of these traits on higher participation.

The *reinforcement perspective* agrees that IT can facilitate political participation. However, from this perspective, IT primarily serves as an enabler for those who are already politically mobilized. Such people tend to be those who are advantaged in socioeconomic terms, and they also tend to be those on the advantaged side of the current "digital divide." Thus, it is concluded that IT has actually increased the gap between those who are politically active and those who are not, thereby reinforcing existing inequalities in participation.

There is some empirical evidence in support of each perspective. On the one hand, some evidence points to the emergence of new online configurations of political mobilization. The insurgency presidential campaigns of Democrat Howard Dean in 2003–2004 and Republican John McCain in 2000 were dramatically boosted by their websites, which collected tens of millions of dollars, especially from those less politically active in offline political settings. To some extent these new participants displayed more comfort in an online political world. The human computer interaction of such websites has a significant effect. For example, Dean's early success in fund-raising and mobilizing support were linked to a website with an attractive, easy-to-use graphical interface, enabling even inexperienced users to learn about the candidate's positions, contribute money, read or contribute to weblogs, and organize and join local support groups. On the other hand, Richard Davis (1998) and Bruce Bimber (2003), among others, present evidence that supports the reinforcement perspective, revealing that those in positions of power or with higher SES use IT far more extensively and effectively for political purposes. Moreover, neither Dean nor McCain was ultimately successful, as other candidates with greater political resources adopted their IT strategies.

These competing perspectives point to a complex relationship between political participation and HCI. Elements of HCI can both enable and constrain particular users regarding their interactions with government and other political actors. However, what users do when computer-mediated political activity is available is not only a product of the technological and software environment. It is also contingent on political and social factors—on both psychological and structural levels—supplying IT users with reasons and differential opportunities to participate.

Political Parties and IT

Political parties are a key linkage mechanism between citizens and the political system. Parties serve as a communication conduit between leaders and followers, organize political information in understandable bundles, and encourage participation. Helen Margetts (2000) uses the term *cyberparty* to refer to political parties that actively utilize the Internet to mobilize citizens. The Internet can reach citizens at relatively low cost and thus reduce the inequalities in the capacity of different parties to link with interested individuals and groups. A large mainstream party such as the Republican Party in the United States or a fringe party such as the Natural Law Party can each maintain a constant online presence for a fraction of the cost of a national advertising campaign on broadcast media.

Also, political parties can choose to cast their message in more pointed terms over the Internet, which, in contrast to broadcast media, is seen mainly by a relatively selective segment of loyal supporters. Historically, much of the information flow has been from the party to the individual rather than fostering a rich dialogue between parties and their supporters or among supporters in ways that could facilitate greater within-party democracy. Certain HCI designs could alter this pattern. However, to this point few parties, not even cyberparties, have constructed their IT interfaces in a manner that might reduce centralized party control over either the content or functioning of the party.

Contacting Government

Contacting politicians or government agencies is another important source of participatory input into the political system. Effective e-mail communications between citizens and government are an important means of citizen input into the political process. And the political responsiveness of government (G2C) is linked to its handling of citizen contacts. Recent research suggests that U.S. Congress members are struggling under a growing deluge of e-mail from constituents and other political activists and that their staffs currently cannot manage this volume of citizen input. In contrast a related survey concludes that most local elected officials in the United States not only believe they are handling the e-mail they receive but also report favorably that this e-mail helps them stay in closer touch with constituents. An important need of elected officials and government personnel is the design of automated systems that screen incoming e-mail (e.g., many elected officials will respond only to constituents) and that formulate an appropriate response based on content analysis of the message (e.g., noncontroversial replies to messages raising a policy issue or referrals to specific public agencies on requests for service).

Life in the Political Community

Other computer-mediated citizen-to-citizen activities (C2C) have significant political consequences beyond the more familiar forms of political participation. In the early nineteenth century, Alexis de Tocqueville observed a close connection between American associational life (i.e., participation in clubs, social groups, etc.) and the health of its democratic politics. Robert Putnam (2000) links a recent decline in associational life with declines in most forms of political participation. These declines have provoked substantial discussion about whether the Internet and virtual communities can invigorate or even supplant face-to-face forms of associational life.

More broadly, there is growing enthusiasm regarding online deliberation as a mechanism for shaping and discussing public policy issues. Numerous online groups have formed to discuss political events in many regions, including some sponsored by government, such as the Public Electronic Network (PEN) in Santa Monica and Network Pericles in Greece. Such online forums can expand policy dis-

A magazine ad, run by the Burroughs Corporation in October 1964, trumpets the advantages of the B 200 computer, noting that the system will be in action during the television coverage of the 1964 presidential election. Photo courtesy of Marcy Ross

cussions beyond the limited numbers who can assemble in one place at one time, and they can bring to bear considerably more extensive information and data to illuminate the topic. However, there are major design challenges around how to encourage open discussion and yet also moderate content and destructive personal attacks.

These concerns relate to at least three C2C topics at the intersection between the psychological components of political behavior and human computer interaction: how individuals acquire and process information about their political world from networked computer sources, develop and maintain online identities, and selectively attend to online content.

▌▌ Washington Tales of the Internet

Former Vice President Al Gore may always have to live down the claim attributed to him that he invented the Internet. What he actually said in a CNN interview in 1999 was the following:

> During my service in the United States Congress, I took the initiative in creating the Internet. I took the initiative in moving forward a whole range of initiatives that have proven to be important to our country's economic growth and environmental protection, improvements in our educational system. (Urban Legends Reference Page 2000)

The media jumped on Gore's choice of words, and in response Vint Cerf (called by some "The Father of the Internet" for his work on Arpanet and the Internet) explained the vice president's role as follows:

> VP Gore was the first or surely among the first of the members of Congress to become a strong supporter of advanced networking while he served as Senator. As far back as 1986, he was holding hearings on this subject (supercomputing, fiber networks…) and asking about their promise and what could be done to realize them. Bob Kahn, with whom I worked to develop the Internet design in 1973, participated in several hearings held by then-Senator Gore and I recall that Bob introduced the term "information infrastructure'" in one hearing in 1986. It was clear that as a Senator and now as Vice President, Gore has made it a point to be as well-informed as possible on technology and issues that surround it. (Urban Legends Reference Page 2000)

President Bill Clinton seems to have been at the opposite end of the spectrum, as a report from *The Independent*, a British newspaper, pointed out in 2004: "Officials at the Bill Clinton Presidential Library have revealed that, while the archives will eventually contain almost 40 million e-mails sent by his staff, there are only two sent by the former president during his eight-year tenure at the White House." (Buncombe, 2004). One was a test message, the other a message of congratulations to Senator John Glenn (a former astronaut) while he was on a space shuttle mission in 1998.

Marcy Ross

Sources: Buncombe, A. (2004, January 28). Clinton's legacy to the Internet age: One e-mail. *The Independent*. Retrieved January 28, 2004, from http://news.independent.co.uk

Urban Legends Reference Page—Questionable Quotes (Internet of Lies). (2000). Retrieved March 19, 2004, from http://www.snopes.com/quotes/internet.htm

Collective Intelligence

The ease with which individuals can discover, create, share, and merge ideas, information, and documents online creates a fertile environment in which thinking becomes a more distributed process of cognitive interaction involving a diversity of sources and viewpoints (what Pierre Lévy [1997] refers to as "collective intelligence") and less the product of a solitary individual. Some suggest that online political discussion, including such forms as weblogs and wikis, might result in a more productive and democratic process of opinion formation on public affairs. However, critics cite the reduced responsibility for advocacy when there is anonymity, the disconnect between reasoned deliberation and the high speed with which online exchanges typically occur, and the possibility that undesirable "groupthink" processes might actually be exacerbated by such virtual interfaces. The content on these open, relatively anarchic systems is the product of multiple, iterative, asynchronous, and distributed contributions. Thus, they raise many intriguing HCI issues concerning how to facilitate searching, integrate diverse contributions, and control content on the site.

IT and Identity Politics

The Internet mediates the cognitive interface between a user and his/her political world in ways that might have significant consequences in shaping the individual's identity, political beliefs, and associations with others. Unlike face-to-face encounters during which identities are marked by a person's physical presentation of self, online identities take their shape from the markers individuals choose to disclose about themselves and transmit to others. Sherry Turkle (1995) describes how, during personal website construction, the user carefully crafts and projects to the world a particular image of who he/she is. This enables individuals to gain recognition from online groups with which they affiliate and even to explore socially marginalized identities. The political and social consequences of such interactions are fertile areas for further research. While some optimists see this situation as creating a new sense of freedom for users, others raise concerns that this potential undermines the ability to create meaningful identities that can be a basis for the formation of virtual communities with deep and authentic attachments. Will new graphical interfaces, streaming video, and so on be designed in ways that more directly represent the individual's physical and personal qualities on line, and thus more closely resemble face-to-face interaction?

Bridging and Bonding

Finally, the Internet delocalizes users from their physical surroundings and brings them in contact with a wider online world of virtual interactions. Traditionally, newspapers and other broadcast media have served a community-creation function by providing groups of people with both a common source of information and a perspective for framing the issues of the day. Today, the Internet can operate in a similar but significantly more decentralized fashion. Far more than other broadcast media, the Internet allows a user to carve out a community of one's choosing. This is significant for political scientists who make a distinction between interpersonal connections that foster bonding between like-minded individuals and those that foster bridging between persons and groups with divergent identities and interests.

It has generally been assumed that effective democracy, indeed any form of functional politics, needs both bonding and bridging mechanisms, but it is particularly reliant on those that bridge differences. Cass Sunstein's (2001) survey of websites yields an image of the Web that he describes as the "daily me," where people can surf their interests selectively, without the risk of encountering challenges to their beliefs. A subsequent study that more explicitly investigates the bridging and bonding practices of Internet users found that while most online users did both, there was a tendency to favor bonding with like-minded groups. The risks to bridging might increase as IT systems and search engines increasingly provide end users with greater capac-

ity to select only sources and information that reinforce their preferences (that is, biases). The emerging artificial-intelligence–based systems that learn an individual's preferences and then automatically provide only supportive materials seem even more problematic if exposure to diversity is valuable for democratic politics.

Public Administration and Management

Public administration is a subfield of political science that has generally considered how the public sector and its employees function to do the business of government—to make and implement policy decisions. This encompasses aspects of G2C, C2G, G2G, G2B, and B2G, as well as internal government operations.

A list of the stages of public policy analysis captures many of the crucial activities that are associated with the field of public administration. These stages are as follows: agenda setting, problem formulation, information gathering, generation and assessment of policy alternatives, policy selection, policy implementation, and evaluation. At every stage of the policy process, well-designed IT systems can provide a rich information base and powerful tools for analysis. Policymakers are increasingly reliant on computer-based search engines, databases, and decision supports that enable policy actors to measure conditions; analyze trends; undertake projections; perform modeling, simulation, and cost-benefit analyses; monitor changes; and so on. A key area of HCI challenges is the development of improved visualization techniques for data displays and data searches. The development of more powerful and multifunctional geographic information systems (GISs), viewed by some as the "killer application" in support of most stages of the public policy process, is another domain with major possibilities for HCI research. There are also many applications of computer-supported cooperative work (CSCW) and other groupware on which improved software and interfaces could enhance communication, coordination, and decision making by groups who make and implement public policy.

Government–Citizen Links

Many e-government applications emphasize G2C— applications that deliver government services to citizens, presumably in a more efficient and effective manner. Governments in advanced democratic societies, with the Scandinavian countries at the forefront, are expanding web portals that enable citizens and other clients to identify and contact the governmental unit they need in order to locate information or engage in a transaction. First-Gov in the United States and ukonline.direct.gov.uk in Great Britain are among the most ambitious national-level attempts to facilitate identification of and connection to the relevant government agency. Even nondemocracies such as China and Cuba are implementing e-gov schemes that link users with government.

A major HCI challenge is how to design user-friendly computer interfaces that enable the average citizen— an individual with only modest understanding of the complex structures and functions of government— to navigate government websites in order to locate comprehensible information and interact with appropriate agencies. There is also rapid growth in the applications that allow citizens and clients of government to complete C2G and B2G transactions online, whether paying a traffic ticket, applying for a permit, completing a government purchase order, submitting a report, or any of the myriad of operational activities that occur between government and either a citizen or a business. Thus, governments are experimenting with web portals that aim for greater ease of use by employing improved keyword search engines, frequently asked questions (FAQs), graphic displays, touch screens, and multilanguage interfaces.

Government–Government Links

In most advanced democracies, the internal administrative processes of governments— generally G2G or intragovernmental linkages are characterized by the features of a "Weberian" (after the research of sociologist Max Weber) bureaucracy. The hallmark features of such bureaucracies include hierararchical organization, specialization of labor, and specific rules of behavior insuring rational, consistent action. Such bureaucratic behavior, while generally pre-dictable, has been strongly criticized as lacking in flexibility and responsiveness and as producing "stovepipe" agencies that fail to coordinate and share functions with each other. Thus advocates of the "new public management" envision a more flexible, cooperative, and entrepreneurial style of government administration.

Various applications of IT, especially web-based systems and other modes of information sharing, are assumed to be crucial facilitators of a reformed, increasingly virtual government in which traditional boundaries between bureaucratic units are bridged. This occurs as web-based systems result in pervasive cross-unit information sharing and more fluid forms of cooperative behavior, both vertically among actors within a unit and horizontally across units (G2G). The current obstacles to the successful design and implementation of such systems are generally grounded in bureaucratic and political resistance more than in sociotechnical issues. However, there are challenging HCI issues in the creation of functional, interoperable information systems within which data generated and used by multiple agencies with different operating routines and different information needs are of high quality, are easily shared, and increase productivity.

Government–Business Links

While e-government's interfaces with citizens have political importance, the government–business aspects of e-gov (G2B and B2G) arguably have the greatest economic significance. Governments have extensive dealings with private businesses as both customers and suppliers, and the systems of bidding, purchasing, and payment are now highly automated. In addition many businesses are subject to government regulation and need approvals, licensing, and diverse forms of information from government. Thus, there is a particular effort to make the digital transactions between government and business more transparent, efficient, and easier to use. There are also concerns regarding authenticity, digital signatures, widespread use of Smart Cards, and so on. And given the public disclosure laws regulating government behavior, there are many challenges in insuring that privacy and confidentiality are assured at the same time as public accountability is maintained.

International Relations

Traditionally, international relations, one of the main subfields of political science, has focused primarily on the interactions between "states" (countries). It examines how individual states behave in relation to other states; how sets of states engage in a variety of cooperative, competitive, and conflictual behaviors; and how the international system of states functions. The Internet bears a special relationship to the field of international relations because its precursor was the Department of Defense's Cold-War–era Advanced Research Project Agency program (ARPANET) to create a communications network that could survive a nuclear attack.

IT applications support some of the conventional capabilities of states in the international system. States utilize IT to manage their personnel (e.g., diplomats, military) outside of the state's borders, to communicate with other states, to gather intelligence about the actions of other states, and to expand their capacity for engaging in conflict (e.g., weapons guidance systems).

Information Age Warfare

Recently, IT has become a much more potent force in the international system. Substantial funding involving HCI issues has been directed to creation of the "electronic battlefield." Success in shaping the behavior of other states, both by the use force and also by the threat to use force, is increasingly linked to the state's ability to engage in "network-centric warfare." In this approach all members of the military force are connected to a robust and extraordinarily rich digital network of shared information. From the central field commander to the bomber pilot to the foot soldier, everyone is continuously provided with the information and visualization tools enabling each to operate with field awareness, speed, synchronization of action, lethality, and survivability that are unmatched in the history of warfare. Insuring the ease of use and the effective interfaces among all this digitized equipment for everyone in the network, as well as improving the functionality of all the smart weapons systems, provides extensive HCI challenges. The major military powers have allocated high levels of research and development support to this area. These capabilities have been applied most fully and

successfully by the U.S. military in the Iraq invasion of 2003.

Globalization

More broadly, current applications of IT have been at the center of a set of technologies that are reshaping the international system. IT has dramatically increased the speed, scale, and distance at which information can be transmitted. This development has affected the world economy in powerful ways, by accelerating and intensifying the flow of goods, capital, and people and by facilitating the multinational functioning of firms. It has also affected culture and behaviors, as diverse ideas have penetrated every corner of the world. These and associated phenomena are generally summarized as *globalization*.

Among the most significant political impacts of globalization is the reduction of the power and autonomy of the state. Globalized IT makes it more difficult for a state to maintain its sovereignty—the right of the state to control all activities within its borders. Major economic actors (e.g., transnational corporations and international regimes such as the World Trade Organization) now use IT to manage operations that are largely unconstrained by national governments or borders. A rapidly expanding number of transborder groups and social movements are also utilizing IT to recruit members and coordinate political actions that pressure national governments or serve as alternatives to governments. These range from humanitarian groups, such as the International Campaign to Ban Landmines (whose founder received the 1997 Nobel Peace Prize for her Internet-based campaign against landmines), to violent groups, such as al-Qaeda.

Thus, sovereign states and other transborder actors are all attempting to use IT as a key resource in the competitive struggle for advantage and control within the international system. The forms of human computer interaction will be critical in determining, on any given international issue, which actors are best able to take advantage of this powerful resource. Many public and private actors are deeply concerned about such HCI-related issues as the security of their own information systems, the growing dangers of cyberterrorism, and the positive and negative uses of encryption. And many political regimes, especially the less democratic ones like China, Singapore, and many Middle Eastern countries, struggle with the need to maintain IT interfaces that are open to the global economy but limit their citizens' online activities and access to information.

Stability or Transformation?

Both political scientists and those who are engaged in HCI work share a need to understand more fully the relationships between information technology and politics. Some posit that the appropriation of information technology capabilities by political actors will produce "politics as usual" because those with political power will use that power to structure the ways in which IT is designed and applied. Others suggest that the emerging information technologies are creating new political beliefs and behaviors and new political relationships that will fundamentally reshape the interactions between governments, citizens, and private sector actors. It seems clear that those designing the interfaces between political actors and the information technology supporting those actors will contribute importantly to shaping the politics of the coming decades. It is less clear what political values the technology-in-use will serve. Will those in the HCI field be primarily influenced by issues of technical possibility and sociotechnical design? Or will they alternatively (or also) be influenced by a vision of how IT *should* affect political phenomena? In either case, will political scientists and HCI professionals be able to discover and be guided by a rich understanding of the implications of IT systems for politics?

James N. Danziger and Michael J. Jensen

See also Digital Government; Online Voting

FURTHER READING

Alberts, D. S., Gartska, J. J., & Stein, F. P. (2001). *Understanding information age warfare* (2nd ed.). Washington, DC: Command and Control Research Program.

Alison, J. E. (2002). *Technology, development, and democracy: International conflict and cooperation in the information age.* Albany, NY: State University of New York Press.

Anderson, D. M., & Cornfield, M. (2003). *The civic web: Online politics and democratic values.* Lanham, MD: Rowman and Littlefield Publishers.

Barber, B. R. (1998). *A passion for democracy: American essays.* Princeton, NJ: Princeton University Press.

Becker, T., & Slaton, C. (2000). *The future of teledemocracy.* Westport, CN: Praeger.

Bimber, B. (2003). *Information and American democracy: Technology in the evolution of political power.* New York, NY: Cambridge University Press.

Brawley, M. R. (2003). *The politics of globalization.* Toronto, Canada: Broadview Press.

Brewer, G., & de Leon, P. (1983). *The foundations of policy analysis.* Chicago: Dorsey Press.

Budge, I. (1996). *The new challenge of direct democracy.* Cambridge, UK: Polity.

Danziger, J. N. (2003). *Understanding the political world: A comparative introduction to political science* (6th ed.). New York: Longman.

Davis, R. (1998). *The web of politics.* London: Oxford University Press.

de Tocqueville, A. (1945). *Democracy in America.* New York: Knopf. (Originally published 1835)

Dreyfus, H. L. (2001). *On the Internet.* New York: Routledge.

Fountain, J. E. (2001). *Building the virtual state: Information technology and institutional change.* Washington, DC: Brookings Institution Press.

Gibson, R., Nixon, P., & Ward, S. (Eds.). (2003). *Political parties and the Internet: Net gain?* New York, NY: Routledge.

Goldschmidt, K. (2001). Email overload in Congress: Managing a communications crisis. *Congress Online Project.* Retrieved October 1, 2003, from www.congressonlineproject.org/emailoverload.pdf.

Hill, K. A., & Hughes, J. E. (1998). *Cyberpolitics: Citizen activism in the age of the Internet.* Lanham, MD: Rowman and Littlefield.

Kamarck, E. C., & Nye, J. S., Jr. (Eds.). (2002). *Governance.com: Democracy in the information age.* Washington, DC: Brookings Institution Press.

Larson, E., & Raine, L. (2002). Digital town hall: How local officials use the Internet and civic benefits they cite from dealing with constituents online. *Pew Internet and American Life Project.* Retrieved on October 1, 2003, from www.pewinternet.org/reports/toc.asp?Report=74.

Lévy, P. (1997). *Collective intelligence: Mankind's emerging world in cyberspace.* Cambridge, MA: Perseus Books.

Margetts, H. (2000). *The cyber party.* Paper to the Democratic Audit, London School of Economics.

Norris, P. (2001). *The digital divide: Civic engagement, information poverty, and the Internet worldwide.* New York: Cambridge University Press.

Norris, P. (2002). The bridging and bonding role of online communities. *The Harvard International Journal of Press-Politics.* Retrieved on October 1, 2003, from http://ksghome.harvard.edu/~.pnorris.shorenstein.ksg/ACROBAT/Bridging.pdf.

Osborne, D., & Gaebler, N. (1992). *Reinventing government.* New York: Penguin.

Poster, M. (2001). *What's the matter with the Internet?* Minneapolis, MN: University of Minnesota Press.

Putnam, R. (2000). *Bowling alone: The collapse and revival of American community.* New York: Simon and Schuster.

Sunstein, C. (2001). *Republic.com.* Princeton, NJ: Princeton University Press.

Tsagarousianou, R., Tambini, D., & Bryan, C. (Eds.). (1998). *Cyber-democracy: Technology, cities and civic networks.* New York, NY: Routledge.

Turkle, S. (1995). *Life on the screen: Identity in the age of the Internet.* New York: Simon and Schuster.

Verba, S., Schlozman, K., & Brady, H. (1995). *Voice and equality: Civic volunteerism in American politics.* Cambridge, MA: Harvard University Press.

PRIVACY

Privacy, often defined as the state of being free from observation, is a matter of concern for many people in this information age. Widely used technologies such as the personal computer, wireless telephones, local area networks, global positioning systems, and the Internet have augmented the amount, types, frequency, and accuracy of information that governments, corporations, and others can obtain about people. For example, recent surveys have found that U.S. companies use electronic techniques to observe, store, and analyze the on-the-job behavior of at least 26 million employees. Nearly three-quarters of major U.S. companies responding to a survey administered by the American Management Association said that they record and review employees' telephone calls, e-mail messages, and Internet activities.

A large body of research suggests that many people worry about these new capabilities. A 1991 survey by the Society for Human Resources Management found that 48.8 percent of participating companies had handled at least one employee complaint concerning an organizational invasion of privacy. Marketing research has suggested that companies often inaccurately judge the intensity of consumers' reactions concerning the use of personal information. Many software manufacturers have had to withdraw products or features of products after hearing an outcry from consumers about invasive data collection of viewing or purchasing habits. Corporate decision-makers appear to underestimate the perceived harm of sharing personal employee information with other parties. Numerous legal actions in the United States have sprung from perceived violations of privacy—for example, *Dallas v. England* (1994); *Shahar v. Bowers* (1993); *Soroka v. Dayton Hudson Corp.* (1991); *Thorne v. El Segundo* (1984).

Many institutions fail to plan appropriately for the privacy implications of computerized collection, storage, and distribution of data until legal action or commercial harm threatens them. One researcher provided documentation suggesting that a majority of Fortune 500 companies lacked sufficient security controls over the personal data they collect. U.S. legal protections for privacy, such as the Privacy Act of 1974, which pertains to government uses of personal data, have done little to protect personal information as companies use it in the private sector. In order to understand how to strike an appropriate balance between the beneficial functions of new technologies and the privacy rights of individuals it is important to consider the legal, philosophical, economic, technical, and social aspects of privacy.

Legal and Philosophical Perspectives

Despite the simplicity of the dictionary definition, philosophers continue to wrestle with the concept of privacy, and social scientists sometimes measure and study invasions of privacy without explicitly defining the term. Practical guides to privacy exist, such as the fair use principles in the 1977 U.S. privacy commission report and the Organisation for Economic Co-operation and Development (OECD) guidelines for data protection, but these documents provide little guidance to those who wish to understand exactly what privacy means to people. Part of the difficulty with defining privacy stems from its cultural embeddedness. Shaped by environment and upbringing, individuals base their expectations and beliefs about privacy on their culture. Even within one country, for example, the United States, opinions about privacy and preferences for it vary widely, because they depend, in part, on religion, occupation, socioeconomic status, and area of residence. Nonetheless, people in Western societies share a core set of values that include the right of individuals to keep some or many aspects of their lives and activities out of the view of the public, the press, private corporations, and the government.

The importance of privacy as an individual right in the United States traces its modern connection to Supreme Court judges Samuel D. Warren and Louis D. Brandeis, who, in an 1890 article in the *Harvard Law Review*, decried the invasive examination of individuals' personal lives by the press. In the ensuing century, law and philosophy scholars defined privacy and discussed its functions and benefits. One noteworthy contributor was Ruth Gavison, a legal scholar who reviewed privacy case law and legislation, refined a coherent definition for the term, and discussed relationships among the concepts of personal information, control, and freedom. Many other scholars have weighed in with definitional discussions of privacy, or criticisms of privacy's legal status as a separate right.

A common thread running through these works is the exploration of the meaning and function of privacy within the legal system and society. This exploration is important because it underscores the importance of balancing the rights and needs of individuals with those of collectives such as the government, the public at large, and private organizations. A society in which individuals have the right to withhold all information about their actions probably could not function properly (imagine if criminals had the right to commit their crimes privately), but a society in which institutions could observe and record everyone's activities all the time would seem repugnant to most people.

Privacy and freedom seem inextricably linked in this perspective, and just as there are legal and ethical limits on freedom—even in democratic societies—the same appears to be true for privacy as well. Legal and philosophical discussions of privacy thus provide a foundation for further analysis, but they do not necessarily provide a clear account of the thoughts and feelings of people who are potentially affected by the privacy invasions resulting from new technologies. Put differently, legal and philosophical writings do not show how privacy works in the minds of people who are affected by new forms of technology. Law and philosophy can draw boundaries around legal and ethical usage, but they cannot provide much guidance about how the design of a technology may affect users' perceptions of privacy.

Technological Perspectives

Many well-known techniques exist both for invading and for protecting privacy. For any given technological measure for observing the behavior of others (for instance, wireless audio transmitters or network packet sniffers), a corresponding collection of countermeasures usually exists (for instance, radio jamming or encryption). Computer scientists and electrical engineers, with their focus on information systems, networks, and digital data, comprise the latest in a long chain of technologists whose inventions have either helped or hindered (or sometimes both) personal rights such as privacy. To examine the privacy implications of technology, an interdisciplinary academic area has developed that is devoted to an analysis of the social and organizational impacts of new technologies. Academic scholars including Enid Mumford, Pelle Ehn, Rob Kling, Paul Attewell, and Phillip Agre have recently addressed aspects of the impact of technology on privacy and related issues. A good deal of this work finds its foundations in social science. For example, both Phillip Agre in reviewing technology and privacy and Victoria Bellotti in examining privacy in multimedia groups drew on the work of 1960s sociologist Erving Goffman. Goffman microanalyzed social interactions between people, and although his work did not focus on privacy per se, it has often been used to explain privacy preferences and behaviors.

Researchers examining privacy and other impacts of technology have also drawn on economic, social, and political analyses. For example, Robert Kraut examined economic arguments for the adoption of "telework" technology by organizations, which raises privacy concerns due to its ability to track and monitor the activities of workers in the home. Rebecca Grant and her colleagues documented ways that electronic monitoring systems designed to improve the bottom line could instead adversely affect it. Paul Attewell contrasted the economic motives for technological innovations with the political motives of individuals who support such innovations. As Pelle Ehn described, put it, technology can consolidate and amplify the control that the powerful have over those who are less powerful (1989, 460–461). Other researchers have used aspects of feminist theory to examine technology designs.

A 1996 collection of articles, *Computerization and Controversy*, demonstrates the variety of ways in which reactions to technology and privacy issues are embedded within the social context of families, work groups, organizations, and society. Drawing on the disciplinary perspectives discussed above to examine the technological transformation of work and connections between privacy and social control, the authors of these articles emphasized the ethical imperatives incumbent on those who design and implement technological innovations. One of the contributors to this book, Andrew Clement, analyzed the privacy implications of multimedia communication "spaces" and provided a guide—based in part on the Organization for Economic Cooperation and Development's (OECD) principles of fair information practice—that multimedia system designers might use to ensure privacy protections for end users of their systems.

Psychological Perspectives

Social psychology and its cognate fields of sociology and anthropology provide psychological perspectives on privacy. In his 1970 book, *Privacy and Freedom,* the privacy scholar Alan Westin drew on all three fields to define four facets of privacy—solitude, intimacy, anonymity, and reserve—and four psychological functions of privacy— personal autonomy, emotional release, self-evaluation, and limited and protected communication. The facets distinguish between different types of privacy. For example, solitude refers to privacy by isolation from others, but intimacy refers to a "reserved space" for enjoyment by two or more people who choose to be together. The psychological functions of privacy distinguish between the different needs that privacy can serve. The two needs that receive the most contemporary attention are personal autonomy—the ability to choose one's own actions—and limited and protected communication—the ability to ensure control over what one communicates to others. These two needs are arguably the most threatened by new forms of information technology. Ubiquitous video surveillance is an example of a technology that may threaten personal autonomy and e-mail is an example of a technology in which limited and protected communication is relevant.

Another researcher whose work extensively explores the psychological underpinnings of privacy is Irwin Altman. In his 1975 book, *The Environment and Social Behavior*, he developed a dialectic theory of privacy that generated an enormous volume of subsequent research. Using "dialectical" to refer to two dynamic, opposing forces that influence privacy, Altman synthesized research from anthropology, sociology, and psychology to develop his analysis. His theories continue to spawn studies in architecture, environmental design, urban planning, communications research, and other fields. Part of the enduring appeal of Altman's formulation is that he presented privacy as a *boundary regulation process*, rather than as an event or state.

The dialectic nature of privacy, Altman claimed, was a function of the inherent tension and necessary balance between closing/protecting and opening/sharing of the self. Altman suggested that basic human nature contained both of these opposing needs: The social nature of human beings makes it incumbent upon people to share themselves with others, but at the same time makes them vulnerable, and therefore motivated to protect themselves in some situations. Note that this insight resolves the apparent paradox implied by the prevalence of people who expose the innermost details of their lives (for example, autobiographical authors and web-loggers) and others who seem intent on isolating themselves (for example, recluses). Because Altman's theory takes both time and situation into account, the processes of opening and closing personal boundaries vary with the surrounding context and changes in one's relationships to others. Altman also discussed the consequences of too much privacy in addition to the problems of too little privacy. Other work based on Altman's theory has highlighted the importance of perceived personal control on privacy and privacy violations: If individuals feel that they can *control* the flow of personal or intimate information about themselves, they are less likely to feel that their privacy has been violated.

Drawing on Altman, Westin, and other sources, many researchers began examining privacy in earnest during the 1960s and 1970s. For example, studies have focused on privacy invasions of physical space, of social space, in personnel selection, in the storage and use of personal data, and in the monitoring of communications and employee performance. Others have compared perceptions of privacy invasion for different data handling practices and beliefs about the types of personal information stored in databases, as well as privacy as it pertains to drug testing. Eugene Stone and Diana Stone-Romero suggested that personal values about privacy are shaped primarily by societal norms. These authors described four prevalent norms that are relevant to privacy: (1) norms about the types of data that it is reasonable for an institution to collect about individuals, (2) norms about freedom from control (that is, by the government), (3) norms about redemption (that is, a belief in the ability to overcome one's past mistakes), and (4) norms about social justice (that is, a belief that personal information should not be used to maintain or exacerbate socioeconomic disparities). All four norms share many similarities with the psychological functions of privacy suggested by Westin.

Sociotechnical Frameworks

Putting the technological and social perspectives together, it appears certain that a thorough understanding of both the technological and the social psychological concerns must inform the design of new technologies. From a purely technical standpoint, specific remedies to ensure the security of data (for example, authentication, access control, and encryption have long been available, and innovations continue to expand and enhance the repertoire of available techniques. From a socio-technical point of view, however, these techniques comprise a toolbox; the difficult work lies in knowing when a particular privacy tool is needed and why. Thus, in designing or administering a form of technology that handles personal information, it is important to understand the perspectives and needs of those individuals whose privacy is at stake—the workers, clients, customers and others whose personal information is collected, transmitted, and stored by the new technology. Armed with the knowledge of the needs of users for privacy, informed and ethical technology designers can create the appropriate controls for their innovations.

To these ends, some frameworks for information privacy combine both social and technical viewpoints. Such frameworks can provide a perspective on how information collection, storage, and dissemination strategies affect people's attitudes, beliefs, and behaviors toward the institutions that seek to obtain the data and the technology they use to do so. Such frameworks have particular relevance for information systems designs that have as their goal the development, implementation, and administration of digital government systems, e-commerce, customer relations management systems, human resource information systems, collaboration software, cooperative work systems, and other information technologies that handle sensitive personal information.

One example of such a framework includes contributions from a variety of different fields. Sandra Petronio, a communications researcher, proposed and tested a "communication boundary management" model built on the work of Altman and others to explain privacy regulation in marital, family, and other interpersonal contexts. In a separate development, other writers have argued for the importance of fairness and justice as explanatory factors in understanding people's reactions to having other people or institutions collect information about them. This work suggests that the intended and actual uses of personal information must respect people's expectations of fair treatment.

Socio-technical researcher Norhayati Zakaria knitted these two perspectives together to provide a lens through which one might examine the privacy implications of modern communications and data management practices. This perspective, called information boundary theory, suggests that technology and privacy concerns collide whenever information and communications technologies mediate the communication of personally relevant information. People will actively use the available features of these technologies to try to control the flow of personally relevant or "intimate" information by means of dynamic processes of boundary opening and boundary closure. Message "senders" try to regulate the flow of information by deciding what information to reveal to message "receivers." Senders make these decisions based on their beliefs about how the information might be used and whether it will be used in a beneficial or harmful manner. Boundary regulation may be manifest in verbal behavior (for instance, "flaming" in an e-mail) or nonverbal behavior (for instance, closing a chat session).

The ideas of boundary opening and closure are particularly applicable to communicative forms of information technology. E-commerce serves as one possible prototype: Customer transactions require revelations of personally relevant information (for example, creditworthiness) to an institutional audience. Information boundary theory would predict an individual's preferences and choices regarding the amount and type of personal information that the individual would be willing to reveal in various e-commerce scenarios. Other communicative applications of information technology are also relevant here. The successful application of knowledge management software in organizations; list servers, bulletin boards and newsgroups in professional organizations; and e-mail and chat for personal purposes all depend upon the degree to which individuals feel comfortable revealing sensitive or intimate information. Such information can relate to any of a variety of domains including work (for example, job performance), personal (for example, information about family members), and health, and depends upon the communicative situation and its goals.

Information boundary theory provides one perspective on the relationship between information technology and privacy. Other perspectives exist as well, and each one provides a different view on the interplay among the functions and capabilities of the technology itself, people's preferences for controlling the flow of information about themselves, and the needs and obligations of the institutions—corporations, governments, and so on—that wish to obtain information about them. Privacy is a prototypical socio-technical problem: Privacy concerns arise at the junction between the new capabilities for observation afforded by technological innovations and the human values and practices relevant to the uses of these new technologies.

Jeffrey M. Stanton

See also Law and HCI; Security; Sociology and HCI; Social Psychology and HCI

FURTHER READING

Adler, P. A., Parson, C. K., & Zolke, S. B. (1985). Employee privacy: Legal and research developments and implications for personnel administration. *Sloan Management Review, 26,* 13–25.

Agre, P. E., & Rotenberg, M. (1997). *Technology and privacy, the new landscape.* Cambridge, MA: MIT Press.

Alder, G. S., & Tompkins, P. K. (1997), Electronic performance monitoring: An organizational justice and concertive control perspective. *Management Communication Quarterly, 10,* 259–288.

Altman, I. (1975). *The environment and social behavior.* Monterey, CA: Brooks/Cole.

Attewell, P. (1987). Big brother and the sweatshop: Computer surveillance in the automated office. *Sociological Theory, 5,* 87–99.

Bellotti, V. (1997). Design for privacy in multimedia computing and communication environments. In P. E. Agre & M. Rotenberg (Eds.), *Technology and privacy, the new landscape* (pp. 63–98). Cambridge, MA: MIT Press.

Clement, A. (1996). Considering privacy in the development of multimedia communications. In R. Kling (Ed.), *Computerization and controversy* (pp. 848–869). San Diego: Academic Press.

Culnan, M. J. (1993, September). How did they get my name? An exploratory investigation of consumer attitudes toward secondary information use. *MIS Quarterly,* 341–361.

Ehn, P. (1989). *Work-oriented design of computer artifacts.* Stockholm: Arbetlivscentrum.

Freedman, W. (1987). *The right of privacy in the computer age.* New York: Quorum.

Gavison, R. (1980). Privacy and the limits of law. *Yale Law Journal, 89,* 421–471.

Goffman, E. (1959). *The presentation of the self in everyday life.* Garden City, N.Y.: Doubleday.

Grant, R. A., Higgins, C. A., & Irving, R. H. (1988). Computerized performance monitors: Are they costing you customers? *Sloan Management Review, 29,* 39–45.

Hacker, S. L. (1987). Feminist perspectives on computer based systems. In G. Bjerknes, P. Ehn, & M. Kyng (Eds.), *Computers and Democracy* (pp. 177–190). Aldershot: Avebury.

Johnson, C. A. (1976). Privacy as personal control. In D. H. Carson (Ed.), *Man-Environment Interactions: Selected Papers Presented at EDRA 5* (pp. 83–100). Stroudsberg, PA: Dowden, Hutchinson, & Ross.

Kling, R. (1996). *Computerization and controversy.* San Diego: Academic Press

Kraut. R. E. (1987). Predicting the use of technology: The case of telework. In R. Kraut (Ed.), *Technology and the Transformation of White Collar Work* (pp. 113–133). Hillsdale, NJ: Erlbaum.

Marx, G. T., Moderow, J., Zuboff, S., Howard, B., & Nussbaum, K. (1990, March/April). The case of the omniscient organization. *Harvard Business Review, 68*(2), 12–30.

Milberg, S. J., Burke, S. J., Smith, H. J., & Kallman, E. A. (1995). Values, personal information, privacy and regulatory approaches. *Communications of the ACM, 38,* 65–74.

Mumford, E. (1987). Sociotechnical systems design: Evolving theory and practice. In G. Bjerknes, P. Ehn, & M. Kyng (Eds.), *Computers and democracy* (pp. 59–76). Aldershot: Avebury.

Newell, P. B. (1995). Perspectives on privacy. *Journal of Environmental Psychology, 13,* 87–104.

Petronio, S. (1991). Communication boundary management: A theoretical model of managing disclosure of private information between marital couples. *Communication Theory, 1,* 311–335.

Rehnquist, W. H. (1974). Is an expanded right to privacy consistent with fair and effective law enforcement? *Kansas Law Review, 23,* 1–15.

Stanton, J. M. (2002). Information technology and privacy: A boundary management perspective. In S. Clarke, E. Coakes, G. Hunter, & A. Wenn (Eds.), *Socio-Technical and Human Cognition Elements of Information Systems* (pp. 79–103). London: Idea Group.

Stone, E. F., & Stone, D. L. (1990), Privacy in organizations: Theoretical issues, research findings and protection mechanisms. *Research in Personnel and Human Resources Management, 8,* 349–411.

U.S. Congress, Office of Technology Assessment. (1987). *The electronic supervisor: New technology, new tensions.* (OTA-CIT-333). Washington, DC: U.S. Government Printing Office.

Warren, S. D., & Brandeis, L. D. (1890). The right to privacy: The implicit made explicit. Reprinted in F. D. Schoeman (Ed.), (1984), *Philosophical dimensions of privacy: An anthology* (pp. 75–103). Cambridge: Cambridge University Press.

Westin, A. F. (1970). *Privacy and freedom.* New York: Atheneum.

Zakaria, N., Stanton, J. M., & Sarkar-Barney, S. (2003). Designing and implementing culturally sensitive IT applications: he interaction of culture values and privacy issues in the Middle East. *Information Technology and People, 16,* 49–75.

PROGRAMMING LANGUAGES

The world of computing has long been concerned about the software problem, sometimes called the "software crisis." The nature of the problem is that building software is difficult, labor intensive, and expensive. Furthermore, the problem is becoming worse as the size and complexity of computer systems increase and as system environments become more demanding because of factors such as concurrency, distributed or network-based computing, and the spreading use of graphical interfaces.

Another aspect of the software problem is that large software systems tend to be buggy (prone to software errors or failures), fragile, and insecure and to require enormous investments to address these deficiencies.

Today's programming languages—the languages that computer programmers use to write software—are part of the software problem. Programming languages are error prone and weak in terms of expressiveness and support for those features that make programming more efficient and reliable. Part of the solution to the software problem will be inventing and deploying better programming languages.

The Purpose of Programming Languages

Programming languages are the medium of expression in programming. They are used for communication with computers, but they are also used for communication between humans because programs are usually read, understood, and modified by communities of programmers. The Open Source movement is a prominent example of a community based on the shared medium of program code.

Computer systems process data, and thus programming languages must describe both how data are structured and represented and how the processing of data is performed.

Computer systems have grown enormously large and complex, consisting of many parts that interact, combine, and so forth. Programming languages must have features that help manage this complexity. The aspects of programming that concern the local requirements of individual procedures are called "programming in the small," whereas those aspects that deal with the construction of large programs out of their component parts are called "programming in the large."

A good programming language should support both programming in the small and programming in the large. The features that support programming in the large deal with abstraction and modularity, although some kinds of abstraction (e.g., procedural abstraction) also play a role in programming in the small.

Programming languages can help deal with the issue of bugs. Certain features of programming languages can eliminate classes of failures or limit their effects. For instance, static type checking detects certain common errors when a program is compiled (translated to machine language for execution), allowing the errors to be corrected before the program is run. Mandatory dynamic checks such as array bounds checking can catch other errors at run-time, and exception handling can allow such errors to be managed in a disciplined manner to avoid catastrophic failure of the program.

Languages that have clear, well-specified meanings, such that their features are well characterized in isolation and in terms of their interactions with other features, lend themselves to formal reasoning about programs. Simple semantics can support useful logics for reasoning about how programs behave and make it possible to formally relate programs with logical specifications of their function.

What Should a Programming Language Do?

What tasks should programming languages support? First, they must provide features for the precise description of structured information (data structures and data types). Typically certain primitive data types such as integers (whole numbers), floating point numbers (decimal fractions), characters (letters, digits, punctuation marks), and Booleans (true, false) are provided as the basis for building more complex structures. These more complex structures are built using forms such as records and tuples for heterogeneous collections; arrays, vectors, and strings for linear sequences; and linked data structures for lists, trees, and general graphs. In most conventional programming languages, these structures are thought of as organizing chunks of computer memory, and they can be modified by operations that update memory. In other programming languages (e.g., functional or declarative languages), these structures behave more like abstract mathematical entities that do not change during a computation.

Next, programming languages must provide the means for processing data. The most elementary operations combine primitive values, for example, adding two integers. In most programming languages, primitive operations also alter parts of memory, for example, variable assignment or array update.

The elementary operations can be combined in various ways:

- forming compound expressions, such as $(x+3)^*y$, that involve several basic operations
- performing several operations one after another in sequence
- testing a condition (e.g., if $x < 3$) and deciding what to do next based on the outcome of the test (conditionals)
- repeating certain processing steps until a condition is achieved (for or while loops)
- detecting exceptional conditions (errors or failures, interrupts from outside the computation) and changing the course of processing to deal with them
- defining and calling procedures or functions that capture some common actions

Beyond these common control constructs, some programming languages provide support for more advanced program control involving concurrency, communication, and synchronization.

An important tool in programming is the ability to abstract and parameterize a segment of program code that performs a general processing action that one would like to use repeatedly. The abstracted code is usually called a "function" or a "procedure," or, in object-oriented languages, a "method."

These features are the building blocks of basic programs or program components (the domain of programming in the small). When the scale of a program becomes large enough, we need to break it into manageable pieces that perform separate, well-defined roles. Some programming languages provide features to make it convenient for us to define and then combine program components, which are often called "modules."

Programming languages also address the management of memory. At the simplest level, this management involves the allocation and layout of memory for a fixed set of global data structures. However, most programming languages also support various forms of dynamically created memory structures. These dynamic structures introduce the problem of reclaiming and recycling memory when the dynamic structures are no longer needed.

Some dynamic structures are managed by the stack discipline associated with procedure calls; they belong to a particular invocation of the procedure and are created when a procedure is called and disappear when the procedure returns. Other dynamically created data structures outlive the procedure invocation that created them and are allocated in a special memory pool called a "heap." Heap-allocated data can be reclaimed either manually or automatically by a process called "garbage collection." Because manual reclamation is a complex and error-prone task, more advanced (or higher-level) programming languages use the more reliable automatic method of garbage collection.

Many other aspects of programming may or may not be directly supported by features of a programming language. For instance, input/output is an area of functionality that might be incorporated in a programming language, but it is more commonly handled by a program library. Standard libraries address many other concerns and can be arbitrarily extended to cover more tasks as time passes and as the demands of programming grow. For instance, libraries support graphical user interfaces. However, the simplicity and flexibility of libraries are influenced by the programming language, particularly by how it supports abstractions and modularity.

Safety is another general property that programming languages should have. Having "safety" roughly means that programs will behave in a sensible, predictable way even if they contain bugs. In other words, the behavior of programs adheres to a well-defined model that covers behaviors of incorrect programs as well as correct programs. Safety is the result of a number of factors, such as automatic memory management (to prevent data structures from being reclaimed and their space recycled while they are still in use), static type checking (to prevent nonsensical combinations of operators and arguments), and dynamic checking of necessary conditions that cannot be enforced by static checking (e.g., the condition that when accessing an array, the index satisfies the array bounds). Safety is a desirable property in its own right, but it is also relevant to software system security because many exploits take advantage of lack of safety in low-level programming languages (e.g., buffer overflow).

Finally, the principle of economy of means should apply to programming languages. A programming language should be as simple as possible, but no simpler, to paraphrase the U.S. physicist Albert Einstein. A programming language is too complex if a typical experienced user has to confine himself or herself to a subset of the language. Another aspect of simplicity is that the various features of the language work well together without special cases or obscure interactions. We sometimes call this aspect "orthogonality."

A Historical Survey

In surveying a representative sample of programming languages, we can organize them by chronology and by paradigm (framework).

The first programming languages were numeric machine languages, which were soon enhanced with symbolic notation for operation codes, labels, and memory locations, leading to assembly language. The first high-level programming language is FORTRAN (1957), which was designed to support scientific and engineering computations of a numeric character. Other first-generation programming languages from around 1960 are ALGOL 60 and COBOL (designed for business data processing). We call these "procedural languages" because they all support some form of subroutine or procedure mechanism. We also call them "imperative languages" because a program consists of a sequence of imperative commands that alter the state of the computation.

During the mid- to late 1960s a second generation of procedural programming languages followed. PL/I (1966) was an IBM-sponsored language meant to be a successor to FORTRAN, COBOL, and ALGOL 60. ALGOL 68 and Pascal were two competing successors to ALGOL 60. ALGOL 68 was a complex design, whereas Pascal strove for simplicity and was originally designed as a vehicle for teaching programming. Simplicity won out, and Pascal became the first of a family of programming languages.

During the late 1960s through the early 1970s programmers designed several languages specifically for low-level systems programming (e.g., for the implementation of operating systems, database systems, and networking software). These systems implementation languages included BCPL, BLISS, and C, which, as the "native" language of the UNIX operating system, eventually became the most widely used programming language. These low-level languages permit a fairly direct and precise control of resources such as memory space, at the cost of extra detail to be managed and more opportunities to introduce bugs. Higher-level languages were also developed for systems programming, including Modula 2, Mesa, Ada, and Modula 3 (all in the Pascal family).

Outside of the programming mainstream dominated by imperative, procedural languages, a number of alternative paradigms were developed, with each paradigm embodying a distinct style or metaphor of programming. These paradigms included functional programming, object-oriented programming, and logic programming.

Functional programming started with the language LISP in 1960. LISP (for "list processing") was oriented toward symbolic programming tasks and became popular in the field of artificial intelligence. It exploited the idea of functions as a kind of first-class data, although in an imperfect form. Scheme (1975) is a technically perfected version of LISP with static (or lexical) variable binding replacing LISP's dynamic binding. ML (1978) and Haskell (1985) are more modern versions of functional languages that differ from LISP and Scheme by incorporating sophisticated static type systems. Haskell is a pure functional language, meaning that it does not permit side effects such as updating of the state of variables, whereas ML is an impure functional programming language because it permits side effects. Functional programming languages promote a style called "value-oriented programming" in which computation consists of transforming one (complex) value into another one without altering or destroying the original value.

Functional programming languages also provided the basis for development of a sophisticated theory of types. Type systems in functional programming languages such as ML and Haskell support safety through static type checking while providing much of the flexibility of dynamically typed languages through the mechanism of parametric polymorphism. They also provide the convenience of automatic inference of types to keep the type system from becoming a burden on the programmer.

Object-oriented programming started with the Simula 67 language (1967), which was a modified form of ALGOL 60. Object-oriented programming is based, naturally enough, on the metaphor of "objects," by which an object is a self-contained unit consisting of private data or state, together with a set of procedures (called "methods") belonging to the object and through which the outside world interacts with the object. For instance, an object representing a circle would contain data defining the position of the center and the radius of the circle, and it might provide methods for moving the center point, for drawing the circle, and for determining whether the circle overlaps with another circle. In most object-oriented programming languages, objects are defined as particular instances of templates called "classes," and classes form a hierarchy in which one class is typically a specialized variant (or subclass) of another, called its "superclass." The relation between subclasses and their superclasses is called "inheritance," and it allows a specialized class of object to be defined incrementally from a more general one by expressing only the differences between the specialized and the general cases. A relation usually also exists between the interfaces or types of a class and its subclasses that allows a specialized object belonging to the subclass to be used anywhere an object of the superclass is acceptable. If the object-oriented language has static typing, this relation between interface types is called "subtyping" or "interface inheritance."

Simula 67 was followed by Smalltalk (1972), and object-oriented features were added to C to produce C++ during the 1980s. Other object-oriented programming languages include Eiffel, Oberon, Java, Objective C, C#, Object Pascal, Modula 3, Python, and Objective Caml. Some of these languages, such as Smalltalk and Java, attempt to adhere to the pure object-oriented approach in which all values are objects, but most of these languages, such as C++ and Simula 67 itself, consist of a base procedural language (e.g., C, ALGOL 60) augmented with object-oriented features. In these mixed languages one can use either the object-oriented or classical procedural style of programming or a mixture of the two.

Logic programming was developed as a byproduct of research during the early 1970s on resolution theorem proving, when Bob Kowalski of the University of Edinburgh noticed that proofs using certain kinds of logical formulae (Horn clauses) could be thought of as computing members of a relation defined by the formulae. This idea was developed into the Prolog programming language during the early 1970s. The Mercury language is a modern version of logic programming.

Besides the members of these major paradigm families, more specialized classes of programming languages exist. APL is the most prominent of a family of array-processing languages. SNOBOL, Icon, and Perl belong to the class of string- or text-processing languages.

A class of relatively small languages is called "scripting languages." This class includes the various UNIX shell languages (the Bourne shell, bash, csh, ksh), tcl, Python, Ruby, and Applescript. Scripting languages tend to have good string-processing facilities but otherwise relatively limited data structure support. They have capabilities for launching external programs (e.g., UNIX commands) and performing system calls for manipulating the file system and other operating system services. Scripting languages are suitable for providing glue to connect a collection of programs and commands into a system, but they do not scale well because they typically have poor support for abstraction and modularity and lack static type checking.

Another category of programming languages that has received more attention lately is domain-specific languages (DSLs). Classical examples of domain-specific languages include database query languages (e.g., SQL), statistical analysis languages (e.g., S), and many command languages or specification languages. Some domain-specific languages are independent, self-contained designs. However, many others are "embedded," meaning that they are implemented as a library of specialized data structures and functions within a general purpose language (such as Scheme or Haskell), perhaps with some syntactic support provided using language facilities such as macros, overloaded function names, and user-defined infix operators.

Spreadsheets also incorporate a kind of domain-specific language in the equations used to define the contents of computed cells. Viewed as rudimentary programming languages, spreadsheets are related to a class of languages called "constraint programming languages." In these languages a computational problem is posed as a set of constraints, and the program performs the computation by invoking algorithms (procedures for solving a mathematical problem in a finite number of steps) that find solutions to the constraints. We can also consider logic programming languages to be constraint programming languages.

Sometimes we speak of text markup languages such as SGML, XML, and HTML as programming languages, but they deal only with expressing the structure of partially structured text. Thus, although they can be said to express the structure of a kind of information, they do not have features that allow one to express how the information is processed. Programs in other languages (CGI scripts in Perl, for instance) are needed to perform the processing and transformation of the data expressed in XML or HTML.

How Programming Languages Work

Programming languages require implementations to enable programs written in the languages to execute on computers. We can take several approaches to implementation. The simplest implementations use interpreters, which are programs that examine the code to be executed and directly perform the specified operations. This approach tends to be fairly simple but results in slow execution.

The next level of sophistication involves the use of a virtual machine (also known as an "abstract machine"), which is an idealized machine for a given language. Programs are translated into virtual machine code, which is then executed by an interpreter for the virtual machine. This approach is used in the Java Virtual Machine (JVM).

The most efficient method of executing a program is to use a tool called a "compiler" to translate the program code to actual machine code for a particular hardware platform (e.g., Pentium or PowerPC). A compiler can perform a deep analysis of the program and translate it in many stages to highly optimized machine code.

Whether an implementation is based on a virtual machine or a full compiler, the first task is to translate the program source code into some internal representation. This internal representation is then analyzed to make sure that it is well formed—that it makes sense. For example, the use of names or variables has to obey certain scoping rules, and in statically typed languages the consistency of operators and their arguments can be checked by a type checker.

Whichever mode of execution is used, it will also require a runtime system that manages the details of memory management, low-level input/output, and so forth, for the user's program. Runtime systems can be minimal programs, or they can be quite sophisticated programs or program libraries, as in the case of languages that require automatic memory management (garbage collection).

The Evolution of Programming Languages

During the long term the advances embodied in novel programming languages gradually filter out the wider programming community. These advances generally involve one of the following factors: (1) increased expressive power, meaning the same functionality can be expressed more simply, with fewer lines of code, (2) higher level of abstraction, meaning fewer low-level details to worry about, and (3) improved safety and robustness, meaning additional classes of errors can be eliminated by the language.

Programming language design has other tradeoffs, such as conciseness of notation versus readability, mathematical rigor versus ease of learning for novices, and power and versatility versus simplicity. The argument between advocates of static typing and dynamic typing goes on, but the advantages of static typing for program design and error detection become increasingly important as the size of programs grows.

The limitations on progress concern various design tradeoffs. Increasing expressiveness and the level of abstraction is perceived to be at odds with efficiency and with the predictability of performance.

However, this tradeoff can be softened by the ever-increasing sophistication of compiler technology and the exponential improvement in hardware capabilities.

One other factor affects the evolution of programming languages. As more and more of the functionality of a system is provided by program libraries or APIs (application programmer interfaces), the programming language itself tends to play the role of a medium for accessing a particular collection of APIs. Because the development of APIs can involve many millions of dollars of investment, this situation works against adopting better programming languages. This situation means that new programming languages need to provide interoperability facilities for calling library functions from old APIs.

In general the progress of programming languages is Darwinian: Good ideas eventually are recognized and have an impact, improving the programmer's intellectual toolset. However, progress is slower than one might expect because the most elegant and technically valuable designs often do not triumph in the marketplace.

David B. MacQueen

See also Compilers; Markup Languages; Open Source Software

FURTHER READING

Begin, T. J., & Gibson, R. G. (1996). *History of programming languages.* Boston: Addison-Wesley.

Bird, R., & Wadler, P. (1988). *Introduction to functional programming.* Upper Saddle River, NJ: Prentice Hall International.

Bruce, K. B. (2002). *Foundations of object-oriented languages.* Cambridge, MA: MIT Press.

Mitchell, J. C. (1996). *Foundations of programming languages.* Cambridge, MA: MIT Press.

Mitchell, J. C. (2003). *Concepts in programming languages.* Cambridge, UK: Cambridge University Press.

Pierce, B. C. (2002). *Types and programming languages.* Cambridge, MA: MIT Press.

Reynolds, J. C. (1998). *Theories of programming languages.* Cambridge, UK: Cambridge University Press.

Sethi, R. (1996). *Programming languages: Concepts and constructs.* Boston: Addison-Wesley.

Stirling, L., & Shapiro, E. (1986). *The art of Prolog.* Cambridge, MA: MIT Press.

PROTOTYPING

In the context of human-computer interaction, a prototype is a preliminary version of a computerized system. The prototype models certain aspects of the final system, but is limited in other ways. Prototyping is a system development approach that involves the construction and testing of prototypes in collaboration with the prospective users. It is often suggested as a mechanism for improving analysis and design in loosely structured high-technology development projects. Prototyping alleviates many of the practical problems posed by the need to define requirements, and it improves design effectiveness by integrating users directly into the design process. In heavily computerized organizations, systems prototyping can be a key mechanism for organizational change.

Categories of Prototypes

There are different categories of prototypes. The simplest is a mock-up that models physical aspects of the final system. Mock-ups are often made of cardboard, wood, or plastic, and for this reason they are non-executable (you cannot use them for actual computing tasks). Instead, overhead projectors and projector screens are used to simulate the output from the system. People manipulate the projectors, thereby carrying out the simulation.

A throwaway prototype is executable; it is developed to inquire into, and to express, requirements. The throwaway is probably the most common and widely used category of prototype. Within this category are user interface prototypes, which have limited functionality and precede the specification process, and specification prototypes, which provide a throwaway working model of an entire system prior to specification and construction.

A quick-and-dirty prototype is an early implementation without prior analysis and design. For practical reasons it often becomes the final system, being revised until the users are satisfied. If revisions continue, they tend to become very complicated and maintenance is exceedingly expensive.

A design-driven prototype is an implementation of a design that is as close to the final system as possible. It is usually made and used for technical experiments. Such a prototype provides a "test-drive" of a traditionally developed system prior to finalization.

An evolutionary prototype is a modifiable, running model of part of a system. It is gradually developed into the final version, which then becomes the system. This form of prototyping underlies many release-oriented software products.

Advantages and Disadvantages of Prototyping

The advantages of prototyping are widely acknowledged. Systematic use of prototypes relieves many of the problems that occur when information systems development is based on extensive use of specifications. Prototypes provide users with a concrete understanding of the proposed computer system, and they eliminate the confusion and potential for misunderstanding that arise from the interpretation of abstract specifications, replacing it with meaningful and direct communication between systems developers and users. As a result, prototypes are a good mechanism for coping with requirements uncertainty.

Because the prototyping concept is so broad, it can accommodate various system development approaches. Prototypes are especially useful when development agility (responsiveness to changing requirements and rapid deployment of systems) is paramount. In such situations, prototyping is often completed with little or no written requirements or software documentation, the prototype becoming a form of operational specification.

Prototyping does have certain disadvantages, however, which have prevented many system development organizations from achieving the maximum benefits of prototyping. They include the inefficiency of prototyped computer systems, the impracticality of large prototypes, the unrealistic expectations created by prototypes, the need to implement a significant part of the system in order to entice real user interaction, and the lack of effective development environments.

More-powerful computers and development environments have helped in alleviating problems with inefficient and ineffective prototypes. The advent of Web development environments has drawn many prototyping projects onto a Web-based foundation, which has made up for the lack of better environments offline. To some extent, these innovations will enable larger prototypes and help developers to satisfy both their own and their users' expectations.

Combining Prototypes and Specifications

Prototyping is sometimes contrasted to specifying, when *specifying* is understood as a development effort divided into phases. The specifications developed in one phase form the primary basis for the subsequent phase. The specifications are an abstract formal listing of the expected system characteristics; developed in isolation from any system construction. Collaboration with users is only undertaken to provide input to and validation of specifications. Because the specifications are abstract, construction issues are postponed and users have no real opportunity to engage their expected "experience" with the final artifacts.

Specifying and prototyping have been compared on an empirical basis in order to identify their relative strengths and weaknesses. One result of this comparison was the software engineer Barry Boehm's 1988 formulation of the spiral model, which combines the use of specifications with user interface or design-driven prototypes. The spiral model employs risk analysis to determine the relevance of either a specification or a prototype. This analysis is conducted regularly, since the relevance of a specification or a prototype is assumed to change as the risks of the project change. However, the spiral model has the disadvantage of fully integrating risk analysis in an essentially specification-based method. Furthermore, although the spiral model allows user interface design and design-driven prototypes, it makes no use of evolutionary prototyping.

When to Use Prototyping

The problems that have been experienced in prototyping processes indicate that it may not always be the proper approach. This observation raises a difficult question: When should prototyping be used? Some attempts to answer this question have focused on the type of the system being developed. Yet it has turned out to be virtually impossible to identify a certain class of software systems that are particularly suited for prototyping. A more elaborate solution is to limit the use of prototyping to certain situations. But classifications of such "ideal" situations are not easy. Indeed, the main problem with the majority of work regarding ideal prototyping situations is the mechanistic manner in which such situations have been classified.

A contingency approach to deciding when to prototype has been suggested. With a contingency approach, a decision about whether prototyping is relevant is made based on factors such as clarity and stability of requirements; project duration, size, and innovativeness; the impact of the development process on the developing organization; performance requirements for the system; user participation; developer experience, particularly with prototyping; the number of intended users of the proposed system; the system's predicted impact on users; and management support.

Risk analysis can also play a part in the decision to use or not to use prototyping. There are known risk factors that need to be considered before undertaking an information system development project. They include the stability, experience, and quality of the development group; the role of information systems in current and future decision-support and corporate services; and recent major information system fiascos. The strength of the contingency approach to decision making is that it detaches the developer from slavish loyalty to particular methods (like prototyping methods or specification methods) that might be inappropriate for a particular setting. Its main drawback is that it determines the relevance of prototyping or specifying from an evaluation of the software project as a whole. It lacks the decision granularity to decide prototyping methods for one part of a large project and specifying methods for another part of the project.

Managing Prototype Development

It can be difficult to manage prototyping because of the process's dependence on iterative activities. The basic management functions of planning and control are complicated because plans are supposed to change with each cycle, and control can be hampered by lack of meaningful progress measurement coupled with the uncontrolled dependence on user cooperation.

There are at least four key issues to resolve in successful prototype management. First, managers, analysts, programmers, and users must agree on the exact objectives of the process. Second, the project management has to come to grips with its limited control over users and users' interactions with designers. Third, because each iteration involving development and subsequent evaluation of a prototype may uncover a multitude of potential revisions and directions for further improvement, developers must have a way of focusing their work. Fourth, developers must find a way to measure the "fit" of each iteration of a prototype, and thus to measure project progress.

Currently, two simple mechanisms are used to resolve the problems. The first is to impose strict limits on the time spent on prototyping. The second is to limit the scope of prototyping by applying prototypes only to very narrow areas of the development process. Both of these mechanisms are simple, but they limit the potentials of prototyping significantly. They preclude the use of prototyping as an overall approach to systems development, which means they preclude evolutionary prototyping. Essentially, one is limited to narrow design and design-driven prototypes in what is otherwise a traditional project.

Risk management is a much stronger approach, because decisions about time and scope are made dynamically on the basis of project risks. Risk analysis also provides a focus on the dangers inherent in moving from system design into system production. This approach not only constrains the role of prototypes in systems development, but also expands the potential benefits by requiring the consideration of risks regarding both functionality and data storage facilities.

Prototyping Tools

A large variety of tools are available to support prototype development. The suite of tools selected will often represent a trade-off between system execution efficiency and development labor. Straightforward software development tools will lead to very efficient prototypes, but the cost of development and iterative redevelopment will be high. Usually prototyping will take advantage of labor-saving software development environments that require less programming time but produce more inefficient prototypes. This trade-off can generally guide selection among tools such as those mentioned below.

Office Suites

Very simple tools can be used with prototyping projects where the prototype is expendable, as is the case with mock-ups and throwaways. Screens and reports can even be represented and partly simulated using word processors, spreadsheets, or graphics packages.

Editors and Compilers

Prototypes can be built using a simple editor and a compiler, just as any other program.

Software Studio Suites

More sophisticated compilers include extensively integrated suites of tools for managing software projects, including special-purpose editors, debuggers, wizards that generate program skeletons, screen painters that build program code from a screen image, and so forth.

Application Generators

These high-level compilers operate from very high-level code, essentially generating prototype programs from specification languages.

Web Development Suites

These development environments allow developers to build websites using WYSIWYG ("what you see is what you get") Web screens, with labor-saving support for interactive forms, formats, graphics, images, templates, and database access.

Database Application Suites

Most major database packages provide (at least optionally) screen generators, report generators, application generators, and Web development facilities as an integrated tool suite for building applications that access data in the database.

Computer-Aided Software Engineering (CASE)

These tool suites, also often available with database packages, provide (at least optionally) code generators that build functioning programs and databases directly from design drawings and specifications. These are the most expensive tool suites, and usually generate pretty inefficient programs. CASE tools are sometimes used as a design suite, with the program code then being developed in another environment.

Bolt-on Enterprise Resource Planning Development Suites

Major enterprise resource planning (ERP) packages will have optional development environments. There may be application generators, special-language environments, and website development tools.

Economics can dominate decisions about tool selection. Where good programming labor is inexpensive and computing machinery is expensive, prototyping with normal compiler tools may prove most attractive. The more efficient code minimizes the production computing resources required to operate the prototype. Where good programming labor is expensive and computing machinery is inexpensive, prototyping with application generators or Web development suites may prove most effective. The more extensive production-computing resources may be justified by the cost savings in development labor. Training costs must be considered, however. CASE tools, and to a lesser extent application generators, database suites, and Web suites, can be complex and unique settings, and may involve extensive training costs for developers.

Economics can sometimes yield to expediency. Developers may choose to develop prototypes with whatever tools are well known to the developers. Such a reduction in the tool learning curve has its benefits when speed is of the essence. When it becomes urgent to assemble a prototype, the developers may well grab whatever tools are at hand, rather than spend time making a rational tool selection decision.

Future Directions

Because of its many benefits, prototyping has become a widely practiced technique and a component in many broader systems development methodologies. It remains a strong alternative to specifying approaches and will likely remain as one of the central techniques for systems analysis in the foreseeable future.

Richard Baskerville and Jan Stage

See also Beta Testing; User-Centered Design

FURTHER READING

Alavi, M. (1984). An assessment of the prototyping approach to information systems development. *Communications of the ACM, 27*(6), 556–563.

Baskerville, R., & Stage, J. (1996). Controlling prototype development through risk analysis. *MIS Quarterly, 20*(4), 481–504.

Boar, B. H. (1984). *Application prototyping: A requirements definition strategy for the 80s.* New York: John Wiley & Sons.

Boehm, B. W. (1988). A spiral model of software development and enhancement. *Computer, 21*(5), 61–72.

Boehm, B., Gray, T., & Seewaldt, T. (1984). Prototyping versus specifying: A Multiproject experiment. *IEEE Transactions on Software Engineering SE-10*(3), 290–302.

Budde, R., Kuhlenkamp, K., Mathiassen, L., & Züllighoven, H. (Eds.). (1984). *Approaches to prototyping.* Berlin, Germany: Springer-Verlag.

Burns, R. & Dennis, A. (1985). Selecting the appropriate application development methodology. *Data Base, 17*(1), 19–23.

Cockburn, A. (2001). *Agile software development.* Reading, MA: Addison-Wesley.

Connell, J. L., & Schafer, L.B. (1989). *Structured rapid prototyping.* Englewood Cliffs, NJ: Yourdon Press.

Davis, G. B. (1982). Strategies for information requirement determination. *IBM Systems Journal, 21*(1), 4–30.

Ehn, P. (1988). *Work-oriented design of computer artifacts.* Stockholm: Arbetslivscentrum.

Grønbæk, K. (1990). Supporting active user involvement in prototyping. *Scandinavian Journal of Information Systems, 2*, 3–24.

Hardgrave, B. C., Wilson, R. L., & Eastman, K. (1999). Toward a contingency model for selecting an information system prototyping strategy. *Journal of Management Information Systems, 16*(2), 113–137.

Iivari, J., & Karjalainen M. (1989). Impact of prototyping on user information satisfaction during the IS specification phase. *Information & Management, 17*(1), 31–45.

Lantz, K. E. (1988). *The prototyping methodology.* Englewood Cliffs, NJ: Prentice Hall.

Mason, R., & Carey, T. Prototyping interactive information systems. *Communications of the ACM, 26*(5), 347–354.

Moynihan, T. (2000). Coping with requirements-uncertainty: The theories-of-action of experienced IS/software project managers. *The Journal of Systems and Software, 53*(2), 99–109.

Naumann, J., & Jenkins, A. (1982). Prototyping: The new paradigm for systems development. *MIS Quarterly, 6*(3), 29–44.

Porra, J. (1999). Colonial systems. *Information Systems Research, 10*(1), 38–70.

Snyder, C. (2003). *Paper prototyping: The fast and easy way to design and refine user interfaces.* New York: Morgan Kaufmann.

Vonk, R. (1990). *Prototyping: The effective use of CASE technology.* New York: Prentice Hall.

PSYCHOLOGY AND HCI

Human-computer interaction (HCI) is intimately intertwined with psychology. The field of HCI emerged as a special blend of human factors, cognitive psychology, engineering psychology, design, and computer science. The advent of generally available computing in the 1970s and the personal computer in the 1980s brought with them a concern that the interfaces were difficult to use, making people miserable and their work slow and frustrating. Psychologists were involved in human-factors research (research into designing equipment and environments for optimum human functioning) since World War II, so their interest in the problems of design in computing was a natural extension.

Psychology is the study of human behavior, ranging from the study of how neurons and physical structures determine behavior, to individual cognitive and emotional mechanisms, to the behavior of small groups and large organizations. Psychologists are interested in understanding both how computers are affecting people and how to design computers to fit better with human needs and capabilities. Because the computer is a very malleable and interactive tool, there has been a great interest in studying both its design and the effects of computer use on human behavior at all levels.

HCI and Organizational Psychology

Traditional HCI focuses on individuals and their interactions with the functionality offered through computer interfaces. Computer-supported cooperative work (CSCW) is an HCI specialty that focuses on group- and organizational-level issues.

For example, a key research finding at the organizational level is what is called the productivity paradox. Since the early 1990s, researchers have found zero correlation between the amount a company spent on information technology and the resulting productivity. Thomas Landauer, a psychologist, attributed this to poor design: The technologies are so difficult to learn and use that although they speed up some aspects of work, they slow down others. More recently Eric Brynjolfsson, a professor of management, has shown a small but positive correlation between money spent on information technology and productivity. Landauer would attribute that to an increase in user-centered design, which makes the technology easier to use.

In the late 1980s, the computer scientist Jonathan Grudin examined why people do not adopt various technologies that are intended to help them coordinate their work (like group calendars, for example). He found that many technologies benefited people other than the ones who had to expend the effort to enter information and keep it up to date. For example, a group calendar requires people to enter their meetings and appointments and keep them up to date so that others, such as their managers, can schedule more meetings. The cost is to the individual, but the benefit is to the manager. When calendars added features that benefited the person who had to expend the effort, they were suddenly widely adopted.

This issue of technology adoption ties in with issues of organizational change and change agents (technology being one such agent). Research may reveal remedies that facilitate technology adoption, either through suggesting changes in the design of the technology itself or in the design of the introduction of the technology to the people. There is a great deal known in organizational psychology that can be applied to the successful design and adoption of information technology.

Researchers in a related field, management information systems (MIS) in business schools, have researched important HCI-like topics, such as the effect of monitoring employee performance by computer (loss of control, the occasional lack of fit of the measure to the intended behavior) and the kinds of organizational structures that are helped most by various technologies.

HCI and Small-Group Behavior

Social psychology has long studied group dynamics, trust, and impression formation, which are relevant to the study of how technology changes the behavior in groups. For example, there are a number of studies that show that people who communicate over video have little advantage over those with only audio in getting their work done. However, people prefer the video format to the audio-only format. Audio-only is hard. Without video, people lose valuable cues to turn taking and cannot discern whether their points are being understood or agreed with or not. People talk longer when they have no feedback about whether they are understood or not.

Trust is another relevant phenomenon that social psychologists have investigated. The old adage says "Trust needs touch." Many people insist that a team needs to meet face-to-face in order to establish and maintain trust. Work in 2000 has shown, however, that if the team members engage in a social activity, even if they are not face-to-face, trust can and does form. It forms a bit more slowly, but in time it reaches the same levels as it would have had the team members met face-to-face.

Unfortunately, if a group contains both people who are collocated and people who are remote, those at a distance may be ignored and in some cases disadvantaged. Theories from social psychology suggest that this is because when dealing with people at a distance we lose the social cues, it takes more effort to communicate remotely, and any wrong step can cost a person membership in an "in-group." Stud-

ies of telecommuting show that the principle of "out of sight, out of mind" applies. People who work remotely are passed over for promotion and not informed of important information.

The psychological concept of distributed cognition has similarly been embraced by those in HCI, especially those in CSCW. The core idea in distributed cognition is that the things that make us smart are in our environment; they include artifacts, other people, and the placement of both in space, not just in our heads. Studies of teams of pilots or ship controllers have shown that they construct cheat sheets and other aids and/or place team members in clear sight of each other to make their cognition easy at various stressful points. This recognition leads us to construct computer-based aids to team or individual performance, in particular looking at ways to use visual displays, for example, to help decision making or problem solving.

Researchers in HCI and CSCW have also worked with the concepts from psycholinguistics, primarily looking at the nature of conversations and the achievement of common ground. Common ground is people's shared understanding of what they all know so that conversations include the right vocabulary and level of detail. Analysis of conversations with and without video, for example, show that it is easier to achieve common ground if you can see the visual cues of understanding or not. Without the visual cues of heads nodding or furrowed brows, people have to explicitly check with one another to see if they have understood or not.

Much of the work in social psychology relating to group dynamics has also been extended to the world of technology support for teamwork. The psychologist Joseph McGrath and his colleagues studied how groups form over time when they are not collocated and how moving people in and out of the collocated workspace affected trust buildup and people's attention to one another and. Others have studied how different types of personalities affect the progress of groups, and that research too can be applied to the world of remote work. Researchers and practitioners in the business world are trying to assess which types of people would be good at working from home or telecommuting, and which would not.

A Personal Story— Human Factors Come into the Forefront

As part of the Berkshire Publishing team working on this encyclopedia, I've seen the field of human factors engineering mentioned a number of times as an important foundation in the history of HCI. Each time, I thought about my uncle, Allan Stave, who entered this field when it was relatively new in 1958.

Allan was a navy pilot, who went on to study psychology after he was discharged from the service. He combined his experience in the cockpit with his academic training to become a human factors engineer for an aerospace company. It was always hard to wrap our minds around what Uncle Allan actually did. But eventually we got it. His job was to influence the design of equipment and procedures so that people using these devices would not make errors. Or, if an error is made, the resulting situation would be: (1) obvious to the person that an error had been made, and (2) the problem could be "put right" without serious consequences.

With an always-inquiring mind and a keen insight into human nature, Allan was a natural in this field. To get his firsthand view of the field, I asked him to describe the need for a human factors attitude in the design process. His response follows below:

> During the early years of human factors, designers' major problems (as they saw them) were to accomplish the job as inexpensively as possible and within the time frame allowed. They didn't concern themselves with possible problems that users would encounter once the design and production process was complete. They didn't understand that equipment which was easy to design and build might not be easy to use. Whereas the design and construction of a piece of equipment might require one or two years to complete, the people who had to use this equipment would have to live with it (and maintain it) for twenty or so years. To this end, it is cheaper in the long run if effort is expended in the design process to make equipment easy to use and maintain. In many cases the cost of design and construction is dwarfed by the cost of operation and maintenance. It may be a lot more work for engineers and production people, but it always pays off in the end. The basic task of human factors personnel is to find out what's required by the people who'll be operating the system and get it designed properly the first time—rather than getting it out the door and fixing it later.

Like I said, it's not an easy field to wrap your mind around, but once you do, it becomes clear how essential it is that human factors engineers have a hand in the design of equipment ranging from cockpit instrument panels to medical devices.

Marcy Ross

In 2000, the HCI scholars Judy and Gary Olson published their findings on remote work, called "Distance Matters." They highlighted the human aspects of teamwork that will never be solved with technology, such as cultural misunderstandings and circadian rhythms. The more we connect with people who are remote, the more likely we are to encounter people very different from us—the cultural distance will always be there. With large cultural differences, it is harder to achieve common ground and talk efficiently and effectively. Too much has to be explained. In addition, time zones and circadian rhythms cannot be overcome with technology. The Olsons noted that although when people travel they normally accommodate to the place visited, in videoconferencing, no one travels, and so less accommodation happens. Misunderstandings ensue.

HCI and Individual Psychology

In 1983, Stuart Card, Tom Moran and Alan Newell wrote a seminal book called *The Psychology of Human Computer Interaction*. In it, they compiled the findings about individual cognition that had to be attended to if computers were going to be easy to learn to use and then to use. This included facts about visual and auditory sensation, recognition, memory, problem solving, motor movement, and decision making.

In addition, they created a composite model called GOMS. GOMS has two parts: a knowledge base, and an engine that uses that knowledge base to act. The knowledge base consists of goals, operators, methods, and selection rules (hence the name GOMS); these four components specify what knowledge someone has to have in order to use a particular computer system. The engine, called the model human processor, uses parameters of human behavior (such as how long it takes to type, to point with a mouse, and so forth) in conjunction with this knowledge base and particulars of the environment (for example, the task to be performed) to predict behavior. The researchers also created a simplified version of this model called the keystroke-level model that helps predict how long it will take someone to do a task, taking into account both the physical (keystrokes) and mental (choosing between methods, retrieving a method) steps. In the mid-1990s, David Meyer and David Kieras added new components to the model to create EPIC (Executive Process, Interactive Control). EPIC focuses heavily on the perceptual motor aspects of using a computer and predicts well with complex multimodal tasks.

On a more practical level, many of the guidelines for designing computer systems and the methods for evaluating them rely on findings from cognitive psychology. Gestalt principles of perception (broadly, that people perceive things as unified wholes rather than as collections of parts) guide the layout of visual displays. Fitts's Law, which concerns how rapidly a person can move from one point to another, guides keyboard design and the on-screen areas that can be selected or clicked on. An evaluation method called Cognitive Walkthough instructs the evaluator to ask questions about what users know how to do, whether they can find what they are looking for easily on the screen, whether they can perform the correct action easily, and whether they will understand what they just did. The method gets inside of the head of the users and assesses their knowledge, recognition, action, and understanding.

A recent addition to our understanding of how people behave with computers comes from a psychological construct of moment-by-moment analysis of the costs and benefits of doing various things. Stuart Card and Peter Pirolli have investigated and modeled people's search behavior on the Web, noting how long they will continue with the results of a search, when they will quit and start a new search, and so forth. They call this behavior information foraging, with the analogy being to animals' foraging for food. People make assessments of the likelihood that the next item will be good based on their assessment of the fit of the items up to that point, much the way a bird will continue in an orchard if he has success finding fruit. They use a concept called information scent to characterize that assessment.

The personality psychologist Sherry Turkle takes a very different approach to understanding the psychological aspects of human-computer interaction. Her books *Life on the Screen: Identity in the Age of the Internet* and *The Second Self: Computers and the Human Spirit* explore the feelings people have about their identity when taking a false persona in a chat room, or, in her case, finding that someone else was taking her identity. She also explores the thought patterns of the new generation of children, who refer to real life as RL and exclaim that some natural things look "realistic."

Although not much has been done at the neural psychological level with computer interfaces, there have been a few intriguing experiments. People have been successful in manipulating a computer interface through their brain waves. The performance artist Stelarc went one step further, making it possible through a neural connection for someone to send a command to Stelarc's muscle over the Internet, causing muscles to move. Stelarc has explored a number of other direct connections as well, including a robotic exoskeleton and a third ear and arm that are controlled by his brain.

Methods from Psychology

One of the earliest contributions psychologists made to the field of HCI was their set of methods. In HCI, we observe people at work to find out not just what they do at the computer but also how they organize their work setting. We observe them using the computer and note all the pausing, fumbling, going down wrong paths that occurs when they are having difficulty. In psychology this is called naturalistic observation.

Methods from experimental psychology have given computer designers the ability to evaluate various features, comparing people's times and errors with various designs. Usability studies are similar to psychology experiments: Users are given a standardized task to do with a computer and monitored for their time, errors, and attitudes, just as subjects in traditional psychology experiments are give a task to perform and monitored as they perform it. HCI has adopted psychology's rigorous standards for experimentation when it comes to testing both individual interface designs and general principles. For example, research into Fitts's Law (which says that a user's speed and accuracy selecting objects on a computer screen depends on the object's size and how far the user has to move the pointer) has generated ideas about different kinds of computer menu designs, including circular menus and menus in which the further down the menu you go, the larger the area you click in.

Methods that ask people to sort items into categories have been used by computer designers to guide menu organization. Experiments have also been used to determine readability of fonts, color contrast, and other features of visual display. Additionally, experiments have helped determine how quickly things can move on the screen and still be successfully followed by the user. When windows open on the computer, they do not open instantly; you can see them get bigger—this is because the user sees the casual tie between their action (clicking on the file name) and the reaction (the enlarging window). Research also reveals what many of us know instinctively: that people are not very good at labeling files to be recognized by others or even by themselves at a later time.

What HCI Gives Back to Psychology

HCI is often thought of as an applied field, with psychology and other disciplines contributing to it. We believe, however, that in attempting to solve practical problems of design, HCI uncovers fundamental psychological phenomena, thereby contributing to both the practical and scientific world. Three big contributions HCI has made to psychology are integrated cognitive modeling (EPIC, inspired by GOMS), the theory of information foraging, and new methods for collecting data over the Internet.

As mentioned earlier, EPIC grew from the GOMS model, putting known component cognitive processes and stores together to predict complex behavior. In the spirit of other cognitive modeling efforts, the authors set a cognitive architecture and then program tasks using that architecture. A cognitive architecture is a set of assumptions about aspects of cognition that are relatively stable over time and relatively independent of the task. The architecture has an unlimited working memory in which information decays over time, a rehearsal process with particular time constants, separate perceptual and motor processors that have different time constants, and so forth. The model already has accounted for a wide variety of known phenomena in psychology. Because the model is programmed, it is easier to discover conflicting accounts of phenomena; the model makes thinking precise.

Information-foraging theory uses mathematically based ideas from biological food foraging to describe how people search for information. When some of the behaviors that Stuart Card and Peter Pirolli wanted to specify could not be easily put into mathematical terms, they turned to computer simulation. They also observed real people doing searches, both at their computers and in the library noting how information, books, stacks of

Virtual Flight for White-Knuckled Travelers

ATLANTA (ANS)—An estimated 25 million Americans are afraid of flying. Some are so paralyzed by the thought of getting on a plane that they're willing to forego vacations, and even career advancements, just to stay on the ground.

Now these white-knuckled infrequent flyers can get on a simulated airplane as part of a new therapy designed to treat anxiety disorders.

Developed by a psychologist and computer scientist, the virtual airplane ride feels like the real thing, with earphones and goggles creating the visual and sound environment and a special vibrating chair creating the feeling of being in a plane in flight.

Meanwhile, a therapist sits nearby at a computer and, by pushing a few buttons, simulates take-off, taxiing, smooth and turbulent flights, landings—whatever element of a flight a person finds most daunting.

"When they look around, they're immersed in this virtual airplane," said Barbara Rothbaum, developer of the virtual flight and a professor in the department of psychiatry at the Emory University School of Medicine.

It works as well as more traditional therapies, she said. In a controlled study of the system, participants who boarded the virtual airplane were as likely to feel better about flying afterward as those who were given what is called exposure therapy, which involves actually getting on a flight.

Experts say fear of flying is a common phobia. Confronting the fear head-on by getting on a plane with a therapist after a series of counseling sessions has proved effective, but it is time consuming, expensive and simply impossible for those whose fear is extreme.

The virtual flight is far less intimidating, Rothbaum said, much less expensive and potentially more useful to busy therapists. The whole system will cost less than $5,000, and Rothbaum expects it to be popular among social workers, hospitals and therapists.

"It does translate into real life," the professor said.

She is so enthused about the technology's possibilities that she is now planning a study that will test a slightly altered version of the therapy on those with a fear of heights, public speaking and highway driving.

Source: Virtual flight holds promise for white-knuckled travelers. American News Service, August 17, 2000.

paper, etc. were physically arranged. The theory predicted that a particular type of interface would support more effective searching, so Card and Pirolli built and tested it, confirming the design's value. Their research is an excellent example of a multi-method investigation such as one rarely sees in psychology.

The last contribution is the design of Web-based experiments. It is now possible to collect data from thousands of people cheaply over the Internet. Questionnaires and surveys can be posted to sites such as SurveyMonkey.com, which will then send it out to a sample the researcher specifies and compile the results. Experiments can also be run online: Social psychologist Mahzarin Banaji, for example, has people download a small applet that then tests their reaction times to various pairs of words that can indicate people's stereotypes and prejudices. More than 1.5 million responses have been collected at the site, a sample size far larger than any laboratory experiment could ever hope to collect.

Internet chat rooms are good places to observe interesting behavior—for example, researchers have been interested in seeing the reactions people get when they adopt a persona with a gender that is different from their own. Weblogs, or blogs, which are online journals or diaries, are also interesting sources of psychological data.

Psychologists and HCI in the Twenty-First Century

It is hard to think of any new technology that will *not* have psychological ramifications. In the twenty-first century, technology makes it possible for robots to be members of caretaker teams for the elderly; repair people can have the repair manual for the device they are repairing directly projected into their eyes by projectors mounted on glasses, the computer itself embedded in their clothing. Computers can sense tension in the user and suggest activities to reduce it. People can hear again thanks to cochlear implants—basically microchips that translate sound into neural pulses. As soon as children can reach a keyboard, there are educational and entertainment

programs for them. People deeply care about robot pets. The World Wide Web is changing how we educate ourselves, both in the classroom and everyday life.

Sherry Turkle continues her study of identity and what it means to be human as the twenty-first century unfolds. For example, she is uncomfortable with an elderly person saying "I love you" to a robot and the robot saying "I love you" back. Although computers can be reactive in appropriate ways to people, she feels the emotion expressed in that instance is inauthentic, and thus troubling. Psychologists and people in HCI are likely to continue to be kept busy as the world embraces new information technology as fast as it is developed.

Judith S. Olson

See also Collaboratories; Cognitive Walkthrough; Social Psychology and HCI

FURTHER READING

Brynjolfsson, E. (2003). The IT productivity gap. *Optimize, 7*(21). Retrieved December 16, 2003, from http://ebusiness.mit.edu/erik/Optimize/pr_roi.html

Card, S. K., Moran, T. P., & Newell, A. (1983). *The psychology of human computer interaction.* Hillsdale, NJ: Lawrence Erlbaum Associates.

Clark, H. H., & Brennan, S. E. (1991). Grounding in communication. In L. Resnick, J. M. Levine, & S. D. Teasley (Eds.), *Perspectives on socially shared cognition* (pp. 127–149).Washington, DC: American Psychological Association.

Finn, K., Sellen, A., & Wilbur, S. (Eds.). (1997). *Video-mediated communication.* Hillsdale NJ: Lawrence Erlbaum Associates.

Grudin, J. (1988). Why CSCW applications fail: Problems in the design and evaluation of organizational interfaces. *Proceedings of the ACM Conference on Computer Supported Cooperative Work* (pp. 85–93). Portland, OR: ACM Press.

Hollingshead, A. B., McGrath, J. E., and O'Connor, K. M. (1993). Group performance and communication technology: A longitudinal study of computer-mediated versus face-to-face work. *Small Group Research, 24*(3), 307–333.

Hutchins, E. (1991). The social organization of distributed cognition. In L. B. Resnick, J. M. Levine, & S. D. Teasley (Eds.*)*, *Perspectives on socially shared cognition.* (pp. 283–307). Washington: American Psychological Association.

Kieras, D. E., Wood, S. D., and Meyer, D. E. (1995). Predictive engineering models using the EPIC architecture for high-performance task. In *Proceedings of the ACM Conference on Human Factors in Computing Systems, CHI '95.* (pp. 11–18). Denver, CO: ACM Press.

Landauer, T. K. (1997). *The trouble with computers: Usefulness, usability, and productivity.* Cambridge, MA: MIT Press.

McGrath, J. E., & Hollingshead, A. B. (1994). *Groups interacting with technology.* Thousand Oaks, CA: Sage.

Olson, G. M., & Olson, J. S. (2000). Distance matters. *Human-Computer Interaction, 15*(2–3), 139–178.

Sproull, L., & Kiesler, S. (1991*). Connections: New ways of working in the networked organization.* Cambridge, MA: MIT Press.

Turkle, S. (1984*) The second self: Computers and the human spirit.* New York: Simon & Schuster.

Turkle, S. (1995). *Life on the screen: Identity in the age of the Internet.* New York: Simon & Schuster.

Veinott, E. S., Olson, J. S., Olson, G. M., and Fu, X. (1997). Video matters! When communication ability is stressed, video helps. In S. Pemberton (Ed.), *Proceedings of the ACM Conference on Human Factors in Computing Systems, CHI '97* (pp. 315–316). New York: ACM Press.

PUNCH CARDS

See Atanasoff-Berry Computer; Hollerith Cards

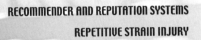

RECOMMENDER AND REPUTATION SYSTEMS

Recommender and reputation systems draw on the experiences of some people to make recommendations to other people. The recommendations may be about movies, cars, messages on computer bulletin boards, or businesses. In short, any time the past is predictive of the future, recommender and reputation systems can help people make informed choices about what to pay attention to or consume and with whom to interact.

Of course, recommending based on the experiences of other people did not originate with computer systems. Word of mouth and gossip surely predate the written word. In the modern era institutions such as credit reporting agencies, the Better Business Bureau, and Zagat's restaurant guides have emerged to gather and distribute recommendations about people and businesses.

Information and communication technologies such as the Internet, however, have enabled new ways for people to gather information about past experiences, aggregating that information into recommendations and distributing the recommendations. In short, recommender and reputation systems involve more people and provide recommendations on more topics than were possible during the pre-Internet era.

Examples of Recommender Systems

The website Amazon.com uses multiple recommender systems to help people choose among vast selections of books and other products. For example, when a customer looks at the sales page for a book, Amazon finds in its database other purchasers of that book. A system then recommends other products based on what those people purchased. Amazon displays the products under the heading, "Customers who bought this book also bought:."

The website MovieLens (http://movielens.umn.edu) is a movie recommender system maintained by researchers at the University of Minnesota. Users rate movies, and the system makes predictions about how well they will like other movies.

The website eBay.com is a large online auction site that uses a reputation system to provide feedback about users who buy and sell goods. Because purchasing goods from a stranger can be risky, the reputation system collects comments on previous interactions. This system gives a potential buyer some sense of whether a seller's previous customers were satisfied.

The website Slashdot.org is a news site dedicated to stories about technology issues. As each story is posted, users can comment on it, and other users rate those comments as good or bad. This system acts as a recommender for which comments are worth reading. Also, as comments are moderated, the authors of the comments accrue or lose "karma." Karma scores act as a reputation system to provide information about who is a valuable contributor to the site.

The website Google.com is one of the most widely used Web search engines in the world and uses a recommender system called "PageRank" to order results in response to search queries. PageRank treats a link from another website as an indicator that the author of the other site found a page valuable. Google incorporates the number of incoming links as one factor in its decision about which pages to recommend and in what order.

The History of Recommender Systems

Recommender systems have a long history in non-technical settings, including restaurant guides and movie reviews. The development of computer-supported recommender systems is a more recent phenomenon.

Several ways exist to select information based on text matching of contents, but they are most effective at detecting relevance rather than quality. During the early 1990s several prototype recommender systems were developed that shared quality evaluations among users. Important systems during this time period recommended Usenet (a worldwide distributed discussion system) news articles, movies, and songs, among other things. These systems pioneered the concepts and algorithms (procedures for solving a mathematical problem in a finite number of steps that frequently involve repetition of an operation) that would form the basis of future recommender systems.

With the advent of the World Wide Web recommender systems left the research laboratory and became widely used by the public. Early manifestations of recommender systems on the Web included "cool links" pages, which created lists of recommendations of other sites that were considered worth visiting. Eventually these lists became unwieldy because of the large numbers of users, and automated forms of recommenders became more prevalent, especially in electronic commerce (e-commerce) applications. An early example was Amazon.com, which received wide attention, for both the successes and the failures of its book recommendation system.

Now recommender systems are so common on the World Wide Web that they no longer attract attention: They have become almost invisible. Recommender systems are used to help people purchase everything from clothes to travel to wine. Online communities use recommender systems liberally in trying to build trust and recognition among their members.

Types of Recommender Systems

Recommender systems have become increasingly familiar during the past several years, although often they go by different names, such as "social filtering," "collaborative filtering," and "reputation systems."

People's tastes differ for many products. Recommender systems can cater to varying tastes by tailoring recommendations to each person. The latest *Star Wars* movie will be highly recommended for some people but not for others. To make personalized recommendations, collaborative filtering systems first identify neighbors with similar preferences. The users' preferences may be inferred from their actions, such as reading an article or buying a book, or the user is required to explicitly enter subjective reviews or evaluations. For example, people who rate the same movies highly would be close neighbors, but those people whose ratings are frequently in conflict would not be. The system then recommends movies that were highly rated by close neighbors, ignoring the ratings of people with different tastes.

Reputation Systems: Incentives and Selection Effects

Sometimes what is being recommended is another user rather than a service or product. Analogous to other recommender systems, a reputation system informs people about who has been trustworthy so the people can choose whom to trust. For example, at eBay, buyers may avoid bidding on items from sellers who have received a lot of negative feedback.

When meeting face to face, people use small cues to determine characteristics of each other. Visual channels provide cues to age, gender, ethnicity, even status. Auditory cues are used to determine emotion, trustworthiness, and intent, among other things. When operating through the Internet or other contemporary computer technologies, these channels of information are usually lost, and people have difficulty determining if another person online can be trusted. Reputation systems aggregate the history of others' interactions to act as a proxy for those lost cues.

In addition to merely informing people, reputation systems perform two functions that are not so prominent in other recommender systems. First, they provide incentives for good behavior. Knowing that they will be rated, people may choose to be more honest or offer a better service than they otherwise would.

Second, reputation systems can discourage a phenomenon that economists call "adverse selection." Consider eBay, for example. If buyers were unable to distinguish reliable from unreliable sellers, then reliable sellers would get paid the same amount as unreliable sellers. However, the best sellers might find that price too low and thus would not participate in the market. High-quality sellers are more likely to participate in a market where they know buyers will be able to recognize their quality.

Entities in the system need to be long lived. A person needs to have a history of interactions in order for other people to be able to tell anything about that person. If it's too easy to switch identities, it's hard to build up that history.

Feedback about current interactions is captured and distributed. New users in the system should be able to see what others have found out about other users.

Past feedback guides the decisions of others. The system should help users make decisions about whom to trust and how much. Without this help, no incentive effect for good seller behavior would exist, nor any antidote to the problem of adverse selection.

Design Issues

The successful implementation of recommender systems requires attention to many design issues. One of the issues is the design of appropriate user interfaces. These interfaces include interfaces for inputting preferences or ratings as well as interfaces that return the results of the recommender back to the end user. First, on the input side, users should understand what it is that they are rating. They should understand whether they are rating a user or a piece of content, for instance. Users should also be able to tell how their ratings will be used and interpreted. For example, on a numeric scale, is a five a good score and a one a bad score, or the opposite? Does rating an item "up" mean that the user perceived it as good on some absolute scale or as better than the current score assigned to the item?

On the output side as well users need to understand the intended meaning of recommendations, and users generally prefer to understand how the recommendations were generated. Amazon, for example, has links to explain how recommendations were generated. The interface often allows the end users to change the structure of the information they receive based on the recommendations. Slashdot, for example, allows users to hide comments below a certain score threshold.

In general, systems can either suggest one or more items that are recommended or they can provide numeric scores. A high score is a prediction that the user will like an item; a low score acts as a negative recommendation.

Prediction scores might be displayed either numerically or visually with bar graphs or a number of stars. Predictions can also be used to sort items, so that the most highly recommended items appear first. Finally, low-scoring items can be filtered out, as with Slashdot's threshold system for hiding low-scoring comments.

Designers of recommender systems need to determine how the systems will elicit ratings from users. This determination includes both the form that the ratings will take and how the ratings will enter the system. Ratings can take many forms, including written reviews, simple votes, scaled ratings, or categorization. All of these forms have their own implications for the implementation of the system.

One method of eliciting ratings is to depend on explicit feedback by which users make the conscious choice to enter their preferences and ratings into the system. This method has the benefit of allowing richer personalization but often requires too much effort from users, especially if many ratings are required from users. In addition, some users may "free ride"—simply use data provided by other users without providing any of their own. Designers have responded to these issues by keeping instances of explicit user feedback simple and easy for any single user. For example, eBay solicits a relatively simple vote from a single user and depends on the aggregate data of many users to generate reputations. Less often, designers of recommender systems tie the provision of feedback to a user's own reputation within the system. Slashdot adds points to users' reputations when the users use all of their assigned votes.

Another way to avoid burdening users is to estimate what their preferences are by mining traces of their behavior in the system. Amazon does this mining by capturing which products people search for or buy, without requiring the people to explicitly rate things.

Another problem that can occur in designing systems to elicit feedback is the improper use of rating privileges. This problem can occur either because the system is not sensitive to errors in the rating mechanism or because users are trying to use loopholes in the system to acquire advantages over other users. In the first instance, numerous ways exist by which a system might engender errors in eliciting feedback. If too few users enter ratings into the system, sometimes users come to an early, negative consensus on what is being rated. In systems that allow unlimited ratings, users sometimes engage in "vote dumping"—rating large numbers of items without carefully considering their actual preference for those items.

Users often have some incentive to bend the rules of the recommender system to meet their own personal goals. Users of eBay might create false identities to vote up a main identity and hence seem more dependable than they are. Slashdot users often create multiple identities to be able to write comments that they know would negatively affect their reputation.

Recommender systems continue to grow in both prevalence and complexity. As more users come online, and as information sources become richer, the challenge will be to make ever more effective use of people's experiences to guide other users while keeping the systems easy to understand and use.

Cliff Lampe and Paul Resnick

See also Information Retrieval; Online Questionnaires

FURTHER READING

Avery, C., Resnick, P., & Zeckhauser, R. (1999). The market for evaluations. *American Economic Review, 89*(3), 564–584.

Doctorow, C. (2003). *Down and out in the Magic Kingdom.* New York: Tor Books.

Friedman, E. J., & Resnick, P. (1997). The social cost of cheap pseudonyms. *Journal of Economics and Management Strategy, 10*(2), 173–179.

Raymond, E. S. (2000). *The cathedral and the bazaar: Musings on Linux and Open Source by an accidental revolutionary.* Sebastopol, CA: O'Reilly & Associates.

Resnick, P., & Varian, H. (1997). Recommender systems [Special issue]. *Communications of the ACM, 40*(3).

Resnick, P., Zeckhauser, R., Friedman, E., & Kuwabara, K. (2000, December). Reputation systems. *Communications of the ACM, 3*(12), 45–48.

Rheingold, H. (2003). *Smart mobs: The next social revolution.* Cambridge, MA: Perseus.

Riedl, J., Vrooman, E., Gladwell, M. (2002). *Word of mouse: The marketing power of collaborative filtering.* New York: Warner Books.

Terveen, L., & Hill, W. (2001). Beyond recommender systems: Helping people help each other. In J. M. Carroll (Ed.), *HCI in the new millennium* (p. 273). New York: Addison-Wesley.

REPETITIVE STRAIN INJURY

Chronic musculoskeletal disorders (MSDs) associated with computer work have increased since the early 1990s. These disorders range in severity from mild symptoms to functional impairment and can occur in any job with repetition, force, awkward postures, vibration, and cold. Both prevention and treatment of these disorders rely heavily on interventions based on a holistic approach to human-computer interaction. These interventions include the specific designs of the input devices used as well as the design and organization of the human-computer interaction (HCI) workstation.

HCI Health

Musculoskeletal disorders, also known as "repetitive strain injuries" or "cumulative trauma disorders," are prevalent in today's office, with more than 50 percent of newly hired computer users experiencing MSDs within the first year on a job. Problems include eyestrain, neck and shoulder pain, low back pain, elbow pain (tendinitis), forearm pain (muscles), and nerve entrapments. Specific diagnoses include deQuervain's tenosynovitis (inflammation of a tendon sheath), medial and lateral epicondylitis (tennis elbow), carpal tunnel syndrome, radial tunnel syndrome, cubital tunnel syndrome, and thoracic outlet syndrome. Carpal tunnel syndrome is often inappropriately diagnosed and should be accompanied by a series of tests completed by an appropriately trained physician, such as a neurologist and/or rheumatologist. More details about these disorders can be obtained through the U.S. National Library of Medicine and the National Institutes of Health.

Treatments of such disorders range from simple work modification to surgery. Because early intervention is best in reducing severity, computer workers who feel pain while they work should consult a medical professional as soon as possible. Modifying the workstation is a necessary step to reduce the stressors and to prevent the injury from reoccurring.

Workstation modification should address two components: reducing the stress on the musculoskeletal system and allowing the tissues to rest, including during microbreaks. These two components are based on possible pathology associated with injury mechanisms. First, an injury occurs when the physical load on the tissue is above the tolerance for that tissue. Second, an injury occurs when the rate of tissue damage exceeds the rate of repair. For each repetitive loading of a tissue, a small amount of damage normally goes unnoticed. For chronic disorders the body may not be able to keep up with the small damage processes taking place with each repetitive loading. For example, wearing splints at night allows for this repair process to take place for carpal tunnel syndrome by maintaining a neutral and relaxed wrist posture.

The risk factors for musculoskeletal disorders—force, repetition, and awkward postures—are all present in human-computer interaction. Many factors in the office can affect a worker's exposure to these risk factors. Time at the computer is the most commonly reported risk factor. Steve Sauter (1991), a researcher at the National Institute for Occupational Safety and Health, reported arm discomfort increased with increases in keyboard height above elbow level, and Michelle Marcus (2002), an epidemiologist at Emory University, reported discomfort increased with the keyboard being closer to the edge of the work surface. The research by Marcus and associates also indicated that traditionally recommended HCI workstation designs may not be appropriate and that workstation designs should allow for more flexibility in use and in general should provide opportunities for the body to be supported while working.

Visual Access: Lighting, Vision, and the Monitor

Visual access is a key ergonomic component in any workstation design. The body follows the eyes in order to obtain visual access. For HCI, visual access requires reducing glare on the monitor screen, properly positioning the monitor, and having proper corrective vision.

General overhead lighting is not optimal for computer work environments because it often creates glare on the glass monitor screen, blocking visual access. Diffuse (indirect) lighting is appropriate for most computer work environments. Computer monitors should be placed at a right angle to the direct light source, such as windows and other lights. The new flat-panel LCD monitors reflect much less light than their glass counterparts and therefore significantly reduce glare.

Lack of proper corrective vision can create many types of MSDs. For example, people who use bifocals or progressive lenses may suffer neck strain due to positioning their head to view the monitor through the bottom part of their lenses. Hence, a single-vision prescription for computer work is preferred. Workers should provide to an optometrist a description of their computer workstation as well as the location of their monitor relative to their sitting position to obtain a proper prescription.

The monitor should be positioned such that the top of the screen does not exceed the user's eye level (preferably 2.54–5 centimeters below) and should be placed 45–60 centimeters from the user. The viewing angle should be 15–30 degrees downward with respect to horizontal. The monitor should be directly in front of the user, minimizing twisting and asymmetric support of the body. Flat-panel screens can be easily mounted on an adjustable monitor arm, allowing for greater flexibility.

HCI Workstation Designs

HCI encompasses many daily activities, and as a result interaction mechanics differ. Hence, adjustability accommodates the HCI workstation both for different workers and for different interaction mechanics.

HCI workstation designs need to be comfortable by supporting key components of the body, such as the low back and the forearms, and to allow for movement of workstation components between alternating HCI tasks. Support of the forearms is especially important with interaction that does not involve input devices. Armrests allow the forearms to rest during short durations of input device inactivity. New workstation designs provide support of the forearms on the desk surface. Sit-stand workstations allow users to both sit and stand while working, allowing users with back pain to alternate between different postures throughout the day.

A Personal Story—The Complexities of Repetitive Strain

During my days as a graduate student in California I spent many hours working on the computer, programming, writing, or communicating with friends back home on the East Coast. Unfortunately, I had limited resources for extra medical expenses not covered by my bare-bones student health insurance policy. So into my third year of graduate school, my eyes had changed considerably since my last prescription for corrective lenses. I started to have headaches at the end of the day; but the headaches started earlier and earlier each day. They started to interfere with my work. I was unable to complete all my tasks and responsibilities.

So I went to the optometry school, where I could get low cost care and a discount on glasses. Since the optometrist was a student, the exam took a couple hours, and they checked for everything. I got a new prescription and ordered a new pair of glasses. A week later, I had my new glasses. The first day of wearing the glasses the headaches were gone. I was thrilled. I was able to work throughout the day. My productivity improved, and I was looking forward to finishing my graduate studies without the headaches.

After about two weeks of high productivity, my wrist started to hurt. I had developed a mild case of wrist extensor tendonitis. The headaches had reduced my time at the computer and therefore protected my wrists. Now I had to pay attention and remember to take breaks to keep my wrists healthy. This story always reminds me of the complex and integrated nature of computer-related repetitive strain injuries.

Jack Dennerlein

Chairs provide the majority of support in a workstation. Chairs should have a five-leg base for stability and a swivel and wheels for ease of reaching and getting in and out. The seat pan supports body weight through the body's legs and the bottom of the body's back. The seat pan should be slightly concave and padded and have a rounded waterfall edge to reduce edge compression at the back of the body's legs. The backrest should support the entire back of the user from the head to the lumbar (low back) region. Ideally the backrest should contain a lumbar support so that no gap exists between the backrest and the spine, supporting the complete spine. For smaller workers, this support is often achieved with smaller or adjustable seat pan depths.

The chair should be adjusted such that when the person's feet are flat on the floor the knees are at approximately a 90-degree angle. This angle allows for even distribution of pressure on the back side of the person's legs. If the seat pan depth is adjustable, with the person's back supported by the backrest, four fingers should fit between the edge of the seat pan and the back of the knees. The stiffness of the backrest should be balanced such that it is high enough to support the person's back but low enough to allow extension of the person's back without excessive effort. Vertically, the armrests should be at elbow height with the shoulders relaxed. Horizontal adjustments allow the armrests to be moved closer to the body, alleviating shoulder abduction (spreading away from a position near or parallel to the median axis of the body). Armrests should be padded and contain no sharp edges.

Positioning the Keyboard and Mouse

Vertically, the keyboard and mouse should be placed at a height that keeps the forearms level and the wrists straight. The height of the *g* and *h* keys on the keyboard should be the same height as the elbows after the chair has been adjusted accordingly. The mouse should be at the same level. Ideally, the keyboard should be placed on an adjustable-height work surface such that the workstation can be adjusted to fit different workers.

The keyboard and mouse should be placed on a large horizontal work surface, that is, the desk or table, allowing for many configurations to accommodate variations in HCI tasks. For example, the keyboard can be moved away from the edge of the work surface to allow workers to rest their forearms on the table in front of the keyboard during an interactive task such as editing a document or navigating a browser through the Internet. The conventional position for the mouse is at the right side of the keyboard (even for left-handed people); however, the keyboard design with a numeric pad places the mouse farther from the body. A simple intervention is to move the mouse to the left side of the keyboard. This relocation accomplishes two goals. First, it moves the mouse closer to the center line of the body, and second, it transfers the mouse activity to the left hand, allowing the right hand to rest. Another intervention is to position the mouse directly in front of the user between the keyboard and the edge of the work surface, providing a more neutral shoulder position and support for the forearm. A large work surface allows the user to vary configurations with the tasks.

Keyboard trays can provide vertical adjustment and can provide excellent relief for users suffering from wrist pain due to awkward wrist postures associated with keyboard use. However, trays do not always accommodate a mouse, do not provide support for the body, and often push users away from other equipment with which they may require repetitive interaction.

Keeping the Wrists Relaxed and Straight

The slope of the keyboard and the use of wrist rests affect wrist angle and can help reduce wrist strain. First, the slope of the keyboard should prevent the wrists from extending. Relative to the position of the forearms the keyboard should be flat or slope slightly downward, with the far side of the keyboard a bit lower. Keyboard trays often allow for a sloping keyboard. On nonadjustable surfaces the feet on the back of the keyboard can be lowered, allowing for less wrist extension. Second, wrist rests remind users to keep their wrists straight. Wrist rests elevate the wrists, preventing extension resulting from resting the wrists below input devices. Wrist rests can, however, create contact pressures, thus exposing users to a risk factor. Users would do better to rest their arms on a larger area to distribute the weight, decreasing pressures.

Alternative Device Designs

The design of input devices affects user exposure to MSD risk factors associated with HCI. For the keyboard the design of the key switch and the shape of the keyboard are factors. For the mouse the motion sensor technology (optical versus the ball-and-rollers) and the shape have been the most common improvements in design. For users, having access to a library of alternative keyboards and mice can be useful in determining which devices work best.

The key switch design of a keyboard requires a certain force, with a corresponding displacement of keys, to be achieved for switch activation. This force is low, in the range of 56 to 85 grams; however, when the force is higher the incidence of musculoskeletal disorders increases. Furthermore, when the mechanism within the key switch acts like a spring, both muscle activity and MSD symptoms decrease.

The layout of the keys affects the posture of wrists and forearms, and therefore many alternative keyboards change the physical dimensions and layout. Split keyboards, which divide the keyboard into two parts, one for each hand, are the most common and have two designs—fixed and adjustable. Adjustable split keyboards can be adjusted to individual configurations; however, such keyboards can be complicated to use. Pat Tittiranonda, a researcher at the Lawrence Livermore Laboratories (1999), reported that users preferred fixed split keyboards compared with adjustable split keyboards.

Excessive mouse use has been associated with carpal tunnel syndrome; however, no studies have linked MSDs with specific design aspects. Mouse use often requires awkward postures and precise motor control. Shoulder pain and neck pain often occur when an unsupported arm manipulates a mouse for long periods of time. Therefore, most interventions either change arm support or provide alternative pointing devices. Many alternative mouse designs attempt to alter the posture of the hand and fingers through shape.

The primary alternative pointing devices are trackballs, touch pads, isometric joy sticks (the eraser head-like controls in the middle of a keyboard), and

pen and tablets. In performance tests only pen and tablets do as well as the mouse; however, the other devices do require different motor control strategies, altering the distribution of forces on the musculoskeletal system and providing relief to users.

The technology of the mouse has recently improved with the advent of the cordless mouse and the optical mouse. The cordless mouse allows a user to easily move the mouse to different areas in the workspace. The optical mouse works on almost any surface without movement sensors becoming dirty and frustrating the user. The scroll wheel also has added functionality to the mouse, helping to remove the drag process for scrolling down windows. Unlike keyboard switches, the mouse does not provide tactile information about the virtual desktop environment. Hence, a new generation of mice adds vibration and force feedback technology, which provide the user with tactile cues through electromechanical actuators.

Both the keyboard and the pointing device have software settings in the operating system that can assist users. Keyboard mapping, by which keys are given specific functions, and keyboard shortcuts can reduce users' dependence on a mouse. Through the control panels of the operating system or hardware-specific software, users can create keyboard shortcuts for highly repetitive mouse functions. Software programs often have macro programs that allow users to record and play back repetitive keystrokes and mouse movements, thus alleviating mouse usage. Switch and movement sensitivity also can be adjusted through the operating system's control panels. The mouse control panel often has a drag-lock feature so that users do not have to continuously hold the mouse button as well as options to change the speed of the double click feature and the acceleration feature.

Speech recognition programs are a good alternative for physically and/or visually challenged persons and persons with advanced disorders. Software and hardware vary widely with regard to ease of use, reliability, and cost. Accuracy rates are still low for recognizing spoken language. Speech recognition programs may not be suitable for highly interactive tasks (e.g., multiple software, Web browsing, etc.).

Another alternative is the laptop computer. When used as a main computer, a laptop should be used with an external keyboard and mouse. Most manufacturers sell port replicators and docking stations, which allow for easy access and portability of the computer. The keyboard, monitor, and mouse should be used in accordance with the preceding desktop guidelines. Without a port, external keyboard, and monitor setup, one should avoid using a laptop in one position for prolonged periods.

Reducing Work-Related Stress

Because we can perform many activities of daily living through HCI, we often sit at a computer workstation for hours on end. However, the human body is designed for motion. Users should take short breaks every hour. Research indicates that these breaks do not decrease productivity. Software exists to remind users to take frequent breaks.

Software usability is crucial in reducing stress. Application software that frustrates users can increase their exposure to risks and increase their job stress.

Jack Dennerlein

See also Ergonomics; Keyboard

FURTHER READING

American National Standards Institute. (1988). *American national standard for human factors engineering of visual display terminal workstations* (Standard No. 100-1988). Santa Monica, CA: Human Factors Society.

Andersen, J. H., Thornsen, J. F., Overgaard, E., Lassen, C. F., Brandt, L. P. A., Vilstrup, I., Kryger, A. I., & Mikkelsen, S. (2003). Computer use and carpal tunnel syndrome: A 1-year follow-up study. *JAMA, 289*(22), 2963–2969.

Armstrong, T. J., & Silverstein, B. A. (1987). Upper-extremity pain in the workplace—Role of usage in causality. In N. M. Hadler (Ed.), *Clinical concepts in regional musculoskeletal illness* (pp. 333–354). Orlando, FL: Grune & Stratton.

Bergqvist, U., Wolgast, E., Nilsson, B., & Voss, M. (1995). The influence of VDT work on musculoskeletal disorders. *Ergonomics, 38*(4), 754–762.

Bureau of Labor Statistics (BLS). (2001). *Reports on survey of occupational injuries and illnesses in 1977–2000.* Washington. DC: Bureau of Labor Statistics, U.S. Department of Labor.

Dennerlein, J. T., Becker, T., Johnson, P., Reynolds, C., & Picard, R. (2003). Frustrating computer users increases exposure to physical factors. *Proceedings of the 15th triennial congress of the International Ergonomics Association (IEA 2003).* CD-ROM.

Dennerlein, J. T., & Yang, M. C. (2001). Haptic force-feedback devices for the office computer: Performance and musculoskeletal loading issues. *Human Factors, 43*(2), 278–286.

Faucett, J., & Rempel, D. (1994). VDT-related musculoskeletal symptoms: Interactions between work posture and psychosocial work factors. *American Journal of Industrial Medicine, 26*(5), 597–612.

Franzblau, A., Flashner, D., Albers, J. W., Blitz, S., Werner, R., & Armstrong, T. (1993). Medical screening of office workers for upper extremity cumulative trauma disorders. *Archives of Environmental Health, 48,* 164–170.

Galinsky, T. L., Swanson, N. G., Sauter, S. L., Hurrell, J. J., & Schleifer, L. M. (2000). A field study of supplementary rest breaks for data-entry operators. *Ergonomics, 43*(5), 622–638.

Gerard, M. J., Armstrong, T. J., Franzblau, A., Martin, B. J., & Rempel, D. M. (1999). The effects of keyswitch stiffness on typing force, finger electromyography, and subjective discomfort. *American Industrial Hygiene Association Journal, 60*(6), 762–769.

Gerr, F., Marcus, M., Ensor, C., Kleinbaum, D., Cohen, S., Edwards, A., Gentry, E., Ortiz, D. J., & Monteilh, C. (2002). A prospective study of computer users: I. Study design and incidence of musculoskeletal symptoms and disorders. *American Journal of Industrial Medicine, 41,* 221–235.

Honan, M. M., Serina, E., Tal, R., & Rempel, D. (1995). Wrist postures while typing on a standard and split keyboard. In *Proceedings of the Human Factors and Ergonomics Society 39th annual meeting.* Santa Monica, CA: Human Factors and Ergonomics Society.

Johnson, P. W., Tal, R., Smutz, W. P., & Rempel, D. M. (1994). Fingertip forces measured during computer mouse operation: A comparison of pointing and dragging. In *Proceedings of the 12th congress of the International Ergonomics Association* (pp. 208–210). Toronto, Canada: International Ergonomics Association.

Marcus, M., Gerr, F., Monteilh, C., Ortiz, D. J., Gentry, E., Cohen, S., Edwards, A., Ensor, C., & Kleinbaum, D. (2002). A prospective study of computer users: II. Postural risk factors for musculoskeletal symptoms and disorders. *American Journal of Industrial Medicine, 41,* 226–249.

Rempel, D., Tittiranonda, P., Burastero, S., Hudes, M., & So, Y. (1999). Effect of keyboard keyswitch design on hand pain. *Journal of Occupational and Environmental Medicine, 41*(2), 111–119.

Sauter, S. L., Schleifer, L. M., & Knutson, S. J. (1991). Work posture, workstation design, and musculoskeletal discomfort in a VDT data entry task. *Human Factors, 33*(2), 151–167.

Silverstein, B. A., Fine, L. J., & Armstrong, T. J. (1986). Hand wrist cumulative trauma disorders in industry. *British Journal of Industrial Medicine, 43,* 779–784.

Sommerich, C. M., Starr, H., Smith, C. A., & Shivers, C. (2002). Effects of notebook computer configuration and task on user biomechanics, productivity, and comfort. *International Journal of Industrial Ergonomics, 30*(1), 7–31.

Tittiranonda, P., Rempel, D., Armstrong, T., & Burastero, S. (1999) Effect of four computer keyboards in computer users with upper extremity musculoskeletal disorders. *American Journal of Industrial Medicine, 35*(6), 647–661.

U.S. Occupational Safety and Health Administration. (1997). *Working safely with video display terminals* (OSHA Publication No. 3092). Retrieved January 8, 2004, from http://www.osha.gov/

Wahlstrom, J., Hagberg, M., Johnson, P. W., Svensson, J., & Rempel, D. (2002). Influence of time pressure and verbal provocation on physiological and psychological reactions during work with a computer mouse. *European Journal of Applied Physiology, 87*(3), 257–263.

SCENARIO-BASED DESIGN

In the 1960s, increasing scale and complexity in software overtook management practices in software development. The resulting failures—cost overruns, late delivery, and ineffective and unreliable systems—were labeled the "software crisis." There is still no comprehensive resolution of the software crisis. Early approaches attempted to specify designs systematically before implementing them; this was particularly ineffective for interactive software systems. More recent approaches have encouraged designers to iteratively redesign until they identify and meet all requirements. However wise, this is an implicit acknowledgement that no software development methods exist.

Scenario-based design is a third alternative: Narrative representations of the use of a software system are created and maintained as a central technique for designing the software itself. In other words, scenarios of use are developed before the system whose use they describe is itself designed, implemented, or used at all. This is a somewhat obvious idea from a human-computer interaction perspective: After all, the use of software, the experience of using it, and its impact on people and their organizations is the ultimate determinant of the success of the software. And indeed, as software increasingly becomes an end-user product and/or service, this fundamental value orientation of driving software design and development by describing its envisioned use is increasingly more appropriate.

It is also more pervasive in contemporary system-development practice. Scenario-based design was debated and seen as somewhat radical as recently as the early 1990s. However, through the past decade, it has seeped into every facet of the system-development life cycle. Scenarios are a major tool in conveying vivid system visions and product proposals, in capturing, organizing, and analyzing system requirements, in developing functional specifications, in describing and hand-simulating software architectures and models (where they are sometimes called "use cases"), in identifying and developing user interface metaphors, in expressing usability specifications, in guiding prototyping and creating a medium for rough prototypes, in designing or classifying usability evaluation test tasks, in creating task-oriented documentation, and in contextualizing design rationales. During the past decade, planning and managing the use, the user experience, the work activity, and the organizational impacts of software as it is developed have become standard software design practices.

An Example

Scenarios are stories in which characters interact with tools and information, and with one another. The characters typically have attributes that distinguish them—knowledge and skills, interests and motivations, job roles and objectives. They behave in a context that is also distinct and that both constrains and facilitates their activity. The plot or action of the scenario describes how the characters plan and pursue goals, improvise and make sense of courses of action, and experience consequences.

Scenario-based design typically starts with a problem scenario in which the characters are supported by current technology. Analyzing such scenarios helps to identify challenges, conflicts, and opportunities in the current situation, guiding the development of solution scenarios. Suppose we were interested in the design of new educational technology to facilitate collaborative, project-based learning in middle-school science. We might construct a character named Marissa, a girl who likes helping other students even more than she likes science itself and who likes to use instant messaging after dinner. Marissa is interested in planetary motion. She wonders whether smaller planets always move faster, and how the size and density of a sun alters plane-

tary motions. These questions were not addressed in her class or in her textbook. She has two friends who are also interested in this question, but both are boys. She'd like to work with them on this problem, but only if the interaction can be fairly casual and she can keep her own work at least partially distinct.

The point of such a common scenario, from the standpoint of human-computer interaction (HCI) design and software development, is to vividly depict how people do or try to do things that might be better facilitated by new systems and applications in order to better understand how they use, and perhaps misuse, currently available systems and applications. In our example, the students can chat and send e-mail, but these are inadequate tools for their purposes. A better approach might be to view and annotate Web pages collaboratively, to find and adapt or just create simulation models of solar systems, and to edit notes and reports of their investigation jointly. In our project, we developed such approaches. The scenario helps designers to analyze requirements and envision solutions by focusing on concrete cases instead of on demographic or normative summaries. Some of the special strengths of scenario-based methods are the following:

1. Story narratives are particularly vivid and memorable, as can be seen in Freud's case studies or the research of the French structural anthropologist Claude Levi-Strauss;
2. Scenarios evoke empathetic, elaborative, and interrogative cognitive processes, helping designers to "reflect in action";
3. Scenarios are highly malleable, facilitating what-if reasoning, lowering the perceived cost of changes, and reducing the risk of premature commitment, a common failure pattern in professional design;
4. Scenarios describe other people's work and activity, and thereby discourage designers from taking themselves and their own concerns as typical;
5. Keeping the focus of the design work on people and organizations also helps designers balance their own concerns with external factors like popular design paradigms, technology zeitgeist, and business perceptions;

A Personal Story—The Value of a Devil's Advocate

In the spring of 1989, I was attending a brown bag research lunch meeting at the IBM Watson Center, along with a dozen or so other members of the User Interface Institute. We were talking about design, and about how technical representations—like functional specifications—are used to guide software design projects. I was holding forth on the virtues of user interaction scenarios as useful adjuncts to these more traditional design representations, and my colleague Linda Tetzlaff was pointing out every flaw in my line of reasoning. To regain the initiative, I shifted ground and suggested that scenarios might be *better* as a design representation. Perhaps functional specifications should be re-conceptualized as an adjunct to scenarios!

Linda, who had years of experience as a software developer and as a manager, did not like this suggestion. And she had many reasons for why it was a bad idea. Still, what started out as a half-baked proposal came to seem more serious and more interesting to me as we chatted further. Later that summer, and thanks to a great deal of support—and devil's advocacy—from Linda and other colleagues, we wrote our first paper on what is now known as scenario-based design.

John M. Carroll

6. Scenarios are a level of design description that is accessible to all stakeholders in a design, allowing seriously participatory design methods, including the direct involvement of users in all design discussions; and
7. Because they help to broaden the design space through literary abstraction mechanisms like genre, style, and theme, scenarios are very effective brainstorming tools.

Technical Challenges

A testimony to the importance of scenario-based methods in contemporary HCI design is the striking fact that younger designers often take these practices for granted. This popularity also serves to emphasize the many remaining open questions and technical challenges. First, merely writing scenarios is not a guarantee of their usability or usefulness. Scenarios are tools to investigate, analyze, and describe HCI issues and possibilities. The actions that are carried out in creating a scenario and subsequently making use of it are as important as the scenario itself. Scenarios are most useful if they are systematically grounded in the realities of use, if they are rigorously questioned, and if they are shared among all stakeholders in a design project.

Second, scenarios are not a uniform category. Some scenarios describe use at the level of individuals and others describe use at the level of organizations. Some describe the subjective goals and experiences of users; others describe only public and objective events. All scenarios are both rich and incomplete, but they vary greatly in what aspects are emphasized and detailed, and what aspects are elided. Finally, scenarios are codified in many media, including text, videos, and semiformal notations like the unified modeling language (UML). Notations have substantial effects on how information can be used, yet the effects of notations on the utility of scenarios has not been investigated.

Third, scenario-based practices are poorly supported with tools. One way to think about this is in terms of using generic tools to support version management and the indexing, retrieval, and reuse of scenario libraries, and using representational formats to support the verification and testing of scenarios. Such initiatives are widely discussed currently, and definitely should be pursued and investigated, but they might well turn out to be paradoxical: To the extent that scenarios are fundamentally different from other design representations (for example, from functional specifications), they may require entirely different tool strategies. For example, scenarios encourage brainstorming through essentially literary mechanisms like genre, style, and themes. If such properties are central to their utility in design, then instead of generic information-management tools we need to develop tool strategies that support these special properties. However, tools to support the unique cognitive opportunities of scenarios have not yet been widely investigated.

Finally, scenario-based design is complementary to many other design approaches and techniques, such as specification-driven design, task-analytic design, design patterns, and extreme programming. However, the specific contrasts among these approaches have not been thoroughly analyzed. For example, task-analytic design focuses singularly on requirements identification by representing work objectively and comprehensively through recursive hierarchical decomposition. Scenario-based design focuses on expanding the design space, identifying fundamental misconceptions about work, involving and empowering stakeholders, and narrowing the gap between requirements analysis and design. While these contrasts are often conceived of narrowly and competitively, it may be that the best utilization of scenario-based design is to develop broad, composite methods. To date, such methods have only been discussed programmatically.

At the outset of HCI, the two central technical challenges were to understand user activities and experiences more deeply and more efficiently, and to support designers more powerfully, more flexibly, and more broadly across the system-development life cycle. Scenario-based methods address both these challenges and bring them together in ways that have proved both practical and intellectually fruitful.

John M. Carroll

See also Cognitive Walkthrough; Iterative Design; Socio-Technical Design; Software Engineering; Value Sensitive Design

FURTHER READING

Carroll, J. M. (Ed.). (1995). *Scenario-based design: Envisioning work and technology in system development.* New York: Wiley.

Carroll, J. M. (1997). Human-computer interaction: Psychology as a science of design. *International Journal of Human-Computer Studies, 46,* 501–522.

Carroll, J. M. (2000). *Making use: Scenario-based design of human-computer interactions.* Cambridge, MA: MIT Press.

Carroll, J. M., Chin, G., Rosson, M.B., & Neale, D. C. (2000). The development of cooperation: Five years of participatory design in the virtual school. In D. Boyarski & W. Kellogg (Eds.), *DIS'2000: Designing Interactive Systems* (pp. 239–251). New York: Association for Computing Machinery.

Carroll, J. M., Rosson, M. B., Chin, G., & Koenemann, J. (1998). Requirements development in scenario-based design. *IEEE Transactions on Software Engineering, 24*(12), 1156–1170.

Cross, N. (2001). Design cognition: Results from protocol and other empirical studies of design activity. In C. Eastman, M. McCracken, & W. Newstetter (Eds.), *Design knowing and learning: Cognition in design education* (pp. 79–103). Amsterdam: Elsevier.

Freud, S. (1900). The interpretation of dreams. In J. Strachey (Ed. & Trans.), *The standard edition of the complete psychological works of Sigmund Freud, 4.* London: Hogarth Press.

Isenhour, P. L., Carroll, J. M., Neale, D. C., Rosson, M. B., & Dunlap, D. R. (2000). The virtual school: An integrated collaborative environment for the classroom. *Educational Technology and Society, 3*(3), 74–86.

Kahneman, D., & Tversky, A. (1972). Subjective probability: A judgement of representativeness. *Cognitive Psychology, 3,* 430–454.

Kyng, M. (1995). Creating contexts for design. In J. M. Carroll (Ed.), *Scenario-based design: Envisioning work and technology in system development* (pp. 85–107). New York: Wiley.

Lévi-Strauss, C. (1967). *Structural anthropology.* Garden City, NY: Anchor Books.

Muller, M. J., Tudor, L. G., Wildman, D. M., White, E. A., Root, R. A., Dayton, T., et al. (1995). Bifocal tools for scenarios and representations in participatory activities with users. In J.M. Carroll (Ed.), *Scenario-based design: Envisioning work and technology in system development* (pp. 135–163). New York: Wiley.

Robertson, S. P., Carroll, J. M., Mack, R. L., Rosson, M. B., Alpert, S. R., & Koenemann-Belliveau, J. (1994). ODE: A self-guided, scenario-based learning environment for object-oriented design principles. In Proceedings of OOPSLA'94: Conference on Object-Oriented Programming Systems, Languages and Applications (*ACM SIGPLAN Notices, 29*(10), 51–64). New York: ACM Press.

Rosson, M. B., & Carroll, J. M. (1996). The reuse of uses in Smalltalk programming. *ACM Transactions on Computer-Human Interaction, 3*(3), 219–253.

Rosson, M. B., & Carroll, J. M. (2002). *Usability engineering: Scenario-based development of human-computer interaction.* San Francisco: Morgan-Kaufmann.

Schön, D. A. (1983). *The reflective practitioner: How professionals think in action.* New York: Basic Books.

SCIENCE FICTION

See Literary Representations; Movies

SEARCH AND RESCUE

Urban Search and Rescue (USAR) workers have forty-eight hours to find trapped survivors in a collapsed structure; after that, the likelihood of finding victims still alive is nearly zero. As recently seen in Turkey, Taiwan, New York, and Iran, the magnitude of the devastation of urban environments usually exceeds the resources—USAR specialists, USAR dogs, and sensors—needed to rescue victims within the critical first forty-eight hours. Moreover, the mechanics of how large structures pancake often prevent rescue workers from searching buildings due to the unacceptable personal risk from further collapse. Finally, both people and dogs are frequently too big to enter voids, limiting a typical search to no more than a few feet from a perimeter.

Robots, on the other hand, can bypass these dangers and difficulties and can therefore expedite the search for victims immediately after a collapse. They can be used for USAR in a number of ways—for example, they can search for survivors, assess structural damage, deposit radio transmitters, leave small amounts of food and medication, guide the insertion of jaws-of-life tools, and identify the location of limbs to prevent workers from damaging a victim's arm or leg with rescue equipment.

Robotic Search and Rescue

Advanced robotic technology can assist rescue workers in four ways: (1) by entering unstable structures, it can reduce the personal risk to workers and dogs; (2) by penetrating ordinarily inaccessible voids, it can increase the speed of response; (3) by methodically searching areas with multiple sensors (using algorithms guaranteed to provide a complete search in three dimensions), it can increase efficiency and reliability; and (4) by being able to enter spaces that were otherwise inaccessible, it can extend the reach of USAR workers. Appropriate hardware platforms—for example, small robots, shape-shifting robots, and flexible snake robots—already exist, but these robotic platforms will not be usable by USAR personnel unless software is developed to reduce or eliminate the burden of teleoperating unfamiliar technology for long periods of time under conditions of emotional and physical stress.

Both robot mechanisms and software development are important areas of research on urban search and rescue robots. For instance, while autonomous navigation in difficult outdoor terrain has been achieved by numerous researchers, many issues remain in automating the full sensory sweeps of a robot that can "see" all locations of unknown spaces. The critical open research questions revolve around developing formal methods for guaranteeing the completeness of a search in three dimensions with different sensors (especially vision, range, acoustic, and thermal sensors); characterizing a volume of space in order to aid exploration decisions and structural assessments; mobile sensing, where the mobile base actively moves to optimize an articulated sensor; and navigation with manipulation, where the robot pushes small pieces of rubble aside in order to proceed with the search. Answering these questions will make fundamental contributions to motion planning and multisensor functionality-based perception.

It is usually a given that the assets of a city (including personnel and equipment) will not be sufficient to rescue all people, and that a situation will require triage instead. Therefore, the first thing rescue workers do is attempt to assess the structural characteristics of a site to determine entry points that might lead to pockets of survivors. As a search progresses, workers constantly attempt to locate survivors and to assess the effort and risk involved in a rescue due to the physical characteristics of the surrounding structure. When rescuers find survivors, they often try to talk to them to determine if there may be other victims nearby, in which case they would make that area a higher priority for excavation. Continuing communication may also be important to provide some emotional comfort to the victim and to help workers locate the whole body during removal. The most important information to a rescue worker is where the survivors are and what the characteristics of the surrounding structure are.

Gathering information about survivors and damaged structures is difficult in the USAR environment, which is characterized by extremely small clearances (less than two feet of headroom) and piles of rubble. Often a search proceeds from the top down— a hole is cut in the roof and rescue workers attempt to lower and guide equipment into a void. A major concern is whether the weight and movement of rescue workers will trigger a further collapse as they go into or onto the building to deploy sensors manually. This is especially true for situations like the one in Taiwan, where a sixteen-story apartment building was left intact but tilting. The structure was easy for workers to work in, but there was an unacceptable risk of collapse. And large commercial buildings are even more difficult to work in because of the amount of potential pancaking; workers can only access these buildings via their roofs, which limits access to most of the lower levels and presents another danger because parts of the structure may not support the weight of the rescuers.

Sensing conditions are challenging, because little or no natural light enters the voids. Rescue workers often have to use proctoscopes with fish-eye lenses to look into voids, but the fish-eye perspective is disorienting and fatiguing and may result in an unconscious victim being missed or a surrounding structure being misidentified. Also, because there is no easy way to turn the proctoscope tube dynamically to see all through the void, important viewpoints may be missed. Acoustics can be used to detect cries of help or sounds of breathing, but noise from power generators and machinery being used to remove rubble can interfere with sensing unless the sensor is near the victim.

In office and apartment buildings, the rubble is often covered with gray dust from crumbled cinderblocks and sheetrock. Anything not gray is treated as a potential survivor, since human movement will knock off the dust and blood will show up well.

Although USAR is frequently cited as a possible beneficiary of mobile robot technology, platforms and algorithms specifically for search and rescue activities are relatively new. The first published technology specifically for USAR appears to be the efforts of John Blitch for his master's thesis under the direction of Robin Murphy. Blitch's work, which was motivated by his experiences helping with the rescue after the Oklahoma City bombing, created an expert system to advise rescue workers on what type of asset (human, dog, or robot type) to deploy given a particular void or entry into a collapsed building.

Murphy's group has followed two simultaneous paths toward field-able USAR robots: first, the creation of the marsupial cooperative team concept, where a mother robot carries daughter robots to be deployed, and second, the development of biomimetic sensing and behavioral sensor fusion algorithms for detecting survivors. Her group has developed a new mobile platform, called Silver Bullet, that is capable of traversing the uneven terrain characteristic of collapsed buildings, as well as two micro-robots for USAR. Silver Bullet contains a wide variety of sensors: monocular, stereovision, thermal, sonar, acoustic (to hear survivors scream), GPS, inclinometers, and a radio Ethernet link. This work is ready to be integrated into a coherent platform and with more deliberative functions such as path planning.

Open Areas of Research

A number of demands made by USAR on mobile robots are still unmet. First of all, sensing is needed for two USAR-specific (non-navigational) tasks: to detect possible survivors and to categorize volumes of space for preliminary structural assessment.

A second need is for multiple sensors to cope with the unfavorable conditions for pure vision sensing and to improve the overall quality of sensing through sensor fusion. And algorithms that can guarantee complete sensor coverage of a 3-D space are critical for reliable detection. Because the volumes of space to be searched are often confined, unstable, and difficult to negotiate, another need is for a robot that can avoid triggering slides and further collapses by minimizing direct contact with nearby surfaces.

At the same time, a robot may need to physically move a small obstacle to make progress, and therefore voids will have to be categorized in terms of composition (clutter, stability, and grade), rubble attribute (whether the void through the rubble is predominately horizontal or vertical), and hazard to the robot (wetness, corrosion potential, and the possibility of creating an electrical hazard). Finally, new devices are needed, such as serpentine robots that can use their many degrees of freedom to reach deeply into a convoluted structure without contacting it, just as a surgeon can use an arthroscopic surgical instrument to make repairs deep inside the body without causing damage to the surrounding tissue.

Previous work in general navigation has produced mobile robots capable of reactive navigation, path planning, and localization in real-time in structured indoor environments and some outdoor terrains. However, the demands of USAR remain unmet and, with the noticeable exception of Murphy's group, the associated issues are not being considered in a coherent context.

Howie Choset

See also Human-Robot Interaction

FURTHER READING

Center for Robot Assisted Search and Rescue (CRASAR). (2004). Retrieved April 6, 2004, from http://crasar.org

Urban search and rescue (USAR). (2000). Sensor Based Planning Lab, Carnegie Mellon University. Retrieved April 6, 2004, from http://voronoi.sbp.ri.cmu.edu/projects/prj_search_rescue.html

SEARCH ENGINES

Although the term *search engines* is sometimes applied to information retrieval systems for other types of data, it is most commonly applied to information retrieval systems for the World Wide Web (Web). Web search engines have become a part of everyday life for millions of people because the Web has become such an important medium of communication throughout the world. However, the same properties that make the Web useful also present a unique information organization problem because anyone, anywhere in the world, may add information to the Web at any time. In addition, much of the information present on the Web today is gone tomorrow. Finally, no regulatory body exists to govern the content of the Web. The Web is, therefore, a disorganized, dynamic, and unmoderated body of useful information jumbled together with junk. Which information is useful and which is junk depend on one's perspective and needs. These factors combine to make the development of successful Web search engines among the most challenging of problems. The problem of building a search engine is further compounded by the fact that the technology must be effective not only for librarians and information scientists, but also for anyone, from a child to that child's grandparents. To be effective, a search engine must be proactive in discovering newly available information, it must be able to easily change as Web content comes and goes, and it must embody an understanding of the people who will use it—it must be user friendly.

Fundamentals

Modern search engines consist of three principal components: a Web spider, an indexing and retrieval system, and a user interface. Initial approaches to building search engines focused on the first of these components. Three such early engines were the RBSE (Repository Based Software Engineering) Web spider, Jumpstation, and the World-Wide Web Worm The term *Web spider* derives from the fact that such engines "walk" around the Web cataloging the documents they find. A Web spider automatically navigates from one webpage to another, following each hyperlink it finds in turn to explore the network of documents that composes the Web as it develops. As early Web spiders crawled the Web they indexed the webpages they discovered using simple keyword-based techniques. For example, for a webpage containing the words "Bill," "Clinton," and "president," a searcher, having typed those words as a query, would find that page as well as every other page containing those three words. The problem was that early search engines/spiders provided only rudimentary search functionality. In most cases the pages retrieved in response to a query such as the preceding were not ranked in any way, so that much of what was retrieved was often of little interest to the searcher. At the time, however, the Web was not so big, so scanning through all search results to discover whether the Web held the information one sought was usually not an insurmountable task.

One difference between the Web of the early 1990s and the Web of ten years later is that then topic coverage was spotty at best, whereas now it is nearly comprehensive in scope. Then the question was whether anyone had posted the information that a searcher wanted. Now the question is whether one can find the information that will satisfy his or her need. Most people assume that it is there somewhere—an assumption that is probably correct for a high percentage of queries. As the Web grew from hundreds of sites in 1993 to hundreds of thousands of sites in 1996, the simple indexing and retrieval techniques employed by these early systems became ineffective. As the Web began to exhibit the value that its creators had predicted, useful information became harder and harder to find.

Relevance of Webpages

Initial efforts to solve the problems of early search engines/spiders focused on developing systems that embodied better measures of query relevance, so that searchers were more likely to find needed information. These efforts focused on indexing and retrieval systems, the second primary component of search engines. An indexing and retrieval system maintains and organizes a set of documents called a "collection." For a search engine the collection of interest may comprise billions of webpages. A search engine collection is continually updated through the use of Web spiders that gather and download copies of documents to be processed by the indexing and retrieval system. The indexing half of this search engine subsystem processes the documents gathered by Web spiders, associating each document with a set of terms (words and phrases) that identifies to some degree what that document is about.

Such indexing and retrieval systems create a data structure that is similar to the kind of index one finds at the end of a book, where specific terms are listed in alphabetical order, with the page numbers of passages relevant to each term nested beneath. In a search engine index, the relationship between each document and a particular term by which it is indexed is weighted using a value that represents the relative strength of the relationship between the document and the term when compared to the relationship between the same document and other terms. The set of relationships between terms and documents and the associated weights is called the "index" in search engine terminology. The index serves as the fulcrum on which the search engine pivots. All newly discovered webpages are added to the index, old web-

pages are removed, and all queries are matched against the index to identify relevant documents and the order in which they should be presented to the searcher. In response to queries, the retriever component of the indexing and retrieval system locates all documents that have been associated with a set of query terms. Based on the strength of the relationship between the query terms and the documents associated with each term, the retriever ranks the matching documents using some measure of relevance, combining the weights of all query terms as they relate to a document into a single ranking score for each document. The retriever then sorts the documents in descending order on the basis of the ranking scores.

Most search engines are full-text indexing and retrieval systems. This means that the terms used to index a given document are those found in the text of that document. In the first search engines developers borrowed full-text search techniques and tools from the information retrieval and information science communities. Prior to their inclusion in search engines, such techniques and tools had been used for decades in retrieval systems found in libraries and other depositories of information. Such techniques and tools employ statistical measures of word usage within documents; roughly speaking, in response to a query, the documents that rank highest are those that use the search terms most frequently. This means that at a lower level the weight of a given index term in relation to a particular document is directly related to how many times that term appears within the document. The intuition here is that the more frequently the author of a document uses a particular term, the more likely the document is to be related to the ideas that term identifies. Examples of this type of search engine include the original incarnations of AltaVista (www.altavista.com), Info-Seek (www.infoseek.com), and Lycos (www.lycos.com). This new class of search engine, although having the potential to help people find useful information, rarely did so. The primary reason for its failure is that with the volume of information available on the Web, constructing queries that distinguished useful documents containing the search terms from all other documents that happened to contain those terms was difficult.

Because nearly any term is used in a variety of contexts in human language, term-frequency approaches to Web retrieval are poor isolators of the one context in which a given searcher is interested. For example, the term *caterpillar* refers both to fuzzy insect larvae and to a manufacturer of heavy equipment. In addition, a quick search of the Web identifies a variety of books, children's clubs, and games that are relevant to the term *caterpillar*. To effectively distinguish one context from another using a term frequency-based search engine, one required fairly sophisticated query construction skills akin to those employed by reference librarians and other information specialists. Unfortunately, the average search engine user is not an information specialist and, in contrast, enters very simple queries. Several studies indicate that most people simply type two or three words and hit the search button. Given the unconstrained nature of subjects addressed in Web documents, such queries retrieved many irrelevant documents for most queries, making it necessary to sift through hundreds, if not thousands, of documents to find only a few useful ones. Search engine developers tried many approaches to indexing, retrieval, and ranking algorithms to alleviate the problems that most users experienced in trying to find the information they needed; however, little improvement was made until the late 1990s with the advent of Google.

Popularity of Webpages

Serge Brin and Larry Page took a different approach to building search engines in their design of Google. Google replaces the notion of relevance with that of popularity. Instead of a ranking algorithm based on the frequency with which search terms appear in documents, Google selects all documents associated with a particular term and then ranks them on the basis of how easily they can be found by starting at any webpage and wandering randomly by following paths of hyperlinks from that webpage. Imagine, for example, how easy it is to happen upon the Microsoft homepage by starting anywhere. News stories in nearly every publication include links to Microsoft. A variety of programming-related sites, software, and hardware vendors also connects to

Microsoft, as do extremely popular sites such as Yahoo! and Amazon on numerous pages. Google uses an algorithm called "PageRank" that employs what Brin and Page labeled the "random-surfer model" to determine the overall utility of a webpage. The greater the number of unique paths one can travel to find a particular webpage, the more popular and hence more valuable it is.

Although PageRank was a great step forward in the development of indexing and retrieval technology, in many ways Google also was the first search engine to deal effectively with the third and final search engine component: the user interface. PageRank embodies the understanding that when using the Web most people search for pages that many other people have found to be useful in the past and typically associates that information with the words that people most commonly use to describe their need. This technique works especially well for information objects associated with specific names. For example, when one types the query "Microsoft Office XP," he or she usually wants one of a few heavily used sites such as the Microsoft Office homepage, the location where upgrades can be downloaded, or perhaps the Amazon page from which one can purchase a copy of Office online. By preferring the most popular pages associated with a given set of search terms, Google frequently directs people to exactly the information they wish to find, particularly if a single webpage of information will do the trick. Google almost always delivers when one is looking for one specific piece of information.

Google has been the most successful search technology developed for the Web, in large part because it works for a large percentage of the millions of searches that people perform each day. However, Google is not without its shortcomings. Because in ranking search results Google replaces a measure of relevance with a measure of popularity, when one wishes to search for information that is off the beaten path, Google, in effect, pulls the searcher back to more heavily trafficked sites related to the information of interest. For example, imagine that a hobbyist is interested in woodworking and thinking of building a dining room table. The most easily constructed searches for webpages on this topic locate primarily commercial sites selling dining room tables.

Although Google is unquestionably helpful in many search tasks, a number of problems remain to be solved in the space of search engine technology.

Remaining Challenges

After a full decade of research and development of Web search engines we have learned much about the problems of building such engines. The Web is extremely large and changes rapidly. This change occurs faster than the fastest Web spiders can crawl; therefore, we cannot capture a snapshot of the entire Web. In fact, some research has found that an individual search engine indexes only a fraction of the total content of the Web at any given time. These and other findings demonstrate that building effective Web spiders is an extremely challenging technical problem. With regard to indexing and retrieval, Google has demonstrated the value of popularity as a means of distinguishing useful information from information that is less useful. Building on this work, several researchers have suggested indexing and retrieval technologies that combine measures of relevance with measures of popularity to resolve some of the shortcomings of PageRank.

Finally, we have learned much about human search behavior. People naturally assume that the search engine they use shares the context in which they are working. As a result, they often fail to supply sufficient detail to resolve the inevitable ambiguity of a keyword search. No research to date has demonstrated an effective means of encouraging people to supply sufficient detail to effectively narrow the context of their inquiries. Consequently, the burden of resolving query ambiguity is left to the search engine. People by nature type two or three words and hit the search button. Therefore, in all probability, the next generation of Web search technologies will be systems that are tailored to the needs and behaviors of individual users, systems that no longer attempt to be all things to all people, but instead a few things to one person.

Shannon Bradshaw

See also Information Overload; Information Retrieval

FURTHER READING

Bradshaw, S. (2003). Reference directed indexing: Redeeming relevance for subject search in citation indexes. *Proceedings of the 7th European Conference on Research and Advanced Technology for Digital Libraries,* 499–510.

Brin, S., & Page, L. (1998). The anatomy of a large-scale hypertextual Web search engine. *Computer Networks, 30*(1–7), 107–117.

Eichmann, D. (1994). The RBSE spider—Balancing effective search against Web load. *Proceedings of the First International World Wide Web Conference,* 113–120.

Gray, M. (1996). Internet statistics. Retrieved September 30, 2003, from http://www.mit.edu/people/mkgray/net/

Haveliwala, T. (2003, July–August). Topic-sensitive PageRank: A context-sensitive ranking algorithm for Web search. *IEEE Transactions on Knowledge and Data Engineering,* 784–796.

Lawrence, S., & Giles, C. L. (1999). Accessibility of information on the Web. *Nature, 400,* 107–109.

McBryan, O. (1994). GENVL and WWWW: Tools for taming the Web. *Proceedings of the First International World Wide Web* Conference.

Richardson, M., & Domingos, P. (2002). The intelligent surfer: Probabilistic combination of link and content information in PageRank. *Advances in neural information processing systems 14.* Cambridge, MA: MIT Press.

Spink, A., Wolfram, D., Jansen, B., & Saracevic, T. (2001). The public and their queries. *Journal of the American Society for Information Science and Technology, 52*(3), 226–234.

World Wide Web Consortium (W3C). Retrieved September 30, 2003, from http://www.w3.org

SECURITY

The number of computerized databases has increased rapidly over the past three decades, and the advent of the Internet and networking capabilities has made it increasingly easy to access this data. As a result, the need to develop techniques for protecting stored data became urgent in every sphere, from food to infrastructure, including government, industry, and institutions such as hospitals and universities. In the 1970s work on discretionary access control models began, but it was not until the Air Force summer study in 1982 that many of the efforts to develop multilevel secure database management systems were initiated. This resulted in the development of various secure database system prototypes and products. In the 1990s, with the advent of new technologies such as digital libraries, the World Wide Web, and collaborative computing systems, the interest in security became even more urgent.

Access Control

A fundamental concept of information security is *access control*—that is, the set of rules and methods that prevent unauthorized persons from gaining access to information while granting convenient access to authorized users. Access control models include those for discretionary security and mandatory security. In discretionary access control models, users or groups of users are granted access to data objects, which could be files, relations, objects, or even data items. Access control policies include rules such as User U has *read access* (is allowed to obtain and read the information) to Relation R1 and *write access* (is allowed to change the information) to Relation R2. Access control could also include negative control where user U does not have read access to Relation R.

In mandatory access control, subjects that act on behalf of users are granted access to objects based on some policy. A well-known policy is the Bell and La Padula policy where subjects are granted clearance levels and objects have sensitivity levels. The set of security levels forms a partially ordered lattice where Unclassified < Confidential < Secret < Top-Secret. The policy has two properties: (1) A subject has read access to an object if its clearance level dominates that of the object; and (2) A subject has write access to an object if its level is dominated by that of the object.

Other types of access control include role-based access control in which access is granted to users depending on their roles and the functions they perform. For example, personnel managers have access to salary data while project managers have access to project data. The idea here is generally to give access on a need-to-know basis.

While the early access control policies were formulated for operating systems, these policies have been extended to include other systems such as database systems, networks, and distributed systems. For example, a policy for networks includes policies not only for reading and writing but also for sending and receiving messages.

Other security policies include administration policies such as those for ownership of data and how to manage and distribute the data. Database administrators as well as system security officers are generally involved in formulating the administration policies. Security policies also include policies for identification and authentication: Each user or subject acting on behalf of a user has to be identified and authenticated, possibly using some password mechanisms. Identification and authentication become more complex for distributed systems. For example, how can a user be authenticated at a global level?

The steps to developing secure systems include developing a security policy, developing a model of the system, designing the system, and verifying and validating the system. The methods used for verification depend on the level of assurance that is expected. Testing and risk analysis are also part of the process. These activities will assess and perhaps eliminate the risks involved.

Secure Systems

While research on secure database systems was reported in the 1970s and secure operating systems such as Honeywell's SCOMP and MULTICS were developed, it was not until the early 1980s that active research began in this area. Much of the initial focus was on multilevel secure database systems. The security policy for operating systems developed in the 1960s and 1970s was modified slightly. For example, the write policy for secure database systems was modified to state that a subject has write access to an object if the subject's level is that of the object. Since database systems enforced relationships between data and had semantics, there were additional security concerns. For example, data could be classified based on content, context, and time. Also, research was carried out on securing not only relational systems but also object systems.

Based on research on computer networks that began in the late 1970s, networking protocols were eventually extended to incorporate security features. The policies included those for reading, writing, and sending and receiving messages. Research on encryption and cryptography was applied to security problems with networks and the Internet, and security for stand-alone systems was extended to distributed systems, including distributed databases and distributed operating systems. Much of the research on distributed systems now focuses on securing the Internet (Web security) and on securing systems such as distributed-object-management systems.

As new kinds of systems emerge, new security issues need to be investigated, and old solutions may be incapable of scaling up to vastly larger systems without extensive development work. Data warehouses, vast repositories of terabytes (trillions of bytes) or eventually petabytes (quadrillions of bytes), take information storage and retrieval to an entirely new scale. Collaborative computing systems unite geographically dispersed users who may interact using different hardware and software, and the security of a heterogeneous distributed system may depend upon its weakest link. Multimedia systems present many challenges of integration, complicating design to the point that unrecognized vulnerabilities proliferate. Agent systems let software programs act on behalf of the human users, and access control must be handled properly not only for each human being on the systems, but also for each software agent in it. With the advent of the Internet and the World Wide Web, security is being given serious consideration not only by government organizations but also by commercial organizations. With e-commerce it is important to protect the company's intellectual property, the flow of money, and the customer's privacy.

Secure Database Systems

Work on discretionary security for databases began in the 1970s when security was investigated for System R at IBM's Almaden Research Center. Essentially, the security properties specified the read and write access that a user may have to relations, attributes, and data elements. In the 1980s and 1990s security issues were investigated for object systems. Here the security properties specified the access that users had to objects, instance variables, and classes. In addition to read and write, method execution access was also specified.

Since the early 1980s much of the focus has been on multilevel secure database management systems, and various designs, prototypes and commercial products of multilevel database systems have been developed. Illustrative efforts include the SeaView effort by SRI International and the Lock Data Views effort by Honeywell. These efforts extended relational models with security properties. One challenge was to design a model where a user sees different values at different security levels. For example, at the Unclassified level an employee's salary appears to be $20,000 and at the Secret level it appears to be $50,000. In the standard relational model such ambiguous values cannot be represented due to integrity properties.

Note that several other significant developments have been made on multilevel security for other types of database systems, including security for object database systems in which security properties specify read, write, and method execution policies. Much work was also carried out on secure concurrency control and recovery. The idea here was to enforce security properties and still meet consistency without having covert channels. Research was also carried out on multilevel security for distributed, heterogeneous, and federated database systems.

As database systems become more sophisticated, securing these systems will become more difficult. For example, one problem that has existed for decades but takes on new urgency is the *inference problem*. Suppose someone with a relatively low security clearance has limited access to a database that is supposed to be secure, and maliciously wishes to obtain information that is kept at a higher security level. Can that person tease the information out of the system by posing multiple queries and inferring sensitive information from the legitimate responses?

Imagine that the Navy uses a distributed information system to track its ships as they sail on various missions around the world, and for simplicity's sake assume it has only two security levels, Secret and Unclassified. Many personnel will need access to some information about the ships, because they are responsible for the logistics of providing fuel, food, and mail from home along the routes that these ships sail. Thus, every person using the information system will know that ships named Champion, Ohio, and Florida are in the Mediterranean. Let's say the information system is a semantic net—that is, a network of nodes and the links between them. A node can be a concept such as "ship" or an entity such as the Champion. The links are relationships; for example, Champion IS-A ship. The relation "IS-A" means that an entity belongs to a category, in this case that the Champion belongs to the category of ships. Another Unclassified piece of information, expressed by a relationship between two nodes, might be: Champion CARRIES passengers. However, this may be disinformation, and the truth available only to users with Secret clearance is: Champion CARRIES Spark; Spark IS-A weapon. This is an example of "polyinstantiation" in a database, a situation in which users at different security levels see different information.

Champion is sailing under the cover story that it is going to Greece on a peaceful cultural mission, and at the Unclassified level the system may report: Champion HAS-DESTINATION Greece. But on the Secret level, it may report: Champion HAS-DESTINATION Libya. A relation that every ship on the seas must have is HAS-CAPTAIN, and at both the Unclassified and Secret levels, the system reports: Champion HAS-CAPTAIN Smith. The database may include a list of all senior officers, with some Unclassified information about them, such as: Smith IS-SKILLED-IN battle management. Perhaps through an oversight the following sensitive information was not classified Secret as it should have been: Smith TRAINED-ON Spark. However, an espionage agent might not know what the code word Spark stood for.

But perhaps the database has not classified these two pieces of information Secret either: Spark IS-SAME-TYPE-AS Star and Star IS-A weapon. An espionage agent could infer that Spark is also a weapon, but a new one the exact nature of which is classified, and conclude that Smith seems too skilled at warfare to be sent on a cultural mission. The spy would then have the challenge of trying to find Unclassified information that might confirm that Spark was aboard the Champion, and that the cultural delegation expected in Greece might actually be traveling by other means. The final challenge would be to deduce the warship's destination.

The inference problem also arises in statistical databases, because it may be possible to extract confidential information about single individuals from census data by means of a series of statistical analyses. For example, although there are many dentists in Fargo, North Dakota, there may be only one who has three children and is fifty-seven years old. A clever snoop, who is prevented from seeing the original census data but allowed to request a series of statistical analyses, may be able to deduce the annual income of the dentist and even to infer the dentist's identity. These hypothetical examples illustrate the importance of designing databases to provide inferential security—that is, to prevent malicious individuals with partial access to infer other information they do not have a right to see. Unfortunately, if a system has multiple levels of access and very complex data structures, it may not be possible even in principle to provide absolute confidence that inferential attacks cannot succeed. This is a lively area of research, which is made all the more challenging by the fact that the constant development of new tools for information finding and analysis gives potential information thieves more tools to work with.

Emerging Trends

The increasing interest in data mining since the 1990s has resulted in new security concerns. Because a data-mining tool can make correlations and associations that may be sensitive, a user's access to sophisticated data-mining tools could exacerbate the inference problem. On the other hand, data mining could also help with security problems such as intrusion detection and auditing. For instance, it may be possible to monitor the use of an information system and infer when people are attempting to infer information they are not entitled to have. Thus, the tool of the intruders may be used against them, to strengthen rather than to erode security.

The advent of the Web resulted in extensive investigations of security for digital libraries and electronic commerce. In addition to developing sophisticated encryption techniques, security research also focused on securing the Web clients as well as the servers. Programming languages such as Java were designed with security in mind. Much research was also carried out on securing software agents. Organizations such as the Object Management Group (OMG) started working groups to investigate security properties, and as a result, secure distributed object management systems became commercially available.

It is a unique challenge to develop appropriate security policies for the Web because no one person or organization owns it. Various security solutions, starting with encryption, have been proposed to protect information such as credit card numbers and social security numbers. In certain cases tradeoffs will need to be made between security and other important considerations such as the quality of service. And along with technological solutions, legal aspects will also have to be examined. Directions in secure database systems are being driven by developments on the World Wide Web. Databases are no longer stand-alone systems but are being integrated into various applications such as multimedia, electronic commerce, mobile computing systems, digital libraries, and collaboration systems, and security issues for these new generation systems will be very important.

There have been many developments on various object technologies such as distributed object systems and components and frameworks, and eventually the security policies of the various subsystems and components will have to be integrated to form policies for the entire systems. New technologies such as data mining will help solve security problems such as intrusion detection and auditing, but these technologies can also violate the privacy of individuals because adversaries can use the new tools to extract unauthorized information. Another important security challenge that lies ahead is finding a way to protect migrating legacy databases and applications.

Bhavani Thuraisingham

See also Identity Authentication; Privacy; Law and HCI

FURTHER READING

Air Force summer study board report on multilevel secure database systems. (1983). Washington, DC: Department of Defense.

Bell, D., & LaPadula, L. (1975). *Secure computer systems: Unified exposition and multics interpretation* (Tech. Rep. No. ESD-TR-75-306). Bedford, MA: Hanscom Air Force Base.

Ferarri, E., & Thuraisingham, B. (2000). Database security: Survey. In M. Piattini, M. & O. Diaz (Eds.), *Advanced database technology and design.* Boston: Artech House.

Proceedings of the IFIP 1997 and 1998 Conference Series in Database Security (Panel on Data Warehousing and Data Mining Security). North Holland, Amsterdam.

Rubinovitz, H., & Thuraisingham, B. (1994). Security Constraint Processsing in a Distributed Database Environment. *ACM Conference on Computer Science,* 356-363.

Special issue on computer security. (1983). *IEEE Computer.*

Thuraisingham, B. (1989). Security for object-oriented database systems. *Proceedings of the ACM OOPSLA Conference.* New Orleans, LA.

Thuraisingham, B., et al. (1993). Design and implementation of a database inference controller. *Data and Knowledge Engineering Journal,* 8.

SEMANTIC WEB

Beginning in the 1990s, the World Wide Web has evolved into what is now called the *semantic web.* To provide more information more usefully much of the work of data finding and assembling must be automated, which requires that Web pages and information available in other forms on the Web be identified in a way that computers can recognize, evaluate, and work with in complex ways. To understand how this can be done, we need to examine how the semantic web is being created, the relationship between Web services and the semantic web, the layers of the semantic web, and security issues.

Defining the Semantic Web

Many organizations urgently need efficient access to data, ways of efficiently sharing the data, methods for extracting information from the data, and unhindered use of the data. As a result, there have been many efforts to integrate the various data sources scattered across several websites, and extracting information from these databases in the form of patterns and trends has also become important. These data sources may be databases managed by database management systems or data from multiple data sources warehoused in a repository.

The advent of the World Wide Web (WWW) in the mid 1990s resulted in an even greater demand for managing data, information, and knowledge effectively. There is now so much data on the Web that managing it with conventional tools is almost impossible. Therefore, to provide interoperability as well as warehousing between the multiple data sources and systems, and to extract information from the databases and warehouses on the Web, various new tools are being developed.

While the current Web technologies facilitate the integration of information from a syntactic (form) point of view, there is still a lot to be done to integrate the semantics (meaning) of various systems and applications. That is, current Web technologies depend on the human-in-the-loop for information integration. Tim Berners-Lee, the father of the WWW, realized the inadequacies of Web technologies and subsequently strove to make the Web more intelligent. His goal was to have a Web that could liberate humans from having to integrate disparate information sources and to carry out extensive searches. He concluded that to reach his goal he would need machine-understandable Web pages and ontologies (a set of formal definitions of the relations among terms) for information integration. This resulted in the notion of the semantic web.

A semantic web can be thought of as a highly intelligent and sophisticated Web that needs little or no human intervention to carry out tasks such as scheduling appointments, coordinating activities, searching for complex documents, and integrating disparate databases and information systems. While progress has been made toward developing such an intelligent Web there is still a lot to be done.

Technologies such as intelligent agents, ontology matching, and markup languages are contributing to the development of the semantic web. Intelligent agents are software programs that can follow instructions in a somewhat complex way, carrying out tasks like getting information on a book publisher, for example, and being able to deduce that if the company is in Chicago it also is in Illinois. Ontology matching is like fitting alternative sets of terms together, for example, permitting a software agent in search of a com-

pany's zip code to realize that the "postal code" on the company's website is the same thing. A markup language is a standard system for embedding information in a document, for example, machine-readable bytes on a website that tell the agent which numbers are the postal code. Nevertheless, one still needs a human user to make decisions and take actions.

Imagine that a college student is writing a term paper about how computer science is concentrated in certain geographic areas of the United States. The student wants a table of how many computer scientists there are in each state, per 100,000 employed persons, and gives the computerized intelligent agent clear instructions, and the agent searches the Web for the information. Not finding the desired table already on a website anywhere, it assembles the table from other websites. A site at the census bureau gives the populations of the fifty states in a table marked up with computer codes identifying the nature of the data. One column is called StateName, with a reference to an ontology (which may be on a completely different website) that defines these unambiguously as the names of the fifty U.S. states, not the states of Australia or the Canadian provinces. A second column in the same table is tagged as EmployedPopulation. On a different website, the agent finds a table that also has StateName plus a variable called ComputerScientists. One table may have the states in alphabetical order (Alabama to Wyoming), whereas the other has them in order of the geographic regions (Maine to Hawaii). Guided by the ontologies and its own programmed reasoning powers, the intelligent agent creates a new table, correctly calculating computer scientists per 100,000 employed for each of the fifty American states, and presents it (all in the fraction of a second) to the user.

Web Services

Much of the early Web developments focused on search engines and browsers to sift through large quantities of information rapidly. The World Wide Web is essentially a gigantic hypertext system, which has now evolved into a hypermedia system as it handles multiple data types including text, images, video, audio, and animations. The Web also manages structured as well as unstructured data. Structured data could come from relational databases, which can contain very complex sets of relationships among entities and their attributes, as well as from simple files. The challenges are not only to carry out efficient searches but also to integrate the data and information on the Web so that the users see the Web as a seamless system. As the goal is to provide a complete set of services for the human user, the Web must carry out all needed functions, such as doing tedious calculations, managing appointments and schedules, giving guidance on where to purchase something for the best price, and offering advice on which financial analyst or physician to go to. That is, users need a collection of semantic web services, and the Web must understand what this collection provides.

The evolution from the basic Web to the semantic web is under way, yet much more needs to be done. Currently the significant developments include developing markup languages for the common representation of documents and providing some services on the Web. These could include directory services to locate information, publish-and-subscribe services to publish documents as well as to subscribe to documents, security services to ensure secure information integration, real-time services to manage information in real time, and dependable computing services for carrying out computationally intensive work for business, government, or science. Web services description languages (WSDL) are also being developed.

Making Web services more intelligent is challenging because they must not only provide services to human users, they must also make selective decisions depending on the needs of these users. For example, the president of the United States may require certain types of services while a professor at a university may require a different set of services. The semantic web must customize the service. The advice it gives to human users about what types of services to use and when to use them must be appropriate for the context and goals of individual users.

Layers of the Semantic Web

Tim Berners-Lee has specified various layers for the semantic web. At the lowest level are the protocols for communication, including TCP/IP (Transmission Control Protocol/Internet Protocol), HTTP (Hyper-text Transfer Protocol), and SSL (Secure Socket Layer). The next level is the XML (eXtensible Markup Language) layer that also includes XML schemas. The following level is the RDF (Resource Description Framework) layer. After that comes the Ontologies and Interoperability layer and finally, at the highest level, is the Trust Management layer.

TCP/IP, HTTP, and SSL are the protocols for data transmission. They are built on top of more basic communication layers. With these protocols users can transmit the Web pages over the Internet without dealing with syntax or the semantics of the documents. Then comes the XML and XML schemas layer. XML is the standard representation language for document exchange. If a document is not marked-up, then each machine may display the document in its own way. This makes document exchange extremely difficult. If all documents are marked up using the formal rules of XML, then there is uniform representation and presentation of documents. Without some form of common representation of documents, it is impossible to have any sort of communication on the Web. XML schemas essentially describe the structure of the XML documents. Both XML and XML schemas are the invention of Tim Berners-Lee and the World Wide Web Consortium (W3C), which was formed in the mid-1990s.

XML focuses only on the syntax (form) of a document, not on its semantics (meaning). A document can have different interpretations at different sites, which is a major issue for integrating information seamlessly across the Web. In order to overcome this significant limitation, the W3C started discussions on the RDF language in the late 1990s. RDF, which uses XML syntax but has support to express semantics, is essential to integrating and exchanging information in a meaningful way on the Web. However, while XML has received widespread acceptance, RDF is only now beginning to get acceptance. While XML documents are exchanged over protocols such as TCP/IP, HTTP, and SSL, RDF documents are built using XML.

The next layer is the Ontologies and Interoperability layer. RDF is only a specification language for expressing syntax and semantics. What entities need to be specified? How can the community accept common definitions? To solve these issues, various communities such as the medical community, the financial community, the defense community, and even the entertainment community have come up with ontologies. Ontologies can be used to describe the wines of the world or the different types of aircraft used by the United States Air Force, or to specify diseases or financial entities. The idea is that once a community has developed ontologies, the community will publish these ontologies on the Web and everyone interested in the ontologies of the community will use them. Of course, within a community there may be different factions and each faction could come up with its own ontologies. For example, the American Medical Association could come up with its ontologies for diseases while the British Medical Association could come up with different ontologies. This forces the system and, in this case, the semantic web to develop common ontologies. While the goal is for the British and American communities to come up with common ontologies, in the real world, differences do exist. Ideally, ontologies facilitate information exchange and integration. Ontologies specified using RDF syntax are used by Web services so that the Web can provide semantic web services to human users.

The final layer is Logic, Proof, and Trust. How do you trust the information on the Web? Obviously it depends on where it comes from, which means that interested parties have to communicate with each other and determine how to trust each other and how to trust the information obtained on the Web. Logic-based approaches and proof theories are being examined for enforcing trust on the semantic web.

Information Integration and Mining

Information, essentially data that make sense, is everywhere on the Web. The database research and engineering community has been working on database integration for some decades, encountering many challenges, including the interoperability of heterogeneous data sources. The various databases are integrated by means of schemas, which are essentially data that describe the data in the databases.

Integrating the diverse and disparate data sources on the Web is an especially complicated challenge that depends on technologies, many of which will be Web services. For example, the data may not be in databases but in files both structured and unstructured or in the form of tables, text, images, audio, or video. XML, RDF, Web services, and related technologies have brought about new ideas and ways to integrate information.

Some argue that the semantic web should be viewed as a gigantic distributed database with millions of nodes, each containing data that has to be integrated and managed, and that the developments of the 1980s and 1990s should be used to manage its heterogeneous databases. However, we now have XML, RDF, ontologies, Web services, machine learning, intelligent agents, and data-mining technologies. The challenge is to integrate these technologies with what has been done already to provide efficient solutions for information integration on the Web. Integration demands not only representation languages and ontologies, but also techniques and tools to extract, manage, integrate, and exchange information efficiently.

Data mining is the process of extracting information from large collections of data (often previously unknown) through machine learning and statistical reasoning techniques. Researchers are developing techniques to extract information from Web databases. Mining usage patterns can help organizations carry out targeted marketing. It is also possible to mine and obtain the structure of the Web.

Conventional search engines can find only a fraction of the information actually available on the Web, chiefly the parts that consist of ready-made pages that have definite URLs or Web addresses. The so-called Deep Web consists of a vast number of data resources mainly belonging to companies, governments, and universities that can be queried by their own systems and assembled on the fly into the form of a Web page, but which do not exist in the form of static Web pages that can be mined using traditional approaches. They could be among the most valuable parts of the future semantic web.

Semantic-web mining depends on Web mining as well as tools to extract semantics for interoperbility. While data mining can help build the semantic web, the semantic web can facilitate data mining.

Security involves not only preventing malicious or accidental harm to information resources, but also controlling who has access to what information under what circumstances. It cuts across all layers of the semantic web. For example, consider the lowest layer. Security depends on secure TCP/IP, secure sockets, and secure HTTP, and there are now security protocols for these lower-layer protocols. Security also needs end-to-end network security—that is, secure TCP/IP cannot be built on untrusted communication layers. The next layer, XML and XML schemas, must also be secure—that is, access to various portions of the document for reading, browsing, and modifications must be controlled. The next step is securing RDF, which requires security for the interpretations and semantics as well as for the XML. For example, within a certain context, portions of the document may be unclassified while within certain other contexts the document may be classified. Much research and development work has been carried out on security-constraints processing for relational databases, but it remains to be seen whether these results can be applied unchanged to the semantic web.

Once XML and RDF have been secured, the next step is to examine security for ontologies and interoperation. That is, ontologies may have security levels attached to them. Certain parts of the ontologies could be secret while certain other parts may be unclassified. The challenge is how to use these ontologies for secure information integration. Researchers have done some work on the secure interoperability of databases but other work needs to be done so that the information on the Web can be managed, integrated, and exchanged securely.

Closely related to security is privacy. That is, certain portions of a document may be private while certain other portions may be public or semiprivate. Privacy has recently received a lot of attention, partly due to national security concerns, and it may become a critical issue for the semantic web, because it isn't yet clear how users can take advantage of the semantic web while maintaining their own privacy and sometimes anonymity as well as the privacy and anonymity of the people described by the information.

Security must be inserted into a computer or information system right from the beginning, and sim-ilarly, it cannot be an afterthought for the semantic web. However, the system will become inefficient if security must be guaranteed 100 percent at all times. What is needed is a flexible security policy.

Realizing the Semantic Web

Building the semantic web is an evolutionary process, and we are already in the process of migrating from the Web to the semantic web. Web services and XML were, arguably, the first step, and we can safely say that there will be no end. Society has embraced the Web, and all communities would benefit from its becoming more intelligent. Therefore, as technologies emerge they will be incorporated into the semantic web and help to build it.

Different communities are already building their own semantic webs—that is, there will be no one semantic web. The medical community will come up with its own ontologies and XML specifications and build its own semantic web while the financial community will build another one better adapted to its purposes. The underlying principles will remain the same, but the ontologies, tools, and security provisions will differ. The goal is to make the Web more intelligent so it can lift the burden of tedious data-drudgery from human users.

Bhavani Thuraisingham

See also Information Organization; Information Retrieval; Ontology; Website Design

FURTHER READINGS

Berners-Lee, T., Hendler, J., & Lassila, O. (2001). The Semantic Web. *Scientific American, 284*(5), 34–43.

St. Laurent, S. (2000). *XML*. New York: McGraw Hill.

Sheth, A., & Larson, J. (1990). Federated database systems. *ACM Computing Surveys, 22*(3), 183–286.

Thuraisingham, B., & Ford, W. (1995). Security constraint processing in a distributed database management system. *IEEE Transactions on Knowledge and Data Engineering*, 274–293.

Thuraisingham, B. (1998). *Data mining: Technologies, techniques, tools and trends*. Boca Raton, FL: CRC Press.

Thuraisingham, B. (2001). *XML Databases and the Semantic Web*. Boca Raton, FL: CRC Press.

SMART HOMES

We live in an increasingly interconnected and automated society. So-called smart environments—environments that are able to respond to the people within them—embody this trend by linking computers to everyday tasks and settings. Important features of such environments are that they possess a degree of autonomy, adapt themselves to changing conditions, and communicate with humans in a natural way. These systems can be found in offices, airports, hospitals, classrooms, and many other environments. This article discusses automation of our most personal environment: the home.

We define a smart home as one that is able to acquire and apply knowledge about its inhabitants and their surroundings in order to adapt to the inhabitants and meet the goals of comfort and efficiency. Designing and implementing smart homes requires a breadth of knowledge not limited to a single discipline or technical specialty; machine learning, decision sciences, human-machine interfaces, wireless networking, mobile communications, databases, sensor networks, and pervasive computing all make contributions. A smart home can control many aspects of the environment, such as climate, lighting, maintenance, and entertainment. Intelligent automation of these activities can reduce the amount of interaction required by inhabitants and reduce energy consumption and other potential operating costs. The same capabilities can be used to provide important features such as health monitoring and home security through such operations as the detection of unusual activities.

Smart-home operations can be characterized by the following scenario. At 6:45 AM, the home turns up the heat because it has learned that it needs 15 minutes to warm to the inhabitant's favorite waking temperature. The alarm sounds at 7:00, which signals the bedroom light and the coffee maker to go on. The inhabitant, Bob, steps into the bathroom and turns on the light. The home records this manual interaction, displays the morning news on the bathroom video screen, and turns on the shower. While Bob is shaving, the home senses that Bob is four pounds over his ideal weight and adjusts the suggested daily menu that will later be displayed in the kitchen. When Bob finishes grooming, the bathroom light turns off while the kitchen light and display turn on. During breakfast, Bob requests the janitor robot to clean the house. When Bob leaves for work, the home secures all doors behind him and starts the lawn sprinklers despite knowing the 30 percent chance of rain. To reduce energy costs, the house turns down the heat until 15 minutes before Bob is due home. Because the refrigerator is low on milk and cheese, the home places a grocery order. When Bob arrives home, his grocery order has arrived, the house is back at Bob's desired temperature, and the hot tub is waiting for him.

Several smart-home projects have been initiated in research labs. The Georgia Tech Aware Home, the MIT Intelligent Room, and the Microsoft eHome all focus on identifying user movements and activities with an impressive array of sensors. The MavHome Smart Home at the University of Texas at Arlington and the Neural Network House at the University of Colorado at Boulder control aspects of the house such as lighting and temperature in response to an inhabitant's activities (for example, turning on the lights in the kitchen in the morning based on the fact that the inhabitant uses the kitchen at that time.) —an adaptation that goes beyond the abilities of other smart homes. The interest of industrial labs in intelligent environments is evidenced by the creation of standards such as Jini (an open software architecture for adaptive network-centric solutions), Bluetooth (a wireless technology standard for connecting mobile products), and SIP (a signaling protocol to support Internet and remote presence), and by supporting technologies such as Xerox PARC's Zombie Board (a networked multimedia whiteboard), the Cisco Internet Home, and the Verizon Connected Family project (Internet-based services for the home). Perhaps the best way to understand a smart home, however, is to examine a case study.

Case Study: MavHome Smart Home

The MavHome smart home at the University of Texas at Arlington represents an environment that acts as an intelligent agent, perceiving the state of the home through sensors and acting upon the environment through device controllers. The agent's goal is to maximize its inhabitants' comfort while minimizing the cost of running the home. In order to achieve this goal, the house must be able to predict, reason about, and adapt to its inhabitants.

Control of the entire house is performed by an agent. However, the MavHome software is a multi-agent system organized in a hierarchy. Thus, as control of every task within the house may be too great a task for a single software architecture to handle efficiently, the task can be decomposed into subtasks, each handled by a separate subordinate agent, and the subtasks can be further decomposed as necessary. For example, one agent may monitor and control the master bathroom but can assign the task of monitoring and controlling the shower to a separate subordinate agent.

The desired smart-home capabilities, therefore, must be organized into a software architecture that lets them operate seamlessly while allowing improvements to be made to any of the supporting technologies. The supporting technologies are divided into four cooperating layers. The decision layer selects actions for the agent to execute. The information layer collects information and generates inferences useful for decision making. The communication layer routes information and requests between agents. The physical layer contains the environment hardware.

Because controlling an entire house is a very large and complex learning and reasoning process, the process is decomposed into reconfigurable subareas, or tasks. Thus the physical layer for one agent may represent another agent somewhere in the hierarchy, which is capable of executing the task selected by the requesting agent.

In general, information moves from the bottom up: Sensors monitor the environment (keeping track, for example, of lawn moisture levels) and, if necessary, transmit the information to another agent through the communication layer. The database records the information in the information layer, updates its learned concepts and predictions accordingly, and alerts the decision layer to the presence of new data. During action execution, information flows from the top down. The decision layer selects an action (for example, to run the sprinklers) and re-

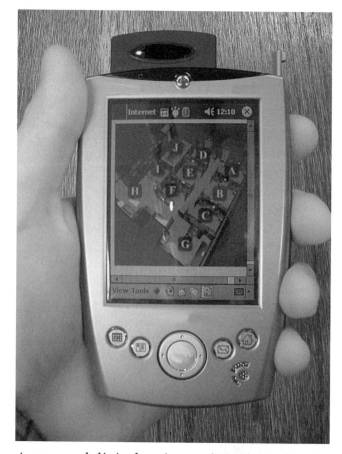

A personal digital assistant (PDA) used in the MavHome smart-home project at the University of Texas, Arlington. Photo courtesy of Michael Youngblood.

lates the decision to the information layer. After updating the database, the communication layer routes the action to the appropriate effector, which executes it. If the effector is actually another agent, the agent receives the command through its effector as perceived information and must decide upon the best method of executing the desired action. Specialized interface agents allow interaction with users, robots, and external resources such as the Internet. Agents can communicate with one another using a hierarchical flow of information based on their functional location in the architecture. At the lowest level in the agent hierarchy, the agent's task is not further decomposed. For example, an effector component would directly control an associated device or piece of hardware (e.g., bathwater), rather than passing execution of a more abstract task to another agent (e.g., provide assistance to the inhabitant for morning grooming in the bathroom).

In order to maximize comfort, minimize cost, and adapt to inhabitants, a smart home must rely on tools from the field of artificial intelligence, such as prediction and automated decision making. Prediction guesses the inhabitant's next action and predicts the behavior of devices in the home. For example, it predicts how much time is needed to warm the house to a specified temperature and how much energy that task requires. MavHome needs to predict the inhabitant's next action in order to automate selected repetitive tasks for the inhabitant (for example, in the scenario described above, prediction would allow MavHome to automate the turning on of the bathroom light for Bob). The home will need to make this prediction based on the current state of the inhabitant and the house, as well as the inhabitant's previous interactions with various devices. The number of prediction errors must be minimal, and the algorithms must be able to deliver predictions with minimal delays for computation. Prediction must then be handed over to a decision layer that will select actions that will let the house meet its goals.

Predicting Inhabitants' Actions

The inhabitant of a smart home typically interacts with various devices as part of his or her routine activities. These interactions may be treated as a sequence of events, with some inherent pattern of recurrence. To predict the inhabitant's actions, the home must first mine the data to identify sequences of actions that are regular and repeatable enough to generate predictions. Then it can use a sequence-matching approach to predict the next action in one of these sequences.

To mine the data, the home can pass an examination window over the history of the inhabitant's actions, looking for sequences within the window that merit attention. Each sequence is evaluated using the minimum description length principle, which favors sequences that can be reduced by replacing each instance of the discovered pattern with a pointer to the pattern's definition. A regularity factor (daily, weekly, monthly) helps compress the data and thus increases the value of a pattern. Action sequences are first filtered by the mined sequences. If the mining algorithm considers a sequence to be significant, then predictions can be made for events within the sequence window. When the mining algorithm is used as a filter for two alternative-prediction algorithms, the accuracy of the prediction increases on average by 50 percent. Using the mining algorithm as a filter ensures that MavHome will not erroneously seek to automate anomalous and highly variable activities.

Automated Decision Making

The goal of MavHome's decision-making algorithm is to enable the home to automate basic functions in order to maximize the comfort of the inhabitants and minimize the cost of operating the home. It is assumed that comfort will be maximized by minimizing the inhabitants' manual interactions with the home; the home's energy usage can be measured to determine its operating cost.

Because the goal is a combination of these two factors, blind automation of all inhabitant actions is frequently not the desired solution. For example, an inhabitant might turn on the hallway light in the morning before opening the blinds in the living room. If MavHome opens the blinds in the living room before the inhabitant leaves the bedroom, it will save the inhabitant time and alleviate the need for the hallway lights, thereby decreasing the home's energy usage. Similarly, if MavHome turns down the air conditioning after the inhabitant leaves the house and turns it back up before the inhabitant returns, it will save more energy than it would if it turned the air conditioning to maximum after the inhabitant arrived home in order to cool the house as quickly as possible.

MavHome uses reinforcement learning to acquire an optimal decision policy. In this framework, the agent learns autonomously from potentially delayed rewards rather than from a teacher, reducing the necessity for the inhabitant to supervise or program the system. (A reward for any agent in the architecture is a numeric response to the selected action, reflecting how well the action achieves the overall goal of the agent—at the top level of the hierarchy, the entire house. Some outcomes of the action deserving reward, such as increasing comfort of the inhabitant, may not be perceivable until several actions in a row are executed. The reward after such a sequence of actions should be distributed among the actions leading up to this outcome, thus in some cases the rewards are delayed.)

The agent explores the effects of its actions over time and uses this analysis to form decision policies that optimize the expected future reward. MavHome learns a policy based on a state space, $S = \{s_i\}$, consisting of the states of the devices in the home, the predictions of the next event, and expected energy utilization over the next time unit. A reward function, r, takes into account the amount of user interaction required, the energy consumption of the house, and other parameters that quantify the performance of the home. This reward function can be tuned to the particular preferences of the inhabitants, thus providing a simple means to customize the home's performance. Q-learning, an algorithm in which Q represents a learned-action function value, is used to approximate an optimal action strategy by estimating the predicted value, $Q(s_t, a_t)$, of executing action a_t in state s_t at time t. After each action, the utility is updated as

$$Q(s_t, a_t) \leftarrow \alpha[r_{t+1} + \gamma \max_{a \in A} Q(s_{t+1}, a) - Q(s_t, a_t)].$$

After learning, the optimal action, a_t, can be determined as

$$a_t = \arg \max_{a \in A} Q(s_t, a).$$

MavHome Implementation

The MavHome smart-home project is in place at the University of Texas at Arlington. Students register their presence in the environment using a fingerprint reader, and data is collected continuously based on their interactions with devices in the environment.

A live demonstration of MavHome was conducted in the fall of 2002. During the previous weeks, activity data was collected for one of the project participants ("MavHome Bob"). Actions included turning on lights en route to his desk in the morning, watching a live news feed on the computer, taking a coffee and TV break, and turning off devices on the way out at the end of the day. Despite the presence of approximately fifty people during the live demonstration (who were setting off motion sensors throughout the environment), MavHome correctly predicted and automated each activity.

Practical Considerations

So how easily can the features of a smart home be integrated into new or existing homes? The software described in the MavHome implementation consists of commercial X10 controllers, a computer, a variety of sensors, and a wireless network. A simple implementation can be integrated into an existing house for under a thousand dollars, in many cases. If robots or customized devices are introduced, the cost increases.

A computer interface in a smart home must be very simple. Manual control of devices must be able to override home decisions, and alternative interfaces, including voice control, are offered. Other than starting or resetting the software, no interaction with the computer is required. In our experiments, the software adapted to user activities in a couple of weeks, but the training time will vary according to the complexity of the users' actions and the number of people in the home. Various types of interaction are possible depending on the needs of the users. The users can vary the certainty threshold at which activities are automated, although this is not necessary because manual resetting of actions selected by the house will eventually cause the house to not automate those particular commands. The users can also request that the home simply make suggestions for automation, which the users then accept or decline on a case-by-case basis.

Introducing intelligent control into a house can result in a number of privacy and safety issues. Safety constraints must be placed on each device to ensure that the house will not select an action that endangers inhabitants. The house may not be allowed, for example, to select a temperature setting below 50 degrees or above 90 degrees. The entire automation can be quickly disabled with one mouse click or voice command—all devices can operate without computer control.

Smart homes typically benefit from collecting information about the health, typical patterns, and other features of their inhabitants. (Such data collection might be performed by researchers or commercial manufacturers of smart homes to improve the architecture or efficiency of the houses). This leads to a number of data privacy and security issues. Data should only be collected with the inhabitants' consent, and shared with other sites only as the inhabitants permit. New smart homes in neighboring locations could, for example, benefit from patterns learned in an older home, but care must be taken to share information in a way that does not violate the privacy of the inhabitants of the older home.

At present, smart-home technologies make it possible to reduce the work required to maintain a home, lessen energy utilization, and provide special benefits for elderly residents and people with disabilities. In the future, it should be possible to generalize these abilities for use in other environments, including offices, hospitals, automobiles, and airports.

Diane J. Cook and Michael Youngblood

See also Ubiquitous Computing

FURTHER READING

Bobick, A., Intille, S., Davis, J., Baird, F., Pinhanez, C., Campbell, L., et al. (2000). The KidsRoom: A perceptually-based interactive and immersive story environment. *Presence, 8*(4), 369–393.

Das, S., Cook, D. J., Bhattacharya, A., Heierman, III, E. O., & Lin, T.-Y. (2003). The role of prediction algorithms in the MavHome smart home architecture. *IEEE Wireless Communications, 9*(6), 77–84.

Demchak, G. (2000). *Towards a post-industrial architecture: Design and construction of houses for the information age.* Unpublished master's thesis, Massachusetts Institute of Technology, Cambridge, MA.

Fox, A., Johanson, B., Hanrahan, P., & Winograd, T. (2000). Integrating information appliances into an interactive space. *IEEE Computer Graphics and Applications, 20*(3), 54–65.

Hedberg, S. After desktop computing: A progress report on smart environments research. *IEEE Intelligent Systems, 15*(5), 7–9.

Kidd, C., Orr, R. J., Abowd, G. D., Atkeson, D., Essa, I., MacIntyre, B., et al. (1999). The Aware Home: A living laboratory for ubiquitous computing. In N. Streitz, J. Seigal, V. Hartkopf, & S. Konomi (Eds.), *Cooperative buildings: Integrating information, organizations and architecture (Second International Workshop, Cobuild '99, Pittsburgh, USA, October 1999, proceedings)* (pp. 191–198). Heidelberg, Germany: Springer.

Lesser, V., Atighetchi, M., Benyo, B., Horling, B., Raja, A., Vincent, R., et al. (1999, January). The Intelligent Home testbed. In *Proceedings of the Autonomy Control Software Workshop.* Seattle, WA.

Mozer, M. (1998). The Neural Network House: An environment that adapts to its inhabitants. In *Proceedings of the AAAI spring symposium on intelligent environments* (pp. 110–114). Menlo Park, CA: AAAI.

Peace, S., & Holland, C. (Eds.). (2001). *Inclusive housing in an ageing society.* Bristol, UK: The Policy Press.

Russell, S., & Norvig, P. (2003). *Artificial intelligence: A modern approach.* Englewood Cliffs, NJ: Prentice Hall.

Torrance, M. C. (1995, May). Advances in human-computer interaction: The intelligent room. *Working notes of the CHI 95 research symposium.* Denver, CO.

Watkins, C. J. C. H. (1989). *Learning from delayed rewards.* Doctoral dissertation, Cambridge University, Cambridge, UK.

Ziv, J., & Lempel, A. (1978). Compression of individual sequences via variable rate coding. *IEEE Transactions on Information Theory, IT-24,* 530–536.

SOCIABLE MEDIA

Sociable media are media that enhance communication and the formation of social ties among people. Such media are not new—letter writing can be traced back thousands of years—but the advent of the computer has brought about an immense number of new forms.

Researchers in the field of sociable media study how existing technologies are used, how they affect the relationships among the people using them, and how they transform society. Researchers also design new technologies, drawing from fields such as cognitive science, sociology, and urban design, to create systems that better support social interaction. They also examine the ways by which social cues are communicated in the real world and the virtual world, discover the limits imposed upon online communities by their mediated nature, and explore directions that virtual societies can take that physical societies cannot take. The goal is to understand and improve the social aspects of mediated communication.

Definition of the Perspective

Mediated communication is any communication in which the participants communicate via some sort of medium, such as written letters, telephone calls, and e-mail. Mediated communication is in contrast to unmediated, face-to-face communication in which the participants are in direct contact with each other. In unmediated communication, social cues are communicated through words, tone of voice, gesture, clothing, facial expression, proximity, and so forth. These cues provide information about a person's age, race, social class, and gender; they reveal emotional state; and they help to choreograph the interaction. In mediated communication, some or most of these cues are absent, and other cues, nonexistent in unmediated communication, may exist. The social information that participants can assess about each other varies greatly from one medium to another. Participants might not know with whom they are speaking or how large their audience is—or they might have access to a detailed history of their partners' interactions or to the assessments others have made about them. They might be communicating in real time (synchronously) or in intervals ranging from seconds to days; the response to a message thus might be an immediate emotional reaction or a well-thought-out reaction.

The sociable media approach to evaluating media differs from the traditional, information theoretical approach. With the latter approach the key measurement of a medium is the amount of information, measured in bits (units of computer information equivalent to the result of a choice between two alternatives), that a particular channel can carry, and the goal is higher capacity and efficiency. The sociable media approach is more subjective and context dependent. For example, given a channel of sufficiently high bandwidth (the capacity for data transfer of an electronic communications system), one might think that videoconferencing, in which many thousands of bits are transmitted per second, would be clearly preferable to text interaction, a medium of much lower bandwidth. Yet, although more information is transmitted by video, we are not sure, from a sociable media perspective, which is preferable. Do we want to know what the participants look like? Do we not want to know their ages, race, weight, and so forth? Is the interaction the focus of everyone's attention, or is it a peripheral activity, one carried out while attending to other tasks?

The sociable media perspective also helps us to understand how social information is encoded in a message. At first glance the text of a message might appear to be its sole source of information. Yet, we can find other important social cues. They are in the style of writing—whether formal or informal, in standard English or in prose peppered with emoti-cons (keyboard characters that typically represent a facial expression or suggest an attitude or emotion and that are used in computerized communications), acronyms, and abbreviations. They are in the recipient list because one can send other people copies of a message, privately as co-conspirators or openly as witnesses. They are in the timing of replies, whether replies are immediate or delayed by days or weeks. The study of sociable media involves the evaluation and interpretation of the social nuances of different media in different situations.

The roots of sociable media reach back about four thousand years. Although the earliest known clay tablets are administrative records, archaeologists have found plaques bearing personal correspondence dating as far back as 2000 BCE. Throughout most of our history, letters (i.e., messages written on physical objects that are conveyed from sender to receiver) have been the dominant form of sociable media. Letter writing has sustained friendships and initiated romances across great distances. Historical accounts of brides being courted across the Atlantic attest to the ability of this medium to convey an impression of the character, personality, and emotional intensity of the writer. Mediated spoken communication became possible only during the late nineteenth century with the invention of the telephone, but since then conversing at a distance has quickly become an indispensable part of daily social life. Visual images have long been an important, if infrequent, medium for social communication (the English king Henry VIII married his fourth wife, Anne of Cleves, on the basis of the German painter Hans Holbein's portrait of her). The development of inexpensive film and cameras and, more recently, the ability to easily send images electronically are making transmitted images an increasingly common yet still evolving form of social communication.

The advent of computer-mediated communication has made possible many new forms of sociable media. The computer brings a great deal of design freedom, allowing many aspects of the medium, such as whether it is ephemeral or persistent, named or anonymous, to be designed rather than technologically determined. E-mail, online chats, newsgroups, simulation games, weblogs (online journals), and virtual reality conferencing are but a few of the existing computer-based sociable media, and more are yet to be invented.

Sociability is an essential part of human nature. We live and thrive in cooperative groups. Social interaction helps us form relationships and coalitions, evaluate status, discourage free riders, and enforce local norms. Much of our conversation is social, either in topic (as in the discussion of others' actions) or form (as in the status messages encoded in tone of voice and grammar). Yet, we often do not recognize the importance of sociability. We often assume that information exchange is the primary purpose of language and that conversations in which no explicit knowledge is imparted are a waste of time. Yet, in any conversation, no matter how seemingly pointless, the participants are exchanging social information, subtly encoded.

People have not necessarily designed communication technologies for sociability. People often design such technologies within the context of engineering and business, domains that prize efficiency and utility. Yet, people, being highly social, quickly find social uses for any communication medium. The history of communication technologies illustrates both the commercial world's underestimation of the importance of social communication and people's readiness to adapt media for social purposes. The telephone was initially marketed as a business tool; several decades passed before people recognized its social use for residential customers. The early planners of networked computers did not envision their social potential, but early users developed e-mail within two years of the initial connection. Developers of the World Wide Web initially conceived it as an academic publishing tool, yet personal homepages with pictures, anecdotes, and hyperlinks to one's friends appeared almost as soon as an accessible Web browser was available. Today people are increasingly aware of the importance of the social uses of media and are making more effort to create sociable media.

Creating sociable media involves understanding the features that affect how they can be used. Among the most important features are rhythm, format, bandwidth, permanence, and identification. For example, e-mail typically is, respectively, asynchronous (not occurring in real time), text based, low bandwidth, persistent, and has a wide range in the participants' identifications. An online game, for comparison, might be, respectively, synchronous, graphical, medium bandwidth, ephemeral, and anonymous.

Rhythm

The rhythm of a medium—whether it is synchronous or asynchronous—describes how quickly messages are exchanged with it.

With synchronous media, the participants communicate at the same time. Face-to-face conversations are synchronous, as are phone calls and some computer-based media such as chat. The participants must be available at the same time, providing a sense of co-presence, even if they are physically far from each other.

With asynchronous media, the participants communicate independently. E-mail and written letters are asynchronous. The time required for a message to be sent ranges from seconds in the case of e-mail to a day to several weeks for letters (even longer before air mail). Participants in an asynchronous discussion are able to compose their messages more carefully. They do not need to be available at the same time; however, this fact also means they do not have the sense of presence that users of synchronous media have.

The rhythm of a conversation—how quickly each participant responds, the length of each utterance or message, and so forth—is itself expressive. Responding to an e-mail within a few seconds conveys a different message than does waiting days or weeks to respond. Rhythm is also roughly correlated with formality; people often use asynchronous media more formally.

The speed at which a medium can convey a message affects the type of information that is exchanged and the communication style. As communication frequency increases, messages become more informal and more intimate. This fact is true even within the same medium—rapidly exchanged papers and notes are more informal than is a letter that requires weeks of travel to its destination. Written letters, which at their fastest are still slower than computational media, are relatively formal, with conventional greetings and closings and a body with at least nominal content. E-mail is usually more informal, with features of both written and oral language; its users may omit greetings and sometimes send messages conversationally, in a series of rapid exchanges. Messages sent by Instant Messaging (IM) are very informal, with many features of oral communication, including a greater use of nonverbal expressions such as emoticons and other representations of embodied action.

Format

People can send messages in a variety of formats, including text, sounds, images, and programs. Some social information requires particular formats. To see what people look like requires an image; to see their gestures and expressions requires a moving image. One can create a list of participants using text, but to present their relationships in a more complex, nonlinear order requires graphics. A medium may translate the format of the message: A textual e-mail that is ordinarily perceived visually, as written text, may be presented as spoken words by a text-to-speech synthesizer. Most of our experience with mediated communication is verbal, whether written or spoken. We are just beginning to explore the potential of communicating within graphical environments, to experiment with sending interactive experiences.

Bandwidth

Bandwidth is the amount of information that a channel can convey. Low-bandwidth media require that a sender transmit relatively few bits per message and require less time to transmit, an especially important feature when using a slow connection. Text is low bandwidth, whereas sound and video are high. The relation between the information bandwidth of a medium—how much information, in the mathematical sense, is sent—and the social bandwidth of a medium—how much social and expressive information is sent—is not simply linear. Text, which is low bandwidth, can be an expressive and effective form of communication. Going from voice-

only communication (i.e., the telephone) to image and voice communication (i.e., the videophone) greatly increases the number of bits conveyed but does not necessarily make for a better social medium.

The bandwidth of network connections has been steadily increasing, but so has the size of the material that people want to send over networks. Compression is the process of making a message smaller without losing important information. What is "important" may vary from application to application. For sociable media, maintaining the integrity of social cues is paramount. With video communication, for example, bandwidth may not be sufficient both to send detailed images and to send them without delays. Experiments have shown that reducing image detail is preferable to maintain the timing of the sequences; such reduction keeps the image in sync with the voice and ensures that gestures and glances are seen as they are made, an important rhythm because the perceived timing of these expressive actions affects their meaning.

Permanence

Media have a range of permanence: They can be persistent or ephemeral. Any physical medium is persistent, as are all asynchronous media because they must be stored in some form. Other media can be made persistent—a phone call is normally ephemeral, but if it is recorded it is persistent.

Persistent conversations among multiple participants are a new phenomena that became feasible on a large scale only with the advent of the computer. In their various formulations (private mailing lists, public newsgroups, bulletin boards, etc.) persistent conversations enable a large number of people, often initially strangers, to converse about any topic. They have become one of the most popular forms of online social interaction, and their role in reshaping society—in redefining how we establish social ties, where we gather information, how we form opinions—is still developing.

The permanence of a medium has important privacy implications. Upon delivery, an ephemeral message is gone, except in the participants' memory. It cannot be subsequently conveyed to others except by creating a new message telling about it. A persistent message, however, can be conveyed to others who were not privy to the original message. For many years participants in newsgroups (large asynchronous online conversations) assumed that their discussions were ephemeral because the discussions disappeared from most servers after a few weeks. Yet, these discussions had been archived and, with the advent of Web-based search engines, were made publicly available, along with the search tools to easily find all the discussion posts ever made by a person. The privacy issues here involve not only the reading of posts by people other than the intended audience, but also the reading of posts outside of their original context.

Identity

Identity is at the core of all social interactions. We care about how others perceive us and devote considerable energy to conveying our own identity to others. Our perception of others' identity is an essential context for understanding their words and actions so that we can know what sort of behavior to expect from them, how to act toward them, and what their role in our lives might be.

Identity plays a key role in virtual communities. In communication, which is the primary activity of such communities, knowing the identity of those people with whom you communicate is essential for understanding and evaluating an interaction. Yet, in the disembodied world of the virtual community, identity is also ambiguous. Many of the basic cues about personality and social role that we are accustomed to in the physical world are absent. Some people claim that the ability to establish an independent and disembodied identity is one of the most valuable aspects of online culture—it allows people to explore roles and relationships that would otherwise be closed to them. Other people claim that anonymity encourages irresponsible, hostile behavior and that the term *anonymous community* is an oxymoron.

People handle the relationship between an online persona and a physical self differently in various online environments, often as a result of interface decisions built into the system technology. Some systems make it impossible to trace a participant's real name; others try to ensure that messages are as-

cribed to their author's physical being—and the cultures that evolve are strikingly different.

In the physical world we typically know something about the identity of people with whom we are speaking. Even if we do not know their name, we can detect cues about their age, race, gender, affiliations, and so forth in their clothing, voice, and face. These cues may not be present online. Participants in an online forum may be anonymous, their real names unknown, with no tie even to an online persona. They may be pseudonymous, their real names unknown, but the persistent record of their actions may be available. Or they may be named, their real names and identity known and verified. Anonymous communication allows people to talk freely about topics that they might otherwise be afraid to discuss, such as personal health issues or politics. Yet, anonymity also allows disruptive and antisocial behavior to flourish. Pseudonymous communication, in which a person participates in online interactions using a persistent persona, allows a person to establish a reputation. To the extent that the person behind the persona values this reputation, the person is encouraged to behave responsibly. Indeed, people have said that one of the benefits of the online world is the possibility of creating communities in which the participants do not know each other's race, age, or gender and in which identity is instead primarily based on one's history of behavior.

The Changing Media of Communication

People now have numerous ways to communicate, including traditional letters, telephone calls, e-mail, instant messaging, and video conferencing. They can participate in mediated games or search online for tennis partners, child-care providers, and potential lifetime mates. Communication media are becoming ubiquitous, meaning they exist everywhere. We are rapidly approaching the time when, for millions of people, mediated sociability will be with them at all times, no matter where they are or what they are doing. The challenge for the field of sociable media is not simply to invent ever-newer ways of communicating, but also to understand the social implications of ubiquitous and omnipresent communication media.

One significant change is the increasing emphasis on subjective and social concepts of place and distance over purely physical distance. Communication media are by definition technologies that allow people to communicate between distant locations; thus, they have always played a role in reducing the significance of physical distance. More recent technologies have accelerated this reduction both in quantity, by making communication faster across ever-greater distances, and in quality, by transmitting immediate presence through synchronous media. Whereas asynchronous media such as letters transmit information from one place to a distant one, synchronous media create a virtual space, a shared nonphysical environment in which the interaction occurs. We have seen this interaction for many years with the telephone, and the effect has become more apparent with the advent of mobile phones. Mobile phone users may move through a physical space, but their attention and reactions are occurring in the virtual space of their conversation. A new phenomenon is the sending of presence information without an accompanying message. Systems show when their users are logged in, how long they have been idle. Users of these systems receive a continuous flow of information about their distant friends, colleagues, or family members, shifting the center of awareness from the physical to the mediated world.

Spatial metaphors have always been part of our concepts of relationship—we have close friends, distant relatives. Social technologies are making these metaphors literal as we move toward a time when the concepts of place and distance will be increasingly based on personal relationships rather than physical location. Are you alone when chatting online in an otherwise vacant apartment? How about when none of your friends is online, although you are in a crowded café? What happens to local ties as associations are increasingly based on affinity and common interests rather than physical proximity? The implications of this change, both for the social realm and the physical realm, are many.

Another significant change is the number of people with whom we keep in contact. Maintaining personal ties by using e-mail is much less costly (in money, time, and effort) than maintaining personal ties by paying personal visits. One challenge that this fact brings to the field of sociable media is to build tools to help people manage this complex personal social world. Not only are we in touch with more people, but also we have fewer cues with which to remember them. When we meet people in the physical world, we see their face and hear their voice, we see them within a spatial context that helps provide us with a well-defined memory. Online we may see little of people (perhaps just an e-mail address) and may encounter them in a social setting (such as a discussion board) with few if any visual memory cues. Designers of new social technologies are developing ways to help people keep track of these relationships by creating visualizations of social information, such as a person's interaction history, the contents of a person's e-mail archive, and the network of connections in a virtual community.

A network's ability to connect us with more and more people may be infinite, but our attention is not. Are these large numbers of weaker ties replacing or supplementing stronger ties? If the former, social theories suggest that we may be moving toward a world where people have greater access to ideas, information, and opportunities, due to the wider range of people with whom we are in contact, but also toward a world where social support is weaker and our sense of responsibility for each other is diminished. The goal for the observer of sociable media is to understand the implications of media as they are built; the goal for the designer is to understand what sort of world he or she hopes to foster and to learn from these observations and create new technologies that lead to this goal.

Judith S. Donath

See also Affective Computing; Chatrooms; E-mail

FURTHER READING

Donath, J. (2002, April). A semantic approach to visualizing online conversations. *Communications of the ACM, 45*(4), 45–49.

Donath, J., & Robertson, N. (1994, October.).The sociable web. *Proceedings of the Second International WWW Conference.* Chicago.

Smith, M. A., & Kollack, P. (1999). *Communities in cyberspace.* London: Routledge.

Sociable Media Group, MIT. (2003). *Artifacts of the presence era.* Retrieved May 27, 2004, from http://smg.media.mit.edu/

Turkle, S. (1995). *Life on the screen: Identity in the age of the Internet.* New York: Simon & Schuster.

SOCIAL INFORMATICS

Social informatics (SI) is a theoretical and empirical approach to the study of information and communication technologies (ICTs) in society. We are surrounded by computers, cell phones, personal data assistants (PDAs), and many other digital devices at work, in school, and at home. The pace of innovation in computing is not slowing down—pervasive computing, broadband wireless networks, massive digital storage devices, and faster and more powerful mobile devices are all on the horizon. We are entering an age of ubiquitous computing where ICTs are increasingly routine and important in our lives.

Basic Assumptions of Social Informatics

One profound question, simple to ask and difficult to answer, is what this immersion in and dependence on ICTs is doing to us. In part, this is because it is always challenging to study something pervasive and routine, especially when what we want to investigate is almost invisible. In addition, we lack reliable approaches to the study of the ways in which our work and social lives are affected by the ICTs we design and use. These approaches must have theories and methods that will allow us to uncover these impacts and to understand the ways in which we are affecting the ICTs on which we rely.

Social informatics is one useful approach to answering this question. According to Rob Kling, a leading scholar of computerization and society: "A serviceable working conception of 'social informatics' is that it identifies a body of research that examines the social aspects of computerization. A more formal definition is 'the interdisciplinary study of the design, uses and consequences of information technologies that takes into account their interaction with institutional and cultural contexts'" (Kling 1999, 1).

This definition has three important implications. The first is that SI is a social science that focuses primarily on social and organizational levels of analysis. As an approach to studying ICTs in their social and organizational contexts, it cuts across many academic disciplines. People working in information systems, information science, sociology, anthropology, or HCI can all be using the ideas and methods of SI.

The second implication is that SI has a specific object of study. While SI researchers share an interest in hardware and software, they are not interested, for the most part, in building or designing ICTs. Instead, they want to understand the complex relationships that are involved when ICTs are designed and used in different types of social (or cultural) and organizational (or institutional) contexts. This means that researchers want to study ICTs, the people who design, implement, maintain, and use them, and the different settings in which they are designed and used. This is why SI is best understood as a problem-based social science.

The third implication is subtler. Researchers who use an SI approach share a basic assumption that influences the conduct of their work. They assume that ICTs, people, and contexts are in relationships of mutual shaping. The key phrase in this assumption, "mutual shaping," means that each influences the other, although not necessarily in equal measures. ICTs affect the contexts in which they are used and, at the same time, are affected by these contexts. Management scholar Stephen Barley explains that "technologies are . . . occasions that trigger social dynamics which, in turn, modify or maintain an organization's contours" (1986, 81). Mutual shaping also means that people shape their uses of ICTs and in turn, are shaped by their uses of these technologies. This means that ICTs provide "both constraints on and resources for" the actions of the people using the technologies (Rammert 1997, 176). An obvious example of mutual shaping is the way in which people's communicative behaviors have changed as they have integrated cell phones into their lives. These three implications pave the way for examining the usefulness of SI for HCI.

The SI Approach to HCI

Social informatics is relevant for human-computer interaction because of a theoretical and methodological trend that has been noticeable in HCI since the late 1990s. This trend, spurred by (among other factors) a technical development, the rise of ubiquitous, pervasive, and mobile computing, is leading many HCI researchers to take a social turn in their thinking. ICTs will not fade into the surroundings and become invisible without a clear theoretical and empirical understanding of the nature of the social and organizational contexts in which they are designed and used, and many researchers are rising to the challenge. An early indication can be seen in the definition of the discipline proposed for the Association for Computing Machinery (ACM) by psychologist Thomas Hewett (1995, 5): "Human-computer interaction is a discipline concerned with the design, evaluation and implementation of interactive computing systems for human use and with the study of major phenomena surrounding them."

The attention to the "major phenomena" surrounding ICTs is also indicative of this social turn. For example, cognitive scientists James Hollan, Edwin Hutchins, and David Kirsh argue for shifting the theoretical base of HCI from individualistic to distributed cognition, because it focuses on "entire environments." They describe a shift from a time when people were, in effect, tethered to single machines that contained the bulk of their digital work to the current state of computing, where we use multiple devices from multiple locations to access our digital work on the network. This is happening in the workplace and in our social lives and is changing the ways in which we interact with our machines and with each other. This approach can help us understand how we interact and coordinate our actions in these environments and can provide a clearer and more appropriate way to support our interactions with ICTs.

Some researchers turn to activity theory to understand how people routinely use ICTs in daily life. They argue that technology use must be studied longitudinally because it is embedded in people's social and organizational worlds and shaped by ongoing interactions among their expectations of the technologies, the tasks at hand, and the changing contexts of use. Other researchers make a similar point, arguing that a long-term research commitment is needed to observe people using technologies in their social domains in order to build a "shared practice" with them. This is a theoretical move from individualistic conceptions of interactions with ICTs to concepts of social interaction.

As empirical attention turns to the importance of the social and organizational contexts, physical location and social space have sometimes been treated as key concepts in understanding how people use ICTs, particularly interactive mobile systems. Some researchers argue that research into new ICTs requires a deeper understanding of people's tasks and contexts. A recent paper pushes this farther, claiming that the "everyday life" of the people using ICTs is a ""stage" and "opportunity" for deeper understanding of the contexts of use (Iacucci and Kuutti 2002, 303). Other researchers are calling for the integration of ethnographic techniques into the methodology of HCI.

Researchers in HCI have been incorporating more of the social and organizational context of ICT design and use into their studies at theoretical and empirical levels. Rather than having to rediscover the complexities of the social and organizational contexts that make a difference in the design and use of ICTs, researchers can turn to the theories, findings, and insights of SI.

HCI Problems that SI Can Solve

The main problem that social informatics can solve that will be important to human-computer interaction has to do with understanding the social and organizational contexts within which people design, implement, manage, and use ICTs. As HCI researchers turn their attention to the social phenomena that surround ICTs, the basic question they ask is what elements of these contexts make a difference for ICT design and use. SI can answer this question because it focuses on "the 'social context' of information technology development and use [assuming that it] plays a significant role in influencing the ways that people use information and technologies, and thus influences their consequences for work, organizations, and other social relationships" (Kling 1999, 1). HCI researchers can take advantage of the detailed analysis and understanding of these contexts that have been at the center of SI research and theorizing for the past fifteen years. In that time some interesting insights have emerged about the complex relationships among ICTs, people, and contexts. Here are four of them: First, ICTs do not exist in social or technical isolation. The discussion above of the embeddedness of ICTs in social and organizational contexts makes it clear that ICTs are sociotechnical systems—that is, they have social as well as technical components. This means that in addition to the hardware and software themselves, we have to pay attention to those who design and maintain them, who manage and pay for them, and who use them in their routine work and play.

Second, ICTs are not value-neutral. The values and beliefs of the designers of ICTs are embedded in the hardware and software. This can be seen in a side-by-side comparison of Macintosh and Windows operating systems. Also, when ICTs are integrated into organizations, they can support or challenge the prevailing organizational values, depending on who uses them and how they are used.

Third, ITC use has moral and ethical outcomes that have social consequences for the contexts in which they are used. The decision to use peer-to-peer software for trading copyrighted music in MP3 files is a clear violation of the intellectual property rights of copyright holders. The authors of the software may not have intended for it to be used for illegal activities, but those who downloaded the software quickly put it to that use. The hundreds of thousands of files exchanged using Napster had clear consequences for the users, the company, the music industry, and the artists who created the music.

Fourth, ICTs co-evolve during design, development, and use, which means that that they undergo changes and modifications over their lifetimes. This is because ICTs are configurable: Their components can be modified and reorganized to meet the needs of the local users. We do this in a small way when we configure software to suit our preferences, and organizations do this in a larger and more complex way when, for example, they reconfigure their computing and communications infrastructures to include an intranet or a wireless network. Also called "design in use," this reminds us that sociotechnical systems are always in a state of change. Sometimes the change is very slow—we are still using mice and keyboards as our main input devices. Other times it is extremely rapid and disruptive—for example, with Napster.

Currently occupying the attention of HCI researchers are some problems that could benefit from the SI approach, such as the design of interfaces for people with special needs. More broadly characterized as universal accessibility, this includes the incorporation of speech into the interface, the design of effective groupware for meetings and decision making, and the creation of digital environments to support collaborative work among virtual groups. While all of this can be studied in isolation, the lesson of SI is that to design an interface to facilitate the work of people with special needs, for example, it is necessary to understand how they routinely interact, communicate, and accomplish work tasks in specific organizational settings.

Limitations of the SI Approach

The main limitation of social informatics is that it adds a layer of complexity to our understanding of human-computer interaction by insisting that the relationships among ICTs, the people who design and use them, and the contexts in which they are designed and used are intricate, dynamic, and situated in social and organizational space. This consequence of the assumption of "mutual shaping" means that it is difficult to predict the outcomes of ICT implementation and use. SI points out that the consequences of the introduction and uses of ICTs vary because their social and organizational contexts are usually much more complex than researchers had thought. In generic form, the question is "If this type of technology is put into this organization, will A or B happen?" To rephrase the question in a more practical way: "If we install a collaborative groupware system in the organization, will it improve the virtual group's productivity?" For an SI researcher, the answer is usually, "It depends on. . . ." The reason for this is that the outcome of any particular implementation of ICTs depends in large part upon the local social and organizational contexts in which they are placed.

To understand why this is, assume that you are the researcher who is going to tackle this problem. You might begin by learning about the groupware hardware and software. However, there is a second and critically important step to take. When faced with this type of problem, you remember the assumption about mutual shaping and realize that you cannot provide a sound and empirically grounded answer to the original question until you investigate a range of questions about the context. What type of work group is it? Is it local, regional, or international? Do they ever meet face to face? Is workgroup membership stable? What type of management structure is in place? How does the chain of command and accountability work? What is the role of the IT department in supporting the group? What levels of expertise and experience do the group members have? How are these ICTs supposed to be used here? How are they actually being used?

Using an SI approach, in addition to the expected focus on the computers, you are paying careful attention to the contexts in which the ICTs are being used and the work practices of the people using them. Understanding the group's social and organizational contexts will in turn allow you to better answer the original question. Based on what you have uncovered, you now know that if certain conditions are present, productivity may be enhanced as a consequence of the introduction of groupware. If other conditions are present, productivity may be hindered. This is why an SI researcher's initial response to a question about the impacts of ICTs on an organization is likely to be, "It depends on...."

SI provides HCI with a sound theoretical and empirical base from which to engage in the detailed and nuanced exploration of the social and organizational contexts of ICT design, implementation, and use; the result of this exploration is an understanding of the elements of these contexts that make a difference in the design and use of computing and other ICTs.

Howard Rosenbaum

See also Computer-Supported Cooperative Work; Groupware; Telecommuting

FURTHER READING

Barley, S. (1986). Technology as an occasion for structuring: Evidence from observations of CT scanners and the social order of radiology departments. *Administrative Science Quarterly, 31,* 8–108.

Bishop, A. P., & Star, S. L. (1996). Social informatics of digital library use and infrastructure. In M. Williams (Ed.), *Annual Review of Information Science and Technology 39* (pp. 301–402). Medford, NJ: Learned Information.

Bowker, G., Star, S. L., Turner, W., & Gasser, L. (Eds). (1997). *Social science, technical networks and cooperative work: Beyond the great divide.* Hillsdale, NJ: Erlbaum.

Dillon, A. (1998). Cultural analysis and what designers need to know—a case of sometimes too much, sometimes too little, and always too late: Why ethnography needs to show its relevance. *ACM SIGDOC Asterisk Journal of Computer Documentation, 22*(1), 13–17.

Dix, A., Rodden, T., Davies, N., Trevor, J., Friday, A., & Palfreyman, K. (2000). Exploiting space and location as a design framework for interactive mobile systems. *ACM Transactions on Computer-Human Interaction (TOCHI), 7*(3), 285–321.

Graham, T. C. N., Watts, L. A., Calvary, G., Coutaz, J., Dubois, E., & Nigay, L. (2000). A dimension space for the design of interactive systems within their physical environments. In *Proceedings of the Conference on Designing Interactive Systems: Processes, Practices, Methods, and Techniques* (pp. 406–416). New York: ACM Press.

Hartswood, M., Procter, R., Slack, R., Soutter, J., Vos, A., & Rouncefield, M. (2002). The benefits of a long engagement: From contextual design to the co-realisation of work affording artefacts. In *ACM International Conference Proceeding Series: Proceedings of the Second Nordic Conference on HCI* (pp. 283–286). New York: ACM Press.

Hewett, T. T., Baecker, R., Card, S., Carey, T., Gasen, J., Mantei, M., et al. (1996). ACM special interest group on computer-human interaction curriculum development group. *ACM SIGCHI Curricula for Human-Computer Interaction.* Retrieved August 19, 2003, from http://www.acm.org/sigchi/cdg

Hollan, J., Hutchins, E., & Kirsh, D. (2000). Distributed cognition: Toward a new foundation for HCI research. *ACM Transactions on Computer-Human Interaction (TOCHI), 7*(2), 174–196.

Iacucci, G., & Kuutti, K. (2002). Everyday life as a stage in creating and performing scenarios for wireless devices. *Personal and Ubiquitous Computing, 6*(4), 299–306.

Jones, M. L. W., Rieger, R. H., Treadwell, P., & Gay, G. K. (2000). Live from the stacks: User feedback on mobile computers and wireless tools for library patrons. In *Proceedings of the Fifth ACM Conference on Digital Libraries* (pp. 95–102). New York: ACM Press.

Kling, R. (1999). What is Social Informatics and why does it matter? *D-Lib Magazine, 5*(1). Retrieved August 19, 2003, from http://www.dlib.org:80/dlib/january99/kling/01kling.html

Kling, R., Rosenbaum, H., & Hert, C. A. (Eds.). (1998). Social Informatics [Special Issue]. *Journal of the American Society for Information Science, 49*(12). Retrieved August 19, 2003, from http:/www.asis.org/Publications/JASIS/v49n1298.html

Kling, R., Rosenbaum, H., & Sawyer, S. (forthcoming). *Information and communication technologies in human contexts: Contributions of Social Informatics.* Medford, NJ: Information Today, Inc.

Petersen, M. G., Madsen, K. H., & Kjær, A. (2002). The usability of everyday technology: Emerging and fading opportunities. *ACM Transactions on Computer-Human Interaction, 9*(2), 74–105.

Rammert, W. (1997). New rules of sociological method: Rethinking technology studies. *British Journal of Sociology, 48*(2), 171.

Sawyer, S., & Rosenbaum, H. (2000). Social Informatics in the information sciences: Current activities and emerging directions. *Informing Science 3*(2). Retrieved August 19, 2003, from http://inform.nu/Articles/Vol3/indexv3n2.htm.

Shneiderman, B. (2003). *Leonardo's Laptop.* Cambridge, MA: MIT Press.

Simonsen, J., & Kensing, F. (1998). Make room for ethnography in design!: Overlooked collaborative and educational prospects. *ACM SIGDOC Asterisk Journal of Computer Documentation, 22*(1), 20–30.

Walsham, G. (1998). IT and changing professional identity: Micro studies and macro-theory. *Journal of the American Society for Information Science, 49*(12), 1081–1089.

Weinberg, J. B., & Stephen, M. L. (2002). Participatory design in a HCI course: Teaching ethnography methods to computer scientists. In *Proceedings of the 33rd SIGCSE Technical Symposium on Computer Science Education* (pp. 237–241). New York: ACM Press.

SOCIAL PROXIES

Humans are social creatures. In the physical world of face-to-face interaction we play close attention to what others do. We speed up a presentation when the audience begins to fidget; we forego stopping at the store when we see that the parking lot is jammed; we decide to eat at the restaurant that is crowded and noisy rather than the suspiciously empty one next door. The physical world is full of such socially salient information, and sociology provides a large literature that testifies to the many ways in which we use such cues to govern our own behavior and coordinate our actions with others (for example, the work of Erving Goffman, William H. Whyte, Christian Heath, and Paul Luff). However, in the digital world, our online tools and environments are almost devoid of socially salient information.

A social proxy is an abstract dynamic graphical representation that portrays socially salient information about the presence and activities of a group of people participating in an online interaction. It is one technique for providing online multi-user systems with some of the cues so prevalent in the face-to-face world. Social proxies are intended to be visible to all those portrayed in them, thus providing a common ground from which users can draw inferences about other individuals, or about the group as a whole.

The shared nature of a social proxy is critical. The knowledge that activity depicted in the social proxy is visible to all participants makes it public, and transforms it into a resource for the group. If I see something, I know that you can see it as well, and furthermore, I know that you know that I know. It is this mutuality that supports people being held accountable for their actions and that underlies the social phenomena, such as feelings of obligation and peer pressure, that enable groups to interact coherently.

The presence and activities of participants in a multiroom persistent chat system called Babble are dynamically reflected in Figure 1. The large circle represents a room that contains a conversation. The small dots within the circle depict people looking at that room's conversation; dots outside the circle depict people who are logged on to Babble but are in a different chatroom. When participants are active—meaning that they either "speak" (that is, type) or "listen" (that is, click or scroll)—their dots move quickly to the inner periphery, and then, when their activity ceases, they gradually drift back out over about twenty minutes. Thus, this proxy depicts a situation in which five people are active in the

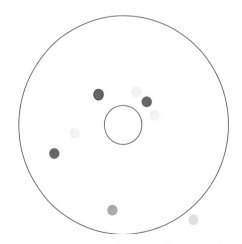

FIGURE 1. *A social proxy for a multiroom chat system that depicts the size of the chat and degree of activity of the participants (via their proximity to the circle's core)* Source: Erickson et al. (1999).

chatroom, two are in the room but idle, and one person is logged on elsewhere.

Social proxies play a number of roles in online systems. One is to create a sense of place or a feeling for the state of the interaction as a whole. For example, when users of the Babble system notice that its social proxy has a cluster of dots in the center, the experience is something like walking down the street and noticing a crowd: People gain a sense that something is happening, and, curious, are drawn into it. Another role of social proxies is to provide information that can indicate opportune moments for interaction. Thus, using the Babble social proxy, Erin Bradner, Wendy Kellogg, and Thomas Erickson have observed a phenomenon that they call "Waylay." The name refers to the fact that a member of a Babble who wants to chat with another person who is currently idle may keep an eye on the Babble proxy, watching for that person's dot to move into the center (which signifies that they have typed or clicked in the Babble application), and will then try to initiate a contact with them (perhaps via the Babble system or perhaps by some other means such as the telephone or dropping by the office).

Waylay works for two reasons: First, the movement in the social proxy alerts the wayler to the activity of the contactee; but second, and more subtly, contactees know that their activity is visible and that the fact of that visibility is itself public. It is something like making eye contact with someone you know has a question for you: Not only do they see you, but they see you seeing them, and thus you feel a greater sense of obligation. Social proxies can play a variety of other roles: By virtue of making that state of a group interaction public, they serve as a general resource that allows individuals, and the group as a whole, to be aware of collective activities and to steer them.

Social proxies come in many forms and emphasize different aspects of online interactions. A number of systems—for instance, Chat Circles (Viegas and Donath 1999), Fugue (Shankar et al. 2000), and Talking in Circles (Roddenstein and Donath 2000)—provide proxies for various forms of online chat. For example, Chat Circles depicts participants as circles in a 2D online space, and their relative positions

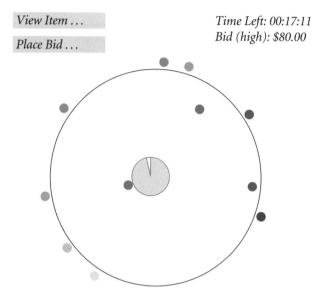

View Item . . .

Place Bid . . .

Time Left: 00:17:11
Bid (high): $80.00

FIGURE 2. *A social proxy for an online auction that depicts the bidders (inside the circle), the viewers (around the outside), and a clock counting down the remaining time left in the auction (center)*

determine who can "hear" whom. Social proxies are not just about supporting online chat. Carl Gutwin and his colleagues designed a "radar view" of a large shared workspace that showed where various participants were looking and pointing. Similarly, Thomas Erickson and Wendy Kellogg show social proxies for supporting online auctions, lectures, and queues. The auction proxy portrays the participants (both viewers and bidders) in an online auction, and aims to recapture some of the drama of face-to-face auctions in which participants often end up bidding not just *for* an item, but *against* other bidders. (See Figure 2.)

Social proxies are a relatively new technique for enriching the context of online interactions. We suspect that as computing power, network bandwidth, and the adoption of the Internet for everyday collaborative activity continues to increase, social proxies will become increasingly common.

Thomas Erickson and Wendy A. Kellogg

See also Chatrooms; Social Psychology and HCI; Sociology and HCI

FURTHER READING

Bradner, E., Kellogg, W., & Erickson, T. (1999). The adoption and use of Babble: A field study of chat in the workplace. *The Proceedings of the European Computer Supported Cooperative Work Conference.* New York: ACM Press.

Erickson, T., & Kellogg, W. A. (2003). Social translucence: Using minimalist visualizations of social activity to support collective interaction. In K. Höök, D. Benyon, & A. Munro (Eds.), *Designing Information Spaces: The Social Navigation Approach* (pp. 17–42). London: Springer-Verlag.

Erickson, T., Smith, D. N., Kellogg, W. A., Laff, M., Richards, J. T., & Bradner, E. (1999). Socially translucent systems: Social proxies, persistent conversation, and the design of "Babble." In *CHI 1999 Conference Proceedings: Conference on Human Factors in Computing Systems* (pp. 72–79). New York: ACM Press.

Goffman, E. (1963). *Behavior in public places: Notes on the social organization of gatherings.* New York: Free Press.

Gutwin, C., Greenberg, S., & Roseman, M. (1996). Workspace awareness in real-time distributed groupware: Framework, widgets, and evaluation. In *People and Computers XI: Proceedings of the HCI'96* (pp. 281–298). Berlin, Germany: Springer-Verlag.

Heath, C. & Luff, P. (2000). *Technology in Action.* Cambridge. MA: Cambridge University Press.

Rodenstein, R., & Donath, J. S. (2000). Talking in circles: Designing a spatially grounded audioconferencing environment. In *CHI 2000 Conference Proceedings: Conference on Human Factors in Computing Systems* (pp. 81–88). New York: ACM Press.

Shankar, T. R., VanKleek, M., Vicente, A., & Smith, B. K. (2000). Fugue: A computer mediated conversational system that supports turn negotiation. In *Proceedings of the Thirty-Third Annual Hawaii International Conference on System Sciences.* Los Alamitos, CA: IEEE Computer Society Press.

Viegas, F. B., & Donath, J. S. (1999). Chat circles. In *CHI 1999 Conference Proceedings: Conference on Human Factors in Computing Systems* (pp. 9–16). New York: ACM Press.

Whyte, W. H. (1988). *City: Return to the center.* New York: Doubleday.

SOCIAL PSYCHOLOGY AND HCI

Social psychology is the study of how people interact with other people—in dyads, small groups, organizations, and entire communities. Social psychology is a broad field that encompasses a range of topics, including how people behave in social groups; how they perceive and reason about one another; the nature of attitudes and how attitudes are related to behavior; the determinants of interpersonal attraction and the development of social relationships; and the social and cultural factors that help shape interpersonal behavior. Although social psychology historically focused on face-to-face interaction, its methods and theories have been readily extended to human-computer interaction (HCI).

Social psychology contributes in three important ways to human-computer interaction—theoretically, methodologically, and practically. Theoretically, social psychology brings to HCI a number of well-established concepts and analytical frameworks that can be applied to the study of people's interaction with computers and their interaction with one another through computers. Methodologically, social psychology brings to HCI a set of research techniques that can be used to better understand the social psychological aspects of computer use. Practically, social psychology contributes to a wide variety of HCI research domains, including computer-supported collaborative work, home and school computing, online communities, social and cultural factors in human-computer interaction, and virtual reality and robotics. Social psychologists often work collaboratively with computer scientists, designers, and members of other disciplines to understand people's use of new computing technologies and to ensure that systems meet the needs of their users.

Theoretical Contributions

The results from many traditional areas of study in classic social psychology have been fruitfully applied to issues in human-computer interaction. Below is a sampling of the major theoretical areas of social psychology and some examples of how they have been applied in HCI.

Group Behavior

A central interest for social psychologists is how people behave in groups—work teams, family units, friendship circles, and other units. Groups are characterized by interdependencies among members such that what one person does affects the others. Social psychologists have developed a number of influential theories of group behavior. One set of theories pertains to how groups function as units, including how they divide up their labor, how they coordinate their respective activities to achieve a group goal, and how they communicate with one another. This category of group-related theories has been applied in HCI to the study of how new technologies change the dynamics of teamwork. For example, teams find it more difficult to coordinate their activities when members are located at a distance from one another and must rely on computer-mediated communication systems such as electronic mail or instant messaging to interact.

Another set of theories pertains to how being with others affects individual behavior. For example, the theory of *social facilitation* describes how the presence of others can improve or harm performance on a task, depending upon how well learned the task is. Similarly, *social loafing* refers to an oft-repeated finding that people work less hard when they are in a group than when they are working by themselves, particularly when their individual contributions cannot be identified. Theories of social loafing have been used to explain HCI phenomena such as the low rates of active participation in Internet bulletin boards and e-mail distribution lists.

Person Perception and Social Cognition

Person perception refers to the process by which people form impressions of others from cues such as physical characteristics, clothing, speech, and nonverbal behavior. Social psychologists have developed theories of the impression-formation process and of the factors influencing the accuracy of people's impressions. Social psychologists have also examined how people manipulate impression-management cues in order to deceive others. Social cognition refers to the processes by which people store, retrieve, and reason about information about others and how they use cognitive devices such as schemas and stereotypes to facilitate reasoning about others. People who are known to be computer programmers, for example, may be assumed to possess a wide range of characteristics such as intelligence or introversion that go beyond their computer expertise per se.

Theories of person perception and social cognition have broad implications for HCI. In group contexts, social psychologists have investigated how different communications technologies (phone,

e-mail, Internet chat, and video conferencing systems) affect how people perceive others. For example, network delays in instant messaging and video conferencing systems can lead people to make negative judgments of their partners' responsiveness and interest. Researchers have also examined how people use the ambiguity inherent in many computer-mediated communications technologies to intentionally mislead their partners. Theories of person perception and social cognition have also been applied to the budding fields of human-avatar and human-robot interaction. Investigators examine how the presence or absence of characteristics like facial features affects people's judgments of the competence and "personalities" of avatars and robots.

Attitudes and Behavior

Another focal area in social psychology is the study of people's attitudes, opinions, and beliefs about objects, events, and environments, and other people. Social psychologists have developed theories of the structure of attitudes and of the relationships between attitudes and actual behavior. Theories of attitudes and behavior are particularly helpful in HCI for understanding how technology is adopted in the community and workplace. For example, research has shown that people's attitudes toward a new technology and the likeliness that they will use that technology depend not only on how good the technology is, in a technical sense, but also on what their friends and community leaders do. If all their friends use a given word processing program, for example, people are much more likely to use the same program than to compare the features of a range of programs to find the most suitable one for their individual needs. The study of attitudes and behavior has also been applied to people's willingness to participate in new arenas of social interaction such as online communities.

Interpersonal Attraction and Close Relationships

Social psychologists have long been interested in what draws people together (and what keeps them apart). Studies have shown, for instance, that people are drawn to those who are *attractive* (that is, have desirable personal characteristics such as physical attractiveness and competence), who are *similar* to them in key aspects (for example, appearance, age, and interests), and who are *familiar* (that is, encountered on a regular basis). A study by Festinger, Schachter, and Back of friendship patterns in an apartment complex showed that people's likelihood of reporting that they were friends with a fellow dweller in the complex decreased as the distance between their apartments increased. Results such as these have had wide application to our understanding of distributed work, particularly why it is so much harder to maintain strong working relationships with remote colleagues. Research on similarity and attractiveness has also shaped HCI's understanding of the development of social relations on the Internet, through e-mail, chatrooms, instant messaging, and other communication tools.

Social and Cultural Dimensions of Interpersonal Behavior

Most of the preceding discussion focused on properties or characteristics of social behavior that are common to all human beings. Clearly, however, not everyone responds in the same way to every social situation. Social psychologists also study the ways that social and cultural attributes such as gender, age group, socio-economic status, nationality, and so forth influence interpersonal attitudes and behavior. One attribute of particular interest for HCI is gender, particularly differences in men's and women's attitudes toward computer technologies. Recently there has also been a growing interest in the attitudes of the elderly towards computers and the development of systems to meet the specific needs of this age group. Theories of gender differences, age differences, and cultural differences can help HCI researchers predict and accommodate group differences in technology needs and usage.

Methodological Contributions

Social psychologists make use of a combination of laboratory and field experimentation, survey research, and observational studies to study social behavior. Each of these methods has been fruitfully applied to our understanding of the social aspects of HCI. Many of these methodologies overlap with those of other physical and social sciences. The unique contribu-

tions of social psychology lie in the use of multiple methods to address the same issue (for example, using a combination of experiments, surveys, and observation to understand teamwork in corporations), and in the applications of these methodologies to the social psychological aspects of HCI.

Laboratory Experimentation

Laboratory experiments allow social psychologists to look closely at how one or more factors ("independent variables") influence other factors ("dependent variables") in a controlled setting in which other variables that might influence the results are taken into account. Imagine, for example, that a researcher is interested in understanding how different modalities of communication (telephone, instant messaging, e-mail, and video conferencing) affect group performance. Although it is possible to collect samples of naturally occurring group interactions in each modality, the contexts of these interactions might differ in ways that affect how well the group performs. People might choose face-to-face meetings for more problematic tasks while relying on e-mail for easier ones. These differences in task difficulty make it difficult to interpret the results. A better approach to this topic is to design a laboratory experiment to test how technologies influence performance when other key factors, such as numbers of participants, type of task, and length of interaction, are determined by the investigator and kept constant across all communication technologies. Because we can control for these and other factors that could influence our results, we know that any performance differences we find between groups using the different communications technologies are due to the technologies themselves.

The major strength of laboratory experiments is the tight control they allow researchers to exercise over the variables of interest in a study. A limitation of this method is that the tasks that people perform in the laboratory may not be representative of real-world tasks so that the findings may not generalize to other settings such as actual workplaces or communities. For this reason, social psychologists often use field experiments, surveys, and observational methods in addition to laboratory experimentation to ensure that their findings have generalizability.

A Personal Story—Love and HCI

I first met Bev Meyrowitz in 1963 at summer camp, where she was the counselor for the nine-year-old girls and I for the nine-year-old boys. It was attraction at first sight, and we spent a happy summer together. Well before the end of it, I (we?) fell in love.

But love is one thing, marriage is another. Was Bev a keeper? (Note to young 'uns: In those days, people expected to marry for life.)

HCI gave me the answer. As a Harvard graduate student in 1964, I took one of the first computing courses offered to sociologists. The human-computer interface then was brutally direct: I would keypunch 20 to 1,000 IBM control cards, walk to the computer center, being careful not to drop or mess up the cards en route (and not bend, spindle, or mutilate them). I would go to the card reader that connected directly to the giant mainframe (an IBM 7094) and feed my card deck into its jaws.

Ten hours later, I got a printout back. With luck, it would give me the results of my *DataText* statistical analysis. Much more frequently, it would give a bunch of error messages, telling me that my logic was silly or that I had carelessly left out semi-colons in my control statements.

This was miserable work. The probability of success was low, and potential gratification was delayed a minimum of ten hours. Always a late riser, I fell into the rhythm of submitting my first computer job at 10 AM, getting output at 8 PM, checking and fixing it, and then resubmitting it at 10 PM for pick-up the next morning.

Yet, although I try not to let my current graduate students discover this, there is more to life than computer runs. In my case, there was Bev, who was commuting from her first teaching job in New York City to visit me in Cambridge.

Tired as she was from the commute and coping with her rough-and-ready students, she spent much romantic time with me in the computer center—where we sublimated our love on keypunches—and trudging to and from the computer center. Moreover, when the inevitable happened and the large box of control cards dropped, she stooped to the occasion and immediately bent down with me to pick up and sort the cards.

It was then that I knew that I had a keeper. What more stringent test could there be?

Forty years later, I still know she's a keeper, although our IBM cards have been replaced by a high-speed Internet interface as Bev Wellman and I sit at our PCs, still side-by-side.

Barry Wellman

Field Experimentation

Field experiments are conducted in people's natural environments, such as their workplace, school, or home. In a field experiment assessing the effects of communications media on team performance, a researcher might assign different work teams at a corporation to different communications media for their projects. The researcher would then measure team coordination and performance. Field studies are similar to laboratory studies in that independent and dependent variables are specified in advance, but typically researchers have less control over other factors than they would in the laboratory. In the hypothetical field study above, for instance, the different teams might be working on different projects, which could influence the outcomes. Field studies thus have the benefit of greater generalizability because they take place in people's normal settings, but they have the disadvantage of lower control over possible intervening factors.

Survey Research

In survey research, a series of oral or, more typically, written questions on a topic of interest are distributed to a sample of individuals. In social psychology, the majority of surveys are *close-ended*, which means that respondents select from among a set of response options. For example, workers in a corporation might be asked to indicate how often they use e-mail on a scale of 1 (never) to 5 (daily), with the values in between reflecting intermediate frequencies, or they might be asked to rate a new video conferencing system on a scale of 1 (dislike very much) to 5 (like very much). Statistical procedures are then used to analyze the data and draw conclusions from the response of many individuals.

Survey methods allow researchers to look at behavior in organizations and in the home at a level of detail that would not be possible using experiments. Longitudinal survey studies, in which the same people are studied over the course of months or years, can be especially valuable for understanding technology adoption. For example, the HomeNet project (homenet.hcii.cs.cmu.edu), conducted by Sara Kiesler, Robert Kraut, and their associates at Carnegie Mellon University, has for nearly eight years used surveys distributed to a large number of households to understand how computers are used in the home—for example, which family members use the Internet most frequently; what sorts of activities they do while online, and how Internet use affects their social networks and overall well-being.

A strength of survey methods is their efficiency—a large number of questions can be asked about a wide range of topics to a large group of respondents in a reasonably short period of time. A major limitation of survey methods is that they do not allow researchers to determine direction of causality. If, for instance, an investigator found that greater time spent online was associated with fewer face-to-face friendships, it would be impossible to tell whether this was because time online hurt face-to-face friendships or because having fewer face-to-face friendships leads people to seek acquaintances online. A second limitation is that surveys use self-report data, and people cannot always report accurately on their behaviors.

Observational Research

Observational research methods are those in which the investigator looks closely at a phenomenon of interest in order to glean insights into the variables that cause the phenomenon or result from it. For example, social psychologists might perform a site visit to a major corporation to observe how its employees use communications technologies as they go about their daily activities. Often social psychologists enhance their observations through audio- and/or video-recordings that can be analyzed in detail.

Observational research is often an important first step in HCI research. By closely observing how people interact with their current technology, social psychologists identify problem areas and new information technology requirements that are useful for system design. Observational techniques can provide in-depth understanding of how particular populations interact with technology, but they suffer from issues of generalizability because it is never clear how typical the sample observed is to the user population in general. Observational research can, however, shape the design of later survey and experimental studies and help ensure that HCI development work is closely intertwined with users' needs.

Practical Contributions

Social psychologists have contributed to a wide range of research and development areas in HCI. This section highlights some of these areas along with some of the prominent social psychologists working in these domains. Many HCI professionals with backgrounds in fields other than social psychology have also made contributions to these areas; their work is covered in other entries in this encyclopedia.

Computer-Mediated Communication

Much of the early impact of social psychologists in HCI came from their participation in studies of computer-mediated communication at the great corporate labs of the 1960s, 1970s, and 1980s. At Bell Laboratories in the 1960s, Robert Krauss and his colleagues investigated how well people could understand one another when telephony introduced a delay between speakers and listeners. Later studies at AT&T Labs and Bell Communications Research (BELLCORE) focused on the new video technologies and communication. At BELLCORE, for example, social psychologists helped design the Cruiser video system that enabled workers in different offices to communicate with one another via video, and even to leave video messages if the other party was not available.

Today social psychologists both in industry

and in academia are engaged in studies of the effects of new technologies on interpersonal communication. At Carnegie Mellon University, for example, Robert Kraut, Susan Fussell, and an interdisciplinary team of colleagues have been investigating ways that novel forms of video conferencing can be used to support communication about three-dimensional objects in the real world. Among their findings have been that video systems that point cameras toward the objects are more valuable for collaboration than head-oriented video systems that simply show partners' faces. Other work in this vein attempts to extend our understanding of face-to-face interaction by comparing it with communication via new technologies involving wearable computers and virtual reality.

Computing in the Workplace

A major focus of social psychologists in HCI has been on understanding how work teams collaborate and on identifying the factors that influence the success of these collaborations. Work teams come in all varieties, from air traffic controllers coordinating in real time to research collaborations that may extend over months or years. Teams vary in size, goals and aims, history, and many other characteristics. In the past, work teams often shared an office, floor, or building in a single location, but today team members may be distributed all around the world. Social psychologists study co-located and distributed teams to understand the ways they assign tasks, communicate with one another, coordinate their individual activities, and maintain leadership.

Joseph E. McGrath, professor emeritus at University of Illinois at Chicago Circle, has spent decades studying the effects of technology on work groups. McGrath has examined the effects of introducing computers into work teams—how technologies affect team processes, coordination of individual activities, leadership, and many other aspects of team dynamics. Andrea Hollinghead, at the University of Illinois at Urbana-Champaign, has also studied the impact of HCI on team processes, including the effects of technology on how information is stored and retrieved by individual team members.

A related line of work examines the effects of technologies specifically designed to support particular types of group interaction—for example, Group Decision Support Systems (GDSS), software tools that facilitate discussion and decision-making among team members. These tools vary in terms of how the interaction is structured (for instance, whether there is a leader or not; whether participants are anonymous or identified by name). Social psychologists Russell Spears, Martin Lea, and Tom Postmes of the University of Amsterdam have conducted substantial research on the effects of GDSS on group interaction. Linda Skitka at University of Illinois at Chicago Circle has looked at how decision-support tools influence the quality of people's decisions. Their work, along with that of others in this area, influences the design of group support systems so that they maximize team effectiveness.

Computing in the Home and School

Another area of investigation concerns the impact of new technologies on the home and school. The ground-breaking research of the HomeNet project demonstrated the heavy reliance of families on the Internet for *communication* (for instance, exchanging e-mail with friends and family members) rather than for *information* (for instance, reading websites). The HomeNet project also investigated how Internet use affected people's well-being and face-to-face relationships. HomeNet has been followed by other extensive studies of home computing, such as the HomeNetToo project (www.homenettoo.org) at Michigan State University. In HomeNetToo, social psychologist Linda Jackson and her colleagues use survey and other methodology to understand the precursors and consequences of Internet use in low-income families. One of the project's most important findings is that Internet use by low-income children appeared to improve their grade-point averages and standardized reading scores.

Social psychologists also study the use of computers and Internet technology in schools. Janet Schofield of the University of Pittsburgh and her collaborators have been investigating how the introduction of computers into the classroom affects the social processes and dynamics of education. Joel Cooper and Kimberlee Weaver of Princeton University have focused on the effects of gender on the effectiveness of computer technologies for schoolchildren, particularly on the factors that create higher levels of computer anxiety in girls and the ways in which the educational system might reduce gender differences. Social psychologists have also been involved in the design and evaluation of distance education programs, wherein students can attend classes from their home or other noncampus location. Of particular interest is how the lack of face-to-face contact with the professors and fellow students affects the learning process.

Online Communities

The interest of social psychologists in how people form collectives extends naturally to the study of online communities such as chatrooms, electronic distribution lists and bulletin boards, and other computer-based social organizations. Online communities can be work-related or they can be social in nature (for instance, oriented toward hobbies, dating, or social support) Of particular interest are the similarities and differences between various types of online communities and similar communities that are not online, and the impact of personality, gender, and cultural factors on community participation.

Katelyn McKenna and her colleagues at New York University have studied factors influencing participation in online communities and the ways that relationships are formed on the Internet. At Microsoft Research, Shelly Farnham and her colleagues in the Social Computing Group investigate people's participation in online communities. They have looked at how online communities are built up over time, the dynamics of communication in online communities, and the types of personalities and social characteristics associated with active participation in these communities. McKenna, Farnham, and others working in this area have provided many insights into online communities that have influenced the design of systems to support these new forms of social life.

Virtual Reality, Robotics, and "Social" Computing Systems

Much of the initial impact of social psychology on HCI focused on human-to-human interaction *through* computers. Computers themselves in this early work were generally conceived of as objects without social properties. Today this is changing. Interfaces to desktop-computer programs incorporate personal properties through the use of *avatars*—software agents with animate forms such as animals, people's faces, or even waggling paper clips. Stanford University sociologist Clifford Nass has pioneered work applying theories of social perception to people's interactions with avatars and other computing devices. His work has shown that the voice and visual image of an avatar have strong effects on people's perceptions of the avatar's "personal" characteristics, such as intelligence and warmth, and therefore on their interactions with it.

Another exciting new direction for social psychology in HCI is the application of theories of social perception and social interaction to human-robot interaction. Sara Kiesler of Carnegie Mellon University and her colleagues have been examining how the visual form of robots, such as the presence and shape of humanoid features such as eyes, ears, and mouths, affects people's inferences about the robots' intelligence, warmth, and other attributes. In related work, Pamela Hinds and her colleagues at Stanford University have been examining how the physical features of robots affect how people interact with them on collaborative tasks. This and other work by social psychologists in robotics complements the growing computer science and artificial intelligence interest in the field of sociable robotics (for instance, the sociable robots project headed by Cynthia Breazeal).

The Research Center for Virtual Environments and Behavior (RECVEB) at University of California at Santa Barbara (www.recveb.ucsb.edu) reflects another new direction for social psychology in HCI. This interdisciplinary project, codirected by James Blascovich, uses immersion in virtual reality to understand social influence and social interaction processes. For example, by using avatars to represent conversational partners in a virtual reality environment, investigators can manipulate partner characteristics, such as appearance and interpersonal distance, to determine their effects on the interaction in ways that would not be possible in face-to-face settings. Studies at the RECVEB span a wide range of social psychological topics and are intended both to inform traditional social psychology theory and to help designers build realistic and useful virtual reality systems.

An Expanding Role

Social psychologists have participated in HCI research and development for many decades. Social psychological theories and methods have been constructively applied to a wide range of topics in HCI. By working closely with computer scientists, engineers, sociologists, anthropologists, and specialists in many other fields, social psychologists help ensure that the tools designed for interacting with computers and through computers meet the needs of the people they are intended to serve. As human-computer interaction becomes increasingly "social" through the use of avatars, robots, and virtual reality systems, the role of social psychology in HCI will continue to expand.

Susan R. Fussell

See also Computer-Supported Cooperative Work; Psychology and HCI; Sociology and HCI

FURTHER READING

Bowker, G. C., Star, S. L., Turner, W., & Gasser, L. (1997). *Social science, technical systems, and cooperative work: Beyond the great divide.* Mahwah, NJ: Erlbaum.

Breazeal, C. (2002) Designing sociable robots. Cambridge, MA: MIT Press.

Cooper, J., & Weaver, K. (2003). *Gender and computers: Understanding the digital divide.* Mahwah, NJ: Erlbaum.

Farnham, S., Cheng, L., Stone, L., Zaner-Godsey, M., Hibbeln, C, Syrjala, K., Clark, A., & Abrams, J. (2002). HutchWorld: Clinical Study of Computer-Mediated Social Support for Cancer Patients and Their Caregivers. In *Proceedings of CHI 2002* (pp. 375–382). NY: ACM Press.

Festinger, L., Schachter, S., & Back, K. (1950). *Social pressures in informal groups.* Stanford, CA: Stanford University Press.

Fiske, S. T., & Taylor, S. E. (1991). *Social cognition* (2nd ed.). New York: McGraw Hill.

Galegher, J., Kraut, R. E., & Egido, C. (Eds.). (1990). *Intellectual teamwork: Social and technological bases for cooperative work.* Hillsdale, NJ: Erlbaum.

Hartmann, H., Kraut, R. E., & Tilly, L. (1986). *Computer chips and paper clips: Technology and women's employment.* Washington, DC: National Academy Press.

Hinds, P., & Kiesler, S. (Eds.) *Distributed work.* Cambridge, MA: MIT Press.

Hinds, P. J., Roberts, T. L., and Jones, H. (2004). Whose job is it anyway? A study of human-robot interaction in a collaborative task. *Human-Computer Interaction, 19*(1-2).

Hollingshead, A. B. (in press). Computer-mediated communication, the Internet, and group research. In M. Hogg and R. S. Tindale (Eds.), *Blackwell handbook of social psychology* (Vol. 3). Oxford, UK: Blackwell.

Huff, C. W., & Finholt, T. (Eds.). (1994). *Social issues in computing: Putting computers in their place.* New York: McGraw-Hill.

Kiesler, S. (Ed.). (1997). *Culture of the Internet.* Mahwah, NJ: Erlbaum.

Kiesler, S., Siegel, J., & McGuire, T. (1984). Social psychological aspects of computer mediated communication. *American Psychologist, 39,* 1123–1134.

Kiesler, S., & Sproull, L. (1997). Social responses to "social" computers. In B. Friedman (Ed.), *Human values and the design of technology.* Stanford, CA: CLSI Publications.

Krauss, R. M., & Weinheimer, S. (1966). Concurrent feedback, confirmation and the encoding of referents in verbal communication. *Journal of Personality and Social Psychology, 4,* 343–346.

Kraut, R. E. (Ed.) (1987). *Technology and the transformation of white-collar work.* Hillsdale, NJ: Erlbaum.

Kraut, R. E. (2003). Applying social psychological theory to the problems of group work. In J. M. Carroll (Ed.), *HCI models, theories and frameworks: Toward a multidisciplinary science* (pp. 325–356). New York: Morgan Kaufman.

Kraut, R. E., Fish, R. S., Root, R. W., & Chalfonte, B. L. (1990). Informal communication in organizations: Form, function, and technology. In S. Oskamp & S. Spacapan (Eds.) *Human reactions to technology: The Claremont Symposium on applied social psychology* (pp. 145–199). Beverly Hills, CA: Sage.

Kraut, R. E., Fussell, S. R., Brennan, S. E., & Siegel, J. (2002). Understanding effects of proximity on collaboration: Implications for technologies to support remote collaborative work. In P. Hinds & S. Kiesler (Eds.) *Distributed work* (pp. 137–162). Cambridge, MA: MIT Press.

McGrath, J. E., & Hollingshead, A. B. (1994). *Groups interacting with technology: Ideas, evidence, issues, and an agenda.* Thousand Oaks, CA: Sage.

McKenna, K. Y. A., & Bargh, J. A. (Eds.). (2002). Interpersonal and group processes on the Internet: Is social life being transformed? *Journal of Social Issues, 58,* 1–206.

Nass, C. & Moon, Y. (2000). Machines and mindlessness: Social responses to computers. *Journal of Social Issues, 56*(1), 81–103

Reeves, B., & Nass, C. (1996). *The media equation: How people treat computers, television, and new media like real people and places.* New York: Cambridge University Press.

Reis, H. T. & Judd, C. M. (Eds.) (2000). *Handbook of research methods in social and personality psychology.* Cambridge, UK: Cambridge University Press.

Schofield, J. W. (1995). *Computers and classroom culture.* New York: Cambridge University Press.

Schofield, J. W., & Davidson, A. L. (2002). *Bringing the Internet to school: Lessons from an urban district.* San Francisco, CA: Jossey-Bass.

Schroeder, R. (2002). *The social life of avatars: Presence and interaction in shared virtual environments.* London: Springer-Verlag.

Short, J., Williams, E., & Christie, B. (1976). *The social psychology of telecommunications.* New York: Wiley.

Skitka, L. J., & Sargis, E. G. (in press). Social psychological research and the Internet: The promise and the perils of a new methodological frontier. In Y. Amichai-Hamburger (Ed.), *The social net:*

The social psychology of the Internet. Oxford, UK: Oxford University Press.

Spears, L., Lea, M., & Postmes, T. (2001). Social psychological theories of computer-mediated communication: Social pain or social gain? In W. Peter Robinson & H. Giles, (Eds.), *The new handbook of language and social psychology* (2nd ed., pp. 601–624).

SOCIOLOGY AND HCI

Sociology tends to focus on large-scale social units, such as societal institutions and whole societies, so it often approaches human-computer interaction as a problem of the general relation of the technology to human users as a collective. Many sociologists study narrowly defined topics using rigorous scientific methodologies, and some of them join social and behavioral scientists from other disciplines in examining aspects of the human meaning of computing. However, sociology's distinctive contribution concerns the possibility that information technology offers humanity the opportunity to create an entirely new kind of society.

The Nature of Sociology

With political science, sociology shares a concern with power, but it does not limit itself to the kinds of power exercised through the system of government. It also examines power relations between genders, age cohorts, social classes, ethnic groups, and individuals. Like anthropology, it often employs the concept of culture, but it does not focus on the proverbially simple and relatively uniform cultures of pre-industrial societies. Rather, it charts cultural variations within modern societies, whether across subcultures, religions, the mass media, or social networks. The concept of interaction links sociology to social psychology, an interdisciplinary field that is the subject of a different essay in this encyclopedia.

Sociologists employ a wide range of methods to explore a bewildering variety of topics from a dazzling constellation of theoretical perspectives. Some of the most popular research areas are groups and social networks; family and sex roles; deviant behavior and crime; community and urban life; formal organizations; occupations and professions; inequality (stratification); race and ethnic relations; religion; social and political movements; social change; and demography (population studies).

Many leading sociologists compare societies across space and time, often working as historians, or they write essays about social issues and processes. Collectively, these areas are sometimes called macrosociology, because they concern societies as a whole and examine large social structures such as social classes or formal organizations. Much of the most influential sociological theory is written by macrosociologists, often in a literate and scholarly style but without formal methodology. Among the more technical areas, a prominent example is demography, the study of population trends, chiefly births (fertility), deaths (mortality), and migration. This form of sociology is highly quantitative but often atheoretical, and it employs computers for both data processing and modeling.

Sociological Use of Computers

Computers enter sociology in two ways: as tools for doing research and as instances of technology that may affect the conditions of human life. Many of those who work on substantive topics employ computers for the statistical analysis of quantitative data, and occasionally they study how cybernetics or computer-mediated communication affects the phenomena they habitually study. Demographers, mathematical sociologists, and social network researchers make very heavy use of computers. They often conceptualize social processes in terms of algorithms, as if society itself were a vast computational system.

The kinds of computer-related topics sociologists study naturally relate to the ways in which sociologists themselves use computers. Some of the most rigorous forms of sociology became computerized in the 1960s and have continued to use the methods available when they first adopted information technology. The unfortunate result may have been a tardiness in exploring more recent approaches. By the time of the 1890 census of the United States, demographers were using card-based data-tabulating machines. In the 1930s and 1940s, opinion polling achieved a level of maturity using similar equipment, and in the 1960s both demography and polling switched over to mainframe computers for statistical analysis.

In an ideal research project, sociologists would identify a theory that needed testing. With care, they would derive empirically testable hypotheses from the theory and change their concepts into variables that could be rigorously measured. This would take weeks or even months. Then data would be collected about the variables, as carefully as possible. In principle, a single computer run of the data would be sufficient to test the hypotheses and thereby evaluate the theory. The fundamental model of computer use that fit this approach was batch processing. In the 1990s, as more and more other sciences became interested in *data mining*, sociologists dismissed any kind of atheoretical *data dredging* that hunted through piles of information for unexpected patterns.

As the 1990s progressed, a few senior sociologists and many graduate students began studying the implications of the rapidly evolving information technology and using the new technology in their own work. The Internet was especially decisive in this transition, but was by no means the only computerized factor. In 1993, the Sociology Program of the National Science Foundation staged a workshop on sociological applications of artificial intelligence and funded a demonstration project to place all the data from the General Social Survey on the World Wide Web for anyone to analyze at no cost. Subsequently, NSF's Sociology Program and the Digital Library Initiative funded forward-looking projects to develop online cyberinfrastructure, such as virtual data centers, network-based group process laboratories, and experimental systems for performing a wide variety of other kinds of sociological research. At the same time, individual researchers throughout the many subspecialties of sociology have been adopting methodologies like computer simulation and Web-based questionnaire administration, which is preparing sociology to play a vital role in the emerging information age.

Post-Industrial Society

Among the most influential macrosociological theories of the implications of information technology for society is Daniel Bell's analysis of *post-industrial society*. Roughly speaking, his theory is based on the commonly held view that humanity has gone through a series of evolutionary stages, in which information has played different roles. No one knows how long ago humans gained the power of language, although one guess is around half a million years ago. Prior to that, we had only a very limited information-processing capacity, possibly greatest in the visual domain because we had to find our way across a complex landscape with animals and other humans. Presumably, language arose to facilitate social interaction, and was eventually applied to other domains. The invention of agriculture and the related emergence of cities, starting more than ten thousand years ago, led to what Bell and others call pre-industrial society. Trade, taxation, and the emergence of formal organizations like governments necessitated the invention of bookkeeping, which evolved into versatile systems of writing that were applied to religious, artistic, and many other purposes. The industrial revolution, beginning more than two centuries ago, expanded the role of information and led to universal schooling, widespread literacy, and a vastly increased scope for science.

Bell rejects the idea that technological innovations directly caused these social and cultural changes, a view often called *technological determinism*. Rather, he believes that the social and political structure shapes the kind of technology people develop and how they respond to it. While technology may sometimes push society in unexpected directions, often a society that is changing as the result of socio-cultural dynamics will demand a new kind of technology. Notably, in the twentieth century, a complex interplay of factors produced a new revolution in which industrial society gave way to post-industrial society.

The shift from industrial to post-industrial society entails an economic reorganization, from an emphasis on producing goods to an emphasis on providing services. The professional and technical class of occupations becomes dominant. Theoretical knowledge becomes central, both in driving innovation and in steering decisions by policymakers in government and elsewhere. Planning for the future emphasizes the control of technology, which requires a scientific assessment of its implications. In order to manage these novel challenges, a new intellectual technology is created, which is centered on computers, information systems, and the analytical concepts through which raw data can be transformed into knowledge and perhaps wisdom.

Bell imagines that post-industrial society will require governments to collect a vast array of information and use it to manage many aspects of the economy, including the development of new technologies. The extensive use of information technology to guide decision making has become central to most modern societal institutions, outside government as well as inside.

One of the most influential sociological analyses of post-industrial society is *The Information Age* trilogy by Manuel Castells, which begins with *The Rise of the Network Society*. For industrial society, Castells says, new sources of energy were the chief factor generating increased productivity. Informational society depends for productivity growth on the generation, processing, and communication of new knowledge. Constant improvements in information technology are therefore absolutely essential for progress in most realms. The key test of performance for industrial society was economic growth, and information technology allows traditional industries to achieve maximum efficiency. However, the informational society has its own distinctive performance principle, which is technological development itself. That requires people to increase knowledge and process it effectively at ever-higher levels of complexity.

The end of the twentieth century saw the collapse of the Soviet Union and the international communist movement, largely because they failed to master information technology and to adopt a distributed, network form of social organization. Informational capitalism triumphed and began building a new world order through an economic globalization that is dependent upon information technology, and through a cultural globalism that is based to a significant degree on Internet. The chief opponent to informational capitalism is religious fundamentalism. According to Castells, the class struggle that marked industrial society has been superceded by a new source of tension between the individual person and the Net, which often takes the form of struggles over personal identity rather than economic issues.

Castells identifies five fundamental features of the informational technology paradigm: (1) technologies process information rather than just matter and energy; (2) technologies affect all human activities; (3) organizations take the form of communication networks; (4) technologies and organizations are continually changing; (5) specific technologies merge into an integrated scientific and engineering system.

The first four of these features have obvious implications for human-computer interaction, as increasing numbers of people work with computerized information in all spheres of human activity in organizations based on computer networks, where technology-enabled change is endemic. Mihail Roco, a leader of the U.S. National Nanotechnology Initiative, and William Bainbridge, a sociologist working with information technology, have shown that technology has entered a period of revolutionary convergence as four major areas combine: nanotechnology, biotechnology, information technology, and new technologies based in cognitive science. The last two fields are intimately connected to human-computer interaction, and in coming years nanotechnology can dissolve the distinction between biology and information technology, through biosensor networks, manufacturing techniques that mimic genetics, and computing and communication devices implanted in the human body. As technologies converge into a single network of knowledge, there will be great pressure for organizations to do so as well.

Bureaucracy as Social Intelligence

For years computer scientists have commented on the fact that the efficiency of software has not increased nearly as rapidly as the efficiency of hardware. Moore's Law, suggested by Gordon Moore of the Intel Corporation around 1968, is a cliché but true: The effective power of computing hardware doubles about every eighteen months. There have been many attempts, largely unsuccessful, to develop software programming approaches that would allow software to be created more cheaply or more reliably. Sociology suggests a fresh perspective that may explain why this is the case.

In a very real sense, much software is embodied bureaucracy. A bureaucracy is a system of roles, rules, and connections, analogous to the modules, algorithms, and data structures of software. New programming approaches often attempt to restructure the flow of work among designers and programmers, essentially to reorganize the bureaucracy that produces the software. Unfortunately, human bureaucracy is not nearly so rational as it pretends to be, and bureaucracies typically contain self-defeating contradictions. These contradictions are written into the software, perhaps without anyone being conscious of the fact. For example, the specifications that a particular software project are supposed to meet should ideally be defined clearly ahead of time and should consist of a consistent set of achievable goals. But bureaucratic organizations have great trouble identifying consistent goals and sticking to them. As programmers are industriously writing code, the organization that employs them may be changing its expectations for the software, and they may be communicating poorly with each other.

In a classic textbook on the sociology of bureaucracies, W. Richard Scott suggested that organizations bring together five main elements: (1) social structure, (2) participants, (3) goals, (4) environments, and (5) technology. The social structure is not merely the formal organization, but also the informal relationships between individuals, and the patterns of interaction of subgroups such as work teams and divisions. The participants are the people themselves, with their great variety of personal goals, abilities, beliefs, and habitual behaviors. The goals are not only the formal aims, but also the informal goals that influential individuals or groups within the organization may have, such as a desire for social status or self-expression. The environment is the larger world of external resources, competitors, and socio-cultural realities that shape opportunities for the organization.

The fifth element, technology, is more than the hardware of the machines that produce the products. Scott stresses that it also includes "software," by which he means not merely computer programs but also the symbols with which human participants communicate. From this perspective, bureaucratic rules themselves are a kind of software, because they are algorithms of a sort, specifying the steps to be taken to accomplish particular tasks. In an organization that creates computer software, some of these bureaucratic algorithms will be incorporated into the computer programs, typically bringing with them all their inconsistencies and contradictions. This is readily visible with complex database systems created for use by bureaucracies, where different people have different levels of authority to change data or to move work forward a given number of steps. Another clear example is commercial operating systems and applications software, where some of the technical decisions result directly from the nature of competition between corporations that want to make it easy to link their own software products together and difficult for competitors' products to work as effectively.

Scott reports that three major perspectives on organizations have been influential in different periods in the recent history of sociology—the rational-systems, natural-systems, and open-systems approaches. The first of these assumed that organizations have specific, well-defined goals and that they pursue these goals through a formalized social structure. This approach is probably the most optimistic and superficially seems well-suited for a company that wants to produce effective, reliable computer hardware or software. This perspective was popular in the 1950s and earlier, and it remains influential throughout bureaucracies in the West.

The second perspective, which gained influence during the 1960s, stresses that the real people inside an organization have their own goals and informal social structure. Often they share the implicit goal of maintaining the survival of their social system, which implies that they cannot ignore official goals like security or profitability altogether, but that they are incompletely committed to them. For example, since industrial sociology began studying work teams in the 1930s, it has been obvious that workers typically trade off increased profits for the corporation against more pleasant working conditions, and they resist changes that they feel uncomfortable about. Thus, the people in an organization are a natural social system that may benefit from a somewhat rational bureaucratic system but may also at times work against it.

Scott himself was influential in developing the open-systems perspective. It views organizations as somewhat unstable coalitions of interest groups that are constantly negotiating and renegotiating with each other about goals and how to attain them. Furthermore, the organization is but one unit in a larger environment of competing and cooperating organizations. Formal organizations are like computer systems in which data flow from one module to another. The closest analog might be neural networks or genetic algorithms, which are constantly readjusting in response to inputs of largely random data. Organizational units are only loosely coupled, and their interactions are of necessity chaotic. Like a computerized data processing system, Scott says, an organization has input, throughput, and output. Information and resources come in. They flow in complex channels inside the organization. And information and resources flow out of the organization into the larger marketplace and world.

These three perspectives offer very different advice about how to improve the management of software creation and other comparable computer-related work. The rational-system perspective says that organizations must be managed hierarchically to achieve formal goals, whereas the natural-system perspective claims that the human-resource management of workers is paramount. The open-systems perspective says there is no one best way to manage an organization, because everything depends on the environment and other contingencies. Ideally, from the open-systems perspective, a successful organization will be a complex, adaptive system, not entirely predictable but generally achieving its diverse goals. However, to the extent that software really is a form of embodied bureaucracy, the open-systems perspective says that perfection is an unachievable goal.

More recent writers have built upon Scott's work. For example, Kathleen Carley conceptualizes human groups as mechanisms for processing information, and she has employed computer simulations to develop a theory of group stability based on three axioms: (1) individuals are continuously engaged in acquiring and communicating information; (2) what individuals know influences their choices of interaction partners; and (3) the behavior of individuals is a function of their current knowledge.

The net effect of these axioms is that groups tend to form around shared knowledge, potentially at many different levels of aggregation. Within a computer software company, for example, groups emerge having distinctive knowledge, both technical and organizational. The company itself is a knowledge system, analogous to a relational database but embodied in people. At a high scale, the computer software industry is a group sharing distinctive knowledge not possessed by other industries. Interaction among individuals within a company tends to increase the uniformity of their knowledge, because data are shared among them and anomalous data are erased to make room for shared assumptions.

This dynamic process of information coordination may also lead to loss of potentially useful diversity in knowledge. At the level of entire industries, Paul DiMaggio and Walter Powell have argued that companies within a particular industry tend to become more uniform than they need to be to achieve their practical goals, and this can mean a decline of innovation. Thus, to the extent that the computer software industry is a large-scale information-processing system, over time it may lose the capacity to find new solutions to problems, according to these information-oriented sociological theories of bureaucratic organizations.

The Challenge of Empirical Research in a Chaotic World

The use of computers to administer interviews and questionnaire surveys has allowed sociologists to carry out many studies of human interaction with computers during such data-gathering activities. In Computer-Assisted Telephone Interviewing (CATI) or Computer-Assisted Personal Interviewing (CAPI), a professional interviewer reads questions aloud from the computer screen and enters the data, but the interaction remains one between a human interviewer and a human respondent. The great cost of sending an interviewer to a person's home and the high rate of refusal in attempted telephone interviews has driven many researchers to experiment with administering questionnaires over the Internet, especially using the versatile interactive capabilities of the World

Wide Web. The shift to computer-mediated questionnaire administration is stimulating not only methodological innovations, but many studies of how differently people behave when interacting with computers through various modalities.

High-quality research on public attitudes toward computers dates back at least to a study by Robert S. Lee based on data collected in 1963. At that time, the public had little direct contact with computers but had two distinctly different images: (1) computers are beneficial tools, and (2) computers are awesome thinking machines that threaten humanity. Forty years later, the majority of people in post-industrial societies had access to personal computers at home, work, or school, and the Internet was rapidly becoming an integral part of everyday life. During such a transition period, public attitudes and the pragmatic impact of new technology will be somewhat unstable, and studies are likely to give conflicting results simply because they capture different particular moments in time. For example, some studies seemed to indicate that when people started using personal computers they cut back on their use of more traditional mass media. However, sociologist John Robinson and his colleagues found in the mid-1990s that people who adopted the new technology were often more heavy users of traditional technology as well, and that the impact of computers on time use was likely to be complex and changing as the new technology diffused, people adapted to it, and new applications emerged.

Thus, the role of computers in society is changing. Or, to put the point more precisely, computers are taking on ever more complex and subtle roles in an increasing variety of social contexts. They become not only a technology but also an emotional force, a stereotype, and a mythology. Computers have sometimes strengthened one side to a policy debate through their mystique rather than through objective results. For example, Paul Henman has analyzed the ways in which computer models of the economic impact of environmental policy served partisan purposes in the Australian debate over greenhouse gas emissions, more because of the prestige associated with computers than because of the objective accuracy of their projections. At other times, advocacy groups have used computer technology to make their cases about changing information technology itself. Sagi Leizerov has reported that groups concerned with privacy used websites effectively to force Intel to change the default settings of the unique identification code in each Pentium III chip.

Internet is an affective world in which users experience sentiments that may be strong or subtle, reflecting the differences (like gender) they bring to the computer and the online contexts that strengthen or weaken the influence of their individual characteristics. Some studies show that Internet strengthens traditional communities, others that it weakens them, and still others that it creates a new kind of community above and beyond those in the conventional world. In the sociology of religion, some studies seem to show that Internet gives tiny sects and cults the opportunity to compete on an equal footing with the conventional mainstream churches, but at the same time other studies suggest that it further strengthens the major denominations or even helps angry groups of ex-members who are organizing against particular religious groups. The effects of computers at work are diverse, with some research suggesting that they de-skill various occupations, requiring less from workers and therefore offering them less pay and inferior working conditions, whereas other research suggests that computation requires increased intellectual skills and therefore better paid personnel.

In cooperation with social and behavioral scientists from other disciplines, sociologists have made progress in understanding the changing role of computers and the emerging online communities. At times, the results seem incoherent, and every finding is contingent upon factors that themselves are fluctuating unpredictably. In part, this chaos represents the revolutionary nature of the technology, but it also reflects the fundamental vitality of society itself, as it migrates online.

Perhaps humanity has entered a transition period, unusually chaotic because transformative information technologies are causing revolutionary changes that may not be completed for many years and that act unevenly across society. Daniel Bell's image of a well-managed post-industrial society may, therefore, describe the end of the twenty-first century, not the beginning. However, Manuel Castell implies that informational society may never fully stabilize, because new innovations will constantly upset any equilibrium that temporarily establishes itself. Thus, sociologists may face the challenge that even when a theory of the social implications of computing is true, it will only be true in some limited domain.

William Sims Bainbridge

See also Anthropology and HCI; Political Science and HCI; Psychology and HCI; Social Psychology and HCI

FURTHER READING

Altman, M., Andreev, L., Diggory, M., King, G., Sone, A., Verba, S., et al. (2001). A digital library for the dissemination and replication of quantitative social science research: The Virtual Data Center. *Social Science Computer Review, 19*(4), 458–470.

Bainbridge, W. S. (1995). Sociology on the World Wide Web. *Social Science Computer Review, 13*, 508–523.

Bainbridge, W. S. (1997). *Sociology.* New York: Barron's.

Bainbridge, W. S. (2002). Validity of Web-based surveys. In O. V. Burton (Ed.), *Computing in the Social Sciences and Humanities* (pp. 51–66). Urbana: University of Illinois Press.

Bainbridge, W. S., Brent, E. E., Carley, K. M., Heise, D. R., Macy, M. W., Markovsky, B. (1994). Artificial social intelligence. *Annual Review of Sociology, 20*, 407–436.

Banks, R., & Laurie, H. (2000). From PAPI to CAPI: The case of the British Household Panel Survey. *Social Science Computer Review, 18*(4), 397–406.

Bell, D. (1973). *The coming of post-industrial society.* New York: Basic Books.

Burton, O. V. (Ed.). (2002). *Computing in the social sciences and humanities.* Urbana: University of Illinois Press.

Cappell, C. L., & Guterbock, T. M. (1992). Visible colleges: The social and conceptual structure of sociology specialties. *American Sociological Review, 57*(2), 266–273.

Carley, K. (1991). A theory of group stability. *American Sociological Review, 56*, 331–354.

Castells, M. (2000). *The rise of the network society* (2nd ed.). Oxford, UK: Blackwell.

Couper, M. P. (2000). Usability evaluation of computer-assisted survey instruments. *Social Science Computer Review, 18*(4), 384–396.

DiMaggio, P. J., & Powell, W. W. (1991). The iron cage revisited: Institutional isomorphism and collective rationality in organizational fields. In W. W. Powell & P. J. DiMaggio (Eds.), *The new institutionalism in organizational analysis* (pp. 63–82). Chicago: University of Chicago Press.

Ennis, J. G. (1992). The social organization of sociological knowledge: Modeling the intersection of specialties. *American Sociological Review, 57*(2), 259–265.

Ferringo-Stack, J., Robinson, J. P., Kestnbaum, M., Neustadtl, A., & Alvarez, A. (2003). Internet and society: A summary of research reported at WebShop 2001. *Social Science Computer Review, 21*(1), 73–117.

Form, W. (1987). On the degradation of skills. *Annual Review of Sociology, 13*, 29–47.

Hadden, J. K., & Cowan, D. E. (Eds.). (2000). *Religion on the Internet: Research prospects and promises.* New York: JAI/Elsevier.

Henman, P. (2002). Computer modeling and the politics of greenhouse gas policy in Australia. *Social Science Computer Review, 20*(2), 161–173.

Howard, P. N., & Jones, S. (Eds.). (2003). *Society online: The Internet in context.* Thousand Oaks, CA: Sage.

King, A. B. (2001). Affective dimension of Internet culture. *Social Science Computer Review, 19*(4), 414–430.

Lee, R. S. (1970). Social attitudes and the computer revolution. *Public Opinion Quarterly, 34*(1), 53–59.

Leizerov, S. (2000). Privacy advocacy groups versus Intel. *Social Science Computer Review, 18*(4), 461–483.

Markovsky, B., Lovaglia, M., & Thye, S. (1997). Computer-aided research at the Iowa Center for the Study of Group Processes. *Social Science Computer Review, 15*(1), 48–64.

Moore, G. E. (1965, April 19). Cramming more components onto integrated circuits. *Electronics, 38*(8), 114–117.

Moretti, S. (2002). Computer simulation in sociology. *Social Science Computer Review, 20*(1), 43–57.

Mulkey, L. M., & Anderson, T. D. (2002). Using online context as a mediating variable in the investigation of sex-role orientation and care-oriented moral reasoning. *Social Science Computer Review, 20*(2), 137–148.

Robinson, J. P., Barth, K., & Kohut, A. (1997). Personal computers, mass media, and use of time. *Social Science Computer Review, 15*(1), 65–82.

Roco, M. C., & Bainbridge, W. S. (2003). *Converging technologies for improving human performance.* Dordrecht, Netherlands: Kluwer.

Smith, V. (1997). New forms of work organization. *Annual Review of Sociology, 23*, 315–339.

Tonn, B. E., Zambrano, P., & Moore, S. (2001). Community networks or networked communities? *Social Science Computer Review, 19*(2), 201–212.

Saunders-Newton, D., & Scott, H. (2001). "But the computer said!" credible uses of computational modeling in public sector decision making. *Social Science Computer Review, 19*(1), 47–65.

Scott, W. Richard. (1981). *Rational, Natural, and Open Systems.* Englewood Cliffs, NJ: Prentice-Hall.

Wellman, B., Salaff, J., Dimitrova, D., Garton, L., Gulia, M., and Haythornthwaite, C. (1996). Computer networks as social networks: Collaborative work, telework, and virtual community. *Annual Review of Sociology, 22*, 213–238.

Witte, J. C. (2003). The case for multimethod design. In P. N. Howard & S. Jones (Eds.), *Society Online* (pp. xv–xxxiv). Thousand Oaks, CA: Sage.

Witte, J. C., Amoroso, L. M., & Howard, P. E. N. (2000). Method and representation in Internet-based survey tools: mobility, community, and cultural identity in Survey 2000. *Social Science Computer Review, 18*(2), 179–195.

"Who's on First" for the Twenty-First Century

*T*he classic comedy routine "Who's on First" by Bud Abbott and Lou Costello focused on baseball. This clever adaptation for the electronic age (author unknown), which is excerpted below, has made the rounds via e-mail.

ABBOTT: Ultimate Super Duper Computer Store. Can I help you?

COSTELLO: Thanks. I'm setting up a home office in the den and I'm thinking of buying a computer.

ABBOTT: Do you want a computer with Windows?

COSTELLO: I don't know. What do I see when I look out the windows?

ABBOTT: Wallpaper.

COSTELLO: Never mind the windows. I need a computer and some software.

ABBOTT: Software that runs on Windows?

COSTELLO: No; on the computer. I need something I can use to write proposals, track expenses. You know; run a business. What have you got?

ABBOTT: Office.

COSTELLO: Yeah, for my office. Can you recommend anything?

ABBOTT: I just did.

COSTELLO: You just did what?

ABBOTT: Recommended something.

COSTELLO: You recommended something?

ABBOTT: Yes.

COSTELLO: For my office?

ABBOTT: Yes.

COSTELLO: Okay; what did you recommend for my office?

ABBOTT: Office.

COSTELLO: Yes; for my office.

ABBOTT: Office for Windows.

COSTELLO: I already have an office and it has windows. Let's say I'm sitting at my computer and want to type a proposal. What do I need?

ABBOTT: Word.

COSTELLO: If I'm writing a proposal, I'm going to need lots of words. But what program do I load?

ABBOTT: Word.

COSTELLO: What word?

ABBOTT: The Word in Office.

COSTELLO: The only word in office is office.

ABBOTT: The Word in Office for Windows.

COSTELLO: Which word in office for windows?

ABBOTT: The Word you get when you click the blue W.

COSTELLO: I'm going to click your big W if you don't give me a straight answer. Let's forget about word for a minute. What do I need if I want to watch a movie on the Internet?

ABBOTT: RealOne.

COSTELLO: Maybe a real movie, maybe a cartoon. What I watch is none of your business. Now what do I need to watch it?

ABBOTT: RealOne.

COSTELLO: If it's a long movie I'll also want to watch reels two, three, and four. Can I watch reel four?

ABBOTT: Of course.

COSTELLO: Great! With what?

ABBOTT: RealOne.

COSTELLO: Okay; so I'm at my computer and want to watch a movie. What do I do?

ABBOTT: You click the blue 1.

COSTELLO: I click the blue one what?

ABBOTT: The blue 1.

COSTELLO: Is that different from the blue W?

ABBOTT: Of course, it is. The blue 1 is RealOne. The blue W is Word.

COSTELLO: What word?

ABBOTT: The Word in Office for Windows.

COSTELLO: But there's three words in office for windows.

ABBOTT: No; just one. But it's the most popular Word in the world.

COSTELLO: It is?

ABBOTT: Yes; although to be fair there aren't many other Words left. It pretty much wiped out all the other Words.

COSTELLO: And that word is the real one?

ABBOTT: No. RealOne has nothing to do with Word. RealOne isn't even part of Office.

COSTELLO: Never mind. I don't want to get started with that again. But I also need something for bank accounts, loans and so on. What do you have to help me with my money?

ABBOTT: Money.

COSTELLO: That's right. What do you have?

ABBOTT: Money.

COSTELLO: I need money to track my money?

ABBOTT: Not really. It comes bundled with your computer.

COSTELLO: What comes bundled with my computer?

ABBOTT: Money.

COSTELLO: Money comes bundled with my computer?

ABBOTT: Exactly and no extra charge.

COSTELLO: I get a bundle of money with my computer at no extra charge? How much money do I get?

ABBOTT: Just one copy.

COSTELLO: I get a copy of money. Isn't that illegal?

ABBOTT: No. We have a license from Microsoft to make copies of Money.

COSTELLO: Microsoft can license you to make money?

ABBOTT: Why not? They own it.

SOCIO-TECHNICAL SYSTEM DESIGN

Socio-technical design advocates the participation of end users in the information system (IS) design process. The information system includes the network of users, the developers, the information technology, and the environments in which the system will be used and supported. The process includes the design of the human-computer interface and patterns of human-computer interaction. Socio-technical design stands in opposition to traditional system or software engineering designs that focus on activities of system engineers who design the computational functions and features of a new system and use computer-aided design tools and notations to capture and formalize the results of such a design process.

The Legacy of Socio-Technical Design

The Tavistock Institute for Human Relations in London is widely credited with originating the concept and practice of socio-technical systems (STS) design in the 1940s, although the institute is still active. The institute's focus was on the design of work systems in factories and offices and initially focused on traditional noncomputing manufacturing systems. STS design, together with social psychology and social ecology, were the three major foci of the institute's concern with improving relations between people who were seen as "dehumanized" by modern industrial society. Viewers of the cinema classics *Metropolis* (1927) by Fritz Lang or *Modern Times* (1936) by Charlie Chaplin have seen how dehumanization and conflicts between labor and management in the industrial age have been dramatized with melancholy resolutions instead of the ongoing strife and restricted assembly line working conditions that gave impetus to the STS design movement. By the 1970s the institute had begun to focus on the design and introduction of computing systems as socio-technical systems for use in organizational settings.

From the 1960s through the 1980s a number of Scandinavian projects emerged following a similar tradition that recognized the design and introduction of computing systems as STS for use in manufacturing organizations and office work. However, these Scandinavian projects broadened the focus of STS not only to include user participation in system design, but also to recognize the need to address the politics of labor conditions and labor-management conflicts through improved workplace democratization.

The results from the Tavistock Institute, Scandinavian projects, and others that followed addressing the design and introduction of computing systems in new settings and situations became associated with this proposition for how best to design computer-based information systems: Information systems development and adoption should involve the participation of end users in the design, introduction, and integration of system features and workflow to make system-based work more satisfying. Key terms used to denote this proposition include *user involvement, participatory design, user satisfaction, human relations,* and, for the political dimension, *workplace democracy.*

Contemporary Socio-Technical Systems Design Issues

Although the STS design movement has been a source of inspiration for many students and designers of contemporary information systems that embody human-computer interaction, the concepts and practices for socio-technical systems design have evolved. Much of the legacy of STS design was prescriptive (offering advice for what should be done during system design), but contemporary scholars of human-computer interaction prefer empirically grounded studies with descriptive results (an empirically grounded record of what was done during system design) or proactive "action research" agenda and thus work toward development of an STS design practice that builds on such grounds. The classic prescription for user involvement in participatory design says little about which users, user representatives, or customers are chosen in practice to participate in a system design effort. Similarly, unless users are trained or already skilled in the design of information systems, their participation may yield little in working toward a system design that increases their satisfaction with their system-based work or enables them to expand their work or occupational skills and career options. Instead, their naïve participation may enable their unwitting revelation of social relations, communication, or discourse patterns that make their system-based work more easily monitored or the boundaries of their privacy more easily traversed by system designers who design system usage and navigational monitoring mechanisms. Finally, researchers are calling into question as problematic the whole notion of what is and is not part of an information "system" based on empirical studies. Instead, researchers are using alternative metaphors suggesting ways of viewing an information system embedded in an organizational workplace as a "web of computing" or "socio-technical interaction network." This points to a reframing from user-participatory STS design to participatory analysis and mapping of socio-technical interaction networks (STINs) that provide one or more views into the embedding context of information system and system-based work design.

IS development is shaped by emergent requirements and contextualized design; it is not something that people get right the first time, and then it is done. Historically STS design seemed predicated on the precept that an IS can somehow be designed to be correct, consistent, and complete prior to its implementation and use. Instead, experts have realized from a variety of studies and sources that IS development is incremental, iterative, and ongoing when situated within a complex organizational setting. Even so-called packaged software that can be bought off the shelf cannot often be installed out of the box without configuration or customization, adaptation, training, and the need to temporarily support parallel (both legacy and new) system versions. Thus, the requirements and design of an organizationally embedded information system are never finished or final but instead are routinely recapitulated, reviewed, and revised in response to how the system is adapted to present circumstances of usage and to the external market, government, and enterprise conditions that impinge on system usage or functionality. Unfortunately, the classic STS design approach does not provide the critical insights, tools, or guidelines beyond "user participation" for how to best stay abreast and engage and empower users, developers, and maintainers of an IS in managing its evolution.

Similarly, the prescription for design of an STS via user participation by itself will not lead to radical changes in the way a given information system is intended to support its users, their workflow, or their workplace. Such participation is necessary but not sufficient to bring changes that address the political order of an organization or its institutional surroundings. Instead, reinvention and transformation of existing organizational information systems and work practices are central to achieving radical changes. Reinvention seeks to discover new ways of doing established work practices, whereas transformation seeks to rearrange workflow, staffing, and related resource configurations. Both reinvention and transformation are most effective when they are participatory throughout their trajectories and most likely to fail when they are simply assigned by others who are not part of existing work practices.

Research Directions

The future of research in STS design seems likely to focus on the following topics. First, the focus of STS design research is evolving toward attention to STINs of people, resources, organizational policies, and institutional rules that embed and surround an information system as well as to how they interact with one another. This focus may be due in part to the growing recognition that a traditional focus on system design as being either system-centric or user-centric leaves the boundary between what is and is not part of the system ambiguous. Such ambiguity means that prescriptive policies toward user participation leave open the question of who is a user of what, thus confounding where user participation is best encouraged and practiced. In contrast, a focus on STINs draws attention to the web of socio-technical relations that interlinks people in particular settings to a situated configuration of IT and organizational resources that must collectively be mobilized in order for a useful information system to be continuously (re)designed to meet evolving user needs.

Second, the focus will likely expand to address both the socio-technical requirements and designs of information systems. The traditional attention to system design assumes that system users have well-defined needs that can be addressed through a proper design discipline and participation strategy. In contrast, experts increasingly recognize that a large set of information systems in complex organizational settings generally has user requirements that are situated in space (organizational, resource configuration, markets, and social worlds) and time (immediate, near term, and long term), meaning that user requirements are continuously evolving rather than fixed. Given the continuous evolution of information system requirements, techniques for continuously engaging system users are needed to determine which of their requirements have changed, which new requirements are at hand, and which requirements are no longer relevant.

Third, experts often do not know, given the first focus mentioned, what an STS or a STIN looks like, how to communicate its form or dynamics to others, and how to systematically reason about it. This uncertainty points to the need to know how to visualize (via text, graphics, or multimedia) an STS or a STIN. Existing approaches to data or information visualization focus on techniques for displaying primarily quantitative data rather than qualitative relationships. In contrast, techniques for mapping an STS or a STIN, such as rich pictures (diagrams of directed graphs that associate text or graphic images as nodes or edges in the graph), social network diagrams (sometimes called "sociograms"; directed graphs that depict a network of relations among a social group), discourse patterns (recurring, ongoing topics and exchanges between people) or social interaction protocols, interactive graphic simulations, or even the virtual worlds of computer games may inspire new ways for communicating the structural conditions and process dynamics that help outline what can be visually represented about an STS or a STIN.

Fourth, the design of STS will evolve away from prescriptive remedies to embodied and collective work practices that can be easily adopted and put into effect. Perhaps the best example of this remedy can be found in the world of free source or Open-Source Software development projects or communities. In this socio-technical world the boundary between software system developers and users is blurred, highly permeable, or nonexistent. Participation in system design, assertion of system requirements, and design decision making are determined by effort, willingness, and public experience in similar situations rather than by assignment by management or some other administrative authority. Similarly, the openness of the source code of a software system enables many forms of transparency, access, and ability to customize a system's design to best address user-developer needs. Furthermore, because people who participate in the design and evolution of open source systems often do so on a voluntary basis, these people quickly recognize the need to find ways to cooperate and to collaborate to minimize individual effort while maximizing collective accomplishment. This recognition is most easily observed in the online (or Web-based) communications, shared source code files and directories, application invocation (which starts an application program or system) or system configuration scripts, Web pages and embedded hyperlinks, and other textual artifacts that people in Open-Source Software project communities employ as the media, content, and hyperlinked context of system design and evolution.

Fifth, the four preceding foci collectively begin to draw attention to matters beyond the design of user-system interaction or human-computer interfaces. Instead, future STS or STIN research will increasingly employ Web analyses, ethnographic (cultural study) methods, and contextualized design techniques to study how people accomplish their work in an organizational setting using the information technology, people, resources, and circumstances at hand. To understand the information system or interaction network, researchers will need to understand the workplace, interorganizational networks, social worlds, and cultural milieu that embed and situate how people interact with and through the information systems at hand in their work. Similarly, researchers need to discover ways that enable information system developers to understand and become users and ways that enable users to understand and become developers to empower and sustain each group in its effort to design and redesign information systems for their work.

Walt Scacchi

See also Ethnography; Social Informatics; User-Centered Design

FURTHER READING

Atkinson, C. J. (2000). Socio-technical and soft approaches to information requirements elicitation in the post-methodology era. *Requirements Engineering, 5*(2), 67–73.

Beyer, H., & Holtzblatt, K. (1997). *Contextual design: A customer-centered approach to systems designs.* San Francisco: Morgan Kaufmann Publishers.

Bjerknes, G., & Bratteteig, T. (1995). User participation and democracy: A discussion of Scandinavian research on system development. *Scandinavian Journal of Information Systems, 7*(1), 73–98.

Ehn, P., & Kyng, M. (1987). The collective resource approach to system design. In G. Bjerknes, P. Ehn, & M. Kyng (Eds.), *Computers and democracy—A Scandinavian challenge* (19–57). Aldershot, UK: Avebury.

Emery, F. E., & Trist, E. L. (1960). Socio-technical systems. In C. W. Churchman & M. Verhurst (Eds.), *Management science, models and techniques: Vol. 2* (pp. 83–97). London: Pergamon Press.

Goguen, J. A. (1996). Formality and informality in requirements engineering. *Proc. 4th. Intern. Conf. Requirements Engineering, IEEE Computer Society,* 102–108.

Greenbaum, J., & Kyng, M. (1991). *Design at work: Cooperative design of computer systems.* Hillsdale, NJ: Lawrence Erlbaum Associates.

Kling, R. (1977, Winter). The organizational context of user-centered software design. *MIS Quarterly, 1,* 41–52.

Kling, R., Kim, G., & King, A. (2003). A bit more to IT: Scholarly communication forums as socio-technical interaction networks. *Journal American Society for Information Science and Technology, 54*(1), 47–67.

Kling, R., & Scacchi, W. (1980). Computing as social action: The social dynamics of computing in complex organizations. *Advances in Computers, 19,* 249–327.

Kling, R., & Scacchi, W. (1982). The web of computing: Computer technology as social organization. *Advances in Computers, 21,* 1–90.

Monk, A., & Howard, S. (1998, March–April). The rich picture: A tool for reasoning about work context. *Interactions 5,* 21–30.

Poltrock, S. E., & Grudin, J. (1994). Organizational obstacles to interface design and development: Two participant observation studies. *ACM Transactions Human-Computer Interaction, 1*(1), 52–80.

Scacchi, W. (2001). Redesigning contracted service procurement for Internet-based electronic commerce: A case study. *Information Technology and Management, 2*(3), 313–334.

Scacchi, W. (2002). Understanding the requirements for developing Open-Source Software systems. *IEE Proceedings—Software, 149*(1), 24–39.

Schuler, D., & Namioka, A. E. (1993). *Participatory design: Principles and practices.* Mahwah, NJ: Lawrence Erlbaum Associates.

Truex, D., Baskerville, R., & Klein, H. (1999). Growing systems in an emergent organization. *Communications ACM, 42*(8), 117–123.

Viller, S., & Sommerville, I. (2000). Ethnographically informed analysis for software engineers. *International Journal of Human-Computer Studies, 53,* 169–196.

SOFTWARE CULTURES

Since the advent of software technology in the 1950s, programmers have created many distinct software cultures. Remembering this fact is important whenever we engage in cross-cultural interactions; for example, when one software development culture is replacing another one, or when programmers trained in one culture maintain legacy programs created within another culture.

Human Culture

Human culture is a shared set of experiences, knowledge, and customs within a specific human community. The unity of the culture facilitates dialogue among members of the culture because it allows people to build on shared assumptions without explicitly formulating and communicating them. Whenever there is a lack of shared culture, resulting cultural differences make dialogue difficult. There are no longer shared assumptions and shared experiences, and communication has to start on a more basic level, becomes more tedious, and the probability of misunderstanding increases. *Culture shock* is a common term that describes the situation of people who suddenly find themselves surrounded by an alien and unfamiliar culture, without clues to help them decipher the signals and symbols that the culture contains. Perhaps the first anthropological examination of human culture was *Primitive Culture* (1871), by a founding father of cultural anthropology, Edward Burnett Tylor.

Knowledge of a culture is necessary for proper interpretation of cultural artifacts. Only those who understand the culture can understand the statues, paintings, buildings, books, and other artifacts created within that culture. Understanding the culture may involve understanding the languages, idioms, way of life, and views of the world prevalent within that culture. If the understanding of the culture is only partial, the understanding of the artifacts will also be only partial.

Defining Software Culture

Communities of programmers develop and maintain software artifacts. Like other human communities, they develop distinct cultures. During the history of software technology, there have been many different, identifiable software cultures, each of which has had a distinct set of characteristics.

Software has been produced and sold as an independent and separate product since the 1950s. Programming existed long before that, but it was tightly bundled with the respective hardware; only in the 1950s did software emerge as a product in its own right. In the decades since the 1950s, software technology has produced numerous software cultures. Some of them have coexisted or overlapped in time, while others succeeded earlier ones. Some of them were universal and dominated mainstream software technology, while others found homes in specialized niches. In order to characterize them, let us look at what constitutes a software culture.

Software culture is determined by the specific technologies, the properties of the computer configurations, the expectations of the users, the processes of software development, and the qualifications and backgrounds of the programmers.

The first significant software culture was based on assembly language and data input through punched cards and punched tape. Assembly language required programming in machine code, with only limited help provided by the symbolic addresses and symbolic names of the machine instructions. The overriding concern of the programmers was the limitation of computer resources; they were hampered by the small size of computer memory and computers' slow speed. Users' expectations were modest, and users (e.g., scientists, accountants) were satisfied with simple inputs and simple printouts. As a result, a significant part of programmers' effort was spent in algorithmic optimizations, and the resulting code was greatly influenced by these optimizations.

In later software cultures, computer resources were cheaper and more powerful, and there was a discernible trend away from efficiency and toward programs that were easier to understand. Increased understandability was facilitated by various innovations that allowed a better structuring of programs. High-level languages with expressions and statements replaced machine instructions. Structured programming superseded the previously tangled flow of control with nested control constructs such as if-then-else and loops. The emphasis on cohesion led to the use of concise functions with an easy-to-explain functionality. Object-oriented programming led to programs that consisted of programming objects that emulated real-world objects. Three-tier program architectures separated programs into three parts, one interacting with the outside, one implementing business rules (formulas and algorithms used by the application for such calculations as taxes and compound interest), and one storing the permanent data. All these developments radically improved the comprehensibility of the programs, though often at the expense of efficiency.

The life cycle of a software culture starts with an innovation in technology, process, or education. There are early adapters of the innovation. If their experience is positive, the innovation may move into the mainstream and serve as the foundation of a new culture. The emergence of a significant culture means that the innovations were successful and provided considerable benefits.

Cultures compete against one another, and the marketplace picks winners and losers. Among software cultures, some were small and were overwhelmed by larger ones because they could not provide sufficient infrastructure. (Infrastructure includes compilers, software tools, training materials, textbooks, and a pool of available programmers.) Once a software culture becomes established, it reigns for a certain time, until an accumulation of new innovations makes it obsolete. Because of the investment that each culture represents, pockets of the old culture generally survive, but these pockets get increasingly smaller and more isolated. Their maintenance becomes increasingly expensive and problematic, and in due time they disappear.

Examples of Specific Software Cultures

As mentioned above, the first widespread software culture was characterized by the use of assembly languages and emphasis on optimization of both program memory and computer speed. The background of the programmers of that era was most likely electrical engineering or mathematics.

The large step forward was the invention of programming languages and compilers (programs that translate programming language code into machine-language instructions that a computer's central processing unit can understand). Programming languages superseded assembly language, with the first widely used programming languages (for example, FORTRAN, COBOL, and ALGOL) appearing in the late 1950s. Their statements and expressions were translated into whole sequences of machine instructions, which made the programming easier but also less optimized, because the automatically generated instructions missed some optimizations that a human programmer might make. Because of that, high-level code was often combined with patches of assembly code wherever the efficiency of the code was of critical importance. High-level programming constructs were more readable and closer to the way people think, and hence the code was easier to understand. It was also during this time that textbooks, training, and college courses in programming were introduced, producing the first cohort of professional programmers.

The culture that developed as a result of those innovations emphasized the use of structured control flow and use of data structures that included pointers and records. At about the same time, computer science majors came into existence. Specialized programming languages for teaching computer science appeared, most notably Pascal, which was developed in the late 1960s. This era was also characterized by the emergence of methodologies of program development, such as stepwise refinement and structured design, that each had a very characteristic subculture associated with it.

The next large software culture emerged around the C programming language (developed in 1972) and the UNIX operating system. C was unlike other high-level languages in that it allowed an extraordinary degree of control over computer resources and displaced many remaining pockets of assembly language programming.

Another large software culture emerged around object-oriented programming. C++, which was developed in the early 1980s as a sequel to C, is an example of an object-oriented programming language. It maintained compatibility with C. Since object-oriented programming allows wider reuse of code than previous programming paradigms, the programs frequently used extensive reusable libraries. Another feature, developed in the early and mid 1980s, was the graphic user interface (GUI), which supports a more natural user interaction with computers, as the user can use graphical menus and buttons rather than having to learn special commands. Users came to expect GUIs, which changed the character of software programs considerably.

Numerous other programming cultures sprouted up around other programming languages or special application domains, or were based on variants of the cultures listed above. Some programming languages, like FORTRAN and COBOL, were continually updated and spanned a sequence of cultures. Each of the mainstream cultures mentioned here had a prime of life of about ten years before a new culture succeeded it (or, in the case of FORTRAN and COBOL, before it was updated).

Communication across Cultures

When software is created, there is extensive communication between the developers and the users in order to elicit requirements. There is also an extensive communication among developers themselves. Since software is complex and has to implement requirements with great precision, these communications are usually very extensive. They are facilitated by shared culture and hindered by a lack of it, as is true for any communication.

Programmers inevitably possess a native software culture in which they are comfortable. Typically, this is the culture they were trained in or worked in for an extended period of time. The problem arises when the programmer tries to interact with a different culture.

The need to change culture arises regularly in programmers' careers. If the programmers are developers of new software, they are likely to face a new culture about every ten years and require retraining if their skills are not to become obsolete.

Special problems arise when software engineers maintain legacy programs that were created within a culture that is not the engineers' current culture. According to the scholar and software engineer Tetsuo Tamai, typical legacy software lasts more than a decade, and hence it is fairly common to maintain software that was created in a previous culture. Often programmers who were schooled in the latest culture find themselves confronting an artifact created in an earlier culture. When new programmers fresh from school encounter such programs, they experience culture shock: It is hard for them to decipher aspects of the program, yet they are supposed to correct and enhance it.

The scholar and software engineer Václav Rajlich described an encounter between a modern programmer and a FORTRAN system from the 1970s. The program under investigation was the FASTGEN geometric modeling system, written in FORTRAN 77. It supports models of solid objects such as vehicles and aircraft from primitive shapes such as triangles, spheres, cylinders, donuts, boxes, wedges, and rods. CONVERT is one of the programs within FASTGEN and consists of 2,335 lines of code.

CONVERT was developed in the 1970s and is the product of the culture of that time. There are several aspects of the program that make it difficult for today's programmers to understand. The first problem is the architecture of the FASTGEN system. The FASTGEN system consists of several programs that simulate, analyze, or display the geometric model. The programs communicate with one another through data files. The user must execute the programs individually and is responsible for running them in the correct sequence and with the correct parameters. The software of the 1970s used these architectures because of the limitations of computer memory at that time.

Another problem is the lack of cohesion in the program modules. Subroutines are large and mix unrelated programming plans. They are not logical pieces of program and thus make comprehension difficult.

CONVERT contains many obsolete program plans that were designed to solve problems in the old operating system. For example, CONVERT reads and processes data in batches of two hundred records. (Batching made execution in old mainframe operating systems more efficient.) This batching, however, does not correspond to the logic of the input data and complicates understanding the program considerably. To understand the related code, the programmer must know about this specific optimization and its rationale, even though it is no longer used in today's applications.

The small local memory that old computers possessed did not allow storing the complete geometric model. Thus, CONVERT uses scratch tapes to store all intermediate forms of the model and constantly rewinds and rewrites those tapes.

None of these techniques are used today, and they surprise the programmer who is unfamiliar with the software culture of the 1970s. But today's programmer must understand all these differences to be able to maintain the program.

Reengineering

Managers have learned that it is difficult to convince talented and ambitious programmers to embed themselves in the obsolete programming cultures of the past. If the programmers do so, they miss out on developments within the mainstream culture and sentence themselves to obsolescence, with potentially serious consequences for their future careers. For that reason, dealing with legacy software has always been considered a serious problem. One of the strategies is cross-cultural reengineering. A reengineered program has attributes of the target culture and it is much easier to maintain.

The purpose of cross-cultural reengineering is to update obsolete software cultures while preserving as much of the original work as possible. The extent to which the reengineering preserves the old program determines the level of reengineering. Code-level reengineering fixes an occasional problem in the code but essentially preserves the software intact.

Preservation at the file or function level preserves the structure of the files and functions but replaces the code. Architecture-level reengineering preserves the architecture of the program and discards everything else. Which level of reengineering is appropriate depends on the difference between the original and target software cultures.

The Future

The 1990s and early 2000s have brought many innovations that will substantially impact future software cultures. It is highly likely that the quick pace of cultural shifts will continue unabated.

A special dilemma arises when planning long-lasting applications. For example NASA is preparing space missions that may last for fifty to a hundred years. These missions will be supported by software, both on board and at ground support. It is very likely that the software will have to be continuously maintained, as is common in most long-lasting applications. In the likely case of a sustained pace of software innovations and culture shifts, the software culture of the original developers and the software maintainers will diverge sharply, making this software a maintenance nightmare. Researchers and software developers who specialize in software cultures, culture transitions, and cross-culture reengineering will have their work cut out for them for the foreseeable future.

Václav Rajlich

See also Anthropology and HCI; Ethnography

FURTHER READING

Rajlich, V., Wilde, N., Buckellew, M., & Page, H. (2001). Software cultures and evolution. *IEEE Computer, 34*(9), 24–29.

Tamai, T., & Torimitsu, Y. (1992). Software lifetime and its evolution process over generations. In *Proceedings of the IEEE International Conference on Software Maintenance* (63–69). Los Alamitos, CA: IEEE Computer Society Press.

Taylor, E. (1958). *Primitive culture.* New York, Harper & Row. (Original work published 1871)

Woods, S. Carrière, S. J. Kazman, R. (1999). A semantic foundation for architectural reengineering and interchange. In *Proceedings of IEEE International Conference on Software Maintenance* (391–398). Los Alamitos, CA: IEEE Computer Society Press.

SOFTWARE ENGINEERING

The fields of software engineering and human-computer interaction (HCI) have had a long, complex, and occasionally troubled relationship. But because they are, for better or worse, inextricably intertwined, it is important to find ways to unify them so they can work together harmoniously. Software engineering is of enormous interest to HCI practitioners and usability engineers, and several attempts have been made recently to integrate the activities of the two fields.

Software Engineering and HCI

The Institute of Electrical and Electronic Engineers (IEEE) defines software engineering as the application of a systematic, disciplined, quantifiable approach to the development, operations, and maintenance of software; that is, the application of engineering to software. Mary Shaw, of Carnegie Mellon University, in her seminal article characterizing software engineering provides a similar definition: The disciplined application of scientific knowledge to resolve conflicting constraints and requirements for problems of immediate, practical significance. Both definitions emphasize the importance of applying disciplined scientific knowledge to software. The difference between them is that the first emphasizes quantification and the second emphasizes practicality. Taken together, these definitions suggest that software engineering is about creating methods, practices, and tools that will enable an engineering professional of average skills to create high-quality solutions to problems of real significance. Therefore, the field strives for repeatability—that is, it tries to define processes, methods, and tools that remove much of the human element (and hence the variability) from the creation of complex systems.

Typically software engineers are in charge of the development, operation, and maintenance of a software-intensive system, and HCI design and usability evaluation is only a part of the overall engineering process. It is, however, an extremely important part of this process. For example, a 1992 survey by Brad Myers and Mary Beth Rosson found that about half of the code and almost half of the effort of software projects was devoted to the user interface portion. Irrespective of the precise percentage of time or effort involved, user interface software is a major component of any modern interactive system and a major determinant of its eventual success. As a consequence, careful attention must be paid to the usability aspects of a software engineering effort, and, conversely, to the engineering implications of usability decisions.

However, the two disciplines do not always work together in complete harmony. Software engineering has its deepest roots in computer science, mathematics, and engineering. HCI, while it also has deep roots in computer science, is heavily influenced by cognitive science, sociology, industrial design, and graphic design. As a result, the two groups approach problems from a different perspective, have different conceptions of a life cycle, and frequently have trouble communicating with each other. A 2003 survey by software engineer and HCI researcher Rick Kazman and his colleagues of the relationships between software engineers and HCI practitioners found mutual mistrust and poor working relationships. The survey noted a number of disturbing practices that could affect the creation of high quality, usable software-intensive systems. For example, software engineers typically have no formal training in HCI, and HCI practitioners typically have no formal training in software engineering. Both groups frequently made design decisions that affected the other group without appropriate advance consultation. The two groups also made dramatically different assumptions on whose responsibility it was to ensure usability and had dramatically different perceptions of how often they had interacted in a project life cycle. And when the two groups did interact, it was frequently too late in the project life cycle to have a significant and cost-effective impact.

Software Engineering Concerns

Software engineering concerns can be categorized from a project-centric view according to a number of dimensions. Looking at the activities in the software (or system) development life cycle (SDLC) provides a temporal view of the activities involved in a software development project, from inception through maintenance and, eventually, retirement.

A typical SDLC, as it is practiced in relatively mature software development organizations, contains the following engineering activities (or "workflows," as they are sometimes known): business needs and constraints modeling, requirements analysis, architecture design, detailed design, implementation testing, deployment, and maintenance. In addition, many software engineering processes, such as the Unified Process, describe a number of supporting activities that occur alongside the engineering activities, including project management, configuration control and change management, and environment. Taken together, these activities form an overall process for developing software, and they occur in different proportions as a product moves through its lifetime, from inception into deployment. Within each activity there is a common substructure or set of subactivities. Each activity involves some analysis, some implementation, some documentation, and some review or validation.

Business Modeling, the first major activity in the SDLC, has two parts: (1) creating the business case for a system, which involves assessing the costs and benefits (and hence return on investment) for the system under consideration, and (2) describing, in a formal way, how a business or market operates, enabling an understanding of the key features and requirements of that domain. The first part involves describing the purpose of the system, who its major stakeholders are, the prospective benefit derived from the system, its most important functional requirements, its technical, managerial, economic, or political constraints, and its architectural drivers (major quality attribute goals that shape the architecture, such as performance, security, and availability). The costs, benefits, schedule, and resource requirements of the project are also taken into consideration here.

The second part involves determining the boundaries, or scope, of the business domain, and this typically results in the creation of a business domain model. The business domain model contains, and is documented by, a collection of business scenarios, or use cases, which describe the anticipated use of the system. From this basis the domain model describes and names the important concepts and entities for the system—the domain objects—as well as identifying and naming the relations between these objects and the important actors who interact with the domain objects (users, administrators, maintainers, and so on).

The second major activity in the SDLC is to capture the system requirements. Such requirements are typically organized into service statements and constraint statements. The service statements are further categorized into functional requirements, data requirements, and system scope. Functional requirements state what the system should do. They are typically captured as textual statements in a formal requirements document or as use cases organized into something called a Unified Modeling Language (UML) use case diagram (which itself is part of a modern requirements document). Data requirements state what data the system should manage, and how the data flows from (sub-)system to (sub-)system. These were traditionally captured as data-flow diagrams, but have more recently been captured in use case diagrams. System scope determines the boundaries of a system's functionality and hence the scope of the requirements.

The constraint statements include the quality attributes of performance, security, availability, maintainability, usability, and so forth, as well as any legal or industrial standards that the system must meet. These statements may also dictate data formats to which the system must adhere, interoperability with other systems, and any mandated software platforms on which the product must be based. Requirements are typically gathered in requirements elicitation activities and are then analyzed for conflicts, overlaps, and risks.

Once the requirements have begun to take shape, the process of architectural design may begin. The software architecture of a program or computing system is commonly defined as the structure or structures of the system, which comprise software elements, the externally visible properties of those elements, and the relationships among them. The focus of architectural design is on making structural decisions that allow the system to satisfy its major functional and quality attribute requirements (typically expressed via the "externally visible" properties of the architectural elements). Architectural design specifically eschews any discussion of data structure, algorithms, or other purely component-internal aspects of software design. The architectural design process determines the framework into which all subsequent development artifacts will be placed, and determines how these components will interact with each other at the time of construction and at run-time. Because of its critical role in software development, an architecture is typically the object of considerable scrutiny and formal review or evaluation. Architectural documentation is different from design documentation and requires different techniques and structures.

Once the architectural design has been established the design of individual components can proceed. Detailed design, unlike architectural design, is focused on the details of specific design elements (in object-oriented design, these are typically classes) so that they can be translated into code—interfaces, algorithms, and data structures. At detailed design time, application logic is finalized, database schemas are determined, and user interfaces are decided upon. Detailed designs are commonly analyzed via code walkthroughs and inspections, and are documented, in the UML, using class diagrams, use cases, activity diagrams, sequence diagrams, collaboration diagrams, and state charts. User interface designs are typically documented in mock-ups or prototypes.

Implementation, Deployment, and Maintenance Concerns

Once the detailed design of at least a portion of the system has been completed implementation may begin. This may include custom software coding, and also commonly includes the installation and configuration of purchased commercial components. Each unit of implementation needs to be tested separately before it is incorporated into the growing fabric of the system. As part of the implementation effort, individual classes and then larger-scale components need to be tested and integrated.

The unit testing activity is typically accompanied by other kinds of testing, such as loading test databases and initial performance testing and tuning. In modern systems development, incremental development means incremental (ongoing) integration and testing. That is, there are no distinct integration and testing phases—this activity occurs continuously.

To accomplish this, dependencies between modules (coupling) need to be managed, typically by creating stubs (which simulate missing modules) and drivers (which call components to be tested without having them integrated into the entire program). Because intelligence is often distributed in modern object-oriented systems (there is no "main" program), object-oriented systems must be designed for integration. Hence, each module must be as independent as possible.

Implementation and test plans are documented as distinct entities in the SDLC. These implementation and test plans are constantly analyzed to compare the plan with the actual, so that project efforts, deliverables, and expectations may be managed, and so that the quality of the product can be assessed as it is maturing.

Once a system has been sufficiently implemented and tested, it must be deployed. In simple systems, this is nothing more than the installation of the software on some hardware. However, in complex systems, deployment involves a wide variety of activities, including managing configurations (and reconfigurations) of the system, managing portability across platforms, managing releases and making different released versions available simultaneously (including packaging and applying bug fixes to released versions), deploying product lines of related systems based upon a common architecture, and managing scalability, reliability, and performance across varying installations and workloads.

Deployments are documented in the UML using deployment diagrams that emphasize the allocation of software to physical resources (computational nodes and networks). These deployment diagrams support the analysis of issues involved with installing a system into production, dependencies among installed systems, and the hardware, software, and network infrastructure of an entire organization.

Although system development is of enormous importance, the fact is that systems, once created, tend to outlive their creators, and most software system budgets and efforts are spent on maintenance

(estimates range from 67 percent to 80 percent). Maintenance is typically categorized into four discrete activities: (1) corrective maintenance—solving everyday problems, providing technical support, and performing minor changes that do not affect the overall functionality of the system; (2) adaptive maintenance—introducing secondary changes to meet performance and throughput demands or to adapt to a changing environment; (3) perfective maintenance—improving the system by redesigning portions of the system to accommodate substantial new requirements; and (4) preventive maintenance—changing the system to ensure that future faults do not occur.

Because maintenance affects all portions of the unified process, it is typically not documented differently than the other portions of the life cycle. Maintenance activities may entail embracing new business modeling and collecting and analyzing new requirements, potentially making architectural changes and detailed design changes. Each of these changes needs to be documented and analyzed using the appropriate techniques and templates. Once made, the changes need to be tested, integrated, and deployed.

Management, Processes, and Methods

Properly managing a software engineering effort is just as important as being technically competent. And the importance of management is even more pronounced when there are different groups of stakeholders with different needs, values, and perspectives (as in the case of software engineers and HCI practitioners). Managing a software project includes careful planning for project deliverables, costs and resources, schedules and milestones, risks, project processes and measurements, engineering and management tools, project standards, and people and team organization.

Management planning operates within a set of fixed constraints, the most important of which are, typically, time and money. A project must be continuously assessed relative to operational issues (how the system affects people, procedures, and the organization), economic issues (costs and benefits), technical issues (skills, expertise, people, and training), and schedule (time to market). All of this is typically documented in a project plan, which specifies the scope of a project, the direction and management of the project, and the tasks and schedule. It describes the management, including the collection of metrics. And it details how resources, including people, are to be allocated and managed.

A process is a way of doing something. Because software can be so enormously complex, software engineering process models have taken an increasingly central role in the theory and practice of software development in the past decade. Quite simply, there are many ways to build software, and the aim of processes and methods is to ensure that software is built predictably, on schedule, on budget, and within quality goals. "The quality of the process determines the quality of the product" is an oft-repeated slogan in the software process community.

Process models state an order of activities in an engineering effort. They specify what is to be delivered, and when, they assign activities and artifacts to developers, and they offer criteria for monitoring progress, measuring outcomes, and planning. The most widespread process models for software include the Software Engineering Institute's Capability Maturity Model (CMM) and its family of variants and related methods, the most important of which are the CMM integration, the team software process, and the personal software process. Another set of process models and standards for managing system quality that has been developed in parallel with the CMM family is the ISO 9000 family, promulgated by the International Organization for Standardization (ISO). One portion of this family has been specialized to software-intensive systems.

Software Quality

An ever-present concern in the engineering of software is the degree to which a software-intensive system will be able to meet its quality goals. These goals have traditionally been given names like performance, availability, maintainability, security, and usability. These "ilities" determine, to a great extent, the eventual success or failure of a software project and shape its architecture.

While only one of these "ilities," usability, is the direct responsibility of the HCI specialist, virtually all qualities can interact with each other. Hence, a change in the performance of a system, or in its security, may greatly affect its usability (for example, by speeding up or slowing down key operations, or by adding additional steps and time to an already complex process). And a change to a system to improve its usability (for example, the addition of a macro recording facility so that users can record useful sequences of commands and invoke them with a special keystroke combination) may inadvertently compromise the security of a system.

Because software qualities interact and trade off one with another, it is crucially important that a software be designed with explicit quality goals in mind and that it be analyzed and inspected for the satisfaction of quality goals.

Attempts at Unification

The application of HCI methods continues to be an afterthought in the development of software despite many suggestions about how to integrate these methods with software development processes. One reason for this is that mismatches between current software engineering processes make it impossible to map these processes directly onto corresponding processes and methods in HCI. The problem of integration is further exacerbated by the misconceptions that software engineers and HCI practitioners have about each other. There have been many attempts at unification, and many communities have focused on increasing understanding and cooperation between the two fields. These attempts at unification can be broadly grouped into four categories: shared tools, shared notations and models, shared processes and methods, and shared curricula.

In a typical software development project, the software engineering group chooses the main development tools—a design documentation tool, a development environment, a source code repository, a testing tool, and so forth. The usability specialists may choose additional tools that are specific to the prototyping, creation, and evaluation of a user interface. Few interface tools are shared or integrated with tools used in the larger software engineering life cycle, and in general, tools for aiding in the prototyping, creation, and evaluation of user interfaces are frequently distinct from the normal software engineering environment, although this situation has improved in recent years with the support for significant application frameworks in most popular development environments and with the widespread adoption of prototyping tools for user interfaces, particularly Web-based interfaces.

The most widely used notation for representing design information in modern systems development is the UML. In addition, there has been considerable research into shared architectures that address both HCI and software engineering considerations. For example, the Model-View-Controller paradigm has pervaded user interface development since it was first introduced in 1984 by Adele Goldberg, one of the creators of the Smalltalk language. This was later enriched by architecture and design patterns.

Software engineering, like any engineering discipline, is enormously dependent on repeatable, standardized, agreed-upon processes and methods, to achieve high quality and repeatable results. For software engineering and HCI to work together, therefore, they must share processes, or at the very least have processes that easily integrate with each other. Numerous efforts have been made to share and bridge processes and methods. Most modern software engineering processes are centered around object-oriented development. The most widely accepted process for object-oriented development is the Rational Unified Process (RUP). Many researchers have noted the disconnect between processes for human-computer interaction and processes for software engineering, and several attempts have been made to extend the RUP to better address HCI concerns. But the fact remains that in official versions of the Unified Process, little attention is given to the specifics of HCI.

The Future of Software Engineering

To have a hope for a better tomorrow, we need to educate tomorrow's practitioners. For this reason, there is a great need for shared curricula that emphasize not only the specific techniques and practices of software engineering and human-computer interaction, but also the most productive ways for these disciples to interact. This curriculum development needs to take into account tools, notations and models, processes, and methods. Such curricula are just now beginning to be developed and promulgated, but given the importance of these two fields, we can expect the widespread acceptance of such curricula in the future.

To unify the usability engineering life cycle and the software engineering life cycle and their attendant communities more closely, attention needs to be paid to the dependencies among the parts, to communication between the stakeholders, to the coordination of the activities between the groups, and to the differences in tools, vocabularies, and methods.

Rick Kazman

See also History of HCI; Programming Languages

FURTHER READING

Anderson, J., Fleek, F., Garrity, K., & Drake, F. (2001). Integrating usability techniques into software development. *IEEE Software, 18*(1), 46–53.

Artim, J., et al. (1998). Incorporating work, process and task analysis into commercial and industrial object-oriented system development. *SIGCHI Bulletin, 30*(4).

Bass, L., Clements, P., & Kazman, R. (2003). *Software architecture in practice* (2nd ed.). New York: Addison-Wesley.

Bass, L., & John, B. E. (2003). Linking usability to software architecture patterns through general scenarios. *Journal of Systems and Software, 66*(3), 187–197.

Booch, G., Rumbaugh, J., & Jacobson, I. (1999). *The unified modeling language user guide.* Reading, MA: Addison-Wesley.

Chrissis, M. B., Konrad, M., & Shrum, S. (2003). *CMMI: Guidelines for process integration and product improvement.* New York: Addison-Wesley.

Clements, P., Kazman, R., & Klein, M. (2001). *Evaluating software architectures: methods and case studies.* New York: Addison-Wesley.

Clements, P., Bachmann, F., Bass, L., Garlan, D., Ivers, J., Little, R., et al. (2002). *Documenting software architectures: Views and beyond.* New York: Addison-Wesley.

Clemmensen, T., & Norbjerg, J. (2004). Separation in theory—coordination in practice: Teaching HCI and SE. *Software Process Improvement and Practice, 8*(2).

Constantine, L., & Lockwood, L. (1999). *Software for use: A practical guide to the models and methods of usage-centred design.* New York: Addison-Wesley.

Constantine, L., & Lockwood, L. (2002). Usage-centered engineering for web applications. *IEEE Software, 19*(2).

Coutaz, J. (1987). PAC, an implementation model for the user interface. *Proceedings of INTERACT'87,* 431–436.

Ferre, X., Juristo, N., Windl, H., & Constantine, L. (2001). Usability basics for software developers. *IEEE Software, 18*(1), 22–29.

Goldberg, A. (1984). *Smalltalk-80: The interactive programming environment.* New York: Addison-Wesley.

Goransson, B., Gulliksen, J., & Boivie, I. (2004). The usability design process—integrating user-centered systems design in the software development process. *Software Process Improvement and Practice, 8*(2).

Gornik, D. (2003). IBM rational unified process: Best practices for software development teams. *IBM Technical Paper TP026B.*

Hefley, W., et al. (1994). Integrating human factors with software engineering practices. *Human-Computer Interaction Institute Technical Report, CMU-CHII,* 94–103.

Hix, D., & Hartson, H. R (1993). *Developing user interfaces: Ensuring usability through product and process.* New York: Wiley.

Humphrey, W. (1996). *Introduction to the personal software process.* New York: Addison-Wesley.

Humphrey, W. (1999). *Introduction to the team software process.* New York: Addison-Wesley.

IEEE Standard Glossary of Software Engineering Terminology. (1990). Piscataway, NJ: IEEE.

IFIP Working Group 2.7/13.4 on user interface engineering. Retrieved March 12, 2004, from http://www.se-hci.org

Jambon, F., Girard, P., & Ait-ameur, Y. (2001). Interactive system safety and usability enforced with the development process. *Engineering for Human-Computer Interaction,* 39–52. New York: Springer-Verlag.

John, B. E., Bass, L., & Adams, R. J. (2003). Communications across the HCI/SE divide: ISO13407 and the rational unified process. *Proceedings of HCI International 2003, 1,* 484–488. Hillsdale, NJ: Erlbaum.

Kazman, R., & Bass, L. (2004). Guest editor's introduction. Software process improvement and practice. *Special Issue on Bridging the Process and Practice Gaps between Software Engineering and Human Computer Interaction, 8*(2).

Kazman, R., Bass, L., & Bosch, J. (2003). Bridging the gaps between software engineering and Human-Computer Interaction. In *Proceedings of the International Conference on Software Engineering,* 777–778.

Kazman, R., Gunaratne, J., & Jerome, B. (2003). Why can't software engineers and HCI practitioners work together? *Human-Computer Interaction Theory and Practice—Part 1 (Proceedings of HCI International '03),* 504–508.

Kehoe, R., & Jarvis, A. (1996). *ISO 9000-3: A tool for software product and process improvement.* New York: Springer-Verlag.

Kruchten, P. (2000). *The rational unified process—An introduction* (2nd ed.). New York: Addison-Wesley/Longman.

Metzker, E., & Offergeld, M. (2001). An interdisciplinary approach for successfully integrating human-centered design methods into development processes practiced by industrial software development organizations. *Engineering for Human-Computer Interaction* (pp. 19–31). Berlin: Springer-Verlag.

Myers, B. (2003). Graphical user interface programming. In A. B. Tucker (Ed.), *CRC Handbook of Computer Science and Engineering (2nd ed.).* Boca Raton, FL: CRC Press.

Myers, B., & Rosson, M.B. (1992). Survey on user interface programming. *Proceedings of CHI '02,* 195–202. New York: ACM Press.

Neumann, P. (1995). *Computer-Related Risks.* New York: Addison-Wesley/ACM Press.

Nielsen, J. (1994). *Usability engineering.* San Francisco: Morgan Kaufmann.

Radle, K., & Young, S. (2001). Partnering usability with development: How three organizations succeeded. *IEEE Software, 18*(1), 38–45.

Schach, S. (1996). *Classical and object-oriented software engineering.* New York: McGraw-Hill/Irwin.

Shaw, M. (1990). Prospects for an engineering discipline of software. *IEEE Software,* 15–24.

Sutcliffe, A. (2003). Scenarios, models and the design process in software engineering and interactive systems design. *Proceedings of HCI International, 1,* 579–583. Hillsdale, NJ: Erlbaum.

Thayer, R. H., & Dorfman, M. (1999). *Software requirements engineering* (2nd ed.). New York: IEEE Computer Society Press.

van Harmelan, M. (2001). *Object modeling and user interface design.* Boston: Addison-Wesley.

Wiegers, K. (1999). *Software requirements.* Redmond, WA: Microsoft Press.

SONIFICATION

Sonification is the presentation of information as non-speech sound. It is useful for helping detect patterns in complex data, for conveying information in situations in which visual displays are not available, and for helping to make information available to the visually impaired.

Often the sounds that naturally accompany events in the physical world are very informative. For example, a car with an automatic transmission makes distinctive sounds as it changes gears. So does the disk drive of a computer; listeners may be able to detect problems by noticing abnormalities in the sounds the disk drive makes. The frequency of the sounds emitted by popcorn as it pops reveals the progress of the process: There are few pops at the beginning, with the rate increasing until much of the popcorn has popped. Then the rate gradually decreases until all of the popcorn is popped.

Unlike the above examples, in which sounds are produced as incidental by-products of physical events, most sonification entails transforming information into sound. An early and highly successful example is the Geiger counter, also known as the Geiger-Müller counter, an instrument that detects and measures radioactivity. It was invented by Hans Wilhelm Geiger and further developed by E. Walther Müller in 1928. This meter emits a series of audible ticks if radiation passes through it; the higher the rate of ticking, the higher the level of radiation.

Acoustical and Perceptual Characteristics of Sounds

Sound is the sensation of pressure variations in the air; these pressure variations can be represented as a waveform. Various aspects of sound can be used to represent information, and the most important for the purposes of sonification (not necessarily in this order) are amplitude, frequency, duration, spatial location, and timbre. Each of these aspects affects the way a sound is perceived.

The loudness of a sound is determined by the amplitude of the waveform: The greater the amplitude, the louder the sound. A waveform with a repeating element is called periodic. The length of a repeating element is the period, and the number of repeating elements that occur within a unit of time, such as a second, is called the frequency of the waveform. The frequency of a waveform is perceived as pitch. High-frequency waveforms have higher pitches than low-frequency waveforms.

The spatial location of a sound is indicated by natural cues such as the differences in loudness perceived by the listener's ears and the difference between the times that the sound reaches the listener's ears. For example, if a sound is coming from the left, the sound will be perceived sooner and louder in the left ear than in the right. For the purposes of sonification, there are at least two methods of simulating these spatial differences. The first method uses differing loudness in each ear to create a two-dimensional sound that is heard inside the head on an axis that connects the two ears. However, this simulation is somewhat unnatural when compared with the other method of simulating spatial location, which creates a sound in three-dimensional space and uses natural cues necessary for sound localization (time differences, loudness differences, and others). Using this method, the sounds will be perceived as coming from outside the listener's head.

Sound waves can also differ in more complex ways. For example a clarinet and a trumpet would sound very different even if the sounds they produced had the same amplitude (volume) and frequency (pitch). These more complex attributes of waveforms are called timbre. Pitch, loudness, and duration are better for presenting continuous

data, whereas timbre is more suitable for categorical variables.

The mapping between the acoustic properties of the waveform and perception is often complex. For example, sounds with frequencies of 1,000 hertz (cycles per second) and 2,000 hertz are perceived as more similar than sounds of 2,000 hertz and 3,000 hertz. The relationship between perception and the physical properties of the stimulus is called the psychophysical function, and the mapping of data to sound displays should take the psychophysical function into account. Musical scales take this psychophysical function into account, and therefore we hear the musical notes as equidistant from one another even though the differences in hertz are not equal. Another difficulty in mapping values to sounds is that sound dimensions often interact, such that change in one dimension alters perception of the other. For example, even if two sounds have the same pitch, the sound that is louder is perceived to have a higher pitch.

It is sometimes important to consider the conceptual dimension in choosing a mapping for the sonification of data. For example, there is evidence that the psychophysical function that maps numeric values to frequencies is different when people are told that the pitch of the sound represents pressure than when it represents velocity. Specifically, the same change in pitch is perceived as representing a bigger change when listeners are judging pressure than when they are judging velocity.

For auditory displays, it is often considered more natural to use dynamically changing sounds than static sounds. A static sound maintains the same loudness and pitch for the duration of the sound. For a dynamically changing sound, the loudness, pitch, or both may change during the duration of the sound. However, dynamic sounds must be used with care because the dimensions may interact and thus the perception of the sounds could be different than it would be if they were static. For instance, the researchers John Neuhoff, Michael McBeath, and Walter Wanzie found that when people listened to a change in loudness with a rising pitch, they perceived the change to be greater than when they heard the same degree of change in loudness with a falling pitch.

Applications of Sonification

Sonification is currently used to detect and display patterns in research data and in other situations where visual data displays are inappropriate. It is also useful in multimedia interfaces and as an aid to the visually impaired.

Displaying Patterns in Data

The auditory system is well suited to detect patterns in research data. An excellent example is described by the researcher Gregory Kramer. Strange events were detected by the flight controllers of the Voyager 2 space probe as it crossed the rings of Saturn. The problem could not be determined even after extensive analyses of visual displays of the data received from spacecraft. However, when the data were sonified by playing them through a music synthesizer, a clear pattern emerged. A "machine-gunning" sound could be heard whenever the spacecraft entered an area of high dust concentration. It turned out that Voyager 2 had been colliding with electromagnetically charged micrometeoroids.

Statistical data are often displayed as graphs, and these too can be sonified. The analog to a visual graph is an auditory graph that presents data using dimensions of sound instead of visual properties. For example, the auditory graph of the correlation between people's height and weight can be represented using a sequence of discrete sounds, with pitch representing height and loudness representing weight. In this auditory graph, as the value of height increases, the pitch increases; similarly as the amount of weight increases, so does the loudness of the sound. Research by the psychologist John Flowers and his colleagues has shown that that auditory versions of graphs such as histograms, frequency polygons, and box plots are perceived much like their visual counterparts.

Alternative Displays of Data

A second important application of sonification is for what are called "eyes-busy" tasks. A surgeon performing an operation needs to concentrate his or her visual attention on the task at hand. Data about the patient's condition, such as heart rate, blood oxygen, and so forth, are better presented auditorily than as visual graphs that would distract the surgeon. It should be understood, however, that the simultaneous presentation of visual and auditory information may sometimes overload cognitive processing capacity. For example, talking on a hands-free cellular phone has been shown to interfere with driving.

Mobile devices such as cellular phones and PDAs (personal digital assistants) have either no visual display or have very limited display space. These devices are better able to present data auditorily than visually. Imagine a physician on call at home asked to help on a difficult diagnosis. Lacking a means of displaying relevant medical information visually, the physician could listen to these data over the phone if they were properly sonified.

Multimedia Interfaces

Sonification can also be used to provide feedback on actions in a computer interface using what are called auditory icons—everyday sounds that convey information about events. The basic idea is to accompany computer events and attributes with sounds associated with these events and attributes. For example, dragging an icon could produce a dragging sound; opening a file could produce a sound indicating that a desk drawer had opened. When possible, it is advantageous to parameterize these sounds. For example, if lower tones were mapped to larger values, then opening a large file would produce a lower-frequency sound than opening a smaller file.

Although auditory icons can provide useful feedback, they are limited in the amount of information they can convey. The use of "earcons" provides a more abstract and therefore more general method to convey information about computer commands. Earcons are musical tones used in structured combinations to create auditory messages. The tones and messages are arbitrarily associated with one another so that a hierarchical family of earcons can be developed. For example if Sound A were the earcon for "File" and Sound B were the earcon for "Open" then the sound AB, consisting of the sequential playing of the two sounds, would represent the command "File Open."

Aids for the Visually Impaired

Sonification has important applications for people with visual disabilities. Navigation aids, display of images, and interaction with computer interfaces can all benefit from sonification.

The Nottingham object detector and its successor, the Sonic Pathfinder, were designed to provide object detection capabilities. The Sonic Pathfinder plays musical tones using pitch to indicate the distance from the nearest object. As an object gets closer, the tone decreases in pitch. The spatial location of the object is indicated by playing a tone louder in one ear than the other.

As an object detector, the Sonic Pathfinder was not intended to provide a representation analogous to the visual image experienced by sighted observers. The KASPA system, developed by the scientist and inventor Leslie Kay, goes a step in that direction, providing a richer representation of the environment. As in the Sonic Pathfinder, distance is represented by pitch, but texture is also represented—by timbre. The physicist Peter Meijer's vOICe system is an ambitious attempt to sonify grayscale images. In this system, vertical position is indicated by pitch, brightness is indicated by loudness, and horizontal position is indicated by temporal parameters. Although the vOICe system shows considerable promise, it is difficult to learn to use.

Allistair Edwards of York University developed an auditory interface to a word processor by arranging auditory objects in a two-dimensional grid. The objects correspond to the top-level items in standard word-processing menus, such as "File" and "Edit." As the user moves the mouse over an auditory object, a sound is played identifying the object by pitch. Pitch decreases as the mouse is moved from left to right in a given row. All objects in the top row have higher pitches than items in the second row, etc. This makes it relatively easy for users to locate the desired object. Double clicking an object allows the user to hear the choices under that object. User testing showed that blind users easily learned to navigate this system.

The Future

Although some applications of sonification, such as the Geiger counter, have been around for quite some time, the vast majority of the work on sonification has been done since 1990. Despite considerable progress, many questions remain unanswered. Research focused on specific design issues, such as which sound dimensions are best for different sonification problems, and in what combination, is currently under way and should lead to a coherent set of design guidelines that will facilitate the development of interfaces using non-speech sounds.

David M. Lane, Anikó Sándor, and S. Camille Peres

See also Musical Interaction; Speech Synthesis

FURTHER READING

Barras, S., & Kramer, G. (1999). Using sonification. *Multimedia Systems, 7,* 23–31.

Blattner, M. M., & Dannenberg, R. B. (Eds.). (1992). *Multimedia interface design.* Reading, MA: ACM Press/Addison-Wesley.

Boff, K. R., Kaufman, L., & Thomas, J. P. (Eds.). (1986). *Sensory processes and perception,* 1. New York: John Wiley and Sons.

Bregman, A. S. (1993). Auditory scene analysis: Hearing in complex environments. In S. McAdams & E. Bigand (Eds.), *Thinking in sound: The cognitive psychology of human audition* (pp. 10–34). Oxford, UK: Oxford University Press.

Deutsch, D. (Ed.). (1982). *The psychology of music.* New York: Academic Press.

Edwards, A. D. N. (1989). Soundtrack: An auditory interface for blind users. *Human-Computer Interaction, 4*(1), 45–66.

Flowers, J., Buhman, D. C., & Turnage, K. D. (1997). Cross-modal equivalence of visual and auditory scatterplots for exploring bivariate data samples. *Human Factors, 39*(3), 341–351.

Flowers, J., & Hauer, T. (1992). The ear's versus the eye's potential to access characteristics of numeric data. Are we too visuocentric? *Behavior Research Methods, Instruments and Computers, 24*(2), 258–264.

Flowers, J., & Hauer, T. (1993). "Sound" alternatives to visual graphics for exploratory data analysis. *Behavior Research Methods, Instruments and Computers, 25*(2), 242–249.

Flowers, J., & Hauer, T. (1995). Musical versus visual graphs: Cross-modal equivalence in perception of time series data. *Human Factors, 37*(3), 553–569.

Gaver, W. W. (1997). Auditory interfaces. In M. Helander, T. K. Landauer, & P. Prabhu (Ed.), *Handbook of human computer interaction* (2nd ed.): Elsevier Science B.V.

Getty, D. J., & Howard Jr., J. H. (1981). *Auditory and visual pattern recognition.* Hillsdale, NJ: Erlbaum.

Handel, S. (1989). *Listening: An introduction to the perception of auditory events.* Cambridge, MA: MIT Press.

International Community for Auditory Display (ICAD). (n.d.) Retrieved December 10, 2003, from http://www.icad.org/

Kramer, G. (1994). An introduction to auditory displays. In G. Kramer (Ed.), *Auditory display: Sonification, audification and auditory interfaces. Proceedings of the First International Conference on Auditory Displays (ICAD) 1992* (pp. 1–77). Reading, MA: Addison-Wesley.

McAdams, S., & Bigand, E. (1993). Introduction to auditory cognition. In S. McAdams & E. Bigand (Eds.), *Thinking in sound: The cognitive psychology of human audition* (pp. 1–9). Oxford, UK: Oxford University Press.

Meijer, P. B. L. (2003). *The vOICe*. Retrieved December 10, 2003, from http://www.seeingwithsound.com/voice.htm

Moore, B. C. J. (1997). *An introduction to the psychology of hearing* (4th ed.). San Diego, CA: Academic Press.

Neuhoff, J., McBeath, M. K., & Wanzie, W. C. (1999). Dynamic frequency change influences loudness perception: A central, analytic process. *Journal of Experimental Psychology: Human Perception and Performance, 25*(4), 1050–1059.

Petrie, H., & Morley, S. (1998). The use of non-speech sounds in non-visual interfaces to the MS-Windows GUI for blind computer users. Paper presented at the 1998 International Conference on Auditory Display (ICAD), Glasgow, UK.

Stevens, S. S. (2000). *Psychophysics: Introduction to its perceptual, neural, and social prospects* (2nd ed.). Oxford, UK: Transaction Books.

Walker, B., Kramer, G., & Lane, D. M. (2000). *Psychophysical scaling of sonification mappings*. Retrieved December 10, 2003, from http://www.icad.org/websiteV2.0/Conferences/ICAD2000/PDFs/WalkerKramerLane.pdf

Warren, R. M. (1999). *Auditory perception: A new analysis and synthesis*. Cambridge, UK: Cambridge University Press.

SPAMMING

Spamming is the practice of sending unsolicited bulk e-mail. The term *spam* originally referred to a spiced ham food product marketed by Hormel. The food product Spam was satirized in a skit on the British television series *Monty Python*. The skit featured a group of Vikings chanting "spam, spam, spam." Whimsical computer users found unsolicited bulk e-mail to be as ubiquitous as the chanting of the term *spam,* and the term stuck.

The first spam was sent on 5 March 1994, by the U.S. immigration law firm Canter & Siegel advertising its services with an immigration lottery. From that humble beginning spam has swollen to become a major problem confronting e-mail users. Experts estimate that 70 percent of all inbound Internet traffic is spam, and that percentage continues to rise. Much spam contains offensive material, including advertising for pornography and illegal substances.

One of the most common types of spam attempts identity theft. In some cases spam purportedly originates from a foreign country and requests that the recipient assist in moving funds out of the country for a fee. The recipient is asked for bank account information. Although spammers in many countries have produced this type of spam, most appears to originate from Nigeria and is called "419 SPAM" (named after section 419 of the Nigerian penal code which prohibits this activity).

Another type of spam that attempts identity theft is phishing—e-mail that is purportedly from a trusted source (such as a bank or online auction house) and that leads to a bogus webpage that collects personal information such as account passwords or credit card numbers. The problem of phishing is often aggravated because the bogus webpage exploits bugs in a Web browser or uses legitimate tools such as Javascript to create a false address bar in a browser. Recipients might believe that they are at a legitimate webpage when in fact they are communicating with a criminal website.

Techniques Used in Spamming

The spamming process consists of four phases: generating a list of e-mail addresses, forming messages, transmitting the spam, and collecting responses. To generate a list of e-mail addresses, spammers originally used spider programs that scoured the World Wide Web and online discussion groups for valid e-mail addresses. Because people increasingly keep e-mail lists secret, spammers have resorted to using a variety of new techniques, including guessing e-mail addresses (by using a standard dictionary of login names such as "sales" or common first names and trying all these names at registered Internet domains) and using viruses that capture users' lists of e-mail addresses.

To transmit spam, spammers often look for open e-mail relays. Standard e-mail software allows computers to run outgoing mail servers that accept e-mail and forward it. These mail servers allow mobile computing users to connect from anywhere in cyberspace back to their home computer. Spammers often scan Internet protocol (IP) addresses at random looking for open relays. Because a number of operating systems (including many versions of Linux) come with mail relays open by default, spammers are frequently able to find many such computers.

A number of emerging Asian economies (including South Korea, Taiwan, and China) are frequent targets for spammers seeking open mail relays.

In forming messages, spammers often attempt to personalize spam by including randomly generated text that evades detection by automated spam filters.

In collecting responses to spam, spammers often attempt to avoid direct detection by using a series of intermediaries. For example, they may refer a consumer to a website that will collect an order, or they may provide a foreign telephone number for communication.

People have attempted to control spam by both legislative and technical means.

Legislative Attempts to Control Spam

In the United States, Congress enacted the Controlling the Assault of Non-Solicited Pornography and Marketing Act of 2003, usually referred to by the acronym *CANSPAM*. When this article was written, people could not yet evaluate the effectiveness of the act, but some people have criticized it as being unenforceable. Whether the act applies to spam originating from non-U.S. sources is not clear. The act requires that spam include valid return e-mail addresses and options for recipients to unsubscribe to spam e-mail lists. However, anecdotal experience suggests that unsubscribing to spam e-mail lists actually results in a recipient receiving more spam; the person who originated the spam can add the recipient's address to a list of people who carefully read the spam. CANSPAM also supercedes state laws that in many cases carried stronger penalties for spamming. Finally, some people have questioned the constitutionality of anti-spam legislation because they feel that regulating spam infringes on free speech.

Technical Attempts to Control Spam

Many e-mail users and Internet service providers use e-mail filters to screen spam. However, these filters can fail by incorrectly identifying a non-spam message as spam (a false positive) or by incorrectly identifying a spam message as non-spam (a false negative).

Techniques for filtering spam include forming a list of IP addresses through which spam has originated or has been forwarded in the past (blacklist filtering); checking for terms that are offensive or are unlikely to occur in ordinary e-mail, such as *Viagra* (content filtering); using statistical learning methods to separate spam from non-spam (Bayesian filtering); and requiring that e-mail be accepted only if the return e-mail address is on a list of approved senders (whitelist filtering).

Use of these techniques has led to an escalating battle between spammers and spam filter creators that is often likened to an arms race. Spammers attempt to avoid being caught by blacklist filtering by sending messages through random computers or spreading viruses that themselves can spread more spam. Spammers attempt to avoid being caught by content filtering and Bayesian filtering by modifying spelling in their spam (for example, the word *Viagra* may be spelled "V1agra") and by inserting random words that prevent their messages from automatically being labeled as spam. Spammers attempt to avoid being caught by whitelist filtering by forging return addresses so that spam appears to be from the recipient's organization. Because spammers usually have access to widely available commercial spam filters, they can experiment until their messages pass detection.

Computer scientists have proposed other techniques for controlling spam, such as "e-mail for a fee," which would require that each delivered piece of e-mail be paid for with a small fee, analogous to stamps used for ordinary postal mail. The hope is that such a fee would make spam too expensive for a spammer to send. Other techniques would modify the e-mail infrastructure to require authentication of the sender using strong cryptographic methods. Unfortunately, such modifications would have to be so extensive (and in some cases would create disadvantages, such as removing the ability to send free and legitimate e-mail and anonymous e-mail) that none of these techniques has achieved wide acceptance, much less implementation.

J. D. Tygar

See also Viruses

FURTHER READING

Graham, P. (2002). *A plan for spam*. Retrieved April 13, 2004, from www.paulgraham.com/antispam.html

Schwartz, A., & Garfinkel, S. (1998). *Stopping spam*. Sebastopol, CA: O'Reilly & Associates.

SPEECH RECOGNITION

The goal of speech recognition research is to develop methods that will allow computers to accept speech input. Research in this area has been active since the 1950s. Excitement about computer speech understanding has been stimulated by science fiction characters such as the computer HAL in Stanley Kubrick's 1968 movie *2001: A Space Odyssey* and the android Data in the television series *Star Trek: The Next Generation*. Although the idea of being able to talk casually with a computer has caught the imagination of many, in reality, speech recognition technology is not yet advanced enough to make possible interactions such as are common in science fiction. Simple but practical applications such as voice command and control and dictation are becoming commonplace, but even in these more focused applications, technical problems can occur.

What Is Speech Recognition?

A speech recognizer uses a computational model to identify spoken words from a speech signal. In general, the speech signal is preprocessed so that the recognition algorithm can match representations for some portion of the signal to an internal representation of a finite set of words. Current systems use a variety of knowledge types to achieve current levels of performance, which are yet to reach those achieved by HAL or Data. The most common knowledge types are phonetic (based on speech sounds), phonological (based on variations in pronunciation, as in the variation between *fish and chips* and *fish 'n' chips* or *idea* and *idear*), and lexical (based on word pronunciation and word co-occurrence patterns). An important challenge for future speech systems is to incorporate more knowledge into speech recognition models.

In the 1970s, speech researchers began applying the principles of statistical pattern recognition with the goal of finding the most likely sequence of words given the acoustic signal and other types of knowledge. This approach has produced more accurate and robust speech recognition systems than the previously used template and rule-based systems. Commercial speech recognition systems based on these statistical techniques have been available since the early 1990s. Speech recognition systems typically include two highly interrelated modules: acoustic model training and speech recognition, as shown in Figure 1. Figure 1 depicts the components that are

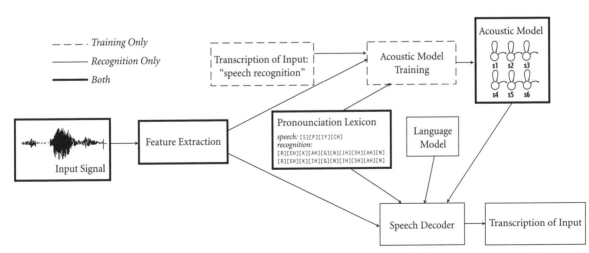

FIGURE 1. *The components that are common to both modules, along with those components that are specific to each module*

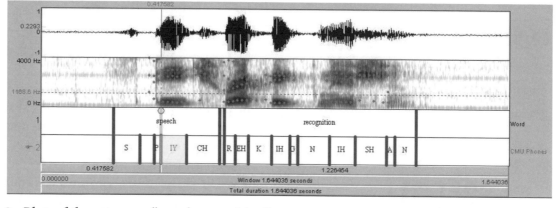

FIGURE 2. *Plots of the utterance "speech recognition"*

common to both modules, along with those components that are specific to each module.

Beginning from the left in Figure 1, the user creates a speech signal by speaking into a microphone. Acoustically, the speech produced is a series of air pressure changes between the sound source (the mouth of the speaker) and the microphone. The microphone then converts these pressure changes into changes in voltage, which if displayed on an oscilloscope, might appear as the speech waveform shown in Figure 1. Figure 2 shows the waveform for the utterance "speech recognition," along with other representations of that speech. The phrase was spoken into a microphone and recorded for display using a software package called the Praat tool. For this waveform, the horizontal axis represents time and the vertical axis represents the amplitude of the signal. The panel labeled "Word" displays the time intervals for each word in the utterance. Although words are an important way to transcribe speech, linguists often also use a phonetic alphabet, which is made up of linguistic subword units called phonemes, to capture the close relationship between the printed characters and the produced sound. The panel labeled "CMU phonemes" displays the time intervals for the phonemes that comprise the pronunciation of each word.

Moving to the next component in Figure 1, the signal undergoes feature extraction, in which it is digitized and further analyzed to extract a more compact representation for the speech signal. One common technique used during feature extraction is spectrum analysis. A spectrum is an estimate of the distribution of the signal energy as a function of frequency over a fixed interval of time (or frame length). A spectrogram is a plot of a spectrum over time. The center panel of Figure 2 shows the spectrogram for the utterance "speech recognition," with frequency on the vertical axis (ranging from 0 to 4,000 hertz, or cycles per second), time on the horizontal axis (in seconds), and intensity represented as darkness of the grayscale image. If the spectrogram is thought of as a three-dimensional plot, then the spectrum at a given point in time (actually over a small fixed interval) is the vertical slice at that point showing intensity as a function of frequency. The spectrum of a vowel sound usually has several obvious peak values: The center frequency and bandwidth of these peak values are called formants and are associated with resonances of the vocal tract and particular speech sounds. The formants are numbered starting with the lowest-frequency formant, called F1, followed by the next-highest, F2, and so on. In the spectrogram shown in Figure 2, the darker horizontal bars with superimposed dots indicate the formant values. The formants are important in speech analysis because they can be used to identify phonemes, which are units commonly used by modern speech recognition systems. For example, during the production of the phoneme *IY*, which corresponds to the vowel sound in the word *speech*, the F1 formant is at about 415 hertz, F2 at about 2,470 hertz, and F3 at about 2,980 hertz. A phone is the acoustical representation of a phoneme; in English there are between forty and fifty phones.

Once the features of a speech signal are extracted, they are passed either to acoustic model training or the speech decoder, depending on whether the acoustic model is being created or is being used to produce a speech transcription. A common acoustic modeling technique used to support both training and recognition is hidden Markov modeling (HMM). To construct a high-quality recognizer using this approach, it is important to construct accurate acoustic models for the various speech sounds (or phones). This acoustic model, once trained, can then be used by the speech decoder to produce a transcription for the input speech signal. The HMM learning algorithm (called Baum-Welch re-estimation) combines features from the feature extraction step with knowledge of what was said (using human-generated transcriptions of the speech) and how it was said using a pronunciation lexicon. The pronunciation lexicon contains the various ways that a word in the vocabulary can be pronounced (e.g., "speech" is pronounced in two different ways in Figure 1). Once an acoustic model is trained, it is used by the decoder in conjunction with other knowledge sources in order to generate the transcription for the input speech signal.

Most decoders produce the most likely word sequence given the match between the speech features extracted from the speech signal and representations of possible speech sounds stored in the acoustic model, aided by lexical knowledge. Current systems usually employ two types of lexical knowledge: the same pronunciation lexicon used during acoustic model training and a language model. The purpose of the language model is to add constraints concerning the likelihood of various sequences of words in order to focus the decoder on the more feasible word sequences. Most language models determine the probability of a word sequence $w_1, w_2 \ldots w_n$ using a small window of words, with bigram and trigram models being the most common. A bigram language model predicts the next word based on the word preceding it, while a trigram language model predicts the next word given the prior two words.

Why Is Speech Recognition So Challenging?

A major problem for speech recognition systems based on pattern recognition is variability in the speech signal. Sources of variability include those introduced by each speaker due to his or her physical state (people sound different, for example, if they have head colds or are fatigued), emotional state, speech rate, age, and dialect (British English, for example, sounds different from U.S. English, and within Great Britain or the United States there are also great variations in how English is spoken). Furthermore, context contributes significantly to variability in speech sounds. For example, in U.S. English the *t* in *butter* sounds different from the *t* in *bet,* and *gas shortage* is pronounced gash shortage. Contextual differences sometimes make it difficult to discern one phoneme from another. Additionally, environmental factors such as background noise and the position of the microphone can affect the recognizer's performance. In Figure 2, there are intervals of silence before speech and after recognition; however, the speech waveform is not entirely flat in those regions because of background noise picked up by the microphone.

A speech system designer may choose to improve the accuracy of a speech recognition application by restricting speaking style, using only limited, task-specific vocabularies with restricted utterance forms, or selecting applications for which noise is less of a concern. Although speech recognition systems are becoming more common, their likelihood of success is affected by a number of choices. Some of these choices are discussed below.

Speaker-Dependent or Speaker-Independent Systems

In order to customize the acoustic models to a user, speaker-dependent recognizers use specific characteristics of that individual's speech rather than features that may generalize more robustly to a wide variety of speakers. In general, speaker-dependent systems are more accurate than speaker independent systems; however, before using a speaker-dependent system, a user must provide samples of his or her speech. This is not necessary for a speaker-independent system, but adapting a speaker-independent recognizer to the characteristics of a given speaker or class of speakers can improve the accuracy of the system.

Isolated-Word or Continuous-Speech Systems

Isolated-word systems require speakers to pause briefly between words, whereas continuous-speech systems have no such restrictions. Isolated-word recognition systems can achieve a high degree of accuracy (above 90 percent for small vocabularies of ten to one hundred words). The absence of silence between words makes continuous-speech recognition more difficult than isolated-word recognition, largely due to speech coarticulation, which is the process by which neighboring sounds in speech influence one another. The pronunciation of phonemes in words and phrases is context-sensitive due to coarticulation. In isolated word recognition, explicit modeling of coarticulation is unnecessary because only single entire words are generated by the speaker, so only word-level models are used. A continuous-speech recognizer must model coarticulation both within and between words. Therefore training data for a continuous-speech recognizer must consist of continuously spoken speech, for which it is difficult, if not impossible, to consistently identify the boundaries dividing the words, let alone the boundaries between segments within words.

Spontaneous-Speech or Read-Speech Systems

Spontaneous speech tends to be pronounced less carefully than read speech, and with less consistent speech rates. Additionally, spontaneous speech is more likely to contain speech repairs (as, for instance, when a person says, "I will walk to, I mean, run to the store") and to suffer from less clearly marked word boundaries (in spontaneous speech a person is more likely to say "wanna" for *want to* than he or she is when reading the phrase) and greater variability in pronunciation, stress, intonation, and structure than speech produced by oral reading.

Small-Vocabulary or Large-Vocabulary Systems

Early systems were designed for small, closed-vocabulary tasks (less than a few hundred words), for example, digit and letter recognition. Modern systems work with large vocabularies often containing more than twenty thousand words. Recognition is generally more difficult when vocabularies are large or when they include many similar-sounding words. Another important problem for large-vocabulary systems is the problem of processing utterances containing out-of-vocabulary words, that is, words not appearing in the pronunciation lexicon. It is not unusual for large-vocabulary systems to produce errors when processing utterances containing out-of-vocabulary words, such as the names of new people and places.

By adding restrictions to the speech model (for example, by making it speaker dependent, limiting the vocabulary, making it an isolated-word model, or limiting the model to read speech), the model becomes simpler and more accurate, but also less natural. To achieve naturalness, many of today's speech recognition systems are speaker independent, use large vocabularies, and support continuous speech. Use of these large-vocabulary continuous-speech recognizers (LVCSR) brings with it problems of greater confusion among the words due to increased vocabulary size and difficulty in building models that capture the coarticulation effects both within individual words and between words. Since it is not feasible to train an acoustic model for each word (or for that matter for each syllable) in an LVCSR, it becomes necessary to work with pieces of words, typically phonemes. To account for the fact that a phoneme may be spoken differently depending on the phonemes surrounding it, many modern systems use context-dependent phone models to model speech more accurately. These LVCSR systems also rely heavily on a language model to choose between a variety of likely mappings between sounds and words. Other factors affecting the feasibility of a speech recognition system include computation time limitations (real-time processing), source characteristics (for example, whether there is environmental noise, the type and the placement of the microphone, types of noise sources, and speaker characteristics), language characteristics, and system characteristics.

Current Uses for Speech Recognition Systems

Speech recognition systems are becoming more and more common, providing functions like voice dialing and call routing, data entry, data access, and command and control. However, not all applications are equally successful. Traditionally, speech recognition research has focused on the transcription of speech into words. This perspective has led system developers to treat reduction of the word error rate as the fundamental measurement of a system's success. However, many alternative measurements may be equally if not more important, especially for consumer speech applications. These measurements include system response time, semantic accuracy, and task success rate. Furthermore, with the current state of speech recognition technology, human factors issues can have a large impact on user satisfaction, which in many cases determines whether an application will succeed or fail.

Speech is something that we often take for granted, but when interacting with a speech recognition system, this assumed familiarity can lead to problems. In his book *The Psychology of Everyday Things,* the computer scientist and writer Donald Norman states that the designer of any system should make sure that the user can figure out what to do, and that the user can tell what is going on. In other words, the designer should focus not just on the task, but also on the user and the user's understanding of the task. For a speech recognition system, this implies that users know when and what to speak, and that they receive feedback that the system is responding as expected.

The use of speech recognition for wireless telephone dialing is a capability that many people, especially those without the ability to use their hands, find very useful. This application permits a user to dial a telephone number by simply uttering one or more user-selected words. The application uses a speaker-dependent recognizer, which is easily trained and affords a user-friendly interface with a high recognition accuracy when used in an acoustical environment similar to that used during training. If, for example, the user had previously trained the recognizer to dial his or her home phone number when the words "phone home" are spoken, then the user can easily dial home by putting the phone in the appropriate mode and speaking "phone home" into the receiver, getting both audible and visual feedback to the effect that the utterance had been recognized and that the correct number is being dialed.

An example of a more complex, telephone-only speech recognition application that supports dialogue is the Jupiter system from the MIT Spoken Language Systems Group. This is an application that allows a user to access current weather information for five hundred or more cities across the world. It is a continuous-speech, speaker-independent system with a vocabulary of about two thousand words. The user speaks into a telephone using words appropriate to the task (that is, asking for weather information for a particular city) with the telephone-quality speech going to the speech recognizer. The recognizer then generates text, which is fed into a language-understanding system that produces a database query. The query is performed, and the result is converted into a natural-language sentence that goes to a synthesizer for playback to the user over the telephone (it closes the loop by supplying the requested weather-related information). From the United States, one can reach the Jupiter system by dialing a toll-free number: 1-888-573-8255.

Although the number of speech applications is increasing, more sophisticated applications will require new techniques yet to be developed.

Future Challenges

Most people, when imagining future speech applications, think about a speech system that has the ability not only to recognize words accurately but also to understand what those words mean in context in order to act on that understanding. To achieve this goal, computer models must be designed to combine fast, robust, high-quality acoustic models with a better model of human language processing. It is important to build acoustic models that show graceful degradation in the presence of noise, that is they should not stop working in the presence of a slight amount of street noise. The models should also have the flexibility to adapt to new microphones, background conditions, and speakers. Furthermore, future acoustic models need to cope with multiple simultaneous speakers in order to handle human-to-human conversations better. Future models must have the ability to handle words for which they have not been trained. Humans can cope with new words, including proper names, newly coined words, and sometimes even nonsense words (as in the poem "Jabberwocky" by Lewis Carroll).

Future speech applications will be characterized by extensive use of natural language and speech processing for man-machine interaction and by advanced systems for handling human knowledge. These systems must understand what is being said and act upon that information in some manner (for example, giving answers in synthetically generated speech). Knowledge sources that can be used to achieve speech understanding include:

- Acoustic or phonetic knowledge, which indicates how words are related to their sounds. Speech sounds such as vowels and consonants function mainly to indicate the identity of words and the regional dialect of a speaker.
- Prosodic knowledge, which is derived from the acoustic characteristics of speech, including the pitch or fundamental frequency, the length or duration of a word, a part of a word, or a stretch of silence, and the loudness or intensity of a word or syllable. For example, speakers use prosody to add structure to an utterance, to emphasize new material, to control turn taking in conversational interactions, to indicate types of utterances (for example, to distinguish questions from statements), and to express their feelings.
- Morphological knowledge, which concerns how words are constructed out of basic meaning units. For example, *un + friend + ly = unfriendly; love + past tense = loved;* and *object + oriented = object-oriented.* This type of knowledge is very important for languages that create new word forms through a morphological process.
- Lexical knowledge (dictionary knowledge), which covers word-level information such as word pronunciations, parts of speech (whether words are

nouns, verbs, and so forth), features (such as number or case), usage patterns, and word meaning. Words and the ways that they are spoken and used are a very important part of human communication.

- Syntactic knowledge, which deals with how words are put together to make legal sentences. For example, the sentence "The cat chased the dog" contains a subject (*The cat*) and predicate (*chased the dog*). These phrases can be further subdivided into subparts: The predicate, for example, contains the verb *chased* and a direct object *the dog.* By understanding the structure of this sentence, we can more easily ascertain its meaning.
- Semantic knowledge, which includes the identification of a word's meaning (for example, being able to distinguish when *post* means the metal stem of a pierced earring and when it means a support fixed in an upright position), how words combine to create a sentence's meaning, and how combining words into a sentence affects both word and overall sentence meaning (compare, for example, "Fred broke the window with the block" with "Fred broke the window with Nadia.").
- Pragmatic knowledge, which explains how context affects the interpretation of a sentence. For example, the sentence "Louise loves him" means one thing when it follows the question "Who loves Fred?" and another when it follows the sentence "Louise has a cat." Another interesting example is "Can you pass the salt?" Although framed as a yes-no question, at the dinner table, it is actually a polite request for someone to pass the salt.
- Task and world knowledge, which include knowledge of a specific task, things in the world, how other people's minds work, what a listener knows or believes, and so forth.

An important problem for future systems is how to integrate all of these knowledge sources with the acoustic model in an effective yet efficient manner. Current systems utilize some of these knowledge sources but do not do so in the general purpose manner that Data in *Star Trek: The Next Generation* does.

More work on speech understanding is needed to make the vision of Data a reality.

Mary P. Harper and V. Paul Harper

See also Dialog Systems; Natural-Language Processing; Speech Synthesis

FURTHER READING

Allen, J. (1995). *Natural language understanding.* Redwood City, CA: Benjamin/Cummings.

Baker, J. K. (1975). The Dragon system: An overview. *IEEE Transactions on Acoustics, Speech and Signal Processing, 23*(1), 24–29.

Boersma, P., & Weenicnk, D. (n.d.). Praat: Doing phonetics by computer. Retrieved August 15, 2003, from http://www.fon.hum.uva.nl/praat

Carnegie Mellon University Pronunciation Dictionary. Retrieved August 15, 2003, from http://www.speech.cs.cmu.edu/cgi-bin/cmudict

Huang, X., Acero, A., & Hon, H.-W. (2001). *Spoken language processing: A guide to theory, algorithm, and system development.* Upper Saddle River, NJ: Prentice Hall.

Jelinek, F. (1976). Continuous speech recognition by statistical methods. *Proceedings of the IEEE, 64,* 532-556.

Jupiter. Retrieved August 15, 2003 from http://www.sls.csail.mit.edu/sls/whatwedo/applications/jupiter.html

Jurafsky, D., & Martin, J. H. (2000). *Speech and language processing: An introduction to natural language processing, computational linguistics, and speech recognition.* Upper Saddle River, NJ: Prentice Hall.

Markowitz, J. A. (1995). *Using speech recognition: A guide for application developers.* Upper Saddle River, NJ: Prentice Hall.

Norman, D. A. (1988). *The psychology of everyday things.* New York: Basic Books.

Stork, D. G. (Ed.). (1997). *HAL's legacy: 2001's computer as dream and reality.* Cambridge, MA: MIT Press.

SPEECH SYNTHESIS

The term *speech synthesis* refers to text-to-speech (TTS) synthesis and involves the generation of speech from textual input by digital computers. Early applications of TTS focused on computers reading aloud scanned or stored text for the visually impaired, but the variety of usages has increased dramatically during the past decade because of advances in the core technologies underlying TTS as well as increases in computer processing power, memory, and storage.

TTS has its roots in so-called talking machines that have been in existence for centuries. However, these machines as well as later analogue electrical devices perform only one of the steps performed by TTS systems, namely the generation of speech from a symbolic representation of speech sounds (phonemes). This step is the final step in the lengthy and complex sequence of steps needed for the conversion of text to speech. Not until the 1970s did TTS in this sense come into existence.

Fundamental Tasks of Text-to-Speech Conversion

A brief example illustrates the challenges faced by TTS. Consider this sentence:

"Does Dr. Smith, our new family doctor, live next to St. John's church at number 9?"
A human effortlessly renders this sentence as:
"does doctor SMITH
\<small pitch rise\>
\<pause\>
\<lower voice\>
our new FAMILY doctor
\<small pitch rise\>
\<pause\>
\<reset voice to normal\>
live next to saint JOHN's church at number NINE
 \<large pitch rise\>"

This example shows that a TTS system has to perform the following steps:

1. Text normalization: Expansion of abbreviations (e.g., "St."), numbers, and other non-words into words
2. Phonetization: Generation of a phoneme sequence that represents the sounds in a word (e.g., pronounce "live" as [l][I][v] and not as [l][aʲ][v])
3. Emphasis: Determination of which words need emphasis, the type of emphasis, and the amount
4. Phrasing: Determination of how a sentence is to be divided into shorter phrases between

which pauses or other markers of phrase boundaries are to be inserted

5. Timing: Determination of the duration of each phoneme, syllable, and word in the output speech
6. Pitch contour: Determination of the melody across the sentence
7. Synthesis: Generation of digital speech output that contains the computed phonemes and has the desired timing and pitch contour

The combination of steps 1–4 is referred to as the "text analysis" or "natural language processing" (NLP) component, and the combination of steps 5–6 is referred to as the "prosody component." The output from the NLP component consists of a symbolic representation of the output speech. This representation consists of linguistic entities such as phonemes, words, and phrases and of tags (labels) attached to these entities, such as "emphasis level" or "parenthetic phrase." We call this representation the "linguistic data structure." The output from the prosody component is numerical and specifies durations, pitch contour, and often additional acoustic features that the output speech should have. We refer to this output as the "target prosody." Finally, the synthesis component generates speech that contains the correct phonemes and whose prosody matches the target prosody.

Three TTS Architectures

Although hybrids exist, TTS systems that have been created during the past three decades fall into three broad architectural categories: synthesis by rule, diphone synthesis, and unit selection synthesis.

In synthesis-by-rule systems the synthesis component creates speech by computing acoustic parameter trajectories—such as energy, pitch, and formant frequencies—that are converted into digital speech. The MITalk system and its commercial version, DECTalk, are the best known of these systems.

As for diphone synthesis, characterizing a signal as complex as speech by rule-based parameter trajectories, even when done as thoroughly as in the MITalk system, is unlikely to capture the full richness of natural speech. After computer storage and

memory became large enough to contain sufficient amounts of recorded speech, researchers were able to perform synthesis by pasting (or concatenating) intervals (or units, typically diphones, that is, sequences consisting of two successive phonemes) of recorded speech. Diphone synthesis became possible not only because of increased computing power, memory, and storage, but also because new linear predictive coding (a method for computing acoustic parameters where the parameters characterize a linear filter) (LPC)-based speech modification methods had been invented in the field of speech compression. LPC allowed researchers to smooth speech units to prevent the "seams" between them from being audible and to modify the duration and pitch of the units in order to make their prosody match the target prosody. The Bell Labs system is the best known of these systems.

Unit selection synthesis bypasses the prosody component and does not modify the prosody of recorded speech units. This system takes advantage of further increases in computer storage and processing power and uses as its key ingredient a large corpus (body) of recorded speech—at least an order of magnitude (factor of 10) larger than what is used in diphone TTS. The recordings are labeled and segmented (i.e., phoneme tags with time stamps are associated with the recorded speech; additional tags, such as for stress, may be present), and the linguistic data structure (a data structure that is computed by the NLP component and consists of a symbolic representation of the output speech) computed from the input text is used to search for a compatible sequence of speech intervals in the speech recordings. When more than one compatible sequence exists, the system selects the sequence that best satisfies additional criteria, such as minimization of the acoustic differences between units at the points where they are to be concatenated. In the same way as LPC was a critical enabling factor for diphone synthesis, new search algorithms developed in related fields, including automatic speech recognition and algorithm research, were a key enabling factor for unit selection synthesis.

Language

The combinatorial complexity of language (the number of combinations that exist) has important implications for TTS. Unit selection synthesis works well in restricted domains, such as monetary amounts, credit card numbers, times, and dates. For example, to generate sixteen-digit credit card numbers in the typical four-four-four-four format, one needs to record each digit in only a relatively small number of contexts as defined in terms of the following contextual factors. First is the location of a four-digit group: Such groups have different intonation patterns. For example, the final group shows a sharp pitch fall. Second is the coarticulatory context: The pronunciation of the [eʲ] phoneme that starts the word for the digit "8" is pronounced differently when preceded by the [u] in the word for the digit "2" than when preceded by the [i] in the word for the digit "3." In combination at most a few hundred contexts have to be differentiated, and hence only a few thousand digits need to be recorded.

In unrestricted domains unit selection seems impractical because of the enormous number of combinations of phoneme sequences and contextual distinctions that are relevant for output speech. Consider that in the United States 1.5 million distinct surnames and at least several hundreds of thousands of words exist. New words can be created by adding prefixes and suffixes (consider *practice, practiced, practices, practical, practically, impractically, practicality, impracticality*).

Any word can occur in a wide variety of word— and, hence coarticulatory—contexts.

A word's temporal pattern (i.e., the pattern of durations of its successive phonemes) and pitch pattern depend on a large number of factors, including the phonemes in preceding and following words, emphasis level of the word and of its neighbors, location of the word in the phrase, and location of the phrase in the sentence.

Based on these considerations, the combinatorics (number of combinations) of language would seem to make unit selection synthesis implausible because the numbers of units and distinct contexts in which these units must be recorded are too large to be practical. Yet, remarkably successful implementations of the system have been produced. How is this possible?

The success of unit selection synthesis is due to at least three factors. The first of these concerns the uneven frequency distribution of units or unit-

context combinations in a language. As a result, the recordings need to contain only a fraction of the total number of unit-context combinations to nevertheless have a high likelihood of covering most combinations needed for an arbitrary input sentence. Any language has constraints on phoneme sequences, word stress patterns, locations of words in phrases, and word sequences. These constraints can be absolute, such as the constraint that [w] cannot be followed by a consonant, or probabilistic, such as the low frequency of three-syllable words with stress on the final syllable.

Although this uneven frequency distribution certainly reduces the amount of recordings needed to attain a certain coverage level of the language, researchers must be cautious for the following reason. Language tends to have the large-number-of-rare-events characteristic, meaning that the number of events (i.e., units or unit-context combinations) that are rare is so large that their combined probability is near certainty. In other words, a randomly selected input sentence is likely to require at least one unit that has not been recorded, even if a large amount of recordings has been made.

However, this problem may be counteracted at least in part by two other factors. One factor is that often a unit might be available that is perceptually similar to the unit that is actually needed but missing. The other factor is that listeners, knowing that they are listening to a computer, may be tolerant to isolated flaws in an utterance when the remainder has a high quality of perceived naturalness.

Diphone synthesis and synthesis by rule are not challenged by the combinatorics of language because of their generative capabilities that allow them to create any sequence of speech sounds with any prosodic pattern. Of course, these generative capabilities come at the expense of speech quality degradation.

Human speech is among the most complex forms of human behavior. It is complex both because of the neural, physiological, acoustical, and mechanical processes involved in its generation and because of the information conveyed.

Speech involves the coordination of multiple muscle systems, including systems that control the pressure of the exhaled air, the characteristics of the vocal chords, the position of the tongue (which itself is a highly complex organ containing hundreds of muscles), the velic flap that determines whether air will pass through the oral cavity or the nasal cavity, and the lips. The complexity of the speech production apparatus is such that one cannot reasonably expect it to be mimicked by a computer model in all its details.

A simplified model of the human speech production apparatus that has played a central role in the history of TTS is the Source-Filter Model. According to this model, the vocal chords are in one of two states. In voiced sounds, such as vowels and nasals, the vocal chords oscillate regularly to produce a sound source with a given frequency that we perceive as pitch. In voiceless sounds, such as voiceless fricatives (e.g., [s], [f], [sh]), they allow air to pass through essentially unobstructed. A constriction elsewhere, such as between the lips or between the tongue and the teeth, creates a turbulent sound source. The sound produced in either state is modified by the shape of the oral cavity, with the position of the tongue playing an important role. In the case of vowels, for example, the position of the tongue uniquely and fully determines which vowel is heard.

To a first order of approximation, the transformation of either sound source by the articulatory system can be modeled as a time-varying linear filter. (A filter is a mathematical operation that predicts the value of the speech signal by the weighted sum of the values of the speech signal during the preceding few milliseconds.) The filter coefficients correspond to the momentary shape of the oral cavity and determine the frequency characteristics of the sound.

Human speech conveys far more than words. In particular, prosody plays a central role in human speech, not only by indicating which syllables are stressed, which words are important, and what the structure of a sentence is, but also by conveying an array of complex interpersonal messages, such as emotions, social standing, and doubt. Humans convey these messages by using several acoustic cues, including pitch pattern, duration, overall speaking rate, loudness, voice quality (tense, raspy, breathy), and lip aperture. Both computing these messages from text and conveying these messages via these acoustic cues are well beyond the capabilities of current TTS technology.

Speech Perception

Understanding human speech production is important for TTS, but the case for the relevance of speech perception is stronger than the case for speech production because the ultimate goal of TTS is not that its internal algorithms and data structures faithfully mimic aspects of human speech production but rather that its output sounds as if it has been produced by a human. Hence, we find a paradox in the fact that relatively little research has been conducted on perception of synthetic speech. Among the few perception studies, the most important have focused on predicting subjective speech quality from an objective measure of the acoustic difference between two units. Objective acoustic difference measures, or acoustic cost functions, are critical for unit selection synthesis because the search algorithms rely on such measures. Current results have not yet produced cost functions that are able to predict human perception accurately, with typical correlations between observed and predicted quality ratings of 50–60 percent.

NLP Component

Traditionally three phonetization methods are used in TTS in combination: human-generated rules, pronunciation dictionaries, and morphemic decomposition (the decomposition of a word into a stem, prefixes, and suffixes). (Morphemes are the smallest units of a language that carry *meaning*.) A typical example of a rule is "If a 't' is preceded by a stressed vowel, followed by a vowel, and word internal, then its pronunciation is a flapped-[t]." English is known for the irregularity of its pronunciation, with long-range dependencies (the pronunciation of a letter or letter group depends on other relatively distant letters in the word) such as in the pronunciation of the initial consonant in the words *though* and *thought*. Hence, rules need to be complemented by pronunciation dictionaries. However, dictionaries are also insufficient because in most languages new words can be formed by adding prefixes, suffixes, and affixes. Morphemic decomposition splits words into morphemes, which are then phoneticized with rules or dictionaries. For example, the word *mishap* is decomposed into "mis"+"hap" instead of "mish"+"app." This process is further amended with stress rules. For example, in English words of Latinate origin, predictable stress shifts occur, such as *TEMpest → temPESTuous.*

Additional phonetization methods are used to address the many problems that remain, including language-specific challenges such as the absence of word boundaries in Mandarin Chinese, the use of multiple scripts in Japanese, or the absence of explicit vowels in Arabic.

Other aspects of the linguistic data structure include tags for prosody generation or, in unit selection synthesis, for prosody-based search. Current systems compute a minimal set of tags, typically binary word emphasis tags (emphasized, not emphasized) and three phrasing tags (approximately corresponding to the comma, period, and question mark).

Computing emphasis from text can be done at a rudimentary level with the function word-content word distinction, a rudimentary level with the distinction between function words and content words. However, in the following sentence a human speaker is likely to strongly emphasize the content words "blue" and "green" but not the content word "house":

"I said blue house, not green house."

Although the contrastive stress in this example can be detected by simple rules, more challenges arise from the distinction between given information and new information. When in a paragraph the same entity is referred to by different terms ("The president," "The commander-in-chief," "The leader of the free world"), human speakers give the first occurrence stronger emphasis than subsequent occurrences. If this is not done, the listener may erroneously perceive these subsequent occurrences as introducing new entities. For a TTS system to mimic this feature of human speech, it would need a vast store of real-world knowledge.

Computation of phrasing tags involves more than detection of punctuation marks because humans insert phrase boundaries at many points that are not so indicated. In parsing methods a sentence is represented as a parse tree containing such entities as verb phrases and noun phrases, and the system uses rules that specify phrase boundary placement as a function of parse tree structure. In statistical methods the probability of a phrase boundary is modeled by the system as a function of the parts-of-speech sequence in a window surrounding a given word juncture.

A major architectural challenge created by the multimethod nature of the NLP component is how to ensure that the corresponding subcomponents interact properly. Researchers are addressing this challenge by increasingly using weighted finite state transducers (WFSTs), which provide a unified formal structure for representations as diverse as parse trees, dictionaries, and morphological decomposition rules. In addition, WFSTs have well-understood mathematical properties that provide further computational advantages.

Prosody Component

The prosody component has as input the linguistic data structure and generates as output target values for timing, pitch, and often additional acoustic features such as energy.

Typically the temporal structure of the output speech is given in the form of phoneme duration. As discussed, phoneme duration depends on many factors, including the identity of the phoneme (e.g., [aʲ] as in *bite* is on average longer than [e] as in *bet*), the identities of the surrounding phonemes, word stress, word emphasis, position of the phoneme in the syllable (e.g., in the word *noon,* the first occurrence of [n] is longer than the second occurrence), position of the syllable in the word (the final syllable tends to be longer than non-final syllables), and position of the word in the phrase. The effects of these factors to some degree interact. For example, the [e] in *bed* is longer than in *bet,* but the difference is substantially larger when the word is phrase final (at the end of the phrase) than when it is not. As a result, mimicking natural durational patterns is a difficult problem for which several approaches have been proposed. Among the earlier approaches is a rule-based approach in which the duration of a phoneme is altered by applying successive rules corresponding to the factors. The availability of larger speech corpora (bodies) in the early 1990s led to improvements by the introduction of statistical approaches in which parameters in statistical models are estimated from observed durations instead of being manually fine tuned in laborious trial-and-error procedures.

Whereas researchers have a substantial consensus on timing, no such consensus exists on pitch. Among the many approaches to pitch, two approaches are most prominent. In the superpositional approach the pitch contour is viewed as being formed by adding underlying, simpler curves that correspond to different classes of linguistic entities. In the best known of these approaches, these underlying curves correspond to phrases and accented syllables. During synthesis these curves are computed from the linguistic data structure and the output from the timing component and added. In the tone sequence approach pitch curves are generated by interpolation between time/frequency points generated by rule. In addition to these older approaches, new statistical approaches, such as the Tilt Model, have been developed.

Synthesis Component

The synthesis component performs different steps depending on whether the TTS system uses synthesis by rule, modifies recorded speech (as in diphone synthesis), or uses search only (as in unit selection synthesis.)

In synthesis by rule the system computes parameter trajectories and converts these trajectories into digital speech, in part by controlling filters that modify the output of a periodic or noise sound source in accordance with the Source-Filter Model or more complex variants of this model. The key challenge in synthesis by rule is to state rules that coordinate the trajectories of this large number of parameters to produce natural-sounding speech without the benefit of few of these parameters being directly observable in human speech. Only with a deep understanding of the human speech apparatus in combination with a substantial effort in manual fine tuning were researchers able to obtain the impressive results exemplified by MITalk and DECTalk.

In LPC-based diphone synthesis, diphones are represented as sequences of filter coefficient vectors, typically at 5- or 10-ms. intervals or pitch-synchronously. During synthesis these vector sequences can be concatenated smoothly and in a straightforward way to reduce discrepancies between units. Once concatenated and smoothed, the timing of these vector sequences can be adjusted to match the target timing by interpolating, deleting, or repeating vectors. A signal is generated that is either noise (to mimic sounds such as "S") or is periodic (to mimic sounds such as vowels that are generated by regular vibrations of the vocal folds. Next the source signal is generated to reflect the phoneme characteristics (voiced versus unvoiced) and the target pitch contour independently of the sequence of filter coefficient vectors.) Finally, the filter vectors are applied to the source signal to create the output speech.

Although LPC synthesis constituted a breakthrough and generated speech quality that in the 1980s was considered adequate, researchers agree that LPC synthesis in this simple form is no longer adequate. Researchers have made progress with several refinements of LPC synthesis, including the use of periodic sources that are based on glottal models (mathematical descriptions of how the vocal folds separate), the use of pitch-synchronous analysis and synthesis, better smoothing methods, and use of filters with more coefficients. Yet, researchers generally consider new methods based on the pitch synchronous overlap add (PSOLA) method to be superior.

The PSOLA method takes advantage of the fact that in voiced regions (regions containing sounds such as vowels, nasals (e.g., *n* and *m*), voice fricatives (e.g., *z* and *v*), liquids (e.g., *r* and *l*), or glides (e.g., *y* and *w*)) the speech signal has an uneven energy distribution over time, with energy concentrated around the time points that correspond to the moments when the oscillating glottis is open. Symmetrical bell-shaped windows are centered on these time points and multiplied by the speech signal to further emphasize these energy concentrations. This results in the original speech signal being represented as a sequence of short-term speech signals. Due to the bell-shaped window, the signals start and end at zero energy levels, so that one can generate new speech signals by recombining these short-term speech signals without too much concern for artifacts caused by overlap (as the result of regions being added that contain parts of the original speech that belonged to temporally separate regions). Pitch can be modified by increasing or decreasing the time intervals between their centers, and the duration of a speech interval can be increased by duplicating them.

The key challenges in unit selection synthesis are corpus design, cost functions, and the search algorithms.

Corpus design attempts to maximize the coverage of the target domain (the collection of all sentences that the system may encounter as input in a given application or range of applications). If the target domain is unrestricted, researchers have several methods to optimize coverage. These methods include construction of a hybrid corpus that contains subcorpora (subsets of the corpus) for important restricted domains (e.g., numbers) or subcorpora that serve fallback purposes. An example of the latter is the inclusion of a diphone corpus recorded with neutral prosody. To optimize frequency-weighted coverage in unrestricted domain applications, researchers can use text selection methods that find the smallest set of sentences in a large text corpus providing the best coverage of the text corpus in terms of the units needed for synthesis. Currently text corpora are available in several languages containing billions of words.

Researchers use cost functions to select unit sequences when multiple unit sequences are available in the speech corpus. Researchers customarily distinguish between target cost and concatenation cost. The former refers to the degree to which a unit represents the target phonemes and prosodic context, and the latter refers to the acoustic difference between two units. As stated, researchers currently have no objective measures that accurately predict perceived speech quality.

Researchers use search algorithms to find the optimal unit sequence based on the linguistic data structure and the cost functions. As speech corpora grow in size, the computational cost increases rapidly. However, researchers have many algorithms for this task, including algorithms developed or refined in speech recognition such as search algorithms.

Applications

The earliest applications of TTS were reading machines for the visually impaired, and applications of TTS for special populations are likely to increase. For example, people can address reading difficulties, whether due to being a nonnative speaker or to developmental disorders such as dyslexia, with interactive language teaching software. TTS provides unlimited flexibility in textual materials, and the ability to modify speech in real time can add capabilities, such as for prosody teaching. Assistive uses for the visually impaired are likely to increase and to include speech-enabled webpages and speech-enabled mobile phones.

For the general population the fact that listening to synthetic speech is not an inherently pleasurable experience remains an important limitation. People will use TTS only if they need access to information but cannot obtain it in a visual form. Thus, telephone applications and in-car applications dominate the space of TTS applications. A further factor confining this space is that many services can be provided by using recorded human speech. Yet, with the explosive increase in mobile telephony, the Internet-fed need for instantaneous information access, the flexibility offered by TTS to service providers, and the ingenuity in developing applications that avoid the weaknesses of TTS, consumer applications for the general population are certain to increase.

Text-to-speech synthesis is not a solved problem, but any side-to-side comparison between current TTS systems and systems from the 1970s shows that substantial progress has been made. This progress has been accompanied by major changes in scientific focus. Rule-based synthesis was closely tied to speech science, in particular articulatory research. Diphone synthesis focused on signal-processing methods while statistical methods for NLP and prosody were enabled by the advent of large online text corpora, the proliferation of mathematical models in related fields such as psychology, and the growth of the field of computational linguistics. Finally, unit selection synthesis is not directly tied to articulatory research, signal processing, or prosodic modeling and emphasizes database construction and search algorithms.

Currently, except for applications that require a small footprint, unit selection synthesis is the dominant system. When a speech corpus contains all the units needed for a given input sentence, the result is indistinguishable from human speech. However, the fundamental problem remains that in unrestricted synthesis the required units are not always available, in which case the resulting speech is audibly flawed. The question is whether researchers can address this problem by using ever-larger corpora or by developing a hybrid method that uses some of the signal-modification technology created for diphone synthesis and is grounded in the knowledge and technologies that have been accumulated during the decades of TTS research.

Jan P. H. van Santen

See also Dialog Systems; Natural-Language Processing; Speech Recognition

FURTHER READING

Allen, J., Hunnicutt, S., & Klatt, D. (1976). *From text to speech: The MITalk system*. Cambridge, MA: Cambridge University Press.

Atal, B., & Hanauer, S. (1971). Speech analysis and synthesis by linear prediction of the speech wave. *Journal of the Acoustical Society of America, 50,* 637–655.

Bailly, G., & Benoit, C. (Eds.). (1992). *Talking machines, theories, models, and designs*. Amsterdam, Netherlands: Elsevier Science Publishers.

Charpentier, F., & Moulines, E. (1989). Pitch-synchronous waveform processing techniques for text-to-speech synthesis using diphones. *Proceedings of Eurospeech 1989, 2,* 13–19.

Dusterhoff, K. E., Black, A. W., & Taylor, P. A. (1999). Using decision trees within the tilt intonation model to predict F0 contours. *Proceedings of Eurospeech 1999*.

Dutoit, T. (1996). *An introduction to text-to-speech synthesis*. Boston: Kluwer Academic Publishers.

Fant, G. (1960). *Acoustic theory of speech production*. The Hague, Netherlands: Mouton.

Flanagan, J. (1972). *Speech analysis synthesis and perception* (2nd ed.). New York: Springer-Verlag.

Fujisaki, H., & Nagashima, S. (1969). Synthesis of pitch contours of connected speech. *Annual Report of the Engineering Research Institute, University of Tokyo, 28,* 53–60.

Huang, X., Acero, A., & Hon, H. (2001). *Spoken language processing: A guide to theory, algorithm and system development*. New York: Prentice Hall.

Hunt, A., & Black, A. (1996). Unit selection in a concatenative speech synthesis system using a large speech database. *Proceedings, International Conference on Audio, Speech, and Signal Processing, 1,* 373–376.

Iwahashi, N., & Sagisaka, Y. (2000). Statistical modeling of speech segment duration by constrained tree regression. *Trans. of Institute of Electronics, Information and Communication Engineers, E83-D,* 1550–1559.

Keller, E., Bailly, G., Monaghan, A., Terken, J., & Huckvale, M. (Eds.). (1994). *Fundamentals of speech synthesis and speech recognition*. New York: Wiley.

Klabbers, E., & Veldhuis, R. (2001). Reducing audible spectral discontinuities. *IEEE Transactions on Speech and Audio Processing, 9*(1), 39–51.

Klatt, D. (1987). Review of text-to-speech conversion in English. *Journal of the Acoustical Society of America, 82,* 737–793. Retrieved September 29, 2003, from http://www.mindspring.com/~ssshp

Kleijn, W. B., & Paliwal, K. (Eds.). (1995). *Speech coding and synthesis*. Amsterdam, Netherlands: Elsevier Science.

Olive, J. P. (1977). Rule synthesis of speech from dyadic units. *Proceedings, International Conference on Audio, Speech, and Signal Processing, 77,* 568–570.

Pierrehumbert, J. (1981). Synthesizing intonation. *Journal of the Acoustical Society of America, 70,* 985–995.

Sagisaka, Y., Campbell, W., & Higuchi, N. (Eds.). (1998). *Computing prosody: Computational models for processing spontaneous speech*. Berlin, Germany: Springer-Verlag.

Sagisaka, Y., Kaiki, N., Iwahashi, N., & Mimura, K. (1992). ATR–TALK speech synthesis system. *Proceedings of the International Conference on Spoken Language Processing, 1,* 482–486.

Spiegel, M. (1985). Pronouncing names automatically. *Proceedings of the American Voice I/O Systems Conference 1985,* 107–132.

Sproat, R. (1997). *Multilingual text-to-speech synthesis: The Bell Labs approach*. Boston: Kluwer Academic Publishers.

Stevens, K. (1999). *Acoustic phonetics*. Cambridge, MA: MIT Press.

van Bezooijen, R., & van Heuven, V. (1997). Assessment of synthesis systems. In D. Gibbon, R. Moore, & R. Winsky (Eds.), *Handbook of standards and resources for spoken language systems* (pp. 481–63). Berlin, Germany: Walter de Gruyter.

van Santen, J. (1994). Assignment of segmental duration in text-to-speech synthesis. *Computer Speech and Language, 8,* 95–128.

van Santen, J., Sproat, R., Olive, J., & Hirschberg, J. (Eds.). (1997). *Progress in speech synthesis*. New York: Springer-Verlag.

SPEECHREADING

Speechreading is the act of recognizing or understanding speech using visual cues. The term "lipreading" is often used as a synonym because the most salient cues for speechreading are lip movements. However, humans usually make use of additional cues such as the movement of the chin and eyebrows, facial mimicry, and even hand gestures and body language. Speechreading has been researched in the context of automatic speech recognition as well as with the goal of improving current acoustic speech recognizers.

Properties of the Visual Information

A message transmitted from a speaker to a listener is typically encoded in several ways. In an information-theoretical sense, these codings can be viewed as separate channels that transmit parts of the same message or all of it. The most obvious and usually most reliable channel is the acoustic signal. It is the one used by telephones and radios and commercially available automatic speech recognizers.

Another channel is the visual signal, which includes lip movements and facial and hand gestures. The biggest advantage of visual information is that it complements acoustic information. For example, a visual signal does not degrade in acoustically noisy environments, whereas an acoustic signal is independent of lighting conditions. The sounds /m/ and /n/ are very similar acoustically, but distinct visually. The sounds /b/ and /p/ are similar both acoustically and visually, but if both channels are taken together, the time difference between the opening of the lips and the beginning of voicing is a very strong cue that helps to make that distinction.

Applications

Speechreading can be used as an additional source of information for automatic speech recognition. But it also has a number of other applications.

- **Speaker recognition.** Speechreading requires finding and tracking a person's face in a sequence of images. The same is true for face recognition. In face recognition, an individual's identity is determined or verified using an image of their face. This recognition can be made more reliable using speechreading because speakers vary in the way their lips move and facial mimicry changes during speech.

- **Speech and video coding.** Video telephony and conferencing systems need to transmit high-bandwidth video over low-bandwidth connections. This requires the use of efficient coding strategies that compress the signal and thus reduce the bandwidth. Speech coding usually makes use of a model of speech production. The parameters used for generating the speech signal are estimated using the model and then transmitted instead of the speech signal. At the receiving end, the same model is used to regenerate the speech signal. In addition, an error signal is transmitted, encoding the difference between the generated and the real speech signal. Speechreading can help to more reliably estimate the parameters needed to correctly configure the model. Furthermore, it can be used to implement the same strategy for video coding. A model of the face is the basis. The parameters to configure this model (such as jaw movement, lip opening, the position of the eyebrows, gaze direction, skin color, and the presence of beards and glasses) are estimated from the video signal and then transmitted. At the receiving end, the face is reconstructed from the model and the parameters.

Voice activity detection. One of the challenges of speech recognition and speech coding is to determine when a signal contains speech. A very simple approach to this is to look in the signal for energy that exceeds some noise-dependent threshold. This approach does not work very well if the background noise varies too much. Using visual cues, a system may look for lip movements or it may check whether the speaker is looking at the system and is close enough.

- **Speaker change detection.** If the system is engaged in a conversation with several speakers, speechreading can help to decide who is speaking—for example, by looking for lip movements.

- **Speaker localization and tracking.** The same strategy can be used to locate and track a speaker. This information can be used very effectively to steer a "beam former." A beam former combines the signals of several microphones in a microphone array in such a way that it has a preferred listening direction. This direction can be determined reliably using visual information. The same information can also be used to steer the camera if panning is possible.

- **Medical applications.** Speech reading can also be used for diagnostic or therapeutic applications. For example, the face and facial movements exhibit a large degree of symmetry along the vertical axis. After a stroke, this symmetry is often destroyed and speechreading can be used to measure the degree of asymmetry. It can also be used to measure the effect of a speech therapy.

Technical Implementation

Extracting visual information requires the use of a camera. Due to their low cost, regular video cameras are often used in speechreading systems. Most acoustic speech recognition systems slice the speech signal into blocks, sometimes called frames, about 100 times per second. In contrast, visual speech recognition must do with a rate of only 25 to 30 frames per second. While this has turned out to be sufficient to represent the visual information, it poses the problem of correctly synchronizing acoustic and visual information.

As the price difference between color and black-and-white cameras diminishes, more and more systems make use of the additional color information for more reliable feature extraction (for example, skin color). However, care must be taken to handle varying lighting conditions, which often have more detrimental effects on color than brightness.

Most modern video cameras use CCD (charge coupled device) elements that are infrared-sensitive. Normally, a filter is inserted which removes infrared light. To improve speechreading in low light conditions, this filter can be replaced and the camera fitted with an infrared light.

A more exotic way to measure lip movements employs ultrasound. On a headset an array of ultrasound elements is located at the microphone near the lips. The elements emit ultrasound in such a way that the sound travels mainly in one direction (beam forming). The sound eventually hits the lips, is reflected, and comes back to the microphone. The direction in which the sound travels can be steered and thus the lips can be scanned along a raster. If the lips are open, the beam can even "look" inside the mouth. The advantage of this approach is that it is completely independent of any lighting or noise conditions.

Outlook

At present, few systems make use of speechreading. A reliable extraction of the necessary features for speechreading requires time-intensive image-processing algorithms. Besides the camera for recording the visual signal, a processor with enough power is needed, which in turn increases the hardware costs of a speech-recognition system. This is the main reason why speechreading has not taken a stronger foothold in the automatic speech-recognition market. However, with more and more computers being equipped with cameras and processing power becoming ever more ubiquitous, it is to be expected that this hurdle will diminish over time.

Another drawback of speechreading is that the technology is not yet in a stage at which most applications work well outside the laboratory. It is difficult to reliably extract the visual cues under all lighting conditions, which is necessary for mobile applications. It is also not yet clear how best to integrate visual and acoustic information. This is especially true for continuous speech recognition such as dictation systems. Nonetheless, the potential benefits of speechreading have sparked interest among research groups around the world, and it is to be expected that these problems will eventually be solved.

Marcus E. Hennecke

See also Dialog Systems; Gesture Recognition; Speech Recognition

FURTHER READING

Petajan, E. D., Brooke, N. M., Bischoff, G. J., & Bodoff, D. A. (1988). An improved automatic lipreading system to enhance speech recognition. In *Proceedings of Human Factors in Computing Systems* (pp. 19–25). New York: ACM.

Stork, D. G., & Hennecke, M. E. (Eds.). (1995). Speechreading by humans and machines, *150 of NATO ASI Series, Series F. Computer and Systems Sciences*. Berlin: Springer Verlag.

SPELL CHECKER

People expect to read correctly spelled documents. However, many people who create documents have difficulties in spelling correctly. For example, people who are learning to read and write, who are learning a foreign language, or who are visually challenged can have difficulties in spelling correctly. To help such people, a spell checker is a computer program that helps users correct spelling errors as they create text.

Spell Checker Uses

Originally spell checkers were used for specialized languages. In 1962 Constance K. McElwain and Martha Evans developed a computer program called "Degarbler" that could correct up to 70 percent of errors in computer-recognized Morse code. Subsequently, James O'Brien (1967) developed an early prototype of a spell checker that corrected optical character reader (OCR) output.

A spell checker is now considered to be a standard feature of word processing programs. Virtually all modern word processors have a spell checker to determine if words are spelled correctly, even as users type them. Spell checkers can also correct a misspelled word before users even realize that they have misspelled it. For this automatic correction feature, spell checkers have a list of commonly misspelled words such as *teh* for *the* or *recieve* for *receive*. As a user types a word that matches one on this list, the spell checker automatically changes the word to the correct spelling. The list of words varies. However, most spell checkers allow users to modify the list to better suit them.

Another common spell checker function is marking a word that the spell checker does not recognize. To correct the spelling, a user can command (e.g., right click on the word) the spell checker to reveal a list of the possible alternatives for the word. The user can choose the correct word, ignore the word completely, or add it to the user dictionary of the spell checker.

However, the most popular method of checking spelling is prompting the spell checker to check the entire document or a selected portion of the document. Users usually click on a toolbar button to invoke the spell checker. When the spell checker flags an unfamiliar word, the spell checker allows the user to ignore that word, change it, or add it to the user dictionary. Most spell checkers also look for double word errors and punctuation errors.

Spelling Error Detection

The most common way a spell checker detects spelling errors is to look up words in an internal dictionary. If a word is not in the dictionary, then the word is considered to be misspelled. However, the majority of spell checkers do not use a complete dictionary with fully spelled words. These dictionaries contain only word stems, for example, the word *help* but not the words *helps, helped, helpful,* or *helping.* Thus, a spell checker uses suffix or prefix removal rules before looking up words. *Un,* which begins the word *unhelpful,* is a prefix, and *ful,* which ends the word *unhelpful,* is a suffix. Thus, a spell checker strips both prefix and suffix from a word before looking up the word in its dictionary. A spell checker can fail in two ways in identifying misspellings. First, a spell checker can identify a word as incorrectly spelled when it is not. This error is referred as a "false alarm." This type of error is caused by infrequently used words and proper nouns. A user can minimize these errors by increasing the number of look-up dictionary entries in the electronic dictionary, used to determine the validity of a word by the spell checker.

However, users cannot include all proper nouns in a dictionary, and thus many spell checkers let users add proper nouns to their dictionary. Second, spell checkers can fail to recognize words that are misspelled in the context of the sentence. For example, the word *knight* in the sentence, "The meeting was held two knights ago" is a misspelling. The use of a bigger dictionary usually worsens this type of error because the dictionary will more likely include obscure words, which tend to match misspellings. However, the use of a smaller dictionary will cause more false alarms.

Spelling Error Correction

In 1964 computer scientist Fred Damerau published a paper showing that 80 percent of spelling errors can be explained by four simple patterns: (1) A correct word and its misspelling are the same length and differ in only one letter—for example, *alphabet* versus *alphibet;* (2) a correct word and its misspelling are the same length and differ in two adjacent letters such that two letters are interchanged—for

A Personal Story—Check the Spell Checker

My daughter often bemoans the fact that, as an editor, I'm on her case about spelling and grammar errors. She complained once too often about it at school, and her teacher asked me to come in to talk to the sixth-grade class about proofreading and editing. I approached the day of my visit with some trepidation. I'd seen one too many sitcoms about parents who flop on Career Day, humiliating themselves and their kids. I had to come up with an angle that would grab the class—and maybe teach them a little something as well.

The kids were all active users of Word, which meant they'd all been introduced to the art of spell checking. I knew the teachers had cautioned them about depending too heavily on spell checkers, so I gave them a handout, which read something like this:

> Weather or knot you dew well in school depends on many thinks. Ewe mite knead too study more hours, four example, or ask you're teacher fore extra help. Their can be sow many weighs to improve yore efforts.

I announced that this messy paragraph had passed the spell check with flying colors, yet it was full of errors. They started calling them out, and I wrote each on the board with the correct word and other homonyms and sound-alike words. Once we'd covered the fifteen errors in my little test, we were on a roll (role). There (their, they're) was no (know) stopping them. I kept writing (righting, riding) until the board (bored) was full. Each one (won) of the kids seemed to think the game was great (grate). Point made (maid).

Marcy Ross

example, *alphabet* versus *alhpabet;* (3) a misspelled word has one letter more in comparison to the correctly spelled word—for example, *alphabet* versus *allphabet;* and (4) a misspelled word has one letter less in comparison to the correctly spelled word—for example, *alphabet* versus *alpabet.* In addition, computer scientists Emmanouel Yannakoudakis and Dave Fawthrop (1983) found that the first letter is usually correct. Thus, the correct spelling of a misspelled word is likely to begin with the same letter and is either the same length or one letter longer or shorter.

Because most misspellings fit these four patterns, a spell checker can compare a misspelling with each entry in the dictionary to determine whether it differs in one of the four patterns. If it does, then the dictionary entry is selected as the correct spelling. However, this process can generate more than one correctly spelled word, and thus further processing will be required to select one true correct spelling. This further processing can be accomplished by a user's manual selection of a word or by another automatic method to rank the candidates according to the degree of similarity.

Another approach to correcting spelling errors is based on the Soundex system (used by some spell checkers), which preserves the important features of pronunciation by discarding the vowels and group consonants if they are likely to be substituted for each other. Thus, in the case of spell checking based on dictionary look-ups, every dictionary entry is given a Soundex code computed from the misspelling. The dictionary entry, which has the same Soundex code as the misspelling, is retrieved as the correct spelling. For example, if *disapont* is a misspelled word, then the Soundex-based spell-correction program will retrieve a set of words in the following to be possible candidates of the correctly spelled word: disband, disbands, disbanded, disbanding, disbandment, disbandments, dispense, dispenses, dispensed, dispensing, dispenser, dispensers, dispensary, dispensaries, dispensable, dispensation, dispensations, deceiving, deceivingly, despondent, despondency, despondently, disobeying, disappoint, disappoints, disappointed, disappointing, disappointedly, disappointingly, disappointment, disappointments, disavowing.

Another approach to correcting spelling errors is matching strings, a method used by almost all spell checkers. One way to compare strings is to count the number of sub-strings, which are present in the longer string. For example, an incorrectly spelled word, *rhithm,* has the *rh* and *thm* of the word *rhythm.* This means that in the incorrectly spelled word five letters out of six (83 percent) match *rhythm.* Either the spell checker automatically replaces "rhithm" with "rhythm" or shows the user "rhythm" as a possible replacement of "rhithm."

Open Source Spell Checkers

Several spell checkers allow users to correct their spelling errors and also to modify the spell checkers' code freely to meet their needs. One well-known open source spell checker called "Ispell" is screen oriented: Users see their errors in the context of the whole text and are guided by some possible corrections. Ispell is fast, easy, and supports languages other than English.

GNU Aspell is another open source spell checker. Some users consider GNU Aspell to be better than other spell checkers, such as Ispell and Microsoft Word's spell checker, at providing good suggestions for misspelled words in the English language.

NetSpell is another open source spell checker. It generates suggestions for a misspelled word using phonetic matching and displays them in a ranked order by a typographical score. NetSpell handles multiple languages.

Problems and Possibilities

Spell checkers are far from ideal. They fail to recognize a fairly high proportion of errors. Users often find that spell checkers' suggestions are inappropriate, obscure, and out of context. However, recent research shows that spelling correction by spell checkers can be improved by using contextual information such as the part of speech of misspelled words. For example, the word *uncer* in the sentence "We find an uncer" is a misspelling. By using one of the described spelling error correction methods, one can come up with an unordered list of candidate corrections such as *under, ulcer,* and *unclear.* The

word that should replace *uncer* has to be a noun because *uncer* is preceded by a determiner. Thus, one can select *ulcer* as the correct spelling because *ulcer* is the only noun from the candidates. *Under* is a preposition, and *unclear* is an adjective.

Woojin Paik

See also Natural-Language Processing

FURTHER READING

Angell, R., Freund, G., & Willett, P. (1983). Automatic spelling correction using a trigram similarity measure. *Information Processing and Management, 19*(4), 255–261.

Atkinson, K. (2003). GNU Aspell 0.50.4.1. Retrieved January 20, 2004, from http://aspell.sourceforge.net/man-html/manual.html

Damerau, F. (1964). A technique for computer detection and correction of spelling errors. *Communications of the ACM, 7*(3), 171–176.

Durham, I., Lamb, D., & Saxe, J. (1983). Spelling correction in user interfaces. *Communications of the ACM, 26*(10), 764–773.

Hendry, D. (2000). Design space of spelling checkers and correctors. Retrieved January 20, 2004, from http://faculty.washington.edu/dhendry/Projects/Spelling/

Joseph, D., & Wong, R. (1979). Correction of misspellings and typographical errors in a free-text medical English information storage and retrieval system. *Methods of Information in Medicine, 18*(4), 228–234

Kernighan, M., Church, K., & Gale, W. (1990). A spelling correction program based on a noisy channel model. In H. Karlgren (Ed.), *COLING-90 13th International Conference on Computational Linguistics* (pp. 205–210). Helsinki, Finland: Helsinki University Press.

Knuth, D. (1973). *The art of computer programming: Vol. 3. Sorting and searching.* Reading, MA: Addison-Wesley.

Kuenning, G. (1996). International Ispell. Retrieved January 20, 2004, from http://fmg-www.cs.ucla.edu/fmg-members/geoff/ispell.html

Kukich, K. (1992). Technique for automatically correcting words in text. *ACM Computing Surveys (CSUR), 24*(4), 377–439.

McElwain, C. K., & Evans, M. E. (1962). The degarbler—a program for correcting machine-read Morse code. *Information and Control, 5*(4), 368–384.

Mitton, R. (1996). Spellchecking by computer. *Journal of the Simplified Spelling Society, 20*(1), 4–11.

O'Brien, J. A. (1967). Computer program for automatic spelling correction (Tech. Rep. RADC-TR-66-696). New York: Rome Air Development Center.

Pollock, J., & Zamora, A. (1984). Automatic spelling correction in scientific and scholarly text. *Communications of the ACM, 27*(4), 358–368.

Ruch, P. (2002). Information access and retrieval: Information retrieval and spelling correction: An inquiry into lexical disambiguation. *Proceedings of the 2002 ACM Symposium on Applied Computing,* 699–703

VanBerkel, B., & DeSmedt, K. (1988). Triphone analysis: A combined method for the correction of orthographical and typographical errors. *Second Conference in Applied Natural Language Processing, 77–83.*

Wagner, R., & Fischer, M. (1974). The string-to-string correction problem. *Journal of the ACM, 21*(1), 168–173.

Welter, P. (2003). NetSpell. Retrieved January 20, 2004, from http://www.loresoft.com/Applications/NetSpell/default.aspx

Yannakoudakis, E. J., & Fawthrop, D. (1983). The rules of spelling errors. *Information Processing and Management, 19*(2), 89–99.

SPHINX

Computer-based speech recognition systems came into existence in the 1950s, shortly after the development of the high-speed analog-to-digital converter. The earliest systems were based on explicit matching of the recorded signal against pre-stored templates. Later advancements included the inclusion of phonotactic rules and dynamic time-warping algorithms for explicit pattern matching. The 1980s saw great advancement in rule-based methods for speech recognition that combined expert knowledge about the signal and spectral characteristics of the speech signal with AI techniques in order to perform recognition. In spite of all these advances, the goal of speaker-independent recognition of continuous speech remained elusive to these early researchers.

Origin of Sphinx

In the early 1970s, James Baker, then a graduate student at Carnegie Mellon University (CMU) working under the supervision of Professor Raj Reddy, proposed an alternative method for automatic speech recognition—a purely statistical approach based on a then-obscure mathematical model called the Hidden Markov Model (HMM). The HMM models sound units as having a sequence of states, where each state has its own unique distribution. The parameters of the state distributions must be learned from training data, and recognition using these models involves a fairly computationally intensive decoding algorithm, where the computer evaluates HMMs for several hypotheses in order to determine the most probable one. The HMM-based recognizer represented a paradigmatic shift from the signal- and rule-based approaches followed by almost all researches until that time, in that it relied almost entirely on statistical knowledge of the speech signal gained through automated analysis of large quantities of speech data, and not on codified human expertise.

It was initially considered that the HMM approach was computationally infeasible, since it required large quantities of data to learn the parameters of the HMMs and large amounts of computation to perform the actual recognition. Soon, however, researchers realized that it also presented a conceptually powerful modeling paradigm for speech sounds, with greater flexibility than any of the then-current techniques. By the 1980s, several research teams around the world were working intensively on this and related statistical paradigms. Notable among these were the teams at AT&T Bell Laboratories and IBM, both based in the United States. By the mid-1980s, these teams had succeeded in developing statistical speech-recognition systems that worked well for narrow acoustic domains, such as for individual speakers (speaker-dependent systems) or in speaker-independent recognition of words that were spoken distinctly apart and recorded as separate speech signals (isolated-word systems).

True speaker-independent recognition of continuously spoken speech still presented a problem. By the late 1980s, researchers were beginning to discover ways to deal with this, although it was still generally felt that the computational resources of the time, which consisted of slow processors and tiny memory by today's standards, could simply not support an HMM-based speaker-independent continuous-speech-recognition system. This belief was shattered in 1988 by the unveiling of the HMM-based Sphinx speech-recognition system at CMU, which incorporated several new innovations in the modeling of spoken sounds and in the engineering of the actual algorithms used for recognition. This was a continuous-speech speaker-independent system that not only recognized speech with high accuracy, but did so at the natural speed at which words are spoken by an average person (real-time recognition), using the best machines of the time, such as the SUN-3 and DEC-3000. The system was developed by

Kai-Fu Lee, then a doctoral student under the supervision of Professor Raj Reddy at CMU. The Sphinx demonstrated to the world that automatic speaker-independent recognition of continuous speech was not only possible, but also achievable with the computational resources of the day. The system achieved unprecedented word recognition accuracies of about 90 percent on 1,000-word vocabulary tasks.

Milestones and the Spirit of Sphinx

Since 1988, as computers and algorithms have grown in sophistication, Sphinx has morphed into a suite of recognition systems, each marking a milestone in HMM-based speech recognition technology. All of these retain the name of Sphinx, and are labeled with different version numbers in keeping with the contemporary style of referencing software. There are currently four versions of Sphinx in existence. Sphinx-1, the first breakthrough version developed in 1988, used the technology of discrete HMMs, that is, HMMs that use discrete distributions or simple histograms to model the distribution of the speech within any state of the HMM. This required quantizing the vectors into a discrete set of symbols.

Sphinx-2 emerged five years later, in 1992, and was developed by Xuedong Huang. It marked another milestone through the use of technology based on semicontinuous HMMs, much of it developed at CMU. Semi-continuous HMMs did not require the quantization of speech vectors. State distributions of the HMM were modeled by mixtures of Gaussian densities. Rather than the speech vectors themselves, it was the parameters of the Gaussian densities that were quantized. To reduce the total number of parameters in the system, it incorporated a decision-tree-based state clustering algorithm invented by Mei-Yuh Hwang at CMU. With these innovations, Sphinx-2 was able to achieve an accuracy of about 90 percent on vocabularies of up to 30,000 words.

Sphinx-3 was developed in 1996 at CMU by Eric Thayer and Mosur Ravishankar. The system incorporated continuous-density HMMS, which allowed the modeling of speech in a fully continuous vector space. Naturally, this resulted in better recognition performance as compared to its predecessors—the system was able to perform open vocabulary recognition tasks with remarkable accuracy, often exceeding 90 percent. Since 1996, the permeation of microprocessors into almost every electronic device, the development of Internet-based applications based on newer protocols, programming, and markup languages, and easy access to multimodal sources of information, have opened up many new applications for automatic speech recognition. This has led to a stream of new innovations in HMM-based speech recognition, permitting modularity at more conceptual levels, comprehensive interfacing capabilities, and the processing of multiple and varying streams of information for improved performance.

Sphinx-4 incorporates many of these innovations. The system was initiated in 2001 by a team of experts from CMU, Mitsubishi Electric Research Labs, and SUN Microsystems. In 2002, experts from Hewlett Packard joined the effort. Sphinx-4 is written entirely in the JAVA programming language, and is being developed on an open-source platform.

Rita Singh

See also Dialog Systems, Natural-Language Processing; N-grams, Speech Recognition

FURTHER READING

Baker, J. K. (1975). Stochastic modeling for automatic speech understanding. In D. R. Reddy (Ed.), *Speech recognition* (pp. 521–542). New York: Academic Press.

Church, K. (1983). Allophonic and phonotactic constraints are useful. Paper presented at the *International Joint Conference on Artificial Intelligence*, Karlsruhe, West Germany.

Forgie, J., & Forgie, C. (1959). Results obtained from a vowel recognition computer program. *Journal of Acoustic Society of America, 31*(11), 1480–1489.

Huang, X., Alleva, F., Hon, H.-W., Hwang, M.-Y., Lee, K.-F. & Rosenfeld, R. (1992). The SPHINX-II speech recognition system: An overview. *Computer Speech and Language, 7*(2), 137–148.

Hwang, M.Y. (1993). Subphonetic acoustic modelling for speaker-independent continuous speech recognition. Unpublished doctoral dissertation, *CMU-CS-93-230*, Carnegie Mellon University, Pittsburgh, PA.

Lamere, P., Kwok, P., Walker, W., Gouvea, E., Singh, R., Raj, B., & Wolf, P. (2003). Design of the CMU Sphinx-4 decoder. *Proceedings of the*

8th European Conference on Speech Communication and Technology (EUROSPEECH 2003).

Lee, K. F., Hon, H.W., & Reddy, R. (1990). An overview of the SPHINX speech recognition system. *IEEE Transactions on Acoustics, Speech and Signal Processing, ASSP,* 38(1), 35–44.

Placeway, P., Chen, S., Eskenazi, M., Jain, U., Parikh, V., Raj, B., et al. (1997). The 1996 Hub-4 Sphinx-3 system. *Proceedings of the 1997 ARPA Speech Recognition Workshop,* 85–89.

Ravishankar, M. K. (1996). *Efficient algorithms for speech recognition.* Unpublished doctoral dissertation, *CMU-CS-96-143,* Carnegie Mellon University, Pittsburgh, PA.

Sakoe, H., & Chiba, S. (1978). Dynamic programming algorithm optimization for spoken word recognition. *IEEE Transactions on Acoustics, Speech and Signal Processing, ASSP,* 26(1), 43–49.

Zue, V. (1985). The use of speech knowledge in automatic speech recognition. *Proceedings of the IEEE,* 73(11), 1602–1615.

STATISTICAL ANALYSIS SUPPORT

Much of the impact that computers have had on the modern world is captured by a statement that Lord Kelvin, the British scientist, made in 1883: "[W]hen you can measure what you are speaking about, and express it in numbers, you know something about it; but when you cannot measure it, when you cannot express it in numbers, your knowledge is of a meagre and unsatisfactory kind." Computers have enabled us to record and manage numerical data for problems in physics, sociology, linguistics, astronomy, geology, politics, journalism, even art history—for almost every field of human endeavor. Much of our lives, both professional and personal, can be described by numerical abstractions. Helping us to make sense of these numbers is the goal of systems for statistical analysis support.

Systems for statistical analysis have superficial resemblances to other interactive software, such as databases and spreadsheets, because they share functionality at the interactive level of data management and manipulation. Nevertheless there are important differences. For example, one difference is that the correctness of a statistical result cannot be determined without inspecting the path of reasoning leading to it, and complex chains of assumptions may be necessary along the way. Such factors limit the extent to which statistical analysis can be automated

and raise several interrelated issues that interface designers must consider:

- Contextual knowledge. Knowledge about the meaning of data is a critical part of sensible data analysis. For example, a given sample of numerical data ranging from 75 to 125 might describe IQ values, candy prices (in cents) in a vending machine, summer temperatures in a desert, or some other possibility. Information about the population from which data values have been collected, how they were collected, known relationships in the data, and so forth can make a difference in what types of analysis operations are reasonable and how apparent patterns should be understood. This kind of contextual information can be difficult or impossible for a system to capture in an automated fashion, because it is not explicit in the data. Instead, a system must accommodate human knowledge in its analysis.

- Statistical knowledge. Another component of effective analysis is knowledge about statistical practice, which includes knowledge about the dependence of analysis techniques on properties of the data and how their results should be interpreted, as well as heuristic knowledge about the applicability of techniques. For example, many statistical modeling techniques assume that unmodeled variation in the data follows a specific distribution. A system for statistical support can help ensure that users are aware of their assumptions in evaluating the validity of results.

- Management of the analysis process. Statistical analysis is almost always incremental, and often it is iterative as well. This means that a system can contribute to analysis by helping manage the growing amount of information that becomes available through the analysis process.

- Management of data and models. Two key activities in data management include manipulation and presentation. Rich manipulation operators allow users to filter and transform the data into appropriate form, while data presentation facilities help make meaningful and interesting patterns stand out rather than being lost in a crowded or possibly deceptive visual display. Often an analysis works not on raw data but on descriptions or models, which means that the same facilities are needed for the manipulation and presentation of these data abstractions.

The inverse order of these issues reflects the difficulty of handling them in a statistical analysis support system. A wide range of commercial systems currently supports effective general-purpose data manipulation and presentation, but on the other end of the spectrum, systems that can intelligently handle real-world contexts in their support of statistical analysis only rarely leave the research laboratory, and are limited to very specialized problem domains. This article discusses ways to address these issues, focusing as much as possible on general concepts rather than specific systems.

Managing Data and Models

The problem of presenting numerical data so that patterns can easily be seen has been explored for centuries for paper-based presentations. Edward Tufte, professor emeritus at Yale University, has written several books on information display and visualization that give a good informal introduction to the history of the topic, mainly from a graphic design perspective. Books by William S. Cleveland, a statistics researcher at Lucent Technologies, and by Stephen Kosslyn, professor of psychology at Harvard University, take a more rigorous approach, explaining the advantages and disadvantages of statistical presentation techniques as well as the relationship between these techniques and human perception and cognition. For example, consider the difference between a bar chart and a pie chart for displaying a set of values. Experiments have shown that if the endpoints of two side-by-side lines are aligned with one another, then we can judge with considerable accuracy which line is longer than the other. This makes bar charts a good choice as a data display for many purposes. In contrast, our judgments about non-aligned angles and areas are not nearly as accurate, which means that pie charts are generally an inferior choice for a presentation.

A number of efforts have been made to incorporate such practical knowledge into automated or semiautomated systems for presentation design;

this remains an active research area in graphics, human-computer interaction, information visualization, and intelligent user interfaces. The range of presentation techniques includes scatter plots and line plots and all their variations (in two or more dimensions), surface plots, hierarchical and network graphs, and many more specialized possibilities, alone or in combination. Many of these techniques are relevant for presenting statistical models, especially those with hierarchical and network structures.

Techniques for data manipulation have also been explored in the literature, with the most attention paid to interactive computer environments. Modern environments, whether command-based or direct manipulation systems, attempt to give the user the ability to modify data and relationships easily (for instance, with spreadsheet-like functionality), to select and filter subsets of data (for example, with database-like functionality), to establish dynamic connections between different data properties such that patterns hidden within and across relationships become apparent, and in general to derive new data for analysis from existing data.

Managing the Analysis Process

In many (perhaps most) common computer tasks, such as writing a computer program or designing a spreadsheet, the end result is what matters: whether the program runs correctly, whether the spreadsheet computes the correct results. In contrast, a statistical analysis does not consist only of, say, a number representing the probability that two sample means are significantly different. Rather, an analysis is closer in form to a legal argument, in which each step in a decision process must be justified by either a reasonable assumption or an explicit test.

Most statistical systems thus provide some kind of journaling capability, allowing users to record the sequence of decisions they make in carrying out an analysis. Journaling can be a separate activity, as is common in statistical support systems with graphical user interfaces, but in the case of command line interfaces, journaling becomes naturally integrated into the interaction process.

Systems can provide organizational assistance for managing the analysis process in a few different ways. They can support independent, ongoing lines of analysis recorded in separate streams. They can allow editing and revision of journal inputs such that they reflect an idealized rational analysis rather than the less relevant fits and starts that may take place. They can produce abstract networks of operations and results, so that the potentially changing relationships between components of the analysis become visible. Some systems can even make inferences about the relationships between results and suggest structures or alterations to be imposed on the analysis process. In applying these techniques, systems must balance the user concerns of flexibility, recording effort, and ease of analysis reconstruction and result retrieval.

Incorporating Statistical Knowledge

An important concept developed and explored over the past two decades is that of statistical strategies. A statistical strategy is a formal description of the actions and decisions involved in applying statistical tools to a problem. A statistical strategy may include knowledge about the mathematical foundations of a statistical technique, how it is commonly used in practice, its strengths and weaknesses in modeling different phenomena, and how its results can be interpreted. The appeal of building statistical strategies into an analysis system is obvious; such a system could reduce the effort of carrying out complex analyses, automatically generate alternative interpretations for analysts to consider, and even make statistical expertise available to novices.

Many current systems for statistical analysis include a very limited form of statistical strategy in their processing. For example, a regression command may produce not only a set of modeling parameters and a graphical display of a regression model, but also a set of diagnostic results that suggest further actions to improve the model (for example, data points with high leverage). Such strategies are only implicit, however, which limits their power considerably: they are relatively inflexible and do not combine automatically; their internal reasoning process

is not available for inspection or evaluation; they cannot be modified to reflect the needs of a particular analysis. The granularity at which the statistical reasoning process is represented, in compiled form, is too low. Statistical programming environments address the difficulties above to some extent, but suffer from the opposite problem: Programs are usually at too detailed a level to reflect statistical reasoning, lacking the appropriate abstractions, which are as often based on abstract knowledge as on properties of data.

Work on representing statistical strategies has tackled these issues by adding to the set of conceptual structures that we usually associate with statistical systems. For example, a statistical analysis can be considered in terms of a hierarchy of operational levels, with general concerns such as experiment design at the most abstract level, semiformalized rules for applying statistical techniques at an intermediate level, and numerical procedures at the lowest level. An open representation allows an analyst to steer the selection and execution of operations at any level in the hierarchy. A stagewise rather than vertical account of statistical analysis leads to a comparable framework.

Research on statistical strategies continues today, although their feasibility for general-purpose statistical support remains an open question.

Integrating Contextual Knowledge

A recurring theme in this article is that a statistical analysis support system provides information and actions that we apply toward understanding some phenomenon or solving some problem. However, although our grasp of context, of what results mean, is a vital part of the analysis, accommodating human judgment and understanding is one of the most difficult issues that a statistical analysis system must face.

One representative way in which this issue has manifested itself in recent research is in the problem of preference elicitation. Imagine a statistical system designed to support the work of a market analyst. Given information about the activities of different companies, the general condition of different sectors of the economy, consumer confidence, and so forth, the system helps the analyst make predictions about market trends by providing models and summaries of the available data. The system's task is complicated by several factors: Conditions change over time, available information is incomplete and uncertain, gathering more information is costly, and the value of the system's results depends on the analyst's judgment. Analyses based on different information will produce different results. If an opportunity to gain new information arises, but at some cost in time or money, the system must help the analyst evaluate whether the new information is worth the cost: Are early, approximate predictions preferable to later, more precise predictions? Is one analysis procedure preferable to another? What is the value of a given high-risk judgment? How should an analysis be modified to reflect a changing situation? Comparable questions can be raised for all types of statistical decision-making, at the level of data presentation and manipulation, the selection and application of modeling techniques, or the interpretation of results. Answers depend on the context, which in principle might include any piece of knowledge available, and can thus be very difficult to establish in explicit terms.

One simple way to solve these problems, though only partially, is to reduce the scope of an analysis as much as possible. Thus, for example, an automated payroll system might produce a statistical summary of workers' punctuality in a store, or a word processor might generate a readability index based on word-count statistics for a text document. Even here, however, context comes into play. A power outage might delay the opening of the store, causing the payroll system to produce an accurate but useless summary for that day. The word processor might not be able to distinguish between an informal newspaper column and a technical article, so that it gives inappropriate recommendations about improving readability. Understanding the best way to integrate statistical results into the context of real world activities is, understandably, receiving a great deal of attention today.

Robert St. Amant

See also Artificial Intelligence; Expert Systems

FURTHER READING

Becker, R. A., & Chambers, J. M. (1984). *S: an interactive environment for data analysis and graphics.* Belmont, CA: Wadsworth Advanced Book Program.

Card, S., Mackinlay, J., & Shneiderman, B. (1999). *Readings in information visualization: Using vision to think.* San Francisco, CA: Morgan Kaufmann.

Cleveland, W. S. (1993). *Visualizing data.* Summit, NJ: Hobart Press.

Cleveland, W. S. (1994). *The Elements of graphing data.* Summit, NJ: Hobart Press.

Daniel, C., & Wood, F. S. (1980). *Fitting equations to data.* New York: Wiley.

Gale, W. A., Hand, D. J., & Kelly, A. E. (1993). Statistical applications of artificial intelligence. In C. R. Rao (Ed.), *Handbook of statistics* (Vol. 9, pp. 535–576). Amsterdam: Elsevier Science.

Hoaglin, D. C., Mosteller, F., & Tukey, J. W. (1985). *Exploring data tables, trends, and shapes.* New York: Wiley.

Huber, P. J. (1986). Data analysis implications for command language design. In K. Hopper & I. A. Newman (Eds.), *Foundations for human-computer communication.* Amsterdam: Elsevier Science.

Kosslyn, S. (1993). *The elements of graph design.* New York: Freeman.

National Research Council. (1991). *The future of statistical software: Proceedings of a forum.* Washington, D.C.: National Academy Press.

Tufte, E. (1990). *Envisioning information.* Cheshire, CT: Graphics Press.

Tufte, E. (1997). *Visual explanations.* Cheshire, CT: Graphics Press.

Tukey, J. W. (1977). *Exploratory data analysis.* Boston, MA: Addison-Wesley.

STRATEGIES FOR USING COMPLEX COMPUTER APPLICATIONS

See Application Use Strategies

SUPERCOMPUTERS

A supercomputer, broadly defined, is one of the fastest computers currently available. Supercomputers are systems that provide significantly greater sustained performance than is available from mainstream computer systems; by performance we mean the rate of execution for floating-point operations per second (flop/s), that is, the rate of execution of a certain type of mathematical operation, such as addition or multiplication of 64 bit numbers. Since the mid-twentieth century, the field of scientific computing has undergone rapid change. There has been a remarkable turnover of technologies, architectures, vendors, and ways in which systems are used. Despite these changes, the long-term improvement in performance seems to be steady and continuous, following what is known as Moore's Law rather closely. In 1965 Gordon Moore, one of the founders of Intel, conjectured that the number of transistors per square inch on integrated circuits would roughly double every year. It turns out that the doubling occurs not every twelve months, but roughly every eighteen months. Moore predicted that this trend would continue for the foreseeable future. Figure 1 shows the peak performance of computers that have been called supercomputers from the 1950s to 2003. Here we chart kiloflops per second (that is, thousands of floating-point operations per second), megaflops per second (millions of floating-point operations per second), gigaflops per second (billions of floating-point operations per second), teraflops per second (trillions of floating-point operations per second), and petaflops per second (quadrillions of float-

ing-point operations per second). This figure shows clearly how well Moore's Law has held over almost the complete lifespan of modern computing.

Historical Development

In the second half of the 1970s, the introduction of vector computer systems marked the beginning of modern supercomputing. A vector computer, or vector processor, is a machine that can efficiently handle arithmetic operations on arrays of numbers These systems offered a performance advantage of at least one order of magnitude over (that is, they were at least ten times faster than) the conventional scientific computing systems of that time

Raw performance was the main, if not the only, selling point for supercomputers of this variety. However, in the first half of the 1980s the integration of vector systems into conventional scientific computing environments became more important. Only those manufacturers that provided high performance and standard programming environments, operating systems, and key applications were successful in getting the industrial customers that became essential for survival in the marketplace. Over time the commodity processors' per-

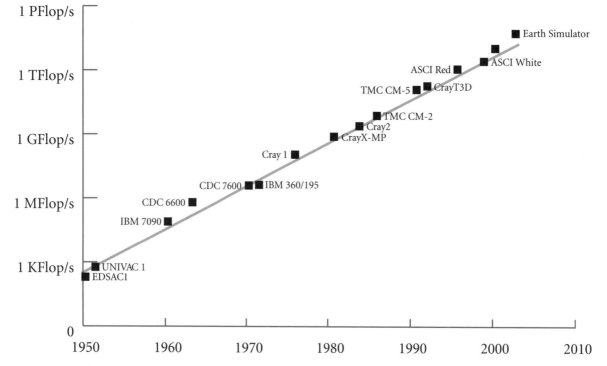

FIGURE 1. *Moore's Law and peak performance of various computers over time*

formance became more enhanced and began to approach the more specialized vector processors. Performance was increased primarily by improved chip technologies and by producing shared-memory multiprocessor systems out of the commodity processors, sometimes referred to as symmetric multiprocessors, or SMPs. An SMP is a computer system that has two or more processors connected in the same box, managed by one operating system, sharing the same memory, and having equal access to input-output devices. Application programs may run on any or all processors in the system; assignment of tasks is decided by the operating system. One advantage of SMP systems is scalability; additional processors can be added as needed up to some limiting factor determined by the rate at which data can be sent to and from memory.

At the end of the 1980s, several U.S. government programs sponsored research into scalable parallel computing using distributed memory. A distributed-memory computer system is one in which several interconnected computers share the computing tasks assigned to the system. Overcoming the hardware scalability limitations of shared memory was the main goal of these new systems. The increased performance of standard microprocessors after the Reduced Instruction Set Computer (RISC) revolution of the late 1980s, together with the cost advantage of large-scale parallelism, formed the basis for the "attack of the killer micros"—that is, for the rise of microcomputers, which can be used in parallel. The eventual result was that computer manufacturers were able to use off-the-shelf, mass-produced microprocessors instead of custom vector processors, and that fact made possible the development of massively parallel processors, or MPPs. The strict definition of MPP is a machine with many interconnected processors, where the actual number of processors is dependent on the state of the art. Currently, the majority of high-end machines have fewer than 256 processors, and machines with the most processors have on the order of 10,000 processors. A more practical definition of an MPP is a machine whose architecture is capable of having many processors—that is, it is scalable. In particular, machines with a distributed-memory design (in comparison with shared-memory designs) are usually synonymous with MPPs, since they are not limited to a certain number of processors. In this sense, *many* is a number larger than the current largest number of processors in a shared-memory machine.

State of Systems Today

The acceptance of MPP systems not only for engineering applications but also for commercial applications and especially for database applications required emphasizing new criteria for market success, such as stability of the system, continuity of the manufacturer, and a good price and performance. Success in commercial environments is now a new important requirement for a successful supercomputer business. Due to these factors and to a decline in the number of vendors in the market, hierarchical systems built with components designed for the broader commercial market are currently replacing homogeneous systems (homogeneous, because previously the users of supercomputers—research institutions—wanted them for more or less the same sorts of applications) at the very high end of performance. Clusters built with off-the-shelf components also gain more and more attention. A cluster is a commonly found computing environment consisting of many PCs or workstations connected together by a network. The PCs and workstations, which have become increasingly powerful over the years, can, when considered together, be viewed as a significant computing resource. This resource is commonly known as a cluster, and the term can be generalized to apply to any heterogeneous collection of processors with arbitrary interconnect network.

At the beginning of the 1990s, as the multiprocessor vector systems were reaching their widest distribution, a new generation of MPP systems came on the market, claiming to equal or even surpass the performance of vector multiprocessors. To provide a more reliable basis for statistics on high-performance computers, the Top 500 list was begun. This report lists the sites worldwide that have the five hundred most powerful installed computer systems. The ranking of the Top 500 is based on the Linpack benchmark, a challenging measure consisting of a dense system of linear equations that must be solved. This measure is widely used to compare computer performance. The Top 500 list has been updated twice a year since June 1993. In the first Top

500 list in June 1993, there were already 156 MPP present (31 percent of the total 500 systems).

The year 1995 saw remarkable changes in the distribution of the systems in the Top 500 according to customer types (academic sites, research labs, industrial and commercial users, vendor sites, and confidential sites). Until June 1995, the trend in the Top 500 data was a steady decrease in industrial customers, matched by an increase in the number of government-funded research sites. This trend reflects the influence of governmental high-performance computing (HPC) programs that made it possible for research sites to buy parallel systems, especially systems with distributed memory. Industry was understandably reluctant to follow this path, since systems with distributed memory have often been far from mature or stable. Hence, industrial customers stayed with their older vector systems, which gradually dropped off the Top 500 list because of low performance.

Beginning in 1994, however, companies such as SGI, Digital, and Sun began selling symmetric multiprocessor (SMP) models in their workstation families. From the very beginning, these systems were popular with industrial customers because of the maturity of the architecture and their superior price-to-performance ratio. However these SMP systems, because their memory systems are not scalable, do not appear in the current Top 500 list. At the same time, IBM SP systems began to appear at a reasonable number of industrial sites. While the IBM SP was initially intended for numerically intensive applications, in the second half of 1995 the system began selling successfully to a larger commercial market, with dedicated database systems representing a particularly important component of sales. It is instructive to compare the growth rates of the performance of machines at fixed positions in the Top 500 list with those predicted by Moore's Law. To make this comparison, we must separate the influence from the increasing processor performance and from the increasing number of processors per system on the total accumulated performance. If we analyze data from 1993 through 2003 to evaluate the relative growth of the total number of processors and the average processor performance, we find that these two factors contribute almost equally to the annual total performance growth, which stands at a factor of 1.82. On average, the number of processors grows by a factor of 1.30 each year, and processor performance increases by a factor of 1.40 per year. (Moore's Law predicted growth doubling every eighteen months.)

Programming Models

Parallel processing in supercomputers decomposes necessary work into many parts that can be done simultaneously. The standard parallel architectures support a variety of decomposition strategies, such as decomposition by task (task parallelism) and decomposition by data (data parallelism). Data parallelism is the most common strategy for scientific programs on parallel machines. In data parallelism, the application is decomposed by subdividing the data space over which it operates and assigning different processors to the work associated with different data subspaces. Typically this strategy involves some data sharing at the boundaries, and the programmer is responsible for ensuring that this data sharing is handled correctly, that is, that data computed by one processor and used by another is correctly synchronized.

Once a specific decomposition strategy is chosen, it must be implemented. At this point, the programmer must choose a programming model to use. The two most common models are the shared-memory model, in which it is assumed that all data structures are allocated in a common space that is accessible from every processor, and the message-passing model, in which each processor (or process) is assumed to have its own private data space and data must be explicitly moved between spaces as needed. In the message-passing model, data is distributed across the processor memories; if a processor needs to use data that is not stored locally, the processor that owns that data must explicitly send the data to the processor that needs it. The latter must execute an explicit "receive" operation, which is synchronized with the send, before it can use the communicated data.

To achieve high performance on parallel machines, the programmer must be concerned with scalability and load balance. Generally, an application is thought to be scalable if larger parallel configurations can solve proportionally larger problems in the same running time as smaller problems on smaller configurations. Load balance typically means that the processors have roughly the same amount of work, so that no one processor holds up the entire solution. To balance the computational load on a machine with processors of equal power, the programmer must divide the work and communications evenly. This can be challenging in applications applied to problems that are unknown in size until run time.

Transforming Effect on Science and Engineering

Supercomputers have transformed a number of science and engineering disciplines, including cosmology, environmental modeling, condensed-matter physics, protein folding, quantum chromodynamics, device and semiconductor simulation, seismology, and turbulence. As an example, consider cosmology—the study of the universe, its evolution and structure—a discipline that has undergone one of the most striking paradigm shifts. A number of new, tremendously detailed observations deep into the universe are available from such instruments as the Hubble Space Telescope and the Digital Sky Survey. However, until recently, it has been difficult, except in relatively simple circumstances, to tease from mathematical theories of the early universe enough information to allow comparison with observations.

However, supercomputers have changed all of that. Now, cosmologists can simulate the principal physical processes at work in the early universe over space-time volumes sufficiently large to determine the large-scale structures predicted by the models. With such tools, some theories can be discarded as being incompatible with the observations. Supercomputing has allowed comparison of theory with observation and thus has transformed the practice of cosmology.

Another example is the U.S. Department of Energy's Accelerated Strategic Computing Initiative (ASCI), which applies advanced capabilities in scientific and engineering computing to one of the most complex challenges in the nuclear era: maintaining the performance, safety, and reliability of the United States' nuclear weapons without physical testing. A critical component of the agency's Stockpile Stew-

> Computers are magnificent tools for the realization of our dreams, but no machine can replace the human spark of spirit, compassion, love, and understanding.
>
> —*Louis Gerstener*

ardship Program (SSP), ASCI research develops computational and simulation technologies to help scientists understand aging weapons, predict when components will have to be replaced, and evaluate the implications of changes in materials and fabrication processes for the design life of aging weapons systems. The ASCI program was established in 1996 as part of the Clinton administration's commitment to pursue a comprehensive ban on nuclear weapons testing. ASCI researchers are developing high-end computing capabilities far above the current level of performance, as well as advanced simulation applications that can reduce the current reliance on empirical judgments by achieving higher-resolution, higher-fidelity, three-dimensional physics and full-system modeling capabilities for assessing the state of nuclear weapons.

Employing parallelism to solve large-scale problems is not without its price. The complexity of building parallel supercomputers with thousands of processors to solve real-world problems requires a hierarchical approach, in which memory is associated closely with central processing units (CPUs). Consequently, the central problem faced by parallel applications is managing a complex memory hierarchy. It is the communication of data and the coordination of processes within this hierarchy that represent the principal hurdles to effective, correct, and widespread acceptance of parallel computing. Today's parallel computing environment has architectural complexity layered upon a multiplicity of processors. Scalability—the ability of hardware and software to maintain reasonable efficiency as the number of processors is increased—is the key metric.

The future will be more complex yet. Distinct computer systems will be networked together into an extremely powerful computational grid. The pieces of this composite whole will be distinct in hardware (they will have their own CPUs), software (they will have their own operating systems), and operational policy (they will determine their own security).

Future Trends

Based on the current Top 500 data (which cover the last thirteen years) and the assumption that the current rate of performance improvement will continue for some time to come, we can extrapolate the observed performance and compare these values with the goals of such programs as the Accelerated Strategic Computing Initiative (ASCI), High Performance Computing and Communications, and the PetaOps initiative. We can extrapolate the observed performance using linear regression on a logarithmic scale. This means that we fit exponential growth to all levels of performance in the Top 500. Based on the extrapolation from these fits, we can expect to see the first 100 teraflop-per-second system by 2005. By 2005, no system smaller than 1 teraflop per second should be able to make the Top 500 ranking.

Looking even further in the future, we speculate that based on the current doubling of performance every year to fourteen months, the first petaflop-per-second system should be available around 2009. Due to the rapid changes in the technologies used in HPC systems, there is currently no reasonable projection possible for the architecture of such systems at the end of the decade.

There are two general conclusions we can draw. First, parallel computing is here to stay. It is the primary mechanism by which computer performance can keep up the demands from computational science problems that want more accuracy and resolution in their solutions. Second, the architecture of high-performance computing will continue to evolve at a rapid rate. Thus, it will be increasingly important to find ways to support scalable parallel programming without sacrificing portability. This challenge must be met by developing software systems and algorithms that promote portability while easing the burden of program design and implementation.

Jack Dongarra

See also Grid Computing

FURTHER READING

Anderson, E., Bai, Z., Bischof, C., Blackford, S., Demmel, J. Dongarra, et al. (1999). *LAPACK users' guide* (3d ed.). Philadelphia: SIAM.

Brooks, E. (1989). *The attack of the killer micros.* Presentation at the Teraflop Computing Panel, Supercomputing '89, Reno, Nevada.

Browne, S., Dongarra, J., Garner, N, Ho, G., & Mucci, P. (2000). A portable programming interface for performance evaluation on modern processors. *International Journal of High Performance Computing Applications, 14*(3), 189–204.

DeRose, L., & Reed, D. A. (1999, September). *SvPablo: A multi-language architecture-independent performance analysis system.* Paper presented at the International Conference on Parallel Processing, Fukushima, Japan.

Dongarra, J. J. (2003). *Performance of various computers using standard linear equations software.* Retrieved August 8, 2003, from http://www.netlib.org/benchmark/performance.pdf

Dongarra, J., London, K., Moore, S., Mucci, P., & Terpstra, D. (2001). Using PAPI for hardware performance monitoring on Linux systems. In *Proceedings of the Conference on Linux Clusters: The HPC Revolution*, Retrieved August 8, 2003, from http://icl.cs.utk.edu/projects/papi/documents/pub-papers/2001/linux-rev2001.pdf

Foster, I., & Kesselman, C. (Eds.). (1998). *The Grid: Blueprint for a new computing infrastructure.* San Francisco: Morgan Kaufmann.

Moore, G. E. (1965). Cramming more components onto integrated circuits. *Electronics, 38*(8), 114–117.

Snir, M., Otto, S., Huss-Lederman, S., Walker, D., & Dongarra, J. (1996). *MPI: The complete reference.* Boston: MIT Press.

Top 500. (2002). *Top 500 Supercomputer Sites.* Retrieved August 8, 2003, from http://www.top500.org

TABLET COMPUTER

Tablets are fully programmable computers similar in many ways to their smaller cousins, personal digital assistants, which are commonly designed to be held in a user's hands and controlled through a stylus rather than a keyboard. They are a fulfillment of the 1968 vision of Alan Kay, one of the pioneers of modern computing who worked together at the Xerox Palo Alto Research Center. Kay imagined a future of portable and versatile personal computers he called DynaBooks, which could enhance many aspects of work, education, and daily life. Over the intervening decades, attempts to bring this dream to reality have fallen short of the goal, and it remains to be seen whether success is finally within reach.

In 1988, Apple Computer held a contest in which university students were asked to imagine what the personal computer of the year 2000 would be like. The winning design, submitted by a team at the University of Illinois, was a tablet computer about 8.5 by 11 by 1.5 inches in size, with a touchscreen on one side that could be used for both input and output. While recognizing that some users would want a conventional keyboard as peripheral equipment, the college students imagined that the chief means of data input would be writing on the screen with a stylus, augmented by tapping on a virtual keyboard graphically displayed on the screen.

Fifteen years after this prediction, real tablet computers were available but relatively unpopular. The Illinois students had gotten some things wrong in predicting what an early-twenty-first-century tablet computer would be like. For example, they imagined the screen would be soft and respond to the touch of fingers, whereas actual tablet computers have hard screens that respond only to a special stylus. They were perhaps too optimistic about how good handwriting recognition software and electric batteries would be by the year 2000. But they recognized correctly many of the characteristics the machines would have, including a wireless connection to the Internet and the approximate size of the devices. In 2003, a major push from Microsoft and products from several manufacturers established tablets as one of the common types of computers with which humans interact.

Many of these machines resemble laptops and can be used in the same general way. It could be said that the Toshiba Portégé is a laptop that can be a tablet, whereas the HP/Compaq TC1000 is a tablet that can be a laptop. Both have 768 by 1024 pixel screens, internal hard disks, wireless connections, USB ports, and room for flash cards, just as many laptops of the same vintage do. However, neither has a drive for removable disks of any kind, although both can be connected to a docking station that has such a device. In both, a slightly undersized keyboard can be turned and folded under the back of the screen when only stylus input is needed, or the screen can be rotated and lifted into the approximate position behind the keys that the screen of a laptop has. The biggest difference between the the Portégé and the TC1000 is that in the former the keyboard holds all the electronics and is permanently affixed by a hinge to the screen, whereas in the latter the electronics are integrated into the back of the screen and the keyboard is merely a peripheral that can be dispensed with.

The stylus of a pocket computer is a passive digitizer that must press against the screen to be detected by the pressure-sensitive top layer. Thus, it has no working parts and can be made of practically anything. In contrast, a tablet computer stylus is an active digitizer, typically containing a battery and electromagnetically detected by a sensor grid hidden behind the light-emitting layer of the screen. For machines running a full-sized version of the Windows operating system, such as XP, the stylus contains two switches that function like the buttons on a mouse. Pressing the tip of the stylus against the screen is equivalent to clicking the left mouse but-

ton, and pressing an area on the side of the stylus is like clicking the right mouse button. In addition, a specially designed stylus can contain a ballpoint pen that makes it possible to write legibly on paper placed over the screen at the same time as the movements of the stylus are digitized and stored in the tablet computer's memory.

Human-computer interaction researchers have begun studying the performance of tablets in various contexts, exploring ways to give them additional functionality. The user of a desktop computer is chained to one location and a very narrow range of postures. In contrast, users of tablet computers can move around their home or office, and can work freely in any posture that allows them to hold the tablet in one hand and the stylus in another. If the task involves only reading or voice recognition software is employed, one hand is sufficient. Experiments have begun on how multiple users, each with their own tablet, may move freely around their workspace while sharing information and graphics.

Perhaps the most distinctive use for which tablets may be better suited than other kinds of computers is serving as a reading appliance or electronic book reader. A tablet is the physical size of many books and almost as comfortable to handle, yet it can hold the texts of twenty thousand books or more. Since Project Gutenberg began digitizing books in 1971, a broadly based movement has been working to replace traditional paper books with electronic books ("e-books"). Among many other such efforts, there is the Million Books Project, an international partnership involving China, India, and the United States with the aim of digitizing one million books in multiple languages.

Digitization efforts are costly in terms of human labor, but each book needs to be scanned in only once before it can be made freely available to everybody. For recent publications there are often difficult copyright challenges, and many companies are selling e-books online in copy-protected formats. In a few years, after millions of publications are available digitally, efficient tablet computers could replace paper books entirely, except for collectors and very specialized uses.

William Sims Bainbridge

FURTHER READING

Crooks, C. E. (2004). *Developing tablet PC applications.* Hingham, MA: Charles River Media.

Hinckley, H. (2003). Distributed and local sensing techniques for face-to-face collaboration. *Proceedings of the 5th international conference on multimodal interfaces* (pp. 81–84). New York: ACM Press.

Kay, A. C. (1972). A personal computer for children of all ages. In *Proceedings of the ACM National Conference* (pp. 1–11). New York: ACM Press.

McClard, A., & Somer, P. (2000). Unleashed: Web tablet integration into the home. *Proceedings of the SIGCHI conference on human factors in computing systems* (pp. 1–8). New York: ACM Press.

Mel, B. W., Omohundro, S. M., Robison, A. D., Skiena, S. S., Thearling, K. H., Young, L. T., et al. (1988). Tablet: Personal computer in the year 2000. *Communications of the ACM, 31*(6), 639–646.

Michalek, G. V. (2003). *Million book universal library project: Manual for metadata capture, digitization, and OCR.* Pittsburgh, PA: Carnegie Mellon University.

Plotkin, W. (2002). Electronic texts in the historical profession. In Orville Vernon Burton (Ed.), *Computing in the social sciences and humanities* (pp. 87–123). Urbana: University of Illinois Press.

Schilit, B. N., Price, M. N., Golovchinsky, G., Tanaka, K., & Marshall, C. C. (1999). The reading appliance revolution. *Computer, 32*(1), 65–73.

TASK ANALYSIS

The purpose of task analysis is to describe tasks, and more particularly, to identify and characterize the fundamental characteristics of a specific activity or set of activities. According to the *Shorter Oxford Dictionary,* a task is "any piece of work that has to be done" and is generally taken to mean one or more functions or activities that must be performed to achieve a specific goal. Since a task always is a directed activity, simply speaking of activities and tasks without taking into account their goals has no methodological merit. Task analysis should therefore be defined as the study of what a person or a team is required to do to achieve a specific goal or, simply put, who does what and why. The contents of the task are usually described in terms of the actions and/or cognitive processes involved. The goal describes the purpose of the task as a specific system, state, or condition that is to be achieved. A goal may, however, also be a psychological state or objective, such as "having done a good job." The task analysis

literature has usually eschewed the subjective and affective aspects of tasks and goals, although they clearly are essential both for understanding human performance and for designing artifacts and work environments.

The Need To Know

Task analysis is necessary because of a practical need to know in detail how things should be done or are done. When dealing with human-machine interaction, and more generally with how people use sociotechnical artifacts, it is necessary to know both what activities (functions) are required to accomplish a specified objective (= *why*) and how people (= *who*) habitually go about doing things—particularly since the latter often is significantly different from the former. Such knowledge is necessary to design, implement, and operate human-machine systems, and is especially important for figuring out how the interaction takes place and how it can be facilitated. Task analysis, however, has applications that go well beyond interface and interaction design and may be used to address issues such as training, performance assessment, event reporting and analysis, function allocation, procedure writing, maintenance, risk assessment, and work management.

The term *task analysis* is commonly used as a generic label. A survey of task analysis methods shows that they represent many different meanings of the term (Kirwan & Ainsworth, 1992). A little closer inspection, however, reveals that they fall into five main categories.

■ the analysis and description of tasks or working situations that do not yet exist or that are based on hypothetical events;

■ the description and analysis of observations of how work is carried out or of event reports (e.g., accident investigations);

■ the representation of either of the above, in the sense that the notation is used to capture the results; this is of interest due to the increasing use of computers to support task analysis;

■ the various ways of further analysis or refinement of data about tasks (from either of the above sources); and finally

Excerpt from *Cheaper by the Dozen*

Frank B. Gilbreth (1868–1924) and Lillian Gilbreth (1878–1972) were management engineers, who did pioneering work in time-and-motion study. They were also the parents of twelve children, whose growing-up years are chronicled in the best-selling memoir Cheaper by the Dozen (1948). As the excerpt below indicates, the Gilbreth children were valued subjects in their father's work on task analysis.

Dad took moving pictures of us children washing dishes, so that he could figure out how we could reduce our motions and thus hurry through the task. Irregular jobs, such as painting the back porch or removing a stump from the front lawn, were awarded on a low-bid basis. Each child who wanted extra pocket money submitted a sealed bid saying what he would do the job for. The lowest bidder got the contract.

Dad installed process and work charts in the bathrooms. Every child old enough to write-and Dad expected his offspring to start writing at a tender age-was required to initial the charts in the morning after he had brushed his teeth, taken a bath, combed his hair, and made his bed. At night, each child had to weigh himself, plot the figure on a graph, and initial the process charts again after he had done his homework, washed his hands and face, and brushed his teeth. Mother wanted to have a place on the charts for saying prayers, but Dad said as far as he was concerned prayers were voluntary.

It was regimentation, all right. But bear in mind the trouble most parents have in getting just one child off to school, and multiply it by twelve. Some regimentation was necessary to prevent bedlam. Of course there were times when a child would initial the charts without actually having fulfilled the requirements. However, Dad had a gimlet eye and a terrible swift sword. The combined effect was that truth usually went marching on.

Yes, at home or on the job, Dad was always the efficiency expert. He buttoned his vest from the bottom up, instead of from the top down, because the bottom-to-top process took him only three seconds, while the top-to-bottom took seven. He even used two shaving brushes to lather his face, because he found that by so doing he could cut seventeen seconds off his shaving time. For a while he tried shaving with two razors, but he finally gave that up.

"I can save forty-four seconds," he grumbled, "but I wasted two minutes this morning putting this bandage on my throat."

It wasn't the slashed throat that really bothered him. It was the two minutes.

Source: Gilbreth, Frank B., Jr., & Carey, Ernestine Gilbreth. (1948). *Cheaper by the Dozen* (pp. 2–3). New York: Thomas Y. Crowell.

■ the modes of presentation of results and the various ways of documenting the outcomes.

Task analysis should in principle be distinguished from task description. A task description produces a generalized account or summary of activities as they have been carried out. It is based on empirical data or observations rather than on design data and specifications. A typical example is link analysis or even Hierarchical Task Analysis (Annett et al. 1971). Properly speaking, task description or performance analysis deals with actions rather than with tasks. This is comparable to the French tradition in cognitive psychology where a distinction is made between tasks and activities. The task is the objective to be attained, while the activity is the actual performance of the task, which, of course, may be different from the prescribed task. Another possible term would therefore be activity analysis.

History

The formal pursuit of task analysis dates to the beginnings of the twentieth century, and is usually linked to the engineer Frederick Taylor's 1911 proposal of a system of scientific management. This approach to work design was based on the notion that tasks should be specified and designed in minute detail and that workers should receive precise instructions about how their tasks should be carried out. In order for this to occur, tasks had to be analyzed unequivocally, or "scientifically," if possible in quantitative terms, so that the most efficient method for each task step and for the distribution of task steps among workers could be determined. The classical methods of analyzing tasks are exemplified by the engineer Frank Gilbreth's 1911 motion-and-time study, which was developed to make work more efficient. (The principles of motion-and-time studies are still applied today in many production and service industries.)

While motion studies were adequate to describe manual work, they were unable to cope with the growing complexity of tasks that followed developments in electronics, control theory, and computing during the 1940s and 1950s. Due to the increasing capabilities of machines, people were required to engage in multiple activities at the same time, either because individual tasks became more complex or because simpler tasks were combined into larger units. An important consequence of this was that tasks changed from being a sequence of activities referring to a single goal to becoming an organized set of activities referring to a hierarchy of goals.

From Sequential to Hierarchical Task Organization

The technological development meant that the nature of work changed from being predominantly manual to becoming more dependent on mental capabilities (comprehension, monitoring, planning). Human factors engineering, or classical ergonomics, soon recognized that traditional methods of breaking a task down into small pieces, which each could be performed by a person, were no longer adequate. They also realized that the human capacity for processing information would determine the capacity of the joint human-machine system and that human capacity for learning and adaptation was insufficient to meet the new technological demands. To capture more complex task organization, Robert Miller developed a method for human-machine task analysis in which main task functions could be decomposed into subtasks. Each subtask could then be described in detail. Miller's method was followed in the late 1960s and early 1970s by the development of hierarchical task analysis (HTA). HTA has in practice become the standard method for task analysis—and task description—and is widely used in a variety of contexts, including human-machine interface design.

The process of HTA is to decompose tasks into subtasks and to repeat this process until a level of elementary tasks has been reached. Each subtask or operation is specified by its goal, the conditions under which the goal becomes relevant or "active," the actions required to attain the goal, and the criteria that mark the attainment of the goal. The relationship between a set of subtasks and the superordinate task is governed by plans expressed as, for instance, procedures, selection rules, or time-sharing principles. The overall aim of HTA is to describe the task in sufficient detail, with the level of resolution required depending on the specific purposes of the analysis (for example, interaction design, training requirements, interface design, risk analysis, and so on). HTA can be seen as a systematic way of searching for how tasks are organized that is adaptable for use in a variety of different contexts and purposes within the field of human factors.

Goals–Means Task Analysis

While HTA focuses on the structure of the tasks or activities needed to attain the goals, another approach to task analysis is to focus on the relations among goals and subgoals, and use that to identify the required tasks. This approach is referred to as goals-means task analysis, or functional task analysis.

The starting point is a goal, which is a specified condition or state of the system. A description of the goal usually includes or implies the criteria of achievement—that is, the conditions that determine when the goal has been reached. In order to achieve the goal, certain means are required. These are typically one or more activities that need to be carried out; hence tasks in their own right. Yet most tasks are only possible if specific conditions are fulfilled. For instance, you can only work on your laptop if you have access to an external power source or if the batteries are sufficiently charged. If these conditions are met, the task can be carried out. If not, bringing about these preconditions becomes a new (sub)goal. In this way, goals are decomposed recursively, thereby defining a set of goal-subgoal dependencies that also serves to structure or organize the associated tasks.

Tasks and Cognitive Tasks

In addition to the change that led from sequential motion-and-time descriptions to hierarchical task organization, a further change occurred in the late 1980s leading to a focus on the cognitive nature of tasks. The need to understand the cognitive activities of the human-machine system, first identified by Hollnagel & Woods (1983), soon developed a widespread interest in cognitive task analysis, defined as the extension of traditional task analysis techniques to yield information about the knowledge, thought processes, and goal structures that underlie observable task performance. The shift represented a change in emphasis from overt to covert activities. Since many tasks require considerable mental effort, in particular retrieving and understanding the information available, and in planning and preparing what to do (including monitoring of what happens), much of what is essential for successful performance is covert. Whereas classical task analysis very much relies on observable actions or activities, the need to find out what goes on in people's minds requires other approaches.

Some of the methods used are think-aloud protocols and introspection, which involve extrapolating from one's own experience to what others may do. The issue of thinking aloud has been hotly debated, as has the issue of introspection (Nisbett & Wilson, 1977). Other structured techniques rely on controlled tasks, questionnaires, and so forth. Yet in the end the issue is one of making inferences from some set of observable data to what goes on behind. This raises interesting questions regarding methods for data collection to support task analysis and leads to increasing reliance on models of the tasks. As long as task analysis is based on observation of actions or performance, it is possible to establish some kind of objectivity or intersubjective agreement or verification. As more and more of the data refer to the unobservable, the dependence on interpretations increases. For an interpretation to be socially acceptable within a scientific community, it must refer to an acknowledged frame of reference, which typically is expressed as a model (Hollnagel 1998).

Task Representation

For some purposes, the outcome of a task analysis may simply be rendered as a written description of the tasks and how they are organized. In most cases this is supplemented by some kind of graphical representation or diagram, since such representations make it considerably easier to grasp the overall relations.

For a number of other purposes, specifically those that have to do with design, it is useful if the task can be represented in different ways, such as some kind of model that can be manipulated. The benefit is clearly that putative changes to the task can be implemented in the model and the consequences explored. This has led to the development of a range of methods that rely on some kind of symbolic model of the task or activity. This development often goes hand in hand with user models—symbolic representations of users that can be used to simulate responses to what happens in the work environment. In principle such models can carry out the task as specified by the task description, but the strength of the results depends critically on the validity of the model assumptions.

Erik Hollnagel

See also Cognitive Walkthrough; Instruction Manuals; Scenario-Based Design

FURTHER READING

Annett, J., & Duncan, K. D. (1967). Task analysis and training design. *Occupational Psychology, 41,* 211–221.

Annett, J., Duncan, K. D., Stammers, R. B., & Gray, M. J. (1971). *Task analysis* (Training Information Paper No. 6). London: HMSO.

Gilbreth, F. B. (1911). *Motion study.* Princeton, NJ: Van Nostrand.

Hollnagel, E. (1998). Measurements and models, models and measurements: You can't have one without the other. In: NATO RTO Meeting Proceedings 4, *Collaborative crew performance in complex operational systems,* April 20–22, 1998, Edinburgh, Scotland (TRO-MP-4 AC/323(HFM)TP/2).

Hollnagel, E., & Woods, D. D. (1983). Cognitive systems engineering: New wine in new bottles. *International Journal of Man-Machine Studies, 18*, 583–600.

Kirwan, B., & Ainsworth, L. K. (1992). *A guide to task analysis*. London: Taylor & Francis.

Leplat, J. (1989). Error analysis, instrument and object of task analysis. *Ergonomics, 32*, 813–822.

Miller, R. B. (1953) *A method for man-machine task analysis* (WADC Tech. Rep. No. 53–137). Dayton, OH: Wright Air Development Center.

Nisbett, R. E., & Wilson, T. D. (1977). Telling more than we can know: Verbal reports on mental processes. *Psychological Review, 74*, 231–259.

Schraagen, J. M., Chipman, S. F., & Shalin, V. L. (Eds.). (2000). *Cognitive task analysis*. Mahwah, NJ: Lawrence Erlbaum Associates.

Shepherd, A. (1998). HTA as a framework for task analysis. *Ergonomics, 41*, (11), 1537–1552.

Taylor, F. W. (1911). *The principles of scientific management*. New York: Harper.

TAXONOMIES

See Digital Libraries; Information Organization; Lexicon Building; Ontology

TELECOMMUTING

What is telecommuting? Definitions vary, but at its most basic it is using telecommunications equipment to gain access to employees or coworkers and materials in the workplace rather than physically traveling to the workplace to do so. This is the definition that is most consistent with the composition of the word itself, and with the intent of the engineer and physicist Jack Nilles, who coined the term in the mid-1970s. Telecommuting is important because, if it could be implemented on a more extensive basis, it would provide substantial benefits for individuals, organizations, and the societies in which they live and function. Up to this point, there has been little research on how human-computer interaction (HCI) affects telecommuting. However an HCI perspective provides insights on why telecommuting has not achieved its potential and suggests ways of overcoming the problems that have hindered telecommuting.

Telecommuting is exemplified by the slogan, "Bring the work to the worker, rather than the worker to the work." This transfer can be facilitated with electronic equipment that may include telephones, fax machines, personal computers, network connections, video and voice teleconferencing equipment, and so forth. This hardware is assisted by communications software, and possibly by group support and by workflow and document management systems. The ultimate telecommuter is a person who performs (almost) all work duties at a remote location, visiting the organizational workplace only on rare occasions.

History

The concept of telecommuting has been around for a long time. E. M. Forster's novella *The Machine Stops* (1909), although it does not use the word telecommuting, portrays a future in which almost everyone lives in isolation and communicates via telephones and the equivalent of video screens. In one scene the protagonist uses this communications system to deliver a lecture in a way that foreshadows some current distance learning implementations.

Since then, a great deal has been written about telecommuting. For example, on 15 July 2003, the Google Internet search engine found approximately 276,000 webpages containing the word. On the same day, a search on the word *telecommuting* at Amazon.com, the Internet department store, found 116 books (although many did not have *telecommuting* in their titles).

In contrast to Forster's anti-utopian vision of the future, much of what has been written about telecommuting since 1950 has been very positive. Telecommuting purportedly will generate substantial societal benefits by reducing traffic congestion, air pollution, and dependence on imported oil. Proponents claim that it will increase people's productivity and predict that these gains will flow through to their organizations. A reduced real estate requirement is another possible benefit at the organizational level, since, if most employees do not have to be concentrated at one location, organizational offices could be reduced.

For individuals, telecommuting unquestionably frees up time otherwise spent commuting and significantly reduces transportation costs and possibly stress. Advocates also suggest that it could reduce the need for child or elder care and increase employment opportunities for persons with disabilities. However, as documented by Kathleen Christensen in *Women and Home-Based Work* (1988), research on this issue indicates that having responsibility for childcare while trying to telecommute generally does not work out satisfactorily.

In 1980, *The Third Wave*, an international best-seller by the futurist Alvin Toffler, devoted a chapter to the "electronic cottage." Toffler suggested that in twenty to thirty years, as much 10 to 20 percent of the population could earn its living by working at home with the assistance of telecommunications equipment. Since then, the steadily increasing capabilities and declining costs of information and telecommunication technologies (ICT) have made working from home much more practical than it was at the time of Toffler's forecast.

Telecommuting in Practice

In spite of all the publicity and the favorable technology trends, work from home is still not very common. Less than 10 percent of the U.S. population substitutes telecommuting for travel to a conventional workplace on a regular basis. Of those who do, the most typical arrangement is telecommuting only one day per week. Multiplying a 10 percent participation by a frequency of 20 percent indicates a traffic reduction of only 2 percent. (More sophisticated analyses, which include persons who telecommute more frequently or less frequently, produce similar results.) To put this into context, traffic volumes in major urban areas often increase by two percent or more annually, thus offsetting in a year or less all the benefits traceable to telecommuting.

This low substitution rate obviously limits the personal and societal benefits resulting from telecommuting, as well as any real estate savings at the organizational level. Although consultants frequently claim that telecommuting increases productivity, the poor quality of much of the research is not adequate to validate this claim for individual employees, much less for whole organizations.

Up to this point, most of the research and publishing on telecommuting has focused on costs and benefits at a relatively superficial level. Some recent research has considered sociological and organizational management factors. Although few if any researchers have looked at human-computer interaction issues related to telecommuting, this perspective could help provide an explanation for why usage is so low. Identifying the HCI problems would be a step toward solving them, and thus would remove at least some of the obstacles to achieving more of the potential societal, organizational, and individual benefits.

HCI Issues and Telecommuting

People who telecommute, especially those who do it more often than the typical one day per week, generally must deal with social, organizational, and mechanical issues that generally do not apply to on-site employees. On the social side, telecommuters' contact with other employees is reduced. On the mechanical side, they have less external structure in their work, and their access to organizational materials is generally impaired.

Social Contact

Human beings are social creatures. Many of us do most of our work in groups that transcend the individual members, and this pattern of human behavior dates back to our earliest days. (Toffler's vision of the electronic cottage failed to recognize that even though work prior to the industrial revolution was accomplished at or near the home, it was generally performed by groups, including multiple generations and collateral relatives, rather than by isolated individuals.)

Telecommuting departs from this historical pattern. Telecommuters are isolated from other employees. They miss much of the camaraderie of a work group. They have fewer opportunities for spontaneous interactions, which are emotionally important and which can lead to new or improved ways of accomplishing the goals of the work group. Other employees may feel that telecommuters are not really members of the team. Telecommuters often report that they believe they have fewer chances of promotion than employees who spend more time in the organizational offices.

From an HCI perspective, the challenge is to use technology in a way that can maintain many of the social aspects of work for people who are not at the physical workplace. E-mail is a means of communication, but it cannot substitute for face-to-face interactions with other employees. Similarly, a telecommuter can talk to (or leave voice messages for) other people via the telephone, but more likely than not, the person receiving the call will not be as ready at the moment for a business-related call as the person initiating the call. Spontaneous interactions in which none of the parties are preoccupied with other matters, such as those that occur regularly in the hallways at the worksite, are even more difficult to achieve with the telephone.

One possible HCI solution is to have large (wall-sized) displays in both the organizational offices and in telecommuters' homes, with each home display showing a video feed from the remote location, and vice versa. This could make it possible for local and remote employees to interact more like they do when at the same physical location. Variations on this approach have been tested in a number of research settings in attempts to increase interaction between groups of employees at separate locations. Although the costs are currently too high to do this in the homes of individual employees, the continuously declining costs and increasing capabilities of hardware and networking technologies may make this a viable option in the near future.

Access to Materials

The high-rise office building originated in Chicago in 1885 and has evolved a great deal since then. It has become a very efficient environment for much of the work in both the service industries and in the administration of other industries. It includes storage of and easy access to large volumes of organizational files, high-speed high-volume copying equipment, fax machines, and other electronic equipment for manipulating and transmitting the materials in those files.

With its layout of a vertical stack of horizontal floors, the high-rise office building makes it possible to assemble employees into manageable work groups on individual floors. Elevators are actually an automated transit system that makes it possible

to travel quickly and to access individuals, groups, and materials located on different floors easily.

Some form of teleconferencing system or wall display system as was mentioned above could become a workable substitute for proximity to other workers in an office building. The need for access to large numbers of paper files, however, still puts many telecommuters at a disadvantage. They must check out files that they might need while working off-site, and they must transport them back and forth to work without losing them in transit or among papers at their residences. If the files must remain at the work location, the telecommuters or other employees may need to spend a substantial amount of time at copying machines or fax machines. If telecommuters discover that they have not brought home everything necessary, they must either return to the office or wait until someone does the extra work of faxing the material to them.

On the other hand, physical access to materials is becoming less important as more organizations implement document management systems and put increasing amounts of organizational information into data warehouses. This transition will be a gradual process, but lower costs and greater capabilities could make telecommuting a more viable option for employees whose work depends heavily on access to documents and information.

Structure

The conventional workplace provides a substantial amount of structure to many work processes. Most employees whose work does not require outside contact arrive at the work location not later than a specified starting time and remain there at least until a specified quitting time. There is usually a pattern of breaks and lunch times, and meetings are often scheduled for around the same time on regular days, weeks, or months. Work comes in from familiar sources, and outputs typically go to a well-known set of recipients. Even in situations where standard times have not been identified for certain outputs, employees generally know how long it should take to generate them and receive implicit as well as explicit signals about when they need to be completed and delivered.

Commuting to and from work may actually be beneficial to employees because it reinforces the structure of work. It provides a temporal and geographical transition between home and employment. Even the dreaded stress of commuting may be helpful in a certain sense, by getting employees emotionally prepared for the challenges of the workplace in the morning and then replacing the tensions of the day with a different form of stress while traveling home.

For some knowledge workers, the relatively new and evolving technology of workflow systems may become an adequate replacement for the structure of the traditional place of employment. These systems have routing capabilities to deliver materials to employees, who can then forward their outputs to other employees. Thus these systems integrate off-site employees into a structured chain of effort that may make the telecommuters feel a part of an ongoing process with other employees. And for employees who have problems with self-discipline, these systems by their very nature provide a complete and detailed record of all outputs and the time it took to produce them.

Workflow systems are often coupled with or facilitated by document management systems. It might even be possible for workflow systems to provide a functionally effective transition between work and home activities, by delivering some form of entertaining organizational or educational material. This could be delivered regularly at the start and end of each workday, and possibly at other times.

Training

Many telecommuters require training to make the best use of the newer technologies that can support them in remote locations. It is a good idea to provide additional training in issues related to telecommuting even if the off-site employees will not use any unfamiliar technologies. This training can include information on coping with and compensating for reduced social contact, limited access to materials, and reduced structure in their work.

There are many materials available to assist both trainers and telecommuters who are seeking information on their own. Many of the recommendations or suggestions have been successfully used by telecommuters and organizations and are easy to implement. For example, some telecommuters find that a fifteen-minute walk before work creates an adequate transition between living at home and working at home. Some try to meet with others for lunch near their homes to compensate for the reduction in social contact at work. Michael Dziak's *Telecommuting Success: A Practical Guide for Staying in the Loop While Working Away from the Office* (2001) provides numerous checklists and a wealth of other material to help telecommuters obtain the benefits of telecommuting and avoid the common pitfalls.

Looking Ahead

Up to this point, telecommuting has not fulfilled the expectations of social analysts, researchers, and policy makers. However it is still possible that telecommuting will become much more common in the future. As an analogy, the fax machine dates back to the nineteenth century, but was not adopted by large numbers of businesses until after 1980. Substantial fax usage in the home did not occur until about a decade later, but has now become very common. It is possible that some combination of new or improved hardware, software, and networking technologies could lead to a similar turning point for telecommuting. Such an upsurge might also be facilitated by new or evolving forms of organizational structure or management, or perhaps by widespread changes in cultural patterns at the societal level.

The prospect of large numbers of people working in physical isolation and connected primarily through electronic mechanisms is disturbingly reminiscent of Forster's "The Machine Stops." On the other hand, our experience to date suggests that telecommuting will not increase substantially until HCI, new technologies, and new organizational practices are successful in mitigating the more repugnant aspects of Forster's vision.

Ralph David Westfall

See also Computer-Supported Cooperative Work; Work

FURTHER READING

Bailey, D. E., & Kurland, N. B. (2002). A review of telework research: Findings, new directions, and lessons for the study of modern work. *Journal of Organizational Behavior, 23*(4), 383–400.

Becker, F. D., & Steele, F. (1995). *Workplace by design: Mapping the high-performance workscape.* San Francisco: Jossey-Bass.

Christensen, K. (1988). *Women and home-based work: The unspoken contract.* New York: Holt.

Bertin, I. (1998). *The teleworking handbook.* Kenilworth, UK: The Telecottage Association.

Dziak, M. J. (2001). *Telecommuting success: A practical guide for staying in the loop while working away from the office.* Indianapolis: Jist Works.

Forster, E. M. (1909). The machine stops. *Oxford and Cambridge Review.* Retrieved August 20, 2003, from http://www.plexus.org/forster.html

Huws, U., Korte, W., & Robinson, S. (1990). *Telework: Toward the elusive office.* New York: John Wiley and Sons.

Igbaria, M., & Tan, M. (Eds.) (1998). *The virtual workplace,* Harrisburg, PA: Idea Group.

Mokhtarian, P. L. (1996). The information highway: Just because we're on it doesn't mean we know where we're going. *World Transport Policy and Practice, 2*(1–2), 24–28.

Nilles, J. M. (1998). *Managing telework: Strategies for managing the virtual workforce.* New York: John Wiley and Sons.

Nilles, J. M., Carlson, F. R., Jr., Gray, P., & Hanneman, G. J. (1976). *The telecommunications-transportation tradeoff.* New York: Wiley.

Prusak, L., & Cohen, D. (2001). *In good company: How social capital makes organizations work.* Boston: Harvard Business School.

Toffler, A. (1980). *The third wave.* New York: William Morrow.

Westfall, R. D. (1997). The telecommuting paradox. *Information Systems Management, 14*(4), 15–20.

Westfall, R. D. (in press). Does telecommuting *really* increase productivity? *Communications of the ACM.*

TELEPRESENCE

Telepresence is the perception of being physically present within a computer-mediated environment (the remote world, or the remote environment). Someone experiencing telepresence loses the sense of being physically present within his or her actual physical environment (the local world, or local environment) and instead has the experience of being part of the remote world.

The ultimate telepresence is depicted in the film *The Matrix* (1999), in which the illusion of presence is so compelling that one must be recruited, "born again," indoctrinated, and trained to recognize that the remote world is not the real world.

Virtual Presence

Teleoperation and virtual reality have been called the two principal aspects of synthetic environments. A synthetic-environment system includes a human user, a computer-mediated human-machine interface, and a remote world. In teleoperation, the remote world is a real place and the user interacts with it by means of remote video, robotic manipulators, unmanned vehicles, and other remotely controlled devices. The user controls the devices by means of a computer, or computer-controlled, interface. In virtual reality the remote world is a computer-generated simulation, and telepresence is often referred to as virtual presence. Virtual presence and telepresence are the same user experience; the difference is only only in the type of remote world being experienced.

Before proceeding, however, it is worth noting one area in which telepresence and virtual presence may differ (and *may* is an important qualifier, as much research still needs to be done before science has a complete understanding of this topic). A user's understanding of the impact of his or her actions in the remote world in teleoperation, particularly in high-risk or potentially high-cost situations such as surgery or military operations, may enhance consciousness of his or her separation from the remote world and therefore result in a weaker experience of telepresence that can be had when the remote world is simulated. It is also worth noting that hybrid combinations of teleoperators and virtual reality are possible, as when a computer graphic is superimposed upon real-world video.

Teleoperation

Telepresence is sometimes used, inaccurately, as a synonym for teleoperation. Telepresence is not the same thing as teleoperation, although the quality of teleoperation may affect telepresence. Teleoperation is the projection of user capabilities into a remote, real-world location through the use of remotely controlled (mostly robotic) devices. This is truly teleoperation, that is, manipulating the remote world from a distance. In the past, telepresence has been used to mean teleoperation, but in modern usage that is inappropriate. Telepresence is the projection of awareness into a remote world, not the projection of capability. Indeed, awareness may be projected without capability (for example, it is possible to feel telepresent during a virtual tour of a museum even if you cannot control the pace or point of view of the tour) and capability may be projected without awareness (users do not necessarily feel telepresent when, for example, performing routine remote maintenance work within a nuclear reactor).

Immersion

Immersion too is sometimes used, inaccurately, as a synonym for telepresence. Telepresence is not the same thing as immersion, although immersion may affect telepresence. Immersion is the degree to which a human-computer interface controls sensory information presented to the human and accepts human actions as inputs. For example, a head-mounted display (HMD) is more immersive than a monitor because the HMD restricts the user's visual inputs to those coming from the HMD. (Some HMDs allow the user to see the local world through the display; these are less immersive than those that do not allow any viewing of the outside world.) Immersion describes how completely an interface controls information flow to and from the user; telepresence describes the user's reaction to the interface and the remote world.

History

The mathematician Marvin Minsky, a pioneer in the field of artificial intelligence and robotics, popularized the term telepresence in a 1980 essay describing his concept of an ideal teleoperator system, one that would immerse the user and be capable of human dexterity. In his essay, Minsky discussed the capabilities of such a machine and only hinted at the human experience of projecting oneself into a remote world through the use of such a machine. Minsky was writing as a futurist and not as a scientist or engineer. He was describing a vision of a future in which robotic devices could extend human capabilities into remote worlds. For the most part, he was reacting to what he perceived to be the inadequacies of the thirty-

five years or so of robotic manipulator development that had preceded his essay.

The displacement of perception of self into a remote area was noticed by robotic manipulator developers at least fifteen years priors to Minsky's essay, but the phenomenon was neither widely studied nor given a unique label. Interestingly, after Minsky's essay the phenomenon came to be strongly associated with the term telepresence, even though the essay does not directly address the perception of projection of self. The dualism of the term has persisted to this day: While the teleoperation community seems to be moving towards the consensus that telepresence refers to the psychological phenomenon, there are still researchers who either relate telepresence to the effectiveness of a teleoperator or fail to adequately distinguish between the teleoperator's performance and the perception of being present in the remote environment. In some quarters, telepresence has been adopted as a design ideal for teleoperators, resulting in the abandonment of a more practical design approach driven by mission requirements. The rationale behind giving primacy to telepresence is that the most flexible system imaginable is the human; therefore, fully reproducing human capabilities must result in the most flexible possible system for teleoperation. This has an appeal that is perhaps more romantic than reasonable; hard-headed engineers note that systems produced by adopting the full telepresence approach are likely to be unnecessarily complex and expensive.

The emergence of virtual reality (beginning before Minsky's essay but becoming important only in the decades succeeding it) included parallel observation of perception of projection of self into virtual worlds. Virtual reality developers began noticing that users sometimes perceived themselves to be present in the remote world rather than the local world. This experience is the same psychological phenomenon as the one noticed by the developers of remote manipulators. In the virtual reality community it was sometimes called immersion and sometimes called virtual presence. The confusion between immersion and virtual presence mirrors the confusion between telepresence used to describe the capabilities of the teleoperator and telepresence used to describe the experience. Again, this dualism persists, although there is movement in the community towards accepting the definition of immersion presented above.

In recent years there have been several interesting developments regarding telepresence. First, the relationship between teleoperation and virtual worlds and between telepresence and virtual presence was clearly delineated by the scientists Nathaniel I. Durlach and Anne S. Mavor. This has encouraged cross-fertilization of research in teleoperation and virtual reality. Second, great progress has been made in developing tools for measuring the strength of telepresence. Third, and perhaps most importantly, new theories about the importance of telepresence and the impact of telepresence on mission performance and human users have been emerging. For many years, particularly in the robotics community, researchers could be divided into telepresence promoters and telepresence opponents. Today, more sophisticated views placing telepresence in the context of mission requirements are being developed. Fourth, the volume of research on telepresence has been increasing, particularly in the 1990s and into the twenty-first century, as virtual presence and telepresence have come to be accepted as synonymous and as researchers have gained greater access to simulators of sufficient quality to do telepresence experiments. (Prior to about 1990, telepresence researchers depended on real robotic manipulators and vehicles, which are expensive and of limited availability.)

Psychological Background

Several attempts have been made to develop a psychological framework for understanding why telepresence occurs and what its implications are for users. Generally, these relate telepresence to known psychological or human-system phenomena. One kind of approach considers cognitive factors. For example, the psychologist John V. Draper and colleagues have studied telepresence as an aspect of human attention: Telepresence is the degree to which users focus their attention on the remote world at the cost of focus within the local world. The strength of telepresence may be defined as the ratio of attention focused on the remote world to attention focused on the local world. The industrial engineer David B. Kaber and his colleagues have framed telepresence in terms of situation awareness (SA). SA is the degree to which users recognize elements in a world (an element can be any important attribute or actor—for example, the aircraft and the ground in a flight simulator), understand the relationships among elements (my airplane is 500 meters above the ground), and can predict future arrangements of elements (if my airplane keeps diving, it will hit the ground). As with attention, the SA approach describes telepresence relative to the focus of cognitive processing. As remote-world SA increases, so does telepresence. But as local-world SA increases, telepresence decreases. Both the attentional and SA approaches can be thought of in terms of human information processing: The more one processes information from the remote world and the less one processes information from the local world, the stronger the experience of telepresence will be.

Another kind of approach considers the efficiency of information transmittal between remote and local worlds. For example, scientist T. J. Smith relates telepresence to sensorimotor perturbation. When the normal human sensory (perception) and motor (movement) relationships are changed, a perturbation may be said to occur. This happens, for example, when one tries to perform some task using a mirror. Because the mirror image is reversed compared to normal images, it can be difficult to translate between perception and action (one goes left when one wanted to go right, for example). Dentists are masters of adaptation to sensorimotor perturbations, and many people learn to adapt to the perturbed images presented by the rear-view mirrors of their automobiles (some do not). Remote systems can have perceptual perturbations in which, for example the point of view is different from the normal one because remote television cameras are set to one side of the task space. They can have motor perturbations in which, for example, a robotic manipulator arm doesn't move exactly as a human arm moves. They can have temporal perturbations in which time lags affect the timing of perception and action. According to the sensorimotor perturbation idea, telepresence is reduced by the sum of all the perturbations present. Stating it another way, the fewer the number and the weaker the strength of perturbations, the stronger people's experience of telepresence, because their perceptions and actions within the remote world match what they would experience if they were actually in the remote world.

The attention, SA, and perturbation concepts can be integrated. It may be that perturbations cause users to think more carefully about their actions; this may have the effect of focusing attention or SA on the user interface itself at the cost of the remote world. In other words, perturbations are limiting factors on the free focus of attention or SA in the remote world.

Telepresence in Telecommunication

While telepresence is most commonly used in the context of synthetic environments, in the last five years or so the term has also started to crop up in the literature regarding telecommunications. Specifically, telepresence has been used to describe the ability of users to participate in meetings held at remote locations. This usage of telepresence in the context of teleconferencing has some merit in that telepresence can be interpreted to mean that a person is present at a meeting held at a remote location (literally, tele + presence). However, it is unfortunate that it recapitulates the old confusion between teleoperation and telepresence. It will be interesting to see how usage evolves within the telecommunications community. Making a prediction based on history, it is likely that researchers and developers will begin to recognize the differences between the ability to interact with remote colleagues (which might be called teleoperation) and the user's perception of being actually present at that meeting (real telepresence).

Telepresence Research

An important question being researched today is whether or not telepresence has an impact on task performance in the remote world. The MIT professor Thomas B. Sheridan, one of the most widely published researchers in this area, has often questioned whether telepresence is a useful construct for designing teleoperators. Advocates have speculated that the experience of telepresence allowed users to respond more naturally and, therefore, more effi-

ciently. Others have speculated that telepresence could be counterproductive, as when a user supervising multiple robots becomes strongly telepresent at one remote site and neglects responsibilities at other sites or in the local world. Insofar as high telepresence is correlated with good performance, what is the causal relationship between telepresence and performance? It is possible that high telepresence leads to good performance; conversely, it is possible that good performance results in a halo effect that causes users to rate telepresence high; and it is also possible that good systems promote both good performance and high telepresence, but that telepresence itself does not affect performance. For entertainment system such as video games, telepresence itself may be a good criterion for the success of the system, but is there a cost associated with becoming too engrossed in a remote world for too long? Much more research must be done to explicate the complex relationship between telepresence and the mission of the synthetic environment system.

Telepresence has also inspired a philosophical debate that addresses fundamental questions of human consciousness. Philosophical issues are outside the purview of the current volume or of this article but illustrate how progress in science and technology can require reappraisal of cultural questions.

John V. Draper

See also Virtual Reality

FURTHER READING

Draper, J. V., Kaber, D. B., & Usher, J. M. (1998). Telepresence. *Human Factors, 40*(3), 354–375.

Draper, J. V., Kaber, D. B., & Usher, J. M. (1999). Speculations on the value of telepresence. *Cyberpsychology & Behavior, 2*(4), 349–362.

Heinlein, R. A. (1950). *Waldo and Magic, Inc.* New York: Signet Books.

IJsselsteijn, W. A., Lombard, M., & Freeman, J. (2001). Toward a core bibliography of presence. *Cyberpsychology & Behavior, 4*(2), 317–320.

Minsky, M. (1980, June). Telepresence. *Omni, 2*(9), 45–51.

Nash, E. B., Edwards, G. W., Thompson, J. A., & Barfield, W. (2000). A review of presence and performance in virtual environments. *International Journal of Human-Computer Interaction, 12*(1), 1–41.

Nichols, S., Haldane, C., & Wilson, J. R. (2000). Measurement of presence and its consequences in virtual environments. *International Journal of Human-Computer Studies, 52*(3), 471–491.

Zelazny, R. (1975, November). Home is the hangman. *Analog Science Fiction and Fact, 95*(11).

TEXT SUMMARIZATION

With increasingly larger amounts of text available to people electronically, text summarization has become an important approach to dealing with information overload. Text summarization is a technique for identifying the key points of a document or a set of related documents and presenting these key points as a brief, integrated, and independent representation. Thus, the goal of text summarization is to output a coherent and concise summary of input text of any size (e.g., a book, a news article, multiple articles, e-mail messages, and transcribed speech).

People apply text summarization to single documents to create a representation of the content of a single textual input. Multiple-document summarization, also known as "multidocument summarization," takes many inputs—possibly of different types and possibly covering different subtopics—and creates a single summary. Examples of input of the same type include documents such as a set of news or journal articles, whereas examples of different types include legal information from different sources, including briefs, textbooks, technical articles, and brochures. Multidocument summaries differ from single-document summaries in that in addition to requiring the presentation of key points, multidocument summaries must identify key similarities and differences across the input document set.

A person can use summaries, also known as "abstracts," as proxies for documents, for example, in large online archives where titles and abstracts are used to represent the full document. A person can then examine the summary to determine whether to view the full text of a document. Among the challenges in automatic summarization (using computers to produce summaries) are (1) determining the key points of a document or document set, which requires sophisticated statistical and rule-based natural language processing, (2) weaving these key points

into a single coherent document to be presented to the user, and (3) tailoring the summary to the needs of the user in a given subject area or domain.

The creation of abstracts or summaries from articles is an established practice in the field of information science. Typically, domain specialists manually create a summary of a given text for a specific purpose. Perhaps the best-known examples of text summarization are newspaper abstracts, summaries of journal articles, and abstracts of books. In these examples domain specialists with a background in the topic synthesize information and create a new summary. Although computational systems might aim for information synthesis, so far they cannot achieve this goal. Automatic summarization is an established practice in the field of natural language processing. The aim of computational systems is not only to achieve levels comparable to those of human performance, but also to provide additional options such as the ability to modify the summary size automatically, browse term frequency occurrences, handle large volumes of input, and visualize across documents and document sets. Experts have developed two basic techniques for automatic summarization—extraction and fusion—with recent hybrid techniques now dominating the field.

Sentence Extraction

The earliest techniques for automatic summarization used a method called "sentence extraction." This method is fundamentally a statistical approach, using varying degrees of symbolic methodology. The basic approach, initiated during the early 1950s, involved single documents only. Each word in a document was stemmed, using simple techniques to permit related words to be counted together, for example, *reduction, reduce, reducing,* and *reduced* are all counted as variants of the stem *reduc-*. If each of these words occurred once in the same document, then the count for the stem *reduc-* would be four. After the elimination of a stop list of highly frequent words—for example, *the, of,* and *fact*—the sentences with the most high-frequency words were selected. Although this technique may seem simplistic, it continues to be effective.

The key limitation of this initial form of sentence extraction was that no control existed for words that were unique to particular documents when compared to a larger document set. In other words, each single document was considered by itself, with no comparison to how it might differ from an average document. Thus, sentences that were about unusual topics might not be selected, although those sentences would be the very ones that could provide a characterization of what was different about the document. This situation led to the introduction of a measure known as "term frequency" as a function of document frequency measure; this measure is known as "tf*idf" (term frequency/inverse document frequency) in the field of information retrieval. The function of tf*idf is to control for words that tend to occur commonly across documents and to favor those words that are truly unique to a particular document or document set, as compared with a larger document set.

In addition to not considering how a document might differ from an average over a large number of documents, early sentence-extraction techniques did not take into account any linguistic or rhetorical structure information. For example, cue phrases—that is, phrases that signal especially important sentences—were ignored. For example, in scientific writing a writer typically precedes the most important conclusion with a phrase such as *In summary . . ., In conclusion, This paper proves that . . .*, or another such phrase to indicate the primary point of the article. By ignoring these phrases, the computational summarizer does not take advantage of the fact that the writer might essentially lead the summarizer to the main points of an article. Later techniques have taken into account cue phrases, which might be specific to a given domain or style, but which allow an automatic summarization system to utilize writers' clues to what are the essential and major points of the text.

In addition to ignoring cue phrases, early techniques did not take into account larger rhetorical structure. For example, newspaper journalists are trained to put the most important point of an article in the lead sentence. Often the writer precedes the lead sentence with an informal "hook" sentence, that is, a sentence that catches the reader's interest.

The main summary sentence of the article will follow this optional attention-getting sentence. Often the writer resummarizes the article in the final sentence. The early purely statistical approaches to word counting ignored the rhetorical structure information that characterizes different genres. Later approaches have tailored summarizers to combine statistical methods with knowledge of how certain stylistically distinct documents might be written in order to take advantage of information provided by rhetorical structure.

Finally, a side effect of extracting sentences from different locations within a document is that often anaphoric (relating to a word or phrase that takes its reference from another word or phrase) resolution and name expansion are not correctly output. For example, the opening sentence of a summary might be *The company decided to terminate production of this product.* In the earlier context of the document the company might have been named, and the product might have been discussed. This sentence, taken out of context, would confuse the reader and would leave the reader with limited information on which company and which product. Later approaches to summarization have incorporated techniques to ensure that anaphoric references are resolved in opening sentences of summaries, but these techniques involve sophisticated reasoning that is more typical of the fusion approach to summarization described in the next section. In addition to checking that anaphoric references are resolved, techniques expand proper names so that the longest version occurs at the start of the summary, for example, *President Abe Lincoln* rather than a shortened version, for example, *Lincoln*.

Language Fusion

In addition to sentence extraction, in which a variety of techniques might be used to determine which sentences to select from a document, later approaches have used sophisticated language generation to create a new text for a summary based on a conceptual analysis of the input text. Language generation, also known as "language fusion," takes phrasal and conceptual input and uses rules to create sentences from the partial input. The use of language fusion for summarization requires a language-generation component that is capable of taking the output of text analysis, which creates abstract semantic representations of articles, and of generating cohesive and concise text, to express the key points of a document. The steps in using language generation for summarization are clustering input documents to identify key points and then using those key points to generate new language for the summary. Research issues in effective summary creation using language generation include temporal ordering of clauses and co-reference resolution (how individual statements are connected within a document). For example, sentence ordering implies a temporal relationship between propositions; it would be unnatural to say *The Lone Ranger rode into the sunset and mounted his horse* instead of *The Lone Ranger mounted his horse and rode into the sunset* even though these two sentences contain the same clausal information. The fact that clause order generally implies temporal precedence makes the first version difficult to process and, indeed, pragmatically incorrect. An automatic language-generation system must contain mechanisms to avoid such errors.

Typically, a single-document fusion-based summarization system will analyze input text to figure out the key points as phrases or concepts. For example, related terms might be linked by the use of semantic relations found in resources such as the online lexical reference system WordNet. The system then inputs the topic and phrases of the article to a language-generation component, which orders the concepts and creates well-formed text from the conceptual input. Language fusion generally requires more overhead because it necessitates an entire language-generation module, but the results tend to justify the overhead. Language fusion overcomes the types of error found in summaries created by sentence extraction—for example, unresolved anaphor, lack of context, and choppiness in style. Thus, a smoother and more coherent output is created.

Single-Document versus Multidocument Summarization

Summarization over single documents is the most common type of summarization because it involves creation of a single summary from a single type of input. Early approaches involved only single documents because they are conducive to simple statistical techniques.

The primary limitation of single-document summarization is that no comparison across documents is possible. People are capable of taking a set of related documents and creating a single summary of the main points across the documents. The goal of multidocument summarization is to model this process. Multidocument summarization involves several phases. First, articles on similar topics must be identified so that the summary applies to only related documents. Given an input set of documents, determining document relatedness is generally achieved with classification techniques. After a document set containing texts on the same topic is formed, two other aspects must be addressed: points of similarity and points of difference across the document set. To start, points of similarity across the document set must be identified and prioritized. These two goals are generally achieved through word, phrase, and phrasal variant overlap. Often conceptual information is used to identify similarities, for example, if one article is about cats and another about dogs, the similarity between the articles can be found through the fact that cats and dogs are mammals. However, similarity has many facets, so the step of ranking which similarities might be of interest to a user is a computational challenge.

A further computational challenge is identification of differences that are significant within the document set. Areas of difference must be identified and ranked. The challenge of identifying differences is highly complex and involves the capability to recognize differences that are significant to a topic. For example, two sentences from related documents might be different on the surface, for example, *The president was assassinated while attending the theater with his wife* is on the surface dissimilar from *Lincoln was fatally shot by Booth in Washington, DC.* Researchers have developed ways to determine semantic similarity using dictionaries and language resources, but this challenge is largely unsolved.

Another challenge in identifying differences is being able to discriminate those differences that affect the accuracy of a summary, for example, *In the most serious earthquake of this century, more than eighty thousand people lost their homes* versus *In the most serious earthquake of this century, more than ten thousand people lost their homes.* By all criteria, these sentences are nearly the same. In fact, they are also logically consistent. However, the scope of the numbers of people differs to the point that any automatic summarization technique might need to contain mechanisms to make judgments on how to reflect accurately these differences. This challenge is especially important when dealing with news articles that report on events with temporal components. For example, an early article might report fifty people wounded in an initial estimate, which then could become twenty-five people in later articles but jump to eighty people in still-later articles. Collecting information on the source of the information, including the time of reporting, would enable an automatic summarization system to generate a comparison sentence, for example, *Initial reports claimed fifty people wounded, whereas later reports confirmed eighty wounded.* In this case, the intermediate report might be judged to be omissible.

Summarization over Single versus Multiple Languages

In 2003 only 57 percent of the information on the Internet was in English. Between 1996 and 2003 more than 450 million non-English-speaking people gained access to electronic information through the Internet. These statistics imply that non-English text on the Internet will continue to increase. This increase will provide new opportunities for automatic summarization techniques to take as input multiple texts in multiple languages. As discussed earlier, the steps in multidocument summarization include first classifying related documents and then determining key similarities and differences. Similarly, multilingual, multidocument summarization must include a translation step. Assuming that the goal is to create a single summary in one language of an entire document set, then translation can occur in several places. However, because robust automatic machine translation is still not a mature technology, degradation of input is a serious problem for summarization.

Consider multilingual, multidocument summarization over news from the World Wide Web. One approach is to collect all the news and to translate all the articles. After translation, topics are then classified and similarities and differences identified over the translated texts. The disadvantage of this approach is that translation introduces unintended ambiguities. Therefore, the quality of classification is affected. Articles on unrelated topics are then difficult to summarize because most of the findings show dissimilarities. Another approach is to collect multiple documents in different languages, along with English articles that are topically related but not necessarily translations of the documents. In this approach the non-English text is translated but is derived within the context of the English text. When similar sentences are identified, extraction of the relevant sentence from the English-original text provides a smoother summary. Yet another approach is to summarize over non-English languages and then translate the summaries into English. In this approach the single summary is created from inputs of summaries rather than from full text. These approaches can be adapted to any language, meaning that concise and coherent text summarization over information from multilingual resources will become a reality in the near future.

Judith L. Klavans

See also Video Summarization

FURTHER READING

Goldstein, J., Kantrowitz, M., Mittal, V., & Carbonell, J. (1999). Summarizing text documents: Sentence selection and evaluation metrics. *Proceedings of the 22nd International Conference on Research and Development in Information Retrieval* (SIGIR'99), 121–128.

Kan, M-Y, & Klavans, J. L. (2002). Using librarian techniques in automatic text summarization for information retrieval. *Proceedings of the Joint Conference on Digital Libraries* (JCDL 2002). Portland, Oregon.

Mani, I., & Maybury, M. T. (1999). Advances in automatic text summarization. Cambridge, MA: MIT Press.

THEORY

Theory is the backbone of all sciences, but many researchers feel that the field of human-computer interaction (HCI) lacks a theory. HCI designers are often skeptical of the contribution that theory makes to their creative work. Engineers can be impatient with the abstract nature and lack of specific guidance provided by theoretical accounts of HCI. In light of these critiques, many people assert that theory has no role in HCI. To answer this assertion, one needs to understand the nature of scientific theories and review the history of theoretical development in HCI before envisaging the prospects for a theory in HCI.

The Role of Theory in Science

Classically, the scientific method follows a cycle in which people observe phenomena within nature and notice regularities. People then infer causal theories about these regularities. People then deduce hypotheses from theories and subject the hypotheses to experimental evaluation, allowing theories to be falsified. The theories are modified or replaced, and the scientific process continues toward ever more accurate and comprehensive theories of nature. Theories have three roles to play in the furtherance of knowledge: They explain what is already known; they predict what will happen in unknown situations, and they generate the discovery of novel situations.

HCI is a particularly challenging domain for the development of scientific theory. It is an interdisciplinary domain, where the sciences of psychology and computer science meet in a context driven by continual advances in electronic engineering, chemistry, and physics. Commercial and technological changes mean that the scope of phenomena is changing at a rate far faster than in any other scientific domain. We can hardly be surprised that theories have had difficulty in fulfilling even their basic explanatory role, let alone predicting the unknown and generating the new. The sciences of psychology and computer science are also comparatively young and

are notably divided within themselves; thus, HCI is faced with the difficulties of communication and conceptual focus between different theorists within these two parent disciplines.

The very difficulty of developing theory within a rapidly changing domain is an attractive feature for many researchers. As an applied field, HCI does hold out the prospect of fruitfully applying theoretical predictions in novel technologies and making a real difference to society. Economically, an HCI technology that has been developed with some theoretical basis is more likely to succeed than one that has been driven by feasibility alone. Attractions also exist for theorists who wish to remain within the parent disciplines but who seek new phenomena to test and to extend existing theories. Psychologists can explore perception, attention, memory, and learning within the context of entirely novel situations or virtual reconstructions of known situations, where many variables can be controlled with much greater precision than in real-world counterparts. Computer scientists can explore the behavior of complex systems when faced with the apparent unpredictability of human operators and organizations, and evaluate the robustness of architectures in the context of technological implementation. These opportunities may be justification for the use of HCI as a domain for scientific investigation, but they do not require a theory of HCI, and without a theory, HCI is not a scientific discipline.

A theory consists of a definition of the phenomenon that it intends to explain and of the things in the world that are thought to be involved in causing the phenomenon or that are affected by it (the theoretical entities). Crucially, a theory also defines the relationships between entities, so that if the states of all of the relevant entities are known for a particular moment, the theory allows predictions to be made about the future for these entities within a certain time frame. The scope of the phenomenon and of the entities involved marks out the domain of the theory: the range of things that it is intended to deal with. These entities can have distinct and measurable states, or values, that vary in time and so define the variables that can be measured and used in experiments.

Theories are abstract rules that people infer from many particular instances or observations but that are thought to hold true in general for all instances. They can therefore be tested by deducing specific hypotheses about situations that have not yet been observed and by applying a general rule to predict what will happen. People can then set up a situation (by controlling the values or states of the variables that a theory defines as causative) and observe the outcome. Such tests of hypotheses are called "experiments," and they provide empirical tests of the applicability of a theory.

If the outcome differs from that predicted by the theory, then it has been falsified and needs to be modified. This result may require a minor alteration to some small part of a theory, or it may require a major alteration. The result may be catered for by a situation-specific additional rule or the incorporation of an additional variable. Over time the incremental addition of specific rules and variables may lead the theory as a whole to become internally contradictory or unable to make clear predictions for as-yet-unobserved situations. At some point the theory will be rejected, and, instead of being modified, it will be replaced by a new theory. The new theory might start with a completely different set of entities and variables to explain the same phenomena as the old theory but in a more economical manner. It might divide the phenomena in a different way, so that the observable events that are thought worth explaining are not the same as those explained by the old theory, even though the domain may be the same.

If the outcome of an experiment is in line with the theoretical prediction, then the theory is supported but cannot logically be said to have been proven true because other reasons may exist for why results turned out as they did. The best that we can say is that the theory has received empirical support. Not all hypothetical predictions provide equally strong empirical tests of a hypothesis: We need to take into account the likelihood of the predicted outcome, compared to the likelihood of outcomes that would falsify the hypothesis. If a large range of outcomes that are consistent with the hypothesis and a small number of potentially falsifying outcomes exist, then the prediction is not very useful because it does not give us much certainty in the particular outcome. The worst theories are those that account for all possible outcomes because such theories cannot be falsified. Theories have to be potentially falsifiable to be accepted scientifically: An unfalsifiable theory may have great explanatory power, but it has no predictive power and cannot generate new discoveries.

The longer that a theory survives without substantial falsification, the more likely it is to be taken as true, especially if supporting evidence for it comes from quite different applications of the theory in apparently different phenomena. Converging evidence from different problems is the strongest support for a theory because it points to its generality and hence its value in economically explaining the behavior of a large number of variables by a smaller number of entities and rules.

The true value of scientific theory for society lies beyond the purely scientific desire to explain causal relationships in nature. Theories' definitions of phenomena, and of entities, provide a conceptual framework that can direct investigations and hence generate the discovery of novel phenomena that also need explanation. Theories, therefore, continually widen the scope of things that need to be explained, potentially leading to their own rejection. The discovery of new phenomena, the construction of new technologies, and the improvement of existing technologies follow from this generative power of theory.

The Development of Theory in HCI

Over time, developments in technology have meant that the interaction between human and computer has taken three forms. Originally, computers were large and expensive machines shared by expert users to perform well-defined tasks in corporate settings. These computers then developed into cheaper personal computers used by a single person to perform many varied tasks. They are now becoming fashionable consumer products, used by individuals to communicate in many settings, not least for entertainment and enjoyment rather than work (mobile phones, electronic organizers, and music players are all small, powerful computers with generic abilities but niche-specific hardware). HCI theory has had to keep pace with these changes.

People could address the first two forms by considering the interaction between a single person and a single computer, often a single software program. Researchers dealt with ergonomic considerations of input and output modalities in isolation, without needing to consider the interaction itself. Psychologists theorized about the human side of the interaction and computer scientists theorized about the computer side of the interaction. Initial HCI theory was thus heavily influenced by the dominant theoretical positions within the parent disciplines and tended to consider the two sides of the interaction independently rather than the interaction itself.

From psychology, information-processing models of cognition provided an attractive way to construct a model of what might be happening in a user's head during an interaction. Psychologists Stuart Card, Thomas Moran, and Alan Newell defined a "model human processor" that, in analogy with computing devices, perceived events on a computer screen, processed the information, formed goals, decided how to carry them out, and executed actions through a keyboard (and later through a mouse). Each cognitive operation required a specified time to execute, estimated from the psychological literature, and by specifying exactly what sequence of operations was required to perform a task, an analyst could work out how long the entire task would take (this results in what has become known as a "keystroke-level model," although what is actually being modeled are the internal mental operations). The model human processor gave rise to the GOMS approach to HCI: Goals are achieved through a sequence of Operators, which are collected into Methods, which are chosen through the use of Selection rules. GOMS models took a well-understood task to be performed by an expert and predicted how long the task should take. They were thus well suited to qualitative evaluations of design alternatives typical during the first phase of HCI, where implementation was expensive and tasks well defined. As the second phase developed, the weaknesses of GOMS models became more apparent. They said little about how information was acquired or structured, and they said little about the interaction at a higher level than task execution. This type of theory tended to have high predictive power within its domain, but as the domain altered to include different types of users and less-understood tasks, its predictive power waned, and its lack of generative ability become more obvious.

Psychologist Don Norman defined a more abstract theory for the second phase of HCI, in which an interaction was seen as a set of seven stages, organized into two gulfs that divided the users' minds from the world in which they were acting. The gulf of execution spanned the stages of goal formation, intention to act, action specification, and action execution and resulted in a person making some change to the state of the world (that is, interacting with a device). The gulf of evaluation spanned the stages of perceiving the new state of the world (or device), interpreting the changes, and evaluating the outcome to compare it with the original goal. The cycle could then continue, with the modification of the original goal or the formation of new goals. This theory was more generative than the GOMS approach because the seven stages corresponded to design questions that researchers could use to guide design as well as evaluate it. Norman listed these questions as asking how easily one could determine a device's function, identify the actions that are possible, infer the relationships between intention and action, perform the actions, identify system states, compare system states and intended states, and define the relationship between system state and interpretation.

Inherent in Norman's theory was the idea of a user's mental model of a device, a recognition that people base their actions not on an immediate evaluation of the observable state of the world but rather on their inferences about unobservable internal states of other entities, derived from previously observed aspects. This recognition held people to be natural scientists who develop causal theories to simplify the complexity of their observable world and help them predict what is about to happen and how they can behave to influence it. This recognition was consistent with the mental models approach in cognitive psychology advocated by Philip Johnson-Laird, along with the literature on errors in human reasoning caused by phenomena such as confirmation bias, by which people fail to search for evidence that will falsify their models of the world and thus can persist with false models. A false model of the state of a computer system will, sooner or later, lead to an interaction error, the learning of an inefficient action execution (in GOMS terms), or the failure to discover system functions. The task of the designer is, in this view, to help the user to build an appropriate model by making the unobservable and observable aspects of the system correspond closely. Norman used this approach to advocate user-centered design, in which design is focused on the needs of users, the tasks that they are to perform, and their ability to understand the device, and also seeks to involve them throughout the design process.

Newer Developments

By the time these theories had matured and had influenced HCI, the pace of change was already moving the field away from the dyad (pairing) of one user and one computer to more socially interactive situations in which technological devices supported communication between humans in a variety of roles, typified by the field of computer-supported cooperative work (CSCW). The models borrowed from cognitive psychology had little to say about such use. Indeed, within psychology itself a divide exists between those people who study the workings of an individual mind and those people who study the social interactions of individuals. During the 1990s HCI researchers turned to social psychology—and to the social sciences in general—to find conceptual methods to suit these wider contexts of interaction.

One method that focused on the contextualized nature of HCI drew from the developmental psychology of Lev Vygotsky. He had proposed that, instead of occurring through a series of maturational stages, competencies develop independently in different domains, with little transfer of skills between domains. Children can be at different stages of development in each domain, and what is critical is their zone of proximal development, the difference between what they are already able to do and what they would be able to learn to do if presented with the challenge. Much of device use is discovering what the device can do, and activity theory applies Vygotsky's ideas about development to knowledge acquisition in general. Scandinavian and eastern European researchers, who had (for political and cultural reasons) a traditional focus upon group and

work psychology, first applied activity theory to HCI. Psychologist Susanne Bødker shaped the approach to focus on the computing device as mediating human activity, where activity can be construed as the development of expertise or knowledge in specific contextual domains.

Sociologist Lucy Suchman compared HCI with other forms of situated action, where people are able to apply sophisticated, situation-specific skills and knowledge without needing to have a mental model or any naïve theory to drive their planning. Suchman proposed that much behavior is fitted to the immediate demands of a situation, rather than being shaped by a higher goal. Behavior that appears to be rationally based and coherently directed to a particular goal is actually determined by local factors, and in particular by the social and cultural context of the moment at which decisions need to be made. Although plans do exist and can be used to guide one's behavior, they are just one resource among many other sources of information about the most appropriate action to take next.

Suchman's work was based in a sociological technique called "ethnomethodology." This technique seeks to understand how people make sense of their world. In this way ethnomethodology is similar to the mental models approach in seeing the person as a theorist, but it takes the social interaction between individuals as its focus rather than causation in general. Applied to HCI, especially by psychologist Paul Dourish and sociologist Graham Button, ethnomethodology addresses the nature of work and the communication between workers who are to use a technological system. Designing the system is not so much an analysis of the functionality required and how best to provide it as an analysis of the flow of information between workers (or in general, people) and how to facilitate it.

Prospects for Theory in HCI

Although the more socially oriented theories of HCI have explanatory power, especially in the hands of their proponents, they have not yet proven themselves in terms of predictive or generative power; it is too early for us to decide whether any of the approaches will survive in their current form or whether they will need to be further adapted to the peculiar demands of HCI, with its rapid progression of technological context. HCI certainly has changed decisively from the simpler information-processing models of the 1980s, and phenomena of social interaction and communication are now key parts of the domain.

We may have to concede that HCI is not a single discipline amenable to a single body of theory and that it will, like other applied sciences, continue to adapt and borrow theories from its parent disciplines, modifying them and applying them even after psychology, sociology, and computer science have moved on to other approaches. This pattern of one-way communication between basic science and applied science would weaken the claim that HCI is a valuable domain for basic scientists to explore and evaluate their theories.

Psychologist Philip Barnard and colleagues have proposed that what HCI needs is not a single theory because the domain includes phenomena that are being described at several levels of systemic complexity. Just as psychology has its own theories for dealing with different levels of analysis of human behavior, ranging from neuropsychology through cognitive psychology to social and organizational psychology, so HCI needs theories that deal with the traditional dyadic interactions of users and their devices, people communicating through devices, and communities interacting as groups. Each level of the system requires its own type of theory, but a new form of theory is needed to map between the concepts at different levels of theorizing. Plenty of competing theories exist for different levels, but little communication exists between them. In recognizing the need to incorporate social psychological and sociological theorizing into HCI, we would make a mistake in discarding the existing body of cognitive and system theory simply because it does not address the new levels of interest.

The task for future HCI researchers is to find ways of communicating between the phenomena explained, predicted, and generated by each different level of theory. If HCI could succeed in this, it would acquire a conceptual unity as a science and would also make a major contribution to science.

Jon May

See also Computer-Supported Cooperative Work; Psychology and HCI; Social Psychology and HCI

FURTHER READING

Barnard, P. J., May, J., Duke, D., & Duce, D. (2000). Systems, interactions and macrotheory. *ACM Transactions on Computer Human Interaction, 7,* 222–262.

Bødker, S. (1991). *Through the interface: A human activity approach to user interface design.* Hillsdale, NJ: Lawrence Erlbaum Associates.

Card, S. K., Moran, T. P., & Newell, A. (1983). *The psychology of human-computer interaction.* Hillsdale, NJ: Erlbaum.

Dourish, P., & Button, G. (1998). On "technomethodology": Foundational relationships between ethnomethodology and system design. *Human-Computer Interaction, 13*(4), 395–432.

Norman, D. A. (1988). *The design of everyday things.* Boston: MIT Press.

Suchman, L. A. (1987). *Plans and situated actions: The problem of human-machine communication.* New York: Cambridge University Press.

THREE-DIMENSIONAL GRAPHICS

Three-dimensional (3D) computer graphics involves the generation of images of 3D objects within a scene. As opposed to two-dimensional (2D) image processing and editing applications, such as Adobe Photoshop and Jasc's Paintshop Pro, 3D computer graphics applications focus on creating output that have objects appear solid or 3D. The resulting images can be found in many everyday products, such as video games, movies, cell phones, and theme park rides.

Three-dimensional computer graphics can be defined as computer output through graphic images that appears "solid" or three-dimensional. Typically, this involves creating a 2D image (on a monitor, a poster, or movie screen, as examples) that represents a view of the 3D scene from some vantage (the viewpoint). There exist true 3D "volumetric" display systems such as holography and uncommon devices such as a verifocal mirror, but they are not yet significant for human computer interaction. The most common technologies that can present dynamic, large 3D computer graphics include monitors, data and movie projectors, televisions, and head mounted displays. Each of these allows different types of interaction and levels of immersion.

Generating 2D Images

The goal of designers is to generate a 2D image of a 3D scene; that is, given a 3D scene, and a position and orientation of a virtual camera, we need to compute the camera's resulting 2D image. The image is composed of discrete elements called *pixels*, and we look to compute the correct color for each pixel. This is similar to taking a virtual camera snapshot of the virtual scene.

A 3D scene is composed of a set of 3D objects. An object is typically described as a set of *geometric primitives* (basic elements understood by the system) that define the surface of the objects (*surface models*) or as volume information (*volumetric models*—typically found in medical applications). Each approach has advantages, though surface models are the most common for interactive and photorealistic applications.

To generate a 2D view of a 3D scene, systems pass the scene objects through a *graphics pipeline*. The different stages in this pipeline depend on the fundamental approaches to the image-generation method being used: forward rendering or backward rendering (*ray tracing*). Ray tracing is commonly used for photorealistic, non-real-time image generation. Ray tracing traces the rays of light that would land on a pixel. Most backward-rendering approaches, while capable of generating extremely realistic looking images, do not operate in real time, and thus do not allow a high level of interaction. For example, watching movies—though they may contain high quality 3D computer graphics—is a passive experience for the audience. More relevant for HCI are forward-rendering approaches used in most interactive applications. The forward-rendering graphics pipeline has several stages through which the scene primitives pass. The pipeline described here is a basic one followed by the common standards OpenGL and DirectX. There exist variations to this pipeline, such as those in multigraphics processor systems, but all share the same basic premise. Each object for the scene is already defined in its own local Cartesian coordinate space, in terms of the relative positions of its features along *x*, *y*, and *z* dimensions. The first stage is to *transform* each object into its appropriate location in a global or world coordinate system. This transformation is done through multiplying the vertices of a model by a model transformation matrix. This transformation, in effect, places each object in the 3D scene. Given a virtual camera's position, orientation, and intrinsic (such as resolution, aspect ratio, etc.) parameters, the 3D scene is then transformed into a viewing or camera coordinate system (another transformation matrix multiplication).

The next stage is to *project* each object primitive onto the virtual camera's image plane. To do this each primitive undergoes a projection (typically a perspective projection, though there are others, such as orthographic projection). Finally, those primitives are labeled as either being within the camera's view frustum (the part of the scene that is inside the camera's field of view), partially in the view frustum (requires *clipping*), or completely out of the view frustum (reject). That is, we know which pixels are being projected onto by a given primitive.

Finally, the primitives are *rasterized*, that is, transformed into a grid of pixels (picture elements) properly arranged in *x* and *y* coordinates to be displayed on a computer screen or similar device. This involves setting pixel color values in a file or, more typically, in a block of memory, such as a *frame buffer*. For a given primitive, the pixels it projects onto have their color values set depending on the lighting and several primitive properties, such as depth (is it the closest primitive to the camera for a given pixel), materials, textures, and transparency. Lighting and texture mapping, applying images such as photos onto a primitive, help increase the perceived realism of the scene by providing additional 3D depth cues.

After each primitive is passed through this pipeline, the scene has been rendered, and the image is complete. The next frame begins completely anew, and each primitive is again passed through the entire pipeline. For interactive applications this process is done several times a second (*frame rate*), at least 10 Hz (10 frames per second), and optimally at 30 or 60 Hz. Other visual presentation properties include: image color, resolution, contrast brightness, field of view (FOV), visual accuracy, and latency (time from receiving input to display of appropriate image).

Perceiving 3D from 2D Images

But how can humans perceive three-dimensional information from these two-dimensional output images? Humans use a variety of cues within images to capture 3D information of the scene. These *depth cues* are divided into cues within a single image (monoscopic), two images of a scene taken at the same time from different positions (stereoscopic), a series of images (motion), and changes in the physical body (physiological). Only a brief summary from Sherman and Craig is included here.

Monoscopic depth cues (cues within a single image) include:

- *Interposition*—an object that occludes another is closer
- *Shading*—interplay of light and shadows on a surface gives shape information
- *Size*—usually, the larger objects are closer
- *Linear perspective*—parallel lines converge at a single point
- *Surface texture gradient*—usually, there is more detail for closer objects
- *Height in the visual field*—usually, the higher (vertically) objects in the image are farther
- *Atmospheric effects*—usually, the blurrier objects are farther
- *Brightness*—usually, the dimmer objects are farther
- *Interposition, shading, and size* are the most prominent depth cues.

Stereoscopic depth cues (cues within two images of the scene, taken at the same time) are based on the fact that each of our eyes sees a different, laterally displaced, image of the world. When we focus on a point, called the *fixation point*, it appears at the center of the retina of both eyes. All other objects will appear at *different* places on the two retinas. The brain correlates the differences in an object's position on the retinas as depth information. Note that this is similar to the computer vision approach of depth from stereo. Stereo depth cues can be simulated by generating two images that mimic the different views of the scene from each eye. Then the user's left eye is presented with *only* the left-eye image, and the right eye with only the right-eye image. Presented with the differing images, the user then *fuses* the images to perceive a 3D scene. Some people have problems with their binocular vision or stereovision and might not be able to perceive a single 3D view from the two stereo images.

In generating the correct image for each eye, the system must take into account many factors, including the distance between user's eyes (interpupilary distance), the fixation point, and distance to display surface. As these factors vary per person—and in the case of the fixation point, the factor is continually varying—always generating the *correct* image is impossible. Fortunately, a simple approximation of always focusing "at infinity" and assuming that the user's view direction is perpendicular to, and passes through the center of, the image plane can create images that work for a majority of situations.

Instead of rendering the user's view from a single point, two images are rendered, typically the left eye with a (interpupilary distance/2) translation applied in the –*x* dimension, and the right eye with (interpupilary distance/2) in the +*x* dimension. This does limit the amount of separation (visual angle) that an object can have between the two images before it can no longer be fused, thus limiting how close an object can be to the user. Further, if any other assumption (such as interpupilary distance) is not measured accurately or updated appropriately, the *perceived* location of an object rendered in stereo will be different than its *modeled* location.

There are several different methods to present these stereo image pairs to the user, such that each eye receives its appropriate image. Time-parallel methods present both images to the user at the same time. Head Mounted Displays (HMD) are devices with two displays mounted within inches of the user's eyes. The stereo images are displayed on the two screens. The old View-Master stereograph viewer operated on similar principles.

Other time-parallel approaches display both images superimposed on one screen. Anaglyph approaches use colored lens (e.g., red and blue) filters fitted into glasses worn by the user. The two images are rendered in either blue (left) or red (right). The red lens filter on the left eye blocks out the red image, and thus the left eye sees only the blue image. The blue lens works similarly for the right image. A similar approach can be achieved using polarized lenses. Images are projected through a polarizing lens (either circular or linear polarized, where one lens is rotated 90 degrees with respect to the other) that allows only light vibrating in a certain axis to pass through. The user wears glasses with similar polarizing lenses that allow only the image for the appropriate eye to pass through. These are *passive stereoscopic* approaches.

Another method is to use time-multiplexed projection, in which the two stereo images are rendered and projected one at a time, in sequence (left eye then the right eye). "Shutter" glasses are worn to channel the correct image to the appropriate eye. Most commercial glasses have LCD panels that are either open to let light through, or when signaled, they activate the LCD panels to block out light. The glasses are synchronized with the display (e.g., using infrared emitters) to ensure the correct image is completely visible before the LCD is open for that eye. This is an *active stereoscopic* approach. There are advantages and disadvantages to the different stereoscopic approaches: 3D fidelity, accuracy, and the dynamics of the rendered scene, and varying costs.

Motion depth cues are signals found in a sequence of images that provide 3D information of the scene. Motion parallax is the fact that objects nearer to the eye will move a greater distance across the retina over some period of time compared with objects farther away. Motion parallax is generated when either the object being viewed moves in relation to the user or vice versa. This can be observed by looking out the passenger-side window of an automobile as it is moving. Nearby cars, signs, and stores will move a greater distance over some time as would objects farther away, such as large skyscrapers, clouds, and mountains.

Finally, physiological depth cues are physical changes in the body when we focus on point in the scene. *Accommodation* is the changing of the shape of the lens of the eye to focus on an object. *Convergence* is the rotation of the eye such that the fixation point or object is in the center of the retina for each eye. These cues are typically weaker than the previously discussed cues and are difficult to simulate with computer graphics.

Interacting with 3D graphics

The most common inputs for interacting with 3D graphics are the following:

- Changing the viewpoint of the scene
- Interacting with the scene
- Issuing a system command

Most methods use traditional 2D devices, such as keyboard, mice buttons, and joystick buttons, to issue commands to the system. More advanced virtual reality systems use complex interaction devices. Examples of commands are toggling a rendering option, loading a model, and deleting a selected object. Typically, these commands are located on a *graphical user interface*—an interface to the program that is a combination of 2D and 3D controls called *widgets*.

Changing the viewpoint, or *navigation*, is typically controlled with an additional device, such as a mouse, keyboard, joystick, tracking system, or haptic feedback device. The viewpoint of most interactive programs either is from a first-person, inside-looking-out perspective or a third-person, outside-looking-in perspective. Referring back to the rendering pipeline, navigation involves simply changing the position and orientation of the camera that is viewing the scene. The new updated pose of the camera is used to render each frame.

A first-person viewpoint is analogous to seeing the virtual scene from the perspective of a virtual character or vehicle. Most of the navigation is to simulate walking or flying. The most common navigation method is to have a set of controls handle the direction the character is facing (e.g., the mouse) and an additional set of controls for translation along the view direction and an axis perpendicular to the view direction. Flying has the viewpoint translate along the view direction. Walking is similar, but the viewpoint is "clamped" to a height range from the ground plane. First-person "shooter" video games typically employ a mouse + keyboard or joystick combination for navigation.

The third-person perspective, or trackball style navigation, has the camera move about a sphere that circumscribes the objects of interest. This movement has the effect of always having the object of interest be in the center of the rendered image. This technique is common in scientific visualization, medical imaging, engineering, and design applications. In these tasks the goal is to provide the user with a broader perspective of the model, as opposed to the first-person perspective, which tries to immerse the user inside the virtual scene.

The final type of system input is interacting with the scene. Examples of scene interaction include selecting an object (*picking*) and affecting objects and systems. Picking, that is, using a cursor to select an object, determines the first object that is intersected by a ray from the camera location through the cursor. Each application has different methods in which a user may to interact with virtual objects and systems (e.g., physics simulation). Typically, most systems try to incorporate interaction mnemonics that are effective, natural, consistent, and make sense.

Future Directions

While the mouse, keyboard, and joystick are the most common devices to interact with the scene, for many tasks, they are not the most *natural*. Is natural interaction important? How can interface designers create natural interactions for potentially complex tasks? Doing so is complicated by tasks that have no physical equivalent, such as deleting or scaling. Researchers are continually evaluating new widgets, controls, and devices. As computer graphics applications work with increasingly more complex data, interaction requirements will increase. Examples include being able to handle 3D environments, haptic feedback, and multisensory output. Poor interaction choices can reduce the efficacy of a system for training, ease of use, immersion, and learning. These are all critical research topics in the short term and long term for computer graphics human-computer interaction.

Benjamin Lok

See also Animation; Virtual Reality

FURTHER READING

Bowman, D., & Hodges, L. (1997). An evaluation of techniques for grabbing and manipulating remote objects in immersive virtual environments. *1997 ACM Symposium on Interactive 3-D Graphics*, 35–38.

Eberly, D. (2000). *3D game engine design: A practical Approach to real-time computer graphics*. San Francisco: Morgan Kaufmann.

Faugeras, O., Vieville, T., Theron, E., Vuillemin, J., Hotz, B., Zhang, Z., et al. (1993). Real-time correlation-based stereo: Algorithm, implementations and applications. *INRIA Technical Report* RR–2013.

Foley, J., van Dam, A., Feiner, S., & Hughes, J. (1995). *Computer graphics: Principles and practice* (2nd ed.). Reading, MA: Addison-Wesley.

Hand, C. (1997). A survey of 3-D interaction techniques. *Computer Graphics Forum, 16*(5), 269–281.

Hearn, D., & Baker, M. (1996). *Computer graphics with OpenGL* (3rd ed). Upper Saddle River, NJ: Prentice Hall.

Lindeman, R., Sibert, J., & Hahn, J. (1999). Hand-held windows: Towards effective 2D interaction in immersive virtual environments. *IEEE Virtual Reality* (pp. 205–212).

Mine, M., Brooks, F., & Sequin, C. (1997). Moving objects in space: Exploiting proprioception in virtual-environment interaction. *Proceedings of SIGGRAPH 97*. Retrieved on November 4, 2003, from http://www.cs.unc.edu/~mine/papers/minecows.pdf.

Sherman, W., & Craig, A. (2003). *Understanding virtual reality: Interface, application, and design*. Boston: Morgan Kaufmann.

Watt, A. (1993). *3D computer graphics* (2nd ed.). New York: Addison-Wesley.

Woo, M., Neider, J., Davis, T., & Shreiner, D. (1999). *OpenGL® programming guide: The official guide to learning OpenGL, version 1.4* (4th ed.). Reading, MA: Addison-Wesley.

THREE-DIMENSIONAL PRINTING

Computer output can take the form of bright images on a monitor screen, printed words on a page, music and other sounds from a loudspeaker or headset, and even physical movements and pressures from a haptic (relating to the sense of touch) device. Thus, not surprisingly many people have imagined that three-dimensional physical objects could be printed. After pioneering research by many groups and individuals, in 1987 Charles Hull and the 3D Systems company produced the first commercial three-dimensional printer. It employed a process called "stereolithography" that constructs objects gradually, building them up layer by layer by using a laser beam to selectively solidify some of the liquid resin or plastic in a vatlike construction chamber. During the next few years many teams developed a range of other processes with different materials and with different advantages and disadvantages.

Applications

At present the most commonly used term for three-dimensional printing technology is "rapid prototyping" because creating prototypes as part of the industrial design process was initially the most significant commercial application. Among the great variety of machines that has been developed are some machines called "concept modelers" because they can rapidly and cheaply produce an object the same shape and size of the final product, but usually from flimsy materials that cannot stand the stresses experienced in performing the function of the final product itself. Concept models are good for assessing the aesthetics of the design because several can be made in a short time with varying shapes, and they can help designers see how well their design fits physically with the other parts that will form the final product.

Functional modelers, in contrast, produce objects that have physical properties close to those of the final mass-produced product, although they often are not as durable and may lack one or more features such as color. Objects produced by functional modelers are often realistic enough to be presented to corporate management for decisions about producing the final product, to be used in test models to refine features of the overall design, and to be photographed for promotional advertising before the assembly line has turned out the first production examples. Functional modelers tend to be slower than concept modelers, and a single object can take hours to print out, but using a functional modeler is much quicker than machining a prototype by hand. Textbooks on rapid prototyping using methods such as stereolithography are filled with examples in which the design team of a manufacturing corporation was able to save weeks and many thousands of dollars by using this technology. In the twenty-first-century commercial world of quickly changing competition and consumer demand, a few weeks can be crucial for success in the market.

In addition to its value in the design process, three-dimensional printing has two related applications in creating the tooling for mass production. In the first application, even flimsy-but-accurate models can be used as patterns for making molds in which to cast manufactured parts. One common method of casting, investment casting, was discovered thousands of years ago and used to great effect by artists in ancient Greece. In the version called the "lost wax technique," a Greek sculptor or artisan would carve a wax model of a statue or piece of jewelry, then encase it in plaster or a similar substance that could endure high temperatures. After the plaster had set, heat would melt the wax, and molten metal could be poured into the mold that held the shape of the lost wax model. Today molds for casting limited test runs, or even major production runs, are often produced from models printed out from computer designs, sometimes made from wax but often from more modern materials. In the second application, not a pattern but rather a tool is printed out to make the part such as a mold, and some three-dimensional printers can make molds directly from metal that is durable enough for injection molding of plastic articles.

Many challenges must be overcome before three-dimensional printing can be used extensively for direct manufacturing of products, rather than just for prototyping and for making tools. How, for example, can stereolithography compete with injection molding in the manufacture of a hundred thousand plastic parts? It is too slow and too costly. A good analogy is ordinary two-dimensional printing. If one wants a hundred copies of a newsletter, one would probably print one copy on a desktop laser printer, then run off the other ninety-nine on a photocopier to save both time and money. If one wants to print a hundred thousand copies of a newspaper, then neither laser printers nor photocopiers are cost effective—although both laser printing and photocopying are used to prepare drafts of today's edition of the newspaper for the high-speed printing press.

However, some functional modelers produce precise objects from fairly strong materials, and significant financial investment almost certainly can transform some of the technologies into good methods for manufacturing certain kinds of products.

Other methods clearly will continue to be more profitable for really large-scale mass production. However, in the modern world significant markets exist for short runs of distinctive manufactured products, including some markets where the ideal would be to manufacture a large number of objects, none of which was exactly identical in shape to another. After three-dimensional printing was further developed by being applied to some initially profitable industries, presumably the technology would evolve into a better competitor in other areas as well.

One apparent success story is the use of stereolithography to produce the orthodontic plastic teeth aligners that are used to gradually move an adult's teeth into proper position. As with more traditional techniques, the process starts when a dentist makes a mold of the patient's crooked teeth. At the dental lab plastic is poured into this mold, and the result is scanned into a computer. Special software calculates how the teeth will have to move, in many tiny steps, during the months of orthodontic treatment. Then stereolithography produces a set of aligners for the patient, one aligner for each of those steps and no two alike. The patient wears each aligner for a month or so, in proper order, and they straighten the teeth without need for wire braces. This application clearly exploits the versatility of stereolithography, and it challenges us to think of all the other near-term applications that might benefit from its advantages.

Methods

The process of three-dimensional printing begins with a computer. All three-dimensional printers are precisely controlled by a computer, and this technology was impossible before the widespread use of small computers in the 1980s. Generally an object is designed using computer-aided design (CAD) software. Surface detail can be added by scanning in artwork, or the specifications for the entire object even can be scanned in from a sample. The most striking examples are the specifications of human skulls, measured without harming their owners by means of computerized tomography (CT) scans, which are entered into computers so that plastic duplicates can help surgeons plan brain surgery.

After the object's shape has been computerized, the data are generally transformed into a format called "STL" (originally developed for stereolithography but now used with other methods as well), which represents the object's surfaces as a large number of connected triangles. Curved surfaces are only approximated by these triangles, and greater accuracy can be achieved by using a greater number of smaller triangles, at the cost of increased file size and slower calculations. The STL representation is then transformed again into what is essentially a pile of cross-sections, the laminations that the printer will actually sculpt.

The original stereolithography method exploits the fact that some liquid resins (several plastic materials, including epoxies) can solidify when a laser beam of the right strength and color is focused on them, a process known as "photopolymerization." Machines have many special features and components that deal with various technical problems, but the fundamental idea is as follows. The object will be built on a platform, set just below the surface of a vat of liquid resin, in a workspace similar in size to that of a household oven. A laser aims downward at the liquid resin while scanning across the surface under computer control, firing at any point where the very bottom slice of the object is supposed to be, solidifying the resin. When the first lamination has been completed, the platform moves downward a short distance, often less than a millimeter, and a new layer of liquid resin is spread over the top of it. The laser goes to work a second time, solidifying the second lamination. This process is repeated again and again, sometimes for several hours, until the very last lamination has been drawn at the top of the object.

Many details have to be handled properly. If parts of the object jut out, supports have to be built up to hold them in position, and these supports may have to be removed by hand later on. The object may still be somewhat soft when it comes out of the stereolithography, so it may need to be cured to its final hardness by shining an ultraviolet light on it for a while. A curved or angled surface on the side of the object unfortunately will look somewhat like a flight of stairs, each step representing one of the laminations. This same problem is often noticeable when diagonal lines are drawn on a computer screen: Because pixels (the small discrete elements that together constitute an image, as on a television or computer screen) are square, a diagonal line cannot be represented accurately. A solution that works for computer screens but not for stereolithography is antialiasing, which is the process of softening the stair-step appearance by placing along the edge of the line pixels that are intermediate in color between the line and the background. The equivalent of pixels in three-dimensional printing are voxels (volume pixels, cubes rather than squares), and three-dimensional printing has no way to make a cube of epoxy that only half exists. Two effective but costly solutions are (1) making the object with a large number of thin laminations, which is extremely time consuming, and (2) making the problematic surfaces slightly too large and then grinding off the stair-step ridges mechanically in an extra process.

Among the many alternatives to resin-solidifying stereolithography, laser sintering (causing to become a coherent mass by heating without melting) has significant advantages. Instead of liquid resin a solid powder is used. A laser heats powder particles just enough for them to soften and blend into each other, not necessarily fully melting them. The untouched powder remains in place, sometimes serving to support extended parts of the growing object, until the process is complete and the untouched powder can be swept away. Laser sintering works well with some metal alloys, allowing the process to make rather strong and durable objects. Some low-cost computerized fabrication devices cut the laminations from solid layers of paper or plastic foam by means of a laser or even a sharp knife blade. Other devices follow the principle of ink-jet printers and squirt controlled droplets of a hardener liquid onto a powder. Researchers are experimenting on approaches that avoid layering altogether, for example, by squirting a hardening liquid from a printing head that can point at the growing object from any direction.

Future Prospects

We have every reason to expect that three-dimensional printing using current methods will gradu-

ally improve and be extended to a wider and wider range of manufacturing jobs. The popular media frequently claim that either a technical breakthrough or inspired engineering is about to launch onto the market a low-cost three-dimensional printer that could be used in schools or homes to manufacture art objects or kitchen crockery. Science fiction postulates that an entirely different method for manufacturing three-dimensional objects, based on nanotechnology (the art of manipulating materials on an atomic or molecular scale, especially to build microscopic devices), will be invented: universal assembler nanoscale robots that can be programmed to grab atoms and put them in the right positions to build absolutely anything.

Such wild ideas aside, even just the gradual progress of current photopolymerization stereolithography and laser sintering is almost certain to increase their scope for human creativity. Computer output is no longer limited to colors, lights, sounds, and spots of ink, but rather now includes physical objects. This progress opens new opportunities for human beings to use computers as the medium for expressing their boundless imaginations.

William Sims Bainbridge

See also Laser Printer; Three-Dimensional Graphics

FURTHER READING

Chua, C. K., Leong, K. F., & Lim, C. S. (2003). *Rapid prototyping: Principles and applications*. River Edge, NJ: World Scientific.

Cooper, K. G. (2001). *Rapid prototyping technology: Selection and application*. New York: Marcel Dekker.

Rise of the replicators. (2004). *Popular Science, 264*(2), 36–37.

Smalley, R. E. (2001). Of chemistry, love and nanobots. *Scientific American, 285*(3), 76–77.

Venuvinod, P. K., & Ma, W. (2004). *Rapid prototyping: Laser-based and other technologies*. Dordrecht, Netherlands: Kluwer.

TOUCHSCREEN

A touchscreen allows users to interact with a computer via touch. Because touchscreens, in essence,

This SMART Board interactive whiteboard uses touch-screen technology to navigate through a website.

merge a pointing device with a monitor, they can effectively eliminate the need for external input devices such as mice, keyboards, trackballs, or joysticks. Moreover, due to the naturalness of interaction through touch, well-designed touchscreen-based interfaces have low learning curves, making them effective devices for a variety of computer-based tasks.

Touchscreens function by converting a user's tactile interactions with a visual display into digital input, communicating the touch's location (e.g., an X coordinate and a Y coordinate). With some technologies, however, a third coordinate is returned providing a measure of the amount of pressure being applied to the surface of the screen or how far the user's finger is above the screen.

Samuel Hurst, a physicist at the University of Kentucky, is credited with the first implementation of a touchscreen in 1971. Hurst's touchscreen used a battery, metallic strips, and two sheets of conductive paper for the purpose of electronically plotting data coordinates. That same year Hurst founded Elographics (now Elo Touchsystems). Today dozens of manufacturers are developing touchscreens using a variety of technologies.

When creating touchscreens, five main technologies are used, each offering capabilities suiting it to specific tasks or environments:

1. Membrane or resistive touchscreens use two separated layers of conductive material. When a user presses on the upper layer, electricity flows between the two layers, allowing the system to determine the location of the user's finger. Resistive touchscreens are often used in tasks requiring high resolution and are particularly useful if users are wearing gloves.
2. Capacitive touchscreens use a single layer of material and detect changes in the amount of electric charge that can be stored to determine where the user is touching. Due to their resiliency, capacitive touchscreens typically find usage in high volume or abusive environments.
3. Surface acoustic wave (SAW) touchscreens use a single layer of material and rely on the energy absorption of the user's finger to sense the location of a touch. SAW touchscreens are an effective alternative if the application could benefit from information about how hard the user's finger is touching the screen or how high the user's finger is above the screen.
4. Infrared touchscreens place a frame containing infrared transmitters and receivers around the monitor. When a user's finger blocks infrared signals, the location of the finger can be computed. Infrared touchscreens are used in situations requiring high image quality, large displays, or functionality with a variety of selection devices. Infrared touchscreens are not an effective solution if high-resolution interactions are necessary.
5. Piezoelectric or strain gauge touchscreens place a pane of glass over a monitor and use pressure sensors at the corners of the monitor to determine the location of the touch. Strain gauge touchscreens allow for quick and inexpensive conversion of traditional monitors into touch-screens.

Which of these technologies is appropriate depends on the intended environment, users, cost, and functionality. Indeed, the adaptability of touchscreens to their intended use allows for their use in a wide variety of applications. Touchscreens can be found in home automation systems, personal digital assistants, automobiles, tablet PCs, interactive games, point-of-sale systems, retail kiosks, track pads, reservation systems, machine controllers, and voting machines.

When designed effectively, touchscreens allow for rapid interactions with minimal errors. When necessary, touchscreens also support high-resolution interactions. The natural style of interactions supported by touchscreens makes them ideal for applications that will be used by novices, such as information kiosks and voting machines. The ability to integrate the input device with the display makes touchscreens an effective alternative when external devices are unlikely to be effective, such as vehicle-based information systems and personal digital assistants. Accordingly, the touchscreen is an integral device in the human-computer interaction toolbox and the subject of both commercial and academic research.

Rich Goldman and Andrew Sears

FURTHER READING

Grebb, M. (2003). *The sleek touch*. Retrieved October 10, 2003, from http://www.ce.org/publications/vision/2003/sepoct/p10.asp

Moore, B. (2003). *Touch screen technology*. Retrieved October 10, 2003, from http://www.idat.com/a-touchtech.html

Sears, A., Plaisant, C., & Shneiderman, B. (1992). A new era for high precision touch screens. In H. R. Hartson & D. Hix (Eds.), *Advances in Human-Computer Interaction, 3*, 1–33. Norwood, NJ: Ablex.

Touchscreens.com. (2003). *What are touchscreens used for?* Retrieved October 10, 2003, from http://www.touchscreens.com/intro-uses.html

UBIQUITOUS COMPUTING

Ubiquitous computing, a relatively new field of computer science, proposes the notion that some form of computing can be present in all aspects of daily life. Also called "pervasive computing," ubiquitous computing seeks to embed computers of some sort everywhere around us in ways that are useful. We could find computation occurring in furniture, walls, electronic equipment, and even the body of humans and animals. Researchers hope that supporting computation away from the bounds of the conventional desktop environment can lead to the discovery of interesting and dynamic user experiences.

This broad definition of *ubiquitous computing* suggests a close relationship between the two fields of ubiquitous computing and mobile computing.

However, the inclusion of the phrases "in all aspects of daily life" and "everywhere around us" in the definition differentiates the two fields in that ubiquitous computing provides for applications within mobile computing and more. A mobile computing experience, for instance, is a traveler sending e-mail at an airport using a cell phone. With ubiquitous computing, however, travelers could use their cell phones to notify the airport's check-in system of their arrival. In turn, the system could provide travelers with directions to appropriate gates, given that the airport is large and contains various distributed sensors for locating people.

Goals

Two general goals of ubiquitous computing are: (1) convenience: to provide more effective ways to complete a task than can be achieved through the conventional way, thus yielding better user experiences, and (2) flexibility: to provide user experiences that are unsupported by conventional computing—or the desktop.

Since the inception of computers, one of their primary goals has been convenience. For example, Charles Babbage, the English mathematician and inventor, built an adding machine that provided a mechanical and automated means to performing arithmetic computations, and it eliminated the human error involved in such computations. Today computers have become smaller and more powerful and have taken on more tasks that were previously performed manually; for instance, we can now write, spell check, and save our compositions on computers. Ubiquitous computing extends this notion of convenience to everyday artifacts and environments, thereby making them smarter and context aware, which can subsequently simplify our interactions with them. It also provides us with the convenience of being able to work at locations beyond our desktops.

Flexibility has also been a key goal of conventional computing. For instance, today computers allow groups of people to simultaneously edit a document during a collaboration session. Embedding computers into artifacts that are found throughout our environment further extends this goal of flexibility because these artifacts are able to perform operations that they could not normally perform without computation power. The next few sections describe some classes of ubiquitous computing interaction. They contain examples that will show how these goals are closely related.

Beyond Desktop Computers

People often work by themselves and in groups away from their desks. This fact is the motivation for certain computing devices, which allow people to work away from their conventional desktop computers. These devices are built in various sizes and forms and serve a variety of purposes. Data and application windows can be transferred between these devices and desktop computers. Examples are mobile computers such as personal digital assistants (PDAs), tabs and pads, and pervasive stationary computing

devices. Tabs and pads are inch-scale devices, which are particularly useful in a meeting. A user could transfer project-specific information to them before attending the meeting, pass them around to other participants in the meeting, and transfer the stored information to other computers available at the meeting location.

Pervasive stationary devices support work though another approach—they are physically embedded in our environments and thus require users to be at their locations to use them. They can serve as electronic whiteboards for: (1) drawing and annotating during a group meeting, (2) large displays of content that must be simultaneously viewed by members of a group, (3) extensions of users' personal desktops or mobile computer screens, and (4) public kiosks for supporting tasks such as e-mail and Web surfing. Furthermore, they can be placed in a variety of locations. For instance, a meeting room could have these devices embedded in its walls, tables, and chairs; additionally, an airport could provide several Web kiosks throughout its sitting areas.

Smart Environments

Embedding computers into appliances and other artifacts within our environment can also allow them to provide smarter and more personal interactions with us. For example, a thermostat in a home could remember the temperature preferences of each of its inhabitants and personalize each room's temperature depending on who is in it. Also, small computers could be embedded into the frames of paintings in an art museum so that when people are near a painting, the computer plays a script describing the history of the painting and its artist. It may even have the ability to answer viewer questions.

Universal Service Interaction

Universal service interaction is the ability to use interactive (client) computers such as cell phones and handheld computers to interact with arbitrary and possibly remote services. Such services can be physical appliances (e.g., TVs, lights, and sensors) or software services. For example, a vacationer at a beach, realizing that it is raining at home, can turn the water sprinklers off using a handheld computer. Additionally, while on vacation, the vacationer is able to use the same handheld computer to control the appliances in a hotel room because it contains various preferences such as favorite TV channels. The airport check-in and directions system described earlier is an example of a software service.

I do not fear computers. I fear the lack of them.

—*Isaac Asimov*

Service composition is an extension of universal service interaction and involves performing operations that compose and connect a set of services together for the purposes of (1) more efficiently performing a task than individually interacting with each service and/or (2) forming a composite unit that provides functionality that is individually unsupported by the services. For example, before going on vacation, the vacationer could use the handheld computer to simultaneously query for all the home appliances that are on. The handheld computer could subsequently provide an operation for simultaneously turning off those appliances that are not essential while away. Also, a person might find it useful to compose a thermostat with sensors that can identify a person in a room to assist the thermostat in appropriately setting temperatures.

Wearable Computers

Small computers can also be embedded into objects that we wear, such as clothes and jewelry. For instance, a ring could contain storage chips that allow its owner to store data from one computer and transfer it to another. A shirt's collar could contain a small computer and microphone that allows the person wearing it to control appliances through speech. It could also support the recording of verbal memos and notes.

Tracking people and monitoring their bodily functions are other applications for wearable computers. For example, a pair of running shoes could contain specialized computers for tracking a runner's form, speed, and distance. Additionally, the run-

ner's watch could contain a computer that monitors heart rate, a feature that is already available today.

Service Discovery

Clearly, users must be aware of the existence of services they wish to interact with before they can use them. Without asking other people, how can users discover the availability of an interactive service in a given a network or physical space? The approaches to achieving this awareness fall between the two extremes of push and pull. In push-based discovery, information about the services that a system provides is automatically delivered (or pushed) to a user's computing device without any user request. For instance, the airport's check-in system could recognize the entry of travelers into the airport and deliver a list of the services it provides to their cell phones. With pull-based discovery, users must explicitly request (or pull) the available services over the network—that is, do a network search. Travelers, for example, would have to connect to the airport's network using their mobile computers that provide interfaces for performing searches for services.

Issues

The applications above raise several issues. In universal service interaction a service should ideally provide user interfaces (UIs) for all possible kinds of client devices. One approach to supporting this ability is to handcraft or manually program one or more UIs of a given service that execute on the set of target client devices. At interaction time, users are able to load these UIs from a remote machine on the fly or from the local storage of their computer. Another approach is to use a client-specific UI generator that creates a UI on the fly. Downloading and generating the UI allows users to interact with services they did not anticipate using and thus did not preinstall on their client computers. However, downloading the UI has the limitation that client devices not in a service's target set cannot be used to interact with it. This limitation is important because numerous kinds of cell phones and mobile computers are available today; furthermore, this set is constantly growing. Client-specific UI generators do not have this limitation and also require less programming. On the other hand, a UI generator can create UIs only in the presentation styles with which it was programmed. Handcrafted UIs, on the other hand, can be designed to the programmer's and device manufacturer's preferences and specifications.

In addition, if pervasive computing devices are to support sharing and moving of data, their builders, too, must address the differences among these devices. For example, supporting the transfer of program windows from desktop computers to tabs and pads involves handling the variability in display sizes and operating systems among them. Similarly, to allow flexible service composition, programmers must allow composition of heterogeneous services.

Heterogeneity also exists in users. Therefore, when implementing UIs for universal service interaction and deploying pervasive computing devices, their builders must address the special needs and differences among the users of their systems. For example, a speech-based UI may be more appropriate than a screen-based UI for a given user and vice versa. Also, people will find it useful for a Web kiosk in an airport to support different languages.

The kinds of network connections that a service uses to support interaction can also affect the kinds of users and tasks it can support. For example, if the water sprinklers were controllable only through a home wireless network, the vacationer could not deactivate them from afar. This raises the related issue of security.

Given the various applications listed earlier, we can generalize security into two aspects—service side and client side. Service-side security protects the service's host machine, such as a computer that hosts a software-based service or an actual device, from executing undesired operations submitted by users. For example, a public kiosk that allows a user to save information and later view it should prevent arbitrary users from accessing that user's information. The appliances in the vacationer's home should prevent strangers from controlling them. Client-side security protects the client machine from downloading "Trojan horse" programs that execute unauthorized or undesirable operations. For example, a traveler's cell phone should prevent arbitrary services from

being pushed onto it that perform operations such as extracting the traveler's call history and phone book.

Several ubiquitous computing applications involve the detection of users and their locations in a given environment. However, some users may not always want this detection; for instance, the example of airports using sensors to locate and track people inside it so that it can provide them with gate directions. Due to privacy concerns, some people in the airport may not wish to be tracked, or they may already know how to get to their gates. Therefore, the airport ideally would provide mechanisms that allow people to choose to be ignored.

Most of the preceding issues are open. For example, no universal service interaction system currently fully addresses the user and client heterogeneity issue while simultaneously incurring reasonably low implementation costs and avoiding limitations such as the users and presentation styles it can support. In conclusion, the open issues that ubiquitous computing presents are one of the reasons why it is currently a hot research area.

Olufisayo Omojokun and Prasun Dewan

See also Mobile Computing; Wearable Computer

FURTHER READING

Gemperle, F., Kasabach, C., Stivoric, J., Bauer, M., and Martin, R. (1998, October). Design for wearability. *Proceedings of the Second International Symposium on Wearable Computers,* 116–123.

Johanson, B., Fox, A., & Winograd, T. (2002, April). The interactive workspaces project: Experiences with ubiquitous computing rooms. *IEEE Pervasive Computing Magazine, 1*(2), 67–74.

Nichols, J., & Myers, B. (2003, May). Studying the use of handhelds to control smart appliances. *Proceedings of the 23rd International Conference on Distributed Computing Systems, Workshops,* 274–279.

Omojokun, O., & Dewan, P. (2003, May). Experiments with mobile computing middleware for deploying appliance UIs. *Proceedings of the 23rd International Conference on Distributed Computing Systems, Workshops,* 375–380.

Omojokun, O., Isbell, C., & Dewan, P. (2002). An architecture for supporting personalized agents in appliance interaction. In *Technical Report of the AAAI Symposium on Personalized Agents* (pp. 40–47). Menlo Park, CA: AAAI Press.

Tandler, P., Streitz, N., & Prante, T. (2002, November). Roomware: Moving toward ubiquitous computers. *IEEE Micro, 22*(6), 36–47.

Want, R., & Hopper, A. (1992, February). Active badges and personal interactive computing objects. *IEEE Transactions of Consumer Electronics* 38(1), 10–20.

Weiser, M. (1991, September). The computer for the twenty-first century. *Scientific American, 265*(3), 94–100.

Weiser, M. (1993, July). Some computer science problems in ubiquitous computing. *Communications of the ACM, 36*(7), 74–84.

UNICODE

The Unicode Standard is the universal character-encoding scheme for written characters and text. It defines a consistent way of encoding multilingual text for international data exchange and is used in all modern software, programming languages, and standards.

As the default encoding for HTML and XML, Unicode provides the character infrastructure of the World Wide Web. Unicode is required in new Internet protocols and implemented in all modern operating systems and computer languages. The emergence of the Unicode Standard and the availability of tools supporting it are among the most significant recent global software technology trends.

Character Coverage

The Unicode Standard encodes the letters, syllables, and ideographs used to write the world's languages, both modern and historic, as well as punctuation, notational systems, and symbols. It also includes the largest set of characters for mathematical and technical publishing in existence, and an extensive set of musical symbols. However, it does not encode logos, graphics, or graphologies unrelated to text. The Unicode Standard is chiefly arranged by individual scripts. (See Table 1.)

The writing systems of many languages have characters in common. To avoid duplicate encoding, the Unicode Standard assigns only one code to each letter, punctuation mark, diacritic, and so on, even when it is used in multiple languages.

The most notable example of character unification in the Unicode Standard is Unified Han, a collection of over seventy thousand ideographic characters used in written Chinese, Japanese, Korean,

TABLE 1. *Selected Scripts and the Languages that Use Them*

Script	Examples of Languages
Arabic	Arabic, Pashto, Persian (Farsi), Sindhi, historic Turkish, Uighur, Urdu
Bengali	Bengali (Bangla), Assamese
Canadian Aboriginal Syllabics	Inuktitut, Cree
Cyrillic	Russian, Bulgarian, Ukrainian
Devanagari	Hindi, Awadhi, Marathi, Nepali, Newari, Sanskrit, Santali
Gujarati	Gujarati
Hangul	Korean
Hebrew	Hebrew, Yiddish, Judezmo (Ladino)
Hiragana	Japanese
Ideographs (Unified Han)	Chinese, Japanese, Korean, historic Vietnamese
Katakana	Japanese
Latin	English, French, German, Indonesian, Italian, Malay, Polish, Portuguese, Spanish, Turkish, Vietnamese
Malayalam	Malayalam
Sinhala	Sinhala, Pali, Sanskrit
Tamil	Tamil, Badaga, Saurashtra
Thai	Thai, Kuy, Lanna Tai, Pali
Telugu	Telugu

and historic Vietnamese. Developed by an international group of experts, this is the largest character collection for East Asian languages in the history of computing. It encompasses over two thousand years of literary usage throughout East Asia, including all the main classical dictionaries.

Character Encoding and Semantics

On a computer, characters are encoded internally as numbers. The numeric range used to code

Relationship of the Unicode Standard to ISO/IEC 10646

The Unicode Standard is code-for-code identical to International Standard ISO/IEC 10646, also known as the Universal Character Set (UCS). ISO/IEC 10646 provides character names and code points; the Unicode Standard provides the same names and code points plus important implementation algorithms, properties, and other useful semantic information. Any implementation that is conformant to Unicode is also conformant to ISO/IEC 10646.

During 1991, the Unicode Consortium and the International Organization for Standardization (ISO) recognized that a single, universal character code was highly desirable. A formal convergence of the two standards was negotiated, and their repertoires were merged into a single character encoding in January 1992. Close cooperation and formal liaison between the Unicode Consortium and the Joint Technical Committee 1 Subcommittee and its Working Group responsible for ISO/IEC 10646 (ISO/IEC JTC 1/SC 2/WG 2) have ensured that all additions to either standard are coordinated and kept synchronized, to maintain exactly the same character repertoire and encoding in both standards.

Unicode Editorial Committee

History and Development of Unicode

The Unicode Standard had its origin in discussions between multilingual experts at Xerox Corporation and Apple Computer in 1987. The term "Unicode" was coined by Joseph D. Becker from *unique, universal,* and *uniform* character encoding.

The Unicode Consortium, a nonprofit organization, was incorporated in 1991 to develop, extend, and promote use of the Unicode Standard. Members include corporations, organizations, and government agencies active in the field of information technology.

The Unicode Technical Committee (UTC) is responsible for the development and maintenance of the Unicode Standard, continuing the work of the original informal Unicode Working Group. Full members of the Unicode Consortium make the decisions of the UTC.

Unicode Editorial Committee

characters is called the *codespace*. A particular integer in this range is called a *code point*. The entire codespace of the Unicode Standard provides 1,114,112 unique code points that can be assigned to characters or designated for other uses. This is more than sufficient for all known requirements.

A *character* is an abstract concept. The Unicode Standard defines an *abstract character* as "a unit of information used for the organization, control, or representation of textual data." (Unicode 4.0, 1363). When an abstract character is mapped or assigned to a particular code point in the codespace, it is then referred to as an *encoded character*.

Code points that are assigned to abstract characters are categorized as graphic, format, control, or private-use. *Graphic characters* are typically associated with a visible-display representation. *Format characters* affect the display representation of surrounding characters. The exact interpretation of most control and all private-use code points is determined by higher-level protocols outside the Unicode Standard.

Version 4.0 of the Unicode Standard encodes 96,248 graphic characters, which are sufficient for textual communication in the world's current languages and for the classical forms of many languages as well. Over 70 percent of these graphic characters (70,207) are Unified Han ideographs.

Character encoding standards define not only the identity of each character and its numeric value, or code point, but also how this value is represented in bits. The Unicode Standard defines three encoding forms that allow the same data to be transmitted in 8, 16, or 32 bits per code unit. All three encoding forms—UTF-8, UTF-16, and UTF-32—encode the same common character repertoire and can be efficiently transformed into each other without any loss of data. The Unicode Consortium fully endorses the use of any of these encoding forms as a way of implementing the Unicode Standard.

The Unicode Standard, unlike other character set standards, views character semantics as inherent in the definition of a character, and so supplies a rich set of character attributes, called *properties*, for each character. The Unicode Character Database, an integral part of the Unicode Standard, contains files defining character properties.

The assignment of the semantics of a character is based on its behavior. In order to implement particular character behaviors, many properties are specified in relation to the processes or algorithms that use them. Examples of properties are those that specify the following:

- the unique name of a character;
- the script of a character is (for example, Latin, Cyrillic, or Thai);
- which characters are letters, punctuation, symbols, white space, and so on;
- what the numeric value of a digit is;
- upper and lower case relations;
- which sequences of characters are equivalent;
- what characters should be used in program-language identifiers;
- the behavior of the text with mixed directions, such as Arabic or Hebrew with English; and
- the behavior of line-breaking in text editors.

Properties are essential for the processing of text; for example, they coordinate with the Unicode Collation Algorithm, which specifies the default sorting behavior of text.

Text Processing

Unicode data is *plain text*, that is, computer-encoded text that consists only of a sequence of code points from the Unicode Standard, without additional formatting or structural information. Additional struc-

ture for representing text with fonts, sizes, and so on is provided by other systems, such as HTML or word processors (which are outside the scope of Unicode).

Glyphs are the shapes that appear on a screen or paper as particular representations of one or more characters. For complex scripts such as Arabic or the various Indic scripts, glyphs change shape or position depending on their context, or may even split across other glyphs. The number of glyphs needed to display text written in a script may be significantly larger than the number of Unicode characters for that script. The Unicode Standard does specify the minimal textual display behavior for individual complex scripts such as Arabic, Syriac, Devanagari, and Tamil.

In computer memory, Unicode characters are stored in a logical order that roughly corresponds to the order in which text is typed in via the keyboard, and often corresponds to phonetic order. In some circumstances, the order of characters differs from this logical order when the text is displayed or printed. The ordering of characters is specified by the Unicode Standard, which allows text to be exchanged between different programs and systems and yet still be comprehensible.

Text processes supporting many languages are often more complex than those for English alone. The Unicode Standard strives to minimize this additional complexity, thus enabling modern computer systems to interchange, render, and manipulate text in multiple languages to facilitate global communication.

Unicode Editorial Committee

The UnicodeConsortium is a registered trademark, and Unicode is a trademark of Unicode Inc.

See also Machine Translation

FURTHER READING

Gillam, R. (2002). *Unicode demystified: a practical programmers guide to the encoding standard.* Boston, MA: Addison-Wesley.
Graham, T. (2000). *Unicode: a primer.* Foster City, CA: MIS:Press.
Lunde, K. (1999). *CJKV information processing.* Beijing: O'Reilly.
Unicode 4.0 (2003). *The Unicode standard, version 4.0.* Boston, MA: Addison-Wesley. Retrieved April 6, 2004, from http://www.unicode.org/versions/Unicode4.0.0/

UNIVERSAL ACCESS

The terms *universal design* and *accessible design* usually bring "designing for disability" to mind. However, people without disabilities also frequently find themselves in diverse environments or situations that require changes to product interfaces. Within a single day—for instance, as a person drives or walks and shops or works—constraints of different environments and activities may require different interfaces, often on the same device. People may also switch preferences within a single environment and activity—for example, someone sitting at a workstation may want to stand up and walk around while continuing to compose. Or someone who is using a keyboard to carry out one task may prefer to use speech or pointing for another. This entry is about designing for the diversity of both users and environments. It applies both to people with disabilities and those without. Common to both is a need for products with flexible interfaces that can change to meet the needs of people in different environments, especially mobile environments.

Designing for Diverse Abilities and Situations

The situational needs of users with disabilities parallel the user needs of people with without disabilities. As a result, both groups have the same needs in different situations. Some examples:

- Products that are operable without vision are required by people who are blind. They are also required by people without disabilities but whose eyes are busy (for instance, driving a car) and by people in the dark.
- Products that are operable with low vision are required by people with partial vision. They are also required by people (without disabilities) who forgot their reading glasses, are using a small, low resolution display, or are working in a smoky environment.
- Products that are operable without sound are required by people who are deaf. They are also required by people in very loud environments,

those whose ears are busy, or individuals that are in the library.

- Products that are operable with limited hearing are required by people who are hard of hearing. They are also required by people in noisy environments.
- Products that are operable with limited manual dexterity are required by people with a physical disability. They are also required by people in gloves or protective equipment or who are in a moving vehicle on uneven roads.
- Products that are operable with limited cognition are required by people with a cognitive disability. They are also required by people who are distracted, panicked, or under the influence of alcohol.
- Products that are operable without reading are required by people with a cognitive disability. They are also required by people who haven't learned to read a language and those who left their reading glasses behind.

Accommodating Diversity Within a Product

In the past, the ability to accommodate individuals with such wide variety of interface requirements was extremely limited by technology. Interfaces were implemented in hardware and the adjustability was mechanical and difficult or expensive. Today it is hard to find any product where the interface is not controlled by a microprocessor and software instructions. As a result, products can exhibit very different behaviors at different times in order to fit the needs or whims of the user. With software, even the appearance, language, and language level used on the buttons can change from one user to the next.

If someone is not able to use the environments and devices they encounter in daily life effectively, there are three things that can be done: (1) Change the world to match their needs (universal design); (2) change the individual so they can use the world (surgery, therapy, training, or personal assistive technologies); or (3) create a "bridge" between the person and the product or environment (adaptive assistive technologies).

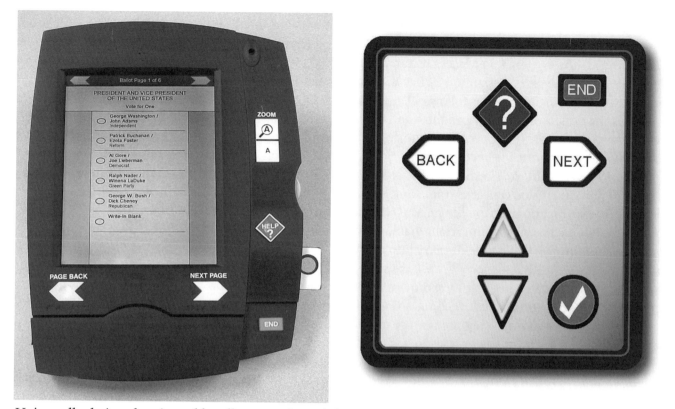

Universally designed voting tablet allows people with low vision, hearing impairments, physical impairments, difficulty or inability to read the ballot for any reason and even many legally blind individuals to vote on the same machine—with voice confirmation of text they touch and what they mark/select. A cable connects an optional keypad with page turn keys, up and down keys to move through candidates and referenda text, and a vote key that allows use by those who cannot use the touchscreen, such as people who are blind or who cannot reach the screen. Photos courtesy of Gregg Vanderheiden.

The first approach, changing the world, is commonly called *universal design, accessible design* or *barrier free design* in the United States; in other countries it often goes by the terms *design for all* or *inclusive design*. It involves designing standard environments and products that are usable by people with a wide a range of abilities (or constraints). The objective of this approach is to make the world as directly usable as possible for people with and without disabilities. In general, this means creating more flexible interfaces and more interface options in standard products.

The second approach includes such things as surgery, rehabilitation, training, and personal assistive technologies, such as glasses, hearing aids, and wheelchairs. In the future, individuals (with and without disabilities) may carry with them specialized interface technologies or devices that could act as universal remote consoles to control other devices as they encounter them.

The third approach (bridge technologies) involves technologies that are used to adapt a particular device or environment to a particular individual. These bridges usually take the form of adaptive assistive technologies such as screen readers or custom modifications to environments or products. They do not usually move around with the individual and are not seen as an extension of the individual. Computers are increasingly being programmed to act as bridge technologies to other information technologies, which decreases the cost and increases the power of the bridge technology approach. Bridge technologies in the cognitive area are also becoming possible for the first time.

Universal Design

The term *universal design* has had many definitions. It was coined, however, by Ron Mace, a researcher at the Center for Universal Design at North Carolina State University. He defined it as follows: "Universal design is the design of different products and environments to be usable by all people, to the greatest extent possible, without the need for adaptation or specialized design" (Mace, Hardie, and Plaice 1992, 2). His definition created concerns from some in industry because it set no practical limits. And what is possible is not necessarily commercially viable—for example, building $2,000 braille displays into every electronic device with a display. Some consumers were also concerned that his definition did not mention compatibility with assistive technology, which many view as key to their being able to use mainstream technology.

Commercial Universal Design

To address these issues and create a practitioner's definition of universal design, a companion definition was proposed by G. C. Vanderheiden. Commercial universal design is "the process of designing products so that they are usable by the widest range of people operating in the widest range of situations as is commercially practical. It includes making products directly accessible and useable (without the need for any assistive technology) and making products compatible with assistive technologies for those who need them."

It is important to emphasize that there are no universally accessible or universally usable products. There simply is too great a range of human abilities and too great a range of situations or limitations that individuals may find themselves in. Thus, universal design is more a function of keeping all of the people and all of the situations in mind and trying to create a product that is as flexible as is commercially practical so that it can accommodate the different users and situations. Universal Design is a process, not an outcome.

Recent Focus on Universal Design

A number of factors have led to the recent interest in universal design. The two primary forces have been disability access and mobile computing. Recent laws have mandated that some products be made more accessible for people with disabilities. For example, section 255 of the Telecommunication Act requires manufacturers of telecommunication products and services to make their products accessible to people with disabilities where it is "readily achievable." And section 508 of the Rehabilitation Act requires the federal government to show preference toward those electronic and information technologies that are accessible to people with disabilities in their purchasing when it is not an "undue burden," thus making accessibility commercially advantageous.

In addition to government action, the rapid increase in the numbers of individuals who are older is also starting to provide a market pull toward more accessible products. As can be seen in Figure 1, functional limitations increase sharply as people age. In addition, a large percentage of these limitations affect vision, hearing, and physical abilities, all of which can directly affect product usability and which can be affected by product design.

Assistive Technologies

Even with the widespread practice of universal design, there will always be a need for assistive technologies to fill the needs of individuals with exceptionally severe or multiple disabilities. In these cases assistive technologies (AT) can provide the needed function or bridge. Assistive technologies can be divided into two types: personal assistive technology (PAT) and adaptive assistive technology (AAT). PAT is used here to refer to technologies that are an extension of a person rather than an adaptation to a particular device or environment. PAT is with users whenever they encounter devices or environments where they need it, and they generally use it for a variety of tasks. Braille-based PDAs, voice access systems that act as keyboards to other devices they encounter, and even devices that directly interpret brain activity and control other devices that users may encounter in their environment are examples of PAT.

Adaptive assistive technology is associated with a particular location, device, or function. Where personal assistive technology is an extension of the individual, adaptive assistive technology can be thought of as a bridge to or an adaptation of a device or environment. Screen readers installed on particular computers for people who are blind or a ramp installed on a building are examples of adaptive assistive technology.

This distinction becomes important when considering the accessibility or usability of a product. In general, a building is considered accessible to people in wheelchairs if they can use it with their wheelchair because they will always have the wheelchair (AT) with them when they encounter the building. On the other hand, a card catalog system in a library that is screen-reader compatible but has no screen reader installed would not be considered accessible to people who are blind because they would not have a screen reader with them when they encountered the computer, and would not be allowed to load foreign software into the system if they did.

Basic Components of Accessible and Usable Design

Whether considering universal design (including the use of personal assistive technology) or access via adaptive assistive technology, the same basic goals must be met if the product is to be usable by people with the full range of abilities. A number of different schemes have tried to capture the different dimensions of accessible and usable design for different product types. The Telecommunication Access Advisory Committee, the Access Board, and FCC came up with twenty-three guidelines. The Electronic and Information Technology Access Advisory Committee came up with over ninety. The Access Board reduced these to just under seventy. In all cases, the guidelines are a combination of general performance-based guidelines and specific design-based guidelines.

An excellent set of principles for application across both environments and technologies was developed at the Rehabilitation Engineering Center at North Carolina State University. Researchers developed a set of seven principles and twenty-nine guidelines, called the Principles of Universal Design, as well as a set of Design Performance Measures.

In order to provide a more information-technology-specific tool, a new approach has been proposed that collapses the various guidelines

into their essential components with regard to information technologies. This collapsing takes the form of identifying the key objectives or requirements for providing more flexible, universally usable interfaces and then identifying key strategies for meeting these objectives. This approach breaks the requirements into three major objectives.

Ensuring Information Is Perceivable

The first objective is ensuring that all information presented by or through the device can be perceived without vision, without hearing, without reading (due to low vision or cognition), without color perception and without causing seizures.

Information presented in a form that is only perceivable with a single sense (for example, only vision or only hearing) is not accessible to people without that sense. It is also not accessible by anyone using a mobile technology that does not present all modalities—for instance, a phone or an automobile audio-only browser.

The basic strategies for doing this include making all information available either in (a) presentation-independent form that can be presented in any sensory form (for instance, electronic text) or (b) sensory parallel form where forms suitable for presentation in different sensory modalities are all provided in synchronized form (for example, a captioned and described movie), and providing a mechanism for presenting information in visual, enlarged visual, auditory, enhanced auditory (louder and if possible better signal to noise ratio) and, where possible, tactile form. To meet these requirements, text formatting must be electronically readable and presentable without vision.

Ensuring Product Is Operable

The second objective is to provide at least one mode for all product features that can be operated without pointing, without vision, without any requirement to respond quickly, without fine motor movement, without simultaneous action, without speech, and without requiring the presence or the use of biological parts (for instance, touch, fingerprints or the iris, etc.).

Interfaces that are technology- or technique-specific cannot be operated by individuals who cannot use that technique (for example, a person who is blind cannot point to a visual target; other people cannot physically use pointers accurately).

The basic strategies for accomplishing this objective include (1) making all interfaces controllable via text input and output, (2) having all text output voiced or compatible with a device that will voice it, (3) making all input and displayed information non-timed, or allowing the user to freeze the timer or to set it to a very long time (five to ten seconds to do single action and two to four seconds to stop an action), and (4) having at least one mode for achieving each and every function of the product that does not require any of the following: no simultaneous activations, no twisting motions, no fine motor control, no biological contact, and no user speech. If biological techniques are used for security, there should be at least two alternatives, one of which should preferably be non-biological.

Ensuring Product Is Understandable

The third basic objective is to facilitate the understanding of content by those without skill in the language used on the product, without a good memory, or without any background information.

People with cognitive difficulties may not be able to use language to access and use complex devices or products. And many other users may find that they are unable to master alternate access techniques if they are layered on top of complex interfaces or content.

The basic strategies for accomplishing this objective include using the simplest, easiest to understand language for the material, site, or situation; making sure that if unexpected languages are used, they are identified to allow translation; and providing a means to determine the meaning of unusual words, phrases, and abbreviations.

Ensuring Product Is Compatible with AT

Finally, it is important that all three objectives be met by technologies that are compatible with the assistive technologies commonly used by people with low vision, without vision, with impaired hearing or deafness, without physical reach and the ability to manipulate, and who have cognitive or language disabilities.

In many cases people coming to a task bring their assistive technologies with them. It is important that those who cannot use products directly have access to products that have been designed to allow them to access and use the products using the tools they carry with them. This also applies to mobile users and to people with glasses, gloves, or other extensions to themselves.

The basic strategies for accomplishing this objective include supporting standard points for the connection of audio amplification devices and alternate input and output devices (or software), and not interfering with the use of assistive technologies such as hearing aids or system-based technologies.

Future Design Directions

With advancing technology, the face of accessible design is changing in dramatic ways that may redefine many of the terms we currently use, including "universal," "accessible," and "assistive technology."

Network-Based Personal Assistive Technology

In the future it may be possible for individuals to have personal assistive technologies that they do not actually carry on their person. We are rapidly approaching a time when it will be practical to have assistive technologies that reside "in the ether" and can be pulled down and made available whenever they are needed. This is already true for Web-based interactions. People with disabilities can use the Web to invoke Web-based virtual assistive technologies from any Web location. This virtual AT capability is not complete today, however, because when using the Web from a library or other public place, the individual has to be able to use the (not personally owned) Web terminal before they can invoke or call up the Web-based assistive technology service. There are also some locations where full Web access may not be available and the AT service may not be reachable or where rerouting of the Web content through the virtual AT or downloading of the virtual AT may not be permitted.

For this virtual personal assistive technology model to be fully effective, a means needs to be provided that will automatically fetch and install the virtual AT software as the person approaches the device, and the devices need to be designed to allow users to substitute their alternate interface or interface modification instead of or as a part of the standard interface on the product. Such virtual AT would be considered a personal assistive technology because users would have it with them or available to them whenever they encountered the products they needed to use it with.

Human Augmentation as a Personal Assistive Technology

Another type of personal assistive technology that is evolving is personal augmentation. Hearing aids are probably the earliest type of electronic augmentation in that they allow their users to hear better than they normally hear. Other common augmentations are prosthetic limbs, cochlear implants, and the beginning stages of artificial vision.

At the present time these human augments fall into the category of artificial partial restorations of ability. They are partial because these augments do not restore the same full function as the original human organ; they are artificial because the restored functionality is not identical to what was lost. For example, when a cochlear implant is provided, it does not provide the same functionality as what was lost. It does not even provide the same type of functionality as is experienced by someone who is hard of hearing. For these reasons, traditional design guidelines for low vision or hard of hearing people may not help people using artificial vision or hearing, or it may not help them as much as design guidelines that take the specific strengths and weaknesses of the artificial restorations or augments into account.

For example, universal designers may create a product that can be used by people with full hearing or people who are hard of hearing. However, to think of people who use cochlear implants as hard of hearing would result in a mischaracterization of their hearing abilities because most people who are hard of hearing will have an ever-increasing drop-off in the high frequencies while retaining mid-to-low frequency hearing. However, someone with a cochlear implant may be able to "hear" equally well at high and low frequencies, depending upon how the cochlear implant is set up to present information to the user. Also, the type of hearing that they have at any frequency may be quite dif-

ferent than that of someone with a hearing impairment. Guidelines designed to provide guidance for addressing individuals with a full range of hearing abilities need to take into account this different type of hearing. Similarly, providing individuals with artificial vision makes it clear that this vision differs from traditional low vision.

If technology continues on its present course, it is likely that in the future people will be augmenting their abilities even if they do not have any functional impairments. Electronic or electromechanical enhancements are drawing nearer every day as advances in biocompatibility continue. These advances may cause us to be dealing with human diversity in still additional dimensions than we have today.

Artificial Agents

Another trend in human interfaces is the increased use of artificial intelligence. The next-next-generation interface for the Web will probably be artificial-agent-based (in addition to having a direct access option). With these interfaces, people would not interact directly with the content on the Web when searching and carrying out other activities. Rather, they could pose their questions or requests to artificial agents who would then interact with the Web. But before such systems would be functional, a number of advances in language comprehension and processing would be required as well as advances in the semantic markup of the Web. Key to this would be the creation of Web content that was machine perceivable, machine operable, and machine comprehendible.

Machine perceivable refers to the ability of a machine to access the information given the current limitations on machine vision and hearing at the time. Today, graphics are accompanied by Alt-Text so that a machine would not need to interpret them but could perceive their meaning through the Alt-Text. In the future, text that is presented graphically might be scanned and read, and some elementary charts or diagrams might also be machine perceivable. Similarly, clear, articulate speech may soon be considered machine perceivable. It is likely to be some time, however, before complex scenes and images or complex auditory information would be machine perceivable unless it were accompanied by text equivalents (Alt-Text or text descriptions or transcripts).

Machine operable means that the interface elements would need to be operable given the perceptual limitations of the device. Interface elements that do not appear until users carry out a visual task (such as pointing), and that would not be evident from examining the content code, would not be machine operable/friendly. Nor would server side image maps (where the machine would have to literally click on every pixel in order to discover the links since it is not able to process the visual image). Client side image maps with proper semantic markup, however, could be easily deciphered, analyzed and operated.

Machine comprehendible is a more difficult area. Using clear and simple language can facilitate the ability of machines to process text and understand it. We already have software that can create summaries and generate indexes by reading clearly written material. Actually understanding the content of most web pages will follow as machine intelligence advances.

Universal Benefits

The need to accommodate the needs and abilities of individuals with diverse abilities, constraints, and preferences has caused us to have to think differently about interface design. This includes thinking about interfaces that can adapt to a wider variety of users and of situations that can vary from user to user, even for the same user at different times in the same day. The fact that the needs of those with disabilities parallel the needs of non-disabled people in different environments, especially mobile environments, makes it much easier to develop and deploy flexible interfaces in mainstream products commercially. The rapidly advancing technologies facilitate this as well as present us with whole new approaches to interface design that promise even more flexible, agent-oriented interfaces that can match varied needs and preferences.

Gregg Vanderheiden

See also Braille; Brain-Computer Interfaces; Keyboard

FURTHER READING

Connell, B. R., et al. (1997). *The principles of universal design: Version 2.0.* Raleigh, NC: The Center for Universal Design.

LaPlante, M. P. (1988). *Data on disability from the National Health Interview Survey, 1983–85: An InfoUse report.* Washington, DC: National Institute on Disability and Rehabilitation Research, US Department of Education.

Mace, R. L., Hardie, G. J., & Plaice, J. P. (1991). Accessible environments: Toward universal design. In W. Preiser, J. Vischer, & E. White (Eds.), *Design interventions: Toward a more human architecture.* New York: Van Nostrand Reinhold

Story, M. F., & Mueller, J. L. (2001). Universal design performance measures for products: A tool for assessing universal usability. In J. Winters, C. Robinson, R. Simpson & G. Vanderheiden, (Eds.), *Emerging and accessible telecommunications, information and healthcare technologies—Emerging challenges in enabling universal access.* Arlington: RESNA Press.

Story, M. F. Mueller, J. L., & Montoya-Weiss, M. (2001). Completion of universal design performance measures. In *Proceedings of the RESNA 2001 Annual Conference.* Arlington: RESNA Press.

Survey of income and program participation (SIPP): Series P-70, #8 Survey. (1984). Washington, DC: Bureau of the Census.

Vanderheiden, G. C. (2000). Fundamental principles and priority setting for universal usability. *Proceedings of the ACM—Universal Usability Conference, Washington, DC* (pp. 32–38). New York: ACM Press.

Vanderheiden, G. C. (2001). Telecommunications—Accessibility and future directions. In C. Nicolle & J. Abascal (Eds.), *Inclusive design guidelines for HCI* (pp. 239–257). London: Taylor & Francis.

Vanderheiden, G. C. (2002). Interaction for diverse users. In J. Jacko and A. Sears (Eds.), *Human-Computer Interaction Handbook* (pp. 397–400). Mahwah, NJ: Erlbaum.

USABILITY EVALUATION

The International Organization for Standardization (ISO) defines *usability* as "the extent to which the product can be used by specified users to achieve specified goals with effectiveness, efficiency, and satisfaction in a specified context of use." Usability has five attributes: learnability, efficiency, memorability, preventing errors, and user satisfaction. Whether one attribute is more critical than another depends on the type of application. For example, if the software will be used infrequently, then memorability will be essential because users will need to remember the actions necessary for tasks that are not often performed. If the application is time-critical, then efficiency and preventing errors will be critical.

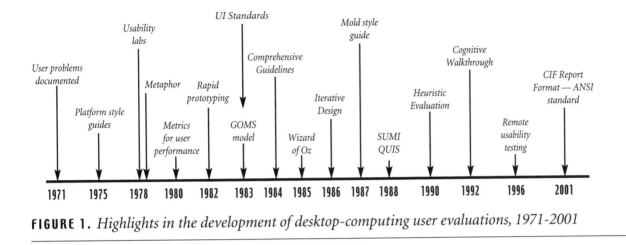

FIGURE 1. *Highlights in the development of desktop-computing user evaluations, 1971-2001*

Usability engineering is the discipline that provides structured methods for achieving usability in user interface design during product development. Usability evaluation is part of this process. While theoretically any software product could be evaluated for usability, the evaluation is unlikely to produce good results if a usability engineering process has not been followed. Usability engineering has three basic phases: requirements analysis, design/testing/development, and installation. Usability goals are established during the requirements analysis. Iterative testing is done during the design/testing/development phases and the results are compared to the usability goals. User feedback is also important after installation as a check on the usability and functionality of the product.

There are three basic methods for evaluating usability. The methods depend on the source used for the evaluation. This source can be users, usability experts, or models. Figure 1 shows a timeline for usability evaluations in the last thirty years. Users were first used as the source of usability feedback but models have been used for over twenty years. Expert feedback was developed in heuristic reviews and cognitive walkthroughs and has been used since the early 1990s. All three methods rely on usability engineers or usability professionals to design, conduct, analyze, and report on the evaluations.

User-Centered Evaluations

User-centered evaluations consist of identifying representative users and tasks, and observing the problems users have using a particular software product to accomplish these tasks. During the design/testing/development cycle of software development, two types of user evaluations are carried out. Formative evaluations are used to inform user interface design. Summative evaluations document the effectiveness, efficiency, and user satisfaction of a product at the end of the development cycle. These two types of evaluation differ in the purpose of the evaluation, the methods used, the formality of the evaluation, the robustness of the software being evaluated, the measures collected, and the number of participants used. In both types of evaluation, representative users are recruited to participate, some method of collecting information is used, and some way of disseminating the results of the evaluation to members of the software development team is devised.

The Role of Usability Laboratories

Usability laboratories are used in some companies to conduct the evaluations. Usability laboratories make a company's commitment to usability visible. Laboratories are usually outfitted with audio and video recording equipment to capture what the user is doing on the computer. The computer screen, the user's hand motions, and the facial expression of the user are usually recorded. In addition, logging software captures keystrokes of what the user is typing and clicking in the interface. Many laboratories are designed with rooms for observers as well as for the users. These rooms can be separated by one-way glass, or the video from the user's computer can

A Personal Story—Is Usability Still a Problem?

Some people express the belief that usability problems belong to the past: "Yes, with the old character-based CRT terminals usability was definitely a problem. But today, we have graphical screens, established design guidelines and powerful interface builders. So we have solved the basic usability problems." When I face this belief, I like to counter-argue by using three of my own recent experiences.

The first counterargument originates from a user-based usability evaluation of an electronic patient record in a hospital. This system was delivered by a large and respected software producer, and a previous version had been used for eight years in a neighbouring country. Nevertheless, we detected seventy-five usability problems of which nine were critical and thirty-nine serious. This evaluation was conducted when the system was being introduced in the hospital. We repeated the evaluation a year later to see how much had been changed with experience. This time we found eighty-six usability problems of which twelve were critical and thirty-eight serious. Some of the problems that were detected in the first evaluation had disappeared or become less serious, but several fundamental problems were still there and new critical problems had emerged. A key problem was that the system registered and presented information in a very fragmented way. Therefore, it was impossible to get an overview of the state of a patient. In addition, it consisted of different sub-systems with different interface designs and very little integration of data between them. Despite graphical screens, established design guidelines and powerful interface builders, developers keep producing software with fundamental usability problems. And that applies even to experienced developers and a classical administrative task.

The second counter-argument originates from a user-based usability evaluation of a service for a WAP enabled mobile telephone. This service would provide the user with a list of used cars for sale. On this simple service we detected thirty-five usability problems of which eight were critical and sixteen serious. The users had problems activating the service in the desired way and they could not interpret the output correctly. This system illustrates how the new mobile technologies with their small screens and limited interaction devices seriously challenge the practices that have developed in human-computer interaction over the last couple of decades.

The third counterargument originates from a user-based usability evaluation of a system for booking operations in a hospital. Again, it seemed to be a reasonably simple administrative system. But we detected fifty-one usability problems of which nineteen were critical and fifteen serious. This usability evaluation was particularly interesting because the developers of the system watched the evaluation, and we had a chance to talk with them between the individual tests. After the first two users, the developers expressed quite clearly that these two users must have been unusually stupid. After the next two users, the developers had gone very quiet. And after the last two users, they immediately said, "We need to collaborate on this." The system reflected a lack of understanding of the work of the users, and when this became apparent, the immediate reaction of the developers was to blame the users.

I think these experiences illustrate in different ways how usability problems are still far from being solved. And if anything, escalating integration of individual systems and rapid development of new and mobile technologies are increasing, rather than decreasing, the necessity of dealing with usability in a conscious and systematic way.

Jan Stage

be piped into a separate room where managers and developers observe the testing. Remote usability labs consist of audio and video recording equipment bundled conveniently to allow usability engineers to travel to users, rather than having users come to them. Digital video software reduces the amount of recording equipment needed.

Formative Evaluations

Formative evaluations obtain user feedback for early concepts or designs of software products. These evaluations are typically informal because the goal is to collect information to be used for design rather than to collect measures of usability. The primary source of data in formative evaluations is verbal data from the user. Early evaluations may use paper prototypes or initial screen designs. Later evaluations can be done on partial prototypes or prototypes of only one portion of a user interface. When possible, logging software is also used to capture user interaction. Additionally, usability engineers often take notes of critical incidents that occur during the evaluation. The debriefing or postevaluation interview is an excellent source of information in formative evaluations. Usability engineers can probe in depth to understand any sources of confusion in the interface.

Formative evaluations need to be conducted at a fairly rapid pace in order to provide design input when it is needed. As a consequence, the evaluations often focus on a small portion of the user interface, involve relatively few user-participants, and have a less formal reporting mechanism than summative evaluations. Ideally, software designers and developers can observe the evaluations and discuss results and potential solutions with the usability engineers after the evaluations.

Summative Evaluations

Summative evaluations are more formal evaluations conducted to document the usability characteristics of a software product. These evaluations involve a number of users—the recommended number is five to seven users per cell, where a cell represents a class of end-users. For example, if a product is being design for both home and small business users, then representative users of both types must be included in the evaluation. If both adults and teenagers will be using the home product, then representatives from both groups need to be included as evaluation participants. Good experimental design is essential for accurate summative evaluation. The metrics of efficiency, effectiveness, and user satisfaction are typically used and the design of the evaluation must include the measures and the collection methodology. Tasks used in the evaluation usually represent the core functionality of the software but may also include new or improved functionality. Directions and materials given to the users need to be designed and tested in a pilot evaluation to make sure that they are understandable.

Usability evaluation has always tried to make the "context-of-use" as realistic as possible. However, a usability laboratory cannot duplicate actual conditions of use within an office or home. Interruptions and other demands for attention do not, and cannot, occur during usability evaluation conditions. As such, these evaluations represent the best-case condition. If the software is not usable in the laboratory, it will certainly not be usable in real-world use. However, usability in the laboratory does not guarantee usability in more realistic conditions.

The desired level of usability is defined early in the usability engineering lifecycle and the actual results from the summative evaluation are then compared to this. If good usability engineering practices have been followed, which would have included a number of formative evaluations, it is likely that the desired level will be achieved. If this is not the case, then a decision must be made to either release the software or redesign and reevaluate its usability.

Advantages and Disadvantages

The chief advantage of user-centered evaluation is the involvement of users. Results are based on actually observing what aspects of the user interface cause problems for representative users. The downside is that user evaluations are expensive and time-consuming. Finding and scheduling an appropriate number of representative users for each user type is difficult. Laboratory and usability engineering resources are needed to conduct the evaluations and analyze the results. The realism of the evaluation is also an issue. Have the correct tasks been selected? How will the product function in real work environments? Beta testing and user feedback after installation are used to gather data about the usability aspects of the product in the actual context of use.

Expert-Based Evaluations

Expert evaluations of usability are similar to design reviews of software projects and code walkthroughs. Inspection methods include heuristic evaluations, guideline reviews, pluralistic walkthroughs, consistency inspections, standards inspections, cognitive walkthroughs, formal usability inspections, and feature inspections.

Guideline and Standards Reviews

Guideline and standard reviews need a basis for making judgments. Standards for user interfaces have been built into graphic user interface development software. For example, standard widgets are used by software applications developed in the Microsoft platform. Some companies have style guides for software applications and compile a checklist to assure that applications conform to this style. Numerous guidelines have been developed to facilitate the design and evaluation of user interfaces. The guidelines have been obtained from many studies and are sometimes contradictory. The use of the guideline depends on many factors including the type of application, the expertise of the end-users, and the environment in which the application will be used. For example, a set of guidelines for websites is maintained by the National Cancer Institute (NCI); evidence supporting the guidelines ranges from research experiments to observational evidence to expert opinion.

Cognitive Walkthroughs

Guidelines are oriented towards a static view of the user interface. Aspects of the design are evaluated separately and not in the context of use in a real-world task. The cognitive walkthrough technique was developed to address this. Cognitive walkthroughs can be performed by individuals or by groups. To conduct a cognitive walkthrough, the usability expert needs a detailed description of the user interface, a scenario for the task, the demographics of the end-user population, the context in which the use would occur, and a successful sequence of actions that should be performed. The evaluator then looks at the actions for each task and evaluates whether the user will be able to select the right action, will be able to determine that the selected action is correct, and will see progress towards the solution. Critical information to capture during the walkthrough is what the user should know prior to performing the task and what the user should learn while performing the task. The developers of the cognitive walkthrough point out that the focus is on the learnability aspect of usability. Thus other evaluation methods must also be applied to assess other aspects of usability.

Heuristic Evaluations

The heuristic evaluation technique is the most widely used inspection method. Heuristic evaluation uses a small set of evaluators who judge a user interface for compliance with usability design principles. Examples of heuristics used in evaluations are as follows:

- Visibility of system status
- Match between system and the real world
- User control and freedom
- Consistency and standards
- Error prevention
- Recognition rather than recall
- Flexibility and efficiency of use
- Aesthetic and minimalist design
- Help users recognize, diagnose, and recover from errors
- Help and documentation

(Nielsen 1993, 20)

Each inspector judges the user interface separately and after the assessments have been made, the inspectors meet to compile their findings. Five evaluators is the recommended number for critical systems and no fewer than three evaluators are recommended for any heuristic review.

Advantages and Disadvantages

Heuristic reviews are less expensive and less time-consuming to conduct than user-centered evaluations. The cognitive walkthrough can be accomplished using only a text description of the user interface and therefore can be used very early in the software development process. However, inspection techniques do not provide possible solutions to the usability problem. Moreover, it is difficult to summarize the findings from multiple evaluators because they report problems differently and at different levels. There is also the issue of severity. Not all usability problems are equal. Development teams need to be able to prioritize what problems get fixed according to the seriousness of the problem. There is currently no agreement on how to judge the severity of usability problems.

An early study comparing heuristic reviews to results from laboratory usability tests found that heuristic reviews were better predictors of problems

Global Usability

At California Polytechnic State University, a multimedia training project—the Africa Learning Network (ALN)—was developed to teach African women to do business in West Africa. Most of the women involved in the development held doctorates in agriculture from European universities. The training was to supplement their agricultural expertise with practical training in business. Many of them were educated in a traditionally French style where the education system is highly structured. The project was designed to give them business skills through interactive CD-ROM tutorials and the Internet. Some of the training modules included overcoming gender bias, raising capital, and learning basic computer skills.

As part of the project, several women came to campus to learn about multimedia tools and to test a preliminary version of the CD-ROM. Extensive usability testing was done. The women were asked to load the CD and exercise the software. There were no "right" or "wrong" answers; the women were simply asked to do what they felt the instruction required. The developers/usability testers looked on as the women worked on the CD. One woman sat as the CD loaded and music played. As the testers watched her at the computer, time passed, and she did nothing. Usability testers traditionally do not interrupt during the middle of a test. However, since she sat there for a period of time, they had to know why she was not continuing with the training. They asked, "How come you're not using the software?" To this she replied, "I'm waiting for the music to stop." In her tradition, one step had to be completed before continuing. For her, the end of the music would have been a signal to begin. This is a great example of how something viewed as so simple can become a development flaw when dealing with other cultures.

Ruth Guthrie

that real users encounter than cognitive walkthroughs and guideline-based evaluations. However, none of these methods found more than 50 percent of the problems discovered in laboratory testing. The last section of this article discusses issues in comparing evaluation methodologies.

Model-Based Evaluations

A model of the human information processor has been developed based on data derived from psychology research on the human systems of perception, cognition, and memory. The model incorporates properties of short-term and long-term memory, along with some capabilities of human visual and audio processing. Times for cognitive processing and motor processing are also included. This allows human-computer interaction researchers to evaluate user interface designs based on predictions of performance from the model.

GOMS Models
The GOMS model consists of Goals, Operators, Methods, and Selection rules. A method is a set of steps or operators that will accomplish a goal, and in any interface more than one method may provide the same result. The user then chooses the method based on selection rules. A GOMS model can be used only for evaluating the efficiency of the procedural aspect of usability and cannot evaluate potential errors due to screen design or terminology. Natural GOMS Language (NGOMSL) has extended the GOMS model to predict learning time. For both these techniques a task analysis must be done to construct the goals, operators, methods, and selection rules.

Other Modeling Techniques
The EPIC (Executive-Process/Interactive Control) system simulates the human perceptual and motor performance system. EPIC can interact as a human would with a simulation of a user interface system.

EPIC is being used to study people engaged in multiple tasks, such as using a car navigation system while driving. Using EPIC involves writing production rules for using the interface and writing a task environment to simulate the behavior of the user interface.

A model of information foraging useful in evaluating information-seeking in websites is based on the ACT-R model. The ACT-IF model was developed to test simulated users interacting with designs for websites and predicts optimal behavior in large collections of web documents. The information-foraging model is being used to understand the decisions that users of the web make in following various links to satisfy information goals.

Advantages and Disadvantages

It is less expensive to use models to predict user behavior than to use empirical, user-centered evaluations because many more iterations of the design can be tested. However, a necessary first step is to produce a model description by conducting a task-level cognitive task analysis. This is time-consuming but can test many user interface designs. Models must then be tested for validity by watching humans perform the tasks and coding their behavior for comparison with the model. This too is time-consuming, but it is necessary in order to determine if the model predictions are accurate.

Current Issues

While the HCI community has come a long way in developing and using methods to evaluate usability, the problem is by no means solved. This chapter has described three basic methods for evaluation but there is not yet agreement in the community about the comparative usefulness of the techniques. Although a number of studies have compared these methods, the comparison is difficult and flaws have been pointed out in several of them. First, there is the issue of using experimental (user-centered) methods to obtain answers to large questions of usability rather than to the more narrow questions that are more traditional for experimental methods. A second issue is what should be used for the comparison. Should user-centered methods be considered the ground truth? All usability tests are not created equal. There can be flaws in the way tests are designed,

conducted, and analyzed. However, while individual methods have limitations and can be flawed in their implementation, it is certain that performing some evaluation is better than doing nothing. The current best practice to provide rich data on usability is to use a number of different methodologies.

Evaluation methodologies were, for the most part, developed to evaluate the usability of desktop systems. The current focus in technology development on mobile and ubiquitous computing presents challenges for current usability evaluation methods. It is difficult to simulate real-world usage conditions for these applications in a laboratory. Going out into the field to evaluate use places constraints on how early evaluations can be done because software must be reasonably robust for these types of evaluations. Mobile and multiuser systems must be evaluated for privacy and for any usability issues entailed in setting up, configuring, and using them. The use of software in the context of doing other work also has implications for determining the context of use. For example, we need to test car navigation systems in the car—not in the usability lab.

User-centered evaluations require the selection of an increasingly wide range of people as more people adopt new technologies. Representative users of mobile phones, for example, would have to include the disabled and people of all ages, from teenagers to senior citizens. Usability evaluation techniques are also being applied to websites, where again, there is a broad user population. Because design and development cycles in website development are extremely fast, extensive usability evaluations are usually not feasible. To more closely replicate the context of website usage for evaluations, usability practitioners are currently looking at remote testing methods. International standards exist for user-centered design processes, documentation, and user interfaces. Usability is becoming a requirement for companies purchasing software because they recognize that unusable software will increase the total cost of ownership. New usability evaluation methodologies need to be developed to meet the demands of our technology-focused society. Researchers and practitioners in usability will need to join forces to meet this challenge.

Jean Scholtz

FURTHER READING

Anderson, J. R., Matessa, M., & Lebiere, C. (1997). ACT-R: A theory of higher level cognition and its relation to visual attention. *Human-Computer Interaction, 12*(4), 439–462.

Behaviour & Information Technology, 13(1–2). (January–April 1994). [Special issue devoted to usability laboratories]

Card, S. K., Moran, T. P., & Newell, A. (1983). *The psychology of human-computer interaction.* Hillsdale, NJ: Erlbaum Associates.

Card, S. K., Moran, T. P., & Newell, A. (1980). The keystroke-level model for user performance time with interactive systems. *Communications of the ACM, 23*(7), 396–410.

Dumas, J., & Redish, J. (1993). *A practical guide to usability testing.* Norwood, NJ: Ablex.

Gray, W. D., John, B. E., & Atwood, M. E. (1993). Project Ernestine: Validating a GOMS analysis for predicting and explaining real-world performance. *Human-Computer Interaction, 8*(3), 237–309.

Gray, W. D., & Salzman, M. D. (1998). Damaged merchandise? A review of experiments that compare usability evaluation methods. *Human-Computer Interaction, 13*(3), 203–262.

Hartson, H. R., Castillo, J. C., Kelso, J., Kamler, J., & Neale, W. C. (1996). Remote evaluation: The network as an extension of the usability laboratory. In *Proceedings ACM CHI'96*, 228–235.

The Industry Usability Reporting (IUSR) Project. Retrieved September 12, 2003, from http://www.nist.gov/iusr

International Organization for Standardization. Retrieved Sept. 12, 2003, from http://www.iso.ch/iso/en/ISOOnline.openerpage

Jeffries, R., Miller, J. R., Wharton, C., & Uyeda, K. M. (1991). User interface evaluation in the real world: A comparison of four techniques. In *Proceedings ACM CHI'91*, 119–124.

Karat, J., Jeffries, R., Miller, J., Lund, A., McClelland, I., John, B., et al. (1998). Commentary on "Damaged Merchandise?" *Human-Computer Interaction, 13*(3), 263–324.

Kieras, D. E. (1997). A Guide to GOMS Model Usability Evaluation Using NGOMSL. In M. Helander & T. Landauer (Eds.), *The Handbook of Human-Computer Interaction* (pp. 733–766). Amsterdam: North-Holland.

Kieras, D., & Meyer, D. E. (1997). An overview of the EPIC architecture for cognition and performance with application to human-computer interaction. *Human-Computer Interaction, 12*, 391–438.

Lewis, C., Polson, P., Wharton, C., & Rieman, J. (1990). Testing a walkthrough methodology for theory-based design of walk-up-and-user interfaces. In *Proceedings ACM CHI'90*, 235–242.

Mack, R., & Nielsen, J. (1994). *Usability inspection methods.* New York: Wiley. Mayhew, D. (1999). *The usability engineering lifecycle.* San Francisco: Morgan Kauffman.

Microsoft Corporation. (1995). *The Windows interface guidelines for software design.* Redmond, WA: Microsoft Press.

Muller, M., Haslwanter, J., & Dayton, T. (1997). In M. Helander & T. Landauer (Eds.), *The Handbook of Human-Computer Interaction* (pp. 255–298). Amsterdam: North-Holland.

National Cancer Institute. (2003). Research-based web design and usability guidelines. Retrieved September 12, 2003, from http://www.usability.gov.

Nielsen, J. (1993). *Usability engineering.* San Diego, CA: Academic Press.

Neilsen, J. (1994). Enhancing the explanatory power of usability heuristics. In *Proceedings ACM CHI'94*, 152–158.

Nielsen, J., & Molich, R. (1990). Heuristic evaluation of user interfaces. In *Proceedings ACM CHI'90*, 249–256.

Pirolli, P., & Card, S. (1995). Information foraging in information access environments. In *Proceedings ACM CHI '95*, 51–58.

Pirolli, P. (1997). Computational models of information scent-following in a very large browsable text collection. In *Proceedings ACM CHI '97*, 3–10.

Section 508 of the Rehabilitation Act (29 U.S.C. 794d), as amended by the Workforce Investment Act of 1998 (P.L. 105–220), August 7, 1998. Retrieved September 12, 2003, from http://www.section508.gov/.

Smith, S. L, & Mosier, J. N. (1986). Guidelines for designing user interface software (Technical Report NTIS No. A177 198). Hanscom Air Force Base, MA: USAF Electronic Systems Division.

Yourdon, E. (1989). *Structured walkthroughs* (4th ed.). Englewood Cliffs, NJ: Yourdon Press.

USER MODELING

A model is a simplified version of a complex thing that is used to make predictions about how the complex thing will behave under different conditions. As an example, a crash test dummy is a model of a real person used to learn what would happen to a real person in a car crash. Automakers use crash test dummies to learn how different people, design decisions, and crash conditions affect what happens in an accident. In this example, different people would be represented by crash test dummies of different weight, height, and flexibility; different design decisions might include (for example) the style of bumper, the type of seatbelts and airbags, or the construction materials used for the body of the vehicle; and different crash conditions could be created by changing the speed of the car at impact or the angle and location of the collision. This information allows automakers to design automobiles that are safe for the greatest number of people under the greatest number of crash conditions.

The user models that will be discussed in this article are used to make predictions about how people interact with computer interfaces. User models can be either physical (for example, a pair of glasses that distorts one's vision to simulate a user with poor eyesight) or theoretical (for example, modeling a person's short-term memory as a set of seven slots, each capable of holding one piece of information). User models can be used when an application is being designed, to determine its default behavior, or during run time, to modify the application's behavior to suit a specific user better. Finally, models can be used to predict behavior that has yet to be observed, or to explain behavior that has already been observed. This article focuses on theoretical models that application designers use for the purpose of rigorously estimating how a range of users are likely to behave and perceive while using a computer system, with the goal being to design systems that are most useful for the greatest number of potential users.

Models of Human Information Processing

The user models we are discussing are often referred to as models of human information processing. Models in this category are all similar in that they assume humans are composed of interacting subsystems and perform tasks by making observations, deciding on a response to the observations, and acting based on this decision.

Models in this category differ based on what disciplines the models emerged from (psychology, physiology, or sociology) and what aspects of human behavior they cover (perceptual, mental, physical, emotional, attentional).

Fitts's Law

Fitts's Law is a physiology-based model that is one of the best-known models used in the field of human-computer interaction (HCI). Fitts's Law predicts the time it takes a person to move his or her hand from a starting point to a target based on the size of the target and the distance between the starting point and target. The law states that the time T required to move the hand from a starting point to a target of size S, which is distance D from the hand, is given by:

$$T = a + b\log_2\left(\frac{2D}{S}\right)$$

where a and b are constants that are adjusted for the specific situation being modeled. In HCI, this model is used for such tasks as estimating the amount of time it will take a person to move his or her hand

from the keyboard to the mouse, or the time required to move the mouse pointer from its current position on the screen to a button at another location on the screen by moving the mouse.

Consider the task of pressing a key when a light is switched on. Fitts's law ignores both perceptual activity (identifying when the light is observed) and mental activity (for example, deciding which of several keys to press), and only describes motor activity. Hence, using Fitts's Law to model this action would provide an estimate of the time to press the key, but would ignore the time required to perceive the light or choose which key to press.

The Model Human Processor

The model human processor (MHP), on the other hand, is a model of human information processing, derived from psychological data, that represents perceptual, mental, and physical phenomena. The MHP represents a person as a collection of interconnected special-purpose memories and processors. The perceptual processor represents the person's sensory input; the cognitive processor the individual's thought processes, and the motor processor controls his or her physical movements.

In addition to specifying a structure composed of memories, processors, and their interconnections, the MHP also specifies properties of these memories and processors, such as the number of items that can be stored in each memory and the amount of time each processor requires to perform a single action. The MHP would model the action of pressing a key in response to a light as follows:

- The perceptual processor observes the light and notifies the cognitive processor.
- The cognitive processor selects the appropriate response and passes this information to the motor processor.
- The motor processor executes the chosen motor command.

The MHP on its own is an unwieldy tool for analyzing user interfaces. Instead, the MHP serves as the basis of a family of user modeling methods called GOMS, which stands for *Goals, Operators, Methods* and *Selection* rules. (See Table 1.) The members of

TABLE 1. Components of the GOMS Framework

Component	Description
Goals	The tasks the user is trying to accomplish.
Operators	Steps performed as part of completing the tasks. Operators can be perceptual, mental, or physical.
Methods	Sequences of operators.
Selection rules	Rules for choosing between potential methods for accomplishing a task or subtask within a task.

the GOMS family vary in their assumptions; there are very simple models that provide quick (but less accurate) estimates of user performance as well as very detailed models that provide labor-intensive (but very accurate) estimates.

A GOMS model uses the components in Table 1 to specify the steps used to complete a task. Two key assumptions in all GOMS models are that the user will perform the task in the exact same way each time (in other words, each time the user performs the task, the user will follow the same steps, each of which will take the same amount of time), and that the user will not make any mistakes along the way or be interrupted at any point during the task.

Because a GOMS model is based on the MHP, the steps within a task can be associated with the actions of specific processors, which allows quantitative predictions of performance time to be made. Hence, the task of pressing a key in response to a light would be modeled as follows:

- one perceptual processor action to observe the light;
- one cognitive processor action to choose the correct response;
- one physical processor action to move the finger to press the key.
- The total time (T_{total}) required for this task would then be calculated as:

$$T_{total} = T_p + T_c + T_m$$

where T_p is the time required for a single cycle of the perceptual processor, T_c is the time required for a single cycle of the cognitive processor and T_m is the time required for a single cycle of the motor (physical) processor.

The Difference Between Estimating and Measuring

It is important to understand that models are used to estimate behavior, which is very different (much less precise) from measuring behavior. To know exactly how a person or group of people will perform a specific task with a specific interface, it is necessary to expose people to the interface and measure their performance. Models, on the other hand, are used to expose lots of virtual people to an interface to estimate how they would perform with it. Obviously, the more detailed the model is, the more accurate the estimate will be. On the other hand, the larger the group of people the model is used to represent, the less accurate the estimate will be. In other words, a detailed model tailored to one specific user can be very accurate, but a less detailed model representing many potential users will be less accurate.

However, even if a model is not accurate in an absolute sense, it can still be useful if it is relatively accurate. In other words, if a software designer wants to compare two interfaces, A and B, it may not be necessary to know precisely how long it would take a user to perform the same task using both interfaces. It may be enough to know that the user will take longer to perform the task using A than it will to perform the same task using B. In other words, the software designer can use a model to learn that B is better *relative to* A.

The uses for which user models are best suited are making relative comparisons between interfaces based on predictions of performance (for example, the number of seconds required to perform a specific task). User models can also be used to identify where errors might occur and to estimate the time required to learn to use an interface. Finally, user models can reduce—but not eliminate—the need to evaluate a user interface with real people. By reducing the amount of testing that must be done with real people, user models can accelerate the process and reduce the cost of designing a user interface.

Richard C. Simpson

See also Adaptive Help Systems; Psychology and HCI; Task Analysis

FURTHER READING

Card, S. K., & Moran, T. P. (1980). The keystroke-level model for user performance time with interactive systems. *Communications of the ACM, 23*(7), 396–410.

Card, S. K., Moran, T. P., & Newell, A. (1983). *The psychology of human-computer interaction*. Hillsdale, NJ: Erlbaum.

Fitts, P. M. (1954). The information capacity of the human motor system in controlling the amplitude of movement. *Journal of Experimental Psychology, 47*, 381–391.

Fitts, P. M., & Posner, M.I. (1967). *Human performance*. Belmont, CA: Brooks-Cole.

Jacko, J. A., & Sears, A. (2003). *The human-computer interaction handbook*. Mahwah, NJ: Lawrence Erlbaum Associates.

John, B. E., & Kieras, D. E. (1996). The GOMS family of user interface analysis techniques: Comparison and contrast. *ACM Transactions on Computer-Human Interaction, 3*, 320–351.

Rasmussen, J. (1986). *Information processing and human-machine interaction*. Amsterdam: North-Holland.

Stephanidis, C. (2001). *User interfaces for all: Concepts, methods and tools*. Mahwah, NJ: Lawrence Erlbaum Associates.

Wickens, C. D. (1992). *Engineering psychology and human performance*. New York: HarperCollins Publishers.

Wood, S. D. (1998, 2001). *GOMSmodel.org*. Retrieved October 28, 2003, from http://www.gomsmodel.org

USER SUPPORT

Users require some kind of support in order to use, develop, and manipulate information systems. Information systems include the hardware, software, computer networks, and the Internet, whether used at home or at the workplace. The concept of user support encompasses the technical and social methods of providing help to users. The types of services provided by support staff typically include assistance with technical problems with hardware, operating systems, and applications; user account management; backup and recovery services; hardware inventory; end user training; software inventory; and answering frequently asked questions. User support staff must have a diverse set of technical skills in order to provide assistance to a heterogeneous end-user population that may include people at multiple levels of technical, business, and organizational proficiency. Furthermore, support staff are expected to provide this help in a cost- and time-effective manner.

Support for Users at Home

According to the U.S. Census Bureau, in August 2000 54 million household, or 51 percent of U.S. households, had one or more computers in their homes. The rapid adoption of computer and Internet technology has meant many more computer users who require some kind of help to solve a variety of technical problems related to hardware, software, and network issues.

Home users get hardware support mainly through the stores from which they purchased the hardware or from the hardware manufacturer. This support may be based on the manufacturer's warranty or on product or service plans that can be acquired at the time of the purchase.

Software support is offered by software companies through interactive tutorials, manuals, websites that list frequently asked questions and their answers, and through direct assistance online or by phone. Software companies also offer access to knowledge databases in which the user can search for words related to their problem and to community newsgroups through which users share their comments and questions with other users. An example of this kind of site is the Microsoft website available at http://support.microsoft.com. Software-oriented online communities encourage users to ask questions and respond to one another regarding software. Open-source software is mainly supported in this way. Users participate actively, motivated by the challenge and by reputation they can gain at those sites based on their technical experience.

For Internet support, users' Internet service providers (ISPs) have support staff that can respond to users' questions online or over the phone. Large providers may also visit homes to check the network connections.

Support for Corporate Users

Today, many organizations have internal user support units known as information centers (IC) or help desks. For instance, IBM operational support services define an incident as a "single request for assistance on a particular product or problem, which may involve multiple calls for resolution" (www-1 .ibm.com/services/its/us/endusersupport.html). Incidents reported to the help desk are usually categorized according to an area of specialization (e.g., user accounts, virus/security issues) in addition to the level of knowledge required to solve it. Less experienced staff make first attempts, with more experienced or specialized staff stepping in to handle problems that the less experienced staff cannot solve. The Help Desk Institute—a membership association for corporate help desk professionals—identified three main reasons for increased numbers of calls and longer calls from corporate users to their own help desks: (1) changes, upgrades, conversions, and installations; (2) more customers; and (3) newer, more complex technologies.

Information centers usually troubleshoot problems over the phone and have automated call distribution systems and specialized software to help create, route, conduct triage on, and resolve incidents. Moreover, help desk software packages can inventory the incidents topic and can keep track of the number of incidents resolved by each staff member,

their average response time, and time taken in resolving the incident.

Additionally, information centers maintain knowledge bases that store possible solutions and comments about problems previously solved. Knowledge bases can be broken down into components. These components include the case base, the vocabulary used to describe cases, the similarity measures used to compare cases, and the rules or

---

KNOWLEDGE BASE A collection of facts, rules, and procedures organized into schemas. The assembly of all of the information and knowledge of a specific field of interest.

---

algorithms used to transfer and integrate new solutions into the case base. Knowledge bases can incorporate hardware and software manuals, frequently asked questions, and newsgroup files. Support staff can search for solutions within the knowledge base when they are troubleshooting. The knowledge base is continually updated as consultants contribute their comments and other personnel review the accuracy of this information.

Some companies prefer to outsource support services in order to cut costs and have a more consistently trained workforce to handle recurring incidents. On the other hand, outsourcing might means transferring ownership and aspects of control from the organization to the service provider: A company must decide what it wants to keep control of and what it feels comfortable giving to service providers. Some organizations choose partial outsourcing, which usually involves hardware and peripheral support. Managers may also take advantage of the support provided by manufacturers as well as online services that make it possible for employees to help themselves.

User Support and User Satisfaction

End users often find it difficult to adapt to the rapid changes in their jobs that result from information systems innovations. Support provided to users is crucial for this adaptation. A 1993 study by Meral

Büyükkurt and Everett Vass showed that end user support contributed to end user satisfaction.

Previous studies of end user support have hoped to discover factors that are particularly influential in affecting user satisfaction. Even if such factors are identified, however, each organization will still need to perform its own studies to assure that those factors are relevant in their particular environment. In research published in 1994, Mirani and King presented an instrument that identified types of support provided by information centers (help desks). Other researches have added or categorized support factors in order to measure end user satisfaction. Factors considered include information system staff response time and technical competence, software upgrades, ease of access to computing facilities for the user, cost effectiveness of the IT systems in the company, user understanding of the organization's IT system, documentation to support training, and data security and privacy.

Managing Support Personnel

Having reliable support is crucial if companies are to use their information systems to accomplish their business goals effectively, yet in the early 2000s, the United States faced a shortage of support workers. The need for people with technical support skills continues to increase. In 2002 the *Journal of Education for Business* noted that computer support specialists report a 97 percent rate of projected job growth between 2000 and 2010.

Companies are facing challenges in recruiting, hiring, developing, compensating, and retaining information technology (IT) staff. Conclusions about recruiting and hiring IT personnel from a study that R. Ryan Nelson and Peter Todd conducted between 1998 and 2001 include that managers concurred that it is better to focus on getting quality applicants than to worry about quantity and that the ability to learn new technologies is critical. User support staff typically spend more than 80 percent of their time on phone duty and the balance researching and working to resolve problems. This does not leave them much time for other activities, such as receiving further training and development. An effective compensation strategy should tie rewards to performance

and be customized to fit specific groups and individuals. Retention is primarily about job satisfaction and fit with the organizational culture. Retention strategies should focus on maximizing three types of satisfaction: personal, professional, and social.

The Future

The increase in support costs witnessed in the early 2000s will continue, especially with increasing security problems (viruses, denial-of-service attacks, and worms) that affect productivity. In addition, users are continually demanding better support services as their computers have more capabilities, they feel more confident with technology, and they consequently have more demands.

Online support will continue to develop as technology does, but demand for support staff is increasing, and IT personnel will be always required. In the last few years, academic programs or courses that would develop such end-user support skills as problem solving, communication skills, and skills in interpersonal relations in addition to technical skills have been suggested as ways to prepare information systems professionals for the increasing demands of end users.

Indira R. Guzman

See also Instruction Manuals; User-Centered Design; User Modeling

FURTHER READING

Beisse, F. (2001). *A guide to computer user support for help desk & support specialists* (2nd ed.). Cambridge, MA: Course Technology.

Berry, R. L., & Yager, S. E. (1999). Preparing IS professionals to support end users: The development of an end user support course. In *Proceedings of the Decision Sciences Institute Conference1999* (pp. 305–307). Atlanta, GA: Decision Sciences Institute.

Bowman, B., Grupe, F. H., Lund, D., & Moore, W. D. (1993). An examination of sources of support preferred by end user computing personnel. *Journal of End User Computing, 5*(4), 4–11.

Büyükkurt, M., & Vass, E. (1993). An investigation of factors contributing to satisfaction with end-user computing process. *Canadian Journal of Administrative Sciences, 10*(3), 212–229.

Doherty, S. (2001). Helpdesk salvation. *Network Computing, 12*(1), 42–48.

Govindarajulu, C., & Lippert, S.K. (June 2002). The status of end-user computing support: An exploratory study. In *Informing science & IT education conference proceedings* (pp. 581–585). Retrieved

January 22, 2004, from http://ecommerce.lebow.drexel.edu/eli/2002Proceedings/papers/Govin163Statu.pdf

Karsten, R. (2002). An analysis of IS professional and end user causal attributions for user-system outcomes. *Journal of End User Computing, 14*(4), 51–73.

Lee, D., Trauth, E., & Farwell, D. (1995). Critical skills and knowledge requirements of IS professionals: A joint academic/industry investigation. *MIS Quarterly, 19*(3), 313–340.

McGill, T. J. (2002). User-developed applications: Can end users assess quality? *Journal of End User Computing, 14*(3), 1–15.

Mirani, R. & King, W.R. (1994). The development of a measure for end-user computing support. *Decision Sciences, 25*(4), 481–498.

Nelson, R. R. & Todd, P. A. (2003). Peopleware: The hiring and retention of IT personnel. In M. Igbaria & C. Shayo (Eds.), *Strategies for managing IS/IT personnel* (pp. 1–17). Hershey, PA: Idea Group Publishing.

Newburger, E. C. (2001). *Home computers and Internet use in the United States: August 2000, Special Studies.* Retrieved January 23, 2004, from http://www.census.gov/prod/2001pubs/p23-207.pdf

Shaw, N. C., DeLone, W. H., & Niederman, F. (2002). Sources of dissatisfaction in end-user support: An empirical study. *Database for Advances in Information Systems, 3*(2), 41–55.

Yager, S. E., & Berry, R. L. (2002). Preparing end user support specialists. *Journal of Education for Business, 78*(2), 92–96.

USER-CENTERED DESIGN

The design of everyday objects is not always intuitive, and at times it leaves the user frustrated and unable to complete a simple task. User-centered design (UCD) is a broad term that describes design processes in which end users influence how a design takes shape. Developers consult users about their needs and involve them at specific times during the design process, typically during requirements gathering and usability testing. Some UCD methods involve users much more completely; recognizing users as partners with designers throughout the design process.

History

The term *user-centered design* originated in the 1980s in the research laboratory of the cognitive psychologist Donald Norman at the University of California at San Diego (UCSD) and became widely used after the 1986 publication of *User-Centered System Design:*

New Perspectives on Human-Computer Interaction, which Norman edited with the psychologist Stephen Draper. Norman built further on the UCD concept in his 1988 book *The Psychology of Everyday Things* (*POET*). (The book was reissued in 2002 as *The Design of Everyday Things.*) In *POET* Norman recognizes the needs and the interests of the user and focuses on the usability of the design. He offers four basic suggestions regarding design:

- Make it easy to determine what actions are possible at any moment (make use of constraints).
- Make things visible, including the conceptual model of the system, the alternative actions, and the results of actions.
- Make it easy to evaluate the current state of the system.
- Follow natural mappings between intentions and the required actions; between actions and the resulting effect; and between the information that is visible and the interpretation of the system state. (Norman 1988, 188)

These recommendations place the user at the center of the design. The role of the designer is to facilitate the task for the user and to make sure that the user is able to use the product as intended, with a minimum of time spent learning how to use it. Telling designers that products should be intuitive is not enough, however. Norman suggested that the following seven principles of design are essential for facilitating the designer's task. These seven tasks are subordinates of the four basic principles mentioned above, and they help to ensure that the designer has a list of guidelines that is intuitive to follow:

1. "Use both knowledge in the world and knowledge in the head." By building conceptual models, write manuals that are easily understood and that are written before the design is implemented.
2. "Simplify the structure of tasks." Make sure not to overload the short-term memory or the long-term memory of the user. On average the user is able to remember five things at a time. Make sure the task in consistent and provide mental aids for easy retrieval of information

from long-term memory. Make sure the user has control over the task.

3. "Make things visible: bridge the gulfs of Execution and Evaluation." The user should be able to figure out the use of an object by seeing the right buttons or devices for executing an operation.

4. "Get the mappings right." One way to make things understandable is to use graphics.

5. "Exploit the power of constraints, both natural and artificial," in order to give the user the feel that there is one thing to do.

6. "Design for error." Plan for any possible error that can be made; this way the user will be allowed the option of recovery from any possible error made.

7. "When all else fails, standardize." Create an international standard if something cannot be designed without arbitrary mappings. (Norman 1998, 189–201)

In 1987 the computer scientist Ben Shneiderman articulated a similar set of principles in the form of eight golden rules. Later the engineer Jakob Nielsen adapted and popularized these same basic concepts to produce heuristics (problem-solving techniques) for usability engineering.

Norman stressed the need to explore users' needs and desires and the product's intended uses fully. Involving actual users, often in the environment in which they would use the product being designed, was a natural evolution in the field of user-centered design. Users became a central part of the development process. Their involvement led to more effective, efficient, and safer products and contributed to the acceptance and success of products.

How to Involve Users in Design

It is necessary to think carefully about who a user is and how to involve users in the design process. Obviously the people who will use the final product or artifact to accomplish a task or goal are users, but there are other users as well. The people who manage the users have needs and expectations too, as do the people who are affected by the product or artifact's use, and those who use the by-products (either services or other products) that the product or artifact produces. Ken Eason, who studies the effect of information technology on organizations, has identified three types of users: primary, secondary, and tertiary. Primary users are those who actually use the artifact; secondary users are those who will occasionally use the artifact or those who use it through an intermediary; tertiary users are those who will be affected by the use of the artifact or make decisions about its purchase. For a product design to be successful, it should take all three levels of user into account.

Once the stakeholders have been identified and a thorough investigation of their needs has been conducted, designers can develop alternative design solutions that users may then evaluate. These design solutions can be simple paper-and-pencil drawings in the beginning phase of the process. Listening to users discuss the alternative designs can amplify designers' understanding of the intended purpose(s) of the artifact and may provide information that does not come out of initial interviews, observations, and needs analysis. As the design cycle progresses, prototypes (limited versions of the product or artifact) can be produced and user tested. At this point, designers should pay close attention to users' evaluations, as the evaluations will help identify measurable usability criteria in the areas of effectiveness, efficiency, safety, utility, learnability, and memorability (how long it takes to remember to perform the most common tasks). Evaluations will also reveal users' satisfaction with the product or artifact. It is only through feedback collected in an interactive, iterative process involving users that products can be refined. The discussion so far indicates the central role of usability testing in UCD, which we examine in more detail in the next section before discussing participatory design, which is a form of UCD that has gained strong acceptance in recent years.

Usability Testing

Usability testing should make a product more usable, involve actual users and real tasks, and generate results that testers can observe, record, and analyze. Usability testing focuses on user needs, relies on empirical measurement, and employs iterative design. Designers of interactive systems are now aware that many pilot tests should be conducted before releasing any product to the public. In this section the discussion is limited to design of

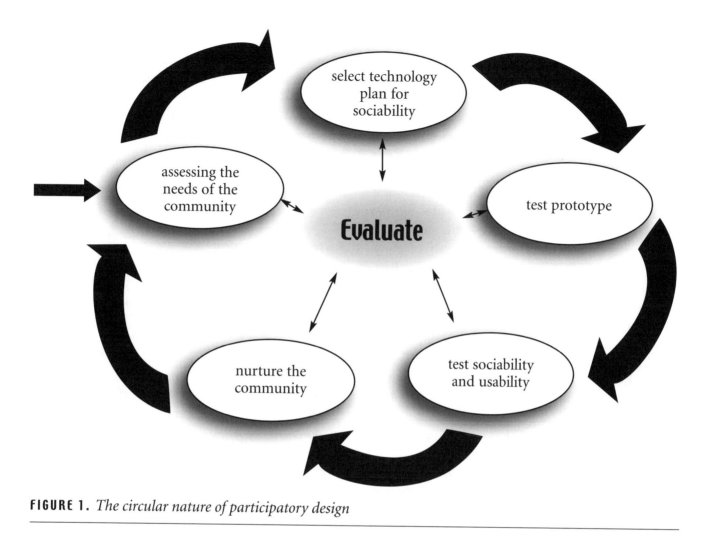

FIGURE 1. *The circular nature of participatory design*

computer-related systems. Shneiderman has observed that an interactive system is like a play: Extensive rehearsals are expected, especially close to opening night. Historically, usability tests are conducted in usability laboratories staffed by experts in user-interface design and testing. These laboratories are set up so that designers can observe the testers unnoticed. While large companies such as Microsoft and IBM still rely on usability laboratories, the cost of running such laboratories and the distributed nature of many systems make it increasingly common for developers to use mobile usability testing kits instead—at a fraction of the cost.

In computer design, before product implementation, paper mock-ups of screen displays can be tested in order to assess the wording and layout. Techniques that are employed in usability testing include thinking aloud (the user is asked to articulate all of his or her actions), videotaping the users in action, and interviewing the users or having them fill out questionnaires to gain insight into how well they liked the design under investigation.

Generally usability tests require typical users to perform typical, standardized tasks in a typical task environment so that the designers can learn how long it takes users to learn a specific function, how fast they perform the task, the type of errors they make, and at what rate they make errors.

After the product is released, it is wise to continue with evaluations. The most common methods for evaluating products after they have been released are interviews and focus groups. Both provide valuable information about user satisfaction and any problems with the product's functionality that might need rethinking. Data logging may also be performed.

Variations on Usability Testing

Usability testing has limitations: It does not cover all the interface features, and because it lasts for only a few hours in the laboratory, it does not reveal how the product is going to perform over long periods of time in the real environment. Furthermore, the small number of participants rarely represents the whole population of users.

The cognitive psychologist Deborah Mayhew recommends the usability engineering lifecycle as a complete approach to developing a human-computer interface. It includes three phases of iterative testing. The first-level evaluation is an iterative conceptual-model evaluation, designed to get feedback before any code has been developed. Formal usability testing is often done at this stage. For each iteration, there should be between three to ten users, the testing should be done in the workplace, and a minimum of instructions should be provided in order to test ease of learning. The next testing stage should be done after the prototype has been coded to get early feedback about its usability. The same evaluation principles used in the first-level evaluations are employed here, except that at this second level, the prototype takes the place of the paper mock-up. The third testing phase occurs after the interface is ready, and its purpose is to evaluate the final product against the usability goals set at the beginning of development.

Website usability testing can also take a user-centered approach. It is recommended that usability testing begin when a paper prototype has been created and continue as the interface is coded, but in reality most websites are not tested before implementation. Usually testing is done with users and with experts through expert reviews. Experts can comment on overall usability issues while users can point out small problems related to tasks. It is advisable to involve users from the target audience and to follow the same procedures as for testing software applications. Testing can take place in a laboratory, in the workplace, or at home with the designer observing the user's interactions with the system.

One problem with usability testing is that it is expensive, which has prompted development of alternative testing techniques, the most well-known of which are heuristic (guidelines for evaluation) and discount usability testing. In heuristic evaluation experts inspect the application or website guided by high-level heuristics such as "reduce load on short-term memory," and based on their knowledge of the target user population, they identify problems with the design. Discount usability evaluation provides a variation on this theme; the claim is that three to five reviewers identify around 80 percent of the usability problems. The low cost of these approaches makes them attractive to developers, but there is concern about their efficacy.

Participatory Design

In participatory design, users are in essence co-designers. The participatory design approach emerged in Scandinavia, born out of labor unions' push for workers to have more democratic control in their work environment. Because of cultural differences that may exist between users and designers (for example, users sometimes may be unable to understand the language of the designers), it is recommended that the team uses prototypes, such as mock-ups or paper-based outlines of the screen of a webpage or of a product. Prototypes are especially important given cultural differences, since they allow for hands-on work and transcend words. Other types of prototyping techniques are PICTIVE (Plastic Interface for Collaborative Technology Initiatives through Video Exploration) and CARD (Collaborative Analysis of Requirements and Design). The PICTIVE prototyping method uses office products, such as pens, papers, and sticky notes. The actions of the users are videotaped. CARD uses playing cards with pictures of specific items on them. They allow the designer to map a layout of the product using a picture of each item to be included in the design. PICTIVE concentrates on the detailed aspects of the system, while CARD looks at the flow of the task.

In recent years the participatory design approach has been used for designing novel systems. For example, Allison Druin (2002), a scholar in the field of information studies, and her team have developed a version of participatory design in which children help develop children's software. Jenny Preece, a scholar of information systems, has developed a form of participatory, community-centered design for developing online communities. In 2003 the scholars Chadia Abras, Diana Maloney-Krichmar, and Jenny

Preece created an online community for a doctoral program using participatory design.

Advantages and Disadvantages of User-Centered Design

The major advantage of user-centered design is that it makes possible a deeper understanding of the psychological, organizational, social, and ergonomic factors that affect the use of computer technology. The involvement of users assures that the product will be suitable for its intended purpose in the environment in which it will be used. This approach leads to the development of products that are more effective, efficient, and safer.

It also helps designers manage user's expectations about a new product. When users have been involved in the design of a product, they know from an early stage what to expect from a product, and they feel that their ideas and suggestions have been taken into account during the process. This is true if the small percentage of users involved in testing is a true representation of the users in the target population. This leads to a sense of ownership of the final product that often results in higher customer satisfaction and smoother integration of the product into the environment. If the process is not user-centered, it could lead to ill-thought-out designs. When users' expectations are not met, users may get frustrated or angry.

The major disadvantage of user-centered design is that is can be quite costly. It takes time to gather data from and about users, especially if you seek to understand the environment in which they will be using the products. The process requires resources, both financial and human. User-centered design teams generally benefit from including people from different disciplines, particularly psychologists, sociologists, and anthropologists, whose jobs are to understand users' needs and communicate them to the technical developers in the team. The downside to this approach is that members of the team have to learn to communicate effectively and to respect one another's contributions and expertise. This can be time consuming and hence adds costs to the process. Management may question whether the added value

is worth the cost, particularly if delivery dates are threatened. Fortunately, the concept of user-centered design is broad, and therefore flexible. As discussed above, certain types of user-centered design are less expensive than others. Given that involving users in design has been shown to result in more usable, satisfying designs, we expect that, despite its costs, user-centered design will continue to be popular.

Chadia Abras, Diane Maloney-Krichmar, and Jenny Preece

See also Cognitive Walkthrough; User Modeling

FURTHER READING

Abras, C. (2003). *Determining success in online education and health communities: Developing usability and sociability heuristics.* Unpublished doctoral dissertation, University of Maryland, Baltimore County.

Abras, C., Maloney-Krichmar, D., & Preece, J. (2003, June). *Evaluating an online academic community: "Purpose" is the key.* Paper presented at the HCI International 2003, Crete, Greece.

Dicks, R. S. (2002). *Mis-usability: On the uses and misuses of usability testing.* Paper presented at the Annual ACM Conference on Systems Documentation, Toronto, Ontario, Canada.

Dix, A., Finlay, J., Abowd, G., & Beale, R. (1997). *Human-Computer Interaction* (2nd ed.). New York: Prentice-Hall.

Druin, A. (2002). The role of children in the design of new technology. *Behaviour and Information Technology, 21*(1), 1–25.

Dumas, J. S., & Redish, J. C. (1993). *A practical guide to usability testing.* Norwood, NJ: Ablex.

Eason, K. (1987) *Information technology and organizational change.* London: Taylor and Francis.

Ehn, P. (1989). *Word-oriented design of computer artifacts* (2nd ed.). Hillsdale, NJ: Lawrence Erlbaum Associates.

Ehn, P., & Kyng, M. (1991). Cardboard computers: Mocking-it-up or hands-on the future. In J. Grenbaum & M. Kyng (Eds.), *Design at work* (pp. 169–196) Hillsdale, NJ: Lawrence Erlbaum Associates.

Gould, J. D., & Lewis, C. (1985). Designing for usability: Key principles and what designers think. Communications of the ACM, 28(3), 300–311.

Kuhn, S. (1996). Design for people at work. In T. Winograd (Ed.), *Bringing design to software* (pp. 273–289) Boston: Addison-Wesley.

Lazar, J. (2001). *User-centered Web development.* Boston: Jones and Bartlett Computer Science.

Mayhew, D. J. (1999). *The usability engineering lifecycle.* San Francisco: Morgan Kaufmann.

Muller, M. J. (1991). PICTIVE-An exploration in participatory design. In *Proceedings of CHI '91* (pp. 225–231). New York: ACM Press.

Nielsen, J. (1993). *Usability Engineering.* San Francisco: Morgan Kaufmann.

Nielsen, J. (1994). *Guerilla HCI: Using discount usability engineering to penetrate the intimidation barrier.* Retrieved December 30, 2003, from http://www.useit.com/papers/guerrilla_hci.html

Nielsen, J. (1999). *Voodoo usability.* Retrieved December 30, 2003, from http://www.useit.com/alertbox/991212.html

Nielsen, J. (2001). *Ten usability heuristics.* Retrieved December 30, 2003, from http://www.useit.com/papers/heuristic/heuristic_list.html

Norman, D. (1988). *The psychology of everyday things.* New York: Doubleday.

Norman, D. A., & Draper, S. W. (Eds.). (1986). *User-centered system design: New perspectives on human-computer interaction.* Hillsdale, NJ: Lawrence Erlbaum Associates.

Preece, J. (2000). *Online communities: Designing usability, supporting sociability.* Chichester, UK: John Wiley & Sons.

Preece, J., Rogers, Y., & Sharp, H. (2002). *Interaction design: Beyond human-computer interaction.* New York: John Wiley & Sons.

Preece, J., Rogers, Y., Sharp, H., Benyon, D., Holland, S., & Carey, T. (1994). *Human-computer interaction.* Essex, UK: Addison-Wesley Longman.

Rubin, J. (1994). *Handbook of usability testing.* New York: John Wiley & Sons.

Shneiderman, B. (1998). *Designing the user interface: Strategies for effective human-computer interaction* (3rd ed.). Reading, MA: Addison-Wesley.

Tudor, L. G. (1993, October). *A participatory design technique for high-level task analysis, critique and redesign: The CARD method.* Paper presented at the Proceedings of the Human Factors and Ergonomics Society, Seattle, WA.

VALUE SENSITIVE DESIGN

Information technologies may either support or undermine enduring human values; sometimes they do both at the same time. For example, surveillance cameras in banks, malls, and airports increase individual and sometimes national security, but often at the expense of individual privacy. Similarly, images and text available on the Web increase access to and use of information, but can lead to infringements of intellectual property rights. In response to such problems, value sensitive design emerged in the mid-1990s as an approach to the design of information and computer systems that accounts for human values in a principled and comprehensive manner throughout the design process. Value sensitive design particularly emphasizes values with moral import, including privacy, trust, informed consent, respect for intellectual property rights, universal usability, freedom from bias, moral responsibility, accountability, honesty, and democracy. Value sensitive design also addresses values of usability (for example, how easy a system is to use), conventions (for example, standardization of protocols), and personal taste (for example, color preferences within a graphical user interface). Methodologically, value sensitive design integrates and iterates on three types of investigations: conceptual, empirical, and technical.

The Tripartite Methodology

Conceptual investigations comprise philosophically informed analyses of the central constructs and issues under investigation. For example, how does the philosophical literature conceptualize certain values and provide criteria for their assessment and implementation? What values have standing? How should we engage in trade-offs among competing values in the design, implementation, and use of information systems (for example, how do we balance autonomy and security, or anonymity and trust)? In addition to addressing these questions, conceptual investigations are concerned with the needs of two types of stakeholders: direct and indirect. Direct stakeholders are those who interact directly with the computer system or its output. Indirect stakeholders are those who are otherwise affected by the use of the system. For example, the direct stakeholders in a computerized medical records system would be doctors, nurses, insurance companies, and hospitals; one group of indirect stakeholders would be the patients. As this example shows, how the information system works can be just as important to indirect stakeholders as to direct stakeholders.

Empirical investigations focus on the human response to the technical artifact, and on the larger social context in which the technology is situated. The entire range of quantitative and qualitative methods used in social-science research may be applicable, including observations, interviews, surveys, focus groups, experimental manipulations, measurements of user behavior and human physiology, contextual inquiry, collection of relevant documents, and heuristic evaluation. Typically, empirical investigations serve to validate and expand key values identified in the conceptual investigations and to assess stakeholders' experience of the value-oriented features of a system at various stages in the design and deployment process.

Technical investigations focus on the design and performance of the technology itself. It is assumed that technologies in general, and information and computer technologies in particular, provide value "suitabilities" that follow from properties of the technology. That is, a given technology is more suitable for certain activities and more readily supports certain values while rendering other activities and values more difficult to realize. For example, an online calendar system that displays individuals' scheduled events in detail readily supports ac-countability within an organization but makes privacy difficult. In one form, technical investigations focus on how existing technological properties and underlying mechanisms support or hinder human values. In a second form, technical investigations involve the proactive design of systems to support values identified in the conceptual or empirical investigations.

The three types of investigations—conceptual, empirical, and technical—are employed iteratively such that the results of one type of investigation are integrated with those of the others, which in turn influence still other investigations of the earlier investigations.

Value Sensitive Design in Practice: An Example

To illustrate the practice of value sensitive design, consider the attempt by the researchers Batya Friedman, Edward Felten, and their colleagues to design web-based interactions that support informed consent in a web browser through the development of new technical mechanisms for cookie management. (A cookie is a small text string—often no more than an ID number—that is sent by a Web server to a browser. The text is then stored by that browser, typically on the user's hard drive, and sent back to a Web server at a later time.)

The team began their project with a conceptual investigation of informed consent itself. They drew on diverse literature, such as the 1987 Belmont Report (which delineates ethical principles and guidelines for the protection of human research subjects), to develop a model for informed consent in online interactions. In the model, *informed* means that the online sites provide adequate information in an intelligible fashion, while *consent* encompasses voluntariness, competence, and agreement. Next, the researchers used the results from their conceptual investigation—the model of informed consent online—to structure a technical investigation, which in this case was a retrospective analysis of how the cookie and web browser technology embedded in Netscape Navigator and Internet Explorer (the two most commonly used Web browsers) changed

AIBO, a robotic dog, moves toward a preschool child who has been petting the dog. Researchers at the University of Washington studying preschool interactions with robotic pets note that the such contacts may impede children's development by substituting for interactions with live animals. Photo courtesy of Kahn, P. H., Jr., Friedman, B., Perez-Granados, D. R., Freier, N. G. (2004). Robotic pets in the lives of preschool children. In Extended Abstracts of CHI 2004. *New York, NY: Association for Computing Machinery Press.*

with respect to informed consent over a five-year period beginning in 1995. Specifically, they used the five criteria of disclosure, comprehension, voluntariness, competence, and agreement to evaluate how well each browser supported informed consent. This technical investigation revealed that while advances were made in providing information so as to elicit informed consent, problems remained. For example, in both Netscape Navigator and Internet Explorer, the information disclosed about a cookie still did not adequately specify what the information would be used for or how the user might benefit or be harmed by its use. Moreover, the default setting, hidden from view on both browsers, was to accept all cookies.

Friedman and her colleagues then used the results from their first two investigations to guide a second technical investigation: a redesign of the Mozilla browser (the open-source code for Netscape Navigator). Specifically, they developed three new types of mechanisms: peripheral awareness of cookies, just-in-time information about individual cookies and cookies in general, and just-in-time management of cookies. (In this case *just-in-time* means that users can call up information with a single mouse click regarding a specific cookie or cookies in general at any time during their Web browsing.) The researchers also conducted empirical investigations—formative evaluations to assess how well their working designs were providing the user with informed consent. The results of the empirical investigation eventually led the researchers to add the criterion of minimizing distraction from the task at hand to their original set of five criteria in the initial conceptual investigation.

This project helps illustrate the iterative and integrative nature of value sensitive design. It also demonstrates that value sensitive design can be applied successfully to mainstream Internet software for a diverse group of users.

What Is Unique About Value Sensitive Design?

At least four other overarching approaches have sought to account for human values in systems design: computer ethics, social informatics, computer-supported cooperative work, and participatory design. Value sensitive design builds on many of the strengths (and techniques) of these approaches, but in addition value sensitive design offers a unique approach based on a constellation of seven features.

First, as described above, value sensitive design builds on the integration and iteration of conceptual, empirical, and technical investigations. Second, value sensitive design seeks to be proactive, to influence the design of technology early in and throughout the design process. Third, while value sensitive design can be employed alongside of existing successful software engineering methodologies, it dovetails particularly well with those that support open, agile, and flexible information architectures that respond quickly to new value considerations as they emerge throughout the design and deployment process. Fourth, value sensitive design enlarges the arena in which values are considered from the workplace (as is traditional in the field of computer-supported cooperative work) to education, the home, commerce, online communities, and public life. Fifth, value sensitive design takes not

only such values as cooperation (as in computer-supported cooperative work), participation, and democracy (as in participatory design) into consideration, but all values, especially those with moral import. Sixth, value sensitive design is an interactional theory: Values are viewed neither as inscribed into technology nor as simply transmitted by social forces. Rather, value sensitive design believes both that people and social systems affect technological development and that new technologies shape (but do not rigidly determine) individual behavior and social systems. Seventh, value sensitive design maintains that certain values (such as those that pertain to human welfare) are universally held, although how such values play out in a particular culture at a particular point in time can vary considerably. For example, even while living in an igloo, Inuits have conventions that ensure some forms of privacy; yet such forms of privacy are not maintained by separated rooms, as they are in most Western cultures. Generally, the more concretely one conceptualizes a value (that is, the more it is captured in actual actions), the more one will recognize cultural variation; conversely, the more abstractly one conceptualizes a value, the more one will recognize universals. Value sensitive design seeks to work on both concrete and abstract levels.

Recent Work and Future Directions

Studies that have successfully drawn on value sensitive design have focused on such topics as bias in computer systems, search engines, privacy in public spaces, informed consent, electronic access to information in the public domain, the human-robotic relationship, autonomy and privacy in hardware design, and the use of simulations to explore the interactions of land use, transportation, and environmental planning in urban development.

Numerous opportunities exist to extend and validate value sensitive design. Here are seven areas in which we can expect to see future work emerge.

1. The integrative and iterative methodology. Value sensitive design builds on an emerging methodology that integrates and iterates on conceptual,

empirical, and technical investigations. Each component needs further development and explication, as does their interaction.

2. Diverse values. Researchers will want to investigate how value sensitive design handles diverse values within the same information or computer system, particularly when those values come into conflict. A subset of this problem is how to balance moral and nonmoral values.

3. Diverse technologies. Value sensitive design should be successful across a wide range of technologies, including ones that involve large systems embedded in the social and political landscape (such as simulations that look at how land use, transportation, and environmental planning interact in urban development).

4. Diverse populations. Value sensitive design should be successful for populations that are diverse in terms of age, culture, and lifestyle. It should be able to account for such diversity while allowing for some universal standardization of design.

5. Industry. Value sensitive design should be able to adapt to an industry context, where economic constraints and the need for fast product development drive much of the technical development.

6. Value-oriented metrics and evaluation. Value sensitive design should provide techniques for evaluating the value-oriented features of information and computer systems.

7. Transfer of methodology. Given its multidisciplinary nature, the methodology behind value sensitive design should be transferable to a larger academic community and industry. Questions still need to be answered about how to apply value sensitive design and to integrate these methods with industry practice

Value sensitive design seeks to offer a response to a pervasive problem in fields related to human-computer interaction, namely, that various approaches do certain things well, but leave out crucial components. For example, Orlikowski and Iacono (2001) reviewed ten years of work in information systems research and found that the technological

artifact itself "tends to disappear from view, be taken for granted, or is presumed to be unproblematic once it is built and installed" (121). Similarly, in reviewing the field of social informatics, Johnson writes: "One aspect that still confounds me is how to reconcile the basic premise of social informatics—that it is critical to gain knowledge of the social practices and values of the intended users—with the basic work of system developers. How, if at all, can programmers practice and apply social informatics?" (Johnson 2000, 18). Value sensitive design answers this question by proposing the iterative integration of conceptual, empirical, and technical investigations, grounded in an overarching theory with intellectual commitments from philosophy, the social sciences, and system design.

Batya Friedman

See also Social Informatics

FURTHER READING

Camp, J. L. (2000). *Trust and risk in Internet commerce.* Cambridge, MA: MIT Press.

Friedman, B. (Ed.). (1997). *Human values and the design of computer technology.* New York and Stanford, CA: Cambridge University Press and CSLI, Stanford University.

Friedman, B., & Nissenbaum, H. (1996). Bias in computer systems. *ACM Transactions on Information Systems, 14*(3), 330–347.

Friedman, B., Howe, D. C., & Felten, E. (2002). Informed consent in the Mozilla browser: Implementing value sensitive design. In *Proceedings of the Thirty-Fifth Annual Hawai'i International Conference on System Sciences* [CD-ROM]. Los Alamitos, CA: IEEE Computer Society.

Friedman, B., & Kahn, Jr., P. H. (2003). Human values, ethics, and design. In J. A. Jacko & A. Sears (Eds.), *The human-computer interaction handbook* (pp. 1177–1201). Mahwah, NJ: Lawrence Erlbaum Associates.

Hagman, J., Hendrickson, A., & Whitty, A. (in press). What's in a barcode: Informed consent and machine scannable driver licenses. In *CHI 2003 Extended Abstracts of the Conference on Human Factors in Computing Systems.* CD-ROM. New York: ACM Press.

Introna, L., & Nissenbaum, H. (2000). Shaping the Web: Why the politics of search engines matters. *The Information Society, 16*(3), 1–17.

Jancke, G., Venolia, G. D., Grudin, J., Cadiz, J. J., & Gupta, A. (2001). Linking public spaces: Technical and social issues. In *CHI 2001 Conference Proceedings* (pp. 530–537). New York: ACM Press.

Johnson, E. H. (2000). Getting beyond the simple assumptions of organization impact. *Bulletin of the American Society for Information Science, 26*(3), 18–19.

Kahn, Jr., P. H., Friedman, B., & Hagman, J. (2002). "I care about him as a pal": Conceptions of robotic pets in online AIBO discussion forums. In *CHI 2002 Extended Abstracts* (pp. 632–633). New York: ACM Press.

Nissenbaum, H. (1998). Protecting privacy in an information age: The problem of privacy in public. *Law and Philosophy, 17,* 559–596.

Orlikowski, W. J., & Iacono, C. S. (2001). Research commentary: Desperately seeking the "IT" in IT research—A call to theorizing the IT artifact. *Information Systems Research, 12*(2), 121–134.

Shneiderman, B. (2000). Universal usability. *Communications of the ACM, 42*(5), 84–91.

Tang, J. C. (1997). Eliminating a hardware switch: Weighing economics and values in a design decision. In B. Friedman (Ed.), *Human values and the design of computer technology* (pp. 259–269). New York: Cambridge University Press and CSLI, Stanford University.

Thomas, J. C. (1997). Steps toward universal access within a communications company. In B. Friedman (Ed.), *Human values and the design of computer systems* (pp. 271–287). New York: Cambridge University Press and CSLI, Stanford University.

VIDEO

Video is the visual element of television and movies. People also use video to communicate with computers, robots, information systems, the Internet, and other media whose displays present video for entertainment or understanding. Understanding of video by such media provides scientific rationale for searchable video databases, robotic navigation, biometric security systems (based on face recognition), industrial inspection systems, and machines commanded by eye gaze or gesture.

Creating Video

Video input devices include analogue and digital cameras and electronic video capture systems. Examples include cameras for television and cinematography and desktop computer video cards that transmit live video streams or store video clips for subsequent retrieval. Multiple or mobile camera systems can provide information for reconstruction of three-dimensional (3D) scenes.

Capture

Video cameras typically scan scenes into regular patterns (rasters) of scanning lines organized into picture elements (pixels) with fixed separation (res-

olution) responding to primary colors (red, blue, green). Each frame is defined by the time it takes the scanning mechanism to complete one scan. In non-interlaced video, each frame is scanned by reading all the lines of each stored image pixel by pixel with electronic circuitry that addresses and determines the charge state of the memory element corresponding to each pixel, retracing the scan to start the next frame. In interlaced video, each frame is scanned by reading certain lines of the image, retracing to scan lines missed on the previous scan. By contrast, the human eye focuses peripheral regions of a scene onto rods of the retina for monochrome vision at low resolution (peripheral vision) while making involuntary movements to focus selected regions of a scene onto centrally located cones of the retina sensitive to primary colors at higher resolution (foveal vision).

Television cameras and movie cameras typically provide electrical signals encoded in standard formats, including those developed by the National Television Standards Committee (NTSC, 29.97 frames per second), primarily used in the United States and Japan; the international committees for the Sequential Couleur Avec Memoire (SECAM [sequential color with memory], 25 frames per second), a system widely used in France and the Commonwealth of Independent States; and Phase Alternating Line (PAL, 25 frames per second) systems that are found in the United Kingdom and West Germany. These electrical signals are often digitized in accordance with the Consultative Committee for International Radio (CCIR) digital standards. Analogue video is captured as the intensity and displacement in time (phase) of an electrical signal relative to a broadcast carrier wave, unlike the logical on and off signals of digital video. Common analogue video storage formats include VHS, Super VHS, and Betacam SP, whereas digital storage formats include the widely used Digital Betacam and DVCPro50.

Animation

Animation is another use of video. Animation relies on the phenomenon of human persistence of vision to create an illusion of continuous motion by displaying a sequence of images (frames).

Animation input devices include pressure-sensitive graphics tablets, styli, light pens, computer mice, and scanners. If animation key frames drawn or directly constructed by the animator are provided, computer systems can generate user-specified motion for animated characters (avatars). In an alternative approach to animation input, live actors perform scripts wearing suits equipped with motion sensors whose recorded movements may be applied to avatars. Facial animation provides realistic avatar expression in response to input speech or phonemes (units of language that correspond to a set of similar speech sounds).

Animation information is often expressed in terms of lines, colors, shading, lighting, and other geometric constructs (vectors) displayed (rendered) by computer graphics techniques. Video streams suitable for television or movies often contain rendered vectors mixed with rasters. Interactive television systems such as OpenTV and Liberate may express animation information as executable content (computer programs) suitable for display by the graphics subsystem of a digital television set top converter box.

The OpenTV system was based on Object Application Kernel (OAK) technology developed by Sun Microsystems to permit computer programs to run effectively on multiple computer operating systems, forerunner to the programming language Java. The Liberate system provides an interactive content development environment similar to Javascript scripting language and the hypertext markup language (HTML) familiar to Internet content developers. Executable content is inserted into video streams by specialized servers in a way that can be recognized or requested by a set top box.

Visualization of models that evolve over time is an additional source of video content. Examples include weather maps, traffic flow patterns, games, and simulations displayed in video form for rapid comprehension.

Coding

Codecs that code, decode, compress, and decompress digital video signals are critical to the storage and retrieval of video information transmitted via media of significantly lower data rate (bandwidth). For example, a 760×480-pixel digital movie stored at 8-bit resolution, which encodes up to 255 levels for each of the red, blue, and green primary colors transmitted at 29.97 frames per second without compression would require about $760 \times 480 \times 8$ by $3 \times 29.97 = 262$ million bits per second (Mbps) bandwidth. Consequently, an 860-megahertz (MHz) cable television system that can switch digital signals on and off no faster than 860 million times per second could deliver at most about three movie channels in continuous use, and the delivery of five hundred channels would require an average signal compression of about 154:1.

The widely used Moving Picture Experts Group (MPEG) standards provide one solution to this dilemma, approximating the video by a reduced bandwidth signal such that the difference between the exact and approximate video is not noticeable by the typical human eye. Since the first MPEG standard (MPEG-1) for the coding of moving pictures and associated audio for digital storage media at up to about 1.5 Mbit per second was released in five parts during the period 1993–1998, several standards (MPEG-2, -4, -7) have addressed the generic coding of moving pictures to enable digital television set-top boxes, Digital Versatile Discs (DVDs), mobile video, and searchable video databases. Researchers have started work on a new standard (MPEG-21) that provides an interoperable framework for everyone involved in the delivery and use of multimedia and that addresses issues such as copyright protection.

Editing Video

Since the Ampex Corporation introduced the analogue video tape recorder in 1956 and the analogue video tape splicer in 1958, concepts familiar to film strip editors have percolated into editing video destined for television and movies. Online editing (creating a finished product ready for distribution) and offline editing (which results in a preview); inserting, changing, and deleting video frames in arbitrary order (nonlinear editing); combining and separating multiple video tracks; and locating frames via control tracks with associated time code have all entered the editor's repertoire. The advent of digital video frame stores in the mid-1970s (which store up to several fames of digital video) led to the development of digital editing systems such as the Abekas A53D and the Grass Valley Group Kaleidoscope.

These expensive room-sized broadcast editing systems require skilled operators who can navigate a complex editing console. Although requiring a high level of artistic skill, desktop video editing has become a reality at greatly reduced price. MPEG video editing inserts, changes, and deletes key frames and associated picture sequences. Software programs such as Adobe Premiere present the user with icons of traditional editing tools, including A/B roll workspaces (allowing switching between two or more video sources), video preview, clip bin, multiple video tracks, key frame tracks, timeline, and effects palettes. OpenTV Author provides a graphical interface for interactive television content by letting the user drag and drop executable elements termed "gadgets" onto a representation of the screen. Using Digital Storage Management carousel extensions to the MPEG standards (which broadcast executable content repeatedly), links to executable content may be mixed with the video and streamed on request.

Special Effects

Video special effects may alter scenes by changing sizes, shapes, colors, textures, lighting, shading, and other geometric properties. Scenes may be superimposed on the screen, accelerated, or decelerated in a timeline. Of special note, the chroma key process allows the user to composite any region of a video frame with another when that region has a specified range (termed a "key") of color (chroma) or luminance (luma). New special effects sometimes result from serendipitous discovery, whereas effects such as fractal geometry (shapes that appear similar to within a geometric distortion at every level of detail) or geometric distortion are based on extensive mathematical analysis. Application of special effects to digital video stretches the limits of data storage capacity and data retrieval rate, spurring developments in data compression (e.g., wavelets) and the advance of desktop video editing systems based on the recent MPEG-4 standard.

A movie is typically referred for post-production editing after it has been produced and captured on camera. A typical postproduction video editing suite comprises at least some of the following components: Edit controllers, linear and nonlinear editing bays with switchers for switching video sources, character generators for titling and captioning, digital video effects generators, downstream keyers for performing dissolves, logos and captioning, chroma key for matteing (e.g., covering the top and bottom of the image to make it look wider), large video friendly hard disk and, graphic workstations for animation and graphical input. In a manner similar to chroma key, the downstream keyer replaces the lightest (or darkest) portions of the downstream keyer video signal with the video source signal, leaving the dark areas showing the original video image. To synchronize these editing systems for processing and displaying video in a stable scanning pattern, a master sync generator sends out horizontal and vertical synchronization signals together with the subcarrier (the basic stabilizing signal) for application by the system components in a process known as "genlocking."

Video databases store and retrieve video content, whereas video servers serve the content to human or machine users on demand. The long-felt need to search and browse video by content is addressed by the MPEG-7 multimedia description standard. Current techniques for automatic indexing by content include scene change detection, key frame selection, and understanding images of located frames.

Using Video

Human interaction with television has been somewhat passive and group oriented since the first public demonstration of mechanical monochrome television by John Logie Baird (1888–1946) on 23 January 1926 and the efforts of Philo T. Farnsworth (1906–1971) and Vladimir Zworykin (1889–1982) to develop electrical television during the 1920s and 1930s. Although technology has advanced from channel changing to Internet-like interaction—and many attempts have been made to increase viewer interactivity—frequent scene changes due to cuts, edits, pans, and zooms seem only to overload, disorient, and tranquilize viewers. Currently based on the MPEG-2 standard, compressed digital television promises to increase the number of channels by more effective utilization of bandwidth than analogue television.

Movies

Movie rental on VHS tape or DVD is widespread, fueled by access to many titles. Cinemas present new titles on big screens with many channels of Surround Sound. Efforts to improve the movie-going experience by adding stereo effects have not yet been spectacularly successful, requiring special glasses to properly deliver the images to the left and right eyes. The advent of digital cinema based on wavelet or advanced MPEG compression solves the problem of movie distribution by facilitating near-simultaneous screening in remote digital theaters.

Video on Demand

Video on Demand (VOD) delivers video on request via cable, broadband, or digital television. Subscription VOD (sVOD) is a marketing framework in which a television viewer subscribes to unlimited access to subscription movies and pays per view for access to premium movies. This causes typical subscribers to browse subscription movies but to watch premium movies all the way through.

Mobile Video Phone

Mobile phone video based on MPEG-4 standards is available over high-bandwidth 2.5G (packet switched) telephone networks. Presenting information by this communication medium requires careful selection and reformatting for the typical short viewing distance (about 40 centimeters) and useable screen size (about 176×182 pixels).

Scientific Systems

Video also can be used to record the behavior of subjects for subsequent analysis in life science experiments. Other sciences, such as astronomy, have also developed large scientific databases with much imaging and video content. Interactive visualization of data from these databases challenges available computing resource, to which a grid of low cost workstations seems a promising answer.

Video Conferencing

Multipoint room-based and desktop video conferencing systems often save travel expense, especially for viewers who have already established trust and are familiar with each other's nonverbal signals.

Viewers typically see a graphical representation of the conference with windows for observing participants and viewing documents or slides and communicate with participants via video, audio, or text chat.

Security Systems

Surveillance systems that record video from multiple cameras also have become a familiar sight. Face-recognition technology promises to enhance security through biometric identification and may soon become widespread at airports and corporate offices.

Command Systems

The recent development of eye gaze- and gesture-commanded systems opens new vistas for the command and control of computers, robots, surgical systems, and other hands-free devices with systems that understand video. The typical user of such systems indicates a location for action by looking or pointing.

Outlook

The outlook for video-based systems is bright. Video conferencing and mobile video phones may become a regular part of daily life, as will the increasing use of hands-free systems that understand video.

Immanuel Freedman

See also Animation; Avatars; Gesture Recognition

FURTHER READING

Farid, M., Murtagh, F., & Starck, J. L. (2002). Computer display control and interaction using eye-gaze. Retrieved January 2, 2004, from http://main.cs.qub.ac.uk/~fmurtagh/papers/fm6.pdf

Grossman, A. (2001, July 9). The rush to SVOD: Not so fast. Retrieved January 2, 2004, from http://www.broadbandweek.com/news/010709/010709_supp_rush.htm

Jain, A. K. (1988). *Fundamentals of digital image processing.* Englewood Cliffs, NJ: Prentice Hall.

Ohanian, T. (1998). *Digital nonlinear editing: Editing film and video on the desktop* (2nd ed.). Boston: Focal Press.

VIDEO SUMMARIZATION

Effective methods of video indexing and video summarization are essential for ubiquitous consumption of video by humans or machines. Video indexing is attaching metadata to video content to facilitate easy searching and browsing. Metadata can be text based or content based in the form of visual or audio descriptors. Such metadata is usually presented in a standard compliant machine-readable format—for example, International Standards Organization (ISO) MPEG-7 descriptions—to facilitate consumption by search engines and intelligent agents. Video summarization is computing an abstract of the video content, which can be in the form of a sequence of key frames (one or more representative frames in a shot) or key-event clips, also known as a "trailer" or "highlight" of the video.

Two applications of video indexing and summarization are television and mobile devices. A user may provide video preferences to an intelligent agent in a TV set. The agent continuously filters through the descriptors in all incoming program streams to find matching content. If the user is away or is watching another channel at the time a match is found, the set-top box (a digital video recorder) can record either the whole program or a customized summary of it computed online by the agent. With the advent of wireless systems, mobile users have faster access to multimedia content. However, live streaming of a complete program may still be impractical. Instead, a mobile user may prefer to receive only summaries of essential events, which are computed automatically in near real time by the service provider.

Video Modeling

Video models serve as foundations of various indexing and summarization methods, and they can be either structural or semantic. Structural video models represent video as a union of coherent temporal or spatio-temporal units, either shots or objects. A shot is a collection of frames recorded by a continuous motion of the camera; hence, frames within a shot represent a continuous action in time and space. The next level in shot-based video structure corresponds to scenes (or sequences). A scene is a collection whose shots share spatial, temporal, perceptual, or thematic content.

A video object is a spatio-temporal entity that corresponds to a semantic real-world object. Objects have shapes and life spans. In contrast to shot-based representations, object representations allow for temporal gaps because objects may disappear from the scene and then reappear. In camera-controlled (computer vision) search and retrieval applications, such as video surveillance, the indexing process generally controls the camera operations. Object-based structural modeling and indexing generally are more difficult in broadcast video applications, where the indexing process often does not have control of the camera operations.

Semantic information can be incorporated in structural models by means of structured or free-text annotations or can be represented at a higher level by semantic models. Annotations can be manual or extracted automatically from closed captions or on-screen text or by face detection and recognition. An important difference between annotations and semantic models is that the latter can support entities, such as objects and events and relations between them, which make processing complex queries possible. Semantic video models can be considered as extensions of entity-relation (ER) models (database models) developed for documents by database- and information-retrieval communities.

A video consists of two main entities: objects and events. Objects can be described by spatial features (color) or spatio-temporal features (motion). Players, referee, ball, and field lines are examples of objects in sports video. An event consists of specific actions and interactions of objects that convey a semantic meaning in a particular domain. For example, goals, corner kicks, and red cards are events in a soccer game. The presence of a moving object is an event in a surveillance application.

A relationship is an association between entities. Examples of relationships include generalization and aggregation. An "is-A" relationship generalizes one entity to another, for example, "a player is a person." An aggregation relationship specifies a "has-A" relationship between entities, for example, "a team has a player."

Attributes are properties of entities or relationships. Two types of attributes exist: identifying attributes (identifiers) and descriptive attributes (descriptors). The former uniquely identifies a specific entity, whereas the latter describes its properties.

Basics of the MPEG-7 Standard

MPEG-7 is an international standard for multimedia content description, published by the Moving Pictures Experts Group. It standardizes the syntax and semantics of textual, visual, and audio descriptions in both textual and binary formats. MPEG-7 has four major components:

- Descriptors (D) describe features, including color, edges, and motion.
- Description schemes (DS) schemes are predefined structures, which specify how descriptors and description schemes can be combined.
- Description definition language (DDL) defines the syntax of MPEG-7 DS.
- Binary format (BiM) enables efficient representation and transmission of MPEG-7 descriptors.

MPEG-7 introduces three major description schemes. The segment DS describes the structure of spatial, temporal, and spatio-temporal video segments, their attributes, and their hierarchical decompositions and structural relationships. The semantic DS defines a generic semantic model to enable semantic retrieval in terms of objects, agent objects, events, concepts, states, places, times, and semantic relations. The summarization DS describes various forms of video abstracts, including key-frame and key-clip summaries. In addition, several low-level descriptors are defined to describe color, texture, shape, motion, and facial features.

Low-Level Video Processing and Key-Frame Summarization

Generic pixel-level video processing, analysis, and pattern recognition methods can be used for shot boundary detection, spatio-temporal object segmentation and tracking, extraction of low-level features such as color, texture, shape, and motion for frames, shots, and video objects, and detection of key frames.

Shot boundary detection methods locate frames, across which large differences are observed in some feature space, usually consisting of a combination of color and motion. Boundaries can be sharp, known as "cuts," or gradual, known as "special effects," such as wipes and fades. It is easier to detect cuts than special effects. The simplest method for cut detection is to check pixel intensity differences between successive frames. If a predetermined number of pixels exhibit differences larger than a threshold value, then a cut can be declared. This approach can be sensitive to presence of noise and compression artifacts in the video.

A more robust approach is to compute the frequency of colors in each frame and then check differences between successive frames. Researchers have developed various measures and tests to quantify similarity or dissimilarity. A closely related approach is to detect changes in the counts of edge pixels in successive frames. Although it effectively detects cuts and fades, this approach cannot usually differentiate between wipes and camera motion, such as pans and zooms. Detection of certain special effects requires a combination of frame difference and camera motion estimation methods.

Shot boundary detection algorithms (procedures for solving a mathematical problem in a finite number of steps that frequently involves repetition of an operation) also exist for specific domains, such as sports video. Sports video is arguably one of the most challenging domains for robust shot boundary detection due to (1) existence of a strong color correlation between successive shots because a single dominant color background, such as the soccer field, may be seen in successive shots, (2) existence of large camera and object motions, and (3) existence of many gradual transitions, such as wipes and dissolves.

Coherent spatio-temporal regions, such as planar objects with rigid motion, can be automatically segmented based on uniformity of low-level features, such as color and motion. For example, VideoQ—a video query system developed at Columbia University—employs color and edge information for segmentation of regions and motion information to track them. The segmentation is reinitialized at each shot boundary; therefore, regions are not linked across shots. Similarly, NeTra-V—a video segmentation and retrieval system developed at the University of California, Santa Barbara—extracts and tracks spatio-temporal regions within shots for object-based indexing and retrieval. The spatio-temporal regions computed in this manner are not necessarily semantically meaningful objects. Segmenting and tracking of semantic objects in an unconstrained setting require user intervention for initialization. However, in some well-constrained settings, semantic objects can be computed fully automatically. For example, in video surveillance systems, where the camera is stationary, objects in the scene can be extracted by simple change detection and background subtraction methods.

Key frames exploit frame-to-frame similarity within a shot for a compact visual representation. Key frames can be automatically selected by low-level feature analysis and employed to generate a visual table of contents. For example, a hierarchy of key frames can be constructed for efficient content-based indexing and browsing. Clustering of adjacent key frames based on low-level color, shape, and luminance projection features has been used to define scenes, which lead to story board representation of video.

High-Level Abstraction and Key-Event Summaries

Semantic analysis of video generally involves use of both cinematic and object-based features. Object-based features allow high-level domain analysis, but their extraction may be difficult and computationally costly for real-time implementation. Cinematic features, which originate from common video composition and production rules such as shot types and transitions, offer a good compromise between the computational requirements and resulting semantics. Different cinematic rules may apply to different domains of content such as action movies, TV sitcoms, TV news, and sports broadcasts.

Replays in sports broadcasts are indicators of important events in the game; hence, replay detection is an important video processing tool in automatic generation of highlights. Three types of slow-motion

replay detection algorithms exist: (1) spatial domain algorithms that detect large fluctuations in frame differences; (2) spatial domain algorithms that detect video editing effects; and (3) compressed domain algorithms that detect when frames are repeated during slow motion.

Cinematographers define three types of shots: long, medium, and close-up shots. In sports broadcasts, long shots are used to capture the global view of the field; medium shots zoom in to particular regions on the field; and close-ups may occur as the camera zooms in on a player.

Shot types can be determined by spatial and spatio-temporal features. Spatial algorithms mainly use color information; however, algorithms also use texture and shape features. An effective approach to distinguish long, medium, and close-up shots is to check the ratio of grass-colored pixels to all pixels in a frame. Because only spatial features are used, a shot type can ideally be determined from a single key frame. In some applications, only detection of long shots may be of interest, so the problem reduces to two-class pattern recognition. For instance, tennis long shots can be detected by verifying that the ratio of court-colored pixels is greater than a threshold. Dominant color and camera motion have also been used to detect long, medium, and close-up shots in tennis. Spatio-temporal features, such as object motion, may also be useful for shot-type classification. Camera motion, color, and edge features have been used for baseball shot classification, where shot types include pitch view, catch overview, catch close-up, running overview, running close-up, audience view, and touch-base close-up.

Cinematic features include shot lengths, shot transition (special) effects, shot types, sequencing of shot types, slow-motion replays, and other shot features, such as on-screen text and some audio features.

Detection of interesting events (also key events) is essential for both semantic video indexing and summarization. Event detection for generic video is an unsolved problem in computer vision. Solutions exist, however, for specific domains such as surveillance and sports video. In surveillance video key events are related to object motion. Key events in sports video are generally related to changes in the score of the game.

Sports video processing systems can be classified as those that require complete control over camera positions, such as LucentVision and ESPN K-Zone, which track tennis ball and baseball, respectively, and postprocessing systems for broadcast video. The postprocessing systems rely on domain-specific rules and may employ cinematic features or object-based features for event detection.

Cinematic descriptors are commonly employed, for example, for the detection of plays and breaks in soccer games by shot types and slow-motion replay detection. Detected slow-motion replays can be concatenated (linked) and presented as interesting event summaries. Scene cuts and camera motion parameters have also been used for soccer event detection. Because basketball video consists of strong and repetitious camera pans, plays can be segmented into Team A offenses and Team B offenses by just analyzing the type of the camera operation and the direction of the dominant camera motion. Camera motion type, direction, and magnitude have also been used to classify shots as wide-angle and close-up shots. The temporal evolution of camera motion parameters may demonstrate similarities for certain events if the broadcasting crews are consistent in capturing an event across multiple games and if different broadcasters use similar camera operations for the same events. Shot-type transitions and camera motion characteristics can be combined to detect several soccer events, such as goals, free kicks, and corner kicks.

Ekin, Tekalp, and Mehrotra (2003) introduced algorithms that use both cinematic and object-based features for automatic detection of (1) goal events, (2) the referee, and (3) the penalty box in soccer videos. Goals are detected based solely on cinematic features resulting from common rules employed by the producers after goal events to provide a better visual experience for TV audiences. The distinguishing jersey color of the referee is used for fast and robust referee detection. Penalty box detection is based on the three-parallel-line rule that uniquely specifies the penalty box area in a soccer field.

A. Murat Tekalp

See also Text Summarization; Video

FURTHER READING

Adali, S., Candan, K. S., Chen, S. S., Erol, K., & Subrahmanian, V. S. (1996). The advanced video information system: Data structures and query processing. *Multimedia Systems, 4*(4), 172–186.

Ahanger, G. & Little, T. D. C. (1996). A survey of technologies for parsing and indexing digital video. *The Journal of Visual Communication and Image Representation, 7*, 28–43.

Antani, S., Kasturi, R., & Jain, R. (2002). A survey on the use of pattern recognition methods for abstraction, indexing and retrieval of images and video. *Pattern Recognition, 35*, 945–965.

Benitez, A. B., Begi, M., & Chang, S. F. (1999). Using relevance feedback in content-based image metadata search. *IEEE Internet Computing* (pp. 59–69).

Bouthemy, P., Gelgon, M., & Ganansia, F. (1999). A unified approach to shot change detection and camera motion characterization. *IEEE Transactions on Circuits and Systems for Video Technology, 9*, 1030–1044.

Brunelli, R., Mich, O., & Modena, C. M. (1999). A survey on the automatic indexing of video data. *The Journal of Visual Communication and Image Representation, 10*, 78–112.

Courtney, J. D. (1997). Automatic video indexing via object motion analysis. *Pattern Recognition, 30*(4), 607–626.

Dagtas, S., Al-Khatip, W., Ghafoor, A., & Kashyap, R. L. (2000). Models for motion-based video indexing and retrieval. *IEEE Transactions on Image Processing, 9*(1), 88–101.

Deng, Y., & Manjunath, B. S. (1998). NeTra-V: Toward an object-based video representation., *IEEE Transactions on Circuits and Systems for Video Technology, 8*(5), 616–627.

Dimitrova, N., Zhang, H., Shahraray, B., Sezan, I., Huang, T., & Zakhor, A. (2002). Applications of video content analysis and retrieval. *IEEE Multimedia, 9*, 42–55.

Divakaran, A., Radhakrishnan, R., & Peker, K. (2001). Video summarization with motion descriptors. *The Journal of Electronic Imaging, 10*(4), 909–916.

Ekin, A., Tekalp, A .M., & Mehrotra, R. (2003). Automatic soccer video analysis and summarization. *IEEE Transactions on Image Processing, 12*(7), 796–807.

Foresti, G. L., Marcenaro, L., & Regazzoni, C. S. (2002). Automatic detection and indexing of video-event shots for surveillance applications. *IEEE Trans. Multimedia, 4*(4), 459–471.

Gargi, U., Kasturi, R., & Strayer, S. H. (2000). Performance characterization of video-shot change detection methods. *IEEE Transactions on Circuits and Systems for Video Technology, 10*, 1–13.

Hacid, M. S., Decleir, C., & Kouloumdjian, J. (2000). A database approach for modeling and querying video data. *IEEE Transactions on Knowledge and Data Engineering, 12*(5), 729–750.

Hampapur, A., Jain, R., & Weymouth, T. E. (1995). Production model based digital video segmentation. *Multimedia Tools Applications, 1*, 9–46.

Hanjalic, A. (2002). Shot-boundary detection: Unraveled and resolved? *IEEE Transactions on Circuits and Systems for Video Technology, 12*, 90–105.

Jeannin, S., Jasinschi, R., She, A., Naveen, T., Mory, B., & Tabatabai, A. (2000, September). Motion descriptors for content-based video representation. *Signal Processing: Image Communication, 16*(1–2), 59–86.

Jiang, H., Helal, A., Elmagarmid, A. K., & Joshi, A. (1998). Scene change detection techniques for video databases. *Multimedia Systems, 6,* 186–195.

Koprinska, I., & Carrato, S. (2001). Temporal video segmentation: A survey. *Signal Processing: Image Communication, 16*(5), 477–500.

Lienhart, R. (2001). Reliable transition detection in videos: A survey and practitioner's guide. *International Journal of Image Graphics, 1,* 469–486.

Manjunath, B. S., & Ma, W. Y. (1996). Texture features for browsing and retrieval of image data. *IEEE Transactions on Pattern Analysis and Machine Intelligence, 8*(11), 679–698.

Manjunath, B. S., Salembier, P., & Sikora, T. (Eds.). (2002). *Introduction to MPEG-7: Multimedia content description interface.* New York: Wiley.

Rui, Y., Huang, T. S., Ortega, M., & Mehrotra, S. (1996). Relevance feedback: A power tool for interactive content-based image retrieval. *IEEE Transactions on Circuits and Systems for Video Technology, 8*(5), 644–655.

Satoh, S., Nakamura, Y., & Kanade, T. (2001). Name-It: Naming and detecting faces in news videos. *Multimedia, 6*(1), 22–35.

Sundaram, H., & Chang, S. F. (2002). Computable scenes and structures in films. *IEEE Transactions on Multimedia, 4,* 482–491.

Tan, Y. P., Kulkarni, S. R., & Ramadge, P. J. (2000). Rapid estimation of camera motion from compressed video with application to video annotation. *IEEE Transactions on Circuits and Systems for Video Technology, 10*(1), 133–146.

Zhang, H. J., Kankanhalli, A., & Smoliar, S. W. (1993). Automatic partitioning of full-motion video. *Multimedia Systems, 1,* 10–28.

Zhong, D., & Chang, S. F. (1999). An integrated approach for content-based video object segmentation and retrieval. *IEEE Transactions on Circuits and Systems for Video Technology, 9*(8), 1259–1268.

VIRTUAL REALITY

The goal of virtual-reality (VR) systems is to immerse the participant within a computer-generated, virtual environment (VE). Interacting with the VE poses unique problems. The ideal VE system would have the participant fully believe he was actually performing a real-life task. Every component of the real-life task would be fully replicated. The environment would be visually identical to a real-world environment: Participants would hear accurate sounds, smell identical odors, and when they reached out to touch an object, they would be able to feel it. For example, an ideal VR system for examining designs for product assembly would present an assembly experience identical to one experienced in the real world. Parts and tools would have mass, feel real, and handle appropriately. Participants would interact with every object as they would if they were doing the task on an actual assembly line. For their part, the virtual objects would respond to participants' action appropriately. Training and simulation would be optimal.

Obviously, current VEs have yet to achieve that level of verisimilitude. Currently, participants use specialized equipment, such as tracked displays and gloves, to track movement, interpret actions, and provide input to the VR system. Interactive three-dimensional computer graphics and audio software generate the appropriate scenes and auditory cues. Finally, the participant receives the VE output (images, sounds, tactile feedback) through visual and audio hardware.

In this article, we focus on immersive VR systems. Immersive VR is characterized—though not universally—by participant head tracking (monitoring the participant's position and orientation) and stereo imagery (providing different views of the VE for each eye).

Interestingly, the issues for human-computer interaction (HCI) in VR can be strikingly different from the issues in traditional two-dimensional or three-dimensional HCI. In VR, the participant views the virtual environment from a first-person perspective. Researchers and developers in VR strive for a high level of fidelity between the virtual action and the corresponding real action being simulated. For example, a VR system for training soldiers in close quarters combat must have the participant perform physical actions and receive visual, audio, and haptic (tactile) inputs that are as similar to those in the actual scenario as possible. Some virtual actions (such as deletion and selection, for example) have no correlate action in real life, so system designers must find a way to make those actions seem as natural as possible. Most if not all objects in the VE are virtual. That is, when a participant reaches out grab a virtual object, there will no physical object to give an appropriate feel. For hands-on tasks, having nothing to feel or handle might be so detrimental to the experience as to make the VR ineffective.

Immersive VR systems that satisfy the high-fidelity interaction requirements can become an important tool for training, simulation, and education for tasks that are too dangerous, expensive, or difficult to re-create in the real world. Modern flight simulators are an example of a near-perfect combination of real and virtual objects. In most state-of-the-art flight simulators, the entire cockpit is real, but a motion platform provides motion sensations, and the visuals of the environment outside the cockpit are virtual. The resulting synergy is so compelling and effective that it is almost universally used to train pilots.

UR Interaction: Technology

Tracking and signaling actions are the primary means of input into VEs. Tracking is the determination of a object's position and orientation. Common objects to track include the participant's head, the participant's limbs, and interaction devices (such as gloves, a computer mouse, or joysticks). Most tracking systems have sensors or markers attached to these objects; other devices then track and report the position and orientation of the sensors.

Commercial tracking systems employ one or a combination of mechanical, magnetic, optical, acoustic, inertial, and global positioning satellite (GPS) approaches. Each method has different advantages with respect to cost, speed, accuracy, robustness, working volume, scalability, wirelessness, and size. No one tracking technology handles all tracking situations.

Depending on the task, the requirements for accuracy, speed, and latency of the tracking system's reports will differ. VEs that aim for a high level of participant sense of presence—a measure of how much the participants believe they are truly present in the VE—have stringent head tracking requirements. Researchers estimate that the VR and tracking systems need to accurately determine the participant's pose and to display the appropriate images in under 90 milliseconds, and preferably under 50 milliseconds. If the lag is too high, the VR system induces a "swimming" feeling, and might make the participant disoriented and hamper the quality of interactivity.

Tracking the participant's limbs allows the VR system to present an avatar, or virtual representation of the user within the virtual environment, as well as rough information on the shape of the participant's body pose. Researchers believe that the presence of an avatar increases a participant's sense of presence. The accuracy and speed requirements for limb tracking are typically lower than those for head tracking.

Finally, object tracking, usually accomplished by attaching a sensor to the object, allows a virtual model of an object to be associated with a real object. For example, attaching a tracker to a dinner plate allows an associated virtual plate to be naturally manipulated. Since each sensor reports the pose information of a single point, most systems use one sensor per object and assume the real object is rigid in shape and appearance.

Since humans use their hands for many tasks, tracking and obtaining inputs from a hand-based controller was a natural evolution for VR controllers. A tracked glove reports information on the position and pose of the participant's hand to the VR system. Gloves can also report pinching gestures, button presses (the buttons can be built into the glove) and finger bends. These glove actions are associated with virtual actions such as grasping, selecting, translation, and rotation. Tracked gloves provide many different kinds of inputs and, most importantly, are very natural to use. Glove disadvantages include sizing problems (most are one-size-fits-all), limited feedback (issues with haptic feedback and detecting gestures), and hygiene complications when there are multiple users.

The most common interaction devices are tracked computer mice (sometimes called bats) and joysticks. To an ordinary mouse or joystick is added a tracking sensor with three or six degrees of freedom (DOF) that reports the device's position and orientation. Tracked mice and joysticks have numerous buttons whereby the participant can provide input, and they are cheap, easily adaptable for different tasks, and familiar to many users. However, they may not provide the required naturalness, feel, and functionality for certain tasks.

One way to achieve ease of use, numerous inputs into a system, and proper feedback is to engineer a specific device to interface with the VR system. For example, the University of North Carolina ultrasound augmented-reality (AR) surgery system attached a tracking sensor to a sonogram wand. The inputs from the sonogram wand buttons were passed to the VR system. This enabled the AR system to provide a natural interface for training and simulation. However, it also required developing software and manufacturing special cables to make possible communication between the sonogram machine and a PC. Creating these special devices is time consuming and the resulting tools are usable only for a limited set of tasks.

Given the system inputs, the resulting VE is outputted to the participant. For example, as the participant changes his or her head position and orientation, the tracking system passes that information to the VR system's rendering engine. Three-dimensional views of the VE are generated from the updated pose information.

The visual output is typically presented either in a head-mounted display (HMD) or a multiple-wall back-projected CAVE (an acronym for "cave automatic virtual environment"; the proprietary name for a system developed by the National Center for Supercomputing Applications, or NCSA). HMDs are helmets with integrated display devices. The helmet has two screens located a short distance from the user's eyes. One can think of a participant who uses an HMD as carrying the VE display around with him or her. There are many commercial HMDs available, including the Virtual Research V8, VFX ForteVR, and Sony Glasstron.

CAVE environments have multiple back-projected display walls and data projectors. The virtual environment is rendered from multiple views (such as forward, right, left, down) and projected onto the display walls. Fakespace, Inc. provides commercial CAVE solutions (www.fakespacesystems .com).

VR systems use either stereo headphones or multiple speakers to output audio to the user, taking into account the user's position, sound sources, and the VE geometry. Common audio packages include Creative Lab's EAX and AuSIM's AuTrak.

VR haptic information is presented to the participant through active feedback devices. Examples of force feedback devices include a vibrating joystick, which vibrates when the user collides with a virtual object), and the Sensible Phantom, which resembles a six-DOF pen. (The pen is connected to motors that push back when the pen is pressed

into a virtual wall.) Two examples of effective systems are the dAb system, which simulates painting on a virtual canvas, and the Immersion CyberGrasp glove, which allows design evaluation and assembly verification of virtual models.

VR Interaction: Locomotion

VR locomotion—movement and navigation within the VE—is one of the primary methods of VR interaction. VE locomotion is different from real-world locomotion in two ways. First, the virtual space can be on a completely different scale from the tracked real space, as is the case with a VE on the molecular or planetary scale. Second, locomotion in the VE might be difficult or undesirable to emulate in the real world. For example, consider the navigation issues in a VE that simulates emergency evacuations on an oil platform to train rescue personnel.

The most common method of locomotion is flying. When some input, such as a button press, is received, the participant is moved in the VE along some vector. Two common choices for this translation vector are the view direction of the user and a vector defined by the position and orientation of an interaction device, such as a tracked joystick or mouse. While easy to use and effective, flying is not very natural or realistic.

In the method of locomotion known as walking in place, when participants make a walking motion (lifting their feet up and down, but not moving forward), the participant moves in the VE along a vector. By monitoring the tracker sensor's reports, the VR system can detect walking motions.

Specific devices have been engineered to simulate long-distance locomotion. Treadmills such as the Sarcos Treadport and ATR ATLAS allow the user to physically walk long distances in the VE. Sometimes a steering device is included to permit direction change in the VE. Unfortunately, treadmills do not handle rotations or uneven terrain well, and they are growing more uncommon. Further, there were safety issues in simulating high speeds and collisions with virtual objects.

Other locomotion devices include specialized motion platforms and exercise cycles. A motion platform is a mechanical stage whose movement is controlled by the VR system. For example, flight simulators use motion platforms to physically move and rotate the participant to simulate the sensations of flight. Of course, there are limitations to the range of motions, but for many applications, motion platforms provide an extremely valuable level of realism.

VR locomotion approaches have to deal with a finite—and typically quite limited—tracked space within which the participant can physically move around. Further, the participant typically has numerous wires connecting the tracking sensors and display devices to the VR system. Motorized methods of VR locomotion also have safety issues with regard to speed and the methods they employ to move the user.

New commercial and research approaches to VR locomotion look to provide more natural and effective locomotion over larger spaces. New tracking systems, such as the WorldViz PPT, Intersense IS-900, and the 3rdTech HiBall, are scalable wide-area trackers with working volumes approaching 12 meters by 12 meters. This allows the participant to physically navigate large VE distances. Studies have shown that real walking is better than walking in place, which in turn is better than flying when it comes to enhancing a participant's sense of presence.

The Naval Research Laboratory's GAITER system is a combination of harnesses and treadmills that allows soldiers to emulate running across large distances in combat simulations. The Redirected Walking project at the University of North Carolina looks to expand the physical tracking volume by subtly rotating the virtual world as the participant walks. This causes participants to walk in a circle in the real world, though in the virtual world it appears as if they have walked along a straight line. This could allow a finite real-world space to provide an infinite virtual walking space.

UR Interaction:
Interacting with Virtual Objects

Training and simulation VR systems, which account for a substantial number of deployed VR systems, aim to re-create real-world experiences. The accuracy with which the virtual experience re-creates the actual experience can be extremely important—for example, in medical and military simulations.

The fundamental problem is that most things are not real in a VE. Having everything virtual removes many of the important cues that we use to perform tasks, such as motion constraints, tactile response, and force feedback. Typically these cues are either approximated or not provided at all. Depending on the task, this can reduce the effectiveness of a VE. Of course, the other end of the spectrum—using all real objects—removes many of the advantages of using a VE, such as quick prototyping and training and simulation for expensive or dangerous tasks.

In a VE, participants interact with virtual objects, with the simulated environment, and with system objects. The methods of interaction will vary depending on the task, participants, and equipment (hardware and software) configuration. For example, the interactions to locate three-dimensional objects in orientation and mobility training for people who are visually impaired are different from those in a surgery planning simulation. Variables to consider include accuracy, lag, intuitiveness, fidelity to the actual task, and feedback.

Interacting with Virtual Objects

The most common interactions with virtual objects are the application of three-dimensional transformations and the issuing of system commands (such as delete or opening a file). VR issues include the lack of a registered physical object that corresponds with the virtual object and limitations in getting inputs to and from the system.

Given that most objects are virtual, can a system without having motion constraints, correct affordance (objects interacting as one would expect), or haptic feedback still remain effective? These are some of the basic research questions that are being explored. It is the system designers' job to provide interaction methodologies that do not impede system effectiveness.

Interacting with the Simulated Environment

VR systems use simulations for tasks as various as calculating physics (for example, collision detection and response), lighting (that is, drawing a scene with correct lighting information), and approximating real-world phenomena. Most VR systems require participants to control objects in the simulation and indeed the simulation itself. For example, in a solider simulation, the participant affects the simulated soldier's view and battlefield location and provides input by (for example) pressing buttons to make the soldier fire his weapon.

Many simulations focus on creating realistic experiences for the participant. Having a natural means of interaction—for example, a prop machine gun instead of a button in the previous example—improves realism, but also increases cost and reduces generality (as the prop has limited uses in other applications). On the other end of the spectrum, sometimes interaction using a generic interaction device such as a joystick is so different from interaction in a real-world setting that the simulation fails to provide any benefit.

Interacting with the VR System

When we speak of interacting with the VR system, we mean interaction with system objects such as menus and dialog boxes. Like traditional users of two-dimensional or desktop three-dimensional systems, VR participants need to be able to open files, change system settings, and accept incoming messages. VR systems have unique issues because of participants' first-person perspective, the need to present the system interface in an unobtrusive, natural way, the desire not to lower participants' sense of presence, and the need to accept participant input. Interacting in 3D VR worlds is inherently different than 2D or 3D desktop interfaces that most computers use. For example, allowing the user to select and move an object in VR typically involves: {1} performing a grasping gesture, (2) physically moving your arm the distance you want to move the object, and (3) releasing the grasping gesture. This is different than using a mouse, icons, and windows, as we are trying to replicate the real task virtually.

Most VR systems provide the system interface as virtual objects attached either to the virtual environment (world coordinate system), to a tracked device (local coordinate system), or to the participant (user coordinate system). Using the world coordinate system (the interface appears as an VE object,

such as a computer panel) provides a way to keep the interaction with the virtual environment (both virtual objects and the system interface) consistent. But for some VEs—such as a solider simulation—the scale (large distances) or the subject matter (realistic combat) do not naturally lend themselves to such a system interface.

Using the local coordinate system (attaching the system interface to a tracked device, such as a participant-carried tablet or mouse) allows the system to provide a consistent virtual world. Previous studies have shown that participants who can use a physical object for interactions perform tasks better than participants who use a purely virtual interface.

When the user interface is attached to the user, menus and dialog boxes appear relatively stationary to the user, even as they navigate around the world. This is similar to implementing a standard 2D desktop interface in a 3D environment. In this case, the interface is always within the participant's reach, but its appearance and integration with the rest of the VE is typically not as seamless as when the interface is attached to a tracked device or to a virtual object.

Future Directions in VR Interaction

New hardware, software, interaction techniques, and VR systems are constantly evolving; the topics covered here are by no means a comprehensive list.

New products, such as the Immersion Haptic Workstation, provide high-quality tracking of the participant's hands coupled with force feedback that allows the participant to "feel" virtual objects. The improved interaction could enable VR to be applied to hands-on tasks that were previously hampered by poor haptic feedback.

VEs populated with multiple participants (often physically distributed over great distances) have unique interaction issues. In a University College London study, two participants, one at UCL (England), and the other at the University of North Carolina at Chapel Hill, (United States of America), must navigate a virtual maze while carrying a stretcher. How do the participants interact in a shared virtual space?

Researchers are interested in how important audio, gestures, and facial expressions are for cooperative interaction.

Combining several interaction methods may lead to solutions that are greater than the sum of their parts. For example, the BioSimMER system seeks to train emergency response medical personnel. The system interprets hand gestures and voice commands, and participants also use traditional methods of interacting with the simulation. Researchers are also investigating passive techniques that use image processing and computer vision to aid in tracking and interpreting the participant's actions and gestures.

There is also research into new types of VR systems. Hybrid environments—VEs that combine real and virtual objects—focus on providing virtual systems with natural physical interfaces as well as intuitive virtual interfaces. There exists a spectrum of environments, from augmented reality, in which displays of the real world are supplemented with virtual objects, to mixed and augmented virtual reality, in which the VE is supplemented with real objects.

Hybrid systems hope to improve participants' performance and sense of presence by having real objects registered with virtual objects. In studies of passive haptics (feedback from devices not actively controlled by the VR system, such as a Styrofoam block in the real world registered with a static object in the virtual world), major virtual objects, such as the walls and unmovable furniture, were registered with stationary physical objects. It was found that passive haptics did improve participants' sense of presence.

New methods to navigate and interact with virtual objects are constantly being developed, and there are movements to formalize the description and evaluation of interaction technologies. Doing so would allow VR system engineers to make interface design decisions confidently and reduce the ad hoc nature of the creation of those technologies. Formal evaluation also promotes a critical review of how and why people interact with VEs.

As the types of interactions grow more complex, higher-order interactions with simulated objects, including deformable objects, and virtual characters are becoming a major research focus. Developing the system's ability to interpret participants' facial expressions, voices, gestures, and poses may make it possible to provide a new level of natural interaction.

As the hardware, interaction technologies, and software advance, VR system designers are increasingly able to develop natural and effective means for participants to interact with a VE. We believe improved HCI will allow VR to fulfill its promise to provide a new paradigm for human interaction with digital information.

Benjamin C. Lok and Larry F. Hodges

See also Augmented Reality; Haptics

FURTHER READING

Baxter, W., Sheib, V., Lin, M., & Manocha, D. (2001). DAB: Interactive haptic painting with 3D virtual brushes. *Proceedings of ACM SIGGRAPH, 461–468.*

Bowman, D., & Hodges, L. (1997). An evaluation of techniques for grabbing and manipulating remote objects in immersive virtual environments. *Proceedings of the 1997 Symposium on Interactive 3-D Graphics, 35–38.*

Fuchs, H., Livingston, M., Raskar, R., Colucci, D., Keller, K., State, et al. (1998). Augmented reality visualization for laparoscopic surgery. *Proceedings of First International Conference on Medical Image Computing and Computer-Assisted Intervention; Lecture Notes in Computer Science 1496, 934–943.*

Hand, C. (1997). A survey of 3-D interaction techniques. *Computer Graphics Forum, 16(5), 269–281.*

Hoffman, H. (1998). Physically touching virtual objects using tactile augmentation enhances the realism of virtual environments. *Proceedings of the IEEE Virtual Reality Annual International Symposium '98, 59–63.*

Hollerbach, J., Xu, Y., Christensen, R., & Jacobsen, S. (2000). Design specifications for the second generation Sarcos Treadport locomotion interface. Haptics Symposium, *Proceedings of ASME Dynamic Systems and Control Division, 69(2), 1293–1298.*

Höllerer, T., Feiner, S., Terauchi, T., Rashid, G., & Hallaway, D. (1999). Exploring MARS: Developing indoor and outdoor user interfaces to a mobile augmented reality system. *Computers and Graphics, 23(6), 779–785.*

Insko, B. (2001). Passive haptics significantly enhances virtual environments. Unpublished doctoral dissertation, University of North Carolina, Chapel Hill.

Lindeman, R., Sibert, J., & Hahn, J. (1999). Hand-held windows: Towards effective 2D interaction in immersive virtual environments. *Proceedings of IEEE Virtual Reality '99, 205–212.*

Lok, B. (2001). Online model reconstruction for interactive virtual environments. *Proceedings of the 2001 Symposium on Interactive 3-D Graphics, 69–72, 248.*

Lok, B., Naik, S., Whitton, M., & Brooks, F. (2003). Effects of handling real objects and avatar fidelity on cognitive task performance in virtual environments. *Proceedings of IEEE Virtual Reality 2003, 125–132.*

Meehan, M., Razzaque, S., Whitton, M., & Brooks, F. (2003). Effect of latency on presence in stressful virtual environments. *Proceedings of IEEE Virtual Reality 2003*, 141–148.

Mine, M., Brooks, F., & Sequin, C. (1997). *Moving objects in space: Exploiting proprioception in virtual-environment interaction.* *Proceedings of SIGGRAPH '97*, 19–26.

Razzaque, S. Kohn, Z., Whitton, M. (2001). Redirected walking. Paper presented at Eurographics 2001, Manchester, UK.

Rickel, J., & Johnson, W. (2000). Task-oriented collaboration with embodied agents in virtual worlds. In J. Cassell, J. Sullivan, and S. Prevost (Eds.), *Embodied Conversational Agents* (pp. 95–122). Boston: MIT Press.

Slater, M., & Usoh, M. (1993). The influence of a virtual body on presence in immersive virtual environments. In *Proceedings of the Third Annual Conference on Virtual Reality* (pp. 34–42). London: Meckler.

Stansfield, S., Shawver, D., Sobel, A., Prasad, M. & Tapia, L. (2000). Design and implementation of a virtual reality system and its application to training medical first responders. *Presence: Teleoperators and Virtual Environments*, 9(6), 524–556.

Sutherland, I. (1965). The ultimate display. *Proceedings of IFIP '65, 2*, 506.

Templeman, J., Denbrook, P., & Sibert, L. (1999). Virtual locomotion: Walking in place through virtual environments. *Presence: Teleoperators and Virtual Environments*, 8(6), 598–617.

Usoh, M., Arthur, K., Whitton, M., Steed, A., Slater, M., and Brooks, F. (1999). Walking > Virtual Walking> Flying, in Virtual Environments. *Proceedings of SIGGRAPH '99*, 359–364.

VanDam, A., Laidlaw, D., & Simpson, R. (2002). *Experiments in immersive virtual reality for scientific visualization, Computers and Graphics*, 26, 535–555.

Welch, G., Bishop, G., Vicci, L., Brumback, S., & Keller, K. (1999). The HiBall tracker: High-performance wide-area tracking for virtual and augmented environments. *Proceedings of the ACM Symposium on Virtual Reality Software and Technology 1999*, 1–10.

Welch, G., & Foxlin, E. (2002). Motion tracking: No silver bullet, but a respectable arsenal. *IEEE Computer Graphics and Applications* Special Issue on Tracking, 22(6), 24–38.

Zachmann, G., & Rettig, A. (2001) Natural and robust interaction in virtual assembly simulation. *Eighth ISPE International Conference on Concurrent Engineering: Research and Applications*, 425–434.

VIRUSES

Viruses and worms are malware: malicious computer programs that electronically spread through a network. A virus must be executed by a user action to spread, whereas a worm spreads simply by direct infection. (The terms *virus* and *worm* are often respectively attributed to a 1974 science-fiction novel by David Gerrold, *When H.A.R.L.I.E. Was One,* and a 1975 science-fiction novel by John Brunner, *Shockwave Rider.*) The first uncontrolled virus, Elk Cloner, appeared in 1982 and infected Apple II computers; today, during the height of recent computer virus attacks, e-mails containing computer viruses have accounted for up to 8 percent of e-mail being transmitted worldwide.

Vectors for Viruses

Computer viruses predate today's nearly universal use of the Internet. The earliest computer viruses were spread through floppy disks that were used to exchange messages. In many cases of early viruses on operating systems such as MS-DOS, the virus would be stored in the boot sector of a hard disk and installed in memory when the computer booted up. As use of the Internet has grown, virus transmission has largely moved to macro viruses and viruses that are spread by e-mail.

Macro viruses install "macros" in applications that allow users to execute code when they access certain document types. For example, popular applications such as Microsoft Word allow users to write macros—short programs that perform operations—and then store those programs both in the applications and in documents produced by the applications. A macro virus for Word installs itself in a Word application and spreads its code in Word documents produced by that application. When a Word document is sent from a user to a recipient, and the recipient opens the infected document, her Word application is infected. As she produces subsequent Word documents, they in turn carry the virus with them. Because most computers run Microsoft operating systems and Microsoft office applications, Microsoft document types are frequent targets of virus writers.

E-mail viruses spread through attachments to e-mail messages. These attachments contain executable code (often the fact that the code is executable is hidden) that causes them to spread when they are executed. Often the virus contains some tantalizing message (a recent virus contained the subject line "I love you"). In many cases e-mail viruses themselves are macro viruses using scripting programs built into popular e-mail programs such as Microsoft Outlook or Qualcomm Eudora. These scripting programs will search through a user's records to find e-mail correspondents and then transmit themselves to those correspondents. In many cases the e-mail virus will forge a return address, making location of the source of the virus difficult (and frustrating uninfected users as they sort through numerous messages that incorrectly report them as a transmitter of the e-mail virus).

Vectors for Worms

Worms spread directly from computer to computer. The first large-scale worm infection occurred on the UNIX operating system in November 1988 and was written by Robert T. Morris, then a graduate student at Cornell University. The Morris worm demonstrated a number of techniques that later became standard for worm authors. In particular, it was the first large-scale worm to exploit a weakness called "buffer overflow." The worm sent messages to other computers requesting information about users on those computers using the UNIX "finger" service. The messages exceeded the expected maximum length of the finger request. Because the receiving computers did not have provisions for overly long messages, data were corrupted. By careful exploitation of this weakness, the author of the worm was able to cause the worm to reproduce itself. Buffer overflow problems turned out to be common in many applications and operating systems, and by 1998 two-thirds of all advisories issued by the U.S. Department of Defense-sponsored Computer Emergency Response Team involved the buffer overflow weakness.

The Morris worm also demonstrated that worms can use multiple methods to spread themselves. The Morris worm attempted to guess passwords using a list of potential passwords; when a username/password infection was found on a given computer, the worm would then try that same username/password combination on remote computers likely to be used by the user (exploiting the fact that users often use a single password on multiple computers).

More recent worms spread at frighteningly fast rates. For example, the "Slammer" (also called "Sapphire") worm of 25 January 2003, infected systems that run Microsoft SQL Server software. The majority of Slammer infections occurred within ten minutes of the worm's release, and during the initial phases of infection, the infected population doubled in size every 8.5 seconds. (As the worm saturated virtually all vulnerable computers on the Internet, the exponential growth of infected computers abated.) The rapid spread of the worm made real-time human response virtually impossible. As a result, Slammer's spread led to serious real-world consequences, including a failure of major automatic teller machine networks, failure of the 911 emergency phone number system in Seattle, Washington, and failure of airline flight reservation systems and subsequent flight cancellations.

Worms, Viruses, and Denial-of-Service Attacks

In many cases worms and viruses are designed to carry out specific malicious attacks, such as destruction of data on infected computers. Perhaps the most serious attack is the backdoor attack, which allows the infected computer to be controlled at will by an outsider. A particularly serious type of backdoor attack is the denial-of-service attack. Denial-of-service attacks (often called "DoS" attacks) attempt to infect a large number of "zombie" computers. On a signal from the attacker (or on a particular date/time), the infected zombie computers start transmitting messages to a victim computer, overwhelming the capability of the victim computer to process the incoming messages. For example, the Code Red worm exploited a buffer overflow weakness in Microsoft software in an attempt to target the www.whitehouse.gov website run by the Office of the President of the United States.

Because denial-of-service attacks involve numerous infected computers, stopping them when they occur is difficult if not impossible—identifying all the infected computers and removing the worm or virus from them are simply unfeasible. Instead, the target of the attack must work with its Internet service provider to block certain types of incoming messages or rename the targeted site. Because these defenses can take hours to implement, waves of denial-of-service attacks can make targeted sites unavailable for extended periods of time.

Varieties

Another type of malware is adware. Adware causes advertising messages to be generated on a user's computer. Although adware can be spread as part of a virus or worm, it is often installed on users' computers by more pedestrian methods: as part of an installed application. A number of free or low-cost applications on the World Wide Web include adware. Adware often is difficult to remove from a computer.

Conventional viruses and worms infect computers with exact copies of themselves. However, more powerful polymorphic viruses and worms modify themselves with each new infection. This modification makes detection of such viruses and worms more difficult because virus-scanning applications must scan for all possible forms. A virus designer can build a polymorphic virus by using a random number generator to generate a random cryptographic key and then using that key to encrypt the virus as it spreads onto a new computer. Because most of the virus will be encrypted, and each encryption will be different, detecting the presence of the virus is difficult.

Computer scientists have described a variety of methods by which backdoors can be installed in computer systems. One method deserves special mention; it was presented by Ken Thompson (one of the original developers of the UNIX operating system) in his acceptance speech for the 1983 Turing Award (the highest academic award in computer science). Thompson explained how one could use a compiler, a program that transforms source code into machine executable object code, to spread a backdoor. Thompson described how a compiler could recognize a login program. The compiler would add a backdoor to the login program, allowing any user who knew a particular secret string to gain access to a computer. Then the compiler would be modified to add the backdoor to any compiler program. After this stage was reached, it would no longer be necessary to include any evidence of the backdoor in source code—whenever a compiler program was itself recompiled, the backdoor would be automatically included.

This method is not merely a theoretical attack but rather was actually implemented by Thompson and by others. Because this kind of backdoor remains benign until actually triggered, detecting it even with full analysis of the source code of a system is impossible.

Defenses against Viruses and Worms

As Ken Thompson demonstrated, no method of virus and worm defense can be completely satisfactory—a clever virus author can defeat any form of defense. As a result, most defenses are reactive—rather than try to anticipate all possible viruses and worms, they try to detect and defend against viruses and worms that are actually observed in practice. After a virus or worm is identified, engineers characterize it by a set of particular features—its signature—that uniquely identifies it. (In the case of polymorphic viruses, finding a virus signature can be difficult.) A virus scanner is programmed to search for the signature, and whenever the signature is found, the virus scanner attempts to isolate or remove the infection. As new viruses are found, updated lists of signatures and removal (or isolation) techniques are published. Commercial virus scanners often use regular updates of these lists from a vendor-provided source.

Similarly, many operating system vendors (including Microsoft and Apple) provide systems for automatically and quickly distributing updates to vulnerable software. Although these systems are certainly useful, their effectiveness is limited if few people use them.

Experts often cite using better computer security (especially turning off unused software features) as a method for defending against viruses and worms. For example, many computer users do not need to use macro (scripting) features in e-mail programs, and if these features are turned off, viruses spread by e-mail will be far less effective. Unfortunately, turning off features is often complicated, limiting this technique's effectiveness for typical users. To maximize the capabilities of their software, vendors are usually motivated to ship software with most (or all) features turned on.

An alternative defense is a firewall, which is software or hardware that isolates a computer on a network. Firewalls vary from complex programs to relatively simple systems that are included in many home network routers. Firewalls can defend against many, but not all, attacks.

Many researchers attribute virus vulnerability to the widespread distribution of a relatively small number of operating systems and application software. For example, a recent report by a team led by computer security researcher Dan Geer described Microsoft software as a monoculture that presents a serious computer security threat. However, viruses and worms have been observed even in software (such as the Linux operating system) that is used by only a small fraction of users.

One proactive (acting in anticipation of future problems) method of virus protection involves statistical techniques. For example, a common characteristic of many worm attacks is that an infected computer will try to contact a large number of other computers. Some researchers have proposed automatically checking for this pattern of communication and temporarily disabling computers that demonstrate it. However, such a technique at best can only slow down an attack—as long as the virus author keeps the attack level below the triggering threshold, the attack will evade detection.

The number of viruses and worms has increased each year since they first became common in the mid-1980s. Although computer security specialists continue to find methods to defeat many viruses and worms, their growing presence suggests that we will continue to struggle with them for many years.

J. D. Tygar

See also Hackers; Spamming

FURTHER READING

Cheswick, W., Bellovin, S., & Rubin, A. (2003). *Firewalls and Internet security: Repelling the wily hacker* (2nd ed.). Boston: Addison-Wesley.

Computer Science and Telecommunications Board. (1999). *Trust in cyberspace*. Washington, DC: National Academy Press.

Geer, D., Pfleeger, P., Schneier, B., Quarterman, J., Metzger, P., Bace, R., & Gutmann, P. (2003). *CyberInsecurity: The cost of monopoly*. Retrieved April 13, 2004, from http://www.ccianet.org/papers/cyberinsecurity.pdf

Moore, D., Paxson, V., Savage, S., Shannon, C., Staniford, S., & Weaver, N. (2003). Inside the Slammer worm. *IEEE Security & Privacy, 1*(4), 33–39.

Spafford, E. (1988). *The Internet worm program: An analysis (Purdue Technical Report CSD-TR-823)*. Retrieved April 22, 2004, from www.protovision.textfiles.com/100/tr823.txt

Spafford, E. (1989). Crisis and aftermath. *Communications of the ACM, 32*(6), 678–687.

Staniford, S., Paxson, V., & Weaver, N. (2002). How to own the Internet in your spare time. *Proceedings of the 11th USENIX Security Symposium* (pp. 149–162).

Thompson, K. (1984). Reflections on trusting trust. *Communications of the ACM, 27*(8), 761–763.

VISUAL PROGRAMMING

Visual programming is programming that uses more than one dimension to convey the semantics of a program. Such additional dimensions can include multiple spatial dimensions or a time dimension or both. This contrasts with traditional textual programming, where semantics can only be conveyed with a single dimension—namely, text. (The syntax of some textual programming languages allow the use of a second dimension, such as the continuation of a linear string across a vertical dimension in limited ways; however, the language must still be expressible via a one-dimensional string grammar.) Just as the one-dimensional words of a textual program are the tokens of a textual program, the tokens of a visual program are any significant, potentially multidimensional object or relationship. Just as textual tokens comprise a textual expression, a *visual expression* is composed of the collection of one or more visual tokens. A *visual programming language* (VPL) is a programming language whose syntax includes one or more visual expressions.

Four Visual Programming Strategies

The goal of visual programming research is not to eliminate text from programming languages. Rather, most VPL research has aimed to accomplish one or more of the following goals: (1) to make programming more accessible to a particular audience; (2) to increase the correctness with which people perform programming tasks; (3) to improve the speed and efficiency with which people perform programming tasks; and (4) to increase a human's ability to learn programming. Four strategies are commonly used in VPL design to achieve these goals:

1. Concreteness: Concreteness allows the programmer to work with particular instances rather than abstract variables. One way in which a language can be concrete is by allowing a programmer to specify some aspect of semantics on a specific object or value.

2. Directness: From a cognitive perspective, the directness of a programming language specifies the distance between the problem a programmer wishes to solve and the actions required to express a solution to that problem through the language. For example, in the context of direct manipulation, this is usually described as "the capacity to manipulate the object of interest directly" (Shneiderman 1983, 62).

3. Explicitness: Explicitness describes a VPL's ability to represent particular program semantics explicitly, rather than requiring the programmer to make inferences. The presence of multiple dimensions provides VPLs with opportunities to make such semantics explicit in ways not practical solely with a sequence of text. One example of explicitness is the communication of dataflow relationships by displaying directed edges among related variables.

4. Liveness: One characteristic of interest in VPL research is the immediacy of semantic feedback provided during the process of editing a program. The immediacy of this feedback is termed the liveness of the language. Steven L. Tanimoto, professor of computer science and engineering at the University of Washington, describes four levels of liveness, the last two of which provide opportunities to VPLs. At level 3, a language automatically provides semantic feedback as soon as an edit is performed to the program, with no need for explicit action by the programmer. For example, spreadsheets support level 3 liveness via their automatic recalcula-

tion. At level 4, feedback is provided to the programmer after any event, not just source code edits such as clock ticks and mouse clicks. By responding to program edits—and in doing so supporting level 3 liveness—in addition to other events, the current state of the system is reflected to a user as computations continue.

Two VPL Paradigms

The form-based paradigm is arguably the most commonly used programming paradigm today due to the widespread use of commercial spreadsheets. However, the dataflow paradigm is currently the most widely used approach to visual programming in industry.

Form-Based Visual Programming

In form-based languages, a program is composed of multidimensional forms. For example, commercial spreadsheets are two-dimensional forms whose contents are specified by cell formulas. The form-based paradigm is used by a VPL called Forms/3. Forms/3 programs are composed of forms (spreadsheets) whose contents are specified in free-floating cells that are not locked into a grid. These cells are placed on a form by the programmer to achieve the desired layout and then given formulas to dictate the program's computations, which can be a mixture of text and graphics. Cell formulas become a network of (one-way) constraints, and the system continuously ensures that all values displayed on the screen satisfy these constraints.

Forms/3 is a research language used to experiment with both programming language and human-computer interaction (HCI) devices to remove spreadsheet limitations. Forms/3 is a "gentle slope" language, intended to allow end users to create spreadsheets with fewer limitations than exist in other spreadsheet languages, while at the same time allowing more sophisticated users and programmers to create more powerful spreadsheets without having to leave the spreadsheet paradigm to do so. To support the software lifecycle beyond the programming phase, Forms/3 also includes an integrated testing methodology that explicitly supports incremental spreadsheet testing during the incremental programming process. Other Forms/3 features to assist users in testing and debugging include assertions, automatic test case generation, and fault localization.

Dataflow-Based Visual Programming

In contrast to traditional programming languages, where instructions determine program execution sequence, in dataflow languages the flow of data determines the execution sequence. One dataflow VPL aimed at professional programmers is LabVIEW. LabVIEW programs are called virtual instruments (VIs), in imitation of physical instruments. Each VI has a front panel serving as the user interface, a block diagram containing the graphical source code that defines the program's functionality, and an icon and connector pane that allows a programmer to use a VI within another VI. (See Figure 1.)

LabVIEW was originally designed as a domain-specific language for laboratory data acquisition. Because LabVIEW VIs model laboratory instruments, there is only a small cognitive distance from data acquisition problems to the LabVIEW programs that handle these problems, giving them a high level of directness in this domain. As with other dataflow VPLs, LabVIEW also features explicit rendering of the edges in a graph, which explicitly communicate the dataflow relationships to the programmer with a minimal requirement of inference.

UPL Specifications

Because textual languages are only expressible via one-dimensional string grammars, only one relationship is possible between the symbols of a sentence: "next to." Hence, the relationship "next to" is implied when one symbol is written next to another in a grammar, and a textual grammar need not specify this relationship.

VPLs, however, can use more than one dimension to convey the semantics of a program. The consequence of this freedom is a large number of possible relationships, such as "overlaps" or "touches." Hence, relationships between symbols must be made explicit in the grammar, which means that traditional conventions for specifying grammars of textual languages such as BNF cannot be used without modifications to support multidimensionality.

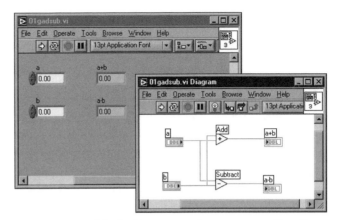

FIGURE 1. *A block diagram and a corresponding front panel*

This means that the non-terminal x can be rewritten to the multiset $X_1, ..., X_n$ if the sentence contains symbols $X_1', ..., X_m'$ (the context) such that the attributes of these symbols satisfy the constraint C. denotes the vector of attributes of x whose values are defined by the vector expression E over attributes of other objects in the production.

As a concrete example, the following is a CMG production taken from the specification of state diagrams:

TR:transition ::= A:arrow, T:text
   where exists R:state, S:state
   where
   T.midpoint close_to A.midpoint,
   R.radius = distance(A.startpoint, R.midpoint),
   S.radius = distance(A.endpoint, S.midpoint)
   and
   TR.from = R.name,
   TR.to = S.name,
   TR.label = T.string.

In this example, = (TR.from, TR.to, TR.label) and E = (R.name, S.name, T.string).

Kim Marriott and Bernd Meyer, professor and senior lecturer (respectively) at Monash University, devised a taxonomy for VPLs using several different classes of CMGs. They summarize the relative expressiveness of classes in the hierarchy, thereby providing a means of comparing VPLs according to their computational properties. They also show that the membership problem for the classes in the taxonomy is inherently complex, indicating that parsing for even the most restrictive class in the taxonomy is very expensive.

Considering the Users of UPLs

The *attention investment model* of abstraction use analyzes the actions that will be taken by a programmer in terms of investments of attentional effort. The model considers human attention as an economic resource that can be invested in programming activities. Attention units provide the basis for modeling the kinds of trade-offs a user might make in an economic system in which the scarce commodity is attention:

■ *Cost*: attention units to get the work done. (Presumably the work itself has value, but this is external to the model.)

■ *Investment*: attention units expended toward a potential reward, where the reward can either be external to the model or a *pay-off*.

■ *Pay-off*: reduced future cost in attention units.

■ *Risk*: probability that additional future cost will result from the way the user has chosen to spend attention.

These concepts can be applied to any programming situation, regardless of whether the programmer is a professionally trained software developer or an end-user programmer engaged in programming aimed at less experienced audiences. The following is an example of these concepts in an end-user programming situation:

Suppose the user is a teacher thinking of creating a spreadsheet to calculate student grades (an end-user "program"). This will *cost* some *attention units*. The cost of creating the spreadsheet is an *investment*, because there is a potential *pay-off*: The teacher could use the spreadsheet on multiple students this term, instead of calculating each one's grades manually, and in future terms as well. But there is a *risk* that she'll get the formulas wrong, and turning in incorrect grades would cost her a lot of future attention units to straighten out. This simple investment model, when applied at multiple levels of granularity, can model many of the actions and decisions made during programming tasks. These applications can help inform the design of visual programming devices.

The model has been validated in a cognitive simulation of programmer behavior for fine-grained decisions, and there is evidence that it is effective in practice for aiding with language design.

A more focused way for language designers to consider relevant aspects of human cognition is via the *cognitive dimensions framework*. The cognitive dimensions framework, as delineated by Thomas R. G. Green, reader in computing at Open University, and Marian Petre, Advanced Research Fellow of the Engineering and Physical Sciences Research Council, is outlined below as a series of questions:

1. Closeness of mapping: What "programming games" need to be learned?
2. Consistency: When some of the language has been learned, how much of the rest can be inferred?
3. Diffuseness: How many symbols or graphic entities are required to express a meaning?
4. Error-Proneness: Does the design of the notation induce "careless mistakes"?
5. Hard Mental Operations: Are there places where the user needs to resort to fingers or penciled annotation to keep track of what's happening?
6. Hidden Dependencies: Is every dependency overtly indicated in both directions? Is the indication perceptual or only symbolic?
7. Premature Commitment: Do programmers have to make decisions before they have the information they need?
8. Progressive Evaluation: Can a partially complete program be executed to obtain feedback on "How am I doing"?
9. Role-Expressiveness: Can the reader see how each component of a program relates to the whole?
10. Secondary Notation: Can programmers use layout, color, or other cues to convey extra meaning above and beyond the "official" semantics of the language?
11. Viscosity: How much effort is required to perform a single change?
12. Visibility: Is every part of the code simultaneously visible (assuming a large enough display), or is it at least possible to compare any two parts side-by-side at will? If the code is dispersed, is it at least possible to know in what order to read it?

Cognitive dimensions can help a language designer identify trouble spots in a VPL or a VPL feature. For example, in considering the fault localization feature of the Forms/3 language, a designer's use of the consistency dimension pointed out the following potential trouble spot: The fault localization feature uses the colors white and red to communicate the fault likelihood of program points (spreadsheet cells). However, red is also used by Forms/3 to communicate the "untestedness" of a program point (spreadsheet cell). The feature therefore assigns a separate meaning to the color red, rendering it inconsistent with the rest of the environment.

Harnessing the Power of Visual Programming

Research such as the cognitive dimensions work helps to align the focus of visual programming researchers on the human programmers. Due to such influences, as visual programming research has matured, researchers have learned that visual programming research is not a matter of learning whether visual expressions are superior to text-only notations because every notation has strengths and weaknesses. The essence of visual programming research is to learn how to harness visual programming's expressive power to support particular properties that assist human cognition.

Joseph R. Ruthruff and Margaret M. Burnett

FURTHER READING

Beckwith, L., Burnett, M., & Cook, C. (2002). Reasoning about many-to-many requirement relationships in spreadsheets. In *IEEE Conference on Human-Centric Computing Languages and Environments*, 149–157.

Blackwell, A. F. (2002). First steps in programming: A rationale for attention investment models. In *IEEE Conference on Human-Centric Computing Languages and Environments*, 2–10.

Burnett, M. M. (1999). Visual programming. In J. G. Webster (Ed.), *Encyclopedia of electrical and electronics engineering.* New York: Wiley. Burnett, M. M., Atwood, J., Djang, R., Gottfried, H., Reichwein, J., & Yang, S. (2001). Forms/3: A first-order visual language to explore the boundaries of the spreadsheet paradigm. *Journal of Functional Programming, 11*, 155–206.

Burnett, M. M., Cook, C., Pendse, O., Rothermel, G., Summet, J., & Wallace, C. (2003). End-user software engineering with assertions in the spreadsheet paradigm. In *International Conference on Software Engineering*, 93–103.

Burnett, M. M., & Gottfried, H. (1998). Graphical definitions: Expanding spreadsheet languages through direct manipulation and gestures. *ACM Transactions on Computer-Human Interaction, 5*(1), 1–33.

Fisher, M., Cao, M., Rothermel, G., Cook, C. R., & Burnett, M. M. (2002). Automated test case generation for spreadsheets. In *International Conference on Software Engineering*, 141–151.

Green, T. R. G., & Petre, M. (1996). Usability analysis of visual programming environments: A "cognitive dimensions" framework. *Journal of Visual Languages and Computing, 7*(2), 131–174.

Hutchins, E., Hollan, J., & Norman, D. (1986). Direct manipulation interfaces. In D. Normal & S. Draper (Eds.), *User centered system design: New perspectives on human-computer interaction* (pp. 87–124). Hillsdale, NJ: Erlbaum. Marriott, K., & Meyer, B. (1997). On the classification of visual languages by grammar hierarchies. *Journal of Visual Languages and Computing, 8*(4), 375–402.

Nardi, B. (1993). *A small matter of programming: Perspectives on end user computing.* Cambridge, MA: MIT Press.

Rothermel, G., Li, L., DuPuis, C., & Burnett, M. M. (1998). What you see is what you test: A methodology for testing form-based visual programs. In *International Conference on Software Engineering*, 198–207.

Ruthruff, J., Creswick, E., Burnett, M. M., Cook, C., Prabhakararao, S., Fisher II, M., & Main, M. (2003). End-user software visualizations for fault localization. In *ACM Symposium on Software Visualization*, 123–132.

Shneiderman, B. (1983). Direct manipulation: A step beyond programming languages. *Computer, 16*(8), 57–69.

Tanimoto, S. (1990). Viva: A visual language for image processing. *Journal of Visual Languages and Computing, 2*(2), 127–139.

Yang, S., Burnett, M. M., DeKoven, E., & Zloof, M. (1997). Representation design benchmarks: A design-time aid for VPL navigable static representations. *Journal of Visual Languages and Computing, 8*(5/6), 563–599.

WEARABLE COMPUTER

By the most liberal definition of the term, a *wearable computer* is simply a computer that can be worn on the body of a person. Such a definition would encompass handheld computers, personal digital assistants (PDAs), and many mobile phones that integrate computation. However, many interfaces for these devices require that users interrupt their task (walking, conversing, repairing a car, etc.) in order to concentrate on the interface whenever they wish to consult the devices. For example, a laptop computer is used while it is on a horizontal surface, and a user can devote both hands to typing on its keyboard. Thus, although laptops are mobile in the sense that they can be carried to a new location, they cannot be accessed effectively while a user is actually moving or performing other tasks. Palm-top devices are more mobile than laptops in that they are more accessible; however, their interfaces still assume that most, if not all, of the user's attention is devoted to the computer application. In addition, palm-tops usually require both hands (one to hold the device and one to manipulate a pointer or keypad) on the device and both eyes to operate, making them difficult to operate while in motion or while performing another task.

Wearable computers, on the other hand, can be operational while the user is mobile. In a manner similar to mobile phones and portable digital music players, wearable computers can provide access to information and computation while the user is occupied with another task. Wearable computers may be integrated into clothing or incorporated into other worn objects, such as wristwatches, so as not to interfere with everyday mobility. They may also offer

797

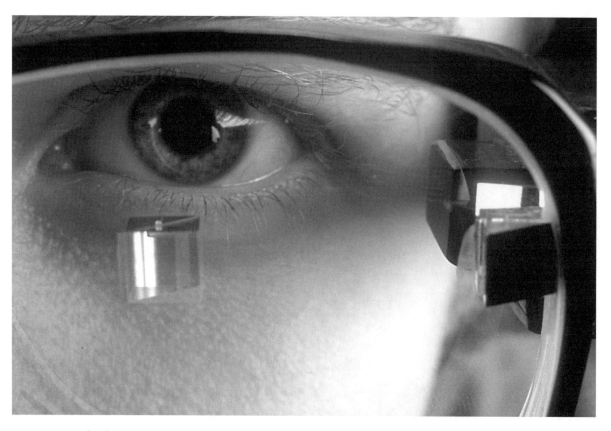

FIGURE 1. *Thad Starner sporting a wearable computer.* Photo courtesy of Georgia Institute of Technology.

hands-free or hands-limited use through speech interfaces, one-handed keyboards, or small pointing devices such as belt-worn trackballs and dials. These input interfaces allow the wearer to occupy his or her hands with another task, be it shaking hands with a colleague, carrying a package, or caring for a wounded patient. Likewise, output interfaces such as visual overlay head-up displays and ambient audio allow the user to gather information while paying attention to another task. Wearable computers are chiefly used in situations where computation, monitoring, or mediated communication (computer annotation or translation of information to assist the user) is needed while a person is simultaneously engaged in another activity. Examples include battlefield communications, medical monitoring, automatic language translation, inspection and repair, and warehouse picking (assisting with filling orders from warehouse inventory), although dual-task applications are common in the general consumer and business worlds as well.

Technical Challenges

One vision of wearable computers is a central computer carried in the pocket and connected to wired or wireless peripherals worn on the body. This central computer would contain the main central processing unit (CPU), memory, disk storage, and the central node for the user's on-body network. Optionally, the central computer might also contain a long-range wireless radio for connection to the Internet or shorter-range wireless for connection to other devices in a room. The user would put on and take off peripherals as needed throughout the day. For example, a pair of earphones might be worn when the user wishes to hear information about artwork in a museum, whereas a pair of eyeglasses with an embedded screen might be worn to convey purchase-history information about customers met at a sales convention. A one-handed chording keyboard, such as HandyKey's Twiddler, might be added to allow rapid editing of a document as the user rides the subway to work or takes notes during conversations.

Task-specific sensors and input devices might also be added. For example, a wearable might be equipped with a radio frequency identification (RFID) tag reader for a package-delivery task or sensors for monitoring a medical condition.

Although such suites of wearable devices are not commonly available, trends in technology indicate their future possibility. By examining the improvement in laptop computer technology between 1990 and 2003, we see that mobile storage density increased by a factor of 4,000, mobile CPU capability by a factor of 900, and the amount of available random-access memory (RAM) by a factor of 256. In addition, wireless Internet connections are available in many countries. Given these technology improvements and the shrinkage of mobile electronic devices, we can easily imagine a wearable device as described earlier with the capabilities of a full desktop computer. In fact, this article's first draft was written with a wearable computer, head-up display, and one-handed keyboard, although all peripherals were wired. However, much of the challenge of wearable computing is not in miniaturizing the technology per but rather in providing appropriate technologies and interfaces that reflect the needs of the user in a mobile environment. In general, wearable computer designs balance four issues:

Power usage and heat dissipation: Given their close proximity to the body, wearable computers, like laptops, are limited in the amount of heat they can dissipate without causing the user discomfort. In addition, the size, weight, and energy density of current batteries place a limit on the power available to a wearable computer. Peripheral devices also need a means to draw power, especially if they are connected to the main wearable computer through a wireless data network.

On- and off-body networking: Communication between devices both on and off the body is an integral part of wearable computing. As with any wireless mobile device, networking is often constrained by the amount of available power and the array of services available.

Privacy: Due to the amount of personal information that may be transmitted and stored on a wearable computer, privacy is an important concern. As with ubiquitous computing, the creation of appropriate, intuitive privacy safeguards that provide the desired functionality is both a technical and a social issue.

Interface: The connection between user and computer at all levels combines to create the user's total experience. This connection includes the human-computer interface, psychophysics, human factors, ergonomics, industrial design, and even fashion. Like clothing, a wearable interface must be customized to both the person wearing the device and the environments in which it will be used. Research in wearable computing seeks common components that can be adapted for many domains and for many users.

Each of these issues affects the others, and wearable device designers must keep these interrelations in mind when constructing their systems.

Augmenting Human Cognition

Sometimes people apply the term cyborg to wearable computer users because of the similarity of their equipment to devices described in twentieth-century science fiction. Coined by Manfred Clynes and Nathan Kline in 1960, the term cyborg refers to a combination of human and machine in which the interface between the two is practically seamless; the machine has become a "natural" extension of the human's mind and body. Although Clynes and Kline envisioned cyborgs in the context of adapting humans for the rigors of space, they also applied the concept to more commonplace environments. When children learn to ride a bicycle, their full concentration is spent on thinking about how to shift their balance, adjust their speed, and so forth. After a few months, however, riding becomes almost like walking: Children think only about turning left, and their body automatically leans into the turn, adjusting for the feel of the road, the speed of the bike, and anything that might be in their path. This familiarity frees up their attention for other tasks such as talking with their fellow bikers or watching the scenery. A large number of wearable interfaces are designed to enable the same kind of easy interaction between human and computer. These wearable interfaces are used in applications designed to achieve what is known generally as "augmented cognition":

the improvement of one's mental ability for a given task.

The most common augmented cognition application is information delivery, in which a person is engaged in a task and needs information about it. Examples of such information include positions of enemy troops on a battlefield, the next step in a repair or inspection task, or the name and purchase history of the customer with whom a sales representative is meeting. The two main challenges for wearables that support such tasks are how to determine what information is valuable given the user's current environment and how to deliver that information in a way that is not distracting.

Some applications give the user an interface for directly requesting information. To limit distraction, such an interface often uses modalities (sight, hearing, touch, etc.) that are not already in use in relation to the primary task. For example, commercially available wearables for warehouse-picking applications allow a picker to speak simple queries about tasks and item locations into a head-worn microphone, leaving his or her hands and eyes unencumbered. Other systems attempt to eliminate the need for a user to ask anything at all by using the environment itself as the query. For example, the Jimminy system displays on a head-mounted display information based on a person's location, people to whom he or she is speaking, and time of day (see Rhodes 1997).

Several methods communicate information in nondistracting ways. Simple yes/no information can be conveyed in what are called "ambient" or "calm" interfaces. Information can also be presented in stages so that the user gets only as much information as he or she wants and no more. Finally, the task environment itself can be used to simplify and disambiguate (to establish a single semantic or grammatical interpretation for) information, as is the case in augmented-reality systems such as the friend-or-foe head-up display used by some military pilots. These systems use an overlay of information on the view port itself so that other jets seen through the window appear to be labeled with their appropriate information. This interface technique has a much lower cognitive load than would a traditional radar screen on the dashboard because the pilot does not need to do the mental calculations to link the icon of a plane on a screen with the actual plane seen through the window.

The idea of creating an information technology device that complements and extends the user's abilities has a long history in computing. In his 1945 article entitled "As We May Think," Vannevar Bush, one of the pioneers of computing, called for a device to aid human memory and thought:

> Consider a future device for individual use, which is a sort of mechanized private file and library. It needs a name, and, to coin one at random, "memex" will do. A memex is a device in which an individual stores all his books, records, and communications, and which is mechanized so that it may be consulted with exceeding speed and flexibility. It is an enlarged intimate supplement to his memory. (Bush 1945, www.theatlantic.com/unbound/flashbks/computer/bushf.htm)

Bush's vision of the future included even the ability for a user to capture information for his or her memex while mobile—foreshadowing research in wearable computing today. Similarly, in 1960 J. C. R. Licklider, who headed the U.S. Advanced Research Projects Agency's Information Processing Technical Office (ARPA IPTO), described the idea of "man-machine symbiosis" with the hope that "human brains and computing machines will be coupled together very tightly, and that the resulting partnership will think as no human brain has ever thought" (Licklider 1960, 1). Licklider's efforts to fund "interactive computing," as opposed to the batch processing common in his day, led to much of modern computing, including windowing, hypertext, multitasking, and the Internet. One can argue that these efforts indeed did augment human cognition. A commonplace Web search engine now allows a user to search more information more quickly than any nonelectronic library, and the personal computer aids in the integration and synthesis of this information into new works more rapidly than the typewriter and paper.

In the future wearable computers will continue to extend today's information support services into the mobile realm, making them even more personal and interactive. Perhaps searches will be performed continuously and automatically based on sensing of the user's context (as with Jimminy), or perhaps the wearable will create automatic personal diaries of the user's life, similar to Bush's idea of the memex. Certainly as new portable sensors and large amounts of on-body storage become possible during the next decade, researchers and the commercial market will explore how such systems can be leveraged to the user's advantage.

Wearable Computer Applications

The earliest wearable computers were designed to gain an advantage secretly in games of chance. As early as 1961, MIT professors Edward Thorp and Claude Shannon created a covert analog wearable computer to predict the outcome of a roulette wheel. Even in these early wearables, the design trade-offs discussed earlier are evident. Because detection could mean being barred from casinos, the networking, interface, and power considerations were designed to minimize detectability. In turn, these trade-offs affected the usability of the system, which, although successfully deployed, could not be used consistently enough to generate the revenue hoped. However, gambling devices have persisted as an underground application of wearable computers to this day, with varying degrees of success.

Another of the oldest applications of wearable computers is enabling technology for the disabled. In 1968 Hubert Upton created an analog wearable computer used as an aid for lip reading. The computer distinguished between fricatives (consonants characterized by frictional passage of the expired breath through a narrowing at some point in the vocal tract), stops (consonants characterized by complete closure of the breath passage in the course of articulation), and voiced phonemes (any of the abstract units of the phonetic system of a language that correspond to a set of similar speech sounds that is perceived to be a single distinctive sound in the language) and lit corresponding LEDs mounted in a pair of eyeglasses. In this way the computer attempted to provide information to the lip reader that could not be recovered from watching a speaker's lips. Current research in this area includes creating mobile sign-language-to-spoken-language translators, wearable navigation aids for the blind, closed captioning displays for deaf movie patrons, and memory aids for the elderly.

With the advent of body-worn and implanted sensors, medical wearable devices have become more commonplace. Embedded computers in pacemakers can monitor a person's level of physical activity and adjust the heart rate accordingly. Some computers can even display their parameters in real time on a PDA screen. Other wearable medical devices simply retain sensor readings for patient studies. For example, a recently developed system monitors a patient's stomach pH level through a sensor temporarily implanted in the esophagus. The sensor transmits its readings wirelessly to a data logger that the patient wears on a hip. After a week the sensor passes harmlessly through the body, and a doctor interprets the sensor readings.

Mobile augmented reality is perhaps the most photogenic of wearable computing applications. Augmented reality overlays information-rich virtual realities on top of the physical world, such that virtual graphical objects seem to co-exist with physical objects. Instead of restricting the World Wide Web to desktop computer monitors, wearable computers with the appropriate support infrastructure can allow any object or location in the physical world to serve as a hypertext link. For example, with current research systems a museum visitor is able to discover more information about an artifact simply by staring at it, triggering associated hypertext presentations. By allowing annotation, friends and colleagues are able to leave private messages for each other at offices, restaurants, or street corners. Similarly, tourists are able to see how a historical district once looked by walking through the district and seeing virtual images of now-destroyed buildings overlaid on current architecture.

Building on early academic successes, commercial wearable computers are being marketed in niche application areas such as information support for maintenance, repair, inspection, shipping, and warehouse picking. For example, a wearable computer might be used as an electronic service manual for a car mechanic while he or she is repairing a car. With a head-up display and a voice- or simple knob-based interface, the wearable can be used while the mechanic is lying under the automobile. This mobility provides a significant time savings over the use of a thousand-page service manual, which would require the mechanic to get out from under the car and find the correct page. Wearable computers have been used for car maintenance, armored tank inspection, and airplane inspection. Equipped with a bar code scanner in a ring, wearable computers are used to track packages in shipping warehouses and to scan tickets at theater events.

Portable consumer electronics, and especially mobile phones, have been steadily approaching the functionality and interaction style of wearable computers. Modern mobile phones, PDAs, and portable digital music players now integrate belt clips, one-handed typing interfaces, audio headsets, individually distinguishable audio cues, and even speech-recognition to allow operation while users are engaged in other activities. As consumer appliances continue to drive improvements in mobile computation, storage, and data networks, today's wearable research applications, such as augmented reality, become more practical. Conversely, as wearables become more common, perhaps mobile consumer electronics applications will begin to be subsumed by general-purpose wearable computers. A similar phenomenon is occurring with desktop computers as consumers are using them as fax machines, stereos, VCRs, and other office and entertainment appliances.

Thad Starner and Bradley Rhodes

See also Augmented Cognition; Augmented Reality; Mobile Computing; Pocket Computers

FURTHER READING

Bush, V. (1945) As We May Think. Atlantic Monthly, 76(1) 101–108. Retrieved March 25, 2004, from http://www.theatlantic.com/unbound/flashbks/computer/bushf.htm

Clynes, M., & Kline, N. (1960). Cyborgs and space. *Astronautics, 14*, 26–27.

Ishii, H., & Ullmer, B. (1997). Tangible bits. In *Conference on Human Factors in Computing Systems (CHI)* (pp. 234–241). Pittsburgh, PA: ACM.

Licklider, J. (1960) Man-Computer Symbiosis. IRE Transaction of Human Factors in Electronics, HFE-1 (1), 4–11.

Rhodes, B. (1997). The wearable remembrance agent: A system for augments memory. *Personal Technologies, 1*(4), 218–224.

Sawhney, N., & Schmandt, C. (1999). Nomadic radio: Scaleable and contextual notification for wearable audio messaging. In *Conference on Human Factors in Computing Systems (CHI)* (pp.96–103). Pittsburgh, PA: ACM.

Smailagic, A., & Siewiorel, D. (1993). A case study in embedded systems design: VuMan 2 wearable computer. *IEEE Design and Test of Computers, 10*(4), 56–67.

Starner, T., Mann, S., Rhodes, B., Levine, J., Healey, J., Kirsch, D., Picard, R., & Pentland A. (1997). Augmented reality through wearable computing. Presence, 6(4), 386–398.

Starner, T. (2001) The challenges of wearable computing: Parts 1 & 2. IEEE Micro, 21(4), 44-67

Stein, R., Ferrero, S., Hetfield, M., Quinn, A., & Krichever, M. (1998). Development of a commercially successful wearable data collection system. In *Proceedings from IEEE International Symposium on Wearable Computers* (pp. 18–24).Pittsburgh, PA:]IEEE Computer Society.

Thorp, E. (1998). The invention of the first wearable computer. In *Proceedings from IEEE International Symposium on Wearable Computers* (pp. 4–8. Pittsburgh, PA: IEEE Computer Society.

Upton, H. (1968). Wearable eyeglass speechreading aid. *American Annals of the Deaf, 113*, 222–229.

WEBSITE DESIGN

It is projected that the World Wide Web (WWW) will grow to 50 billion pages by 2005 and have a billion users by 2010. When the Web was in its infancy, site designers were required to know HTML programming to create a website. Today there are many software programs available to facilitate Web design—for example, Microsoft FrontPage and Macromedia Dreamweaver. These tools provide a visual layout editor that allows designers with little or no programming knowledge to create a site graphically. Advanced tools are also being used to add sophisticated graphics, animation, video, and audio components.

Most websites are either informational sites or e-commerce sites. Informational sites, such as www.cnn.com and www.harvard.edu, provide users with information about a particular area, such as news, education, training, reference, or entertainment. E-commerce sites, such as www.amazon.com and www.landsend.com, are product-based and revenue-focused. Intranet sites are generally informational and restricted to a private network. Intranets are primarily used by corporations to house proprietary information for their employees.

The Design Process

Despite shorter development cycles, the process by which a website is designed is expected to mirror that of quality software application design. This includes gaining a complete understanding of the target user population via user and task analysis, determining site goals, prototyping alternative designs, and testing usability. *User analysis* is an examination of the characteristics, capabilities, goals, and motivation of the targeted end-users. *Task analysis* provides an understanding of how users will work with the site, the tasks they will perform, and their level of importance or criticality. Both these activities help paint an accurate picture of the targeted user audience.

Once this information is collected and the site's goals are defined, the design phase begins. Page designs are prototyped and tested. Low-fidelity prototypes are visual mock-ups showing the site's look-and-feel and basic navigation. These prototypes are purposely done quickly (and can even be done on paper) so that they can be tested with users to determine whether they meet their goals. High-fidelity prototypes are more complete representations of a site and its functionality.

It is recommended that designers test the usability of a prototype with potential users before too much time and effort is invested in the design. Usability testing is an empirical method of measuring a website's ease-of-use. To conduct the test, representative users are observed as they complete a series of tasks with the website. Observational data, user satisfaction data, and performance data are collected, summarized, and used as the basis for redesign. The data gathered in a usability test is both objective and subjective and may include measurements of task success, task completion time, number of links/steps to complete tasks, user perceptions of ease of use and appeal, and overall user satisfaction with the site. The design process of a website is iterative in that the design, prototyping, and usability testing are repeated until the site goals have been met.

For designers as well as for users, the most important page of a website is probably the home page. This is where users get a first impression of a site's organization and begin to build a mental representation of its structure and purpose. Given that users have a choice of websites to visit, first impressions are very important to a site's success. This is different from traditional software applications, which require users to purchase and install them before using. With more invested,

these users may be more reluctant to disregard a program solely on a first impression. Switching to another website, however, is only a mouse click away.

Navigation

Navigating a website is facilitated by the use of links, button bars, menus, and browser buttons (Back and Forward). Pages within a site can be accessed directly by other site pages (or search engines) and therefore should be quickly identifiable with a site logo and headers telling users where they are. Link color is also used to inform users of location and previously visited pages. Links can be embedded within the page content (embedded), directed to other levels of the site structure (structural), or directed to related information (associative). Positioning of links on a text-intense page like a news story) has been found to impact user satisfaction and preference. Users report that embedded links are easier to navigate and that they make it easier to recognize key information and to follow the main idea than links positioned at the bottom of the page, top of the page, or in a left menu.

Structural links can be displayed via menus. Cascading menus have the advantage of requiring less screen real estate than indexed menus. However, it is sometimes difficult for users to control their mouse movements precisely enough to view and select the correct menu item. Research comparing cascading menus and indexed menus (like that used by Yahoo.com) shows that indexed menus yield faster search times and higher levels of satisfaction by users.

Users typically attend to information presented on the visible portion of a Web page (an area referred to as "above the fold") and do not like to scroll. Research has shown that online documents that require paging tend to be superior in both performance and preference to documents that require scrolling on a single page.

Overall Structure

The overall structure of a site must be considered before a site is designed. In a survey of Web users, almost 70 percent of users stated that one of their greatest problems with the Web was not being able to find the information they were looking for. A problem associated with hypertext systems is called the "art museum phenomenon," which states that users often forget important aspects of a hypertext structure because they are overwhelmed by the sheer volume of information provided (like a visitor to an art museum unable to recall details of a specific painting).

Many studies have been done to determine the optimal structure of menu and hypertext systems. Most of these studies show that breadth is better than depth. Other research has shown that the shape of the structure is also important. For larger sites (more than four levels), users are able to find information faster if the structure is concave (breadth of 8 × 2 × 2 × 8 pages). Other studies show a (4 × 4 × 4 × 4) structure to be less efficient than hypertext shapes of the same depth—for example, a (6 × 2 × 2 × 12) structure or structures that are deeper. Thus, the ideal website structure provides users the greatest number of choices at both the top and terminal levels of a site, while constricting the choices between these levels.

Users are accustomed to looking in certain areas on a Web page to find specific navigational elements such as links, a Home button, search capability, and advertisements. Research shows that users expect internal Web links to be located on the upper left side of a Web page, external Web links to be located on the right side or lower left side of a Web page, a "back to home" link to be located at the top-left corner, access to a site search engine to be located at the top-center of the screen, and advertisement banners to be located at the top of the page. This information can help with designing site pages because positioning Web elements in unexpected locations may increase search time and decrease overall site satisfaction.

To define a site's general appearance and maintain an underlying consistency, designers can use style sheets. Font type and size, colors, headers and footers, margins and spacing, and boilerplate content such as copyright statements are all elements that can be defined in a style sheet.

Reading on the Web

Eye-tracking studies show that most users do not read Web pages but rather *scan* them. For this reason, Web page design differs from the design of paper-based materials. Characteristics of the text displayed on a Web page have been shown to influence reading speed and satisfaction in online reading. These characteristics include font type and size, line length, and color contrast.

Font Type and Size

Website designers have a tremendous number of font types and sizes from which to choose. Research investigating the most commonly used online fonts suggests that they all tend to be equally legible at the 10-, 12-, and 14-point size though older adults and children prefer larger font sizes. Studies comparing sans serif fonts (Arial, Comic Sans MS, Tahoma, and Verdana) and serif fonts (Courier New, Georgia, Century Schoolbook, Times New Roman) show no difference in effective reading between font types. However, users generally prefer sans serif fonts over serif fonts when reading online and have been shown to attribute personality characteristics to the different font types. For example, Times New Roman has been reported to appear more "businesslike" while Comic Sans and Bradley fonts are reported to be more "fun." This information can be used by website designers as they consider their target audience and site goals.

Line Length

Studies investigating line lengths have reached mixed conclusions. Some researchers conclude that longer line lengths are read more efficiently from computer screens than narrower ones. Others favor short to medium line lengths. For example, it has been recommended that shorter line lengths (about 60 characters per line (CPL)) be used in place of longer, full-screen lengths, since longer line lengths require greater lateral eye movements, making it more likely that readers will lose their place within the text and possibly find it more tiring to read. In general, researchers recommend limiting line lengths to around 40 to 60 CPL.

Contrast/Backgrounds

Plain backgrounds of online material have been shown to produce faster search times than medium textured backgrounds. The contrast between the foreground text and the background is very important to the readability of text. The highest contrast is black text on a white background or white text on a black background. The more textured the background, the greater the contrast needs to be. Different color settings (true color versus 16-bit color) also affect the contrast. Most studies show that dark characters on a light background are superior to light characters on a dark background. Color vision capabilities of users must also be considered. Approximately 8 percent of males and less than 0.5 percent of females have a color-vision deficit of some kind. Therefore, it is important to note that different font color combinations can have an effect on the readability of a site.

Delay Time/Response Time

Recent surveys show that approximately 75 percent of those who connect to the Internet from home use a 56Kbps modem connection. While this number continues to decrease as the availability of cable and DSL connections increase, download speed is an important consideration in website design. As a rule, long system-response times contribute to user frustration and dissatisfaction. Graphics, animations, audio, and video components all result in increased page download time. The amount of time users will tolerate delays typically depends on how complex they think the task is, their experience, and feedback. Research attempting to quantify acceptable delay time for websites suggests that without feedback, users will wait approximately 8 to 12 seconds. After this point, users will typically lose attention and leave the page.

Designing for Different Populations

Website design may vary depending on the population that tends to use a site. Below are details about the specific design requirements for four distinct user groups.

Children

Children tend to explore a website much differently than adults do. Interested mainly in fun, they tend to be attracted to colorful sites offering animation and sound and have been shown to click repeatedly on areas of a Web page to see and hear special effects. In a usability study with children, Jakob Nielsen found that children prefer sites with simple text and navigation, do not typically scroll on a

page, and are more likely to click on an advertisement than adults. In addition, gender differences were noted in that boys complained more about having to read text on a page than girls. Children also respond well to images that they can relate to, such as a village, playground, or house (rather than a file folder). In addition, young children often have poorer motor coordination and shorter attention spans than adults and should be presented with sites with large buttons, font sizes, and menu options.

Older Adults

Older adults represent one of the fastest growing user groups of the Web. They often have impaired vision, reduced motor coordination, and shorter attention spans than younger adults. In addition, older users generally take more time and need more steps than younger users to find information. For this reason, the use of large font sizes, high foreground to background contrast, simple navigation, and large buttons are necessary.

International Audiences

As the name implies, the World Wide Web is a global environment. Guidelines for the internationalization of websites are similar to those for traditional software applications. This includes the use of appropriate and familiar text, international symbols, quality translation of content, and culturally appropriate symbols and graphics. Designers must be careful when displaying times of day to use formats that are universally understood. Dates should be spelled out since abbreviated notations (for example, 1/5/2003) do not always convey the same meaning in different countries. Usability testing with users from various countries is one way to discover cultural anomalies in a global website.

Disabled (ADA)

The Americans with Disabilities Act (ADA) mandates that all websites offer equal access to users with disabilities. The Web Accessibility Initiative (WAI), started by the World Wide Web Consortium (W3), strives to provide accessibility of the Web through technology, guidelines, tools, education, and research. Its guidelines explain how to make a website accessible to users with a variety of disabilities, including visual, speech, motor, and cognitive. For example, one guideline is "to provide equivalent alternatives to auditory and visual content." Users with visual disabilities typically use screen readers to "read" Web pages. If graphical content does not have alternate text associated with it, these users would not be informed of its presence. Therefore, all graphical and video content, animations, and audio are required to have text (<alt> tags) associated with them so that users can still "see" a representation of the page. In addition, the WAI recommends the use of style sheets, user control of blinking, flashing, and scrolling content, clear and consistent navigational tools, and the use of clear and simple language.

Standards and Guidelines

As the number of websites continues to grow and the general public becomes more dependent on the Internet as a daily source of information, more and more users will demand high quality websites that are easy to use. Increasing numbers of publications on standards and guidelines are available: These include the *Web Style Guide, IBM's Ease of Use Web Guidelines, Research-Based Web Site Design and Usability Guidelines, Nielsen Norman Group's Design Guidelines, and Web Accessibility Guidelines.* Designers can help create usable websites by following a high quality process, adhering to standards and guidelines, and testing a website with users prior to release.

Barbara S. Chaparro and Michael L. Bernard

See also Task Analysis; Universal Access; User Modeling

FURTHER READING

Bernard, M. (2002). Examining the effects of hypertext shape on user performance. *Usability News, 4*(2). Retrieved December 18, 2003, from http://psychology.wichita.edu/surl/usabiliynews/42/onlinetext.htm

Bernard, M., Lida, B., Riley, S., Hackler, T., & Janzen, K. (2002). A comparison of popular online fonts: Which size and type is best? *Usability News, 4*(1). Retrieved December 18, 2003, from http://psychology.wichita.edu/surl/usabilitynews/41/onlinetext.htm

Duchnicky, J. L., & Kolers, P. A. (1983). Readability of text scrolled on visual display terminals as a function of window size. *Human Factors, 25,* 683–692.

Foss, C. L. (1989). Tools for reading and browsing hypertext. *Information Processing Management, 25,* 407–418.

Georgia Tech Research Corporation. *GVU's WWW User Survey.* Retrieved July 27, 2003, from http://www.gvu.gatech.edu/user_surveys/

Hackos, J., & Redish, J. (1998). *User and task analysis for interface design.* New York: Wiley. IBM (2003). *IBM's Ease of Use Web Guidelines.* Retrieved July 29, 2003, from http://www3.ibm.com/ibm/easy/eou_ext.nsf/publish/572

King, A. (2003). *Speed up your site: Web site optimization.* Indianapolis, IN: New Riders Publishing.

Kruk, S., & Black, S. (2000). *Don't make me think: A common sense approach to usability.* Indianapolis, IN: New Riders Publishing.

Lynch, P., & Horton, S. (2002). Web style guide: Basic design principles for creating web site (2nd ed.). New Haven, CT: Yale University Press.

Morrell, R. W., Dailey, S. R., Feldman, C., Mayhorn, C. B., & Echt, K. V. (2002, April). *Older adults and information technology: A compendium of scientific research and web site accessibility guidelines.* Bethesda, MD: National Institute on Aging.

Nielsen, J. (2000). *Designing web usability.* Indianapolis, IN: New Riders Publishing.

Nielsen, J. (2000). *Homepage usability: 50 websites deconstructed.* Indianapolis, IN: New Riders Publishing.

Nielsen, J. (2003). *Nielsen Norman Group's design guidelines.* Retrieved July 29, 2003, from www.useit.com

National Cancer Institute. (2003). *Research-based web site design and usability guidelines.* Retrieved July 27, 2003, from http://usability.gov/guidelines/

Poynter Institute. (2000). *Stanford-Poynter eyetracking online news study.* Retrieved July 27, 2003, from *http://www.poynter.org/content/content_view.asp?id=1676*

Rubin, J. (1994). *Handbook of usability testing.* New York: Wiley.

Cole, J. I., Suman, M., Schramm, P. Lunn, R., & Aquino, J. (2003). *Surveying the digital future—Year three.* Los Angele, CA: UCLA Center for Communication Policy. Retrieved December 18, 2003, from http://www.ccp.ucla.edu

Web Accessibility Initiative (WAI). Retrieved July 27, 2003, from http://www.w3.org/WAI/

Youngman, M., & Scharff, L. (1998). Text width and margin width influences on readability of GUIs. *Southwest Psychological Association.* Retrieved July 27, 2003, from http://hubel.sfasu.edu/research/textmargin.html

WIRELESS SYSTEMS

See Mobile Computing

WORK

Computers are not just on our desktops anymore but rather are everywhere among us: in cars, cash registers, appliances, televisions, and a myriad of other technologies, notably those that we encounter at work.

Although usability issues go hand in hand with computers, so do the promises of computerization that emerged during the twentieth century from the heritage of calculating machines that reached back thousands of years to the abacus. As computerization has spread past simple calculation the promises have expanded to the possibility of computers taking over the drudgery of work, enabling humans to do more interesting things. An accompanying and pervasive fear, as old as the industrial revolution, is that computers will simply take over, not just releasing us from drudgery but eliminating our livelihoods. The reality is somewhere in between, as is the impact.

What Is Work?

However, before we can explore the impact of computers, we must define *work*. For most of us this task seems simple. Work is what we do from 9 A.M. to 5 P.M. (or increasingly from 9 A.M. to 8 P.M.), or it is what we get paid to do. However, a number of social movements have forced society to acknowledge that work is not always paid for. Stay-at-home mothers (and fathers) are both working. However, here we focus on the more traditional view of going off to a job. Our conception of what counts as work has been defined in terms of producing or accomplishing something. Originally this activity was generally interpreted in terms of manual labor. Even with the increasing role of technology during the mid-twentieth century, manufacturing was work, but many "white collar" jobs seemed different. Doctors, lawyers, and businesspeople did something other than what farmers, factory workers, and meat packers did. Peter Drucker, a writer on organization and management, describes how a growing percentage of employees during the last one-quarter of the twentieth century were knowledge workers. In contrast to workers who employ manual skill or muscle, knowledge workers employ concepts, ideas, and theories they have learned in systematic education. Plenty of more "traditional" work still is being done, but such work is relegated to less-educated clerical

Software Prescribes Break Time for Enhanced Productivity

ITHACA, N.Y. (ANS)—People who work at the computer all day need a break or two or three—or more. Researchers at Cornell University have discovered that frequent rest reduces injury and can also make workers better typists.

The researchers found that staff who used a computer software program that reminded them to take many short breaks throughout the day did more accurate work and were more productive.

The computer software, designed to manage workflow and injury risks associate with keyboard and mouse overuse, acted like a visual alarm clock to remind workers that they had been using the keyboard or mouse for too long and needed a break.

"The perception that the more breaks you take the less work you do is not true in this case," said Alan Hedges, professor of ergonomics at Cornell and author of the study. "People need to approach work on the computer like a marathon runner," he said. "What these microbreaks do is to help people pace their work more efficiently throughout the day."

"But most people who work on computers are more like sprinters," he said. "The strange thing about working on a computer is that time just flies, and before you know it you've been working for hours without a break." That can lead to repetitive stress injuries.

Forcing workers to simply take breaks every hour does not help because it does not take into account how hard they are working at the computer, Hedges said. "The software actually monitors how hard you are working on the computer and feeds the information back to you." A little alert bar on the computer screen gradually turns from green to red as a computer worker enters the zone where he or she needs a break. The break does not necessarily have to mean a rest from work, Hedges said. It can mean making a phone call, doing paperwork or having a short meeting with a co-worker. Or it could mean a quick trip to the water fountain, or a simple stretch at your desk.

Source: Computer advises worker to take break when productivity flags. American News Service, October 14, 1999.

workers and others. In 1995 the number of knowledge workers in U.S. corporations was estimated at 31 percent of the workforce and rapidly growing.

Even during the late twentieth- century the automation of many manufacturing processes has further blurred what was manual labor into knowledge work as workers are "less likely to be using their hands and more likely to be using their minds to monitor, manage and control the flow of information" and the production line (Sellen and Harper 2002, 51). Thus, computerization has broadened our notion of work beyond manual labor into a range of other work. This broadening is one of several effects that computers have had on work, but not necessarily the first.

In all of these cases the introduction of technology implies an interface with humans and their work. Thus, the field of human-computer interaction (HCI) is profoundly concerned with how computer technology and work interact.

Computerization and Its Fears

Long before the advent of knowledge workers, however, people had fears of automation and machinery. The Industrial Revolution moved the production of goods from being a matter of art or craft to feeding and monitoring mechanical beasts. The Information Revolution was expected to change work patterns, just as the Industrial Revolution did before it. These changes balanced between fears and promises. Robots would take over manufacturing lines, and a variety of intermediate automation would eliminate other jobs, freeing us from drudgery.

Similarly, the U.S. efficiency engineer F. W. Taylor worked during the late nineteenth and early twentieth centuries to make management a science, including performing time-motion studies in order to determine where changes needed to be made for greater efficiency. The popularization of computers for business was often assumed to be a Taylorist enhancement—that is, a way to make office processes more efficient.

As the information scientist Robert Kling has put it:

> There is no paucity of images to portray the effects of computing on work life. Daniel Bell (1973) and Charles A. Myers (1970) provide enthusiastic and largely systems-rationalist accounts of computing as an aid to "knowledge work." [Systems rationalists view human beings as similar to computer systems, doing a job obediently and cooperatively.] They both emphasize how computer-based technologies enlarge the range and speed at which data are available. Myers, for example, concludes that "computing will help relieve 'specialists and professionals' of the time-consuming and repetitive parts of their work." In contrast, Harry Braverman (1974), a class-politics analyst, argues that managers conceive of workers as general-purpose machines that they operate. He views automation as a managerial strategy to replace unreliable and finicky "human machines" with more reliable, more productive, and less self-interested mechanical or electronic machines. He argues that computerized information systems usually are organized to routinize white-collar work and weaken the power of lower-level participants in an organization. (Kling 1980, 75)

Another approach that Robert Kling presents is that of human-relations analysts who feel that the "effects of computerization are contingent upon the technical arrangements chosen and the way they are introduced into the workplace" (Kling 1980, 76). Many of the empirical studies of the workplace that he cites, including his own, fall into the area of human relations analysis. Those studies discovered that the picture was more complicated. Kling reports that ". . . respondents used computer-based reports and attributed job-enlarging influences to computer use; they also attributed increases in job pressure and task significance to computing" (Kling 1980, 76). Yet, at the time at the time Kling found that computer use did not have a dominant effect on the respondents' jobs.

Decades later our perception is that jobs have changed more significantly. During the economic climate of the 1990s we saw an ultimate goal of computerizing many knowledge-worker jobs. As computers stepped in to automate knowledge work, like

---

It is questionable if all the mechanical inventions yet made have lightened the day's toil of any human being.

John Stuart Mill

manual work before it, many formerly sacred white-collar jobs were eliminated in the name of efficiency and the bottom line. The ability to eliminate these jobs was facilitated first by notions that the knowledge of workers actually belonged to the company and second by notions that such knowledge could be extracted and saved to computers when the workers retired or were downsized. This approach, that of identifying and saving organizational memory and further managing the knowledge of a company, has become an ongoing effort for many of the world's largest businesses. However, at the same time computers have made possible completely new kinds of jobs.

Themes

Computers have made possible work in situations that we would not have dreamed possible, such as geographically distributed work teams, monitoring of sensitive manufacturing processes, and remote scientific explorations such as the Mars Rover of the U.S. space program. In turn, these enabled practices have blurred boundaries between home and work and between who does what, where, and when. In addition, computerization has shifted where the labor is divided between human and computer as well as between human and human. Our expectations have changed as communication and travel have sped up.

Changing Expectations

People have a long history of assuming that computers will make many jobs easier, particularly menial, repetitive jobs. As Kling points out, for every utopian view there is an equally gloomy one. However, the contrasting exaltation and mechanization of workers are not the only expectations that have been affected by computers. Some of their effect is more subtle, such as in the rhythm of written correspondence. We worry when an e-mail is not responded to promptly, even from halfway around the world. Everyone is assumed to have a fax machine and a cell phone, and an increasing percentage of the population takes planes as if planes were buses. At the same time, access to computer infra-

structure has become emblematic of an increasing "digital divide" between the haves and have-nots, both within a particular country and between First World and Third World countries.

Many advances in computer science have been alternately feared and feted for how they might change work. Braverman predicted mechanization of clerical workers did happen to some extent, but not as completely as expected. In contrast, during the 1980s people saw the field of artificial intelligence (AI), particularly expert systems, as a way to spread an expert's knowledge to those people with less experience. During the 1990s this idea evolved into the possibility of reducing the need for experts, putting information back into the hands of knowledge owners—the corporations. Corporate downsizing went along with the move to capture knowledge in electronic data systems. Such systems were expected to provide information at one's fingertips, without one having to worry about retiring experts or laid-off individuals. As well, robotics promised something similar for automating the production line.

In all these cases the reality was more complicated and subtle. Jobs did go away because of automation, but new jobs sprang up. Focusing on the office we see several changes. New technology such as e-mail and the World Wide Web enabled the fast movement of written communication in a way that had not been seen before. Our ability to easily move text digitally began to shift job roles and tasks. Administrative assistants and such phenomena as the typing pool were reduced or eliminated as knowledge workers began to send their own electronic communications. This altering of who does what was forced further as the economic downturn resulted in support staff being further reduced and even eliminated. The advent of the World Wide Web during the mid-1990s using the infrastructure of the Internet from the 1960s made digital information more easily sharable across distance. A person's desktop computer became more powerful, while hypertext markup language (HTML) supported displaying data largely independent of the computer, operating system, or application. This advance allowed business processes to be moved from paper forms to online access. Again, this advance often altered who did the job, not whether the job was done. Corporate reimbursements, for example, have steadily moved away from paper, and thus the timing issues have changed.

Underlying many office automation projects was the desire to use computers for calculation. In order for people to do that, however, data needed to be in a machine-readable format—a process that has moved from dedicated workers (data entry employees and data processors) to general workers the myth of the paperless office arose. However, this myth is a promise that has yet to be fulfilled. As Abigail Sellen and Richard Harper point out in The Myth of the Paperless Office (2002), it is not so much that paper is impossible to get rid of, but rather that we have focused so much on technology that we haven't focused enough on what the technology is replacing—in this case, paper. As we go deeper into the automation of business processes we are discovering how little we know about our own work practice. This discovery in turn has sparked a new set of endeavors to understand the actual practice of work, rather than the synopsized version found in manuals.

Altering Boundaries for Work

Despite the negatives, computerization still holds many promises for changing work in positive ways. Computers have allowed us to work in situations that we would not have dreamed possible. Teleworking is gaining in popularity, although not completely sweeping the world as predicted earlier. Other trends are the increasing distribution and globalization of work on planet Earth, including global software development and scientific collaboratories (distributed research centers in which scientists in disparate geographical locations are able to work together, often on the same data set). The Mars Rover mission is just one example of remote scientific exploration made possible by computers. Computerization may have shifted the division of labor between human and computer, as well as between human and human, through such innovations as telework, global teams (collaboratories), and telemedicine.

Telework, Global Teams, and Telemedicine: Communication and Coordination

Computers have greatly facilitated communication around the globe, not just by enhanced control of phone systems such as mobile phone switching and voice over Internet protocol (VoIP) (telephone calls made over the Internet), but more generally by e-mail and now the Web, both of which facilitate asynchronous communication (where participants are not communicating at the same time, but the persistence of the communication makes it possible to communicate). Computerization has enhanced communication and coordination in three areas. Although distance does still matter, computers are helping to span that distance and change how we work.

The first area is telework. The notion of telework has been around for decades and includes a wide range of work styles, all facilitated by increased communication speed, greater storage capabilities, and the decreasing size of computers. Although many people think of telework in the utopian terms of working at home—eliminating the commute and leading a more balanced life—it also covers nontraditional offices or hot desking (not having to provide regular office space or at least not a dedicated desk) and the notion of virtual business. Virtual business is a notion created as well as facilitated by the Web. Sellen and Harper examined several companies that tried to become paperless. To make being paperless work one company needed to be flexible about both its changing business processes, providing some sense of continuity for its workers, and what constituted being "paperless"—which didn't necessarily mean getting rid of all paper. This flexibility distinguished that company from another company that tried to become paperless but failed without the additional work adjustments.

Computer professionals themselves were some of the earliest candidates for telework (including HCI professionals such as Jean Scholtz, Victoria Bellotti, and Tom Erickson), although not the only ones. National Public Radio (NPR) reporter Brian Molpas describes a virtual marketing company where none of the employees is co-located and whose motto is "working anytime, anyplace, anyway, at any pace" and whose clients include other virtual businesses.

Finally, a report written for the U.S. Department of Energy in 1994 shows how the effects of telework go beyond work and into society, affecting travel and other behavior. Experts expect traffic patterns to shift so as to reduce rush hours, although perhaps not achieving the euphoric notion of eliminating commute traffic implied by the utopia of working at home.

The second area in which computerization has enhanced communication and coordination is scientific collaboratories. William Wulf, while at the U.S. National Science Foundation (NSF), originally described a collaboratory as a "center without walls, in which the nation's researchers can perform their research without regard to geographical location—interacting with colleagues, accessing instrumentation, sharing data, and computational resources, and accessing information in digital libraries." This shared work is made possible by a number of computer-assisted communication and collaboration tools. Studied early by a number of academic institutions—particularly the University of Michigan's CREW (the Collaboratory for Research on Electronic Work) Lab—during the last decade shared work has gained widespread government and scientific support in several areas, including high-energy physics, astrophysics, chemistry, the National Science Foundation, and National Institute of Standards and Technology (NIST). Spurred equally by computerization and the increasing expense of collecting certain kinds of data, collaboratories provide a way to justify expenditures such as the Hubble telescope and the Mars Rover by providing a way to share data more broadly.

The third area is distributed and remote work. Computers are altering the boundaries between work and home through telework and the ability to change where we work. Collaboratories are one example of how work can be done by someone not physically present, allowing scientific collaborations without everyone being in the same physical location and providing a mechanism for a scientist to analyze data that he or she was not present to collect. However, telemedicine and other medical applications provide a different approach, one that extends the collaborative notions of collaboratories to provide access that would otherwise be impossible.

Remote surgery may not be a reality yet, or even around the corner, but telemedicine has been a going concern for at least a decade. The American Telemedicine Association (ATA) was founded in 1993 and continues to promote access to medical care via telecommunications technology. Telemedicine often doesn't replace workers but rather provides ways for limited workers to provide better care with remote consultation and imaging capabilities. As NPR reported, some consultations are done in real time through video and audio links, whereas others are asynchronous—such as distributing still images to specialists in more urban areas. Costs are high (especially in infrastructure) but invaluable in places such as the Navajo reservation in the Four Corners area of the Southwest United States, where resources are limited and distance great. For this reason people tend to use telemedicine in places where government or other agencies, rather than doctors, bear the start-up costs.

Telemedicine is also spreading into an area called "e-health." This area ranges from advice services and community resources such as the website webMD.com and UseNet communities to proprietary online communications systems with one's physician. Like automated medical records, these services are changing not only the job of a doctor but also the expectations of patients. Doctors may spend a significant portion of their day now answering patient requests online, while services such as webMD contract to provide information to the public. In turn, patients now can use such services, or the Internet at large, to search for medical information, enhancing patient knowledge and care.

As the last example shows, changes in work affect not only workers but also the consumers of the products of that work. The areas that we have touched on foreshadow coming changes as wireless networks and ubiquitous computing further change where and how we can work.

Christine A. Halverson

See also Collaboratories; Computer-Supported Cooperative Work; Impacts; Telecommuting

FURTHER READING

Bell, D. (1973). *The coming of post-industrial society: A venture in social forecasting.* New York: Basic Books.

Braverman, H. (1974). *Labor and monopoly capital: The degradation of work in the twentieth century.* New York: Monthly Review Press.

Collaboratories. (2003). University of Michigan, School of Information. Retrieved February 28, 2004, 2004, from http://www.si.umich.edu/research/projects.htm

Digital Divide Network. *Digital divide basics.* Retrieved February 28, 2004, from http://www.digitaldividenetwork.org/content/sections/index.cfm?key=2

Dreyfus, H. L. (1979). *What computers can't do: The limits of artificial intelligence* (Rev. ed). New York: Harper & Row.

Dreyfus, H. L., & Dreyfus, S. L. (1986). *Mind over machine: The power of human intuition and expertise in the era of the computer.* New York: Free Press.

Drucker, P. F. (1973). *Management: Tasks, responsibilities and practices.* New York: Harper & Row.

Hackett, E. J. (2000). Interdisciplinary research initiatives at the U.S. National Science Foundation. In P. Weingart & N. Sterhr (Eds.), *Practicing interdisciplinarity* (pp. 248–259). Toronto, Canada: University of Toronto Press.

Halverson, C. A., Erickson, T., & Sussman, J. (2003). *What counts as success? Punctuated patterns of use in a persistent chat environment.* Paper presented at the Conference on Supporting Group Work, Sanibel Island, FL.

Higa, K., & Shin, B. (2003). Virtual extension: The telework experience in Japan. Communications of the ACM, 46(9), 233–242.

Huston, T. L., & Huston, J. L. (2000). Is telemedicine a practical reality? *Communications of the ACM, 42*(6), 91–95.

Jasanoff, S., Markle, G. E., Petersen, J. C., & Pinch, T. (Eds.). (1995). *The handbook of science and technology studies.* Thousand Oaks, CA: Sage Publications.

Kanter, R. M. (2001). *Evolve!: Succeeding in the digital culture of tomorrow.* Cambridge, MA: Harvard Business School Press.

Kidd, A. (1994). *The marks are on the knowledge worker.* Paper presented at the ACM Conference on Human Factors in Computing Systems, Boston.

Kling, R. (1980). Social analyses of computing: Theoretical perspectives in recent empirical research. *Computing Surveys, 12*(1), 61–110.

Knorr-Cetina, K. (1999). *Epistemic cultures: How the sciences make knowledge.* Cambridge, MA: Harvard University Press.

Kouzes, R. T., Myers, J. T., & Wulf, W. A. (1996). Collaboratories: Doing science on the Internet. *IEEE Computer, 29*(8). Retrieved March 24, 2004, from http://collaboratory.emsl.pnl.gov/presentations/papers/IEEECollaboratories.html

Kraker, D. (2003, October 20). Telemedicine is a success for Navajos. NPR. Retrieved March 2, 2004, from http://www.npr.org/features/feature.php?wfId=1472515

Kyng, M., & Greenbaum, J. M. (1991). *Design at work: Cooperative design of computer systems.* Mahwah, NJ: Lawrence Erlbaum Associates.

Landauer, T. K. (1995). *The trouble with computers: Usefulness, usability, and productivity.* Cambridge, MA: MIT Press.

Molpas, D. (2001*).* The company from nowhere. NPR. Retrieved March 2, 2004, from http://www.npr.org/programs/morning/features/2001/mar/010330.cfoa.html

Myers, C. A. (1970). *Computers in knowledge-based fields.* Cambridge, MA: MIT Press.

Interactions, 5(1), 44–54.

National Academy of Sciences. (1999). *Improving research capabilities in chemical and biomedical sciences: Proceedings of a multi-site electronic workshop.* Washington, DC: National Academy Press.

National Coordination Office for Information Technology Research and Development, National Science and Technology Council. (1999). Networked computing for the 21st century: Collaboratories. *Computing, information, and communications networked computing for the 21st century.* Retrieved February 28, 2004, from http://www.ccic.gov/pubs/blue99/collaboratories.html

Niles, J. S. (1994). Beyond telecommuting: A new paradigm for the effect of telecommunications on travel. Global Telematics for US DOE. Retrieved February 28, 2004, from http://www.lbl.gov/ICSD/Niles/

Nonaka, I., & Takeuchi, H. (1995). *The knowledge creating company.* New York: Oxford University Press.

Olson, G. M., Atkins, D. E., Clauer, R., Finholt, T. A., Jahanian, F., Killeen, T. L., Prakash, A., & Weymouth, T. (1998). The upper atmospheric research collaboratory. Interactions, 5(3), 48–55.

Olson, G. M., & Olson, J. S. (2001). Distance matters. *Human Computer Interaction, 15*(2/3) 1–39.

Rheingold, H. (2000). *Tools for thought* (2nd ed.). Cambridge, MA: MIT Press.

Ruppel, C. P., & Harrington, S. J. (1995). Telework: An innovation where nobody is getting on the bandwagon. *ACM SIGMIS Database, 26*(2–3), 87–104.

Salazar, C. (2001). *Building boundaries and negotiating work at home.* Paper presented at the International Conference on Supporting Group Work, Boulder, CO.

Scholtz, J., Bellotti, V., Schirra, L., Erickson, T., DeGroot, J., & Lund, A. (1998). Telework: When your job is on the line.

Sellen, A. J., & Harper, R. H. (2002). *The myth of the paperless office.* Cambridge, MA: MIT Press.

Spinks, W. A., & Wood, J. (1996). *Office-based telecommuting: An international comparison of satellite offices in Japan and North America.* Paper presented at the Conference on Computer Personnel Research, Denver, CO.

Taylor, F. W. (1998). *The principles of scientific management.* Mineola, NY: Dover Press. (Original work published 1911)

Yates, J. (1993). Control through communication: The rise of system in American management. Baltimore, MD: Johns Hopkins University Press.

WORKFORCE

Information Technology (IT) encompasses a broad array of products and activities related to computing and communications in the modern economy. While many workers make use of IT in the course of their work, the IT workforce may be defined more narrowly as including "workers…engaged primarily in the conception, design, development, adaptation, implementation, deployment, training, support, documentation, and management of information technology systems, components or applications" (National Research Council 2001, 44). This definition includes hardware and software engineers, programmers, database administrators, help desk personnel, and technicians who install and service PCs, networks, and software, but excludes most office workers who use IT products as part of their jobs.

The IT workforce can be further subdivided into two subgroups based largely on skill requirements. What the National Research Council calls category 1 workers, and others have termed the core of the IT workforce, are those professionals involved primarily in the "development, creation, specification, design and testing of IT artifacts." Workers engaged in these activities require a relatively high degree of specialized training and skills. Category 2 workers, by contrast, are employed primarily in the "application, adaptation, configuration, support or implementation of IT products or service designed or developed by others" (Ellis & Lowell 1999, 1). Category 2 workers may also require high levels of technical knowledge, but they do not require the breadth of vision, creativity, or communication skills of category 1 workers.

Size and Location of the IT Workforce

IT has become a global industry with significant employment throughout Western Europe, Asia, and the Indian subcontinent. The industry's origins are in the United States, however, and the United States continues to be the source of most new technologies and remains home to a disproportionate share of IT employment. A 2001 study by the Organization for Economic Co-Operation and Development (OECD) reports that in 2001 the United States accounted for 36 percent of Information and Communications Technologies(ICT) employment among the seventeen countries surveyed. The next largest IT employer, Japan, had roughly half (17 percent) of the employment of the United States, while France and the United Kingdom each accounted for 8 percent of ICT employment.

Two independent sources of statistics are available to measure the size of the IT workforce in the United States—the Current Population Survey (CPS) and the Occupational Employment Statistics Survey (OES). The CPS relies on data gathered from households, while the OES collects information from employers. They yield comparable estimates of the size of the IT workforce, but each source has its particular strengths. The CPS provides the longest running time series of data and a broad array of demographic information not available in the OES. On the other hand, the OES offers more detailed occupational breakdowns than the CPS.

Neither source conforms precisely to the definitions of the IT workforce that scholars have developed, and the rapidly changing character and content of jobs in the IT workforce make it especially hard to track changes in this component of the workforce. Nonetheless, it is possible to assemble reasonably good measurements of the number and characteristics of category 1 IT workers. Although a complete list of occupations that are engaged in IT would be quite large, most category 1 IT workers are found in a relatively small number of occupations. These are (with 2001 U.S. Department of Labor employment numbers in parentheses): software engineers (623,100), programmers (501,550), systems analysts (448,270), network and computer systems administrators (227,840), computer operators (177,990), network systems and data communications analysts (126,060), database administrators (104,250), computer hardware engineers (67,590), operations research analysts (57,520), and computer and information scientists, research (25,620). Together these core occupations account for a little more than 2.5 million workers, or about 2 percent of the total U.S. workforce.

Measuring the size of the category 2 IT workforce is much harder because occupational titles do not adequately capture the IT content of the support activities of many of the technicians and other occupations included in this group. Estimates of the size of this group vary more widely as a result, but most researchers believe that it is approximately the same size as the category 1 IT workforce.

IT has become pervasive throughout the economy, and IT workers are found in all sectors and industries although the largest concentrations remain in computer-related industries. For instance, the computer and data processing services industry employs more IT workers than does all of manufacturing. Other large employers of IT workers include finance, insurance, and real estate companies, wholesale and retail trade, and federal, state, and local governments.

Geographically, IT employment is highly concentrated as well. More than one-third of category 1 IT workers are employed in just five cities—New York, Washington, D.C., San Francisco, Los Angeles, and Boston—and the ten largest U.S. cities account for just over 50 percent of all IT workers.

Characteristics of IT Workers

Because of the rapidly evolving nature of IT occupations, none of the available data sources accurately captures the full scope of the IT workforce. Of the available sources, the U.S. Department of Labor's Current Population Survey (CPS) is the best suited to understanding the characteristics of the IT workforce and tracing its historical evolution over the past two decades.

Contrary to trends in the rest of the labor force, the IT workforce has become increasingly dominated by men over the last decade. In 2002, 70 percent of full-time IT workers were male while only 30 percent were female. In 1992, by comparison, 42 percent of the IT workforce was female. The racial composition of the core IT workforce has also changed substantially in recent years. While 77 percent of category 1 IT workers are white in 2002, this is down from 85 percent in 1992. This decline is accounted for by a more than doubling of the share of Asians (from 6 to 14 percent). Meanwhile the share of African-American workers has held steady at about 8.5 percent.

IT workers are younger than the workforce as a whole. The average age of IT workers in 2002 was 38.2 years, versus 40.5 for all non-IT workers. Part of the relatively younger ages in IT occupations results from the fact that the IT industry itself is relatively young. As the industry has matured average ages have been converging toward those in the rest of the workforce. There has been some suggestion of age discrimination in the IT workforce because of these statistics and the observation that older IT workers (40 years and above) are more likely to lose their jobs than younger workers. However, older and younger IT workers who have lost their jobs take about the same amount of time to find new employment.

Foreign-born IT workers constitute about 17 percent of the core IT workforce but comprise only about 10 percent of the U.S. population. These foreign workers also tend to be highly concentrated in just a few states. As a result of the industry's dependence on

A Personal Story—Cultural Differences

In the early nineties I briefly visited Japan under the auspices of a consortium whose aim was to produce radical advances in HCI. As part of the trip, my host arranged a series of visits to R&D labs, each of which put on a demonstration for me.

One of the demonstrations, at a lab whose identity I will suppress, was of a face and expression recognition system. The researchers were clearly proud of their system and were so confident of it that they proposed to demonstrate it using me as a subject. After I sat down in a chair, they positioned the camera and began the demo. The system promptly crashed!

Now, to me, this was not a big deal. My demos—especially back in those days—crashed so often that I had a stock phrase for the occasion: "Notice the seamless integration with the debugger." However cultures differ, and to my hosts this was quite embarrassing—a loss of "face." Apparently, in Japan, one does not demonstrate buggy software to visitors! After receiving several apologies, I went on to the next demo and forgot the incident.

That, however, was not the end of the matter. A few demos later, the researcher who had run the expression recognition demo returned. He was, if anything, more embarrassed. The problem, he explained, trying with some difficulty to find appropriate words, is that, well, most Japanese have hairlines. (It is difficult to be tactful in a second language!) I, on the other hand, have what I prefer to refer to as "a high forehead," though I will admit that a camera might have difficulty detecting a hairline. Even worse, at least from the gesture recognition software's point of view, is that I also have a beard, something also uncommon in Japan. That gives me a hairline, but one that runs beneath my mouth. The face recognition system, in an interesting example of how cultural biases can be reified in software, had a facial model that assumed that hairlines were always above eyes, and hence was unable to cope with my facial "geography."

While I had known for quite some time that cultural differences are both deep and subtle, I had tended to associate them with ways of thinking and behaving. This was a nice reminder that cultural assumptions lurk everywhere, and that our assumptions about people, whatever they may be, often surface in our designs in very unexpected ways.

Thomas Erickson

foreign workers, the IT workforce is influenced by legislative changes in immigration and visa policy, the most important of which is the H-1B visa program. The H-1B visa is an employer-sponsored, nonimmigrant visa for a foreign worker coming temporarily to the United States to perform services in a specialty occupation. The annual H-1B visa cap rose from 65,000 in the U.S. government's fiscal year 1998 to 115,000 in 1999 and 2000 and then to 195,000 in 2001 and 2002. The cap on the number of new foreign workers entering the U.S. on H-1B visas reverted back to 1998 levels on October 1, 2003 (the start of the federal fiscal year), and there is some indication that the IT industry's reliance on H-1B visas is diminishing. A recent report by the American Electronics Association concluded that the IT industry relied on 65 percent of the capped number in 2001 but only 34 percent in 2002.

As the industry has evolved into a more conceptual field in which the development, creation, specification, and design of IT products becomes increasingly important, employers are requiring higher levels of education. These changes are reflected in high and increasing levels of educational attainment within the IT workforce. Nearly two-thirds of the IT workforce holds a bachelor's degree or higher compared to only 30 percent of the non-IT workforce. Slightly less than half the IT workforce had at least a bachelor's degree just ten years ago.

Training and Education of IT Workers

Career paths into IT occupations have become more complex and less linear even when compared to those traditionally followed only a decade ago. The traditional career path was one in which the prospective IT worker went through formal education, found employment in the industry, and then gradually progressed into higher-level jobs. The place at which one exited the formal educational system largely determined one's initial position within the workforce, and most IT workers remained with one or a small number of employers until retirement.

Today, however, there are many opportunities for training in addition to formal degree programs. For example, there exists a variety of nondegree programs, distance education programs, and employer-based training organizations. Workers now frequently move back and forth between the educational system and the workforce as they continuously retrain throughout their careers. As a result, there is no "most common path" into the IT industry. IT workers with a bachelor's degree might enroll in a community college for a particular certification program or in a four-year college to take courses that will bolster their basic knowledge. Others may take courses or enroll in a degree program at the graduate level in disciplines such as information systems or business. There are still others who will enroll in a doctoral program in computer science or a related discipline. The end result is that there are many paths into a particular IT career.

Anticipated growth in the higher-end IT occupations will require an increasingly educated IT workforce but the pipeline into the more traditional IT training does not show signs of meeting this demand over the coming years. The Computing Research Association's Taulbee Survey is an annual survey of Ph.D.-granting programs in computer science and computer engineering in the United States and Canada. According to the 2001–2002 Taulbee Survey, 849 Ph.D. degrees were awarded by the 182 departments responding to the survey, which was the lowest figure reported since 1989. This may reflect a hangover from the high-tech boom of the late 1990s in which many students who would otherwise have pursued Ph.D. degrees were pulled into the job market. Consistent with this interpretation, the number of students entering Ph.D. programs recently increased by 22 percent, and departments are reporting a record number of applicants to their programs. It is unclear whether these trends will ultimately have a substantial effect on the IT labor supply, since there has also been a shift in the areas of specialization for Ph.D. students who are moving away from industry-related training and toward academic-related training. If this is the case, then the Ph.D. pipeline may not alleviate labor shortages in the industry despite the increased numbers of students. White and nonresident alien men account for a very large percentage of both Ph.D. production and enrollment in the Taulbee Survey, whereas women account for only 19 percent of enrollment and 18 percent of graduates.

Evidence on trends in bachelor's degree enrollment from the Taulbee Survey shows that the period of explosive growth in enrollment is likely over. There were 20,677 bachelor's degrees in computer science

A Personal Story—Employee Resistance to Technology

In our work on organizations and IT change, my research team has found that "resistance to technology" is often not what it seems. In the case of the social service agency described below, it took careful observation of the organizational context and the local history to understand why an IT solution, reasonably designed to decrease paperwork and facilitate the delivery of services, was resented by the staff.

In order to help their agency comply with new government reporting requirements, caseworkers for elderly and needy clients were asked to make a transition toward the use of laptop computers rather than the former system of filling out up to seventy pages of paper forms for each client. The caseworkers were not at all pleased at the prospect. At first, it appeared that employee resistance was based on the perceived inconvenience and difficulty of learning new computer skills. However, interviews and detailed observations revealed that their more salient concerns were altogether different, focused on client interactions, in the short run, and ultimately upon assumptions about the caseworkers' professional identity. One case manager explained her thoughts about client interaction this way,

"I think (my clients) are not going to like it. They are not used to it. The screen thing is like this, in front of your face. They can't see what you are doing."

Concerned about compromising the quality of care, another case manager explained that it is her primary job to listen to the clients:

"I like to have eye-to-eye contact with the client and to me. It's not polite to sit there with a senior and be trying to type and concentrating on your typing errors and just looking at them occasionally. It's almost like a quick insurance salesman coming into the house. It doesn't seem right."

Privacy of clients' information was also a concern. Caseworkers believed that sensitive information such as personal hygiene needed to be recorded for health history, but did not belong in a central database where it might be embarrassing for clients.

The issue of caseworkers' self identify was subtler. This concern arose prior to our study in reaction to another technological innovation. While never articulated, this concern was manifest in our data. Several months before the proposed change to laptop computers, the management had introduced a requirement that caseworkers bring cellular phones to the field. In the caseworkers' view, the main function of these heavy and awkward cellular phones seemed to be to monitor their work. When asked why they had gotten the cellular phones, one caseworker explained, "…so they could find us if they needed us." Another complained, "We [had our personal] cell phones but we're not allowed to use them."

The connection between the cellular phones and the laptops, in the minds of caseworkers, was critical in their attitudes to the new laptop initiative. Consensus was that the cell phones had been introduced as an instrument of administration control and intrusion, and that the laptops were just one more thing that would be used in the same way. In cases like these, the technology itself is almost irrelevant.

Technology acceptance that focuses too much on the details of the technology may be missing the point. Rather, the potential useful qualities of the proposed new technology only matter after the political and emotional issues within an organization have been taken into account.

Our qualitative methodology, which postponed the identification of significant variables until raw interview data had been sorted to reveal its own categories, was well suited to understanding this problem. What resulted was an understanding of the workers' view of the situation and their extra-logical anxieties and needs. These loomed larger than worries about learning about the proposed technology itself. The study pointed to the need to address these management issues before cognitive issues of computer training could be effectively introduced.

Kathryn Stam

The study cited in this personal account was funded in part by a grant from the National Science Foundation (SES9984111/ 0196415), but the ideas and conclusions expressed herein are those of the authors and no necessarily endorsed by the NSF.

and computer engineering awarded in the 2001–2002 academic year. Trends in the undergraduate population also suggest that the share of women in the field may continue to decline: Over 82 percent of bachelor's degrees awarded went to men. These figures are consistent with broader national-level data from the National Center for Education Statistics (NCES), which includes a wider range of IT-related disciplines. The NCES reports that there were a total of 41,954 bachelor's degrees in computer and information sciences awarded in 2001, with 72.3 percent awarded to men. Just over 66 percent of the 16,038 master's degrees conferred in Computer and Information Sciences were awarded to males in 2001, and 82.3 percent of the 768 Ph.D. degrees awarded went to men.

Much of the failure to attract students to IT-related academic disciplines in larger numbers is probably the result of negative perceptions and a general lack of information about these fields. A 1999 survey of eighth grade students and high school juniors in Silicon Valley, the heart of the American IT industry, indicated a greater understanding of the types of training required for professions such as lawyer, doctor/nurse, and sales/marketing than for computer-related occupations. Survey data also indicate that students who do well in mathematics have a positive attitude toward computer-related occupations. But these studies have also shown that student interest in mathematics tends to decline with age. By the time they reach college, many have decided against the further study of mathematics and are thus directed away from technical careers in IT. This has been especially true for female students. Efforts by policymakers to improve the supply of qualified IT workers has thus understandably focused on improving education, access to computers, and changing perceptions of mathematics and IT-related academic fields. These are, of course, long-term strategies for reshaping the pipeline into IT careers and will take some time to start producing tangible results.

Evolution of the IT Workforce

The rapid pace of advances in the power of computing hardware, and in the capabilities of software has been one of the main drivers of economic growth and change in the United States and other advanced economies in the past half century. These changes have produced dramatic shifts in the size and composition of the IT workforce over time. The Bureau of Labor Statistics' Current Population Survey provides the best source of data to measure the growth of a fixed group of core IT occupations (systems analysts, programmers, computer operators, and operations and systems researchers) over time.

Over the past two decades the CPS data indicate that employment in core IT occupations increased by 92.5 percent, rising from about 1.47 million in 1983 to 2.83 million in 2002. At the peak of IT employment in 2000, the total had reached just over 3 million. By comparison, non-IT employment increased only 31.6 percent over the same period. As a result, IT employment increased from 1.45 percent of the labor force in 1983 to 2.16 percent in 2002.

Much of the growth in IT employment has been concentrated in the higher-level occupations, such as systems analysts, whose numbers increased 520 percent from 1983 to 2002. In comparison, the number of programmers has grown much more slowly, and the number of computer operators has fallen considerably. These changes reflect a variety of factors. On the one hand, the relative stagnation of programmers' employment reflects an increased tendency to export the routine work of writing code to lower-cost locations overseas, such as India, while U.S.-based employees focus on the conceptual tasks of specifying software tasks and outlining the procedures necessary to achieve business ends. On the other hand, it reflects the shifting costs of hardware and software. As hardware costs have fallen, programming tools have become much more sophisticated, making it possible to automate many of the steps involved in producing lines of code. Indeed, the increased power of desktop software, such as spreadsheet programs, allows individual users to accomplish tasks that in the past would have required the services of specialized programmers.

The Future of the IT Workforce

The rapid growth of the IT workforce reflects a rising demand for IT workers. Rising relative wages of IT workers indicate that this growth of demand has outstripped increases in supply, creating a relative scarcity of IT workers. Despite the recent technology sector slowdown, all forecasters expect IT employment to grow more rapidly than overall employment. Increasing the supply of qualified IT workers is clearly critical to meeting future industry demands. Rising real wages will attract more workers to the IT sector. The marked changes in IT education in the past decade are a response to the rising demand among workers for IT training that can provide alternative pathways to enter the field. The high cost of IT labor in the United States will also encourage the continued growth of off-shore employment or increase employer pressure for further changes in immigration restrictions, such as higher caps on H-1B visa issuances to allow more foreign workers.

Information technology is a $2.5 trillion global industry. While the United States is the largest single customer of IT products and services, no one country has a dominant position in terms of the human capital or intellectual property needed to design and develop information technology. Unlike other more traditional industries, IT does not derive its value directly from geography-specific natural resources, and much of IT production is not bound by the conventions of time or physical space. As a result, the relocation of IT operations offshore is an important consideration with significant implications for the domestic IT industry. This outsourcing of operations may be undertaken to reduce cost structures or to tap into a labor supply that cannot be found in the United States. According to a recent Information Technology Association of America (ITAA) study, only 6 percent of all firms have moved their IT jobs overseas but 12 percent of IT firms have already moved jobs overseas. While the relocation of jobs offshore is commonly thought to primarily affect category 2 workers who do not have highly specialized skills, the ITAA survey indicates that this is increasingly not the case. In fact, programming and software engineering jobs are the most likely types of IT jobs to be moved offshore, which may indicate an increasing tendency to outsource more sophisticated value-added jobs.

The small and shrinking share of women and minorities in the IT workforce is problematic because it suggests that some potential talent is somehow being discouraged from entering IT occupations. This trend

has serious implications for the domestic IT industry since locating and employing qualified labor is central to a firm's success in the increasingly competitive global economy of the twenty-first century.

Joshua L. Rosenbloom and Brandon Dupont

See also Digital Divide; Education in HCI; Gender and Computing

FURTHER READING

Adelman, C. (1999). *Leading, concurrent, or lagging? The value of IT education in IT careers.* Washington, DC: US Department of Education.

Beniger, J. R. (1986). *The control revolution: Technology and the economic origins of the information society.* Cambridge, MA: Harvard University Press.

Cortada, J. W. (1993a). *Before the computer: IBM, NCR, Burrough, and Remington Rand and the industry they created, 1865–1956.* Princeton, NJ: Princeton University Press.

Cortada, J. W. (1993b). *The computer in the United States: From laboratory to market, 1930 to 1960.* Armonk, NY: ME Sharpe.

Cortada, J. W. (1996*). A bibliographic guide to the history of computer applications, 1950–1990.* Westport, CT: Greenwood Press.

Ellis, R., & Lowell, B. L. (1999). *Core occupations of the U.S. information technology workforce* [IT Workforce Data Project, Report 1]. Retrieved November 12, 2003, from http://www.cpst.org/ITWF_Report.cfm

Fisher, F. M., McKie, J. W., and Mankie, R. B. (1983). *IBM and the U.S. data processing industry: An economic history.* New York: Praeger.

Freeman, P., & Aspray, W. (1999). *The supply of information technology workers in the United States.* Washington, DC: Computing Research Association.

Garfinkel, S. (1999). *Architects of the information society: 35 years of the laboratory for computer science at MIT.* Cambridge, MA: MIT Press.

Grant, G. (2003*). H-1B hearing: Companies say foreign workers needed.* Retrieved November 8, 2003, from http://www.infoworld.com/article/03/09/17/HNh1bhearing_1.html.

Hammer, D. P. (1976). *The Information Age: Its development, its impact.* Metuchen, NJ: Scarecrow Press.

Hilton, M. (2001). Information technology workers in the new economy. *Monthly Labor Review, 124*(6), 41–45.

Information Technology Association of America. (2003). *Workforce survey, May 5, 2003.* Retrieved November 12, 2003, from http://www.itaa.org/workforce/studies/03execsumm.pdf.

Jorgenson, D. (2001). Information technology and the U.S. economy. *American Economic Review, 91*(1), 1–32.

Lee, J. A. N. (1995). *International biographical dictionary of computer pioneers.* Chicago: Fitzroy Dearborn.

Mishel, L., Bernstein, J., & Schmitt, J. (2001). *The state of working America.* Ithaca, NY: Cornell University Press.

National Center for Education Statistics. (2002*). Digest of education statistics.* Washington DC: U.S. Department of Education.

National Research Council. (2001). *Building a workforce for the information economy.* Washington, DC: National Academy Press.

Organization for Economic Co-Operation and Development. (2001). *Measuring the information economy.* Paris: OECD Publications.

Ritchie, D. (1986). *The computer pioneers: The making of the modern computer.* New York: Simon and Schuster.

U.S. Department of Commerce, Economics and Statistics Administration. (2002). *Digital economy 2002.* Washington, DC: U.S. Department of Commerce.

U.S. Department of Commerce, Technology Administration. (1997). *International plans, policies, and investments in science and technology.* Washington, DC: U.S. Department of Commerce.

U.S. Department of Commerce, Technology Administration. (1998). *The new innovators: Global patenting trends in five sectors.* Washington, DC: U.S. Department of Commerce.

U.S. Department of Labor, Bureau of Labor Statistics. (1983–2002). *Current population survey.* Washington, DC: U.S. Department of Commerce.

U.S. Department of Labor, Bureau of Labor Statistics. (2001). *Occupational employment statistics survey.* Washington, DC: U.S. Department of Commerce.

Vardi, M. Y., Finin, T., and Henderson, T. (2003). 2001–2002 Taulbee Survey results. *Computing Research News 15*(2), 6–13.

WORLD WIDE WEB

The World Wide Web (WWW or "the Web") was designed originally as an interactive world of shared information through which people could communicate with each other and with machines. The Web is a global virtual network of information and services hosted on servers that can be accessed by client browsers or other servers. It was built on top of the Internet network and is distinct from it in that the Web uses a specific limited set of protocols to transfer information that go beyond the Internet in providing access from mobile phones and other devices.

The Web came to prominence in the mid 1990s as a hypertext system on which documents were formatted in a language called the HyperText Markup Language (HTML) and transferred using the HyperText Transfer Protocol (HTTP) from unique addresses called Universal Resource Locations (URL). This combination of markup language, transfer protocol, and addressing— together with server software to serve up documents and client browsers to view and navigate between documents—brought to an end an era of incompatibilities between computer systems. The interoperability this combination provides allows users access to a vast amount of information stored across the world and also allows anybody with a server to publish information that can be accessible globally. However, the Web had a history before it gained prominence and has moved on since its rise to popularity.

History of the World Wide Web

The origins of the ideas of hypertext found in the Web can be traced back to Vanevar Bush's famous article, "As We May Think," in *Atlantic Monthly* in 1945, in which he proposed the *Memex* machine that would, by a process of binary coding, photocells, and instant photography, allow microfilms cross-references to be made and automatically followed. It's development continued in 1968 with Doug Englebart's *NLS* system using digital computers and providing hypertext e-mail and documentation sharing. Ted Nelson coined the word *hypertext* in 1965, before proposing his *Xanadu* hypertext system in 1981. In 1978 Andrew Lippman of MIT Architecture Machine Group lead a team of researchers that developed what is argued to be the first *true* hypermedia system called the *Aspen Movie Map*. This application was a virtual ride simulation through the city of Aspen, Colorado.

In 1989 at the particle physics laboratory at CERN in Geneva, new experiments were planned, each involving about 350 researchers at each of 200 locations around the world who would work together for up to fifteen years. To address the information needs of these projects, two scientists independently proposed the development of hypertext systems. Robert Cailliau proposed a hypertext project for handling documentation inside the CERN laboratory, while Tim Berners-Lee proposed a networked hypertext system for project participants. A joint proposal was made to CERN management for a project in 1990 after which Berners-Lee created a prototype server and browser that supported WYSIWYG browsing and authoring on the NeXT machine. Berners-Lee also came up with the name World Wide Web, which was adopted by the two researchers.

Since the NeXT platform was not widely available, a simplified version without editing facilities, which could be easily adapted to any computer, was constructed by Nicola Pellow in 1991: the Portable Line-Mode Browser.

In 1991 the Web was not the only choice of distributed document access tool. There were several others

"Inventing" the World Wide Web

During the 1980s and early 1990s, Tim Berners-Lee, a British software engineer and designer, worked on information-storage projects that evolved into a global hypertext program, which he called the "World Wide Web." Many students now write to Berners-Lee about the origins of the Web, so he has posted a "kids page" on his website that answers the questions frequently asked for school reports. Below is an excerpt from that page.

Did you invent the Internet?

No, no, no!

When I was doing the WWW, most of the bits I needed were already done.

Vint Cerf and people he worked with had figured out the Internet Protocol, and also the Transmission Control Protocol. Paul Mockapetris and friends had figured out the Domain Name System.

People had already used TCP/IP and DNS to make email, and other cool things. So I could email other people who maybe would like to help work on making the WWW.

I didn't invent the hypertext link either. The idea of jumping from one document to another had been thought about lots of people, including Vanevar Bush in 1945, and by Ted Nelson (who actually invented the word hypertext). Bush did it before computers really existed. Ted thought of a system but didn't use the internet. Doug Engelbart in the 1960's made a great system just like WWW except that it just ran on one [big] computer, as the internet hadn't been invented yet. Lots of hypertext systems had been made which just worked on one computer, and didn't link all the way across the world.

I just had to take the hypertext idea and connect it to the TCP and DNS ideas and—ta-da!—the World Wide Web.

Just like that?

No, actually the inventing it was easy. The amazing thing which makes it work is that so many people actually have made web servers, and that they all work the same way, on the Internet. They all use HTTP.

So the difficult bit was persuading people to join in. And getting them to agree to all use the same sort of HTTP, and URLs, and HTML. I'm still doing that sort of thing. The World Wide Web Consortium (W3C) is like a club of people and companies who feel the Web is important, and keeping it working is important, and making it even better and even more powerful is important. I am the director of W3C (I started it) but thousands of people are now working on all kinds of wonderful things.

Source: Berners-Lee, T. Answers for young people. Retrieved March 30, 2004, from http://www.w3.org/People/Berners-Lee/Kids

---

available based on the established File Transfer Protocol (FTP) that served document archives, but also provided content-based search of the documents and shared indexes across archives (e.g., Gopher, WAIS, Veronica and Archie). There was also an established hypertext research community at the time that had produced commercial hypertext tools (e.g., OWL-Guide in 1986, Apple's HyperCard in 1987), as well as hypertext techniques well in advance of those in the Web (e.g., KMS from Carnegie Mellon University or the then draft OSI hypermedia standard HyTime). However, the distributed hypertext in the Web and its universal document-addressing scheme clearly had the advantage.

In 1992 many laboratories, including SLAC (California), DESY (Hamburg), NIKHEF (Amsterdam), FNAL (Chicago), and RAL (UK), established servers, so that by the end of the year there were fifty Web servers worldwide, linked through an index page at CERN. The need to create a browser for the WYSIWYG user interface to the UNIX operating system X-windows was met by Viola (from Pei Wei at O'Reilly Associates, California) and Midas (from SLAC).

In 1993 Viola and Midas were shown to the Software Development Group of the National Center for Supercomputing Applications, Illinois (NCSA). Marc Andreessen and Eric Bina from NCSA then wrote the

Tim Berners-Lee on the Web as Metaphor

"Should we then feel that we are getting smarter and smarter, more and more in control of nature, as we evolve? Not really. Just better connected—conntected into a better shape. The experience of seeing the Web take off by the grassroots effort of thousands gives me tremendous hope that if we have the individual will, we can collectively make of our world what we want."

Source: Berners-Lee, T., with Fischetti, M. (2000). *Weaving the Web*. New York: HarperBusiness.

Mosaic browser, which was made freely available for the three major platforms of UNIX, MS-Windows, and the Apple Macintosh. It was easy to install, robust, and allowed in-line color images through the introduction of the <IMG> tag. With these features, the Mosaic browser was readily adopted so that by the end of 1993 there were 250 Web servers worldwide. To count and index those Web servers, Matthew Gray at MIT (Massachusetts Institute of Technology) developed his World Wide Web Wanderer, which was the first robot on the Web. The database of captured URLs became the first Web database—the Wandex.

In 1994 interest in the Web outside the science community escalated when Jim Clark, previously at SGI, founded Mosaic Communications Corp (later Netscape) and hired Marc Andreessen to develop industry-quality software. In April 1994 two Stanford University Ph.D. candidates, David Filo and Jerry Yang, created the searchable Web directory Yahoo! In the same month Brian Pinkerton at the University of Washington launched the WebCrawler, the first full-text search engine on the Web. As a result of concerns that fragmentation of Web standards would destroy the interoperability that the Web had achieved, Tim Berners-Lee and the Laboratory for Computer Science (LCS) of MIT started the World Wide Web Consortium (W3C) to direct future developments for the Web. Berners-Lee left CERN to join the LCS at MIT. By the end of 1994 there were 2,500 Web servers worldwide.

In July 1995 the first Microsoft Internet Explorer Web browser was released and initiated a period often called the "browser wars," when the Netscape and Microsoft products competed for market position by adding functionality in a series of rapidly released new versions. From 1995 developments in Web technology have been coordinated by the World Wide Web Consortium (W3C). The objectives of W3C remain to promote standards for the evolution of the Web and interoperability between WWW products by producing specifications and reference software. Early issues addressed by W3C included a clear definition of the HTML mark-up language; the definition of a bitmap graphics standard that would not suffer from patent issues that the de-facto standard of GIF were (called PNG); the introduction of synchronised multimedia (e.g., video, audio)—SMIL; a Platform for Internet Content Selection (PICS) to provide a mechanism for ratings services to classify websites and pages in terms of suitability for children, reliability, or by other selection measures; and, most importantly, the division between presentation and content in webpages—XML and CSS.

CERN could no longer list all the servers on the Web, so search engines that updated databases with the location and content of what was available became essential. In December Digital Equipment Corporation's (DEC) AltaVista came online as a robot-driven, full-text-based Web search engine supporting natural language and advanced searching techniques, run on a commercially supported farm of servers. By the end of 1995, there were approximately 73,500 Web servers worldwide and the Web was now clearly the only technology to choose for a distributed document application, so much so that the Web started to be generally mistaken for the Internet.

By the end of 1996, the number of Web servers was at 650,000; by June 2002 this number had risen to 3,080,000 websites. By 1998 W3C had published recommendations on all five issues that it had started to address three years earlier. Since 1998 W3C has been addressing a number of challenges for the Web of tomorrow:

Ensure access to the Web by many devices—The Web is becoming accessible from a wide range of devices including cellular phones, TV, digital cameras, and in-car computers. Interaction with resources on the Web can be achieved through a keypad, mouse, voice, stylus, or other input devices. W3C has activities addressing device independence and multimodal interaction to contribute to W3C's goal of universal access.

Web Services
The Web started as a tool for users to view documents. It is now becoming a tool for computers to communicate with each other and call on services provided by each other in a peer-to-peer manner, rather than only in a browser-to-server one.

Semantic Web
As data and services become more common on the Web, they need to be described in a machine understandable way in order to be discovered, evaluated for fitness for users' purposes, and then called. The Web also needs to support the negotiation of, and commitment to, legal contracts for the use of data and services, as well as supporting long-term trust relationships to limit the growing incidence of cybercrime. To support machine dialogues in these areas, richer representations of vocabularies, rules, and inference, which are collectively termed the Semantic Web, are required.

Account for cultural diversity—In 1999 approximately half of all public websites were located in the United States and no other country accounted for more than 5 percent of public websites. By March 2003 Global Reach reported that only 35.2 percent of webpages were in English, with 26.4 percent in Chinese, Japanese, or Korean. The World Wide Web is moving toward global sourcing of information, and the technologies must ensure access to the Web by people with different languages, writing conventions, and cultures.

User Interface Issues in the Development of Web Technology

Scalability
Web protocols have been designed to operate over vast numbers of servers and clients. Two examples of this design are the distributed addressing protocol and the stateless protocol.

The Web has been designed as a distributed storage system rather than a centralized one. Links from one document to another contain the address of the target document inside the source document. Consequently, if the target document is removed, an error occurs: "Error 404—Document Not Found." This error could be avoided by keeping copies of all versions of all documents centrally rather than distributing them. Such a repository could be created, but it would act as a bottleneck for update and access of information. Hence the design decision to accept the frequent 404 error rather than constrain the webpage update process.

The HTTP protocol makes a single access to a server to retrieve a page and then terminates. It does not maintain a connection throughout a dialogue in the way that a telephone line stays open while parties are talking. The telephone style stateful protocol is more efficient for this class of conversational interaction, than a stateless one would be: it would be akin to having to dial a person's number on the phone for each statement you make and for their reply. However, in a Web, where users access successive pages on different machines, a stateless protocol is more efficient—the design decision has been made in the expectation of users moving between distributed servers frequently while browsing.

Many decisions in the design of the Web are motivated by the need for the solution to be used by a very large population at once. Good individual dialogue design has been sacrificed to allow the Web to scale up to a global level of usage.

Content and Presentation
The HTML language combined markup for both presentation and content into the source document; for example, it includes markup tags for paragraphs and headers as well as stating how those will be displayed in terms of font size and color. This combination prevents the document presentation adapting to different devices, for example, reformatting for a hand-held PC or mobile phone. The HTML language was also constructed to be easy to be written in a plain text editor without inserting all the matching closing tags for each initiating tag. Although this eases writing HTML by hand, it made it harder for other

programs to process or transform it. It was necessary that HTML be easy to write with plain text editors before specialized editors were available, but once the Web was established as an application and such specialized editors were being used, this requirement reduced in importance and the need to transform marked-up documents took a higher priority.

To overcome these problems, W3C developed an eXtensible Mark-up Language (XML) that just defines the content of a document and not its presentation. The presentation is defined separately in a Cascading Style Sheet (CSS) that states how each content tag should be presented. The style sheets are termed cascading because different styles can be created for a document by the author, the designer of the display device, or the end user, and the resulting presentation style gives priority to the one most locally defined to the user. This cascade allows the author's display requirements to be modified for the display device and personal presentation preferences.

XML goes further than just resolving these problems in that it provides a syntax in which a family of languages can then be defined to structure and transform data. XSLT is defined as an XSL Transformation language to modify XML data presented. XML Schema is defined as a language to state the data types (e.g., real or integer number, string) of each data item found in an XML document. XML Schema was developed to meet not only the needs of the document community, but also those of the software engineering and database communities, so that XML would be readily amenable to representing data and being manipulated by programs.

Navigation—Linking, Indexing, and Searching

Most Web browsers allow users to scroll through single pages that they are viewing and select hyperlink anchors embedded behind words, phrases, images, or video. Selecting anchors traverses hyperlinks and brings up new pages to either replace the existing one in the browser or launch a new browser. This model is very powerful, but the user will quickly forget the path that he or she has taken and the alternative anchors that have been considered but rejected. Consequently, it is very easy to get lost in the Web using this navigation model alone.

To overcome this confusion, browser designers include a list to provide a history of the pages that have been recently visited. This list allows users to return to previous pages and follow alternative paths. The history function can usually be operated from either of two mechanisms: first, by the use of forward and backward buttons on the browser to move between the most recent selections, or second, by viewing the whole list and picking an entry point from it. Since the list of all pages visited grows rapidly, this mechanism is limited to a time window (e.g., only pages visited in the current session, today, or in the last two weeks). The design decisions as to which interface tools are used for which mechanism and which time windows to apply are based on studies of the number of sites visited and the frequency of use of each mechanism. For example, visiting the previous page viewed is very common, so the previous and next buttons are large and visible on the browser, while revisiting a site visited last week is less common, so the history mechanism required to access this information will be less prominent. Users can build their own index of favorite locations that can be structured to allow them to jump to entry points into the Web that they judge as being useful. This is a third mechanism used to overcome the problem of lost history.

These three mechanisms support navigation, but none will allow a user to access a webpage about a topic of interest not yet visited. To overcome this initial use problem, some sites will be set as default portals, which will provide indexes or search engines.

Michael Wilson

See also Markup Language; Mosaic; Website Design

FURTHER READING

Bush, V. (1945). As we may think. *The Atlantic Monthly, 176*(1), 101–108.

Berners-Lee, T., Fischetti, M. (1999). *Weaving the Web: The original design and ultimate destiny of the World Wide Web by its inventor.* San Francisco: Harper.

Gillies, J., & Cailliau, R. (2000). *How the Web was born: The story of the World Wide Web.* New York: Oxford Paperbacks.

WYSIWYG

WYSIWYG is an acronym for "what you see is what you get" and refers to the correspondence between the way a document appears in a computer editor and the way it appears when printed. Prior to WYSIWYG editors, formatting commands were interspersed with text in a document. For example, the IBM formatting program CMS Script used the command ".ce" to center text, ".ss" to indicate single spacing, and ".ll" to specify the line length. The user could see the effect of the formatting commands only when the document was previewed or printed. Another disadvantage of non-WYSIWYG editors is that formatting errors are not apparent until printing or previewed. Thus, writing a document was akin to writing and debugging a computer program.

WYSIWYG editors require displays that allow pixels to be controlled individually (called "bitmapped displays") to enable, for example, a section of text to be shown in bold and in a larger size. Therefore, early personal computers and mainframes accessed by text-based terminals were incapable of WYSIWYG. The first WYSIWYG word processor, Bravo, was developed at Xerox's Palo Alto Research Center (PARC) in 1974 and ran on the Xerox Alto minicomputer. Although WYSIWYG word processors and graphics editors were developed for the Xerox Star and the Apple Lisa computers, not until release of the Apple Macintosh in 1984 did WYSIWYG editors receive widespread use. The Macintosh came with a word processor (MacWrite) and a graphics editor (MacPaint), both of which were WYSIWYG.

More recently WYSIWYG has become standard on word processors and graphics editors. However, pure

The Future of HCI: No Need to Do What I Say—Just Do What I Think!

The adage WYSIWYG is well-known and respected in software. It means "What You See Is What You Get." It signals user-friendliness. It is counterposed to inconvenient and cumbersome mark-up adorning one's document or data object. In our work with eye-gaze control of display devices, we are taking this concept very seriously indeed. We are looking at how to implement systems whereby what you gaze at determines how the system responds, and the content with which it responds. Starting with computer displays delivering web content or video streams, we are investigating how the object of desire is provided to the user simply on the basis of the user's gaze. It seems to be straight out of the old sitcom I Dream of Jeanie. It is! Let's have a look at how this can be made to work.

The benefits are evident. We could all go around gazing and/or glaring at each other and inanimate things, and produce all manner of effects. Therefore, we first need to pose the question as to where the immediate benefits are really to be found. Eye-gaze device control is of interest to the motor handicapped, and to surgeons during medical operations when the hands are occupied. Zooming of a large radiology image, or a large astronomy image, can be the result of concentration of the observer's interest, as expressed by his or her eye-gaze behavior. A novel way to view simultaneous video streams—indeed, TV programs—is rendered possible, whereby video is delivered only on the basis of the viewer expressing sufficient interest by continuing to look at it. This last application domain seems to be the most innovative.

The long-term goal of this research is to develop a new way for the human to interact with multimedia data and information streams. Less prosaically it puts you and me in control of what data and information the computer or other machine provides to us. It does this on the basis of our reaction to the data or information we are receiving currently. The computer is doing what we desire, and is using our eye-gaze behavior to divine just what it is that we want.

Evidently we could instead throw a switch, or just take a hammer to the TV set. The novelty, though, is that the machine or display device is monitoring us, and not just through a timer switch. Control of our interaction with machines through the user's eye-gaze is a small step on the road towards making machines increasingly clever.

Fionn Murtagh

WYSIWYG has some disadvantages, and therefore many programs offer options for partial WYSIWYG mode. For example, if a user has only a moderate amount of screen space, the user might prefer to display only the printed portion of the page rather than the whole page including the margins. Documents with many large graphics can be slow and unwieldy to display and scroll through. Therefore, an option to display place holders for graphics rather than the graphics themselves is useful but not WYSIWYG.

Some users prefer to have the option of revealing the formatting codes that are used internally by a word processor to specify formatting. Aficionados of Word-Perfect who change to other word processors often miss its "reveal codes" option. Another option allows users to see nonprinted characters such as spaces to help them to determine, for example, if one or two spaces separate a sentence.

Modern HTML (hypertext markup language) editors typically allow users to switch between editing in a WYSIWYG mode and editing the HTML code itself. For example, Macromedia's Dreamweaver not only allows the user to switch between modes, but also provides the option of splitting the screen so that the user can edit in either mode and have the changes reflected in the other. Similar capabilities are available for programmers using high-level programs such as Java. Elements of the user interface can be created using a WYSIWYG interface, whereas much of the coding is done as straight program code.

David M. Lane

See also Graphical User Interface

FURTHER READING

Baecker, R., Grudin, R., Buxton, W., & Greenberg, S. (1995). *Readings in human-computer interaction: Toward the year 2000*. New York: Morgan Kaufmann.

Hiltzik, M. A. (2000). *Dealers of lightning: Xerox PARC and the dawn of the computer age*. New York: HarperBusiness.

APPENDIX 1

GLOSSARY

Throughout the text, the *Berkshire Encyclopedia of Human-Computer Interaction* includes glossary terms and definitions as sidebars. The full glossary below provides quick and easy access to a particular term, helping to make the articles and content more familiar to the nonexpert and providing a handy resource for knowledgeable professionals in the field as well.

ADAPTIVE HELP SYSTEMS: a specific kind of help system and a recognized area of research in the fields of artificial intelligence and human-computer interaction.

AFFECTIVE COMPUTATIONS: computations that machines make that relate to human emotions.

AGENTS: computational entities that can sense and act, and decide on their actions in accordance with some tasks or goals.

ANDROID: A robot that is designed to closely resemble a human.

ANTHROPOMETRY: the study of human body measurements, which focuses on the comparison of the physical characteristics and physical abilities of people.

APPLICATION: a software program that performs a major computing function (such as word processing or Web browsing).

ARTIFICIAL INTELLIGENCE (AI): the subfield of computer science that is concerned with symbolic reasoning and problem solving.

ASCII: the American Standard Code for Information Interchange, a universally used coding system. ASCII has an initial character set of 128 numbers (from 0 through 127) that stands for letters, numbers, punctuation marks, and characters. ASCII is the most common format for the transfer of text files between computers.

AUGMENTED COGNITION: a field of research that seeks to extend a computer user's abilities via technologies that address information-processing bottlenecks inherent in human-computer interaction.

AUGMENTED REALITY: a field of research that concentrates on integrating virtual objects into the real world.

AVATARS: digital representations of humans in online or virtual environments.

BANDWIDTH: the amount of data that can be sent through a network or modem connection. Generally measured in bits per second, or "bps."

BETA TESTING: a stage in the design and development process of computer software and hardware that uses people outside a company, called "beta testers," to be sure that products function properly for typical end-users outside the firm.

BITMAP: an array of pixels, in a data file or structure, which correspond bit for bit with an image.

BROWSERS: software programs (e.g., Microsoft Internet Explorer, Netscape Navigator) that allow you to view Web pages.

COMPILERS: computer programs that translate one programming language into another.

COOKIE: a small text string—often no more than an ID number—sent by a Web server to a browser. The text is then stored by that browser, typically on the user's hard drive, and sent back to a Web server at a later time.

CYBORG: a technologically enhanced human being.

DATA MINING: the process of information extraction with the goal of discovering hidden facts or patterns within databases.

DATA VISUALIZATION: a discipline that uses computers to make pictures that elucidate a concept, phenomenon, relationship, or trend hidden in a large quantity of data.

DESKTOP METAPHOR: when the interface of an interactive software system is designed such that its objects and actions resemble objects and actions in a traditional office environment (e.g., directories called "folders" and text documents called "files").

DOCUMENT CLUSTER: documents that are considered to be alike, and therefore potentially all of relevance to an information retrieval query.

EMBEDDED SYSTEMS: systems that use computers to accomplish specific and relatively invariant tasks as part of a larger system function—as when, for example, a computer in a car controls engine conditions.

EXPERT SYSTEM: a computer system that captures and stores human problem-solving knowledge or expertise so that it can be used by other, typically less-knowledgeable people.

FUNCTIONALITY: the capabilities of a given program or parts of a program.

GROUPWARE: any software system that is designed to facilitate group work and interaction, used for systems such as e-mail, mailing lists, bulletin boards, newsgroups, instant messaging, and wikis.

HELP SYSTEMS: computer-based systems that answer user questions on a program's functions and help users learn how to accomplish given tasks using the program.

HYPERTEXT: text that uses hyperlinks to present text and static graphics. Many websites are entirely or largely hypertexts.

INFORMATION SPACES: representations, most often spatial or similar (e.g. locations and interconnections in graph form), that can facilitate finding and using information.

INTELLIGENT AGENT: software program that actively locates information for you based on parameters you set. Unlike a search engine or information filter, it actively seeks specific information while you are doing other things.

INTERFACE: Interconnections between a device, program, or person that facilitate interaction.

KNOWLEDGE BASE: a collection of facts, rules, and procedures organized into schemas; the assembly of all of the information and knowledge of a specific field of interest.

MACHINE LEARNING: any one of a range of algorithms that aim at deriving associations, e.g. the appropriate class or category for a set of measurements.

MARKUP LANGUAGES: text encoding that tags an electronic document to indicate how the text should look when it is printed or displayed or to describe the logical structure and meaning of data contained in the document.

METADATA: information about the actual source of the data: the author, the period when or the context within which the data got provided; the age of the author, and the title of the document.

MOORE'S LAW: a theory first posed in 1965 by Gordon Moore, one of the founders of Intel, that the number of transistors per square inch on integrated circuits would roughly double every year. It has come to mean that the effective power of computing hardware doubles about every eighteen months.

MOTION CAPTURE: computerized methods of recording the movements of a human body that filmmakers use to create realistic movement in animated virtual actors.

MUDS: computer-moderated, persistent virtual environments through which multiple persons interact simultaneously.

MULTIAGENT SYSTEMS: the scientific field that studies the behavior of multiple agents when they interact with each other and with their environment in various scales and forms of organization.

NEURAL NETWORK: any one of a family of algorithms, originally felt to reflect the type of processing carried out by the human brain, and targeting such applications as categorization or classification; or learning of associations.

OPEN SOURCE SOFTWARE: open source software permits sharing of a program's original source code with users, so that the software can be modified and redistributed to other users.

OPERATING SYSTEM: software (e.g., Windows 98, UNIX, or DOS) that enables a computer to accept input and produce output to peripheral devices such as disk drives and printers.

PERSONALITY CAPTURE: methods of uploading aspects of a person's character to a computer or information system.

SEMANTIC WEB: a common framework that allows data to be shared and reused across application, enterprise, and community boundaries.

UBIQUITOUS COMPUTING: a field of computer science that proposes the notion that some form of computing can be present in all aspects of daily life by embedding computers of some sort everywhere around us in ways that are useful.

UNIX: a widely used operating system, improved and enhanced by many people since its development in 1969 by Bell Laboratories.

USENET – An international system of online discussion groups, known as newsgroups.

USER INTERFACE: the environment (e.g., Windows, MacIntosh, DOS, UNIX) allowing a person to interact with a computer.

VIRTUAL REALITY: a type of system that immerses a participant in a computer-generated, virtual environment.

VOICE OVER INTERNET PROTOCOL (VOIP): transmitting telephone calls (voice, fax) over the Internet, as opposed to using the publicly switched telephone network (PSTN) that most businesses and consumers use.

WIKI: server software that allows users to write and edit Web documents collectively using a Web browser.

Compiled by Marcy Ross, with thanks to the HCI contributors who provided so many useful definitions within their articles.

MASTER BIBLIOGRAPHY OF HUMAN– COMPUTER INTERACTION

The Further Reading sections at the end of each article provide citations to what the authors of the articles think are the key publications on the topic. These include journal articles, chapters in books, dissertations, conference papers, edited works, manuals, books, and websites. As one might expect, many significant papers and journal articles are also available online, accessible to all Web users. When possible, we have listed where these publications are available online.

Of course, the literature on HCI is vast and growing quickly, but the list of 2,600 references below provides a comprehensive guide to both historical and cutting edge sources.

Aberg, J. (2002). *Live help systems: An approach to intelligent help for Web information systems* (Linkopings Studies in Science and Technology, Dissertation No. 745). Linkopings, Sweden: Department of Computer and Information Science, Linkopings University.

Abrams, D., Baecker R., & Chignell, M. (1998). Information archiving with bookmarks: Personal Web space construction and organization. In Proceedings of CHI'98 Conference on Human Factors in Computing Systems (pp. 41-48). New York: ACM Press.

Abramson, M. A., & Means, G. E. (Eds.). (2001). *E-government 2001* (ISM Center for the Business of Government). Lanham, MD: Rowman & Littlefield.

Abras, C. (2003). *Determining success in online education and health communities: Developing usability and sociability heuristics.* Unpublished doctoral dissertation, University of Maryland, Baltimore County.

Abras, C., Maloney-Krichmar, D., & Preece, J. (2003, June). *Evaluating an online academic community: "Purpose" is the key.* Paper presented at the HCI International 2003, Crete, Greece.

Accot, J., & Zhai, S. (1997). Beyond Fitts' Law: Models for trajectory-based HCI tasks. In Proceedings of CHI 1997: ACM Conference on Human Factors in Computing Systems (pp. 295-302).

Accot, J., & Zhai, S. (2002). More than dotting the i's—Foundations for crossing-based interfaces. In *Proceedings of CHI 2002: ACM Conference on Human Factors in Computing Systems, CHI Letters 4*(1), 73–80.

Ackerman, M. S. (2002). The intellectual challenge of CSCW: The gap between social requirements and technical feasibility. In J. M. Carroll

(Ed.), *Human-computer interaction in the new millennium* (pp. 303–324). New York: ACM Press.

Adali, S., Candan, K. S., Chen, S. S., Erol, K., & Subrahmanian, V. S. (1996). The advanced video information system: Data structures and query processing. *Multimedia Systems, 4*(4), 172–186.

Adam, A. (2001). Gender and computer ethics. In R. A. Spinello & H. T. Tavani (Eds.), *Readings in cyberethics* (pp. 63–76). Sudbury, MA: Jones and Bartlett.

Adam, A. (2002). Cyberstalking and Internet pornography: Gender and the gaze. *Ethics and Information Technology, 2*(2), 133–142.

Adam, J. (1996, November). Geek gods: How cybergeniuses Bob Kahn and Vint Cerf turned a Pentagon project into the Internet and connected the world. *Washingtonian Magazine, 66.*

Adams, J. (2002). *Programming role playing games with DirectX.* Indianapolis, IN: Premier Press.

Adar, E., & Huberman, B. A. (2000). Free riding on gnutella. *First Monday.* Retrieved January 29, 2004, from http://www.firstmonday.dk/issues/issue5_10/adar/

Adelman, C. (1999). *Leading, concurrent, or lagging? The value of IT education in IT careers.* Washington, DC: US Department of Education.

Adler, P. A., Parson, C. K., & Zolke, S. B. (1985). Employee privacy: Legal and research developments and implications for personnel administration. *Sloan Management Review, 26,* 13–25.

Adobe Systems. (1999). *PostScript language reference, 3E.* Reading, MA: Addison-Wesley.

Agel, J. (Ed.). (1970). *The making of Kubrick's 2001.* New York: New American Library.

Agrawal, D. P., & Zeng, Q-A. (2003) *Introduction to wireless and mobile systems.* Pacific Grove, CA: Brooks/Cole-Thompson Learning.

Agre, P. E., & Rotenberg, M. (1997). *Technology and privacy, the new landscape.* Cambridge, MA: MIT Press.

Agricola, G. (1950). *De re metallica* (H. C. Hoover & L. H. Hoover, Trans.). New York: Dover.

Ahanger, G. & Little, T. D. C. (1996). A survey of technologies for parsing and indexing digital video. *The Journal of Visual Communication and Image Representation, 7,* 28–43.

Aho, A. V., & Ulman, J. D. (1977). *Principles of compiler design.* Reading, MA: Addison-Wesley.

Aho, A. V., Sethi, R., & Ulman, J. D. (1986). *Compilers: principles, techniques and tools.* Reading, MA: Addison-Wesley.

Ahrend, K. (2001). *Die Nutzung der maschinellen Übersetzung in der Europäischen Kommission* (The use of machine translation in the European Commission). Retrieved on February 12, 2004 from http://europa.eu.int/comm/translation/reading/articles/tools_and_workflow_en.htm#mt

Aidemark, J., Vinter, J., Folkesson, P., & Karlsson, J. (2002). Experimental evaluation of a time-redundant execution for a brake-by-wire application. In *Proceedings of the International Conference on Dependable Systems and Networks (DSN02)* (pp. 210–218). Cupertino, CA: IEEE CS Press.

Air Force summer study board report on multilevel secure database systems. (1983). Washington, DC: Department of Defense.

Alavi, M. (1984). An assessment of the prototyping approach to information systems development. *Communications of the ACM, 27*(6), 556–563.

Albers, M. J., & Kim, L. (2000). User web browsing characteristics using palm handhelds for information retrieval. In *Proceedings of IEEE professional communication society international professional communication conference* (pp 125–135). Piscataway, NJ: IEEE Educational Activities Department.

Alberts, D. S., Gartska, J. J., & Stein, F. P. (2001). *Understanding information age warfare* (2nd ed.). Washington, DC: Command and Control Research Program.

Alder, G. S., & Tompkins, P. K. (1997), Electronic performance monitoring: An organizational justice and concertive control perspective. *Management Communication Quarterly,* 10, 259–288.

Aldhous, P. (1993). Managing the genome data deluge. *Science,* 262, 502–3.

Alexander, C., et al. (1977). *A pattern language.* New York: Oxford.

Aliaga, D. G. (1997). Virtual objects in the real world. *Communications of the ACM, 40*(3), 49–54.

Alison, J. E. (2002). *Technology, development, and democracy: International conflict and cooperation in the information age.* Albany, NY: State University of New York Press.

Allen, B. P. (1994). Case-based reasoning: Business applications. *Communications of the ACM, 37*(3), 40–42.

Allen, J. (1995). *Natural language processing.* Boston: Addison-Wesley.

Allen, J. (1995). *Natural language understanding.* Redwood City, CA: Benjamin/Cummings.

Allen, J. F., Schubert, L. K., Ferguson, G., Heeman, P., Hwang, C. H., Kato, T., et al. (1995). The TRAINS project: A case study in building a conversational planning agent. *Journal of Experimental and Theoretical Artificial Intelligence, 7,* 7–48.

Allen, J., Byron, D., Dzikovska, M., Ferguson, G., Galescu, L., & Stent, A. (2001). Towards conversational human-computer interaction. *AI Magazine, 22*(4), 27–37.

Allen, J., Hendler, J., & Tate, A. (Eds.). (1990). *Readings in planning.* San Mateo, CA: Morgan Kaufmann.

Allen, J., Hunnicutt, S., & Klatt, D. (1976). *From text to speech: The MITalk system.* Cambridge, MA: Cambridge University Press.

Allen, R. B. (1990). User models: Theory, method, and practice. *International Journal of Man-Machine Studies, 32,* 511–543.

Allwood, C. M. (1984). Error detection processes in statistical problem solving. *Cognitive Science, 8,* 413–437.

Allwood, C. M., & Bjorhag, C. G. (1990). Novices debugging when programming in Pascal. *International Journal of Man-Machine Studies, 33*(6), 707–724.

Allwood, C. M., & Bjorhag, C. G. (1991). Training of Pascal novices error handling ability. *Acta Psychologica, 78*(1–3), 137–150.

Allwood, C. M., & Hakken, D. (2001). "Deconstructing use": Diverse discourses on "users' and "usability" in information system development and reconstructing a viable use discourse. *AI & Society, 15,* 169–199.

Alpert, S., Karat, J., Karat, C.-M., Brodie, C., & Vergo, J. G. (2003). User attitudes regarding a user-adaptive e-commerce web site. *User Modeling and User-Adapted Interaction, 13*(4), 373–396.

Alterman, R., Feinman, A., Introne, J., & Landsman, S. (2001, August). *Coordinating Representations in Computer-Mediated Joint Activities.* Paper presented at the 23rd Annual Conference of the Cognitive Science Society, Edinburgh, United Kingdom. Retrieved August 7, 2003, from http://www.hcrc.ed.ac.uk/cogsci2001/pdf-files/0015.pdf

Altman, I. (1975). *The environment and social behavior.* Monterey, CA: Brooks/Cole.

Altman, M., Andreev, L., Diggory, M., King, G., Sone, A., Verba, S., et al. (2001). A digital library for the dissemination and replication of quantitative social science research: The Virtual Data Center. *Social Science Computer Review, 19*(4), 458–470.

BIBLIOGRAPHY

Altmann, E. M., & Trafton, J. G. (2002). Memory for goals: an activation-based model. *Cognitive Science, 26*(1), 39–83.

Alvarez, R. M. (2002). *Ballot design options, California Institute of Technology*. Retrieved February 17, 2004, from http://www.capc.umd.edu/rpts/MD_EVote_Alvarez.pdf

Alvarez, R. M., & Nagler, J. (2001). The likely consequences of Internet voting for political representation. *Loyola of Los Angeles Law School Review, 34*(3), 1115–1153.

Amant, R. (1999). User interface affordances in a planning representation. *Human-Computer Interaction, 14*(3), 317–354.

Amento, B., Terveen, L., & Hill, W. (2003) Experiments in social data mining: The TopicShop system. *ACM Transactions on Computer-Human Interaction, 10*(1), 54–85.

American Association of University Women (AAUW). (2000). *Tech-savvy: Educating girls in the new computer age.* Washington, DC: AAUW Educational Foundation.

American Council of the Blind. (2001). *Braille: History and use of Braille.* Retrieved May 10, 2004, from http://www.acb.org/resources/braille.html

American National Standards Institute. (1988). *American national standard for human factors engineering of visual display terminal workstations* (Standard No. 100-1988). Santa Monica, CA: Human Factors Society.

Ames, C., & Comino, M. (1992). Cybernetic composer: An overview. In M. Balaban, K. Ebcioglu, & O. Laske (Eds.), *Understanding music with AI* (pp.186–205). Cambridge, MA: AAAI Press/MIT Press.

An empirical study. *Post-Proceedings of the Conference of Gestures: Meaning and Use.* Porto, Portugal, April 2000.

Andersen, J. H., Thornsen, J. F., Overgaard, E., Lassen, C. F., Brandt, L. P. A., Vilstrup, I., Kryger, A. I., & Mikkelsen, S. (2003). Computer use and carpal tunnel syndrome: A 1-year follow-up study. *JAMA, 289*(22), 2963–2969.

Anderson, C. A., & Bushman, B. (2001). Effects of violent video games on aggressive behavior, aggressive cognition, aggressive affect, physiological arousal, and pro-social behavior: A meta-analytic review of the scientific literature. *Psychological Science, 12*, 353–359.

Anderson, C. A., & Dill, K. E. (2000). Video games and aggressive thoughts, feelings, and behavior in the laboratory and in life. *Journal of Personality & Social Psychology, 78*, 772–790.

Anderson, D. M., & Cornfield, M. (2003). *The civic web: Online politics and democratic values.* Lanham, MD: Rowman and Littlefield Publishers.

Anderson, D., Anderson, E., Lesh, N., Marks, J., Mirtich, B., Ratajczak, D., et al. (2000). Human-guided simple search. In *Proceedings of the National Conference on Artificial Intelligence (AAAI)* (pp. 209–216). Cambridge, MA: MIT Press.

Anderson, E., Bai, Z., Bischof, C., Blackford, S., Demmel, J. Dongarra, et al. (1999). *LAPACK users' guide* (3d ed.). Philadelphia: SIAM.

Anderson, J. (1998*). Arabizing the Internet.* Emirates Occasional Papers # 30. Abu Dhabi, United Arab Emirates: Emirates Center for Strategic Studies and Research

Anderson, J. R., & Lebiere, C. (Eds.). (1998). *Atomic components of thought.* Hillsdale, NJ: Erlbaum.

Anderson, J. R., Bothell, D., Byrne, M. D., & Lebiere, C. (2002). An integrated theory of the mind. Retrieved October 17, 2002, from http://act-r.psy.cmu.edu/papers/403/IntegratedTheory.pdf

Anderson, J. R., Matessa, M., & Lebiere, C. (1997). ACT-R: A theory of higher level cognition and its relation to visual attention. *Human-Computer Interaction, 12*(4), 439–462.

Anderson, J., & Eikelman, D. (Eds.). (2003). *New media in the Muslim world: The emerging public sphere* (Indiana Series in Middle East Studies). Bloomington: Indiana University Press.

Anderson, J., & Fickas, S. (1989). A proposed perspective shift: Viewing specification design as a planning problem. *ACM SIGSOFT Software Engineering Notes, 14*(3), 177–184.

Anderson, J., Fleek, F., Garrity, K., & Drake, F. (2001). Integrating usability techniques into software development. *IEEE Software, 18*(1), 46–53.

Anderton, C. (1998). *Digital home recording.* San Francisco: Miller Freeman Books.

Angell, R., Freund, G., & Willett, P. (1983). Automatic spelling correction using a trigram similarity measure. *Information Processing and Management, 19*(4), 255–261.

Annett, J., & Duncan, K. D. (1967). Task analysis and training design. *Occupational Psychology*, 41, 211–221.

Annett, J., & Duncan, K. D. (1967). Task analysis and training design. *Occupational Psychology*, 41, 211–221.

Annett, J., Duncan, K. D., Stammers, R. B., & Gray, M. J. (1971). *Task analysis* (Training Information Paper No. 6). London: HMSO.

Annis, J. F. (1989). An automated device used to develop a new 3-D database for head and face anthropometry. In A. Mital (Ed.), *Advances in industrial ergonomics and safety* (pp. 181–188). London: Taylor & Francis.

Annis, J. F., Case, H. W., Clauser, C. E., & Bradtmiller, B. (1991). Anthropometry of an aging work force. *Experimental Aging Research, 17*, 157–176.

Anobile, R. J. (Ed.). (1980*). Star Trek, the motion picture: The photostory*. New York: Pocket Books.

Antani, S., Kasturi, R., & Jain, R. (2002). A survey on the use of pattern recognition methods for abstraction, indexing and retrieval of images and video. *Pattern Recognition, 35*, 945–965.

Apple Computer Company. (1993). *Macintosh Japanese input method guide.* Cupertino, CA: Apple.

Apple Computer. Apple developer connection—Icons. (2003). Retrieved January 4, 2004, from http://developer.apple.com/ue/aqua/icons.html

Apple Computer. Apple human interface guidelines. (2003). Retrieved January 7, 2004, from http://developer.apple.com/documentation/UserExperience/Conceptual/OSXHIGuidelines/index.html#//apple_ref/doc/uid/20000957

Ardissono, L., & Goy, A. (1999). Tailoring the interaction with users in electronic shops. In J. Kay (Ed.), *Proceedings of the 7th International Conference on User Modeling* (pp. 35–44). New York: Springer-Verlag.

Aristotle. (350 BCE). *Categories* .Retrieved March 8, 2004, from http://www.classicallibrary.org/aristotle/categories

Armstrong, T. J., & Silverstein, B. A. (1987). Upper-extremity pain in the workplace—Role of usage in causality. In N. M. Hadler (Ed.), *Clinical concepts in regional musculoskeletal illness* (pp. 333–354). Orlando, FL: Grune & Stratton.

Aronson, J. E., Turban, E., & Liang, T. P. (2004). *Decision support systems and intelligent systems* (7th ed). Upper Saddle River, NJ: Prentice Hall.

Arrison, S. (2002, April 19). *Why digital dividers are out of step.* Retrieved July 17, 2003, from http://www.pacificresearch.org/press/opd/2002/opd_02-04-19sa.html

Artim, J., et. al. (1998). Incorporating work, process and task analysis into commercial and industrial object-oriented system development. *SIGCHI Bulletin, 30*(4).

Asher, R. E., & Simpson, J. M. Y. (Eds.). (1994). *The encyclopedia of language and linguistics.* Oxford, UK: Pergamon.

Asimov, I. (1950). *I, robot.* New York: Grosset and Dunlap.

Asimov, I. (1954). *The caves of steel.* Garden City, NY: Doubleday.

Asimov, I. (1956). *The naked sun.* New York: Bantam.

Asimov, I. (1983). *The robots of dawn.* New York: Ballantine.

Aspray, W. (1985). The scientific conceptualization of information: A survey. *IEEE Annals of the History of Computing, 7,* 117–140.

Associated Press. (2002, June 22). U.N. warns on global digital divide. Retrieved July 18, 2003, from http://lists.isb.sdnpk.org/pipermail/comp-list/2002-June/001053.html

Association for Computing Machinery's special interest group on knowledge discovery and data mining. Retrieved August 21, 2003, from http://www.acm.org/sigkdd.

Atal, B., & Hanauer, S. (1971). Speech analysis and synthesis by linear prediction of the speech wave. *Journal of the Acoustical Society of America, 50,* 637–655.

Atanasoff, J. V. (1984). Advent of electronic digital computing. *Annals of the History of Computing, 6*(3), 229–282.

Atkins, D. (1999). Visions for digital libraries. In P. Schauble & A. F. Smeaton (Eds.), *Summary report of the series of joint NSF-EU working groups on future directions for digital libraries research* (pp. 11–14). Washington, DC: National Science Foundation.

Atkins, D. E., Drogemeier, K. K., Feldman, S. I., Garcia-Molina, H., Klein, M. L., Messerschmitt, D. G., Messina, P., Ostriker, J. P., & Wright, M. H. (2003). *Revolutionizing science and engineering through cyberinfrastructure.* Arlington, VA: National Science Foundation.

Atkinson, C. J. (2000). Socio-technical and soft approaches to information requirements elicitation in the post-methodology era. *Requirements Engineering, 5*(2), 67–73.

Atkinson, K. (2003). GNU Aspell 0.50.4.1. Retrieved January 20, 2004, from http://aspell.sourceforge.net/man-html/manual.html

Attewell, P. (1987). Big brother and the sweatshop: Computer surveillance in the automated office. *Sociological Theory, 5,* 87–99.

Attneave, F. (1959). *Applications of information theory to psychology: A summary of basic concepts, methods, and results.* New York: Henry Holt.

Aura, T., Nikander, P., & Leiwo, J. (2000). DoS-resistant authentication with client puzzles. *Security Protocols—8th International Workshop.*

Austrian, G. D. (1982). *Herman Hollerith: Forgotten giant of information processing.* New York: Columbia University Press.

Avery, C., Resnick, P., & Zeckhauser, R. (1999). The market for evaluations. *American Economic Review, 89*(3), 564–584.

Awad, E. M. (1996). *Building expert systems: Principles, procedures, and applications.* Minneapolis/St. Paul, MN: West Publishing.

Ayers, E., & Stasko, J. (1995). Using graphic history in browsing the World Wide Web. In *Proceedings of the Fourth International World Wide Web Conference* (pp. 451–459). Retrieved January 19, 2004, from http://www.w3j.com/1/ayers.270/paper/270.html

Azuma, R. (1997). A survey of augmented reality. *Presence: Teleoperators and Virtual Environments, 6*(3), 355–385.

Baase, S. (1997). *A gift of fire: Social, legal and ethical issues in computing.* Upper Saddle River, NJ: Prentice Hall.

Baba, M. L. (1995). The cultural ecology of the corporation: Explaining diversity in work group responses to organizational transformation. (1995). *Journal of Applied Behavioral Science, 31*(2), 202–233.

Baba, M. L. (1999). Dangerous liaisons: Trust, distrust, and information technology in American work organizations. *Human Organization, 58*(3), 331–346.

Backs, R. W. (2002). *Engineering Psychophysiology.* Mahwah, NJ: Erlbaum.

Badler, N., Phillips, C., & Webber, B. (1993). *Simulating humans: Computer graphics, animation, and control.* Oxford, UK: Oxford University Press.

Baecker, R. M. (1993). *Readings in groupware and computer-supported cooperative work: Assisting human-human collaboration.* San Francisco: Morgan-Kaufmann.

Baecker, R. M., & Marcus, A. (1990). *Human factors and typography for more readable programs.* Reading, MA: Addison-Wesley.

Baecker, R. M., Grudin, J., Buxton, W. A. S., & Greenberg, S. (Eds.). (1995). *Readings in human-computer interaction: Toward the year 2000* (2nd ed.). Los Altos, CA: Morgan Kaufmann.

Baecker, R. M., Nastos, D., Posner, I. R., & Mawby, K. L. (1993). The user-centered iterative design of collaborative writing software. In *Proceedings of InterCHI'93* (pp. 399–405). New York: ACM Press.

Baecker, R., & Small, I. (1990). Animation at the interface. In B. Laurel (Ed.), *The art of human-computer interface design* (pp. 251–267). Reading, MA: Addison-Wesley.

Baeza-Yates, R., & Rubiero-Neto, B. (1999). *Modern information retrieval.* Reading, MA: Addison Wesley.

Bailenson, J. N., Beall, A. C., Blascovich, J., & Rex, C. (in press). Examining virtual busts: Are photogrammetrically generated head models effective for person identification? *PRESENCE: Teleoperators and Virtual Environments.*

Bailenson, J. N., Beall, A. C., Loomis, J., Blascovich, J., & Turk, M. (in press). Transformed social interaction: Decoupling representation from behavior and form in collaborative virtual environments. *PRESENCE: Teleoperators and Virtual Environments.*

Bailenson, J. N., Blascovich, J., Beall, A. C., & Loomis, J. M. (2001). Equilibrium revisited: Mutual gaze and personal space in virtual environments. *PRESENCE: Teleoperators and Virtual Environments, 10,* 583–598.

Bailey, D. E., & Kurland, N. B. (2002). A review of telework research: Findings, new directions, and lessons for the study of modern work. *Journal of Organizational Behavior, 23*(4), 383–400.

Bailey, K. D. (1994). *Typologies and taxonomies: An introduction to classification techniques.* Thousand Oaks, CA: Sage Publications.

Bailly, G., & Benoit, C. (Eds.). (1992). *Talking machines, theories, models, and designs.* Amsterdam, Netherlands: Elsevier Science Publishers.

Bainbridge, L. (1983). Ironies of Automation. *Automatica, 19*(6), 775–779.

Bainbridge, L. (1991). Verbal protocol analysis. In J. Wilson & E. Corlett (Eds.), *Evaluation of human work: A practical ergonomics methodology* (pp. 161–179). London: Taylor and Francis.

Bainbridge, W. S. (1919). *Report on medical and surgical developments of the war.* Washington, DC: Government Printing Office.

Bainbridge, W. S. (1984). Religious insanity in America: The official nineteenth-century theory. *Sociological Analysis, 45,* 223–240.

Bainbridge, W. S. (1986). *Dimensions of science fiction.* Cambridge, MA: Harvard University Press.

Bainbridge, W. S. (1995). Sociology on the World Wide Web. *Social Science Computer Review, 13,* 508–523.

Bainbridge, W. S. (1997). *Sociology.* New York: Barron's.

BIBLIOGRAPHY

Bainbridge, W. S. (2000). Religious ethnography on the World Wide Web. In J. K. Hadden & D. Cowan (Eds.), *Religion and the Internet*. Greenwich, CT: JAI Press.

Bainbridge, W. S. (2002). Validity of Web-based surveys. In O. V. Burton (Ed.), *Computing in the Social Sciences and Humanities* (pp. 51–66). Urbana: University of Illinois Press.

Bainbridge, W. S. (2003). Massive questionnaires for personality capture. *Social Science Computer Review, 21*(3), 267–280.

Bainbridge, W. S. (2003). The future of Internet: Cultural and individual conceptions. In P. N. Howard & S. Jones (Eds.), *The Internet and American life*. Thousand Oaks, CA: Sage Publications.

Bainbridge, W. S. (in press). The evolution of semantic systems. *Annals of the New York Academy of Science*.

Bainbridge, W. S., Brent, E. E., Carley, K. M., Heise, D. R., Macy, M. W., Markovsky, B. (1994). Artificial social intelligence. *Annual Review of Sociology, 20*, 407–436.

Baird, B., Blevins, D., & Zahler, N. (1993). Artificial intelligence and music: Implementing an interactive computer performer. *Computer Music Journal, 17*(2), 73–79.

Bajura, M., Fuchs, H., & Ohbuchi, R. (1992). Merging virtual objects with the real world: Seeing Ultrasound imagery within the patient. *Computer Graphics (Proceedings of SIGGRAPH'92), 26*(2), 203–210.

Baker, J. K. (1975). Stochastic modeling for automatic speech understanding. In D. R. Reddy (Ed.), *Speech recognition* (pp. 521–542). New York: Academic Press.

Baker, J. K. (1975). The Dragon system: An overview. *IEEE Transactions on Acoustics, Speech and Signal Processing, 23*(1), 24–29.

Balka, E., & Smith, R. (Eds.) (2000). *Women, work and computerization*. Boston: Kluwer.

Ballard, D. H., Hayhoe, M. M., Pook, P. K., & Rao, R. P. N. (1997). Deictic codes for the embodiment of cognition. *Behavioral and Brain Sciences, 20*(4), 723–742.

Banks, R., & Laurie, H. (2000). From PAPI to CAPI: The case of the British Household Panel Survey. *Social Science Computer Review, 18*(4), 397–406.

Bannon, L. (1991). From human factors to human actors: The role of psychology and human-computer interaction studies in system design. In J. Greenbaum & M. Kyng (Eds.), *Design at work* (pp. 25–44). Hillsdale, NJ: Erlbaum.

Baraff, D. (1994, July). Fast contact force computation for non-penetrating rigid bodies. *Computer Graphics, Proceedings of SIGGRAPH*, 23–34.

Baranek, B., & Newman. (1981, April). *A history of the ARPANET: The first decade*. NTIS No. AD A 115440). Retrieved March 23, 2004, from http://www.ntis.gov

Barber, B. R. (1998). *A passion for democracy: American essays*. Princeton, NJ: Princeton University Press.

Barber, W., & Badre, A. (1998). Culturability: The merging of culture and usability. *Human Factors and the Web*. Retrieved March 1, 2004, from http://www.research.att.com/conf/hfweb/proceedings/barber/index.htm

Barfield, W., & Danas, E. (1996). Comments on the use of olfactory displays for virtual environments. *Presence, 5*(1), 109–121.

Barkai, D. (2002). *Peer-to-peer computing: Technologies for sharing and collaborating on the Net*. Santa Clara, CA: Intel Press.

Barker, T. T. (2003). *Writing software documentation: A task-oriented approach* (2nd ed.). New York: Longman.

Barley, S. (1986). Technology as an occasion for structuring: Evidence from observations of CT scanners and the social order of radiology departments. *Administrative Science Quarterly, 31*, 8–108.

Barnard, P. (1991). Bridging between basic theories and the artifacts of human-computer interaction. In J. M. Carroll (Ed.), *Designing interaction: Psychology at the human-computer interface* (pp. 103–127). Cambridge, UK: Cambridge University Press.

Barnard, P. J., May, J., Duke, D., & Duce, D. (2000). Systems, interactions and macrotheory. *ACM Transactions on Computer Human Interaction, 7*, 222–262.

Barnes, B. A. (1977). Discarded operations: Surgical innovation by trial and error. In J. P. Bunker, B. A. Barnes, & F. Mosteller (Eds.), *Costs, risks, and benefits of surgery* (pp. 109–123). New York: Oxford University Press.

Barras, S., & Kramer, G. (1999). Using sonification. *Multimedia Systems, 7*, 23–31.

Barrett, L. F., & Barrett, D. J. (2001). An introduction to computerized experience sampling in psychology. *Social Science Computer Review, 19*(2), 175–185.

Barron, T., & LostLogic. (2002). *Multiplayer game programming*. Roseville, CA: Prima Tech.

Bartle, R. (1990). *Early MUD history*. Retrieved July 31, 2003, from http://www.ludd.luth.se/mud/aber/mud-history.html

Bartle, R. A. (2003). *Designing virtual worlds*. Indianapolis, IN: New Riders Publishing.

Bartlett, M. S., Hager, J. C., Ekman, P., & Sejnowski, T. J. (1999). Measuring facial expressions by computer image analysis. *Psychophysiology, 36*(2), 253–263.

Barzilay, R. & Lee, L. (2002). Bootstrapping lexical choice via multiple-sequence alignment. *Proceedings of Empirical Methods in Natural Language Processing*, 164–171.

Basalla, G. (1988). *The evolution of technology*. Cambridge, UK: Cambridge University Press.

Basili, V., & Turner, A. (1975). Iterative enhancement: A practical technique for software development. *IEEE Transactions on Software Engineering, SE-1*(4), 390–396.

Baskerville, R. L., & Stage, J. (1996). Controlling prototype development through risk management. *Management Information Systems Quarterly, 20*(4), 481–504.

Baskerville, R., & Pries-Heje, J. (in press). Short cycle time systems development. *Information Systems Journal, 14*(2).

Bass, L., & John, B. E. (2003). Linking usability to software architecture patterns through general scenarios. *Journal of Systems and Software, 66*(3), 187–197.

Bass, L., Clements, P., & Kazman, R. (2003). *Software architecture in practice* (2nd ed.). New York: Addison-Wesley.

Bassili, J. (1978). Facial motion in the perception of faces and of emotional expression. *Journal of Experimental Psychology, 4*, 373–379.

Bates, B. (2001). *Game design: The art and business of creating games*. Roseville, CA: Prima Tech.

Bates, M. (1979). Information search tactics. *Journal of the American Society for Information Science, 30*(4), 205–214.

Bates, M. J. (1998). Indexing and access for digital libraries and the Internet: Human, database, and domain factors. *Journal of the American Society for Information Science, 49*(13), 1185–1205.

Batteau, A. (2000). Negations and ambiguities in the cultures of organization. *American Anthropologist, 102*(4), 726–740.

Batteau, A. (2001). A report from the Internet2 'Sociotechnical Summit.' *Social Science Computing Review, 19*(1), 100–105.

BIBLIOGRAPHY

Baudisch, P., DeCarlo, D., Duchowski, A. T., & Geisler, W. S. (2003, March). Focusing on the essential: Considering attention in display design. *Communications of the ACM, 46*(3), 60–66.

Bauer, A. (2003). *Compilation of functional programming languages using GCC—Tail Calls.* Retrieved January 20, 2004, from http://home.in.tum.de/~baueran/thesis/baueran_thesis.pdf

Baum, L. F. (1900). *The wonderful wizard of Oz.* Chicago: G. M. Hill.

Baum, L. F. (1904). *The marvelous ozama of Oz.* Chicago: Reilly and Britton.

Baxter, W., Sheib, V., Lin, M., & Manocha, D. (2001). DAB: Interactive haptic painting with 3D virtual brushes. *Proceedings of ACM SIGGRAPH,* 461–468.

Bayley, A. (2000). *KDE user interface guidelines.* Retrieved January 11, 2004, from http://developer.kde.org/documentation/design/ui/index.html

Bayliss, J. D., & Ballard, D. H. (2000). Recognizing evoked potentials in a virtual environment. *Advances in Neural Information Processing Systems, 12,* 3–9.

Baym, N. K. (2000). *Tune in, log on: Soaps, fandom, and online community.* Thousand Oaks, CA: Sage.

BBC News. (2002, March 10). *Digital divisions split town and country.* Retrieved July 18, 2003, from http://news.bbc.co.uk/2/hi/science/nature/1849343.stm

Beall, A. C., Bailenson, J. N., Loomis, J., Blascovich, J., & Rex, C. (2003). Non-zero-sum mutual gaze in immersive virtual environments. In *Proceedings of HCI International 2003* (pp. 1108–1112). New York: ACM Press.

Bear, G. (2002). *Blood music.* New York: ibooks.

Beaudouin-Lafon, M. (Ed). (1999). *Computer supported co-operative work.* Chichester, UK: John Wiley & Sons.

Becker, F. D., & Steele, F. (1995). *Workplace by design: Mapping the high-performance workscape.* San Francisco: Jossey-Bass.

Becker, R. A., & Chambers, J. M. (1984). *S: an interactive environment for data analysis and graphics.* Belmont, CA: Wadsworth Advanced Book Program.

Becker, T., & Slaton, C. (2000). *The future of teledemocracy.* Westport, CN: Praeger.

Beckwith, L., Burnett, M., & Cook, C. (2002). Reasoning about many-to-many requirement relationships in spreadsheets. In *IEEE Conference on Human-Centric Computing Languages and Environments,* 149–157.

Begin, T. J., & Gibson, R. G. (1996). *History of programming languages.* Boston: Addison-Wesley.

Behaviour & Information Technology, 13(1–2). (January–April 1994). [Special issue devoted to usability laboratories]

Beisse, F. (2001). *A guide to computer user support for help desk & support specialists* (2nd ed.). Cambridge, MA: Course Technology.

Belkin, N. (2000). Helping people find what they don't know. *Communications of the ACM, 43*(8), 58–61.

Belkin, N., & Croft, B. (1992). Information filtering and information retrieval: Two sides of the same coin? *Communications of the ACM, 35*(12), 29–38.

Belkin, N., Cool, C., Stein, A., & Thiel, U. (1995). Cases, scripts, and information-seeking strategies: On the design of interactive information retrieval systems. *Expert Systems with Applications, 9*(3), 379–395.

Bell, D. (1973). *The coming of post-industrial society: A venture in social forecasting.* New York: Basic Books.

Bell, D., & LaPadula, L. (1975). *Secure computer systems: Unified exposition and multics interpretation* (Tech. Rep. No. ESD-TR-75-306). Bedford, MA: Hanscom Air Force Base.

Bell, G., & Gray, J. (2001). Digital immortality. *Communications of the ACM, 44*(3), 29–30.

Bellotti, V. (1997). Design for privacy in multimedia computing and communication environments. In P. E. Agre & M. Rotenberg (Eds.), *Technology and privacy, the new landscape* (pp. 63–98). Cambridge, MA: MIT Press.

Bellovin, S. M., & Merritt, M. (1991). *AT&T Bell Labs limitations of the Kerberos authentication system.* Retrieved February 17, 2004, from http://swig.stanford.edu/pub/summaries/glomop/kerb_limit.html

Belson, K., & Richtel, M. (2003, May 5). America's broadband dream is alive in Korea. *The New York Times,* p. C1.

Ben-Arie, J., Wang, Z., Pandit, P., & Rajaram, S. (2002). Human activity recognition using multidimensional indexing. *IEEE Transactions on Pattern Analysis and Machine Intelligence, 24*(8), 1091–1104.

Benedikt, M. (Ed.). (1992). *Cyberspace: First steps.* Cambridge, MA: MIT Press.

Benford, S., Brown, C., et al. (1996). Shared spaces: Transportation, artificiality, and spatiality. In *Proceedings of the ACM Conference on Computer Supported Cooperative Work.* New York.

Beniger, J. R. (1986). *The control revolution: Technology and the economic origins of the information society.* Cambridge, MA: Harvard University Press.

Benitez, A. B., Begi, M., & Chang, S. F. (1999). Using relevance feedback in content-based image metadata search. *IEEE Internet Computing,* 59–69.

Bennett, K. B., Toms, M. L., & Woods, D. D. (1993). Emergent features and configural elements: Designing more effective configural displays. *Human Computer Interaction, 35,* 71–97.

Benoit, C., Martin, J. C., Pelachaud, C., Schomaker, L., & Suhm, B. (1998). Audio-visual and multimodal speech systems. In D. Gibbon, R. Moore & R. Winski (Eds), *Handbook of Standards and Resources for Spoken Language Systems* (Supplement Vol.). Berlin, Germany: Mouton de Gruyter.

Bentham, J. (1986). *Doctor Who: The early years.* London: W. H. Allen.

Benzécri, J.-P. (1992). *Correspondence analysis handbook.* Basel, Switzerland: Marcel Dekker.

Benzeev, T. (1995). The nature and origin of rational errors in arithmetic thinking: Induction from examples and prior knowledge. *Cognitive Science, 19*(3), 341–376.

Bergman, M., & Paavola, S. (2001). *The Commens dictionary of Peirce's terms.* Retrieved December 19, 2003, from http://www.helsinki.fi/science/commens/terms/icon.html

Bergquist, M., & Ljungberg, J. (2001). The power of gifts: Organizing social relationships in open source communities. *Information Systems Journal, 11*(4), 305–320.

Bergqvist, U., Wolgast, E., Nilsson, B., & Voss, M. (1995). The influence of VDT work on musculoskeletal disorders. *Ergonomics, 38*(4), 754–762.

Beringer, D. B., & Scott, J. (1985). The long-range light pen as a head-based user-computer interface: Head-mounted 'sights' versus head positioning for computer access by the disabled, progress for people. *Proceedings of the Human Factors Society 29th Annual Meeting,* Baltimore, MD.

Berkelman, P. J., & Hollis, R. L. (2000, July). Lorentz magnetic levitation for haptic interaction: Device design, performance, and in-

BIBLIOGRAPHY

tegration with physical simulations. *International Journal of Robotics Research, 19*(7), 644–667.

Berman, F., Fox, G., & Hey, T. (2002). *Grid computing—Making the global infrastructure a reality.* Indianapolis, IN: Wiley.

Bernard, M. (2002). Examining the effects of hypertext shape on user performance. *Usability News, 4*(2). Retrieved December 18, 2003, from http://psychology.wichita.edu/surl/usabiliynews/42/onlinetext.htm

Bernard, M., Lida, B., Riley, S., Hackler, T., & Janzen, K. (2002). A comparison of popular online fonts: Which size and type is best? *Usability News, 4*(1). Retrieved December 18, 2003, from http://psychology.wichita.edu/surl/usabilitynews/41/onlinetext.htm

Berners-Lee, T. (1991). World Wide Web seminar. Retrieved August 7, 2003, from http://www.w3.org/Talks/General.html

Berners-Lee, T., & Fischetti, M. (1999). *Weaving the Web.* New York: HarperCollins.

Berners-Lee, T., Hendler, J., Lassila, O. (2001). The semantic web. *Scientific American, 284*(5), 34–43, Retrieved January 22, 2004, from http://www.sciam.com

Bernsen, N. O., Dybkjaer, H., & Dybkjaer, L. (1998). *Designing interactive speech systems: From first ideas to user testing.* New York: Springer Verlag.

Bernstein, M. (1991). Deeply intertwingled hypertext: The navigation problem reconsidered. *Technical Communication, 38* (1), 41–47.

Berry, D. C. (1993). Slips and errors in learning complex tasks. In G. M. Davies & L. R. H. (Eds.), *Memory in everyday life. Advances in psychology* (pp. 137–159). Amsterdam: North-Holland/Elsevier.

Berry, R. L., & Yager, S. E. (1999). Preparing IS professionals to support end users: The development of an end user support course. In *Proceedings of the Decision Sciences Institute Conference1999* (pp. 305–307). Atlanta, GA: Decision Sciences Institute.

Berry, W. T., & Poole H. E. (1966). Annals of printing. London: Blandford Press.

Berson, A. (1992). *Client/server architecture.* New York: McGraw-Hill.

Berson, A. (1995). *Sybase and client/server computing.* New York: McGraw-Hill.

Berthoz, A. (2000). *The brain's sense of movement.* Cambridge, MA: Harvard University Press.

Bertin, I. (1998*). The teleworking handbook.* Kenilworth, UK: The Telecottage Association.

Bester, A. (1974). *The computer connection.* New York: ibooks.

Bester, A. (1997). *Virtual unrealities: The short fiction of Alfred Bester.* New York: Vintage.

Betts, M. (1994, April 18). Computer matching nabs double dippers. *Computerworld,* 90.

Bevan, P. (2002). *The circadian geography of chat.* Paper presented at the conference of the Association of Internet Researchers, Maastricht, Netherlands.

Beyer, H., & Holtzblatt, K. (1997). *Contextual design: A customer-centered approach to systems designs.* San Francisco: Morgan Kaufmann Publishers.

Bhavnani, S. K. (2002). Domain-specific search strategies for the effective retrieval of healthcare and shopping information. In *Proceedings of CHI'02* (pp. 610–611). New York: ACM Press.

Bhavnani, S. K. (in press). The distribution of online healthcare information: A case study on melanoma. *Proceedings of AMIA '03.*

Bhavnani, S. K., & John, B. E. (2000). The strategic use of complex computer systems. *Human-Computer Interaction, 15*(2–3), 107–137.

Bhavnani, S. K., Bichakjian, C. K., Johnson, T. M., Little, R. J., Peck, F. A., Schwartz, J. L., et al. (2003). Strategy hubs: Next-generation

domain portals with search procedures. In *Proceedings of CHI'03* (pp. 393–400). New York: ACM Press.

Bhavnani, S. K., Reif, F., & John, B. E. (2001). Beyond command knowledge: Identifying and teaching strategic knowledge for using complex computer applications. In *Proceedings of CHI' 01* (pp. 229–236). New York: ACM Press.

Bianchi-Berthouze, N. (2002). Mining multimedia subjective feedback. *Journal of Intelligent Information Systems, 19*(1), 43–59.

Biber, D. (1988). *Variation across speech and writing.* Cambridge, UK: Cambridge University Press.

Bier, E. A., Stone, M. C., Pier, K., Buxton, W., & DeRose, T. D. (1993). Toolglass and magic lenses: the see-through interface. In *Proceedings of SIGGRAPH 93* (pp. 73–80).

Bigmore, E. C., & Wyman, C. W. H., (Eds.). (1978). *A bibliography of printing.* New Castle, DE: Oak Knoll Books.

Bijker, W. E., & Law, J. (Eds.). (1992). *Shaping technology/building society: Studies in sociotechnical change.* Cambridge, MA: MIT Press.

Bikson, T. K., & Eveland, J. D. (1996). Groupware implementation: Reinvention in the sociotechnical frame. In *Proceedings of the Conference on Computer Supported Cooperative Work: CSCW '96* (pp. 428–437). New York: ACM Press.

Bilal, D. (1998). Children's search processes in using World Wide Web search engines: An exploratory study. *Proceedings of the 61st ASIS Annual Meeting, 35,* 45–53.

Bilal, D. (1999). Web search engines for children: A comparative study and performance evaluation of Yahooligans!, Ask Jeeves for Kids, and Super Snooper. *Proceedings of the 62nd ASIS Annual Meeting, 36,* 70–82.

Bilal, D. (2000). Children's use of the Yahooligans! Web search engine, I: Cognitive, physical, and affective behaviors on fact-based tasks. *Journal of the American Society for Information Science, 51*(7), 646–665.

Bilal, D. (2001). Children's use of the Yahooligans! Web search engine, II: Cognitive and physical behaviors on research tasks. *Journal of the American Society for Information Science and Technology, 52*(2), 118–137.

Bilal, D. (2002). Children's use of the Yahooligans! Web search engine, III: Cognitive and physical behaviors on fully self-generated tasks. *Journal of the American Society for Information Science and Technology, 53*(13), 1170–1183.

Bilal, D. (2003). Draw and tell: Children as designers of Web interfaces. *Proceedings of the 66th ASIST Annual Meeting, 40, 135–141.*

Bilal, D. (In press). Research on children's use of the Web. In C. Cole & M. Chelton (Eds.), *Youth Information Seeking*: Theories, Models, and Approaches. Lanham, MD: Scarecrow Press.

Biles, J. A. (1994). GenJam: A genetic algorithm for generating jazz solos. In *Proceedings of the 1994 International Computer Music Conference* (pp. 207–210). San Francisco, CA: International Computer Music Association.

Billings, C. E. (1997). *Issues concerning human-centered intelligent systems: What's "human-centered" and what's the problem?* Retrieved July 21, 2003, from http://www.ifp.uiuc.edu/nsfhcs/talks/billings.html

Billings, D. E. (1997). *Aviation automation: The search for a human-centered approach.* Mahwah, NJ: Lawrence Erlbaum Associates.

Bimber, B. (2003). *Information and American democracy: Technology in the evolution of political power.* New York, NY: Cambridge University Press.

Bin, Q., Chen, S., & Sun, S. (2003). Cultural differences in e-commerce: A comparison between the U.S. and China. *Journal of Global Information Management, 11*(2), 48–56.

Binder, E. (1965). *Adam Link—Robot.* New York: Paperback Library.

Binmore, K. (1997). *Fun and games: A text on game theory.* Lexington, MA: D. C. Heath.

Birbaumer, N., Kubler, A., Ghanayim, N., Hinterberger, T., Perelmouter, J. Kaiser, J., et al. (2000). The thought translation device (TTD) for completely paralyzed patients. *IEEE Transactions on Rehabilitation Engineering, 8*(2), 190–193.

Birch, G. E., & Mason, S. G. (2000). Brain-computer interface research at the Neil Squire Foundation. *IEEE Transactions on Rehabilitation Engineering, 8*(2), 193–195.

Bird, R., & Wadler, P. (1988). *Introduction to functional programming.* Upper Saddle River, NJ: Prentice Hall International.

Birnholtz, J., & Bietz, M. (2003). Data at work: Supporting sharing in science and engineering. In *Proceedings of Group 2003.* New York: ACM Press.

Bisantz, A. M., Roth, E. M., Brickman, B., Lin, L., Hettinger, L., & McKinney, J. (2003). Integrating cognitive analysis in a large scale system design process. *International Journal of Human-Computer Studies, 58,* 177–206.

Bishop, A. P., & Star, S. L. (1996). Social informatics of digital library use and infrastructure. In M. Williams (Ed.), *Annual Review of Information Science and Technology 39* (pp. 301–402). Medford, NJ: Learned Information.

Bistarelli, S., Montanari, U., & Rossi, F. (1997). Semiring-based constraint satisfaction and optimization. *Journal of the ACM, 44*(2), 201–236.

Bjerknes, G., & Bratteteig, T. (1995). User participation and democracy: A discussion of Scandinavian research on system development. *Scandinavian Journal of Information Systems, 7*(1), 73–98.

Bjerknes, G., Ehn, P., & Kyng, M. (Eds.). (1987). *Computers and democracy: A Scandinavian challenge.* Aldershot, UK: Avebury.

Black, M. J., & Yacoob, Y. (1997). Recognizing facial expressions in image sequences using local parameterized models of image motion. *International Journal of Computer Vision, 25*(1), 23–48.

Blackburg Electronic Village. (n.d.) *About BEV.* Retrieved August 12, 2003, from http://www.bev.net/about/index.php

Blackmon, M. H., Kitajima, M., & Polson, P. G. (2003). Repairing usability problems identified by the cognitive walkthrough for the web. In *CHI 2003: Proceedings of the Conference on Human Factors in Computing Systems,* 497–504.

Blackmon, M. H., Polson, P. G., Kitajima, M., & Lewis, C. (2002). Cognitive walkthrough for the Web. In *CHI 2002: Proceedings of the Conference on Human Factors in Computing Systems,* 463–470.

Blackwell, A. F. (2002). First steps in programming: A rationale for attention investment models. In *IEEE Conference on Human-Centric Computing Languages and Environments,* 2–10.

Blair, D. C. (1990). *Language and representation in information retrieval.* Amsterdam: Elsevier Science.

Blair, K., & Takayoshi, P. (Eds.). (1999). *Feminist cyberspace: Mapping gendered academic spaces.* Stamford, CT: Albed.

Blank, J. (2001). *Mullahs on the mainframe: Islam and modernity among the Daudi Borhas.* Chicago: University of Chicago Press.

Blascovich, J. (2001). Social influences within immersive virtual environments. In R. Schroeder (Ed.), *The social life of avatars.* Berlin, Germany: Springer-Verlag.

Blascovich, J., Loomis, J., Beall, A. C., Swinth, K. R., Hoyt, C. L., & Bailenson, J. N. (2001). Immersive virtual environment technol-ogy as a methodological tool for social psychology. *Psychological Inquiry, 13,* 146–149.

Blattner, M. M., & Dannenberg, R. B. (Eds.). (1992). *Multimedia Interface design.* Reading, MA: ACM Press/Addison-Wesley.

Blindness Resource Center. (2002). *Braille on the Internet.* Retrieved May 10, 2004, from http://www.nyise.org/braille.htm

Blomberg, J. (1998). *Knowledge discourses and document practices: Negotiating meaning in organizational settings.* Paper presented at the annual meeting of the American Anthropological Association, Philadelphia, PA.

Blythe, J. (1999). Decision-theoretic planning. *AI Magazine, 20*(2), 37–54.

Boar, B. H. (1984). *Application prototyping: A requirements definition strategy for the 80s.* New York: John Wiley & Sons.

Bobick, A. F., & Davis, J. W. (1996, August). *An appearance-based representation of action.* Paper presented at the Thirteenth International Conference on Pattern Recognition, Vienna, Austria. Retrieved August 19, 2003, from http://www.cis.ohio-state.edu/~jwdavis/Publications/TR-369.pdf

Bobick, A. F., & Davis, J. W. (2001, March). The recognition of human movement using temporal templates. *IEEE Transactions on Pattern Analysis and Machine Intelligence, 23*(3), 257–267.

Bobick, A., Intille, S., Davis, J., Baird, F., Pinhanez, C., Campbell, L., et al. (2000). The KidsRoom: A perceptually-based interactive and immersive story environment. *Presence, 8*(4), 369–393.

Bobrow, D. G. (1965). *Natural language input for a computer problem solving system* (Doctoral dissertation, MIT, 1965), source number ADD X1965.

Bødker, S. (1991). *Through the interface: A human activity approach to user interface design.* Hillsdale, NJ: Lawrence Erlbaum Associates.

Bødker, S., Ehn, P., Sjögren, D., & Sundblad, Y. (2000). *Co-operative design: Perspectives on 20 years with "the Scandinavian IT design mode"* (Report No. CID-104). Retrieved June 16, 2003, from http://cid.nada.kth.se/pdf/cid_104.pdf

Bødker,, S., Gronbaek, K., & Kyng, M. (1993) Cooperative design: Techniques and experiences from the Scandinavian scene. In D. Schuler and A. Noamioka (Eds.), *Participatory design: Principles and practices* (pp. 157–176). Hillsdale, NJ: Lawrence Erlbaum Associates.

Boehm, B. W. (1988). A spiral model of software development and enhancement. *Computer, 21*(5), 61–72.

Boehm, B., Gray, T., & Seewaldt, T. (1984). Prototyping versus specifying: A Multiproject experiment. *IEEE Transactions on Software Engineering* SE-10(3), 290–302.

Boersma, P., & Weenicnk, D. (n.d.). *Praat: Doing phonetics by computer.* Retrieved August 15, 2003, from http://www.fon.hum.uva.nl/praat

Boff, K. R., Kaufman, L., & Thomas, J. P. (Eds.). (1986). *Sensory processes and perception,* 1. New York: John Wiley and Sons.

Boguraev, B., & Pustejovsky, J. (Eds.). (1996). *Corpus processing for lexical acquisition.* Cambridge, MA: MIT Press.

Boiko, B. (2002). *Content management bible.* New York: Hungry Minds. Retrieved January 22, 2004, from http://metatorial.com/index.asp

Bolanowski, S. J., Gescheider, G. A., Verillo, R. T., & Checkosky, C. M. (1988). Four channels mediate the mechanical aspects of touch. *Journal of the Acoustical Society of America, 84*(5), 1680–1694.

Bollinger, T. (1999). Linux and open-source success: Interview with Eric. S. Raymond. *IEEE Computer,* 85–89.

Bolt, R. A. (1980). Put-that-there: Voice and gesture at the graphic interface. *Computer Graphics, 14*(3), 262–270.

BIBLIOGRAPHY

Bolt, R. A. (1985). Conversing with computers. *Technology Review, 88*(2), 34–43.

Bolter, J. D. (1991). *Writing space: The computer, hypertext, and the history of writing.* Hillsdale, NJ: Lawrence Erlbaum Associates.

Booch, G., Rumbaugh, J., & Jacobson, I. (1999). *The unified modeling language user guide.* Reading, MA: Addison-Wesley.

Bordia, P. (1997). Face-to-face versus computer-mediated communication. *Journal of Business Communication, 34,* 99–120.

Borgman, C. L. (2000). *From Gutenberg to the Global Information Infrastructure: Access to information in the networked world.* Cambridge, MA: MIT Press.

Borgman, C. L., Bates, M. J., Cloonan, M. V., Efthimiadis, E. N., Gilliland-Swetland, A., Kafai, Y., Leazer, G. H., & Maddox, A. B. (1996). *Social aspects of digital libraries: Final report to the National Science Foundation.* Los Angeles: Graduate School of Library & Information Studies, UCLA. Retrieved January 26, 2004, from http://dlis.gseis.ucla.edu/DL/UCLA_DL_Report.html

Borning, A., & Duisberg, R. (1986). Constraint-based tools for building user interfaces. *ACM Transactions on Graphics, 5*(4), 345–374.

Borofsky, R. (1994). Introduction. In R. Borofsky (Ed.), *Assessing cultural anthropology.* New York: McGraw-Hill.

Bosnjak, M., & Tuten, T. (2001). Classifying response behaviors in Web-based surveys. *Journal of Computer Mediated Communication, 6*(3). Retrieved May 11, 2004, from http://www.ascusc.org/jcmc/vol6/issue3/boznjak.html

Boulanger, R., Thompson, G., & Saleh, J. (2003). Shedding some light on "dark matter." In *Proceedings of the Ninth Biennial Symposium on Arts and Technology* (pp. 12–16). New London, CT: Connecticut College.

Bouthemy, P., Gelgon, M., & Ganansia, F. (1999). A unified approach to shot change detection and camera motion characterization. *IEEE Transactions on Circuits and Systems for Video Technology, 9,* 1030–1044.

Boutilier, C., Dean, T., & Hanks, S. (1999). Decision-theoretic planning: Structural assumptions and computational leverage. *Journal of Artificial Intelligence Research, 11,* 1–94.

Bowen, J. E. (1994). An expert system for police investigations of economic crimes. *Expert Systems with Applications, 7*(2), 235–248.

Bowker, G. C., Star, S. L., Turner, W., & Gasser, L. (1997). *Social science, technical systems, and cooperative work: Beyond the great divide.* Mahwah, NJ: Erlbaum.

Bowman, B., Grupe, F. H., Lund, D., & Moore, W. D. (1993). An examination of sources of support preferred by end user computing personnel. *Journal of End User Computing, 5*(4), 4–11.

Bowman, D., & Hodges, L. (1997). An evaluation of techniques for grabbing and manipulating remote objects in immersive virtual environments. *1997 ACM Symposium on Interactive 3-D Graphics,* 35–38.

Boyle, C., & Encarnacion, A. O. (1994). MetaDoc: An adaptive hypertext reading system. *User Modeling and User-Adapted Interaction, 4*(1), 1–19.

Bradner, E., Kellogg, W. A., & Erickson, T. (1999). The adoption and use of Babble: A field study of chat in the workplace. In S. Bodker, M. Kyng, & K. Schmidt (Eds.), *ECSCW 99: Proceedings of the Sixth European Conference on Computer Supported Cooperative Work* (pp. 139–158). Dordrecht, The Netherlands: Kluwer.

Bradshaw, S. (2003). Reference directed indexing: Redeeming relevance for subject search in citation indexes. *Proceedings of the 7th European Conference on Research and Advanced Technology for Digital Libraries,* 499–510.

Brahan, J. W., Lam, K. P., & Chan, H. L. W. (1998). AICAMS: Artificial Intelligence Crime Analysis and *Management System. Knowledge-Based Systems, 11, 335–361.*

Brain, M., & Tyson, J. (1998–2003). *How cell phones work.* Retrieved July 28, 2003, from http://electronics.howstuffworks.com/cell-phone.htm

Braman, S. (2004). *Change of state: An introduction to information policy.* Cambridge, MA: MIT Press.

Bransford, J. D., Brown, A. L., & Cocking, R. R. (Eds.). (2000). *How people learn: Brain, mind, experience, and school* (Exp. ed.). Washington, DC: National Academy Press.

Braverman, H. (1974). *Labor and monopoly capital: The degradation of work in the twentieth century.* New York: Monthly Review Press.

Brawley, M. R. (2003). *The politics of globalization.* Toronto, Canada: Broadview Press.

Breazeal, C. (2002) Designing sociable robots. Cambridge, MA: MIT Press.

Bregman, A. S. (1993). Auditory scene analysis: Hearing in complex environments. In S. McAdams & E. Bigand (Eds.), *Thinking in sound: The cognitive psychology of human audition* (pp. 10–34). Oxford, UK: Oxford University Press.

Brennen, V. A. *A basic introduction to Kerberos.* Retrieved February 17, 2004, from http://www.cryptnet.net/fdp/crypto/basic_intros/kerberos/

Brewer, G., & de Leon, P. (1983). *The foundations of policy analysis.* Chicago: Dorsey Press.

Brey, P. (1997). Philosophy of technology meets social constructivism. *Techne: Journal of the Society for Philosophy and Technology, 2*(3–4). Retrieved March 24, 2004, from http://scholar.lib.vt.edu/ejournals/SPT/v2n3n4/brey.html

A Brief History of FORTRAN /fortran. (1998). Retrieved January 20, 2004, from http://www.ibiblio.org/pub/languages/FORTRAN /ch1-1.html

Briere, D., & Traverse, P. (1993). AIRBUS A320/A330/A340 electrical flight controls: A family of fault-tolerant systems. *Proceedings of the Fault-Tolerant Computing Symposium (FTCS-23)* (pp. 616–623). Cupertino, CA: IEEE CS Press.

Brin, S., & Page, L. (1998). The anatomy of a large-scale hypertextual web search engine. 7th International World Wide Web Conference (WWW7). *Computer Networks and ISDN Systems, 30*(XXX). Retrieved January 22, 2004, from www-db.stanford.edu/~backrub/google.html, www7.scu.edu.au/programme/fullpapers/1921/com1921.htm, decweb.ethz.ch/WWW7/00/

Bringhurst, R. (1992). *The elements of typographic style.* Vancouver, Canada: Hartley and Maerks.

Briscoe, T., & Carroll, J. (1997). Automatic extraction of subcategorization from corpora. *Proceedings of the 5th Conference on Applied Natural Language Processing ANLP-97.* Retrieved February 9, 2002, from http://acl.ldc.upenn.edu//A/A97/A97-1052.pdf

Brockmann, R. J. (1998). *From millwrights to shipwrights to the twenty-first century: Explorations in the history of technical communication in the United States.* Creskill, NJ: Hampton Press.

Brooke-Wavell, K., Jones, P. R. M., & West, G. M. (1994). Reliability and repeatability of 3-D body scanner (LASS) measurements compared to anthropometry. *Annals of Human Biology, 21,* 571–577.

Brooks, E. (1989). *The attack of the killer micros.* Presentation at the Teraflop Computing Panel, Supercomputing '89, Reno, Nevada.

BIBLIOGRAPHY

Brooks, Jr., F., Ouh-Young, M., Batter, J. J., & Kilpatrick, P. (1990). Project GROPE: Haptic displays for scientific visualization. *Computer Graphics, 24*(4), 177–185.

Brosnan, M. J. (1998). *Technophobia: The psychological impact of information technology.* London: Routledge.

Brosnan, M. J., & Lee, W. (1998). A cross-cultural comparison of gender differences in computer attitudes and anxiety: The U.K. and Hong Kong. *Computers in Human Behavior, 14*(4), 359–377.

Brown R. (1967). Review of research and consultancy in industrial enterprises: A review of the contribution of the Tavistock Institute of Human Relations to the development of industrial sociology. *Sociology, 1,* 33–60.

Brown, J. S., & Duguid, P. (2000). *The social life of information.* Boston: Harvard Business School Press.

Brown, P., et al. (1990). A statistical approach to machine translation. *Computational Linguistics, 16*(2), 79–85.

Brown, R. D. (1996). Example-based machine translation in the Pangloss system. *Proceedings of the 6th International Conference on Computational Linguistics (COLING-96)* (pp. 169–174).

Browne, D. (1993). Experiences from the AID Project. In M. Schneider-Hufschmidt, T. Kühme, & U. Malinowski (Eds.), *Adaptive user interfaces: Principles and practice* (pp. 69–78). Amsterdam, Netherlands: Elsevier.

Browne, S., Dongarra, J., Garner, N, Ho, G., & Mucci, P. (2000). A portable programming interface for performance evaluation on modern processors. *International Journal of High Performance Computing Applications, 14*(3), 189–204.

Bruce, K. B. (2002). *Foundations of object-oriented languages.* Cambridge, MA: MIT Press.

Bruce, V., & Burton, M. (1992) *Processing images of faces.* Norwood, NJ: Ablex Publishing.

Brunelli, R., Mich, O., & Modena, C. M. (1999). A survey on the automatic indexing of video data. *The Journal of Visual Communication and Image Representation, 10,* 78–112.

Brunner, J. (1975). *Shockwaver rider.* New York: Ballantine Books.

Brusilovsky, P., Kobsa, A., & Vassileva, J. (Eds.). (1998). *Adaptive hypertext and hypermedia.* Dordrecht, Netherlands: Kluwer.

Brynjolfsson, E. (2003). The IT productivity gap. *Optimize, 7*(21). Retrieved December 16, 2003, from http://ebusiness.mit.edu/erik/Optimize/pr_roi.html

BSR/HFES 100. (2002). *Human factors engineering of computer workstations.* Santa Monica, CA: Human Factors and Ergonomics Society.

Buck, L. B., & Axel, R. (1991). A novel multigene family may encode odorant receptors: A molecular basis for odor recognition. *Cell, 65,* 175–187.

Budde, R., Kautz, K., Kuhlenkamp, K., & Züllighoven, H. (1992). What is prototyping? *Information Technology & People, 6*(2–3, 89–95).

Budde, R., Kuhlenkamp, K., Mathiassen, L., & Züllighoven, H. (Eds.). (1984). *Approaches to prototyping.* Berlin, Germany: Springer-Verlag.

Budge, I. (1996). *The new challenge of direct democracy.* Cambridge, UK: Polity.

Burdea, G. C. (1996). *Force and touch feedback for virtual reality.* New York: John Wiley and Sons.

Bureau of Labor Statistics (BLS). (2001). *Reports on survey of occupational injuries and illnesses in 1977–2000.* Washington. DC: Bureau of Labor Statistics, U.S. Department of Labor.

Burks, A. R. (2003). *Who invented the computer? The legal battle that changed computing history.* Amherst, NY: Prometheus Books.

Burks, A. R., & Burks, A. W. (1989). *The first electronic computer: The Atanasoff story.* Ann Arbor: University of Michigan Press.

Burl, M. C., Doleman, B. J., Schaffer, A., & Lewis, N. S. (2001). Assessing the ability to predict human percepts of odor quality from the detector responses of a conducting polymer composite-based electronic nose. *Sensors and Actuators B: Chemical 72*(2), 149–159.

Burnett, M. M. (1999). Visual programming. In J. G. Webster (Ed.), Encyclopedia of electrical and electronics engineering. New York: Wiley. Burnett, M. M., Atwood, J., Djang, R., Gottfried, H., Reichwein, J., & Yang, S. (2001). Forms/3: A first-order visual language to explore the boundaries of the spreadsheet paradigm. Journal of Functional Programming, 11, 155–206.

Burnett, M. M., & Gottfried, H. (1998). Graphical definitions: Expanding spreadsheet languages through direct manipulation and gestures. *ACM Transactions on Computer-Human Interaction, 5*(1), 1–33.

Burnett, M. M., Cook, C., Pendse, O., Rothermel, G., Summet, J., & Wallace, C. (2003). End-user software engineering with assertions in the spreadsheet paradigm. In *International Conference on Software Engineering,* 93–103.

Burns, R. & Dennis, A. (1985). Selecting the appropriate application development methodology. *Data Base, 17*(1), 19–23.

Burton, O. V. (Ed.). (2002). *Computing in the social sciences and humanities.* Urbana: University of Illinois Press.

Busey, A. (1995). *Secrets of the MUD wizards: Playing and programming MUDs, MOOs, MUSHes, MUCKs and other Internet role-playing games.* Indianapolis, IN: Sams.net Publishing.

Bush, V. (1945) As We May Think. Atlantic Monthly, 76(1) 101–108. Retrieved March 25, 2004, from http://www.theatlantic.com/unbound/flashbks/computer/bushf.htm

Bush, V. (1945). As we may think. In J. Nyce & P. Kahn (Eds.), *From Memex to hypertext: Vannevar Bush and the mind's machine* (pp. 85–110). San Diego, CA: Academic Press.

Bush, V. (1996). As we may think. *Interactions, 3*(2), 35–46.

Buxton, W. (1986). There is more to interaction than meets the eye: Some issues in manual input. In D. A. Norman & S. W. Draper (Eds.), *User Centered System Design* (pp. 319–337): Lawrance Erlbaum Associates.

Buxton, W., Billinghurst , M., Guiard, Y., Sellen, A., & Zhai, S. (1994/2002). *Human Input to Computer Systems: Theories, Techniques and Technology (book manuscript).* Retrieved April 6, 2004, from http://www.billbuxton.com/inputManuscript.html.

Buyukkokten, O., Kaljuvee, O., Garcia-Molina, H., Paepcke, A., & Winograd, T. (2002). Efficient web browsing on handheld devices using page and form summarization. *ACM Transactions on Information Systems, 20*(1), 82–115.

Büyükkurt, M., & Vass, E. (1993). An investigation of factors contributing to satisfaction with end-user computing process. *Canadian Journal of Administrative Sciences, 10*(3), 212–229.

Buyya, R. (2002). *Economic based distributed resource management and scheduling for grid computing.* Retrieved February 2, 2004, from http://www.cs.mu.oz.au/~raj/

Buyya, R., Abramson, D., & Giddy, J. (2000a). An economy driven resource management architecture for global computational power grids. *Proceedings of the 2000 International Conference on Parallel and Distributed Processing Techniques and Applications (PDPTA 2000).* Las Vegas, NV: CSREA Press.

Buyya, R., Abramson, D., & Giddy, J. (2000b). Nimrod-G: An architecture for a resource management and scheduling system in a global computational grid. *The 4th International Conference on*

BIBLIOGRAPHY

High Performance Computing in Asia-Pacific Region (HPC Asia 2000). New York: IEEE Computer Society Press.

Bynum, T. (2000). Ethics and the information revolution. In G. Colllste (Ed.) *Ethics in the age of information technology* (pp. 32–55). Linköping Sweden: Linköping University Press.

Bynum, T. W. (2001). Computer ethics: Its birth and its future. *Ethics and Information Technology, 3*(2), 109–112.

Byrne, M. D. (2001). ACT-R/PM and menu selection: applying a cognitive architecture to HCI. *International Journal of Human-Computer Studies, 55*(1), 41–84.

Byrne, M. D., & Bovair, S. (1997). A working memory model of a common procedural error. *Cognitive Science, 21*(1), 31–61.

Byrne, M., John, B., Wehrle, N., & Crow, D. (1999). The tangled Web we wove: A taskonomy of WWW Use. In *Proceedings of CHI'99 Conference on Human Factors in Computing Systems* (pp. 544–551). New York: ACM Press.

Cabeza, R., & Nyberg, L. (2000). Imaging cognition II: An empirical review of 275 PET and fMRI studies. *Journal of Cognitive Neuroscience, 12*(1), 1–47.

Caidin, M. (1972). *Cyborg.* New York: Arbor House.

California Internet Voting Task Force. (2000). *A report on the feasibility of Internet voting.* Retrieved August 1, 2003, from http://www.ss.ca.gov/executive/ivote/final_report.htm

Callon, M. (1980). The state and technical innovation: A case study of the electrical vehicle in France. *Research Policy, 9,* 358–376.

Caltech/MIT Voting Technology Project. (2001). *Voting: What is, what could be.* Retrieved August 1, 2003, from http://www.vote.caltech.edu/Reports/

Camp, J. L. (2000). *Trust and risk in Internet commerce.* Cambridge, MA: MIT Press.

Camp, T. (1997). The incredible shrinking pipeline. *Communications of the ACM, 40*(2), 103–110.

Campbell, J. E. (2004). *Getting it on online: Cyberspace, gay male sexuality and embodied identity.* Binghamton, NY: The Haworth Press.

Campbell, M., Hoane, A. J., & Hsu, F. (2002). Deep Blue. *Artificial Intelligence, 134*(1-2), 57–83.

CAN-SPAM legislation. Retrieved March 31, 2004, from http://www.spamlaws.com/federal/108s877.html

Capek, K. (1990). *Toward the radical center: A Karel Capek reader.* New York: Catbird.

Caplin, S. (2001). *Icon design: Graphic icons in computer interface design.* New York: Watson-Guptill Publications.

Cappell, C. L., & Guterbock, T. M. (1992). Visible colleges: The social and conceptual structure of sociology specialties. *American Sociological Review, 57*(2), 266–273.

Capurro, R., & Hjorland, B. (2003). The concept of information. *Annual Review of Information Science and Technology, 37,* 343–411.

Carbonell, J., Mitamara, T., & Nyberg, E. H. (1992). The KANT perspective: a critique of pure transfer (and pure interlingua, pure statistics,…). In *Proceedings of the Fourth International Conference on Theoretical and Methodological Issues in Machine Translation— TMI-92* (pp. 225–235).

Card, S. K., & Moran, T. P. (1986). User technology: From pointing to pondering. *Proceedings of the Conference on History of Personal Workstations,* 183–198.

Card, S. K., English, W. K., & Burr, B. J. (1978). Evaluation of mouse, rate controlled isometric joystick, step keys and text keys for text selection on a CRT. *Ergonomics, 21,* 601–613.

Card, S. K., Mackinlay, J. D., & Robertson, G. G. (1991). A morphological analysis of the design space of input devices. *ACM Transactions on Information Systems, 9*(2), 99–122.

Card, S. K., Moran, T. P., & Newell, A. (1980). The keystroke-level model for user performance time with interactive systems. *Communications of the ACM, 23*(7), 396–410.

Card, S. K., Moran, T. P., & Newell, A. (1983). *The psychology of human computer interaction.* Hillsdale, NJ: Lawrence Erlbaum Associates.

Card, S., Mackinlay, J., & Shneiderman, B. (1999). *Readings in information visualization: Using vision to think.* San Francisco, CA: Morgan Kaufmann.

Cardigan, P. (Ed.). (2002). *The ultimate cyberpunk.* New York: ibooks.

Carley, K. (1991). A theory of group stability. *American Sociological Review, 56,* 331–354.

Carnegie Mellon University Pronunciation Dictionary. Retrieved August 15, 2003, from http://www.speech.cs.cmu.edu/cgi-bin/cmudict

Carnes, P. J. (1983). *Out of the shadows.* Minneapolis, MN: CompCare.

Carnes, P. J., Delmonico, D. L., Griffin, E., & Moriarty, J. (2001). *In the shadows of the Net: Breaking free of compulsive online behavior.* Center City, MN: Hazelden Educational Materials.

Carr, J. J., Brown, J. M. (1981). *Introduction to biomedical equipment technology.* New York: Wiley.

Carroll, J. M. (1990). *The Nurnberg funnel: Designing minimalist instruction for practical computer skills.* Cambridge: MIT Press.

Carroll, J. M. (Ed.). (1995). *Scenario-based design: Envisioning work and technology in system development.* New York: Wiley.

Carroll, J. M. (1997). Human-computer interaction: Psychology as a science of design. *International Journal of Human-Computer Studies, 46,* 501–522.

Carroll, J M. (Ed.). (1998). *Minimalism beyond the Nurnberg funnel.* Cambridge: MIT Press.

Carroll, J. M. (2000). *Making use: Scenario-based design of human-computer interactions.* Cambridge, MA: MIT Press.

Carroll, J. M. (Ed.). (2003). *HCI models, theories and frameworks.* San Francisco: Morgan Kaufmann.

Carroll, J. M., & Campbell, R. L. (1986). Softening up hard science: Response to Newell and Card. *Human-Computer Interaction, 2*(3), 227–249.

Carroll, J. M., & Rosson, M.B. (2001). Better home shopping or new democracy? Evaluating community network outcomes. In *Proceedings of Human Factors in Computing Systems: CHI 2001* (pp. 372–379). New York: ACM Press.

Carroll, J. M., Chin, G., Rosson, M .B., & Neale, D. C. (2000). The development of cooperation: Five years of participatory design in the virtual school. In *Designing interactive systems: DIS 2000* (pp. 239–251). New York: ACM Press.

Carroll, J. M., Rosson, M. B., Chin, G., & Koenemann, J. (1998). Requirements development in scenario-based design. *IEEE Transactions on Software Engineering, 24*(12), 1156–1170.

Carroll, J., & Rosson, M. B. (1989). The paradox of the active user. In J. Carroll (Ed.), *Interfacing thought: Cognitive aspects of human-computer interaction* (pp. 80–111). Cambridge, MA: MIT Press.

Carter, J., & Stephenson, M. (1999). *Initial flight test of the production support flight control computers at NASA Dryden Flight Research Center* (NASA Technical Memorandum TM-1999-206581). Washington, DC: NASA.

Carter, R., Day, B., & Meggs, P. (2002). *Typographic design: Form and communication.* Hoboken, NJ: John Wiley & Sons.

Carvin, A. (2000). Mind the gap: The digital divide as the civil rights issue of the new millenium. *Multimedia Schools, 7*(1), 56–58. Retrieved July 17, 2003, from http://www.infotoday.com/mm-schools/jan00/carvin.htm

Casacuberta, F., Vidal, E., & Vilar, J. M. (2002). Architectures for speech-to-speech translation using finite-state models. In *Proceedings of the ACL Workshop on Speech-to-Speech Translation, Algorithms and Systems* (pp. 39–44).

Casati, R. & Varzi. A. (1994). *Holes and Other Superficialities.* Cambridge, MA: MIT Press.

Cassell, J. (Ed.). (2000). *Embodied conversational agents.* Cambridge, MA: MIT Press.

Cassell, J., & Jenkins, H (Eds.). (1998). *From Barbie to Mortal Kombat: Gender and computer games.* Cambridge: MIT.

Cassell, J., & Vilhjálmsson, H. (1999). Fully embodied conversational avatars: Making communicative behaviors autonomous. *Autonomous Agents and Multi-Agent Systems, 2*(1), 45–64.

Cassell, J., Bickmore, T., Billinghurst, M., Campbell, L., Chang, K., Vilhjálmsson, H., et al. (1999). Embodiment in conversational interfaces: REA. In *Proceedings of the ACM Conference on Human Factors in Computing Systems (CHI)* (pp. 520–527). New York: ACM Press.

Cassell, J., Torres, O., & Prevost, S. (1999). Turn taking vs. discourse structure: How best to model multimodal conversation. In Y. Wilks (Ed.), *Machine conversations* (pp.143–154). The Hague, Netherlands: Kluwer.

Castelliano, J. (1992). *Handbook of display technology.* San Diego, CA: Academic Press.

Castells, M. (2000). *The rise of the network society* (2nd ed.). Oxford, UK: Blackwell.

Castells, M. (2001). *The Internet galaxy: Reflections on Internet, business, and society.* Oxford, UK: Oxford University Press.

Castells, M., Tubella, I., Sancho, T., & Wellman, B. (2003). *The network society in Catalonia: An empirical analysis.* Barcelona, Spain: Universitat Oberta Catalunya.

Cataldo, A., Liu, X., & Chen, Z. (2002). *Soft walls: Modifying flight control systems to limit the flight space of commercial aircraft.* Retrieved July 18, 2003, from http://buffy.eecs.berkeley.edu/ResearchSummary/03abstracts/acataldo.1.html

Catalog of free compilers and interpreters. (1998). Retrieved January 20, 2004, from http://www.idiom.com/free-compilers/

Cater, J. P. (1994). Approximating the senses. Smell/taste: Odors in virtual reality. In *Proceedings of the IEEE International Conference on Systems, Man and Cybernetics* (p. 1781). Washington, DC: IEEE Computer Society Press.

Catledge, L., & Pitkow, J. (1995). Characterizing browsing strategies in the World Wide Web. In *Computer systems and ISDN systems: Proceedings of the Third International World Wide Web Conference, 27*, 1065–1073.

Cattagni, A., & Farris, E. (2001). *Internet access in U.S. public schools and classrooms: 1994–2000* (NCES No. 2001-071). Retrieved July 18, 2003, from http://nces.ed.gov/pubsearch/pubsinfo.asp?pubid=2001071

Ceaparu, I. (2003). Finding governmental statistical data on the Web: A case study of FedStats. *IT & Society, 1*(3), 1–17. Retrieved February 17, 2004, from http://www.stanford.edu/group/siqss/itandsociety/v01i03/v01i03a01.pdf

Center for Robot-Assisted Search and Rescue. (n.d.). Retrieved July 21, 2003, from http://www.crasar.org/

Chadabe, J. (2003). *Electric sound: The past and promise of electronic music.* Upper Saddle River, NJ: Prentice Hall.

Chapin, J., & Nicolelis, M. (2002). Closed-loop brain-machine interfaces. In J. R. Wolpaw & T. Vaughan (Eds.), *Proceedings of Brain-Computer Interfaces for Communication and Control: Vol. 2. Moving Beyond Demonstration, Program and Abstracts* (p. 38). Rensselaerville, NY.

Chapman, N. P. (2003). Digital media tools. Chichester, UK; Hoboken, NJ: Wiley Ed.

Charles, J. (1998). Open source: Netscape pops the hood. *IEEE Software,* 79–82.

Charlton, S. G., & O'Brien, T. G. (2002). *Handbook of human factors testing and evaluation.* Mahwah, NJ: Erlbaum.

Charniak, E. (1994). *Statistical language learning.* Cambridge, MA: MIT Press.

Charpentier, F., & Moulines, E. (1989). Pitch-synchronous waveform processing techniques for text-to-speech synthesis using diphones. *Proceedings of Eurospeech 1989, 2*, 13–19.

Chastrette, M. (1997). Trends in structure-odor relationships. *SAR and QSAR in Environmental Research 6*, 215–254.

Chatty, S., & Lecoanet, P. (1996). Pen computing for air traffic control. CHI 96–common ground. In M. J. Tauber, V. Bellotti, R. Jeffries, J. D. Mackinlay, & J. Nielsen (Eds.), *Proceedings of the Conference on Human Factors in Computing Systems* (pp. 87–94). Reading, MA: Addison-Wesley.

Chaum, D., Fiat, A., & Naor, M. (1990). Untraceable electronic cash. In G. Blakley & D. Chaum (Eds.), Advances in cryptology (pp. 319–327). Heidelberg, Germany: Springer-Verlag.

Chen, W., & Wellman, B. (2004). "Charting Digital Divides: Within and Between Countries." In W. Dutton, B. Kahin, R. O'Callaghan, & A. Wyckoff (Eds.), *Transforming Enterprise.* Cambridge, MA: MIT Press.

Cherny, L. (1999). *Conversation and community: Chat in a virtual world.* Stanford, CA: CSLI Publications.

Cherry, C. (1957). *On human communication: A review, a survey, and a criticism.* Cambridge: MIT Press.

Cheswick, W., Bellovin, S., & Rubin, A. (2003). *Firewalls and Internet security: Repelling the wily hacker* (2nd ed.). Boston: Addison-Wesley.

Chetty, M., & Buyya, R. (2002). Weaving computational grids: How analogous are they with electrical grids? *Computing in Science and Engineering, 4*, 61–71.

Chi, E., Pirolli, P., & Pitkow, J. (2000). The scent of a site: A system for analyzing and predicting information scent, usage, and usability of a Web site. In *Proceedings of CHI'2000 Conference on Human Factors in Computing Systems* (pp.161–168). New York: ACM Press.

Children's Partnership. (2000). Online content for low-income and underserved Americans: The digital divide's new frontier. Retrieved July 17, 2003, from http://www.childrenspartnership.org/pub/low_income/

Choudhary, R., & Dewan, P. (1995). A general multi-user undo/redo model. In *Proceedings of European Conference on Computer Supported Work.* Dordrecht, Netherlands: Kluwer.

Chrisman, N. R. (1997). *Exploring geographic information systems.* New York: Wiley.

Chrissis, M. B., Konrad, M., & Shrum, S. (2003). *CMMI : Guidelines for process integration and product improvement.* New York: Addison-Wesley.

Christensen, K. (1988). *Women and home-based work: The unspoken contract.* New York: Holt.

Chu, H. (2003). *Information representation and retrieval in the digital age*. Medford, NJ: Information Today.

Chua, C. K., Leong, K. F., & Lim, C. S. (2003). *Rapid prototyping: Principles and applications*. River Edge, NJ: World Scientific.

Chung, G., & Dewan, P. (2001). Flexible support for application-sharing architecture. In *Proceedings of European Conference on Computer Supported Cooperative Work, Bonn*. Dordrecht, Netherlands: Kluwer.

Church, K. (1983). *Allophonic and phonotactic constraints are useful*. Paper presented at the International Joint Conference on Artificial Intelligence, Karlsruhe, West Germany.

Cinkosky, M. J., Fickett, J. W., Gilna, P., & Burks, C. (1991). Electronic data publishing and GenBank. *Science, 252*, 1273–1277.

Clancy, T., & Pieczenik, S. (1998). *Net force*. New York: Berkley.

Clark, H. H., & Brennan, S. E. (1991). Grounding in communication. In L. Resnick, J. M. Levine, & S. D. Teasley (Eds.), *Perspectives on socially shared cognition* (pp. 127–149). Washington, DC: American Psychological Association.

Clark, J., & Edwards, O. (1999). *Netscape time*. New York: St. Martin's Press.

Clark, R. E. (1983). Reconsidering research on learning from media. *Review of Educational Research, 53*(4), 445–459.

Clarke, A. C. (1953). *The city and the stars*. New York: Harcourt, Brace and Company.

Clarke, K. C. (1999). *Getting started with geographic information systems* (2nd ed.). Upper Saddle River, NJ: Prentice-Hall.

Clauser, C., Tebbetts, I., Bradtmiller, B., McConville, J., & Gordon, C. (1998). *Measurer's handbook: U.S. Army anthropometric survey* (Technical Report No. TR-88/043). Natick, MA: U.S. Army Natick Research, Development and Engineering Center.

Clement, A. (1996). Considering privacy in the development of multimedia communications. In R. Kling (Ed.), *Computerization and controversy* (pp. 848–869). San Diego: Academic Press.

Clements, P., Bachmann, F., Bass, L., Garlan, D., Ivers, J., Little, R., et al. (2002). *Documenting software architectures: Views and beyond*. New York: Addison-Wesley.

Clements, P., Kazman, R., & Klein, M. (2001). *Evaluating software architectures: methods and case studies*. New York: Addison-Wesley.

Clemmensen, T., & Norbjerg, J. (2004). Separation in theory—coordination in practice: Teaching HCI and SE. *Software Process Improvement and Practice, 8*(2).

Cleveland, W. S. (1993). *Visualizing data*. Summit, NJ: Hobart Press.

Cleveland, W. S. (1994). *The elements of graphing data*. Summit, NJ: Hobart Press.

Clifford, J., & Marcus, G. (Eds.). (1986). *Writing culture: The poetics and politics of ethnography*. Berkeley and Los Angeles: University of California Press.

Clodius W. (1997). *Re: History and evolution of compilers*. Retrieved January 20, 2004, from http://compilers.iecc.com/comparch/article/97-10-008

Clute, J., & Nicholls, P. (1995). *The encyclopedia of science fiction*. New York: St. Martin's Griffin.

Clynes, M., & Kline, N. (1960). Cyborgs and space. *Astronautics, 14*, 26–27.

CNNIC (China Internet Network Information Center). (2003, July). *12th statistical survey report on the Internet development in China*. Retrieved January 23, 2004, from http://www.cnnic.org.cn/download/manual/en-reports/12.pdf

Cockburn, A. (2001). *Agile software development*. Reading, MA: Addison-Wesley.

Cockburn, A., & Jones, S. (1996). Which way now? Analysing and easing inadequacies in WWW navigation. *International Journal of Human-Computer Studies, 45*(1), 105–129.

Cockburn, A., & McKenzie, B. (2001). What do Web users do? An empirical analysis of Web use. International Journal of Human-Computer Studies, 54(6), *903–922.*

Cockburn, A., Greenberg, S., McKenzie, B., Jason Smith, M., & Kaasten, S. (1999). WebView: A graphical aid for revisiting Web pages. In *Proceedings of the 1999 Computer Human Interaction Specialist Interest Group of the Ergonomics Society of Australia (OzCHI'91)* (pp. 15–22). Retrieved January 19, 2004, from http://www.cpsc.ucalgary.ca/Research/grouplab/papers/1999/99-WebView.Ozchi/Html/webview.html

Cockburn, A., McKenzie, B., & Jason Smith, M. (2002). Pushing Back: Evaluating a new behaviour for the Back and Forward buttons in Web browsers. *International Journal of Human-Computer Studies, 57*(5), 397–414.

CoCo, D. (1995). Real-time 3D games take off. *Computer Graphics World, 8*(12), 22–33.

Cohen, M. (2003). *The Sims superstar expansion pack*. Roseville, CA: Prima Games.

Cohen, P. R. (1995). *Empirical methods for artificial intelligence*. Cambridge, MA: MIT Press.

Cohen, P. R., & Levesque, H. J. (1991). Teamwork. *Nous, 35*.

Cohn, J., Zlochower, A., Lien, J., & Kanade, T. (1999). Automated face analysis by feature point tracking has high concurrent validity with manual faces coding. *Psychophysiology, 36*, 35–43.

Colby, K. M., Watt, J. B., & Gilbert, J. P. (1966). A computer method of psychotherapy: Preliminary communication. *The Journal of Nervous and Mental Disease, 142*(2), 148–152.

Cole, J. I., Suman, M., Schramm, P. Lunn, R., & Aquino, J. (2003). *Surveying the digital future—Year three*. Los Angele, CA: UCLA Center for Communication Policy. Retrieved December 18, 2003, from http://www.ccp.ucla.edu

Cole, M., & O'Keefe, R. M. (2000). Conceptualizing the dynamics of globalization and culture in electronic commerce. *Journal of Global Information Technology Management, 3*(1), 4–17.

Cole, R. E. (2002). From continuous improvement to continuous innovation. *Total Quality Management, 13*(8), 1051–1056.

Cole, R., Mariani, J., Uszkoriet, H., Zaenen, A., and Zue, V. (1997). *Survey of the state of the art in human language technology*. Cambridge, UK: Cambridge University Press.

Colin, B. J. (1992). *Regulating privacy: Data protection and public policy in Europe and the United States*. Ithaca, NY: Cornell University Press.

Coll, R., Zia, K., Coll, J. H. (1994). A comparison of three computer cursor control devices: Pen on horizontal tablet, mouse and keyboard. *Information & Management, 27*(6), 329–339.

Collaboratories. (2003). University of Michigan, School of Information. Retrieved February 28, 2004, 2004, from http://www.si.umich.edu/research/projects.htm

Collins, W. R., Miller, K., Spielman, B., & Wherry, P. (1994). How good is good enough? An ethical analysis of software construction and use. *Communications of the ACM, 37*(1), 81–91.

Colton, K. (1978). *Police computer systems*. Lexington, MA: Lexington Books.

Comer, D. (1994). *Internetworking with TCP/IP: Vol. 3. Client-server programming and applications*. Englewood Cliffs, NJ: Prentice Hall.

Comiskey, B., Albert, J. D., Yoshizawa, H., & Jacobson, J. (1998). An electrophoretic ink for all-printed reflective electronic displays. *Nature, 394*(6690), 253–255.

Compaine, B. (2001). *The digital divide: Facing a crisis or creating a myth.* Cambridge, MA: MIT Press.

Compiler Connection. (2003). Retrieved January 20, 2004, from http://www.compilerconnection.com/index.html

Compiler Internet Resource List. (n.d.). Retrieved January 20, 2004, from http://www.eg3.com/softd/compiler.htm

Computer Science and Telecommunications Board. (1999). *Trust in cyberspace.* Washington, DC: National Academy Press.

Conati, C., Gertner, A., & VanLehn, K. (2002). Using Bayesian networks to manage uncertainty in student modeling. *User Modeling and User-Adapted Interaction, 12*(4), 371–417.

Cone, C. (2001). Technically speaking: Girls and computers. In P. O'Reilly, E. M. Penn, & K. de Marrais (Eds.), *Educating young adolescent girls* (pp. 171–187). Mahwah, NJ: Lawrence Erlbaum Associates.

Conklin, J. (1988). Hypertext: An introduction and survey. In I. Greif (Ed.), *Computer supported cooperative work: A book of readings* (pp. 423–475). San Mateo, CA: Morgan-Kauffman.

Conklin, J., & Begeman, M. (1988). gIBIS: A hypertext tool for exploratory discussion. *ACM Transactions on Office Information Systems, 6*(4), 303–313.

Connell, B. R., et al. (1997). *The principles of universal design: Version 2.0.* Raleigh, NC: The Center for Universal Design.

Connell, J. L., & Schafer, L.B. (1989). *Structured rapid prototyping.* Englewood Cliffs, NJ: Yourdon Press.

Conrad, F. G. (n.d.). *Usability and voting technology: Bureau of Labor Statistics.* Retrieved February 17, 2004, from http://www.capc.umd.edu/rpts/MD_EVote_Conrad.pdf

Constantine, L., & Lockwood, L. (1999). *Software for use: A practical guide to the models and methods of usage-centred design.* New York: Addison-Wesley.

Constantine, L., & Lockwood, L. (2002). Usage-centered engineering for web applications. *IEEE Software, 19*(2).

Cooper, A. (Ed.). (2002). *Sex and the Internet: A guidebook for clinicians.* New York: Brunner-Routledge.

Cooper, A, Delmonico, D. & Burg, R. (2000). Cybersex users, abusers, and compulsives: New findings and implications. *Sexual Addiction & Compulsivity: Journal of Prevention and Treatment, 7,* 5–29.

Cooper, A., Scherer, C. R., Boies, S. C., & Gordon, B. L. (1999). Sexuality on the Internet: From sexual exploration to pathological expression. *Professional Psychology: Research and Practice, 30,* 154–164.:

Cooper, J., & Weaver, K. (2003). *Gender and computers: Understanding the digital divide.* Mahwah, NJ: Erlbaum.

Cooper, K. G. (2001). *Rapid prototyping technology: Selection and application.* New York: Marcel Dekker.

Cooper, K., & Torczon, L. (2003). *Engineering a Compiler.* Burlington, MA: Morgan Kaufmann.

Cooper, K., Kennedy, K., and Torczon, L. (2003). *COMP 412 Overview of the course.* Retrieved January 20, 2004, from http://www.owlnet.rice.edu/~comp412/Lectures/L01Intro.pdf

Cooper, R. B. (1994). The inertia impact of culture on IT implementation. *Information and Management, 17*(1), 17–31.

Corbett, A. T., & Trask, H. (2000). Instructional interventions in computer-based tutoring: Differential impact on learning time and accuracy. *Proceedings of ACM CHI' 2000 Conference on Human Factors in Computing Systems* (pp. 97–104).

Corbin, J. R. (1991). *The art of distributed applications: Programming techniques for remote procedure calls.* New York: Springer-Verlag.

Cornell University Common Front Group. (n.d.). *Concepts of user interface design.* Retrieved January 11, 2004, from http://cfg.cit.cornell.edu/cfg/design/concepts.html

Corra, W. T., Jensen, R. J., Thayer, C. E., and Finkelstein, A. (1998). Texture mapping for cel animation. In *Proceedings of SIGGRAPH' 98, Computer Graphics Proceedings, Annual Conference Series* (pp. 435–446).

Cortada, J. W. (1993a). *Before the computer: IBM, NCR, Burrough, and Remington Rand and the industry they created, 1865–1956.* Princeton, NJ: Princeton University Press.

Cortada, J. W. (1993b). *The computer in the United States: From laboratory to market, 1930 to 1960.* Armonk, NY: ME Sharpe.

Cortada, J. W. (1996). *A bibliographic guide to the history of computer applications, 1950–1990.* Westport, CT: Greenwood Press.

Costigan, P., & Elder, S. (2003). Does the questionnaire implement the specification? Who knows? In R. Banks, et al. (Eds.), *The impact of technology on the survey process: Proceedings of the 4th International Conference on Survey and Statistical Computing.* Chesham Bucks, UK: Association for Survey Computing.

Cotin, S., & Delingette, H. (1998). Real-time surgery simulation with haptic feedback using finite elements. *IEEE International Conference on Robotics and Automation, 4,* 3739–3744.

Coulouris, G., & Thimbleby, H. (1992). *HyperProgramming.* Wokingham, UK: Addison-Wesley Longman.

Couper, M. P. (2000). Usability evaluation of computer-assisted survey instruments. *Social Science Computer Review, 18*(4), 384–396.

Cournia, N., Smith, J. D., & Duchowski, A. T. (2003, April). Gaze- vs. hand-based pointing in virtual environments. In *Proceedings of CHI '03: Short talks and interactive posters* (pp. 772–773). Fort Lauderdale, FL: ACM.

Courtney, J. D. (1997). Automatic video indexing via object motion analysis. *Pattern Recognition, 30*(4), 607–626.

Coutaz, J. (1987). PAC, an implementation model for the user interface. *Proceedings of INTERACT'87,* 431–436.

Cover, T. M., & Thomas, J. A. (1991). *Elements of information theory.* New York: Wiley.

Crabtree, A. (1998). *Ethnography in participatory design.* Paper presented at the Participatory Design Conference, Seattle, WA.

Cranor, L. F. (1996). Electronic voting. *ACM Crossroads, 2*(4). Retrieved August 1, 2003, from http://www.acm.org/crossroads/xrds2-4/voting.html

Cranshaw, J. (1997). *Let's build a compiler.* Retrieved January 20, 2004, from http://compilers.iecc.com/crenshaw/

Crawford, G. P. (2000). A bright new page in portable displays. *IEEE Spectra, 37*(10), 40–46.

Crawford, G. P., & Escuti, M. J. (2002). Liquid crystal display technology. In J. P. Hornak (Ed.), *Encyclopedia of imaging science and technology* (pp. 955–969). New York: Wiley Interscience.

Crichton, M. (2002). *Prey.* New York: HarperCollins.

Crocker, D. *E-mail history.* Retrieved March 31, 2004, from www.livinginternet.com.

Crooks, C. E. (2004). *Developing tablet PC applications.* Hingham, MA: Charles River Media.

Crooks, C. E., & Crooks, I. (2002). *3D game programming with Direct X 8.0.* Hingham, MA: Charles River Media.

Cross, N. (2001). Design cognition: Results from protocol and other empirical studies of design activity. In C. Eastman, M. McCracken,

BIBLIOGRAPHY

& W. Newstetter (Eds.), *Design knowing and learning: Cognition in design education* (pp. 79–103). Amsterdam: Elsevier.

Cross, R., & Parker, A. (2004). *The hidden power of social networks: Understanding how work really gets done in organizations.* Boston: Harvard Business School Press.

Cruse, D. A. (1986). *Lexical semantics.* Cambridge, UK: Cambridge University Press.

Cruz-Neira, C., Sandin, D., & DeFanti, T. A. (1993). Virtual reality: The design and implementation of the CAVE. *Proceedings of the SIGGRAPH 93 Computer Graphics Conference, USA, 135*–142.

Cuban, L. (1986). *Teachers and machines: The classroom use of technology since 1920.* New York: Teachers College Press.

Culnan, M. J. (1993, September). How did they get my name? An exploratory investigation of consumer attitudes toward secondary information use. *MIS Quarterly,* 341–361.

Culy, C., & Riehemann, S. (2003). The limits of n-gram translation evaluation metrics. *Proceedings of MT Summit IX.* Retrieved February 12, 2004 from http://www.amtaweb.org/summit/MTSummit/papers.html

Cusumano, M. A., & Yoffie, D. B. (1998). *Competing on Internet time.* New York: Free Press.

Cypher, A., (Ed.). (1993). *Watch what I do: Programming by demonstration.* Cambridge, MA: MIT Press.

Czernuszenko, M., Pape, D., Sandin, D., DeFanti, T., Dawe, G. L., & Brown, M. D. (1997). The ImmersaDesk and Infinity Wall projection-based virtual reality displays [Electronic version]. *Computer Graphics, 31*(2), 46–49.

Dagtas, S., Al-Khatip, W., Ghafoor, A., & Kashyap, R. L. (2000). Models for motion-based video indexing and retrieval. *IEEE Transactions on Image Processing, 9*(1), 88–101.

Dahlbom, B. (1995). Göteborg informatics. *Scandinavian Journal of Information Systems, 7*(2), 87–92.

Dahling, R. L. (1962). Shannon's Information Theory: The spread of an idea. In Stanford University, Institute for Communication Research, *Studies of Innovation and of Communication to the Public* (pp. 117–139). Palo Alto: Stanford University Press.

Dalley, S. (Ed.). (1998). *Myths from Mesopotamia: Creation, the flood, Gilgamesh, and others.* New York: Oxford University Press.

Daly, J. (1994, December). For beta or worse. *Forbes ASAP,* 36–40.

Damer, B. (1998). *Avatars!* Berkeley, CA: Peachpit Press.

Damerau, F. (1964). A technique for computer detection and correction of spelling errors. *Communications of the ACM, 7*(3), 171–176.

Damon, A., & Stout, H. (1963). The functional anthropometry of old men. *Human Factors, 5,* 485–491.

Danby, J. M. A. (1997). *Computer modeling: From sports to space flight, from order to chaos.* Richmond, VA: William-Bell.

Daniel, C., & Wood, F. S. (1980). *Fitting equations to data.* New York: Wiley.

Daniels, P. (1986). Cognitive models in information retrieval: An evaluative review. *Journal of Documentation, 42*(4), 272–304.

Dannenberg, R. (1984). An on-line algorithm for real-time accompaniment. In *Proceedings of the 1994 International Computer Music Conference* (pp. 193–198). San Francisco, CA: International Computer Music Association.

Dannenberg, R. (1989). Real-time scheduling and computer accompaniment. In M. Mathes & J. Pierce (Eds.), *Current directions in computer music research* (pp. 225–261). Cambridge, MA: MIT Press.

Dannenberg, R. (2003). Sound synthesis from video, wearable lights, and "the watercourse way." In *Proceedings of the Ninth Biennial Symposium on Arts and Technology* (pp. 38–44). New London, CT: Connecticut College.

Dannenberg, R., & Mont-Reynaud, B. (1987). Following an improvisation in real time. In *Proceedings of the 1987 International Computer Music Conference* (pp. 241–248). San Francisco, CA: International Computer Music Association.

Danziger, J. N. (2003). *Understanding the political world: A comparative introduction to political science* (6th ed.). New York: Longman.

Darrell, T., Essa, I., & Pentland, A. (1996). Task-specific gesture modeling using interpolated views. *IEEE Transaction on Pattern Analysis and Machine Intelligence, 18*(12).

Darwin, C. (1890). *The expression of the emotions in man and animals* (2nd ed.). London: John Murray.

Das, H. (Ed.). (1994). *Proceedings of the SPIE—The International Society for Optical Engineering.* Bellingham, WA: International Society for Optical Engineering.

Das, S., Cook, D. J., Bhattacharya, A., Heierman, III, E. O., & Lin, T.-Y. (2003). The role of prediction algorithms in the MavHome smart home architecture. *IEEE Wireless Communications, 9*(6), 77–84.

David, R. (1999). *The web of politics: The Internet's impact on the American political system.* New York: Oxford University Press.

Davis, G. B. (1982). Strategies for information requirement determination. *IBM Systems Journal, 21*(1), 4–30.

Davis, J. A., Smith, T. W., & Marsden, P. V. (2001). *General social surveys, 1972–2000: 3rd version.* Storrs, CT: Roper Center for Public Opinion Research, University of Connecticut, and Ann Arbor, MI: Inter-University Consortium for Political and Social Research.

Davis, R. (1998). *The web of politics.* London: Oxford University Press.

Davis, R. (2002). Sketch understanding in design: Overview of work at the MIT AI lab. In R. Davis, J. Landay & T. F. Stahovich (Eds.), *Sketch understanding: Papers from the 2002 AAAI Symposium* (pp. 24–31). Menlo Park, CA: American Association for Artificial Intelligence (AAAI).

Davis, S. M., & Botkin, J. W. (1994). *The monster under the bed.* New York: Simon & Schuster.

Davis, W. S., & Benamati, J. (2003). *E-commerce basics: Technology foundations and e-business applications.* New York: Addison-Wesley.

Dean, T., Allen, J., & Aloimonos, Y. (2002). *Artificial intelligence: Theory and practice.* Upper Saddle River, NJ: Pearson Education POD.

Deal, T., & Kennedy, A. (1999). *The new corporate cultures.* Reading, MA: Perseus Books.

Dean, T., & Wellman, M. (1991). *Planning and control.* San Mateo, CA: Morgan Kaufmann.

Deb, K., & Gulati, S. (2001). Design of truss-structures for minimum weight using genetic algorithms. *Finite Elements in Analysis and Design, 37*(5), 447–465.

DeCarlo, D., & Metaxas, D. (2000). Optical flow constraints on deformable models with applications to face tracking. *International Journal of Computer Vision, 38*(2), 99–127.

Dechter, R. (2003). *Constraint processing.* San Francisco: Morgan Kaufmann.

DeFanti, T. A., Brown M. D., & Stevens, R. (Eds.). (1996). Virtual reality over high-speed networks. *IEEE Computer Graphics & Applications, 16*(4), 14–17, 42–84.

DeFanti, T., Sandin, D., Brown, M., Pape, D., Anstey, J., Bogucki, M., et al. (2001). Technologies for virtual reality/tele-immersion applications: Issues of research in image display and global networking. In R. Earnshaw, et al. (Eds.), *Frontiers of Human-Centered Computing, Online Communities and Virtual Environments* (pp. 137–159). London: Springer-Verlag.

deGroot, A., Hooman, J., Kordon, F., Paviot-Adet, E., Iounier, Lemoine, M., et al. (2001). A survey: Applying formal methods to a software-intensive system. In *6th IEEE International Symposium on High Assurance Systems Engineering* (HASE '01) (pp. 55–64). Cupertino, CA: IEEE CS Press.

Deibert, R. J. (2002). Dark guests and great firewalls: The Internet and Chinese security policy. *Journal of Social Issues, 58*(1), 143–159.

Delmonico, D. L. (1997). *Internet sex screening test.* Retrieved August 25, 2003, from http://www.sexhelp.com/

Delmonico, D. L., Griffin, E. J., & Moriarity, J. (2001). *Cybersex un-hooked: A workbook for breaking free of compulsive online behavior.* Wickenburg, AZ: Gentle Path Press.

Delmonico, D. L., & Miller, J. A. (2003). The Internet sex screening test: A comparison of sexual compulsives versus non-sexual compulsives. *Sexual and Relationship Therapy, 18*(3), 261–276.

DeLoura, M. (Ed.). (2000). *Game programming gems.* Hingham, MA: Charles River Media.

DeLoura, M. (Ed.). (2001). *Game programming gems II.* Hingham, MA: Charles River Media.

Demchak, G. (2000). *Towards a post-industrial architecture: Design and construction of houses for the information age.* Unpublished master's thesis, Massachusetts Institute of Technology, Cambridge, MA.

DeMers, M. N. (2000). *Fundamentals of geographic information systems* (2nd ed.). New York: Wiley.

Dempski, K. (2002). *Real-time rendering tricks and techniques in DirectX.* Indianapolis, IN: Premier Press.

Dempster, W. T., Gabel, W. C., & Felts, W. J. L. (1959). The anthropometry of the manual work space for the seated subject. *American Journal of Physical Anthropometry, 17,* 289–317.

Deng, Y., & Manjunath, B. S. (1998). NeTra-V: Toward an object-based video representation., *IEEE Transactions on Circuits and Systems for Video Technology, 8*(5), 616–627.

Dennerlein, J. T., Becker, T., Johnson, P., Reynolds, C., & Picard, R. (2003). Frustrating computers users increases exposure to physical factors. *Proceedings of the 15th triennial congress of the International Ergonomics Association (IEA 2003).* CD-ROM.

Dennerlein, J. T., & Yang, M. C. (2001). Haptic force-feedback devices for the office computer: Performance and musculoskeletal loading issues. *Human Factors, 43*(2), 278–286.

Dennett, D. C. (1995). *Darwin's dangerous idea.* New York: Simon & Schuster.

Denning, P. J. (1992): Educating a new engineer. *Communications of the ACM,* 35(12), 83–97.

DeRose, L., & Reed, D. A. (1999, September). *SvPablo: A multi-language architecture-independent performance analysis system.* Paper presented at the International Conference on Parallel Processing, Fukushima, Japan.

Dertouzos, M. L., Berners-Lee, T., Fischetti, M. (1999). *Weaving the Web: The original design and ultimate destiny of the World Wide Web by its inventor.* San Francisco: Harper.

Desurvire, H. W. (1994). Faster, cheaper!! Are *usability inspection methods* as effective as empirical testing? In J. Nielsen & R. L. Mack (Eds.), Usability inspection methods (pp. 173–202). New York: Wiley.

Deutsch, D. (Ed.). (1982). *The psychology of music.* New York: Academic Press.

Dewan, E. M. (1967). Occipital alpha rhythm eye position and lens accommodation. *Nature, 214,* 975–977.

Dewan, P. (1993). Tools for implementing multiuser user interfaces. *Trends in Software: Issue on User Interface Software, 1,* 149–172.

Dewan, P. (1998). Architectures for collaborative applications. *Trends in Software: Computer Supported Co-operative Work, 7,* 165–194.

Dewan, P., & Choudhary, R. (1991). Flexible user interface coupling in collaborative systems. In *Proceedings of the ACM CHI'91 Conference.* New York.

Dewan, P., & Shen, H. (1998). Flexible meta access-control for collaborative applications. In *Proceedings of ACM Conference on Computer Supported Cooperative Work.* New York.

Dibbell, J. (1999). *My tiny life: Crime and passion in a virtual world.* London: Fourth Estate.

DiBona, C., Ockman, S., &and Stone, M. (Eds.). (1999). *Open sources.* Sebastopol, CA: O'Reilly.

Dicks, R. S. (2002). *Mis-usability: On the uses and misuses of usability testing.* Paper presented at the Annual ACM Conference on Systems Documentation, Toronto, Canada.

Diderot, D., & le Rond D' Alembert, J. (Eds.). (1758–1776). *Encyclopedie ou dictionnaire raisonne des sciences, des arts et des métiers, par une societe de gens de letteres* [Encyclopedia or rational dictionary of sciences, arts, and the professions, by a society of people of letters](2nd ed.). Luca, Italy: André Le Breton.

Dieli, M. (1989). The usability process: Working with iterative design principles. *IEEE Transactions on Professional Communication, 32*(4), 272–279.

Digital Divide Network staff. (2003). *Digital divide basics fact sheet.* Retrieved July 18, 2003, from http://www.digitaldividenetwork.org/content/stories/index.cfm?key=168

Dillman, D. (2000). *Mail and Internet surveys: The tailored design method.* New York: John Wiley & Sons.

Dillon, A. (1998). Cultural analysis and what designers need to know—a case of sometimes too much, sometimes too little, and always too late: Why ethnography needs to show its relevance. *ACM SIG-DOC Asterisk Journal of Computer Documentation, 22*(1), 13–17.

DiMaggio, P. J., & Powell, W. W. (1991). The iron cage revisited: Institutional isomorphism and collective rationality in organizational fields. In W. W. Powell & P. J. Dimaggio (Eds.), *The new institutionalism in organizational analysis* (pp. 63–82). Chicago: University of Chicago Press.

Dimitrova, N., Zhang, H., Shahraray, B., Sezan, I., Huang, T., & Zakhor, A. (2002). Applications of video content analysis and retrieval. *IEEE Multimedia, 9,* 42–55.

Dinh, H. Q., Walker, N., Song, C., Kobayashi, A., & Hodges, L. F. (1999). Evaluating the importance of multi-sensory input on memory and the sense of presence in virtual environments. In *Proceedings of IEEE Virtual Reality* (pp. 222–228). Washington, DC: IEEE Computer Society Press.

Divakaran, A., Radhakrishnan, R., & Peker, K. (2001). Video summarization with motion descriptors. *The Journal of Electronic Imaging, 10*(4), 909–916.

Dix, A. (1997). *Human-Computer interaction.* New York: Prentice-Hall.

Dix, A., Finlay, J., Abowd, G., & Beale, R. (1993). *Human-computer interaction.* Hillsdale, NJ: Prentice Hall.

Dix, A., Rodden, T., Davies, N., Trevor, J., Friday, A., & Palfreyman, K. (2000). Exploiting space and location as a design framework for interactive mobile systems. *ACM Transactions on Computer-Human Interaction (TOCHI), 7*(3), 285–321.

Do, E. Y.-L. (2002). Drawing marks, acts, and reacts: Toward a computational sketching interface for architectural design. *AIEDAM*

(Artificial Intelligence for Engineering Design, Analysis and Manufacturing), 16(3), 149–171.

Doctorow, C. (2003). *Down and out in the Magic Kingdom.* New York: Tor Books.

Doctorow, C., Dornfest, R., Johnson, J. S., Powers, S., Trott, B., & Trott, M. G. (2002). *Essential blogging.* Sebastopol, CA: O'Reilly.

Dodds, D. (2001*). Professional XML metadata.* Hoboken, NJ: Wrox.

Dodge, M., & Kitchin, R. (2001). *Atlas of cyberspace.* London: Addison-Wesley.

Doherty, S. (2001). Helpdesk salvation. *Network Computing, 12*(1), 42–48.

Dolan, R. J., & Matthews, J. M. (1993). Maximizing the utility of consumer product testing: Beta test design and management. *Journal of Product Innovation Management, 10,* 318–330.

Donath, J. (2002, April). A semantic approach to visualizing online conversations. *Communications of the ACM, 45*(4), 45–49.

Donath, J., & Robertson, N. (1994, October.).The sociable web. *Proceedings of the Second International WWW Conference.* Chicago.

Donchin, E. (1989). The learning strategies project. *Acta Psychologica, 71*(1–3), 1–15.

Donchin, E., Spencer, K., & Wijesinghe, R. (2000). The mental prosthesis: Assessing the speed of a P300-based brain-computer interface. *IEEE Transactions on Rehabilitation Engineering, 8*(2), 174–179.

Dongarra, J. J. (2003). *Performance of various computers using standard linear equations software.* Retrieved August 8, 2003, from http://www.netlib.org/benchmark/performance.pdf

Dongarra, J., London, K., Moore, S., Mucci, P., & Terpstra, D. (2001). Using PAPI for hardware performance monitoring on Linux systems. In *Proceedings of the* Conference on Linux Clusters: The HPC Revolution, Retrieved August 8, 2003, from http://icl.cs.utk.edu/projects/papi/documents/pub-papers/2001/linux-rev2001.pdf

Douglas, S. A., & Mithal, A. K. (1997). *The ergonomics of pointing devices.* London: Springer-Verlag.

Dourish, P., & Bellotti, V. (1992). Awareness and coordination in shared workspaces. In *Proceedings of the Conference on Computer Supported Cooperative Work: CSCW '92* (pp. 107–114). New York: ACM Press.

Douthitt, E. A., & Aiello, J. R. (2001). The role of participation and control in effects of computer monitoring on fairness perceptions, task satisfaction, and performance. *Journal of Applied Psychology, 86*(5), 867–874.

Dowding, G. (1961). *An introduction to the history of printing types.* London: Wace.

Downey, G. (1998). *The machine in me: An anthropologist sits among computer engineers.* New York: Routledge.

Doyle, L. B. (1961). Semantic road maps for literature searchers. *Journal of the ACM, 8,* 553–578.

Drabenstott, K. (2000). Web search strategies. In W. J. Wheeler (Ed.), *Saving the user's time through subject access innovation: Papers in honor of Pauline Atherton Cochrane* (pp. 114–161). Champaign: University of Illinois Press.

Draper, J. V., Kaber, D. B., & Usher, J. M. (1998). Telepresence. *Human Factors, 40*(3), 354–375.

Draper, J. V., Kaber, D. B., & Usher, J. M. (1999). Speculations on the value of telepresence. *Cyberpsychology & Behavior, 2*(4), 349–362.

Dreyfus, H. L. (1979). *What computers can't do: The limits of artificial intelligence* (Rev. ed). New York: Harper & Row.

Dreyfus, H. L. (1999). Anonymity versus commitment: The dangers of education on the Internet. *Ethics and Information Technology, 1*(1), 15–21.

Dreyfus, H. L. (2001). *On the Internet.* New York: Routledge.

Dreyfus, H. L., & Dreyfus, S. L. (1986). *Mind over machine: The power of human intuition and expertise in the era of the computer.* New York: Free Press.

Droste, C. S., & Walker, J. E. (2001). *The general dynamics case study on the F-16 fly-by-wire flight control system.* Reston, VA: American Institute of Aeronautics and Astronautics.

Drucker, P. F. (1973). *Management: Tasks, responsibilities and practices.* New York: Harper & Row.

Druin, A. (2002). The role of children in the design of new technology. *Behaviour and Information Technology, 21*(1), 1–25.

Druin, A., Bederson, B., Hourcade, J. P., Sherman, L., Revelle, G., Platner, M., et al. (2001). Designing a digital library for young children. In *Proceedings of the first ACM/IEEE-CS Joint Conference on Digital Libraries* (pp. 398–405). New York: ACM Press.

Dubrovsky, V. J., Kiesler, S., & Sethna, B. N. (1991). The equalization phenomenon: Status effects in computer-mediated and face-to-face decision-making groups. *Human-Computer Interaction, 6,* 119–146.

Dubuoe, P., & McKeown, K. R. (2001) Empirically estimating order constraints for content planning in generation In *Proceedings of the ACL-EACL 2001,* July 6–11, Toulouse, France.

Duchenne, G.-B. (1990). The mechanism of human facial expression: *Studies in emotion and social interaction.* Cambridge University Press; Editions de la Maison des Sciences de l'Homme.

Duchnicky, J. L., & Kolers, P. A. (1983). Readability of text scrolled on visual display terminals as a function of window size. *Human Factors, 25,* 683–692.

Duchowski, A. T. (2003). *Eye tracking methodology: Theory & practice.* London: Springer-Verlag.

Duckham, M., Goodchild, M. F., & Worboys, M. F. (2003). *Fundamentals of geographic information science.* New York: Taylor and Francis.

Dumas, J. S., & Redish, J. C. (1993). *A practical guide to usability testing.* Norwood, NJ: Ablex.

Dunham, M. H. (2002). *Data mining: Introductory and advanced topics.* Upper Saddle River, NJ: Prentice Hall.

Durham, I., Lamb, D., & Saxe, J. (1983). Spelling correction in user interfaces. *Communications of the ACM, 26*(10), 764–773.

Durndell, A., & Haag, Z. (2002). Computer self-efficacy, computer anxiety, attitudes toward the Internet and reported experience with the Internet, by gender, in an East European sample. *Computers in Human Behavior, 18,* 521–535.

Dusterhoff, K. E., Black, A. W., & Taylor, P. A. (1999). Using decision trees within the tilt intonation model to predict F0 contours. *Proceedings of Eurospeech 1999* (pp. 1627–1630). Budapest, Hungary.

Dutoit, T. (1996). *An introduction to text-to-speech synthesis.* Boston: Kluwer Academic Publishers.

Dutton, W. H. (1999). *Society on the line: Information politics in the digital age.* Oxford, UK: Oxford University Press.

Dutton, W. H., & Peltu, M. (1996). *Information and communication technologies—Visions and realities.* Oxford, UK: Oxford University Press.

Dyson, F. (1979). *Disturbing the universe.* New York: Harper & Row.

Dziak, M. J. (2001). *Telecommuting success: A practical guide for staying in the loop while working away from the office.* Indianapolis: Jist Works.

Eason, K. (1987) *Information technology and organizational change.* London: Taylor and Francis.

BIBLIOGRAPHY

Eastman Kodak Company. (2003). *Ergonomic design for people at work* (2nd ed.). New York: Wiley.

Eberly, D. (2000). *3D game engine design: A practical Approach to real-time computer graphics*. San Francisco: Morgan Kaufmann.

Echt, K. V. (2002). Designing Web-based health information for older adults: Visual considerations and design directives. In R. W. Morrell (Ed.), *Older adults, health information, and the World Wide Web* (pp. 61–88). Mahwah, NJ: Lawrence Erlbaum Associates.

Edelstein, H. (1994). *Unraveling client/server architecture*. Redwood City, CA: M & T Publishing.

Edwards, A. D. N. (1989) Soundtrack: An auditory interface for blind users. *Human-Computer Interaction, 4*(1), 45–66.

Edwards, P. N (1996). *Closed world: Computers and the politics of discourse in Cold War America*. Cambridge: MIT Press.

eEurope. (1995–2002). *An information society for all*. Retrieved July 18, 2003, from http://europa.eu.int/information_society/ eeurope/index_en.htm

Egan, G. (1994). *Permutation City*. New York: Harper.

Ehn, P. (1988). *Work-oriented design of computer artifacts*. Stockholm, Sweden: Almqvist & Wiksell.

Ehn, P. (1989). The art and science of designing computer artifacts. *Scandinavian Journal of Information Systems, 1*, 21–42.

Ehn, P., & Kyng, M. (1987). The collective resource approach to system design. In G. Bjerknes, P. Ehn, & M. Kyng (Eds.), *Computers and democracy—A Scandinavian challenge* (pp. 19–57). Aldershot, UK: Avebury.

Ehn, P., & Kyng, M. (1991). Cardboard computers: Mocking-it-up or hands-on the future. In J. Grenbaum & M. Kyng (Eds.), *Design at work* (pp. 169–196) Hillsdale, NJ: Lawrence Erlbaum Associates.

Ehud Reiter, E., Sripada, S., & Robertson, R. (2003). Acquiring correct knowledge for natural language generation. *Journal of Artificial Intelligence Research, 18*, 491–516.

Eichmann, D. (1994). The RBSE spider—Balancing effective search against Web load. *Proceedings of the First International World Wide Web Conference, 113–120*.

Eisert, P., & Girod, B. (1998). Analyzing facial expression for virtual conferencing. *IEEE Computer Graphics & Applications, 18*(5).

Ekin, A., Tekalp, A .M., & Mehrotra, R. (2003). Automatic soccer video analysis and summarization. *IEEE Transactions on Image Processing, 12*(7), 796–807.

Ekman, P. (1978). Facial signs: Facts, fantasies and possibilities. In T. Sebeok, (Ed.), *Sight, Sound and Sense*. Bloomington: Indiana University Press.

Ekman, P. (1991). *Telling lies: Clues to deceit in the marketplace, politics, and marriage*. New York: Norton. Ekman, P., & Friesen, W. (1978). *Facial action coding system*. Palo Alto, CA: Consulting Psychologists Press.

Ekman, P. (Ed.). (1982). *Emotion in the human face* (2nd ed.). New York: Cambridge University Press.

Ekman, P., & Friesen, W. V. (1978). *Facial action coding system: Investigator's guide*. Palo Alto, CA: Consulting Psychologists Press.

Electoral Commission. (2002). *Modernising elections: A strategic evaluation of the 2002 electoral pilot schemes*. Retrieved August 1, 2003, from http://www.electoralcommission.org.uk/templates/ search/document.cfm/6170

Electronic Privacy Information Center. (2003). *Privacy and human rights 2003*. Washington, DC: Author.

Elkerton, J., & Palmiter, S. L. (1991). Designing help using a GOMS model: An information retrieval evaluation. *Human Factors, 33*(2), 185–204.

Elkin-Koren, N. (1996). Cyberlaw and social change: A democratic approach to copyright law in cyberspace. *Cardozo Arts & Entertainment Law Journal, 14*(2), 215–end.

Ellis, C. A., Gibbs, S. J., & Rein, G. L. (1991) Groupware: Some issues and experiences. *Communications of the ACM, 34*(1), 38–58.

Ellis, D. (1990). *New horizons in information retrieval*. London: The Library Association.

Ellis, R., & Lowell, B. L. (1999). *Core occupations of the U.S. information technology workforce* [IT Workforce Data Project, Report 1]. Retrieved November 12, 2003, from http://www.cpst.org/ ITWF_Report.cfm

Ellman, T. (1993). Abstraction via approximate symmetry. In *Proceedings of the 13th IJCAI* (pp. 916–921). Chambéry, France.

Elting, C., Zwickel, J., & Malaka, R. (2002). Device-dependant modality selection for user-interfaces: An empirical study. In *Proceedings of the 7th international conference on intelligent user interfaces* (pp. 55–62) New York: Association for Computing Machinery.

Elvins, T. T. (1998, February). Augmented reality: "The future's so bright I gotta wear (see-through) shades." Computer Graphics, 32(1), 11–13.

Elzinga, C. D., Hallmark, T. M., Mattern Jr., R. H., & Woodward, J. M. (1981). Laser electrophotographic printing technology. *IBM Journal of Research and Development*, 25(5), 767–773.

Emery, F. E., & Trist, E. L. (1960). Socio-technical systems. In C. W. Churchman & M. Verhurst (Eds.), *Management science, models and techniques: Vol. 2* (pp. 83–97). London: Pergamon Press.

Emery, F., & Trist, E. (1965). The causal texture of organizational environments. *Human Relations, 18*, 21–31.

Encarnação, L. M., & Stoev, S. L. (1999). An application-independent intelligent user support system exploiting action-sequence based user modeling. In J. Kay (Ed.), *Proceedings of 7th International Conference on User Modeling, UM99, June 20–24, 1999* (pp. 245–254). Vienna: Springer.

Endsley, M., & Kaber, D. B. (1999). Level of automation effects on performance, situation awareness and workload in a dynamic control task. *Ergonomics, 42*(3), 462–492.

Engel, W. F. (Ed.). (2002). *Direct3D ShaderX: Vertex and pixel shader tips and tricks*. Plano, TX: Wordware Publishing.

Engelbart, D. (1963). A conceptual framework for the augmentation of man's intellect. In P. Howerton & D. Weeks (Eds.), *Vistas in information handling* (pp. 1–29). Washington, DC: Spartan Books.

Engelbart, D., & English, W. (1968). A research center for augmenting human intellect. *AFIPS Conference Proceedings, 33*, 395–410.

Engen, T. (1982). *The perception of odors*. New York: Academic Press.

Ennis, J. G. (1992). The social organization of sociological knowledge: Modeling the intersection of specialties. *American Sociological Review, 57*(2), 259–265.

Erickson, T., & Kellogg, W. (2000) Social translucence: An approach to designing systems that support social processes. *ACM Transactions on Computer-Human Interaction (TOCHI), 7*(1), 59–83.

Erickson, T., & Kellogg, W. A. (2003). Social translucence: Using minimalist visualizations of social activity to support collective interaction. In K. Höök, D. Benyon, & A. Munro (Eds.), *Designing Information Spaces: The Social Navigation Approach* (pp. 17–42). London: Springer-Verlag.

Erickson, T., Smith, D. N., Kellogg, W. A., Laff, M., Richards, J. T., & Bradner, E. (1999). Socially translucent systems: Social proxies, persistent conversation, and the design of "Babble." In *CHI 1999 Conference Proceedings: Conference on Human Factors in Computing Systems* (pp. 72–79). New York: ACM Press.

Essa, I., & Pentland, A. (1997). Coding, analysis, interpretation, and recognition of facial expressions. *IEEE Transaction on Pattern Analysis and Machine Intelligence, 19*(7), 757–763.

Essa, I., Basu, S., Darrell, T., & Pentland, A. (1996). Modeling, tracking and interactive animation of faces and heads using input from video. In *Proceedings of Computer Animation Conference 1996* (pp. 68–79). New York: IEEE Computer Society Press.

European Union. (2002, May 4). *e-Government and development: Bridging the*

Evans, D., & Schmalensee, R. (2000). *Paying with plastic: The digital revolution in buying and borrowing.* Cambridge, MA: MIT Press.

Evenson, L. (1997, March 16). Present at the creation of the Internet: Now that we're all linked up and sitting quietly, Vint Cert, one of its architects, describes how the Internet came into being. *San Francisco Chronicle* (p. 3ff).

Fano, R., & Corbato, F. (1966). Time-sharing on computers. *Scientific American, 214*(9), 129–140.

Fant, G. (1960). *Acoustic theory of speech production.* The Hague, Netherlands: Mouton.

Farid, M., Murtagh, F., & Starck, J. L. (2002), Computer display control and interaction using eye-gaze. *Journal of the Society for Information Display, 10,* 289–293.

Farkas, D. K. (1999). The logical and rhetorical construction of procedural discourse. *Technical Communication, 46*(1), 42–54.

Farkas, D. K., & Farkas J. B. (2002). *Principles of Web design.* New York: Longman.

Farnham, S., Cheng, L., Stone, L., Zaner-Godsey, M., Hibbeln, C, Syrjala, K., Clark, A., & Abrams, J. (2002). HutchWorld: Clinical Study of Computer-Mediated Social Support for Cancer Patients and Their Caregivers. In *Proceedings of CHI 2002* (pp. 375–382). NY: ACM Press.

Faucett, J., & Rempel, D. (1994). VDT-related musculoskeletal symptoms: Interactions between work posture and psychosocial work factors. *American Journal of Industrial Medicine, 26*(5), 597–612.

Faugeras, O., Vieville, T., Theron, E., Vuillemin, J., Hotz, B., Zhang, Z., et al. (1993). Real-time correlation-based stereo: Algorithm, implementations and applications. *INRIA Technical Report RR-2013.* Retrieved June 7, 2004, from http://www.inria.fr/rrrt/rr-2013.html

Federal Voting Assistance Program. (2001). *Voting over the Internet Pilot Project Assessment Report.* Washington DC: Author.

Feigenbaum, E., & McCorduck, P. (1983). *The fifth generation.* Reading, MA: Addison-Wesley.

Feldman, S. (1999). NLP Meets the Jabberwocky: Natural language processing in information retrieval. *ONLINE, May 1999.* Retrieved January 22, 2004, from www.onlinemag.net/OL1999/feldman5.html

Feldman, S. (2000). The answer machine. *Searcher, 8*(1), 1–21, 58–78. Retrieved January 22, 2004, from http://www.infotoday.com/searcher/jan00/feldman.htm

Fellbaum, C. (1998). *WordNet: An electronic lexical database.* Cambridge, MA: MIT Press.

Feller, J. (2004). *Open source resources.* Retrieved April 16, 2004, from http://opensource.ucc.ie/

Feller, J., & Fitzgerald, B. (2002). *Understanding open source software development.* London: Addison-Wesley.

Fensel, D., Hendler, J., Lieberman, H., & Walster, W. (Eds.). (2002). *Spinning the semantic Web: Bringing the World Wide Web to its full potential.* Cambridge, MA: MIT Press.

Ferarri, E., & Thuraisinham, B. (2000). Database security: Survey. In M. Piattini, M. & O. Diaz (Eds.), *Advanced database technology and design.* Boston: Artech House.

Ferre, X., Juristo, N., Windl, H., & Constantine, L. (2001). Usability basics for software developers. *IEEE Software, 18*(1), 22–29.

Ferringo-Stack, J., Robinson, J. P., Kestnbaum, M., Neustadtl, A., & Alvarez, A. (2003). Internet and society: A summary of research reported at WebShop 2001. *Social Science Computer Review, 21*(1), 73–117.

Festinger, L., Schachter, S., & Back, K. (1950). *Social pressures in informal groups.* Stanford, CA: Stanford University Press.

Fickas, S., & Helm, B. (1992). Knowledge representation and reasoning in the design of composite systems. *IEEE Transactions on Software Engineering, 18*(6), 470–482.

Fidel, R., & Crandall, M. (1997). Users' perception of the performance of a filtering system. In *Proceedings of the 20th annual ACM SIGIR Conference on Research and Development in Information Retrieval* (pp. 198–205). New York: ACM Press.

Fidel, R., Davies, R. K., Douglass, M. H., Holder, J. K., Hopkins, C. J., Kushner, E. J., et al. (1999). *A visit to the information mall: Web searching behavior of high school students.* Journal of the American Society for Information Science, *50(1),* 24–37.

Fielding, C. (2001). The design of fly-by-wire flight control systems. Retrieved July 18, 2003, from http://www.shef.ac.uk/acse/ukacc/activities/flybywire.pdf

Fielding, R. T. (1999). Shared leadership in the Apache project. *Communications of the ACM, 42*(4), 42–43.

Fikes, R., & Nilsson, N. (1971). STRIPS: A new approach to the application of theorem proving to problem solving. *Artificial Intelligence, 2*(3,4), 189–208.

Fikes, R., & Nilsson, N. (1993). STRIPS: A retrospective. *Artificial Intelligence, 59*(1,2), 227–232.

Fillmore, C. J. (1992). Corpus linguistics vs. computer-aided armchair linguistics. *Directions in corpus linguistics: Proceedings from a 1991 Nobel Symposium on Corpus Linguistics* (pp. 35–66). Stockholm: Mouton de Gruyter.

Finger, R., & Bisantz, A. M. (2002). Utilizing graphical formats to convey uncertainty in a decision-making task. *Theoretical Issues in Ergonomics Science, 3*(1), 1–24.

Finholt, T. A. (2002). Collaboratories. In B. Cronin (Ed.), *Annual Review of Information Science and Technology, 36,* 74–107. Washington, DC: American Society for Information Science and Technology.

Finholt, T. A., & Olson, G. M. (1997). From laboratories to collaboratories: A new organizational form for scientific collaboration. *Psychological Science, 8*(1), 28–36.

Fink, D., & Laupase, R. (2000). Perceptions of web site design characteristics: A Malaysian/Australian comparison. *Internet Research, 10*(1), 44–55.

Finn, K., Sellen, A., & Wilbur, S. (Eds.). (1997). *Video-mediated communication.* Hillsdale NJ: Lawrence Erlbaum Associates.

Fischer, C. S. (1940). *America calling: A social history of the telephone to 1940.* Berkeley and Los Angeles: University of California Press.

Fischer, G. (1998). Making learning a part of life: Beyond the 'gift-wrapping' approach of technology. In P. Alheit & E. Kammler (Eds.), *Lifelong learning and its impact on social and regional development* (pp. 435–462). Bremen, Germany: Donat Verlag.

Fischer, G. (2001). User modeling in human-computer interaction. *User Modeling and User-Adapted Interaction, 11*(1–2), 65–86.

Fisher, F. M., McKie, J. W., and Mankie, R. B. (1983). *IBM and the U.S. data processing industry: An economic history.* New York: Praeger.

Fisher, M., Cao, M., Rothermel, G., Cook, C. R., & Burnett, M. M. (2002). Automated test case generation for spreadsheets. In *International Conference on Software Engineering*, 141–151.

Fisher, R. A. (1935). *The design of experiments.* London: Oliver & Boyd.

Fisher, W. M., Zue, V., Bernstein, J., & Pallett, D. (1987). An acoustic-phonetic data base. *113th Meeting of the Acoustical Society of America*, Indianapolis, IN.

Fiske, S. T., & Taylor, S. E. (1991). *Social cognition* (2nd ed.). New York: McGraw Hill.

Fitts, P. M. (1954). The information capacity of the human motor system in controlling the amplitude of movement. *Journal of Experimental Psychology, 47,* 381–391.

Fjallbrant, N. (1997). *Scholarly communication: Historical development and new possibilities.* Retrieved July 28, 2003, from http://internet.unib.ktu.lt/physics/texts/schoolarly/scolcom.htm

Flanagan, J. (1972). *Speech analysis synthesis and perception* (2nd ed.). New York: Springer-Verlag.

Fleischer, J. M., Latta, M. R., & Rabedeau, M. E. (1977). Laser-optical system of the IBM 3800 printer. *IBM Journal of Research and Development, 21,* 479.

Floridi, L. (1999). Information ethics: On the philosophical foundations of computer ethics. *Ethics and Information Technology, 1*(1), 37–56.

Flowers, J., Buhman, D. C., & Turnage, K. D. (1997). Cross-modal equivalence of visual and auditory scatterplots for exploring bivariate data samples. *Human Factors, 39*(3), 341–351.

Flowers, J., & Hauer, T. (1992). The ear's versus the eye's potential to access characteristics of numeric data. Are we too visuocentric? *Behavior Research Methods, Instruments and Computers, 24*(2), 258–264.

Flowers, J., & Hauer, T. (1995). Musical versus visual graphs: Cross-modal equivalence in perception of time series data. *Human Factors, 37*(3), 553–569.

Foley, J., van Dam, A., Feiner, S., & Hughes, J. (1995). *Computer graphics:* Principles and practice (2nd ed.). Reading, MA: Addison-Wesley.

Fong, T., & Nourbakhsh, I. (2003, March). Socially interactive robots [Special issue]. *Robotics and Autonomous Systems, 42.*

Fontenelle, T. (2003). Special issue on FrameNet. *International Journal of Lexicography, 16*(3).

Forbus, K., Usher, J., & Chapman, V. (2003). Sketching for military courses of action diagrams. In *International Conference on Intelligent User Interfaces* (pp. 61–68). San Francisco: ACM Press.

Foresti, G. L., Marcenaro, L., & Regazzoni, C. S. (2002). Automatic detection and indexing of video-event shots for surveillance applications. *IEEE Trans. Multimedia, 4*(4), 459–471.

Forgie, J., & Forgie, C. (1959). Results obtained from a vowel recognition computer program. *Journal of Acoustic Society of America, 31*(11), 1480–1489.

Form, W. (1987). On the degradation of skills. *Annual Review of Sociology,* 13, 29–47.

Forster, E. M. (1909). The machine stops. *Oxford and Cambridge Review.* Retrieved August 20, 2003, from http://www.plexus.org/forster.html

Forsythe, D. (2001). *Studying those who study us: An anthropologist in the world of artificial intelligence.* Stanford, CA: Stanford University Press.

Fortunati, L., & Manganelli, A. M. (2002). A review of the literature on gender and ICTs in Italy. In K. H. Sørensen & J. Steward (Eds.), *Digital divides and inclusion measures: A review of literature and statistical trends on gender and ICT* (STS Report 59-02). Trondheim, Norway: Centre for Technology and Society.

Foss, C. L. (1989). Tools for reading and browsing hypertext. *Information Processing Management, 25,* 407–418.

Foster, I., & Kesselman, C. (2003). *The grid Blueprint for a new computing infrastructure* (2nd ed.). Burlington, MA: Morgan Kaufmann.

Foster, I., Kesselman, C., & Tuecke, S. (2001). The anatomy of the grid: Enabling scalable virtual organizations. *International Journal of Supercomputer Applications, 15*(3).

Fountain, J. E. (2001). *Building the virtual state: Information technology and institutional change.* Washington, DC: Brookings Institution Press.

Fountain, J. E. (2002). *Information, institutions and governance: Advancing a basic social science research program for digital government.* Cambridge, MA: National Center for Digital Government, John F. Kennedy School of Government.

Fountain, J. E., & Osorio-Urzua, C. (2001). The economic impact of the Internet on the government sector. In R. E. Litan & A. M. Rivlin (Eds.), *The economic payoff from the Internet revolution* (pp. 235–268). Washington, DC: Brookings Institution Press.

Fox, A., Johanson, B., Hanrahan, P., & Winograd, T. (2000). Integrating information appliances into an interactive space. *IEEE Computer Graphics and Applications, 20*(3), 54–65.

Fox, E. A., & Urs, S. R. (2002). Digital libraries. *Annual Review of Information and Science and Technology (ARIST), 46,* 503–589.

Fox, E. A., Gonçalves, M. A., & Kipp, N. A. (2002). Digital libraries. In H. Adelsberger, B. Collis, & J. Pawlowski (Eds.), *Handbook on information systems* (pp. 623–641). Berlin: Springer-Verlag.

Foxall, G. R. (1997). *Marketing psychology: The paradigm in the wings.* London: Macmillan.

Frakes, W. B., & Baeza-Yates, R. (Eds.). (1992). *Information retrieval: Data structures and algorithms.* Englewood Cliffs, NJ: Prentice Hall.

Franklin, J. (2002). Improvisation and learning. In T. Dietterich, S. Becker, & Z. Ghahramani (Eds.), *Neural information processing systems (NIPS)* 14. Cambridge, MA: MIT Press.

Franzblau, A. Flashner, D., Albers, J. W., Blitz, S., Werner, R., & Armstrong, T. (1993). Medical screening of office workers for upper extremity cumulative trauma disorders. *Archives of Environmental Health, 48,* 164–170.

Fraser, N. (1997). Assessment of interactive systems. In D. Gibbon, R. Moore, and R. Winski (Eds.), *Handbook of standards and resources for spoken language systems* (pp. 564–614). New York: Mouton de Gruyter.

Free Software Foundation. (1991). GNU General Public License. Retrieved January 20, 2004, from http://www.fsf.org/licenses/gpl.html

Freedman, W. (1987). *The right of privacy in the computer age.* New York: Quorum.

Freeman, F. G., Mikulka, P. J., Prinzel, L. J., & Scerbo, M. W. (1999). Evaluation of an adaptive automation system using three EEG indices with a visual tracking task. *Biological Psychology, 50*(1), 61–76.

Freeman, P., & Aspray, W. (1999). *The supply of information technology workers in the United States.* Washington, DC: Computing Research Association.

Freiberger, P., & Swaine, M. (1999). *Fire in the valley: The making of the personal computer* (2nd ed.). New York: McGraw-Hill.

Freud, S. (1900). The interpretation of dreams. In J. Strachey (Ed. & Trans.), *The standard edition of the complete psychological works of Sigmund Freud, 4.* London: Hogarth Press.

Freuder, E. C. (1982). A sufficient condition for backtrack-free search. *JACM, 29*(1), 24–32.

Freuder, E. C. (1985). A sufficient condition for backtrack-bounded search. *JACM, 32*(4), 755–761.

Freuder, E. C. (1991). Eliminating interchangeable values in constraint satisfaction problems. In *Proceedings of AAAI-91* (pp. 227–233). Anaheim, CA.

Frey, P. W. (Ed.). (1983). *Chess skill in man and machine.* New York: Springer-Verlag.

Frick, A., Bächtiger, M. T., & Reips, U.-D. (2001). Financial incentives, personal information, and drop-out in online studies. In U.-D. Reips & M. Bosnjak (Eds.), *Dimensions of Internet science* (pp. 209–220) Lengerich, Germany: Pabst.

Friedman, B. (Ed.). (1997). *Human values and the design of computer technology.* London: Cambridge University Press.

Friedman, B., & Kahn, Jr., P. H. (2003). Human values, ethics, and design. In J. A. Jacko & A. Sears (Eds.), *The human-computer interaction handbook* (pp. 1177–1201). Mahwah, NJ: Lawrence Erlbaum Associates.

Friedman, B., & Kahn, P. H. (in press). A value sensitive design approach to augmented reality. In W. Mackay (Ed.), *Design of augmented reality environments,* Cambridge MA: MIT Press.

Friedman, B., & Nissenbaum, H. (1996). Bias in computer systems. *ACM Transactions on Information Systems, 14*(3), 330–347.

Friedman, B., Howe, D. C., & Felten, E. (2002). Informed consent in the Mozilla browser: Implementing value sensitive design. In *Proceedings of the Thirty-Fifth Annual Hawai'i International Conference on System Sciences* [CD-ROM]. Los Alamitos, CA: IEEE Computer Society.

Friedman, E. J., & Resnick, P. (1997). The social cost of cheap pseudonyms. *Journal of Economics and Management Strategy, 10*(2), 173–179.

From sexual exploration to pathological expression. *Professional Psychology: Research and Practice, 30*(2), 154–164.

Frutiger, A. (1980). *Type, sign, symbol.* Zürich, Switzerland: ABC Verlag.

Frutiger, A. (1989). *Signs and symbols: Their design and meaning.* New York: Van Nostrand Reinhold.

Fry, C. (1993). Flavors band: A language for specifying musical style. In S. Schwanauer & D. Levitt (Eds.), *Machine models of music.* Cambridge, MA: MIT Press.

Fuchs, H., Livingston, M., Raskar, R., Colucci, D., Keller, K., State, et al. (1998). Augmented reality visualization for laparoscopic surgery. *Proceedings of First International Conference on Medical Image Computing and Computer-Assisted Intervention*; Lecture Notes in Computer Science 1496, 934–943.

Fujii, H., & Croft, W. B. (1993). A comparison of indexing techniques for Japanese text retrieval. In *Proceedings of the 16th annual ACM SIGIR Conference on Research and Development in Information Retrieval* (pp. 237–246). New York: ACM Press.

Fujisaki, H., & Nagashima, S. (1969). Synthesis of pitch contours of connected speech. *Annual Report of the Engineering Research Institute, University of Tokyo, 28,* 53–60.

Fujiyoshi, H., & Lipton, A. J. (1998, October). *Real-time human motion analysis by image skeletonization.* Paper presented at the Fourth IEEE Workshop on Applications of Computer Vision, Princeton, New Jersey. Retrieved August 19, 2003, from http://www.dcs.ex.ac. uk/people/wangjunl/fujiyoshi_hironobu_1998_1.pdf

Gabor, D. (1946). Theory of communication. *Journal of the Institution of Electrical Engineers, Pt. III, 93,* 429–459.

Gajendar, U. (2003). Learning to love the pixel: Exploring the craft of icon design. Retrieved January 11, 2004, from http://www.boxe-sandarrows.com/archives/learning_to_love_the_pixel_exploring_the_craft_of_icon_design.php

Galata, A., Johnson, N., & Hogg, D. (2001). Learning variable-length Markov models of behavior. *Computer Vision and Image Understanding, 81*(3), 398–413.

Gale, W. A. (ed.) (1986). *Artificial intelligence and statistics.* Reading, MA: Addison-Wesley.

Gale, W. A., Hand, D. J., & Kelly, A. E. (1993). Statistical applications of artificial intelligence. In C. R. Rao (Ed.), *Handbook of statistics* (Vol. 9, pp. 535–576). Amsterdam: Elsevier Science.

Galegher, J., Kraut, R. E., & Egido, C. (Eds.). (1990). *Intellectual teamwork: Social and technological bases for cooperative work.* Hillsdale, NJ: Erlbaum.

Galinsky, T. L., Swanson, N. G., Sauter, S. L., Hurrell, J. J., & Schleifer L. M. (2000). A field study of supplementary rest breaks for data-entry operators. *Ergonomics, 43*(5), 622–638.

Gallagher, J. C., & Vigraham, S. (2002). A modified compact genetic algorithm for the intrinsic evolution of continuous time recurrent neural networks. In W. B. Langdon, E. Cantú-Paz, K. Mathias, R. Roy, D. Davis, R. Poli et al. (Eds.), *GECCO 2002: Proceedings of the Genetic and Evolutionary Computation Conference* (pp. 163–170). San Francisco: Morgan-Kaufmann.

Garau, M., Slater, M., Vinayagamoorhty, V., Brogni, A., Steed, A., & Sasse, M. A. (2003). The impact of avatar realism and eye gaze control on perceived quality of communication in a shared immersive virtual environment. In *Proceedings of the SIGCHI Conference on Human Factors in Computing Systems* (pp. 529–536). New York: ACM Press.

Gardner, J. W., & Bartlett, P. N. (1999). *Electronic noses: Principles and applications.* New York: Oxford University Press.

Garfinkel, H. (1967). *Studies in ethnomethodology.* Englewood Cliffs, NJ: Prentice-Hall.

Garfinkel, S. (1999). *Architects of the information society: 35 years of the laboratory for computer science at MIT.* Cambridge, MA: MIT Press.

Gargi, U., Kasturi, R., & Strayer, S. H. (2000). Performance characterization of video-shot change detection methods. *IEEE Transactions on Circuits and Systems for Video Technology, 10,* 1–13.

Garman, N. (1996). Caught in the middle: Online professionals and beta testing. *Online, 20*(1), 6.

Garson, J. (1885). The Frankfort Craniometric Agreement, with critical remarks thereon. *Journal of the Anthropological Institute of Great Britain and Ireland, 14,* 64–83.

Garton, L. & Wellman, B. (1995). Social impacts of electronic mail in organizations: A review of the research literature. In B. R. Burleson (Ed.), *Communications Yearbook, 18.* Thousand Oaks, CA: Sage.

Garud, R., Sanjay, J., & Phelps, C. (n.d.). *Unpacking Internet time innovation.* Unpublished manuscript, New York University, New York.

Gashnig, J. (1979). *Performance measurement and analysis of certain search algorithms.* Pittsburgh, PA: Carnegie-Mellon University.

Gavan, J. (1950). The consistency of anthropometric measurements. *American Journal of Physical Anthropometry, 8,* 417–426.

Gaver, W. W. (1997). Auditory interfaces. In M. Helander, T. K. Landauer, & P. Prabhu (Ed.), *Handbook of human computer interaction* (2nd ed.): Elsevier Science B.V.

Gavison, R. (1980). Privacy and the limits of law. *Yale Law Journal, 89,* 421–471.

Gavrila, D. M. (1999). The visual analysis of human movement: A survey. *Computer Vision and Image Understanding,* 73(1), 82–98.

GCC Homepage. (2004). Retrieved January 26, 2004, from http://gcc.gnu.org/

Geer, D., Pfleeger, P., Schneier, B., Quarterman, J., Metzger, P., Bace, R., & Gutmann, P. (2003). *CyberInsecurity: The cost of monopoly.* Retrieved April 13, 2004, from http://www.ccianet.org/papers/cyberinsecurity.pdf

Gemmell, J., Bell, G., Lueder, R., Drucker, S., & Wong, C. (2002). MyLifeBits: Fulfilling the Memex vision. In *ACM Multimedia* (pp. 235–238). New York: Association for Computing Machinery.

Gemperle, F., Kasabach, C., Stivoric, J., Bauer, M., and Martin, R. (1998, October). Design for wearability. *Proceedings of the Second International Symposium on Wearable Computers,* 116–123.

Georgia Tech Research Corporation. *GVU's WWW user survey.* Retrieved July 27, 2003, from http://www.gvu.gatech.edu/user_surveys/

Gerard, M. J., Armstrong, T. J., Franzblau, A., Martin, B. J., & Rempel, D. M. (1999). The effects of keyswitch stiffness on typing force, finger electromyography, and subjective discomfort. *American Industrial Hygiene Association Journal,* 60(6), 762–769.

Gerr, F., Marcus, M., Ensor, C., Kleinbaum, D., Cohen, S., Edwards, A., Gentry, E., Ortiz, D. J., & Monteilh, C. (2002). A prospective study of computer users: I. Study design and incidence of musculoskeletal symptoms and disorders. *American Journal of Industrial Medicine,* 41, 221–235.

Gerstner, K. (1974). Compendium for literates: A system of writing. Cambridge, MA: MIT Press.

Getty, D. J., & Howard Jr., J. H. (1981). *Auditory and visual pattern recognition.* Hillsdale, NJ: Erlbaum.

Gevins, A., Leong, H., Du, R., Smith, M. E., Le, J., DuRousseau, D., Zhang, J., & Libove, J. (1995). Towards measurement of brain function in operational environments. *Biological Psychology, 40,* 169–186.

Giarratano, J. C. (1998). *Expert systems: Principles and programming.* Pacific Grove, CA: Brooks Cole.

Gibson, J. J. (1966). *The senses considered as perceptual systems.* Boston: Houghton Mifflin.

Gibson, R., Nixon, P., & Ward, S. (Eds.). (2003). *Political parties and the Internet: Net gain?* New York, NY: Routledge.

Gibson, W. (1984). *Neuromancer.* New York: Ace Books.

Gibson, W., & Sterling, B. (1991). *The difference engine.* New York: Bantam.

Gilbreth, F. B. (1911). *Motion study.* Princeton, NJ: Van Nostrand.

Gilbreth, F., & Gilbreth, L. (1919). *Applied motion study.* London: Sturgis and Walton.

Gildea, D., & Jurafsky, D. (2002). Automatic labeling of semantic roles. *Computational Linguistics,* 28(3), 245–288.

Gillam, R. (2002). *Unicode demystified: a practical programmers guide to the encoding standard.* Boston, MA: Addison-Wesley.

Gilleade, K., & Allanson, J. (2003). *A tollkit for exploring affective interface adaptation in video games.* Human-Computer International (HCII03). Crete, Greece: Lawrence Erlbaum Associates.

Gillies, J., & Cailliau, R. (2000). *How the Web was born: The story of the World Wide Web.* New York: Oxford Paperbacks.

Ginsparg, P. (2001). *Creating a global knowledge network.* Retrieved July 28, 2003, from http://arxiv.org/blurb/pg01unesco.html

Gladwin, T. (1970). *East is a big bird.* Cambridge, MA: Harvard University Press.

Glaisher, J. W. L. (1874). On the problem of the eight queens. *Philosophical Magazine,* 4(48), 457–467.

Gligor, V. D. (1983). A note on the denial of service problem. *Proceedings of 1983 Symposium on Security and Privacy* (pp. 139–149).

Gligor, V. D. (1986). On denial of service in computer networks. *Proceedings of International Conference on Data Engineering* (pp. 608–617).

Gligor, V. D. (2003). Guaranteeing access in spite of service-flooding attacks. *Proceedings of the Security Protocols Workshop.*

Global Reach. Retrieved on February 27, 2004, from www.glreach.com/globstats/index.php3

Globe. (2004). *The Globe program.* Retrieved March 9, 2004, from http://www.globe.gov/globe_flash.html

Glover, F. (1989). Tabu Search—Part I. *ORSA Journal on Computing,* 1(3), 190–206.

Godfrey, M. W., & Tu, Q. (2000). *Evolution in open source software: A case study.* Paper presented at the tThe 2000 International Conference on Software Maintenance.

Goel, V. (1995). *Sketches of thought.* Cambridge MA: MIT Press.

Goffman, E. (1959). *The presentation of the self in everyday life.* Garden City, N.Y.: Doubleday.

Goffman, E. (1963). *Behavior in public places: Notes on the social organization of gatherings.* New York: Free Press.

Goguen, J. A. (1996). Formality and informality in requirements engineering. *Proceedings of the 4th International Conference on Requirements Engineering,* IEEE Computer Society, 102–108.

Goldberg, A. (1984). *Smalltalk-80: The interactive programming environment.* New York: Addison-Wesley.

Goldberg, J. H., & Kotval, X. P. (1999). Computer interface evaluation using eye movements: Methods and constructs. *International Journal of Industrial Ergonomics, 24,* 631–645.

Goldberg, J. H., Stimson, M. J., Lewenstein, M., Scott, N., & Wichansky, A. M. (2002). Eye tracking in web search tasks: Design implications. In *Proceedings of Eye Tracking Research & Applications* (ETRA) (pp. 51–58). New Orleans, LA: ACM.

Goldschmidt, K. (2001). Email overload in Congress: Managing a communications crisis. *Congress Online Project.* Retrieved October 1, 2003, from www.congressonlineproject.org/emailoverload.pdf.

Golle, P., Leyton-Brown, K., & Mironov, I. (2001). Incentives for sharing in peer-to-peer networks. In *Proceedings of the 20001 ACM Conference on Electronic Commerce* (pp. 264–267). New York: ACM Press.

Gomer, F. (1980). *Biocybernetic applications for military systems.* Chicago: McDonnell Douglas.

Gomes, C. P. (2004). Randomized backtrack search. In M. Milano (Ed.), *Constraint and Integer Programming: Toward a Unified Methodology* (pp. 233–291). Boston: Kluwer Academic Publishers.

Goodman, B. A., & Litman, D. J. (1992). On the interaction between plan recognition and intelligent interfaces. *User Modeling and User-Adapted Interaction,* 2(1), 83–115.

Goodman, E. D., Seo, K., Rosenberg, R. C., Fan, Z., Hu, J., & Zhang, B. (2002). Automated design methodology for mechatronic systems using bond graphs and genetic programming. In *2002 NSF Design, Service, and Manufacturing Grantees and Research Conference* (pp. 206–221). Arlington, VA: National Science Foundation.

Goransson, B., Gulliksen, J., & Boivie, I. (2004). The usability design process—integrating user-centered systems design in the software development process. Software Process Improvement and Practice, 8(2).

BIBLIOGRAPHY

Gordon, C., & Bradtmiller, B. (1992). Interobserver error in a large scale anthropometric survey. *American Journal of Human Biology, 4,* 253–263.

Gordon, C., Bradtmiller, B., Clauser, C., Churchill, T., McConville, J., Tebbetts, I., & Walker, R. (1989). *1987–1988 anthropometric survey of U.S. Army personnel: Methods and summary statistics* (Technical Report No. TR-89/027). Natick, MA: U.S. Army Natick Research, Development and Engineering Center.

Gordon, D. (1990). *The justice juggernaut: Fighting street crime, controlling citizens.* New Brunswick, NJ: Rutgers University Press.

Gornik, D. (2003). IBM rational unified process: Best practices for software development teams. *IBM Technical Paper TP026B.*

Gorriz, C., & Medina, C. (2000). Engaging girls with computers through software games. *Communications of the Association of Computing Machinery, 43*(1), 42–49.

Gorski, P. (Fall, 2002). Dismantling the digital divide: A multicultural education framework. *Multicultural Education, 10*(1), 28–30.

Gotterbarn, D. & Rogerson, S. (2001). The ethics of software project management. In G. Colllste (Ed.), *Ethics in the age of information technology* (pp. 278–300). Linköping Sweden: Linköping University Press.

Gotterbarn, D. (1995). Computer ethics: Responsibility regained. In D. G. Johnson & H. Nissenbaum (Eds.), *Computers, ethics, and social values* (pp. 18–24). Englewood Cliffs, NJ: Prentice Hall.

Gotterbarn, D. (2002). Reducing software failures: Addressing the ethical risks of the software development lifecycle. *Australian Journal of Information Systems, 9*(2). Retrieved December 10, 2003, from http://www.inter-it.com/articles.asp?id=195

Gould, J. D., & Lewis, C. (1985). Designing for usability: Key principles and what designers think. *Communications of the ACM, 28*(3), 300–311.

Gould, J. D., Boies, S. J., & Lewis, C. (1991). Making usable, useful, productivity-enhancing computer applications. *Communications of the ACM, 34*(1), 74–86.

Govindarajulu, C., & Lippert, S.K. (June 2002). The status of end-user computing support: An exploratory study. In *Informing science & IT education conference proceedings* (pp. 581–585). Retrieved January 22, 2004, from http://ecommerce.lebow.drexel.edu/eli/2002Proceedings/papers/Govin163Statu.pdf

Graham, P. (2002). *A plan for spam.* Retrieved April 13, 2004, from www.paulgraham.com/antispam.html

Graham, T. (2000). *Unicode: a primer.* Foster City, CA: MIS: Press.

Graham, T. C. N., Watts, L. A., Calvary, G., Coutaz, J., Dubois, E., & Nigay, L. (2000). A dimension space for the design of interactive systems within their physical environments. In *Proceedings of the Conference on Designing Interactive Systems: Processes, Practices, Methods, and Techniques,* (pp. 406–416). New York: ACM Press.

Grant, G. (2003). *H-1B hearing: Companies say foreign workers needed.* Retrieved November 8, 2003, from http://www.infoworld.com/article/03/09/17/HNh1bhearing_1.html.

Grant, R. A., Higgins, C. A., & Irving, R. H. (1988). Computerized performance monitors: Are they costing you customers? *Sloan Management Review, 29,* 39–45.

Gray, M. (1996). *Internet statistics.* Retrieved September 30, 2003, from http://www.mit.edu/people/mkgray/net/

Gray, W. D. (1995). VCR-as-paradigm: A study and taxonomy of errors in an interactive task. In K. Nordby, P. Helmersen, D. J. Gilmore, & S. A. Arnesen (Eds.), *Human-Computer Interaction—Interact'95* (pp. 265–270). New York: Chapman & Hall.

Gray, W. D. (2000). The nature and processing of errors in interactive behavior. *Cognitive Science, 24*(2), 205–248.

Gray, W. D., & Altmann, E. M. (2001). Cognitive modeling and human-computer interaction. In W. Karwowski (Ed.), *International encyclopedia of ergonomics and human factors* (pp. 387–391). New York: Taylor & Francis.

Gray, W. D., & Boehm-Davis, D. A. (2000). Milliseconds matter: An introduction to microstrategies and to their use in describing and predicting interactive behavior. *Journal of Experimental Psychology: Applied, 6*(4), 322–335.

Gray, W. D., & Fu, W.-t. (2001). Ignoring perfect knowledge in-the-world for imperfect knowledge in-the-head: Implications of rational analysis for interface design. *CHI Letters, 3*(1), 112–119.

Gray, W. D., & Fu, W.-t. (in press). Soft constraints in interactive behavior: The case of ignoring perfect knowledge in-the-world for imperfect knowledge in-the-head. *Cognitive Science.*

Gray, W. D., & Salzman, M. D. (1998). Damaged merchandise? A review of experiments that compare usability evaluation methods. *Human-Computer Interaction, 13*(3), 203–261.

Gray, W. D., John, B. E., & Atwood, M. E. (1993). Project Ernestine: Validating a GOMS analysis for predicting and explaining real–world performance. *Human-Computer Interaction, 8*(3), 237–309.

Gray, W. D., Palanque, P., & Paternò, F. (1999). Introduction to the special issue on: interface issues and designs for safety-critical interactive systems. *ACM Transactions on Computer-Human Interaction, 6*(4), 309–310.

Graybill, R., & Melhwm, R. (2002). *Power aware computing.* New York: Kluwer Academic/Plenum.

Grebb, M. (2003). *The sleek touch.* Retrieved October 10, 2003, from http://www.ce.org/publications/vision/2003/sepoct/p10.asp

Green, T. R. G., & Petre, M. (1996). Usability analysis of visual programming environments: A "cognitive dimensions" framework. *Journal of Visual Languages and Computing, 7*(2), 131–174.

Greenbaum, J. (1979). *In the name of efficiency.* Philadelphia: Temple University Press.

Greenbaum, J., & Kyng, M. (1991). *Design at work: Cooperative design of computer systems.* Hillsdale, NJ: Lawrence Erlbaum Associates.

Greenwald, A. G., & Farnham, S. D. (2000). Using the Implicit Association Test to measure self-esteem and self-concept. *Journal of Personality and Social Psychology, 79*(6), 1022–1038.

Greenwald, A. G., McGhee, D. E., & Schwartz, J. L. K. (1998). Measuring individual differences in implicit cognition: The Implicit Association Test. *Journal of Personality and Social Psychology, 74*(6), 1464–1480.

Gregory, R. L. (1997). *Eye and brain: The psychology of seeing.* Oxford, UK: Oxford University Press.

Gregory-Huddleston, K. (1994). Culture conflict with growth: Cases from Silicon Valley. In T. Hamada & W. Sibley (Eds.), *Anthropological Perspectives on Organizational Culture.* Washington, DC: University Press of America.

Griffiths, J.-M. (1998). Why the Web is not a library. In B. Hawkins & P. Battin (Eds.), *The mirage of continuity: Reconfiguring academic information resources for the twenty-first century* (pp. 229–246). Washington, DC: Council on Library and Information Resources, Association of American Universities.

Grishman, R., Mcleod, C., & Meyers, A. (1994). COMLEX syntax: Building a computational lexicon. Proceedings of the 15th International Conference on Computational Linguistics (COLING-94), Kyoto, Japan.

BIBLIOGRAPHY

Gritzalis, D. (Ed.). (2003). *Secure electronic voting*. Boston: Kluwer Academic Publishers.

Grodzinsky, F. S. (1999). The practitioner from within: Revisiting the virtues. *Computers and Society, 29*(1), 9–15.

Grønbæk, K. (1990). Supporting active user involvement in prototyping. *Scandinavian Journal of Information Systems, 2*, 3–24.

Gross, M. D., & Do, E. Y.-L. (2000). Drawing on the back of an envelope: A framework for interacting with application programs by freehand drawing. *Computers and Graphics, 24*(6), 835–849.

Grossman, A. (2001, July 9). The rush to SVOD: Not so fast. Retrieved January 2, 2004, from http://www.broadbandweek.com/news/010709/010709_supp_rush.htm

Grossnickle, J., & Raskin, O. (2001). *Handbook of online marketing research*. New York: McGraw Hill.

Grossnickle, J., & Raskin, O. (n.d.). Supercharged beta test. *Webmonkey: Design*. Retrieved January 8, 2004, from http://hotwired.lycos.com/webmonkey.

Grosz, B. J. (1978). Discourse analysis. In D. Walker (Ed.), *Understanding spoken language* (pp. 235–268). New York: Elsevier North-Holland.

Grosz, B. J., & Kraus, S. (1996). Collaborative plans for complex group actions. *Artificial Intelligence, 86*, 269–358.

Grosz, B. J., & Kraus, S. (1999). The evolution of SharedPlans. In M. Wooldridge & A. Rao (Eds.), *Foundations and theories of rational agency* (pp. 227–262). Amsterdam: Kluwer.

Grosz, B. J., & Sidner, C. (1986). Attention, intention, and the structure of discourse. *Computational Linguistics, 12*(3), 175–204.

Grosz, B. J., & Sidner, C. L. (1990). Plans for discourse. In P. R. Cohen, J. Morgan, & M. Pollack (Eds.), *Intentions in communication* (pp. 417–445). Cambridge, MA: MIT Press.

Grubb, L., & Dannenberg, R. (1998). Enhanced vocal performance tracking using multiple information sources. In *Proceedings of the 1998 International Computer Music Conference* (pp. 34–44). San Francisco, CA: Computer Music Association.

Grudin, J. (1988). Why CSCW applications fail: Problems in the design and evaluation of organizational interfaces. *Proceedings of the ACM Conference on Computer Supported Cooperative Work* (pp. 85–93). Portland, OR: ACM Press.

Grudin, J. (1990) Groupware and cooperative work. In B. Laurel (Ed.), *The art of human-computer interface design* (pp. 171–185). Reading, MA: Addison-Wesley.

Grudin, J. (1990). The computer reaches out: The historical continuity of interface design. In *Proceedings of the SIGCHI conference on human factors in computing systems '90* (pp. 261–268). New York: ACM Press.

Grudin, J. (1994). Groupware and social dynamics: Eight challenges for developers. *Communications of the ACM, 37*(1), 92–105.

Grudin, J., & MacLean, A. (1984). Adapting a psychophysical method to measure performance and preference tradeoffs in human-computer interaction. In *Proceedings of INTERACT '84* (pp. 338–342). Amsterdam: North Holland.

Guarino, N. (1998). Formal Ontology in Information Systems. In *Proceedings of the International Conference on Formal Ontology in Information Systems* (pp. 3–15). Trento, Italy.

Guiard, Y. (1987). Asymmetric division of labor in human skilled bimanual action: the kinematic chain as a model. *Journal of Motor Behavior, 19*(4), 486–517.

Guillaume, D., & Murtagh, F. (2000). Clustering of XML documents. *Computer Physics Communications, 127*, 215–227.

Guo, X. (1999). *Eye contact—Talking about non-verbal communication: A corpus study*. Retrieved April 29, 2004, from http://www.languagemagazine.com/internetedition/ma99/sprpt35.html

Gupta, S., Kaiser, G., Neistadt, D., & Grimm, P. (2003). DOM-based content extraction of HTML documents. In *Proceedings of the twelfth international conference on World Wide Web* (pp. 207–214). New York: Association for Computing Machinery.

Gustafson, J. (2000). Reconstruction of the Atanasoff-Berry computer. In R. Rojas & U. Hashagen (Eds.), *The first computers: History and architectures* (91–106). Cambridge, MA: MIT Press.

Gutierrez-Osuna, R. (2002). A self-organizing model of chemotopic convergence for olfactory coding. In *Proceedings of the 2nd Joint EMBS-BMES Conference* (pp. 236–237). Houston, TX: IEEE.

Gutierrez-Osuna, R. (2002). Pattern analysis for machine olfaction: A review. *IEEE Sensors Journal, 2*(3), 189–202.

Gutwin, C., & Greenberg, S. (1998). Design for individuals, design for groups: Tradeoffs between power and worskpace awareness. In *Proceedings of ACM Conference on Computer Supported Cooperative Work*. New York: ACM.

Gutwin, C., & Greenberg, S. (1999). The effects of workspace awareness support on the usability of real-time distributed groupware. *ACM Transactions on Computer-Human Interaction, 6*(3), 243–281.

Gutwin, C., Greenberg, S., & Roseman, M. (1996). Workspace awareness in real-time distributed groupware: Framework, widgets, and evaluation. In *People and Computers XI: Proceedings of the HCI'96* (pp. 281–298). Berlin, Germany: Springer-Verlag.

Haber, R. (1970). How we remember what we see. *Scientific American, 222*, 104–112.

Hacid, M. S., Decleir, C., & Kouloumdjian, J. (2000). A database approach for modeling and querying video data. *IEEE Transactions on Knowledge and Data Engineering, 12*(5), 729–750.

Hacker, B. (1978). *On the shoulders of Titans: A history of Project Gemini*. Washington, DC: NASA Scientific and Technical Information Office.

Hacker, S. L. (1987). Feminist perspectives on computer based systems. In G. Bjerknes, P. Ehn, & M. Kyng (Eds.), *Computers and Democracy* (pp. 177–190). Aldershot, UK: Avebury.

Hackett, E. J. (2000). Interdisciplinary research initiatives at the U.S. National Science Foundation. In P. Weingart & N. Sterhr (Eds.), *Practicing interdisciplinarity* (pp. 248–259). Toronto, Canada: University of Toronto Press.

Hackos, J. T., (1994). *Managing your documentation projects*. New York: Wiley.

Hackos, J., & Redish, J. (1998). *User and task analysis for interface design*. New York: Wiley.

Hadden, J. K., & Cowan, D. E. (Eds.). (2000). *Religion on the Internet: Research prospects and promises*. New York: JAI/Elsevier.

Haddon, A. (1934). *The history of anthropology*. London: Watts & Co.

Hafner, K. (2001). *The Well: A story of love, death & real life in the seminal online community*. Berkeley, CA: Carroll & Graf.

Hafner, K., & Lyon, M. (1996). *Where wizards stay up late: The origins of the Internet*. New York: Simon & Schuster.

Hagel, J., & Brown, J. S. (2002). *Service grids: The missing link in web services*. Retrieved February 2, 2004, from http://www.johnhagel.com/paper_servicegrid.pdf

Haggerty, K. D., & Ericson, R. V. (1999). The militarization of policing in the information age. *Journal of Political and Military Sociology, 27*(2), 233–255.

Hagman, J., Hendrickson, A., & Whitty, A. (in press). What's in a barcode: Informed consent and machine scannable driver licenses. In

BIBLIOGRAPHY

CHI 2003 Extended Abstracts of the Conference on Human Factors in Computing Systems. CD-ROM. New York: ACM Press.

Haining, P. (Ed.). (1983). *Doctor Who: A celebration.* London: W. H. Allen.

Hakken, D. (1991). Culture-centered computing: Social policy and development of new information technology in England and the United States. *Human Organization, 50*(4), 406–423.

Hakken, D. (1999). *Cyborgs@cyberspace?: An ethnographer looks to the future.* New York: Routledge.

Hakken, D. (2003). *The knowledge landscapes of cyberspace.* New York: Routledge.

Hakken, D., & Andrews, B. (1993). *Computing myths, class realities.* Boulder, CO: Westview Press.

Hall, C. (1994). *Technical foundations of client/server systems.* New York: Wiley.

Haller, S., Kobsa, A., & McRoy, S. (Eds.). (1999). *Computational models for mixed-initiative interaction.* Dordrect, Netherlands: Kluwer Academic.

Hallford, N., & Hallford, J. (2001). *Swords and circuitry: A designers guide to computer role-playing games.* Roseville, CA: Prima Tech.

Halverson, C. A., Erickson, T., & Sussman, J. (2003). *What counts as success? Punctuated patterns of use in a persistent chat environment.* Paper presented at the Conference on Supporting Group Work, Sanibel Island, FL.

Hammer, D. P. (1976). *The Information Age: Its development, its impact.* Metuchen, NJ: Scarecrow Press.

Hampapur, A., Jain, R., & Weymouth, T. E. (1995). Production model based digital video segmentation. *Multimedia Tools Applications, 1,* 9–46.

Hampton, K. (2001). *Living the wired life in the wired suburb: Netville, glocalization and civil society.* Unpublished doctoral dissertation, University of Toronto, Ontario, Canada.

Hampton, K., & Wellman, B. (2003). Neighboring in Netville: How the Internet supports community and social capital in a wired suburb. *City and Community, 2*(3), 277–311.

Han, J., & Kamber, M. (2000). *Data mining: Concepts and techniques.* San Francisco, CA: Morgan Kaufman.

Hand, C. (1997). A survey of 3-D interaction techniques. *Computer Graphics Forum, 16*(5), 269–281.

Hand, D. J., Mannila, H., & Smyth, P. (2001). *Principles of data mining.* Cambridge, MA: MIT Press.

Handel, S. (1989). *Listening: An introduction to the perception of auditory events.* Cambridge, MA: MIT Press.

Hanjalic, A. (2002). Shot-boundary detection: Unraveled and resolved? *IEEE Transactions on Circuits and Systems for Video Technology, 12,* 90–105.

Haralick, R. M., & Elliott, G. L. (1980). Increasing tree search efficiency for constraint satisfaction problems. *Artificial Intelligence, 14,* 263–313.

Haramundanis, K. (1997). *The art of technical documentation* (2nd ed.). Woburn, MA: Butterworth-Heinemann.

Harasim, L. M. (Ed.). (1990). *Online education: perspectives on a new environment* (pp. 39–64). New York: Praeger.

Haraway, D. (1991). *Simians, cyborgs, and women— The reinvention of nature.* London: Free Association Books.

Hardgrave, B. C., Wilson, R. L., & Eastman, K. (1999). Toward a contingency model for selecting an information system prototyping strategy. *Journal of Management Information Systems, 16*(2), 113–137.

Hardy, I. R. (1996). *The evolution of ARPANET e-mail.* History Thesis, University of California at Berkeley. Retrieved March 31, 2004, from http://www.ifla.org/documents/internet/hari1.txt.

Harel, D., Carmel, L., & Lancet, D. (2003). Towards an odor communication system. *Computational Biology and Chemistry, 27,* 121–133.

Haritaoglu, I., Harwood, D., & Davis, L. S. (2000, August). W4: Real-time surveillance of people and their activities. *IEEE Transactions on Pattern Analysis and Machine Intelligence, 22*(8), 809–830.

Harnad, S. (2001). *For whom the gate tolls? How and why to free the refereed research literature online through author/institution self-archiving, now.* Retrieved July 28, 2003, from http://cogprints.soton.ac.uk/documents/disk0/00/00/16/39/index.html

Harold, E. R. (1998). *XML: Extensible markup language.* San Francisco: Hungry Minds.

Harrison, S., & Dourish, P. (1996). Re-placing space: The roles of place and space in collaborative systems. In *Proceedings of the Conference on Computer Supported Cooperative Work: CSCW '96* (pp. 67–76). New York: ACM Press.

Harrison, T. M., & Zappen, J. P. (2003). Methodological and theoretical frameworks for the design of community information systems. *Journal of Computer-Mediated Communication, 8*(3). Retrieved February 17, 2004, from http://www.ascusc.org/jcmc/vol8/issue3/harrison.html

Harrison, T. M., Zappen, J. P., & Prell, C. (2002). Transforming new communication technologies into community media. In N. W. Jankowski & O. Prehn (Eds.), *Community media in the information age: Perspectives and prospects* (pp. 249–269). Cresskill, NJ: Hampton Press Communication Series.

Hars, A., & Ou, S. (2001). Working for free? Motivations of participating in open source projects. Paper presented at the Hawaii International Conference on Systems Sciences.

Hart, A. (1992). *Knowledge acquisition for expert systems.* New York: McGraw-Hill.

Hartley, R. V. L. (1928). Transmission of information. *Bell System Technical Journal, 7,* 535–563.

Hartmann, H., Kraut, R. E., & Tilly, L. (1986). *Computer chips and paper clips: Technology and women's employment.* Washington, DC: National Academy Press.

Hartson, H. R., Castillo, J. C., Kelso, J., Kamler, J., & Neale, W. C. (1996). Remote evaluation: The network as an extension of the usability laboratory. In *Proceedings ACM CHI'96,* 228–235.

Hartswood, M., Procter, R., Slack, R., Soutter, J., Vos, A., & Rouncefield, M. (2002). The benefits of a long engagement: From contextual design to the co-realisation of work affording artefacts. In *ACM International Conference Proceeding Series: Proceedings of the Second Nordic Conference on HCI* (pp. 283–286). New York: ACM Press.

Hauben, M. (2003). *History of ARPANET.* Retrieved August 7, 2003, from http://www.dei.isep.ipp.pt/docs/arpa.html

Hauck, R. V., Atabakhsh, H., Ongvasith, P., & Chen, H. (2002). Using Coplink to analyze criminal-justice data. *IEEE Computer, 35*(3), 30–37.

Hauptmann, G., & McAvinney, P. (1993) Gesture with speech for graphics manipulation. *International Journal of Man-Machine Studies, 38*(2), 231–249.

Haveliwala, T. (2003, July–August). Topic-sensitive PageRank: A context-sensitive ranking algorithm for Web search. *IEEE Transactions on Knowledge and Data Engineering,* 784–796.

Haydon, L. M. (1995). *The complete guide to writing and producing technical manuals.* New York: Wiley.

Haythornthwaite, C., & Wellman, B. (1998). Work, friendship and media use for information exchange in a networked organization. *Journal of the American Society for Information Science, 49*(12), 1101–1114.

Hayward, T. (1995). *Info-rich, info-poor: Access and exchange in the global information society.* London: K. G. Saur.

Hearn, D., & Baker, M. (1996). *Computer graphics with OpenGL* (3rd ed). Upper Saddle River, NJ: Prentice Hall.

Hearnshaw, H. M., & Unwin, D. J. (Eds.). (1994). *Visualization in geographical information systems.* New York: Wiley.

Heath, C. & Luff, P. (2000). *Technology in Action.* Cambridge. MA: Cambridge University Press.

Hecker, F. (1999). Setting up shop: The business of open-source software. *IEEE Software,* 45–51.

Heckhausen, H., & Beckmann, J. (1990). Intentional action and action slips. *Psychological Review, 97*(1), 36–48.

Hedberg, S. After desktop computing: A progress report on smart environments research. *IEEE Intelligent Systems, 15*(5), 7–9.

Heeks, R. (Ed.). (1999). *Reinventing government in the information age: International practice in IT-enabled public sector reform.* London and New York: Routledge.

Hefley, W., et al. (1994). Integrating human factors with software engineering practices. *Human-Computer Interaction Institute Technical Report,* CMU-CHII, 94–103.

Hegner, S. J., Mc Kevitt, P., Norvig, P., & Wilensky, R. L. (Eds.). (2001). *Intelligent help systems for UNIX.* Dordrecht, Netherlands: Kluwer.

Heidner, F. (1915). Type-writing machine. *Letter's Patent 1,* 138–474. United States Patent Office.

Heinlein, R. A. (1950). *Waldo and Magic Inc.* Garden City, NY: Doubleday.

Heinlein, R. A. (1966). *The moon is a harsh mistress.* New York: Orb.

Helander, M., Landauer, T. K., & Prabhu, P. V. (1997). *Handbook of human-computer interaction* (2nd ed.). Amsterdam: Elsevier Science-North Holland.

Helmreich, S. (1999). *Silicon second nature: Culturing artificial life in a digital world.* Berkeley and Los Angeles: University of California Press.

Hendry, D. (2000). *Design space of spelling checkers and correctors.* Retrieved January 20, 2004, from http://faculty.washington.edu/dhendry/Projects/Spelling/

Henman, P. (2002). Computer modeling and the politics of greenhouse gas policy in Australia. *Social Science Computer Review, 20*(2), 161–173.

Herbst, S. (1993). *Numbered voices: How opinion polling has shaped American politics.* Chicago: University of Chicago Press.

Herring, S. C., with D. Johnson & T. DiBenedetto. (1995). "This discussion is going too far!" Male resistance to female participation on the Internet. In M. Bucholtz & K. Hall (Eds.), *Gender articulated: Language and the socially constructed self* (pp. 67–96). New York: Routledge.

Hert, C. A. (1997). *Understanding information retrieval interactions: Theoretical and practical applications.* Stamford, CT: Ablex.

Hertzum, M., & Jacobsen, N. E. (2003). The evaluator effect: A chilling fact about usability evaluation methods. *International Journal of Human–Computer Interaction, 15*(1), 183–204.

Herz, J. C. (1995). *Surfing on the Internet: A net-head's adventures on-line.* New York: Little, Brown.

Herz, R. S. (1998). Are odors the best cues to memory? A cross-modal comparison of associative memory stimuli. *Annals of the New York Academy of Sciences, 855,* 670–674.

Heterick, R. C. (2001). Some can't, Some Kant. *The Learning MarketSpace.* Retrieved March 9, 2004, from http://www.center.rpi.edu/LForum/lm/Apr01.html

Hewett, T. T., Baecker, R., Card, S., Carey, T., Gasen, J., Mantei, M., et al. (1992). *ACM SIGCHI curricula for human-computer interaction.* New York: ACM. Retrieved July 24, 2003, from http://www.acm.org/sigchi/cdg/

Higa, K., & Shin, B. (2003). Virtual extension: The telework experience in Japan. *Communications of the ACM, 46*(9), 233–242.

Hilbert, D. M. (1999). *Large-scale collection of application usage date and user feedback to inform interactive software development.* Unpublished doctoral dissertation, University of California, Irvine.

Hill, K. A., & Hughes, J. E. (1998). *Cyberpolitics: Citizen activism in the age of the Internet.* Lanham, MD: Rowman & Littlefield.

Hill, W., & Hollan, J. (1994). History-enriched digital objects: Prototypes and policy issues. *Information Society, 10*(2), 139–145.

Hilton, M. (2001). Information technology workers in the new economy. *Monthly Labor Review, 124*(6), 41–45.

Hiltz, S. R., & Turoff, M. (1993). *The network nation* (2nd ed.). Cambridge, MA: MIT Press.

Hiltzik, M. A. (2000). *Dealers of lightning: Xerox PARC and the dawn of the computer age.* New York: HarperBusiness.

Hinckley, H. (2003). Distributed and local sensing techniques for face-to-face collaboration. In *Proceedings of the 5th international conference on multimodal interfaces* (pp. 81–84). New York: ACM Press.

Hinckley, K., & Sinclair, M. (1999). Touch-sensitive input device. In *Proceedings of CHI'99: ACM Conference in Human Factors in Computing Systems* (pp. 223–230). New York: ACM Press.

Hinckley, K., Cutrell, E., Bathiche, S., & Muss, T. (2002). Quantitative Analysis of Scrolling Techniques. In *Proceedings of CHI 2002: ACM Conference on Human Factors in Computing Systems* (pp. 65–72). New York: ACM Press.

Hinds, P. J., Roberts, T. L. and Jones, H. (2004). Whose job is it anyway? A study of human-robot interaction in a collaborative task. *Human-Computer Interaction, 19*(1–2).

Hinds, P., & Kiesler, S. (Eds.). (2002). *Distributed work.* Cambridge, MA: MIT Press.

Hirsh, S. G. (1999). Children's relevance criteria and information seeking on electronic resources. *Journal of the American Society for Information Science, 50*(14), 1265–1283.

Hix, D., & Hartson, H. R (1993). *Developing user interfaces: Ensuring usability through product and process.* New York: Wiley.

Ho, F.-C. (2002). An analysis of reading errors in Chinese language. In L. Jeffrey (Comp.), *AARE 2002 conference papers* (n.p.). Melbourne, Australia: Australian Association for Research in Education.

Hoaglin, D. C., Mosteller, F., & Tukey, J. W. (1983). *Understanding robust and exploratory data analysis.* New York: Wiley.

Hoaglin, D. C., Mosteller, F., & Tukey, J. W. (1985). *Exploring data tables, trends, and shapes.* New York: Wiley.

Hobson, D., & Molenbroek, J. (1990). Anthropometry and design for the disabled: Experiences with seating design for cerebral palsy population. *Applied Ergonomics, 21*(1), 43–54.

Hochmuth, P. (2002, December 12). IBM's open source advocate. *Network World.* Retrieved April 16, 2004, from http://www.nwfusion.com/power/2002/frye.html

Hockey, G. R. J., Briner, R. B., Tattersall, A. J., & Wiethoff, M. (1989). Assessing the impact of computer workload on operator stress: The role of system controllability. *Ergonomic, 32*, 1401–1418.

Hodges M. E., & Sasnett, R. M. (1993). *Multimedia computing: Case studies from MIT Project Athena*. Reading, MA: Addison Wesley.

Hoekstra, P. (1997). On postures, percentiles and 3D surface anthropometry. *Contemporary Ergonomics* (pp. 130–135). London: Taylor & Francis.

Hof, R., Green, H., & Himmelstein, L. (1998, October 5). Now it's YOUR WEB. *Business Week* (pp. 68–75).

Hoffman, D. L., & Novak, T. P. (1998, April). Bridging the racial divide on the Internet. *Science, 280*, 390–391.

Hoffman, D. L., Novak, T. P., & Schlosser, A. E. (2000). The evolution of the digital divide: How gaps in Internet access may impact electronic commerce. *Journal of Computer Mediated Communication, 5*(3), 1–57.

Hoffman, E. T. A. (1885). The sand-man. In *Weird Tales* (J. T. Bealby, Trans.). New York: Scribner's. (Original work published 1817)

Hoffman, H. (1998). Physically touching virtual objects using tactile augmentation enhances the realism of virtual environments. *Proceedings of the IEEE Virtual Reality Annual International Symposium '98*, 59–63.

Hoffman, P. E., & Grinstein, G. G. (2002). A survey of visualizations for high-dimensional data mining. In U. Fayyad, G. G. Grinstein, & A. Wierse (Eds.), *Information visualization in data mining and knowledge discovery* (pp. 47–82). San Francisco: Morgan Kaufmann.

Hoffman, R. R., Crandall, B., & Shadbolt, N. (1998). Use of the critical decision method to elicit expert knowledge: A case study in the methodology of cognitive task analysis. *Human Factors, 40*(2), 254–276.

Hofstede, G. (1980). *Culture's consequences: International differences in work-related values*. Beverly Hills, CA: Sage.

Hogg, T., Huberman, B. A., & Williams, C. P. (Eds.). (1996). Special volume on frontiers in problem solving: Phase transitions and complexity. *Artificial Intelligence, 81*(1–2). Burlington, MA: Elsevier Science.

Hollan, J., & Stornetta, S. (1992). Beyond being there. *ACM CHI'92 Proceedings*.

Hollan, J., Hutchins, E., & Kirsh, D. (2000). Distributed cognition: Toward a new foundation for HCI research. *ACM Transactions on Computer-Human Interaction (TOCHI), 7*(2), 174–196.

Holland, J. H. (1975). *Adaptation in natural and artificial systems*. Cambridge, MA: MIT Press.

Hollerbach, J., Xu, Y., Christensen, R., & Jacobsen, S. (2000). Design specifications for the second generation Sarcos Treadport locomotion interface. Haptics Symposium, *Proceedings of ASME Dynamic Systems and Control Division, 69*(2), 1293–1298.

Höllerer, T., Feiner, S., Terauchi, T., Rashid, G., & Hallaway, D. (1999). Exploring MARS: Developing indoor and outdoor user interfaces to a mobile augmented reality system. *Computers and Graphics, 23*(6), 779–785.

Hollingshead, A. B. (in press). Computer-mediated communication, the internet, and group research. In M. Hogg and R. S. Tindale (Eds.), *Blackwell handbook of social psychology* (Vol. 3). Oxford, UK: Blackwell.

Hollingshead, A. B., McGrath, J. E., and O'Connor, K. M. (1993). Group performance and communication technology: A longitudinal study of computer-mediated versus face-to-face work. *Small Group Research, 24*(3), 307–333.

Hollnagel, E. (1998). Measurements and models, models and measurements: You can't have one without the other. In: NATO RTO Meeting Proceedings 4, *Collaborative crew performance in complex operational systems*, April 20–22, 1998, Edinburgh, Scotland (TRO-MP-4 AC/323(HFM)TP/2).

Hollnagel, E., & Woods, D. D. (1983). Cognitive systems engineering: New wine in new bottles. *International Journal of Man-Machine Studies, 18*, 583–600.

Holt, B. J., & Morrell, R. W. (2002). Guidelines for website design for older adults: The ultimate influence of cognitive factors. In R. W. Morrell (Ed.), *Older adults, health information, and the World Wide Web* (pp. 109–129). Mahwah, NJ: Lawrence Erlbaum Associates.

Honald, P. (1999). Learning how to use a cellular phone: Comparison between German and Chinese users. Technical Communication: *Journal of the Society for Technical Communication, 46*(2), 196–205.

Honan, M. M., Serina, E., Tal, R., & Rempel, D. (1995). Wrist postures while typing on a standard and split keyboard. In *Proceedings of the Human Factors and Ergonomics Society 39th annual meeting*. Santa Monica, CA: Human Factors and Ergonomics Society.

Hooker, J. (2000). *Logic-based methods for optimization: Combining optimization and constraint satisfaction*. New York: Wiley.

Hoos, H. H., & Stützle, T. (2004). *Stochastic local search*. San Francisco: Morgan Kaufmann.

Hornby, G. S., & Pollack, J. B. (20012). Evolving L-systems to generate virtual creatures. *Computers and Graphics, 25*(6), 1041–1048.

Hornby, G. S., & Pollack, J. B. (2002). Creating high-level components with a generative representation for body-brain evolution. *Artificial Life, 8*(3), 223–246.

Horton, W. (1993). Let's do away with manuals before they do away with us. *Technical Communication, 40*(1), 26–34.

Horton, W. (1994). *Designing and writing online documentation: Hypermedia for self-supporting products* (2nd ed.). New York: Wiley.

Horvitz, E., Breese, J., Heckerman, D., Hovel, D., & Rommelse, K. (1998). The Lumière project: Bayesian user modeling for inferring the goals and needs of software users. In *Proceedings of Fourteenth Conference on Uncertainty in Artificial Intelligence* (pp. 256–265). San Francisco: Morgan Kaufmann.

Horvitz, E., Pavel, M., & Schmorrow, D. D. (2001). *Foundations of augmented cognition*. Washington, DC: National Academy of Sciences.

Hove, D. (Ed.). *The Free online dictionary of computing*. Retrieved March 10, 2004, from http://www.foldoc.org.

Hovy, E. H. (1988). *Generating natural language under pragmatic constraints*. Hillsdale, NJ: Lawrence Erlbaum.

How Stuff Works. (1998–2004). *How do digital signatures work?* Retrieved March 18, 2004, from http://www.howstuffworks.com/question571.htm

Howard, D. L., & Crosby, M. (1993). Snapshots from the eye: Towards strategies for viewing bibliographic citations. In G. Salvendy & M. Smith (Eds.), *Advances in human factors/ergonomics: Human-computer interaction: Software and hardware interfaces* (Vol. 19B, pp. 488–493). Amsterdam: Elsevier Science.

Howard, P. N., & Jones, S. (Eds.). (2003). *Society online: The Internet in context*. Thousand Oaks, CA: Sage.

Howe, A., von Mayrhauser, A., & Mraz, R. (1997). Test case generation as an AI planning problem. *Automated Software Engineering, 4*(1), 77–106.

Hrdlicka, A. (1918). Physical anthropology; its scope and aims, etc. *American Journal of Physical Anthropometry, 1,* 3–23.

Hsu, F. (2002). *Behind Deep Blue: Building the computer that defeated the world chess champion.* Princeton, NJ: Princeton University Press.

Huang X. D., Alleva, F., Hon, H. W., Hwang, M. Y., Lee, K. F., and Rosenfeld, R. (1993). The Sphinx II Speech Recognition System: An overview. *Computer Speech and Language, 7*(9), 137–148.

Huang, W., Olson, J. S., & Olson, G. M. (2002). Camera angle affects dominance in video-mediated communication. In *Proceedings of CHI 2002, short papers* (pp. 716–717). New York: ACM Press.

Huang, X., Acero, A., & Hon, H. (2001). *Spoken language processing: A guide to theory, algorithm and system development.* New York: Prentice Hall.

Huang, X., Alleva, F., Hon, H.-W., Hwang, M.-Y., Lee, K.-F. & Rosenfeld, R. (1992). The SPHINX-II speech recognition system: An overview. *Computer Speech and Language, 7*(2), 137–148.

Huber, P. J. (1986). Data analysis implications for command language design. In K. Hopper & I. A. Newman (Eds.), *Foundations for human-computer communication.* Amsterdam: Elsevier Science.

Hudson, J. M., & Bruckman, A. S. (2002). IRC Francais: The creation of an Internet-based SLA community. *Computer Assisted Language Learning, 1*(2), 109–134.

Huff, C. W. (1996). Practical guidance for teaching the social impact statement. In C. W. Huff (Ed.), *Proceedings of the 1996 Symposium on Computers and the Quality of Life* (pp. 86–90). New York: ACM Press.

Huff, C. W., & Finholt, T. (Eds.). (1994). *Social issues in computing: Putting computers in their place.* New York: McGraw-Hill.

Huff, C. W., & Martin, C. D. (1995, December). Computing consequences: A framework for teaching ethical computing. *Communications of the Association for Computing Machinery, 38*(12), 75–84.

Hughes, J., King, V., Rodden, T., & Andersen, H. (1994). Moving out from the control room: Ethnography in system design. In *Proceedings of the Conference on Computer Supported Cooperative Work: CSCW '94* (pp. 429–439). New York: ACM Press.

Hughes, T. J. (1998). *Rescuing Prometheus.* New York: Pantheon Books.

Huhns, M. N., & Singh, M. P. (Eds.). (1997). *Readings in agents.* San Francisco: Morgan Kaufmann.

Humphrey, D. G., & Kramer, A. F. (1994). Toward a psychophysiological assessment of dynamic changes in mental workload. *Human Factors, 36*(1), 3–26.

Humphrey, W. (1996). *Introduction to the personal software process.* New York: Addison-Wesley.

Humphrey, W. (1999). *Introduction to the team software process.* New York: Addison-Wesley.

Hunt, A., & Black, A. (1996). Unit selection in a concatenative speech synthesis system using a large speech database. *Proceedings, International Conference on Audio, Speech, and Signal Processing, 1,* 373–376.

Huston, T. L., & Huston, J. L. (2000). Is telemedicine a practical reality? *Communications of the ACM, 42*(6), 91–95.

Hutchby, I. (2001). *Conversation and technology: From the telephone to the Internet.* Malden, MA: Blackwell.

Hutchins, E. (1991). The social organization of distributed cognition. In L. B. Resnick, J. M. Levine, & S. D. Teasley (Eds.), *Perspectives on socially shared cognition.* (pp. 283–307). Washington: American Psychological Association.

Hutchins, E. (1994). How a cockpit remembers its speeds. *Cognitive Science, 19,* 265–288.

Hutchins, E. (1995). *Cognition in the wild.* Cambridge, MA: MIT Press.

Hutchins, E. (1995). *Distributed cognition.* Cambridge, MA: MIT Press.

Hutchins, E. L., Hollan, J. D., & Norman, D. A. (1986). Direct manipulation interfaces. In D. A. Norman & S. W. Draper (Eds.), *User centered system design* (pp. 87–124). Hillsdale, NJ: Lawrence Erlbaum.

Hutchins, J. (1986). *Machine translation: Past, present, future.* Chichester, UK: Horwood.

Hutchins, J. (2003). Machine translation: general overview. In R. Mitkov (Ed.), *The Oxford handbook of computational linguistics* (pp. 501–511). Oxford, UK: Oxford University Press.

Huws, U., Korte, W., & Robinson, S. (1990). *Telework: Toward the elusive office.* New York: John Wiley and Sons.

Hwang, M.Y. (1993). *Subphonetic acoustic modelling for speaker-independent continuous speech recognition.* Unpublished doctoral dissertation, CMU-CS-93-230, Carnegie Mellon University, Pittsburgh, PA. .

Iacucci, G., & Kuutti, K. (2002). Everyday life as a stage in creating and performing scenarios for wireless devices. *Personal and Ubiquitous Computing, 6*(4), 299–306.

IBM. (2002). *Websphere MQ application message interface. (SC34-6065-00).* Armonk, NY: IBM.

IBM (2003). IBM's Ease of Use Web Guidelines. Retrieved July 29, 2003, from http://www3.ibm.com/ibm/easy/eou_ext.nsf/publish/572

ICONOCAST. (1999). *More concentrated than the leading brand.* Retrieved August 29, 2003, http://www.iconocast.com/issue/1999102102.html

Ide, N., & Véronis, J. (1998). Word sense disambiguation: The state of the art. *Computational Linguistics, 24*(1), 1–40.

IEEE 802.11 Working Group for Wireless Local Area Networks. Retrieved February 25, 2004, from http://grouper.ieee.org/groups/802/11/

IEEE Robotics & Automation Society. (1995). *Proceedings of the IEEE/RSJ international conference on intelligent robots and systems: Human robot interaction and cooperative robots.* Piscataway, NJ: IEEE Robotics & Automation Society.

IEEE Standard Glossary of Software Engineering Terminology. (1990). Piscataway, NJ: IEEE.

IFIP Working Group 2.7/13.4 on user interface engineering. Retrieved March 12, 2004, from http://www.se-hci.org

Igarashi, T., & Hughes, J. F. (2001). A suggestive interface for 3-D drawing. In *Proceedings of the ACM Symposium on User Interface Software and Technology (UIST)* (pp. 173–181). New York: ACM Press.

Igarashi, T., Matsuoka, S., & Tanaka, H. (1999). Teddy: A sketching interface for 3-D freeform design. In *Proceedings of the SIGGRAPH 1999 Annual Conference on Computer Graphics* (pp. 409–416). New York: ACM Press/Addison-Wesley Publishing Co.

Igbaria, M., & Tan, M. (Eds.) (1998). *The virtual workplace,* Harrisburg, PA: Idea Group.

IHMC. (2003). *IHMC Cmap tools.* Retrieved March 9, 2004, from http://cmap.ihmc.us/

Iivari, J., & Karjalainen M. (1989). Impact of prototyping on user information satisfaction during the IS specification phase. *Information & Management, 17*(1), 31–45.

IJsselsteijn, W. A., Lombard, M., & Freeman, J. (2001). Toward a core bibliography of presence. *Cyberpsychology & Behavior, 4*(2), 317–320.

Ikeuchi, K., Sato, T., Nishino, K., & Sato, I. (1999). Appearance modeling for mixed reality: photometric aspects. In *Proceedings of the 1999 IEEE International Conference on Systems, Man, and Cybernetics (SMC'99)* (pp. 36–41). Piscataway, NJ: IEEE.

ILEX. (n.d.). *Intelligent labeling explorer: A project at the University of Edinburgh into dynamic hypertext generation.* Retrieved March 23, 2004, from http://www.hcrc.ed.ac.uk/ilex/

Information power grid: NASA's computing and data grid. (2002). Retrieved February 2, 2004, from http://www.ipg.nasa.gov/ipgusers/globus/1-globus.html

Information Technology Association of America. (2003). *Workforce survey, May 5, 2003.* Retrieved November 12, 2003, from http://www.itaa.org/workforce/studies/03execsumm.pdf.

Insko, B. (2001). *Passive haptics significantly enhances virtual environments.* Unpublished doctoral dissertation, University of North Carolina, Chapel Hill.

Interaction and Presentation Laboratory. (n.d.). *Human-robot interaction at IPLab.* Retrieved July 21, 2003, from http://www.nada.kth.se/iplab/hri/

International Community for Auditory Display (ICAD). (n.d.) Retrieved December 10, 2003, from http://www.icad.org/

International Organization for Standardization. (Ed.). (1992–2003). *Ergonomics requirements for office work with visual display terminals (VDTs), (ISO Standard 9241).* Geneva, Switzerland: International Organization for Standardization.

International Organization for Standardization. (Ed.). (1996). *Basic human body measurements for technical design (ISO Standard 7250).* Geneva, Switzerland: International Organization for Standardization.

International Organization for Standardization. (Ed.). (2000). *Ergonomic design for the safety of machinery (ISO Standard 15534).* Geneva, Switzerland: International Organization for Standardization.

International Organization for Standardization. (Ed.). (2002). *Safety of machinery—Anthropometric requirements for the design of workstations at machinery (ISO Standard 14738).* Geneva, Switzerland: International Organization for Standardization.

International Organization for Standardization. (Ed.). (2003). *General requirements for establishing an anthropometric database (ISO Standard 15535).* Geneva, Switzerland: International Organization for Standardization.

International Organization for Standardization. Retrieved Sept. 12, 2003, from http://www.iso.ch/iso/en/ISOOnline.openerpage

Internet Policy Institute. (2001). *Report of the National Workshop on Internet Voting: Issues and research agenda.* Retrieved August 1, 2003, from http://www.diggov.org/archive/library/doc/ipi_onlinevoting.jsp

Introna, L. D. (2001). Virtuality and morality: On (not) being disturbed by the other. *Philosophy in the Contemporary World, 8*(1), 31–39.

Introna, L. D., & Nissenbaum, H. (2000). Shaping the Web: Why the politics of search engines matters. *The Information Society, 16*(3), 169–185.

IRC.Net. *IRC net: Our history.* Retrieved July 30, 2003, from http://www.irc.net/

Isaacs, E., Kamm, C., Schiano, D., Walendowski, A., & Whittaker S. (2002, April) *Characterizing instant messaging from recorded logs.* Paper presented at the ACM CHI 2002 Conference on Human Factors in Computing Systems, Minneapolis, MN. Retrieved August 7, 2003, from http://hci.stanford.edu/cs377/nardi-schiano/CHI2002. Isaacs.pdf

Isen, A. M., Ashby, F. G., & Waldron, E. (1997). The sweet smell of success. *Aroma-Chology Review, 4*(3), 1.

Isenhour, P. L., Carroll, J. M., Neale, D. C., Rosson, M. B., & Dunlap, D. R. (2000). The virtual school: An integrated collaborative environment for the classroom. *Educational Technology and Society, 3*(3), 74–86.

Ishii, H., & Ullmer, B. (1997). Tangible bits. In *Conference on Human Factors in Computing Systems* (CHI) (pp. 234–241). Pittsburgh, PA: ACM.

Ito, M. (Ed.). (2004). Portable, personal, intimate: Mobile phones in Japanese life. Cambridge, MA: MIT Press.

Ivanov, Y. A., & Bobick, A. F. (2000, August). Recognition of visual activities and interactions by stochastic parsing. *IEEE Transactions on Pattern Analysis and Machine Intelligence, 22*(8), 852–871.

Iwahashi, N., & Sagisaka, Y. (2000). Statistical modeling of speech segment duration by constrained tree regression. *Trans. of Institute of Electronics, Information and Communication Engineers,* E83-D, 1550–1559.

Jackson, L. A., Ervin, K. S., Gardner, P. D., & Schmitt, N. (2001). Gender and the Internet: Women communicating and men searching. *Sex Roles, 44*(5–6), 363–380.

Jackson, L. A., Ervin, K. S., Gardner, P. D., & Schmitt, N. (2001a). The racial digital divide: Motivational, affective, and cognitive correlates of Internet use. *Journal of Applied Social Psychology, 31*(10), 2019–2046.

Jackson, L. A., von Eye, A., Biocca, F., Barbatsis, G., Fitzgerald, H. E., & Zhao, Y. (2003, May 20–24). *The social impact of Internet Use: Findings from the other side of the digital divide.* Paper presented at the twelfth International World Wide Web Conference, Budapest, Hungary.

Jackson, P. (1999). Introduction to expert systems (3rd ed.). Reading, MA: Pierson Addison-Wesley.

Jackson, P., & Moulinier, I. (2002). *Natural language processing for online applications: Text retrieval, extraction, and categorization.* Amsterdam: John Benjamins.

Jacob, R. J. (1990). What you look at is what you get: Eye movement-based interaction techniques. In *Proceedings of CHI '90* (pp. 11–18). Seattle, WA: ACM.

Jacob, R. J. K. (1991). The use of eye movements in human-computer interaction techniques: What you look at is what you get. *ACM Transactions on Information Systems, 9*(3), 152–169.

Jacob, R. J. K., & Sibert, L. E. (1992). The perceptual structure of multidimensional input device selection. In *Proceedings of CHI'92: ACM Conference on Human Factors in Computing Systems* (pp. 211–218).

Jain, A. K. (1988). *Fundamentals of digital image processing.* Englewood Cliffs, NJ: Prentice Hall.

Jambon, F., Girard, P., & Ait-ameur, Y. (2001). Interactive system safety and usability enforced with the development process. In *Engineering for Human-Computer Interaction* (pp. 39–52). New York: Springer-Verlag.

James, D. L., & Pai, D. K. (1999, August). ArtDefo, accurate real time deformable objects. *Computer Graphics, Proceedings of SIGGRAPH,* 66–72.

James, W. (1890). *The principles of psychology.* New York: Henry Holt.

James, W. (1985). *Psychology: The briefer course.* Notre Dame, IN: University of Nortre Dame Press. (Original work published 1892.)

Jancke, G., Venolia, G. D., Grudin, J., Cadiz, J. J., & Gupta, A. (2001). Linking public spaces: Technical and social issues. In *CHI 2001 Conference Proceedings* (pp. 530–537). New York: ACM Press.

BIBLIOGRAPHY

Janssens, M., Brett, J. M., & Smith, F. J. (1995). Confirmatory cross-cultural research: Testing the viability of a corporate-wide safety policy. *Academy of Management Journal, 38,* 364–382.

Jansson, G., Billberger, K., Petrie, H., Colwell, C., Kornbrot, D., Fänger, J. F., et al. (1999). Haptic virtual environments for blind people: Exploratory experiments with two devices. *The International Journal of Virtual Reality, 4*(1), 10–20.

Jasanoff, S., Markle, G. E., Petersen, J. C., & Pinch, T. (Eds.). (1995). *The handbook of science and technology studies.* Thousand Oaks, CA: Sage Publications.

Jaspan, B. (1995). *Kerberos users' frequently asked questions 1.14.* Retrieved February 17, 2004, from http://www.faqs.org/faqs/kerberos-faq/user/.

Jaspert, W., Pincus, B., Turner, W., & Johnson, A. F. (1970). *The encyclopaedia of type faces.* New York, NY: Barnes & Noble.

Jeannin, S., Jasinschi, R., She, A., Naveen, T., Mory, B., & Tabatabai, A. (2000, September). Motion descriptors for content-based video representation. *Signal Processing: Image Communication, 16*(1–2), 59–86.

Jeffrey, K. (2001). *Machines in our hearts: The cardiac pacemaker, the implantable defibrillator, and American health care.* Baltimore: Johns Hopkins University Press.

Jeffries, R., Miller, J. R., Wharton, C., & Uyeda, K. M. (1991). User interface evaluation in the real world: A comparison of four techniques. In *Proceedings ACM CHI'91,* 119–124.

Jelinek, F. (1976). Continuous speech recognition by statistical methods. *Proceedings of the IEEE, 64,* 532–556.

Jenkins, J. M., Oatley, K., and Stein, N. L. (Eds.). (1998). *Human emotions: A reader.* Malden, MA: Blackwell.

Jennings, N., Sycara, K., & Georgefi, M. (1998). A roadmap of agent research and development. *Journal of Autonomous Agents and Multi-Agent Systems, 1*(1), 7–38.

Jiang, H., Helal, A., Elmagarmid, A. K., & Joshi, A. (1998). Scene change detection techniques for video databases. *Multimedia Systems, 6,* 186–195.

Joch, A. (January 22, 2001). *Compilers, interpreters and bytecode.* Retrieved January 20, 2004, from http://www.computerworld.com/softwaretopics/software/story/0,10801,56615,00.html

Johanson, B., Fox, A., & Winograd, T. (2002, April). The interactive workspaces project: Experiences with ubiquitous computing rooms. *IEEE Pervasive Computing Magazine, 1*(2), 67–74.

John B. E., & Marks, S. J. (1997). Tracking the effectiveness of usability evaluation methods. *Behaviour & Information Technology, 16*(4/5), 188–202.

John, B. E. (1990). Extensions of GOMS analyses to expert performance requiring perception of dynamic visual and auditory information. In J. C. Chew & J. Whiteside (Eds.), *ACM CHI'90 Conference on Human Factors in Computing Systems* (pp. 107–115). New York: ACM Press.

John, B. E. (1996). TYPIST: A theory of performance in skilled typing. *Human-Computer Interaction, 11*(4), 321–355.

John, B. E., & Mashyna, M. M. (1997). Evaluating a multimedia authoring tool. *Journal of the American Society for Information Science, 48*(11), 1004–1022.

John, B. E., Bass, L., & Adams, R. J. (2003). Communications across the HCI/SE divide: ISO13407 and the rational unified process. In *Proceedings of HCI International 2003,* 1, 484–488. Hillsdale, NJ: Erlbaum.

Johnson, A. F. (1966). *Type designs: Their history and development.* London: Deutsch.

Johnson, A., Leigh, J., & Costigan, J. (1998). Multiway tele-immersion at Supercomputing '97. *IEEE Computer Graphics and Applications, 18*(4), 6–9.

Johnson, A., Sandin, D., Dawe, G., Qiu, Z., Thongrong, S., & Plepys, D. (2000). Developing the PARIS: Using the CAVE to prototype a new VR display [Electronic version]. *Proceedings of IPT 2000.* [CD-ROM]

Korab H., & Brown, M. D. (Eds.). (1995). *Virtual environments and distributed computing at SC'95: GII Testbed and HPC challenge applications on the I-WAY.* Retrieved November 5, 2003, from http://www.ncsa.uiuc.edu/General/Training/SC95/GII.HPCC.html

Johnson, B. (1989). *The design and analysis of fault-tolerant digital systems.* New York: Addison-Wesley.

Johnson, C. A. (1976). Privacy as personal control. In D. H. Carson (Ed.), *Man-Environment Interactions: Selected Papers Presented at EDRA 5* (pp. 83–100). Stroudsberg, PA: Dowden, Hutchinson, & Ross.

Johnson, C., & Parker, S. (1995). Applications in computational medicine using SCIRun: A computational steering programming environment. In *The 10th International Supercomputer Conference* (pp. 2–19). New York: IEEE.

Johnson, D. (2001). *Computer ethics* (3rd. ed.). New York: Prentice Hall.

Johnson, D. G. (2004). Computer ethics. In H. Nissenbaum & M. E. Price (Eds.), *Academy and the Internet* (pp. 143–167). New York: Peter Lang.

Johnson, E. H. (2000). Getting beyond the simple assumptions of organization impact. *Bulletin of the American Society for Information Science, 26*(3), 18–19.

Johnson, P. W., Tal, R., Smutz, W. P., & Rempel, D. M. (1994). Fingertip forces measured during computer mouse operation: A comparison of pointing and dragging. In Proceedings of the 12th Congress of the International Ergonomics Association (pp. 208–210). Toronto, Canada: International Ergonomics Association.

Johnson, R. C. (1997). Science, technology, and black community development. In A. H. Teich (Ed.), *Technology and the future* (7th ed.; pp. 270–283). New York: St. Martin's Press.

Johnston, K, & Johal, P. (1999). The Internet as a "virtual cultural region": Are extant cultural classifications schemes appropriate? *Internet Research: Electronic Networking Applications and Policy, 9*(3), 178–186.

Jonassen, D. H., Beissner, K., & Yacci, M. (1993). *Structural knowledge: Techniques for representing, conveying and acquiring structural knowledge.* Hillsdale, NJ: Lawrence Erlbaum.

Jones, M. L. W., Rieger, R. H., Treadwell, P., & Gay, G. K. (2000). Live from the stacks: User feedback on mobile computers and wireless tools for library patrons. In *Proceedings of the Fifth ACM Conference on Digital Libraries* (pp. 95–102). New York: ACM Press.

Jones, S. (Ed.). (1995). *Cybersociety: Computer-mediated communication and community.* Thousand Oaks, CA: Sage.

Jones, S. (Ed.). (1997). *Virtual culture: Identity and communication in cybersociety.* London: Sage.

Jordan, S. (Ed.). (1971). *Handbook of technical writing practices.* New York: Wiley-Interscience.

Jorgenson, D. (2001). Information technology and the U.S. economy. *American Economic Review, 91*(1), 1–32.

Joseph, D., & Wong, R. (1979). Correction of misspellings and typographical errors in a free-text medical English information storage and retrieval system. *Methods of Information in Medicine, 18*(4), 228–234

Joshi, A. K. (1987). The relevance of tree adjoining grammar to generation. In G. Kempen (Ed.), *Natural language generation: Recent advances in artificial intelligence, psychology, and linguistics* (pp. 233–252). Dordrecht, Netherlands: Kluwer Academic Publishers.

Jurafsky, D., & Martin, J. (2000). *Speech and language processing: An introduction to natural language processing, computational linguistics, and speech recognition.* Upper Saddle River, NJ: Prentice Hall.

Jurgen, R. (1995). *Automotive electronics handbook.* New York: McGraw-Hill.

Kaasten, S., & Greenberg, S. (2001). Integrating Back, History and bookmarks in Web browsers. In *Proceedings of CHI'01* (pp. 379–380). New York: ACM Press.

Kaelbling, L., Littman, M., & Cassandra, A. (1998). Planning and acting in partially observable stochastic domains. *Artificial Intelligence, 101,* 99–134.

Kafai, Y. B., & Bates, M. J. (1997). Internet Web-searching instruction in the elementary classroom: Building a foundation for information literacy. *School Library Media Quarterly, 25*(2), 103–111.

Kahn, Jr., P. H., Friedman, B., & Hagman, J. (2002). "I care about him as a pal": Conceptions of robotic pets in online AIBO discussion forums. In *CHI 2002* Extended Abstracts (pp. 632–633). New York: ACM Press.

Kahneman, D., & Tversky, A. (1972). Subjective probability: A judgement of representativeness. *Cognitive Psychology, 3,* 430–454.

Kamarck, E. C., & Nye, J. S., Jr. (2001). *Governance.com: Democracy in the information age.* Washington, DC: Brookings Institution Press.

Kaminka, G. A., Pynadath, D. V., & Tambe, M. (2002). Monitoring teams by overhearing: A multi-agent plan recognition approach. *Journal of Artificial Intelligence Research, 17.* 83–135.

Kan, M-Y, & Klavans, J. L. (2002). Using librarian techniques in automatic text summarization for information retrieval. *Proceedings of the Joint Conference on Digital Libraries* (JCDL 2002). Portland, Oregon.

Kanawati, R., & Malek, M. (2002). A multi-agent system for collaborative bookmarking. In P. Georgini, Y. L'Espèrance, G. Wagner, & E. S. K. Yu (Eds.), *Proceedings of the Fourth International Bi-Conference Workshop on Agent-Oriented Information Systems* (pp. 1137–1138). Retrieved December 16, 2003, from http://sunsite.informatik.rwth-aachen.de/Publications/CEUR-WS/Vol-59/8Kanawati.pdf

Kandel, E., Schwartz, J., & Jessell, T. (2000). *Principles of neural science* (4th ed.). New York: McGraw-Hill Health Professions Division.

Kantardzic, M. (2002). *Data mining: Concepts, models, methods, and algorithms.* Somerset, NJ: Wiley-IEEE Press.

Kanter, R. M. (2001). *Evolve!: Succeeding in the digital culture of tomorrow.* Cambridge, MA: Harvard Business School Press.

Kaplan, B. (Ed.). (1961). *Studying personality cross-culturally.* New York: Harper and Row.

Karat, J., Jeffries, R., Miller, J., Lund, A., McClelland, I., John, B., et al. (1998). Commentary on "Damaged Merchandise?" *Human-Computer Interaction, 13*(3), 263–324.

Karow, P. (1994). *Digital typefaces: Description and formats.* New York: Springer-Verlag.

Karow, P. (1994). *Font technology: Methods and tools.* New York: Springer-Verlag.

Karsten, R. (2002). An analysis of IS professional and end user causal attributions for user-system outcomes. *Journal of End User Computing, 14*(4), 51–73.

Kasturi, R., Gorman, L. O., & Govindaraju, V. (2002). Document image analysis: A primer. *Saadhana, 27*(1), 3–22.

Katz, J. E., & Rice, R. E. (2002). *Social consequences of Internet use: Access, involvement, and interaction.* Cambridge, MA: MIT Press.

Katz, J., & Aakhus, M. (2002). *Perpetual contact: Mobile communications, private talk, public performance.* Cambridge, UK: Cambridge University Press.

Kavanaugh, A., & Cohill, A. (1999). *BEV research studies, 1995–1998.* Retrieved August 12, 2003, from http://www.bev.net/about/research/digital_library/docs/BEVrsrch.pdf

Kay, A. (1993). The early history of Smalltalk. *ACM SIGPLAN Notices, 28*(3), 69–95.

Kay, A. C. (1972). A personal computer for children of all ages. In *Proceedings of the ACM National Conference* (pp. 1–11). New York: ACM Press.

Kay, A., & Goldberg, A. (1977). Personal dynamic media. *IEEE Computer, 10*(3), 31–41.

Kay, J., & Kummerfeld, B. (1994). User models for customized hypertext in J. Mayfield and E. C. Nicholas (Eds.). *Advances in hypertext for the World Wide Web* (47–69). New York: Springer-Verlag.

Kay, L. (2000). *Who wrote the book of life? A history of the genetic code.* Palo Alto: Stanford University Press.

Kaye, J. N. (2001). *Symbolic olfactory display.* Unpublished master's thesis, MIT, Cambridge, MA. Retrieved December 31, 2003, from http://web.media.mit.edu/~jofish/thesis/symbolic_olfactory_display.html

Kazman, R., Bass, L., & Bosch, J. (2003). Bridging the gaps between software engineering and human-computer interaction. In *Proceedings of the International Conference on Software Engineering,* 777–778.

Kazman, R., Gunaratne, J., & Jerome, B. (2003). Why can't software engineers and HCI practitioners work together? *Human-Computer Interaction Theory and Practice—Part 1 (Proceedings of HCI International '03),* 504–508.

Keeter, S.,Miller, C., Kohut, A., Groves, R., & Presser, S. (2000). Consequences of reducing nonresponse in a national telephone survey. *Public Opinion Quarterly, 64*(2), 125–148.

Kehoe, R., & Jarvis, A. (1996). *ISO 9000-3: A tool for software product and process improvement.* New York: Springer-Verlag.

Keller, E., Bailly, G., Monaghan, A., Terken, J., & Huckvale, M. (Eds.). (1994). *Fundamentals of speech synthesis and speech recognition.* New York: Wiley.

Keller, H. (1954). *The story of my life.* Garden City, NY: Doubleday.

Keller, P. A. (1997). *Electronic display measurement.* New York: Wiley SID.

Kendall, L. (2002). *Hanging out in the virtual pub.* Berkeley, CA: University of California Press.

Kendon, A. (1980). Gesticulation and speech: Two aspects of the process of utterance. *Relationship Between Verbal and Nonverbal Communication,* 207–227.

Kennedy, M. (1996). *The Global Positioning System and GIS: An introduction.* Chelsea, MI: Ann Arbor Press.

Kennedy, P. R., Bakay, R. A. E., Moore, M. M., Adams, K., & Goldwaithe, J. (2000). Direct control of a computer from the human central nervous system. *IEEE Transactions on Rehabilitation Engineering, 8*(2), 198–202.

Kerlow, I. V. (2000). *The art of 3-D computer animation and imaging* (2nd ed.). New York: Wiley.

Kernighan, M., Church, K., & Gale, W. (1990). A spelling correction program based on a noisy channel model. In H. Karlgren (Ed.),

COLING-90 13th International Conference on Computational Linguistics (pp. 205–210). Helsinki, Finland: Helsinki University Press.

Kettebekov, A., M. Yeasin, & Sharma, R. (2003). Improving continuous gesture recognition with spoken prosody. *Proceedings of the IEEE Conference on CVPR, 1,* 565–570.

Kettebekov, S., & Sharma, R. (2001). Toward natural gesture/speech control of a large display. In L. Nigay (Ed.), *Engineering for human computer interaction* (pp. 133–146). Berlin: Springer-Verlag.

Kettebekov, S., Yeasin, M., & Sharma, R. (2003). Improving continuous gesture recognition with spoken prosody. In *Proceedings of the IEEE Conference on Computer Vision and Pattern Recognition (CVPR'03)* (Vol 1.pp. 565–570). New York: IEEE.

Khanna, N., Fortes, J. A. B., & Nof, S. Y. (1998). A formalism to structure and parallelize the integration of cooperative engineering design tasks. *IIE Transactions, 30*(1), 1–16.

Kidd, A. (1994). *The marks are on the knowledge worker.* Paper presented at the ACM Conference on Human Factors in Computing Systems, Boston.

Kidd, C., Orr, R. J., Abowd, G. D., Atkeson, D., Essa, I., MacIntyre, B., et al. (1999). The Aware Home: A living laboratory for ubiquitous computing. In N. Streitz, J. Seigal, V. Hartkopf, & S. Konomi (Eds.), *Cooperative buildings: Integrating information, organizations and architecture (Second International Workshop, Cobuild '99, Pittsburgh, USA, October 1999, proceedings)* (pp. 191–198). Heidelberg, Germany: Springer.

Kidder, T. (1981). *The soul of a new machine.* Boston: Little, Brown.

Kieras, D. E. (1997). A Guide to GOMS Model Usability Evaluation Using NGOMSL. In M. Helander & T. Landauer (Eds.), *The Handbook of Human-Computer Interaction* (pp. 733–766). Amsterdam: North-Holland.

Kieras, D. E., & Meyer, D. E. (1997). An overview of the EPIC architecture for cognition and performance with application to human-computer interaction. *Human-Computer Interaction, 12*(4), 391–438.

Kieras, D. E., Wood, S. D., and Meyer, D. E. (1995). Predictive engineering models using the EPIC architecture for high-performance task. In *Proceedings of the ACM Conference on Human Factors in Computing Systems, CHI '95.* (pp. 11–18). Denver, CO: ACM Press.

Kiesler, S. (1997). Culture of the Internet. Mahwah, NJ: Lawrence Erlbaum Associates.

Kiesler, S., & Sproull, E. (1986). Response effects in the electronic survey. *Public Opinion Quarterly, 50,* 402–413.

Kiesler, S., & Sproull, L. (1997). Social responses to "social" computers. In B. Friedman (Ed.), *Human values and the design of technology.* Stanford, CA: CLSI Publications.

Kiesler, S., & Sproull, L. S. (1992). Group decision-making and communication technology. *Organizational Behavior and Human Decision Processes, 52,* 96–123.

Kiesler, S., Siegel, J., & McGuire, T. (1984). Social psychological aspects of computer mediated communication. *American Psychologist, 39,* 1123–1134.

Kim, A. J. (2000). *Community building on the Web.* Berkeley, CA: Peachpit Press.

Kim, G., & Govindaraju, V. (1997). A lexicon driven approach to handwritten word recognition for real-time applications. *IEEE Transactions on Pattern Analysis and Machine Intelligence, 19*(4), 366–379.

Kim, G., & Govindaraju, V. (1997). Bank check recognition using cross validation between legal and courtesy amounts. *International Journal on Pattern Recognition and Artificial Intelligence, 11*(4), 657–674.

Kim, G., Govindaraju, V., & Srihari, S. (1999). Architecture for handwritten text recognition systems. *International Journal of Document Analysis and Recognition, 2*(1), 37–44.

King, A. (2003). *Speed up your site: Web site optimization.* Indianapolis, IN: New Riders Publishing.

King, A. B. (2001). Affective dimension of Internet culture. *Social Science Computer Review, 19*(4), 414–430.

King, D. W., & Tenopir, C. (2001). Using and reading scholarly literature. In M. E. Williams (Ed.), *Annual review of information science and technology: Vol. 34. 1999–2000* (pp. 423–477). Medford, NJ: Information Today.

Kirkpatrick, H., & Cuban, I. (1998). Should we be worried? What the research says about gender differences in access, use, attitudes and achievement with computers. *Educational Technology, 38*(4), 56–61.

Kirkpatrick, S., Gelatt, J. C. D., & Vecchi, M. P. (1983). Optimization by simulated annealing. *Science, 220*(4598), 671–680.

Kirschenbaum, S. S., & Arruda, J. E. (1994). Effects of graphic and verbal probability information on command decision-making. *Human Factors, 36*(3), 406–418.

Kirwan, B., & Ainsworth, L. K. (1992). *A guide to task analysis.* London: Taylor & Francis.

Kittredge, R., Korelsky T., & Rambow, O. (1991). On the need for domain communication language. *Computational Intelligence, 7*(4), 305–314.

Klabbers, E., & Veldhuis, R. (2001). Reducing audible spectral discontinuities. *IEEE Transactions on Speech and Audio Processing, 9*(1), 39–51.

Klatt, D. (1987). Review of text-to-speech conversion in English. *Journal of the Acoustical Society of America, 82,* 737–793. Retrieved September 29, 2003, from http://www.mindspring.com/~ssshp

Kleijn, W. B., & Paliwal, K. (Eds.). (1995). *Speech coding and synthesis.* Amsterdam, Netherlands: Elsevier Science.

Klein, S. (1965). Automatic paraphrasing in essay format. *Mechanical Translation, 8*(3), 68–83.

Kling, R. (1977, Winter). The organizational context of user-centered software design. *MIS Quarterly, 1,* 41–52.

Kling, R. (1980). Social analyses of computing: Theoretical perspectives in recent empirical research. *Computing Surveys, 12*(1), 61–110.

Kling, R. (1993): Broadening computer science. *Communications of the ACM, 36*(2), 15–17.

Kling, R. (1999). What is Social Informatics and why does it matter? *D-Lib Magazine, 5*(1). Retrieved August 19, 2003, from http://www.dlib.org:80/dlib/january99/kling/01kling.html

Kling, R. (Ed.). (1996). *Computerization and controversy: Value conflicts and social choices* (2nd ed.). San Diego, CA: Academic Press.

Kling, R., & Callahan, E. (2003). Electronic journals, the Internet, and scholarly communication. In B. Cronin (Ed.), *Annual review of information science and technology: Vol. 37.* 2003 (pp. 127–177). Medford, NJ: Information Today.

Kling, R., & Scacchi, W. (1980). Computing as social action: The social dynamics of computing in complex organizations. *Advances in Computers, 19,* 249–327.

Kling, R., & Scacchi, W. (1982). The web of computing: Computer technology as social organization. *Advances in Computers, 21,* 1–90.

Kling, R., Kim, G., & King, A. (2003). A bit more to IT: Scholarly communication forums as socio-technical interaction networks. *Journal*

American Society for Information Science and Technology, 54(1), 47–67.

Kling, R., Rosenbaum, H., & Hert, C. A. (Eds.). (1998). Social Informatics [Special Issue]. *Journal of the American Society for Information Science, 49*(12). Retrieved August 19, 2003, from http://www.asis.org/Publications/JASIS/v49n1298.html

Kling, R., Rosenbaum, H., & Sawyer, S. (forthcoming). *Information and communication technologies in human contexts: Contributions of Social Informatics.* Medford, NJ: Information Today, Inc.

Klockenberg, E. A. (1926). *Rationalisierung der Schreibmaschine und ihrer Bedienung (Rationalization of typewriters and their operation).* Berlin: Springer.

Knight, J. C. (2002). Safety-critical systems: Challenges and directions. In *24th International Conference on Software Engineering (ICSE '02)* (pp. 547–550). Cupertino, CA: IEEE CS Press.

Knight, K., & Hatzivassiloglou, V. (1995). Two-level, many paths generation. In *Proceedings of the 33rd annual meeting of the Association for Computational Linguistics* (pp. 252–260). San Francisco: Morgan Kaufmann.

Knorr-Cetina, K. (1999). *Epistemic cultures: How the sciences make knowledge.* Cambridge, MA: Harvard University Press.

Knuth, D. (1973). *The art of computer programming: Vol. 3. Sorting and searching.* Reading, MA: Addison-Wesley.

Ko, A. J., Burnett, M. M., Green, T. R. G., Rothermel, K. J., & Cook, C. R. (2002). Improving the design of visual programming language experiments using cognitive walkthroughs. *Journal of Visual Languages and Computing, 13*, 517–544.

Kobsa, A. (2002). Personalized hypermedia and international privacy. *Communications of the ACM, 45*(5), 64–67. Retrieved August 29, 2003, from http://www.ics.uci.edu/~kobsa/papers/2002-CACM-kobsa.pdf

Kobsa, A. (Ed.). (2001). Ten year anniversary issue. *User Modeling and User-Adapted Interaction, 11*(1–2).

Kobsa, A., & Schreck, J. (2003). Privacy through pseudonymity in user-adaptive systems. *ACM Transactions on Internet Technology, 3*(2), 149–183. Retrieved August 29, 2003, from http://www.ics.uci.edu/~kobsa/papers/2003-TOIT-kobsa.pdf

Kobsa, A., Koenemann, J., & Pohl, W. (2001). Personalized hypermedia presentation techniques for improving customer relationships. *The Knowledge Engineering Review, 16*(2), 111–155. Retrieved August 29, 2003, from http://www.ics.uci.edu/~kobsa/papers/2001-KER-kobsa.pdf

Koch, S. (Ed.). (2004). Free/open source software development. Hershey, PA: Idea Group Publishing.

Koch, S., & Schneider, G. (2002). Effort, co-operation and co-ordination in an open source software project: GNOME. *Information Systems Journal, 12*(1), 27–42.

Kocher, P., Jaffe, J., & Jun, B. (1999). Differential power analysis. In M. Weiner (Ed.), *Advances in cryptology* (pp. 388–397). Heidelberg, Germany: Springer-Verlag.

Koenig, S. (2001). Agent-centered search. *AI Magazine, 22*(4), 109–131.

Kogut, B., & Metiu, A. (2001). Open source software development and distributed innovation. *Oxford Review of Economic Policy, 17*(2), 248–264.

Kohl, J. T. (1991). The evolution of the Kerberos authentication service. *Proceedings of the Spring 1991 EurOpen Conference.* Retrieved February 17, 2004, from http://www.cmf.nrl.navy.mil/CCS/people/kenh/kerberos-faq.html#whatis

Kohonen, T. (2001). *Self-organizing maps* (3rd ed.). New York: Springer-Verlag.

Kolonder, J. (1993). *Case-based reasoning.* Mountain View, CA: Morgan Kaufmann.

Koprinska, I., & Carrato, S. (2001). Temporal video segmentation: A survey. *Signal Processing: Image Communication, 16*(5), 477–500.

Koskenniemi, K. (1983). *Two-level morphology: A general computational model for word-form recognition and production.* Helsinki, Finland: University of Helsinki Department of General Linguistics.

Kosslyn, S. (1993). *The elements of graph design.* New York: Freeman.

Kouzes, R. T., Myers, J. T., & Wulf, W. A. (1996). Collaboratories: Doing science on the Internet. *IEEE Computer, 29*(8). Retrieved March 24, 2004, from http://collaboratory.emsl.pnl.gov/presentations/papers/IEEECollaboratories.html

Kowtha, N. R., & Choon, W. P. (2001). Determinants of website development: A study of electronic commerce in Singapore. *Information & Management, 39*(3), 227–242.

Koza, J. R. (1992). *Genetic programming.* Cambridge, MA: MIT Press.

Koza, J. R., Keane, M. A., & Streeter, M. J. (2003). Evolving inventions. *Scientific American, 288*(2), 52–59.

Kraker, D. (2003, October 20). Telemedicine is a success for Navajos. NPR. Retrieved March 2, 2004, from http://www.npr.org/features/feature.php?wfId=1472515

Kramer, G. (1994). An introduction to auditory displays. In G. Kramer (Ed.), *Auditory display: Sonification, audification and auditory interfaces.* In *Proceedings of the First International Conference on Auditory Displays (ICAD) 1992* (pp. 1–77). Reading, MA: Addison-Wesley.

Krantz, S. R. (1995). *Real world client server: Learn how to successfully migrate to client/server computing from someone who's actually done it.* Gulf Breeze, FL: Maximum Press.

Kraus, B. (1979). *Encyclopedia galactica.* New York: E. P. Dutton.

Krauss, R. M., & Weinheimer, S. (1966). Concurrent feedback, confirmation and the encoding of referents in verbal communication. *Journal of Personality and Social Psychology, 4*, 343–346.

Kraut, R. E. (2003). Applying social psychological theory to the problems of group work. In J. M. Carroll (Ed.), *HCI models, theories and frameworks: Toward a multidisciplinary science* (pp. 325–356). New York: Morgan Kaufman.

Kraut, R. E. (Ed.) (1987). *Technology and the transformation of white-collar work.* Hillsdale, NJ: Erlbaum.

Kraut, R. E., Fish, R.S., Root, R.W., & Chalfonte, B.L. (1990). Informal communication in organizations: Form, function, and technology. In S. Oskamp & S. Spacapan (Eds.) *Human reactions to technology: The Claremont Symposium on applied social psychology* (pp. 145–199). Beverly Hills, CA: Sage.

Kraut, R. E., Fussell, S. R., Brennan, S. E., & Siegel, J. (2002). Understanding effects of proximity on collaboration: Implications for technologies to support remote collaborative work. In P. Hinds & S. Kiesler (Eds.) *Distributed work* (pp. 137–162). Cambridge, MA: MIT Press.

Kraut, R., Kiesler, S., Boneva, B., Cummings, J., Helgeson, V., & Crawford, A. (2002). *Internet Paradox Revisited. Journal of Social Issues, 58*(1), 49–74.

Kraut. R. E. (1987). Predicting the use of technology: The case of telework. In R. Kraut (Ed.), *Technology and the Transformation of White Collar Work* (pp. 113–133). Hillsdale, NJ: Erlbaum.

Kretchmer, S., & Carveth, R. (2001). The color of the Net: African Americans, race, and cyberspace. *Computers and Society, 31*(3), 9–14.

BIBLIOGRAPHY

Krishna, C. M., & Shin, K. G. (1997). *Real-time systems.* New York: McGraw-Hill.

Krishnamurthy, S. (2002). An empirical examination of 100 mature open source projects. *First Monday, 7*(6).

Kroemer, K. H. E. (1972). Human engineering the keyboard. *Human Factors, 14,* 51–63.

Kroemer, K. H. E. (2001). Keyboards and keying: An annotated bibliography of literature from 1878 to 1999. *UAIS, 1,* 99–160.

Kroemer, K. H. E., Kroemer, H. J., & Kroemer-Elbert, K. E. (1997). Engineering anthropometry. In K. H. E. Kroemer (Ed.), *Engineering physiology* (pp. 1–60). New York: Van Nostrand Reinhold.

Kruchten, P. (2000). *The rational unified process—An introduction* (2nd ed.). New York: Addison-Wesley/Longman.

Kruk, S., & Black, S. (2000). *Don't make me think: A common sense approach to usability.* Indianapolis, IN: New Riders Publishing.

Krull, R. (2000). Is more beta better? *Proceedings of the IEEE Professional Communication Society,* 301–308.

Kübler, A., Kotchoubey, B., Hinterberger, T., Ghanayim, N., Perelmouter, J., Schauer, M., et al. (1999). The thought translation device: A neurophysiological approach to communication in total motor paralysis. *Experimental Brain Research 124*(2), 223–232.

Kuenning, G. (1996). *International Ispell.* Retrieved January 20, 2004, from http://fmg-www.cs.ucla.edu/fmg-members/geoff/ispell.html

Kuhn, S. (1996). Design for people at work. In T. Winograd (Ed.), *Bringing design to software* (pp. 273–289) Boston: Addison-Wesley.

Kuhn, T. (1962). *The structure of scientific revolutions.* Chicago: University of Chicago Press.

Kukich, K. (1983). Knowledge-based report generations: A technique for automatically generating natural language reports from databases. In *Sixth ACM SIGIR Conference* (pp. 246–250). New York: ACM Press.

Kukich, K. (1992). Technique for automatically correcting words in text. *ACM Computing Surveys (CSUR), 24*(4), 377–439.

Kunda, G. (1992). *Engineering culture: Control and commitment in a high-tech corporation.* Philadelphia: Temple University Press.

Kurtoglu, T., & Stahovich, T. F. (2002). Interpreting schematic sketches using physical reasoning. In R. Davis, J. Landay, & T. Stahovich. (Eds.), *AAAI Spring Symposium on Sketch Understanding* (pp. 78–85). Menlo Park, CA: AAAI Press.

Kurzweil, R. (1999). *The age of spiritual machines.* New York: Penguin.

Kushniruk, A. W., Kaufman, D. R., Patel, V. L., Lévesque, Y., & Lottin, P. (1996). Assessment of a computerized patient record system: A cognitive approach to evaluating medical technology. *M D Computing, 13*(5), 406–415.

Kusserow, R. P. (1984). The government needs computer matching to root out waste and fraud. *Communications of the ACM, 27*(6), 542–545.

Kuwabara, K. (2000). Linux: A bazaar at the edge of chaos. *First Monday, 5*(3), 1–68.

Kyng, M. (1995). Creating contexts for design. In J. M. Carroll (Ed.), *Scenario-based design: Envisioning work and technology in system development* (pp. 85–107). New York: Wiley.

Kyng, M., & Greenbaum, J. M. (1991). *Design at work: Cooperative design of computer systems.* Mahwah, NJ: Lawrence Erlbaum Associates.

Kyng, M., & Mathiassen, L. (Eds.) (1997). *Computers and design in context.* Cambridge, MA: MIT Press.

Lackner, J. R., & DiZio, P. (2000). Human orientation and movement control in weightlessness and artificial gravity environments. *Experimental Brain Research, 130,* 2–26.

Lai, J. (Ed.). (2000). Conversational interfaces. *Communications of the ACM, 43*(9), 24–73.

Laird, J. E., & van Lent, M. (2000). Human-level AI's killer application: Interactive computer games. *AI Magazine, 22*(2), 15–26.

Lamere, P., Kwok, P., Walker, W., Gouvea, E., Singh, R., Raj, B., & Wolf, P. (2003). Design of the CMU Sphinx-4 decoder. *Proceedings of the 8th European Conference on Speech Communication and Technology (EUROSPEECH 2003),* Geneva, Switzerland.

Lamm, E. (December 8, 2001). *Lambda the Great.* Retrieved January 20, 2004, from http://lambda.weblogs.com/2001/12/08

LaMotte, R. H., & Srinivasan, M. A. (1990). Surface microgeometry: Tactile perception and neural encoding. In D. Franzen & J. Westman (Eds.), *Information processing in the somatosensory system* (pp. 49–58). New York: Macmillan.

Lancaster, F. W. (1972). *Vocabulary control for information retrieval.* Washington, DC: Information Resources Press.

Landauer, T. K. (1995). *The trouble with computers: Usefulness, usability, and productivity.* Cambridge, MA: MIT Press.

Landay, J. A., & Myers, B. A. (1995). Interactive sketching for the early stages of interface design. In *CHI '95—Human Factors in Computing Systems* (pp. 43–50). Denver, CO: ACM Press.

Landow, G. P. (1997). *Hypertext 2.0.* Baltimore, MD: Johns Hopkins University Press.

Landsbergen, J. (1987). Isomorphic grammars and their use in the Rosetta translation system. In M. King (Ed.), *Machine translation today: The state of the art* (Proceedings of the Third Lugano Tutorial) (pp. 351–377). Edinburgh, Scotland: Edinburgh University Press.

Lang, P. (1995). The emotion probe: Studies of motivation and attention. *American Psychologist, 50*(5), 372–385.

Langston, C. G. (Ed.). (1989). *Artificial life* (Santa Fe Institute Studies in the Sciences of Complexity, Proceedings, Volume 6). Redwood City, CA: Addison-Wesley.

Lantz, K. E. (1988). *The prototyping methodology.* Englewood Cliffs, NJ: Prentice Hall.

LaPlante, M. P. (1988). *Data on disability from the National Health Interview Survey, 1983–85: An InfoUse report.* Washington, DC: National Institute on Disability and Rehabilitation Research, US Department of Education.

Large, A., & Beheshti, J. (2000). The Web as a classroom resource: Reactions from the users. *Journal of the American Society for Information Science And Technology, 51*(12), 1069–1080.

Large, A., Beheshti J., & Moukdad, H. (1999). Information seeking on the Web: Navigational skills of grade-six primary school students. *Proceedings of the 62nd ASIS Annual Meeting, 36,* 84–97.

Large, A., Beheshti, J., & Rahman, R. (2002). Design criteria for children's Web portals: The users speak out. *Journal of the American Society for Information Science and Technology, 53*(2), 79–94.

Larkin, J., & Simon, H. (1987). Why a diagram is (sometimes) worth 10,000 words. *Cognitive Science, 11,* 65–99.

Larson, E., & Raine, L. (2002). Digital town hall: How local officials use the Internet and civic benefits they cite from dealing with constituents online. *Pew Internet and American Life Project.* Retrieved on October 1, 2003, from www.pewinternet.org/reports/toc.asp?Report=74.

Larson, K., & Czerwinski, M. (1998). Web page design: Implications of structure, memory, and scent for information retrieval. In *Proceedings of ACM CHI '98 Human Factors in Computing Systems* (pp. 25–32). Los Angeles, CA: ACM Press.

Larsson, S., & Traum, D. (2000). Information state and dialogue management in the TRINDI Dialogue Move Engine Toolkit [Special issue on best practice in spoken dialogue systems]. *Natural Language Engineering, 6*(3–4), 323–340.

Laser printing. (1979). *SPIE Proceedings, 169,* 1–128.

Lassiter, J. (1987). *Principles of traditional animation applied to 3D computer animation. SIGGRAPH '87* (pp. 35–44).

Lauer, R. T., Peckham, P. H., Kilgore, K. L., & Heetderks, W. J. (2000). Applications of cortical signals to neuroprosthetic control: A critical review. *IEEE Transactions on Rehabilitation Engineering, 8*(2), 205–207.

Lave, J., & Wenger, E. (1991). *Situated learning: Legitimate peripheral participation.* Cambridge, UK: Cambridge University Press.

Lavendel, G. (1980). *A decade of research: Xerox Palo Alto Research* Center. New York: Bowker.

Law, J. (1987). Technology and heterogeneous engineering: The case of Portuguese expansion. In W. E. Bijker, T. P. Hughes, &T. Pinch (Eds.), *The social construction of technological systems* (pp. 111–134). Cambridge, MA: MIT Press.

Lawrence, S., & Giles, C. L. (1999). Accessibility of information on the Web. *Nature, 400,* 107–109.

Lawson, A. S. (1971). *Printing types: An introduction.* Boston: Beacon Press.

Lazar, J. (2001). *User-centered Web development.* Boston: Jones and Bartlett Computer Science.

Lederman, S. J., & Klatzky, R. L. (1999). Sensing and displaying spatially distributed fingertip forces in haptic interfaces for teleoperator and virtual environment systems. *Presence, 8*(1), 86–103.

Lee, D., Trauth, E., & Farwell, D. (1995). Critical skills and knowledge requirements of IS professionals: A joint academic/industry investigation. *MIS Quarterly, 19*(3), 313–340.

Lee, J. A. N. (1995). *International biographical dictionary of computer pioneers.* Chicago: Fitzroy Dearborn.

Lee, J. D., & Moray, N. (1994). Trust, self-confidence, and operators' adaptation to automation. *International Journal of Human-Computer Studies, 40,* 153–184.

Lee, K. F., Hon, H.W., & Reddy, R. (1990). An overview of the SPHINX speech recognition system. *IEEE Transactions on Acoustics, Speech and Signal Processing, ASSP, 38*(1), 35–44.

Lee, R. S. (1970). Social attitudes and the computer revolution. *Public Opinion Quarterly, 34*(1), 53–59.

Lee, W. B., & Grice, R. A. (2003). An adaptive viewing application for the web on personal digital assistants. In *Proceedings of the 21st annual international conference on documentation* (pp. 125–132). New York: Association for Computing Machinery.

Leganchuk, A., Zhai, S., & Buxton, W. (1998). Manual and cognitive benefits of two-handed input: An experimental study. *ACM Transactions on Computer-Human Interaction, 5*(4), 326–359.

Lehner, V. D., & DeFanti, T. A. (1997). Distributed virtual reality: Supporting remote collaboration in vehicle design. *IEEE Computer Graphics & Applications, 17*(2), 13–17.

Leick, A. (1995). *GPS satellite surveying.* New York: Wiley.

Leigh, J., DeFanti, T. A., Johnson, A. E., Brown, M. D., & Sandin, D. J. (1997). Global tele-immersion: Better than being there. *ICAT '97, 7th Annual International Conference on Artificial Reality and Tele-Existence,* pp. 10–17. University of Tokyo, Virtual Reality Society of Japan.

Leigh, J., Johnson, A., Brown, M., Sandin, D., & DeFanti, T. (1999, December). Tele-immersion: Collaborative visualization in im-mersive environments. *IEEE Computer Graphics & Applications,* 66–73.

Leizerov, S. (2000). Privacy advocacy groups versus Intel. *Social Science Computer Review, 18*(4), 461–483.

Lenhart, A. (2000). *Who's not online: 57% of those without Internet access say they do not plan to log on.* Washington, DC: Pew Internet & American Life Project. Retrieved July 18, 2003, from http://www.pewinternet.org/reports/pdfs/Pew_Those_Not_Online_Report.pdf

Lenhart, A., Rainie, L., & Lewis,O., (2001) *Teenage life online: The rise of instant-message generation and the Internet's impact on friendships and family relations.* Retrieved August 7, 2003, from http://www.pewinternet.org/reports/pdfs/PIP_Teens_Report.pdf

Lenhart, A., Simon, M., & Graziano, M. (2001). *The Internet and education: Findings of the Pew Internet & American Life Project.* Washington, DC: Pew Internet and American Life Project. Retrieved January 4, 2004, from http://www.pewinternet.org/reports/pdfs/PIP_Schools_Report.pdf

Leonard, A. (1997). *Bots: The origin of new species.* San Francisco: HardWired.

Leonard, V. A. (1980). *The new police technology: Impact of the computer and automation on police staff and line performance.* Springfield, IL: Charles C. Thomas.

Leone, A. O., & Ticca, A. (1994). Towards a user environment integrating hypermedia browsers, scientific visualization programs and numerical simulation programs. *Proceedings of the Workshop on Advanced Visual Interfaces* (pp. 234–236). New York: Association for Computing Machinery.

Leplat, J. (1989). Error analysis, instrument and object of task analysis. *Ergonomics, 32,* 813–822.

Lesh, N., Rich, C., & Sidner, C. L. (1999). Using plan recognition in human-computer collaboration. *Proceedings of the Seventh International Conference on User Modelling (UM-99).* Banff, Canada, June 1999.

Lesk, M. (1997). *Practical digital libraries: Books, bytes and bucks.* San Francisco: Morgan Kaufmann.

Lesser, V., Atighetchi, M., Benyo, B., Horling, B., Raja, A., Vincent, R., et al. (1999, January). The Intelligent Home testbed. In *Proceedings of the Autonomy Control Software Workshop.* Seattle, WA.

Lester, J. (Ed.). (1999). Special issue on intelligent user interfaces. *AI Magazine, 22*(4).

Leuf, B. (2002). *Peer to peer: Collaboration and sharing over the Internet.* Boston: Addison-Wesley.

Leuf, B., & Cunningham, W. (2001). *The wiki way: Collaboration and sharing on the Internet.* New York: Addison-Wesley.

Leveson, N. (1995). *Safeware: System safety and computers.* Reading, MA: Addison-Wesley.

Leveson, N., & Turner, C. S. (1993). An investigation of the Therac-25 accidents. *IEEE-Computer 26*(7), 18–41.

Levine, S. P., Huggins, J. E., BeMent, S. L., Kushwaha, R. K., Schuh, L. A., Rohde, M. M., et al. (2000). A direct-brain interface based on event-related potentials. *IEEE Transactions on Rehabilitation Engineering, 8*(2), 180–185.

Lévi-Strauss, C. (1967). *Structural anthropology.* Garden City, NY: Anchor Books.

Lévy, P. (1997). *Collective intelligence: Mankind's emerging world in cyberspace.* Cambridge, MA: Perseus Books.

Levy, S. (1984). *Hackers: Heroes of the computer revolution.* New York: Dell.

Lewis, C., & Wharton, C. (1997). Cognitive walkthroughs. In M. Helander, T. K. Landauer, & P. Prabhu (Eds.), *Handbook of human-computer interaction* (2nd ed., rev., pp. 717–732). Amsterdam: Elsevier.

Lewis, C., Polson, P., Wharton, C., & Rieman, J. (1990). Testing a walk-through methodology for theory-based design of walk-up-and-use interfaces. In *CHI '90: Proceedings of the Conference on Human Factors in Computing Systems,* 235–242.

Lewis, S. G., & Samoff, J. (Eds.). (1992). *Microcomputers in African development: Critical perspectives.* Boulder, CO: Westview Press.

Lhomme, O. (1993). Consistency techniques for numeric CSPs. In *Proceedings from the International Joint Conference on Artificial Intelligence* (pp. 232–238).

Li, Y, Rangaiah, G. P., & Ray, A. K. (2003). Optimization of styrene reactor design for two objectives using a genetic algorithm. *International Journal of Chemical Reactor Engineering, 1,* A13.

Li, Y., Ding, X., & Tan, C. L. (2002). Combining character-based bigrams with word-based bigrams in contextual postprocessing for Chinese script recognition. *ACM Transactions on Asian Language Information Processing, 1*(4), 297–309.

Licklider, J. (1960). Man-computer symbiosis. *IRE Transactions of Human Factors in Electronics, 1*(1), 4–11.

Licklider, J., & Clark, W. (1962). On-line man-computer communication. *AFIPS Conference Proceedings,* 21, 113–128.

Lieberman, H. (1995). Letizia: An agent that assists Web browsing. In *Proceedings of the International Joint Conference on Artificial Intelligence (IJCAI)* (pp. 924–929). San Francisco: Morgan Kaufmann.

Lieberman, H. (Ed.). (2001). *Your wish is my command.* San Francisco: Morgan Kaufmann.

Lienhart, R. (2001). Reliable transition detection in videos: A survey and practitioner's guide. *International Journal of Image Graphics, 1,* 469–486.

Light, J. (2001). Rethinking the Digital Divide. *Harvard Educational Review, 71*(4), 709–733.

Lin, W., & Hauptman, A. G. (2002, July 14–18). A wearable digital library of personal conversations. In *Joint Conference on Digital Libraries* (pp. 277–278), Portland, OR. Retrieved July 30, 2003, from http://www.informedia.cs.cmu.edu/documents/jcdl02_wearable.pdf

Linde, C. (1988). The quantitative study of communicative success: Politeness and accidents in aviation discourse. *Language in Society, 17,* 375–399.

Lindeman, R., Sibert, J., & Hahn, J. (1999). Hand-held windows: Towards effective 2D interaction in immersive virtual environments. *Proceedings of IEEE Virtual Reality '99,* 205–212.

Linton, F., & Schaefer, H.-P. (2000). Recommender systems for learning: Building user and expert models through long-term observation of application use. *User Modeling and User-Adapted Interaction, 10*(2–3), 181–208.

Littlewood, D., Popov, P., & Strigini, L. (2001). Modeling software design diversity: A review. *ACM Computing Surveys, 33*(2), 177–208.

Liu, J., Jing, H., & Tang, Y. Y. (2002). Multi-agent oriented constraint satisfaction. *Artificial Intelligence, 136*(1), 101–144.

Lizza, C., & Banks, S. (1991). Pilot's Associate: A cooperative, knowledge-based system application. *IEEE Intelligent Systems, 6*(3), 18–29.

Local Futures. (2001) *Local futures research: On the move—mobile and wireless communications.* Retrieved July 18, 2003, from http://www.localfutures.com/article.asp?aid=41

Lok, B. (2001). Online model reconstruction for interactive virtual environments. *Proceedings of the 2001 Symposium on Interactive 3-D Graphics,* 69–72, 248.

Lok, B., Naik, S., Whitton, M., & Brooks, F. (2003). Effects of handling real objects and avatar fidelity on cognitive task performance in virtual environments. *Proceedings of IEEE Virtual Reality 2003,* 125–132.

Lok, S., & Feiner, S. (2001). A survey of automated layout techniques for information presentations. In *Proceedings of the First International Symposium on Smart Graphics* (pp. 61–68). New York: ACM Press.

Long, A. C., Landay, J., Rowe, L. A., & Michiels, J. (2000). Visual similarity of pen gestures. In *Proceedings of the SIGCHI conference on human factors in computing systems* (pp. 360–367). New York: Association for Computing Machinery.

Long, J. (1989). Cognitive ergonomics and human-computer interaction. In J. Long & A. Whitefield (Eds.), *Cognitive ergonomics and human-computer interaction* (pp. 4–34). Cambridge, UK: Cambridge University Press.

Longley, P. A., Goodchild, M. F., Maguire, D. J., & Rhind, D. W. (2001). *Geographic information systems and science.* New York: Wiley.

Loomis, J. M., Golledge, R. D., & Klatzky, R. L. (2001). GPS-based navigation systems for the visual impaired. In W. Barfield & T. Caudell (Eds.), *Fundamentals of wearable computers and augmented reality* (pp. 429–446). Mahwah, NJ: Erlbaum.

Lorek, L. (2001, April 30). March of the A.I. robots. *Interactive Week, 8*(17), 46. Retrieved August 29, 2003 from http://cma.zdnet.com/texis/techinfobase/techinfobase/+bwh_qr+sWvKXX/zdisplay.html

Ludi, S., & Wagner, M. (2001). Re-inventing icons: Using animation as cues in icons for the visually impaired. In M. J. Smith, G. Salvendy, D. Harris, & R. J. Koubeck (Eds.), *Proceedings of the Ninth International Conference on Human-Computer Interaction.* New Orleans, LA: HCI International.

Luebke, D., Hallen, B., Newfield, D., & Watson, B. (2000). *Perceptually driven simplification using gaze-directed rendering* (Technical Report CS-2000-04). Charlottesville: University of Virginia.

Lueder, E. (2001). *Liquid crystal displays.* New York: Wiley SID.

Lunde, K. (1999). *CJKV information processing.* Beijing: O'Reilly.

Luperfoy, S. (Ed.). (1998). *Automated spoken dialog systems.* Cambridge, MA: MIT Press.

Lyman, P., & Varian, H. R. (2000). *How much information.* Retrieved March 31, 2004, from http://www.sims.berkeley.edu/how-much-info.

Lynch, C. A. (2002). Digital collections, digital libraries, and the digitization of cultural heritage information. *First Monday, 7*(5).

Lynch, P., & Horton, S. (2002). *Web style guide: Basic design principles for creating Web sites* (2nd ed.). New Haven, CT: Yale University Press.

Ma, K. L. (2000). Visualizing visualizations: Visualization viewpoints. *IEEE Computer Graphics and Applications, 20*(5), 16–19.

Ma, K.-L. (2004). Visualization—A quickly emerging field. *Computer Graphics, 38*(1), 4–7.

MacDonald, L. W., & Lowe, A. C. (1997). *Display systems: Design and applications.* New York: Wiley SID.

Mace, R. L., Hardie, G. J., & Plaice, J. P. (1991). Accessible environments: Toward universal design. In W. Preiser, J. Vischer, & E. White (Eds.), *Design interventions: Toward a more human architecture.* Van Nostrand Reinhold, New York.

MacEachren, A. M. (1995). *How maps work: Representation, visualization, and design.* New York: Guilford Press.

B
I
B
L
I
O
G
R
A
P
H
Y

Machlup, F., & Mansfield, U. (Eds.). (1983). *The study of information: Interdisciplinary messages.* New York: Wiley.

Mack, R., & Nielsen, J. (1994). *Usability inspection methods.* New York: Wiley. Mayhew, D. (1999). The usability engineering lifecycle. San Francisco: Morgan Kauffman.

MacKay, D. M. (1969). *Information, mechanism, and meaning.* Cambridge: MIT Press.

Mackay, W. E., Pothier, G., Letondal, C., Bøegh, K., & Sørensen, H. E. (2002). The missing link: Augmenting biology laboratory notebooks. In *Proceedings of the 15th annual ACM symposium on user interface software and technology* (pp. 41–50). New York: Association for Computing Machinery.

Mackintosh, A. R. (1988, August). Dr. Atanasoff's computer. *Scientific American* (pp. 72–78).

Madden, M., & Rainie, L. (2003). *America's online pursuits.* Washington, DC: Pew Internet and American Life Project.

Madden, T., Smith, R., Wright, M., & Wessel, D. (2001). Preparation for interactive live computer performance in collaboration with a symphony orchestra. In *Proceedings of the 2001 International Computer Music Conference* (pp. 310–313). San Francisco, CA: Computer Music Association.

Madey, G., Freeh, V., &and Tynan, R. (2004). Modeling the F/OSS community: A quantitative investigation. In S. Koch (Ed.), *Free/open source software development.* Hershey, PA: Idea Group Publishing.

Madhvanath, S., & Govindaraju, V. (2001). The role of holistic paradigms in handwritten word recognition. *IEEE Transactions on Pattern Analysis and Machine Intelligence, 23*(2), 149–164.

Madhvanath, S., Kim, G., & Govindaraju, V. (1999). Chain code processing for handwritten word recognition. *IEEE Transactions on Pattern Analysis and Machine Intelligence, 21*(9), 928–932.

Madhvanath, S., Kleinberg, E., & Govindaraju, V. (1999). Holistic verification of handwritten phrases. *IEEE Transactions on Pattern Analysis and Machine Intelligence, 21*(12), 1344–1356.

Maes, P. (1994). Agents that reduce work and information overload. *Communication of the ACM, 37*(7), 30–40.

Maglio, P. P., Barrett, R., Campbell, C. S., & Selker, T. (2000). *SUITOR: An attentive information system.* New York: ACM Press.

Mahach, K. R. (1989). A comparison of computer input devices: Linus pen, mouse, cursor keys and keyboard, perspectives. Proceedings of the Human Factors Society 33rd Annual Meeting, Denver, CO. In *The Human Factors Society, 1* (pp. 330–334). Santa Monica, CA: Human Factors and Ergonomics Society.

Majaranta, P., & Raiha, K.-J. (2002). Twenty years of eye typing: Systems and design issues. *In Proceedings of Eye Tracking Research & Applications* (ETRA) (pp. 15–22). New Orleans, LA: ACM.

Malnic, B., Hirono, J., Sato, T., & Buck, L. B. (1999). Combinatorial receptor codes for odors. *Cell, 96,* 713–723.

Malone, T. W., & Crowston, K. (1994). The interdisciplinary study of coordination. *ACM Computing Surveys, 26*(1), 87–119.

Malone, T. W., Grant, K. R., Turbak, F. A., Brobst, S. A., & Cohen, M. D. (1987). Intelligent information sharing systems. *Communications of the ACM, 30*(5), 390–402.

Maltin, L. (1987). *Of mice and magic—A history of American animated cartoons.* New York: Penguin Books.

Maltz, M. D., Gordon, A. C., & Friedman, W. (2000). *Mapping crime in its community setting: Event geography analysis.* New York: Springer-Verlag.

Manaris, B., & Dominick, W. (1993). NALIGE: A user interface management system for the development of natural language

interfaces. *International Journal of Man-Machine Studies, 38*(6), 891–921.

Mani, I., & Maybury, M. T. (1999). Advances in automatic text summarization. Cambridge, MA: MIT Press.

Manjunath, B. S., & Ma, W. Y. (1996). Texture features for browsing and retrieval of image data. *IEEE Transactions on Pattern Analysis and Machine Intelligence, 8*(11), 679–698.

Manjunath, B. S., Salembier, P., & Sikora, T. (Eds.). (2002). *Introduction to MPEG-7: Multimedia content description interface.* New York: Wiley.

Mankoff, J., Dey, A., Moore, M., & Batra, U. (2002). Web accessibility for low bandwidth input. In *Proceedings of ASSETS 2002* (pp. 89–96). Edinburgh, UK: ACM Press.

Mankoff, J., Hudson, S. E., & Abowd, G. D. (2000). Providing integrated toolkit-level support for ambiguity in recognition-based interfaces. In *Proceedings of the Human Factors in Computing (SIGCHI) Conference* (pp. 368–375). The Hague, Netherlands: ACM Press.

Manmatha, R., & Croft, W. B. (1997). Word spotting: Indexing handwritten manuscripts. In M. Maybury (Ed.), *Intelligent multi-media information retrieval* (pp. 43–64). Cambridge, MA: AAAI/MIT Press.

Mann, R., & Winn, J. (2002). *Electronic commerce.* Gaithersburg, MD: Aspen Publishers.

Mann, W. C., & Matthiessen, C. M. I. M. (1985). Demonstration of the Nigel text generation computer program. In J. D. Benson & W. S. Greaves (Eds.), *Systemic Perspectives on Discourse, 1,* 50–83. Norwood, NJ: Ablex.

Manning, C. D., & Schütze, H. (1999*). Foundations of statistical language processing.* Cambridge, MA: MIT Press.

Manning, P. K. (1992). Information technologies and the police. *Crime and Justice, 15,* 349–398.

Manovich, L. (2002). *The language of new media.* Cambridge, MA: MIT Press.

Mansour, S. (June 5, 1999). *A Tao of Regular Expressions.* Retrieved January 20, 2004, from http://sitescooper.org/tao_regexps.html

Manzoor, K. (2001). *Compilers, interpreters and virtual machines.* Retrieved January 20, 2004, from http://homepages.com.pk/kashman/jvm.htm

Marcus, M., Gerr, F., Monteilh, C., Ortiz, D. J., Gentry, E., Cohen, S., Edwards, A., Ensor, C., & Kleinbaum, D. (2002). A prospective study of computer users: II. Postural risk factors for musculoskeletal symptoms and disorders. *American Journal of Industrial Medicine, 41,* 226–249.

Margetts, H. (2000). The cyber party. Paper to the Democratic Audit, London School of Economics.

Margolis, J. & Fisher, A. (2002). *Unlocking the clubhouse: Women in computing.* Cambridge, MA: MIT.

Margolis, M., & Resnick, D. (2000). *Politics as usual: The cyberspace "revolution."* Thousand Oaks, CA: Sage.

Markovsky, B., Lovaglia, M., & Thye, S. (1997). Computer-aided research at the Iowa Center for the Study of Group Processes. *Social Science Computer Review, 15*(1), 48–64.

Markowitz, J. A. (1995). *Using speech recognition: A guide for application developers.* Upper Saddle River, NJ: Prentice Hall.

Markus, M. L. (1994). Finding a happy medium: Explaining the negative effects of electronic communication on social life at work. *ACM Transactions on Information Systems, 12*(2), 119–149.

Marras, W., & Kim, J. (1993). Anthropometry of industrial populations. *Ergonomics, 36*(4), 371–377.

Marsland, T. A., & Schaeffer, J. (Eds.). (1990). *Computers, chess, and cognition.* New York: Springer-Verlag.

Martin, I., & Venables, P. H. (1980). *Techniques in psychophysiology.* New York: Wiley.

Martin, J. (1973). *Design of man-computer dialogues.* Englewood Cliffs, NJ: Prentice Hall.

Martinez, S. G., Bennett, K. B., & Shattuck, L. (2001). Cognitive systems engineering analyses for army tactical operations. In *Proceedings of the human factors and ergonomics society 44th annual meeting* (pp. 523–526). Santa Monica, CA: Human Factors and Ergonomics Society.

Marx, G. T., Moderow, J., Zuboff, S., Howard, B., & Nussbaum, K. (1990, March/April). The case of the omniscient organization. *Harvard Business Review, 68*(2), 12–30.

Mase, K. (1991). Recognition of facial expressions for optical flow. *IEICE Transactions,* Special Issue on Computer Vision and its Applications, E 74(10).

Mason, R., & Carey, T. Prototyping interactive information systems. *Communications of the ACM, 26*(5), 347–354.

Mason, S. G., & Birch, G. E. (2003, March). A general framework for brain-computer interface design. *IEEE Transactions on Neural Systems and Rehabilitation Technology, 11*(1), 70–85.

Massie, T. H., & Salisbury, J. K. (1994).The PHANToM haptic interface: A device for probing virtual objects. *Proceedings of ASME Winter Annual Meeting, Dynamic Systems and Control, 55,* 295–301.

Mathiassen, L., & Stage, J. (1999). Informatics as a multi-disciplinary education. *Scandinavian Journal of Information Systems, 11*(1), 13–22.

Maybury, M. T., & Wahlster, W. (Eds.). (1998). *Readings in intelligent user interfaces.* San Francisco: Morgan Kaufmann.

Mayer, R. E. (1988). From novice to expert. In M. Helander (Ed.), *Handbook of human-computer interaction* (pp. 781–796). Amsterdam: Elsevier Science.

Mayhew, D. J. (1999). *The usability engineering lifecycle.* San Francisco: Morgan Kaufmann.

McAdams, S., & Bigand, E. (1993). Introduction to auditory cognition. In S. McAdams & E. Bigand (Eds.), *Thinking in sound: The cognitive psychology of human audition* (pp. 1–9). Oxford, UK: Oxford University Press.

McBryan, O. (1994). GENVL and WWWW: Tools for taming the Web. *Proceedings of the First International World Wide Web Conference.*

McCartney, S. (1999). *ENIAC: The triumphs and tragedies of the world's first computer.* New York: Walker.

McClard, A., & Somer, P. (2000). Unleashed: Web tablet integration into the home. *Proceedings of the SIGCHI conference on human factors in computing systems* (pp. 1–8). New York: ACM Press.

McCormick, B., DeFanti, T., & Brown, M. (1987). Visualization in scientific computing. *Computer Graphics, 21*(6).

McDonough, J. (1999). Designer selves: Construction of technologically-mediated identity within graphical, multi-user virtual environments. *Journal of the American Society for Information Science, 50*(10), 855–869.

McDonough, J. (2000). *Under construction.* Unpublished doctoral dissertation, University of California at Berkeley.

McElwain, C. K., & Evans, M. E. (1962). The degarbler— a program for correcting machine-read Morse code. *Information and Control, 5*(4), 368–384.

McGill, T. J. (2002). User-developed applications: Can end users assess quality? *Journal of End User Computing, 14*(3), 1–15.

McGrath, J. E., & Hollingshead, A. B. (1994). *Groups interacting with technology.* Thousand Oaks, CA: Sage.

McGrew, M. (1993). *American metal typefaces of the twentieth century.* New Castle, DE: Oak Knoll Books.

McKenna, K. Y. A., & Bargh, J. A. (Eds.). (2002). Interpersonal and group processes on the Internet: Is social life being transformed? *Journal of Social Issues, 58,* 1–206.

McKeown, K., Jordan, D., Feiner, S., Shaw, J., Chen, E. Ahmad, S., et al. (2002). *A study of communication in the cardiac surgery intensive care unit and its implications for automated briefing.* Retrieved March 23, 2004, from http://www1.cs.columbia.edu/~shaw/papers/amia00.pdf.

McKeown, K. R. (1985). Text generation: Using discourse strategies and focus constraints to generate natural language text. Cambridge, UK: Cambridge University Press.

McKnight, C., Dillon A., & Richardson J. (1991). *Hypertext in context.* Cambridge, UK: Cambridge University Press.

McLaughlin, M. L., Hespanha, J. P., & Sukhatme, G. S. (Eds.). (2002). *Touch in virtual environments.* Upper Saddle River, NJ: Prentice Hall.

McLean, R. (1980). *The Thames & Hudson manual of typography.* New York: Thames & Hudson.

McLuhan, M., Fiore, Q., & Agel, J. (1996). *The medium is the massage: An inventory of effects.* San Francisco: HardWired.

McNeill, D. (1992). *Hand and mind: What gestures reveal about thought.* Chicago: University of Chicago Press.

McNeill, D., Quek, F., et al. (2001). Catchments, prosody and discourse. *Gesture 1,* 9–33.

McRoy, S. W. (Ed.). (1998). Detecting, repairing, and preventing human-machine miscommunication [Special issue]. *International Journal of Human-Computer Studies, 48*(5).

McRoy, S. W., Channarukul, S., & Ali, S. S. (2001). Creating natural language output for real-time applications intelligence. *Intelligence: New Visions of AI in Practice, 12*(2), 21–34.

McRoy, S. W., Channarukul, S., & Ali, S. S. (2003). An augmented template-based approach to text realization. *Natural Language Engineering, 9*(2), 1–40.

McTear, M. F. (2002). Spoken dialogue technology: Enabling the conversational user interface. *ACM Computing Surveys, 34*(1), 90–169.

Meadows, A. J. (1998). *Communicating research.* New York: Academic Press.

Medyckyj-Scott, D., & Hearnshaw, H. M. (Eds.). (1993). *Human factors in geographical information systems.* London: Belhaven Press.

Meehan, M., Razzaque, S., Whitton, M., & Brooks, F. (2003). Effect of latency on presence in stressful virtual environments. *Proceedings of IEEE Virtual Reality 2003,* 141–148.

Meijer, P. B. L. (2003). *The vOIce.* Retrieved December 10, 2003, from http://www.seeingwithsound.com/voice.htm

Mel, B. W., Omohundro, S. M., Robison, A. D., Skiena, S. S., Thearling, K. H., Young, L. T., et al. (1988). Tablet: Personal computer in the year 2000. *Communications of the ACM, 31*(6), 639–646.

Mel'cuk, I. A., & Polguere, A. (1987). A formal lexicon in the meaning-text theory (or how to do lexica with words). *Computational Linguistics, 13*(3–4), 261–275.

Melnick, D., Dinman, M., and Muratov, A. (2003). *PDA Security: Incorporating Handhelds into the Enterprise.* New York: McGraw-Hill.

Memon, A. M., Pollack, M. E., Soffa, M. L. (2001). Hierarchical GUI test case generation using automated planning. *IEEE Transactions on Software Engineering, 27*(2), 144–155.

Memon, A., Pollack, M., & Soffa, M. (1999). Using a goal-driven approach to generate test cases for GUIs. *Proceedings of the International Conference on Software Engineering*, 257–266.

Messick, P. (1998). *Maximum MIDI*. Greenwich, CT: Manning.

Metcalfe, R. M., & Boggs, D. R. (1976). Ethernet: Distributed packet switching for local computer networks. *Communications of the ACM, 19*(5), 395–404.

Metiu, A., & Kogut, B. (2001). *Distributed knowledge and the global organization of software development.* Unpublished manuscript, Wharton School of Business, University of Pennsylvania, Philadelphia.

Metropolis, N., Howlett, J., & Rota, G.-C. (Eds.). (1980). *A history of computing in the twentieth century.* New York: Academic Press.

Metzker, E., & Offergeld, M. (2001). An interdisciplinary approach for successfully integrating human-centered design methods into development processes practiced by industrial software development organizations. In *Engineering for Human-Computer Interaction* (pp. 19–31). Berlin, Germany: Springer-Verlag.

Meyer, A. (1995). Pen computing: A technology overview and a vision. *SIGCHI Bulletin, 27*(3), 46–90.

Michalek, G. V. (2003). *Million book universal library project: Manual for metadata capture, digitization, and OCR.* Pittsburgh, PA: Carnegie Mellon University.

Microsoft Corporation. (1995). *The Windows interface guidelines for software design.* Redmond, WA: Microsoft Press.

Microsoft Corporation. (2003). *Manual of style for technical publications.* Redmond, WA: Microsoft Press.

Microsoft Corporation. *Microsoft Windows XP—Guidelines for applications.* (2002). Retrieved December 20, 2003, from http://www.microsoft.com/whdc/hwdev/windowsxp/downloads/default.mspx

Mikulka, P. J., Scerbo, M. W., & Freeman, F. G. (2002). Effects of a biocybernetic system on vigilance performance. *Human Factors, 44,* 654–664.

Milberg, S. J., Burke, S. J., Smith, H. J., & Kallman, E. A. (1995). Values, personal information, privacy and regulatory approaches. *Communications of the ACM, 38,* 65–74.

Milgram, P., & Kishino, F. (1994, December). A taxonomy of mixed reality visual displays. *IEICE Transactions on Information Systems,* E77-D(12), 1321–1329.

Miller, D., & Slater, D. (1999). *The Internet: An ethnographic approach.* Oxford, UK: Berg.

Miller, G. (2000). Technological evolution as self-fulfilling prophecy. In J. Ziman (Ed.), *Technological innovation as an evolutionary process* (pp. 203–215). Cambridge, UK: Cambridge University Press.

Miller, G. A. (1956). The magical number seven, plus or minus two: Some limits on our capacity for processing information. *Psychological Review, 63,* 81–97.

Miller, G. A., Beckwith, R., Fellbaum, C. D., Gross, D., & Miller, K. J. (1990). WordNet: An on-line lexical database. *International Journal of Lexicography, 3,* 235–244.

Miller, M. (1992, August 9). Patients' records are a treasure trove for a budding industry. *Wall Street Journal,* p. A21.

Miller, M. (2001). *Discovering P2P.* Marina del Rey, CA: Cybex.

Miller, R. B. (1953) *A method for man-machine task analysis* (WADC Tech. Rep. No. 53–137). Dayton, OH: Wright Air Development Center.

Milstead, J., & Feldman, S. (1999). *Metadata: Cataloging by any other name . . . Metadata projects and standards. Online, 23*(1), 24–40. Retrieved January 22, 2004, from www.infotoday.com/online/OL1999/milstead1.html

Mims, F. M. (1985, January). The tenth anniversary of the Altair 8800. *Computers & Electronics, 23*(1), 58–60, 81–82.

Mine, M., Brooks, F., & Sequin, C. (1997). Moving objects in space: Exploiting proprioception in virtual-environment interaction. *Proceedings of SIGGRAPH 97.* Retrieved on November 4, 2003, from http://www.cs.unc.edu/~mine/papers/minecows.pdf

Ministry of Public Management, Home Affairs, Posts, and Telecommunications (Japan). (2003). *Building a new, Japan-inspired IT society.* Tokyo: Author.

Minker, W., Bühler, D., & Dybkjær, L. (??). *Spoken multimodal human-computer dialog in mobile environments.* Dordrect, Netherlands: Kluwer Academic.

Minsky, M. (1980, June). Telepresence. *Omni, 2*(9), 45–51.

Minton, S., et al. (1992). Minimizing conflicts: A heuristic repair method for constraint satisfaction and scheduling problems. *Artificial Intelligence, 58,* 161–205.

Mirani, R. & King, W.R. (1994). The development of a measure for end-user computing support. *Decision Sciences, 25*(4), 481–498.

Mishel, L., Bernstein, J., & Schmitt, J. (2001). *The state of working America.* Ithaca, NY: Cornell University Press.

MIT Kerberos. (n.d.). *Kerberos: The network authentication protocol.* Retrieved March 18, 2004, from http://web.mit.edu/kerberos/www/

MIT/Sloan. (2004). *Free/open source research community,* 2002. Retrieved April 16, 2004, from http://opensource.mit.edu/

Mitchell, C. M., & Miller, R. A. (1986). A discrete control model of operator function: A methodology for information display design. *IEEE Transactions on Systems, Man, and Cybernetics, SMC-16*(3), 343–357.

Mitchell, J. C. (1996). *Foundations of programming languages.* Cambridge, MA: MIT Press.

Mitchell, J. C. (2003). *Concepts in programming languages.* Cambridge, UK: Cambridge University Press.

Mitchell, W. J. (2003). *ME++: The cyborg self and the networked city.* Cambridge, MA: MIT Press.

Mittal, V., Moore, J., Carenini, G., & Roth, S. F. (1998). Describing complex charts in natural language: A caption generation system. *Computational Linguistics, 24*(3), 431–467.

Mitton, R. (1996). Spellchecking by computer. *Journal of the Simplified Spelling Society, 20*(1), 4–11.

Mockus, A., Fielding, R. T., & Herbsleb, J. (2002). Two case studies of open source software development: Apache and Mozilla. *ACM Transactions on Software Engineering and Methodology, 11*(3), 309–346.

Moeslund, T. B., & Granum, E. (2001, March). A survey of computer vision-based human motion capture. *Computer Vision and Image Understanding, 82*(3), 231–268.

Mokhtarian, P. L. (1996). The information highway: Just because we're on it doesn't mean we know where we're going. *World Transport Policy and Practice, 2*(1–2), 24–28.

Molenbroek, J. (1987) Anthropometry of elderly people in the Netherlands: Research and applications. *Applied Ergonomics, 18,* 187–194.

Mollenhoff, C. R. (1988). *Atanasoff: Forgotten father of the computer.* Ames: Iowa State University Press.

Molpas, D. (2001). The company from nowhere. NPR. Retrieved March 2, 2004, from http://www.npr.org/programs/morning/features/2001/mar/010330.cfoa.html

BIBLIOGRAPHY

Mondeca topic organizer. Retrieved January 22, 2004, from http://www.mondeca.com/

Monk, A., & Howard, S. (1998, March–April). The rich picture: A tool for reasoning about work context. *Interactions 5*, 21–30.

Montanari, U. (1974). Networks of constraints: Fundamental properties and application to picture processing. *Information Sciences, 7*, 95–132.

Moor, J. H. (1985). What is computer ethics? *Metaphilosophy, 16*(4), 266–275.

Moore D., & Habeler J. (2002). *Peer to peer: Building secure, scalable and manageable networks*. Berkley, CA: McGraw Hill /Osborne.

Moore, B. (2003). *Touch screen technology*. Retrieved October 10, 2003, from http://www.idat.com/a-touchtech.html

Moore, B. C. J. (1997). *An introduction to the psychology of hearing* (4th ed.). San Diego, CA: Academic Press.

Moore, D., Paxson, V., Savage, S., Shannon, C., Staniford, S., & Weaver, N. (2003). Inside the Slammer worm. *IEEE Security & Privacy, 1*(4), 33–39.

Moore, G. E. (1965). Cramming more components onto integrated circuits. *Electronics, 38*(8), 114–117.

Moore, J. T. S. (2002). Revolution OS [DVD]. United States: Worldview Productions.

Moore, M., Mankoff, J., Mynatt, E., & Kennedy, P. (2002). Nudge and shove: Frequency thresholding for navigation in direct brain-computer interfaces. In *Proceedings of SIGCHI 2001Conference on Human Factors in Computing Systems* (pp. 361–362). New York: ACM Press.

Morahan-Martin, J. (1998). Males, females and the Internet. In J. Gackenbach (Ed.), *Psychology and the Internet* (pp. 169–198). San Diego, CA: Academic Press.

Moretti, S. (2002). Computer simulation in sociology. *Social Science Computer Review, 20*(1), 43–57.

Morgan, B. J. (1990). *The police function and the investigation of crime*. Brookfield, VT: Avebury.

Morgan, K., Satava, R. M., Sieburg, H. B., Matteus, R., & Christensen, J. P. (Eds.). (1995). *Interactive technology and the new paradigm for healthcare*. Amsterdam: IOS Press and Ohmsha.

Morimoto, D., & Flickner, M. (2000). Pupil detection using multiple light sources. *Image and Vision Computing, 18*, 331–335.

Morison, S. (1999). *A tally of types*. Boston: David R. Godine.

Morita, M., & Shinoda, Y. (1994). Information filtering based on user behavior analysis and best match text retrieval. In *Proceedings of the Seventh Annual ACM-SIGIR Conference on Research and Development in IR.* (pp. 272–281). New York: Springer-Verlag.

Morningstar, C., & Farmer, F. R. (1991). The lessons of Lucasfilm's Habitat. In M. Benedikt (Ed.), *Cyberspace: First steps* (pp. 273–302). Cambridge, MA: The MIT Press.

Morrell, R. W., Dailey, S. R., Feldman, C., Mayhorn, C. B., & Echt, K. V. (2002, April). *Older adults and information technology: A compendium of scientific research and web site accessibility guidelines*. Bethesda, MD: National Institute on Aging.

Morris, P. (1993). The breakout method for escaping from local minima. In *Eleventh National Conference on Artificial Intelligence* (pp. 40–45). Menlo Park, CA: MIT Press

Mostow, J., Roth, S. F., Hauptmann, A., & Kane, M. (1994). A prototype reading coach that listens. In *Proceedings of the Twelfth National Conference on Artificial Intelligence* (AAAI-94) (pp. 785–792). Seattle, WA: AAAI Press.

Moxon, J. (1958). *Mechanick exercises on the whole art of printing, 1683–84*. London: Oxford University Press.

Moynihan, T. (2000). Coping with requirements-uncertainty: The theories-of-action of experienced IS/software project managers. *The Journal of Systems and Software, 53*(2), 99–109.

Mozer, M. (1998). The Neural Network House: An environment that adapts to its inhabitants. In *Proceedings of the AAAI spring symposium on intelligent environments* (pp. 110–114). Menlo Park, CA: AAAI.

MPEG. (1999). Overview of the MPEG-4 standard. *Technical Report ISO/IEC JTC1/SC29/WG11 N2725*. International Organisation for Standardization (ISO), Seoul, South Korea. Retrieved April 8, 2004, from http://drogo.cselt.stet.it/mpeg/standards/mpeg-4/mpeg-4.htm.

Muir, B. M. (1987). Trust between humans and machines, and the design of decision aids. *International Journal of Man-Machine Studies, 27*, 527–539.

Muir, P. H., & Carter, J. (Eds.). (1983). *Printing and the mind of man*. Munich, Germany: Karl Pressler.

Mukherjea, S., & Foley, J. (1995). Visualizing the World Wide Web with the navigational view builder. *Computer Systems and ISDN Systems, 27*(6), 1075–1087.

Mulder, A. (1994, July). *Human movement tracking technology*. Retrieved August 19, 2003, from http://www.cs.sfu.ca/people/ResearchStaff/amulder/personal/vmi/HMTT.pub.html#mary

Mulholland, A., & Hakal, T. (2001). *Developer's guide to multiplayer games*. Plano, TX: Wordware Publishing.

Mulkey, L. M., & Anderson, T. D. (2002). Using online context as a mediating variable in the investigation of sex-role orientation and care-oriented moral reasoning. *Social Science Computer Review, 20*(2), 137–148.

Muller, M. J. (1991). PICTIVE-An exploration in participatory design. In *Proceedings of CHI '91* (pp. 225–231). New York: ACM Press.

Muller, M. J., Tudor, L. G., Wildman, D. M., White, E. A., Root, R. A., Dayton, T., et al. (1995). Bifocal tools for scenarios and representations in participatory activities with users. In J.M. Carroll (Ed.), *Scenario-based design: Envisioning work and technology in system development* (pp. 135–163). New York: Wiley.

Muller, M., Haslwanter, J., & Dayton, T. (1997). In M. Helander & T. Landauer (Eds.), The Handbook of Human-Computer Interaction (pp. 255–298). Amsterdam: North-Holland.

Müller-Brockman, J. (1985). *Grid systems in graphic design*. New York: Hastings House.

Mumford, E. (1987). Sociotechnical systems design: Evolving theory and practice. In G. Bjerknes, P. Ehn, & M. Kyng (Eds.), *Computers and democracy* (pp. 59–76). Aldershot, UK: Avebury.

Mumford, E. (1996). *Systems design: Ethical tools for ethical change*. London: MacMillan.

Mumford, E., & MacDonald, B. (1989). *XSEL's progress*. New York: Wiley.

Munson, J., & Dewan, P. (1994). A flexible object merging framework. In *Proceedings of the ACM Conference on Computer Supported Cooperative Work*. New York.

Munson, J., & Dewan, P. (1996). A concurrency control framework for collaborative systems. In *Proceedings of the ACM Conference on Computer Supported Cooperative Work*. New York.

Murphy, K. L., & Collins, M. P. (1997). Communication conventions in instructional electronic chats. *First Monday, 11*(2).

Murray, J. H. (1997). *Hamlet on the Holodeck: The future of narrative in cyberspace*. New York: Free Press.

Murtagh, F., & Heck, A. (1987). *Multivariate data analysis.* Dordrecht, Netherlands: Kluwer.

Murtagh, F., Taskaya, T., Contreras, P., Mothe, J., & Englmeier, K. (2003). Interactive visual user interfaces: A survey. *Artificial Intelligence Review, 19,* 263–283.

Musciano, C., & Kennedy, B. (2002). *HTML and XHTML: The definitive guide* (5th ed.). Cambridge, MA: O'Reilly & Associates.

Myers, B. (2003). Graphical user interface programming. In A. B. Tucker (Ed.), *CRC Handbook of Computer Science and Engineering (2nd ed.).* Boca Raton. FL: CRC Press.

Myers, B., & Rosson, M.B. (1992). Survey on user interface programming. *Proceedings of CHI '02,* 195–202. New York: ACM Press.

Myers, B., Ioannidis, Y., Hollan, J., Cruz, I., Bryson, S., Bulterman, D., et al. (1996). Strategic directions in human computer interaction. *ACM Computing Survey, 28*(4), 794–809.

Myers, B., Lie, K. P., & Yang, B.-C. (2000). Two-handed input using a PDA and a mouse. In *Proceedings of the SIGCHI conference on human factors in computing systems* (pp. 41–48). New York: Association for Computing Machinery.

Myers, C. A. (1970). *Computers in knowledge-based fields.* Cambridge, MA: MIT Press.

Nagle, H. T., Schiffman, S. S., & Gutierrez-Osuna, R. (1998). The how and why of electronic noses. *IEEE Spectrum, 35*(9), 22–34.

Nardi, B. (1993). *A small matter of programming: Perspectives on end user computing.* Cambridge, MA: MIT Press.

Nardi, B. A. (Ed.). (1996). *Context and consciousness: Activity theory and human-computer interaction.* Cambridge, MA: MIT Press.

Nardi, B. A., Whittaker, S., & Bradner E. (2000). Interaction and outeraction: Instant messaging in action. In Campbell, M. (Ed.), *Proceeding of the ACM 2000 conference on computer-supported cooperative work* (pp. 79–88). Philadelphia: ACM.

Nash, E. B., Edwards, G. W., Thompson, J. A., & Barfield, W. (2000). A review of presence and performance in virtual environments. *International Journal of Human-Computer Interaction, 12*(1), 1–41.

Nass, C. & Moon, Y. (2000). Machines and mindlessness: Social responses to computers. *Journal of Social Issues, 56*(1), 81–103

Nass, C. (1996). *The media equation: How people treat computers, televisions, and new media like real people and places.* New York: Cambridge University Press.

National Academy of Sciences. (1999). *Improving research capabilities in chemical and biomedical sciences: Proceedings of a multi-site electronic workshop.* Washington, DC: National Academy Press.

National Aeronautics and Space Administration (NASA). (n.d.). *Robotics.* Retrieved July 21, 2003, from http://spacelink.nasa.gov/ Instructional.Materials/Curriculum.Support/Technology/Robotics/

National and international grid projects. Retrieved February, 2, 2004, from http://www.escience-grid.org.uk/docs/briefing/nigridp.htm

National Cancer Institute. (2003). *Research-based web site design and usability guidelines.* Retrieved July 27, 2003, from http://usability.gov/guidelines/

National Center for Education Statistics. (2002*). Digest of education statistics.* Washington DC: U.S. Department of Education.

National Coordination Office for Information Technology Research and Development, National Science and Technology Council. (1999). Networked computing for the 21st century: Collaboratories. *Computing, information, and communications networked computing for the 21st century.* Retrieved February 28, 2004, from http://www.ccic.gov/pubs/blue99/collaboratories.html

National Research Council. (1991). *The future of statistical software: Proceedings of a forum.* Washington, D.C.: National Academy Press.

National Research Council. (1993). *Toward a coordinated spatial data infrastructure for the nation.* Washington, DC: National Academy Press.

National Research Council. (1999). *Distributed geolibraries: Spatial information resources.* Washington, DC: National Academy Press.

National Research Council. (2001). *Building a workforce for the information economy.* Washington, DC: National Academy Press.

National Science Foundation. (1996). *Culture, society, and advanced information technology* (Report of a workshop held on June 1–2, 1995). Washington, DC: U. S. Government Printing Office.

National Science Foundation. (2003) *Revolutionizing science and engineering through cyberinfrastructure: Report of the National Science Foundation blue-ribbon panel on cyberinfrastructure.* Retrieved December 24, 2003, from http://www.communitytechnology.org/ nsf_ci_report/

National Science Foundation. (2003, June). *Report of the NSF workshop on digital library research directions.* Chatham, MA: Wave of the Future: NSF Post Digital Library Futures Workshop.

National Telecommunications and Information Administration (2002). *A nation online: How Americans are expanding their use of the Internet.* Washington, DC: U.S. Department of Commerce. Retrieved July 18, 2003, from http://www.ntia.doc.gov/ntia-home/dn/html/toc.htm

National Telecommunications and Information Administration, Economics and Statistics Administration. (n.d.) *A nation online: How Americans are expanding their use of the Internet.*

National Telecommunications and Information Administration. (1999). Falling through the Net: Defining the digital divide. Washington, DC: U.S. Department of Commerce.

Nature Webdebates. (2001). *Future e-access to the primary literature.* Retrieved July 28, 2003, from http://www.nature.com/nature/debates/e-access/

Naumann, J., & Jenkins, A. (1982). Prototyping: The new paradigm for systems development. *MIS Quarterly, 6*(3), 29–44.

Neff, G., & Stark, D. (2003). Permanently beta: Responsive organization in the Internet era. In P. Howard and S. Jones (Eds.), *Society Online.* Thousand Oaks, CA: Sage.

Negnevitsky, M. (2001). *Artificial intelligence: A guide to intelligent systems.* Reading, MA: Addison Wesley.

Negroponte, N. (1973). Recent advances in sketch recognition. In *AFIPS (American Federation of Information Processing) National Computer Conference, 42,* 663–675. Boston: American Federation of Information Processing.

Neilsen, J. (1994). Enhancing the explanatory power of usability heuristics. In *Proceedings ACM CHI'94,* 152–158.

Neilsen, J. (1994). *Usability engineering.* Boston: Academic Press.

Neilsen, J. (2002). *Kids' corner: Website usability for children.* Retrieved January 4, 2004, from http://www.useit.com/alertbox/20020414.html

Nelson, R. R. & Todd, P. A. (2003). Peopleware: The hiring and retention of IT personnel. In M. Igbaria & C. Shayo (Eds.), *Strategies for managing IS/IT personnel* (pp. 1–17). Hershey, PA: Idea Group Publishing.

Nelson, T. (1965). A file structure for the complex, the changing, and the indeterminate. In *Proceedings of the ACM National Conference* (pp. 84–100). New York: ACM Press.

Nelson, T. (1973). A conceptual framework for man-machine everything. In *AFIPS Conference* proceedings (pp. M21-M26). Montvale, NJ: AFIPS Press..

Nelson, T. H. (1974). *Dream machines: New freedoms through computer screens—A minority report* (p. 144). Chicago: Nelson.

Nelson, T. H. (1990). *Literary Machines 90.1.* Sausalito, CA: Mindful Press.

Nelson, T. H. (1992). *Literary machines 93.1.* Sausalito, CA: Mindful Press.

Nervous TV newscasters blink more. (1999). Retrieved April 29, 2004, from http://www.doctorbob.com/news/7_24nervous.html

Neteler, M., & Mitasova, H. (2002). *Open source GIS: A GRASS GIS approach.* The Kluwer International Series In Engineering And Computer Science (SECS), 689. Boston: Kluwer.

Neuhoff, J., McBeath, M. K., & Wanzie, W. C. (1999). Dynamic frequency change influences loudness perception: A central, analytic process. *Journal of Experimental Psychology: Human Perception and Performance, 25*(4), 1050–1059.

Neumann, P. (1995). *Computer-Related Risks.* New York: Addison-Wesley/ACM Press.

Neumann, U., & Majoros, A. (1998). Cognitive, performance, and systems issues for augmented reality applications in manufacturing and maintenance. In *Proceedings of the IEEE 1998 Virtual Reality Annual International Symposium* (pp. 4–11). Los Alamitos, CA: IEEE.

Neuwirth, C. M., Chandok, R., et al. (1992). Flexible diff-ing in a collaborative writing system. In *Proceedings of ACM Conference on Computer Supported Cooperative Work.* New York.

Newborn, M. (2003). *Deep Blue: An artificial intelligence* milestone. New York: Springer-Verlag.

Newburger, E. C. (2001). *Home computers and Internet use in the United States: August 2000, Special Studies.* Retrieved January 23, 2004, from http://www.census.gov/prod/2001pubs/p23-207.pdf

Newell, A. (1992). Precis of unified theories of cognition. *Behavioral and Brain Sciences, 15*(3), 425–437.

Newell, A., & Card, S. K. (1985). The prospects for psychological science in human-computer interaction. *Human-Computer Interaction, 1*(3), 209–242.

Newell, A., & Simon, H. (1972). *Human problem solving.* Englewood Cliffs, NJ: Prentice-Hall.

Newell, P. B. (1995). Perspectives on privacy. *Journal of Environmental Psychology, 13,* 87–104.

Nichols, J., & Myers, B. (2003, May). Studying the use of handhelds to control smart appliances. *Proceedings of the 23rd International Conference on Distributed Computing Systems, Workshops,* 274–279.

Nichols, S., Haldane, C., & Wilson, J. R. (2000). Measurement of presence and its consequences in virtual environments. *International Journal of Human-Computer Studies, 52*(3), 471–491.

Nicolelis, M. A. L., & Srinivasan, M. A. (2003). Human-machine interaction: Potential impact of nanotechnology in the design of neuroprosthetic devices aimed at restoring or augmenting human performance. In M. C. Roco & W. S. Bainbridge (Eds.), *Converging technologies for improving human performance* (pp. 251–255). Dordrecht, Netherlands: Kluwer.

Nielsen, J. (1990). The art of navigating through HyperText: Lost in hyperspace. *Communications of the ACM, 33*(3), 296–310.

Nielsen, J. (1993). Iterative user-interface design. *IEEE Computer, 26*(11), 32–41.

Nielsen, J. (1993). *Usability engineering.* San Diego, CA: Academic Press.

Nielsen, J. (1993, April). The next generation GUIs: Non-command user interfaces. *Communications of the ACM, 36*(4), 83–99.

Nielsen, J. (1994). *Guerilla HCI: Using discount usability engineering to penetrate the intimidation barrier.* Retrieved December 30, 2003, from http://www.useit.com/papers/guerrilla_hci.html

Nielsen, J. (1994). *Multimedia and hypertext: The Internet and beyond.* Boston, MA: Academic Press.

Nielsen, J. (1994). *Usability . engineering.* San Francisco: Morgan Kaufmann.

Nielsen, J. (1999). *Voodoo usability.* Retrieved December 30, 2003, from http://www.useit.com/alertbox/991212.html

Nielsen, J. (2000). *Designing web usability.* Indianapolis, IN: New Riders Publishing.

Nielsen, J. (2000). *Homepage usability: 50 websites deconstructed.* Indianapolis, IN: New Riders Publishing.

Nielsen, J. (2001). *Ten usability heuristics.* Retrieved December 30, 2003, from http://www.useit.com/papers/heuristic/heuristic_list.html

Nielsen, J. (2003). *Nielsen Norman Group's design guidelines.* Retrieved July 29, 2003, from www.useit.com

Nielsen, J. (n.d.). *Icon usability.* Retrieved December 20, 2003, from http://www.useit.com/papers/sun/icons.html

Nielsen, J., & Molich, R. (1990). Heuristic evaluation of user interfaces. In *Proceedings ACM CHI'90,* 249–256.

Nietzsche, F. (1967). *The birth of tragedy.* New York: Random House (Original work published 1872).

Niles, J. S. (1994). Beyond telecommuting: A new paradigm for the effect of telecommunications on travel. Global Telematics for US DOE. Retrieved February 28, 2004, from http://www.lbl.gov/ICSD/Niles/

Nilles, J. M. (1998). *Managing telework: Strategies for managing the virtual workforce.* New York: John Wiley and Sons.

Nilles, J. M., Carlson, F. R., Jr., Gray, P., & Hanneman, G. J. (1976). *The telecommunications-transportation tradeoff.* New York: Wiley.

Nirenburg, S., Somers, H. L., & Wilks, Y. A. (2003). *Readings in machine translation.* Cambridge, MA: MIT Press.

Nisbett, R. E., & Wilson, T. D. (1977). Telling more than we can know: Verbal reports on mental processes. *Psychological Review, 74,* 231–259.

Nissenbaum, H. (1998). Protecting privacy in an information age: The problem of privacy in public. *Law and Philosophy, 17,* 559–596.

Nissenbaum, H. (2004). Privacy as contextual integrity. *Washington Law Review, 79,* 119–158.

Nonaka, I., & Takeuchi, H. (1995). *The knowledge creating company.* New York: Oxford University Press.

Nooteboom, S. G. (1980). Speaking and unspeaking: Detection and correction of phonological and lexical errors in spontaneous speech. In V. A. Fromkin (Ed.), *Errors in linguistic performance: Slips of the tongue, ear, pen, and hand* (pp. 87–95). San Francisco: Academic Press.

Norberg, A., & O'Neill, J. (1997). *Transforming computer technology.* Ann Arbor, MI: Scholarly Publishing Office, University of Michigan Library.

Norman, D. (1988). *The psychology of everyday things.* New York: Basic Books.

Norman, D. (2001). *How might humans interact with robots?* Retrieved July 21, 2003, from http://www.jnd.org/dn.mss/Humans_and_Robots.html

Norman, D. A. (1981). Categorization of action slips. *Psychological Review, 88*(1), 1–15.

Norman, D. A. (1983). Design principles for human-computer interfaces. In *Proceedings of the SIGCHI Conference on Human Factors in Computing Systems* (pp. 1–10). New York: ACM Press.

Norman, D. A. (1988). *The design of everyday things.* Boston: MIT Press.

BIBLIOGRAPHY

Norman, D. A. (2003). *Emotional design: Why we love (or hate) everyday things.* New York: Basic.

Norman, D. A., & Draper, S. W. (Eds.). (1986). *User-centered system design: New perspectives on human-computer interaction.* Hillsdale, NJ: Lawrence Erlbaum Associates.

Norris, P. (2001). *Digital divide: Civic engagement, information poverty, and the Internet worldwide.* Cambridge, UK: Cambridge University Press.

Norris, P. (2002). The bridging and bonding role of online communities. *The Harvard International Journal of Press-Politics.* Retrieved on October 1, 2003, from http://ksghome.harvard.edu/~.pnorris.shorenstein.ksg/ACROBAT/Bridging.pdf

Northrop, A., Kraemer, K. L., & King, J. L. (1995). Police use of computers. *Journal of Criminal Justice, 23*(3), 259–275.

Nua Internet (2004). *How many online?* Retrieved January 23, 2004, from http://www.nua.com/surveys/how_many_online/index.html

Nyce, J. M., & Kahn, P. (Eds.). (1991). *From Memex to hypertext: Vannevar Bush and the mind's machine.* Boston: Academic Press.

Nyce, J., & Løwgren, J. (1995). Toward foundational analysis in human-computer interaction. In P. J. Thomas (Ed.), *The social and interactional dimensions of human-computer interfaces* (pp. 37–46). Cambridge, UK: Cambridge University Press

O'Gorman, L., & Kasturi, R. (1998). *Document image analysis.* New York: IEEE Computer Society Press.

O'Looney, J. A. (2002). *Wiring governments: Challenges and possibilities for public managers.* Westport. CT: Quorum Books.

O'Sullivan, C., Dingliana, J., & Howlett, S. (2002). Gaze-contingent algorithms for interactive graphics. In J. Hyönä, R. Radach, & H. Duebel (Eds.), *The mind's eye: cognitive and applied aspects of eye movement research* (pp. 555–571). Oxford, UK: Elsevier Science.

Oard, D. (1997). The state of the art in text filtering. *User Modeling and User-Adapted Interaction, 7,* 141–178.

O'Brien, J. A. (1967). *Computer program for automatic spelling correction* (Tech. Rep. RADC-TR-66-696). New York: Rome Air Development Center.

O'Connor, C., Sceiford, E., Wang, G., Foucar-Szocki, D., & Griffin, O. (2003). Departure, abandonment, and dropout of e-learning: Dilemma and solutions. *Report for the Masie Center eLearning Consortium.* Retrieved March 9, 2004, from www.masie.com/researchgrants/2003/JMU_Exec_Summary.pdf

O'Day, V., & Jeffries, R. (1993). Orienteering in an information landscape: How information seekers get from here to there. In *Proceedings of CHI '93* (pp. 438–445). New York: ACM Press.

Office machines and supplies—alphanumeric machines—alternate keyboard arrangement (revision and redesignation of ANSI X4.22-1983) (formerly ANSI X3.207-1991 (R1997)). Washington, DC: American National Standards Institute.

Office of Justice Programs. (2000). Office of Justice Programs Integrated Justice Information Technology Initiative. Retrieved November 4, 2003, from http://www.ojp.usdoj.gov/archive/topics/integrated-justice/welcome.html

Ogburn, W. F. (1922). *Social change.* New York: Huebsch.

Ohanian, T. (1998). *Digital nonlinear editing: Editing film and video on the desktop* (2nd ed.). Boston: Focal Press.

Ohlsson, S. (1996a). Learning from error and the design of task environments. *International Journal of Educational Research, 25*(5), 419–448.

Ohlsson, S. (1996b). Learning from performance errors. *Psychological Review, 103*(2), 241–262.

Ohshima, T., Sato, K., Yamamoto, H., & Tamura, H. (1998). AR2 hockey: A case study of collaborative augmented reality. In *Proceedings of the IEEE 1998 Virtual Reality Annual International Symposium* (pp. 268–275) Los Alamitos, CA: IEEE.

Oja, E., & Kaski, S. (1999). *Kohonen maps.* Amsterdam, Elsevier.

O'Keefe, R., Cole, M., Chau, P., Massey, A., Montoya-Weiss, M., & Perry, M. (2000). From the user interface to the consumer interface: Results from a global experiment. *International Journal of Human Computer Studies, 53*(4), 611–628.

Olive, J. P. (1977). Rule synthesis of speech from dyadic units. *Proceedings, International Conference on Audio, Speech, and Signal Processing, 77,* 568–570.

Olson, G. M., Atkins, D. E., Clauer, R., Finholt, T. A., Jahanian, F., Killeen, T. L., Prakash, A., & Weymouth, T. (1998). The upper atmospheric research collaboratory. *Interactions, 5*(3), 48–55.

Olson, G. M., Finholt, T. A., & Teasley, S. D. (2000). Behavioral aspects of collaboratories. In S. H. Koslow & M. F. Huerta (Eds.), *Electronic collaboration in science* (pp. 1–14). Mahwah, NJ: Lawrence Erlbaum Associates.

Olson, G. M., & Olson, J. S. (2000). Distance matters. *Human Computer Interaction, 15*(2–3), 139–179.

Olson, G. M., & Olson, J. S. (2003). Human-computer interaction: Psychological aspects of the human use of computing. *Annual Review of Psychology, 54,* 491–516.

O'Mahony, D., Peirce, M., & Tewari, H. (2001). *Electronic payment systems for e-commerce* (2nd ed.). Norwood, MA: Artech House.

O'Mahony, S. (2002). *The Emergence of a new commercial actor: Community managed software projects.* Unpublished doctoral dissertation, Stanford University, Palo Alto, CA. Retrieved on January 8, 2004, from http://opensource.mit.edu/.

Ombwatch. (2002, August 18). *Divided over digital gains and gaps.* Retrieved July 18, 2003, from http://www.ombwatch.org/article/articleview/1052/

Omojokun, O., & Dewan, P. (2003, May). Experiments with mobile computing middleware for deploying appliance UIs. *Proceedings of the 23rd International Conference on Distributed Computing Systems, Workshops,* 375–380.

Omojokun, O., Isbell, C., & Dewan, P. (2002). An architecture for supporting personalized agents in appliance interaction. In *Technical Report of the AAAI Symposium on Personalized Agents* (pp. 40–47). Menlo Park, CA: AAAI Press.

O'Neill, E. T., Lavoie, B. F., & Bennett, R. (2003, April). Trends in the evolution of the public web. *D-Lib Magazine, 9*(4). Retrieved June 7, 2004, from http://www.dlib.org/dlib/april03/lavoie/04lavoie.html

Ong, K. C., Teh, H. C., & Tan, T. S. (1998). Resolving occlusion in image sequence made easy. *Visual Computer, 14*(4), 153–165.

Oppermann, R. (Ed.). (1994). *Adaptive user support: Ergonomic design of manually and automatically adaptable software.* Hillsdale, NJ: Lawrence Erlbaum Associates.

Oram, A. (2001). *Peer-to-peer: Harnessing the power of disruptive technologies.* Sebastopol, CA: O'Reilly Press.

O'Reilly, T. (1999). Lessons from open-source software development. *Communications of the ACM, 42*(4), 33–37.

Organization for Economic Co-Operation and Development. (2001). *Measuring the information economy.* Paris: OECD Publications.

Orlikowski, W. J. (1992). Learning from notes: Organizational issues in groupware implementation. In *Proceedings of the Conference on Computer Supported Cooperative Work: CSCW '92* (pp. 362–369). New York: ACM Press.

Orlikowski, W. J., & Iacono, C. S. (2001). Research commentary: Desperately seeking the "IT" in IT research—A call to theorizing the IT artifact. *Information Systems Research, 12*(2), 121–134.

O'Rourke, M. (1995). *Principles of three-dimensional computer animation.* New York: W. W. Norton.

Orr, J. (1996). *Talking about machines: An ethnography of a modern job.* Ithaca, NY: Cornell University Press.

Osborne, D., & Gaebler, N. (1992). *Reinventing government.* New York: Penguin.

O'Sullivan, D., & Unwin, D. J. (2002). *Geographic information analysis.* Hoboken, NJ: Wiley.

Overholt, D. (2001). The MATRIX: A new musical instrument for interactive performance. In *Proceedings of the 2001International Computer Music Conference* (pp.243–246). San Francisco, CA: Computer Music Association.

Oviatt, S. (2000). Taming speech recognition errors within a multimodal interface. *Communications of the ACM, 43*(9), 45–51.

Oviatt, S. L., Cohen, P. R., Wu, L., Vergo, J., Duncan, L., Suhm, B., et al. (2002). Designing the user interface for multimodal speech and gesture applications: State-of-the-art systems and research directions. In J. Carroll (Ed.), *Human-computer interaction in the new millennium* (pp. 419–456). Reading, MA: Addison-Wesley.

Oviatt, S., & Cohen, P. (2000). Multimodal interfaces that process what comes naturally. *Communications of the ACM, 43*(3), 45–53.

Oviatt, S., Angeli, A. D., & Kuhn, K. (1997). Integration and synchronization of input modes during multimodal human-computer interaction. In *Proceedings of the Conference on Human Factors in Computing Systems (CHI'97),* (pp. 415–422). New York: ACM Press.

Oz, E. (2002). Foundations of e-commerce. Upper Saddle River, NJ: Pearson Education.

Page, G., Campbell, R., & Meadows, A. J. (1997). *Journal publishing* (2nd ed.). Cambridge, UK: Cambridge University Press.

Panteli, N., Stack, J., & Ramsay, H. (2001). Gendered patterns in computing work in the late 1990s. *New Technology, Work and Employment, 16*(1), 3–17.

Pantic, M., & Rothkrantz, L. J. M. (2000). Automatic analysis of facial expressions: The state of the art. *IEEE Transactions on Pattern Analysis and Machine Intelligence, 22*(12), 1424–1445.

Papert, S. (1980). *Mindstorms.* New York: Basic Books.

Papineni, K., Roukos, S., Ward, T., & Zhu, W.-J. (2002). BLEU: A method for automatic evaluation of machine translation. *Proceedings of the 40th Meeting of the Association for Computational Linguistics (ACL)* (pp. 311–318).

Paquet, V. (Ed.). (2004). Anthropometry and disability [Special issue]. *International Journal of Industrial Ergonomics, 33*(3).

Paquette, S., Case, H., Annis, J., Mayfield, T., Kristensen, S., & Mountjoy, D. N. (1999). *The effects of multilayered military clothing ensembles on body size: A pilot study.* Natick, MA: U.S. Soldier and Biological Chemical Command Soldier Systems Center.

Parasuraman, R., Sheridan, T., & Wickens, C. D. (2000). A model for types and levels of human interaction with automation. *IEEE Transacctions on Systems, Man, and Cybernetics, 30*(3), 286–297.

Parent, R. (2001). *Computer animation: Algorithms and techniques.* San Francisco: Morgan-Kaufmann.

Pargman, D. (2000). *Code begets community: On social and technical aspects of managing a virtual community.* Linkoping, Sweden: Linköping University, Department of Communication Studies.

Parke, F., & Waters, K. (1996). *Computer facial animation.* Wellesley, MA: AK Peters.

Parker, D. (1968). Rules of ethics in information processing. *Communications of the ACM, 11*(3), 198–201.

Parunak, H. V. D. (1991). Ordering the information graph. In E. Berk & J. Devlin (Eds.), *Hypertext/hypermedia handbook* (pp. 299–325). New York: McGraw-Hill.

Patrovsky, B., & Mulligan, J. (2003). *Developing online games: An insider's guide.* Indianapolis, IN: New Riders Publishing.

Payne, S. J., & Squibb, H. R. (1990). Algebra mal-rules and cognitive accounts of error. *Cognitive Science, 14*(3), 445–481.

Peace, S., & Holland, C. (Eds.). (2001). *Inclusive housing in an ageing society.* Bristol, UK: The Policy Press.

Pearce, T. C. (1997). Computational parallels between the biological olfactory pathway and its analogue 'the electronic nose': Part I, biological olfaction. *Biosystems, 41*(2), 43–67.

Pearce, T. C., Schiffman, S. S., Nagle, H. T., & Gardner, J. W. (Eds.). (2003). *Handbook of machine olfaction: Electronic nose technology.* Weinheim, Germany: Wiley-VCH.

Peek, R. P., & Newby, G. B. (1996). *Scholarly publishing: The electronic frontier.* Cambridge, MA: MIT Press.

Peirce, C., Hartshorne, C., Weiss, P., & Burks, A. (Eds.). (1935). *Collected papers I–VIII.* Cambridge, MA: Harvard University Press.

Pelachaud, C., Badler, N., & Viaud, M. (1994). *Final report to NSF of the standards for facial animation workshop.* Philadelphia: National Science Foundation, University of Pennsylvania. Retrieved April 8, 2004, from http://www.cis.upenn.edu/hms/pelachaud/workshop_face/workshop_face.html.

Pelham, B. W. (1993). The idiographic nature of human personality: Examples of the idiographic self-concept. *Journal of Personality and Social Psychology, 64*(4), 665–677.

Pellom, B., Ward, W., Hansen, J., Hacioglu, K., Zhang, J., Yu, X., & Pradhan, S. (2001, March). *University of Colorado dialog systems for travel and navigation.* Paper presented at the Human Language Technology Conference (HLT-2001), San Diego, CA.

Pelosi, P., & Persaud, K. C. (2000). Physiological and artificial systems for odour recognition. In F. Mazzei & R. Pilloton (Eds.), *Proceedings of the 2nd Italian Workshop on Chemical Sensors and Biosensors* (pp. 37–55). Retrieved March 5, 2004, from

Peng, Z. R., & Tsou, M. H. (2003). *Internet GIS: Distributed geographic information services for the Internet and wireless networks.* Hoboken, NJ: Wiley.

Perelmouter, J., & Birbaumer, N. (2000). A binary spelling interface with random errors. *IEEE Transactions on Rehabilitation Engineering, 8*(2), 227–232.

Perin, C. (1991). Electronic social fields in bureaucracies. *Communications of the ACM, 34*(12), 74–82.

Perkins, R., Keller, D., & Ludolph, F. (1997). Inventing the Lisa user interface. *Interactions, 4*(1), 40–53.

Perrow, C. (1999). *Normal accidents.* Princeton, NJ: Princeton University Press.

Persaud, K. C., & Dodd, G. H. (1982). Analysis of discrimination mechanisms of the mammalian olfactory system using a model nose. *Nature, 299,* 352–355.

Petajan, E. D., Brooke, N. M., Bischoff, G. J., & Bodoff, D. A. (1988). An improved automatic lipreading system to enhance speech recognition. In *Proceedings of Human Factors in Computing Systems* (pp. 19–25). New York: ACM.

Petersen, M. G., Madsen, K. H., & Kjær, A. (2002). The usability of everyday technology: Emerging and fading opportunities. *ACM Transactions on Computer-Human Interaction, 9*(2), 74–105.

Peterson, I. (1996). *Fatal defect: Chasing killer computer bugs.* New York: Vintage Books.

Petrelli, D., De Angeli, A, & Convertino, G. (1999). A user-centered approach to user modeling. *Proceedings of the 7th International Conference on User Modeling,* 255–264.

Petrie, H., & Morley, S. (1998). *The use of non-speech sounds in non-visual interfaces to the MS-Windows GUI for blind computer users.* Paper presented at the 1998 International Conference on Auditory Display (ICAD), Glasgow, UK.

Petronio, S. (1991). Communication boundary management: A theoretical model of managing disclosure of private information between marital couples. *Communication Theory, 1,* 311–335.

Peuquet, D. J. (2002). *Representations of space and time.* New York: Guilford.

Pew Internet & American Life Project. (2003). *Internet activities* (Chart). Retrieved July 31, 2003, from http://www.pewinternet.org/reports/index.asp.

Pew Internet & American Life Project. (2003). *Unpublished data from June-July 2002 on chat rooms.* Author.

Pfurtscheller, G., Neuper, C., Guger, C., Harkam, W., Ramoser, H., Schlögl, A., et al. (2000). Current trends in Graz brain-computer interface (BCI) research. *IEEE Transactions on Rehabilitation Engineering, 8*(2), 216–218.

Picard, R. W. (1997). *Affective computing.* Cambridge, MA: MIT Press.

Picard, R. W., Vyzas, E., & Healey, J. (2001). Toward machine emotional intelligence: Analysis of affective physiological state. *IEEE Transactions Pattern Analysis and Machine Intelligence, 23*(10), 1175–1191.

Pierce, B. C. (2002). *Types and programming languages.* Cambridge, MA: MIT Press.

Pierrehumbert, J. (1981). Synthesizing intonation. *Journal of the Acoustical Society of America, 70,* 985–995.

Pinelle, D., & Gutwin, C. (2002). Groupware walkthrough: Adding context to groupware usability evaluation. In *CHI 2002: Proceedings of the Conference on Human Factors in Computing Systems,* 455–462.

Pinto-Albuquerque, M., Fonseca, M. J., & Jorge, J. A. (2000). Visual languages for sketching documents. In *Proceedings, 2000 IEEE International Symposium on Visual Languages* (pp. 225–232). Seattle, WA: IEEE Press.

Pirolli, P. (1997). Computational models of information scent-following in a very large browsable text collection. In *Proceedings ACM CHI '97,* 3–10.

Pirolli, P., & Card, S. (1995). Information foraging in information access environments. In *Proceedings ACM CHI '95,* 51–58.

Pirolli, P., & Card, S. (1999). Information foraging. *Psychological Review, 106*(4), 643–675.

Pirolli, P., James, P., & Rao, R. (1996). Silk from a sow's ear: Extracting usable structures from the Web. *Proceedings of the SIGCHI Conference on Human Factors in Computing Systems: Common ground* (pp. 118–125). Retrieved December 16, 2003, from http://www.acm.org/sigchi/chi96/proceedings/papers/Pirolli_2/pp2.html

Pirolli, P., Pitkow, J., & Rao, R. (1996). Silk from a sow's ear: Extracting usable structures from the Web. In R. Bilger, S. Guest, & M. J. Tauber (Eds.), *Proceedings of CHI'96 Conference on Human Factors in Computing Systems* (pp. 118–125). New York: ACM Press.

Pitkow, J. (n.d.). GVU's WWW User Surveys. Retrieved January 19, 2004, from http://www.gvu.gatech.edu/user_surveys/

Pizka, M. (1997). Design and implementation of the GNU INSEL Compiler gic. *Technical Report TUM–I 9713.* Munich, Germany: Munich University of Technology.

Placeway, P., Chen, S., Eskenazi, M., Jain, U., Parikh, V., Raj, B., et al. (1997). The 1996 Hub-4 Sphinx-3 system. *Proceedings of the 1997 ARPA Speech Recognition Workshop,* 85–89.

Plaisant, C., Marchionini, G., Bruns, T., Komlodi, A., & Campbell, L. (1997). Bringing treasures to the surface: Iterative design for the Library of Congress National Digital Library Program. In *Proceedings of Human Factors in Computing, CHI `97* (pp. 518–525). New York: ACM Press.

Plamondon, R., & Srihari, S. N. (2000). On-Line and off-line handwriting recognition: A comprehensive survey. *IEEE Transactions on Pattern Analysis and Machine Intelligence, 22*(1), 63–84.

Pliant, L. (1996). High-technology solutions. *The Police Chief, 5*(38), 38–51.

Plotkin, W. (2002). Electronic texts in the historical profession. In Orville Vernon Burton (Ed.), *Computing in the social sciences and humanities* (pp. 87–123). Urbana: University of Illinois Press.

Podio, F. L., & Dunn, J. S. *Biometric authentication technology: From the movies to your desktop.* Retrieved March 18, 2004, from http://www.itl.nist.gov/div895/biometrics/Biometricsfromthemovies.pdf

Poinçot, P., Murtagh, F., & Lesteven, S. (2000). Maps of information spaces: Assessments from astronomy. *Journal of the American Society for Information Science, 51,* 1081–1089.

Polana, R., & Nelson, R. (1994). Recognizing activities. In *Proceedings of the IEEE Conference on Computer Vision and Pattern Recognition* (pp. 815–818) Seattle, WA.

Pollack, J. B., Lipson, H., Hornby, G., & Funes, P. (2001). Three generations of automatically designed robots. *Artificial Life, 7*(3), 215–223.

Pollock, J., & Zamora, A. (1984). Automatic spelling correction in scientific and scholarly text. *Communications of the ACM, 27*(4), 358–368.

Polson, P., Lewis, C., Rieman, J., & Wharton, C. (1992). Cognitive walkthroughs: A method for theory-based evaluation of user interfaces. *International Journal of Man-Machine Studies, 36,* 741–773.

Poltrock, S. E., & Grudin, J. (1994). Organizational obstacles to interface design and development: Two participant observation studies. *ACM Transactions Human-Computer Interaction, 1*(1), 52–80.

Pope, A. T., Bogart, E. H., & Bartolome, D. S. (1995). Biocybernetic System evaluates indices of operator engagement in automated task. *Biological Psychology, Special Edition: EEG in Basic and Applied Settings, 40,* 187–195.

Porra, J. (1999). Colonial systems. *Information Systems Research, 10*(1), 38–70.

Porter, D. (1997). *Internet culture.* New York: Routledge.

Poster, M. (2001). *What's the matter with the Internet?* Minneapolis, MN: University of Minnesota Press.

Potter, C. D. (1995). Anatomy of an animation. *Computer Graphics World, 18*(3). 36–43.

Powell, T. A. (2000). *Web design: The complete reference.* Berkeley, CA: Osborne: McGraw-Hill.

Poynter Institute. (2000). *Stanford-Poynter eyetracking online news study.* Retrieved July 27, 2003, from http://www.poynter.org/content/content_view.asp?id=1676

Prakash, A., & Knister, M. J. (1992). Undoing actions in collaborative work. In *Proceedings of the ACM Conference on Computer Supported Cooperative Work.* New York.

BIBLIOGRAPHY

Preece, J. (2000). *Online communities: Designing usability, supporting sociability.* Chichester, UK: John Wiley & Sons.

Preece, J., Rogers, Y., & Sharp, H. (2002). *Interaction design: Beyond human-computer interaction.* New York: John Wiley & Sons.

Preece, J., Rogers, Y., Sharp, H., Benyon, D., Holland, S., & Carey, T. (1994). *Human-computer interaction.* Essex, UK: Addison-Wesley Longman.

Preece, R. S. (2002). *Interaction design: Beyond human-computer interaction.* New York: John Wiley & Sons.

President's Information Technology Advisory Committee, Panel on Digital Libraries. (2001). *Digital libraries: Universal access to human knowledge,* report to the president. Arlington, VA: National Coordination Office for Information Technology Research and Development.

President's Council on Bioethics. (2003). *Beyond therapy: Biotechnology and the pursuit of happiness.* Washington, DC: President's Council on Bioethics.

Prestianni, J. (Ed.). (2002). *Calligraphic type design in the digital age: An exhibition in honor of the contributions of Hermann and Gudrun Zapf.* Corte Madera, CA: Gingko Press.

Price, J., & Korman, H. (1993). *How to communicate technical information: A handbook of software and hardware documentation.* Redwood City, CA: Benjamin/Cummings.

Prinzel, L. J., Freeman, F. G., Scerbo, M. W., Mikulka, P. J., & Pope, A. T. (2000). A closed-loop system for examining psychophysiological measures for adaptive task allocation. *International Journal of Aviation Psychology, 10,* 393–410.

Proceedings of the fifty-second annual conference of the American Association for Public Opinion Research. (1997). *Public Opinion Quarterly, 61*(3), 519–551.

Proceedings of the fifty-third annual conference of the American Association for Public Opinion Research. (1998). *Public Opinion Quarterly, 62*(3), 434–473.

Proebstring, T. (n.d.). Todd Proebsting's home page. Retrieved January 20, 2004, from http://research.microsoft.com/~toddpro/

Prosser, P. (1993). Hybrid algorithms for the constraint satisfaction problem. *Computational Intelligence, 9*(3), 268–299.

Prusak, L., & Cohen, D. (2001). *In good company: How social capital makes organizations work.* Boston: Harvard Business School.

Prust, Z. A. (1997). *Graphic communications: The printed image.* Tinley Park, IL: Goodheart-Willcox.

Puerta, A.R. (1997). A model-based interface development environment. *IEEE Software, 14*(4), 41–47.

Pullinger, D., & Baldwin, C. (2002*). Electronic journals and user behaviour.* Cambridge, UK: Deedot Press.

Putnam, R. (2000). *Bowling alone: The collapse and revival of American community.* New York: Simon & Schuster.

Quek, F. (in press). The Catchment Feature Model: A device for multimodal fusion and a bridge between signal and sense. *EURASIP Journal of Applied Signal Processing.*

Quek, F., McNeill, D., et al. (2002). Multimodal human discourse: Gesture and speech. *ACM Transactions on Computer-Human Interaction, 9*(3), 171–193.

Quine, W.V.O. (1969). *Ontological Relativity and Other Essays.* New York: Columbia University Press.

Quintana, C., Soloway, E., & Krajcik, J. (2003). Issues and approaches for developing learner-centered technology. In M. Zelkowitz (Ed.), *Advances in computers: Vol. 57. Information Repositories* (pp. 272–323). New York: Academic Press.

Quiroga, L., & Mostafa J. (2002). An experiment in building profiles in information filtering: The role of context of user relevance feedback. *Information Processing and Management, 38,* 671–694.

Rabiner, L. R., & Juang, B. H. (1986,). An introduction to hidden Markov models. *IEEE ASSP Magazine, 3*(1), 4–16.

Radle, K., & Young, S. (2001). Partnering usability with development: How three organizations succeeded. *IEEE Software, 18*(1), 38–45.

Raghavan, V., Molineros, J., & Sharma, R. (1999). Interactive evaluation of assembly sequences using augmented reality. *IEEE Transactions on Robotics and Automation, 15*(3), 435–449.

Rahimi, M., & Karwowski, W. (Eds.) (1992). *Human-robot interaction.* London: Taylor & Francis.

Rajlich, V., Wilde, N., Buckellew, M., & Page, H. (2001). Software cultures and evolution. *IEEE Computer, 34*(9), 24–29.

Ralston, A. & Reilly, E. D. (Eds.) (1993). *Encyclopedia of computer science* (3rd ed.). New York: Van Nostrand Reinhold.

Rammert, W. (1997). New rules of sociological method: Rethinking technology studies. *British Journal of Sociology, 48*(2), 171.

Randell, R. (Ed.). (1982). *The origins of digital computers* (pp. 305–325). New York: Springer-Verlag.

Raper, J. (2000). *Multidimensional geographic information science.* New York: Taylor and Francis.

Raphael, C. (2001). Music plus one: A system for expressive and flexible musical accompaniment. In *Proceedings of the 2001 International Computer Music Conference* (pp. 159–162). San Francisco, CA: Computer Music Association.

Rash, W. (1997). *Politics on the nets: Wiring the political process.* New York: Freeman.

Raskin, J. (2000). *The humane interface—New directions for designing interactive systems.* New York: Addison-Wesley.

Rasmusen, E. (2001). *Games and information: An introduction to game theory.* Malden, MA: Blackwell Publishing.

Rasmussen, J. (1987). The definition of human error and a taxonomy for technical system design. In J. Rasmussen, K. Duncan, & J. Leplat (Eds.), *New technology and human error* (pp. 23–30). New York: Wiley.

Rasmussen, J., Pejtersen, A. M., & Goodstein, L. P. (1994). *Cognitive systems engineering.* New York: Wiley and Sons.

Rath, T. M., & Manmatha, R. (2003). Word image matching using dynamic time warping. In *Proceedings of the IEEE conference on Computer Vision and Pattern Recognition* (pp. 521–527). Los Alamitos, CA: IEEE.

Ravishankar, M. K. (1996*). Efficient algorithms for speech recognition.* Unpublished doctoral dissertation, CMU-CS-96-143, Carnegie Mellon University, Pittsburgh, PA.

Ray, E. (2003). *Learning XML* (2nd ed.). Sebastopol, CA: O'Reilly

Raymond, E. (1999). *The cathedral and the bazaar: Musings on Linux and Open Source by an accidental revolutionary.* Sebastopol, CA: O'Reilly.

Rayner, K. (1998). Eye movements in reading and information processing: 20 years of research. *Psychological Bulletin, 124*(3), 372–422.

Razzaque, S. Kohn, Z., Whitton, M. (2001). *Redirected walking.* Paper presented at Eurographics 2001, Manchester, UK.

Reason, J. (1990). *Human error.* New York: Cambridge University Press.

Reconstruction of the Atanasoff-Berry Computer. (n.d.). Retrieved on January 27, 2004, from http://www.scl.ameslab.gov/ABC

Redd, W., & Manne, S. (1995). Using aroma to reduce distress during magnetic resonance imaging. In A. Gilbert (Ed.), *Compendium of olfactory research, 1982–1994* (pp. 47–52). Dubuque, IA: Kendall/Hunt.

Reddick, A., & Boucher, C. (2002). *Tracking the dual digital divide.* Ottowa, Canada: Ekos Research Associates. Retrieved January 23, 2004, from http://olt-bta.hrdc-drhc.gc.ca/resources/digital-divide_e.pdf

Reed, M., Manary, M., & Schneider, L. (1999). *Methods for measuring and representing automobile occupant posture* (SAE Technical Paper No. 1999-01-0959). Arlington, VA: Rehabilitation Engineering and Assistive Technology Society of North America, Working Group on Body and Seat Measures.

Reed, M., Manary, M., Flannagan, C., & Schneider, L. (2000). Effects of vehicle interior geometry and anthropometric variables on automobile driving posture. *Human Factors, 42,* 541–552.

Reeves, B., & Nass, C. (1996). *The media equation: How people treat computers, television, and new media like real people and places.* New York: Cambridge University Press.

Régin, J.-C. (1994). A filtering algorithm for constraints of difference in constraint satisfaction problems. In *Proceedings from the National Conference on Artificial Intelligence* (AAAI 1994) (pp. 362–437). Seattle, WA.

Rehnquist, W. H. (1974). Is an expanded right to privacy consistent with fair and effective law enforcement? *Kansas Law Review, 23,* 1–15.

Reid, E. M. (1994). *Cultural formation in text-based virtual realities.* Unpublished doctoral dissertation, University of Melbourne, Australia. Retrieved July 31, 2003, from http://www.aluluei.com/cult-form.htm

Reis, H. T. & Judd, C. M. (Eds.) (2000). *Handbook of research methods in social and personality psychology.* Cambridge, UK: Cambridge University Press.

Reiser, B. J. (2002). Why scaffolding should sometimes make tasks more difficult for learners. *Proceedings of CSCL 2002,* 255–264.

Rempel, D., Tittiranonda, P., Burastero, S., Hudes, M., & So, Y. (1999). Effect of keyboard keyswitch design on hand pain. *Journal of Occupational and Environmental Medicine, 41*(2), 111–119.

Renninger, K. A., & Shumar, W. (Eds.). (2002). *Building virtual communities.* Cambridge, UK: Cambridge University Press.

Resnick, P., & Varian, H. (1997). Recommender systems [Special issue]. *Communications of the ACM, 40*(3).

Resnick, P., Zeckhauser, R., Friedman, E., & Kuwabara, K. (2000, December). Reputation systems. *Communications of the ACM, 3*(12), 45–48.

Revesz, P. (2002). *Introduction to constraint databases.* New York: Springer.

Reynolds, J. C. (1998). *Theories of programming languages.* Cambridge, UK: Cambridge University Press.

Reynolds, M. (1967). *Computer war.* New York: Ace.

Rheingold, H. (1993). *The virtual community: Homesteading on the electronic frontier.* Cambridge, MA: MIT Press.

Rheingold, H. (1998). *Building fun online learning communities.* Retrieved July 30, 2003, from http://www.rheingold.com/texts/education/moose.html

Rheingold, H. (2000). *Tools for thought* (2nd ed.). Cambridge, MA: MIT Press.

Rheingold, H. (2002). *Smart mob: The next social revolution.* New York: Perseus.

Rhodes, B. (1997). The wearable remembrance agent: A system for augments memory. *Personal Technologies, 1*(4), 218–224.

Rice compiler group. (n.d.). Retrieved January 20, 2004, from http://www.cs.rice.edu/CS/compilers/index.html

Rice, R., & Love, G. (1987). Electronic emotion: Socioemotional content in a computer-mediated communication. *Communication Research, 14*(1), 85–108.

Rich, C., & Sidner, C. L. (1997). COLLAGEN: When agents collaborate with people. In W. L. Johnson (Ed.), *Proceedings of the First International Conference on Autonomous Agents (Agents-97)* (pp. 284–291). Marina del Rey, CA: ACM Press.

Rich, E. (1979). User modeling via stereotypes. *Cognitive Science, 3,* 329–354.

Rich, E. (1983). Users are individuals: Individualizing user models. *International Journal of Man-Machine Studies, 18,* 199–214.

Richardson, M., & Domingos, P. (2002). The intelligent surfer: Probabilistic combination of link and content information in PageRank. *Advances in neural information processing systems 14.* Cambridge, MA: MIT Press.

Rickel, J., & Johnson, W. (2000). Task-oriented collaboration with embodied agents in virtual worlds. In J. Cassell, J. Sullivan, and S. Prevost (Eds.), *Embodied Conversational Agents* (pp. 95–122). Boston: MIT Press.

Riedl, J., & Konstan, J. (2002). *Word of mouse: The marketing power of collaborative filtering.* New York: Warner Books.

Riedl, J., Vrooman, E., Gladwell, M. (2002). *Word of mouse: The marketing power of collaborative filtering.* New York: Warner Books.

Rieser, J. J., & Garing, A. E. (1994). Spatial orientation. In *Encyclopedia of human behavior* (Vol. 4, pp. 287–295). San Diego, CA: Academic Press.

Rieser, J. J., & Pick, H. L., Jr. (2002). The perception and representation of human locomotion. In W. Prinz & B. Hommel (Eds.), *Attention and performance XIX: Common mechanisms in perception and action.* Oxford, UK: Oxford University Press.

Sobel, D. (1995). *Longitude: The true story of a lone genius who solved the greatest problem of his time.* New York: Penguin Books.

Rigoll, G., Kosmala, A., & Eickeler, S. (1997). High performance real-time gesture recognition using hidden Markov Models. In *Proceedings of the International Gesture Workshop.* Bielefeld, Germany, September 1997.

Rise of the replicators. (2004). *Popular Science, 264*(2), 36–37.

Rist, R. (1995). Program structure and design. *Cognitive Science, 19,* 507–562.

Ritchie, D. (1986). *The computer pioneers: The making of the modern computer.* New York: Simon and Schuster.

Ritchie, G. D., Russell, G. J., Black, A. W., & Pulman, S. G. (1992). *Computational morphology: Practical mechanisms for the English lexicon.* Cambridge, MA: MIT Press.

Riter, R. (1995). Modeling and testing a critical fault-tolerant multi-process system. In *Proceedings of the Fault-Tolerant Computing Symposium* (pp. 516–521). Cupertino, CA: IEEE CS Press.

Ritter, F. E., & Young, R. M. (Eds.). (2001). Special issue on cognitive modeling for human-computer interaction. *International Journal of Human-Computer Studies, 55*(1).

Roads, C. (1996). *The computer music tutorial.* Cambridge, MA: MIT Press.

Rob, P., & Coronel, C. (2004). *Database systems: Design, implementation, and management* (6th ed.). Boston: Course Technology.

Robert Starch Worldwide, Inc. (1999). *The America Online/Roper Starch Youth Cyberstudy.* Author. Retrieved on December 24, 2003, from http://www.corp.aol.com/press/roper.html/

BIBLIOGRAPHY

Roberts, H. E., & Yates, W. (1975). Altair minicomputer. *Popular Electronics, 7*(1), 33–38.

Robertson, M., Newell, S., Swan, J., Mathiassen, L., & Bjerknes, G. (2001). The issue of gender within computing: Reflections from the UK and Scandinavia. *Information Systems Journal, 11*(2), 111–126.

Robertson, S. P., Carroll, J. M., Mack, R. L., Rosson, M. B., Alpert, S. R., & Koenemann-Belliveau, J. (1994). ODE: A self-guided, scenario-based learning environment for object-oriented design principles. In Proceedings of OOPSLA'94: Conference on Object-Oriented Programming Systems, Languages and Applications (*ACM SIG-PLAN Notices, 29*(10), 51–64). New York: ACM Press.

Robinette, K. (1998). Multivariate methods in engineering anthro-pometry. In *Proceedings of the Human Factors and Ergonomics Society 42nd Annual Meeting* (pp. 719–721). Santa Monica, CA: Human Factors and Ergonomics Society.

Robinette, K. (2000). CAESAR measures up. *Ergonomics in Design, 8*(3), 17–23.

Robinson, J. P., Barth, K., & Kohut, A. (1997). Personal computers, mass media, and use of time. *Social Science Computer Review, 15*(1), 65–82.

Rocco, E. (1998). Trust breaks down in electronic contexts but can be repaired by some initial face-to-face contact. In *Proceedings of CHI 1998* (pp. 496–502). New York: ACM Press.

Rocheleau, B. (1993). Evaluating public sector information systems. *Evaluation and Program Planning, 16,* 119–129.

Roco, M. C., & Bainbridge, W. S. (2001). *Societal implications of nanoscience and nanotechnology.* Dordrecht, Netherlands: Kluwer.

Roco, M. C., & Bainbridge, W. S. (2003). *Converging technologies for improving human performance.* Dordrecht, Netherlands: Kluwer.

Roco, M. C., & Montemagno, C. D. (Eds.). (2004). The coevolution of human potential and converging technologies. *Annals of the New York Academy of Sciences, 1013.* New York: New York Academy of Sciences.

Rodahl, K. (1989). *The physiology of work.* London: Taylor & Francis.

Rodenstein, R., & Donath, J. S. (2000). Talking in circles: Designing a spatially grounded audioconferencing environment. In *CHI 2000 Conference Proceedings: Conference on Human Factors in Computing Systems* (pp. 81–88). New York: ACM Press.

Roe, D. B., & Wilpon, J. G. (Eds.). (1995). *Voice communication between humans and machines.* Washington, D.C.: National Academy Press.

Roebuck, J., Kroemer, K. H. E., & Thomson, W. (1975). *Engineering anthropometry methods.* New York: Wiley.

Rogers, C. (1951). *Client centered therapy: Current practice, implications and theory.* Boston: Houghton Mifflin.

Rogers, E., & Murphy, M. (2001, September). *Human-robot interaction: Final report of the DARPA/NSF Study on Human-Robot Interaction.* Retrieved July 21, 2003, from http://www.csc.calpoly.edu/~erogers/HRI/HRI-report-final.html

Rohall, S. L., & Gruen, D. (2002). Re-mail: A reinvented e-mail prototype. In *Proceedings of Computer-Supported Cooperative Work 2002.* New York: Association for Computer Machinery.

Rollings, A., & Morris, D. (2000). *Game architecture and design.* Scottsdale, AZ: Coriolis Group.

Roseman, M., & Greenberg, S. (1996). Building real time groupware with Groupkit, a groupware toolkit. *ACM Transactions on Computer Human Interaction, 3*(1), 66–106.

Rosenberg, R. S. (1997). *The social impact of computers* (2nd ed.). San Diego, CA: Academic Press.

Rosenbloom, B., & Larsen, T. (2003). Communication in international business-to-business marketing channels: Does culture matter? *Industrial Marketing Management, 32*(4), 309–317.

Rosenblum, L. (2000, January–February). Virtual and augmented reality 2020. *IEEE Computer Graphics and Applications, 20*(1), 38–39.

Rosenfeld, L., & Morville, P. (2002). *Information architecture for the World Wide Web: Designing large-scale web sites* (2nd ed.). Sebastopol, CA: O'Reilly.

Ross, R. (2002). Born-again Napster takes baby steps. *Toronto Star,* E04.

Rosson, M. B., & Carroll, J. M. (1996). The reuse of uses in Smalltalk programming. *ACM Transactions on Computer-Human Interaction, 3*(3), 219–253.

Rosson, M. B., & Carroll, J. M. (2002). *Usability engineering: Scenario-based development of human-computer interaction.* San Francisco: Morgan-Kaufmann.

Roth, E. M., Patterson, E. S., & Mumaw, R. J. (2002). Cognitive Engineering: Issues in User-centered System Design. In J. J. Marciniak (Ed.), *Encyclopedia of software engineering* (2nd ed., pp. 163–179). New York: Wiley Interscience, John Wiley and Sons.

Rothermel, G., Li, L., DuPuis, C., & Burnett, M. M. (1998). What you see is what you test: A methodology for testing form-based visual programs. In *International Conference on Software Engineering,* 198–207.

Rouet, J., Levonen, J. J., Dillon, A., & Spiro, R. J. (Eds.). (1996). *Hypertext and cognition.* Mahwah, NJ: Lawrence Erlbaum.

Rouse, R. (2001). *Game design, theory and practice.* Plano, TX: Wordware Publishing.

Rowe, R. (1993). *Interactive music systems.* Cambridge, MA: MIT Press.

Rowley, D. E., & Rhoades, D. G. (1992). The cognitive jogthrough: A fast-paced user interface evaluation procedure. In *CHI '92: Proceedings of the Conference on Human Factors in Computing Systems,* 389–395.

Rubin, A. D. (2001, October). *Security considerations for remote electronic voting.* Paper presented at the 29th Research Conference on Communication, Information and Internet Policy, Alexandria, VA. Retrieved August 1, 2003, from http://avirubin.com/e-voting.security.html

Rubin, J. (1994). *Handbook of usability testing.* New York: John Wiley & Sons.

Ruch, P. (2002). Information access and retrieval: Information retrieval and spelling correction: An inquiry into lexical disambiguation. *Proceedings of the 2002 ACM Symposium on Applied Computing,* 699–703.

Rucker, R. (1982). *Software.* New York: Avon.

Ruder, E. (1981). *Typographie: A manual of design.* New York: Hastings House.

Ruegg, R., & Frölich, G. (1972). *Basic typography.* Zürich, Switzerland: ABC Verlag.

Rui, Y., Huang, T. S., Ortega, M., & Mehrotra, S. (1996). Relevance feedback: A power tool for interactive content-based image retrieval. *IEEE Transactions on Circuits and Systems for Video Technology, 8*(5), 644–655.

Ruppel, C. P., & Harrington, S. J. (1995). Telework: An innovation where nobody is getting on the bandwagon. *ACM SIGMIS Database, 26*(2–3), 87–104.

Rusch-Feja, D. (2002). The Open Archives Initiative and the OAI protocol for metadata harvesting: Rapidly forming a new tier in the scholarly communication infrastructure. *Learned Publishing, 15*(3), 179–186.

Russell, S., & Norvig, P. (1995). *Artificial intelligence: A modern approach.* Englewood Cliffs, NJ: Prentice-Hall.

Russell, T. L. (1999). *The no significant difference phenomenon.* Montogomery, AL: IDECC (International Distance Education Certification Center).

Ruthruff, J., Creswick, E., Burnett, M. M., Cook, C., Prabhakararao, S., Fisher II, M., & Main, M. (2003). End-user software visualizations for fault localization. In *ACM Symposium on Software Visualization,* 123–132.

Rutledge, J., & Selker, T. (1990). Force-to-motion functions for pointing. In *Proceedings of Human-Computer Interaction—INTERACT'90* (pp. 701–705).

Ryan, A. M., McFarland, L., Baron, H., & Page, R. (1999). An international look at selection practices: Nation and culture as explanations for variability in practice. *Personnel Psychology, 52,* 359–391.

Sagisaka, Y., Campbell, W., & Higuchi, N. (Eds.). (1998). *Computing prosody: Computational models for processing spontaneous speech.* Berlin, Germany: Springer-Verlag.

Sagisaka, Y., Kaiki, N., Iwahashi, N., & Mimura, K. (1992). ATR–n-TALK speech synthesis system. *Proceedings of the International Conference on Spoken Language Processing, 1,* 482–486.

Sakoe, H., & Chiba, S. (1978). Dynamic programming algorithm optimization for spoken word recognition. *IEEE Transactions on Acoustics, Speech and Signal Processing, ASSP, 26*(1), 43–49.

Salazar, C. (2001). *Building boundaries and negotiating work at home.* Paper presented at the International Conference on Supporting Group Work, Boulder, CO.

Salus, P. (1995). *Casting the Net.* Reading, MA: Addison-Wesley.

Salvendy, G. (Ed.). *Handbook of human factors.* New York: Wiley and Sons.

Salvucci, D. D., & Goldberg, J. H. (2000). Identifying fixations and saccades in eye-tracking protocols. In *Proceedings of Eye Tracking Research & Applications (ETRA)* (pp. 71–78). Palm Beach Gardens, FL: ACM.

Sammet, J. (1992). Farewell to Grace Hopper—End of an era! *Communications of the ACM, 35*(4), 128–131.

Sanders, M. (2000). *World Net commerce approaches hypergrowth.* Retrieved March 1, 2004, from http://www.forrester.com/ER/Research/Brief/0,1317,9229,FF.html

Sandin, D. J., Margolis, T., Dawe, G., Leigh, J., and DeFanti, T. A. (2001). The VarrierTM auto-stereographic display. *Proceedings of Photonics West 2001: Electronics Imaging,* SPIE. Retrieved on November 5, 2003, from http://spie.org/web/meetings/programs/pw01/home.html

Sanfilippo, A., Briscoe, E., Copestake, A., Marti, M., Taule, M., & Alonge, A. (1992, January). Translation equivalence and lexicalization in the ACQUILEX LKB. In *Proceedings of the Fourth International Conference on Theoretical and Methodological Issues in Machine Translation—TMI92,* 1–11.

Sanger, J., Wilson, J., Davies, B., & Whittaker, R. (1997). *Young children, videos and computer games.* London: Falmer.

Sarin, S., & Greif, I. (1985). Computer-based real-time conferencing systems. *IEEE Computer, 18*(10), 33–49.

Satoh, S., Nakamura, Y., & Kanade, T. (2001). Name-It: Naming and detecting faces in news videos. *Multimedia, 6*(1), 22–35.

Saund, E., & Moran, T. P. (1994). *A perceptually supported sketch editor.* Paper presented at the ACM Symposium on User Interface Software and Technology, Marina del Rey, CA.

Saunders-Newton, D., & Scott, H. (2001). "But the computer said!" credible uses of computational modeling in public sector decision making. *Social Science Computer Review, 19*(1), 47–65.

Sauter, S. L., Schleifer, L. M., & Knutson, S. J. (1991). Work posture, workstation design, and musculoskeletal discomfort in a VDT data entry task. *Human Factors, 33*(2), 151–167.

Savage, S., Wetherall, D., Karlin, A., & Anderson, T. (2000). Practical network support for IP traceback. *Proceedings of ACM SIGCOMM 2000* (pp. 295–306).

Sawhney, N., & Schmandt, C. (1999). Nomadic radio: Scaleable and contextual notification for wearable audio messaging. In In *Conference on Human Factors in Computing Systems* (CHI) (pp.96–103). Pittsburgh, PA: ACM.

Sawyer, R. J. (1995). *The terminal experiment.* New York: HarperCollins.

Sawyer, S., & Rosenbaum, H. (2000). Social Informatics in the information sciences: Current activities and emerging directions. *Informing Science, 3*(2). Retrieved August 19, 2003, from http://inform.nu/Articles/Vol3/indexv3n2.htm.

Saygin, A. P., Cicekli, I., & Akman, V. (2000). Turing test: 50 years later. *Minds and Machines, 10*(4), 463–518.

Scacchi, W. (2001). Redesigning contracted service procurement for Internet-based electronic commerce: A case study. *Information Technology and Management, 2*(3), 313–334.

Scacchi, W. (2002). Understanding the requirements for developing Open-Source Software systems. *IEE Proceedings—Software, 149*(1), 24–39.

Scerri, P., Johnson, L., Pynadath, D., Rosenbloom, P., Si, M., Schurr, N., & Tambe, M. (2003). A prototype infrastructure for distributed robot-agent-person teams. *Proceedings of the Second International Joint Conference on Autonomous Agents and Multi-Agent Systems (AAMAS-02).* Melbourne, Austrailia, July 2003.

Scerri, P., Pynadath, D. V., & Tambe, M. (2002). Towards adjustable autonomy for the real-world. *Journal of Artificial Intelligence Research, 17,* 171–228.

Schaap, F. (n.d.). *Cyberculture, identity and gender resources* (online hyperlinked bibliography). Retrieved July 31, 2003, from http://fragment.nl/resources/

Schach, S. (1996). *Classical and object-oriented software engineering.* New York: McGraw-Hill/Irwin.

Schacter, J., Chung, G. K. W. K., & Dorr, A. (1998). Children's Internet searching on complex problems: Performance and process analyses. *Journal of the American Society for Information Science, 49*(9), 840–849.

Schaefer, D. R., & Dillman, D. A. (1998). Development of a standard e-mail methodology: Results of an experiment. *Public Opinion Quarterly, 62*(3), 378–397.

Schaeffer, J. (2001). A gamut of games. *AI Magazine, 22*(3), 29–46.

Schaeffer, J., & van den Herik, J. (Eds.). (2002). *Chips challenging champions: Games, computers, and artificial intelligence.* New York: Elsevier.

Schatz, B. (1991). Building an electronic community system. *Journal of Management Information Systems, 8*(3), 87–107.

Schauder, D. (1994). Electronic publishing of professional articles: Attitudes of academics and implications for the scholarly communication industry. *Journal of the American Society for Information Science, 45*(2), 73–100.

Schein, E. H. (1999). *The corporate culture survival guide: Sense and nonsense about cultural change.* San Francisco: Jossey-Bass.

Schiano, D. J., Chen C. P., Ginsberg, J., Gretarsdottir, U., Huddleston, M., & Issacs, E. (2002, April). *Teen use of messaging media.* Paper presented at the ACM CHI 2002 Conference on Human Factors in Computing Systems, Minneapolis, MN. Retrieved August 7, 2003, from http://hci.stanford.edu/cs377/nardi-schiano/CHI2002.Schiano.pdf

Schiffman, S. S. (1995). Use of olfaction as an alarm mechanism to arouse and alert sleeping individuals. *Aroma-Chology Review, 4*(1), 2–5.

Schilit, B. N., Price, M. N., Golovchinsky, G., Tanaka, K., & Marshall, C. C. (1999). The reading appliance revolution. *Computer, 32*(1), 65–73.

Schlenzig, J., Hunter, E., & Jain, R. (1994). Recursive identfication of gesture inputs using hidden Markov models. *In Proceedings of the second IEEE workshop on Applications of Computer Vision (pp. 187–194).* Pacific Grove, CA.

Schlosberg, H. (1954). Three dimensions of emotion. *Psychological Review, 61*(2), 81–88.

Schmitt, V., Morris, J. W., & Jenney, G. (1998). *Fly-by-wire: A historical and design perspective.* Warrendale, PA: Society of Automotive Engineers.

Schneider, J. P. (1994). Sex addiction: Controversy within mainstream addiction medicine, diagnosis based on the DSM-III-R and physician case histories. *Sexual Addiction & Compulsivity: The Journal of Treatment and Prevention, 1*(1), 19–44.

Schneider, J. P., & Weiss, R. (2001). *Cybersex exposed: Recognizing the obsession.* Center City, MN: Hazelden Educational Materials.

Schneider, S. C. (1987). Information overload: Causes and consequences. *Human Systems Management, 7,* 143–153.

Schofield, J. W. (1995). *Computers and classroom culture.* New York: Cambridge University Press.

Schofield, J. W., & Davidson, A. L. (2002). *Bringing the Internet to school: Lessons from an urban district.* San Francisco, CA: Jossey-Bass.

Scholtz, J., Bellotti, V., Schirra, L., Erickson, T., DeGroot, J., & Lund, A. (1998, January/February). Telework: When your job is on the line. *Interactions,* 44–54.

Schön, D. A. (1983). *The reflective practitioner: How professionals think in action.* New York: Basic Books.

Schonlau, M., Fricker, Jr., R. D., & Elliott, M. N. (2001). *Conducting research surveys via e-mail and the Web.* Santa Monica, CA: Rand.

Schraagen, J. M., Chipman, S. F., & Shalin, V. L. (Eds.). (2000). *Cognitive task analysis.* Mahwah, NJ: Lawrence Erlbaum Associates.

Schriver, K. A. (1997). *Dynamics of document design. Creating texts for readers.* New York: Wiley.

Schroeder, R. (2002). *The social life of avatars: Presence and interaction in shared virtual environments.* London: Springer-Verlag.

Schuler, D., & Namioka, A. E. (1993). *Participatory design: Principles and practices.* Mahwah, NJ: Lawrence Erlbaum Associates.

Schwartz, A., & Garfinkel, S. (1998). *Stopping spam.* Sebastopol, CA: O'Reilly & Associates.

Schwartz, E. (1996). *Netactivism: How citizens use the Internet.* Sebastopol, CA: Songline Studios.

Schwartz, M. S. (1995). *Biofeedback: A practitioner's guide.* New York: Guilford Press.

Scott, W. Richard. (1981). *Rational, Natural, and Open Systems.* Englewood Cliffs, NJ: Prentice-Hall.

Sears, A., & Hess, D. J. (1999). Cognitive walkthroughs: Understanding the effect of task description detail on evaluator performance. *International Journal of Human-Computer Interaction, 11*(3), 185–200.

Sears, A., Plaisant, C., & Shneiderman, B. (1992). A new era for high precision touch screens. In H. R. Hartson & D. Hix (Eds.), *Advances in Human-Computer Interaction, 3,* 1–33. Norwood, NJ: Ablex.

Section 508 of the Rehabilitation Act (29 U.S.C. 794d), as amended by the Workforce Investment Act of 1998 (P.L. 105–220), August 7, 1998. Retrieved September 12, 2003, from http://www.section508.gov/

Selker, T., & Burleson, W. (2000). Context-aware design and interaction in computer systems. *IBM Systems Journal, 39*(3–4), 880–891.

Sellen, A. J., & Harper, R. H. (2002). *The myth of the paperless office.* Cambridge, MA: MIT Press.

Selman, B., Kautz, H. A., & Cohen, B. (1994). Noise strategies for improving local search. In *Twelfth National Conference on Artificial Intelligence ,* 337–343. Seattle, WA.

Sendov, B. (2003). *John Atanasoff: The electronic Prometheus.* Sofia, Bulgaria: St. Kliment Ohridski University Press.

Seneff, S., & Polifroni, J. (2000). *Dialogue management in the Mercury flight reservation system.* Paper presented at the Satellite Workshop, ANLP-NAACL 2000, Seattle, WA.

Seneff, S., Hurley, E., Lau, R. Pau, C., Schmid, P., & Zue, V. (1998). Galaxy II: A reference architecture for conversational system development. *Proceedings of the 5th International Conference on Spoken Language Processing,* 931–934.

Seow, K. (1988). Physiology of touch, grip, and gait. In J. G. Webster (Ed.), *Tactile sensors for robotics and medicine* (pp. 13–40). New York: John Wiley and Sons.

Servicios de Telecomunicaciones. (2003). *Usuarios estimados de Internet en México* [Estimated Internet users in Mexico]. Retrieved January 23, 2004, from http://www.cft.gob.mx/html/5_est/Graf_internet/estimi1.pdf

Sethi, R. (1996). *Programming languages: Concepts and constructs.* Boston: Addison-Wesley.

Setlur, S., Lawson, A., Govindaraju, V., & Srihari, S. N. (2002). Large scale address recognition systems: Truthing, testing, tools, and other evaluation issues. *International Journal of Document Analysis and Recognition, 4*(3), 154–169.

Shackel, B. (1959). Ergonomics for a computer. *Design, 120,* 36–39.

Shackel, B. (1962). Ergonomics in the design of a large digital computer console. *Ergonomics, 5,* 229–241.

Shackel, B. (1997). Human-computer interaction: Whence and whither? *JASIS, 48*(11), 970–986.

Shade, L. (1996). Is there free speech on the Net? Censorship in the global information infrastructure. In R. Shields (Ed.), *Cultures of the Internet: Virtual spaces real histories, living bodies.* Thousand Oaks, CA: Sage.

Shankar, T. R., VanKleek, M., Vicente, A., & Smith, B. K. (2000). Fugue: A computer mediated conversational system that supports turn negotiation. In *Proceedings of the Thirty-Third Annual Hawaii International Conference on System Sciences.* Los Alamitos, CA: IEEE Computer Society Press.

Shannon, C. (1950). Programming a computer for playing chess. *Philosophical Magazine, 41,* 256–275.

Shannon, C. E. (1993). A mathematical theory of communication. In N. J. A. Sloane & A. D. Wyner, (Eds.), *Claude Elwood Shannon, collected papers* (pp. 5–83). New York: IEEE Press. (Original work published 1948)

Shapiro, C., & Varian, H. (1998). *Information rules: A strategic guide to the network.* Boston: Harvard Business School Press.

BIBLIOGRAPHY

Sharma, R., Pavlovi´c, V. I., Huang, T. S., Lo, Z., Chu, S., Zhao, Y., et al. (2000). Speech/gesture interface to a visual-computing environment. *IEEE Computer Graphics and Applications, 20*(2), 29–37.

Sharma, R., Yeasin, M., Krahnstoever, N., Rauschert, Cai, G., Brewer, I., et al. (2003). Speech-gesture driven multimodal interfaces for crisis management. *Proceedings of the IEEE, 91*(9), 1327–1354.

Shattuck, J. (1984). Computer matching is a serious threat to individual rights. *Communications of the ACM, 27*(6), 538–541).

Shaw, A. (2001). *Real-time systems and software.* New York: John Wiley & Sons.

Shaw, M. (1990). Prospects for an engineering discipline of software. *IEEE Software*, 15–24.

Shaw, N. C., DeLone, W. H., & Niederman, F. (2002). Sources of dissatisfaction in end-user support: An empirical study. *Database for Advances in Information Systems, 3*(2), 41–55.

Shen, H., & Dewan, P. (1992). Access control for collaborative environments. In *Proceedings of the ACM Conference on Computer Supported Cooperative Work.* New York.

Shenton, A. K., & Dixon, P. (2003). A comparison of youngsters' use of CD-ROM and the Internet as information resources. *Journal of the American Society for Information Science and Technology, 54*(11), 1049–2003.

Shepard, R. N. (1967). Recognition memory for words, sentences and pictures. *Journal of Verbal Learning and Verbal Behavior, 6,* 156–163.

Shepherd, A. (1998). HTA as a framework for task analysis. *Ergonomics, 41*(11), 1537–1552.

Sheridon, N. K.; Richley, E. A.; Mikkelsen, J. C.; Tsuda, D.; Crowley, J. C.; Oraha, K. A., et al. (1999). The gyricon rotating ball display. *Journal for the Society for Information Display, 7*(2), 141.

Sherman, W., & Craig, A. (2003). *Understanding virtual reality: Interface, application, and design.* Boston: Morgan Kaufmann.

Sheth, A., & Larson, J. (1990). Federated database systems. *ACM Computing Surveys, 22*(3), 183–286.

Shi, D., Damper, R. I., & Gunn, S. R. (2003). Offline handwritten Chinese character recognition by radical decomposition. *ACM Transactions on Asian Language Information Processing, 2*(1), 27–48.

Shiel, B. A. (1981). The psychological study of programming. *ACM Computing Surveys, 13*(1), 101–120.

Shirky, C. (2000). *In praise of freeloaders.* Retrieved January 29, 2004, from http://www.openp2p.com/pub/a/p2p/2000/12/01/shirky_freeloading.html

Shneiderman, B. (1980). *Software psychology: Human factors in computer and information systems.* Cambridge, MA: Winthrop.

Shneiderman, B. (1983). Direct manipulation: A step beyond programming languages. *Computer, 16*(8), 57–69.

Shneiderman, B. (1990). Human values and the future of technology: A declaration of empowerment. *Computers & Society, 20*(3), 1–6.

Shneiderman, B. (1992). *Designing the user interface: Strategies for effective human-computer interaction.* Reading, MA: Addison-Wesley.

Shneiderman, B. (1997). A grander goal: A thousand-fold increase in human capabilities. *Educom Review, 32*(6), 4–10. Retrieved July 21, 2003, from http://www.ifp.uiuc.edu/nabhcs/abstracts/shneiderman.html

Shneiderman, B. (2000). Universal usability. *Communications of the ACM, 42*(5), 84–91.

Shneiderman, B. (2002). *Leonardo's laptop: Human needs and the new computing technologies.* Cambridge, MA: MIT Press.

Shneiderman, B. (2003). *Leonardo's Laptop.* Cambridge, MA: MIT Press.

Shneiderman, B., & Maes, P. (1997). Debate: Direct manipulation vs. interface agents. *Interactions, 4*(6), 42–61.

Shneiderman, B., & Rose, A. (1996). Social impact statements: Engaging public participation in information technology design. In C. Huff (Ed.), *Computers and the quality of life: The proceedings of the Symposium on Computers and the Quality of Life* (pp. 90–96). New York: ACM Press.

Short, J., Williams, E., & Christie, B. (1976). The social psychology of telecommunications. New York: Wiley.

Shute, S., & Smith, P. (1993). Knowledge-based search tactics. *Information Processing & Management, 29*(1), 29–45.

Siegel, J., Dubrovsky, V., Kiesler, S., & McGuire, T. W. (1986). Group processes in computer-mediated communication. *Organizational Behavior and Human Decision Processes, 37,* 157–186.

Siegler, R. S., & Jenkins, E. (1989). *How children discover new strategies.* Hillsdale, NJ: Lawrence Erlbaum Associates.

Silag, W. (1984). The invention of the electronic digital computer at Iowa State College, 1930–1942. *The Palimpsest, 65*(5), 150–177.

Silverstein, B. A., Fine, L. J., & Armstrong, T. J. (1986). Hand wrist cumulative trauma disorders in industry. *British Journal of Industrial Medicine, 43,* 779–784.

Simeon, R. (1999). Evaluating domestic and international web-sites strategies. *Internet Research: Electronic Networking Applications and Policy, 9*(4), 297–308.

Simon, H. A. (1956). Rational choice and the structure of the environment. *Psychological Review, 63,* 129–138.

Simonsen, J., & Kensing, F. (1998). Make room for ethnography in design!: Overlooked collaborative and educational prospects. *ACM SIGDOC Asterisk Journal of Computer Documentation, 22*(1), 20–30.

Sims, O. (1994). *Business objects: Delivering cooperative objects for client-server.* New York: McGraw-Hill.

Simsarian, K. (2000). *Towards human-robot collaboration.* Unpublished doctoral dissertation, Swedish Institute of Computer Science, Kista, Sweden. Retrieved July 21, 2003, from http://www.sics.se/~kristian/thesis/

Simson, H., & Casey, S. A. (1988). *Developing effective user documentation: A human-factors approach.* New York: McGraw-Hill.

Sinding-Larsen, H (1987). Information technology and management of knowledge. *AI & Society, 1,* 93–101.

Singh, Push (n.d.). *Open mind common sense.* Retrieved December 22, 2003, from http://commonsense.media.mit.edu/cgi-bin/search.cgi

Singley, M., & Anderson, J. (1989). *The transfer of cognitive skill.* Cambridge, MA: Harvard University Press.

Sinha, I. (1999). *The cybergypsies: A frank account of love, life and travels on the electronic frontier.* London: Scribner.

Skemp, R. R. (1987). *The psychology of learning mathematics.* Hillsdale, NJ: Lawrence Erlbaum.

Skitka, L. J., & Sargis, E. G. (in press). Social psychological research and the Internet: The promise and the perils of a new methodological frontier. In Y. Amichai-Hamburger (Ed.), *The social net: The social psychology of the Internet.* Oxford, UK: Oxford University Press.

Skov, M. B., & Stage, J. (2003). Enhancing usability testing skills of novice testers: A longitudinal study. In *Proceedings of the 2nd Conference on Universal Access in Computer-Human Interaction.* Mahwah, NJ: Lawrence-Erlbaum.

BIBLIOGRAPHY

Slater, M., & Usoh, M. (1993). The influence of a virtual body on presence in immersive virtual environments. In *Proceedings of the Third Annual Conference on Virtual Reality* (pp. 34–42). London: Meckler.

Slater, M., Howell, J., Steed, A., Pertaub, D., Garau, M., & Springel, S. (2000). Acting in virtual reality. *ACM Collaborative Virtual Environments, CVE'2000*, 103–110.

Slater, M., Sadagic, A., Usoh, M., & Schroeder, R. (2000). Small group behaviour in a virtual and real environment: A comparative study. *PRESENCE: Teleoperators and Virtual Environments, 9*, 37–51.

Slepian, D. (1973). Information theory in the fifties. *IEEE Transactions on Information Theory, 19*(2), 145–148.

Slepian, D. (Ed.). (1973). *Key papers in the development of Information Theory.* New York: IEEE Press.

Slocum, W., Bennet, J., Bear, J., Morgan, M., & Root, R. (1987). METAL: THE LRC machine translation system. In S. Michaelson & Y. Wilks (Eds.), *Machine translation today: The state of the art* (pp. 319–350). Edinburgh, Scotland: Edinburgh University Press.

Slone, D. J. (2002). The influence of mental models and goals on search patterns during Web interaction. *Journal of the American Society for Information Science and Technology, 53*(13), 1152–1169.

Smailagic, A., & Siewiorel, D. (1993). A case study in embedded systems design: VuMan 2 wearable computer. *IEEE Design and Test of Computers, 10*(4), 56–67.

Smalley, R. E. (2001). Of chemistry, love and nanobots. *Scientific American, 285*(3), 76–77.

Smeraldi, F., & Bigun, J. (2002). Retinal vision applied to facial features detection and face authentication. *Pattern Recognition Letters, 23*(4), 463–475.

Smith, B. & Welty, C. (2001). Ontology: Towards a new synthesis. In *Proceedings of the International Conference on Formal Ontology in Information Systems* (pp. iii–ix). Ogunquit, Maine.

Smith, D. C., & Alexander, R. C. (1988). Fumbling the future: How Xerox invented, then ignored the first personal computer. New York: William Morrow.

Smith, H. T., & Green, T. R. G. (Eds.). (1980). *Human interaction with computers.* New York: Academic.

Smith, M. A., & Kollack, P. (1999). *Communities in cyberspace.* London: Routledge.

Smith, R., & Hipp, D. R. (1995). *Spoken natural language dialog systems: A practical approach.* New York: Oxford University Press.

Smith, R., & van Kuppevelt, J. (Eds.). (2003). *Current and new directions in discourse and dialogue.* Dordrect, Netherlands: Kluwer Academic.

Smith, S. L., & Mosier, J. N. (1986). *Guidelines for designing user interface software.* Bedford, MA: MITRE.

Smith, V. (1997). New forms of work organization. *Annual Review of Sociology, 23*, 315–339.

Snir, M., Otto, S., Huss-Lederman, S., Walker, D., & Dongarra, J. (1996). *MPI: The complete reference.* Boston: MIT Press.

Snyder, C. (2003). *Paper prototyping: The fast and easy way to design and refine user interfaces.* New York: Morgan Kaufmann.

Snyder, J. P. (1997). *Flattening the earth: Two thousand years of map projections.* Chicago: University of Chicago Press.

Sociable Media Group, MIT. (2003). *Artifacts of the presence era.* Retrieved May 27, 2004, from http://smg.media.mit.edu/

Soe, Y. (2002). *The digital divide: An analysis of Korea's Internet diffusion.* Unpublished master's thesis, Georgetown University, Washington, DC.

Soergel, D. (1974). *Indexing languages and thesauri: Construction and maintenance.* New York: Wiley.

Soergel, D. (1985). *Organizing information: Principles of database and retrieval systems.* Orlando, FL: Academic Press.

Soergel, D. (1994). Indexing and retrieval performance: The logical evidence. *Journal of the American Society for Information Science, 4*(8), 589–599.

Soergel, D. (2000). ASIST SIG/CR Classification Workshop 2000: Classification for user support and learning: Report. *Knowledge Organization, 27*(3), 165–172.

Soergel, D. (2002). A framework for digital library research: Broadening the vision. *D-Lib Magazine, 8*(12). Retrieved January 26, 2004 from http://www.dlib.org/dlib/december02/soergel/12soergel.html

Soergel, D. (2003). *Thesauri and ontologies in digital libraries.* Retrieved January 22, 2004, from http://www.clis.umd.edu/faculty/soergel/SoergelDLThesTut.html

Solomon, C. (1994). *The history of animation: Enchanted drawings.* New York: Wings Books.

Soloway, E., Guzdial, M., & Hay, K. E. (1994). Learner-centered design: The challenge for HCI in the 21st century. *Interactions, 1*(2), 36–48.

Sommerich, C. M., Starr, H., Smith, C. A., & Shivers, C. (2002). Effects of notebook computer configuration and task on user biomechanics, productivity, and comfort. *International Journal of Industrial Ergonomics, 30*(1), 7–31.

Soto, M. (2003, August 8). The toll of information overload: Too much technology diminishes work relationships. *Seattle Times*, p. C1.

Soto, R. (1999). Learning and performing by exploration: Label quality measured by Latent Semantic Analysis. In *CHI '99: Proceedings of the Conference on Human Factors and Computing Systems*, 418–425.

Sowa, J. F. (2000). *Knowledge representation: Logical, philosophical and computational foundations.* Pacific Grove, CA: Brooks/Cole.

Sowa, T., & Wachsmuth, I. (2000). Coverbal iconic gestures for object descriptions in virtual environments:

Spafford, E. (1988). *The Internet worm program: An analysis* (Purdue Technical Report CSD-TR-823). Retrieved April 22, 2004, from www.protovision.textfiles.com/100/tr823.txt

Spafford, E. (1989). Crisis and aftermath. *Communications of the ACM, 32*(6), 678–687.

Sparck Jones, K., & Willett, P. (1997). *Readings in information retrieval.* San Francisco, CA: Morgan Kaufmann.

Spears, L., Lea, M., & Postmes, T. (2001). Social psychological theories of computer-mediated communication: Social pain or social gain? In W. Peter Robinson & H. Giles, (Eds.), *The new handbook of language and social psychology* (2nd ed., pp. 601–624). New York: Pfeiffer.

Specht, M., & Kobsa, A. (1999). *Interaction of domain expertise and interface design in adaptive educational hypermedia.* Retrieved March 24, 2004, from http://wwwis.win.tue.nl/asum99/specht/specht.html

Spencer, R. (2000). The streamlined cognitive walkthrough method, working around social constraints encountered in a software development company. In *CHI 2000: Proceedings of the Conference on Human Factors in Computing Systems*, 353–359.

Spiegel, M. (1985). Pronouncing names automatically. *Proceedings of the American Voice I/O Systems Conference 1985*, 107–132.

Spiller, N. (Ed.). (2002). *Cyber reader: Critical writings for the digital era.* New York: Phaidon.

Spinello, R. A., & Tavani, H. T. (Eds.). (2001). *Readings in cyberethics.* Sudbury, MA: Jones and Bartlett.

Spink, A., Wolfram, D., Jansen, B., & Saracevic, T. (2001). The public and their queries. *Journal of the American Society for Information Science and Technology, 52*(3), 226–234.

Spinks, W. A., & Wood, J. (1996). *Office-based telecommuting: An international comparison of satellite offices in Japan and North America.* Paper presented at the Conference on Computer Personnel Research, Denver, CO.

Spohrer, J. (1996). WorldBoard. *The Apple Research Lab Review, 10.*

Spohrer, J. (1999). Information in places. *The IBM Systems Journal, 38*(4). Retrieved March 9, 2004, from http://www.research.ibm.com/journal/sj/384/spohrer.html

Spool, J. M., Scanlon, T., Schroeder, W., Snyder, C., & DeAngelo, T. (1999). *Web site usability.* Los Altos, CA: Morgan Kaufmann.

Spooner, T., & Rainie, L. (2000). African-Americans and the Internet. Washington, DC: Pew Internet & American Life Project. Retrieved July 18, 2003, from http://www.pewinternet.org/reports/pdfs/PIP_African_Americans_Report.pdf

Sproat, R. (1997). *Multilingual text-to-speech synthesis: The Bell Labs approach.* Boston: Kluwer Academic Publishers.

Sproull, L. & Kiesler, S. (in press). Public volunteer work on the Internet. In B. Kahin & W. Dutton (Eds.), *Transforming enterprise.* Cambridge, MA: MIT Press.

Sproull, L., & Faraj, S. (1995). Atheism, sex, and databases: The Net as a social technology. In B. Kahin & J. Keller (Eds.), *Public access to the Internet* (pp. 62–81). Cambridge, MA: MIT Press.

Sproull, L., & Kiesler, S. (1991). *Connections: New ways of working in the networked organization.* Cambridge, MA: MIT Press.

Sproull, L., Conley, C., & Moon, J. Y. (in press). Pro-social behavior on the net. In Y. Amichai-Hamburger (Ed.), *The social net: The social psychology of the Internet.* New York: Oxford University Press.

St. Amant, R., & Healey, C. G. (2001). Usability guidelines for interactive search in direct manipulation systems. In *Proceedings of the International Joint Conference on Artificial Intelligence (IJCAI)* (pp. 1179–1184). San Francisco, CA: Morgan Kaufman.

St. Laurent, S. (2000). XML. New York: McGraw Hill.

Staab, S., & Studer, R. (Eds.). (2004). *Handbook on ontologies in information systems.* Heidelberg, Germany: Springer.

Stajano, R. (2002). *Security for ubiquitous computing.* West Sussex, UK: John Wiley & Sons.

Stammers, R. B., & Shephard, A. (1995). Task analysis. In J. R. Wilson & E. N. Corlett (Eds.), *Evaluation of human work* (pp. 144–168). London: Taylor and Francis.

Standage, T. (2002). *The Turk: The life and times of the famous eighteenth-century chess-playing machine.* New York: Walker & Company.

Staniford, S., Paxson, V., & Weaver, N. (2002). How to own the Internet in your spare time. *Proceedings of the 11th USENIX Security Symposium* (pp. 149–162).

Stansfield, S., Shawver, D., Sobel, A., Prasad, M. & Tapia, L. (2000). Design and implementation of a virtual reality system and its application to training medical first responders. *Presence: Teleoperators and Virtual Environments, 9*(6), 524–556.

Stanton, J. M. (2002). Information technology and privacy: A boundary management perspective. In S. Clarke, E. Coakes, G. Hunter, & A. Wenn (Eds.), *Socio-Technical and Human Cognition Elements of Information Systems* (pp. 79–103). London: Idea Group.

Star, S. L. (Ed.). (1995). *The cultures of computing.* Oxford, UK: Blackwell Publishers.

Star, S. L., & Ruhleder, K. (1994). Steps towards an ecology of infrastructure: Complex problems in design and access for large-scale collaborative systems. In *Proceedings of CSCW 94* (pp. 253–264). New York: ACM Press.

Stark, R., & Bainbridge, W. S. (1987). *A theory of religion.* New York: Toronto/Lang.

Starker, I., & Bolt, R. A. (1990). A gaze-responsive self-disclosing display. In *Proceedings of CHI '90* (pp. 3–9). Seattle, WA: ACM.

Starkweather, G. K. (1980). High speed laser printing systems. *Laser Applications, 4,* 125–189.

Starkweather, G. K. (1985). A high resolution laser printer. *Journal of Imaging Technology, 11*(6), 300–305.

Starner, T. (2001). The challenges of wearable computing: Parts 1 & 2. *IEEE Micro, 21*(4), 44–67

Starner, T., Mann, S., Rhodes, B., Levine, J., Healey, J., Kirsch, D., Picard, R., & Pentland A. (1997). Augmented reality through wearable computing. *Presence, 6*(4), 386–398.

State, A., Chen, D. T., Tector, C., Brandt, A., Chen, H., Ohbuchi, R., et al. (1994). Observing a volume rendered fetus within a pregnant patient. In *Proceedings of IEEE Visualization '94* (pp. 364–368). Los Alamitos, CA: IEEE.

Stauder, J. (1999, June). Augmented reality with automatic illumination control incorporating ellipsoidal models. *IEEE Transactions on Multimedia, 1*(2), 136–143.

Steehouder, M., Jansen, C., van der Poort, P., & Verheijen, R. (Eds.). (1994). *Quality of technical documentation.* Amsterdam: Rodopi.

Steenbekkers, L., & Molenbroek, J. (1990). Anthropometric data of children for non-specialized users. *Ergonomics, 33*(4), 421–429.

Stefik, M., Foster, G., et al. (1987). Beyond the chalkboard: Computer support for collaboration and problem solving in meetings. *CACM, 30*(1), 32–47.

Stein, R., Ferrero, S., Hetfield, M., Quinn, A., & Krichever, M. (1998). Development of a commercially successful wearable data collection system. In *Proceedings from IEEE International Symposium on Wearable Computers* (pp. 18–24). Pittsburgh, PA: IEEE Computer Society.

Steinberg, S. H. (1996). *Five hundred years of printing.* New Castle, DE: Oak Knoll Books.

Stephenson, N. (1992). *Snow crash.* New York: Bantam.

Stephenson, R. S. (2000). The Harvey project: Open course development and rich content. In L. Petrides (Ed.), *Case Studies on Information Technology in Higher Education* (pp. 185–194). Hershey, PA: Idea Group Publishing.

Stephenson, R. S. (in press). Enhancing learning outcomes. *Journal on Excellence in College Teaching* [Special issue on Web-Based Teaching and Learning].

Sterling, B. (1986). *Mirrorshades: The cyberpunk anthology.* New York: Ace.

Stern, N. (1981). *From ENIAC to UNIVAC: An appraisal of the Eckert-Mauchly computers.* Bedford, MA: Digital Press.

Sternberg, S. (1966). High-speed scanning in human memory. *Science, 153,* 652–654.

Stevens, K. (1999). *Acoustic phonetics.* Cambridge, MA: MIT Press.

Stevens, R., & DeFanti, T. A. (1999). Tele-immersion and collaborative virtual environments. In I. Foster & C. Kesselman (Eds.), *The grid: Blueprint for a new computing infrastructure* (pp. 131–158). San Francisco: Morgan Kaufmann.

Stevens, S. S. (2000). *Psychophysics: Introduction to its perceptual, neural, and social prospects* (2nd ed.). Oxford, UK: Transaction Books.

BIBLIOGRAPHY

Stirling, L., & Shapiro, E. (1986). *The art of Prolog.* Cambridge, MA: MIT Press.

Stone, A. R. (1995). *The war of desire and technology at the close of the mechanical age.* Cambridge, MA: MIT Press.

Stone, E. F., & Stone, D. L. (1990), Privacy in organizations: Theoretical issues, research findings and protection mechanisms. *Research in Personnel and Human Resources Management, 8,* 349–411.

Storey, N. (1996). *Safety-critical computer systems.* New York: Addison-Wesley.

Stork, D. G. (Ed.). (1997). *Hal's legacy: 2001's computer as dream and reality.* Cambridge, MA: MIT Press.

Stork, D. G., & Hennecke, M. E. (Eds.). (1995). *Speechreading by humans and machines.* 150 of NATO ASI Series, Series F. Computer and Systems Sciences. Berlin, Germany: Springer Verlag.

Story, M. F., & Mueller, J. L. (2001). Universal design performance measures for products: A tool for assessing universal usability. In J. Winters, C. Robinson,, R. Simpson & G. Vanderheiden, (Eds..), *Emerging and accessible telecommunications, information and healthcare technologies—Emerging challenges in enabling universal access.* Arlington, VA: RESNA Press.

Story, M. F. Mueller, J. L., & Montoya-Weiss, M. (2001). Completion of universal design performance measures. In *Proceedings of the RESNA 2001 Annual Conference.* Arlington, VA: RESNA Press.

Strachan, L., Anderson, J., Sneesby, M., & Evans, M. (2000). Minimalist user modeling in a complex commercial software system. *User Modeling and User-Adapted Interaction, 10*(2–3), 109–146.

Straub, D., Keil, M., & Brenner, W. (1997). Testing the technology acceptance model across cultures: A three country study. *Information & Management, 31*(1), 1–11.

Strauss, A. L., Schatzman, L., Bucher, R., Erlich, D., & Sabshin, M. (1981). *Psychiatric ideologies and institutions.* New Brunswick, NJ: Transaction.

Streiter, O., Carl, M., & Haller, J. (Eds.). (1999). Hybrid approaches to machine translation. *Working Paper No. 35, Institute of Applied Information Sciences.* Saarbruecken, Germany. Retrieved February 12, 2004 from http://www.iai.uni-sb.de/iaien/iaiwp.

Streitz, N. A., Geißler, J., Haake, J., & Hol, J. (1994). DOLPHIN: Integrated meeting support across local and remote desktop environments and liveboards. In *Proceedings of the Conference on Computer Supported Cooperative Work: CSCW '94* (pp. 345–358). New York: ACM Press.

Stuckey, K. M. (1998). Programming with constraints: An introduction. Cambridge, MA: MIT Press.

Suchman, L. (1987). *Plans and situated actions: The problem of human-machine communication.* Cambridge, UK: Cambridge University Press.

Suchman, L. (2002). *Located accountabilities in technology production.* Retrieved on January 8, 2004, from http://www.comp.lancs.ac.uk/sociology/soc039ls.html. Centre for Science Studies, Lancaster University.

Suchman, L., & Trigg, R. (1992) Understanding practice: Video as a medium for reflection and design. In J. Greenbaum & M. Kyng (Eds.), *Design at work: cooperative design of computer systems* (pp. 65–89). Hillsdale, NJ: Lawrence Erlbaum Associates.

Sullivan, J. W., & Tyler, S. W. (Eds.). (1991). *Intelligent user interfaces.* New York: ACM Press.

Sullivan, K. (1996). The Windows® 95 user interface: A case study in usability engineering. *Proceedings of Human Factors in Computing Systems, CHI '96,* 473–480. New York: ACM.

Sullivan, T. E., Warm, J. S., Schefft, B. K., Dember, W. N., O'Dell, M. W., & Peterson, S. J. (1998). Effects of olfactory stimulation on the vigilance performance of individuals with brain injury. *Journal of Clinical and Experimental Neuropsychology, 20*(2), 227–236.

Sun Microsystems Incorporated. (2001). *Java look and feel design guidelines.* Retrieved January 4, 2004, from http://java.sun.com/products/jlf/ed2/book/

Sun, C., & Chen, D. (2002). Consistency maintenance in real-time collaborative graphics editing systems. *ACM Transactions on Computer Human Interaction, 9*(1), 1–41.

Sun, C., & Ellis, C. (1998). Operational transformation in real-time group editors: Issues, algorithms, and achievements. In *Proceedings of the ACM Conference on Computer Supported Cooperative Work '98.* New York: ACM Press.

Sundaram, H., & Chang, S. F. (2002). Computable scenes and structures in films. *IEEE Transactions on Multimedia, 4,* 482–491.

Sunstein, C. (2001). *Republic.com.* Princeton, NJ: Princeton University Press.

Surkan, K. (n.d.). *The new technology of electronic text: Hypertext and CMC in virtual environments.* Retrieved July 31, 2003, from http://english.cla.umn.edu/GraduateProfiles/Ksurkan/etext/etable.html

Survey of income and program participation (SIPP): Series P-70, #8 Survey. (1984). Washington, DC: Bureau of the Census.

Sutcliffe, A. (2003). Scenarios, models and the design process in software engineering and interactive systems design. *Proceedings of HCI International, 1,* 579–583. Hillsdale, NJ: Erlbaum.

Sutherland, I. (1963). Sketchpad: A man-machine graphical communication system. *AFIPS, 23,* 329–346.

Sutherland, I. (1965). The ultimate display. *Proceedings of IFIP '65, 2,* 506.

Sutton, J., & Bartram, A. (1968). *An atlas of typeforms.* New York: Hastings House.

Suwa, M., & Tversky, B. (1997). What architects and students perceive in their sketches: A protocol analysis. *Design Studies,* 18, 385–403.

Swezey, R. W. (Ed.). *The Human Factors Society, 1,* 114–118. Santa Monica, CA: Human Factors and Ergonomics Society.

Swindells, C., Inkpen, K. M., Dill, J. C., & Tory, M. (2002). That one there! Pointing to establish device identity. In Proceedings of the 15th annual ACM symposium on user interface software and technology (pp. 151–160). New York: Association for Computing Machinery.

Swinyard, W. R., Rinne, H., & Keng Kau, A. (1990). The morality of software piracy: A cross cultural analysis. *Journal of Business Ethics, 9,* 655–664.

Syverson, P., Y Cevesato, I. (2001). The logic of authentication protocols. In R. Focardi & R. Gorrieri (Eds.), *Foundations of security analysis and design* (pp. 63–136). Heidelberg, Germany: Springer Verlag

Szekely, P., Sukaviriya, P., Castells, P., Muthukumarasamy, J., & Salcher, E. (1996). Declarative interface models for user interface construction tools: The Mastermind approach. In L. Bass & C. Unger (Eds.), *Engineering for human-computer interaction* (pp. 120–150). London and New York: Chapman & Hall.

Takeda, H., Kobayashi, N., Matsubara, Y., & Nishida, T. (1997). *Towards ubiquitous human-robot interaction.* Retrieved July 21, 2003, from http://ai-www.aist-nara.ac.jp/papers/takeda/html/ijcai97-ims.html

Talk mode (n.d.). *The jargon file.* Retrieved November 1, 2002, from http://www.tuxedo.org/~esr/jargon/html/entry/talk-mode.html

BIBLIOGRAPHY

Tamai, T., & Torimitsu,Y. (1992). Software lifetime and its evolution process over generations. In *Proceedings of the IEEE International Conference on Software Maintenance* (63–69). Los Alamitos, CA: IEEE Computer Society Press.

Tambe, M. (1997). Towards flexible teamwork. *Journal of Artificial Intelligence Research, 7,* 83–124.

Tan, H. Z., Lim, A., & Traylor, R. M. (2000). A psychophysical study of sensory saltation with an open response paradigm. *Proceedings of the 9th International Symposium on Haptic Interfaces for Virtual Environments and Teleoperator Systems,* ASME Dynamic Systems and Control Division, 69(2), 1109–1115.

Tan, Y. P., Kulkarni, S. R., & Ramadge, P. J. (2000). Rapid estimation of camera motion from compressed video with application to video annotation. *IEEE Transactions on Circuits and Systems for Video Technology, 10*(1), 133–146.

Tandler, P., Streitz, N., & Prante, T. (2002, November). Roomware: Moving toward ubiquitous computers. *IEEE Micro, 22*(6), 36–47.

Tanenhaus, M., Spivey-Knowlton, M., Eberhard, K., & Sedivy, J. (1995). Integration of visual and linguistic information during spoken language comprehension. *Science, 268,* 1632–1634.

Tang, J. C. (1997). Eliminating a hardware switch: Weighing economics and values in a design decision. In B. Friedman (Ed.), *Human values and the design of computer technology* (pp. 259–269). New York: Cambridge University Press and CSLI, Stanford University.

Tang, J., Yankelovich, N., Begole, J., Van Kleek, M., Li, F., & Bhalodia, J. (2001). Connexus to awarenex: Extending awareness to mobile users. In *Proceedings of Human Factors in Computing Systems: CHI 2001* (pp. 221–228). New York: ACM Press.

Tanimoto, S. (1990). Viva: A visual language for image processing. *Journal of Visual Languages and Computing, 2*(2), 127–139.

Tannen, R. S. (1998). Breaking the sound barrier: Designing auditory displays for global usability. *Human Factors and the Web.* Retrieved March 1, 2004, from http://www.research.att.com/conf/hfweb/proceedings/tannen/index.htm

Tanriverdi, V., & Jacob, R. J. K. (2000). Interaction with eye movements in virtual environments. In *Proceedings of CHI '00* (pp. 265–272). The Hague, Netherlands: ACM.

Tao, H., Chen, H., Wu, W., & Huang, T. (1999). Compression of mpeg-4 facial animation parameters for transmission of talking heads. *IEEE Transactions on Circuits and Systems for Video Technology, 9*(2), 264.

Tapscott, D. (1998). *Growing up digital: The rise of the Net generation.* New York: McGraw-Hill.

Task Force on DSM-IV. (1994). *Diagnostic and statistical manual of mental disorders.* Washington, DC: American Psychiatric Association.

Tatham, E. W. (1999). Getting the best of both real and virtual worlds. *Communications of the ACM, 42*(9), 96–98.

Tatham, E. W., Banissi, E., Khosrowshahi, F., Sarfraz, M., Tatham, E., & Ursyn, A. (1999). Optical occlusion and shadows in a "see-through" augmented reality display. In *Proceedings of the 1999 IEEE International Conference on Information Visualization* (pp. 128–131). Los Alamitos, CA: IEEE.

Tauscher, L., & Greenberg, S. (1997). How people revisit Web pages: Empirical findings and implications for the design of history systems. International Journal of Human Computer Studies, 47(1), 97–138.

Tavani, H. (2003). *Ethics and technology: Ethical issues in an age of information and communication technology.* Hoboken, NJ: John Wiley & Sons.

Taylor, A. G. (2003). *The organization of information* (2nd ed.). Westport, CT: Libraries Unlimited.

Taylor, E. (1958). *Primitive culture.* New York, Harper & Row. (Original work published 1871)

Taylor, F. W. (1911). *The principles of scientific management.* New York: Harper.

Taylor, T. L. (2002). Living digitally: Embodiment in virtual worlds. In R. Schroeder (Ed.), *The social life of avatars: Presence and interaction in shared virtual environments.* London: Springer Verlag.

Taylor, T.L. (1999). Life in virtual worlds: Plural existence, multimodalities and other online research challenges. *American Behavioral Scientist, 4*(3).

Teague, G. J. (2002). Women in Computing: What brings them to it, what keeps them in it? *SIGCSE Bulletin, 34*(2), 147–158.

Teasley, S., & Wolinsky, S. (2001). Scientific collaborations at a distance. *Science, 292,* 2254–2255.

Techweb (n.d.). *Beta testing.* Retrieved on January 8, 2004, from http://www.techweb.com/encyclopedia

Teltzrow, M., & Kobsa, A. (2004). Impacts of user privacy preferences on personalized systems—A comparative study. In C.-M. Karat, J. Blom, & J. Karat (Eds.), *Designing personalized user experiences for e-commerce* (pp. 315–332). Dordrecht, Netherlands: Kluwer Academic Publishers.

Templeman, J., Denbrook, P., & Sibert, L. (1999). Virtual locomotion: Walking in place through virtual environments. *Presence: Teleoperators and Virtual Environments, 8*(6), 598–617.

Tenopir, C., & King, D. W. (2000). *Towards electronic journals: Realities for scientists, librarians, and publishers.* Washington, DC: Special Libraries Association.

Tenopir, C., King, D. W., Boyce, P., Grayson, M., Zhang, Y., & Ebuen, M. (2003). Patterns of journal use by scientists through three evolutionary phases. *D-Lib Magazine, 9*(5). Retrieved July 29, 2003, from http://www.dlib.org/dlib/may03/king/05king.html

Tepper, M. S., & Owens, A. (2002). Access to pleasure: Onramp to specific information on disability, illness, and other expected changes throughout the lifespan. In A. Cooper (Ed.), *Sex and the Internet: A guidebook for clinicians.* New York: Brunner-Routledge.

Terranova, T. (2000). Free labor: Producing culture for the digital economy. *Social Text 18*(2), 33–58.

Terry, P. D. (1997). *Compilers and compiler generators— an introduction with C++.* London: International Thomson Computer Press.

Terveen, L., & Hill, W. (2001). Beyond recommender systems: Helping people help each other. In J. M. Carroll (Ed.), *HCI in the new millennium* (p. 273). New York: Addison-Wesley.

Tews, A. D., Mataric, M. J., & Sukhatme, G. S. (2003). A scalable approach to human-robot interaction. *Proceedings of the 2003 IEEE International Conference on Robotics and Automation.* Taipei, Taiwan, May 2003.

Text REtrieval Conference (TREC), cosponsored by the National Institute of Standards and Technology (NIST) and the Defense Advanced Research Projects Agency (DARPA). Retrieved January 22, 2004, from http://trec.nist.gov/

Thalmann, M. N, & Thalmann D. (Eds). (1999). *Computer Animation and Simulation 99.* Vienna, Austria: Springer-Verlag.

Thalmann, N. M., Kalra, P., & Escher, M. (1998). Face to virtual face. *Proceedings of the IEEE, 86*(5), 870–883.

Thayer, R. H., & Dorfman, M. (1999). *Software requirements engineering* (2nd ed.). New York: IEEE Computer Society Press.

The relevance of ICT in development. (2002, May-June) *The Courier ACP-EU*, 192, 37–39. Retrieved 17 July 2003, from http://europa.eu.int/comm/development/body/publications/courier/courier192/en/en_037_ni.pdf

Thom, B. (2003). Interactive improvisational music companionship: A user-modeling approach. *User Modeling and User-Adapted Interaction Journal, 13*(1–2).

Thomas, D. (2002). *Hacker culture*. Minneapolis: University of Minnesota Press.

Thomas, F., & Johnson, O. (1981). *The illusion of life*. New York: Abbeville Press.

Thomas, J. C. (1997). Steps toward universal access within a communications company. In B. Friedman (Ed.), *Human values and the design of computer systems* (pp. 271–287). New York: Cambridge University Press and CSLI, Stanford University.

Thomas, L. C. (1984). *Games, theory, and applications*. New York: Halsted Press.

Thomas, M., & Ormsby, B. (1994). On the design of side-stick controllers in fly-by-wire aircraft. *ACM SIGAPP Applied Computing Review, 2*(1), 15–20.

Thomasson, J., Foster, W., & Press, L. (2002). *The diffusion of the Internet in Mexico*. Austin: University of Texas at Austin, Latin America Network Information Center.

Thompson, K. (1984). Reflections on trusting trust. *Communications of the ACM, 27*(8), 761–763.

Thompson, W., Pick, H., Bennett, B., Heinrichs, M., Savitt, S., & Smith, K. (1990). Map-based localization: The "drop-off" problem. *Proceedings DARPA Image Understanding Workshop*, 706–719.

Thorp, E. (1998). The invention of the first wearable computer. In *Proceedings from IEEE International Symposium on Wearable Computers* (pp. 4–8). Pittsburgh, PA: IEEE Computer Society.

Thuraisingham, B. (1989). Security for object-oriented database systems. *Proceedings of the ACM OOPSLA Conference*. New Orleans, LA.

Thuraisingham, B. (1998). *Data mining: Technologies, techniques, tools and trends*. Boca Raton, FL: CRC Press.

Thuraisingham, B. (2001). *XML.Databases and the Semantic Web*. Boca Raton, FL: CRC Press.

Thuraisingham, B., & Ford, W. (1995). Security constraint processing in a distributed database management system. *IEEE Transactions on Knowledge and Data Engineering*, 274–293.

Thuraisingham, B., et al. (1993). Design and implementation of a database inference controller. *Data and Knowledge Engineering Journal, 8*.

Tittiranonda, P., Rempel, D., Armstrong, T., & Burastero, S. (1999) Effect of four computer keyboards in computer users with upper extremity musculoskeletal disorders. *American Journal of Industrial Medicine, 35*(6), 647–661.

TNS Interactive. (2001). *Asia-Pacific M-commerce report*. Retrieved January 23, 2004, from http://www.tnsofres.com/apmcommerce/

Tocqueville, A,. de. (1945). *Democracy in America*. New York: Knopf. (Original work published 1835)

Toffler, A. (1980). *The third wave*. New York: William Morrow.

Tominaga, K., Honda, S., Ohsawa, T., Shigeno, H., Okada, K., & Matsushita, Y. (2001). Friend Park: Expression of the wind and the scent on virtual space. In *Proceedings of the Seventh International Conference on Virtual Systems and Multimedia* (pp. 507–515). Berkeley, CA: IEEE.

Tomori, O., & Moore, M. (2003). The neurally controllable Internet browser. In *Proceedings of SIGCHI 03* (pp. 796–798).

Tonn, B. E., Zambrano, P., & Moore, S. (2001). Community networks or networked communities? *Social Science Computer Review, 19*(2), 201–212.

Top 500. (2002). Top 500 supercomputer sites. Retrieved August 8, 2003, from http://www.top500.org

Torgerson, W. S. (1958). *Theory and methods of scaling*. New York: Wiley.

Torrance, M. C. (1995, May). Advances in human-computer interaction: The intelligent room. *Working notes of the CHI 95 research symposium*. Denver, CO.

Torvalds, L., & Diamond, D. (2001). *Just for fun: The story of an accidental revolutionary*. New York: Harper Business.

Touchscreens.com. (2003). *What are touchscreens used for?* Retrieved October 10, 2003, from http://www.touchscreens.com/intro-uses.html

Trafton, J. G., Altmann, E. M., Brock, D. P., & Mintz, F. E. (2003). Preparing to resume an interrupted task: Effects of prospective goal encoding and retrospective rehearsal. *International Journal of Human-Computer Studies, 58*(5), 583–603.

Translation Service of the European Commission. (2002). *Translating for a multilingual community*. Retrieved February 12, 2004 from http://europa.eu.int/comm/translation/reading/articles/tools_and_workflow_en.htm.

Treasury Board of Canada. (2001, 2003). *PKI questions and answers for beginners*. Retrieved March 18, 2004, from http://www.cio-dpi.gc.ca/pki-icp/beginners/faq/faq_e.asp

Trist E. (1981). *The evolution of socio-technical systems*. Ontario, Canada: Ontario Quality of Working Life Center.

Truex, D., Baskerville, R., & Klein, H. (1999). Growing systems in an emergent organization. *Communications ACM, 42*(8), 117–123.

Trujillo, A. (1999). *Translation engines: Techniques for machine translation*. London: Springer.

Tsagarousianou, R., Tambini, D., & Bryan, C. (Eds.). (1998). *Cyberdemocracy: Technology, cities and civic networks*. New York, NY: Routledge.

Tsang, E. (1993). *Foundations of constraint satisfaction*. London, UK: Academic Press.

Tudor, L. G. (1993, October). *A participatory design technique for high-level task analysis, critique and redesign: The CARD method*. Paper presented at the Proceedings of the Human Factors and Ergonomics Society, Seattle, WA.

Tufte, E. (1983). *The visual display of quantitative information*. Cheshire, CT: Graphics Press.

Tufte, E. (1990). *Envisioning information*. Cheshire, CT: Graphics Press.

Tufte, E. (1997). *Visual explanations*. Cheshire, CT: Graphics Press.

Tukey, J. W. (1977). *Exploratory data analysis*. Boston, MA: Addison-Wesley.

Turing, A. (1950). Computing machinery and intelligence. *Mind, 59*, 433–460.

Turing, A. M. (1981). Computing machinery and intelligence. In D. R. Hofstadter & D. C. Dennett (Eds.), *The mind's I—Fantasies and reflections on self and soul* (pp. 53–68). New York: Bantam Books. (Reprinted from Mind, 49[236], 433–460)

Turk, M., & Kolsch, M. (in press). Perceptual Interfaces. In G. Medioni & S. B. Kang (Eds.), *Emerging topics in computer vision*. Upper Saddle River, NJ: Prentice Hall.

Turkle, S. (1984) *The second self: Computers and the human spirit*. New York: Simon & Schuster.

BIBLIOGRAPHY

Turkle, S. (1995). *Life on the screen: Identity in the age of the Internet.* New York: Simon & Schuster.

Turkle, S., & Papert, S. (1990). Epistemological pluralism: Styles and cultures within the computer culture. *Signs: Journal of Women in Culture and Society, 16*(1), 128–148.

Turner, A., Chapman, D., & Penn, A. (2000). Sketching space. *Computers and Graphics, 24,* 869–876.

Tushman, M. L., & Nadler, D. A. (1978). Information processing as an integrated concept on organizational design. *Academy of Management Review, 3,* 613–624.

Tygar, J. D. (1998). Atomicity in electronic commerce. *Networker, 2*(2), 23–43.

Tyson, J. (2003). *How instant messaging works.* Retrieved August 7, 2003, from http://www.howstuffworks.com/instant-messaging.htm

U.S. Congress Office of Technology Assessment. (1986). *Technology and structural unemployment: Reemploying displaced adults* (OTA-ITE-250). Washington, DC: U.S. Government Printing Office.

U.S. Congress, Office of Technology Assessment. (1987). *The electronic supervisor: New technology, new tensions.* (OTA-CIT-333). Washington, DC: U.S. Government Printing Office.

U.S. Department of Commerce, Economics and Statistics Administration. (2002). *Digital economy 2002.* Washington, DC: U.S. Department of Commerce.

U.S. Department of Commerce, Technology Administration. (1997). *International plans, policies, and investments in science and technology.* Washington, DC: U.S. Department of Commerce.

U.S. Department of Commerce, Technology Administration. (1998). *The new innovators: Global patenting trends in five sectors.* Washington, DC: U.S. Department of Commerce.

U.S. Department of Commerce. (2000). *Falling through the Net: Toward digital inclusion.* Retrieved July 18, 2003, from http://search.ntia.doc.gov/pdf/fttn00.pdf

U.S. Department of Commerce. (2002). *A nation online: How Americans are expanding their use of the Internet.* Retrieved July 18, 2003, from http://www.ntia.doc.gov/ntiahome/dn/anationonline2.pdf

U.S. Department of Justice. (2000). *Uniform crime reporting: National Incident-Based Reporting System, data collection guidelines: Vol. 1. Data collection guidelines.* Retrieved February 17, 2004, from http://www.fbi.gov/ucr/nibrs/manuals/v1all.pdf

U.S. Department of Labor, Bureau of Labor Statistics. (1983–2002). *Current population survey.* Washington, DC: U.S. Department of Commerce.

U.S. Department of Labor, Bureau of Labor Statistics. (2001). *Occupational employment statistics survey.* Washington, DC: U.S. Department of Commerce.

U.S. Occupational Safety and Health Administration. (1997). *Working safely with video display terminals* (OSHA Publication No. 3092). Retrieved January 8, 2004, from http://www.osha.gov/

UCLA Center for Communication Policy. (2000). *The UCLA Internet report: Surveying the digital future.* Retrieved July 18, 2003, from http://www.ccp.ucla.edu/UCLA-Internet-Report-2000.pdf

UCLA Center for Communication Policy. (2003). *The UCLA Internet report: Surveying the digital future year three.* Retrieved January 8, 2004, from http://ccp.ucla.edu/pdf/UCLA-Internet-Report-Year-Three.pdf

Ulijaszek, S., & Mascie-Taylor, C. G. N. (Eds.). (1994). *Anthropometry: The individual and the population.* Cambridge, UK: Cambridge University Press.

Ullman, D., Wood, S., & Craig, D. (1990). The importance of drawing in the mechanical design process. *Computers and Graphics, 14*(2), 263–274.

Ummelen, N. (1996). *Procedural and declarative information in software manuals: Effects on information use, task performance, and knowledge.* Amsterdam: Rodopi.

Unicode 4.0 (2003). *The Unicode standard, version 4.0.* Boston, MA: Addison-Wesley. Retrieved April 6, 2004, from http://www.unicode.org/versions/Unicode4.0.0/

Updike, D. B. (1980). *Printing types: Their history, forms, and use.* New York: Dover.

Upton, H. (1968). Wearable eyeglass speechreading aid. *American Annals of the Deaf, 113,* 222–229.

Urbach, J. C., Fisli, T. S., & Starkweather, G. (1982). Laser scanning for electronic printing. *Proceedings of the IEEE, 70*(6).

Urban search and rescue (USAR). (2000). Sensor Based Planning Lab, Carnegie Mellon University. Retrieved April 6, 2004, from http://voronoi.sbp.ri.cmu.edu/projects/prj_search_rescue.html

Usoh, M., Arthur, K., Whitton, M., Steed, A., Slater, M., and Brooks, F. (1999). Walking > Virtual Walking> Flying, in Virtual Environments. *Proceedings of SIGGRAPH '99,* 359–364.

Vahid, F., & Givargis, T. (2002). *Embedded systems design: A unified hardware/software introduction.* New York: John Wiley & Sons.

van Bezooijen, R., & van Heuven, V. (1997). Assessment of synthesis systems. In D. Gibbon, R. Moore, & R. Winsky (Eds.), *Handbook of standards and resources for spoken language systems* (pp. 481–63). Berlin, Germany: Walter de Gruyter.

van den Hoven, J. (1994). Towards principles for designing political-administrative information systems.

van den Hoven, J. (1994). Towards principles for designing political-administrative information systems. *Information and Public Sector, 3,* 353–373.

van Eimeren, B., Gerhard, H., & Frees, B. (2002). ARD/ZDF-Online-Studie 2002. *Entwicklung der Online-Nutzung in Deutschland: Mehr Routine, Wengier Entdeckerfreude* [The development of Internet use in Germany: More routine, less fun of discovery]. Media Perspektiven, 8, 346–362.

van Harmelan, M. (2001). Object modeling and user interface design. Boston: Addison-Wesley.

van Kuppevelt, J, Heid, U., & Kamp, H. (Eds.). (2000). Best practice in spoken dialog systems [Special issue]. *Natural Language Engineering, 6*(3–4).

Van Mannen, J. (1983). The fact of fiction in organizational ethnography. In J. Van Maanen (Ed.), *Qualitative methodology* (pp. 37–55). Newbury Park, CA: Sage.

van Santen, J. (1994). Assignment of segmental duration in text-to-speech synthesis. *Computer Speech and Language, 8,* 95–128.

van Santen, J., Sproat, R., Olive, J., & Hirschberg, J. (Eds.). (1997). *Progress in speech synthesis.* New York: Springer-Verlag.

VanBerkel, B., & DeSmedt, K. (1988). Triphone analysis: A combined method for the correction of orthographical and typographical errors. *Second Conference in Applied Natural Language Processing,* 77–83.

VanDam, A., Laidlaw, D., & Simpson, R. (2002). *Experiments in immersive virtual reality for scientific visualization,* Computers and Graphics, 26, 535–555.

Vanderheiden, G. C. (2000). Fundamental principles and priority setting for universal usability. *Proceedings of the ACM—Universal Usability Conference, Washington, DC* (pp. 32–38). New York: ACM Press.

Vanderheiden, G. C. (2001). Telecommunications—Accessibility and future directions. In C. Nicolle & J. Abascal (Eds.), *Inclusive design guidelines for HCI* (pp. 239–257). London: Taylor & Francis.

Vanderheiden, G. C. (2002). Interaction for diverse users. In J. Jacko and A. Sears (Eds.), *Human-Computer Interaction Handbook* (pp. 397–400). Mahwah, NJ: Erlbaum.

VanLehn, K. A. (1990). *Mind bugs: The origins of procedural misconceptions.* Cambridge, MA: MIT Press.

Vardi, M. Y., Finin, T., and Henderson, T. (2003). 2001–2002 Taulbee Survey results. *Computing Research News 15*(2), 6–13.

Vassileva J. (2002) Supporting Peer-to-Peer User Communities. In R. Meersman, & Z. Tari et al. (Eds.), *On the move to meaningful internet systems 2002: CoopIS, DOA, and ODBASE, Coordinated International Conferences Proceedings* (pp. 230–247). LNCS 2519. Berlin-Heidelberg: Springer Verlag Press.

Veinott, E. S., Olson, J. S., Olson, G. M., and Fu, X. (1997). Video matters! When communication ability is stressed, video helps. In S. Pemberton (Ed.), *Proceedings of the ACM Conference on Human Factors in Computing Systems, CHI '97* (pp. 315–316). New York: ACM Press.

Venuvinod, P. K., & Ma, W. (2004). *Rapid prototyping: Laser-based and other technologies.* Dordrecht, Netherlands: Kluwer.

Verba, S., Schlozman, K., & Brady, H. (1995). *Voice and equality: Civic volunteerism in American politics.* Cambridge, MA: Harvard University Press.

Vercoe, B. (1984). The synthetic performer in the context of live performance. In *Proceedings of the 1984 International Computer Music Conference* (pp. 199–200). San Francisco, CA: International Computer Musical Association.

Vercoe, B., & Puckette, M. (1985). Synthetic rehearsal: Training the synthetic performer. In *Proceedings of the 1984 International Computer Music Conference* (pp. 275–278). San Francisco, CA: International Computer Musical Association.

Verdú, S. (Ed.). (1998). Information Theory: 1948–1998. *IEEE Transactions on Information Theory, 44*(6), 2042–2272.

Vertegaal, R. (1999). The GAZE groupware system: Mediating joint attention in multiparty communication and collaboration. In *Proceedings of CHI '99* (pp. 294–301). Pittsburgh, PA: ACM.

Vertegaal, R., Weevers, I., Sohn, C., & Cheung, C. (2003). GAZE-2: Conveying eye contact in group video conferencing using eye-controlled camera direction. In *Proceedings of CHI '03* (pp. 723–730). Fort Lauderdale, FL: ACM.

Vezza, A. (1978). Applications of information networks. *Proceedings of the IEEE, 66*(11).

Vicente, K. J. (1999). *Cognitive work analysis.* Mahwah, NJ: Erlbaum.

Vicente, K. J. (2002). Ecological interface design: Progress and challenges. *Human Factors, 44*(1), 62–78.

Vickery, B. C. (1960). *Faceted classification: A guide to construction and use of special schemes.* London: Aslib.

Vickery, B. C. (2000*). Classification and indexing in science.* Burlington, MA: Butterworth-Heinemann.

Viegas, F. B., & Donath, J. S. (1999). Chat circles. In *CHI 1999 Conference Proceedings: Conference on Human Factors in Computing Systems* (pp. 9–16). New York: ACM Press.

Viller, S., & Sommerville, I. (2000). Ethnographically informed analysis for software engineers. *International Journal of Human-Computer Studies, 53*, 169–196.

Vinciarelli, A., Bengio, S. & Bunke, H. (2003). Offline recognition of large vocabulary cursive handwritten text. In *Proceedings of the Seventh International Conference on Document Analysis and Recognition* (pp. 1101–1107). Los Alamitos, CA: IEEE.

Viterbi, A. J. (1973). Information theory in the Sixties. *IEEE Transactions on Information Theory, 19*(3), 257–262.

Vitruvius, P. (1950). *The ten books on architecture* (M. H. Morgan, Trans.). New York: Dover Publications.

Voas, J. (1999). A world without risks: Let me out! In *4th IEEE International Symposium on High Assurance Systems Engineering (HASE '99)* (p. 274). Cupertino, CA: IEEE CS Press.

Vonk, R. (1990). *Prototyping: The effective use of CASE technology.* New York: Prentice Hall.

Vonnegut, K. (1952). *Player piano.* New York: Delta.

W3C. (1995–2004). *Hypertext markup language (HTML) home page.* Retrieved March 17, 2004, from http://www.w3.org/MarkUp/

Wactlar, H., & Gong, Y. (1999). Informedia experience-on-demand: Capturing, integrating and communicating experiences across people, time, and space. *ACM Computing Surveys, 31*(9).

Wagner, R., & Fischer, M. (1974). The string-to-string correction problem. *Journal of the ACM, 21*(1), 168–173.

Wahlstrom, J., Hagberg, M., Johnson, P. W., Svensson, J., & Rempel, D. (2002). Influence of time pressure and verbal provocation on physiological and psychological reactions during work with a computer mouse. *European Journal of Applied Physiology, 87*(3), 257–263.

Waibel, A., et al. (2003). Speechalator: two-way speech-to-speech translation on a consumer PDA. In *Proceedings of Eurospeech* (pp. 369–372).

Waldrop, M. M. (2001). *The dream machine: J. C. R. Licklider and the revolution that made computing personal.* New York: Viking.

Waldrop, M. M. (2002, May). Grid computing could put the planet's information-processing power on tap. *Technology Review.*

Walker, B., Kramer, G., & Lane, D. M. (2000). *Psychophysical scaling of sonification mappings.* Retrieved December 10, 2003, from http://www.icad.org/websiteV2.0/Conferences/ICAD2000/PDFs/WalkerKramerLane.pdf

Walker, M. A., Kamm, C. A., & Litman, D. J. (2000). Towards developing general models of usability with PARADISE [Special issue on best practice in spoken dialogue systems]. *Natural Language Engineering, 6*(3–4).

Walker, M., Litman, D., Kamm, C., & Abella, A. (1998). Evaluating spoken dialogue agents with PARADISE: Two case studies. *Computer Speech and Language, 12*(3), 317–347.

Wallace, D., Hughes, B., & Vigil, T. (1999). Star Wars: *The essential guide to droids.* New York: Ballantine.

Wallace, R. M., Kupperman, J., and Krajcik, J. (2002). Science on the Web: Students on-line in a sixth-grade classroom. *The Journal of the Learning Sciences, 9*(1), 75–104.

Walsh, P. (2001). *The Zen of Direct3D game programming.* Roseville, CA: Prima Tech.

Walsham, G. (1998). IT and changing professional identity: Micro studies and macro-theory. *Journal of the American Society for Information Science, 49*(12), 1081–1089.

Walther, J. B. (1996). Computer-mediated communication: Impersonal, interpersonal, and hyperpersonal interaction. *Communication Research, 23*, 3–43.

Wang, J. (2003). Human-computer interaction research and practice in China. *ACM Interactions, 10*(2), 88–96.

Wang, J., Zhai, S., & Su, H. (2001). Chinese input with keyboard and eye-tracking. In *Proceedings of the SIGCHI Conference on*

B I B L I O G R A P H Y

Human Factors in Computing Systems (pp. 349–356). New York: ACM Press.

Wang, X., & Reiter, M. K. (2003). Defending against denial-of-service attacks with puzzle auctions. *Proceedings of the 2003 IEEE Symposium on Security and Privacy* (pp. 78–92).

Want, R., & Hopper, A. (1992, February). Active badges and personal interactive computing objects. *IEEE Transactions of Consumer Electronics, 38*(1), 10–20.

Wargin, J., & Dobiey, D. (2001). E-business and change: Managing the change in the digital economy. *Journal of Change Management, 2*(1), 72–83.

Warm, J. S., Dember, W. N., & Parasuraman, E. (1992). Effects of olfactory stimulation on performance and stress in a visual sustained attention task. *Journal of the Society of Cosmetic Chemists, 42,* 199–210.

Warren, R. M. (1999). *Auditory perception: A new analysis and synthesis.* Cambridge, UK: Cambridge University Press.

Warren, R., & Wertheim, A. H. (1990). *Perception and control of self-motion.* Hillsdale, NJ: Erlbaum.

Warren, S. D., & Brandeis, L. D. (1890). The right to privacy: The implicit made explicit. Reprinted in F. D. Schoeman (Ed.), (1984), *Philosophical dimensions of privacy: An anthology* (pp. 75–103). Cambridge: Cambridge University Press.

Warren, W. H. (1995). Self-motion: Visual perception and visual control. In W. Epstein & S. Rogers (Eds.), *Perception of space and motion* (pp. 263–325). San Diego, CA: Academic Press.

Warshauer, S. C. (1998). Multi-user environment studies: Defining a field of study and four approaches to the design of multi-user environments. *Literary and Linguistic Computing, 13*(4).

Warwick, K. (2000). Cyborg 1.0. *Wired, 8*(2), 144–151.

Waterman, T. H. (1989). *Animal navigation.* New York: Freeman and Scientific American Library.

Waters, D. J. (1998). *The Digital Library Federation: Program agenda.* Washington, DC: Digital Libraries, Council of Library and Information Resources.

Watkins, C. J. C. H. (1989). *Learning from delayed rewards.* Unpublished doctoral dissertation, Cambridge University, Cambridge, UK.

Watson, J. S. (1998). If you don't have it, you can't find it: A close look at students' perceptions of using technology. *Journal of the American Society for Information Science, 49*(11), 1024–1036.

Watt, A. (1993). *3D computer graphics* (2nd ed.). New York: Addison-Wesley.

Watt, A. H., & Watt, M. (1992). *Advanced animation and rendering.* New York: Addison-Wesley.

Watt, A., & Policarpo, F. (2001). *3D games: Real-time rendering and software technology, 1.* New York: ACM Press.

Watts, D. J. (2003). *Six degrees: The science of a connected age.* New York: W. W. Norton.

Wayner, P. (1997). *Digital cash: Commerce on the Net* (2nd ed.). San Francisco: Morgan-Kaufmann.

Weaver, W. (1949). Recent contributions to the mathematical theory of communication. In C. E. Shannon & W. Weaver, *The mathematical theory of communication* (pp. 93–117). Urbana: University of Illinois Press.

Web Accessibility Initiative (WAI). Retrieved July 27, 2003, from http://www.w3.org/WAI/

Webster, F. (1995). *Theories of the information society.* London: Routledge.

Webster, J. G. (1998). *Medical instrumentation application and design* (3rd ed.). New York: Wiley.

Wehner, R., Lehrer, M., & Harvey, W. (Eds.). (1996). Navigation [Special issue]. *Journal of Experimental Biology, 199.*

Weik, M. H. (1961, January/February). The ENIAC story. *Ordnance,* 3–7.

Weinberg, G. (1971). *The psychology of computer programming.* New York: Van Nostrand Reinhold.

Weinberg, J. B., & Stephen, M. L. (2002). Participatory design in a HCI course: Teaching ethnography methods to computer scientists. In *Proceedings of the 33rd SIGCSE Technical Symposium on Computer Science Education* (pp. 237–241). New York: ACM Press.

Weiner, N. (1948). *Cybernetics, or control and communication in the animal and the machine.* Cambridge, MA: MIT Press.

Weiser, E. B. (2002). The functions of Internet use and their social and psychological consequences. *Cyberpsychology and Behavior, 4*(2), 723–743.

Weiser, M. (1991, September). The computer for the twenty-first century. *Scientific American, 265*(3), 94–100.

Weiser, M. (1993, July). Some computer science problems in ubiquitous computing. *Communications of the ACM, 36*(7), 74–84.

Weiss, G. (Ed.). (2000). *Multiagent systems: A modern approach to distributed artificial intelligence.* Cambridge, MA: MIT Press.

Weizenbaum, J. (1966). ELIZA—A computer program for the study of natural language communication between man and machine. *Communications of the ACM, 9*(1), 36–45.

Weizenbaum, J. (1967). Contextual understanding by computers. *Communications of the ACM, 10*(8), 474–480.

Weizenbaum, J. (1976). *Computer power and human reason: From judgment to calculation.* New York: Freeman.

Welch, G., & Foxlin, E. (2002). Motion tracking: No silver bullet, but a respectable arsenal. *IEEE Computer Graphics and Applications* [Special Issue on Tracking], *22*(6), 24–38.

Welch, G., Bishop, G., Vicci, L., Brumback, S., & Keller, K. (1999). The HiBall tracker: High-performance wide-area tracking for virtual and augmented environments. *Proceedings of the ACM Symposium on Virtual Reality Software and Technology 1999,* 1–10.

Weld, D. (1994). An introduction to least commitment planning. *AI Magazine, 15*(4), 27–61.

Weld, D. (1999). Recent advances in AI planning. *AI Magazine, 20*(2), 93–122.

Welk, G. J. (2002). *Physical activity assessments for health-related research.* Champaign, IL: Human Kinetics.

WELL, The. (2002). About the WELL. Retrieved August, 2003, from http://www.well.com/aboutwell.html

Weller, A. C. (2001). *Editorial peer review: Its strengths and weaknesses.* Medford, NJ: Information Today.

Wellman, B. (2001). Physical place and cyberspace: The rise of personalized networks. *International Urban and Regional Research, 25*(2), 227–252.

Wellman, B. (2001). *The persistence and transformation of community: From neighbourhood groups to social networks.* Report to the Law Commission of Canada. Retrieved August 12, 2003, from http://www.chass.utoronto.ca/~wellman/publications/lawcomm/lawcomm7.htm

Wellman, B., & Haythornthwaite, C. (Eds.). (2002). *The Internet in everyday life.* Oxford, UK: Blackwell.

Wellman, B., Boase, J., & Chen, W. (2002). The networked nature of community online and offline. *IT & Society, 1*(1), 151–165.

Wellman, B., Salaff, J., Dimitrova, D., Garton, L., Gulia, M., and Haythornthwaite, C. (1996). Computer networks as social networks: Collaborative work, telework, and virtual community. *Annual Review of Sociology, 22,* 213–238.

Wells, H. G. (1938). *World brain*. Garden City, NY: Doubleday, Doran.

Welter, P. (2003). NetSpell. Retrieved January 20, 2004, from http://www.loresoft.com/Applications/NetSpell/default.aspx

Wenger, E. (1998). *Communities of practice: Learning, meaning, and identity*. Cambridge, UK: Cambridge University Press.

Westfall, R. D. (1997). The telecommuting paradox. *Information Systems Management, 14*(4), 15–20.

Westfall, R. D. (in press). Does telecommuting *really* increase productivity? *Communications of the ACM*.

Westin, A. F. (1970). *Privacy and freedom*. New York: Atheneum.

Wexelblat, A. (1997). Research challenges in gesture: Open issues and unsolved problems. In I. Wachsmuth &M. Fröhlich (Ed.), *Gesture and sign language in human-computer interaction* (pp. 1–12). Berlin, Germany: Springer-Verlag.

Wharton, C., Rieman, J., Lewis, C., & Polson, P. (1994). The cognitive walkthrough method: A practitioner's guide. In J. Nielsen & R. L. Mack (Eds.), *Usability inspection methods* (pp. 105–140). New York: Wiley.

Whitelock, P. (1992). Shake-and-bake translation. In *Proceedings of the 14th International Conference on Computational Linguistics (COLING)* (pp. 784–791).

Whittaker, S. & Sidner, C. (1996). E-mail overload: Exploring personal information management of e-mail. In *Proceedings of Computer-Human Interaction*. New York: ACM Press.

Why compilers are doomed. (April 14, 2002). Retrieved January 20, 2004, from http://www.equi4.com/jcw/wiki.cgi/56.html

Whyte, W. F. (1991). *Participatory action research*. Newbury Park, CA: Sage.

Whyte, W. H. (1988). *City: Return to the center*. New York: Doubleday.

Wiegers, K. (1999). *Software requirements*. Redmond, WA: Microsoft Press..

Wiener, N. (1948). *Cybernetics: Or control and communication in the animal and the machine*. New York: Wiley.

Wiener, N. (1950). *The human use of human beings*. New York: Da Capo Press.

Wiggins, J. S. (Ed.). (1996). *The five-factor model of personality*. New York: Guilford.

Wikipedia. (2004). Retrieved March 9, 2004, from http://www.wikipedia.org/

Wilensky, R., Chin, D., Luria, M., Martin, J., Mayfield, J., & Wu, D. (1988). The Berkeley UNIX Consultant project. *Computational Linguistics, 14*(4), 35–84.

Wilheim, A. G. (2000). *Democracy in the digital age: Challenges to political life in cyberspace*. New York: Routledge.

Wilks, Y. (Ed.). (1999). *Machine conversations*. Dordrect, Netherlands: Kluwer Academic.

Wilks, Y., Slator, B., & Guthrie, L. (1996). *Electric words: Dictionaries, computers and meanings*. Cambridge, MA: MIT Press.

Williams, R. (2001). *The animator's survival kit*. New York: Faber & Faber.

Williams, T. (1998). *City of golden shadow*. New York: DAW Books.

Williamson, J. (1950). *The humanoids*. New York: Grosset and Dunlap.

Wilson, A. D., Bobick, A. F., & Cassell, J. (1996). Recovering temporal structure of natural gesture. *Proceedings of the International Conference on Face and Gesture Recognition*. Killington, VT

Wilson, D. A., & Stevenson, R. J. (in press). Olfactory perceptual learning: The critical role of memory in odor discrimination. *Neuroscience and Biobehavioral Reviews*.

Wilson, E. O. (1998). *Consilience: The unity of knowledge*. New York: Knopf.

Wilson, G. F. (2001). Real-time adaptive aiding using psychophysiological operator state assessment. In D. Harris (Ed.), *Engineering psychology and cognitive ergonomics* (pp. 175–182). Aldershot, UK: Ashgate.

Wilson, M. (2002). Six views of embodied cognition. *Psychonomic Bulletin & Review, 9*(4), 625–636.

Wilson, P. (1973). Situational relevance. *Information Storage and Retrieval, 9*(8), 457–471.

Wilson, R. A., & Keil, F. C. (Eds.). (2001). *The MIT encyclopedia of the cognitive sciences (MITECS)*. Cambridge, MA: MIT Press.

Winkels, R. (1992). *Explorations in intelligent tutoring systems and help*. Amsterdam: IOS Press.

Winkler, T. (1998). *Composing interactive music*. Cambridge, MA: MIT Press.

Wright, M., Freed, A., Lee, A., Madden, T., and Momeni, A. (2001). Managing complexity with explicit mapping of gestures to sound control with OSC. In *Proceedings of the 2001International Computer Music Conference* (pp. 314–317). San Francisco, CA: International Computer Musical Association.

Winograd, T. (1972). *Understanding natural language*. New York: Academic Press.

Winograd, T. (1987/1988). A language/action perspective on the design of cooperative work. *Human-Computer Interaction, 3*(1), 3–30.

Winograd, T., & Flores, F. (1986). *Understanding computers and cognition: A new foundation for design*. Norwood, NJ: Ablex.

Winston, A. (1992). *Artificial intelligence* (3rd ed.). Reading, MA: Addison-Wesley.

Wise, J. A. (1999). The ecological approach to text visualization. *Journal of the American Society for Information Science, 50*, 1224–1233.

Witte, J. C. (2003). The case for multimethod design. In P. N. Howard & S. Jones (Eds.), *Society Online* (pp. xv–xxxiv). Thousand Oaks, CA: Sage.

Witte, J. C., & Howard, P. E. N. (2002). Technological & methodological innovation in survey instruments: The future of polling. In F. Cook & J. Manza (Eds.), *Navigating public opinion* (pp. 272—289) Oxford, UK: Oxford University Press.

Witte, J. C., & Pargas, R. P. (2003). The OnQ survey database system: Architecture and implementation. *The impact of technology on the survey process:* In R. Banks, et al. (Eds.), *Proceedings of the 4th International Conference on Survey and Statistical Computing* (pp. 121–132). Chesham Bucks, UK: Association for Survey Computing.

Witte, J. C., Amoroso, L. M., & Howard, P. E. N. (2000). Method and representation in Internet-based survey tools: mobility, community, and cultural identity in Survey 2000. *Social Science Computer Review, 18*(2), 179–195.

Witten, I. H., & Frank, E. (1999). *Data mining: Practical machine learning tools and techniques with Java implementations*. San Francisco, CA: Morgan Kaufmann.

Witten, J., & Bainbridge, D. (2002). *How to build a digital library*. San Francisco, CA: Morgan Kaufmann.

Wobbrock, J. (2003). The benefits of physical edges in gesture-making: Empirical support for an edge-based unistroke alphabet. In *Proceedings of the SIGCHI Conference on Human Factors and Computing Systems* (pp. 942–943). New York: Association for Computing Machinery.

Wolbring, G. (2003). Science and technology and the triple D (Disease, Disability, Defect). In M. C. Roco & W. S. Bainbridge (Eds.), *Converging technologies for improving human performance* (pp. 232–243). Dordrecht, Netherlands: Kluwer.

Wolf, W. (2001). *Computers as components*. San Francisco: Morgan Kaufmann Publishers.

Wolfman, S. A., Lau, T. A., Domingos, P., & Weld, D. S. (2001). Mixed initiative interfaces for learning tasks: SMARTedit talks back. In *Proceedings of the International Conference on Intelligent User Interfaces* (pp. 67–174). New York: ACM Press.

Wolpaw, J. R., Birbaumer, N., McFarland, D., Pfurtscheller, G., & Vaughan, T. (2002). Brain-computer interfaces for communication and control. *Clinical Neurophysiology, 113*, 767–791.

Wolpaw, J. R., McFarland, D. J., & Vaughan, T. M. (2000). Brain-computer interface research at the Wadsworth Center. *IEEE Transactions on Rehabilitation Engineering, 8*(2), 222–226.

Woo, M., Neider, J., Davis, T., & Shreiner, D. (1999). *OpenGL® programming guide: The official guide to learning OpenGL, version 1.4* (4th ed.). Reading, MA: Addison-Wesley.

Woods, D. D., & Roth, E. M. (1988). Cognitive systems engineering. In M. Helander (Ed.), *Handbook of human computer interaction* (pp. 3–35). Amsterdam: Elsevier.

Woods, S. Carrière, S. J. Kazman, R. (1999). A semantic foundation for architectural reengineering and interchange. In *Proceedings of IEEE International Conference on Software Maintenance* (391–398). Los Alamitos, CA: IEEE Computer Society Press.

Worboys, M. F. (1995). *GIS: A computing perspective*. New York: Taylor and Francis.

World Internet Project Japan. (2002*). Internet usage trends in Japan: Survey report*. Tokyo: Institute of Socio-Information and Communication Studies, Tokyo University.

World-Wide Web Consortium (W3C). Retrieved September 30, 2003, from http://www.w3.org

Wresch, W. (1998). Disconnected: Haves and have-nots in the information age. In K. Schellenberg (Ed.), *Computers in society* (7th ed.; pp. 207–212). Guilford, CT: Dushkin/McGraw Hill.

Wu, M. W., & Lin, Y. D. (2001). Open source development: An overview. *IEEE Computer*, 33–38.

Wu, S. T., & Yang, D. K. (2001). *Reflective liquid crystal displays*. New York: Wiley SID.

Wulf, W.A. (1993). The collaboratory opportunity. *Science, 261*, 854–855.

Wurman, R. S. (1989). *Information anxiety*. New York: Doubleday.

Yaar, A., Perrig, A., & Song, D. (2003). Pi: A path identification mechanism to defend against DDoS attacks. *IEEE Symposium on Security and Privacy* (pp. 93–107).

Yacoob, Y., & Davis, L. (1994). Computing spatio-temporal representations of human faces. In *Proceedings of the Computer Vision and Pattern Recognition Conference* (pp. 70–75). New York: IEEE Computer Society.

Yager, S. E., & Berry, R. L. (2002). Preparing end user support specialists. *Journal of Education for Business, 78*(2), 92–96.

Yakel, E. (in press). The social construction of accountability: Radiologists and their recordkeeping practices. *Information Society*.

Yamada, K., & Knight, K. (2001). A syntax-based statistical translation model. In *Proceedings of the 39th Meeting of the Association for Computational Linguistics (ACL)* (pp. 523–530).

Yamamoto, H. (1999). Case studies of producing mixed reality worlds. In *Proceedings of the 1999 IEEE International Conference on Systems, Man, and Cybernetics (SMC'99)* (pp. 42–47). Piscataway, NJ: IEEE.

Yamanaka, T., Matsumoto, R., & Nakamoto, T. (2003). Study of recording apple flavor using odor recorder with five components. *Sensors and Actuators B: Chemical, 89*(1–2), 112–119.

Yamato, J., Ohya, J., & Ishii, K. (1992). Recognizing human action in time-sequential images using hidden Markov Model. *Proceedings of the IEEE Conference on Computer Vision and Pattern Recognition*, 379–385.

Yamato, J., Ohya, J., & Ishii, K. (1993). Recognizing human action in time-sequential images using hidden Markov models. *Transactions of the Institute of Electronics, Information and Communication Engineers, J76D-II*(12), 2556–2563.

Yanco, H. A., Drury, J. L., &. Scholtz, J. (2004) Beyond usability evaluation: Analysis of human-robot interaction at a major robotics competition. *Human-Computer Interaction, 19*(1–2).

Yang, M.-H., & Ahuja, N. (1999, June). *Recognizing hand gesture using motion trajectories*. Paper presented at the IEEE Conference on Computer Vision and Pattern Recognition, Ft. Collins, CO. Retrieved August 19, 2003, from http://vision.ai.uiuc.edu/mhyang/papers/cvpr99.pdf

Yang, Q. (1997). *Intelligent planning: A decomposition and abstraction based approach*. New York: Springer-Verlag.

Yang, S., Burnett, M. M., DeKoven, E., & Zloof, M. (1997). Representation design benchmarks: A design-time aid for VPL navigable static representations. *Journal of Visual Languages and Computing, 8*(5/6), 563–599.

Yannakoudakis, E. J., & Fawthrop, D. (1983). The rules of spelling errors. *Information Processing and Management, 19*(2), 89–99.

Yates, J. (1993). *Control through communication: The rise of system in American management*. Baltimore, MD: Johns Hopkins University Press

Yee, N. (2002). *Befriending ogres and wood elves: Understanding relationship formation in MMORPGs*. Retrieved January 16, 2004, from http://www.nickyee.com/hub/relationships/home.html

Yeffeth, G. (Ed.). (2003). *Taking the red pill: Science, philosophy, and religion in* The Matrix. Dallas, TX: Benbella.

Yeh, P., & Gu, C. (1999). *Optics of liquid crystal displays*. New York: John Wiley and Sons.

Yeh, Y.C. (1998). Design considerations in Boeing 777 fly-by-wire computers. In *3rd IEEE High Assurance Systems Engineering Conference (HASE)* (pp. 64–73). Cupertino, CA: IEEE CS Press.

Yeo, A. (1996). World-wide CHI: Cultural user interfaces, a silver lining in cultural diversity. *SIGCHI Bulletin, 28*(3), 4–7. Retrieved March 1, 2004, from http://www.acm.org/sigchi/bulletin/1996.3/international.html

Yokoo, M. (1998). *Distributed constraint satisfaction*. New York: Springer.

York, D. G., Adelman, J., Anderson, J. E., Jr., Anderson, S. F., Annis, J., Bahcall, N. A., et al. (2000, September). The Sloan Digital Sky Survey: Technical summary. *The Astronomical Journal, 120*(3), 1579–1587.

Young, J. R. (1994). *Textuality and cyberspace: MUD's and written experience*. Retrieved July 31, 2003, from http://ftp.game.org/pub/mud/text/research/textuality.txt

Young, K. S. (1998). *Caught in the Net*. New York: Wiley.

Young, K. S. (2001). *Tangled in the web: Understanding cybersex from fantasy to addiction*. Bloomington, IN: 1st Books Library.

Young, R., & Simon, T. (1988). Planning in the context of Human-Computer Interaction. *Proceedings of the Conference of the British Computer Society Human-Computer Interaction Specialist Group*, 363–370.

Youngman, M., & Scharff, L. (1998). *Text width and margin width influences on readability of GUIs*. Southwest Psychological Association.

BIBLIOGRAPHY

Retrieved July 27, 2003, from http://hubel.sfasu.edu/research/textmargin.html

Yourdon, E. (1989). *Structured walkthroughs* (4th ed.). Englewood Cliffs, NJ: Yourdon Press.

Zachmann, G., & Rettig, A. (2001) Natural and robust interaction in virtual assembly simulation. *Eighth ISPE International Conference on Concurrent Engineering: Research and Applications, 425–434.*

Zahedi, F. (1993). *Intelligent systems for business.* Belmont, CA: Wadsworth.

Zakaria, N., Stanton, J. M., & Sarkar-Barney, S. (2003). Designing and implementing culturally sensitive IT applications: he interaction of culture values and privacy issues in the Middle East. *Information Technology and People, 16,* 49–75.

Zakon, R. H. (1993). *Hobbes' Internet timeline.* Retrieved March 31, 2004, from http://www.zakon.org/robert/internet/timeline

Zapthink. (2002). *Key XML specifications and standards.* Retrieved January 22, 2004, from http://www.oasis-open.org/committees/download.php/173/xml%20standards.pdf

Zelazny, R. (1975, November). Home is the hangman. *Analog Science Fiction and Fact, 95*(11).

Zeleznik, R., Herndon, K. P., & Hughes, J. F. (1996). SKETCH: An interface for sketching 3-D scenes. In *SIGGraph '96 Conference Proceedings* (pp. 163–170). New York: ACM Press.

Zhai, S. (1995). *Human performance in six degree of freedom input control.* Unpublished Ph.D. Thesis, University of Toronto.

Zhai, S. (1998). User performance in relation to 3D input device design. *Computer Graphics, 32*(4), 50–54.

Zhai, S., & Smith, B. A. (1999). An experimental study of document scrolling methods. *IBM Systems Journal, 38*(4), 642–651.

Zhai, S., Kristensson, P.-O., & Smith, B. A. (2004). In search of effective text input interfaces for off the desktop computing. *Interacting with Computers, 16*(3).

Zhai, S., Morimoto, C., & Ihde, S. (1999). Manual and gaze input cascaded (MAGIC) pointing. In *Proceedings of CHI '99* (pp. 246–253). Pittsburgh, PA: ACM.

Zhang, H. J., Kankanhalli, A., & Smoliar, S. W. (1993). Automatic partitioning of full-motion video. *Multimedia Systems, 1,* 10–28.

Zhang, J. X., & Goodchild, M. F. (2002). *Uncertainty in geographical information.* New York: Taylor and Francis.

Zhang, P., Benbadsat, I., Carey, J., Davis, F., Galleta, D., & Strong, D. (2002). Human-computer interaction research in the MIS discipline. *Communications of the Association. for Information Systems, 9,* 334–355.

Zhong, D., & Chang, S. F. (1999). An integrated approach for content-based video object segmentation and retrieval. *IEEE Transactions on Circuits and Systems for Video Technology, 9*(8), 1259–1268.

Zicarelli, D. (1987). M and jam factory. *Computer Music Journal, 11*(4), 13–29.

Ziv, J., & Lempel, A. (1978). Compression of individual sequences via variable rate coding. *IEEE Transactions on Information Theory*, IT-24, 530–536.

Zue, V. (1985). The use of speech knowledge in automatic speech recognition. *Proceedings of the IEEE, 73*(11), 1602–1615.

BIBLIOGRAPHY

HCI IN POPULAR CULTURE

The HCI in Popular Culture appendix to the *Berkshire Encyclopedia of Human-Computer Interaction* brings together 300 novels, nonfiction books, movies, and television programs—and even some music and plays—that explore imaginative perspectives on our relationship with technology. These popular creations show another side of the world covered in the encyclopedia, and provide historical background as well. Scholars and professionals will find the list thought provoking, and teachers will be able to use it to encourage analysis and discussion. Besides that, it's just plain fun.

We've chosen to be inclusive as we compiled this list. The field now called HCI used to be "man-machine" studies so we've felt free to include a wide variety of early novels and other writings that looked at the relationship between humans and machines. The novel *The Time Machine*, for example, examines the ways people might use technologies to enhance and alter their experience. If some choices seem more obvious than others, this is indicative of the complexity and variety of the field. In some selections, a mechanized world forms the backdrop to the story; in others, the computer is itself a character.

Criticisms of technology and HCI are included here, too. In the science fiction universe of *Dune*, for example, an event known as the Butlerian Jihad creates the noncomputerized world of Herbert's series. The Jihad, occurring ten thousand years before the events of *Dune*, was when the last remaining vestiges of free humanity managed to defeat the thinking machines that threatened to destroy them all. Indeed, the plots of many contemporary science fiction books center on highly evolved computers that turn on their human developers or overseers. We've included a range of these works.

In certain cases, we have taken representative examples of large bodies of works. Most of the novels of H. G. Wells, for example, provide detailed depictions of humans using machines to advance their experiences. Likewise, a number of Philip K. Dick's works have focused on the perils of misused or out-of-control technology. In these cases, a few works have been chosen to represent the many.

Concepts such as virtual reality and visual display screens naturally appear in recent books and films, but our popular culture list also includes some surprising children's classics. After all, can't Alice's adventures in Wonderland, depicted in Lewis Carroll's *Through the Looking Glass* (1872), be seen as examples of virtual reality? And in Disney's *Snow White and the Seven Dwarfs* (1937), the wicked queen's question of "Mirror, mirror on the wall, who's the fairest of them all?" is posed to the cinema's first visual display screen with intelligence—making it an HCI classic as well.

Authors of novels and nonfiction books are noted with these entries. In dramatic stage productions, the author's name is given; however, for musicals, the composer, lyricist, and author are generally included. In movie entries, the director's name is given, while documentaries may include the name of the producer or the director. For television shows, the creator is listed; in music entries, the composer is noted. Dates given generally represent the year the work was first published, produced, or shown. In the case of television programs, the year or years that the show aired are noted.

HCI in Popular Culture is a continuing project that can be accessed by visiting www.berkshirepublishing.com/hcipc/, and we welcome additions. Please visit the current online version and add your favorite works.

FICTION

1984

George Orwell
U.S.A.
1949

Long before the advent of wide-screen television, George Orwell imagined that we'd all have giant screens in our homes by 1984. Unfortunately, instead of watching sports events and movies, the people of 1984 are themselves watched by "Big Brother"—making this novel a classic dystopian view of how technology could invade our lives.

Adam Link—Robot

Eando Binder
U.S.A.
1965

A series of stories about the robot hero, Adam Link, originally written in the late 1930s, presenting the robot as sensitive, humane, courageous, and even romantic.

Blood Music

Greg Bear
U.S.A.
2002

A combination of genetic and electronic technologies create noocytes, viruslike molecular computers that absorb the minds and dissolve the bodies of human beings.

Call Me Joe

Poul Anderson
U.S.A.
1957

A crippled scientist on a Jovian moon uses psionic controls to "inhabit" a humanoid on Jupiter's surface, specially engineered to withstand the planet's climate. His persona gradually merges with the humanoid so that he continues to live on Jupiter even when his human body dies on the moon.

Caves of Steel, The

Isaac Asimov
U.S.A.
1954

Two detectives team up, one human and the other robot, to solve a murder mystery in a future world where no human can psychologically tolerate being outdoors, the only way the killer could have entered, and no robot could kill a human. An important exemplar of the "good robot" genre, with an implicit plea for the cherishing of racial diversity and brotherhood.

Cheaper by the Dozen

Frank B. Gilbreth, Jr., Ernestine Gilbreth Carey
U.S.A.
1948

The best-selling memoir about twelve children and their loving, highly efficient parents—the management engineers Frank and Lillian Gilbreth—who did pioneering work in time-and-motion study.

City and the Stars, The

Arthur C. Clarke
U.S.A. / Sri Lanka
1956

Utopian novel of a society where computerization and robots allow people to concentrate on pleasurable things. Written in dialogue with the "The Machine Stops". Yet life has become meaningless in such a utopia, and when the first new human in millennia is born, he searches for a more meaningful life.

Codgerspace

Alan Dean Foster
U.S.A.
1992

A melting cheese sandwich fouls up the artificial intelligence of household appliances being manufactured. Suddenly, toasters, dishwashers, and vacuum cleaners revolt, as they search for meaning of life. Five senior citizens (along with their food processor) wind up with the fate of the galaxy in their hands.

Computer Connection, The

Alfred Bester
U.S.A.
1974

Trauma transfers the personality of a scientist into his supercomputer, where he proves to be a not very nice person.

Computer War

Mack Reynolds
U.S.A.
1967

The rules of a technologically advanced nation mistakenly believe their computer analyses will allow them to triumph over a less bellicose and industrialized nation.

Cryptonomicon

Neal Stephenson
U.S.A.
1999

A novel of codes and cyphers and unraveling them, from breaking Nazi codes in World War II to supposedly unbreakable codes of modern times. Features a supposedly secure data haven in the Pacific, and electronic eavesdropping of computer keys through a wall. Heroes and villains are all very computer-literate.

Diamond Age, The

Neal Stephenson
U.S.A.
1995

The air around the protagonists—and the novel—are permeated with nanotechnology robots that see, sniff, and kill.

FICTION

Diaspora

Greg Egan
U.S.A.
1999

It's the thirtieth century, and most of the population is no longer human, but rather beings downloaded into virtual reality software or robots.

Difference Engine, The

William Gibson, Bruce Sterling
U.S.A.
1992

What if Charles Babbage had actually gotten to build his "Analytical Engine" computer in the nineteenth century? This mystery novel describes the steam-driven cyber society that might have arisen in late Victorian England, 1885.

Down and Out in the Magic Kingdom

Cory Doctorow
U.S.A.
2003

Disney World lives into the future, and so do humans since death has been conquered. The main character takes up residence in Disney World, and he is dismayed to find out that the quaint technology of the Hall of Presidents is to be changed. Now a direct-to-brain interface will allow people to have the illusion of being Washington and Lincoln, rather than watching a life-size animatron.

Dune

Frank Herbert
U.S.A.
1987

Computers, as such, don't exist in this classic science-fiction story set in essentially pre-industrial societies of the distant future. Yet, certain human "mentats" have computer-like reasoning skills (which doesn't prevent them from doing foolish things), the only ones who can navigate space are members of the Guild who have developed the computational ability to see the currents of space at the cost of human form, and a motion-seeking missile that almost kills the hero must have computer-linked sensors to work.

Ender's Game

Orson Scott Card
U.S.A.
1977

In a world on the brink of interstellar war, young geniuses are collected in a space station and trained using a computer game designed to use images from the child's subconscious mind.

Exit Strategy

Douglas Rushkoff
U.S.A.
2002

Originally published as an open source novel online, in which readers could add things. Set in the near future (2008), the plot is about a man caught between venture capitalists and hackers.

Feeling of Power, The

Issac Asimov
U.S.A.
1957

In the future, only computers know how to do math, including simple times tables and long division. It seems pointless for humans to know how. When Earth is threatened by alien invasion and its computers aren't working, one nostalgic fellow who has kept his math skills alive saves the planet. A neat tale of the human ingenuity genre.

Friday

Robert Heinlein
U.S.A.
1969

A rare event: the cyborg is a woman—a secret courier with enhanced intelligence, fighting, and lovemaking ability.

Humanoids, The

Jack Williamson
U.S.A.
1950

Robots become such perfect servants of human beings that human life itself loses all purpose.

FICTION

I, Robot

Isaac Asimov
U.S.A.
1950

The first of Asimov's influential stories about the ethical imperatives, limitations and dilemmas of human-robot interactions. Sets forth The Three Laws of Robotics that are wired into their "positronic" brains: 1. A robot may not injure a human being or, through inaction, allow a human being to come to harm. 2. A robot must obey the orders give it by human beings except where such orders would conflict with the First Law. 3. A robot must protect its own existence as long as such protection does not conflict with the First or Second Law. Influential in urging the acceptance of robots and technology as potentially benign.

Marvelous Land of Oz, The

L. Frank Baum
U.S.A.
1904

Dorothy returns to magical Oz, gaining a friend who is among the very first robots of literature: Tik-Tok, a mechanical man.

Microserfs

Douglas Coupland
U.S.A.
1995

Life as a computer person in a (fictionalized) Microsoft and then in a small Silicon Valley dot-com startup.

Mind Readers

Margery Allingham
U.S.A.
1965

Two boys stir controversy and drama when it is discovered they have a device to communicate telepathically.

Moon Is a Harsh Mistress, The

Robert A. Heinlein
U.S.A.
1966

On the Moon, a computer gains so much processing power that it becomes conscious and leads the oppressed residents of the Moon in a rebellion against the Earth.

Naked Sun, The

Issac Asimov
U.S.A.
1957

A murder mystery set in the future on the planet of Solaria. Residents have a strong norm of never seeing each other in person. They communicate by 3D hologram, and they are tended to by robots. But one day, a resident is killed. Who could have done it, if robots are hard-wired not to kill and residents are soft-wired not to have in-person contact?

Net Force

Tom Clancy, Steve R. Pieczenik
U.S.A.
1998

The first of a series of novels by various authors (under the Tom Clancy brand) about a government agency that defends Internet against criminals, spies, and terrorists.

Neuromancer

Wiliam Gibson
U.S.A.
1984

The seminal human-computer interaction novel which developed the notion of people "jacking in" to the Web through electrodes that connect directly to the brain. The term "cyberspace" was popularized (and possibly invented) here. Contains pioneering depictions of virtual reality, Internet-like communication, and visual data structures.

FICTION

Nine Billion Names of God, The

Arthur C. Clarke
U.S.A.
1953

In this short story, lamas in an isolated Tibetan monastery acquired a sequence analyzing computer to speed up compiling the nine billion names of God from 15,000 years to 100 days. As the computer finishes on the 100th day, the world comes to an end.

Pattern Recognition

William Gibson
U.S.A.
2003

Folks in this book communicate as much by 1:1 e-mail and group chat as they do in-person. The group chat is about a mysterious set of computer-rendered videos that keep appearing online, with aficionados wanting to piece together their plot and their meaning. One of the few novels showing contemporary technologically adept people who are not government or criminal warriors.

Permutation City

Greg Egan
U.S.A.
1994

Experiments uploading human personalities to computers produce unexpected and dramatic results.

Player Piano

Kurt Vonnegut
U.S.A.
1952

Automation has already eliminated all working class jobs, and now it begins to eliminate the need for middle class jobs, including those of the engineers who created the technology. The result is not utopia.

Prey

Michael Crichton
U.S.A.
2002

A chiller in which the union of biotechnology and nanotechnology produces a monster that consists of microscopic specks floating in the air that possess

collective intelligence like that currently explored with swarm robots.

Robots and Empire

Isaac Asimov
U.S.A.
1985

Concluding volume in the Spacer-Earth struggle that started with Caves of Steel. Earth is saved from destruction when a robot formulates a new Zeroth law: The prevention of harm to human beings in groups and to humanity as a whole comes before the prevention of harm to any specific individual.

Robots Have No Tails

Lewis Padgett
U.S.A.
1952

Lewis Padgett is a pseudonym for the husband and wife team of Henry Kuttner and C.L. Moore. All of their robot stories are germane to HCI. One, "The Proud Robot," features a robot that opens beer cans. His lazy and brilliant inventor also stops a corporate giant from driving video watchers from their homes and into large theaters. This is accomplished by inventing a subliminal sound system that only bothers people when amplified in large theaters.

Robots of Dawn

Isaac Asimov
U.S.A.
1983

In the future, the planet Solaria is peopled by humans and humanoid robots. Having the robots do everything means that the humans do not know how to fulfill many everyday tasks. That is why only the people of Earth—who have resisted robots—can undertake journeys to unexplored new worlds.

Shade's Children

Garth Nix
U.S.A.
1997

In a grim future, sadistic overlords rule the world. A group of children with special powers fight back, led by the single adult surviving the disaster, whose per-

FICTION

sonality was downloaded into a computer, where he is slowly going mad.

Ship Who Sang, The

Anne McCaffrey
U.S.A.
1969

Helva is born deformed, but her advanced society has a solution: she is encapsulated in a titanium shell, her brainstem wired directly into the controls of a starship. She can only see and hear via the cameras and microphones of her ship.

Shockwave Rider, The

John Brunner
U.S.A.
1975

A prophetic early novel of home computers, Internet, and information warfare in cyberspace.

Snow Crash

Neal Stevenson
U.S.A.
1992

Finely detailed (and often funny) novel of life in which both cyberspace and "real life" interpenetrate. Foreshadowed much of virtual community and the Web, and influencing thinking about their development.

Software

Rudy Rucker
U.S.A.
1982

Intelligent robots take over the Moon, then return to Earth in order to reward their inventor by transforming him into a robot as well.

Starship Troopers

Robert Heinlein
U.S.A.
1959

The first scenes of this novel vividly depict how a soldier of the future fights aliens while encased in full, computer-assisted body armor that gives him enhanced sensory perception, mobility, and targeting ability. Not in the (poor) movie version.

Survival Ship and Other Stories

Judith Merril
Canada
1973

"The Lady Was A Tramp" is told from the point of view of a woman who has spaceman lovers. Yet this woman is a spaceship (with all of its controls) who has sensual symbiotic relationships with her crew.

Terminal Experiment, The

Robert J. Sawyer
U.S.A.
1995

A computer scientist uploads copies of himself to his computer system, experimenting with removing some of his characteristics, thereby creating a murderer.

The Machine Stops

E.M. Forster
U.K.
1909

This anti-utopian short story by the author of *A Passage to India* describes a future society in which people rarely leave their apartments and all needs and interactions are mediated by The Machine (anticipating a super-super-computer). Civilization falls and most of the world dies when The Machine breaks down. The earliest, and still one of the best, cautionary tales of over-technologization.

FICTION

This Perfect Day

Ira Levin
U.S.A.
1991

A world with a global government, where super-computers are combined into one colossus—UniComp. Personal characteristics are programmed before birth, and UniComp decides every facet of one's life. The main character of the story, Chip, starts to question life as he knows it.

Through the Looking Glass

Lewis Carroll
U.K.
1872

Alice steps through the looking-glass portal and has many virtual reality adventures, some quite Jabberwocky. Sequel to *Alice's Adventures in Wonderland*.

Time Machine, The

H.G. Wells
U.K.
1934

The original influential time-travel story in which a contemporary man travels to the future and finds utopia and dystopia.

True Names

Vernor Vinge
U.S.A.
1981

This science fiction story invents an ultimate human-computer interface and tells a rich story of the life of human hackers and their battle with an artificial intelligence for mastery of a world-spanning computer network. This novella was so visionary but yet so close to upcoming scientific developments that it became both an accurate predictor and an inspiration for new research and developments.

Two Faces of Tomorrow, The

James P. Hogan
U.S.A.
1979

In this futuristic novel, life on Earth is controlled by a worldwide computer network that is logical but lacking in common sense. A powerful, self-aware and self-programming supercomputer, endowed with judgment, is tested out. Unfortunately for humanity, the computer proves all too powerful.

Unnatural Exposure

Patricia Cornwell
U.S.A.
1997

Best-selling chiller-thriller author has made computers and e-mail an integral part of her novels. Cybercrime and cyber insecurity crop up frequently. In this installment of the series about medical examiner Kay Scarpetta, Dr. Scarpetta is stalked in cyberspace by a killer who in the real world is using a store of deadly viruses to commit a string of murders.

Vulcan's Hammer

Philip K. Dick
U.S.A.
1960

Vulcan III, a supercomputer, is given control of the world after a nuclear war. However, when humans try to take back that control, Vulcan isn't eager to oblige.

Waldo and Magic Inc

Robert A. Heinlein
U.S.A.
1950

A physically disabled genius compensates for his weakness by means of teleoperation of robotic arms and other devices.

When H.A.R.L.I.E. Was One

David Gerrold
U.S.A.
1974

A computer named H.A.R.L.I.E. (Human Analog Robot, Life Input Equivalents) is the recipient of all human knowledge. However, H.A.R.L.I.E.'s mission of reproducing the human brain's capacity to the nth degree is becoming decidedly compromised by some human emotions that appear to be creeping into the robot.

FICTION

When the Tripods Came

John Christopher
U.S.A.
1988
Aliens take over the world using a sinister technique—mind control helmets wired to keep the wearer docile and unthinking.

With Folded Hands

Jack Williamson
U.S.A.
1954
Perfect humanoids take over all aspects of human life, for their Prime Directive is "to serve and obey, and guard men from harm"—whether people like it or not.

Worthing Saga, The

Orson Scott Card
U.S.A.
1990
Short stories chronicle the rise and fall of a space-going civilization in which the elite store their minds in machines for decades while their bodies are preserved, making long-term plans feasible once the memories have been re-uploaded into the brain.

NON-FICTION

Age of Spiritual Machines, The

Ray Kurzweil
U.S.A.
1999
Kurzweil gives a nonfiction perspective to a favorite topic of sci-fi, high-tech fiction: What happens when computers go beyond the computational powers of human intelligence. According to Kurzweil, it's due to happen around 2020.

As We May Think

Vannevar Bush
U.S.A.
1945
This July 1945 article by the Director of the Office of Scientific Research and Development lays out a post World War II research agenda, focusing on making more accessible stores of knowledge. Foresees in broad detail the Web and personal digital assistants, forerunners of 2004's Palms.

Atlas of Cyberspace

Martin Dodge, Rob Kitchin
U.S.A.
2002
A visual feast of maps that show the rich and varied landscapes of the Internet, the Web and other emerging cyberspaces. This comprehensive catalog reviews the last thirty years of cyberspace research and motivates and explains major mapping and visualization techniques. The continuously updated online version of the Atlas of Cyberspaces can be found at http://www.cybergeography.org/atlas/atlas.html

Avatars!

Bruce Damer
U.S.A.
1998
This book and the CD-ROM take you on a guided tour to eight virtual world systems: Worlds Chat Space Station, The Palace, AlphaWorld, WorldsAway, OnLine! Traveler, Virtual Places, Comic Chat, and Oz Virtual. You learn how to design an avatar—as a virtual representation of yourself—and how to create your very own virtual world. Besides you will find out about the technical features, cultures, and social etiquette of diverse virtual worlds. The book is a great introduction and documentation of the beginnings of a global brave new world that may soon become our virtual home.

Building the Virtual State: Information Technology and Institutional Change

Jane Fountain
U.S.A.
2001
Describes the implications of how governments use—and could use—the Internet to relate to citizens. Questions such as who pays for government websites, which agencies will maintain the sites, and who will ensure that the privacy of citizens is respected reveal the obstacles that confront efforts to create a virtual state.

Caught in the Net

Kimberly S. Young
U.S.A.
1998
The subtitle to this book explains its mission: How to recognize the signs of Internet Addiction, and a winning strategy for recovery.

Changing Connectivity: A Future History of Y2.03K

Barry Wellman
U.K.
2000
The social implications of probable or possible human computer interfaces to the year 2030.

Code and Other Laws of Cyberspace

Lawrence Lessig
U.S.A.
1999
Describes the implicit and explicit norms that govern design and use of software and the Internet. The argument of this book is that the invisible hand of cyberspace is building an architecture that is quite the opposite of what it was at cyberspace's birth. It is constructing an architecture that makes possible efficient regulation and control.

Cognitive Style of Power Point, The

Edward Tufte
U.S.A.
2003
This short book argues that Power Point slide presentations inherently oversimplify arguments by reducing them to linear, hierarchial sets of bullets. Moreover, they are often badly done.

Communities in Cyberspace

Peter Kollock, Marc Smith
U.S.A.
1998
A collection of accounts of how people find community online.

Community Building on the Web

Amy Jo Kim
U.S.A.
2000
An experienced practitioner gives practical advice on how to build and maintain virtual communities.

Connections

Lee Sproull, Sara Kiesler
U.S.A.
1991
An integrated account of early laboratory experiments comparing computer mediated communication with other forms of communication, especially face-to-face. The focus is on social psychology and small group interactions.

Culture of the Internet

Sara Kiesler
U.S.A.
1997
A collection of descriptions of how people are using the Internet for work and community.

Cyborg: Digital Destiny and Human Possibility in the Age of the Wearable Computer

Steve Mann, Hal Niedzviecki
Canada
2001
Mann, one of the first inventors of wearable computing, presents the humanistic case for humankind to become computer-enhanced cyborgs. He also describes his quest to level the playing fields between humans and bureaucracies.

Designing Web Usability: The Practice of Simplicity

Jakob Nielsen
U.S.A.
1999

Discusses of Web usability in terms of page, content, site, and intranet design. Emphasizes good engineering for usability over self-expression.

Digital Divide

Pippa Norris
U.K.
2001

How the digital divide in computer and Internet use can widen or narrow the gap between social classes and social groups. Examines the evidence for access and use of the Internet in 179 nations across the world. Argues that a global divide is evident between industrialized and developing societies. There is also a social divide between rich and poor within each nation. And a democratic divide is emerging between those who do and do not use Internet resources to engage, mobilize and participate in public life.

Digital Illusion: Entertaining the Future with High Technology

Clark Dodsworth
U.S.A.
1997

This book is summed up well in the following quote from Bran Ferren of Walt Disney Imagineering Research and Development: "In worlds where storytelling is a science, the 'Big Idea' is king, and fantasy makes good business sense, this is an excellent overview, not just of the technology, but of the personal points of view of many of the professionals who make it happen."

Digital Sublime, The: Myth, Power, and Cyberspace

Vincent Mosco
U.S.A.
2004

Explores the myths constructed around new digital technologies, such as the dot-com stock frenzy. Argues for a cultural analysis that such myths are

stories to lift people out of everyday life into the possibility of the sublime.

Distributed Work

Pamela Hinds, Sara Keisler
U.S.A.
2002

A number of scholars write reasonable essays describing how people work together online.

DOS for Dummies

Dan Goodkin
U.S.A.
1993

This guide to IBM's Disk Operating System (DOS) created a new category of books for "dummies," "idiots," and other folks who wanted basic guides to computers and other complexities of life.

Elements of User Experience: User-Centered Design for the Web, The

Jesse James Garrett
U.S.A.
2002

Explanations and illustrations for user-centered web design that focus on ideas rather than tools or techniques. Discussion ranges from strategy and requirements to information architecture and visual design.

e-Living: Life in a Digital Europe

Ben Anderson, et al.
U.K.
2004

A European consortium providing a large number of readable reports about the intersection of computer mediated communication and everyday life in a number of European countries.

Encyclopedia of Community
Karen Christensen, David Levinson
U.S.A.
2003
The four large volumes include fifty articles about the Internet and community, defined quite broadly.

Feminism Confronts Technology
Judy Wajcman
U.K.
1991
Argues that there is a need to understand the gendered design, use, and control of technology: how it differs between women and men. States that cultural and ideological differences often situate women as technologically incompetent. Within the context of a feminist analysis, she examines the relations of power between men and women in how technology is discussed and developed.

Future of Ideas, The
Lawrence Lessig
U.S.A.
2001
Argues that corporations, governments and other forces are using law and technology to control the use of the Internet and limit creativity. Discusses copyright and open source development.

Hanging Out in the Virtual Pub
Lori Kendall
U.S.A.
2002
Rich account of life in a virtual community.

History of Modern Computing, A
Paul Ceruzzi
U.S.A.
2003 (2d ed)
This well-written, comprehensive history of computing since 1945 shows how humans, corporations, and governments shaped computer hardware, software, and uses.

I Owe Russia $1200
Bob Hope
U.S.A.
1963
"Back in the [United] States a reporter asked [comedian Bob Hope] if they had television in Russia, and without thinking, [he] replied, 'Yes. But it watches you.'"

In the Age of the Smart Machine
Shoshana Zuboff
U.S.A.
1988
Ethnographic depiction of how large-scale computerization was introduced to a large organization in the era just before the advent of personal computing.

Information Age (2nd ed.), The
Manuel Castells
U.K.
2000-2004
Trilogy of three major books considering the social, economic, interpersonal, political, and cultural transformations associated with the Internet and information. The books are: *The Rise of the Network Society*; *The Power of Identity*; *End of Millennium*.

Information Anxiety 2
Richard Saul Wurman, David Sume, et al.
U.S.A.
2000
Describes better ways to design and present information clearly. Stresses avoiding data clutter.

Information Utility and Social Choice, The
Sackman Harold, Nie Norman
U.S.A.
1970
A classic work that postulates the notion of a central source for all kinds of information via a terminal that would hook into a TV. The development of the Internet and the World Wide Web has proven the authors prescient.

Inmates Are Running the Asylum, The

Alan Cooper
U.S.A.
1999

Many high-tech applications fail because they are driven by aggressive techies who have little appreciation of what people want and how they are going to use such applications. Subtitled "Why High Tech Products Drive Us Crazy and How To Restore the Sanity," the book argues that programmers need to reevaluate the many user-hostile concepts deeply within the software development process.

Internet Galaxy, The: Reflections on the Internet, Business, and Society

Manuel Castells
U.S.A.
2001

Summarizes the history, social implications and likely future of the Internet, including its ability to simultaneously liberate and exclude

Internet in Everyday Life

Barry Wellman, Caroline Haythornthwaite
U.K.
2002

A collection of essays showing how the Internet is affecting community and community among ordinary people. Unlike most in this genre, looks at non-American as well as American situations.

Internet, The: An Ethnographic Approach

Daniel Miller, Don Slater
U.K.
2000

Fieldwork based story of how the Internet is actually used by a specific society: in this case, Trinidadians—on the island and emigrated abroad.

Leonardo's Laptop: Human Needs and the New Computing Technologies

Ben Shneiderman
U.S.A.
2003

Wondering how Leonardo da Vinci would use a laptop, the book suggests new ways to think about computer use. Emphasizes universal usability. Discusses human relationships and society, and the computer's potential to support creativity, consensus-seeking, and conflict resolution.

Libraries of the Future

J.C.R. Licklider
U.S.A.
1965

A prescient forecast of the Internet by the then-Pophead of the U.S. Advanced Projects Research Agency (ARPA) who funded and encouraged much of the early research.

Life on the Screen

Sherry Turkle
U.S.A.
1995

Case studies of people whose second lives and selves are based on immersive interactions online. Fascinating, but some readers overgeneralized that most people related to computer mediated communication in similar fashion.

Machine in the Garden, The

Leo Marx
U.S.A.
1964

Scene-setting historical account of nineteenth-century concerns about the introduction of machinery into pastoral America. Suggests that concerns about computerization reflect a longstanding tradition.

Monster Under the Bed

Stan David, Jim Botkin
U.S.A.
1994

This book explores the importance of organizations jumping on the "knowledge company" bandwagon as a competitive strategy, as well as the value of training employees to be "knowledge workers."

Myth of the Paperless Office, The

Abigail Sellen, Richard Harper
U.S.A.
2001

Why do people use paper in the digital age? Addresses this question as an entry point into considering the nature of modern work and organizations, and the myths around supposedly obsolete paper and supposedly modern digitization.

NetLab

Barry Wellman, et al.
Canada
2004

Variety of reports about how the Internet is affecting social relations, focusing on the turn of community, work and household ties to "networked individualism."

Network Nation, The

S. Roxanne Hiltz, Murray Turoff
U.S.A.
1993

The second edition of the first scholarly book (1978) to talk about human computer social interactions on the Internet.

Online Communities: Designing Usability and Supporting Sociability

Jenny Preece
U.S.A.
2000

Textbook summarizing knowledge about designing and living in online communities. Covers sociology, design and humanistic practice.

Pew Internet and American Life Project

Lee Rainie, John Horrigan, et al.
U.S.A.
2004

Releases fifteen to twenty reports a year, based on empirical (mostly survey-based) studies of aspects of the Internet and American life, including rural life, teens, politics, religion, strong and weak ties, leisure, music and other downloads.

Readings in Human-Computer Interaction

Ronald Baecker, Jonathan Grudin, et al.
U.S.A.
1995

The editors provide an authoritative, comprehensive, research-based compendium of how people and computers interact. About 1,000 pages.

Simians, Cyborgs, and Women: The Reinvention of Nature

Donna Haraway
U.K.
1991

Collected set of essays that critiques the implicitly masculinist approach to thinking about information and communication technology. Proposes with detailed examples an alternative feminist approach.

Smart Mobs: The Next Social Revolution

Howard Rheingold
U.S.A.
2002

How portable communication and computing—cell phones, wireless, etc.—are going to change society as individuals take their access to connectivity and intelligence with them.

Social Consequences of Internet Use: Access, Involvement, and Interaction

James Katz, Ronald Rice
U.S.A.
2002

Argues that the Internet is a "syntopia" embodying both positive and negative characteristics. Summarizes research into the interplay between the Internet and society, drawing on large U.S. national surveys and case studies.

Soul of a New Machine, The

Tracy Kidder
U.S.A.
1981

Engrossing account of how a Data General team sank their souls and time into designing a new mini-computer.

Surveillance Society

David Lyon
U.K.
2001

Critically examines the nature and potential of monitoring technologies of governments, corporations, and other organizations.

Technology and Social Inclusion: Rethinking the Digital Divide

Mark Warschauer
U.S.A.
2003

Presents different forms of access to—and use of—information and communication technologies. Takes a global perspective and uses case studies to show why different types of people—in less-developed and developed societies—have differential access and use.

Third Wave, The

Alvin Toffler
U.S.A.
1980

Back in 1980, futurist Alvin Toffler accurately predicted the huge effect the "electronic office" would have on society.

Trapped in The Net: The Unanticipated Consequences of Computerization

Gene Rochlin
U.S.A.
1997

Stories about disasters caused by over-computerization and the lack of attention to people's needs, practices, and social structures.

Virtual Community, The

Howard Rheingold
U.S.A.
2000

Second edition of an influential 1993 book that introduced the concept of the virtual community and provided many engrossing details.

Visual Display of Quantitative Information, The

Edward Tufte
U.S.A.
2001 (2d ed)

This classic devotes several hundred pages on how to present information clearly and avoid foolish and misleading uses.

Visual Interfaces to Digital Libraries: Motivation, Utilization, and Socio-Technical Challenges

Katy Borner, Chaomei Chen
U.S.A.
2003

The book presents the state of the art on visual interfaces to digital libraries that aim to exploit the power of human vision and spatial cognition to help individuals mentally organize and electronically access and manage large and complex information spaces.

Weaving the Web

Tim Berners-Lee, Mark Fischetti
U.S.A.
2000

Tim Berners-Lee was the moving force in "weaving" together the many pieces that became the World Wide Web. His story of how that happened is told in this absorbing account written with Mark Fischetti.

World Internet Project

Jeffrey Cole, et al.
U.S.A.
2004

International consortium that provides clear, readable reports about Internet use in a number of countries.

STAGE

Desk Set

William Marchant
U.S.A.
1955

In this comedy, a male efficiency expert tries to computerize the very book-based reference department of a large broadcasting company.

Dryad, The

Robert Lepage
Canada
2005

Solo performance piece, with a 100-year's reverse timeline to the dawn of the modern world where technical inventions interact with the poetic universe of Danish children's writer Hans Christen Andersen. Based on Andersen's visit to the 1867 Paris World Expo.

R.U.R.

Karel Capek
Czechoslovakia
1922

The short play that invented the concept and the word "robot." R.U.R. stands for "Rossom's Universal Robots." And the second major work, after E.M. Forster's "The Machine Stops," to caution against over-computerization (robotization).

Rent

Jonathan Larson
U.S.A.
1996

In this updating of the opera La Boheme (now set in the Manhattan's East Village), a yuppy landlord plans to evict the struggling artists in an East Village building and the homeless inhabitants of the tent city in the vacant lot next door. The landlord plans to use the space for a more lucrative venture: a high-tech "cyber-arts" center.

MOVIES

2001: A Space Odyssey

Stanley Kubrick
U.K.
1968

In the longest section of this movie, two spacemen, exploring the outer solar system, have HAL, the computer, as their crewmate. HAL runs the ship, and has a voice interface with the men. Except HAL malfunctions, gets paranoic, and attacks the men through manipulating their oxygen supply, etc. An earlier section shows travel to the Moon and life on the Moon colony, complete with videophones and lots of computer controls.

2010: The Year We Make Contact

Peter Hyams
U.S.A.
1984

Sequel to *2001*, but more technical and less mystical. A mission to Jupiter seeks to find out what happened to the first expedition and tries to communicate with HAL the computer.

A.I.

Steven Spielberg
U.S.A.
2001

A young android learns to bond with a human family, only to be rejected.

Android

Aaron Lipstadt
U.S.A.
1982
A quite humanlike android finds a creative way to avoid winding up on the scrap heap.

Apollo 13

Ron Howard
U.S.A.
1995
Three astronauts are trapped thousands of miles from earth in a disabled spacecraft.

Back to the Future Series

Robert Zemeckis
U.S.A.
1985
A young man uses a time machine-equipped sports car to travel back and forward in time.

Batteries Not Included

Matthew Robbins
U.S.A.
1987
A tenement of retirees face eviction, only for a pair of small robots to come and save them.

Battle Beyond the Stars

Jimmy Murakami
U.S.A.
1980
Adaptation of the *Seven Samurai* to futuristic space warfare in which mercenaries in small, agile computerized ships defend a farm colony against a huge armada of invaders. Overtones of *Star Wars*.

Battlestar Galactica

Richard A. Colla, Alan J. Levi
U.S.A.

Facing extinction at the hands of the robotic Cylons, the inhabitants of twelve distant human colonies band together under the protection of the Battlestar Galactica, in order to find the thirteenth colony, Earth.

Beautiful Mind, A

Ron Howard
U.S.A.
2001
The story of John Nash, Nobel-prize-winning mathematician, whose Nash Equilibrium theory has become an important concept in the field of multiagent systems

Bicentennial Man, The

Chris Columbus
U.S.A.
1999
Based on one of Isaac Asimov's *I, Robot* stories, this film is the biography of a machine that gradually becomes a human being.

Blade Runner

Ridley Scott
U.S.A.
1982
A detective has to hunt for rogue robots in futuristic Los Angles. The catch is that the robots look human.

Brazil

Terry Gillam
U.K.
1985
The oppression of a bureaucratic state of the near future, where people use curvaceous art deco-ish personal computers.

Center of the World, The

Wayne Wang
U.S.A.
2001

A shy (but attractive) computer genius about to make millions in the dot.com boom of the late 1990s pays a thoughtful prostitute to spend four days with him in a luxury Las Vegas hotel suite. She agrees to erotic play but no sexual penetration. But erotic play and conversation leads to interpersonal attraction. The theme is another variation on the computer expert as a nerd who finds himself as a person, with overtones of *Pretty Woman* and *Indecent Proposal*. (In real

MOVIES

life, a Shyness Institute in Silicon Valley, staffed by psychologists, helps dot-com'ers to learn interpersonal skills.)

Chapman Report, The

George Cukor
U.S.A.
1962
Male survey researchers go to a California town to study intimate relationships and romantically interface with their respondents. Adapted from a novel.

Charly

Ralph Nelson
U.S.A.
1968
The first movie of its genre: retarded person (Cliff Roberston) becomes cyborg-like genius, with tragic results. Overtones of Pygmalion theme of mentoring a superior human and Faustian theme of overreaching oneself. Based on Daniel Keyes' 1959 story, "Flowers for Algernon."

Clear and Present Danger

Phillip Noyce
U.S.A.
1994
The CIA Deputy Director (Harrison Ford) uses computerized voice print analysis to track a Colombian drug cartel leader (Joaquim de Almeida). The U.S. president orders a rogue government element to eliminate the cartel. They use a laser-guided bomb. Based on a novel by Tom Clancy, who is always fascinated with technology.

Close Encounters of the Third Kind

Steven Spielberg
U.S.A.
1977
The only way to communicate with benign alien visitors to earth is via computer-generated musical codes. One of the purest examples of the "good alien" genre (along with Spielberg's *E.T.*).

Colossus: The Forbin Project

Joseph Sargent
U.S.A.
1969
A serious drama in which a computer tries to take control of the world, and its creator attempts to prevent it. Especially interesting are the ways the computer transforms human-computer interaction.

Computer Beach Party

Gary Troy
U.S.A.
1988
The ultimate bikini-human-computer interface movie. Reportedly one of the worst movies ever made.

Computer Wore Tennis Shoes

Robert Butler
U.S.A.
1970
Minor comedy about a university student who receives a major shock while fixing a computer, becomes linked with it, and omniscient.

Conspiracy Theory

Richard Donner
U.S.A.
1997
A New York taxi driver develops conspiracy theories about many things and researches and publishes them on the Internet. But one turns out to be true, and the chase ensues!

Contact

Robert Zemeckis
U.S.A.
1997
Astronomer Jodi Foster uses radiotelescopes operated by advanced signal processing computers to lead the search for extra-terrestrial life. When her team receives a message, Earth's most advanced spaceship takes her to their planet, where the aliens' advanced techniques allow her to perceive paradise.

MOVIES

Conversation, The

Francis Ford Coppola
U.S.A.
1974

A mild-mannered surveillance expert (Gene Hackman) is hired to use advanced electronics to eavesdrop on two members of a corporation. He discovers more than he wants to know, and dangerous situations develop. An underlying theme is the extent to which privacy and autonomy should be protected.

Core, The

Jon Amiel
U.S.A.
2003

The Earth's core is stopping its rotation, causing natural disasters. The only way to stop it is to send a team of scientists burrowing to the core to detonate some Nukes. The "brilliant young anti-establishment hacker" in the control room is key.

Cube

Vincenzo Natali
U.S.A.
1997

Six people are trapped in a mysterious and deadly machine, and must try to understand its secrets in order to escape.

Dark City

Alex Proyas
U.S.A.
1998

An instant classic of visual imagination, this futuristic thriller features John Murdoch waking up to find he is wanted for brutal murders. Without any personal memories and haunted by mysterious beings who stop time and alter reality, he goes on to unravel the riddle of his identity.

Dark Star

John Carpenter
U.S.A.
1974

Parodic dark comedy of a spaceship (Mother) that must cope with a runaway alien, faulty computer systems, and the very smart bomb that thinks it is God and wants to destroy things. John Carpenter's first feature film.

Day the Earth Stood Still, The

Robert Wise
U.S.A.
1951

A space ambassador accompanied by a robot visit Washington, D.C., in a flying saucer to warn humanity to make peace.

Demolition Man

Marco Brambilla
U.S.A.
1993

In this comedy-action movie, Sylvester Stallone is a cop from our era revived in the future to fight the only violent criminal left in a hyper-ordered non-violent society (Wesley Snipes). Public-space communications are anachronistic: Although people use videophones in their homes and cars, on the street they rely on public phone booths rather than on private mobile phones. A subplot extols the unrepressed life of the underground fighting against bureaucratic repression, somewhat similar to the much more frightening *Brazil*.

Demon Seed

Donald Cammell
U.S.A.
1977

A computer scientist creates a super-computer that falls in love with his wife (Julie Christie) and rapes her. Then, she bears the computer's child. Like *The Terminator*, an example of the evils of over-computerization, with machines running amok.

MOVIES

Desk Set

Walter Lang
U.S.A.
1957

An efficiency expert (Spencer Tracy) tries to rationalize and computerize the reference section of a corporation. He's resisted on humanistic terms by chief librarian Katherine Hepburn, and love conquers all. Based on an eponymyous Broadway show. An early, influential argument that human ingenuity can outperform computers. (For a later, more violent, example, see *Soldier*).

Disclosure

Barry Levinson
U.S.A.
1994

The new boss of a male computer expert (Michael Douglas) is a woman (Demi Moore) with whom he had an affair in the past and who harasses him into resuming it. When he files charges, the corporate bosses turn against him, but he uses his computer expertise to triumph and make honest ambition prevail. It is how he uses his expertise that lifts the movie above routine. The "Digicon" corporation, way aPophead of its time in 1994, has a beautiful, functional virtual reality database that the hero wanders through (sumptuous virtual hallways), gathering evidence out of VR files. (Shades of *Neuromancer* and aPophead of *Minority Report*.) When stymied, the hero is helped by a VR assistant, dressed as an "Angel." The hero even meets the avatar of his opponent (Demi) in VR, who is deleting the files that will vindicate him. Yet, the hero soon realizes that backup files are available elsewhere—in this case Malaysia.

Donovan's Brain

Felix Feist
U.S.A.
1953

The Pophead of a rich tycoon, severed from its body, lives in a big jar. It is kept alive and sentient through its connections to a computer. Indeed, the Pophead's forceful personality comes to dominate his keeper. In short, computerization makes people less human. The same story was filmed earlier in *The Lady and the Monster*, and the genre was spoofed in *Mars Attacks*.

Dr Strangelove: Or How I Learned to Stop Worrying and Love the Bomb

Stanley Kubrick
U.K.
1963

In this dark comedy, human stupidity and computer malfunctions and dumb programming lead to World War III, set off by a doomsday bomb whose software is unalterable. The U.S. and Russian war rooms are dominated by huge computer-generated displays. The implicit argument is that foolish people have led the world to war, but computerization makes their actions out of control.

Electric Dreams

Steve Barron
U.S.A.
1984

An architect and his computer each vie for the affections of the same woman.

Eternal Sunshine of the Spotless Mind

Michel Gondry
U.S.A.
2004

A computerized Lacuna program does a brain scan and obliterates selected memories so that you can forget that you ever had a lover who left you. Jim Carrey and Kate Winslet use Lacuna to restart their failing love affair. As the process continues, the movie follows his memories of her back in time. Written by Charlie Kaufman.

eXistenZ

David Cronenberg
Canada
1999

A designer creates an electronic game that taps directly into the players' minds. The game is realistic enough as to blur the boundary between the game and reality. The players exist in a simulacra (copy without an original). Premiered the biological computer aesthetic and blurred the line between game and reality.

Fail-Safe

Sidney Lumet
U.S.A.
1964

An electrical malfunction in the Strategic Air Command's mainframe computer causes a disastrous error, sending a U.S. Air Force bomber squadron to drop a nuclear bomb on Moscow. The President of the United States must convince the Russian leader that the mission is an accident rather than an act of war.

Fantastic Voyage

Richard Fleischer
U.S.A.
1966

Raquel Welch and associates are computer-shrunk to fit into the bloodstream of an important terminally ill person so that they may treat and save him. The battle with the phagocytes is epic, and the visuals are always outstanding. A good example of how computer technology can benefit the world.

Fifth Element, The

Luc Besson
France
1997

The plot is about saving the world from evil in this witty, science-fiction comedy. More to the point are the visuals, both the costumes and the mise-en-scene. Although the plot is outrageously absurd, the movie incorporates much HCI into everyday life 250 years from now, including databases, 3D traffic control, computer-aided whole body reconstruction from a fragment, scanner blockers, and videophones.

Flash Gordon

Frederick Stephani, Ray Taylor
U.S.A.
1936

Flash Gordon himself is boring, but Ming the Merciless, the evil emperor of the planet Mongo, has a wonderful TV camera that provides detailed real-time pictures of anywhere and anyone on earth. Way aPophead of NASA. Originally a movie serial in thirteen episodes.

Flatliners

Joel Schumacher
U.S.A.
1990

Medical students (notably Kiefer Sutherland, Julia Roberts and Kevin Bacon) create near-death experiences for themselves until they go too far and cross the interface with tragic results.

Forbidden Planet

Fred Wilcox
U.S.A.
1956

In this free adaptation of Shakespeare's *The Tempest*, a space crew (led by Leslie Nielsen in a dramatic role) lands on a planet to find only a father (Walter Pidgeon) and daughter (Anne Francis) surviving, attended by their overly faithful servant, Robby the Robot. In the end, the computer robot proves to be dangerous, a cautionary message against losing humanity.

Galaxina

William Sachs
U.S.A.
1980

Famous for starring Dorothy Stratten as an android sex slave with feelings, dealing with the men on her space ship. (Stratten was a *Playboy* magazine centerfold of 1980, but is, alas, best known for being brutally murdered in real life by her jealous husband, as depicted in the *Star 80* movie.)

Gattaca

Andrew Nichol
U.S.A.
1997

In this cautionary tale of avoiding over-perfection, one of the last natural men (i.e., with defects) in a eugenicized world must use a variety of stratagems to avoid being caught by computerized detection devices.

MOVIES

General's Daughter, The

Simon West
U.S.A.
1999

Soldier-detective (John Travolta) solves the murder of a woman soldier, using computerized image enhancement and his deductive intuition. He realizes that while image enhancement can identify 256 shades of gray, the human heart can identify infinite shades.

Ghost in the Machine

Rachel Talalay
U.S.A.
1993

A serial killer escapes into cyberspace at the moment of his death. He continues his killing and harassment from there.

Hackers

Ian Softley
U.S.A.
1995

A young boy is arrested by the Secret Service for writing a virus, and banned from using a computer until his eighteenth birthday. Years later, he and his new-found friends discover a plot to unleash a dangerous computer virus, but must use their computer skills to find the evidence while being pursued by the Secret Service and the evil computer genius behind the virus.

Hedwig and the Angry Inch

John Cameron Mitchell
U.S.A.
2001

The story of a German transgender man-woman who tours the U.S. with a rock group. One character, played by Andrea Martin, has a mobile phone implanted in her Pophead that she turns on by touching her tongue to a front tooth.

Hot Millions

Eric Till
U.K.
1968

Hot Millions, released in 1968, when mainframe computers filled a room and PCs were just a gleam in Steve Wozniak's soldering iron, is a light-hearted crime caper that presages hacking techniques of a generation to come. Peter Ustinov plays an ex-con computer whiz who defeats the security system that protects his company's computer. He then reprograms the computer to issue checks to his several aliases and to mail the checks to bogus companies all over Europe, where Ustinov receives them.

Hunt for Red October, The

John McTiernan
U.S.A.
1990

It's a battle of computers and sonar as a U.S. and a Soviet submarine hunt for each other towards the end of the Cold War. A hymn by author Tom Clancy to the technology of war.

I, Robot

Alex Proyas
U.S.A.
2004

Will Smith stars as a detective in the year 2035 who is called on to investigate a crime allegedly committed by a robot in this movie, supposedly based on the Isaac Asimov stories. However, the film version loses Asimov's sympathy toward robots.

Independence Day

Roland Emmerich
U.S.A.
1996

Earth wins when hero Jeff Goldblum defies all known operating systems by using an Apple PowerBook to create a virus and turn it destructively loose on the alien invaders' mainframe network. This is not even credible if it were Linux or Windows.

MOVIES

Johnny Mnemonic

Robert Longo
Canada
1995

A cyborg courier(Keanu Reaves) is hunted by a pharmaceutical conglomerate that wants to stop his uploading to the world the contents of his life-saving memory chip. The forces of good get important help from two cyborg dolphins, originally trained by the U.S. Navy. A cautionary tale of how corporate forces can dominate uses of technology, although fought by a technologically adept alternative society.

Lawnmower Man 2: Beyond Cyberspace

Farhad Mann
U.S.A.
1995

A legless man gets greater intelligence and tries to create the city of the future in cyberspace, where he can rule.

Lawnmower Man, The

Brett Leonard
U.S.A.
1992

Drugs and computer technology make a super-genius out of a retarded gardener, with the usual ambiguous and cautionary results of science messing with the natural order of things. Follows the same genre as *Charly*.

Mars Attacks

Tim Burton
U.S.A.
1996

Martians attack and conquer the earth. In a subplot, probably modeled after *Donovan's Brain*, a captive man (Pierce Brosnan) and woman (Sarah Jessica Parker) are brought to the Martian spaceship where their severed Popheads live in a bottle and are kept alive.

Masala

Srinivas Krishna
Canada
1991

In this romantic comedy of migrant assimilation to multicultural Toronto, an (East) Indian grandmother converses with the god Krishna, who appears to her on a TV screen, dressed as a hockey goalie.

Matrix, The

Larry Wachowski, Andrew Wachowski
U.S.A.
1999

A young hacker, named Neo, discovers that the world is actually a computer program, and that he has been chosen to rescue humanity from it.

Max Popheadroom

Rocky Morton, Annabel Jankel
U. K.
1986

This British cyberpunk film concerns a news reporter whose personality is uploaded into a computer, while he is trying to discover the truth about subliminal advertisements through which the television network plans to control viewers.

Mercury Rising

Harold Becker
U.S.A.
1998

This thriller implausibly contends that a nine-year old autistic boy can crack secret government codes, ten years in the making, merely by reading the numbers on a computer screen. A celebration of the individual versus the ruthless, computerized government.

Metropolis

Fritz Lang
Germany
1926

In the first great science-fiction movie, workers in a hyper-modern city (set in the year 2000) rebel against wage slavery. A mad scientist creates a beautiful robot (Maria) to calm them down. A more widely seen early warning against artificial computerized humanity than the even earlier "The Machine Stops" story and "R.U.R." play.

Minority Report

Stephen Spielberg
U.S.A.
2002

Tom Cruise plays a wrongly accused detective in the near American future. He and his confreres make extensive use of data visualization (displayed on a huge screen), navigating through the data with dance-like hand gestures. As is common in the genre, human ingenuity and gumption outwit computerized apparatchiks.

Mission: Impossible

Brian de Palma
U.S.A.
1996

Among the many plot twists, secret agents (led by Tom Cruise) use human ingenuity to break into a vault guarded by many computer-based security devices.

Monsoon Wedding

Mira Nair
India
2001

Modern urban upper-class India is a mix of modern and traditional, as signified in a classical dance done by the bride's sister—holding a mobile phone.

My Science Project

Jonathan Beteul
U.S.A.
1995

High school students find a UFO containing a machine that can materialize objects from past and future.

Negotiator, The

F. Gary Gray
U.S.A.
1998

In an unintentional parody of human-computer interaction in a climactic scene, when the bad cop wants to destroy computer-based evidence of his corrup-

tion, he shoots and destroys the video monitor instead of the hard disk. Earlier scenes show an interesting interface, in which audio is translated directly into written text, accompanied by a voice-stress analysis.

Net, The

Irwin Winkler
U.S.A.
1999

Shy female computer expert discovers a conspiracy that allows criminals to gain secret data from government computers.

Patriot Games

Phillip Noyce
U.S.A.
1992

In one episode of this Tom Clancy story, U.S. intelligence and military agencies combine to use computer-enhanced visuals to identify and bomb a militant base in a Middle Eastern country.

Pi

Darren Aronofsky
U.S.A.
1998

A reclusive genius builds a supercomputer in his tiny New York apartment in order to augment his own intelligence and find the hidden truth buried in the digits of the transcendental number pi.

Poltergeist

Tobe Hooper
U.S.A.
1982

In this horror story, a young girl releases evil forces that come through her TV screen from the ancient cemetery below. She must be rescued from the "TV people." Almost a primer for ensuing warnings about how the Internet will alienate users from real life.

Revenge of the Nerds

Jeff Kanew

U.S.A.

1984

Computer-using studious outcasts are harassed by preppy college students, but exact scientifically aided revenge. One of the few "good computer" stories foreshadowing the making of dot-com heroes in the 1990s, led by Microsoft's bespectacled Bill Gates.

Robocop

Paul Verhoeven

U.S.A.

1987

In the near future, a slain policeman is revived as a cyborg: a human brain in an enhanced, almost indestructible robotic body. His emotions and values unstably oscillate between human and machine, with human values winning out in the end. His "good" human side uses his robotic strength and technology to triumph over the evil organization. The privatization of the police force adds another moral complication.

Silent Running

Douglas Trumbull

U.S.A.

1972

A loner crew member (Bruce Dern) serves on a spaceship that is Earth's last nature reserve. He loves his forests, and when ordered to return to eco-devasted Earth, he kills his fellow crew members but finds company with his three cute (an)droids who better share his philosophy: Huey, Dewey and Louie. A poignant, pioneering eco-space film in which the robots seem more human than the world-destructive humans. Its 1960s sensibility includes music by Joan Baez.

Simone

Andrew Niccol

U.S.A.

2002

Al Pacino plays a fading Hollywood director, who has dealt with one too many temperamental actresses. He revives his career by creating a digital film star that he names "Simone" (Simulation One). Simone and her films are huge successes, loved by the world. But the world also wants to see Simone in the flesh, which becomes quite a problem when an actress is a simulation.

Sleeper

Woody Allen

U.S.A.

1973

In this comedy, a nerdish clarinet player (Woody Allen) revives 200 years in the future to become a revolutionary leader and takes the disguise of a robotic house servant. He finds solace in a robotic confessional booths and he finds sex in an instantly effective Orgasmatron booth (in a scene much funnier than Sylvester Stallone and Sandra Bullock's experience in *Demolition Man*). The movie is doubly Keaton: It is a modern equivalent of a Buster Keaton comedy, and it costars Diane Keaton (no relation).

Sliver

Philip Noyce

U.S.A.

1993

This murder mystery is set in a skinny, sliver of a New York apartment building, where the voyeur-owner has secret video cameras installed throughout all the apartment buildings. He can see everything and everybody, including new tenant Sharon Stone. Foreshadows the surveillance society with video cameras permeating public and private places.

Sneakers

Phil Alden Robinson

U.S.A.

1992

Technologically adept heroes use their computer skills. Robert Redford, Sydney Poitier, and Dan Ackroyd lead a lovable renegade band of hackers who penetrate secret computer defenses and transfer billions to their bank accounts. The map tracing of files routing globally through complex sets of nodes popularized the field of cyber-geography and colonizing others' computers to hide one's tracks.

MOVIES

Snow White and the Seven Dwarfs

David Hand
U.S.A.
1937

The movie contains the first visual display screen with intelligence although not much survival skill: "Mirror, mirror on the wall. Who is the fairest of them all?" the wicked Queen asks. And is told that it is not her but Snow White.

Soldier

Paul Anderson
U.S.A.
1998

Kurt Russell, "Sergeant Todd 3465" is a cyber-enhanced, but largely human, soldier. Deemed obsolete by military bureaucracy and abandoned on a pariah world, his ingenuity helps lead fellow outcasts in defeating a largely robotic invasion force.

Space Children

Jack Arnold
U.S.A.
1958

A glowing brain-like creature arrives on a beach near a rocket test site via a teleportation beam and takes control of the children.

Space Cowboys

Clint Eastwood
U.S.A.
2000

Four aged former astronauts are recalled into service to deal with a space emergency when a Russian satellite with 1950s technology threatens to crash. Having trained in the old technology of a generation ago, they have to learn and come to terms with contemporary computer skills for space travel in 2000. Starring James Garner, Clint Eastwood, Tommy Lee Jones and Donald Sutherland.

Spaceballs

Mel Brooks
U.S.A.
1987

The hero in this Brooksian parody of Star Wars is protected by the wisdom of Yogurt, a hologram, who gives him powers of "The Schwartz." The heroine's virginity is constantly checked by her robot, Dot Matrix (with the voice of Joan Rivers).

Spy Kids 3-D: Game Over

Robert Rodriguez
U.S.A.
2003

In this sequel, the Spy Kids enter a virtual reality videogame. Most of the film is in three dimensions, and many of the scenes suggest what a three-dimensional version of contemporary videogames might really be like.

Star Trek: The Motion Picture

Robert Wise
U.S.A.
1979

The first of the *Star Trek* series of movies, this film depicts a human encounter with a robot space probe that has gained vast power from a machine civilization but understands neither compassion nor its own nature.

Star Wars Series

George Lucas
U.S.A.
1979

A young farmboy finds himself embroiled in a galactic war between the evil Empire and the heroic Alliance.

Stepford Wives, The

Bryan Forbes
U.S.A.
1975

In this quietly-building horror story, boring suburban men create even more boring and subservient computerized wives to replace their original, too independent, human wives. A critique of male chauvanism and human conformity. Remade in 2004 for the George W. Bush era as a comedy, starring Nicole Kidman, directed by Frank Oz, and released by Paramount. This time around, the engineering of the Stepford wives is done by a former Microsoft employee (played by Christopher Walken).

Swordfish

Dominc Sena
U.S.A.
2002

Ace computer hacker (Hugh Jackman) is blackmailed by mastermind (John Travolota) and his sidekick of ambiguous loyalties (Halle Berry) to steal nine billion dollars in unnoticed government funds. The hacker, of course, performs incredible feats despite the distractions of a gun held to his Pophead and sexual ministrations of Ms. Berry.

Technical Writer, The

Scott Saunders
Canada
2003

The hero is a technical writer of computer manuals (twitchy and agoraphobic of course), who is seduced by artist Tatum O'Neal with much less benign purposes than the similar nerd genre of *The Center of the World*.

Terminator 2: Judgment Day

James Cameron
U.S.A.
1991

In this sequel to the original time-travel story, the Terminator robot returns, but as the hero rather than the villain.

Terminator 3: Rise of the Machines

Jonathan Mostow
U.S.A.
2003

Another action thriller about conflict between humans and nearly invulnerable machines that raises the question whether we can control technological innovation or it is destined to overwhelm us.

Terminator, The

James Cameron
U.S.A.
1984

An invincible cyborg is sent from the future to kill the mother of its master's greatest foe.

Things to Come

William Cameron Menzies
U.K.
1936

An alternative world history of 1936-2036. First, war reduces the world to small, warring villages. Eventually, hyper-rational, high-tech, computer-aided scientists bring progress and world government. On the eve of the first trip to the moon, riots break out, as people fear that scientific modernism may lead to war again. From H.G. Wells, *The Shape of Things to Come*. Visually original and stunning and beautifully acted, with Ralph Richardson (village "Boss") and Raymond Massey (scientific "airman") standing out.

Thirteenth Floor, The

Josef Rusnak
U.S.A.
1999

To solve a murder mystery, the hero enters a virtual reality world where the computer-generated agents think they are real. A good exploration of realities within realities, and the ambiguities of human personality.

Total Recall

Paul Verhoeven
U.S.A.
1990

In the near future, a computer process has replaced the hero's memory and personality with another, going from tough fighter to wimp. How does the old personality communicate with the new? Via a taped message on a digital videophone.

Tron

Steven Lisberger
U.S.A.
1982

A computer expert is kidnapped into a computer world and can only escape with the aid of a heroic security program. The first feature movie that was completely computer generated.

MOVIES

Under Siege 2: Dark Territory

Geoff Murphy
U.S.A.
1995

At the end of this Steven Seagal action-thriller, the mad scientist, computer genius villain is thwarted in his attempt to blow up the Pentagon when Seagal disables the laser launch software by firing a bullet through the scientist's laptop with just seconds to go.

Universal Soldier

Roland Emmerich
U.S.A.
1992

Jean-Claude Van Damme is a super soldier who was killed in Vietnam but resurrected. He is part of a secret elite robot unit. When the other robots do evil, his competitive spirit and thirst for justice lead him to use his still-human ingenuity to defeat them.

Until the End of the World [Bis ans Ende der Welt]

Wim Wenders
Germany, France, Australi
1991

A woman (Solveig Dommartin) and a man (William Hurt) travel across much of the world, communicating with others by computer-mediated videophone. They wind up in the Australian desert where the man's father (Max von Sydow) has worked with aborigines to invent a machine that records dreams and visions, and enables blind people to see.

Videodrome

David Cronenberg
Canada
1983

The ultimate human-video interface movie: *Videodrome* is an experiment that uses TV transmissions to alter viewers' perceptions by permanently altering their brain.

Virtual Sexuality

Nick Hurran
U.K.
1999

In this teenage comedy, a gorgeous seventeen-year-old young woman goes with her boyfriend to a virtual reality conference. There, she uses a computer to clone herself as the gorgeous young man of her dreams, who has her personality. Romantic complications ensue.

Virtuosity

Brett Leonard
U.S.A.
1995

A computer-created psychopathic killer enters the real world. Starring Denzel Washington.

War Games

John Badham
U.S.A.
1983

Matthew Broderick is a teenager who uses his home computer to impress Ally Sheedy, but taps into the Pentagon's main war computer and almost starts World War III when he plays the "real" war game on the screen. In short, *Dr. Strangelove* from a teen's viewpoint, suggesting the dangers of over-computerization.

Warriors of the Net

Tomas Stephansson
Sweden
1999

The thirteen-minute-long animated film provides an unique and powerful imaginative view of the inner workings of the Internet.

Weird Science

John Hughes
U.S.A.
1985

A teenage movie with a cyber difference: Two boy nerds build a robot as their love slave—the beautiful Kelly LeBrock.

MOVIES

Westworld

Michael Crichton
U.S.A.
1973

In a community (and holiday resort) populated by robots, there is a bug in the programming and one becomes a killer. Part of the "you can't trust computers" genre, but with the reassurance that human ingenuity will make things right in the end.

When Worlds Collide

Rudolph Mate
U.S.A.
1951

In this tale about a scientist who tries to convince the world that the Earth is in the destructive path of a planet, the state-of-the-art computer doing the analysis in the story lacks a keyboard or screen.

Who Is Julia?

Walter Grauman
U.S.A.
1986

A made-for-TV movie with an unbelievable premise for its time (1986)—a brain transplant—that becomes less and less fantastical as science and technology advance. The movie is actually a well-written and thoughtful exploration of the implications for the person whose body is receiving the transplant and the person whose brain still lives in that body, as well as for the families of the two women involved. The ethical and values-based issues that come up for professionals using this kind of amazing medical technology are also dealt with in the film.

You've Got Mail

Nora Ephron
U.S.A.
1998

Tom Hanks and Meg Ryan get romantic by e-mail. They own two competing nearby bookstores, but aren't aware of their "real life" rivalry when they e-mail. The premise of separate e-mail and real lives is seldom met in actual situations. However, it is one of the few movies that tries to show Internet use as a Body Text C (Pophead 1&2 first para) part of contemporary everyday life.

DOCUMENTARIES

Almost Real: Connecting in a Wired World

Ann Shin
Canada
2003

A snapshot of life in the Internet age circa 2002. Focuses on a few persons for whom the Internet has become an essential community, and the many ways (sometimes intimate) that they connect with others. Its concentration on the extreme and exotic distorts perceptions of how most people use the Internet.

Capturing the Friedmans

Andrew Jarecki
U.S.A.
2003

Child molestation in a suburban U.S. computer class. The dangers of hanging out with computer mavens.

Cyberman

Peter Lynch
Canada
2001

Steve Mann is one of the world's first cyborgs (and a University of Toronto computer engineer professor). The movie presents his humanistic and technical ideas, including thoughts on surveillance (and counter-sousveillance) and wearable computing.

Digital Divide

Debra Chasnoff, Lorna Thomas
U.S.A.
1999

Shows some uses of the Internet in developing countries, including a Kenyan health, a Zimbabwean dissident website, and Indian fishermen getting weather information.

Fog of War, The: Eleven Lessons from the Life of Robert McNamara

Errol Morris
U.S.A.
2003

This Oscar winner focuses on McNamara's 1960s role as U.S. Secretary of Defense during much of the

Vietnam War. Shows the limits of overly relying on seemingly rational computerized counts and models, which didn't accurately portray the situation on the ground.

Game Over: Kasparov and the Machine

Vikram Jayanti
Canada/U.K.
2004
Epic tale of the 1977 battle between the world's greatest chess player, Garry Kasparov, and the IBM computer, Deep Blue. Kasparov lost because, ironically, Deep Blue was less of a pure computer than its predecessors. Not only did it rationally anticipate moves, but its software was filled with lessons learned from previous grandmasters. It was able to adjust to Kasparov's evolving moves.

Hi-Tech War

Phil Craig
U.S.A.
2004
Examines the successes and failures of computer-based weapons and communications systems, including guided JDAM missles. Interviews with the weapons' designers and soldier-users, but not with those who were hit by the weapons. Focus is on the U.S.-led war in Iraq.

No Maps for These Territories

Mark Neale
U.K.
2000
Science-fiction writer William Gibson converses about his experiences and views of contemporary life. Cameos by Bruce Sterling, Jack Womack, Bono, and The Edge. Music video style editing makes it visually interesting.

Takedown

Joe Chappelle
U.S.A.
2000
Fictionalized account of the pursuit and capture of hacker Kevin Mitnick. Based on the book by New York Times reporter John Markoff.

TV/RADIO

Astro Boy [Tetsuwan Atom]

Osamu Tezuka
Japan
1951
Famous cartoon robot that helped launch Japanese anime, and made into TV series in Japan, the U.S., and elsewhere. Later the basis for video games. Tezuka gave Astro Boy's birthday as 7 April 2003 because he believed that robots would be everywhere by then. Highly expressionistic drawing style.

Batman

Stanley Ralph Ross, Charles Hoffman
U.S.A.
1966
Batman, Robin, and their valet Alfred use a map display in their Batmobile (pre-satellite GIS) and Batphones to communicate

Battlestar Galactica

Michael Rymer
U.S.A.
2003
The last stand of humans against the Cylons, robots who have turned on them and declared war. The humans flee towards mother Earth in a motley space odyssey, fighting battles and on the lookout for Cylon spies who look like humans. A formula movie of the genre that robots are evil and will turn on humans. With some spy robots posing as humans, there are echoes of McCarthyistic paranoia in the 1950s U.S.

Bionic Woman, The

Harve Bennett
U.S.A.
1976
Like the *Six Million Dollar Man*, the Bionic Woman was filled with computerized implants and organs. She too could run, fight, etc. better than humans, but in the person of Lindsay Wagner, she was also charming and intelligent.

Captain Video and His Video Rangers

Scudder Boyd, Pat Fay
U.S.A.
1949–1955

The first widely distributed space show on TV, with special effects that seem primitive today. (The camera would shake to show blast-off.) Aimed at preteen kids. As the Captain and the Video Rangers patrolled space and protected us from the evil Dr. Pauli, they used such futuristic devices as the Opticon Scillometer, a long-range, x-ray machine that saw through walls; the Discatron, a portable TV portable intercom; and the Radio Scillograph, a palm-sized, two-way radio.

CSI: Crime Scene Investigation

Jerry Bruckheimer
U.S.A.
2000

Forensic evidence investigation agents in Las Vegas routinely use a variety of computer-based techniques to solve crimes. Whereas the *MacGyver* show of the late 1980s showed a resourceful man ingeniously rigging physical (non-computer) devices to foil crime, *C.S.I.* shows ingenious professionals using computer-based devices as part of their repertoire.

Doctor Who

Sydney Newman
U.K.
1963

Long running British children's adventure serial. Dr Who is an unassuming shaggy man who is really a "Time Lord" with great powers and a time-traveling computer hidden in an old-fashioned British phone booth. With spunky child companions, he battles the evil, soul-less Dalek robots. Many actors have played the doctor, and generations of children have been taught from it that soulless robots are evil, but will always be defeated by resourceful and spunky human amateurs.

Doogie Howser, MD

Steven Bochko, David E. Kelley
U.S.A.
1989–1993

Long before there were blogs, Doogie Howser, a sitcom child prodigy who became a doctor at age fourteen, used his trusty PC to keep an electronic journal. Each episode would conclude with Doogie keyboarding a pithy wrap-up on the life lessons he was learning.

Friends

Kevin Bright, Marta Kauffman, et al.
U.S.A.
1994-2004

Although the apartments of the friends are oddly free of computers except for the rare scene with a laptop, Chandler—the most financially solvent of the group—clearly works as some sort of data processing supervisor. However, no one really understands what he does, an all-too-common situation for the friends of anyone who works in a computer-related field.

Futurama

Matt Groening
U.S.A.
1999

A pizza delivery guy from 1999 awakes in 2999. Among his companions is the drunken robot, Bender. Much less successful than Groening's *The Simpsons*.

Game Over

David Sacks
U.S.A.
2004

Animated sitcom depicting the everyday lives of video game heroes in their off-hours: the Smashenburns family. Also a good introduction to video games for the uninitiated.

Get Smart

Mel Brooks, Buck Henry, et al.
U.S.A.
1965–1969

This sitcom popularized the use of the cell phone before it was invented. However, the "shoe-phone" as

TV/RADIO

it was then called was inconveniently located. Starred Don Adams as Secret Agent Maxwell Smart and Barbara Feldon as Agent 99. The Cone of Silence was an early analog privacy device.

Inspector Gadget

Jean Chalopin, Andy Heyward, et al.
Canada
1983
Comic cartoon series of a bumbling bionic police officer trying to cope with the evil empire of M.A.D. using implanted gadgets, such as pop-up roller skates, extensible arms, and a helicopter-hat. His dog and girlfriend do all the work: human common sense is more important than computerized gadgets. Starring (the voice of) *Get Smart* similar comedy hero, Don Adams, with echoes of Peter Sellers' "Inspector Clouseau" character in the *Pink Panther* series.

Jetsons, The

Joseph Barbera, Oscar Dufau, et al.
U.S.A.
1962
A family lives in the future in this cartoon comedy modeled after the prehistoric cartoon series, *The Flintstones*. There's a video terminal on every desk.

Knight Rider

Tom Greene, Glen Larson
U.S.A.
1982–1986
Detective (pre *Baywatch* David Hasselhof) solves crimes, greatly aided by a super car with artificial intelligence. There is an intimate relationship between the male detective and his (male-voiced) car. Like the Asimov robot stories, it suggests the synergistic advantages of a human-computer team.

Law & Order

Dick Wolf
U.S.A.
1990-

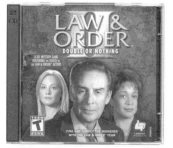

The dramas in the Law & Order "franchise"— *Law & Order, Law & Order: SVU*, and *Law & Order: Criminal Intent*—all periodically have plot lines involving the Internet. Online pornography, e-mail and chatroom relationships, and websites that teach people how to make weapons or commit suicide are among the topics covered in episodes through the years.

Lexx

Paul Donovan, Lex Gigeroff, et al.
Canada/Germany
1997
Fugitives on a starship include a zombie warrior, a former sex worker, and a sexually excitable computer. Preposterous plot and over-arch acting, but often a different take on the science-fiction genre. And it portrays computers that can have feelings.

Lost in Space

Irwin Allen
U.S.A.
1965–1968
The Space Family Robinson get lost in space and trapped on an alien planet. They are greatly aided by their human-sized robot servant, that in the Asimovian spirit, can only do good things for them, and is often wiser and more resourceful, like a good uncle or nanny.

Max Headroom

Francis Delia, Janet Greek, et al.
U.S.A.
1987
A roving reporter for "Network 23" in a futuristic U.S. does his job with the aid of a computerized version of himself. It's a battle of computer smarts and resources, as bureaucratic and evil forces use

T V / R A D I O

computerized surveillance to harass him. Matt Frewer plays both the real and computerized versions.

NetForce

Robert Lieberman
U.S.A.
1999
In the near future (2005), the "NetForce" division of the FBI protects the Internet from a criminal who resembles Bill Gates. "The one who controls the Internet controls the world." Made-for-TV movie.

Nikita

Reza Badiyi, George Bloomfield
Canada
1997
Nikita and the rest of her physically active team of government agents are greatly aided by the wheel-chair-bound Berkoff, who is their computer expert (especially databases and mapping) and informs them through radio communication.

Now and Again

Glenn Gordon Caron
U.S.A.
1999
A government experiment rescues the brain of Michael Wiseman, a middle-aged insurance executive, after he dies in a subway accident. Wiseman, originally played by John Goodman, is put into a new perfect body (played by Eric Close) that is enhanced to give Wiseman great speed and heightened senses. In return for the favor, the government requires that Wiseman stay away from his much-loved wife and daughter (a requirement he, of course, circumvents) and act as a government agent.

Outer Limits [II], The

Pen Densham
Canada
1995
In the spirit of the original 1960s *Outer Limits* this is more an anthology of short stories than a linked series. Common themes are diversity, brotherhood and the unexpected, with heavy use of computers and advanced communication.

Pee-Wee's Playhouse

Paul Reubens
U.S.A.
1986–1991
This popular Saturday morning children's show included vintage cartoon clips, puppets, and state-of-the-art 3D animation, all presented via Pee-Wee's "magic screen."

Prisoner, The

Patrick McGoohan
U.K.
1967–1968
In this cult classic, the hero is a former spy who gets spirited away to a quaint village that is really a high-tech prison. Supercomputers figure among the many technological wonders used to make "the prisoner" crack and reveal the secret reason he has resigned from espionage work.

ReBoot

Gavin Blair, Phil Mitchell, et al.
Canada
1994
Guardian human-like programs have adventures keeping the residents of Mainframe safe from the evil Megabyte and his hench-programs. Kids' cartoon series, with characters such as Dot Matrix, Glitch, and Captain Capacitor. Anthropomorphizes the inner workings of the computer, but does not portray them accurately.

Sex and the City

Darren Star, Michael Patrick King, et al.
U.S.A.
1998-2004
Newspaper columnist Carrie (Sarah Jessica Parker) chatters away with three friends about her romantic crises and other New York events, but she puts her deepest thoughts down on her Apple laptop as she writes her column. Her computer use is more casual than her sex, showing how routine word processing had become by the late 1990s.

TV/RADIO

T
U
/
R
A
D
I
O

Six Million Dollar Man, The

Martin Caidin, Tom Greene
U.S.A.
1973–1978
After astronaut Steve Austin's body was wrecked in a crash, he is resurrected with ultrahuman bionic parts that enable him to run, swim, jump, etc. faster than anyone. Alas, his brain remains dull.

Small Wonder

Howard Leeds
U.S.A.
1985–1989
In this sci-fi sitcom, a robotics engineer brings home a robot known as a Voice Input Child Indenticant (nicknamed Vicki). Vicki, fashioned as a ten-year-old girl, becomes part of the family. Her robotic origins, though, need to be hidden from the world, especially from snoopy neighbors.

Star Trek (original)

Gene Roddenberry
U.S.A.
1966
The crew of the Starship Enterprise use both voice-activated and button-pushing computer interfaces. Their hand-held "tricorders" are very advanced personal digital assistants, providing a variety of aids such as translation and medical diagnosis. However, they never use seat belts, so storms and enemy attacks bounce them around the ship.

Star Trek Voyager

Rick Berman, Michael Piller, et al.
U.S.A.
1995
The chief enemy is The Borg. A cyborg entity, which not only merges human and computer capacity in one body, but links all into a collective consciousness—"The Borg". The beautiful Borg, "7 of 9" (played by Jeri Ryan), joins the Star Trek crew, and repeatedly tries to balance her collective consciousness with her emerging human individualism.

Another character, the balding "Doctor" is a hologram equipped with artificial intelligence that allows him to prescribe the correct treatment with great assurance and success.

Star Trek: The Next Generation

Gene Roddenberry, Rick Berman
U.S.A.
1987–1994

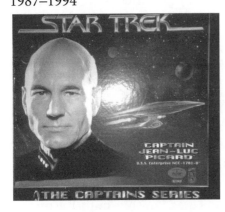

"Data," a lovable human-like robot, is a leading officer of the crew with many responsibilities. He is forever trying to develop human-like emotional capabilities. Despite the many scientific advances of his time, he has very pasty skin and unreal eyeballs. Surprisingly, despite Data's virtues, no robot shows up prominently on the crew of the later *Star Trek Voyager* series.

Time Tunnel, The

Irwin Allen
U.S.A.
1966

Two scientists, working on perfecting a government-financed, computer-assisted "time tunnel," rush Pophead long into the tunnel to prove its potential. Each episode finds the time travelers at the heart of a significant event in the past or future.

Twilight Zone, The

Rod Serling
U.S.A.
1959–1962

Although this classic science fiction series—which ran from 1959 to 1964 (and was revived in the late 1980s and in 2003) seems somewhat low-tech in comparison to shows like *Star Trek*, a number of episodes focused on humans versus machines, space travel, and artificial intelligence.

Whiz Kids

Joe Gannon, Bob Shayne
U.S.A.
1983

A teenage computer whiz and his tech-savvy pals solve mysteries with the help of a talking computer named RALF.

Wire, The

Brad Anderson, et al.
U.S.A.
2002

Set in the Baltimore drug/homicide scene, this detective series featured electronic surveillance. It graphically depicts the lives of everyone in the drug food chain, on both sides of the law.

X-Files, The

Chris Carter
U.S.A.
1993-2002

Mulder and Skully, the FBI agents around whom this show focused, spent much more time out in the field looking for aliens than in front of a computer. However, they relied on three computer geeks (who were also conspiracy theorists), known as The Lone Gunmen, to help them unravel mysteries that involved computer disks, chips, and the like.

MUSIC

Are You Ready, Eddie

Emerson, Lake, and Palmer
U.K.
1996

An ode to Emerson, Lake, and Palmer's sound engineer, Eddie. The song's lyrics ask, "Well, are you ready, Eddie, to turn your sixteen tracks on?"

TV/RADIO

MUSIC

Blue Danube Waltz

Johann Strauss
Austria
1867

This nineteenth-century waltz forms the perfect musical background as the ship in *2001: A Space Odyssey* floats through space.

Computer World

Kraftwerk
U.S.A.
1981

The song's lyrics include, "Interpol and Deutsche Bank, FBI and Scotland Yard. Time, travel, communication, entertainment. Computer World. Computer World." Kraftwerk's songs also included such titles as "Computer Love," "Home Computer," and "Pocket Calculator."

Deeper World

Kate Bush
U.K.
1989

Singer-songwriter Kate Bush looks to her computer for love and understanding: "I turn to my computer. And spend my evenings with it. Like a friend. . . . I turn to my computer like a friend. I need deeper understanding. Give me deeper understanding."

I'm Going to Be an Engineer

Peggy Seeger
U.S.A.
1979

In this feminist folk song, Peggy Seeger tells the story of a girl who is determined to be an engineer despite the fact that this is not an acceptable career for young ladies (at least in the 1970s). As the song goes, "When I went to school I learned to write and how to read. Some history, geography and home economy. And typing is a skill that every girl is sure to need, to while away the extra time until the time to breed. And then they had the nerve to say: What would you like to be. I says, I'm gonna be an engineer."

Mr. Roboto

Dennis DeYoung
U.S.A.
1983

In this cryptic song, "I've got a secret I've been hiding under my skin. My heart is human, my blood is boiling, my brain I.B.M. So if you see me acting strangely, don't be surprised. I'm just a man who needed someone, and somewhere to hide. . . . The problem's plain to see: too much technology. Machines to save our lives. Machines dehumanize."

Pacman Fever

Jerry Buckner, Gary Garcia
U.S.A.
1982

The singer of this anthem to the power of Pacman moans that "I got Pacman Fever. It's Driving me Crazy. I got Pacman Fever. I'm goin' outta my mind."

She Blinded Me With Science

Thomas Dolby
U.K.
1982

A love song to a teacher? As the lyrics go, "She blinded me with science! And hit me with technology. Good heavens Miss Sakamoto—you're beautiful! . . . Mmm—but it's poetry in motion. And when she turned her eyes to me. As deep as any ocean. As sweet as any harmony. Mmm—but she blinded me with science. And failed me in geometry."

Space Oddity

David Bowie
U.K.
1969

Although computers are not specifically mentioned in this David Bowie classic, how else could Ground Control be monitoring Major Tom who is "stepping through the door" of his space capsule and "floating in a most peculiar way."

MUSIC

Star Trekkin

The Firm
U.S.A.
1987
A comic tribute to *Star Trek*, the lyrics note that the starship Enterprise is "Star Trekkin' across the universe. Boldly going forward and things are getting worse!"

The Typewriter

Leroy Anderson
U.S.A.
1952
A stylized music rendition of a pre-computer word processor, who also wrote "The Syncopated Clock," without which no computer could flourish.

Thus Spake Zarathustra

Richard Strauss
Germany
1896
This opus, based on the literary work of the same name by Fredric Nietsche, is the epic opening theme for the dawn of humankind in the *2001: A Space Odyssey* soundtrack.

Virtual Concerto

George Lewis
U.S.A.
2004
A Yamaha Disklavier digital-acoustic player piano is the soloist. It is "played" by a computer program that reacts to the live orchestra's performance. Both the computer-driven piano and the orchestra work from a score that in parts is fully notated while in other parts there are only suggested parameters for improvisation. The choices made by the piano and the orchestra affect the music performed by the other in real time.

Where Would I Be Without IBM

Information Society
U.S.A.
1992
In this song, a rock group croons, "Where would I be without my PC? Where would I be without MTV? Where would I be without CNN? Where would I be—without IBM?"

Contributors: William Sims Bainbridge, Katy Borner, Karen Christensen, Rachel Christensen, Tom Christensen, Emily Colangelo, Sarah Conrick, Tom Erickson, Francesca Forrest, Jonathan Grudin, Bernie Hogan, David Levinson, John May, Ed McBride, Mike Nichols, Marcy Ross, Mark Schane-Lydon, Phuoc Tran; Barry Wellman, Eric Wilson, David Wolf. Special thanks to Barry Wellman for his dedication to making this a varied and comprehensive list.

MUSIC

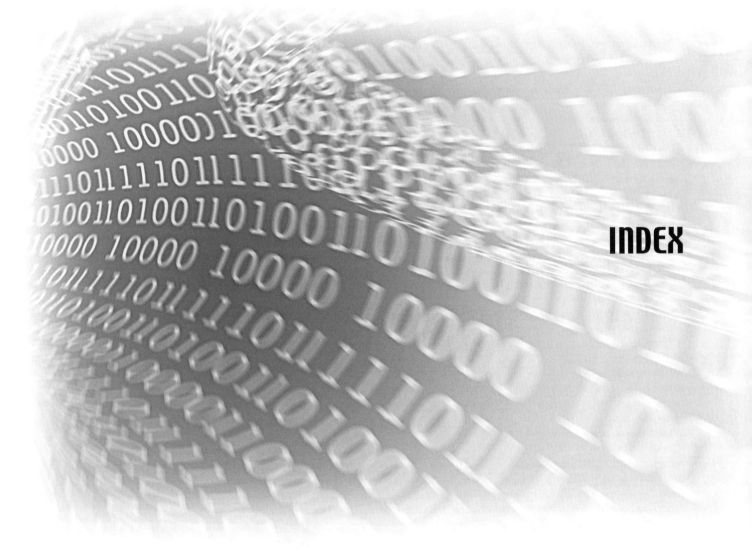

INDEX

Notes: 1) Bold entries and page numbers denote encyclopedia entries; 2) Page numbers followed by (v1) denote volume 1 and (v2) denote volume 2.

A

AATs (adaptive assistive technologies), 746–747(v2)

ABC (Atanasoff-Berry Computer), 50–51(v1)

Abekas A53D, 776(v2)

Abstract characters, 742(v2)

Abstraction
  attention investment model, 794–795(v2)
  classification and, 225(v1)

Abstraction hierarchy models, 225(v1)

Accelerated Strategic Computing Initiative (ASCI),
  703–704(v2)

Acceptance tests, 261(v1)

Access control, 615(v2)

Accessible design, 744–750(v2)

Accessible graphic interfaces, 295(v1)

Accommodation, 730(v2)

ACE (actuator control units), 262–263(v1)

ACM (Association for Computing Machinery), 198–200(v1),
  238(v1)

Acquired knowledge, 248(v1)

ACT-IF and ACT-R models, 755–756(v2)

Active *vs.* passive AHSs (adaptive help systems), 2–3(v1)

Active *vs.* passive reading, 74–75(v1)

Active *vs.* passive stereographic approaches, 730(v2)

Active Worlds, 137(v1), 138(v1)

Activism and hacking, 308(v1)

Actor-network theory, 18(v1)

Actuator control electronics (ACE), 262–263(v1)

Ad hoc networks, 454(v2)

ADA (Americans with Disabilities Act), 805–806(v2)

Adaptive assistive technologies (AATs), 746–747(v2)

Adaptive help systems (AHSs), 1–3(v1), 827(v2)

Adaptive interfaces, 3–7(v1)

Adaptive *vs.* adaptable systems, 4(v1)

Adjustable-angle split keyboards, 404(v1)

Adobe Acrobat, 383–384(v1)

Adobe Systems, 265–267(v1)

Notes: 1) Bold entries and page numbers denote encyclopedia entries; 2) Page numbers followed by (v1) denote volume 1 and (v2) denote volume 2.

A
B

Notes: 1) Bold entries and page numbers denote encyclopedia entries; 2) Page numbers followed by (v1) denote volume 1 and (v2) denote volume 2.

Notes: 1) Bold entries and page numbers denote encyclopedia entries; 2) Page numbers followed by (v1) denote volume 1 and (v2) denote volume 2.

C
D

Notes: 1) Bold entries and page numbers denote encyclopedia entries; 2) Page numbers followed by (v1) denote volume 1 and (v2) denote volume 2.

E

Notes: 1) Bold entries and page numbers denote encyclopedia entries; 2) Page numbers followed by (v1) denote volume 1 and (v2) denote volume 2.

G

Notes: 1) Bold entries and page numbers denote encyclopedia entries; 2) Page numbers followed by (v1) denote volume 1 and (v2) denote volume 2.

Notes: 1) Bold entries and page numbers denote encyclopedia entries; 2) Page numbers followed by (v1) denote volume 1 and (v2) denote volume 2.

K
L

---

*Notes: 1) Bold entries and page numbers denote encyclopedia entries;
2) Page numbers followed by (v1) denote volume 1 and (v2) denote
volume 2.*

m

n

o

Notes: 1) Bold entries and page numbers denote encyclopedia entries;
2) Page numbers followed by (v1) denote volume 1 and (v2) denote
volume 2.

O

P

P

*Notes: 1) Bold entries and page numbers denote encyclopedia entries;
2) Page numbers followed by (v1) denote volume 1 and (v2) denote
volume 2.*

Q
R
S

S

S

*Notes: 1) Bold entries and page numbers denote encyclopedia entries;
2) Page numbers followed by (v1) denote volume 1 and (v2) denote
volume 2.*

T
U

Notes: 1) Bold entries and page numbers denote encyclopedia entries; 2) Page numbers followed by (v1) denote volume 1 and (v2) denote volume 2.

W
X
Y
Z

Notes: 1) Bold entries and page numbers denote encyclopedia entries; 2) Page numbers followed by (v1) denote volume 1 and (v2) denote volume 2.